International BUSINESS

Introduction and Essentials

Donald A. Ball
Nova University

Wendell H. McCulloch, Jr.
California State University, Long Beach

Fourth Edition

**BPI
IRWIN**

Homewood, IL 60430
Boston, MA 02116

Sponsoring editor: *Craig Beytien*
Developmental editor: *Libby Rubenstein*
Project editor: *Carol Goodfriend Schoen*
Production manager: *Bette K. Ittersagen*
Designer: *Maureen McCutcheon*
Cover, part, and chapter illustrator: *Jill Smith*
Artist: *Alice B. Thiede*
Compositor: *The Clarinda Company*
Typeface: *10/12 Sabon*
Printer: *Von Hoffmann Press, Inc.*

Library of Congress Cataloging-in-Publication Data

Ball, Donald A.
    International business: introduction and essentials / Donald A.
Ball, Wendell H. McCulloch, Jr.—4th ed.
      p. cm.
   ISBN 0-256-08010-0
    1. International business enterprises—Management.
  2. International business enterprises.   3. International economic
relations. I. McCulloch, Wendell H. II. Title.
  HD62.4.B34   1990
  658'.049—dc20
                                                    89–39746
                                                      CIP

Printed in the United States of America

1 2 3 4 5 6 7 8 9 0 VH 7 6 5 4 3 2 1 0

To Vicky and Sally
Don, Jr., Dulce, Lianne, and Malinda

About the Authors

Don Ball is professor and coordinator of international business at Nova University in Ft. Lauderdale, Florida, and a consultant to international companies. He has a degree in mechanical engineering from Ohio State University and a Ph.D. in business administration from the University of Florida. Ball has published articles in the *Journal of International Business Studies* and other publications. He is a member of the review boards of *Multinational Management Review* and *Issues in International Business*. Before obtaining the doctorate, he spent 15 years in various marketing and production management positions in Latin America and Europe.

Wendell McCulloch is professor of international finance and law at California State University, Long Beach. He earned a bachelor's degree in economics and political science from George Washington University and a J.D. from Yale University. He has published articles in *The Wall Street Journal*, the *Journal of International Business Studies*, and the *Collegiate Forum*. The results of McCulloch's research have appeared in publications by the Joint Economic Committee of the U.S. Congress and the Heritage Foundation. Before beginning his academic career, McCulloch spent 19 years as an executive for American and European multinationals that offered banking, insurance, and investment products in many countries. While teaching and writing, he continues to act as an international business consultant.

A Note to the Student

Throughout the process of preparing the fourth edition of this text, we kept you, the student, uppermost in our minds. The result is a "student-friendly" text with numerous unique features.

1. Students tell us it is eminently readable. You can understand what is written.

2. Each chapter begins with a list of learning objectives and key words and concepts. These help you find the important points that you should understand.

3. The book is practical. Each chapter begins with a Business Incident, each has margin definitions to help you learn the meanings of important terms, and most contain a Worldview reading. Throughout the book, we explain the significance of the material to the businessperson. Many pictures and examples from industry help animate the book.

4. The text contains numerous tables and figures, many of which we constructed so as to present the data in a more useful form for businesspeople. We interpret the tables and graphs to help you understand their importance.

5. Much of a manager's success depends on the ability to find data. We provide long lists of data sources at various points in the book.

6. You will find information in this text that is not usually found in international business books: complete chapters on the physical forces, production, and exporting and importing, for example.

7. Because it is so comprehensive, this is a book that you will want to keep for your personal library. Many businesspeople buy it for that reason.

Donald A. Ball
Wendell H. McCulloch, Jr.

Preface

We are pleased with the outstanding response to our third edition. Many colleges and universities added their names to a growing list of those who had adopted the first and second editions. It was also gratifying that so many professors took the time to call or write to us about material and improvements that they and their students wished to see in the next edition, the one you are now using.

You will note that this fourth edition has come out after only two years. This is because significant changes in all aspects of international business are occurring so rapidly that we felt it was necessary to bring this information to you sooner. You need to know about the globalization of companies and strategies, Europe 1992, the U.S.–Canada Free Trade Agreement, *glasnost* and *perestroika* in the Eastern bloc, eruptions in China, and the growing competition among the United States, Japan, the NICs, and Europe, all of which are major forces reshaping international business.

Purpose and Scope of This Text

The text is written for the first course in international business taken either at the undergraduate level or in an M.B.A. program. A growing number of schools are permitting students to take the international business course *before* they have all the required basic courses so they are better prepared to discuss the worldwide aspects of each business function. This enables professors to take a more global approach in the presentation of their material.

In schools that do not yet require an international business course, many professors recommend this text as a supplementary book for international courses in finance, management, marketing, and so forth. Numerous executive seminars include this book as part of their handouts in programs on the various aspects of international business, and many business executives buy it as a reference book.

We begin the text by describing the nature of international business and the three environments in which an international businessperson works. In Section Two, we examine the increasingly important international organizations, and the international monetary system, and their impact on business. Next, in Section Three, we discuss the uncontrollable forces that make up the foreign environments and illustrate their effect on business practices. In the final section, we reverse the procedure and deal with the functions of management, showing how managers deal with the uncontrollable forces. The final chapter describes the trends and new directions of worldwide companies. There are many business examples throughout the book.

Changes in the Fourth Edition

Suggestions for improving this edition came from a number of sources: mail questionnaires, detailed chapter-by-chapter reviews by a number of international business professors, calls and letters from professors and students, comments by businesspeople who attended executive seminars or bought the book for their personal libraries, and students in our own classes, both graduate and undergraduate.

Our research confirms that the readability is good, which enables students to read and understand the material. Professors are thus freed of the task of explaining what was read and can use the class time to expand on topics of their choice and to discuss the latest happenings in this rapidly changing field.

We continue to begin each chapter with a quotation, followed by a Business Incident that relates to the material in the chapter. To assist students in learning the language of international business, we now have margin definitions. Another new feature is the Worldview, a reading that is pertinent to the text material. Reviewers have commented favorably on the use of indented materials as examples, and we have increased their use. Some are our own experiences gathered from a combined 34 years as executives for worldwide firms, both in the United States and in various foreign countries. The supplementary reading list has been greatly expanded. Several new end-of-chapter minicases have been added, and there are three new comprehensive cases at the end of the book. You will notice that we have used every effort, including calling government officials, to bring you the latest information. We invite you to compare data in our tables with those of other textbooks published in the same year.

We have incorporated many pictures into the text, because they often can show you something better than we can describe it. Now and then, we include a cartoon—international business does have its lighter side. There are also more graphs to supplement the tables.

Areas of Substantive Change

More changes have been made in this edition than in previous editions.

1. You learn in chapter 1 about the importance that business executives give to the study of international business, the importance they give to learning a foreign language, and how they acquired their international business experience. There is considerable discussion about the use of *global, multinational,* and other terms.

2. In Chapter 3, we now show the gains from trade. The section on trade restrictions has been rewritten, and includes a table that illustrates what important restrictions cost you, the consumer.

3. We describe a new trend in the World Bank and IMF—that of more encouragement of and support for investment by the private sector. Project EC 1992 is discussed in Chapter 5. In Chapter 6, we examine the debt situation of developing countries and the United States and show the differences between them. Chapter 7 is now the economic forces chapter. Many tables useful to businesspeople are included, and their significance is explained.

4. Chapter 8 has been rewritten to illustrate the pervasive influence of the physical forces on international business. We discuss the consequences for worldwide firms of the Alaskan oil spill, the Rhine spill, and other ecological disasters.

5. Chapter 9 has been changed considerably to illustrate more forcibly how culture impacts all business functions. We look at corporate cultures as well as regional cultures. There is more discussion about

Confucianism and Islam and their relevance to management. We have included new sections on technology transfer, the brain drain, the reverse brain drain, and women's education.

6. Chapter 10 now includes a discussion on *glasnost* and *perestroika.* The material on country risk assessment has been expanded. Chapter 12 offers new material on labor mobility and more information on gender discrimination.

7. The information on competition has been completely rewritten to show the struggle among companies in the United States, Japan, Europe, and the NICs. There is new information on counterfeiting and the analysis of the competitive forces, including sources of information. The discussion of environmental scanning has been expanded in Chapter 14.

8. Chapter 15 has been rewritten to reflect the new emphasis on global marketing. We discuss total product versus physical product in this context. A section on services has been added. Greater emphasis has been given in Chapter 16 to sources of assistance to exporters, and a section on importing was added.

9. Chapter 17 has been expanded to include East-West relations. We discuss attempts by the People's Republic of China, the Soviet Union, and other communist countries to liberalize and modernize their agriculture and business—and perhaps their politics. There is more information on countertrade and a discussion of the political upheaval in China.

10. A discussion of just-in-time, its problems, and the newer, synchronized manufacturing process has been added to Chapter 19. We give numerous examples of American and European efforts to improve product quality while lowering costs. There is new information on union-management relations in Chapter 20.

11. We have completely rewritten Chapter 21, "Strategic Planning and Organizational Design," to show how global firms think globally but act locally. There is a detailed discussion of 3M's global strategic planning process and its organization. We have restructured the planning model, and have expanded the discussion on the matrix organizational form. In Chapter 22, we have added a discussion of the working relationships among people of different cultural backgrounds. This has assumed greater importance with the increased globalization of firms. We also examine women's opportunities and their foreign postings.

12. A completely new Chapter 23 describes the future of global and multinational firms.

The Advantages of Using This Book in Your Class

This book is the result of teamwork between many professors and their students who have used previous editions. One aspect constantly mentioned is its readability. Because students understand what they read in this book, the professor can spend less time clarifying basic points and more time discussing emerging issues, of which there is no lack in this fast-moving field. However, don't be misled by the writing style. We have compared this book with others and have yet to find one as comprehensive. Note that we have included a complete chapter on the physical forces, to strengthen what is generally a weak area of students' education. There are also complete chapters on exporting-importing and production. We invite comparisons of our treatment of marketing, financial management, and international organizations, all important topics for international businesspeople. The many tables and their analyses enable students to make important comparisons of markets, and the numerous listed sources of additional information facilitate the research process when you wish to assign them projects.

Our 34 combined years in international business, in both the home offices of worldwide firms and their subsidiaries, have influenced our writing. We wanted a book that would describe what managers have to face in international business and how they respond to the uncontrollable environmental forces; in short, the kind of book people would like to have if they were suddenly told by the boss that they were going overseas. In fact, this happened to one of us—who found no such book at that time.

The Ball and McCulloch International Business Package

1. Instructor's Manual. We have worked to make a manual that will (1) help you save valuable time preparing for the course and (2) provide suggestions for heightening your students' interest in the material. Each chapter-by-chapter discussion presents the learning objectives, an overview, suggestions and comments, student involvement exercises, suggestions for guest lecturers, and a detailed chapter lecture outline, including references to tables when appropriate. Suggestions for videotapes and films are included. There are numerous transparency masters, including many for important tables.

2. Student Resources Manual. Professor Basel Janavaras of Mankato State University has prepared a *Student Resources Manual* that includes additional questions for review, outlines, summaries, and other material to enrich the study of international business. Some professors require their students to have a manual; others recommend that they have it.

3. Test Bank. The test bank is available in three formats: (1) a printed manual, (2) Computest—a floppy disk for the extremely rapid preparation of examinations on your own IBM-compatible computer, and (3) Teletest—a customized, phone-in service available from Richard D. Irwin, Inc. The test bank has been improved and expanded for this edition.

Acknowledgments

To the long list of people to whom we are indebted, we want to add Professors Toivo Aijo, California State University, Long Beach; Robert T. Aubey, University of Wisconsin-Madison; Mark C. Baetz, Wilfrid Laurier University; Rufus Barton, Murray State University; S. A. Billon, University of Delaware; James R. Bradshaw, Brigham Young University; Sharon Browning, Northwest Missouri State University; Dennis Carter, University of North Carolina-Wilmington; Mark Chadwin, Old Dominion University; Refik Culpan, Pennsylvania State University; Peter DeWitt, University of Central Florida; Galpira Eshigi, Illinois State University; Jeff Fadiman, San Jose State University; Prem Gandhi, State University of New York-Plattsburgh; Stanley D. Guzell, Youngstown State University; Gary Hankem, Mankato State University; Paul Jenner, Southwest Missouri State University; Bruce H.

Johnson, Gustavus Adophus College; Michael Kublin, University of New Haven; Eddie Lewis, University of Southern Mississippi; Lois Ann McElroy Lindell, Wartburg College; Carol Lopilato, California State University, Dominguez Hills; Lynn B. Robinson, University of South Alabama; John Setnicky, Mobile College; Jesse S. Tarleton, William and Mary College; John Thanopoulos, Akron University; Kenneth Tillery, Middle Tennessee State University; Hsin-Min Tong, Redford University; Dennis Vanden Bloomen, University of Wisconsin-Stout; and George Westacott, State University of New York-Binghamton. We continue to invite your suggestions for making this a more useful text and thank you for your interest and input.

Donald A. Ball
Wendell H. McCulloch, Jr.

Contents

Section Three
Foreign Environment   162

Chapter 6
Financial Forces   164

Chapter 7
Economic and Socioeconomic Forces   188

Chapter 8
Physical Forces   222

Chapter 9
Sociocultural Forces   254

Chapter 19
Production Systems   **594**

Chapter 20
Labor Relations Policies and Management   **622**

International
BUSINESS

Introduction and Essentials

Section One

The Nature of International Business

S ection One describes the nature and scope of international business and introduces the three environments in which international business managers must operate. How well they perform in their undertakings will depend in great measure on their understanding of the domestic, international, and foreign environments.

Chapter 1 presents the concept of the three environments and their forces. From the history of international business, we learn that although the international firm existed before the Civil War, it differed markedly from the present-day

global company, which is characterized by its explosive growth and closer central control of foreign operations. Managers, realizing that more company personnel must acquire some knowledge of international business, turned to the colleges and universities for assistance in training. From an original base of international trade theory, educators, through intensive research and study, came to include related material from other disciplines, and a new field of study, international business, emerged.

In Chapter 2, information is presented to help you comprehend the dynamic growth and the magnitude of both international trade and foreign investment. We discuss why firms go abroad, and we examine the many ways in which they do it.

An overview of the theories of international trade and economic development is given in Chapter 3 because a basic understanding of this material not only will help explain the actions already taken by government officials but also will provide insight into what they plan to do.

Chapter 1

Introduction to International Business

On the internationalization of markets . . .

There is no longer any such thing as a purely national economy. The rest of the world is just too big to ignore, either as a market or as a competitor. If business schools do nothing other than to train their students to think internationally, they would have accomplished an important task.

John Young, CEO, Hewlett-Packard

The failure to recognize that we're in a global economy is the biggest failing of American chief executives today. It's a fact of life and it doesn't make any difference if you're making shoes or making cars.

Douglas D. Danforth, former CEO, Westinghouse

LEARNING OBJECTIVES

In this chapter, you will study:

1. The distinctions between firms of the early 1900s and present-day global companies.

2. Why international business must be a separate field of study.

3. The three environments—domestic, foreign, and international—in which the multinational or global company operates.

4. The forces in these environments that are categorized as controllable and uncontrollable.

5. The many terms used to describe a firm that has substantial operations in more than one country.

KEY WORDS AND CONCEPTS

- Global company
- Expropriation
- Host nation
- Environment
- Uncontrollable forces
- Controllable forces
- Domestic environment
- Foreign environment
- International environment
- Self-reference criterion
- Multinational company
- Worldwide company

BUSINESS INCIDENT

The statements by the CEOs of two Fortune 500 global companies cited at the beginning of this chapter exemplify what business leaders all over the world are saying about the rapid internationalization of markets. They arrived at this conclusion because companies have matured internationally over the past three decades, and many that used to see themselves as national companies with some foreign business now perceive themselves as firms that operate in an international or global market. This perceptual change raises some interesting questions for both you—the student—and your professors about your preparation for working in this new environment:

1. Do business leaders perceive a need for *all* business students to study the international aspects of business?
2. How should the study of the international aspects be incorporated into the business curriculum?
3. How important is it to learn a foreign language?
4. How do most managers acquire international expertise?
5. What are the opportunities for overseas employment after graduation from college?
6. What are the implications for business education?

To answer these questions, a number of business professors have surveyed the nation's top executives for their opinions. Among their findings were the following:

1. A need to teach the international aspects of business was reflected in a nationwide study of business leaders. Ninety percent of those surveyed responded that "most business firms, domestic as well as international corporations, will be affected directly or indirectly by economic and political developments in the international scene, and most businessmen will, therefore, need an ability to understand and anticipate these effects." Seventy percent of the same respondents *disagreed* with the statement that employees need training in the basic

BUSINESS INCIDENT (concluded)

business disciplines but will learn all the international aspects of business on the job.[1]

Another, nationwide study by Professor Kobrin found that "the odds that *any* manager will be involved internationally have risen dramatically. People in domestic jobs find themselves involved in a number of cross-border and cross-cultural interactions." Two thirds of the respondents reported an increase in the number of Americans involved internationally during the past decade, and 57 percent expected this number to increase.[2] These results are borne out by a third study of executives at 100 large corporations that showed 97 percent felt that pressure to compete internationally would increase substantially in the next five years. However, a majority (66 percent) said American managers were "woefully ignorant of foreign markets."[3]

2. The accreditation agency for business schools, AACSB, recognizing the need for increasing the international content of the business curriculum, changed its standards in 1974 to require that the *worldwide* as well as the domestic aspects of business be taught to all business students. How these aspects were to be included in the curriculum was not specified.

However, executives of large firms in the Southeast and in southern California were very clear as to their preference: 98.8 percent and 96.4 percent, respectively, felt that taking a "Principles of International Business" course was desirable.[4] There are indications that their preference is being heeded by schools of business. A study of AACSB-member schools reported that "the schools surveyed are making an effort to meet the 'worldwide requirement' by offering courses in international business rather than trying to internationalize existing courses."[5]

3. Although the vast majority of those interviewed in the Kobrin study believed that the ability to speak a foreign language is an important asset, they did not regard it as critical. However, Kobrin feels strongly that competency in at least one foreign language must become the norm for managers. "Language training can help simulate experience abroad by providing an intuitive understanding of international differences. The interviews strongly suggested that one needs to have some competency in another language to appreciate its value."[6]

4. Most managers have acquired international expertise through business experience/business travel (92 percent) and overseas assignments (71 percent). But interestingly, those interviewed in the Kobrin study said that opportunities for Americans to be stationed abroad as long-term managers have decreased and will continue to do so. Also important in contributing to their knowledge of other countries is information found in publications such as *Business Week, The Economist, The New York Times,* and *Business International* (63 percent of the respondents).[7]

5. With the possible exception of international banking, there are few opportunities for recent graduates to be assigned overseas even when they have the basic business skills and language ability. The reason is that they must first learn how their employer does business and they must become skilled in some functional area of the firm. International business has become so significant for many companies that they can no longer afford to use overseas assignments for training to the extent that they used to. Although some graduates who want to go overseas may be fortunate to find employment with the division or group in the home office that is responsible for overseas business, others may have to first acquire the technical expertise in the domestic operation. If you are in this second group, we recommend that after working for the company for two to three years, you inform both the personnel department and the head of the international group in your functional area that you are interested in working with them. Some people have been successful in getting into international business by first acquiring industrial experience in the domestic operations of one company and then obtaining employment in the international operations of another firm in the same industry.

6. We learned from the Kobrin survey that while the need for international expertise is increasing dramatically, there are fewer opportunities to obtain it experientially. For this reason, educational institutions and companies must find ways to substitute education for experience.

One way to do this is to take an international business course, as you are doing. This course will help you develop the basis for acquiring international expertise while you still are in college. By the end of this course, you should have a systematic understanding of the various uncontrollable environmental forces and their impact on the firm. An additional benefit: because many of the topics you will be studying are the important issues facing governments and world leaders, you will become a better-informed citizen.

If you have any doubts as to your involvement in a global economy, take a moment to remember how you began your day. After you awoke, you may have looked at your Timex watch for the time and turned on your RCA TV for the news and weather while you showered. After drying your hair with a Conair dryer, you quickly swallowed some Carnation Instant Breakfast and Sanka coffee, brushed your teeth with Close-Up toothpaste, and drove off to class in your Honda with its Firestone tires and a tank full of Shell gasoline.

Meanwhile, on the other side of the world, a group of Japanese students dressed in Lacoste shirts, Levi's™ jeans, and Adidas shoes may be turning off their IBMs in the computer lab and debating whether they should stop for hamburgers and Cokes™ at McDonald's or coffee and doughnuts at Mister Donut. They get into their Ford Probe with Goodyear tires and drive off.

What do you and the Japanese students have in common? You are both consuming products made by *foreign-owned companies*. This is international business.

To further emphasize the point we're making, answer this question: Which of the following companies or brands are foreign owned?

1. Norelco (electric razors).
2. Chesebrough-Pond's (personal care articles).
3. Brooks Brothers (suits).
4. Electrolux (household appliances).
5. Lever Brothers (Lux, Wisk, Close-Up).
6. Lipton Tea.
7. Liggett Group (L&M, Lark, and Eve cigarettes, Alpo dog food).
8. General Tire (tires).
9. Keebler (baked goods).
10. Mack Trucks.
11. RCA records.
12. CBS records.
13. Bantam Books.
14. Moore Business forms.
15. Seagrams.
16. A&P supermarkets.
17. Nabisco (baked goods).[8]

The quotations, the Business Incident, and all that you have read so far illustrate the dramatic internationalization of the world economy. In fact, almost half of the economic activity in the world is international.[9] Moreover, business leaders and academicians predict that events such as Europe 1992 (when the European Community removes most of the remaining barriers between member states) and the U.S.–Canada Free Trade Agreement (which went into effect in 1989) will cause market internationalization to proceed at an even faster pace. All of this points to one salient fact: *There is an emphatic need for businesspeople to have some knowledge of international business.*

Is international business new? Are the practices of exporting and establishing operations overseas of recent origin? Let us take a brief look at the history of international business.

HISTORY OF INTERNATIONAL BUSINESS

International trade and the international firm are not new aspects of business. Even before the time of Christ, merchants were sending representatives abroad to sell their goods. The British East India Company, a trading firm chartered in 1600, established foreign branches, as did a number of American colonial traders in the 1700s. Early examples of American foreign direct investment are the English plants set up by Colt Fire Arms and Ford* (vulcanized rubber), which were established before the Civil War. Both operations failed, however, after only a few years.

The first successful American venture into foreign production was the Scotch factory built by Singer Sewing Machine in 1868. By 1880, Singer had become a worldwide organization with an outstanding foreign sales organization and several overseas manufacturing plants. Other firms soon followed, and by 1914, at least 37 American companies had production facilities in two or more overseas locations. At that time, the book value of U.S. foreign direct investment was $2.65 billion, or about 7 percent of the nation's gross national product (GNP).[10] Note that although the book value of American foreign direct investment had risen to $309 billion by 1987, its percentage of the U.S. GNP was still about 7 percent. During the same period, American exports, the other aspect of international business, rose from $2 billion to $425 billion.

Among those firms already established overseas were national Cash Register and Burroughs, with manufacturing plants in Europe; Parke-Davis, with a plant near London (1902); and Ford Motor Company, which had assembly plants or distribution outlets in 14 countries. General Motors and Chrysler followed soon afterward, so that by the 1920s, all three companies had sizable foreign operations. Interestingly, and quite the reverse of today's situation, in the 1920s, *all* cars sold in Japan were made in the United States by Ford and General Motors and sent to Japan in knocked-down kits to be assembled locally. Another early overseas investor was General Electric, which, by 1919, had plants in Europe, Latin America, and Asia.[11]

Although American firms were by far the largest foreign investors, European companies were also moving overseas. Friedrich Bayer purchased an interest in a New York plant in 1865, two years after setting up his plant in Germany. Then, because of high import duties in his overseas markets, he proceeded to establish plants in Russia (1876), France (1882), and Belgium (1908).[12] Bayer, now one of the three largest chemical companies in the world ($21 billion in sales), has operations in 70 countries. Its annual sales in the U.S. alone are over $4 billion. Other European concerns such as Unilever (Dutch-English), Nestlé (Swiss), Philips (Dutch), and Imperial Chemical (English) were also becoming established in various foreign countries.

This clearly illustrates that multinational firms of a sort existed well before World War I. Why then have they only recently become the object of much discussion and investigation? What differences, if any, are there between the international business firm of the early 1900s and the present-day **global company**?

global company   an organization that attempts to standardize operations worldwide in all functional areas

---

* This Ford was no relation to Henry Ford.

Explosive growth

One important difference is the explosive growth in both the size and the number of U.S. and foreign multinational concerns in the last three decades. Although current data as to their number and size do not exist, a study made by the European Community (EC) in 1976 estimated that approximately 10,000 multinational firms existed worldwide—4,534 in Europe and 2,570 in the United States.[13] A good surrogate variable as to the growth of globals and multinationals is the increase in total *foreign direct investment* (FDI).* It has gone from $105 billion in 1967 to $776 billion in 1987—a sevenfold increase in just 20 years.[14] During the same period, U.S. FDI rose from $59 billion to $260 billion—4.5 times the 1967 amount.

We also have estimates of the importance of the globals and multinationals in the world economy. The United Nations Centre on Transnational Corporations states that although most are medium-size companies with annual sales of less than $1 billion, the 56 largest have sales ranging from $10 billion to $100 billion. Moreover, the 600 largest multinational or global firms account for between one fifth and one fourth of the value added in the production of *all the goods in the world's market economies*. The Centre further states that their importance as exporters and importers is even greater. For example, between 80 and 90 percent of U.S. and U.K. exports are associated with multinational or global firms.[15] In Japan, just nine general trading companies account for 45.1 and 76.7 percent of all the country's exports and imports, respectively.[16]

As a result of this expansion, the foreign company's subsidiaries have become increasingly important in the industrial and economic life of many nations, developed and developing. This situation is in sharp contrast to the one that existed when the dominant economic interests were in the hands of local citizens. The expanding importance of foreign-owned firms in local economies is viewed by a number of governments as a threat to their autonomy. However, the 1980s have seen a marked liberalization of government policies and attitudes toward foreign investment in both developed and developing nations. One of the most important reasons for this change in attitude is the realization that most modern commercial technology originates with the multinationals and globals. To be competitive in world markets, firms in these countries must obtain this technology in the form of direct investment, purchase of capital goods, and the right to use the global or multinational firm's expertise.†[17]

Despite this change in attitude, there are still critics of large global firms who cite such statistics as the following to "prove" that host governments are powerless before them:

1. Only 18 nations have gross national products greater than the total annual sales of General Motors, the world's largest worldwide company.

---

* *Foreign direct investment* is sufficient investment to obtain significant management control. In the United States, 10 percent of the stockholders' equity is sufficient; in other countries, it is not considered a direct investment until a share of 20 or 25 percent is reached.

† Granting the right to use a firm's expertise for a fee is called licensing. See Chapter 2 for more details.

■ **TABLE 1–1**

Ranking of Worldwide Companies and Nations according to GNP or Total Sales

Rankings	Nation or Firm	GNP or Total Sales for 1987 ($ billions)
18.	Austria	$116.7
19.	*General Motors*	101.8
20.	Denmark	97.9
21.	Finland	86.3
22.	Norway	81.7
23.	*Royal Dutch Shell*	78.3
24.	South Africa	77.3
25.	*Exxon*	76.4
26.	Argentina	75.8
27.	*Ford Motor*	71.6
28.	Saudi Arabia	68.7
29.	Indonesia	66.0
30.	Turkey	65.4
31.	Poland	63.8
32.	Algeria	63.1
33.	Yugoslavia	60.5
34.	*IBM*	54.2
35.	*Mobil*	51.2
36.	Venezuela	48.3
37.	Thailand	46.8
38.	Greece	46.7
39.	Hong Kong	46.2
40.	*British Petroleum*	45.2
41.	Peru	44.6
42.	*Toyota Motor*	41.5
43.	*IRI* (Italy)	41.3
44.	*General Electric*	39.3
45.	*Daimler-Benz*	37.5
46.	Portugal	34.9
47.	Pakistan	34.6
48.	*Texaco*	34.4
49.	Philippines	34.3
50.	Colombia	33.6

2. GM's total sales surpass the *sum* of the gross national products of 52 nations.[18]

As Table 1–1 illustrates, these statements are certainly true. In fact, if nations and industrial firms are ranked by gross national product and total sales respectively, 48 of the first 100 on the list are industrial firms. We must point out, however, that regardless of the parent company's size, its subsidiaries operate under the authority of the host nation's government. Their affiliates must comply with local laws or be subject to legal action or even **expropriation.*** Notable examples are the loss of Pfizer's and ITT's Chilean

expropriation government seizure of foreign-owned assets for which prompt, adequate, and effective compensation must be made

---

* Expropriation and related subjects are discussed in Chapters 10 and 11.

■ TABLE 1-1
(concluded)

Rankings	Nation or Firm	GNP or Total Sales for 1987 ($ billions)
50.	AT&T	33.6
50.	Israel	33.6
53.	Egypt	32.8
54.	New Zealand	30.6
55.	DuPont	30.5
56.	Volkswagen	30.4
57.	Hitachi	30.3
58.	Fiat	29.6
59.	Malaysia	29.2
60.	Siemens	27.5
61.	Matsushita	27.3
62.	Unilever	27.1
63.	Chrysler	26.3
64.	Philips	26.0
64.	Chevron	26.0
66.	Ireland	25.8
67.	Nissan Motor	25.7
68.	Kuwait	25.6
69.	Hungary	25.1
70.	Renault	24.5
71.	ENI (Italy)	24.2
72.	Syria	23.7
73.	Nestlé	23.6
74.	Nigeria	23.4
75.	U.A.E.	23.3
76.	BASF (Germany)	22.4
77.	Phillip Morris	22.3
78.	CGE (France)	21.2
78.	Elf Aquitaine	21.2
79.	Samsung (Korea)	21.1
80.	Bayer	20.7

Note: Does not include nations that do not report GNPs to World Bank (some communist nations).

Sources: World Bank, *World Tables*, 1988–89 (Washington, D.C.: 1989); "The World's 50 Biggest Industrial Corporations," *Fortune*, August 1, 1988, pp. D3–D4.

subsidiaries and the seizure of Dow Corning's assets in Venezuela. Interestingly, the threat of expropriation has diminished in the 1980s. During the 1970–75 period, there were 336 acts of expropriation, but between 1980 and 1985, there were only 15. Most differences are now being settled by arbitration.[19]

Closer Central Control

A second important difference between the modern global firm and the earlier international company is the much closer control now exercised by headquarters. Even though the subsidiaries are scattered over the globe, management in the home office coordinates and integrates their activities. Such control has been made possible by fast air travel and by the ability to rapidly transmit and analyze large amounts of information via telephone, telex, and computers.

In earlier days, overseas travel was by ship, communications were handled primarily by letter, and once information arrived in the home office, several days were required for processing before top management could act on it. Under those conditions, there was little possibility of closely coordinating foreign operations and the local subsidiaries had to be given considerable independence. In addition, poor transportation facilities between countries and the presence of tariff and nontariff trade barriers made it difficult for a firm in one country to market its products in another. This meant that there was less need for close integration; thus each subsidiary tended to operate in its own local market.

However, these conditions were changing. The formation of regional marketing groups such as the European Community and the European Free Trade Association and the improvements in transportation facilities made intercountry sales much more feasible. Thus, closer central control became both possible and necessary.

Host Nations' Reaction

host nation   nation in which a foreign affiliate is located

As early as the 1950s, **host nation** governments began to realize that the establishment of an increasing number of businesses controlled by managements outside their jurisdiction was resulting in local firms (subsidiaries) that could pursue objectives in conflict with their own. This, they believed, would weaken national sovereignty.

For example, if government leaders believed it necessary to institute a tight monetary policy and thus restrict the amount of capital available for industrial expansion, they feared that foreign-owned subsidiaries might upset their plans by bringing in capital from abroad. If they attempted to raise taxes to reduce purchasing power, absentee owners might shift production elsewhere, and thus sources of employment might be lost.

As governments strove to provide more infrastructure, such as highways, educational facilities, housing, and all the myriad elements of a higher level of living, they required more foreign exchange. These efforts would be weakened by anything that reduced the availability of foreign exchange, such as fees paid to outsiders for management services and technological assistance or rules by home offices prohibiting subsidiaries from exporting or buying lower-priced raw materials in the open market rather than from the parent company.

Just how pervasive these practices were was not clear. The worldwide company was a new concept, and its operations were not fully understood. To be able to cope with such practices, governments had to know more about them. By the early 1970s, various national and international organizations were studying this new kind of business organization. The United Nations established a Commission on Transnational Corporations and an Information and Research Center at UN headquarters to deal on a continuous basis with issues relating to MNE activities. Workshops were set up to train government officials who negotiate with these firms. A U.S. Senate foreign affairs subcommittee conducted an in-depth investigation. All over the world, government technicians, academicians, and business writers were publishing books and studies on the various aspects of the worldwide company.[20]

INTERNATIONAL BUSINESS AS A SEPARATE FIELD OF STUDY

The growing importance of foreign markets to international firms—plus the fact that thousands of concerns were venturing overseas for the first time—made it imperative for managers to know something about the intricacies of doing business abroad. International business was becoming too significant to allow managements to continue to train personnel by sending promising but inexperienced persons to the overseas "minor leagues," and so industry turned to the colleges and universities for assistance in training. This put the responsibility on educators, who soon realized that the teaching tools, which had come primarily from the study of international trade, were inadequate. To rectify this situation, academicians intensified their study and research from which the new field of international business emerged. It has been much expanded from its initial emphasis on international economics and now includes related material from many disciplines, such as sociology, anthropology, jurisprudence, political science, geography, and business administration; today's international business managers must have some knowledge of all of these fields.

Adding international aspects as an appendage to the study of a domestic business function does not provide an adequate framework for examining the differences between the domestic and foreign environments in order to understand how these dissimilarities influence management decisions. International business as a separate field of study provides not only this framework but also a way to study the principal means of conducting international business—the worldwide company, whose management requires an expertise in handling situations rarely found in a purely domestic operation.

However, there are those who argue that a separate field of study is unnecessary because the concepts learned in the functional areas of business are universal and can be applied in any part of the world. Our experience leads us to believe that this argument has some foundation. Certain concepts and business practices can be transferred intact, but herein lies a trap—*not all of them can*. Because of the differences among the foreign environments and the presence of an international environment, some concepts and business practices must be modified, while others cannot be used at all.

WHY IS INTERNATIONAL BUSINESS DIFFERENT?

International business differs from domestic business in that a firm operating across borders must deal with the forces of three kinds of environments—domestic, foreign, and international. In contrast, a firm whose business activities are carried out within the borders of one country needs to be concerned essentially with only the domestic environment. However, no domestic firm is entirely free from foreign or international environmental

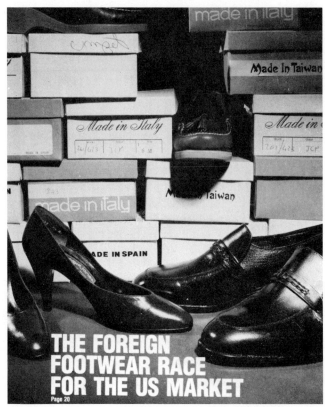

Financial Times of London, World Business Weekly.

forces because the possibility of having to face competition from foreign imports or from foreign competitors that set up operations in its own market is always present. Let us first examine these forces and then see how they operate in the three environments.

Forces in the Environments

environment all the forces surrounding and influencing the life and development of the firm

Environment as used here is the sum total of all the forces surrounding and influencing the life and development of the firm. The forces themselves can be classified as *external* or *internal*. Furthermore, inasmuch as management has no direct control over them (though it can exert an influence), the external forces are commonly called **uncontrollable forces.** They consist of the following forces:

uncontrollable forces external forces over which management has no direct control

1. Competitive.
2. Distributive.
3. Economic.
4. Financial.
5. Legal.

6. Physical.
7. Political.
8. Sociocultural.
9. Labor.
10. Technological.

The elements over which management does have some command are the internal forces, such as the factors of production (capital, raw material, and

controllable forces internal forces that management administers to adapt to changes in the uncontrollable forces

people) and the activities of the organization (personnel, finance, production, and marketing). These are the **controllable forces** that management must administer in order to adapt to changes in the uncontrollable environmental variables. Look at how one change in the political force—the European Community's passage of the Single European Act in 1986—is impacting *all* of the controllable forces of firms worldwide that do business with Western Europe.

This law will eliminate physical (border controls), technical (product standards), and fiscal (different tax and excise duty levels) barriers, thus creating a single internal market of the 320 million inhabitants of the 12 EC member-nations.[21] Although many doubt this goal will be reached by 1992 (the target date), companies are already feeling the impact of this legislation, which some claim is creating a "Fortress Europe."[22]

Hyster Co., a U.S. firm that makes forklift trucks in Europe, had to make changes in its product, suppliers, and shipping pattern to Europe because of a directive on product standards issued to implement the Single European Act. The company was forced to stop shipping certain U.S.-built forklifts directly to its European dealers because the directive requires that they first be certified on EC soil. Now the company must send the forklifts to its Scottish plant to be certified and adorned with a large "E" (for EC) at extra cost. Hyster can no longer use American battery cables because of a required product test—which only one German supplier uses. Altogether, the company has made 15 design changes to conform to the new product standards.[23]

The process of adaptation does not imply that managers must wait passively for changes to occur, to which they then react as Hyster did. As a rule, the most successful administrators are those who are so knowledgeable about the environmental forces that not only are they prepared and waiting, but they may even contribute to these changes. This is, in fact, what the U.S. Department of Commerce has urged businesspeople to do in the case of Europe 1992. They must be so well informed about it that they can alert the government about their problems and concerns, thus enabling officials to discuss those concerns with the EC while there is still time to affect its actions.[24]

The Domestic Environment

domestic environment all the uncontrollable forces originating in the home country that surround and influence the firm's life and development

The **domestic environment** is composed of all the uncontrollable forces originating in the home country that surround and influence the life and development of the firm. Obviously, these are the forces with which managers are most familiar. Being domestic forces does not preclude their affecting foreign operations, however. For example, if the home country is suffering from a shortage of foreign currency, the government may place restrictions on overseas investment to reduce its outflow. As a result, managements of multinationals find that they cannot expand overseas facilities as they would like to do. In another instance from real life, a labor union striking the home-based plants learned that management was supplying parts from its foreign subsidiaries. The strikers contacted the foreign unions, which pledged not to work overtime to supply what the struck plants could not. The impact of this domestic environmental force was felt overseas as well as at home.

Foreign Environments

foreign environment all the uncontrollable forces originating outside the home country that surround and influence the firm

The forces in the **foreign environment** are the same as those in the domestic environment except that they occur in foreign nations.* However, they operate differently for several reasons, including the following:

Different force values.   Even though the kinds of forces in the two environments are identical, their values often differ widely, and at times they are completely opposed to each other. A good example of diametrically opposed political force values and the bewilderment they create for multinational managers is the case of Dresser Industries and the Soviet pipeline. In June 1982, President Reagan extended the American embargo against shipments of equipment for the pipeline to include foreign companies manufacturing equipment under U.S. license. The Dresser home office instructed its French subsidiary to stop work on an order for compressors. In August, however, the French government ordered Dresser-France to defy the embargo and begin scheduled deliveries under penalty of both civil and criminal sanctions. As Dresser's vice president for finance put it, "The order put Dresser between a rock and a hard place."

Changes difficult to assess.   Another problem with the foreign forces is that they are frequently difficult to assess, especially their legal and political elements. A highly nationalistic law may be passed to appease a section of the population. To all outward appearances, a government may appear to be against foreign investment, yet pragmatic leaders may actually encourage it. A good example is Mexico. Legislation was enacted that prohibited foreign firms from having wholly owned subsidiaries, but there was a clause permitting exceptions "if the investment contributes to the welfare of the nation." IBM was successful in obtaining permission to establish a wholly owned subsidiary under this clause.

Forces interrelated.   In the chapters that follow, it will be evident that the forces are often interrelated. This in itself is no novelty, because the same situation confronts the domestic manager. Often different, however, are the types and degrees of interaction that occur. For instance, the combination of high-cost capital and an abundance of unskilled labor in many developing countries may lead to the use of a lower level of technology than would be employed in the more industrialized nations. In other words, given a choice between installing costly, specialized machinery needing few workers or less expensive, general-purpose machinery requiring a larger labor force, management will frequently choose the latter when faced with high interest rates and a large pool of available workers. Another example of interaction is that of the physical and sociocultural forces. Barriers to the free movement of a nation's people, such as mountain ranges or deserts, help maintain pockets of distinct cultures within a country.

* *Foreign* has multiple definitions according to the *American Heritage Dictionary*, including (1) originating from the outside—external, (2) from a country other than one's own, and (3) conducted or involved with other nations or governments. *Extrinsic* is a synonym. Note that we are not using another definition—unfamiliar or strange. Some writers have this last definition in mind when they state that overseas markets in which the firm does business are not foreign because their managers know them well. However, according to any of the first three definitions, the degree of familiarity has no bearing.

The International Environment

international environment
interaction between the domestic and foreign environmental forces

The **international environment** is the interaction between (1) the domestic environmental forces and the foreign environmental forces and (2) the foreign environmental forces of one country and those of another country. This agrees with the definition of *international business*— business whose activities involve the crossing of national borders.

For example, personnel at the headquarters of a multinational or global company work in the international environment if they are involved in any way with another nation, whereas those in a foreign subsidiary do not unless they too are engaged in international trade through exporting or management of other foreign affiliates. In other words, the sales manager of Goodyear-Chile does *not* work in the international environment if he or she sells tires only in Chile. Should Goodyear-Chile export tires to Bolivia, then the sales manager is affected by forces of both the domestic environment of Chile and the foreign environment of Bolivia and therefore is working in the international environment. International organizations whose actions affect the international environment are also properly part of it. These organizations include (1) worldwide bodies (e.g., World Bank), (2) regional economic groupings of nations (e.g., European Community), and (3) organizations of nations bound by industry agreements (e.g., Organization of Petroleum Exporting Countries).

Decision Making More Complex

Those who work in the international environment find that decision making is more complex than it is in a purely domestic environment. Consider managers in the home office who must make decisions affecting subsidiaries in just 10 different countries (many multinationals or globals are in 20 or more countries). They must not only take into account the domestic forces, but they must also evaluate the influence of 10 foreign national environments. Instead of having to consider the effects of a single set of 10 forces, as do their domestic counterparts, they have to contend with 10 sets of 10 forces, *both individually and collectively,* because there may be some interaction.

For example, if management agrees to labor's demands at one foreign subsidiary, chances are it will have to offer a similar settlement at another subsidiary because of the tendency of unions to exchange information across borders. Furthermore, as we shall observe throughout the text, not only are there many sets of forces, but there are also extreme differences among them.

Another common cause of the added complexity of foreign environments is managers' unfamiliarity with other cultures. To make matters worse, they will ascribe to others their own preferences and reactions. Thus, the foreign production manager, facing a backlog of orders, offers the workers extra pay for overtime. When they fail to show up, the manager is perplexed. "Back home, they always want to earn more money." What this manager has failed to understand is that the workers preferred time off to more money. This *unconscious* reference to the manager's own cultural values, called **self-reference criterion,** is probably the biggest cause of international business blunders. Successful administrators are careful to examine a problem in terms of the local cultural traits as well as their own.

self-reference criterion
unconscious reference to one's own cultural values when judging behavioral actions of others in a new and different environment

FORMAT OF THIS BOOK

The three environments and their forces that we have been examining provide the format for this book. After describing the nature of international business in Section One, we examine the international organizations and monetary aspects of the international environment in Section Two. In Section Three, we analyze the uncontrollable forces that make up the foreign environments and illustrate their effect on management practices. Finally, we reverse the procedure in Section Four and discuss management functions, demonstrating how they are influenced by the uncontrollable forces.

Let us now take a moment to clarify some of the international business terminology.

INTERNATIONAL BUSINESS TERMINOLOGY

International business, like every field of study, has its own terminology. To assist you in learning the special vocabulary, an important function of every introductory course, a glossary has been included at the end of the book and the most important terms are listed at the beginning of each chapter.

As with any new discipline, a number of words are employed whose definitions vary among users. *Global,* for example, is becoming the most widely accepted term to describe an organization that produces in, markets in, and obtains the factors of production from multiple countries for the purpose of furthering overall enterprise benefits. Yet some people use such terms as *transnational, supranational,* and *multinational* for global. Furthermore, *multinational* may have two distinct meanings, depending on whether the user is describing *ownership* or the *areas of operation.* For example, multinational usually describes a firm that operates in more than one country; however, government officials in the developing nations and some international organizations use multinational to indicate a joint venture whose owners (governments or groups of stockholders) come from three or more nations.[25] These same officials call a firm operating in two or more countries a *transnational.*[26] This adds to the confusion because for years, Europeans have used transnational to describe a company formed by a merger of two firms of approximately the same size that are from different countries. It is not a joint venture. Four of the largest are (1) Unilever (Dutch-English), (2) Shell (Dutch-English), (3) Azko-Enka (Dutch-German), and (4) ABB, a merger of ASEA (Swedish) and Brown-Boveri (Swiss).

Multinational, Global, and Worldwide

Some people use the words *world* and *global* interchangeably with *multinational,* but increasingly, *global* is being used to describe a firm that attempts to standardize operations in all functional areas, but that responds to national market differences when necessary.

A global firm's management:

1. Searches the world for (*a*) market opportunities, (*b*) threats from competitors, (*c*) sources of products, raw materials, and financing, and (*d*) personnel. In other words, it has global vision.

2. Seeks to maintain a presence in key markets.

3. Looks for similarities, not differences, among markets.

multinational company an organization with multicountry affiliates, each of which formulates its own business strategy based on perceived market differences

Those who use *global* in this manner are defining a **multinational company** as a kind of holding company with a number of overseas operations, each of which is left to adapt its products and marketing strategy to what local managers perceive to be unique aspects of their individual markets.[27] *Multidomestic* has also been suggested as a synonym for multinational.[28] We shall use **worldwide company (WWC)** to mean either a global or a multinational firm.

worldwide company either a global or a multinational company

Perhaps the Japanese have the solution to the usage of terms with multiple definitions; they call the technique of adapting to local conditions, *dochakuka*, meaning "global localization," which comes from Japanese agriculture where it means adjusting the planting, fertilizing, and harvesting methods to meet local soil conditions.[29]

To complete this discussion, we need to mention that the term *supranational corporation* was described in a publication of the United Nations as one in which *both* the operation and ownership are multinational; yet many reserve this term for a corporate form that does not now exist—one that would be chartered by an international agency such as the United Nations.

Definitions Used in This Text

In this text, we will employ the definitions listed below, which are generally accepted by businesspeople. Although we primarily use the terms *global* and *worldwide*, at times multinational enterprise (MNE) may be used interchangeably with worldwide company (WWC), inasmuch as both terms are employed in the literature and in practice.

1. *International business* is business whose activities involve the crossing of national borders. This definition includes not only international trade and foreign manufacturing but also the growing service industry in such areas as transportation, tourism, banking, advertising, construction, retailing, wholesaling, and mass communications.

2. *Foreign business* denotes the domestic operations within a foreign country. This term is sometimes used interchangeably with international business by some writers.

3. *Multinational company (MNC)* with multicountry affiliates, each of which formulates its own business strategy based on perceived market differences. (See Figure 1–1.)

4. *Global company (GC)* is an organization that attempts to standardize operations worldwide in all functional areas.

5. *Worldwide company (WWC)* refers to both global and multinational companies.

CENTRAL THEME OF THIS BOOK

A solid understanding of the business concepts and techniques employed in the United States and other advanced industrial nations is a requisite for success in international business. However, because transactions take place across national borders, three environments—domestic, foreign, and international—

WORLDVIEW

Executives Cite Globalization As Major Concern of U.S. Companies

A recent *Fortune* survey of top American chief executive officers listed progress toward globalization as one of their major concerns.

The United States has been slow in its move toward globalization, however, according to Nolan, Norton & Co., KPMG Peat Marwick's international specialists in information technology. "This lack of progress has occurred despite the fact that the necessary components of the communications infrastructure have been improving rapidly over the past decade," says John L. Daniels, a Nolan Norton principal. "Businesses fail to comprehend that globalization is important, what globalization means, or how to become global.

Doing Business—How, Not Where

Daniels explains that many companies confuse the term "global" with "multinational," "multidomestic," or "worldwide." "Globalization is not an easy idea to grasp because it is more of a business concept—*how* you do business—than a geographic notion—*where* you do business," he says.

"A global company has a sphere of activity and awareness that stretches beyond where it operates to where it earns revenues, where its sources are, and wherever it carries out activities or has a relationship with an outside party. In a global business, relationships with suppliers, distributors, and customers are coordinated across functions and across geographical boundaries."

According to Daniels, recent research on Japanese manufacturing concerns indicates that Japanese firms have an edge over U.S. firms because they tend to coordinate cross-functionally better than their U.S. counterparts. "Canon, of Japan, supplies products to many

high tech companies around the world; they also act as distributors to many of these same companies within Japan. They expand their business relationships with one company by sharing the knowledge of their relationship with that company cross-functionally," he explains.

Wired to the World

Daniels and Caroline Frost, a manager at the Nolan Norton Institute, have helped foreign and domestic companies explore global business opportunities offered by information technology.

To be global, businesses shouldn't be concerned about which functions are centralized and which are decentralized, Daniels and Frost point out. While most companies have not yet made the required investment, it is possible today to wire the world to allow members of a company to connect with everyone else in that company, as well as anyone needed outside the company.

Daniels cites the example of IBM. "Its three Nobel prize winners in the past two years were Europeans. Two are working in IBM's Zurich, Switzerland, lab on superconductivity and a powerful new microscope; and Benoit Mendelbroit, a Frenchman, is working in a U.S. lab on fractal geometry. IBM certainly believes that not all good ideas are found within 25 miles of Armonk, New York."

The Nolan Norton team emphasizes that becoming global is one of the most important transformations that companies will make in the information age. Daniels and Frost predict that companies that succeed in globalization will be viable well into the 21st century.

may be involved instead of just one; and thus in international business, the concepts and techniques employed in domestic operations must often be adapted to local conditions. International managers who have discovered that there are differences in the environmental forces are better prepared to decide when such adaptations are necessary. To be sure, no one can be an expert on these forces for all nations, but just knowing that there may be differences will cause people to "work with their antennas extended." In other words, they will be aware that when they enter the international business scene, they must be

■ FIGURE 1–1   Overseas Locations of a Service WWC, Hospital Corporation of America

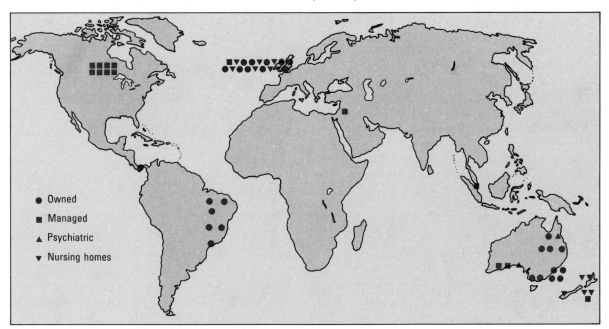

● Owned
■ Managed
▲ Psychiatric
▼ Nursing homes

Source: Hospital Corporation of America, 1988.

on the lookout for important variations in many of the forces that they take as given in the domestic environment. It is to the study of the three environments that this text is directed.

SUMMARY

Among the most significant business developments in the last 40 years have been the rapid growth of international business and the proliferation of multinational and global firms. Although a number of companies have been engaged in this area for nearly a century, the explosive growth in the size and number of international firms is a recent phenomenon, as is the much closer central control exercised by managements. This growth has brought about a need for more managers who can function effectively in the international business environment. To supply this need, industry has turned to colleges and universities for assistance in training. A separate field of study, international business, has evolved from an initial emphasis on international economics and now includes material from many academic disciplines.

International business differs from its domestic counterpart in that it involves three environments rather than one. This makes decision making more complex. Although the kinds of forces are the same in the domestic and foreign environments, their values often differ. Changes in foreign environments are at times more difficult to assess.

QUESTIONS

1. What are the differences between worldwide, global, and multinational companies?

2. Give examples to show how an international business manager might manipulate one of the control-lable forces in answer to a change in the uncontrol-lable forces.

3. A nation whose GNP is smaller than the sales volume of a global firm is in no position to enforce

its wishes on the local subsidiary of that firm. True or false? Please explain.

4. We know that a number of firms have been active in international business for nearly a century. Why, then, has the international firm attracted so much attention in the last two decades?

5. Business is business, and every firm has to produce and market its goods. Why, then, cannot the managers apply the techniques and concepts they have learned in their own country to other areas of the world?

6. What do you believe makes foreign business activities more complex than purely domestic ones?

7. Discuss some possible conflicts between host governments and foreign-owned companies.

8. "International Business" is just a new name for the old "International Trade" course. True or false? Discuss.

9. Why, in your opinion, do the authors regard the use of the self-reference criterion as "probably the biggest cause of international business blunders?" Can you think of an example?

10. You have decided to take a job after graduation in your hometown. Why should you study international business?

MINICASE 1–1

Dansk Manufacturing (Galawi) Limited

In the developing nation of Galawi,* the president and his cabinet are discussing the results of a meeting with Dick Petersen, managing director of Dansk Manufacturing (Galawi) Limited.

President:
Petersen insists that our proposed law to increase company-paid benefits to employees will raise their costs so much they won't be able to compete in the export market anymore. He says that if they can't export, their sales volume will be so low they won't make enough profit to keep the company going. He thinks the home office may order him to close the Galawi operation down. What's your opinion, Mojabum?

Mr. Mojabum, secretary of labor:
Don't forget—we've promised the leaders of the union that we are going to obtain higher benefits for their people. We can't go back on our word.

President:
Also, Mojabum, have you considered what the reaction of the workers might be if they don't get the benefits that this law will provide?

Mojabum:
That's another concern, Mr. President. This proposed law has received quite a bit of publicity. If it doesn't go into effect, we may face a strike or worse.

President:
Such as?

* Although Galawi is fictitious, the conditions are not.

Mojabum:
Perhaps some civil unrest, even public demonstrations.

Mr. Akam, secretary of commerce:
That could be serious, I admit, but on the other hand, Galawi needs this company. It provides jobs for over 300 people.

Mr. Bonat, secretary of the treasury:
Dansk provides a lot more. We know from their tax return that their total sales were over 25 million Galawi francs (Gf) last year. Even with the special tax concession we offered to get them to locate in Galawi, they still paid 2.5 million Gf. Furthermore, Dansk brought in $1 million from their exports last year, and we need that foreign exchange to help pay for oil imports. Think about it—that's 5 million Gf worth of dollars they earned for this country.

Mr. Sassou, secretary of the interior:
Yes, but they also consume foreign exchange, don't they? They certainly have to import some raw materials, spare parts, and machinery that they can't find here. How much does that amount to?

Bonat (treasury):
Yes, they do use some of what they earn—about 40 percent. But it is still a net gain for the country. In fact, you may have forgotten that when they asked to come here, we stipulated that they would have to earn, as a minimum, sufficient foreign exchange to cover their import needs *and* any profits they wished to return to Denmark.

Sassou (interior):

Well, I didn't take part in the negotiations so I don't know all of the details. You mentioned profits. You know that some leaders of the opposition are making speeches about the fact that Dansk is bleeding our country with all the money they're taking out of Galawi. This could cause political unrest. As the one responsible for law and order in this country, this bothers me.

Akam (commerce):

That just isn't so. Dansk agreed not to take out any profits for five more years. They're reinvesting their profits as they said they would. Their operation is growing, they're hiring more people, reducing imports because they're making more components of their products locally, and they're expanding their exports.

Bonat (treasury):

Also, their tax concession runs out in five years, and then they'll pay a 50 percent higher rate, the same as our local businesses.

Akam (commerce):

That's good, because I've had a lot of complaints from businesspeople about the tax preference Dansk gets. By the way, another complaint is about the higher wages they pay. A number of local companies say they're losing their good people to Dansk.

Mojabum (labor):

Yes, but the unions love it. Not only do their members at Dansk get better pay, but so do those working in other places because those other firms have been forced to compete in the labor market.

President:

Nevertheless, this may be getting out of hand. Akam, you'd better talk to Petersen about keeping his pay scales closer to what others are offering. We don't want an inflation on our hands.

Akam (commerce):

I shall, but I do want to remind you that Dansk is not robbing all of the good people from the others. For example, they bring labor trainers from the home plant to train many unskilled people they hire, and they continuously send young supervisors, technical people, and middle managers to Denmark for training.

Dr. Boya (secretary of education):

Let me remind you of one development that I'm enthusiastic about. Dansk is now going to offer six scholarships annually to sons and daughters of local employees to study engineering or business administration in Denmark. It seems to me, Akam, that Dansk is helping educate our people, many of whom will go to work in the firms that are complaining about losing employees to Dansk. They have also brought in technology that this country had never seen before. One thing, though, we've got to find ways to inform the public about the benefits Dansk is bringing to Galawi. What Sassou told us alarms me.

Akam (commerce):

I agree—it is alarming. By the way, I forgot to tell you about a study our economists finished yesterday. They calculate that every Gf spent by a company such as Dansk has a multiplier effect of almost two; that is, if Dansk is spending locally 13 or 14 million Gf for labor, local purchases, and taxes, this is worth perhaps 25 million Gf to the economy as the workers spend their wages in stores, whose owners in turn make purchases, and so forth. We need to consider this effect when we try to calculate the contribution of companies like Dansk to our economy.

Mojabum (labor):

You're right, and this is something the public needs to know. But let's get back to the proposed labor law. Why, do you suppose, haven't Galawi Manufacturing and Inland Steel Products complained about it?

President:

Probably because they're locally owned and not able to move like Dansk can. Don't forget, Dansk is a subsidiary of a multinational, and Galawi is just one of their markets. Also, these firms don't export either, so they're not worrying about keeping costs down to compete in the world market. Well, that's it, gentlemen. We can (1) get the law passed to satisfy the union and perhaps lose a company that hires 300 workers and earns valuable foreign exchange, among other things, (2) stop the law from being passed so as not to lose Dansk, but damage our relations with the union, or (3) come up with some sort of compromise. Let's meet again next week with your recommendations.

1. What are the advantages and the disadvantages for Galawi of Dansk's presence in the country?

2. Can Dansk do anything to improve its situation in Galawi?

3. What do you recommend the government do with respect to the proposed law?

SUPPLEMENTARY READINGS

"Ad Fad." *The Wall Street Journal,* May 12, 1988, p. 1.

Boddewyn, J. J.; Robin Soehl; and Jacques Picard. "Standardization in International Marketing: Is Ted Levitt in Fact Right?" *Business Horizons,* November–December 1986, pp. 69–75.

Cecchini, P. *The Benefits of a Single Market.* London: Wildwood House, 1988.

"Commerce Launches FTA Outreach Program." *Business America,* January 30, 1989, pp. 26–27.

"Community's Goal: A State of Oneness." *Insight,* June 20, 1988, pp. 8–13.

"Corporate Needs and Their Implications for an International Business Curriculum." *Issues in International Business,* Summer–Fall 1985, pp. 33–37.

"Europe's Global Clout Is Limited by Divisions 1992 Can't Paper Over." *The Wall Street Journal,* February 13, 1989, p. 1.

"Europe Will Become Economic Superpower as Barriers Crumble." *The Wall Street Journal,* December 29, 1988, p. 1.

Europe without Frontiers—Completing the Internal Market. Luxembourg: European Community, 1987.

"Fortress Europe." *International Management,* December 1988, pp. 24–30.

"Goodbye Global Ads: Global Village Is Fantasy Land for Big Marketers." *Advertising Age,* November 16, 1987, pp. 22–23.

Japan 1989. Tokyo: Keizai Koho Center, 1989.

Levitt, Theodore. "The Globalization of Markets." *The McKinsey Quarterly,* Summer 1984, pp. 2–29.

"1992: The Bad News." *International Management,* September 1988, pp. 22–26.

Quelch, John A., and Edward J. Hoff. "Customizing Global Marketing." *Harvard Business Review,* May–June 1986, pp. 59–68.

"Scrambling for 1992." *Business Marketing,* February 1989, pp. 49–59.

"The European Community Comes of Age with Its Single Market." *Business International,* June 27, 1988, pp. 193–94

"The Issue Globals Don't Talk About." *International Management,* September 1987, pp. 37–42.

"The Single Market: Europe Looks to the Future." *Deutsche Bank Bulletin,* June 1988, p. 1–5.

"The 21st-Century Executive." *U.S. News & World Report,* March 7, 1988, pp. 48–51.

Transnational Corporations in World Development. New York: United Nations Centre on Transnational Corporations, 1988.

"U.S. Business Should Prepare Now for EC 1992." *Business America,* October 24, 1988, pp. 12–16.

"U.S.–Canada Free Trade Agreement." *Business America,* October 26, 1987, pp. 2–8.

Wilkins, Myra. *The Emergence of Multinational Enterprise: American Business Abroad from the Colonial Era to 1914.* Cambridge, Mass.: Harvard University Press, 1970.

————. *The Maturing of the Multinational Enterprise, 1914–1970.* Cambridge, Mass.: Harvard University Press, 1974.

ENDNOTES

1. Lee Nehrt, *Business and International Education* (Washington, D.C.: American Council on Education, May 1977).

2. Stephen J. Kobrin, *International Expertise in American Business* (New York: Institute of International Education, 1984).

3. "Business Bulletin," *The Wall Street Journal,* November 6, 1986, p. 1.

4. "Corporate Employment Needs and Their Implications for an International Business Curriculum," *Issues in International Business,* Summer/Fall 1985, pp. 33–37.

5. Donald Mulvihill, "How AACSB Schools Are Meeting the International Business Requirements," paper presented at the Annual Meeting of AIB, Montreal, October 15–17, 1981.

6. Kobrin, *International Expertise in American Business,* p. 54. There is a popular saying, "The best language of business is the language of the customer."

7. Ibid., p. 39.

8. All the companies and brands listed are foreign owned except Nabisco.

9. Warren Keegan, "Global Competition: Strategic Alternatives," paper presented on January 31, 1989.

10. Mira Wilkins, *The Emergence of Multinational Enterprise: American Business Abroad from the Colonial Era to 1914* (Cambridge, Mass.: Harvard University Press, 1970), pp. 1–212. This is a classic history of the early multinational firms.

11. Mira Wilkins, *The Maturing of the Multinational Enterprise, 1914–1970* (Cambridge, Mass.: Harvard University Press, 1974), pp. 1–83.

12. Christopher Tugendhat, *The Multinationals* (New York: Random House, 1972), p. 12.

13. "More Multinationals in the EEC than in the U.S.," *Business International,* August 6, 1976, p. 254.

14. Sidney E. Rolfe, *The Multinational Corporation* (New York: Foreign Policy Association, 1969), p. 38; and *Japan 1989* (Tokyo: Keizai Koho Center, 1989), p. 58.

15. *Transnational Corporations in World Development* (New York: United Nations Centre on Transnational Corporations, 1988), p. 16.

16. *Japan 1989*, p. 46.

17. *Transnational Corporations in World Development*, pp. 6–10.

18. See Table 1, Basic Indicators, pp. 222–23, and Box A, p. 289, in *World Development Report 1988* (Washington, D.C.: World Bank, 1988).

19. *Transnational Corporations in World Development*, pp. 314–16.

20. There are literally dozens of these studies. Among those with heavy impact were Vernon's *Sovereignty at Bay*, Tugendhat's *Multinationals*, Servan-Schreiber's *American Challenge*, and the continuing reports published by the United Nations Centre on Transnational Corporations.

21. European Community, *Europe without Frontiers—Completing the Internal Market*, p. 29.

22. "Scrambling for 1992," *Business Marketing*, February 1989, pp. 49–59.

23. "Obstacle Course," *The Wall Street Journal*, January 19, 1989, p. 1.

24. "U.S. Business Should Prepare Now for EC 1992," *Business America*, October 24, 1988, p. 12–16.

25. A shipping company, Multinational Shipping of the Caribbean, has been formed by eight Latin American governments.

26. There has been much discussion in the United Nations over whether to use multinational or transnational. In the first study prepared by the UN Secretariat for the Group of Eminent Persons who were chosen to study multinationals, the term *multinational* was used. However, the report by the Group of Eminent Persons noted that *"Transnational* would better convey the notion that these firms operate from home bases across national borders." During discussion of this report, Latin American representatives noted that multinational was already being used in a different context. The UN Economic and Social Council replaced multinational with transnational in resolutions 1908 and 1913, when it established the Commission on Transnational Corporations. The commission then decided it should work on the definition of transnational. As yet, no decision has been reached. Other UN-affiliated organizations, such as the International Labor Organization, still use *multinational enterprise*. From *Multinational Production Enterprises*, UN Industrial Development Organization, September 10, 1985, pp. 1–3.

27. Warren Keegan, "Global Competition: Strategic Alternatives," paper for the Lubin Graduate School of Business, Pace University, New York, January 24, 1989, pp. 6-13.

28. Thomas Hout, Michael E. Porter, and Eileen Rudden, "How Global Companies Win Out," *Harvard Business Review*, September-October 1982, pp. 98-110.

29. "Business Buzzwords," *International Management*, February 1989, p. 15.

30. The supranational firm is discussed in *The Development of Management Consultancy* (New York: United Nations, 1973), p.15.

Chapter 2

International Trade and Foreign Investment

Exporting isn't always possible . . .

Usually our approach has been to begin with direct export of goods and services. With the EC, we began with direct investment. EC restrictions are very efficient at controlling trade.

> Kim Song Whan, international finance director, Lucky-Goldstar (a Korean conglomerate ranked 32nd in the Fortune International 500 with sales of $14 billion)

Everything here is so cheap!

> Japanese real estate agent visiting Manhattan

LEARNING OBJECTIVES

In this chapter, you will study:

1. The magnitude of international trade and how it has grown.

2. The direction of trade (who trades with whom).

3. The value of analyzing trade statistics.

4. The growth, magnitude, and direction of foreign investment.

5. The reasons for going abroad.

6. The weaknesses in using GNP/capita as a basis for comparing economies.

7. The international market entry methods.

8. The importance of international licensing.

KEY WORDS AND CONCEPTS

- Portfolio investment
- Direct investment
- GNP/capita
- Multinational economic unions
- Twin factories
- Indirect exporting
- Direct exporting
- Sales company
- Joint venture
- Competitive alliance
- Management contract
- Licensing
- Franchising
- Contract manufacturing

BUSINESS INCIDENT

Du Pont, a true global company . . .

Du Pont (total sales—$32.92 billion, 9th in the Fortune 500 and 24th in Forbes' international ranking) is a huge global company by any standard of measurement. The company manufactures in 35 countries and markets in more than 150. One of every four employees works outside the United States. In addition to having wholly owned subsidiaries, it is a partner with Philips-Holland in a joint venture that is the world's largest producer of audio compact discs. A joint venture with Mitsubishi Rayon is an important synthetic fiber manufacturer in Japan. In 1988 alone, Du Pont entered into nine joint ventures in countries such as Korea, Thailand, India, France, and the United Kingdom.

In 1988, Du Pont's exports from the United States amounted to $4.20 billion (12.7 percent of total sales), and its sales from foreign plants reached $12.9 billion (39.2 percent of total sales). Overseas investment was $1.6 billion, an increase of 15 percent over the previous year, and represented 37 percent of its total capital expenditures. According to Richard Heckert, Du Pont's chairman, his company's goal is to expand what he calls international sales (by foreign affiliates) to 50 percent of total sales by 1995. Presently, the company's international business (U.S. exports plus sales by foreign subsidiaries) composes 51.9 percent of total sales, up from 43.2 percent just four years before.

Source: Du Pont, Annual Report, 1988.

Du Pont's experience in augmenting both aspects of its international business—*exports* and *sales by overseas subsidiaries*—is representative of the performance of many global and multinational companies. However, involvement in international business activities is not confined to Fortune 500 manufacturing firms such as Du Pont. Exports and overseas production of services and exports of raw materials have also grown, as has the participation of smaller firms in world markets.

As you saw in the case of Du Pont, to increase sales by their foreign affiliates, these firms must continue to invest in their production and marketing facilities. In this chapter, we shall examine the two topics that are directly related to exports and sales by foreign affiliates: (1) foreign trade, which includes exports and imports, and (2) foreign direct investment that must be made in these affiliates. We shall also look at the various ways that firms enter foreign markets.

INTERNATIONAL TRADE

Volume of Trade

By 1987, the volume of international trade in goods and services measured in current dollars had surpassed $3 trillion.[1] Of this amount, exports of merchandise were $2.48 billion, 19 times what they were in 1960 (see Table 2–1). To be sure, a large part of this increase was the result of inflation, but even in constant dollars, the dollar volume increased 4.35 times (5.8 percent annually).[2] You can appreciate its magnitude by noting that this figure is larger than the gross national product of every country in the world except the United States. One fourth of everything grown or made on earth is exported.

How even has this growth been? Have some nations fared better than others? Generally, the exports of most nations have grown at or near the world average. However, Germany, Japan, France, and Italy have exceeded the world average, as has OPEC; but due to greatly lower oil prices, the value of OPEC's exports is only 40 percent of what it was in 1980, when oil prices were much higher. Much of the EC's increase has come from the admission of six new members, while the relatively low growth rate of EFTA is the result of losing Denmark, Great Britain, and Portugal to the EC. The export growth of the United States and LAIA lagged considerably behind the world average.

The quadrupling of world exports in the relatively short period of 27 years is an indication to business people that their opportunities to export are increasing, but the export growth of individual nations signifies that they must also expect greater competition from imports in their own markets. Figures 2–1a and 2–1b illustrate how the internationalization of competition has affected the United States in certain industries. Note, for example, that while computer exports are 36 percent of U.S. production, imports make up 31 percent of U.S. consumption. Over half (65 percent) of the U.S. consumption of footwear is provided by imports, but only 4 percent of American footwear is sent abroad.

Direction of Trade

What are the destinations of these $3 trillion in exports? If you have never examined trade flows, you may believe that they consist mainly of manufac-

■ TABLE 2-1
World Trade in
Merchandise Exports
(FOB values; in billions
of current U.S. dollars)

	1960	1970	1980	1986	1987	Average Annual Percentage Increase
Total	$128	$314	$2,003	$2,117	$2,480	11.58%
Developed countries	86	225	1,268	1,471	1,747	11.78
West Germany[a]	12	35	193	246	298	12.61
United States	20	43	221	206	245	9.70
Japan	4	19	129	209	229	17.16
France	7	18	111	119	142	11.77
Great Britain	10	19	110	107	131	10.00
Italy	4	13	78	98	117	13.29
Developing countries	27	56	213	422	489	11.28
OPEC	n.e.	18	307	115	120	11.78[b]
Centrally planned economies						
Europe and Russia	13	31	157	190	205	10.73
USSR	6	13	76	97	102	11.06
EC	30[c]	88[c]	662[d]	790[e,f]	951	13.63
EFTA	18[g]	51[h]	117[i]	133[j]	160	8.40
LAIA	9	13	81	71	77	8.25

Notes: n.e. = Nonexistent.
EC = European Community.
EFTA = European Free Trade Association.
LAIA = Latin American Integration Association (formerly LAFTA).
[a]Includes exports to East Germany.
[b]For years 1970 through 1987.
[c]Original 6 members only (Belgium, Luxembourg, France, West Germany, Italy, and the Netherlands).
[d]Includes original 6 plus Denmark, Ireland, and Great Britain.
[e]And beyond includes Greece.
[f]And beyond includes Spain and Portugal.
[g]Original 7 members (Austria, Denmark, Norway, Portugal, Sweden, Great Britain, and Switzerland).
[h]Includes Finland as associate member.
[i]Includes Iceland and excludes Great Britain and Denmark.
[j]And beyond excludes Portugal.
Sources: United Nations *Bulletin of Statistics,* June 1988, pp. 112–273, and various earlier issues.

tured goods exported by the industrialized nations to developing countries in return for raw materials. Note, though, that this is not so. Over three fourths of the developed nations' trade is with one another. However, it is true that the major part (65 percent) of the LDCs' exports also go to the industrialized countries. The main exceptions to this generality are Japan, the United States, and the centrally planned economies.

Japan and the United States—Exceptions.   Japan, being entirely dependent on foreign sources for raw materials, must import to survive. In fact, until the 1980s, Japan behaved more like a resource-poor developing nation than a rich one. It imported raw materials, processed them, and exported the finished products. The distribution system for imports, dominated by large, well-established general trading companies, was designed to provide industry with the raw materials and components it needed and to secure outlets for its production. As other industrialized nations have imposed import restrictions on Japanese exports to protect their home industries, the trading companies

■ **FIGURE 2–1a   Exports—Percent of Total U.S. Production**

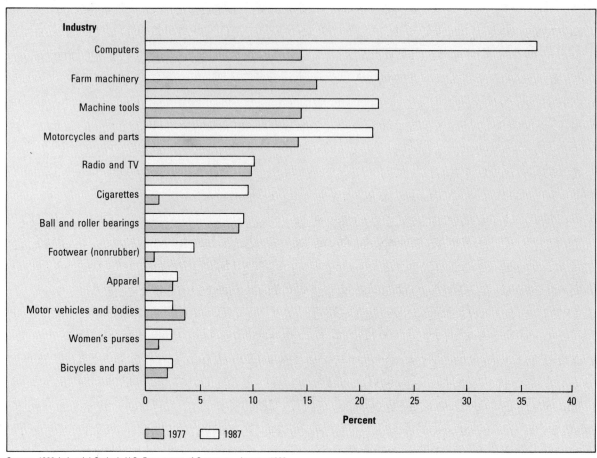

Source: *1988 Industrial Outlook,* U.S. Department of Commerce, January 1988.

have increased their efforts to sell to the LDCs.* You can see the results of these efforts in Table 2–2. While the developed countries as a whole sent 77.9 percent of their exports to other developed countries (DCs) and only 17.9 percent to the LDCs, just 62.6 percent of Japan's exports went to the DCs, and 32.2 percent went to developing nations.

Interestingly, U.S. exports were in about the same proportions, but for somewhat different reasons. American companies have a significantly greater presence in these areas in the form of subsidiaries that are captive customers for their American owners, and in some Southeast Asian countries, buyers still remember that Japan was an aggressor nation.

Centrally planned economies—Another exception.†   In the case of the centrally planned economies, the reasons for their direction of trade are

---

* The nine largest Japanese trading companies, called *sogo shoshas,* account for nearly half of Japan's exports and 70 percent of its imports. See Chapter 13 for more discussion of the *sogo shoshas.*

† *Centrally planned economies* is the name given by the UN to nations where there is little free market activity and the government owns all major factors of production. The governments attempt to plan all activity.

■ **FIGURE 2–1b   Imports—Percent of Total U.S. Consumption**

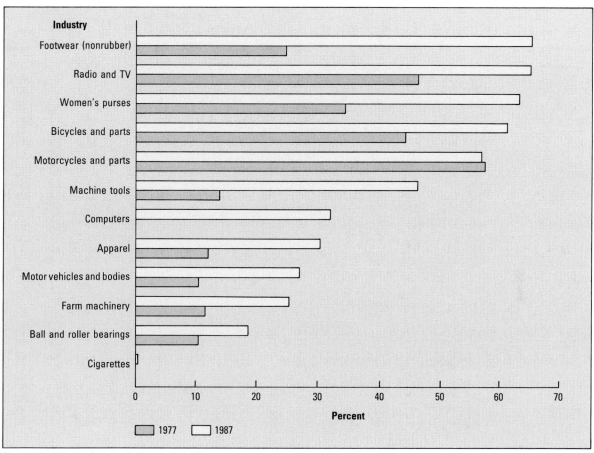

Source: *1988 Industrial Outlook*, U.S. Department of Commerce, January 1988.

essentially political. These countries as a group have attempted to be as self-sufficient as possible and tend to trade with the West only for goods and services that are unavailable within the Eastern bloc. However, even this trade has been somewhat restricted by their lack of foreign exchange. The Eastern-bloc nations have simply not been able to produce the kinds and quality of goods that the Western nations will pay for. Furthermore, the West, for political and security reasons, has placed restrictions on the kinds of products that it will sell to the East. For example, most Western nations refuse to sell any high-tech products, such as super computers and sophisticated electronic equipment, that they believe will aid the Eastern-bloc military effort. You may recall that Mitsubishi, a Japanese firm, was severely criticized for selling to Russia the machinery to produce more silent-running submarine propellers. The United States claimed that this was a severe setback to its submarine detection methods.

The changing direction of trade.   The percentages in Table 2–2 also indicate how the direction of trade changes. In 1980, only 47.5 percent of Japan's exports went to the developed countries while the LDCs received 45.4 percent.

■ **TABLE 2–2   Direction of Trade for Selected Regions and Countries (Percentage of region's or country's total merchandise exports to regions or country in columns)**

| Exports from | Year | Exports to | | | | | | | | | | | | |
		DC	U.S.	Can.	Jap.	USSR	EC	EFTA	LDC	D.A.	D.Am.	OPEC	CPE	CPEA
Developed countries	1960	70.5%	10.3%	5.7%	2.9%	1.2%	24.4%	18.8%	25.5%	6.2%	11.0%	n.e.	2.9%	0.5%
(DC)	1970	76.9	12.8	5.1	3.9	5.2	39.5	9.4	18.7	4.1	8.3	3.4%	3.1	0.6
	1980	71.2	9.7	3.4	3.2	1.9	41.1	9.0	23.3	5.2	6.0	7.9	3.6	1.1
	1987	77.9	14.9	4.4	3.7	1.2	43.3	8.3	17.9	2.6	4.0	3.6	2.2	1.3
United States (U.S.)	1960	63.8	—	18.3	7.1	0.2	19.3	11.9	34.7	2.4	17.4	n.e.	1.0	0.0
	1970	69.5	—	20.7	10.8	0.3	26.6	4.0	29.6	2.3	15.2	4.8	0.8	0.0
	1980	59.8	—	15.7	9.5	0.7	24.8	3.7	36.2	2.9	17.6	8.1	1.8	1.7
	1987	64.1	—	23.4	11.0	0.6	23.3	2.5	30.9	1.7	13.8	4.3	0.9	1.4
Canada (Can.)	1960	91.7	56.6	—	3.3	0.2	8.2	19.5	7.6	0.5	3.5	n.e.	0.7	0.2
	1970	90.7	65.4	—	4.7	0.6	16.4	1.8	7.4	0.7	4.3	1.1	0.8	0.8
	1980	85.2	63.4	—	5.7	2.0	12.8	1.5	10.5	1.4	5.1	2.9	2.7	1.1
	1987	90.0	75.5	—	5.4	0.6	7.4	0.8	8.1	0.7	3.4	1.3	0.8	1.2
Japan (Jap.)	1960	47.7	27.4	3.0	—	1.5	4.3	5.7	50.6	8.6	6.8	n.e.	1.6	0.2
	1970	54.6	31.1	2.9	—	1.8	11.2	3.0	40.0	5.6	5.8	5.1	2.3	3.1
	1980	47.5	24.5	1.9	—	2.1	13.2	2.7	45.4	4.6	6.6	14.2	2.8	4.3
	1987	62.6	36.7	2.4	—	1.1	15.9	3.1	32.2	1.6	3.5	5.0	2.5	3.8
USSR	1960	19.2	0.4	0.1	1.4	—	6.7	6.2	6.6	1.8	1.8	n.e.	56.1	17.3
	1970	21.2	0.5	0.1	3.0	—	10.8	4.2	21.0	4.5	5.1	2.9	52.8	5.0
	1980	36.1	0.3	neg.	1.9	—	21.9	7.3	18.5	1.8	4.8	2.3	42.1	3.2
	1987	21.2	0.4	neg.	1.4	—	14.9	4.4	14.7	1.5	6.3	1.0	51.5	6.0
European Community	1960	71.9	7.5	1.0	0.7	1.4	34.5	21.7	22.4	9.8	5.2	n.e.	4.1	0.8
(EC)*	1970	80.5	8.1	1.3	1.2	1.2	48.9	16.8	14.0	4.9	3.9	3.4	4.0	0.4
	1980	77.7	5.6	0.7	1.0	1.6	53.6	11.9	17.6	6.5	3.0	7.8	3.5	0.4
	1987	83.7	8.7	1.1	1.7	1.1	57.9	11.0	12.7	3.4	2.2	4.0	2.3	0.7
European Free Trade	1960	71.3	8.7	3.7	0.7	1.2	24.1	21.9	24.6	6.7	4.9	n.e.	3.5	0.7
Association	1970	82.2	6.6	1.3	1.3	2.8	26.4	26.4	10.8	3.5	3.6	1.8	6.6	0.4
(EFTA)†	1980	79.6	4.9	0.7	1.3	3.4	53.1	15.3	13.3	3.6	2.9	5.0	6.6	0.5
	1987	82.6	7.7	1.1	2.1	2.9	55.1	14.8	11.2	1.8	2.5	2.6	5.3	0.7

Note: n.e. = Nonexistent.

neg. = Less than 0.05%.

*1980 data include Denmark and Great Britain; Ireland, Greece, Spain, and Portugal are included in 1987 data.

†Excludes Denmark and Great Britain and includes Iceland in 1980.

Sources: *Monthly Bulletin of Statistics* (New York: United Nations, June 1988), pp. 270–73; and *Statistical Yearbook, 1969* (New York: United Nations), pp. 376–83.

However, by 1987, 63 percent (a one-third increase) of its exports were for the DCs, and only 32 percent went to the LDCs. The national debts that many of the developing countries incurred while the industrial economies were expanding were a salient factor.

Note that Russia had shifted a considerable amount of its trade to the West—to the detriment of its Eastern-bloc partners—but the data for 1987 indicate this trend has changed. In the case of the EC, the table demonstrates that its members continue to increase their trade with each other—a trend that is causing apprehension in the United States and Japan, as we mentioned in the first chapter.

Another interesting observation is that the LDCs as a group are selling a smaller percentage of their exports to the DCs—with the exception of the United States and the centrally planned economies—but more to each other. This is due in part to their increasing ability to export manufactured goods. Their scarcity of convertible currency is also a factor.

■ **TABLE 2–2** (concluded)

Exports from	Year	DC	U.S.	Can.	Jap.	USSR	EC	EFTA	LDC	D.A.	D.Am.	OPEC	CPE	CPEA
Less developed	1960	72.3%	10.3%	1.8%	5.1%	1.9%	22.8%	16.2%	22.3%	3.2%	3.9%	n.e.	3.5%	1.0%
countries (LDC)‡	1970	72.4	18.4	1.8	10.8	3.1	22.9	3.0	20.2	2.8	6.7	1.9%	5.1	0.7
	1980	70.2	20.5	1.3	14.0	1.7	27.1	2.7	24.9	2.4	8.0	3.7	2.9	0.7
	1987	65.8	25.8	1.5	11.7	2.8	23.3	2.0	25.7	2.4	5.5	4.4	4.5	3.2
Developing Africa	1960	79.2	7.9	0.4	1.5	2.7	43.8	21.7	12.8	6.6	0.7	n.e.	5.7	1.4
(D.A.) (South Africa	1970	81.1	6.7	0.7	4.0	4.1	61.4	4.3	10.7	5.6	2.0	1.2	6.5	1.0
and Zimbabwe	1980	83.6	31.1	0.2	2.1	0.8	42.8	2.9	12.6	3.1	6.4	1.1	2.6	0.4
excluded)	1987	81.0	16.7	0.6	2.2	1.2	58.2	2.2	12.8	4.8	2.9	1.5	4.8	0.4
Developing America	1960	78.9	42.1	1.7	2.8	1.6	18.5	11.8	18.0	0.7	7.9	n.e.	3.1	0.5
(D.Am.) (United	1970	74.2	32.4	3.4	5.4	3.5	26.3	3.3	19.1	0.7	17.3	0.9	5.8	0.6
States and Canada	1980	64.6	32.2	2.6	4.2	4.8	18.9	2.3	26.5	2.2	21.4	3.3	6.5	0.7
excluded)	1987	67.7	37.8	1.7	5.1	7.0	20.4	1.9	20.9	1.2	15.8	3.0	8.9	1.2
Organization of	1960	n.e.	n.e.	n.e.	n.e.	n.e.	n.e.	n.e.	n.e.	n.e.	n.e.	n.e.	n.e.	n.e.
Petroleum	1970	75.3	9.7	2.5	12.2	0.9	43.5	2.0	19.3	2.3	9.1	0.7	1.6	0.1
Exporting	1980	75.8	18.4	1.5	17.3	0.3	30.8	3.1	22.2	1.4	8.5	1.3	1.2	0.1
Countries (OPEC)§	1987	66.4	17.3	0.7	18.0	0.5	28.4	1.4	30.1	2.3	9.4	3.4	2.6	0.3
Centrally planned	1960	19.4	0.6	0.1	0.2	17.1	7.2	6.8	6.5	1.9	1.8	n.e.	62.3	10.6
economies (CPE)‖	1970	23.0	0.7	0.2	1.5	21.7	12.7	4.6	13.2	3.3	3.1	2.9	60.2	3.4
(Eastern Europe	1980	31.1	0.9	0.2	1.1	17.4	18.7	6.5	14.9	2.8	3.3	3.2	50.7	2.7
and USSR)	1987	21.5	0.9	0.1	0.9	20.4	14.3	5.1	11.9	1.8	4.0	1.9	58.1	3.9
Centrally planned	1960	13.8	0.1	0.3	1.4	48.5	6.6	4.6	20.4	2.0	0.5	n.e.	66.0	n.e.
economies in Asia	1970	31.6	neg.	0.7	12.3	10.2	14.2	2.5	47.3	6.5	4.1	5.0	21.1	n.e.
(CPEA) (excludes	1980	43.8	5.3	0.6	21.5	6.1	13.0	1.5	43.1	5.6	1.9	6.6	13.1	n.e.
intertrade)#	1987	43.3	8.7	1.2	18.2	7.5	12.6	1.7	43.8	1.3	1.4	1.7	11.8	1.1

Note: n.e. = Nonexistent.
neg. = Less than 0.05%.
‡Excludes Zimbabwe exports.
§OPEC members include Algeria, Ecuador, Gabon, Indonesia, Iran, Iraq, Kuwait, Libya, Nigeria, Qatar, Saudi Arabia, United Arab Emirates, and Venezuela.
‖Includes Albania, Bulgaria, Czechoslovakia, East Germany, Hungary, Poland, Romania, and Russia.
#Includes People's Republic of China, Mongolia, North Korea, and Vietnam. Intertrade not reported until 1987.

Major Trading Partners

An analysis of the major trading partners of the firm's home country and those of the nations where it has affiliates that export can provide valuable insights to management.

Why focus on major trading partners?   There are a number of advantages in focusing attention on a nation that is already a sizable purchaser of goods coming from the would-be exporter's country:

1. There are probably no political factors impeding exports from the exporter's country.
2. There should be no strong cultural objections to buying that nation's goods.
3. Satisfactory transportation facilities have already been established.
4. Import channel members (merchants, banks, and customs brokers) are experienced in handling import shipments from the exporter's area.
5. Foreign exchange to pay for the exports is available.
6. The government of a trading partner may be applying pressure on importers to buy from countries that are good customers for that

■ **TABLE 2–3   Major Trading Partners of the United States ($ billion)**

1965		1987		1965		1987	
Imports from	**Amount**	**Imports from**	**Amount**	**Exports to**	**Amount**	**Exports to**	**Amount**
1. Canada	$4.83	1. Japan	$83.07	1. Canada	$5.64	1. Canada	$59.81
2. Japan	2.41	2. Canada	71.50	2. Japan	2.08	2. Japan	28.25
3. UK	1.41	3. W. Germany	28.03	3. W. Germany	1.65	3. UK	17.34
4. W. Germany	1.34	4. Taiwan	26.41	4. UK	1.62	4. Mexico	14.58
5. Venezuela	1.02	5. Mexico	20.27	5. Mexico	1.11	5. W. Germany	11.75
6. Mexico	0.64	6. UK	17.99	6. Netherlands	1.09	6. Netherlands	8.21
7. Italy	0.62	6. Korea	17.99	7. France	0.97	7. S. Korea	8.10
8. France	0.62	8. Italy	11.70	8. India	0.93	8. France	7.94
9. Brazil	0.51	9. France	11.18	9. Italy	0.89	9. Taiwan	7.41
10. Bel. & Lux.	0.49	10. Hong Kong	10.49	10. Australia	0.80	10. Bel. & Lux.	6.19
11. Philippines	0.37	11. Brazil	7.87	11. Bel & Lux.	0.65	11. Australia	5.53
12. India	0.35	12. China (PR)	6.91	12. Venezuela	0.63	11. Italy	5.53
13. Hong Kong	0.34	13. Singapore	6.40	13. Spain	0.47	13. Singapore	4.06
14. Neth. Ant.	0.32	14. Venezuela	6.58	14. S. Africa	0.44	14. Brazil	4.04
15. Australia	0.31	15. Sweden	4.98	15. Switzerland	0.37	15. Hong Kong	3.98

Notes: 1. Exports are stated on an f.a.s. (free alongside ship) value basis. Services not included.
    2. Imports are stated on CIF (Cost, Insurance, Freight) value basis. Services not included.
    3. UK = United Kingdom
    4. Bel. & Lux. = Belgium and Luxembourg. Their export and import statistics are reported jointly.
    5. Neth. Ant. = Netherlands Antilles.
Sources: Bureau of the Census, *Statistical Abstract of the United States* (Washington, D.C.: 1979), pp. 862–65; and *World Almanac, 1989,* p. 183.

nation's exports. We have seen the efforts of the Japanese, Korean, and Taiwanese governments to persuade their citizens to buy more American goods. They have also sent buying missions to the United States.

Major trading partners of the United States.   An example of such an analysis is shown in Table 2–3. We learn from these data that the United States, an industrialized nation, generally follows the tendency we found in Table 2–2; that is, developed nations trade with one another, but there are some exceptions. Two countries, Mexico and Canada, are trading partners because of their geographic proximity. Freight charges are lower, delivery times are shorter, and it is easier and less expensive for buyers and sellers to make contact.

Of course, the importance of Canada as a trading partner will be further heightened with the U.S.–Canada Free Trade Agreement (FTA), which went into effect in 1989. Although about 75 percent of the nearly $150 billion in goods that flow between the partners is already duty free, the removal of import duties from the remaining 25 percent will make a significant increase in cross-border trade.[3]

Note that in just two decades, there as been a marked change in the ranking of America's trading partners. Not only have the rankings changed, but nations have been added while others have become relatively less important.

The newly industrializing nations of Korea, Taiwan, and Singapore are supplying the United States with huge quantities of electronic products and components and other labor-intensive products, much of which is produced by affiliates of American worldwide companies. China's addition to the list is evidence of the new trade relations with this country. These same countries appear as major importers of American goods as well because (1) their rising levels of living enable their people to afford more imported products, and the countries' export earnings provide the foreign exchange to buy them; (2) they are purchasing large amounts of capital goods to further their industrial expansion; and (3) their governments, pressured by the American government to lower their trade deficits with the United States, have sent buying missions to this country to look for products to import, as we mentioned in the previous section.

Utility of These Data

The analysis of foreign trade that we have described would be helpful to anyone just starting to search outside the home market for new business opportunities. The preliminary steps of (1) studying the general growth of trade (Table 2–1) and (2) analyzing major trading partners (Tables 2–2 and 2–3) would provide an idea of where the trading activity is located. After noting the addition of newcomers to the list, the analyst could check the *FT 990*—published monthly by the Department of Commerce—to learn which kinds of products these partners are importing. If the firm's goods are on this list, examining another Commerce publication, the *FT 410,* will tell the researcher the quantities, dollar values, and destinations of specific products.[4] We shall discuss this in greater detail in Chapter 14.

The topic that we have been examining, international trade, exists because firms export. As you know, however, exporting is only one aspect of international business. The other, overseas production, generally requires foreign investment, our next subject of discussion.

FOREIGN INVESTMENT

portfolio investment the purchase of stocks and bonds to obtain a return on the funds invested

Foreign investment may be divided into two components: **portfolio investment,** which is the purchase of stocks and bonds solely for the purpose of obtaining a return on the funds invested, and **direct investment,** by which the investors participate in the management of the firm in addition to receiving a return on their money.

Portfolio Investment

direct investment the purchase of sufficient stock in a firm to obtain significant management control

Although portfolio investors are not directly concerned with control of a firm, they invest immense amounts in stocks and bonds from other countries. Data from the U.S. Department of Commerce show that persons residing outside the United States hold American stocks and bonds valued at $344 billion ($173 billion in stocks). Although there are stockholders in virtually every country in the world, six countries—Canada, France, the Netherlands, Switzerland, Japan, and the United Kingdom—account for over three fourths of the foreign holdings. More than 11 percent of U.S. stocks held abroad are owned by

■ TABLE 2–4
Direct Overseas
Investment (1985 and
1986)

| | 1986 | | 1985 | | |
	Amount (US$ billion)	Share (percent)	Amount (US$ billion)	Share (percent)	1986/1985 (percent)
United States	$259.9	33.5%	$232.7	36.1%	11.7%
United Kingdom	139.5	18.0	116.9	18.1	19.3
West German	73.3	9.5	52.4	8.1	39.9
Netherlands	66.1	8.5	55.5	8.6	19.1
Japan	58.1	7.5	44.0	6.8	32.0
Canada	40.6	5.2	33.5	5.2	21.2
Other	138.0	17.8	109.6	17.0	25.9
World total	$775.5	100.0%	$644.6	100.0%	20.3

Sources: *Japan 1989: An International Comparison* (Tokyo: Japan Institute for Social and Economic Affairs, 1989), p. 58; and *Japan, 1988,* p. 58.

American citizens living abroad. While the ownership of American bonds is evenly divided between private and official owners (foreign governments), nearly all of the foreign-owned stock is held privately.[5] As you can see, this kind of investment is sizable, and it will continue to grow as more American companies list their bonds and equities on foreign stock exchanges.

Foreign Direct Investment

Volume.   Attempts have been made to estimate the total book value of foreign direct investment by summing yearly totals of new investments, but this procedure understates the present value because of the effects of appreciation and inflation.

In Chapter 1, we stated that the book value of all foreign investments is about $776 billion. Table 2–4 indicates how this total is divided among the largest investor nations. Note that the United States has twice the investment of the next largest, Great Britain, who in turn has invested twice as much as Germany, the third largest, although this country experienced the largest percentage increase from 1985 to 1986.

Direction.   Even though it is impossible to make an accurate determination of the present value of foreign investments, we can get an idea of the rate and amounts of such investments and of the places in which they are being made. This is the kind of information that interests managers and government leaders. It is analogous to what is sought in the analysis of international trade. If a nation is continuing to receive appreciable amounts of foreign investment, its investment climate must be favorable. This means that the political forces of the foreign environment are relatively attractive and that the opportunity to earn a profit is greater there than elsewhere. Other reasons for investing exist, to be sure, but if the above are absent, foreign investment is not likely to occur.

In which countries are investments being made, and where do the investments come from? Table 2–5 indicates that the industrialized nations invest primarily in one another just as they trade more with one another.

■ TABLE 2–5
Direction of Foreign
Direct Investment for
Selected Regions and
Countries (Current US$
billion)

	1973	1979	1987
Where funds originate (net investment)			
World	$23.44	$ 48.37	$150.38*
Industrial nations	23.13	48.08	149.00
United States	11.53	24.84	48.46
United Kingdom	4.01	5.91	28.25
Japan	1.92	2.95	21.22
West Germany	1.69	4.73	10.10
France	0.94	2.07	9.96
Netherlands	0.93	2.35	8.60
Canada	0.77	1.89	5.56
Belgium and Luxembourg	0.27	1.36	3.03
Italy	0.26	0.55	2.56
Switzerland	0.30	0.64	1.33
Developing nations (oil export)	0.16	−0.15	0.10
Developing nations (nonoil)	0.15	0.41	1.27
Where funds go (net investment)			
Industrial nations	10.62	24.60	90.59
United States	2.85	9.92	46.04
United Kingdom	1.80	2.76	10.31
France	1.14	2.59	5.58
Spain	0.39	1.43	5.00
Canada	0.83	1.50	4.55
Italy	0.63	0.37	4.47
Belgium and Luxembourg	0.73	1.08	2.59
Netherlands	0.87	1.24	2.58
West Germany	2.06	1.13	2.14
Japan	0.21[†]	0.24	1.30
Developing nations (oil export)	0.27	0.09	−1.71
Developing nations (nonoil)	4.04	8.42	14.34
Africa	0.32	0.36	0.71
Asia	0.80	2.14	6.51
People's Republic of China	n.a.	0.43[‡]	2.54
Singapore	0.39	0.83	1.27
Malaysia	0.17	0.89	0.65
Western hemisphere	2.50	4.38	5.85
Mexico	0.46	0.68	3.54
Brazil	1.39	2.46	0.54[§]
Colombia	0.02	0.16	0.42
Argentina	0.01	0.18	−0.02

n.a. = Not available.
*Amounts do not coincide because of reporting lag.
[†]1974.
[‡]1982.
[§]1986.
Sources: International Monetary Fund, *Balance of Payments Yearbook Supplement to Volumes 31 and 33* (Washington, D.C.: December 1980); and *Balance of Payments Statistics Yearbook,* vol. 38, part 2, 1988, pp. 68–69.

Actually, foreign investment follows foreign trade. Managements observe that the kinds of products they manufacture are being imported in sizable quantities by a country, and they begin to study the feasibility of setting up production facilities there. They are spurred to action because it is common knowledge that competitors are making similar analyses and may arrive at the same conclusion. Often the local market is not large enough to support local production of all the firms exporting to it, and the situation becomes one of seeing who can become established first. Experienced managers know, too, that governments often limit the number of local firms producing a given

■ **TABLE 2–6**   U.S. Direct Investment Position Overseas (Current US$ billion)

| Country or Region | 1960 | | 1987 | | | | | | | |
	Total	Percent of Total	Total	Percent of Total	Manufac-turing	Percent of Manufac-turing	Petroleum	Percent of Petroleum	Other[a]	Percent of Other
Total	$31.87	100 %	$308.79	100%	$126.64	100%	$66.38	100%	$115.77	100%
Developed countries	19.32	61	233.32	76	104.76	83	43.76	66	84.80	73
Canada	11.18	35	56.88	18	25.80	20	11.93	18	19.15	17
Europe[b]	6.69	21	148.95	48	67.48	53	25.79	39	55.68	48
EC[c]	2.65	8	122.25	40	64.91	51	19.10	29	38.24	33
Bel. & Lux.[d]	0.23	0.7	7.80	3	3.68	3	S	—	S	—
France	0.74	2	11.48	4	8.37	7	0.53	1	2.58	2
West Germany	1.01	3	24.45	8	15.97	13	3.32	5	5.16	4
Italy	0.38	1	8.45	3	6.08	5	0.25	<1	2.12	2
Netherlands	0.28	0.9	14.16	5	5.32	4	3.08	5	5.76	5
Great Britain	3.23	10	44.67	14	18.27	14	11.01	17	15.39	13
Denmark and Ireland	n.a.	—	6.59	2	4.36	3	0.15	<1	S	—
Greece	n.a.	—	0.22	<1	0.09	<1	0.00	0	S	—
Japan	0.25	0.8	14.27	5	7.07	6	2.56	4	4.64	4
Aust. and S.A.[e]	1.20	4	13.21	4	4.41	3	3.48	5	5.32	5
Developing countries	11.13	35	71.17	23	21.88	17	19.01	29	30.28	26
Latin America	7.48	23	42.34	14	15.90	13	5.77	9	20.67	18
Brazil	0.95	3	9.96	3	7.73	6	0.27	<1	1.96	2
Venezuela	2.57	8	2.12	1	1.06	1	0.53	<1	0.53	<1
Mexico and Central America	1.54	5	10.43	3	4.55	4	0.84	1	5.04	4
Other western hemisphere	0.88	3	12.59	4	0.26	<1	1.91	3	10.42	9
Africa[f]	0.64	2	5.09	2	0.07	<1	4.24	6	0.78	<1
Middle East	1.14	4	4.76	2	0.41	<1	2.81	4	1.54	1
Other Asia and Pacific	0.98	3	18.99	6	5.26	4	6.19	9	7.54	7
International[g]	1.42	4	4.30	1	n.a.	—	3.61	5	0.69	<1

Notes: n.a. = Not applicable.

S = Suppressed to avoid disclosure of individual firm.

[a]Other includes transportation, communications, public utilities, trade, finance, insurance, real estate, mining, banking, and wholesale trade.

[b]No East European investment included.

[c]Great Britain, Ireland, Denmark, and Greece not in EC in 1960. Are included in 1983.

[d]Belgium and Luxembourg.

[e]Australia, New Zealand, and South Africa.

[f]Does not include South Africa.

[g]Shipping companies operating under flags of convenience primarily those of Panama and Liberia and investments not allocated to any specific country by reporting firms.

Sources: *Survey of Current Business,* June 1988, p. 81; and *Statistical Abstract of the United States 1977,* p. 755.

product so that those who do set up operations will be assured of having a profitable and continuing business.

U.S. Foreign Investment

The United States is by far the largest investor abroad (over 36 percent of the total; see Table 2–4), and as you can see from Table 2–6, American firms have invested much more in the developed than in the developing countries. Also, as with international trade, the relative importance of regions and countries has been changing. In a period of 27 years, the percentage of American foreign investment in the developed nations has risen from 61 percent to 76 percent. Europe's share has more than doubled, and of the European countries, Great Britain and West Germany have obtained the

■ **FIGURE 2–2   Distribution of Japanese Manufacturers' Factory Sites in the United States (as of May 1988)**

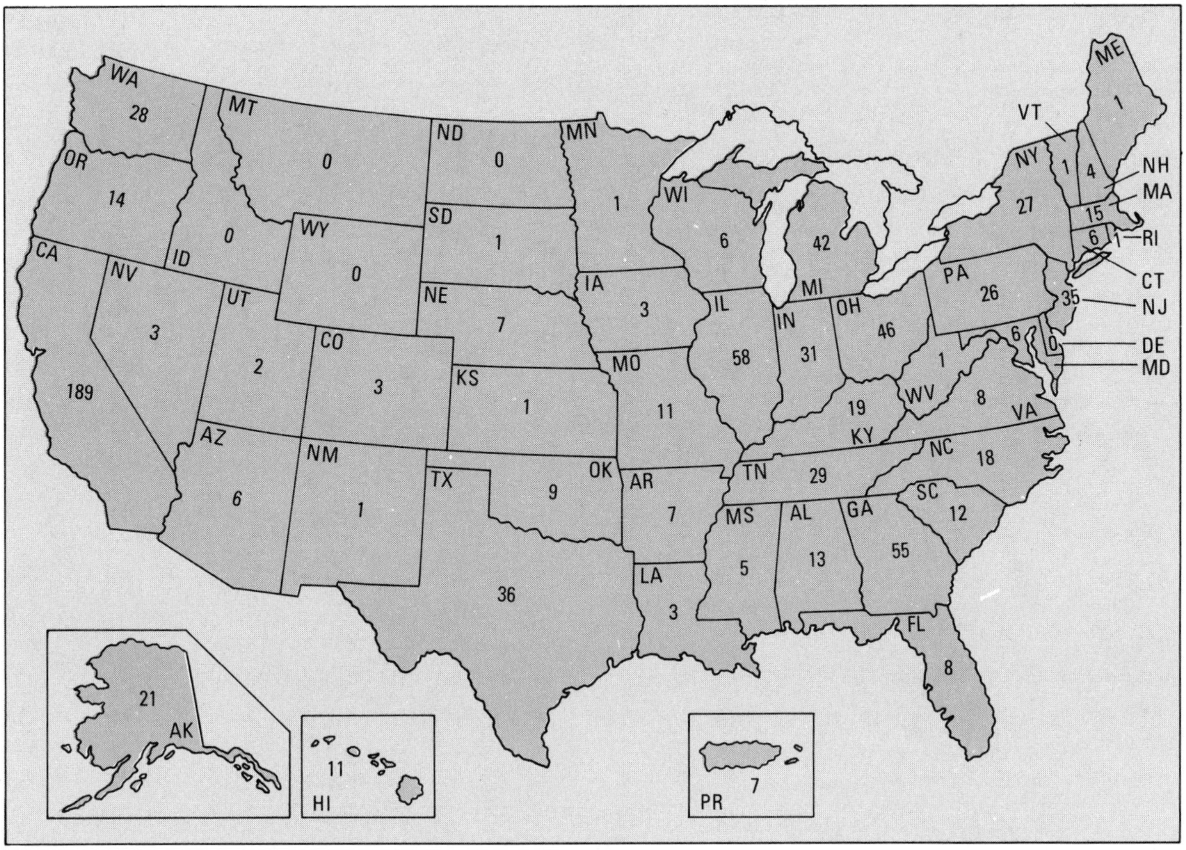

Japanese corporations were operating 837 plants in the United States as of May 1988.
Source: JETRO Survey.

greatest dollar increase. Note that although the developing nations as a group have suffered a large percentage decease, the percentage of investment in the Other Asia and Pacific region—which includes newly industrializing countries (NICs) such as Singapore and Hong Kong—has doubled.

Foreign Direct Investment in the United States

Foreign direct investment in the United States has risen rapidly, from about $6.9 billion in 1960 to $262 billion in 1987. Of the 68 percent of the total foreign investment accounted for by Europe, MNEs in Great Britain and the Netherlands owned 29 and 18 percent, respectively. Although American investments by German and Japanese firms have been expanding rapidly (see Figure 2–2), their U.S. investment levels of $19.64 and $33.36 billion are still way below the Netherlands $47.05 billion and Great Britain's $74.94 billion. (See Table 2–7.) Only four nations—Great Britain, the Netherlands, Japan, and West Germany—account for 70 percent of all foreign direct investment in the United States.

The 15 largest investors in the United States are ranked by revenue in Table 2–8. Although a few firms, such as Shell, Nestlé and Bayer, have been in this

■ **TABLE 2–7   Foreign Direct Investment Position in United States, 1987 ($ billion)**

	All Industries	Petroleum	Manufacturing	Trade	Finance	Insurance	Real Estate
All countries	$261.93	$35.40	$91.03	$47.13	$ 21.80	$15.95	$24.48
Canada	21.73	1.43	7.48	3.58	2.86	1.61	3.36
Europe	177.96	32.79	70.60	25.61	12.21	13.10	10.71
European Community (12)	157.71	32.24	58.83	22.68	10.77	10.95	10.18
Belgium	2.60	S	0.67	0.41	S	0.0	0.01
France	10.20	S	8.91	0.64	−0.25	0.12	0.06
West Germany	19.64	0.3	9.00	5.97	1.00	1.62	1.12
Italy	1.23	S	0.25	0.18	0.33	S	S
Luxembourg	0.15	S	0.05	S	−0.02	0.0	0.02
Netherlands	47.05	S	16.12	4.01	5.11	3.11	3.31
Great Britain	74.94	S	23.51	10.84	S	6.06	5.51
Other EC	1.91	S	0.33	S	S	S	S
Other Europe	20.25	0.55	11.77	2.93	1.44	2.15	0.53
Sweden	4.70	0.35	3.02	1.14	S	S	*
Switzerland	14.34	0.14	8.32	1.54	S	1.86	0.39
Other	1.21	0.06	0.43	0.24	0.19	S	0.13
Japan	33.36	0.03	5.23	14.99	6.02	S	4.43
Australia, New Zealand, and South Africa	6.63	0.10	3.12	0.23	0.13	S	0.33
Latin America	15.29	0.69	3.67	2.39	0.63	1.07	4.19
Middle East	5.05	S	0.25	0.08	0.77	0.0	0.87
Other Africa, Asia, and Pacific	1.90	S	0.69	0.26	0.18	*	0.60

Note: S = Suppressed to avoid disclosure of individual companies.
*Less than $10 million.
Source: *Survey as Current Business*, June 1988, p. 83.

country for many years, most of these investments are recent. You can tell from the names of the American affiliates that their major investment strategy has been to acquire existing firms rather than start from the ground up. In 1987, foreign investors spent $25.6 billion on acquisitions and only $4.9 billion to establish new companies.[6]

WHY GO ABROAD?

International firms go abroad for a number of reasons, all of which are linked to the desire to either increase profits and sales or protect them from being eroded by competition. Any reason, depending on the firm's situation, may achieve either goal.

Increase Profits and Sales

Open up new markets.   Managers are always under pressure to increase the sales and profits of their firms, and when they face a mature, saturated market at home, they begin to search for new markets outside their home country.

GNP/capita   an arithmetic mean derived by dividing a nation's gross national product by its population

They find that (1) a rising **GNP/capita** and population growth appear to be creating markets that are reaching the "critical mass" necessary to become viable candidates for their operations and (2) the economies of some nations where they are not doing business are growing at a considerably faster rate than is the economy of their own market.

New market creation.   Table 2–9 illustrates the great variety in growth rates among the top and bottom countries ranked by GNP/capita. Note the disparity among and between the two groups.

Although nearly everyone looks to GNP/capita as a basis for making comparisons of nations' economies, extreme care must be exercised to avoid drawing unwarranted conclusions. In the first place, because the statistical systems in many developing nations are deficient, the reliability of the data provided by such nations is questionable.

Second, to arrive at a common base of U.S. dollars, the World Bank converts local currencies to dollars. World Bank officials admit that their method of using official exchange rates for the conversion does not accurately reflect the purchasing power of currencies. They say, "The differences in real income between developing and industrialized economies are likely to be exaggerated."[7]

Finally, you must remember that GNP/capita is merely an arithmetic mean obtained by dividing GNP by the total population. However, a nation with a lower GNP but more evenly distributed income may be a more desirable market than one whose GNP is higher. On the other hand, as you will note in the chapter on the economic forces, a skewed distribution of income in a nation with a low GNP/capita may indicate that there is a viable market, especially for luxury goods. People do drive Cadillacs in Bolivia.

The data from Table 2–9 indicate that, from a macro viewpoint, markets around the world are growing, but this does not mean that equally good opportunities exist for all kinds of business. Perhaps surprisingly, economic growth in a nation causes markets for some products to be lost forever while simultaneously markets for other products are being created. Take the case of a country in the initial stage of development. With little local manufacturing, it is a good market for exporters of consumer goods. As economic development continues, however, businesspeople see profit-making opportunities in (1) producing locally the kinds of consumer goods that require simple technology or (2) assembling from imported parts the products that demand a more advanced technology. Given the tendency of governments to protect local industry, the importation of goods being produced in that country will normally be prohibited. Thus, the exporters of the easy-to-manufacture consumer goods, such as paint, adhesives, toilet articles, clothing, and almost anything made of plastic, will begin to lose this market, which now becomes a new market to producers of the inputs to these "infant industries."

> Typical of the simple production facilities for producing consumer goods is the case of a Mexican firm that manufacturers a number of products under licenses from American firms, among which are Listerine toothpaste and McCormick spices. The production line that supplies Listerine toothpaste for all of Mexico consists of one 50-gallon mixing tank, into which the imported ingredients are dumped. A mixer looking like an electric outboard motor is clamped to the tank's side. The mixed contents are discharged by gravity to a tube-filling machine, and the whole operation is handled by one man. The McCormick spice

■ **TABLE 2–8   Sixteen Largest Foreign Investments in the United States ($ million)**

Foreign Investor	Country	U.S. Investment	Industry	Revenue	Assets
1. Seagram Co. Ltd.	Canada	E.I. Du Pont (23%)	Chemicals	$32,657	$30,719
		Seagram (100%)	Alcoholic beverages	2,540	7,946
		Tropicana (100%)	Beverages	741	n.a.
				35,938	
2. Royal Dutch Shell	Netherlands/ United Kingdom	Shell Oil (100%)	Energy, chemicals	21,070	27,169
3. British Petroleum	United Kingdom	BP America (100%)	Energy	14,378	22,452
4. BAT Industries	United Kingdom	BATUS (100%)	Multicompany	6,251	3,788
Imasco Ltd.	Canada	Farmers Group	Insurance	1,191	7,704
		Peoples Drug (100%)	Drugstores	1,498	n.a.
		Imasco USA (100%)	Fast food	1,431	n.a.
				10,371	
5. Tenglemann Group	Germany	A&P (53%)	Supermarkets	10,068	2,640
6. Grand Metropolitan Plc.	United Kingdom	Pillsbury (100%)	Food processors	6,191	3,840
		Grand Met. USA (100%)	Retailing, beverages	2,700	n.a.
				8,891	
7. Campeau	Canada	Allied Stores (100%)	Retailing	6,220	10,784
		Federated Dept. Stores (100%)	Retailing		
		Ralphs Grocery (100%)	Supermarkets	1,842	1,112
				8,062	

Notes: n.a. = Not available.
  e = estimated.
Source: "The 100 Largest Foreign Investments in the U.S.," *Forbes,* July 24, 1989, pp. 313–18.

production area is made up of a machine that fills small metal cans with ground pepper imported in bulk, plus two girls who sit with 50-pound cardboard drums of imported spices between their legs and fill by hand the familiar paper boxes for whole spices, such as cloves, cinnamon, and pepper. The entire production area is smaller than a basketball court.

Multinational economic unions.   The fact that the great majority of nations have experienced population and GNP/capita growth does not necessarily mean they have attained sufficient size to warrant investment in an organization for either handling exports or producing locally. For many products, many of these nations still lack sufficient market potential. However, when such nations have formed **multinational economic unions** (for example, the European Community and the European Free Trade Association), the new markets have been so much larger that a number of firms have bypassed what is often the initial step of exporting and have made their initial market entry by manufacturing locally.

---

multinational economic union   a group of nations that have reduced barriers to intragroup trade and are cooperating in economic matters

■ **TABLE 2–8**   (concluded)

Foreign Investor	Country	U.S. Investment	Industry	Revenue	Assets
8. Nestlé	Switzerland	Nestlé Enterprises (100%)	Food processing	$ 6,089	$4,863 n.a.
		Alcon Lab. (100%)	Optical	500	
				6,589	
9. Hanson Plc.	United Kingdom	Hanson Ind. (100%)	Multicompany	6,030	5,772
10. Pechiney	France	American National Can	Packaging	4,320	3,120
		Pechiney	Metal castings	1,398	1,228
				5,718	
11. Petroleos de Venezuela	Venezuela	Citgo Petroleum (50%)	Refining, marketing	4,110	1,343
		Champlin Refining (100%)	Refining, marketing	1,600	550
				5,710	
12. Unilever NV Unilever Plc.	Netherlands United Kingdom	Unilever U.S.	Food processing	5,688	6,449
13. Hoechst AG	Germany	Hoechst Celanese (100%)	Chemicals	5,679	5,703
14. NV Philips	Netherlands	North American Philips (100%)	Electronics	5,424	3,423
15. BASF AG	Germany	BASF (100%)	Chemicals	5,000	2,956
16. Bayer AG	Germany	Mobay (100%)	Chemicals	2,017	1,493
		Miles (100%)	Health care	1,706	1,229
		Agfa (100%)	Photography	818	759
		Other co. (100%)	Foods, brewing	178	147
				4,719	

Notes: n.a. = Not available.
e = Estimated.

Faster-growing foreign markets. Not only are new markets appearing overseas, but many of these markets are growing at a faster rate than the home market. One outstanding example has been the growth of the Japanese gross national product and GNP/capita, which increased from $43 billion and $458 in 1960 to $1,925 billion and $15,770 in 1987. Table 2–9 shows that Japan's real growth rate averaged 3.1 percent annually, one of the highest among the large industrial countries. Check the annual growth rates of some of the newly industrializing countries (NICs): Singapore, 5.6 percent and Hong Kong, 5.5 percent. Another group of high-growth markets—the OPEC nations, especially those of the Middle East—came into being almost overnight when crude oil prices quadrupled. Managements suddenly found these new markets to be worth billions of dollars. Iran's imports, for example, increased by eight times in only six years. Interestingly, of the 152 nations in the World Bank table on which Table 2–9 is based, 31 had average annual GNP/capita growth rates higher than the American growth rate for the 1980–87 period.

■ **TABLE 2–9**
**Population (1987), GNP/
Capita (1987), and
Average Growth Rates of
GNP/capita (1980–1987)
and Population (1980–
1987) (Countries with
populations of 1 million
or more)***

Ranking	Country†	1987 GNP/Capita (current US$)	1987 Population (millions)	Annual Growth Rates (Percentage) GNP/Capita‡	Annual Growth Rates (Percentage) Population
1.	Switzerland	$21,250	6.5	1.5%	0.3%
2.	United States	18,430	243.4	2.0	1.0
3.	Norway	17,110	4.2	3.5	0.3
4.	Japan	15,770	122.1	3.1	0.6
5.	Sweden	15,690	8.4	1.8	0.1
6.	United Arab Emirates	15,680	1.5	−9.5	5.3
7.	Canada	15,080	25.9	1.9	1.0
8.	Denmark	15,010	5.1	2.4	0.0
9.	Kuwait	14,870	1.8	−3.0	4.2
10.	West Germany	14,460	60.8	1.9	−0.2
11.	Finland	14,370	4.9	2.2	0.5
12.	France	12,860	55.6	0.7	0.5
13.	Austria	11,970	7.6	1.7	0.0
14.	Netherlands	11,860	14.6	0.8	0.5
15.	Belgium	11,360	9.9	1.0	0.0
16.	Australia	10,900	16.2	1.5	1.4
17.	United Kingdom	10,430	56.9	2.5	0.1
18.	Italy	10,420	57.3	1.3	0.2
19.	Hong Kong	8,260	5.5	5.5	1.2
20.	New Zealand	8,230	3.3	0.9	0.9
21.	Singapore	7,940	2.6	5.6	1.1
22.	Israel	6,810	4.4	0.3	1.7
23.	Ireland	6,030	3.6	−1.4	0.8
24.	Spain	6,010	38.9	1.6	0.5
25.	Oman	5,780	1.3	8.7	4.5

Notes: n.a. = Not available.
*The World Bank does not include GNP/capita estimates for most centrally planned economies, such as the USSR and Poland, because there is a dispute as to the methodology that should be employed.
†Only countries for which data were reported to the World Bank are listed.
‡GNP/capita growth rates are real.
Source: *The World Bank Atlas, 1988* (Washington, D.C.: 1988).

Faster growth in the markets of developing nations frequently occurs for another reason. When a firm that has supplied the market by exports builds a factory for local production, the host government generally prohibits imports. The firm, which may have had to share the market with 10 or 20 competitors during its exporting days, now has the local market all to itself or shares it with only a small number of other local producers. Before General Tire began manufacturing tires in Chile, probably a dozen exporters, including General Tire, were competing in the market. However, once local production got under way, there was only one supplier for the entire market—General Tire. That is growth.

■ TABLE 2–9
(concluded)

| Ranking | Country[†] | 1987 | | Annual Growth Rates (Percentage) | |
		GNP/Capita (current US$)	Population (millions)	GNP/ Capita[‡]	Population
128.	Sudan	$330	23.2	−4.0%	2.8%
129.	Rwanda	310	6.5	−3.1	3.3
130.	Sierra Leone	300	3.8	−2.5	2.4
130.	China	300	1,068.7	9.1	1.2
130.	Togo	300	3.3	−3.5	3.4
130.	India	300	797.1	2.6	2.1
130.	Benin	300	4.3	−0.6	3.2
135.	Somalia	290	5.7	−0.8	2.9
136.	Niger	280	6.8	−5.3	3.0
137.	Uganda	260	15.7	−2.4	3.1
138.	Burundi	240	5.0	−0.4	2.7
138.	Zambia	240	7.2	−4.4	3.5
140.	Tanzania	220	23.9	−1.8	3.5
141.	Mali	200	7.8	−0.0	2.4
141.	Madagascar	200	10.9	−4.0	3.3
143.	Burkina Faso	170	8.3	−0.6	2.6
144.	Lao, PDR	160	3.8	n.a.	2.1
144.	Nepal	160	17.4	2.0	2.5
144.	Zaire	160	32.7	−2.8	3.1
144.	Malawi	160	7.6	−0.3	3.3
144.	Bangladesh	160	105.9	1.0	2.6
149.	Mozambique	150	14.6	−9.5	2.7
149.	Chad	150	5.3	2.5	2.4
149.	Bhutan	150	1.3	n.a.	2.1
152.	Ethiopia	120	44.8	−1.6	2.4

Notes: n.a. = Not available.
[†]Only countries for which data were reported to the World Bank are listed.
[‡]GNP/capita growth rates are real.

Obtain greater profits.   As you know, greater profits may be obtained by either increasing total revenue or decreasing the cost of goods sold, and often conditions are such that a firm can do both.

Greater revenue.   Rarely will all of a firm's domestic competitors be in every foreign market in which it is located. Where there is less competition, the firm may be able to obtain a better price for its goods or services. For example, General Tire had only three competitors in Spain for its V-belt line when dozens of brands were available in the United States.

In addition, firms are sometimes able to introduce new products overseas sooner than in the home country. This is especially true in the pharmaceutical industry. Robert Dean of Smith-Kline Beckman (sales, $4.75 billion) claims that delays by the Food and Drug Administration in approving new products were responsible for the industry's going abroad. "This industry would not have its international business if not for FDA regulations. We had to have a broader market to pay for the enormous expense of getting a drug on the market."[8]

Lower cost of goods sold.   Going abroad, whether by exporting or by producing overseas, can frequently lower the cost of goods sold. Increasing total sales by exporting will not only reduce R&D costs per unit, but will also make other economies of scale possible. The president of a Westinghouse division stated, "The people who can spread their R&D and engineering and manufacturing development costs across those three markets [Europe, Japan, and North America] have a substantial advantage." Westinghouse, like many companies, obtains lower unit costs through long production runs made possible by having one factory supply one product internationally.[9]

Producing in other countries can also be less expensive when labor, raw materials, or energy costs are lower. Moreover, some governments offer special inducements to attract new investment, which greatly lowers the cost of investment and thus the size of the risk. For example, Greece, one of the newest members of the European Community, offers the following: (1) investment grants of up to 50 percent of the investment, (2) interest subsidies to cover up to 50 percent of the interest cost of loans from banks, and (3) reduction of up to 90 percent of a firm's taxable profits. While incentives alone are not considered a sufficient motive for investing overseas, they are certainly a contributing factor. Incentives also exert an influence on where investments will be made. It is obvious, too, that they will positively affect the cost of goods sold.

Improved communications.   This might be considered a supportive reason for opening up new markets overseas, because certainly the ability to communicate with subordinates and customers by telex and telephone has given managers confidence in their ability to control foreign operations if they should undertake them. Managers also know that because of improved transportation, they can either send home-office personnel to help with local problems or be there themselves within a few hours if need be.

> Good communication is so important for multinationals that Barbados has been able to attract industry on the basis of its excellent communications. American Airlines does all of its data processing there, for example.

Shorter traveling time has also been responsible for numerous business opportunities because foreign businesspersons have come to the home country to look for new products to import or new technology to buy.[10] The Department of Commerce, in *Business America,* regularly publishes a list of arrivals who desire to contact suppliers.

Overseas profits as an investment motive.   There is no question that greater profits on overseas investments were a strong motive for going abroad in the early 1970s and 1980s. *Business International* reported that 90 percent of 140 Fortune 500 companies surveyed had achieved higher profitability on foreign net assets in 1974. This, of course, was an incentive for firms not yet in foreign markets to go abroad.

However, profits from foreign operations suffered in 1975, when oil prices were quadrupled, European labor was making increased demands, and governments were initiating costly welfare programs.

This situation lasted through 1977, but the ratio of foreign earnings to total earnings (FEBIT/TEBIT) turned up again in 1978 (see Figure 2–3, Part II) and reached a high in 1980. Then foreign profitability dropped in 1981 as the recessionary downturn that began in the United States about mid-1980 appeared overseas. The ratio of foreign earnings to total earnings turned up sharply in 1983, and foreign earnings as a percentage of assets continued to be higher than the U.S. earnings (see Figure 2–3, Part I).

Note that over the 1978–85 period the average growth in foreign earnings outpaced foreign sales growth (5.9 percent versus 4.1 percent), whereas domestic earnings were down an average of 27 percent despite a domestic sales growth of 5.2 percent (Figure 2–3, Part III).

Acquire products for the home market.   The relative ease of foreign travel has both created markets for new products and facilitated the search for new products to be introduced in the U.S. market. Americans have traveled abroad in unprecedented numbers since WW II, and in their travels they have encountered products and customs previously unknown to them. Those who acquired the European habit of drinking wine with their meals, for example, returned home wanting to continue this custom. American marketers, sensitive to this trend, have sent buyers around the world to bring back these new products, and many manufacturers have begun to produce them here.

> Minnetonka executives were browsing in a German supermarket when they came across an intriguing product—toothpaste in a pump dispenser, which had not yet appeared in the United States—so they contacted the German manufacturer. This was the beginning of Check-Up toothpaste. A marketing vice president stated, "We make grocery shopping a regular part of our business trips to Europe. It helps give us a jump on our bigger competitors."
>
> American firms have found products such as aseptic beverage cartons (which permit storage without refrigeration), hair-styling mousses, and body fragrance sprays. "The search across oceans and borders for new products is heating up," said the president of General Food's international division.[11]

Satisfy management's desire for expansion.   The faster growth mentioned previously helps fulfill management's desire for expansion. Stockholders and financial analysts also expect firms to continue to grow, and those companies operating only in the domestic market have found it increasingly difficult to sustain that expectation. As a result, many firms have expanded into foreign markets. This, of course, is what companies based in small countries, such as Nestlé (Switzerland), SKF Bearing (Sweden), and Shell (Great Britain and the Netherlands), discovered decades ago.

Another aspect of this reason sometimes motivates a company's top managers to begin searching for overseas markets. Being able to claim that the firm is a "multinational" creates the impression of importance, which can influence its customers. Sun Microsystems, a manufacturer of computer work stations, recently opened a technical center in Germany and is building a factory in Scotland. "To be a major player in the marketplace, you have to be internationally recognized," said the head of Sun's European operations.[12]

We also know of instances where a company has examined and then entered

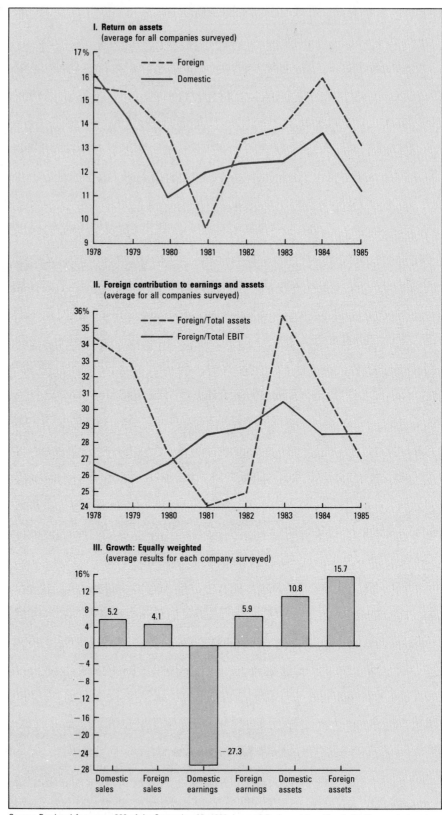

I. **Return on assets**
(average for all companies surveyed)

- - - - Foreign
——— Domestic

II. **Foreign contribution to earnings and assets**
(average for all companies surveyed)

- - - - Foreign/Total assets
——— Foreign/Total EBIT

III. **Growth: Equally weighted**
(average results for each company surveyed)

Domestic sales	5.2
Foreign sales	4.1
Domestic earnings	−27.3
Foreign earnings	5.9
Domestic assets	10.8
Foreign assets	15.7

Source: Reprinted from page 309 of the September 29, 1986, issue of *Business International* with the permission of
the publisher, Business International Corporation (New York).

a market because the president brought it to the attention of the market planners after enjoying a pleasant vacation there.

> How else can you explain the fact that in pre-Castro Cuba, there were three American tire factories in Havana, the "fun capital" of the world, with Miami just 90 miles away? Delivery of tires to Cuba could have been made in hours and at better prices. One of the authors found out why when he spent a winter in Akron working for a tire company. Not surprisingly, the Cuban subsidiary had financial, marketing, and production problems that required the presence of Akron executives—usually in the wintertime.

Let's now look at some reasons for going abroad that are more related to the protection of present markets, profits, and sales.

Protect Markets, Profits, and Sales

Protect domestic market. Frequently, a firm will go abroad to protect its home market. Service companies (accounting, advertising, marketing research, banks, law) will establish foreign operations in markets where their principal accounts are, to prevent competitors from gaining access to those accounts. They know that once a competitor has been able to demonstrate to top management what it can do by servicing a foreign subsidiary, it may be able to take over the entire account. Similarly, suppliers to original equipment manufacturers (for example, battery manufacturers to automobile producers) often follow their large customers. These suppliers have an added advantage in that they are moving into new markets with a guaranteed customer base.

Japanese auto parts suppliers have followed the Japanese car manufacturers to the United States. Tokyo Seat has established a subsidiary to make seats, exhaust systems, and other parts for Honda, who also asked Nippodenso, a Japanese producer of radiators and heaters, to set up an American plant. In addition to Mitsubishi's captive suppliers (firms within the Mitsubishi Group, such as Diamond Star, a Chrysler–Mitsubishi joint venture) who are following Mitsubishi to the United States, nonaffiliated Japanese suppliers are also coming. In Indiana, a cooperative of 16 Mitsubishi suppliers, called Eagle Wings, has built a $36 million factory to produce such components as engine mounts and bumpers. "We had a direct request from Mitsubishi to build this project here in the United States," said Eagle Wings president Isamu Kawasaki,[13] But not only auto parts manufacturers are involved. Mitsubishi Bank, the lead bank for Honda, opened an office in Columbus, Ohio, to serve Honda's Ohio plant.[14]

Occasionally, a firm will set up an operation in the home country of a major competitor with the idea of keeping it so occupied defending that market that it will have less energy to compete in the home country of the first company. Although Kodak claimed its recent decision to open a manufacturing plant in Japan had nothing to do with its Japanese competitor (Fuji), its announcement came just 10 days after Fuji began construction of its first manufacturing facility in the United States.[15]

A company may also go abroad to protect its domestic market when it faces competition from lower-priced foreign imports. By moving part or all of its production facilities to the countries from which its competition is coming, it can enjoy the same advantages, such as less costly labor, raw materials, or energy. Management may decide to manufacture certain components abroad and assemble them in the home country; or, if the product requires considerable labor in the final assembly, it may decide to send components elsewhere for this final operation. A whole new concept, twin factories on the Mexican-American border, came into being because of lower-cost Mexican labor.

Twin factory concept.   Some American companies with labor-intensive assembly operations have established **twin factories**—production facilities on each side of the Mexican-American border, a short distance apart. The American plant produces components requiring capital-intensive processes and delivers them to a plant on the Mexican side, which assembles them. Because the Mexican wage, after various devaluations of the peso, is only one sixth of what Americans would receive or one half of the wage paid to workers in Korea, Hong Kong, Singapore, and Taiwan, American firms are competing successfully with the low-cost operators in Asia. General Motors, for example, has 17 plants performing such labor-intensive tasks as cutting and sewing car seats and assembling electrical wire harnesses. Japanese plants that manufacture in the United States, such as Panasonic (TV) and Sanyo (refrigerators), are also taking advantage of Mexico's low wage rates and its proximity to the United States. About 270,000 workers in 1,050 assembly plants (called *maquiladoras* in Mexico) assemble products ranging from clothing to computer keyboards. Assembly operations now earn more foreign exchange for Mexico than any other export except petroleum. They surpassed tourism in 1985.[16]

Caribbean nations enjoy similar benefits from the Caribbean Basin Initiative. The American apparel industry sends precut pieces to these countries, where they are "assembled" and returned for sale in the United States. This work has created over 100,000 jobs in Haiti, the Dominican Republic, Jamaica, and other nearby countries. Assembly operations such as this and that of Mexico are possible because special laws were passed for these countries that levy duty only on the value added outside of the United States. Normally, an import duty would be assessed on the value of the entire finished product.[17]

Protect foreign markets.   Changing the method of going abroad from exporting to overseas production is often necessary to protect foreign markets. The management of a firm supplying a profitable overseas market by exports may begin to note some ominous signs that this market is being threatened.

Lack of foreign exchange.   One of the first signs is a delay in payment by the importers. They have sufficient local currency but are experiencing delays in obtaining foreign exchange from the government's central bank. The credit manager, by checking with the firm's bank and other exporters, learns that this condition is becoming endemic—a reliable sign that the country is facing a lack of foreign exchange. In examining the country's balance of payments, the financial manager may find that its export revenue has declined, while the import volume remains high. Experienced exporters know that import and foreign exchange controls are in the offing and that there is a good chance of losing the market, especially if they sell consumer products. In times of foreign exchange scarcity, governments will invariably give priority to the importation of raw materials and capital goods.

twin factories production facilities on each side of the Mexican-American border

If the advantages of making the investment outweigh the disadvantages, the company may decide to protect this market by producing locally. Managers know that once the company has a plant in the country, the government will do its utmost to provide foreign exchange for raw materials to keep the plant, a source of employment, in operation. Because imports of competing products are prohibited, the only competition, if any, will have to come from other local manufacturers.

Local production by competitors.   Lack of foreign exchange is not the only reason why a company might change from exporting to manufacturing in a market. Its export business may be growing and payments may be prompt, but still the firm may be forced to set up a plant in the market. The reason is that competitors are also enjoying good profits on a volume that may be reaching a point at which it will support local production.

Should a competing firm decide to put up a factory in the market, management must decide rapidly whether to follow suit or risk losing the market forever. Managers know that many governments, especially those in developing nations, will not only prohibit further imports once the product is produced in the country but will also permit only two or three other companies to enter so as to maintain a sufficient market for these local firms. General Motors tried for years to enter Spain, but the Spanish government, believing there were already enough automobile manufacturers in the country, refused the company entry. Only recently, on the eve of Spain's joining the European Community, was General Motors permitted to enter.

Downstream markets.   A number of OPEC nations have invested in refining and marketing outlets, such as filling stations and heating oil distributors, to guarantee a market for their crude oil at more favorable prices. As you saw in Table 2–8, Petroleos de Venezuela is one of the largest foreign investors in the United States. Kuwait bought Gulf Oil's refining and marketing network in three European countries and also owns 20 percent of British Petroleum, which has the third-largest foreign investment in this country. These are just two examples.[18]

Protectionism.   When a government sees that local industry is threatened by imports, it may erect import barriers to stop or reduce them.* Even threats to do this can be sufficient to induce the exporter to invest in production facilities in the importing country. This and the high-priced yen, which makes it difficult for Japanese exports to compete with American products, are the principal reasons for Japanese investment in the United States.

Guarantee supply of raw materials.   Few developed nations possess sufficient domestic supplies of raw materials. Japan and Europe are almost totally dependent on foreign sources, and even the United States depends on imports for more than half of its aluminum, chromium, manganese, nickel, tin, and zinc. Furthermore, the Department of the Interior estimates that by the end of the century, iron, lead, tungsten, copper, potassium, and sulfur will be added to the critical list.

To ensure a continuous supply, manufacturers in the industrialized countries are being forced to invest primarily in the developing nations, where

---

* See Chapter 3 for a discussion of import barriers.

most new deposits are being discovered.[19] Incidentally, even the United States is seen as a source of raw materials for some resource-poor nations. Shigeo Muraoka, Japanese deputy general consul, states:

> The United States offers an abundance of raw materials. Because Japan has long depended on the United States for various materials, such as grain, coking coal, and lumber, it is entirely logical for Japanese firms to establish facilities close to the sources of these essential raw materials.[20]

Acquire technology and management know-how.   A reason often cited by foreign firms investing in this country is the acquisition of technology and management know-how. The president of the Korean conglomerate Samsung Group ($21.1 billion in sales), speaking of his expansion plans, said, "When it comes to computers and semiconductors, it would be difficult to bring the technology to our country. If we set up our own plant in the United States, we can more easily gain knowledge."[21] The German chemical giant Bayer ($20.7 billion in sales) gave this reason for purchasing Miles Laboratories: "to gain access to the company's well-established distribution, marketing, and research and development."[22]

Geographic diversification.   Many managements have chosen geographic diversification as a means of maintaining stable sales and earnings when the domestic economy or their industry goes into a slump. Generally, when one economy or industry (building materials, for example) is in a trough, it is at its peak elsewhere in the world. In the early 1980s, the foreign operations of American multinationals were outperforming their domestic counterparts. Sunbeam and Ford, for example, reported that their Mexican business was unusually strong, and Twin-Disc, a transmission manufacturer, said that the slowdown in the European market "wasn't nearly as bad as in the United States."[23] In 1987, earnings jumped 32 percent for Hoechst, the German chemical producer, solely because of the earnings of its American subsidiary, Celanese. "Without those earnings, the company would have shown a profit decline," declared Hoechst's chairman.[24]

Political stability.   U.S.-based multinationals have not been motivated by political stability to go overseas, although it is often the prime factor in their choice of where to go. However, European and Third World* firms may actually make foreign investments (usually in the United States) for that reason. An owner of a small German firm that opened a plant in Georgia had this to say as he considered the situation in Europe: "I'm uneasy. I like the Americans and want to retire there. America will be the last country to lose its freedom.[25]

HOW TO ENTER FOREIGN MARKETS

As you learned in Chapter 1, all of the means for becoming involved in overseas business may be subsumed in just two activities: (1) exporting to a

---

* Third World countries are those that belong neither to the Eastern bloc dominated by Russia or to the Western industrialized nations.

foreign market or (2) manufacturing in it.

Exporting

Most firms have begun their involvement in overseas business by exporting—that is, selling some of their regular production overseas. This method requires little in the way of investment and is relatively free of risks. It is an excellent means of getting a feel for international business without committing any great amount of human or financial resources. If management does decide to export, it must choose between *direct* and *indirect* exporting.

indirect exporting the exporting of goods and services through various types of home-based exporters

Indirect exporting.   **Indirect exporting** is simpler than direct exporting because it requires neither special expertise nor large cash outlays. Exporters based in their home country will do the work. Management merely follows instructions. Among the exporters available are (1) *manufacturers' export agents,* who sell for the manufacturer; (2) *export commission agents,* who buy for their overseas customers; (3) *export merchants,* who purchase and sell for their own account; and (4) *international firms,* which use the goods overseas (mining, construction, and petroleum companies are examples).

Indirect exporters, however, pay a price for such service: (1) they will pay a commission to the first three kinds of exporters; (2) foreign business can be lost if exporters decide to change their sources of supply; and (3) firms gain little experience from these transactions. This is why many managements that begin in this manner generally change to direct exporting.

direct exporting the exporting of goods and services by the firm that produces them

Direct exporting.   To engage in **direct exporting,** management must assign the job of handling the export business to someone within the firm. The simplest arrangement is to give someone, usually the sales manager, the responsibility for developing the export businesss. Domestic employees may handle the billing, credit, and shipping initially, and if the business expands, a separate export department may be set up. A firm that has been exporting to wholesale importers in an area and servicing them by visits from either home office personnel or foreign-based sales representatives frequently finds that sales have grown to a point that will support a complete marketing organization.

sales company a business established for the purpose of marketing goods and services, not producing them

Management may then decide to set up a **sales company** in the area. The sales company will import in its own name from the parent and will invoice in local currency. It may employ the same channels of distribution, though the new organization may permit the use of a more profitable arrangement. This type of organization can grow quite large, often invoicing several millions of dollars annually. Before building a plant in Mexico, for many years Eastman Kodak imported and resold cameras and photographic supplies while doing a large business in local film developing. Many firms that began with local repair facilities later expanded to produce simple components. Gradually, they produced more of the product locally until, after a period of time, they were manufacturing all of the components in the country.

Foreign business may evolve sequentially over the path just traced (Singer Sewing Machine's experience), or a company may be forced to move directly to local production (nonsequential) for any of the reasons discussed above in the section "Why Go Abroad?"

■ **FIGURE 2–4**
Share of Acquisitions in Total U.S. Investment for Selected Countries, 1987

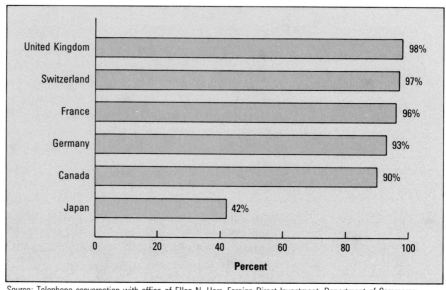

Source: Telephone conversation with office of Ellen N. Herr, Foreign Direct Investment, Department of Commerce, April 7, 1989.

Foreign Manufacturing

When management does decide to become involved in foreign manufacturing, it generally has five distinct alternatives available, though not all of them may be feasible in a particular country. These are:

1. Wholly owned subsidiary.
2. Joint venture.
3. Licensing agreement.
4. Franchising.
5. Contract manufacturing.

A sixth arrangement, the *management contract,* is utilized by both manufacturing and service companies to earn income by providing management expertise for a fee.

Wholly owned subsidiary.   The company that wishes to own a foreign subsidiary outright may (1) start from the ground up by building a new plant, (2) acquire a going concern, or (3) purchase its distributor, thus obtaining a distribution network familiar with its products. In this case, of course, production facilities will have to be built. American companies certainly prefer wholly owned subsidiaries, but they do not have a marked preference for any of the three means of obtaining them.

However, this is not the case for Canadian and European investors in the United States. In 1987, of the $30.5 billion spent, $25.6 billion (84 percent) went to acquire 306 existing businesses, and only $4.9 billion was spent to establish 251 new businesses.[26] As one expert put it, "Buying someone else's strong brands may be the easiest way to expand."[27] Figure 2–4 indicates national preferences.

joint venture a cooperative effort among two or more organizations who share a common interest in a business enterprise or undertaking

Joint venture. A **joint venture** may be (1) a corporate entity between a worldwide company (WWC) and local owners, (2) a corporate entity between two or more WWCs that may or may not be foreign to the area where the joint venture is located, or (3) a cooperative undertaking between two or more firms of a limited-duration project. Large construction jobs are frequently handled by this last form.

Ford and Volkswagen formed a novel joint venture in which their operations in Argentina and Brazil were merged into a holding company, Autolatina, in an effort to eliminate losses suffered by both. The new company, owned 51 percent by VW and 49 percent by Ford (although the venture is considered by both to be an equal partnership), has $4 billion in sales, 76,600 employees, and 15 plants (10 in Brazil). "While Ford will still be Ford and VW will still be VW," said the president of Ford-Brazil, "the merger will provide greater efficiency and technical capacity, a sort of pooling of resources that will help us both." Autolatina uses the facilities and parts of both partners and is developing a new version of a car produced by VW-Brazil, which is called Fox when exported to the United States and Canada.[28]

When the government of a host country requires companies to have some local participation, foreign firms must engage in a joint venture with local owners to do business in that country. In some situations, however, a foreign firm will seek local partners even when there is no local requirement to do so.

Strong nationalism.   Strong nationalistic sentiment may cause the foreign firm to try to lose its identity by joining with local investors. Care must be taken with this strategy, however. Although a large number of people in many developing countries dislike multinationals for "exploiting" them, they still believe, often with good reason, that the products of the foreign companies are superior to the products of purely national firms. One solution to this ambivalence has been to form a joint venture in which the local partners are highly visible, give it an indigenous name, and then advertise that a foreign firm (actually the partner) is supplying the technology. Even wholly owned subsidiaries have followed this strategy.

> Eastman Kodak has eliminated the word *Kodak* from the names of its 100 percent-owned subsidiaries in Venezuela, Mexico, Chile, Peru, and Colombia. Kodak-Venezuela has become Foto Interamericana, and Kodak's large manufacturing company in Mexico is now called Industria Fotografica Interamericana.

Other joint venture benefits.   Other factors that influence managements to enter joint ventures are the tax benefits that some nations (Zimbabwe, for example) extend to companies with local partners or a lack of finances, personnel, or local marketing expertise.

> Merck, the largest U.S. maker of ethical drugs, spent $313 million to acquire 50.5 percent of Banyu Pharmaceutical in Japan. Management had been dissatisfied with the performance of Merck's Japanese subsidiary in the world's second-largest ethical drug market. With this acquisition, the 600-person sales force of Merck-Japan was augmented by Banyu's 350 sales representatives. Merck's chairman said, "To bring new products effectively to market in Japan required a larger and more effective marketing organization. With a controlling interest in Banyu, I would hope for a better penetration of the Japanese market."[29]
>
> To take advantage of Israel's lower labor costs and the 1985 U.S.–Israel Trade Agreement, which (1) reduced import duties on Israeli-made shirts and

(2) permits them quota-free access to the United States, Van Heusen decided to buy the production facilities of an insolvent Israeli clothing manufacturer. When the government refused to sell on Van Heusen's terms, the company formed a joint venture with another Israeli textile-and-apparel conglomerate. Van Heusen will purchase the plant's output for five years, with the option to extend the agreement if satisfied with the local partner's performance, and will have exclusive control over marketing. Although it has trained Israeli engineers and will maintain its own engineers at the operation, the Israeli partner has had to invest all of the capital to expand an existing plant.[30]

Worldwide companies may also enter into joint ventures as a matter of policy so as to reduce investment risk. Their strategy is to enter into a joint venture with either native partners or another worldwide company. Still others, such as Ford and Volkswagen, have joined together to achieve economies of scale. Incidentally, any division of ownership in a joint venture is possible unless there are specific legal requirements.

competitive alliance cooperation between competitors
that may take one of various
forms

Competitive alliances.   Increasingly, companies have been establishing **competitive alliances** (also called strategic alliances) that may include one or more of the forms we have been discussing. The arrangements of Britain's International Computers Limited (ICL) with Japan's Fujitsu are an example.

ICL felt that it needed assistance in two areas—mainframes and office equipment—to share costs, expand access to complementary technologies and markets, and speed product development. It chose Fujitsu for the mainframes, and four distinct agreements were reached:

1. Collaboration with Fujitsu's computer division. ICL provides chip and board design, while Fujitsu contributes chip technology and the expertise in mounting chips in the current boards. Fujitsu assembles and ships the systems to ICL for design and distribution.

2. Cooperation with Fujitsu's semiconductor division to develop dense CMOS technology with 8000 gates. Although this technology did not yet exist, ICL felt that Fujitsu's present technology was more advanced than its own and thus entrusted the design work to Fujitsu.

3. Annual technology meetings to discuss recent developments and search for new areas of cooperation.

4. Commitment to each other as preferential suppliers. When either firm seeks outside sources for components, it gives the other firm the opportunity to bid first.

Although ICL did not establish any joint ventures with Fujitsu, it did form one with General Electric's information services division to work on office equipment.

There is a danger to Fujitsu's partners inherent in such arrangements, as Professor C. K. Prahalad of the University of Michigan warns: "Fujitsu is soaking up a large number of players in the communications and computer industry." He claims that the Japanese are experts in tunneling into the organizations of other people. "We are amazed when they send 25 people to visit a joint partner here and we take pride in saying that we sent 2 people."[31]

In forming competitive alliances with Mitsubishi, Westinghouse took steps to keep its ally from becoming its competitor in the U.S. market, as you will see. Since the 1930s, the two firms have had a licensing agreement to exchange technology. After working together for over 50 years, they formed a 50–50 joint venture to produce components for circuit breakers. Headquartered in Japan, the joint venture supplies components only to the two shareholders. Each partner assembles, tests, and markets the final product.

When the expensive dollar destroyed Westinghouse's competitiveness in circuit breakers, the company formed another joint venture with Mitsubishi that took charge of marketing as well as production and development. The joint venture, located in Pittsburgh, sells in the U.S. market products made in Japan, but it plans to build a factory in this country when the demand is sufficient. To protect its market from being taken over by Mitsubishi, Westinghouse has a service agreement with the joint venture, under which the Westinghouse sales staff markets and services the venture's products.[32]

Disadvantages.   While the joint venture arrangement offers the advantage of less commitment of financial and managerial resources, and thus less risk, there are some disadvantages for the foreign firm. One, obviously, is the fact that profits must be shared. Furthermore, if the law allows the foreign investors to have no more than a 49 percent participation (common in developing countries), they may not have control. This is because the stock markets in these countries are either small or nonexistent, so it is generally impossible to distribute the shares widely enough to permit the foreign firm with its 49 percent to be the largest stockholder.

Lack of control over the joint venture is the reason why many managements resist making such arrangements. They feel that they must have tight control of their foreign subsidiaries to obtain an efficient allocation of investments and production and to maintain a coordinated marketing plan worldwide. For example, local partners might wish to export to markets that the global company serves from its own plants, or they might want to make the complete product locally when the global company's strategy is to produce only certain components there and import the rest from other subsidiaries.[33]

In recent years, numerous governments of developing nations have passed laws requiring local majority ownership for the purpose of giving control of firms within their borders to their own citizens. In spite of these laws, control with a minority ownership is still feasible.

Control with minority ownership.   There have been occasions when the foreign partner has been able to circumvent the spirit of the law and ensure its control by taking 49 percent of the shares and giving 2 percent to its local law firm or some other trusted national.

Another method is to take in a local majority partner, such as a government agency, an insurance company, or a financial institution, that is content to invest merely for a return while leaving the venture's management to the foreign partner. If neither arrangement can be made, the foreign company may still control the joint venture, at last in the areas of major concern, by means of a *management contract.*

management contract an arrangement by which one firm provides management in all or specific areas to another firm

Management contract.   The **management contract** is an arrangement under which a company provides managerial know-how in some or all functional areas to another party for a fee that ranges from 2 to 5 percent of sales. International companies make such contracts with (1) firms in which they have no ownership (examples: Hospital Corporation of America manages hospitals overseas, and Pan American provides management assistance to foreign

WORLDVIEW
How Two Chemical Giants Are Winning in the European Market

Joint ventures are becoming an increasingly common way for companies to exchange complementary strengths. Himont, the 50:50 joint venture formed in 1983 between Italy's Montedison and the US's Hercules, brought together the global marketing strength of Hercules with the world-beating technology of Montedison. As a result, Himont has become the world's leading producer of polypropylene. In Europe, the company has exploited its strong production base in Italy to gain a 20 percent market share in the face of stiff European competition.

Gaining economies of scale and marketing clout. Polypropylene is a flexible plastic substitute for a number of traditional materials such as wood and glass. In the 1970s, the lapse of industry patents attracted a number of LDC producers to the polypropylene market. Faced with the risk of losing both profits and market share, Montedison and Hercules decided to combine forces in a 50:50 joint venture in order to improve economies of scale and gain additional marketing clout. By creating Himont in 1983, the two chemical giants pooled a hefty $900 million in assets and created an enviable annual production capacity of more than 1 million tons.

Why join forces? The complementary strengths of the two partners created a formidable synergy. The marriage of Montedison's technological prowess to Hercules' significant global distribution network enabled both companies to overcome their weaknesses and better exploit their abilities. According to one industry analyst, Hercules' worldwide distribution channels solved Montedison's marketing problems and helped the Italian company translate its laboratory achievements into

market success. At the same time, Montedison's technology rejuvenated Hercules' outdated, costly production facilities.

Technological breakthrough. Montedison, in conjunction with Mitsui Petrochemical Industries, developed a catalyst-process technology for polypropylene production. This process offered Himont a production advantage by slashing costs and creating a superior product. The Italian MNC transferred to Himont both the rights to the catalyst technology and responsibility for the Mitsui relationship.

According to a Himont spokesman, the joint venture's inception coincided with an upturn in the polypropylene market, making it vital to begin operations quickly. Through carefully drafted agreements with its parents, Himont was able to tap their extensive recources for administrative and operational functions and to circumvent the delays and high start-up costs that can plague a joint venture.

Getting down to a winning business. With the venture firmly in place, management was ready to launch its attack on the global market. To clinch the premier position of the global polypropylene market, management realized that it needed to accomplish two feats. First, Himont needed to ensure that it was the lowest-cost producer in the market. Second, it had to develop as many markets and uses for polypropylene as possible. A two-prong strategy is helping Himont fulfill these tasks.

Source: *Business Europe*, BI/Ideas in Action, June 8, 1987.

---

airlines), (2) joint venture partners, and (3) wholly owned subsidiaries. The last arrangement is made solely for the purpose of allowing the parent to siphon off some of the subsidiary's profits. This becomes extremely important when, as in many foreign exchange–poor nations, the parent firm is limited in the amount of profits it can repatriate. Moreover, because the fee is an expense, the subsidiary receives a tax benefit.

Used in joint ventures. Management contracts can enable the global partner to control many aspects of a joint venture even when holding only a minority position. If it supplies key personnel, such as the production and technical managers, the global company can be assured of product quality with which its name may be associated as well as be able to earn additional income by selling the joint venture inputs manufactured in the home plant. This is possible because the larger global company is more vertically integrated. A local paint factory, for example, might have to import certain semiprocessed pigments and driers that the foreign partner produces in its home country for domestic operations. If these can be purchased elsewhere at a lower price, the local majority could insist on other sources of supply. This rarely happens, because the production and technical managers can argue that only inputs from their employer will produce a satisfactory product. They are the experts, and they generally have the final word.

Purchasing commission.   There is another source of income that the global or multinational company derives not only from firms with which it has a management contract but also from joint ventures and wholly owned subsidiaries. That source is a commission for acting as purchasing agent of imported raw materials and equipment. This relieves the affiliates of having to establish credit lines with foreign suppliers and assures them that they will receive the same materials used by the foreign partner. The commission received for this service averages about 5 percent of invoice value and is in addition to the management contract fee.

Licensing.   Frequently, worldwide companies are called on to furnish technical assistance to firms that have sufficient capital and management strength. By means of a **licensing** agreement, one firm (the licensor) will grant to another firm (the licensee) the right to use any kind of expertise, such as manufacturing processes (patented or unpatented), marketing procedures, and trademarks for one or more of the licensor's products.

licensing a contractual arrangement in which one firm grants access to its patents, trade secrets, or technology to another for a fee

> General Tire, for example, has licensed some firms to use its tire technology and others to use its know-how to produce plastic film. At the same time, it has made licensing agreements with V-belt, conveyor belt, and battery manufacturers to use their technology in General Tire subsidiaries.

The licensee generally pays a fixed sum when signing the licensing agreement and then pays a royalty of from 2 to 5 percent of sales over the life of the contract (five to seven years, with option for renewal). The exact amount of the royalty will depend on the amount of assistance given and the relative bargaining power of the two parties.

In the past, licensing was not a primary source of income for globals and multinationals. This has changed, however, especially in this country, because (1) the courts are upholding patent infringement claims more than they used to, (2) patentholders are more vigilant in suing violators, and (3) the Reagan and Bush administrations are pressing foreign governments to enforce their patent laws.[34]

This is forcing foreign companies to obtain licenses instead of making illegal copies. Texas Instruments, for instance, expects to collect over $250 million in royalties through 1990—almost as much as the company's 1987 total profit.[35] It is estimated that Union Carbide, which has a special division to sell its technology and services, added 5 percent to its pre-tax profit just by licensing its process to make a single product—polyethylene, a plastic. According to the Department of Commerce, American firms received $9 billion from the overseas sale of royalties and license fees in 1987 and paid out only $1.33 billion.[36]

However, more than know-how is licensed. In the fashion industry, a number of designers license the use of their names. Pierre Cardin, the largest such licensor, has 840 licenses worldwide on everything from skis to frying pans. These earn him $75 million annually, including $12 million from 32 American licensees. Even Russia pays him $.75 million every year.

Are you giving Coca-Cola free advertising on your T-shirt? The company's manager for merchandise licensing expects the company to make millions from an agreement with the founder of Gloria Vanderbilt. He says the firm agreed to the arrangement because "clothes enhance our image. The money is not important." Inasmuch as the multinational's sales were $7.644 billion (54 percent were foreign revenues) in 1987, perhaps he is right.[37]

Another industry, magazine publishing, is licensing overseas editions. You can buy *Cosmopolitan* in the native language in over a dozen countries, *Playboy* in 10, and *Penthouse* in 5. For some reason, *High Technology* appears only in Japan.

Despite the opportunity to obtain a sizable income from licensing, many firms, especially those that produce high-tech products, will not grant licenses. They fear that a licensee will become a competitor upon expiration of the agreement or that the licensee will aggressively seek to market the products outside of its territory. At one time, licensors routinely inserted a clause in the licensing agreement that prohibited exports, but most governments will not accept such a prohibition. Minicase 2–2 at the end of this chapter presents the opinions of one executive who blames the trade deficit on the earlier licensing practices of American foreign firms.

Franchising.   In recent years, American firms have gone overseas with a new kind of licensing—**franchising.** Franchising permits the franchisee to sell products or services under a highly publicized brand name and a well-proven set of procedures with a carefully developed and controlled marketing strategy. Of the 31,626 overseas outlets operated by 354 American franchising companies, fast-food operations (such as McDonald's, Kentucky Fried Chicken, and Tastee Freeze) are the most numerous—McDonald's alone has about 2,500 outlets in 40 countries (see Figure 2–5). As Table 2–10 indicates, Canada is the dominant market with 9,031 units, Japan is second with 7,366, and Australia is third with 2,816.[38]

Other types of franchisors are hotels (Hilton, Holiday Inn), business services (Muzak, Manpower), soft drinks (Coca-Cola, Orange Crush), home maintenance (Servicemaster, Nationwide Exterminating), and automotive products (Midas).

franchising   a form of licensing in which one firm contracts with another to operate a certain type of business under an established name according to specific rules

contract manufacturing an arrangement in which one firm contracts with another to produce products to its specifications but assumes responsibility for marketing

Contract manufacturing.   International firms employ **contract manufacturing** in two ways. One way is as a means of entering a foreign market without investing in plant facilities. The firm contracts with a local manufacturer to produce products for it according to its specifications. The firm's sales organization markets the products under its own brand, just as Montgomery Ward sells washing machines made by Norge.

The second way is to subcontract assembly work or the production of parts to independent companies overseas. Although the international firm has no equity in the subcontractor, this practice does have some resemblances to

■ **FIGURE 2–5   International Franchising (U.S. Firms) in 1986**

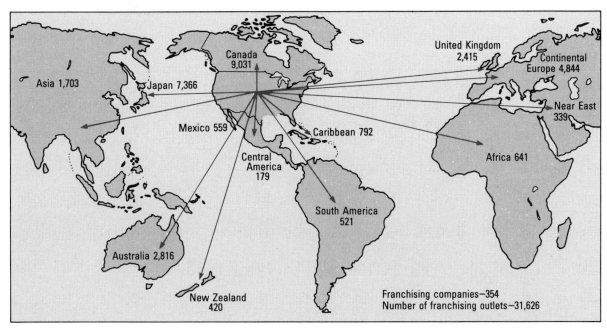

■ **TABLE 2–10**
Where U.S. Franchisors
Operate

Country or Foreign Region	Number of Franchisors
Canada	237
Caribbean	87
Australia	79
Asia (other than Japan and Middle East)	79
Continental Europe	75
United Kingdom	74
Japan	69
Middle East	41
South America	31
Mexico	30
Africa	29
Central America	29
New Zealand	27

Source: *Franchising in the Economy,* 1988, p. 10.

foreign direct investment. When the international firm is the largest or only customer of the subcontractors, it has in effect created in another country a new company that generates employment and foreign exchange for the host nation. Frequently, the international firm will lend capital to the foreign contractor in the same way that a global or multinational firm will lend funds to its subsidiary. Because of these similarities, this practice has gained the name of "foreign direct investment without investment."

Matsushita's Panasonic division is entering the U.S. major appliance market by buying products made by Canadian and U.S. manufacturers, thus avoiding large capital investment initially. If the appliance line is a success, Panasonic is expected to set up its own factories in the United States.[39]

PATHS TO MULTINATIONALISM

Many large global and multinational firms with numerous manufacturing subsidiaries all over the world began their foreign operations by exporting. As this stage became successful, they established sales companies overseas to market their exports. Where the sales company was able to develop a sufficiently large market, a plant to assemble imported parts was set up. Finally, the complete product was manufactured locally. However, this sequence should not be construed as the only way to become involved in foreign markets. In some countries, conditions may require a complete manufacturing plant as the means of initial entry. Worldwide companies today are simultaneously employing all of the methods we have discussed to reach their worldwide markets.[40]

SUMMARY

The volume of international trade in goods and services now amounts to $3 trillion, 19 times its value in 1960. Foreign investment, which has also grown rapidly, now totals about $775 billion. Although there have been some changes in the directions of trade and investment, developed nations still tend to trade with and invest in one another. A noteworthy development of foreign investment has been its rapid increase in the United States ($6.9 billion in 1960 to $262 billion in 1987). Only four nations—Great Britain, the Netherlands, Japan, and West Germany—account for 70 percent of all foreign investment in the United States.

Companies go abroad (exporting and foreign investment) to increase profits and sales and to protect markets, profits, and sales.[41]

The two basic means of going overseas are exporting to markets or producing in them. Exporting may be done directly or indirectly. A firm may become involved in foreign production through various methods: (1) wholly owned subsidiaries, (2) joint ventures, (3) licensing, (4) contract manufacturing, and (5) franchising.

Foreign investment is increasing. Some firms enter overseas markets by exporting, and as they gain experience, they begin to manufacture in these markets. Others bypass exporting and go directly to foreign production. In this case, they may set up wholly owned subsidiaries, but if the costs are too high or if foreign governments prohibit such investment, firms may still become involved in foreign manufacturing through licensing, joint ventures, contract manufacturing, or franchising.

QUESTIONS

1. The greater part of international trade consists of an exchange of raw materials from the developing nations for the manufactured goods from the developed nations. True or false? Explain.

2. The volume of exports has increased, but the ranking of U.S. trading partners in order of importance remains the same year after year. True or false? Of what use is this information to a businessperson?

3. The text suggested that managers can make a preliminary investigation that will give them a "feel" for international trade. Name four publications that they can use for this purpose.

4. Although trade between the Eastern-bloc nations and the West is increasing, why do you believe that the volume of such trade is still a small percentage of world trade?

5. Zaire, according to Table 2–9, has a GNP/capita 33 percent greater than Ethiopia's. It follows that Zaire is a better market than Ethiopia because its inhabitants are richer. Discuss.

6. How can a firm protect its domestic market by investing overseas?

7. Why might management decide to bypass indirect

exporting and go to direct exporting right from the start?

8. Under what conditions might a company prefer a joint venture to a wholly owned subsidiary when making a foreign investment?

9. *a.* Why would the foreign partner in a joint venture wish to have a management contract with the local partner?

b. Why would a global or multinational require a wholly owned foreign subsidiary to sign a management contract when it already owns the subsidiary?

10. What is the purpose of twin factories?

 ## MINICASE 2–1

Method of Entry for Local Manufacturing—The McGrew Company

The McGrew Company, a manufacturer of peanut combines, has for years sold an appreciable number of machines in Brazil. However, a Brazilian firm has begun to manufacture them, and McGrew's local distributor has told Jim Allen, the president, that if McGrew expects to maintain its share of the market, it will also have to manufacture locally. Allen is in a quandary. The market is too good to lose, but McGrew has had no experience with foreign manufacturing operations. Because Brazilian sales and repairs have been handled by the distributor, no one in McGrew has had any firsthand experience in the country.

Allen has made some rough calculations that indicate the firm can make money by manufacturing in Brazil, but the firm's lack of marketing expertise in the country troubles him. He calls in Joan Beal, the export manager, and asks her to prepare a list of all the options open to McGrew, with their advantages and disadvantages. Allen also asks Beal to indicate her preference.

1. Assume you are Joan Beal. Prepare a list of all the options, and give the advantages of each.

2. Which of the options would you recommend?

3. Assuming the president's calculations are correct and a factory to produce locally the number of machines that McGrew now exports to Brazil will offer a satisfactory return on the investment, what special information about Brazil will you want to gather?

MINICASE 2–2

Quick Research—Thomas Seed Company

The Thomas Seed Company grows and markets seeds in the United States. Its specialty is grass seeds. Bob Thomas, the president, has become dissatisfied with his company's growth and has been wondering if exporting might be possible to increase sales. Thomas attended a seminar recently where he heard about the exporting successes of some small firms whose total sales are about the same as Thomas Seeds' ($15 million annually). He also learned that the U.S. Department of Commerce gathers statistics on exports and publishes them in a publication called *FT410,* a copy of which is in the university library nearby.

He called in Mary Adams, the marketing manager, and asked her to do some quick research. "Mary, there may be a way to increase our sales by exporting. I heard that the university has a publication, *FT410,* published by the Department of Commerce, which gives the cumulative totals by product and importing country. It's a monthly, but there

is an issue with the annual totals. Please check the exports of grass seeds. Find out who imports them and how much. Compare the latest year available with, say, 1985. That way we can see if there are any kinds whose exports are growing or countries that are increasing their purchases from the United States. Please let me see the results as soon as you have them."

(Hint: Ask your professor for a copy of the relevant pages of the *FT410.*)

(Hint to the professor: The pages are with the transparency masters in your *I.M.*)

1. Which countries seem to be good markets?

2. Do these countries import any other kinds of seeds from the United States?

SUPPLEMENTARY READINGS

Competitive alliances

"ABB: The New Energy Powerhouse." *International Management,* June 1988, pp. 24–30.

"Business without Borders." *U.S. News & World Report,* June 20, 1988, pp. 48–53

"Collaborative Marketing." *Business Marketing,* April 1987, pp. 33–34.

"Competitive Alliances: Forging Ties Abroad." *International Management,* March 1987, p. 57.

"Competitive Alliances: From the ICL–Fujitsu Link." *Business International,* October 13, 1986, pp. 321–22.

"Competitive Alliances: Westinghouse–Mitsubishi Fuse in Power Market." *Business International,* November 24, 1986, pp. 369–70.

"Facing the Realities of Global Alliances." *International Management,* April 1986, pp. 22–30.

"How Business Is Creating Europe, Inc." *Business Week,* September 7, 1987, pp. 40–41.

"The Down Side of Competitive Alliances and How to Cut Your Risks." *Business International,* January 12, 1987, p. 15.

"With Allies Like These." *The Economist,* November 19, 1988, pp. 75–76.

Foreign investment

"America Still Buys the World." *The Economist,* September 17, 1988, pp. 71–72.

"Are the Japanese Hollowing Out Their Economy?" *International Management,* February 1989, pp. 36–39.

Constantinos, C. Markides, and Norman Berg. "Manufacturing Offshore Is Bad Business." *Harvard Business Review,* September–October 1988, pp. 113–20.

"Foreign Direct Investment in Developing Countries." *Kredietbank Weekly Bulletin,* June 5, 1987, pp. 1–6.

"Foreign Investment Regulations at a Glance." *Business Latin America,* February 29, 1988, pp. 68–69.

"If You Can't Beat 'Em, Buy 'Em: Takeovers Arrive in Japan." *Business Week,* September 29, 1986, pp. 80–81.

"Let's Make a Deal Goes Global." *The Economist,* February 22, 1988, pp. 66–69.

"On the Move Again." *The Economist,* November 5, 1988, p. 83.

"The International Investment Position of the United States in 1987." *The Survey of Current Business,* June 1988, pp. 76–82.

Foreign investment in the United States

"A Cash-Rich Europe Finds the U.S. Ripe for Picking." *Business Week,* January 12, 1988, pp. 48–58.

"For Sale: America." *Time,* September 14, 1987, pp. 52–62.

"How Japan Will Spend Its Cash." *Fortune,* November 21, 1988, pp. 195–210.

"Japanese Firms Hunt Big Foreign Game." *The Wall Street Journal,* November 10, 1988, p. A20.

"U.S. Business Enterprises Acquired or Established by Foreign Direct Investors in 1987." *Survey of Current Business,* May 1988, pp. 50–58.

Franchising

"European Franchisors Go Global." *Europe,* June 1988, pp. 18–19.

Franchising in the Economy. U.S. Department of Commerce, 1987.

"International Franchising." *INC,* April 1988, pp. 116–19.

"McWorld?" *Business Week,* October 13, 1986, pp. 78–86.

Joint ventures

Beamish, Paul. "The Characteristics of Joint Ventures in Developed and Developing Countries." *Columbia Journal of World Business,* Fall 1985, pp. 13–15.

Contractor, Farok J. "Strategies for Structuring Joint Ventures." *Columbia Journal of World Business,* Winter 1984, pp. 30–36.

————. "The Advantages of Joint Ventures as a Way of Doing Business Overseas." *Management Research from Rutgers,* Fall 1986, p. 4.

"How Bry-Air Benefited by 'Thinking Small' in Its Indian JV." *Business Asia,* July 20, 1987, p. 226.

"Japan, U.S. Steelmakers Link Up." *The Wall Street Journal,* November 18, 1988, p. A8.

O'Reilly, Anthony. "Establishing Successful Joint Ventures in Developing Nations: A CEO's Perspective." *Columbia Journal of World Business,* Spring 1988, pp. 10–16.

"Risks of East–West Joint Ventures." *Euromoney,* September 1987, pp. 476–79.

"Soviet Business without Borders." *U.S. News & World Report,* June 20, 1988, pp. 48–53.

Licensing

"How Caterpillar China Coped with Key Obstacles in Major Licensing Deal." *Business International,* July 13, 1987, pp. 217–19.

"How One International Firm Manages a Licensee Network in Latin America." *Business Latin America,* October 3, 1988, p. 314.

"Licensing." *CFO,* June 1987, pp. 43–48.

"Licensing Regulations in 18 Nations." *Business International,* March 7, 1988, pp. 68–69.

"New Profits from Patents." *Fortune,* April 25, 1988, pp. 185–90.

"Running a Licensing Department: The Critical Keys to Success." *Business International,* June 13, 1988, pp. 177–78.

Market entry

"Investing in India: RJR-Nabisco's Success via an Indirect Route." *Business Asia,* August 10, 1987, pp. 255–56.

"Three Consumer Firms Find Ways into India." *Business Asia,* February 8, 1988, pp. 50–51.

"Turning the Tables on the Japanese." *U.S. News & World Report,* June 30, 1986, p. 46.

"Why W. R. Grace Opted to Go It Alone in Its China Investment." *Business Asia,* September 7, 1987, pp. 282–83.

Why go overseas?

Constantinos, C. Markides, and Norman Berg. "Manufacturing Offshore Is Bad Business." *Harvard Business Review,* September–October 1988, pp. 113–20.

DeWitt, R. Peter. "Factors Influencing U.S. Investment Abroad. *CSU Los Angeles Business Forum,* Summer 1986, pp. 12–19.

"Japanese Firms Hunt Big Game." *The Wall Street Journal,* November 10, 1988, p. A20.

"Taking the Sting out of the Plunging Dollar." *Business Week,* December 7, 1987, pp. 72–73.

"Who Made Your Underwear?" *Forbes,* July 25, 1988, pp. 56–58.

"Why the Kings of Crude Want to Be Pump Boys." *Business Week,* March 21, 1988, pp. 110–12.

"Why Unilever Wants to Buy America." *Business Week,* October 21, 1985, p. 118.

"Worldwide Connections." *Forbes,* June 27, 1988, pp. 78–82.

ENDNOTES

1. The value of service exports is estimated to be roughly $900 billion. Service data are very incomplete, and estimates vary according to how they are defined.

2. This illustrates an interesting point concerning data provided by supranational organizations and governments. The UN claims that the volume of international trade for 1981 was $1,962 billion, whereas the International Monetary Fund states that it was only $1,832 billion. When queried by telephone, the head of the IMF statistical department explained that because nonmember communist countries did not report to the IMF, he had to use data that came from communist trading partners that were members. Also, when countries are slow in reporting, the IMF and the UN often estimate by extrapolation. Later, when data do arrive, corrections are made. These charges are made continuously and for previous periods. As late as July 1982, the UN made changes in data for the year 1975. Compare the June and July 1982 issues of the *UN Monthly Bulletin of Statistics,* table 52.

3. "U.S.–Canada Agreement Eliminates Trade Barriers," *Peat Marwick Executive Newsletter,* March 1989, p. 1.

4. One of the writers was given the job of searching for countries where production facilities for industrial rubber products might be set up. Included in the preliminary study was an investigation of the amounts of these goods that were currently being imported. It was evident that certain countries could not have local manufacturing facilities because of the magnitude of their imports. This provided an initial list of prospects, which were then investigated according to other criteria established by management.

5. "The International Investment Position of the United States in 1987," *Survey of Current Business,* June 1988, pp. 76–84; and telephone conversation with the U.S. Treasury.

6. *Peat Marwick Executive Newsletter,* October 1988, p. 3.

7. "Technical Notes," *World Development Report, 1982* (Washington, D.C.: World Bank, 1982), p. 162.

8. "Overhauling the Drug Laws to Promote Competition," *Business Week,* September 4, 1978, p. 65.

9. "The Pitfalls in Global Restructuring," *Dun's Business Month,* June 1988, p. 41.

10. Of the eight licensing agreements in which one of the writers was involved, five came about as a result of unexpected visits from foreign businessmen. Vernon, a professor of international business, noted in a 1968 study that U.S. foreign investment in developed nations increased at the same 10 percent rate as did the arrivals and departures of international travelers in North America and Europe from 1953 to 1965. He suggested that there was a direct relationship. From Christopher Tugendhat,*The Multinationals* (New York: Random House, 1972), p. 25.

11. "U.S. Concerns Seek Inspiration for Products from Overseas," *The Wall Street Journal,* January 3, 1984, p. 15.

12. "U.S. Companies See 1992 as Opportunity," *San Jose Mercury News,* March 26, 1989, p. 1.

13. "A Hard Road for Auto Parts Makers," *Fortune,* March 7, 1983, p. 110.

14. *The Columbus Dispatch,* March 20, 1987, p. 12.

15. "Kodak Will Open Its First Plant in Japan," *The Modesto Bee,* October 1988, p. B5.

16. *Banamex Review* (Mexico City: Banco Nacional de Mexico, January 1988 and December 1977), p. 17 and pp. 415–18.

17. "Who Made Your Underwear?" *Forbes,* July 25, 1988, pp. 56–58.

18. "Why the Kings of Crude Want to Be Pump Boys," *Business Week,* March 21, 1988, pp. 110–12.

19. It is not only the producers of metals and petroleum products that import a large part of the raw materials they use. Such diverse firms as A&P, Anderson Clayton, and Unilever also maintain large foreign operations to ensure a constant supply of coffee (A&P), cotton and coffee (Anderson Clayton), and vegetable oils (Unilever).

20. "Japan's Foreign Direct Investment: Trends and Outlook," *Japan Report* (New York: Japan Information Service, April 16, 1977), p. 2.

21. "Bargain Hunter," *Fortune,* September 6, 1982, p. 11.

22. "Foreigners Grab for Value in the U.S.," *Business Week,* November 14, 1977, pp. 178–79.

23. "As Recession Bites, Many Multinationals Get Lift from Abroad," *The Wall Street Journal,* July 23, 1980, p. 1.

24. "Taking the Sting out of the Plunging Dollar," *Business Week,* December 7, 1987, pp. 72–73.

25. "The New Migration—of Money," *Newsweek,* May 3, 1976, p. 65.

26. "U.S. Business Enterprises Acquired or Established by Foreign Direct Investors in 1987," *Survey of Current Business,* May 1988, p. 52.

27. "Why Unilever Wants to Buy American," *Business Week,* October 21, 1985, p. 16.

28. "Brazil," *International Management,* June 1987, p. 4; and "New Cars," *Brasil,* July 1987, p. 9.

29. From "A Japanese Tonic for Merck," *Business Week,* August 22, 1983, p. 39.

30. "Van Heusen–Polgat JV First to Take Advantage of U.S.–Israel FTA," *Business International,* August 18, 1986, p. 262.

31. "Use a Long Spoon," *Forbes,* December 15, 1986, p. 122.

32. "Westinghouse–Mitsubishi Fuse in Power Market," *Business International,* November 24, 1986, p. 370.

33. One of the writers, who was employed by the Mexican affiliate of an American company, which held 33 percent equity in the affiliate, was asked by the Mexican secretary of commerce why the Mexican plant was not exporting to Guatemala. The reason, which he could not disclose, was that the company served the Guatemalan market from wholly owned plants in the United States and thus kept all the profits. A hurried call to Akron gave him permission to do some exporting to Guatemala to appease the Mexican government, but he was asked "not to try too hard."

34. Telephone conversation with Pfizer executive, April 6, 1989.

35. "New Profits from Patents," *Fortune,* April 25, 1988, pp. 185–90.

36. "U.S. International Transactions," *Survey of Current Business,* September 1988, pp. 33–38.

37. "What's in a Name? Millions if It's Licensed," *Business Week,* April 8, 1985, pp. 97–98.

38. *Franchising in the Economy* (Washington, D.C.: U.S. Department of Commerce, 1988), p. 10.

39. From "Here They Come Again," *Forbes,* June 17, 1985, p. 54.

40. Gillette, in a recent annual report, states that its products are sold in more than 200 countries. It manufacturers in 28 countries and markets through agents or distributors elsewhere.

41. For a good analysis of the factors that have influenced U.S. foreign investment, read R. Peter DeWitt's "Factors Influencing U.S. Investment Abroad," *CSU, Los Angeles Business Forum,* Summer 1986, pp. 12–19.

Chapter 3

Economic Theories on International Trade, Development, and Investment

Protectionist barriers are to economics what steroids are to athletes—a temporary fix and a long-term disaster.

Robert Allen, chairman, AT&T

What one does oneself is fair trade and what the other fellow does is unfair.

Sir Ray Denman, EC ambassador to the United States

LEARNING OBJECTIVES

In this chapter, you will study:

1. Some of the theories that attempt to explain why certain goods are traded internationally.

2. The basic arguments for imposing trade restrictions.

3. Tariff and nontariff trade barriers.

4. The weaknesses of GNP/capita as an economic indicator.

5. The common characteristics of developing nations.

6. The new definition of economic development, which includes more than economic growth.

7. Why some governments are changing from an import substitution strategy of development to one of export promotion and the implications of this change for businesspeople.

8. Some of the theories of foreign direct investment.

KEY WORDS AND CONCEPTS

- Mercantilism
- Absolute advantage
- Comparative advantage
- Factor endowment
- Exchange rate
- Devalue a currency
- International Product Life Cycle (IPLC)
- Dumping
- Countervailing duties
- Tariffs
- Ad valorem, specific, and compound duties
- Variable levy
- Nontariff barriers (NTBs)
- Quotas
- Voluntary export restraints (VERs)
- Orderly marketing arrangements
- Countertrade
- Developed, developing
- Newly industrializing countries (NICs)
- Nonmarket economy
- Underground economy
- Purchasing power parity
- Third World
- Human needs approach
- Unbalanced growth theory
- Import substitution
- Monopolistic advantage theory
- Cross investment
- Internalization theory

BUSINESS INCIDENT

A Practical Application of the Law of Comparative Advantage . . .

After the Marxist government in Chile was overthrown in 1973, the Chicago Boys (a group of conservative Chilean economists educated at the University of Chicago) began decreasing import duties, which averaged about 94 percent, to force local manufacturers to lower their prices and become competitive in the export market. As Chile's economy improved, Chileans began to experience the benefits of lower duties. Shoppers could buy Heinz catsup and Schlitz beer in the supermarkets and then wheel them in German shopping baskets to their Italian cars. Chilean-made products were cheaper also—suits that had cost $100 were selling for $80.

The disadvantage of this action was that a number of local firms either went out of business or contracted their operations. For example, when import duties on appliances were reduced from 100 percent to 32 percent, one of the principal local manufacturers suffered a 75 percent loss in sales. "We're going to lose a large part of our appliance industry," conceded Alvaro Bardon, a 37-year-old Chicago Boy, then head of the Central Bank of Chile, "and also our electronics industry and our automobile assembly plants." Mr. Bardon is hardly disappointed however. "Those are products we should be importing," he says. "We have other things based on our own farm products, our timberlands, our fisheries, and our mineral resources that we should be making because they give us a natural advantage over other countries."

In effect, this Chilean economist was admitting, as were policymakers and academicians worldwide, that the country's trade policy of *import substitution* (manufacturing goods locally to reduce their importation) was not helping to reduce its financial problems and attain higher economic growth rates. Import substitution had lost much of its former respect, and many governments were instituting a policy of *export promotion*. Government leaders

BUSINESS INCIDENT (concluded)

were noting the successes of the newly industrializing countries.

Any businessperson in Chile who knew anything about economic theory could have predicted what was about to happen. To increase exports, the economists were establishing policies to assist the industrial sectors, which had, as Bardon stated, a natural advantage; that is, because of a plentiful supply of the production factors, producers could compete pricewise in international markets. But, for this natural advantage to be effective, the exporters needed a more stable economy in which to operate. The economists responded with the traditional solutions: reduce public expenditure, lower the horrendous inflation rate of 131 percent (the annual rate between 1971 and 1980), and remove the protection from imports that many local manufacturers had enjoyed. A lower inflation rate enables exporters to quote reasonably stable prices and helps keep their costs down. Reducing public expenditure aids in reducing inflation and should reduce government bureaucracy, often the cause of considerable additional expense to business. Reducing protection from imports can force local manufacturers to lower their costs, which will contribute to lower inflation, provide a local source of competitively priced inputs to exporters, and can, as happened in Chile, actually turn some of these manufacturers into exporters themselves.

How successful were these measures? Exports certainly increased—from 14 percent of the gross domestic product (GDP) in 1965 to 30 percent in 1987. This percentage was higher than that of Germany, the world's largest exporter. Much of this export growth is in agricultural products to the United States. Because of opposite seasons, Chile has a natural advantage in this market. Remember the anguish in 1989 among Chilean producers when just two grapes sent to the United States were found to contain cyanide? That single act of terrorism (a political force) might have drastically affected Chile's economic forces by wiping out a multimillion-dollar market for the country's agricultural exports. Increased attention to agriculture also resulted in a huge decrease in Chile's agricultural imports. Grain imports dropped from 1.7 million tons in 1974 to only .26 million tons in 1986. Imagine the savings in foreign currency from this decrease.

Although still excessive, removing price controls, reducing public spending, and increasing competition for local manufacturers helped reduce the annual inflation rate from 131 percent to 19.7 percent over the 1980–87 period. An indicator of the increased efficiency of industry is the doubling of the 1970 gross output per employee.

Source: "Capitalistic Catch," *The Wall Street Journal*, December 12, 1977, p. 1; "Trade Policy Reform" *World Development Report, 1987* (Washington, D.C.: World Bank, 1987), pp. 95–112; and various tables from *World Development Report, 1988.*

The Business Incident illustrates a practical application of the keystone of international trade theory—the law of comparative advantage. Note, too, the education of the head of Chile's central bank, which is typical of government policymakers and advisors worldwide. When they have a particularly strong influence in government affairs, they are frequently dubbed with such names as the "Chicago Boys" in Chile, "tecnicos" in Mexico, or "Berkeley Mafia" (economists educated at the University of California–Berkeley) in Indonesia.

What is the significance for international businesspeople? For one thing, since they frequently will be dealing with government officials trained in economics, they must be prepared to speak their language. When they present plans requiring governmental approval, businesspeople must take care to see that the plans are written in terms that are economically sound, for they are almost certain to be studied by economists and will often need to be approved by them. Marketers proposing large projects to government planners need to be aware that the key determinant now is economic efficiency rather than mere financial soundness.[1] Moreover, as you have seen in the case of Chile, a knowledge of economic concepts, especially in the areas of international trade, development, and investment, frequently will provide an insight as to future government action.

INTERNATIONAL TRADE THEORY

Why do nations trade? This question and the equally important proposition of predicting the direction, composition, and volume of goods traded are what international trade theory attempts to answer. Interestingly, as is the case with numerous economic writings, the first formulation of international trade theory was politically motivated. Adam Smith, incensed by government intervention and control over both domestic and foreign trade, published *An Inquiry into the Nature and Causes of the Wealth of Nations* (1776) in which he tried to destroy the mercantilist philosophy.

Mercantilism

mercantilism an economic philosophy that a government can improve the well-being of its citizens through laws and regulations and that wealth can be obtained by promoting exports and stifling imports

Mercantilism, the object of his attack, was an economic philosophy which held that the government could improve the well-being of a nation's people by means of laws and regulations. Mercantilists also believed it was essential to the nation's welfare to accumulate a stock of precious metals, which were, in their view, the only source of wealth. Because England had no mines, the mercantilists looked to international trade to supply the gold and silver. Exports were promoted and imports were stifled so that the positive balance of trade that resulted would be settled in precious metals. To reduce the need for imports, domestic industry was encouraged and protected by subsidies and import duties. Although the mercantilist era ended in the late 1700s, its arguments live on. A "favorable" trade balance still means that a nation exports more goods and services than it imports. In balance-of-payment accounting, an export that brings dollars to this country is called "positive," but imports that cause dollar outflow are labeled "negative."

An example of modern-day mercantilism was the new industrial policy based on heavy state intervention that the socialists were creating for France. They nationalized key industries and banks so as to use the power of the state as both (1) stockholder and financier and (2) customer and marketer to revitalize the nation's industrial base. With nearly one third of France's productive capacity and 70 percent of its high-tech electronic capabilities in the hands of the government, its power was approaching the level of state intervention in the 17the century. Some writers were calling this high-tech mercantilism. In 1986, after five years of little growth and high unemployment, the government reversed its policy when Jacques Chiroc, a conservative, won the election for premier against President Mitterand's Socialist candidate. Chiroc proceeded to denationalize $23 billion worth of government holdings in banking, insurance, and industry.

In the United States, there is a growing opinion that Japan is the present-day "Fortress of Mercantilism." American businesspeople are concerned that its trade barriers to their imports are the result of Japanese insularity, traditional preoccupation with self-sufficiency, and an "us against them" mentality. The U.S. Secretary of Commerce recently stated, "They tell us they have to protect their markets because of their culture. They haven't joined the world yet." Comments from the Japanese seem to confirm what some Americans are saying. "The public is not in favor of perfect markets," says a Japanese bank manager. "We would like to preserve the substance of our culture. If we move to free trade, we may lose Japanese virtue in the process."[2]

Theory of Absolute Advantage

Adam Smith claimed that market forces, not government controls, should determine the direction, volume, and composition of international trade. He argued that under free trade, each nation should specialize in producing those goods that it could produce most efficiently (had an absolute advantage). Some of these would be exported to pay for the imports of goods that could be produced more efficiently elsewhere. Smith showed by his example of **absolute advantage** that both nations would gain from trade.

absolute advantage   when one nation can produce a good at a lower cost than another nation can

An example.   Suppose that for each unit of input, the following quantities of rice and automobiles can be produced in the United States and Japan:

Commodity	Output per Unit of Input	
	United States	Japan
Tons of rice	3	1
Automobiles	2	4

In the United States, three tons of rice can be produced per unit of input as can two automobiles. Therefore, in the United States, three tons of rice should have the same price as two automobiles. In Japan, however, only one ton of rice can be produced with the unit of output needed to produce four automobiles, therefore, one ton of rice should be as costly as four automobiles. The United States has an absolute advantage in rice production (3 to 1), while Japan's absolute advantage is in automobile manufacturing (4 to 2). Will anyone anywhere give the Japanese automaker more than one ton of rice for his four automobiles? According to the example, a number of American rice producers should because they can get only two automobiles for three tons of rice at home. Similarly, Japanese automakers, once they learn that they can obtain more than one ton of rice for every four automobiles in the United States, will be eager to trade Japanese autos for American rice.

Gains from trade.   Suppose the American rice growers and the Japanese automakers realize that they are more efficient in these products and decide to specialize. The United States shifts all of its units of input to rice, and Japan makes only automobiles. Japan has an exportable surplus of four automobiles, and the United States has a surplus of three tons of rice.

Suppose each nation makes a straight swap of its surplus-three tons of rice for four automobiles. The rice grower receives three fourths of an automobile for each ton of rice, which is more than the two thirds of an automobile received from domestic automakers. The Japanese automakers gained also because they now receive three fourths of a ton of rice per car through trade instead of one fourth of a ton of rice from Japanese growers. Both have gained through specialization. Each now has the following quantities:

Commodity	United States	Japan
Tons of rice	3	3
Automobiles	4	4

Terms of trade.   Although the rate of one ton of rice per three fourths of an automobile in our example was the result of each nation swapping its surplus, the rate of exchange could have been anything between the limits of the U.S. local exchange rate of three tons of rice for two autos to the Japanese internal rate of one ton of rice for four autos. Clearly, both nations have gained by trading. But what if one country has an absolute advantage in the production of *both* rice and automobiles? Will there still be a basis of trade?

Theory of Comparative Advantage

Ricardo demonstrated in 1817 that even though a nation held an absolute advantage in the production of both goods, trade could still take place between two countries with advantages for each as long as the less efficient nation was not *equally* less efficient in the production of both goods.[3] Let us slightly change our first example so that now the United States has an absolute advantage in producing *both* rice and automobiles. Note, too, that compared to the United States, Japan is less inefficient in automaking than in producing rice. Therefore, it has a relative advantage (or **comparative advantage,** according to Ricardo) in producing automobiles. In other words, compared to the U.S., it is not as *inefficient* in making automobiles as it is in producing rice.

comparative advantage although one nation has an absolute disadvantage with respect to another nation in the production of two goods, its absolute disadvantage is less in one of the goods

	Output per Unit of Input	
Commodity	United States	Japan
Tons of rice	6	3
Automobiles	5	4

In the absence of trade, then, 1 ton of rice would be exchanged in the United States for 5/6 of an automobile; in Japan, the exchange rate would be 1 ton of rice for 1 1/3 automobiles. If American rice growers can obtain more than 5/6 of an automobile somewhere for a ton of rice (the local rate of exchange), it would pay them to trade. Obviously, they could do better by trading with Japanese automakers, who must pay 1 1/3 automobiles for 1 ton of Japanese rice.

Gains from trade.   Suppose the United States and Japan again specialize in rice (U.S.) and automobiles (Japan). The American exportable surplus is now 6 tons of rice gained from shifting its inputs to rice production, and Japan has a surplus of 4 automobiles to export. However, a straight swap of 6 tons of rice for 4 automobiles would result in worse terms for the rice growers than they can get domestically. But, remember that a trade is beneficial to both sides if each can get more by trading with each other than by trading at home.

Locally, the American rice growers get 5/6 of an automobile for a ton of rice, but the Japanese automakers have to give 1 1/3 automobiles for a ton of Japanese rice. They split the difference at 1 ton of rice for one automobile. After the trade, each has the following:

Commodity	United States	Japan
Tons of rice	8	4
Automobiles	4	4

Note that this trade left the United States with some surplus rice and one less automobile than it had before the trade. Japan has more rice and the same number of automobiles. However, the U.S. rice growers should be able to trade the 2-ton rice surplus for two automobiles elsewhere. The final result will be:

Commodity	United States	Japan
Tons of rice	6	4
Automobiles	6	4

This simple concept is the basis for international trade.

Notice that in our examples we mentioned a unit of input. This is a more modern version of the examples of Ricardo and Smith, who used only labor input. They did so because at that time only labor was considered important in calculating production costs.[4] Also, no consideration was given to the possibility of producing the same goods with different combinations of factors. Furthermore, no explanation was given as to why production costs differed. Not until 1933 did Ohlin, a Swedish economist building on work begun by the economist Heckscher, develop the theory of **factor endowment**.[5]

Heckscher-Ohlin Theory of Factor Endowment

The Heckscher-Ohlin theory states that international and interregional differences in production costs occur because of differences in the supply of production factors. Those goods that require a large amount of the abundant—and thus less costly—factor will have lower production costs, enabling them to be sold for less in international markets. For example, China, which is relatively well endowed with labor compared to the Netherlands, ought to concentrate on producing labor-intensive goods; the Netherlands, with relatively more capital than labor, should specialize in capital-intensive products. When these countries trade, each will obtain the goods that require large amounts of the production factor in relatively short supply at a lower price, and both will benefit from the transaction.

How useful is this theory for explaining present-day trading patterns? Countries with relatively large amounts of land (such as Australia) do export land-intensive products (such as grain and cattle) whereas Hong Kong exports labor-intensive goods.[6] There are exceptions, however, due in part to the assumptions made by Ohlin. One was the fact that the prices of the factors depend only on the factor endowment. We know this is untrue. Factor prices are not set in a perfect market. Legislated minimum wages and benefits force the cost of labor to rise to a point greater than the value of the product that many workers can produce. Investment tax credits reduce the cost of capital

factor endowment Heckscher-Ohlin theory that countries export products requiring large amounts of their abundant production factors and import products requiring large amounts of their scarce production factors below market cost, and so forth. The result is factor prices that do not fully reflect their supply.

Ohlin also assumed that the same technology was universally available, but this is not so. There is always a lag between the introduction of a new production method and its worldwide application. As a result, superior technology often permits a nation to produce goods at a cost lower than that of a country that is better endowed with the required factor. Closely related to this assumption was another that presumed a given product to be labor or capital intensive. Yet anyone who has watched construction methods in less developed nations knows that wet concrete can be poured either by a gang of laborers with buckets or a crane and its operator. Transportation costs were ignored, but there are goods for which freight charges are so high that the landed cost (export sales price plus transportation charges) is greater than local costs. In this case, there will be little trade. Why not say there will be no trade?

It is because of a demand-side construct that is always difficult to deal with in economic theory and that we have so far neglected—*differences in taste*. As businesspeople, however, we cannot neglect this difference, which enables trade to flow in a direction completely contrary to that predicted by the theory of comparative advantage—from high- to low-cost nations. France sells us wine, cosmetics, clothing, and even Perrier drinking water, all of which are produced here and generally sold at lower prices. Germany and Italy send Porsches and Maseratis to one of the largest automobile producers in the world. We buy these goods not only on the basis of price, the implied independent variable in the theory we have been examining, but also because of taste preferences.

Finally, one other point to note is that these theories have been presented without the mention of money. It could have been introduced earlier, but it really would have added nothing to the explanation. It can, however, change the direction of trade. Let us introduce money to see how this may occur.

Introducing Money

Suppose the total cost of land, labor, and capital to produce either the daily output of rice or automobiles in the example on absolute advantage is $10,000 in the United States or 2.5 million yen in Japan. The cost per unit is as follows:

| Commodity | Price per Unit | |
	United States	Japan
Tons of rice	$\dfrac{\$10,000}{3} = \$3,330/\text{ton}$	$\dfrac{2.5 \text{ million yen}}{1} = 2.5 \text{ million yen/ton}$
Automobiles	$\dfrac{\$10,000}{2} = \$5,000/\text{auto}$	$\dfrac{2.5 \text{ million yen}}{4} = 0.625 \text{ million yen/auto}$

For the traders to know if it is more advantageous to buy locally or to import, they need to know the prices in their own currencies. To convert from foreign to domestic currency, they must have the *exchange rate*.

exchange rate the price of one currency stated in terms of another currency

Exchange rate.   The **exchange rate** is the price of one currency stated in terms of the other. If the prevailing rate is $1 = 250 yen, then 1 yen must be worth

0.004 dollar.* Using the exchange rate of $1 = 250 yen, the prices in the preceding example appear to the U.S. trader as follows:

Commodity	Price per Unit (Dollars) United States	Japan
Tons of rice	$3,330	$10,000
Automobile	5,000	2,500

The American rice producers can earn $6,670 more by exporting rice to Japan than they can by selling locally; but can the Japanese automakers gain by exporting to the United States? To find out, they must convert the American prices to Japanese yen.

Commodity	Price per Unit (Yen) United States	Japan
Ton of rice	0.83 million yen	2.5 million yen
Automobile	1.25 million yen	0.625 million yen

It is apparent that the Japanese automakers will export cars to the United States because a greater profit, 0.625 million yen, can be earned. The American automobile manufacturers, however, will need some very strong sales arguments to sell in the United States if they are to overcome the $2,500 price differential. Ricardo *did not consider* this possibility; in his time, products were considered homogeneous and therefore were sold primarily on the basis of price.

Influence of exchange rate.   Rice to Japan and cars to the United States will be the direction of trade as long as the exchange rate remains in a range around $1 = 250 yen. But if the dollar strengthens to $1 = 750 yen, the American rice will cost as much in yen as the Japanese rice, and importation will cease. On the other hand, should the dollar weaken to $1 = 125 yen, then a Japanese car will cost $5,000 to American traders, and they will have little reason to import. Incidentally, when the dollar did reach 125 yen in 1988, Japanese automakers were forced to accept less yen on their sales to the United States in order for their dollar prices to remain competitive with American car prices.

Another way a nation can avoid losing markets and regain competitiveness in world markets is to **devalue** its currency (lower its price in terms of other currencies). Notice that this leaves the domestic prices unchanged.

devalue a currency   lower its price in terms of other currencies

Mexico, which depends on American tourists for a large part of its foreign exchange earnings, was faced with losing this business because inflation had driven peso prices so high that at the rate of 12.5 pesos = $1, dollar prices to the Americans were excessive. Mexican officials had three alternatives: (1) deflate to drive peso prices down (time consuming and painful to the Mexicans); (2) lower prices by government edict (bureaucratic difficulties as with any system of price controls); or (3) devalue the peso. Overnight the rate was decreased to

---

*If $1 = 250 yen, to find the value of 1 yen in dollars, divide both sides of the equation by $\frac{250 \text{ yen}}{\text{dollar}}$. Then 1 yen $= \frac{2}{250} = \$0.004$.

25 pesos = $1, and without disturbing the peso prices, the prices in dollars were halved. Suddenly, trips to Mexico were a bargain for Americans.

The international trade theory that we have been discussing was the only explanation of trade available to us until the 1960s, when a new concept—the International Product Life Cycle—was formulated.[7]

International Product Life Cycle (IPLC)

This approach, related to the product life cycle, concerns the role of innovation in trade patterns. The concept can be applied to new product introduction by firms in any of the industrialized nations, but because more new products have been successfully introduced on a commercial scale in the United States, let us examine the **IPLC** as it applies to this country. The four stages through which a new product is said to pass are the following:

1. *U.S. exports.* Because the United States possesses the largest population of high-income consumers in the world, competition for their patronage is intense. Manufacturers are therefore forced to search constantly for better ways to satisfy their customers' needs. To provide new products, companies maintain large research and development laboratories, which must be in constant contact with suppliers of the materials they need for product development. The fact that their suppliers are also in this country facilitates the contact.[8] In the early stages of the product life cycle, the design and the production methods are changing. By being close to the market, management can react quickly to customer feedback. These factors combine to make the United States a leader in new product introduction. For a while, American firms will be the only manufacturers of the product; overseas customers, as they learn of the product, will therefore have to buy from American firms. The export market develops.

2. *Foreign production begins.* Overseas consumers, especially those in developed nations, have similar needs and also have the capability to purchase the product. Export volume grows and becomes large enough to support local production. If the innovator is a multinational firm, it will be sending its subsidiaries new product information with complete details on how to produce it. Where there are no affiliates, foreign businesspeople, as they learn of the product, will obtain licenses for its production. Foreign production will begin. The American firm will still be exporting to those markets where there is no production, but its export growth will diminish.

3. *Foreign competition in export markets.* Later, as early foreign manufacturers gain experience in marketing and production, their costs will fall. Saturation of their local markets will cause them to look for buyers elsewhere. They may even be able to undersell the American producers if they enjoy an advantage in labor or raw material costs. In this stage, foreign firms are competing in export markets, and as a result, American export sales will continue to decline.

4. *Import competition in the United States.* If domestic and export sales enable foreign producers to attain the economies of scale enjoyed by the American firm, they may reach a point where they can compete in quality and undersell American firms in the American market. From that point on, the U.S. market will be ser̥ed by imports only. Black-and-white television sets are an example of such a product.

The authors of the IPLC concept also claim that this cycle may be repeated as the less developed countries with still lower labor costs obtain the technology and thus acquire a cost advantage over the more industrialized nations. Although little research has been done to substantiate the IPLC concept, the World Bank study mentioned previously seems to provide a plausible reason for these changes in production locations.

> With countries progressing on the comparative advantage scale, their exports can supplement the exports of countries that graduate to a higher level. . . . A case in point is Japan, whose comparative advantage has shifted towards highly capital-intensive exports. In turn, developing countries with a relatively high human capital endowment, such as Korea and Taiwan, can take Japan's place in exporting relatively human capital-intensive products, and countries with a relatively high physical capital endowment, such as Brazil and Mexico, can take Japan's place in exporting relatively physical capital-intensive products. Finally, countries at lower levels of development can supplant the middle-level countries in exporting unskilled labor-intensive commodities.[9]

Summary of International Trade Theory

In summary, we can say that international trade occurs primarily because of price differences among nations. These differences stem from differences in production costs, which are the result of differences in the endowment of the factors of production and the level of efficiency at which they are utilized. However, taste differences, a demand variable, can reverse the direction of trade predicted by the theory.

International trade theory clearly shows that nations will attain a higher level of living by specializing in goods for which they possess a comparative advantage and importing those for which they have a comparative disadvantage. Generally, trade restrictions that stop this free flow of goods will be harmful to a nation's welfare. If this is true, why is every nation in the world surrounded by trade restrictions?

TRADE RESTRICTIONS

This apparent contradiction occurs because both national and international procedures for making decisions about import restrictions are particularly sensitive to the interest groups who will be hurt by the international competition. These groups consist of a small, easily identified body of people—as contrasted to the huge, widespread number of consumers who gain from free trade. In any political debate over a proposed import restriction, the protectionist group will be united in exerting pressure on government officials, whereas an organized effort by pro-trade consumers is rarely mounted. For example, steel companies and steelworker unions have protested vehemently to Congress and government officials about lower-priced imported steel, yet consumer organizations have said nothing. In other words, if you are employed by a chemical manufacturer, you probably are not going to fight for unrestricted steel imports even though you may believe they contribute to a lower price for your automobile.

In the next section, note the importance of special interest groups.

Arguments for Trade Restrictions and Their Rebuttal

One argument for trade restrictions involves national defense.

National defense.   Certain industries need protection from imports because they are vital to the national defense and must be kept operating even though they are at a comparative disadvantage with respect to foreign competitors. If competition from foreign firms drives these companies out of business and leaves this country dependent on imports, those imports may not be available in wartime.

One problem with this argument is that the armed forces require hundreds of products ranging from pantyhose to bombs.

> In 1984, the U.S. shoe industry, after failing to obtain relief from imports with arguments about loss of jobs, requested Congress to impose restrictions based on the fact that growing reliance on imported footwear is "jeopardizing the national security of the United States." In the event of war, shoemakers claim that there would be insufficient manufacturing capacity in this country.
>
> A Defense Department spokesman said he knew of no plan to investigate the prospects of a wartime shoe crisis. Furthermore, federal law already requires the armed forces to buy U.S.-made footwear exclusively.[10]

Critics of this argument claim it would be far more efficient to pay a subsidy to a number of firms to maintain sufficient capacity for wartime use only. The output of these companies could be varied according to the calculated defense needs. Moreover, a subsidy would clearly indicate the cost to the nation of maintaining these companies in the name of national security. Currently, most American steamship companies receive government subsidies to compensate for their higher operating costs. In this way, we have a merchant marine ready in case of hostility, and we know what this state of readiness costs us.

Protect infant industry.   Advocates for the protection of an infant industry claim that in the long run, the industry does have a comparative advantage but needs protection from imports until the labor force is trained, production techniques are mastered, and the firm achieves economies of scale. When these objectives are achieved, import protection will no longer be necessary. Without the protection, they argue, the firm will not be able to survive because lower-cost imports from more mature foreign competitors will underprice it in its local market.

The protection is meant to be temporary; but realistically, a firm will rarely admit it has matured and no longer needs this assistance. Protected from foreign competition by high import duties, the company's managers have little reason to improve efficiency or product quality.

International businesspeople will find that the infant-industry argument is readily accepted by the governments of most LDCs. The first firm in an industry new to the country generally gets protection with no date stipulated for its removal. However, some of the larger developing nations, such as Brazil and Mexico, have begun to reduce their protection to force these companies to lower their prices and become more competitive in world markets. This approach has been particularly successful in Brazil, which now exports more than $15 billion in goods and services annually.

Protect domestic jobs from cheap foreign labor.   The protectionists who use this argument will compare lower foreign hourly wage rates to those paid here and conclude that exporters from these countries can flood the United States with low-priced goods and put America out of work. The first fallacy of this argument is that wage costs are not all of the production costs nor are they even all of the labor costs. In many LDCs, the legislated fringe benefits are a much higher percentage of the direct wages than they are in this country. Furthermore, the productivity per worker is frequently so much greater in the developed countries because of more capital per worker, superior manage-ment, and advanced technology that the labor cost is lower even though wages are higher.

The second fallacy results from failure to consider the costs of the other factors of production. Where wage rates are low, the capital costs are usually high, and thus production costs may actually be higher in a low-wage nation. Ironically, one of the arguments for protection used by manufacturers in developing nations is that they cannot compete against the low-cost, highly productive firms in the industrialized countries. Those who might be persuaded by this argument to stop imports to save domestic jobs should remember that American exports create jobs—every $1 billion in exports creates 25,000 new jobs. If we stop a country's imports, its government may retaliate with greater import duties on our exports. The result could be a net loss of jobs rather than the gain that was anticipated.

Scientific tariff or fair competition.   Supporters of this argument say they believe in fair competition. They simply want an export duty that will bring the cost of the imported goods up to the cost of the domestically produced article. This will eliminate any "unfair" advantage that a foreign competitor might have because of superior technology, lower raw material costs, lower taxes, or lower labor costs. It is not their intent to ban exports; they wish only to equalize the process for "fair" competition. If this were law, no doubt the rate of duty would be set to protect the least efficient American producer, thereby enabling the more efficient domestic manufacturers to earn large profits. The efficient foreign producers would be penalized, and, of course, their compar-ative advantage would be nullified.

Retaliation.   Representatives of an industry whose exports have had import restrictions placed on them by another country may request their government to retaliate with similar restrictions. An example of how retaliation begins is the ban by the European Community (EC) on imports of hormone-treated beef from the United States on January 1, 1989. Because the use of hormones is considered a health hazard in the EC, it closed the market to $100 million worth of beef (12 percent of total U.S. meat exports). American beef producers complained that no scientific evidence supports the claim, and the United States promptly retaliated by putting import duties on about $100 million worth of EC products, including boneless beef and pork, fruit juices, wine coolers, tomatoes, French cheese, and instant coffee. The EC then threatened to ban U.S. imports of honey, canned corn, walnuts, and dried fruit worth $140 million. The American reply to that threat was an announcement that it would then follow the EC ban with an American ban of all European meat. If that had happened, about $500 million in U.S.–EC trade would have been affected. A joint EC–U.S. task force has been meeting to try to find a solution to end a situation that could escalate into a trade war.[11] U.S. cattle producers are particularly suspicious of the ban because they know that the Europeans routinely use dangerous drugs in the $384 million of pork and beef annually exported to the United States.[12]

dumping selling a product abroad for less than either the cost of production or the price in the home market

Dumping.   Another cause for retaliation is **dumping,** which is selling a product abroad for less than (1) the cost of production or (2) the price in the home market. A foreign manufacturer may take this action because it wishes to sell excess production without disrupting prices in its domestic market, or it may have lowered the export price to force all domestic producers in the importing nation out of business. The exporter expects to raise prices in the market once that objective is accomplished. This is *predatory dumping.*

In the United States, when a manufacturer believes a foreign producer is dumping a product, it can ask the Department of Commerce to make a preliminary investigation. If Commerce finds that products have been dumped, the case goes to the International Trade Commission* to determine if the imports are injuring U.S. producers. If the Commission finds that they are, the U.S. Customs is authorized to levy antidumping duties.

Most governments retaliate when dumping injures local industry. The EC, for example, levied dumping duties ranging from 23 to 43 percent on Japanese computer printers when investigators found that they were priced 20 percent lower in the EC than in Japan.[13]

countervailing duties taxes on an import that has benefited from an export subsidy

Export subsidies.   To encourage exports, governments will often offer export subsidies, such as tax rebates on export income, reduced transportation rates on government carriers, preferential exchange rates to exporters when they import capital equipment, and low-cost loans to foreign buyers. Such actions may prompt competitors in the importing nation to request their governments to impose **countervailing duties** equal to the amount of the subsidy or to the difference between the dumping and home market prices.[14]

Other arguments.   The arguments we have examined are probably the most often quoted. Others that are sometimes given are the use of protection from imports to (1) permit diversification of the domestic economy or (2) improve the balance of trade. You should have gathered from this discussion that protection from imports generally serves the narrow interests of a special group at the expense of many. While their application can sometimes buy time for the protected industry to modernize and become more competitive in the world market, a real danger exists that a nation's trading partners will retaliate with restrictions causing injury to industries that have received no protection. Let's examine these restrictions.

Kinds of Restrictions

Import restrictions are commonly classified as *tariff* (import duties) and *nontariff* barriers.

tariffs taxes on imported goods for the purpose of raising their price to reduce competition for local producers or stimulate their local production

Tariff barriers.   **Tariffs,** or import duties, are taxes levied on imported goods primarily for the purpose of raising their selling price in the importing nation's market in order to reduce competition for domestic producers. A few smaller nations also use them to raise revenue on both imports and exports. Export of

---

*The International Trade Commission is a government agency that provides technical assistance and advice to the president and Congress on matters of international trade and tariffs.

commodities such as coffee and copper are commonly taxed in the developing nations.

Ad valorem, specific, and compound duties.   Import duties are either *ad valorem, specific,* or a combination of the two called *compound.* An **ad valorem duty** is stated as a percentage of the invoice value. For example, the U.S. Tariff Schedule states that flavoring extracts and fruit flavors not containing alcohol are subject to a 6 percent ad valorem duty. Therefore, when a shipment of flavoring extract invoiced at $10,000 arrives in the United States, the importer is required to pay $600 to U.S. Customs before taking possession of the goods. A **specific duty** is a fixed sum of money charged for a physical unit. If you were to import dynamite in cartridges or sticks suitable for blasting, you would have to pay $.37 per pound irrespective of the invoice value. When the flavoring extracts and fruit flavor just mentioned contain over 50 percent alcohol by weight, they are charged $.12 per pound plus 3 percent ad valorem. On a $10,000 shipment weighing 5,000 pounds, you would have to pay a **compound duty** of $900 ($.12 × 5,000 pounds + 0.03 × $10,000 = $600 + $300). Note that a specific duty, unless changed frequently in an inflationary period, soon loses its importance, whereas the amount collected from an ad valorem duty increases as the invoice price rises. Sometimes, however, an exporter may charge prices so much lower than domestic prices that the ad valorem duty fails to close the gap. Some governments set *official prices* or use variable levies to correct this deficiency.

Official prices.   These prices are included in the customs tariff of some nations and are the basis for ad valorem duty calculations whenever the actual invoice price is lower. The official price guarantees that a certain minimum import duty will be paid irrespective of the actual invoice price. It thwarts a fairly common arrangement that numerous importers living in high-duty nations have with their foreign suppliers whereby a false low invoice is issued to reduce the amount of duty to be paid. The importer sends the difference between the false invoice price and the true price separately.

Variable levy.   One form of **variable levy**, which guarantees that the market price of the import will be the same as that of domestically produced goods, is used by the European Community for imported grains. Calculated daily, the duty level is set at the difference between world market prices and the support price for domestic producers.

Lower duty for more local input.   Import duties are set by many nations in such a way as to encourage local input. For example, the finished product ready for sale to the consumer may have a 70 percent ad valorem duty. However, if the product is imported in bulk so that it must be packaged in the importing nation, the duty level may be at 30 percent. To encourage some local production, the government may charge only 10 percent duty on the semifinished inputs. These situations can provide opportunities for foreign manufacturers of low-technology products, such as paint and toilet articles, to get behind a high tariff wall with very modest investments.

Nontariff barriers.   **Nontariff barriers (NTBs)** are the name given to all forms of discrimination against imports other than the import duties we have been examining. As nations have reduced duties, the nontariff barriers, which are either quantitative or nonquantitative, have assumed greater importance. To

---

ad valorem duty an import duty levied as a percentage of the invoice value of imported goods

specific duty a fixed sum levied on a physical unit of an imported good

compound duty a combination of specific and ad valorem duties

variable levy an import duty set at the difference between world market prices and local government-supported prices

nontariff barriers (NTBs) all forms of discrimination against imports other than import duties

WORLDVIEW
A Letter from Europe: Straight Thinking on Trade

Some of the debate [about protectionism and a new trade bill] reminds me of the story of a certain southern congressman who got a letter from a constituent demanding to know where he stood on the issue of whiskey. The constituent did not have to wait long for an answer.

"Sir," replied the congressman, "you raise one of the most important issues of our time, one about which I feel deeply and on which my position is clear. If, by whiskey, you mean the devil's brew, the poison scourge, the bloody monster that defiles innocence, destroys the home, creates misery and poverty, then I am against it with all my power.

"But if you speak of whiskey as the elixir of life that is consumed when good fellows get together, that puts a song in their hearts, laughter on their lips, and the warm glow of contentment in their eyes, the stimulation that puts a little spring into the step of an elderly gentleman—then certainly I am in favor of it.

"My stand is unequivocal and I will not compromise."

So it is with much of the debate about trade. Should the United States take a "firm line" with its trading partners? If by this is meant protectionism, and a return to Hawley-Smoot (the very mention of which causes weak men to fall under the table and strong men to jump out of second-floor windows), then (almost) everyone is firmly against it.

But if it means forcing the cunning foreigner to remove his unfair trade barriers and let American goods into their markets, that is a different matter. The United States should stop pussyfooting around with foreigners, goes the cry. Let them at long last open up their markets . . . or else.

Let me simply give one reason why the second course of action would be unwise. Foreigners are not the only ones to have unfair trade practices. This is illustrated by a Commission list of U.S. trade practices that impede EC exports, given to U.S. Trade Representative Clayton Yeutter in Brussels in December.

The list identifies more than 30 such measures, including some of the following.

High tariffs: The U.S. tariff on certain textiles and glassware is up to 38 percent—three times the EC rate. Two practices (customs user fees—tantamount to imposing an additional tariff—and superfund taxes—a discriminatory tax on imports of petroleum products) have been ruled by the General Agreement on Tariffs and Trade (GATT) to be illegal. On machine tools, the United States has established unilateral limits on European exports, which we consider to be inconsistent with GATT rules.

In the very important area of telecommunications, EC suppliers of switches and transmission equipment experience difficulties in selling into the U.S. market because of lengthy and costly approval procedures.

U.S. law requires that vessels registered in the United States for use between U.S. ports be constructed in the United States, and that only U.S.-registered vessels may be used in U.S. territorial waters for dredging, towing, and salvaging. Only vessels constructed in the United States are eligible. The value of the U.S. market in this area is estimated at about $1.3 billion.

Government procurement is also mentioned. Here the number of Buy America provisions adopted is growing at an alarming rate. Some are plain violations of the GATT Code on Government Procurement—for example, the procurement restrictions on Voice of America or machine tools for the Department of Defense. Others represent an improvement of the U.S. negotiating position (at a time when we are entering into negotiations on a possible extension of the code to new sectors), which is contrary to the standstill commitment entered into by the United States.

Source: Delegation of the Commission of the European Communities, Washington, D.C.

illustrate that this trend has been occurring for some time, an English study found that while 40.3 percent of all world trade was under some kind of control in 1973, by 1979, it had risen to 45.7 percent.[15]

A World Bank study found that over 88,500 NTBs covered $230 billion in merchandise imports of just 16 industrialized nations. However, the estimate is low because it covers actual imports, not the products that were kept out.[16]

quotas numerical limits placed on specific classes of imports

Quantitative. The quantitative barrier, **quotas,** are numerical limits for a specific kind of good that a country will permit to be imported without restriction during a specified period. If the quota is *absolute,* once the specified amount has been imported, further importation for the rest of the period (usually a year) is prohibited.

> K mart ordered a million dollars in wool sweaters from China. Before they arrived in this country, the quota was filled for the year, and K mart had to wait until the following year to bring them in. By that time, they were out of fashion and had to be deeply discounted. The company expected to recover only 60 cents on a dollar.

Some goods are subject to *tariff quotas,* which permit a stipulated amount to enter the country duty free or at a low rate, but when that quantity is reached, a much higher duty is charged for subsequent importations. This process is repeated annually.

Quotas are generally *global;* that is, a total amount is fixed without regard to source. They may also be *allocated,* in which case, the government of the importing nation assigns quantities to specific countries. For example, the United States allocates quotas for specific tonnages of sugar to 25 nations. Because of their nature, allocated quotas are sometimes called *discriminatory* quotas. More recently, because of the general agreement among nations against imposing quotas unilaterally, governments have negotiated **voluntary export restraints(VERs)** with other countries. To avoid formal restrictions on automobile imports by the United States, the Japanese government limits its exports to 2.3 million units. Interestingly, although fewer Japanese cars were imported into this country after the quotas were imposed, sales revenues did not suffer because the Japanese automakers began to export more expensive models.[17]

voluntary export restraints (VERs) export quotas imposed by the exporting nation

Orderly marketing arrangements. Orderly marketing arrangements also restrict international competition and preserve some of the national market for local producers. They differ from unilaterally imposed quotas and other trade barriers in that they are formal agreements resulting from negotiations between exporting and importing countries. Usually, they stipulate the size of import or export quotas that each nation will have for a particular good.

orderly marketing arrangements formal agreements between exporting and importing countries that stipulate the import or export quotas each nation will have for a good

The largest and oldest such arrangement is the Multifiber Arrangement (MFA), which began in 1973 and has subsequently been renewed every four years. The pact includes 54 exporting and importing nations. About 80 percent of the world's textile and clothing exports to the industrialized nations is regulated by this agreement.

In 1986, Japanese computer chip manufacturers slashed prices on a common chip, the DRAM, because of high inventories. The two American producers appealed to the government for help, and an accord was made that fixed minimum prices and established voluntary import quotas. While the American chip manufacturers increased their profits, the makers of products containing the chips and the consumers who buy those products lost. The Brookings Institution, a famous "think tank," estimates that the DRAM's price rose from $2.50 in 1986 to $10 in 1988 and, as a result, added more than $100 to the price of a $500 personal computer. The arrangement has helped American firms, but it has benefited Japanese chip makers much more. Instead of having to cut their prices to compete, they have been able to put their

"To all department heads: While barter agreements
are not opposed per se, caution must —
I repeat, must — be observed."

Rotarian, September 1985.

monopoly profits into research on higher-technology products where Americans still lead. Even lobbyists for the two American beneficiaries are working to have the agreement changed.[18] "What we did was pretty stupid," said a trade analyst at the Institute for International Economics.[19]

countertrade a transaction in which goods are exchanged entirely or partially for goods

Countertrade. Another barrier to free trade is **countertrade.** This is essentially a transaction in which goods are exchanged for goods. The simplest form of countertrade, barter, dates from ancient times, but in recent years various other kinds of countertrade have been used in East–West trade. Because of shortages of foreign exchange and a lack of markets for their products, many noncommunist nations have also been engaging in countertrade. Iraq obtained warships from Italy in exchange for crude oil, for example. Another example was the purchase by Spain of Colombian coffee in exchange for Spanish buses. Countertrade is a barrier to free trade because the sellers are forced to take goods that they would not otherwise buy, and in doing so, they close off another market from free and open competition. It is estimated that this type of transaction now accounts for about 25 percent of all world trade. We shall examine countertrade in greater depth in later chapters and see that it also facilitates trade.

Nonquantitative nontariff barriers. Many international trade specialists claim that the nonquantitative nontariff barriers are the most significant nontariff barriers. Governments have tended to establish nontariff barriers to obtain the protection formerly afforded by import duties. A study of the nontariff nonquantitative barriers revealed over 800 distinct forms, which may be classified under three major headings: (1) direct government participation in trade, (2) customs and other administrative procedures, and (3) standards.

1. *Direct government participation in trade.* The most common direct government participation is the *export subsidy,* one form of which is a cash

payment to the exporter. It is considered an unfair trade practice because it enables exporters to sell at lower prices than they could otherwise and still earn a profit. The European Community, for example, extends subsidies of $196 per metric ton of broilers and $93.76 per metric ton of wheat in order to reduce inventories resulting from high domestic support prices. Importing nations frequently retaliate by levying countervailing duties in the amount of the subsidy. Other kinds of export subsidies include inexpensive credit offered to the exporter's foreign customer by government-owned export banks (most major exporting nations have one; the Export-Import Bank in the United States is an example), lower income taxes on profits earned on exports, and special low freight charges when exports are shipped on domestically owned ship and air lines.

2. *Customs and other administrative procedures.* These cover a large variety of government policies and procedures that either discriminate against imports or favor exports. For example, in France, the time of the year when delays occur in processing the import documentation necessary to import sweaters happens to coincide with the buying season. Italy permits textiles to be imported through only 10 specified ports. The Japanese customs authority changed the classification of a processed food product that an American firm had been importing at a 16 percent duty rate to a category with a rate of 35 percent. U.S. Customs ruled in 1989 that it would treat imported sport utility vehicles, such as the Suzuki Samurai, as trucks subject to a 25 percent duty instead of the 2.5 percent that they had been charged. While this will raise the price of vehicles in the United States, it will permit Suzuki to use its quota under Japan's voluntary export restraint to import more automobiles in their place.[20]

As the exportation of services has increased, governments have found ways to discriminate against them. Data processing has been especially singled out. In Japan, the company that holds a monopoly on international telephone lines refused to lease lines to American companies that wished to connect Japanese clients to data bases in the United States. Brazil requires governmental approval to use international telephone circuits for computers; naturally, foreign companies rarely obtain access to these circuits. In Europe, a number of governments are searching for ways to tax incoming information flows. A major problem, of course, is how to put a commercial value on them. Other examples of discrimination are the Canadian government's giving tax deductions to local businesses who advertise on Canadian TV—but not when they use American stations across the border—or West Germany's allowing only German agencies to hire models to appear in TV advertising.[21]

3. *Standards.* Both governmental and private standards to protect the health and safety of a nation's citizens certainly are desirable, but for years exporting firms have been plagued by many that are complex and discriminatory. France, for example, prohibits the advertising of bourbon, alleging that grain spirits are injurious to health; but of course, spirits made from grapes are exempt from the ban. Australia, like most countries, requires imported livestock to be quarantined but has no quarantine facilities.

Even beer is not free of regulations. Germany has a 16th-century law requiring German beer to be made only of hops, malt, yeast, and water. Beer containing other ingredients, such as corn or rice, that are common in other countries could not cross the border. The law is still in effect in Germany, but it has been struck down by the European Community on behalf of a French brewery that wanted to enter the German market. Although the law no longer affects beer exports to Germany, the French minister of trade has another problem. She claims to have read in German newspapers that drinking French beer can make a person impotent. The beer issue, however, is only 1 of more than 800 protectionist measures that the EC is studying.[22]

Denmark uses a packaging rule to protect its soft-drink industry from foreign competition. All beverages must be sold in returnable bottles. This deters French mineral water producers, because it is too costly to ship the returned bottles back to France for refilling. The European Court of Justice recently ordered Belgium to stop requiring margarine to be packaged as cubes. This rule had been effective in stopping importation from EC countries whose producers used round or rectangular packaging. Japan ruled some imported canned goods unacceptable under its agricultural standards because the figures for the day, month, and year of canning were spaced too far apart on the labels. "Uniqueness" is another ground that Japan has used to shut out foreign imports. The skin of the Japanese is different, so foreign cosmetics companies must test their products in Japan before selling there. Imports of American tangerines have been limited because the stomachs of the Japanese are small and thus have room only for the local tangerines. Probably the strangest claim that has been advanced is that the snow of Japan is different, and therefore its ski equipment should also be different. A private industry group drafted a new set of standards for ski equipment, including one that increased the thickness of the ski under the binding. It argued that wetter snow and narrower slopes made these standards necessary. Only manufacturers meeting them would be able to use the mark SG, which stands for safety goods. Foreign manufacturers, which have 50 percent of the $400 million Japanese market, argued that the standards set by the International Organization for Standardization were adequate and the Japanese standards were unnecessary. Only after considerable pressure were the standards canceled.

Denmark, Finland, Norway, and Sweden each apply separate standards for electrical equipment and require individual testing in the country prior to certifying imports. Imagine the plight of the American manufacturer that must make up special products for each of these countries in order to comply with its special standards. The cost of compliance may price the company out of the market. This could be and frequently is the reason why such standards were set up in the first place.

These few examples will give the reader an idea of the complexity involved in trying to eliminate nontariff barriers. Some progress is being made, but it is slow. Meanwhile, the knowledge that such barriers exist should prompt the international businessperson to look for them before attempting to conduct business in a foreign country.

Costs of Barriers to Trade

You read previously that the computer chip voluntary trade restraint accord has proven costly to the final consumer, and you might have been amazed at how costly it was. But this is a small part of what trade restraints cost you. A study by economists of the Institute for International Economics of 31 product groups for which trade volume exceeds $100 million annually estimated that

■ **TABLE 3–1**
Annual Costs to American Consumer for Import Protection

Product Group	Annual Costs ($ million)	Cost per American Job Saved
1. Textiles and apparel	$27,000	$ 42,000
2. Petroleum	6,900	160,000
3. Carbon steel*	6,800	750,000
4. Automobiles	5,800	105,000
5. Dairy products	5,500	220,000
6. Maritime industries	3,000	270,000
7. Benzenoid chemicals[†]	2,650	1,000,000
8. Meat	1,800	160,000
9. Sugar	930	60,000
10. Nonrubber footwear	700	55,000

*Used in car bodies.
[†]Used in insecticides, detergents, and motor fuels.
Source: Gary Clyde Hufbauer, Diane T. Berliner, and Kimberly Ann Elliott, *Trade Protection in the United States: 31 Case Studies* (London: Institute for International Economics, 1986).

it costs the American consumers *more than $100 million annually* in 25 of the 31 groups. Table 3–1 is a summary of their findings for the 10 product groups most affected. This is why your jeans cost what they do. Even sugar costs twice as much because of American sugar quotas. Note, too, how much it costs to save one American job! Studies done in other countries show similar results.[23]

ECONOMIC DEVELOPMENT

When businesspeople move from domestic to international business, they encounter markets with far greater differences in levels of economic development than those in which they have been working. It is important to understand this because a nation's level of economic development affects all aspects of business—marketing, production, and financial. Although nations vary greatly with respect to economic development levels, we commonly group them into the categories of developed, newly industrializing, developing, less developed, or least developed.

developed a classification for all industrialized nations, which are more technically developed

newly industrializing countries (NICs) the middle-income economies of Brazil, Mexico, South Korea, Taiwan, Hong Kong, and Singapore

developing a classification for the world's lower-income nations, which are less technically developed

nonmarket economy the World Bank's designation for a communist nation

Categories Based on Levels of Economic Development

Developed is the name given to industrialized nations of Western Europe, Japan, Australia, New Zealand, Canada, South Africa, and the United States. A comparatively new category, **newly industrializing countries (NICs)**, includes Brazil, Mexico, South Korea, Taiwan, Hong Kong, and Singapore. These countries (1) have what the United Nations considers middle-income economies with GNP/capita ranging from $2,000 to $5,000, (2) possess a heavy concentration of multinational investment, and (3) export appreciable quantities of manufactured goods, including high-tech products. **Developing**, less developed (LDCs), and least developed are names used to categorize the rest of the world except the communist nations, which are usually placed in a separate **nonmarket economy** classification. Intergovernmental agencies such as the UN and the World Bank tend to employ low-, middle-, and high-income designations rather than developed and less developed. However, since the latter are commonly used in industry as a kind of shorthand to describe the characteristics of two distinct groups of nations, we shall also use them in this text. Note that GNP/capita is the basis for both methods of classification.

GNP/Capita as an Indicator

We mentioned in Chapter 2 that although GNP/capita is widely used to compare countries with respect to the well-being of their citizens and for market or investment potential, businesspeople must use it with caution. What does this value signify? Is a country with an $800 GNP/capita a better market for a firm's products than one whose GNP/capita is only $750? To assume this gives excessive credence to its accuracy. For example, to arrive at the GNP, government economists must impute monetary values to various goods and services not sold in the marketplace, such as food grown for personal consumption. Moreover, many goods and services are bartered in both low-income nations (because people have little cash) and high-income countries (because they wish to reduce reported income and thus pay less income tax). Transactions of this type are said to be part of the *underground economy*.

underground economy the part of a nation's income that, because of unreporting or underreporting, is not measured by official statistics

Underground economy. Much has been written about the part of the national income that is not measured by official statistics because it is either underreported or unreported. Included in this **underground** (black, parallel, submerged, shadow) **economy** are undeclared legal production, production of illegal goods and services, and concealed income in kind (barter).

Figure 3–1 shows a compilation of estimates that vary widely because different methodologies were used and also those who have undeclared income obviously are not going to admit it and be liable to prosecution for tax evasion. But there are many humorous incidents that people tell about others.

> In Bonn, a gardener completes a large landscaping job and when asked for a bill replies, "If you want one, it will be DM1,500 plus 14 percent tax. If you don't need one, just pay me DM1,400 cash." In Greece, when a patient tries to pay with a check, the physician is reluctant to accept one or to give a receipt, and when he opens his desk drawer, it is crammed with cash. A visitor to an Italian company was talking to the chief executive when his secretary announced the unexpected arrival of a tax inspector. He told her to stall the inspector and then called the company's financial director. A few minutes later, the visitor looked out the window and saw the financial director running across the field with an armload of ledgers.[24]

In addition to reducing the total taxes paid to government, the underground economy is responsible for all kinds of distortions of economic data. In Italy, for example, there was no record that a single pair of gloves was produced in Naples, yet it is now known that Naples is one of Italy's biggest glovemaking centers—the unreported output is produced by small groups of workers in kitchens and garages. The official government statistical agency estimates that the GDP is at least 15 percent greater than the official figure. The Italians are proud to say that, because of their underground economy, their per capita

■ **FIGURE 3–1**
Underground Economies

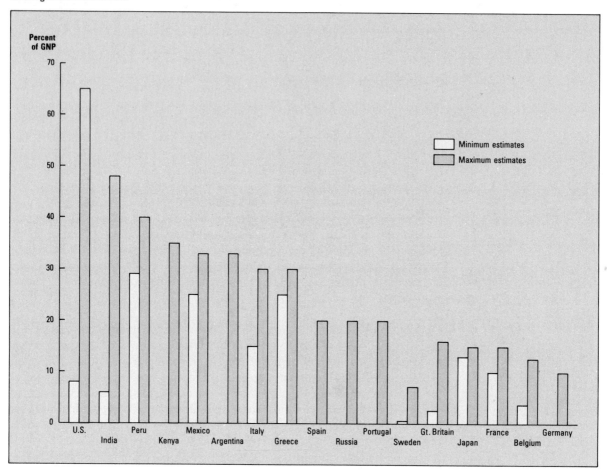

income has now overtaken that of the British. The *black work* in France is believed to be the reason why 50 percent of all the cement produced vanishes into thin air as far as official records are concerned. Even the USSR has its "second economy." Moonlighting workers form work brigades and rent themselves out at triple the prevailing wage at construction projects that are behind schedule. In one case, they were paid from funds officially recorded as payment for 1,000 spare wrenches![25]

Currency conversion.   Another problem with GNP estimates is that to compare them, values of GNP components expressed in the local currency must be converted into a common currency—conventionally the dollar—by using the prevailing exchange rate. If the relative values of the two currencies accurately reflect consumer purchasing power, this conversion would be acceptable, but often they do not. World Bank economists do make some adjustments of the official exchange rates but recognize that "their use to convert national currency values to the U.S. dollar does not attempt to measure the relative *domestic* purchasing powers of currencies."[26]

TABLE 3–2
GNP/Capita Based on UN ICP for Selected Countries

Country	GNP/Capita in US$s Converted at World Bank Adjusted Exchange Rates	GNP/Capita in US$s Based on Purchasing Power Parity
United States	$16,690	$16,690
Luxembourg	14,260	15,272
Japan	11,300	13,266
Finland	10,890	12,894
Canada	9,976	11,941
Botswana	840	3,080
Bolivia	470	1,540
Sri Lanka	380	1,933
Pakistan	380	1,702
India	270	972

Note: The method to make comparisons in Table 3–2 is based on that used by the OECD for its February 9, 1987, press release; factors and GNP from *World Development Report 1987,* p. 270 and Table 1, pp. 202–3.

purchasing power parity
the exchange rate of two currencies expressed as a ratio equals the ratio of prices of goods in the two countries

To overcome this deficiency, the United Nations International Comparison Program (ICP) has developed a method of comparing real GDP* based on **purchasing power parities** rather than on the international demand for currency (exchange rates). These comparisons result in GDP/capita that are considerably higher than those regularly given for LDCs and lower for most developed nations: that is, there are smaller GDP/capita differences between developed and developing nations than what are normally published (see Table 3–2).

More than GNP/Capita Is Required

Even if the problems we have examined did not exist, businesspeople still would not obtain a true picture of the relative strengths of markets by comparing GNP/capita alone. Remember that GNP/capita is a mean, which infers that every inhabitant receives an equal share of the national income. This is patently untrue, especially in the developing nations, where the national income is much less evenly divided than it is in the developed countries. Thus, businesspeople who conclude from a low GNP/capita that a nation is too poor to buy their products will certainly miss some lucrative markets.

The dissatisfaction with GNP/capita as an indicator of a nation's level of living (it is an index of production, not consumption) has led to various attempts to create indexes by combining variables such as the consumption of steel, concrete, newsprint, and electricity with the ownership of automobiles, telephones, TVs, and radios. In chapter 14 on market analysis, we shall examine an index to compare market size that *Business International* has constructed by combining population and GDP with the consumption and production of certain key commodities. Although GNP/capita is an imperfect yardstick for comparing the purchasing power and market size of nations, it does serve as a rough indicator of whether a country is in the developed or

*GDP, unlike GNP, excludes factor income from abroad.

developing category. This is valuable because it gives a set of common characteristics that provide some insight to the approximately 140 nations belonging to the **Third World*** of developing nations.

Third World   the developing nations

Characteristics of Developing Nations

Although there is great diversity among the many developing nations, most share the following common characteristics:

1. GNP/capita of less than $2,000.
2. Unequal distribution of income, with a very small middle class.
3. *Technological dualism*—a mix of firms employing the latest technology and companies using very primitive methods.
4. *Regional dualism*—high productivity and incomes in some regions and little economic development in others.
5. A preponderance (80 to 85 percent) of the population earning its living in a relatively unproductive agricultural sector.
6. Disguised unemployment or underemployment—two people doing a job that one person can do.
7. High population growth (2.5 to 4 percent annually).
8. High rate of illiteracy and insufficient educational facilities.
9. Widespread malnutrition and a wide range of health problems.
10. Political instability.
11. High dependence on a few products for export, generally agricultural products or minerals.
12. Inhospitable topography, such as deserts, mountains, and tropical forests.
13. Low saving rates and inadequate banking facilities.

You can see from these characteristics that a tremendous gap exists between the levels of living of Third World inhabitants and those of industrialized nations. Although economists have studied and theorized about the various aspects of economic development for over two centuries, their preoccupation with the poor nations of the world really began only after World War II.[27]

A Human-Needs Approach to Economic Development

Until the 1970s, economists generally considered economic growth synonymous with economic development. A nation was considered to be developing economically if its real output per capita as measured by GNP/capita was increasing over time. However, the realization that economic growth does not necessarily imply development—because the benefits of this growth so often have occurred to only a few—has led to the widespread adoption of a new, more comprehensive definition of economic development.

The **human-needs approach** defines economic development as the reduction of poverty, unemployment, and inequality in the distribution of income. The definition of poverty also has been broadened. Instead of being defined in terms

human-needs approach defines economic development as the elimination of poverty and unemployment as well as an increase in income

---

*First World refers to industrial nations, Second World to the communist bloc, Third World to developing nations, and Fourth World to the bottom 30 nations of the Third World.

of income, as is common in developed countries, a reduction in poverty has come to mean less illiteracy, less malnutrition, less disease and early death, and a shift from agricultural to industrial production.[28] Note that while economic growth considers only economic change measured by GNP/capita, economic development is concerned also with social changes. To date, there is no single accepted index of economic development, although various attempts are being made to create one.

No accepted general theory.   The inclusion of noneconomic variables has made it impossible to formulate a widely accepted general theory of development. Instead of pursuing a general theory, development economists are concentrating on specific problem areas, such as population growth, income distribution, unemployment, transfer of technology, the role of government in the process, and investment in human versus physical capital.

Relevance for businesspeople.   What is the relevance of a lack of consensus among specialists with respect to development theory? If a particular theory has fallen into disfavor among the experts, does this mean you can neglect it when dealing with government officials? That depends. It may be that those you are contacting still subscribe to it. In that case, you will want to emphasize the parts of your proposal that are germane to the theory, which is generally not too difficult because nearly every proposal will provide not only for investment in physical capital but also for training of employees, providing employment, and transferring technology. There will even be some redistribution of income through the creation of a middle class composed of managers and highly skilled technicians. As an example, let's look at how you might handle your proposal with respect to the unbalanced growth theory.

unbalanced growth theory attaining economic growth by deliberately creating an imbalance in the economy through investment in one industry that will require further investment in supporting industries to reduce the imbalance

Unbalanced growth theory.   Government officials may adhere to the **unbalanced growth theory,** which calls for deliberately creating imbalances by investing in an industry that will then require further investment in related areas to reduce the imbalance.

Will your proposal for an automobile assembly plant, for example, create such an imbalance? Of course it will. There will be an immediate need for such inputs as tires, batteries, fabric-backed vinyl sheeting for upholstery, and so forth. Suppose a tire plant is built. Then nylon fabric must either be imported or made locally. If made locally, a need is created for nylon cord, which will require a chemical plant for nylon fiber. Like the automobile assembly plant, there are many manufacturing processes that, when started, will create "imbalances"; that is, a need for manufactured and semiprocessed inputs not presently available locally. However, this situation will change as others are stimulated to invest when they perceive these marketing opportunities. Automobile manufacturing in Brazil and Mexico began in this manner.

Investment in human capital.   This recent development in theory recognizes that more than just capital accumulation is needed for growth. There must also be investment in the education of people so there will be managers to ensure that the capital is productive and skilled workers to operate and maintain the capital equipment.

If managers know that this theory has strong acceptance in the country where they have an operation or are seeking permission to establish one, they should emphasize this aspect of their investment. A multinational or global firm that does not have training programs for workers is rare, and nearly all send local managers to the home office to update their skills.

Import substitution versus export promotion.   Although developing nations have long considered the exporting of primary products (agricultural and raw materials) an important facet of their development strategy, they have not aggressively promoted the exporting of manufactured goods. Instead, they have concentrated on substituting domestically manufactured products for imports as a way to lessen their dependence on the developed countries.

Unfortunately, **import substitution** has not reduced their dependence on developed nations as much as it has changed the composition of imports from finished products to capital and semiprocessed inputs. Dependence on the developed nations has increased because the inability to obtain these imports due to, for example, a lack of foreign exchange now stops entire industries and throws thousands of people out of work. An example was the closing of automobile and agricultural machinery plants when the Turkish government could not obtain foreign exchange for importing the necessary intermediate products.

Another serious problem with the import substitution strategy stems from the protection to local industry that governments grant by levying high import duties on goods that are also made domestically. With this umbrella, local manufacturers are under no pressure to either lower their costs or improve their quality. Without such pressure, they rarely become competitive in world markets and thus cannot export. Furthermore, other domestic firms that must buy imports from these high-priced, protected industries cannot export either because their costs are excessive.

Problems such as these have caused numerous governments to change from a strategy of import substitution to one of promoting exports of manufactured goods. Spurring them on to this decision has been the rapid export growth of the newly industrializing nations, which we mentioned earlier. To force companies to become competitive in world markets, some governments are limiting the amount and duration of the protection.

This change in strategy affects the worldwide firm in a variety of ways. First, its local affiliate managers must be prepared for demands to export by government officials. They may even be handed an ultimatum, as were automobile manufacturers in Mexico: "If you need to import parts for your output, you must earn the foreign exchange to pay for them by exporting part of your production." A company asking for permission to set up a plant now will certainly be asked about its plans for exporting. This is a new phenomenon to longtime managers accustomed to restricting an affiliate's sales to its internal market to save the export market for home country production. Second, managers can no longer count on having permanent protection from competing imports, as they once could. In some countries, they are likely to be told that after a certain date, they will lose their protection and will be expected to compete internationally. Last, in a situation where two firms are competing for permission to establish a plant, the deciding factor may be that one offers its multinational channels of distribution to the affiliate's exports.

The importance of keeping current.   These few examples illustrate (1) some of the concepts that underlie the strategies and policies of developing nations and (2) the relationship between the theories of international trade and development. Moreover, they show why experienced international business-people keep abreast of developments in both areas.

import substitution the local production of goods to replace imports

INTERNATIONAL INVESTMENT THEORIES

This third set of theories attempts to explain why international investment takes place. The contemporary theory has been expanded considerably from the classical theory, which postulated that differences in interest rates for investments of equal risk are the reason why international capital moves from one nation to another. For this to happen, there had to be perfect competition, but as Kindleberger, a noted economist, stated, "Under perfect competition, foreign direct investment would not occur, nor would it be likely to occur in a world wherein the conditions were even approximately competitive."[29]

Contemporary Theories of Foreign Direct Investment

monopolistic advantage theory foreign direct investment is made by firms in oligopolistic industries possessing technical and other advantages over indigenous firms

Monopolistic advantage theory.   The modern **monopolistic advantage theory** stems from Stephen Hymer's dissertation in the 1960s, in which he demonstrated that foreign direct investment occurred largely in oligopolistic industries rather than in industries operating under near-perfect competition. This meant that the firms in these industries must possess advantages not available to local firms. Hymer reasoned that the advantages must be economies of scale, superior technology, or superior knowledge in marketing, management, or finance. Foreign direct investment took place because of these product and factor market imperfections.[30]

Product and factor market imperfections.   Caves, a Harvard economist, expanded Hymer's work to show that superior knowledge permitted the investing firm to produce differentiated products that the consumers would prefer to similar locally made goods and thus would give the firm some control over the selling price and an advantage over indigenous firms. To support these contentions, he noted that companies investing overseas were in industries that typically engaged in heavy product research and marketing effort.[31]

International product life cycle (IPLC).   We have already examined this theory to help explain international trade flows, but as we said, there is a close relationship between international trade and international investment. As you saw, the IPLC concept also explains that foreign direct investment is a natural stage in the life of a product. To avoid losing a market that it services by exporting, a company is forced to invest in overseas production facilities when other companies begin to offer similar products. This move overseas will be heightened during the third and fourth stages as the company that introduced the product strives to remain competitive, first in its export markets (stage 3) and later in its home market (stage 4), by locating in countries where the factors of production are less expensive. Twin factories on the Mexican-American border are an example.

Other theories.   Another theory was developed by Knickerbocker, who noted that when one firm, especially the leader in an oligopolistic industry, entered a market, other firms in the industry followed. The follow-the-leader theory is considered defensive because competitors are investing to avoid losing the markets served by exports when the initial investor begins local production. They may also fear that the initiator will achieve some advantage of risk diversification that they will not have unless they also enter the market.[32] In addition, there is always the suspicion that the competitor knows something that they do not and the feeling that it is better to be safe than sorry.

cross investment   foreign
direct investment by oligopolistic firms in each other's
home country as a defense
measure

Graham noted a tendency for **cross investment** by European and American firms in certain oligopolistic industries; that is, European firms tended to invest in the United States when American companies had gone to Europe. He postulated that such investments would permit the American subsidiaries of European firms to retaliate in the home market of U.S. companies if the European subsidiaries of these companies initiated some aggressive tactic, such as price cutting, in the European market.[33] Of course, as we noted in Chapter 2, there are a number of other reasons why investment in the United States by foreign multinationals takes place, such as *following the customer* (Japanese parts manufacturers following Japanese auto manufacturers), *seeking knowledge* (Japanese and European investment in the Silicon Valley), and *benefiting from the stability of the American government.*

internalization theory   (an
extension of the market imperfection theory) to obtain a
higher return on its investment, a firm will transfer its
superior knowledge to a foreign subsidiary rather than
sell it in the open market

The **internalization theory** is an extension of the market imperfection theory. The firm has superior knowledge, but it may obtain a higher price for that knowledge by using it than by selling it in the open market. By investing in a foreign subsidiary rather than licensing, the company is able to send the knowledge across borders while maintaining it within the firm, where it presumably yields a better return on the investment made to produce it.[34]

Other theories relate to financial factors. Aliber believes the imperfections in the foreign exchange markets may be responsible for foreign investment. Companies in nations with overvalued currencies are attracted to investment where currencies are undervalued.[35] Although empirical tests are inconclusive, it does seem that a sizable number of U.S. takeovers by European globals and multinationals occurred during the late 1970s, when the dollar was relatively weak. One other financially based theory (portfolio theory) suggests that international operations allow for a diversification of risk and therefore tend to maximize the expected return on investment.[36]

Note that there is one commonality to nearly all of these theories that is supported by empirical tests—the major part of direct foreign investment is made by large, research-intensive firms in oligopolistic industries. Note also that these theories offer reasons why companies find it *profitable* to invest overseas. However, as we stated in Chapter 2, all motives can be linked in some way to the desire to increase or protect not only profits, but also *sales* and *markets.*

SUMMARY

Why do nations trade? Mercantilist nations did so to build up storehouses of gold. Later, Adam Smith showed that a nation would export goods that it could produce with less labor than other nations. Ricardo proved that even though less efficient than other nations, a nation could still profit by exporting goods. All that was necessary was to hold a comparative advantage in the production of the goods.

The idea that a nation would tend to export products requiring a large amount of a relatively abundant factor was offered by Heckscher and Ohlin in their theory of factor endowment. Finally, the International Product Life Cycle theory states that many products that are first produced in the United States or other developed

countries are eventually manufactured in less developed countries and become imports to the very countries where their production began.

Although international trade theory argues for free, unrestricted trade for the benefit of everyone, restrictions on trade still exist because of the pressure of local interest groups. The industries and new industries are given as reasons why protection is required. In response to demands for protection, governments impose such restrictions on trade as import duties and quotas and other nontariff barriers.

A useful tool for international managers is an understanding of economic development theory. This will help them realize that in market analysis, a comparison of

GNP/capita is not enough. They need to investigate the distribution of income and various indexes of consumption as well. Since many government officials are well versed in economic growth theory and are guided by it in their decision making, a knowledge of some of the most popular theories can be advantageous to managers. They must be aware, however, that today development includes not only economic growth but also political and social factors.

International investment theory attempts to explain why foreign direct investment takes place. Product and factor market imperfections provide firms, primarily in oligopolistic industries, with advantages not open to indigenous companies. The International Product Life Cycle theory explains international investment as well as international trade. Some firms follow the industry leader, and the tendency of European firms to invest in the United States (and vice versa) seems to indicate that cross investment is done for defensive reasons. The internalization theory states that WWCs will seek to invest in foreign subsidiaries rather than license their superior knowledge to receive a better return on the investment used to develop that knowledge. There are also two financially based explanations of foreign direct investment. The first holds that foreign exchange market imperfections resulting in overvalued and undervalued currencies attract investors from nations with overvalued currencies to nations with undervalued currencies. The second is the portfolio theory, which postulates that foreign direct investment is made to diversify risk. Empirical tests indicate that most foreign direct investment is made by large, research-intensive firms in oligopolistic industries.

QUESTIONS

1. *a.* Explain Adam Smith's theory of absolute advantage.
   b. How does Ricardo's theory of comparative advantage differ from the theory of absolute advantage?

2. What is the relationship between the Heckscher-Ohlin factor endowment theory and the theories in question 1?

3. Name some products that you believe have passed through the four stages of the International Product Life Cycle.

4. It seems that free, unrestricted international trade in which each nation produces and exports products for which it has a comparative advantage will enable everyone to have a higher level of living. Why, then, does every country have import duty restrictions?

5. We certainly need defense industries, and we must protect them from import competition by placing restrictions on competitive imports. True or false? Is there an alternative to trade restrictions that might make more economic sense?

6. What is the "infant industry" argument? What is one problem with this argument?

7. "Workers are paid $20 an hour in the United States but only $4 in Taiwan. Of course we can't compete. We need to protect our jobs from cheap foreign labor." What are some possible problems with this statement?

8. *a.* What are the two general kinds of import restrictions?
   b. Describe the various types of tariff barriers.
   c. What are some of the nontariff barriers?

9. Of what importance to marketers is a nation's level of economic development?

10. *a.* Although GNP/capita is commonly used to compare countries' market potentials, what are some of the problems associated with using this indicator?
    b. Is anything better than GNP/capita?

11. How does the present-day definition of economic development differ from the definition of economic growth?

12. What problems with the import substitution strategy have caused some governments to increase their emphasis on export promotion?

13. If countertrade permits nations that lack foreign exchange to trade, how can it be called a barrier to free trade?

14. What are the characteristics of most firms that invest overseas? What makes it possible for these firms to compete with local companies, according to the monopolistic advantage theory?

15. Describe two theories of foreign investment that are related to financial factors.

MINICASE 3–1

The Ricardo Case

Suppose that the output per man-day for wine and cloth in Portugal and England are the following:

Commodity	Output per Man-Day	
	Portugal	England
Barrels of wine	2	1
Bolts of cloth	4	3

Suppose also that the total cost of land, labor, and capital to produce the daily output of either wine or cloth is 20 pounds in England or 1,600 escudos in Portugal and that the exchange rate is 1 pound = 50 escudos.

1. What are the prices for the English and Portuguese products in escudos?

2. What are they in English pounds?
3. What will be the direction of trade?
4. What are the upper and lower limits of the terms of trade?
5. The present exchange rate in this example is 1 pound = 50 escudos, but exchange rates do change.

    a. What will the exchange rate have to be to discourage Portuguese traders from importing English products?

    b. What will the exchange rate have to be to discourage English traders from importing Portuguese products?

6. What did you learn about comparative advantage from point 5?

MINICASE 3–2

Tarus Manufacturing

John Baker, vice president of Tarus Manufacturing, called in Ed Anderson, the export manager, to discuss the sales results for the new adhesive that Tarus was exporting to its sales subsidiary in Ecuador.

Baker:
Ed, how is Tarus Equatoriana doing with the new adhesive we're sending them?

Anderson:
Pretty well, John. They've sold 5,000 quarts at 81 sucres, or $3 a quart, in the last six months.

Baker:
Not bad for a small operation. If they keep that up, that product is going to become a best-seller.

Anderson:
That's true, and although our profit is good, I think I can improve it.

Baker:
Great. How are you going to do that?

Anderson:
Well, you know that they have to pay a 40 percent ad valorem import duty on our $1.50 invoice price plus 2.7 sucres per quart specific duty. I've been studying Ecuador's import tariff, and I found that if our subsidiary imports the adhesive in 55-gallon drums, the import duty

is only 30 percent ad valorem plus 180 sucres per drum.

Baker:
Yes, but they'll have to buy cans and labels and fill them. This adds to their expense.

Anderson:
True, but because we won't have to fill the cans or charge them for cans and labels, we will save 20 cents per quart, which we can pass on to them.

Baker:
How much will it cost to fill the cans locally?

Anderson:
They tell me that the cans, labels, and labor will come to 6.75 sucres, which is 25 cents per can, and the only investment required is a shutoff valve, which they screw in the drum head when the cans are filled.

Baker:
I'm not sure I see the advantage, Ed. The cans, labels, and labor are more expensive in Ecuador than they are here. Where is the advantage?

Anderson:
Let me show you, John.

Show Ed Anderson's calculations. Disregard any possible freight savings for shipping in bulk.

SUPPLEMENTARY READINGS

Economic Development

Bornstein, Morris. *Comparative Economic Systems*. Homewood, Ill.: Richard D. Irwin, 1989.

Hagen, Everett E. *The Economics of Development*. Homewood, Ill.: Richard D. Irwin, 1980.

Todaro, Michael P. *Economic Development in the Third World*. New York: McGraw-Hill, 1981.

International Investment

Abdullah, Fuad A. *Financial Management for the Multinational Firm*. Englewood Cliffs, N.J.: Prentice-Hall, 1987.

Barrone, Robert N. "Risk and International Diversification: Another Look." *Financial Review*, Spring 1983, pp. 184–94.

Boddewyn, Jean J. "Foreign and Domestic Divestment and Investment Decisions: Like or Unlike?" *Journal of International Business Studies*, Winter 1983, pp. 23–35.

Caves, Richard. "International Corporations: The Industrial Economics of Foreign Investment." *Economica*, February 1971, pp. 5–6.

Davidson, Kenneth. "Strategic Investment Theories." *The Journal of Business Studies*, Summer 1985, pp. 16–28.

Hymer, Stephen. *The International Operations of International Firms: A Study in Direct Investment*. Cambridge, Mass.: MIT Press, 1976.

Madura, Jeff. *International Financial Management*. St. Paul, Minn: West Publishing, 1986.

Rugman, Alan M. "Internalization Is Still a General Theory of Foreign Direct Investment: A Reappraisal of the Literature." *Review of World Economics*, September 1985, pp. 570–75.

International Trade

"Currency Depreciation and Imports." *Finance & Development*, June 1987, pp. 18–20.

Heckscher, Eli F. *Mercantilism*. Winchester, Mass.: Allen & Unwin, 1934.

"How to Solve the Trade Problem." *Newsweek*, January 12, 1987, p. 40.

"Japan Habla Español." *World Monitor*, January 1989, pp. 29–30.

"Let down by the Drooping Dollar." *Fortune*, June 9, 1986, pp. 95–98.

"1988 List of U.S. Trade Barriers Published by European Community." *European Community News*, December 18, 1987.

Smith, Adam. "An Inquiry into the Nature and Causes of the Wealth of Nations." In *International Trade Theory: Hume to Ohlin*, ed. William R. Allen. New York: Random House, 1965.

"The Extent of Nontariff Barriers to Industrial Countries' Imports." Washington, D.C.: World Bank, 1985.

Wells, Louis Jr. "A Product Life Cycle for International Trade." *Journal of Marketing*, July 1968, pp. 1–6.

World Development Report 1988. Washington, D.C.: World Bank, 1988.

Protectionism

Bhagwati, Jagdish. *Protectionism*. Cambridge, Mass.: MIT Press, 1988.

"Coping with the 'New Protectionism': How Companies Are Learning to Love It." *International Management*, September 1986, pp. 20–26.

Costs and Benefits of Protection. Paris: OECD, 1985.

"Despite Record Profits, Big Three Auto Firms Seek More Protection." *The Wall Street Journal*, January 24, 1989, p. 1.

Eliminating Barriers to International Trade. New York: The Conference Board, 1986.

"Fortress of Mercantilism Still Wary of Competitors." *Insight*, July 18, 1988, pp. 15–17.

Hufbauer, Gary Clyde; Dianne T. Berliner; and Kimberly Ann Elliott. *Trade Protection in the United States: 31 Case Studies*. London: Institute for International Economics, 1986.

"Is Japan Using the U.S. as a Back Door to Europe?" *Business Week*, November 14, 1988, p. 57.

"Protectionism and Economic Integration." *EFTA Bulletin*, 4/87, pp. 6–8.

"Protectionism Can't Protect Jobs." *Fortune*, May 11, 1987, pp. 121–28.

"Protectionist Trade Policies: A Survey of Theory, Evidence, and Rationale." *Federal Reserve Bank of St. Louis Review*, January 1988, pp. 12–29.

"The New Protectionism." *Weekly Bulletein*. Brussels: Kredietbank, June 12, 1987.

Underground Economy

De Soto, Hernando. *The Other Path*. New York: Harper & Row, 1989. An excellent book on the underground economy of Peru.

"Europe's Booming Black Economy." *International Management*, July–August 1987, pp. 24–30.

Houston, Joel F. "The Underground Economy: A Troubling Issue for Policymakers." *Business Review*. Philadelphia: Federal Reserve Bank of Philadelphia, September/October 1987, pp. 3–12.

"How to Make Poor Countries Rich." *Fortune*, January 16, 1989, pp. 101–06.

"Spain's Thriving Underground Economy Spurs Growth but Saps the State Treasury." *The Wall Street Journal*, September 22, 1988, p. 32.

ENDNOTES

1. Government administrators involved in project evaluation are increasingly applying socioeconomic rather than purely financial criteria. For example, social rates of discount and opportunity costs are considered rather than the pure costs of borrowing money. While marketing managers do not have to be development economists any more than they need to be specialists in marketing research, they should have a knowledge of the basic concepts.

2. "Fortress of Mercantilism," *Insight*, July 18, 1988, pp. 15–17.

3. David Ricardo, "The Principles of Political Economy and Taxation," in *International Trade Theory: Hume to Ohlin*, ed. William R. Allen (New York: Random House, 1965), pp. 62–67.

4. The idea that only hours of labor determine production costs is known as the *labor theory of value*. In fairness to Ricardo, we must admit that he included the cost of capital as "embodied labor" in his labor costs. Actually, as shown in the section "Introducing Money," the theory of comparative advantage can be explained by the cost of all factors of production.

5. Eli F. Heckscher, "The Effect of Foreign Trade on the Distribution of Income," *Economisk Tidskrift, XXI*, 1919, pp. 497–512; and Bertil Ohlin, *Interregional and International Trade* (Cambridge, Mass.: Harvard University Press, 1933).

6. The economist, Bela Belassa, in his *Stages Approach to Comparative Advantage* published by the World Bank in 1977, found in a study of 26 developed and developing countries that "the intercountry differences in the structure of exports are in a large part explained by differences in physical and human capital endowments."

7. Louis Wells, "A Product Life Cycle for International Trade," *Journal of Marketing*, July 1968, pp. 1–6.

8. Many new products come not from the manufacturer's laboratories but from its suppliers of machinery and raw materials. Du Pont, an important supplier to the rubber industry, maintains a large laboratory in Akron to give service to the laboratories of the tire manufacturers.

9. Belassa, *Stages Approach to Comparative Advantage*, pp. 26–27.

10. "Footwear Industry Tells Congress 'Shoe Gap' Threatens U.S. Defense," *The Wall Street Journal*, August 24, 1984, p. 21.

11. "Brie and Hormones," *The Economist*, January 7, 1989, pp. 21–22; and "No Solution in Sight," *The Modesto Bee*, March 23, 1989, p. B4.

12. "Double Your Standard," *Forbes*, March 6, 1989, p. 14.

13. "E. C. Imposes Antidumping Duties on Japanese Printers," *Europe*, October 1988, p. 42.

14. Countervailing duties on imported goods may be imposed under U.S. law when the production or export of such goods is subsidized by the government of the exporting country and when U.S. manufacturers of similar goods are injured as a result of the subsidy. The Department of Commerce is responsible for determining if an import is being illegally subsidized or dumped in the U.S. market. Before countervailing or antidumping duties may be imposed, it must also be shown that the U.S. industry has sustained or may sustain damages from these unfair practices. The International Trade Commission is responsible for the injury investigation and determination. See *International Letter*, September 10, 1982, published by the Federal Reserve Bank of Chicago.

15. Sheila A. B. Page, "The Increased Use of Trade Control by Industrial Countries," *Intereconomics* (London: National Institute of Economic and Social Research, 1980).

16. "The Extent of Nontariff Barriers to Industrial Countries' Imports," *Development Research Department Discussion Paper No. 115* (Washington, D.C.: World Bank, 1985).

17. "Japan Continues Self-Imposed Quota on Car Exports," *The Modesto Bee*, January 12, 1989, p. 10.

18. "Managed Trade Is Just a Chip off Protectionism," *The Wall Street Journal*, April 8, 1988, p. 14.

19. "A Hidden Tax on All Our Houses," *U.S. News & World Report*, March 21, 1988, pp. 51–52.

20. "U.S. Designates Suzuki Samurai as Truck Import," *The Wall Street Journal*, January 5, 1989, p. A4.

21. "U.S. Textile Quotas," *Business Week*, September 10, 1984, pp. 20–25.

22. "1988 List of U.S. Trade Barriers Published by European Community," *European Community News*, December 18, 1987, p. 11.

23. The OECD published *Costs and Benefits of Protection*, which evaluates a wide range of studies on import restrictions of manufactured goods in OCED countries.

24. "Everybody's Doing It," *International Management*, July–August 1987, p. 27.

25. "'Shadow Economy' Translates into Every Language," *Business Week*, April 5, 1982, p. 68; and "Europe's Booming Black Economy," *International Management*, July–August 1987, pp. 24–30.

26. "Technical Notes," *World Development Report, 1988*, p. 290.

27. Michael Todoro, *Economic Development in the Third World* (New York: Longman, 1981), p. 57.

28. Charles Kindleberger and Bruce Herrick, *Economic Development* (New York: McGraw-Hill, 1977), p. 1.

29. Charles Kindleberger, *American Business Abroad* (New Haven: Yale University Press, 1969).

30. Stephen Hymer, *The International Operations of International Firms: A Study in Direct Investment* (Cambridge, Mass.: MIT Press, 1976).

31. Richard Caves, "International Corporations: The Industrial Economics of Foreign Investment," *Economica*, February 1971, pp. 5–6.

32. F. T. Knickerbocker, *Oligopolistic Reaction and Multinational Enterprise* (Boston: Harvard Business School, 1973).

33. E. M. Graham, "Transatlantic Investments by Multina-

tional Firms: A Rivalistic Phenomenon," *Journal of Post-Keynesian Economics,* Fall 1978, p. 82–99.

34. P. Buckley and M. Casson, *The Future of Multinational Enterprise* (New York: Macmillan, 1976).

35. R. Z. Aliber, "A Theory of Direct Investment," in *The*

International Corporation (Cambridge, Mass.: MIT Press, 1970), pp. 17–34.

36. A. Rugman, *International Diversification and the Multinational Enterprise* (Lexington, Mass.: Lexington Books, 1979).

Section Two

The International Environment: Organizations and Monetary System

The world is becoming increasingly bureaucratized. National governments have grown as new agencies have been formed, and individuals and businesses must deal with bureaucracies for more and more permits, licenses, clearances, and so on.

This development has spread beyond national borders, and the same phenomenon has been occurring on an international scale. Individuals and businesses may not enjoy the delays and red tape involved in dealing with bureaucracies, but if they are to function successfully, they must learn to do so.

The truth is that dealing with international organizations has some positive features. Some of these organizations, such as the World Bank, the United Nations, the International Monetary Fund, and the Organization for Economic Cooperation and Development, are excellent sources of information for business executives and students. In addition, the World Bank, regional development banks, and private development companies are sources of billions of dollars and other currencies for financing government purchases from businesses.

A positive feature of the bureaucracies from the point of view of students and executives is that they are all sources of many good jobs. Not only do the national governments and international organizations hire thousands of people to

be bureaucrats, but businesses must hire thousands more to deal with the bureaucrats.

As a result of huge foreign debt problems, which came to a head in the early 1980s, Poland and other Soviet-bloc countries, Argentina, Brazil, Mexico, and other Latin American countries, and countries elsewhere were unable to meet even interest, much less principal, payments on their debts. The International Monetary Fund was thrust into new prominence as a source of money and as an adviser and enforcer of how it would be spent. The Bank for International Settlements found itself in the unprecedented and unwanted position of making bridge loans.

In the late 1980s, the European Community and its 12 member-countries launched the extremely ambitious "Project 1992," the objective of which is to create a border-free market of some 320 million people by the end of 1992. At about the same time, the General Agreement on Tariffs and Trade began its Uruguay Round of negotiations aimed at nontariff barriers to trade plus restrictions on services, agriculture, and government procurement.

All of these reasons make international organizations an important subject for business executives and students. Therefore, we devote an entire chapter (Chapter 4) to these organizations.

The international monetary system is discussed in Chapter 5. This system is developing and changing constantly, and the international business student and executive must know where it is and where it has been. The past is important because some influential people and governments want to revive certain practices that are not presently in use.

Whenever you do business or travel internationally, you need different moneys, which are called currencies. Of course, you need U.S. dollars in the United States, but you must have pounds in Britain, francs in France, yen in Japan, and so forth.

Even if you don't travel or conduct any international business, it can be beneficial to know about the relative values of currencies. Currencies fluctuate in value constantly during one day, and over longer periods, their values can change significantly. On the forward, futures, or options markets, you can trade currencies for profit, just as you trade such commodities as wheat and silver. You would buy a currency if you thought its value was going up and sell it if you forecast a drop in its price. If you are in international business, you can use the same currency markets, or banks, to protect yourself against changes in currency values.

Also discussed in Chapter 5 are the gold standard, the gold exchange standard, nations' balances of payments, and fixed and floating currency exchange regimes.

Chapter 4

International Organizations

The United States gets back $3 in the form of sales by private firms for every $1 it contributes to the IDB.

James Bass, economist, Inter-American Development Bank

The $64,000 question is whether or not there will be a Fortress Europe—where they'll be free traders internally and protectionist externally.

Clayton Yeutter, secretary of agriculture

LEARNING OBJECTIVES

In this chapter, you will study:

1. The United Nations (UN), which is extremely active in the economic and social fields and is the source of much business for sellers of goods and services.

2. The new UN member-countries, which are almost all less developed countries (LDCs), are almost all poor, and comprise a majority of the UN membership.

3. World Bank loans, which provide borrowing countries with billions of dollars (and other currencies) and are used by these countries to buy goods and services from businesses in member-countries.

4. The International Finance Corporation (IFC), which is called the investment banker of the World Bank group because it encourages private investment in LDCs by LDC residents.

5. The International Development Association (IDA), which extends credits to the poorest countries.

6. The International Monetary Fund (IMF), whose size, powers, and activities have been expanding.

7. The General Agreement on Tariffs and Trade (GATT), which has had considerable success in reducing tariffs and quotas in international trade and in 1986 began a new (Uruguay) round of negotiations.

8. The Bank for International Settlements, which got unwanted publicity and activity as a result of the 1982 country debt crises.

9. The European Community (EC), which is the most extensive and successful regional economic grouping of nations, and which is now well along with "Project 1992."

10. The Organization of Petroleum Exporting Countries, (OPEC), which formed a cartel that was very effective for a time and may again become a powerful force.

11. The Organization for Economic Cooperation and Development (OECD), which is an excellent source for economic research and statistics.

KEY WORDS AND CONCEPTS

- Less developed countries (LDCs)
- Developed countries (DCs)
- Hard loans
- Soft loans
- Firm surveillance
- Debt default
- Debt rescheduling
- Managed trade
- Uruguay Round
- Marshall Plan

BUSINESS INCIDENT

Michael Barth has learned that experts can be wrong. In the early 1980s, he helped organize a fund in the United States for investing in South Korean stocks. Wall Street experts said the fund would fail for want of investor interest.

Wall Street was wrong. Investors liked the potential of the South Korean economy and bought Korea Fund shares. It was listed on the New York Stock Exchange in 1984 and has since been one of the best-performing country investment funds.

Mr. Barth works for the International Finance Corporation (IFC) capital markets department. The Korea Fund has been followed by a $50 million emerging-markets growth fund, a $30 million Thailand Fund, and an $86 million Malaysia Fund. More are in the works.

Source: Cheah Cheng Hye, "IFC's Pioneering Investment Funds Funnel Capital to Asian Equity Markets," *Asian Wall Street Journal,* September 21, 1987, p. 28.

Given the immense and growing numbers and importance of private and governmental international transactions, it is not surprising that a variety of international organizations have sprung up to facilitate, regulate, measure, or finance them. It behooves the business student—who is likely to be exposed to international opportunities and problems soon after graduation—to be aware of the existence and functions of a number of these organizations.

Some are worldwide organizations, and some are regional organizations with members from only one geographic area. Some are large, some small. Most are groupings of governments, but some are private.

The element common to all the organizations discussed in this chapter is that they all can be important to businesses. They may be sources of orders or sources of financing. They may be regulatory, or they may aim at standardization of weights and measurements. And, last but not least, they may be sources of jobs for you (see Figure 4–1).

THE UNITED NATIONS

Possibly the best-known worldwide organization is the United Nations (UN). Conceived and born amid the idealism and hopes that came with peace following World War II (1939–45), the UN has been a disappointment to many of its original supporters. Others foresaw more accurately what the UN's strengths and weaknesses would probably be.

> During the early UN years, one international law scholar, Professor Edwin Borchard of Yale Law School, cautioned his classes, which contained a number of World War II veterans, not to be too sanguine about enduring peace resulting from the UN. He told them, in effect, to keep their powder dry, and indeed the education or early careers of many of them were interrupted by the Korean War. In fact, one side in that war fought in the name of the UN.

Of course, there have been many other wars, declared and undeclared, between nations, colonies, provinces, tribes, and ethnic groups since the days of great expectation in the mid-1940s. These wars were waged despite the UN's peace-keeping efforts, and until recently many despaired of the UN as a keeper of the peace. However, during the late 1980s, the UN was involved in negotiations that resulted in the reduction or cessation of armed conflicts between the Soviet Union and the freedom fighters in Afghanistan and between Iran and Iraq.

In addition to its peace-keeping functions, the UN also conducts many activities potentially of great importance to businesspeople and students. It spends over $750 million annually for goods and services from businesses worldwide, and its agencies advise member-countries as they contract to buy goods and services in amounts that annually exceed $20 billion.

The UN is characterized by decentralization, which can be a source of frustration for the student or businessperson. To help you better understand the UN's structure, Figure 4–2 presents an organizational chart. To help businesses approach the UN, the Interagency Procurement Services Unit (IAPSU) was established in 1985. It is an information clearinghouse that helps match up suppliers and UN customers.[*]

---

[*] To contact IAPSU and other UN agencies directly, see the Fax, telephone, and telex numbers and addresses in *Business International*, August 15, 1988, p. 254.

■ **FIGURE 4–1**
International Organization Job Opportunities

The World Health Organization (WHO)
is an inter-governmental agency internationally recognized for its efficiency
integrity and numerous lasting achievements, including the eradication of smallpox.
Guided by humanitarian concerns, WHO works to direct and coordinate global and
national efforts to improve the health of peoples in more than
160 member countries at all levels of development. To meet its objectives
WHO depends on staff members with special qualities of leadership,
dedication and commitment.

Our Regional Office for the Eastern Mediterranean is looking for a qualified

Medical Officer
(MANAGER, HEALTH AND BIOMEDICAL INFORMATION-HBI)
to be stationed in Alexandria, Egypt.

He/She will be responsible for planning, organizing, developing and controlling the work of the regional Health and Biomedical Information Program, which consists of the Translation Unit, Library, Reports Unit, Public Information Unit, to ensure the availability to Member States of valid scientific, technical, managerial and other information relating to health and will provide expert advice on HBI issues and policies on health matters in general.

Applicants should have a medical degree from a recognized medical school, post-graduate degree in public health or a related field, extensive progressive experience in the field of health and biomedical information including supervisory, administrative and advisory functions, with several years in a senior post, related experience in an international organization and a very good knowledge of Arabic and English with a working knowledge of French.

Please send your detailed curriculum vitae no later than February 15, 1988 to Personnel (MPR),

World Health Organization
CH-1211 Geneva 27, quoting MPR/EMRO/87/HT.
Applications from women are encouraged. Only candidates under serious consideration will be contacted.

Source: *International Herald Tribune,* January 21, 1988, p. 7.

---

unicef
THE UNITED NATIONS CHILDREN'S FUND
With headquarters in New York
and offices throughout the world, seeks:

SENIOR INTERNAL AUDITOR

RESPONSIBILITIES: To perform financial, operational, program and special audit assignments. To furnish management with analysis, appraisals, recommendations and comments concerning the activities reviewed. To contribute to the overall objective of the Internal Audit.

LOCATION & TRAVEL: The incumbent will be based either in New York or one of our Regional Offices and will be required to travel extensively.

QUALIFICATIONS: Masters degree in Accountancy or Business/Public Administration, or Certified Public/Chartered Accountant qualification. Specialized training in modern audit techniques (computers, others). At least ten years substantive experience in operational and financial auditing preferably with non-profit organizations in progressively responsible positions; experience in analytical and management auditing and supervisory responsibility for the work of other auditors; working or travelling experience in developing countries. Readiness to accept functional missions to field offices as required. Fluency in English is required. Spanish, French or Arabic as a second language would be an asset.

SALARY: Around U.S. $60,000.–. Excellent benefits package.

Qualified women are encouraged to apply.

Send detailed resumé to:
Nowrang Persaud (Ref. VN-88-001)
Recruitment & Staff Development Section
United Nations Children's Fund (UNICEF)
3 United Nations Plaza (H-5F)
New York, N.Y. 10017
United States of America
(Closing date for receipt of applications February 29, 1988.)

Source: *International Herald Tribune,* January 21, 1988, p. 7.

WRITER
Division of Information

The UNITED NATIONS DEVELOPMENT PROGRAMME seeks candidates with extensive writing experience to develop interesting and stimulating photo feature articles on UNDP's worldwide activities. The position is based in New York and requires travel to developing countries. UNDP has 112 field offices and is the world's leading provider of multilateral grant technical assistance to developing countries.

In this multifaceted position you will write articles on development issues for in-house magazines and for placement in outside publications, as well as take responsibility for producing individual booklets or publications.

Qualifications:
■ a minimum of 5 years' professional experience as a writer for a major English language publication;
■ proven mastery of the English language, written and oral; working knowledge of Arabic, French or Spanish an asset;
■ Master's degree in English, journalism, communications, economics, political science or other relevant discipline;
■ ability to take quality photographs an asset;
■ ability to work harmoniously with individuals from diverse national and cultural backgrounds.

Please send detailed resume to: Chief, Recruitment Section IH1027, Division of Personnel, UNDP, One UN Plaza, Room 1824, New York NY 10017 USA.

Source: *The Economist.* October 29, 1988, p. 98.

UN Growth and Change

All UN member-nations are members of the General Assembly, in which each nation has one vote regardless of its size, wealth, or power. The number of members has grown rapidly since the UN's establishment in 1945, and new nations continue to join as they gain independence and become sovereign in

■ **FIGURE 4–2   UN Organizational Chart**

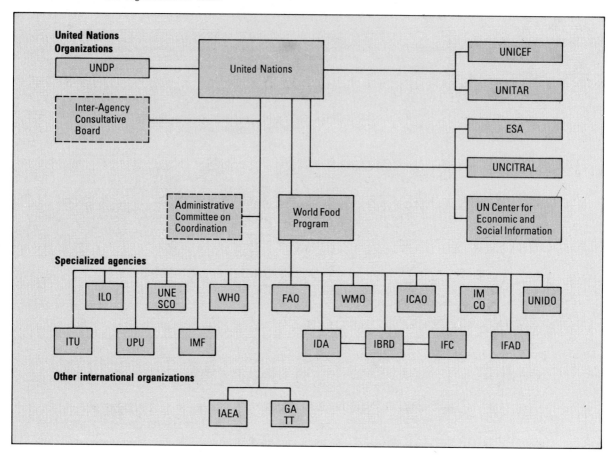

their territory. To understand recent, current, and probable future developments at the UN, it is necessary to bear in mind one fundamental fact about almost all the new members: they are poor.

Their relative poverty, combined with their numbers (they have far more votes than the wealthier, more developed countries can muster) has radically altered the UN's complexion and operational directions. These alterations are being expressed in the multiplication of projects aimed at raising the income of the **less developed countries (LDCs)**. Among the many such projects are education, irrigation, health, agriculture, raw materials, industrialization, and technological transfers from the **developed countries (DCs)**.

United Nations Conference on Trade and Development (UNCTAD).   As indicated, the newer LDC members of the UN are almost all poor countries, and they constitute a majority of UN membership. They are generally dissatisfied with their economic growth, and the UN Conference on Trade and Development (UNCTAD) is an expression of that dissatisfaction.[1] It was established as a permanent organ of the UN General Assembly in 1964.[*][2]

less developed country (LDC) commonly used designation for countries with low per capita income, high illiteracy, and little industrialization

developed country (DC) commonly used designation for countries with relatively high per capita income, low illiteracy, and well-developed industry

---

[*]   In the General Assembly, the LDC majority is not subject to a veto, as it is in the UN Security Council.

UNCTAD has become a forum and rather effective advocate for the LDCs. It has succeeded in convincing countries and international agencies to make low-interest loans or monetary grants to LDCs and to transfer technology to them.

UN Specialized Agencies

UNCTAD is one of these agencies whose functions are frequently highly specialized. UNCTAD was brought into being for the specific purpose of helping the UN's LDC members. Most of the other agencies were created to study and publish information in particular subject areas, but all are now involved with aid to the LDCs.

We shall name these agencies here without discussion. Their names indicate their areas of activity, and if they interest you as potential customers for your company or for research, you can easily find considerable information about them. The UN's specialized agencies are:

UN Children's Fund.
World Health Organization.
Food and Agriculture Organization.
UN Industrial Development
    Organization.
International Labor Organization.
UN Educational, Scientific, and
    Cultural Organization.
UN Development Program.
International Civil Aviation
    Organization.

International
    Telecommunications Union.
Universal Postal Union.
World Meteorological
    Organization.
International Atomic Energy
    Agency.
International Fund for
    Agricultural Development.

Career Opportunities

Having read the list of UN specialized agencies, you can imagine that they hire thousands of people as do the UN Secretariat and the national delegations. The medium- to high-level jobs at these places pay very well and frequently carry tax, travel, and prestige perquisites. You should not ignore them when job hunting. (Recall the three ads in Figure 4–1.)

THE WORLD BANK

The International Bank for Reconstruction and Development is usually referred to—in its own publications and elsewhere—as the World Bank. The World Bank Group consists of the Bank itself, the International Finance Corporation (IFC), and the International Development Association (IDA).

Applicable to the entire group is the preference of most, if not all, governmental borrowers for multinational or international agency loans and assistance rather than bilateral loans or aid. Visions of imperialism, real or imagined, are less likely if the lender/donor is multinational or international.[3] The great majority of group loans or credits* are made to LDCs.

---

* In World Bank terminology, moneys lent by the bank are called *loans,* while those lent by the IDA are referred to as *credits.*

Importance to Business

There are a number of reasons why business should be aware of the World Bank Group's activities:

1. Many companies are suppliers to borrowers in group-financed projects, and these borrowers spend billions of dollars each year buying goods and services from businesses.
2. The development finance institutions (discussed below) in LDCs, which are partly financed and technically assisted by the group, are potential capital sources for businesses selling or working in LDCs.
3. The World Bank's center for arbitration may be able to resolve difficulties encountered by business in a foreign country.
4. Projects financed by the group tend to be mutually supportive (for example, general benefits resulting from improved infrastructure, and better economic resource inventories).
5. The information that the group gathers about a nation's or a project's finances, uses of funds, management abilities, and so forth tends to be more complete and accurate than the information likely to be available to a private, foreign business.

In June 1986, the United States signed an agreement to become involved with a new international body that would insure investors in foreign countries against loss from war, riot, and other risks. This new body is the Mulilateral Investment Guarantee Agency (MIGA), which is affiliated with the World Bank.

MIGA will give advice to investors and try to promote international commercial agreements. Among the risks against which it will insure are breach of contract, expropriation, or a freezing of funds by the host government.

Hard Loans

hard loans made and repayable in hard, convertible currencies at market interest rates with normal market maturities

The World Bank makes **hard loans.** This means its loans are at prevailing market interest rates and are granted only to sound borrowers for periods not exceeding 25 years. The Bank must make relatively safe loans with high assurance of repayment because its own funds are acquired through the sale of securities offerings that must compete with government and private business offerings of all sorts. Investors would not buy World Bank securities at economical interest rates if they felt that the Bank's loans were insecure, because the Bank must repay the buyers of its securities out of proceeds and profits on its loans.

To date, there have been no defaults on loans made by the World Bank, and its bonds carry the highest quality rating available, that is, AAA. The World Bank has operated at a profit every year since 1947. That profit has been used to make additional loans and to furnish funds for the IDA.

Although no World Bank loans have been officially declared to be in default, some countries have been unable to make payments when called for by the original loan terms. Many of those loans have been rescheduled, giving the debtor countries more time to repay them, but it is quite possible that unless economic conditions improve for debtor LDCs, some World Bank loans will have to be recognized as in default.

Business Opportunities and Information Sources

The billions of dollars and other currencies lent by the World Bank create many opportunities for businesses to sell their products and services to the borrowers. International competitive bidding is a Bank requirement. However, although the Bank announces the signing of each loan, it does not invite bids or tenders from potential suppliers to the financed projects. Such invitations are the responsibility of the government or agency executing the project. Thus, a company desiring to sell to a project must watch for the loan announcements and then contact appropriate officials in the borrowing country or at that country's embassy in its own country.[4]

Quite evidently, that procedure poses difficulties for firms, particularly smaller ones, which would like to sell their products or services to a Bank-financed project. In recognition of this, the UN began in 1978 to furnish procurement information. The UN Center for Economic and Social Information in Geneva publishes *Development Forum Business Edition,* a biweekly newspaper that gives details of all major business opportunities opened by World Bank loans. The newspaper publishes requirements for each project and instructions on how to bid for the business.

Among World Bank reports and publications that can be helpful to business and students are its *Annual Report, Statement of Loans* (quarterly), *Guidelines Relating to Procurement under World Bank Loans and IDA Credits, Uses of Consultants by the World Bank and Its Borrowers,* and *World Bank Atlas of Per Capita Product and Population.* Also available are reports of the World Bank's various General Survey Missions regarding certain countries or areas.

International Finance Corporation (IFC)

The International Finance Corporation (IFC) is the World Bank Group's investment banker. Its sphere is exclusively private risk ventures in the LDCs. The purpose of the IFC is to further economic development by encouraging the growth of productive enterprise in member-countries, thus supplementing the activities of the World Bank.[5]

Joint ventures favored.   The IFC's policy is to favor joint ventures that have some local capital committed at the outset, or at least the probability of local capital involvement in the foreseeable future.[6] This is not to say that the IFC will not cooperate with capital sources outside the host country (the country in which the investment is being made), and there are many examples of such cooperation. Among the industries thus capitalized have been fertilizers, synthetic fibers, tourism, paper, and cotton fabric. The outside capital sources, if in related lines of business, are usually worldwide companies (WWCs). A few WWCs that have cooperated with the IFC have been Phillips Petroleum, AKV Netherlands, ICI, Intercontinental Hotels, and Pechiney-Gobain.

Creation of local capital markets.   In return for its investment in a company, the IFC takes securities in the form of stock (equity ownership) or bonds (debt). One objective of the IFC is to sell its securities into a local capital market. To do that, it will help create and nurture such a market. For example, the IFC extended a $5 million credit line to a syndicate of private Brazilian investment banks to provide support for those banks' securities underwriting activities. The banks work with Fondo do Desenvolvimento do Mercado de

Capitais, a revolving capital market development fund maintained by the Brazilian central bank. The objectives are (1) to induce the investment banks to assume a greater role in underwriting Brazilian securities in Brazil, (2) to improve the access of Brazilian companies to long-term domestic source capital, and (3) to encourage Brazilians to invest in sound domestic securities.

Liaison with development finance companies.   The IFC is the liaison within the World Bank Group for the numerous development finance companies (DFCs)—sometimes called development banks, as in Ecuador—that have sprung up, primarily in the LDCs. These DFCs are in many ways local versions of the IFC. Each DFC seeks potentially profitable ventures within its country and assists with feasibility studies. If a venture proceeds, the DFC helps along the way with advice on plant, property, financing, management, or equipment. Finally, the DFC attempts to establish or enlarge a domestic capital market for securities of the venture.[7]

As you saw in this chapter's Business Incident, thanks to the IFC, investors from both poor and rich countries can now buy and sell securities (stocks and bonds) of companies operating in the developing countries. In addition, due to the IFCs catalytic role in direct foreign investment, some $1 billion of IFC 1988 investment supported total foreign investment of over $5 billion.[8]

Like the World Bank, the IFC is reluctant to admit default of a loan or failure of an investment and has rescheduled some loans. Unlike the World Bank, however, the IFC has written off a few investments that it judged could not be revived.

Nevertheless, the IFC has continued to grow. At the end of 1988, its number of projects, incomes, and portfolio commitments were all up (see Figure 4–3).

International Development Association (IDA)

The IDA is the "soft" loan (or "credit," as an IDA loan is called) section of the World Bank. Although it shares the Bank's administrative staff and grants credits for projects covering the same sorts of projects in the LDCs as the Bank's loans, its **soft loans** differ from the "hard" loans of the bank in several important ways. They have 50-year maturities, compared to 15- and 25-year maturities of the Bank. The IDA may grant 10-year grace periods before repayment of principal or interest must begin, whereas the grace periods of the World Bank usually do not exceed 5 years. The IDA charges only three fourths of 1 percent as a service charge on disbursed loan balances plus one half of 1 percent on undisbursed balances.[9] As is evident from these differences, borrowers from the IDA are the poorest of the poor LDCs, which need credit for development projects but cannot carry the burden on their economies or foreign exchange reserve positions that would result from normal commercial term loans. To the maximum extent possible, the credits are made in the currency of the borrowing member-country.[10]

soft loans   may be repayable in soft, nonconvertible currencies; carry low or no interest obligations; are frequently long term, up to 50 years; and may grant grace periods of up to 10 years during which no payments are required

IDA capital sources.   Unlike the World Bank, the IDA cannot raise capital in competitive capital markets and depends instead on subscriptions donated by the DCs and some LDCs. Generally, the DC members make contributions in convertible currencies; the LDC members donate their own currencies.

IDA resources are renewed periodically by a process called "replenishment," whereby 33 supporting nations donate money. The replenishment for

■ **FIGURE 4–3   Increasing Number of IFC Projects**

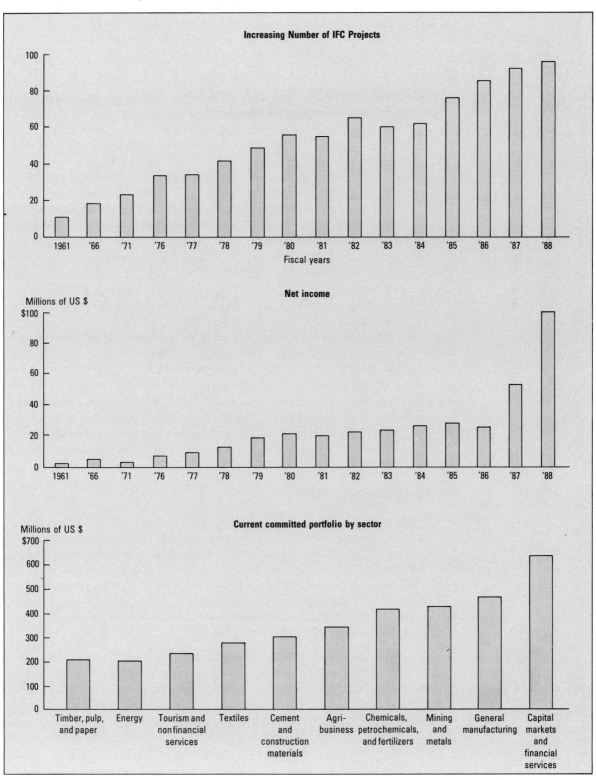

Source: *Finance & Development,* December 1988, p. 40.

1985–87 was in the amount of $9 billion, but that was increased by about $2 billion when drought and political turmoil caused famine in Africa. That was the seventh replenishment; the IDA raised $12.4 billion in the eighth.

INTERNATIONAL MONETARY FUND (IMF)

Although the IMF deals solely with governments, its policies and actions have profound impact on business worldwide. Its influence and impact may become even greater. Before explaining that statement, we should look briefly at the objectives and activities of the Fund and how they developed. Most of them continue to be important.

The IMF Articles of Agreement were adopted at the Bretton Woods Conference in 1944.[11] In general terms, the Fund's objectives were, and continue to be, to foster (1) orderly foreign exchange arrangements, (2) convertible currencies, and (3) a shorter duration and lesser degree of balance-of-payments disequilibria. The premise of the Fund is that the common interest of all nations in a workable international monetary system far transcends conflicting national interests.[12] One of the Fund's original objectives, since abandoned, was the maintenance of fixed exchange rates among member-countries' currencies, with par value related to the U.S. dollar, which was valued at $35 per ounce of gold.

Each member-country has a quota equal to the amount it subscribes to the IMF. Votes at Fund meetings are weighted according to quota size, and the amount a member can draw is related to its quota.[13]

The IMF agreement was entered prior to the founding conference of the United Nations, and when the UN was formed, the Fund was brought into relationship with the UN by an agreement. This agreement preserved the Fund's independence, which was justified by the need for independent control of monetary management. This need results from the temptations of every government to overspend and cause inflation.[14]

Changes in the IMF

The 1970s and 1980s saw some fundamental changes in the IMF's activities and roles. As stated above, the IMF abandoned the objective of maintaining the fixed exchange rate system. More accurately stated, the obligation of maintaining such a system remained in the Fund's Articles of Agreement, but the IMF was powerless to uphold it in the face of a situation in which all major currencies were floating* rather than fixed in value. In recognition of reality, the articles were amended to legalize the actual current practice, that is, floating exchange rates.

Greater power for the IMF?   The amended articles also included a new Article IV, which among other things, empowers the IMF to "exercise **firm surveillance** over the exchange rate policies" of members. There are those who feel that this new surveillance power may permit the Fund to move toward the position in the world occupied by central banks nationally.[15] That, of course, would require the surrender of a great deal of sovereignty by the member-countries, which many governments will stoutly resist.

firm surveillance   may permit the IMF to influence or even dictate fiscal and monetary policies of member-countries if the economically strong countries permit such intrusion

* Discussion of floating exchange rates as compared to fixed exchange rates will be found in Chapter 5.

A development lender.   Due in large part to the big increase in the cost of petroleum, the nonoil LDCs' balance-of-payments deficits soared during the late 1970s and early 1980s. The IMF stepped into this situation, making larger loans for longer periods of time and for purposes other than temporary balance-of-payments corrections. Loans used for long-term development projects will be evaluated by the World Bank, which has been making such loans for years.[16]

A market borrower.   Prior to 1981, the IMF got all of its capital from member-country contributions or from direct borrowing from member-countries. The Fund's financial resources from member quotas grew from about $65.9 billion in 1980 to approximately $150 billion by the end of 1988. In 1981, the Fund was authorized to borrow money in the world's capital markets.

World Debt Crisis and the IMF.   Over the years, countries have occasionally been unable or unwilling to pay their debts. When countries were unable to pay debts that came due (**debt default**), the debts were sometimes rescheduled to give them more time to pay (**debt rescheduling**). Debts of Peru, Zaire, and Turkey are among those that were rescheduled.

Usually due to government changes, countries sometimes refuse to pay the debts of previous governments; the new government repudiates the old debt. This occurred when communist governments assumed power in the Soviet Union, the People's Republic of China, and Cuba.

Before 1981, such reschedulings and repudiations were relatively unusual. Suddenly that all changed. First Poland and other Soviet-bloc countries, then Mexico, followed by Brazil, Argentina, and other Latin American countries as well as countries in Africa and Asia found themselves short of money to repay their debts.

debt default occurs when a debtor will not or cannot repay a loan when payment is due

debt rescheduling involves the debtor and creditor agreeing to permit a longer repayment period, lower interest rate, and/or forgiveness of some of the debt

Financial and economic disaster?   Some observers foresaw massive debt repudiations, bank failures, world trade breakdown, and deep depressions with high unemployment. The debts of the non-OPEC developing countries totaled some $520 billion at the end of 1982, and the disaster scenario had all of them defaulting at once—perhaps after forming a debt "OPEC" to coordinate their debt repudiation.

Enter the IMF.   While Mexico was negotiating its emergency IMF loan in November 1982, it was preparing to inaugurate a new president in December. The outgoing president wanted no part of the austerity programs being insisted on by the IMF, and the incoming president had no official power until December. Jacques de Larosiere, the IMF's managing director, prodded both presidents into cooperation.

De Larosiere's problems did not end there. The some 1,400 large and small creditor banks of Mexico wanted no more to do with Mexico, so he called a creditors' meeting in New York, at which he bluntly warned them that unless they came up with $5 billion more for Mexico, the IMF would pull out. They would lose their entire loans if it did that. The creditors went along with the IMF plan.

Such aggressiveness by the IMF was a sharp departure from its previous low-key approach.[17] Add to that the large increases in the IMF lending resources provided by industrial member-countries between 1981 and 1986, and the Fund had become a major new world force. Lord Harold Lever, an

■ TABLE 4–1
The 17 Major Debtor
Countries

Country	Total Debt Outstanding ($billions)		Interest as Percent of Exports		GDP-Average Annual Growth (percent)		Per Capita Consumption Average Annual Growth (percent)	
	End 1985	End 1987	1985*	1987†	1980–1984	1984–1987	1980–1984	1984–1987
Argentina	$ 50.8	$ 49.4	25.4%	33.1%	−1.6%	2.2%	−2.7%	0.7%
Bolivia	4.0	4.6‡	43.0	31.5	−4.7	−1.9	−7.8	−1.4
Brazil	107.3	114.5	38.2	30.2	0.1	8.0	−1.2	4.2
Chile	21.0	20.5	42.9	29.5	−1.4	4.0	−2.1	−2.3
Colombia	11.3	15.1	16.4	16.6	1.8	4.1	−0.1	0.6
Costa Rica	4.2	4.5‡	24.0	18.9	−0.4	4.1	−4.8	3.3
Ecuador	8.5	9.0‡	24.8	24.4	1.1	1.8	−2.3	−2.1
Ivory Coast	8.0	9.1	18.4	17.1	−2.3	1.7	−6.6	−1.1
Jamaica	3.4	3.8	12.5	17.4	1.3	−1.3	−1.4	−1.4
Mexico	99.0	105.0	34.1	32.7	1.3	−1.0	−1.4	−4.4
Morocco	14.0	17.3	12.7	25.4§	2.5	4.6	−0.2	2.2
Nigeria	19.3	27.0	12.1	11.6	−4.7	−1.6	−4.3	−9.4
Peru	13.4	16.7	7.9	29.0	−0.7	2.6	−3.7	4.7
Philippines	24.8	29.0	12.3	19.0	0.8	−2.2	0.0	−2.3
Uruguay	3.6	3.8‡	21.8	15.3	−3.7	1.8	−4.7	0.8
Venezuela	33.6	33.9	10.4	22.5	−1.8	0.8	−6.4	−2.1
Yugoslavia	19.6	21.8	12.4	7.7	0.6	1.8	−0.5	−0.5
Total	$445.9	$485.0	23.5%	23.8%	−0.3%	2.8%	−1.8%	−1.3%

* Based on estimated interest paid on total external liabilities in 1985.
† Based on interest due in 1987 on long-term debt outstanding at the end of 1986.
‡ End 1986.
§ Excluding private debt.
Source: World Bank.

economist and a senior adviser to the British Labor governments of 1974–79, suggested in 1983 that the IMF become the monitor of national export credit agencies to ensure exports of credits as well as exports of goods.[18]

Despite efforts of the IMF, private banks, and debtor and creditor countries and businesses, progress in solving the world debt problem has been slow and spotty. One development was that the United States became the world's biggest net debtor in 1986, with foreigners holding $107.4 billion more in American assets than U.S. investors held abroad. By the end of 1987, this amount had increased to $368.2 billion. Leaving the United States out of the picture, the 17 major debtor countries had external debt of $445.9 billion at the end of 1987 (see Table 4–1).

You will note some additional information available from Table 4–1. One set of figures represents annual interest payments on the loan as a percentage of the country's exports per year. Of course, the higher that percentage, the more difficult it is for the debtor country to service the loan. Another set of figures shows the average annual growth of gross domestic product. The higher that growth figure the better. And finally, the table shows the growth of annual average consumption. The more rapid the growth of consumption, the less there remains to service debt.

INTERNATIONAL MONETAR'

"OK, I'm sorry we called you a dirty capitalist imperialist swine – now can we have the money?"

From *The Wall Street Journal*, with permission of Cartoon Features Syndicate.

IMF gold sales benefit LDCs.   One intended effect of enhanced IMF power and the availability of special drawing rights (SDRs are discussed in Chapter 5) was the diminished role of gold and the U.S. dollar. A step in that direction was taken in 1976, when the IMF held the first of a series of sales from its gold stock. Those sales continued over a four-year period ending in May 1980, and one sixth of the Fund's gold stock was sold. Another sixth was returned to the members.

The money derived from the IMF gold sales was placed in an account called the Special Trust Fund, which used those moneys as another aid to LDCs.[19] The trust fund was terminated in 1981, at which time the approximately $400 million of repaid loans and interest were transferred to the fund's supplementary financing facility. Those moneys, plus the proceeds of further trust fund loan repayments through 1991, were turned over to the Structural Adjustment Facility (SAF) in 1986, to be managed in collaboration with the World Bank, which was contributing its IDA funds to the SAF.

This marked the first formal collaboration between the World Bank and the IMF. Moneys of the SAF are not simply lent to the poorer LDCs; the Bank and Fund work closely with the borrowing governments to develop medium-term macroeconomic and structural adjustment programs that will help correct distortions in their economies, restore viable payment positions, and promote faster economic growth.[20]

Publications

IMF publications that can be of value to international business students and to businesses include *International Financial Statistics, Balance of Payments Yearbook, Direction of Trade, Government Financial Statistics Yearbook, Annual Report of Exchange Restrictions, Annual Reports of the IMF,* and

Summary Proceedings of Annual Meetings. Mention should also be made of *IMF Staff Papers* on individual countries and of the quarterly publication *Finance & Development.*

REGIONAL DEVELOPMENT BANKS

Regional development banks (DBs) are regional versions of the World Bank. There are three major ones: The African Development Bank, the Asian Development Bank, and the Inter-American Development Bank (IDB). Their function is to lend money in the less developed countries to build infrastructure, support agriculture and industry, and create jobs. The sources of their funds are several. All DBs get contributions from their member-countries, and all get money from developed countries that are permitted to be members even though they are not located in the geographic areas. DBs also raise money in the international capital markets, in the Eurocurrency market, and in the Eurobond market.

In 1987, the African DB's capital was increased 200 percent from $6.9 billion to $20.8 billion, while the African Development Fund replenishment was doubled to $3 billion. The Fund is analogous to the World Bank's IDA in lending to the poorest of the poor.

Although the majority of the African DB's loans have gone to governments, there is change in the wind. Due to the enormous problems engendered by public-sector mismanagement of finances and resources, the African DB and even some of the governments are moving to favor loans to private companies, including some privatized by those governments.[21]

At the Asian DB—the senior management of which is dominated by the Japanese—there is disagreement between Japan and the United States, the two largest shareholders. Washington wants to bring the Asian DB more in line with the World Bank, requiring borrowers to reform their economic policies before loans are granted, especially in countries where bloated government financial institutions are perpetuating inefficiency. While Tokyo pays lip service to this, it appears most interested in turning the Asian DB into a better channel for recycling its huge trade surplus and financing Japanese exports.[22]

The IDB disposes of about $34 billion in resources and would like to increase that by some $25 billion. However, speaking through Secretary James Baker, the United States—which provides most of the IDB's money—says no, unless the IDB gives the lending countries greater influence in the Bank's procedure for approving loans.

Insane Asylum?

"I know it sounds like having the inmates run the insane asylum," says the bank official, "but when the Bank was set up, the United States happily went along with vesting power over policy and practice in the Latin American borrowing nations and not, as in any other bank, with the lenders."

Currently the Bank works in the following way: There are 44 shareholders, all governments represented by their ministers of finance or officials of comparable importance. These are the governors of the Bank. They in turn are represented by 12 executive directors. Of these, eight are from borrowing countries, with 53.5 percent of the vote on their board, and four are from nonborrowing countries. The nonborrowing members are the United States, which has 34.5 percent of the vote, and Canada, Japan, 16 European countries, and Israel, whose combined share of the vote comes to 12 percent.

Attempts within the Bank to meet Baker's demands have involved a variety of proposals that would have enabled any one, two, or three executive directors to delay consideration of a loan proposal for periods of three months to two years. None of the proposals found a consensus on the board. Helping to reconcile the Latin American countries and the United States will top the agenda of the newly elected Bank president.[23]

Reconciliation was achieved through compromises reached during meetings in Rotterdam in March 1989. The proposals that one, two, or three directors could delay Bank lending decisions for 2, 7, or 12 months were accepted, and a $26.5 billion capital increase was agreed upon.

In 1986, the Inter-American Development Bank was midwife to the birth of the Inter-American Investment Corporation as an affiliated organization. The corporation is to support the Latin American private sector with loans, investment, and technical and managerial assistance.

For our purposes, the importance of the regional development bank loans in less developed countries is that the LDC borrowers use much of the borrowed money to purchase goods and services from companies in other countries. The alert business management can earn some of that money.

BANK FOR INTERNATIONAL SETTLEMENTS (BIS)

The Bank for International Settlements (BIS), located in Basel, Switzerland, has become a second home for central bankers of the world's major industrial countries except for the People's Republic of China, the Soviet Union, and East Germany. It was created in 1930 to handle reparations payments from Germany stemming from World War I. Oddly enough, Hitler's National Socialist government continued to make the agreed reparations payments through part of World War II.

The BIS is such a convenient meeting place for central banker groups that one needs a program to sort them out. The BIS board of directors consists of the governors of several European central banks. A second group that meets in Basel consists of the central bank governors of the Group of Ten—which has 11 members now that Switzerland has joined but is still called the Group of Ten. The original 10 are Belgium, Britain, Canada, France, Holland, Italy, Japan, Sweden, West Germany, and the United States. A third group is that of the European Community (Common Market) countries. Yet another group is the annual general meeting of the governors of the 29 central banks that are BIS shareholders.

In addition to providing a congenial and confidential meeting place for central bankers, the BIS provides secure, anonymous cover for shareholder countries as they transfer large amount of currency or gold among themselves. When they do this through the BIS, the currency and gold traders may not be able to figure out the identity of the real buyers and sellers.

The world financial strains in 1982 that enhanced the IMF's role also caused some changes for the BIS. In 1982 and 1983, the BIS made loans to cash-strapped Hungary, Mexico, Argentina, Brazil, and Yugoslavia. These were called "bridge" loans because they were intended to bridge those debtor countries over a period until IMF, government, and private bank loans could be mobilized. The BIS had never made such loans before, and by early 1983 its chairman, Fritz Leutwiler, was announcing that it would make no more of them. There were several reasons for his decision. One was that the bridge loans were potentially long term and therefore potentially dangerous due to the short-term nature of deposits at the BIS. Another was that the small BIS staff was inadequate to evaluate and administer such loans.[24]

In 1984, Leutwiler was replaced as chairman and president by Jean Godeaux of Belgium. The BIS invests conservatively and regularly reports profits. It announced a profit of 106,213,792 gold francs for the 1988–89 year, down from 118,901,393 the previous year due to lower securities trading profits.[*25]

GENERAL AGREEMENT ON TARIFFS AND TRADE (GATT)

How GATT Was Conceived

Arising from the optimism among the Western allies following World War II was the ideal of an international organization that would function in the trade areas much as it was hoped the UN would function in the political and peace-keeping areas. A charter was drawn for an International Trade Organization (ITO) at the Havana Conference in 1948. However, the ITO never came into existence because not enough governments ratified its charter.

At what were thought of as preliminaries to and preparations for an ITO, the American negotiators presented what they envisioned as a step toward an acceptable ITO treaty, which was to embody the numerous bilateral trade treaties into one multilateral treaty. They suggested, in the absence of any established international trade rules, that the commercial policy rules of the draft ITO charter be incorporated into a general agreement on tariffs and trade as an interim measure pending ITO ratification. The American suggestions were accepted, and so the General Agreement on Tariffs and Trade (GATT) was born in 1947.[26] Differently stated, the ITO was not ratified as a de jure organization, and GATT became a de facto international trade organization.[27]

Some observers felt GATT to be a "slender reed" on which to base world progress toward free international trade.[28] Nevertheless, it still exists and has been extremely successful in some areas of tariff reduction as well as in other fields.[29]

GATT Successes

The 96 GATT members include all the OECD countries (Organization for Economic Cooperation and Development, covered later in this chapter), almost 70 developing countries, and a few small communist countries. Together they account for almost 90 percent of world trade. Nine out of 10 disputes brought to GATT have been settled satisfactorily. Average tariffs in industrial countries have tumbled to around 5 percent from an average of 40 percent in 1947, and the volume of trade in manufactured goods has multiplied 20-fold.

[*]A gold franc is worth about $2.

GATT Entirely Successful?

Despite these successes, the future of GATT is very much in question. Growing protectionism—usually by nontariff means—nurtured by the world's economic difficulties of the 1970s and 1980s has served to undermine GATT's credibility and threaten the open trading system it advocates.

managed trade special treatment of certain trade partners

Cars, steel, videos, semiconductors, and shoes have followed textiles and clothing into **managed trade.** In agriculture, where America, the European Community (EC, covered later in this chapter), and Japan are spending a total of some $70 billion a year on subsidies, GATT rules have had no effect. GATT has never covered services (nearly 30 percent of world trade), foreign investment, or intellectual properties (patents, copyrights, and so on).

The principle of equal treatment of all trade partners is much violated. The LDCs are permitted to protect their industries and discriminate among trade partners. The EC has abolished many of the tariffs on intra-EC trade, but tariffs are levied on goods from outside the community. In 1989, Canada and the United States formally began creation of a tariff-free trade area; goods from outside the area will be subject to tariff.

Will GATT Survive?

In 1986, GATT members met in Uruguay to begin the eighth round of negotiations aimed at reviving and strengthening the organization and broadening its scope. These negotiations are referred to as the **Uruguay Round** and are generally agreed to be a make-or-break affair for GATT.

Uruguay Round GATT negotiations in the eighth round, so named because the first meeting was in Uruguay

It was hoped to bring under GATT's auspices new trade areas, including agriculture, services, intellectual properties, and managed trade. The timetable called for a four-year negotiation with final agreements in 1992. A midterm meeting was held in Montreal to measure progress in December 1988. There had been very little.

The Montreal meeting achieved nothing but an agreement to go back to Geneva (GATT's headquarters) and keep trying. The meeting broke up in an acrimonious disagreement between the United States and the EC on agriculture subsidies. The U.S. Congress had given U.S. negotiators authority to agree to reduce U.S. subsidies in stages if the EC and others would agree to reduce theirs in similar stages, all to reach zero at an agreed date. The EC would not discuss a zero possibility, and the negotiators left Montreal with GATT's future more dubious than when they arrived.

Is GATT Irrelevant?

So argues one school of thought, which holds that only the Anglo-American system is rooted in a free-and-fair trade approach. This school identifies five competing systems: Anglo-American, centrally planned, developing, mixed, and plan-driven. Countries identified with these systems are the United States (Anglo-American), the Soviet Union (centrally planned), Mexico (developing), France (mixed), and Japan (plan-driven).

tailored trade results from bilateral free trade agreements to eliminate trade barriers

Some economists and politicians believe the Anglo-American system is at great disadvantage in playing by its free/fair trade rules against the other systems. **Tailored trade** is advocated, of which the Canadian–U.S. trade agreement is an example. In a *Harvard Business Review* article, it is stated,

"American companies can't compete if foreign markets remain closed and the U.S. market remains open."[30] Access to the huge U.S. market would be the incentive for other countries to open theirs.

ORGANIZATION OF PETROLEUM EXPORTING COUNTRIES (OPEC)

Realizing that if the oil-exporting countries were united they could bargain more effectively with the large oil companies, Iran and Venezuela joined the Arab Petroleum Congress at a Cairo meeting in 1959. Discussions and secret agreements at that meeting became the seeds for the Organization of Petroleum Exporting Countries (OPEC).[31]

Oil Companies Should Have Listened

Early in 1960, the Venezuelan minister of mines and hydrocarbons and the Saudi oil minister wrote to the oil companies operating in Venezuela and the Middle East, requesting that they consult with the host governments before making any price changes. In August 1960, the oil companies reduced oil prices, and it is said that the host governments learned of it only when they read it in the newspapers. In any event, they had not been consulted. This made them angry and also increased their anxiety about the control and conservation of their natural resources. In that atmosphere, they called a meeting on September 14, 1960, in Baghdad.

Attending the meeting were representatives of Iran, Iraq, Kuwait, Saudi Arabia, and Venezuela. OPEC was formed, and the OPEC members took charge of pricing.

> This first headquarters of OPEC was in a relatively small apartment in Geneva. There was general skepticism as to the durability of the new organization and hesitancy on the part of some potential employees to take what they feared would be short-term jobs.
>
> Clearly, the skeptics have been proved wrong. OPEC's headquarters have been moved to Vienna, and its members, in addition to the founders named above, include Qatar, Libya, Indonesia, Abu Dhabi, Algeria, Ecuador, and Gabon.[32]

Economic Muscle and Political Strength

OPEC soon began to test its strength, and the price of petroleum began to rise. At the end of 1973 and in early 1974, OPEC demonstrated its potentially devastating strength with the oil embargo by its Arab members against the Netherlands and the United States, accompanied by very large price increases to all customers. Its strength stemmed from the comparative cohesiveness of the members and from the fact that it controlled some 68 percent of the world's known petroleum reserves.[33] OPEC supplied some 84 percent of the European Community's oil needs and over 90 percent of Japan's.[34]

Was OPEC Too Greedy?

Using its strength, OPEC drove up petroleum prices from about $3 a barrel in 1973 to close to $35 in 1980. Such a drastic increase in energy prices caused recession and unemployment in oil-importing countries, but it also sparked conservation measures, increased oil exploration in non-OPEC countries, and research for alternate energy sources.

Thanks to these initiatives, OPEC's market weakened, but its members refused to cut their production and thus an oversupply developed. OPEC had seized control of pricing in the mid-1970s, but by the early 1980s, the free markets were setting prices with major markets in Rotterdam, New York, and Chicago.[35] Prices fell to under $13 a barrel in 1987 and traded between that price and $19 into 1989.

These lower oil prices reversed conservation measures and greatly reduced both oil exploration and research into alternate forms of energy. There are those who worry that such trends may cause the world to become dependent on OPEC once again.

The accompanying cartoon of oil derricks topped with question marks symbolizes the many question marks surrounding the future of OPEC and OPEC's effects on the rest of the world.

THE EUROPEAN COMMUNITY (EC)

Background

In the aftermath of the Second World War Europe was in shambles as a result of the fighting and the devotion of all efforts and investments to the war. In order to assist Europeans back to their feet and to encourage strong, friendly governments, U.S. Secretary of State George C. Marshall recommended the United States give financial aid to and work with European countries in their reconstruction.

Thus was born the **Marshall Plan,** which was immensely successful. It swung into action in 1948, and by the first quarter of 1950, European industrial production was already 138 percent ahead of the level reached in the last year of peace, 1938. Europeans achieved this success by working together, and they continued to do so. One milestone in this relationship was the Treaty

Marshall Plan named for American Secretary of State George C. Marshall, who suggested using U.S. capital and cooperation in Europe's reconstruction after WW II

of Rome, which was signed in 1957 and created the European Community (EC), sometimes called the European Economic Community (EEC) or the European Common Market. The first six Common Market members were Belgium, the Federal Republic of Germany, France, Italy, Luxembourg, and the Netherlands. Chronologically, the next to sign the treaty were Denmark, Ireland, the United Kingdom, Greece, Portugal, and Spain, making a total of 12 member-nations.

EC objectives were to remove trade obstacles among members and to cooperate in many other ways. Brussels was established as headquarters, housing the EC Commission. The 17 commissioners are each responsible for a subject area somewhat similar to U.S. cabinet positions: labor, transportation, trade, and so forth.

The policy-setting body of the EC is the Council of Ministers. The foreign ministers of the 12 member-nations meet periodically to establish policy to be executed by the commissioners and the other Eurocrats as the bureaucrats who work in Brussels are called.

The European Parliament (part of the EC) has its seat in Strasbourg and is popularly elected by voters in each member-country. It has broad but very blunt powers (e.g., it can fire all the commissioners but not fewer than all, and it can veto the entire EC budget but not a portion thereof). On one occasion, it did veto the budget—much to everyone's astonishment—and since then the commission and others have taken the parliament more seriously. Some feel if the parliament is given wider and more discreet powers, it could become the heart of an ultimate United States of Europe. The Single European Act of 1987 gave the European Parliament some power to amend legislation drafted by the commission.

The EC Court of Justice decides all cases arising under the Treaty of Rome, and its authority supersedes that of the member-countries' courts. Because the treaty covers many subjects and more and more cases are being decided by the Court of Justice, its influence is growing steadily.

From 1957 until the early 1970s, cooperation continued and measurable progress was made in eliminating tariff barriers among EC countries. Then the Bretton Woods currency exchange regime collapsed; the OPEC price increases hit; inflation, unemployment, and recession gripped the EC; and progress slowed considerably. The community languished for several years until it was jolted to life by Project 1992.

The EC joins most of the economic and industrial might of Western Europe and most of its population. The EC is the largest import and export market in the world. It is second only to the United States in the size of its gross domestic product, and it accounts for 20 percent of world trade, compared with 14 percent for the United States and 9 percent for Japan. Table 4–2 gives some comparisons between the EC, the United States, Japan, the Soviet Union, and the People's Republic of China.

EC 1992

As indicated, the EC is a major world force. It has now embarked on Project 1992, which will likely make it an even more formidable force. The objectives are to eliminate all boundaries between the 12 member-countries so that people, capital, and goods can move freely and settle, work, and be used or sold anywhere from Greece in the east to Ireland in the west.

■ TABLE 4–2
The Superpower
Contenders Compared

	United States	Soviet Union	Japan	European Community	China
Population (in millions)	243.8	284.0	122.0	323.6	1,074.0
Gross national product (in billions of 1987 U.S. dollars*)	$4,436.1	$2,375	$1,607.7	$3,782	$293.5
Per capita GNP (1987 U.S. dollars*)	$18,200	$8,360	$13,180	$11,690	$270
GNP growth rate					
1966–70 (annual average)	2.8%	5.1%	11%	4.6%	N.A.
1971–75 (annual average)	2.3%	3.1%	4.3%	3%	5.5%
1976–80 (annual average)	3.3%	2.2%	5%	3%	6.1%
1981–85 (annual average)	3%	1.8%	3.9%	1.5%	9.2%
1987	2.9%	0.5%	4.2%	2.9%	9.4%
Inflation (change in consumer prices)	3.7%	−0.9%	0.1%	3.1%	9.2%
Total labor force					
(in millions)	121.6	154.8	60.3	143	512.8
Agricultural	3.4	33.9	4.6	11.9	313.1
Nonagricultural	118.2	120.9	55.7	131.1	199.7
Unemployment rate	6.1%	N.A.	2.8%	11%	N.A.
Foreign Trade					
Exports (in millions of U.S. dollars)	$250.4	$107.7	$231.2	$953.5[†]	$44.9
Imports (in millions of U.S. dollars)	$424.1	$96	$150.8	$955.1[†]	$40.2
Balance (in millions of U.S. dollars)	$173.7	$11.7	$80.4	−$.6	$4.7
Energy					
Consumption (in bbl. of oil equiv. per capita)	55.6	37.3	22.7	24.4	4.8
Oil reserves (in billions of bbl.)	33.4	59	0.1	7.6	18.4
Oil production (in millions of bbl. a day)	9.9	12.7	Negligible	3.1	2.7
Natural gas reserves (in trillions of cu. ft.)	186.7	1,450	1	112.9	30.7
Coal reserves (in billions of metric tons)	263.8	244.7	1	90.5	170
Agriculture					
Grain production (in kilograms per capita)	1,150	740	130	480	402
Meat production (in kilograms per capita)	109	65	31	82	18
Military					
Active armed forces	2,163,200	5,096,000	245,000	2,483,400	3,200,000
Ready reserves	1,637,900	6,217,000	46,000	4,565,800	1,200,000
Defense expenditures' share of GNP	6.5%	15%–25%	1.6%	3.3%	4%–5%

(*continued*)

■ **TABLE 4–2**
(concluded)

	United States	Soviet Union	Japan	European Community	China
Living standard					
Life expectancy (years)	75	69	78	76	68
Automobiles (registrations per thousand)	570	42	235	347	Negligible

Note: The data presented here—with a few exceptions—are for 1987, the latest year for which comparable data are available for all countries.

N.A. = Not available.

* Data were converted at U.S. purchasing power equivalents.

† Data include trade between EC members.

Source: *The Wall Street Journal*. January 23, 1989. p. A8.

This offers great promise to European companies and possibly to companies from countries such as Japan and the United States, which are established in the EC. It also raises great fears outside the EC that as internal barriers are lowered, external ones may be raised, thus creating a Fortress Europe. Existing relationships between the EC and the outside world, particularly the United States, may mitigate Europe's protectionist urges.

EC–U.S.: A symbiotic web.   Well before 1992, the United States and the EC are of major importance to each other. For example, the 12-nation EC bloc bought over 25 percent of total U.S. exports in 1987—more than Canada and more than twice as much as Japan. In world trade, the EC is America's biggest customer; 1988 trade between the EC and the United States was some $160 billion. The U.S. trade deficit with the EC declined from $26.4 billion in 1986 to $24.3 billion in 1987, which is a bright spot in the generally dark U.S. trade deficit picture. On the investment front, over 40 percent of U.S. external investment is in the EC. These are America's most rewarding overseas investments.

The European money and capital markets have become major sources of U.S. corporate funds, rivaling U.S. domestic markets. Going the other direction, so many European companies raise money in U.S. markets that over $200 billion of transatlantic capital swaps each year have created a transatlantic financial network. Companies on both continents rely on this network for capital raising, risk diversification, debt management, import/export financing, and other purposes.[36]

Such symbiosis must be appreciated before we can intelligently forecast the impact of EC 1992 on America. Also, as the world's biggest traders, the EC and the United States share the major responsibilities for the future growth of free trade under the auspices of GATT. For a report on how well they are meeting those responsibilities, see the discussion of GATT, earlier in this chapter.

Fortress Europe?

Although the EC's existing ties with the United States and other countries point away from isolationism, there are powerful forces of protectionism at work in the EC. Some say the big Japanese and American companies should not be beneficiaries of a 323-million-European market created by Europeans. Auto, textile, and other businesses are lobbying for protection, and the countries with

FORTRESS EUROPE: the defences fall into place

Courtesy *International Management*

weaker economies (such as Greece, Ireland, Portugal, and Spain) argue that their industries must be protected "temporarily."

Willy de Clercq, the EC commissioner for external trade, says nonmember countries must grant "reciprocal" rights to EC companies in their markets before the EC will permit their companies to operate in the EC market. There is as yet no clear definition of "reciprocal."

The best guess is there will be a Fortress Europe, but it will not be impregnable. Companies from nonmember countries that are established in the EC by the end of 1992 will probably be permitted to compete as if they were European, but companies' home countries may have to grant some reciprocal rights to EC companies.

Will Project 1992 Succeed?

The obstacles to success are formidable. Each of the 12 nations has its own unique history and loyalties, languages, and cultures. Their tax systems and levels are diverse. There are 12 sovereign governments, each with its own powers, policies, and currencies.

WORLDVIEW
Europe 1992: A Swiss Banker's View
Europe's Internal Market and the "Outsiders"

All the major corporations in the Common Market are positioning themselves for a "great leap forward" in the economic integration of Europe. The same goes for Switzerland's corporate sector—with the big difference that Switzerland is a nonmember country in the heart of EC territory. While we may be "on the outside looking in," we have also been involved in EC Europe for decades; if some Swiss appear unimpressed, they may be thinking about how slowly the Common Market moved in the first 30 years.

But that's not the general view. Most of us take the challenge seriously. Switzerland lives on trade, and we ship more than 55 percent of our merchandise exports to Common Market countries.

I can sketch out my perspective by answering three questions:

1. What is actually *new* about the current politics of integration in Europe?
2. What can we expect? What are the main *consequences*?
3. What do "outsiders" need to know?

The New Approach
The "fresh start" dates back to 1985, with the European Commission's white paper and the Single European Act. The Single European Act facilitates more *qualified majority voting* in the Council of Ministers, where so many initiatives were previously blocked by insistence on unanimity. However, tax harmonization still requires a unanimous decision: the EC cannot impose tax changes on any of its members unless that country concurs. Disputes over tax matters are likely to be the major impediment to meeting the 1992 deadline. But another *institutional* change in integration policies is more important: the principle of *"mutual recognition"* instead of strict harmonization (and all the fine print that implied). Where national regulations have traditionally vied with one another to block foreign competition, they can now be used to gain competitive entry into foreign markets.

"Europe Inc."
What are the *consequences* going to be? What should we really expect? To start with the negative side: 1992, as a deadline, will definitely not be met. The Common Market is also a long distance away from a European Monetary Union with a European Central Bank.

At the same time, the EC has never actually moved backwards, and the general emphasis on regulatory aspects of integration should not obscure another positive aspect: The *business community* has come to see Europe as a true home market. The entrepreneurs are out to *build* "Europe Inc." Shareholders, boards of directors, and even public opinion are willing to countenance the merging of their national standard-bearers with competitors or other partners abroad. The new Europe is not being built by

Nevertheless, real progress has been made, and Project 1992 has momentum. Companies are merging, buying competitors, or creating joint ventures in order to be large enough to compete effectively in the vastly enlarged market. In June 1988, the 12 member-governments committed themselves to free capital movements within the EC in stages to be completed by 1990. The European Monetary System (see Chapter 5) has been in place since 1979. Its value unit, called the European Currency Unit, could become the standard EC currency, replacing national currencies.

The best guess is there will be no United States of Europe by the end of 1992, but much unification will have been achieved. More important, the efforts toward more unification will continue. EC 1992 will be an enhanced power with which Japan, the United States, and the rest of the world must come to terms.[37]

bureaucrats alone; on the contrary: forward-looking managements are already including the impact of a more "congruent" legal environment in their future planning.

In short, whether or not perfect regulatory unification is achieved, we still have to get used to the idea that the EC—with its population of 320 million—will become the largest single market in the industrialized world. A sophisticated market with enormous reserves of labour and offering new opportunities for transborder education and training in almost all industries and sectors.

The question remains: What does it all mean for *outsiders?* The first point is that internal unification and integration automatically implies making distinctions. For example, if an American joins me on my next flight from Zurich to London's Heathrow, we will both have the opportunity to watch our friends from West Germany or France breezing through the "EC members" line while we have our passports inspected with everybody else in the "all others" category: just a logical consequence of EC integration.

Outsider Options

The same goes for the *stronger position* of the EC in international *trade negotiations.* We simply have to accept this—and insist on strict adherence to GATT principles. But even more forceful application of "reciprocity" might produce some remarkable changes in relations between the Common Market and third countries. *Reciprocity,* in practice, is always open to a wide range of interpretations. I would not be too optimistic on the prospects for a level playing field beyond the European Community's borders if the need for a pretext grows. So it's a good idea to have an *affiliated company* in at least one EC country. I would say we "outsiders" should also think about *stronger marketing*—a more deliberate focus on the needs of the internal market.

An important step in harmonizing the rules on *trademarks* was taken in June of this year, when regulations for a European Community trademark were drafted. A single European Trade Mark Office will be responsible for the recognition and equal protection of proprietary marks in all Common Market countries— including trademarks from nonmembers as well. So the community trademark will also make it easier for "outsiders"—provided EC standards are met.

I would like to make a final observation about the *acquisitions* we can expect as a way of buying into the future pan-European market. Mergers across the borders still involve the bridging of wide cultural differences between *European* partners. Sometimes, in fact, these differences even seem larger to the participants than their differences with partners from outside.

Source: Franz Galliker, "Prospects," Swiss Bank Corporation, June 1988.

OTHER REGIONAL GROUPINGS OF NATIONS

The success of the EC has led nations to form a number of other groupings with similar, but usually more limited, objectives. None of those groupings has come as close to being a true common market as the EC; however, some have become customs unions and others free trade areas. A free trade area exists when a group of countries abolishes restrictions on mutual trade but each country keeps its own quotas and tariffs on trade with countries outside the group. An *industrial* free trade area, such as the European Free Trade Association, has free trade in industrial products only.

There are many such groupings and other international organizations, and we shall not take the space required to name them all here. For a list of international organizations, complete with names of officers, addresses, and phone numbers, see *The Europe Yearbook, 1988, A World Survey,* Volume 1, pp. 1567–79. Together with Volume 2, they give a variety of information about most countries of the world.

ORGANIZATION FOR ECONOMIC COOPERATION AND DEVELOPMENT (OECD)

The members of the Organization for Economic Cooperation and Development (OECD) are the noncommunist DCs. The OECD originated in Europe, and most of its members are European. However, among its members now are Australia, Canada, Japan, New Zealand, Turkey, and the United States.

You should be familiar with the OECD because it produces and publishes extensive research and statistics on numerous international business and economic subjects. Also, it produced a declaration of guidelines of good business practices for firms operating in OECD countries.[38]

Material from and about the OECD may be obtained from OECD Publications and Information Center, 1750 Pennsylvania Avenue, N.W., Washington, D.C. 20006.

SUMMARY

The United Nations (UN) is probably the best known of the worldwide organizations. It is active in social and political matters. Its General Assembly, where each country has one vote, is dominated by the many less developed countries (LDCs). The UN's specialized agencies aid the LDCs in their fields such as agriculture, telecommunications, and so on.

The World Bank lends to LDCs for projects and has begun to insist that LDCs put their economic house in order as a condition to making loans. The International Finance Corporation (part of the World Bank) encourages private enterprise in LDCs.

The International Monetary Fund (IMF) helps countries with balance of payments deficits and has moved to the center of efforts to solve LDC debt problems. It is also working with the World Bank on LDC economic policies.

There are also regional development banks which make the same kinds of loans as the World Bank in their geographic regions. The regions are the Western Hemisphere, Africa, and Asia.

The Bank for International Settlements in Switzerland has become a sort of club for central bankers and national treasurers. It played a hand in helping LDC debtors.

The General Agreement on Tariffs and Trade (GATT) attempts to lower trade barriers. Its Uruguay Round of negotiations began in 1986.

The Organization of Petroleum Exporting Countries (OPEC) was for a time a successful cartel controlling the world's oil supply. There are those who fear it may regain control.

The European Community (EC) is a grouping of 12 Western European countries. They are engaged in Project 1992, whose aim is to abolish all barriers among them to the movement of people, money, and goods by the end of 1992. Besides the EC, there are many other but less ambitious groupings of nations.

The Organization for Economic Cooperation and Development (OECD) is an excellent source of research on many topics of value to business. The OECD has developed a code of conduct for firms operating internationally.

QUESTIONS

1. What are some reasons why businesspeople and business students should be aware of the more important international organizations?
2. What is the feature common to all or almost all new UN member-countries?
3. When the World Bank makes a loan, how can a business, which would like to sell products or services to the borrower, go about making sales?
4. *a.* Which part of the World Bank Group is referred to as its investment banker?
   b. Why?
5. How do IDA credits differ from World Bank loans?

6. *a.* The agreement between the IMF and the UN reserves considerable independence for the Fund.
   b. Why?

7. What new authority did the revised Article IV of the IMF Articles of Agreement give the Fund?

8. What changes have occurred at the IMF as a result of multinational debt repayment problems?

9. What are the aims of the Uruguay Round?

10. *a.* What group of nations brought about the creation of UNCTAD?
    b. Why?

11. What is the EC?

12 What is Project 1992?

13. Why do outsiders fear a Fortress Europe?

14. What is the importance of the OECD for business and students?

15. *a.* Where did the Structural Adjustment Facility get its money?
    b. Why is the facility a landmark for the IMF and the World Bank?
    c. For whose benefit is the facility, and what will the Bank and the Fund do with and for the borrowers?

16. What are the purposes of the World Bank's Multilateral Investment Guarantee Agency?

✗ MINICASE 4–1

Use of International Organizations—Setting up a 100 Percent-Owned Subsidiary

You are an international business consultant in the United States. Your specialty is exporting to and investing, licensing, or franchising in LDCs.

One of your clients is a hotel company that wants to build, operate, and 100 percent own a hotel in Guatemala. Your client is willing to put up about half of the original capital but wants to be assured that its share of the profits can be converted to U.S. dollars and repatriated as dividends.

To what organizations discussed in Chapter 4 might you look for assistance in raising the rest of the needed capital? To what organizations might you look for information concerning a Guatemalan company's ability to convert profits into U.S. dollars and remit them to the United States?

MINICASE 4–2

Use of International Organizations—Establishing a Franchise Operation

Suppose this client wanted to put up little or none of the initial capital and wanted no ownership interest in the Guatemalan hotel. Your client will supply plans and knowledge for the design, construction, and furnishing of the hotel. It will publicize the hotel and sell rooms to tourists and conventions.

Your client will provide management and wants to be paid fees to compensate for its know-how, advertising, sales, and management.

Would you proceed any differently than in Minicase 4–1?

MINICASE 4–3

Use of Information from the World Bank to Determine Whether to Invest in a Country

Turn to Table 4–1. Choose any two or more countries and, using the information given in the table, decide which country or countries would be the best, better, not so good, and worst in which to (1) invest your money and (2) expect to be able to collect interest or dividends in hard currencies from your investment.

SUPPLEMENTARY READINGS

Anjaria, S. J. "A New Round of Global Trade Negotiations." *Finance & Development,* June 1986, pp. 2–6.

Burki, Shahid Javed, and Norman Hicks. "International Development Association in Retrospect." *Finance & Development,* December 1982, pp. 22–25.

Dunne, Nancy. "New GATT Round Opens This Month." *Europe;* September 1986, pp. 12–13.

"Evolution of the European Community." *Finance & Development,* September 1986, pp. 30–31.

Hein, John. "What Will the GATT Beget?" *Across the Board,* September 1985, pp. 9–20.

"IFC Foreign Portfolio for Development: An IFC Initiative." *Finance & Development,* June 1986, p. 23.

"IMF's Structural Adjustment Facility." *Finance & Development,* June 1986, p. 39.

Kelly, Margaret. "Fiscal Deficits and Fund-Supported Programs." *Finance & Development,* September 1983, pp. 37–39.

Mehnert, Ralph J. "The ECU's Growing Role in Private Transactions." *Europe,* May 1986, pp. 31–34.

Morrison, Ann. "The Uruguay Round and the GATT: What They Are and What They Do." *Business America,* June 20, 1988, pp. 2–5.

Nakagama, Sam. "The Benefits of OPEC's Misery." *Euromoney,* December 1984, pp. 124–28.

"1992—Europe Without Frontiers." *Europe,* April 1988, pp. 6–9.

"OECD Economic Outlook." *OECD Observer,* January 1986, pp. 27–33.

Russell, Ruth B. *A History of the United Nations Charter.* Washington, D.C.: Brookings Institution, 1958.

Shihata, Ibrahim. "Increasing Private Capital Flows to LDCs." *Finance & Development,* December 1984, pp. 6–9.

"Take Advantage of the EC Market Now." *Business America,* August 1, 1988, pp. 1–6.

"World Bank: Soul Searching in Washington." *Euromoney,* December 1985, pp. 122–31.

ENDNOTES

1. Pierre Lortie, *Economic Integration and the Law of GATT* (New York: Praeger Publishers, 1975), p. X.

2. United Nations General Assembly Resolution 1975 (XIX).

3. Alec Cairncross, *The International Bank for Reconstruction and Development,* Princeton University Essays in International Finance, no. 33 (March 1949), p. 27.

4. Maurice Wolf and Eiting Arnold, *Doing Business with the International Development Organizations in Washington, D.C.* Tax Management, Inc., Bureau of National Affairs, 1982, pp. 20–88.

5. Article I of the Articles of Agreement of the International Finance Corporation (Washington, D.C., June 20, 1956), p. 3.

6. IFC General Policies (Washington, D.C.: IFC, 1970).

7. *Private Development Finance Companies* (Washington, D.C.: IFC, 1964).

8. Sir William Ryrie, "IFC Growth and Diversification," *Finance & Development,* December 1988, p. 22.

9. *Finance & Development,* March 1982, pp. 7–8.

10. Eugene H. Rotberg, "The World Bank: A Financial Appraisal, II," *Finance & Development,* December 1976, pp. 36–39.

11. United Nations Monetary and Finance Conference, Bretton Woods, New Hampshire, July 1 to 22, 1944, Department of State Publication 287, Conference Series 55 (Washington, D.C.: Department of State, 1944).

12. A. Acheson et al, *Bretton Woods Revisited* (Toronto: University of Toronto Press, 1972).

13. Oscar L. Altman, "Quotas in the International Monetary Fund," *International Monetary Fund Staff Papers 5,* no. 2 (1956).

14. Leland M. Goodrich and Edward Hambro, *Charter of the United Nations: Commentary and Documents,* rev. ed. (Boston: World Peace Foundation, 1949), p. 349.

15. For a discussion of how surveillance is working, see G. G. Johnson, "Enhancing the Effectiveness of Surveillance," *Finance & Development,* December 1985, pp. 2–5.

16. Margaret Garritsen de Vries, "The IMF: 40 Years of Challenge and Change," *Finance & Development,* September 1985, pp. 7–10.

17. Art Pine, "IMF Becomes Leader," *The Wall Street Journal,* January 11, 1983, p. 56.

18. *The Economist,* July 9, 1983, pp. 14–16.

19. *Finance & Development,* March 1980, p. 2.

20. *Finance & Development,* June 1986, p. 39.

21. Nicholas Woodsworth, "African Energy and Inertia," *Financial Times,* April 18, 1988, p. 5.

22. Richard Gourlay, "A Time for Critical Self-Study at the ADB," *Financial Times,* February 22, 1988, p. 3; and Cheah Cheng Hye, "ADB Goes Begging for Borrowers, " *The Asian Wall Street Journal,* February 10, 1986, p. 5.

23. Derk Kinnane-Roelofsma, "Bank's Mission Mired in Loan War," *Insight,* February 15, 1988, pp. 34–36.

24. Peter Norman, "BIS Backs Off," *The Wall Street Journal,* February 2, 1983, p. 29.

25. *Bank for International Settlements, 59th Annual Report, 1st April 1988–31st March 1989,* p. 264.

26. Richard N. Gardner, *Sterling-Dollar Diplomacy* (New York: Oxford Univ. Press, 1956).

27. Gerard Curzon, *Multilateral Commercial Diplomacy* (New York: Praeger Publishers, 1965).

28. Gardner, *Sterling-Dollar Diplomacy,* pp. 379–80.

29. Bernard Norwood, "The Kennedy Round: A Try at Linear Trade Negotiations," *Journal of Law and Economics,* October 12, 1966, pp. 297–319; Ernest M. Preeg, *Traders and Diplomats* (Washington, D.C.: Brookings Institution, 1970); John W. Evans, *The Kennedy Round in American Trade Policy: The Twilight of GATT?* (Cambridge, Mass.: Harvard University Press, 1971); Sidney Golt, *The GATT Negotiations, 1973–1974; A Guide to the Issues* (London, Washington, and Ottawa: British-North America Committee, 1974); and B. Balassa and M. E. Dreinin, "Trade Liberalization under the Kennedy Round: The Static Effects," *Review of Economics and Statistics,* May 1967, pp. 125–37.

30. Pat Choate and Jayne Linger, "Tailored Trade: Dealing with the World as It Is," *Harvard Business Review,* January–February 1988, pp. 86–93.

31. Perez Alfonze, "The Organization of Petroleum Exporting Countries," (Caracas) *Monthly Bulletin,* no. 2 (1966).

32. Wendell H. McCulloch, Jr., notes of interviews and conversations with OPEC employees and others in Geneva.

33. *International Petroleum Encyclopedia,* 1979, pp. 194–95, table 6.

34. Luis Vallenilla, *Oil: The Making of a New Economic Order* (New York: McGraw-Hill, 1975).

35. James Cook, "Comeuppance," *Forbes,* May 9, 1983, pp. 55–56.

36. Wendell H. McCulloch, Jr., "United State of Europe 1992?" *Backgrounder,* no. 706, The Heritage Foundation, May 5, 1989, p.2.

37. Ibid, p. 4.

38. OECD, International Investment and Multinational Enterprises, adopted June 21, 1976, OECD Doc. 21 (76)4/I (1976).

Chapter 5

International Monetary System and Balance of Payments

Ninety percent of what we do is based on perception. It doesn't matter if that perception is right or wrong or real. It only matters that other people in the market believe it. I may know it's crazy. I may think it's wrong. But I lose my shirt by ignoring it. This business turns on decisions made in seconds. If you wait a minute to reflect on things, you're lost.

James Hohorst, head of foreign exchange trading in North America, Manufacturers Hanover Trust

LEARNING OBJECTIVES

In this chapter, you will study:

1. The fact that almost every country in the world has its own currency, and that wherever you travel or do business, you need some of the local currency.

2. The fact that the currencies of a few of the wealthier countries are convertible relatively freely into other currencies, but that most currencies are not freely convertible.

3. The international monetary system, which was fashioned at Bretton Woods and was based on international cooperation, using such new institutions as the International Monetary Fund (IMF).

4. The fact that the United States has run a balance-of-payments deficit in most years since 1958, which resulted in billions of U.S. dollars being held by nonresidents of the United States.

5. The fact that in 1971, the fixed currency exchange rate system established at Bretton Woods began to come apart, the currencies began to float in relation to each other.

6. The fact that London, New York, and Tokyo are major money markets, but that many other money markets have developed around the world—in the Middle East, Asia, and the Caribbean.

7. Special drawing rights (SDRs), which may become the main reserve asset for nations and possibly even an international currency.

8. The European Monetary System (EMS), which is a step toward the reimposition of fixed currency exchange rates and has established gold as one of its official reserve assets.

9. The European Currency Unit (ECU), a value unit established by the EMS. Many bonds on the Eurobond markets are now denominated in ECUs, and the usefulness of ECUs is increasing.

10. The balance-of-payments (BOP) accounts.

KEY WORDS AND CONCEPTS

- Convertible currencies
- Gold standard
- Fixed currency exchange rates
- Bretton Woods
- Central reserve asset
- Market measures
- Nonmarket measures
- Monetary policies
- Fiscal policies
- Central bank
- Gold exchange standard
- Floating currency exchange rates
- Money markets
- Special drawing rights (SDRs)
- European Monetary System (EMS)
- European Currency Unit (ECU)

BUSINESS INCIDENT

One of the phone line lights flashed and was quickly answered by a currency dealer. As soon as the caller spoke, the dealer responded quietly, "1010," and replaced his phone on its hook. He then stated in a voice that could be heard around the trading room, "I've got 2 million at 1010."

Another trader was on her phone and said "1000." She then announced, "Got a million at 1000."

In the course of a few seconds, two customers had traded their French francs for 3 million U.S. dollars. The trades were made at exchange rates of 8.1010 and 8.1000 francs per dollar. The action took place in the trading room of a bank in the City, London's financial center, shortly after the news was flashed that a Soviet plane had shot down a Korean passenger jet. The customers felt that the U.S. dollar would appreciate in value if hostilities escalated in the aftermath of the Soviet missiles.

When the U.S. dollar began to drop in value on the foreign exchange markets in early 1985, traders and investors scrambled to make money on the changes. Wall Street brokerage houses came up with ways to play further drops in the dollar's quotes. Some recommended the stocks of companies with large European or Japanese operations. Others touted currency futures or options contracts—for instance, buying deutsche marks or yen for profit if they gained in value against the dollar. A more conservative approach was to buy short-term notes or bonds payable in European Currency Units (ECUs).

Although the American consumer pays U.S. dollars (US$s) for the German car or Scotch woolens purchased in the United States, the car manufacturer in Germany and the wool processor in Scotland must have, respectively, deutsche marks (DM) and pounds sterling (£) in order to meet their local expenses. At some point, the US$s must be exchanged for the necessary DM and £. Underlying the mechanics and rates of exchange (both of which are discussed in some detail in Chapter 6) is the international monetary system. The currencies mentioned above are **convertible currencies** (that is, they are readily convertible in the market), but most currencies are not. For example, the currencies of most less developed countries (LDCs) and communist countries are either not convertible or legally convertible only at artificial, government-established rates.

The international businessperson or student should have some knowledge of the history and current state of the international monetary system. History is important because of its lessons and also because a vocal minority wants to resurrect varieties of it, namely the **gold standard** and **fixed currency exchange rates**. Post-gold standard, 20th-century developments should be studied for the same reasons, while current practices are, by definition, what businesspeople, economists, governments, and institutions are doing now. Informed guesses about the future are necessary ingredients of the forecasting and planning in which each of those groups must be involved.

convertible currencies also called hard currencies, are exchangeable for any other currency at uniform rates at financial centers worldwide

gold standard when a country agrees to buy or sell gold for an established number of currency units

fixed currency exchange rates when two or more countries agree as to the exchange rate(s) of their currencies and undertake to maintain those rates

A BRIEF GOLD STANDARD HISTORY AND COMMENT

From about A.D. 1200 to the present, the direction of the price of gold has been generally up.[1] True, there have been wide fluctuations in that price, and an investor in gold should have steady nerves, though law-abiding American investors were for a time spared that source of nervousness because it was illegal for them to own gold bullion between 1933 and 1976. During that period, the price of gold rose from about $21 per ounce to just under $200 in December 1976, when Americans were again legally free to own gold in bullion form. As it developed, Americans did not rush into the market, and the price has fluctuated between a bit over $100 and over $800 per ounce since 1976.

On December 22, 1717, Sir Isaac Newton, master of the mint, established the price of gold at 3 pounds, 17 shillings, 10.5 pence per ounce. England was then on the gold standard and stood willing to convert gold to currency, or vice versa, until World War I, except during the Napoleonic Wars. During that period, London was the dominant center of international finance. It has been estimated that more than 90 percent of world trade was financed in London.[2]

Most trading or industrial countries adopted the gold standard. Each country set a certain number of units of its currency per ounce of gold, and the comparison of the numbers of units per ounce from country to country was the exchange rate between any two currencies on the gold standard.

The financial burdens of WW I forced Britain to sell a substantial portion of its gold, and the gold standard ended. Between WW I and WW II, there was a short-lived flirtation with the gold standard, but it was not successfully reestablished.

Return to the Gold Standard?

Although the gold standard has not been the international monetary system for many years, it has had some ardent and influential advocates in recent years. One of the staunchest was Jacques Rueff, who until his death in 1978 was a member of the French Academy and an adviser to the French government. The heart of Rueff's argument may be expressed by one word: *discipline*.

Under the gold standard, a government cannot create money that is not backed by gold. Therefore, no matter how great the temptation to create more money for political advantage, without regard for economic results, a government cannot do so without the established amount of gold. This is the discipline that Jacques Rueff argued is the only effective means of avoiding inflation.[3]

One argument for a return to the gold standard, thus making gold the reserve asset of nations, is based on the premise that the current situation, in which the U.S. dollar (US$) is the reserve asset, is unsustainable. As world trade, investment, and economies grow, countries need more reserves. With the US$ as the reserve asset, other countries can increase their reserves only if the United States increases its net reserve indebtedness with a balance-of-payments (BOP) deficit. The United States can increase its liquidity only at the expense of other countries; a U.S. BOP surplus would drain US$ reserves from other countries. Thus, under the present system, the reserves of other countries can increase only if the largest debtor nation in the world—the United States— goes further into debt.

It has been suggested that the five nations with the largest economies should agree to settle their accounts with one another in gold, not US$s.[4] If a gold standard were established, what should be the price of gold? Lewis Lehrman advocates $500 an ounce, based on production costs. Arthur Laffer picks a price in the $200 range, based on the increase in the consumer price level since gold was $35 an ounce. A third school of thought, identified with Robert Mundell, suggests pegging the price where it happens to be on the day that the five nations agree to institute a gold standard.[5]

BRETTON WOODS AND THE GOLD EXCHANGE STANDARD

During WW II, the countries of the world were much too involved with the hostilities to consider the gold standard or any other monetary system. However, many officials realized some system must be established to operate when peace returned. Actually, consideration of it did not await the firing of the last shot. Before that, in 1944, representatives of the major Allied powers,

Bretton Woods a New Hampshire town where treasury and central bank representatives met near the end of WWII. They established the IMF, the World Bank, and the gold exchange standard

with the United States and Britain assuming the dominant roles, met at **Bretton Woods,** New Hampshire, to plan for the future.

There was general consensus that (1) stable exchange rates were desirable, but experience might dictate adjustments; (2) floating* or fluctuating exchange rates had proved unsatisfactory, though the reasons for this opinion were little discussed; and (3) the government controls of trade, exchange, production, and so forth that had developed from 1931 through WW II were wasteful, discriminatory, and detrimental to expansion of world trade and investment. In spite of (3), the conferees recognized that some conditions—for example, reconstruction from war damage or development of less developed countries (LDCs)—would require government controls.

To achieve its goals, the Bretton Woods Conference established the International Monetary Fund (IMF). Article I of the IMF Articles of Agreement set forth its purposes, which reflected the consensus referred to above.[6] The IMF Articles of Agreement entered into force in December 1945.

The IMF agreement was the basis for the international monetary system from 1945 until 1971. It is doubtful, however, that the future role assumed by, or thrust upon, the US$—which became the major **central reserve asset**—was fully foreseen.[7]

central reserve assets are nations' savings accounts in which are held dollars and other hard currencies, gold, and SDRs

The US$ was agreed to be the only currency directly convertible into gold for official monetary purposes. An ounce of gold was agreed to be worth US$35, and other currencies were assigned so-called par values in relationship to the US$. For example, the British pound's par value was US$2.40, the French franc's was US$0.18, and the German mark's was US$0.2732.[8]

It was recognized that each member-country would be subject to different pressures at different times. The pressures could be caused by political or economic events or trends and could render the par values (currency exchange rates) established at Bretton Woods unrealistic. A major force that affects currency exchange rates is the balance of payments (BOP) of the member-countries.

Balance of Payments

One task assumed by the IMF was assistance to member-countries having difficulty keeping their balance of payments (BOP) out of deficit.[†] A country's BOP is a very important indicator for business management of what may happen to the country's economy, including what the government may cause to happen. If the BOP is in deficit, inflation is often the cause, and the company must adjust its pricing, inventory, accounting, and other practices to inflationary conditions. The government may take measures to deal with inflation and the deficit. These may be so-called **market measures** (such as deflating the economy or devaluing the currency) or **nonmarket measures** (such as currency controls, tariffs, or quotas).

market measures to end a BOP deficit include deflation of the economy and devaluation of the currency

nonmarket measures to end a BOP deficit include tariffs, quotas, and currency exchange controls

Even if a company does not consider itself international, it will be affected by inflation and by the government's methods of combating inflation and a BOP deficit. All of those methods have the common goals of causing the

---

* A currency is said to float freely when the governments do nothing to affect its value in the world currency markets. Other varieties of floating are discussed later in this chapter.

† A deficit occurs when the residents of a country are paying nonresidents more than they are earning or otherwise getting from nonresidents. The opposite is a surplus.

■ **TABLE 5-1**
Balance-of-Payments
Accounts

	Debits	Credits
1. Current account		
A. Merchandise imports and exports		
B. Services		
Net goods and services balance		
C. Unilateral transfers		
To abroad		
From abroad		
Net current account balance		
2. Capital account		
A. Direct investment		
To abroad		
From abroad		
B. Portfolio investment		
To abroad		
From abroad		
C. Short-term capital		
To abroad		
From abroad		
Net capital account balance		
3. Official reserves account		
A. Gold export or import (net)		
B. Increase or decrease in foreign exchange (net)		
C. Increase or decrease in liabilities to foreign central banks (net)		
Net official reserves		
4. Net statistical discrepancy		

country's residents to buy fewer foreign goods and services and to sell more to foreigners.

Debits and credits in international transactions.   International debit transactions involve payments by domestic residents to foreign residents, and international credit transactions are the opposite. Taking America as the domestic economy, a list of debit transactions would include:

1. Dividend, interest, and debt repayment services on foreign-owned capital in America.
2. Merchandise imports.
3. Purchases by Americans traveling abroad.
4. Transportation services bought by Americans on foreign carriers.
5. Foreign investment by Americans.
6. Gifts by Americans to foreign residents.
7. Imports of gold.

The opposite would be examples of credit transactions. For example, dividend, interest, and debt repayment services on American-owned capital abroad are credits on the American ledger.

Double-entry accounting.   While writers use debit and credit transaction language, each international transaction is an exchange of assets with a debit and credit side. Thus, the BOP is presented as a double-entry accounting statement in which total credits and debits are always equal. The statement of a country's BOP is divided into several accounts (see Table 5–1).

Current account.   Three subaccounts are included in the current account: (A) goods or merchandise, (B) services, and (C) unilateral transfers. A and B are sometimes treated together, and they include the real (as opposed to the financial) international transactions—exports and imports.

A. The goods or merchandise account deals with "visibles," such as autos, grain, machinery, or equipment, that can be seen and felt as they are exported or imported. The net balance on merchandise transactions is referred to as the country's trade balance.

B. The services account deals with "invisibles" that are exchanged or bought internationally. Examples include (1) dividends or interest on foreign investments, (2) royalties on patents or trademarks held abroad, (3) travel, (4) insurance, (5) banking and (6) transportation.

C. Unilateral transfers are transactions with no quid pro quo; some of these transfers are made by private persons or institutions, and some by governments. Some private unilateral transfers are for charitable, educational, or missionary purposes; others are gifts from migrant workers to their families in their home countries and bequests or the transfer of capital by people migrating from one country to another. The largest government unilateral transfers are aid—which may be in money or kind—from developed countries to developing countries. Pension payments to nonresidents and tax receipts from nonresidents are two other government-related unilateral transfers.

Capital account.   The capital account records the net changes in a nation's international financial assets and liabilities over the BOP period, which is usually one year. A capital inflow—a credit entry—occurs when a resident sells stock, bonds, or other financial assets to nonresidents. Money flows in to the resident, while at the same time the resident's long-term international liabilities are increased, because dividends (profit) may be paid on the stock, rent will be paid on other assets, and interest must be paid on the bonds. And at maturity the bonds' face amounts must be repaid.

Subaccounts under the capital account are (A) direct investment, (B) portfolio investment, and (C) international movements of short-term capital.

A. Direct investments are investments in enterprises or properties located in one country that are "effectively controlled" by residents of another country. Effective control is assumed for BOP purposes (1) when residents of one country own 50 percent or more of the voting stock of a company in another country or (2) when one resident or an organized group of residents of one country own 25 percent or more of the voting stock of a company in another country.

B. Portfolio investments include all long-term—more than one year—investments that do not give the investors effective control over the object of the investment. Such transactions typically involve the purchase of stocks or bonds of foreign issuers for investment—not control—purposes, and they also include long-term commercial credits to finance trade.

C. Short-term capital flows involve changes in international assets and liabilities with an original maturity of one year or less. Some of the fastest-growing types of short-term flows are for currency exchange rate and interest rate hedging in the forward, futures, option, and swap markets. (These subjects are dealt with in Chapter 18, Financial Management.) Among the more traditional types of short-term capital flow are payments and receipts for international finance and trade, short-term borrowings from foreign banks, exchanges of foreign notes or coins, and purchases of foreign commercial paper or foreign government bills or notes.

The volatility, private nature, and wide varieties of short-term capital flows make them the most difficult BOP items to measure—and therefore the least reliable. The wide fluctuations of currency exchange rates and interest rates during the 1980s have caused the surge in hedging activities mentioned above, with attendant surges in short-term capital movements.

Official reserves account.   The official reserves account deals with gold imports and exports, increases or decreases of foreign exchange (foreign currencies) held by the government, and decreases or increases in liabilities to foreign central banks. The last item in this account is the statistical discrepancy entry.

Total BOP credits and debits must be equal because of the double-entry accounting system used to report the BOP. Because some BOP figures are inaccurate and incomplete (this is notably true of the short-term capital flows item), the statistical discrepancy item is plugged in to bring total credits and debits into accounting balance.

Balance-of-Payment Equilibrium and Disequilibrium

While the BOP is always in accounting balance, the odds are astronomical that it would be so without the statistical discrepancy item. There would be a surplus or a deficit in almost every case, but the BOP would nevertheless be considered in equilibrium if over a three- to five-year period the surpluses more or less canceled out the deficits.

Temporary and fundamental BOP deficits.   In IMF terminology, the deficit years for a country in equilibrium are referred to as temporary if they are corrected by the country's monetary and fiscal policies and perhaps by short-term IMF loans and advice.

The fundamental BOP deficit is too severe to be repaired by any **monetary policies** or **fiscal policies** that the country can apply; there are economic, social, and political limits to how much a country can deflate its economy, which causes unemployment, or devalue its currency, which causes higher prices for imports.

In these cases, the IMF rules permitted the countries' currencies to be devalued from the par values per US$ set at Bretton Woods; the amount of the devaluation was agreed by the country and the IMF. Although many par value changes occurred between 1946 and 1971, none led to international financial crises of the kind that followed the devaluations of 1931. This was due at least in part to the performance of the IMF; it was able to maintain generally stable exchange rates, and when changes became necessary, it was able to prevent the competitive devaluations that proved so futile and destructive in the 1930s.

The devaluations of the 1946–71 period were in terms of the US$, so its relative value went up in terms of the devalued currencies. This caused the prices of American goods and services to go up in terms of other currencies, because after devaluation, more units of those currencies were required to buy US$s. This, in turn, was one cause of an American BOP deficit that began in 1958.

monetary policies   regulate the amount of growth or contraction of a nation's monetary stock

fiscal policies   regulate a government's money receipts through taxes and its expenditure

American BOP Deficit

From the end of WW II until about 1958, there was a shortage of US$s for the development of world trade and investment. Even during that era, many dollars flowed abroad due to government aid, private investment, and tourism. Around 1958, the United States began to run a series of BOP deficits, the flow of dollars became a flood, and the US$ shortage ended. The United States could have tried market methods (deflate the economy or devalue the US$) to slow or reverse the deficit, but it did not, and its trading partner countries did not urge it to do so.

Why market methods were not attempted.   Vivid recollections of the hunger and hardships of the 1930s depression caused U.S. leaders to see deflation as the greater danger, and not until the late 1960s was inflation perceived by the U.S. government as a possible cause of another depression. The US$ had been enshrined at Bretton Woods as the key currency in the gold exchange standard and had become, along with gold, the central reserve asset of most countries. Those countries were understandably reluctant to see a reduction in the value of part of their reserves, and U.S. authorities seemed to feel that this nation's prestige would be tarnished by a devaluation of the US$.[9]

Moreover, foreign competitors of U.S. exports derived a price advantage from the overvaluation of the US$. As pointed out above, almost all of the 1946–71 currency value changes were devaluations in terms of the US$. Thus, foreign goods and services became relatively less expensive for holders of US$s; but at the same time, U.S. exports were becoming relatively more expensive for holders of other currencies, who bought fewer of those more expensive goods and services. The foreign competitors of U.S. firms did not want to lose that advantage, and their governments discouraged any U.S. inclination to devalue the US$.

Raising the US$ price of gold would amount to a dollar devaluation in terms of other currencies unless they also devalued. It was generally recognized that the US$ was overvalued and that, if permitted to float, its value would fall vis-à-vis the currencies of most industrialized countries.

The United States had thousands of troops stationed in Europe and Asia and could have saved billions of dollars in expenditures abroad by bringing them home. But the host countries—for example, Germany, Japan, South Korea, and South Vietnam—brought strong pressures on the U.S. government not to reduce its forces, and the United States felt obliged to maintain them.

central bank of a country manages the monetary policy

Gold Exchange Standard

As the United States failed to even try market methods to end its BOP deficit, and other rather halfhearted attempts had little success, dollars piled up in foreign hands, including those of government **central banks**. At this point, beginning in 1958, the "exchange" part of the **gold exchange standard** began to function.

gold exchange standard cast the U.S. dollar as the central currency at $35 per ounce of gold. The U.S. agreed to buy or sell gold from or to other central banks at that price

Gold for dollars.   The exchange feature agreed on at Bretton Woods required the United States to deliver an ounce of gold to any central bank of an IMF member-country that presented US$35 to the U.S. Treasury. As dollars accumulated in foreign hands in amounts greater than were needed for trade

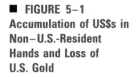

■ **FIGURE 5–1**
Accumulation of US$s in Non–U.S.-Resident Hands and Loss of U.S. Gold

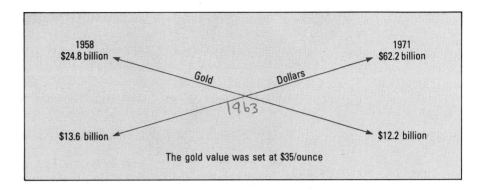

and investment, the central banks began turning them in to the U.S. Treasury for gold.

Gold and dollars go abroad.   From 1958 through 1971, the United States ran up a cumulative deficit of $56 billion. The deficit was financed partly by use of the U.S. gold reserves, which shrank from $24.8 billion to $12.2 billion,[10] and partly by incurring liabilities to foreign central banks. During this period, those liabilities increased from $13.6 billion to $62.2 billion.[11] This is illustrated by Figure 5–1.

The main reason the foreign central banks were willing to accept so many dollars was that those dollars were treated as a central reserve asset; they provided liquidity growth to support growing world trade and finance. But in the late 1960s and into 1971, the central banks became increasingly nervous at the volume of US$ accumulation. A number of them turned in excess dollars for gold, but by the mid-1960s, more dollars were held by the banks than there was gold left in the U.S. Treasury. By 1971, the Treasury held only 22 cents' worth of gold for each US$ held by those banks.[12]

As indicated, another reason foreigners accepted so many US$s was that these dollars provided liquidity to support world trade and investment, which grew rapidly in the post-WW II era. Of course, this meant liquidity growth depended on U.S. BOP deficits, but such deficits could not continue indefinitely without deterioration of confidence in the strength of the U.S. economy and of the US$. Here is illustrated the inherent contradiction of the gold exchange standard. Foreigners needed and wanted growing numbers of dollars for many purposes but became nervous when the amounts of dollars they held exceeded the amount of gold held by the United States at the established price of $35 per ounce of gold.[13]

AUGUST 15, 1971, AND THE NEXT TWO YEARS

As noted above, by 1971, many more dollars were in the hands of foreign central banks than the gold held by the U.S. Treasury could cover. The event said to have triggered the drastic decisions made at Camp David* on the

---

* Camp David is a relatively isolated retreat in the Maryland mountains that U.S. presidents frequently use to escape the pressures of Washington.

weekend beginning Friday, August 13, 1971, was a request by the British government that the United States cover US$3 billion of its reserve against loss.[14] President Nixon, with Treasury Secretary John Connally, Treasury Undersecretary Paul Volcker, and others, made the decisions that the president announced on Sunday night (the 15th). Those decisions shook the international monetary system to its roots.[15]

The president announced that the United States would no longer exchange gold for the paper dollars held by foreign central banks. He was said to have "closed the gold window."

The shock caused currency exchange markets to remain closed for several days, and when they reopened, they began playing a new game for which few rules existed. Currencies were floating, and the stated US$ value of 35 dollars per ounce of gold was now meaningless because the United States would no longer exchange any of its gold for dollars. The gold exchange standard was ended.

The president also imposed and announced a 10 percent surcharge on imports from all industrial countries except Canada. He demanded those countries lower their obstacles to imports from the United States in return for canceling the surcharges. Agreement on trade obstacles was reached in December 1971 along with new currency exchange rates that devalued the US$. The agreement was called the Smithsonian Accord because the final negotiations and signing ceremonies were held at the Smithsonian Institution in Washington, D.C. The new rates could not be maintained, and by 1973, currencies were floating.

Politicians versus Speculators

Two attempts were made to agree on durable, new sets of fixed exchange rates, one in December 1971 and the other in February 1973. Both times, however, banks, businesses, and individuals (collectively referred to as speculators by unhappy politicians) felt that the central banks had pegged the rates incorrectly, and the speculators proved correct each time. Of course, the speculators' prophecies could be said to have been self-fulfilling in that they put billions of units of the major currencies into the currencies they felt to be strong—for example, the deutsche mark (DM), the Dutch guilder, and the Swiss franc—thereby making them even stronger. The speculators profited, and one writer commented, "It wasn't a holdup. It was more like an invited robbery."[16]

floating currency exchange rates values are not set by governments but by markets, although governments intervene frequently

In March 1973, the major currencies began to float in the foreign exchange markets, and the system of **floating currency exchange** rates still prevails.[17] However, Western Europe has moved back toward a fixed system, the European Monetary System, which is discussed later in this chapter.

1973 TO THE PRESENT

The two kinds of currency floats are referred to by various commentators as free or managed or as clean or dirty. The free (clean) float is one of the world's closest approaches to perfect competition, because there is no government intervention and because billions of the product (units of money) are being traded by thousands of buyers and sellers. Buyers and sellers may change sides on short notice as information, rumors, or moods change or as their clients' needs differ. In the managed (dirty) float, governments intervene in the currency markets as they perceive their national interests to be served. Nations may explain their interventions in the currency market in terms of "smoothing market irregularities" or "assuring orderly markets."[18]

Beginning in September 1985, governments' reasons for intervening in currency markets have been expressed more forthrightly. The US$ soared in value from 1981 to its peak in February 1985, gaining some 80 percent against a trade-weighted basket of other major currencies. Although there were many other reasons for the huge growth of the American trade deficit, the powerful US$ was probably the biggest single reason.[19]

The unprecedented U.S. trade deficit, which was $134 billion in 1985 and reached $170 billion at its peak in 1987, greatly concerned the United States and its trading partners. To seek a solution, the finance ministers of the Group of 5 (Britain, France, Germany, Japan, and the United States) met at the Plaza Hotel in New York in September 1985. Although the US$ exchange rate had begun to move down in March, they decided it was still too high and agreed in the so-called Plaza Accord to cooperate in bringing its rate lower. The Plaza meeting was the first of several—including one at the Louvre in Paris in February 1987—whose objective was to set the US$ at the "right" exchange rate, particularly in terms of the Japanese yen and the German deutsche mark (the currencies of the other two major world economies). And so, since 1985, the governments of the Group of 5 have been intervening in currency markets in order to maintain their currencies' exchange rates at the "right" levels or within "target zones."

Not everyone believes government officials really know the right levels or target zones. Professor Jacob Frenkel of the University of Chicago says,

> Some officials seem to think they know exactly what the dollar should be worth in terms of marks, yen, francs, and pounds. The exchange markets have been mulling over this question for several years without reaching lasting conclusions. Are the officials really smarter than the markets?[20]

Currency Areas

The U.S. dollar, Canadian dollar, Japanese yen (¥), Swiss franc, British pound (£), and several other currencies are floating in value against one another and against the European Currency Unit (ECU), a grouping of eight Western European currencies. Most currencies of developing countries (LDCs) are pegged (fixed) in value to one of the major currencies or to currency baskets such as the ECU, special drawing rights (SDRs), or some specially chosen currency mix or basket (see Figure 5–2).[21]

Current developments may make the growth of currency areas, trading blocs, and currency blocs more likely. The most important of those developments are the EC 1992 project, the Canadian–American Free Trade Area, and the alleged attempts by Japan to use the Asian Development Bank to stimulate Japanese goods and services sales throughout Asia. They are all discussed in Chapter 4.

■ **FIGURE 5–2**
Pegged LDC Currencies

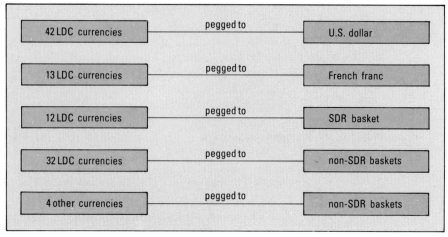

Source: *International Financial Statistics,* September 1988, p. 18.

Snake

In Europe during the mid-1970s, a currency grouping called the snake was created. The snake comprised several European currencies, led by the German deutsche mark. There was an agreed central exchange rate, but currencies' values could fluctuate up or down to a ceiling or floor exchange rate shown by the solid lines.

The snake was so called because of how it appeared in a graph showing the member currencies floating against nonmember currencies, such as the yen or the Canadian or U.S. dollar.

The reptile's health was damaged by the departure of several currencies, including the pound sterling, the Italian lira, and the Swedish krona, and by the in-and-out relationship of the French franc.[22] The system's inflexibility, the major reason those currencies were removed, explains the snake's ultimate demise. Each member-country was responsible for keeping its currency's value within the agreed relationship to the other members' currencies, but each country had different inflation rates, fiscal and monetary policies, and BOP balances. Thus market pressures pushed currency exchange rates out of the agreed ranges, and the countries lacked the political will or resources to restore the agreed exchange rate. Then, the currency automatically fell out of the system.

The snake was the forerunner of the European Monetary System (EMS), discussed later in this chapter.

Experience with Floating

Such immense amounts of major currencies were being bought and sold each trading day that governments' efforts to keep their currencies at fixed exchange rates failed. The central banks stopped trying to peg the major currencies' exchange rates in 1973. OPEC hiked the price of petroleum over 400 percent early in 1974, and there were fears that the banking and monetary systems would not be able to handle the resulting changes in the amounts and directions of currency flows.[23]

■ **FIGURE 5–3   The Dollar's Summer Rally Didn't Last**

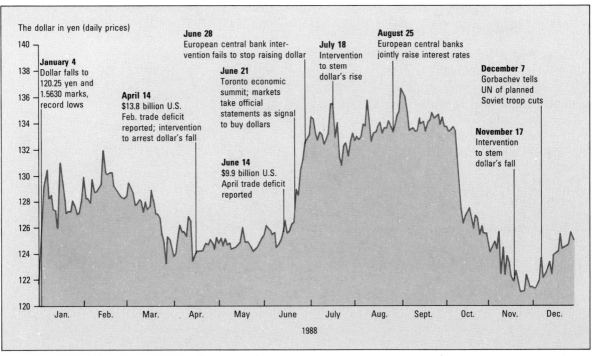

Source: *The Wall Street Journal,* January 3, 1989, p. 6R.

Fears not realized.   However, despite occasional flare-ups and occasional sharp changes in the relative values of currencies, the system did not collapse. Indeed, the volatility of exchange rate movements diminished after a period of uncertainty with the new system, in 1973–74. Uncertainty was heightened by the sudden, drastic increase of oil prices by OPEC. In those days, it could be difficult and costly to engage in a foreign exchange transaction. By 1977, the cost of undertaking foreign exchange transactions was about the same as it had been under the Bretton Woods system.[24]

The system has still not collapsed, even though the value of the US$ fluctuated widely between 1977 and 1989. Beginning in June 1977, the US$ fell in value about 28 percent against the Swiss franc, 20 percent against the Japanese yen, and some 15 percent against the deutsche mark within a year. Many laid the blame for the dollar's weakness on inflationary American fiscal and monetary policies, particularly the latter.

In 1979, the American Federal Reserve System (Fed) slowed the rate of monetary growth, and the US$ began to move up in value. The new administration that took office in 1981 continued the anti-inflationary policies instituted by Fed Chairman Paul A. Volcker in 1979, and indeed inflation did fall. As it fell, the value of the US$ rose, and by the beginning of 1985, it had risen about 80 percent against a trade-weighted basket of other major currencies.

Then, beginning in March 1985, the dollar exchange rate reversed its climb, and by 1988, it had dropped about 40 percent. For an illustration of the US$'s volatility in relation to the yen during 1988, see Figure 5–3. This figure also indicates some of the major causes of the dollar's frequent rises and falls.

WORLDVIEW
On the Hamburger Standard

Depressing though it may be to gourmets, the "Big Mac" hamburger sold by McDonald's could well oust the basket of currencies as an international monetary standard. After all, it is sold in 41 countries, with only the most trivial changes of recipe. That ought to say something about comparative prices. Think of the hamburger as a medium-rare guide to whether currencies are trading at the right exchange rates.

Big Mac watchers will rely on the theory of purchasing power parity (PPP) for currencies. This argues that an exchange rate between two currencies is in equilibrium (i.e., at PPP) when it equates the prices of a basket of goods and services in both countries—or, in this case, the rate of exchange that leaves hamburgers costing the same in each country. Comparing actual exchange rates with PPP is one indication of whether a currency is under- or overvalued.

The Economist's correspondents around the world have been gorging themselves in a bid to test Mac-PPPs. In Washington, a Big Mac costs $1.60; in Tokyo, our *Makudonarudo* correspondent had to fork out ¥370 ($2.40). Dividing the yen price by the dollar price yields a Mac-PPP of $1 = ¥231; but on September 1, the dollar's actual exchange rate stood at ¥154. The same method gives a Mac-PPP against the deutsche mark of DM2.66, compared with a current rate of DM2.02. Conclusion: on Mac-PPP grounds, the dollar looks undervalued against the yen and the deutsche mark.

Sterling is different. The Mac-PPP for the pound is $1.45 (69p to the dollar), within a whisker of the actual rate of around $1.49. But the pound's Mac-PPP against

Source: *The Economist*, September 6, 1986, p. 77.

Currency dealers get younger by the day.

the deutsche mark is DM3.86, suggesting that sterling is undervalued at DM3.02. British industrialists, who squeal about the pound's current "strength," will now like hamburgers even less.

The Australian dollar appears to have been heavily oversold; it is 34 percent below its Mac-PPP rate against the American dollar. Meanwhile, the Irish pound seems to be spot on. However, our correspondent in Ireland has uncovered an opportunity for arbitrage. This month, a Big Mac can be enjoyed in Dublin for just 20 tokens from milk cartons.

The advocates of floating argued that it would end BOP disequilibria because the value of each currency would float up or down to a point where supply equaled demand. It has not worked that way, at least in part due to governments' reluctance to permit extreme changes in the value of their currencies. Governments have intervened in the currency markets to moderate or prevent value changes. The American BOP deficit set new records in 1985, 1986, and 1987 before turning down in 1988.

Forecasting float direction. Such large changes in short time periods prompted efforts by everyone affected to forecast currency value changes. Such changes have many causes, including political events and expectations and

The hamburger standard provides the United States with strong evidence for its contention that Asian NICs (newly industrializing countries) ought to upvalue their currencies; they are more or less tied to the dollar, so their exchange rates have barely budged during the past 18 months. A hamburger costs 64 percent more in Washington than in Hong Kong—i.e., on Mac-PPP grounds the dollar is 64 percent overvalued against the Hong Kong dollar. It is also 23 percent too high against the Singapore dollar.

Caveat Hamburger

The hamburger standard has its limitations. Using purchasing power parities to forecast movements in exchange rates can produce misleading results. For instance, price differences between countries can be distorted by taxes, transport costs, property costs, or such things as the famously high retail markups in Japan and West Germany.

A more serious objection is that a PPP simply indicates where exchange rates should be in the long run if price levels were the only difference between countries. In fact, there are many other differences. So even though PPPs are handy for converting living standards (GDP per person) into a common currency, they are not necessarily the best way to judge the exchange rate needed to bring the current account of the balance of payments into "equilibrium." Confused? Some economics can be hard to digest.

Big MacCurrencies:
Hamburger Prices around the World

Country	Hamburger Prices in Local Currency*	Implied Purchasing Power Parity of the Dollar†	Actual Exchange Rate, Sept. 1	Percent over (+) or under (−) Valuation of the Dollar
Australia	A$1.75	1.09	1.64	+50
Belgium	BFr90	56	42	−25
Brazil	Cz$2.5	7.80	13.80	+78
Britain	£1.10	0.69	0.67	−3
Canada	C$1.89	1.18	1.39	+18
France	FFr16.4	10.30	6.65	−35
Hong Kong	HK$6.60	4.75	7.80	+64
Ireland	IR£1.18	0.74	0.74	−1
Japan	¥370	231	154	−33
Holland	F14.35	2.72	2.28	−16
Singapore	S$2.80	1.75	2.15	+23
Spain	Ptas260	163	133	−18
Sweden	SKR16.5	10.30	6.87	−33
United States	$1.60	—	—	—
West Germany	DM4.25	2.66	2.02	−24

*Prices may vary slightly between branches.
†Foreign price divided by dollar price.
Source: McDonald's.

government economic policies. A major cause is present and forecast relative inflation from country to country. One means of measuring relative inflation is purchasing power parity (PPP), the theory of which is that an exchange rate between the currencies of two countries is in equilibrium when it equates the prices of a basket of goods and services in both countries.

One product sold worldwide that is—or is supposed to be—the same everywhere is McDonald's Big Mac hamburger. The *Economist* did a PPP study using Big Mac as the basket in 15 countries. The report of that study is in the above Worldview.

WORLDVIEW
The Hamburger Standard

It is time to update our McDonald's hamburger standard. We launched it three years ago as a ready reckoner of whether currencies are at their correct exchange rates. Big-Mac watchers rely on the theory of purchasing-power parity (PPP), which argues that in the long run the exchange rate between two currencies is "in equilibrium" (i.e., at PPP) when it equalises the prices of a basket of similar goods and services in both countries.

Our basket is just a Big Mac. The burger's virtue is that it is produced locally with little change in recipe in 50 countries. So international-distribution costs are not the distorting factor which they would be if we used, say, the price of this newspaper in different countries, as a few readers have suggested.

However, we have made one change. A year ago our estimates of the dollar's Mac-PPPs were based on the New York price of a hamburger. We have now found that the price of a Big-Mac varies much more in America than within other countries. The recommended American price before tax is $1.55; in central Manhattan our correspondent had to fork out a top-of-the-range $2.48 ($2.29 before tax). So this time we have used the average post-tax price in four American cities—$2.02.

In Tokyo a Big Mac costs ¥370. Dividing this by the dollar price yields a Mac-PPP of $1 = ¥183, compared with a current exchange rate of ¥133. In other words, the dollar is undervalued by 27%. The dollar is also 11% undervalued against the D-mark, which has a Mac-PPP of DM2.13, but it is almost spot on against sterling. This in turn implies that the pound's PPP against the D-mark is DM3.44—i.e., its actual rate is 7% too low. British manufacturers thus have little need to squeal. Mr. Nigel Lawson, the chancellor of the exchequer, can safely aim for a stronger pound. In contrast to sterling, most of the EMS currencies, like the French franc and the lira, look overvalued against the D-mark.

The currencies of Hong Kong and Singapore still look too cheap against the dollar—one reason that America's trade deficit remains huge. But Mac-PPPs do not support Washington's call for South Korea to continue to upvalue

Big MacCurrencies:

Country	Hamburger Prices in Local Currency*	Implied PPP† of the Dollar	Actual Exchange Rate 11.04.89	Percent over (+) or under (−) Valuation of the Dollar
Australia	A$2.10	1.04	1.24	+19
Belgium	BFr 90	45	39.5	−12
Britain	£1.26	0.62	0.59	−5
Canada	C$2.15	1.06	1.19	+13
Denmark	DKr 24.75	12.3	7.33	−40
France	FFr 17.70	8.76	6.37	−27
Holland	FL5.10	2.52	2.13	−15
Hong Kong	HK$7.60	3.76	7.78	+107
Ireland	IR£1.30	0.64	0.71	+11
Italy	Lire 3,300	1,634	1,382	−15
Japan	¥370	183	133	−27
Singapore	S$2.80	1.39	1.96	+41
South Korea	Won 2,400	1,188	666	−44
Spain	Ptas 280	139	117	−16
Sweden	SKr 21	10.4	6.41	−38
United States††	$2.02	—	—	—
West Germany	DM 4.30	2.13	1.89	−11
Yugoslavia	Dinar 7,000	3,465	9.001	+160

*Prices may vary between branches
†Purchasing-power parity: foreign price divided by dollar price
††Average of New York, Chicago, San Francisco, and Atlanta
Source: McDonald's

its currency. The dollar appears to be 44% undervalued against the won. Indeed, Seoul has the dearest Big Macs in our sample. American Big-Mac watchers should focus their attention closer to home: Big Macs are 12% dearer in the United States than in its leading trade partner, Canada—i.e., the American dollar needs to fall against the Canadian one.

The Economist updated its hamburger standard in 1989. The Worldview on the preceding page appeared in the April 15, 1989, issue on page 86. Compare the two Big MacCurrency tables and note the changes in three years.

Money Markets, Foreign Exchange

money markets are places where monies can be bought, sold, or borrowed

The daily volume of foreign exchange trading in the world's three leading **money markets** has grown at a rapid pace. London is in the lead, handling some $187 billion; New York comes second, with some $129 billion; and Tokyo is a close third, with some $115 billion. The studies leading to these estimates were conducted in September 1989 by the Bank of England, working with the Federal Reserve Bank of New York and the Bank of Japan.

These studies underscore London's pivotal role in world currency trading. Because the London market shares trading hours with markets in Asia and the Middle East during its morning session and with the New York market during its afternoon session, it has more transaction opportunities than do the New York or Tokyo markets.

However, the Tokyo market is growing steadily, and its trading volume is expected to surpass that of New York by 1990. The reasons are that while the United States has become a debtor nation, Japan has become the largest creditor country; and at the same time, the Japanese banks have become the world's biggest, and thus more and more of the world's financial activity is centered in, or at least affected by, Tokyo markets.

The growth of foreign exchange trading in recent years has greatly outpaced world trade even though trade has also expanded. This has been due to the near explosions in international investment and in hedge and swap transactions. Hedges and swaps are explained in Chapter 18.

Banks, currency brokers, and securities houses are major currency dealers. The Bank of England said that 30 percent of London volume was in sterling (British pounds)–US$ transactions and 28 percent in deutsche mark–US$ transactions. The remainder was between the US$ and other major currencies. The Fed found that in New York the most traded currencies—all with the US$—were deutsche marks, followed by Japanese yen, British pounds, Swiss francs, and Canadian dollars.

London, New York, and Tokyo have the biggest currency markets but by no means the only ones. Other important markets are in Los Angeles and San Francisco, Hong Kong, Singapore, Bahrain, Frankfurt, Zurich, and Paris. Trades can be made 24 hours a day at one or more of these markets.

Billions of US$s are traded around the world in the various currency markets. Smaller—but still large—amounts of the other currencies of major market countries are also traded outside the borders of the issuing countries, and all of these currencies are used as countries' national reserve assets as well as in trade, investments, hedges, and swaps.

Beginning in the 1960s, there was a growing feeling that an asset other than national currencies or gold should be created to replace them at least insofar as they are used as central reserve assets. In 1970, the IMF established special drawing rights for that purpose.

WORLDVIEW
Central Reserve/National Currency Conflict

The US$ has been the most used central reserve asset in the world since the end of WW II. Somewhat analogous to a savings account, the dollars were available when needed to finance trade or investments or to intervene in currency markets. Held in the form of U.S. Treasury bonds, the US$s earn interest, and the more held in the savings/central reserve account, the better. But, the countries don't want their central reserve asset US$s to lose value, and there lies a contradiction: at some point, greater numbers of US$s (or any other product) in supply cause them to lose value—supply and demand.

At the same time, the US$ is the national currency of the United States of America, whose government must deal with inflation, recession, interest rates, unemployment, and other national, internal problems. The U.S. government uses fiscal and monetary policies to meet those problems—higher or lower taxes, decisions as to how to spend available revenue, growth or contraction of

the money supply, and rate of growth or contraction.

It would be only accidental if the national interests of the United States in dealing with its internal problems coincided with the interests of the multitude of countries holding US$s in their central reserve asset accounts. The United States may be slowing money supply growth and raising taxes to combat U.S. inflation while the world needs more liquidity, in the form of US$s, to finance growth, trade, or investment. Or, the United States may be stimulating its economy by faster money supply growth and lower taxes at a time when so many US$s are already outstanding that their value is dropping—not a happy state of affairs for countries holding US$s.

It was a quirk of history that thrust the US$ into this conflicting role. It was the hope of the IMF that a non-national asset, the SDR, would rescue the US$ and the world from the conflict.

SDRs in the Future

special drawing rights (SDRs) were established by the IMF as units of value to replace the dollar as a reserve asset

Special drawing rights (SDRs) may be a step toward a truly international currency. The US$ has been the closest thing to such a currency since gold in the pre-WW I gold standard system, but the US$ must also serve as a national currency, and the roles sometimes conflict.

SDRs, bookkeeping entries at the IMF, were created in 1970 by agreement of the IMF members, whose accounts are credited with certain amounts of SDRs from time to time. The objective was to make the SDR the principal reserve asset in the international monetary system.[25]

Value of the SDR.   The SDR's value is based on a basket of the following five currencies (the percentage of each currency is in parentheses): U.S. dollar (42), German mark (19), Japanese yen (15), British pound sterling (12), and the French franc (12). The weights broadly reflect the relative importance of the currencies in trade and payments, based on the value of the exports of goods and services by the member-countries issuing these currencies. In 1986, the yen weight was increased from 13 to 15, and the pound and franc weights were each lowered from 13 to 12.

The value of the SDR in US$ terms is calculated daily by the Fund as the sum of the values in US$s based on market exchange rates of specified amounts of the currencies in the valuation basket.

■ **TABLE 5–2**
SDR Valuation on
August 31, 1988

Currency	(1) Currency Amount	(2) Exchange Rate on August 31	(3) US$ Equivalent
Deutsche mark	0.5270	1.87470	0.281112
French franc	1.0200	6.36200	0.160327
Japanese yen	33.4000	136.56000	0.244581
Pound sterling	0.0893	1.68150	0.150158
U.S. dollar	0.4520	1.00000	0.452000
SDR 1 = US$			1.28818

Column 1: The currency components of the basket.
Column 2: Exchange rates in terms of currency units per U.S. dollar, except for the pound sterling, which is expressed in U.S. dollars per pound.
Column 3: The U.S. dollar equivalents of the currency amounts in column (1) at the exchange rates in column (2)—that is, column (1) divided by column (2).
Source: IMF Treasurer's Department.

An illustrative calculation of the SDR's value in terms of the US$ is shown in Table 5–2. Inasmuch as exchange rates fluctuate, so too does the SDR value from day to day.[26]

Uses of the SDR

The SDR's value remains more stable than that of any single currency, and that stability has made the SDR increasingly attractive as a unit for denominating international transactions. Future payment under a contract, for example, may be agreed to be made in a national currency at its rate in terms of the SDR on the payment date, and some Swiss and British banks will now accept accounts denominated in SDRs.[27]

Holders of SDRs.   SDRs are held by the IMF, its 151 current members, and 16 official institutions, which typically are regional development or banking institutions that have been prescribed by the IMF. All holders can buy and sell SDRs both spot and forward and receive or use SDRs in loans, pledges, swaps, grants, or settlement of financial obligations. Holders receive interest at a rate that is determined weekly by reference to the weighted-average interest rate on short-term obligations in the money markets of the same five countries whose currencies are included in the SDR valuation basket.

SDRs as central reserve assets.   A major purpose envisioned for SDRs was to replace currencies and gold as central reserve assets of nations. That has not happened. After the first allocation of 9 billion SDRs to members in 1972, they constituted 6.1 percent of the central reserves, while foreign exchange made up 65.3 percent and gold 24.5 percent at $35 per ounce. There was a second SDR allocation in 1979 of 13 billion, but total reserves went up faster, so that by 1983, SDRs constituted only 3.4 percent of the central reserves. Currencies had increased to 78.7 percent, and gold had fallen to 8.2 percent, but that was on the basis of valuing gold at $35 per ounce. In the gold markets, the price of gold had soared to over $800 in 1980, and gold traded between $300 and $465 per ounce from then into 1989.

The most recent SDR allocation to the 141 IMF member-countries at that time was on January 1, 1981, in the amount of SDR 4.1 billion. As of June 1988, the Fund had allocated a total of SDR 21.4 billion in six allocations, but SDR holdings by member-countries amounted to only 3.9 percent of their total nongold reserves.

Such lack of enthusiasm for SDRs as central reserve assets may have several explanations. Dollars and other hard currencies are more flexible and have more uses, usually yield higher interest returns, and can officially be credited and debited by anyone—in contrast to the limited numbers with official access to SDRs.

European Monetary System (EMS)

As evidenced by the snake, the European countries prefer a fixed currency exchange rate regime to a floating one. Due to inflexibility and weaknesses, the snake expired in the mid-1970s. Nothing daunted, a larger group of European countries banded together in 1979 and created the **European Monetary System (EMS),** which is a large step back toward fixed currency exchange rates and an enlarged and improved version of the snake.

The EMS member-countries (Britain, which did not become a full member at the beginning, was still debating membership in 1989) agreed to maintain their currency values within an agreed range in relation to one another. An important feature, not available to the old snake, will be the European Monetary Cooperation Fund (EMCF). It will be composed of dollars, gold, and member-country currencies, and it is to be used to support the efforts of member-countries to keep their currency values within the agreed relationship to the other currencies. The EMCF could carry considerable clout when it comes into being. It is expected to have the equivalent of about $32 billion with which to work.[28]

Another difference between the EMS and its ancestor, the snake, is that the exchange rates of the EMS are flexible. If one currency proves weaker than another and the governments cannot or will not take steps to correct the situation, the EMS exchange rates can be changed. There have been several rate rearrangements since 1979. If a snake member-country could not keep its currency up to the agreed strength, it dropped out and ceased to be a member.

Two of the EMS fathers, former French president Valery Giscard d'Estaing and former West German chancellor Helmut Schmidt, think it's time their child was allowed to grow up. They are pushing hard for the never-implemented second stage of their plan, the economic and monetary union of Europe. This union would be accomplished through a European Central Bank and free use of the European Currency Unit (see the next section) by banks, companies, and consumers in all 12 EC countries.

Despite opposition from the German central bank (the Bundesbank) and the British government, the two men are optimistic the European Bank will be a reality by 1992. Mr. Schmidt says, "All the talk about European union will be rubbish if we don't do anything. We must create a European Central Bank because we must have a currency with which you could as easily buy a dress or a train ticket in Paris or Madrid."[29]

European Monetary System (EMS) is a grouping of most Western European nations cooperating to maintain their currencies at fixed exchange rates

WORLDVIEW
Hamburger Parity

Remember the McDonald's hamburger standard which *The Economist* launched last year? We offered it as a rough and ready guide to whether currencies are at their "correct" exchange rates. It is based on the idea that exchange rates should produce purchasing-power parity (PPP)—i.e., they should equate the prices of similar goods (in this case, a Big Mac) bought in different countries.

Following the EMS realignment, Big-Mac watchers want to know the Mac-PPP cross-rates for the D-mark against other member currencies. In Cologne, for instance, a Big Mac costs DM4.10; in Paris, FFr17.40. Dividing the franc price by the D-mark price gives a Mac-PPP of FFr4.24. This week, the D-mark was trading at FFr3.34. Conclusion: on Mac-PPP grounds, the D-mark is 21% undervalued against the French franc.

The D-mark appears to be undervalued against the Belgium franc, the Danish krone and the Italian lira (see table). It looks about right against the Dutch guilder, but it is 28% overvalued against the Irish Punt. The table also shows the Mac-PPPs for the D-mark against the dollar and sterling. Evidently, both have been heavily oversold: the D-mark rate is 36% overvalued against the dollar and 29% against the pound. Britain should join the EMS at once—and go in at a super-competitive rate.

Big MacCurrencies
Hamburger prices

Country	Price* in local currency	Implied† purchasing power parity of the D-mark	Latest exchange rate	% over (+) or under (−) valuation of the D-mark
Britain	£1.13	0.28	0.36	+29
United States	$1.60	0.39	0.53	+36
Belgium	BFf 90	21.95	20.74	−6
Denmark	DKr 21.50	5.24	3.81	−27
France	FFr 17.40	4.24	3.34	−21
Holland	Fl 4.50	1.10	1.13	+3
Ireland	IRE 1.18	0.29	0.37	+28
Italy	Lire 3,300	805	711	−12
West Germany	DM 4.10	–	–	

Source: © 1989 The Economist Newspaper Ltd.

Earlier in this chapter, we saw the Big Mac hamburger purchasing power parity—the relative cost of McDonald's hamburgers in countries around the world—to learn whether at current exchange rates, hamburgers cost the same in each country. They did not, and it could be argued the exchange rates were wrong. The same Big Mac test has been applied to the EMS countries, and the above Worldview gives the results.

European Currency Unit (ECU)

European Currency Unit is a value established by the EMS for intra-EMS bookkeeping

The **European Currency Unit** (ECU) was established as the EMS bookkeeping currency. Its value is determined by reference to a basket of European currencies. The weights of each currency in the ECU are shown in Figure 5–4. The weights changed in 1989 when Portugal and Spain joined the EMS. The Portuguese escudo was accorded a one percent weight while the Spanish peseta was given five percent. The six percent loss was shared among the other currencies.[30]

■ **FIGURE 5–4   Current Composition of the ECU Currency Weightings**

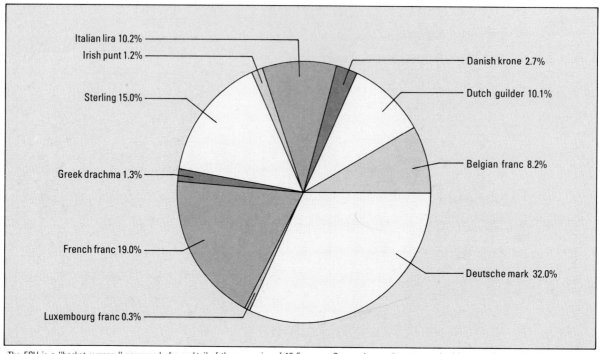

The ECU is a "basket currency" composed of a cocktail of the currencies of 10 European Community member-states, mixed in proportion to the relative strength of each country's economy.

Source: Barclays Briefing, October 1985.

The ECU is becoming more widely used in the Eurobond market and elsewhere; by 1983, the volume of ECU bonds was surpassed only by that of bonds denominated in US$s and deutsche marks. ECU bond issues increased from ECU 190 million in 1981 to about ECU 9.5 billion in 1985; but after 1983, their relative popularity in international financing fell somewhat so that by 1988, international lending by currency showed US$, 64.5 percent; yen, 7.4 percent; Swiss franc, 6.2 percent; pound, 5.7 percent; and the ECU and deutsche mark, tied at 4.1 percent. Figure 5–5 is an announcement of an ECU Eurobond placement.

One reason the ECU has become more popular than the SDR is that neither the US$ nor the yen is included in the currency basket that determines its value. The exchange rates of the US$ and, to a lesser extent, the yen have fluctuated much more widely than have those of the European currencies in the ECU basket. Both the US$ and the yen are in the SDR basket, so the SDR's value has been less stable than that of the ECU.

Another reason the ECU's use has surpassed that of the SDR is active sponsorship of the ECU by European governments, banks, and businesses; the SDR has received no such support. The ECU is being used for various purposes, and support and supplementary networks have been put in place. Bank accounts can be denominated in ECUs, and ECU traveler's checks are

■ FIGURE 5–5
ECU Denominated
Euro-Notes

This announcement appears as a matter of record only. These Securities have not been registered under the United States Securities Act of 1933 and may not, as part of the distribution, be offered, sold or delivered, directly or indirectly, in the United States or to United States persons.

New Issue / April, 1986

ECU 100,000,000

Phibro-Salomon Inc

8½% Series A Note Due February 24, 1996
and 100,000 Warrants to Purchase
ECU 100,000,000 8½% Series B
Notes Due February 24, 1996

Salomon Brothers International Limited

Banque Nationale de Paris   Banque Bruxelles Lambert S.A.

Banque Générale du Luxembourg S.A.   Banque Indosuez

Banque Internationale a Luxembourg S.A.   Bayerische Hypotheken-und Wechsel-Bank
                                                              Aktiengesellschaft
Commerzbank Aktiengesellschaft   Crédit Agricole   Crédit Commercial de France

Crédit Lyonnais   Daiwa Europe Limited   Deutsche Bank Capital Markets Limited

Fuji International Finance Limited   Generale Bank   Goldman Sachs International Corp.

Kredietbank International Group   Morgan Guaranty Ltd.

Morgan Stanley International   Nippon Credit International (HK) Ltd.

Nippon European Bank S.A./LTCB Group   Nomura International Limited

Orion Royal Bank Limited   Shearson Lehman Brothers International

Swiss Bank Corporation International Limited   The Taiyo Kobe Bank (Luxembourg) S.A.

Takugin International Bank (Europe) S.A.   S.G. Warburg & Co. Ltd.

Source: © 1989 The Economist Newspaper Ltd.

available. Between units of some large multinational enterprises, debits and credits are denominated in ECUs as they buy, sell, or borrow from one another.

Countries outside the European Community have begun to utilize ECUs (e.g., the Soviet Union, Cameroon, Romania, Sweden, and New Zealand), and American companies have recently issued bonds denominated in ECUs. ECU futures and options contracts are available at markets in Amsterdam, Chicago, and Philadelphia. And, last but not least, an association of banks together with the European Investment Bank (a unit of the European Community) has begun a multilateral, electronic clearing system for ECU transactions. It will be administered by the Bank for International Settlements, which will perform functions for the ECU similar to the U.S. Federal Reserve's clearing of dollar transactions.

By 1987, enthusiasm for ECU financing had cooled somewhat, and some companies that used the ECU had forsaken it. There seem to be six reasons for this. First, the ECU has proved more volatile than expected because the pound is a component of its value but not subject to EMS rules because Britain is not a member. Another source of volatility is the lira's 6 percent fluctuation band (all other member-currencies have a 2.25 percent band), and in 1989, the

Spanish peseta and the Portuguese escudo became part of the ECU and received 6 percent bands.

Second, inclusion of those two additional weak currencies will make ECU devaluation more likely. Confidence in the ECU had already been undermined by participation of weak currencies such as the Greek drachma.

Third, Germany does not recognize the ECU. Although the Germans are being pressured to accept them, as of now, invoices can't be made in ECUs for transactions with Germany.

Fourth, ECU investments pay uncompetitive interest rates. A Belgian financier switched to Belgian francs for higher yields and lower devaluation risk.

Fifth, in contrast to the major national currencies, there is no central authority to manage the ECU. Creation of the European Central Bank advocated by Messrs. Giscard d'Estaing and Schmidt would solve this problem, but the Bank faces obstacles and is not now in place.

Sixth, there are psychological barriers. Widespread ECU use would carry a loss of sovereignty for national governments, which they are loath to see. In addition, many firms are reluctant to explore this unusual currency.[31]

SUMMARY

Although debate continues about the relative merits of fixed exchange rates compared to the floating (mostly dirty) ones that have been in effect since 1973, many feel that the shocks and strains suffered by the international monetary system since 1971 would have made fixed rates impossible. The inherent contradiction of the gold exchange standard led to the collapse of the fixed, or par, rates established at Bretton Woods. Then the shocks of the OPEC petroleum price increases, the strains of the BOP gyrations of such countries as the United Kingdom and Italy, and the U.S. deficits combined with the German and Japanese surpluses would have made impossible the sustained maintenance of fixed exchange rates during the mid- and late 1970s and the 1980s.

So we find ourselves at the present situation of currency areas, US$, £, Ff, or SDR, with the LDCs pegged to a major currency and those currencies in a managed float. But even with the float, persistent BOP imbalances have not been avoided, and the world is seeking methods to bring about better balance among the important economies. In theory, floating currencies should achieve balance, but they have not. The gold standard is in the past, and the gold exchange standard fell of its own weight.

As matters stand, coordination must be on a nation-by-nation basis, and the policies called for in the world's best interests may be extremely unpopular politically within a country. For example, restraint of monetary base growth may be called for, but fears of depression and unemployment may deter national leaders from implementing such a policy.

Developments mentioned in this chapter may hold some promise of making desirable coordination possible. One possibility is greater use of SDRs, which could permit the growth of world liquidity to be controlled by the IMF instead of being dependent on the size or existence of the U.S. BOP deficit.

Countries measure their BOP on an annual basis; the BOP measures the flows of money from residents of a country to nonresidents, and vice versa. It is in surplus if more money is coming in than is going out; the opposite is a deficit. The BOP contains a current account, a capital account, and an official reserves account, and it is balanced by the statistical discrepancy account.

Another attempt at coordination, and at fixed currency exchange rates, is the European Monetary System (EMS), inaugurated in 1979. Its members include most of Europe's most important economic powers, and it will have a huge fund of gold, U.S. dollars, and European currencies with which to achieve its goals.

The EMS created a unit of value called the European Currency Unit (ECU), the use of which as a denomination for bonds issued by European and other organizations has surpassed that of the SDR. There are bank accounts and traveler's checks in ECUs, and some multinational companies use ECUs for settlement of accounts between company units. The original purpose of the ECU was that it be used for settlement of accounts among EMS members, just as the SDR is used for settlement of accounts among IMF members.

Finally, what about gold? Pulling in one direction have been economists and government officials who want to demonetize gold and substitute for it special drawing rights (SDRs) and national currencies. They point out that SDRs can be controlled in number by the IMF in response to world need for liquidity, while the quantity, not to mention the price, of gold cannot be so controlled. There are other arguments against gold, such as the sources of most newly mined ore—the USSR and South Africa.

Other economists and officials pull in the other direction. They favor keeping gold as a part of reserve assets. The basis of their argument is the discipline that gold imposes on politicians who want to inflate national economies for temporary political advantage.

Now that national governments and central banks can buy gold, it is virtually certain that some of them will. Gold is part of the EMS reserves. It is too soon to write it out of the international monetary system.

QUESTIONS

1. What was Rueff's argument for the gold standard?
2. *a.* Describe the international monetary system devised at Bretton Woods.
   b. What were its strengths?
   c. Discuss the inherent contradiction of the gold exchange standard.
3. How does "dirty" float differ from "clean"?
4. What sorts of currency areas have developed in the post-1973 international monetary system?
5. What institutions make up most of the world's current money markets?
6. *a.* What is a special drawing right?
   b. Discuss its current and potential uses.
7. Why would fixed exchange rates have been difficult to maintain from 1973 to the present?
8. Why might the EMS be able to achieve fixed currency exchange rates among its member-countries?
9. Why should business managers be aware and wary of the BOP of the country in which their business operates?
10. What is the ECU? Why is it used more than the SDR?
11. Explain the central reserve/national currency conflict.

MINICASE 5-1

Payment Terms for an International Contract

You are the financial executive of an American construction company. Your company is about to contract for a multiphase project in Italy. Progress payments will be made, but most of the money will not be due until near the end of the project, eight or nine years in the future.

Your company wants to be paid in US$s. The Italian customer wants to make payments in Italian lira (II). You fear devaluation of the II in terms of the US$ over the term of the contract.

Draft a contract payment clause to be used as a compromise. Use an IMF or EMS developed value discussed in this chapter.

MINICASE 5–2

SDR Exchange Risk

The Bowling Green National Bank has made loans denominated in SDRs to several of its MNE customers. It has built up a portfolio to the amount of SDR 8 million. Management decides to hedge by selling in the forward market the currencies that make up the SDR basket. How much of each currency must be hedged?

"May I have my allowance in Deutsche Marks, Dad?"

Source: From *The Wall Street Journal*, with permission of Cartoon Features Syndicate.

SUPPLEMENTARY READINGS

Auerbach, Robert D. *Money, Banking and Financial Markets*, 2nd ed. New York: Macmillan, 1985.

Bareau, Paul Louis Jean. *The Disorder in World Money: From Bretton Woods to SDRs*. London: Institute of Economic Affairs for the Wincott Foundation, 1981.

Bergel, Clive. "ECU Plays Growing International Role." *Europe*, January–February 1986, pp. 28–29.

Bernholz, Peter. "The Introduction of Inflation-Free Monetary Constitutions (Gold Standard)." *Economic and Financial Prospects*, April–May 1986, pp. 1–5.

Boschen, John F. "Should We Reduce the Role of Banks in the Monetary Policy Process?" (Federal Reserve Bank of Kansas City) *Economic Review*, February 1988.

Coffey, Peter. *The European Monetary System: Past, Present and Future*. Boston: Martinus Nijhoff, 1984.

"Common Currency for Europe in 1992 Looks Good on Paper." *Business Month*, October 1988, p. 26.

Dixon, Joly. "Monetary Reform and the ECU." *Europe*, May 1986, pp. 18–20.

Eiteman, David K., and Arthur I. Stonehill. *Multinational Business Finance*. Reading, Mass.: Addison-Wesley Publishing, 1982, chaps. 2 and 3.

Fekete, Janos. "Do We Need a Monetary System?" *USA Today*, January 1988, pp. 18–21.

Hood, William C. "International Money, Credit and the SDR."

Finance & Development, September 1983, pp. 6–9.

Jager, Henk, and Eelke de Jong. "The Private ECU's Potential Impact on Global and European Exchange Rate Stability." (Banca Nazionale del Lavoro) *Quarterly Review*, March 1988, pp. 33–60.

Kvasnicka, Joseph G. "Why the U.S. Is Trying to Reduce the Dollar's Value." (Federal Reserve Bank of Chicago) *International Letter*, September 1985.

Ludlow, Peter. *The Making of the European Monetary System*, Boston: Butterworth Scientific, 1982.

Mundell, Robert A., and Jacques J. Polak. *The New International Monetary System*. New York: Columbia University Press, 1977.

Pick, Franz. *The U.S. Dollar, 1940–1976: An Advance Obituary*. New York: Pick Publications, 1976.

Root, Franklin R. *International Trade and Investment*. Cincinnati: South Western Publishing, 1984, chaps. 2, 9, and 10.

Safire, William. *Before the Fall*. New York: Belmont City Books, 1975.

Sarcinelli, Mario. "The EMS and the International Monetary System: Toward Greater Stability." (Banca Nazionale del Lavoro) *Quarterly Review;* March 1986, pp. 57–84.

Solomon, Robert. *The International Monetary System, 1945–1981,* 2nd ed. New York: Harper & Row, 1981.

Summer, Michael T., and George Zis. *European Monetary Union: Progress and Prospects.* New York: St. Martin's Press, 1982.

Thanassoulas, Constantine. "A Balance of Payments Mystery—The Case of the Growing Discrepancy." *Barclays Review,* August 1985, pp. 59–62.

Wanniski, Jude. *The Way the World Works: How Economies Fail and Succeed.* New York: Basic Books, 1978.

Williamson, John. *The Lending Policies of the International Monetary Fund.* Washington, D.C.: Institute for International Economics, 1982.

ENDNOTES

1. Charles N. Henning, William Pigott, and Robert Haney Scott, *International Financial Management* (New York: McGraw-Hill, 1978), p. 149.

2. Albert C. Whitaker, *Foreign Exchange,* 2nd ed. (New York: Appleton-Century-Crofts, 1933), p. 157.

3. Jacques Rueff, *The Wall Street Journal,* June 5, 6, and 9, 1969.

4. John Mueller, "The Reserve Currency Curse," *The Wall Street Journal,* September 4, 1986, p. 26.

5. "Sell Some Gold," editorial, *The Wall Street Journal,* September 4, 1986, p. 26.

6. *Articles of Agreement, International Monetary Fund* (Washington, D.C.: IMF, 1944), Article I.

7. Robert Z. Aliber, *The Future of the Dollar as an International Currency* (New York: Praeger Publishers, 1966).

8. For a discussion of how the pars were set, see Henning et al., *International Financial Management,* pp. 108, 218.

9. Theodore Sorenson, *Kennedy* (New York: Harper & Row, 1965), p. 408. See also *Maintaining the Strength of the United States Dollar in a Strong Free World Economy* (Washington, D.C.: U.S. Treasury Department, January 1968), p. xi: and *Economic Report of the President,* January 1964, p. 139.

10. *Federal Reserve Bulletin,* September 1969 and January 1974.

11. Ibid., December 1971 and January 1974.

12. Ibid., January 1974, p. A75.

13. This was perceived by the French economist Jacques Rueff, who also forecast the results; see endnote 3. The contradiction is discussed by Franklin R. Root, *International Trade and Investment* (Cincinnati: South Western Publishing, 1984), pp. 179–80.

14. William Safire, *Before the Fall* (New York: Belmont City Books, 1975), p. 514. The size of the British request has been questioned; see Charles Coombs, *The Arena of International Finance* (New York: John Wiley & Sons, 1976), p. 218, where Coombs says that the Bank of England request was for cover of only US $750 million.

15. Wilson E. Schmidt, "The Night We Floated," International Institute for Economic Research, Original Paper 9, October 1977.

16. Ibid., p. 7.

17. For detailed accounts of the international monetary system during the 1971–73 period, see Coombs, *Arena of International Finance,* chap. 12; and Robert Solomon, *The International Monetary System* (New York: Harper & Row, 1977), chaps. 12–15.

18. For discussions of the varieties and methods of clean or dirty floats plus comparisons of float versus peg, see, for example, Weir M. Brown, *World Afloat: National Policies Ruling the Waves,* Essays in International Finance, no. 116 (Princeton, N.J.: International Finance Section, Department of Economics, Princeton University, May 1976); Harry G. Johnson, *Further Essays in Monetary Economics* (Winchester, Mass.: Allen & Unwin, 1972); Anthony M. Lanyi, *The Case for Floating Exchange Reconsidered,* Essays in International Finance, no. 72 (February 1976); Raymond F. Mikesell and Henry M. Goldstein, *Rules for a Floating Regime,* Essays in International Finance, no. 109 (March 1975); and "Economics Brief: To Fix or Float," *The Economist,* January 9, 1988, pp. 66–67.

19. Wendell H. McCulloch, Jr., "American Exports: Why Have They Lagged?" A Study for the Subcommittee on Trade, Productivity, and Economic Growth of the Joint Economic Committee, Congress of the United States, May 14, 1985.

20. Lindley H. Clark, Jr., "Do We Really Know What the Dollar Exchange Rate Should Be?" *The Wall Street Journal,* November 19, 1985, p. 35.

21. Root, *International Trade and Investment,* chap. 10.

22. Stanley W. Black, *Floating Exchange Rates and National Economic Policy* (New Haven: Yale University Press, 1977), pp. 23–26, 49–50, 129–30, 149–50, 154–56, and 173–74.

23. Charles N. Stabler, "Banks and Their Foreign Loans," *The Wall Street Journal,* January 29, 1976, p. 16.

24. Geoffrey Bell, "The International Financial System and Capital Shortages," in *The World Capital Shortage,* ed. Alan Heslop (Indianapolis: Bobbs-Merrill, 1977), pp. 35–57.

25. Peter Kenen, "Techniques of Central International Reserves," paper presented at the J. Marcus Flemming Memorial Conference, International Monetary Fund, November 12, 1976.

26. *IMF Survey,* September 1988, pp. 5–7.

27. John Parke Young, "Can the Dollar Be as Solid as the Rock of SDRs?" *Los Angeles Times,* April 5, 1978, pt. 4, p. 2.

28. *IMF Survey,* March 1979, p. 99.

29. Philip Revzin, "Fathers of Europe's Monetary System Push Creation of a Joint Central Bank," *The Wall Street Journal,* February 23, 1988, p. 20.

30. "The Definition of the ECU," *Economic and Financial Prospects Supplement,* Swiss Bank Corporation, February/March 1989, pp. 2–3.

31. Dominque Vandercammen, "Why the ECU Still Fails to Attract MNCs Eight Years after Its Debut," *Business International Money Reports,* April 27, 1987, pp. 130–36.

Section Three

Foreign Environment

In Chapter 1, we stated that many of the business practices followed in the home country can be transferred intact and applied in other countries. However, we also mentioned that because of the differences in environmental forces, some ways of doing business must either be adapted to meet local conditions or changed completely.

In Section Three, we shall examine these forces to see how they differ from those that home country businesspeople are accustomed to encountering in this country. Only by such an investigation can we discover whether (1) we can transfer the business practice as is, (2) we must adapt it to local conditions, or (3) we cannot use it at all.

Having examined the international monetary system in Section Two, we begin Section Three with a discussion of the uncontrollable financial forces (Chapter 6) with which international companies must contend. Some of these forces are foreign currency exchange risks, balance of payments, taxation, tariffs, monetary and fiscal policies, inflation, and national accounting rules.

In Chapter 7, we consider the economic forces. Managements must know how the scarce

resources of land, labor, and capital are being allocated to the production and distribution of goods and services and the manner in which they are consumed. We explore important economic and socioeconomic dimensions of the economy.

Next we look at the physical forces—location, topography, and climate (Chapter 8). We offer examples to illustrate their influence on both the controllable and uncontrollable forces. The constantly changing situation in natural resources is emphasized not only because of their importance to firms that consume them but also because the income from new discoveries frequently creates new markets. The "Contamination of Resources" section focuses on the Bhopal and Rhine disasters and the Exxon oil spill and their consequences for WWCs.

Chapter 9 discusses the significance of the sociocultural forces for international businesspeople. It points out that the wide variety of attitudes and values among cultures affects managers of all the business functions. Although executives normally do not have time to become thoroughly immersed in a nation's culture, they should be familiar with at least those aspects that affect their business relationships.

In Chapter 10, we investigate the political forces that are a powerful factor in the success or failure of a foreign venture. Some of these are nationalism, terrorism, unstable governments, international organizations, government-owned businesses, and various ideological forces.

Legal forces, the subject of Chapter 11, reflect a nation's political climate. Managements of international firms must be familiar with the host country's laws because those laws set the constraints within which the managers must operate. In this chapter, we discuss laws concerning taxation, antitrust, imports, price and wage controls, labor, currency, and industrial property.

The composition, skills, attitudes, and union activities of an area's labor pool must be investigated because these labor forces affect productivity and, ultimately, the firm's profitability. Chapter 12 discusses these forces.

Competition is growing in world markets for a number of reasons, including (1) new competitors, (2) slowly growing markets, and (3) contracting markets. As Chapter 13 points out, a firm's ability to compete frequently depends on its ability to obtain adequate channels of distribution.

Chapter 6

Financial Forces

We're getting used to volatility; we're getting good at coping with it now.

> Citicorp foreign exchange
> currency trader

Traders aren't paranoid—there really are people after them.

> Virick Martin, currency trader,
> Merrill Lynch Capital Markets

Countries don't go bust.

> Walter Wriston, chairman,
> Citibank

LEARNING OBJECTIVES

In this chapter, you will study:

1. How to read and understand foreign exchange quotations.

2. The difference between spot and forward rates.

3. Some causes of exchange rate changes.

4. Government intervention in currency exchange markets.

5. How to recognize a currency exchange risk.

6. Government currency controls.

7. Some effects of inflation on business.

8. Monetary and fiscal policies that cause or combat inflation.

9. Why business must watch BOP developments, international monetary reserves, exchange rate forecasts, and comparative inflation rates.

10. The LDC debt crisis and some possible solutions to it.

11. The fact that the United States has the largest net negative international investment position in the world.

KEY WORDS AND CONCEPTS

- Sovereign debt
- Net negative international investment position
- Vehicle currency
- Intervention currency
- Safe haven
- Cross-rates
- Spot rate
- Forward rate
- Trading at a premium
- Trading at a discount
- Currency exchange controls
- Export incentives

BUSINESS INCIDENT

In 1984, after the U.S. dollar (US$) had increased in value against the Japanese yen (¥) in an almost uninterrupted rise since 1981, many "experts," including currency traders, thought that the US$ had peaked. Expecting the dollar's value to fall, the chief trader of Fuji Bank's New York money-dealing operation arranged to sell (short) large amounts of dollars for future delivery, betting that he would earn a huge profit when he purchased the lower-cost dollars for many fewer ¥ on the delivery date.

He lost the bet. Instead of going down, the US$ continued to go up, and he lost $48 million for Fuji over a four-month period.

sovereign debt   the debt of a government or government agency

net negative international investment position   the U.S. Commerce Department's description of what is commonly called the U.S. international debt

The "uncontrollable" financial forces on which we shall touch include foreign currency exchange risks, national balances of payment, taxation, tariffs, national monetary and fiscal policies, inflation, and national business accounting rules. *Uncontrollable* means that these forces originate outside the business enterprise. It does not mean that the financial management of companies is helpless to minimize their disadvantages; those disadvantages may even be turned to the company's advantage.

We shall have a look at what causes exchange rates to change and at how governments sometimes intervene in foreign exchange markets. We shall emphasize the importance for management to remain aware of BOP developments, exchange rate forecasts, inflation forecasts, government fiscal and monetary policies, and other financial forces. And at the end of the chapter, we look at the **sovereign debt** crises of developing countries, such as Brazil and Mexico. And not to be outdone, the United States has run up the biggest **net negative international investment position** in the world.

FLUCTUATING CURRENCY VALUES

An attempt is being made to bind together the values of most of the major European currencies in the European Monetary System (EMS). Although several currency value realignments have been made by EMS members since its inception in 1979, there has been less value fluctuation than was experienced before EMS and less fluctuation than has occurred in the currencies of the major non-EMS countries. The currencies of the other leading trading countries float and fluctuate in value relative to each other and to the EMS. Those countries include Australia, Britain, Canada, Japan, and the United States.

The company financial manager must understand how to protect against losses or optimize gains from such fluctuations. Another level of currency exchange risk is encountered when a nation suspends or limits convertibility of its currency, and the manager must try to foresee and minimize or avoid losses resulting from large holdings of inconvertible and otherwise limitedly useful currencies.

When you have a currency that you want to convert into another currency, the first thing you might do is look for the value of the currency you have in terms of the one you want. The international currency exchange quotations that you would look at are found in business publications such as *The Wall Street Journal* or the *Financial Times* and in the business section of most major newspapers.

FOREIGN EXCHANGE QUOTATIONS

The foreign exchange quotations—the price of one currency expressed in terms of another—can be confusing until you have examined how they are reported. In the world's currency exchange markets, the U.S. dollar (US$) is the common unit being exchanged for other currencies. Even if a holder of Japanese yen (¥) wants British pounds (£), the trade will be to buy US$s with

■ FIGURE 6-1
Key Currency
Cross-Rates
(Late New York trading
January 31, 1989)

	Dollar	Pound	SFranc	Guilder	Yen	Lira	DMark	FFranc	CdnDlr
Canada	1.1838	2.0748	.74089	.55879	.00909	.00086	.63102	.18558	—
France	6.3790	11.180	3.9924	3.0111	.04900	.00465	3.4003	—	5.3886
Germany	1.8760	3.2881	1.1741	.88553	.01441	.00137	—	.29409	1.5847
Italy	1370.5	2402.1	857.74	646.92	10.527	—	730.54	214.85	1157.7
Japan	130.19	228.18	81.481	61.454	—	.09499	69.398	20.490	109.98
Netherlands	2.1185	3.7131	1.3259	—	.01627	.00155	1.1293	.33211	1.7896
Switzerland	1.5978	2.8005	—	.75421	.01227	.00117	.85171	.25048	1.3497
United Kingdom	.57055	—	.35708	.26932	.00438	.00042	.30413	.08944	.48196
United States	—	1.7527	.62586	.47203	.00768	.00073	.53305	.15676	.84474

Source: *The Wall Street Journal*, February 1, 1989, p. C11.

vehicle currency a currency used as a vehicle for international trade or investment

intervention currency a currency used by a country to intervene in the foreign currency exchange markets (e.g., using some of its U.S. dollar reserve to buy—and thus strengthen—its own currency)

safe haven in reference to the U.S. dollar, a political concept based on the belief that the U.S. is less likely than most countries to elect a socialist or communist government or to be subjected to a military coup or revolution

cross-rates currency exchange rates directly between non-US$ currencies; usually determined by buying the US$ with one currency (e.g., the £ and then using those US$s to buy the other currency (e.g., the ¥)

the ¥ and then to buy £s with the US$s. The reasons for this procedure are historical and practical.

Historically, the international monetary system established at Bretton Woods just before the end of World War II set the value of the US$ in terms of gold at $35/ounce. The values of all the other major currencies were then stated in terms of the US$; for example, the yen was worth 0.28 of a U.S. penny, the French franc (Ff) was worth 18 cents, the German mark (DM) was worth 27 cents, and the £ was worth $2.40. In other words, the US$ was established as the keystone currency at the center of the world's monetary system.

The practical reasons for the continuing central position of the US$ are the several functions it has come to perform in the world. It is the main central reserve asset of many countries. It is the most used **vehicle currency** and **intervention currency.**

Among the reasons why the US$ is in great demand worldwide are its so-called **safe haven** aspect and its universal acceptance. Even if U.S. interest rates and investment opportunities were less attractive, there would still be a feeling that money is safe in American securities or property. Inflation has been brought to a low level, and the country is seen as less likely than others to be invaded or to elect a socialist government. It is seen as a safe haven.

As to universal acceptance, if you have traveled internationally with US$s, you have found them welcome everywhere. A dramatic example was the scene in the film *The Killing Fields,* which is based on a true story, in which the Cambodian doctor/prisoner was asked by the Vietnamese officer for whom he worked to take the officer's young son and try to escape with the boy to Thailand. The officer gave the doctor a small emergency kit whose contents included a roll of American $20 bills.

Although the US$ remains the most used currency, the currencies of the other noncommunist, industrial countries are also important in world transactions and growing more so. This is particularly true of the West German deutsche mark (DM) and the Japanese yen (¥). And, although most large currency exchanges go through the US$ (see the ¥–British pound [£] example above), it is also possible to directly trade yen for pounds. The exchange rates for trading directly between non-US$ currencies are called **cross-rates.** See Figure 6–1 for the cross-rate quotes on January 31, 1989.

Exchange Rates

Refer to Figure 6–2 and you will see that the price for one West German deutsche mark at the bottom of the list beside "W. Germany (Mark)" is .5321. This means that one DM costs US$ 0.5321. For a less expensive currency, look at the Japanese yen, which is quoted at .007671, meaning each yen costs that fraction of a dollar. Two currencies that cost more than US$1 on January 31, 1989, were the "Bahrain (Dinar)" at $2.6521 and the "Britain (Pound)" at $1.7515.

DM1.8790 = US$1.00

There is more to be learned from reading the exchange rates quotes. Using Figure 6–2, you will see the figure .5357 to the right of the "W. Germany (mark)" .5321 quote. Now look at the tops of the columns in which those numbers appear, and you will find the abbreviations, "Tues." and "Mon." As you probably have surmised, the .5321 quote is the price at the close of trading on Tuesday, January 31, 1989, while .5357 was the quote at the close of the previous trading day. Those two prices tell you the US$ strengthened a little vis-à-vis the German mark during Tuesday's trading; one DM costs US$.5321 at Tuesday's close, while it had cost fractionally more, US$.5357, at Monday's close.

There is another way of expressing the value relationships between currencies. Look again at the "W. Germany (Mark)" line in Figure 6–2, and move to the right of the number about which we spoke. There you find another "Tues." and another "Mon." column; the quote in the "Tues." column is 1.8740, while it is 1.8665 under "Mon." These quotes inform us how many German marks it took to buy one US$ at the close of trading on each of those days, and they are the mirror images of the two quotes to the left. Observe that about one more German pfennig was needed to buy one US$ after Tuesday's trading than was needed after Monday's trading; in other words, the DM had weakened a little vis-à-vis the US$.

spot rate the exchange rate between two currencies for delivery within two business days

Spot rates.   The **spot rate** is the exchange rate between two currencies for their immediate trade for delivery within two days. The rate on the same line as the name of the country is the spot rate. You will note in Figure 6–2 that the spot rate for German marks was .5321.

forward rate the exchange rate between two currencies for delivery in the future, commonly 30, 60, 90, or 180 days

Forward rates.   The **forward rate** is the cost today for a commitment by one party to deliver to or take from another party an agreed amount of a currency at a fixed, future date. The commitment is a forward contract, and for frequently traded currencies such contracts are usually available on a 30-, 60-, 90-, or 180-day basis. You may be able to negotiate with banks for different time periods or for contracts in other currencies.

Refer to the "W. Germany (Mark) 30-Day Forward" quotation in Figure 6–2, and you will see that it is .5335. Compare that with the spot rate of .5321, and you can see that it would cost more in US$s to buy DMs for delivery in 30 days than for delivery today. Looking at the 90- and 180-day quotes, you can see that the premium grows larger. This means that traders in the forward markets believe the German mark will strengthen in US$ terms for at least six months. The DM is said to be **trading at a premium** in the forward

trading at a premium when a currency's forward rate quotes are stronger than spot

■ FIGURE 6-2   Exchange Rates (Tuesday, January 31, 1989)

The New York foreign exchange selling rates below apply to trading among banks in amounts of $1 million and more, as quoted at 3 P.M. Eastern time by Bankers Trust Co. Retail transactions provide fewer units of foreign currency per dollar.

Country (currency)	US$ Equivalent Tues.	Mon.	Currency per US$ Tues.	Mon.	Country (currency)	US$ Equivalent Tues.	Mon.	Currency per US$ Tues.	Mon.
Argentina (austral)	.058173	.058173	17.19	17.19	Lebanon (pound)	.001897	.001897	527.00	527.00
Australia (dollar)	.8887	.8805	1.1252	1.1357	Malaysia (ringgit)	.36650	.36589	2.7285	2.7330
Austria (schilling)	.07566	.07616	13.21	13.13	Malta (lira)	2.9455	2.9455	.3395	.3395
Bahrain (dinar)	2.6521	2.6521	.37705	.37705	Mexico (peso)				
Belgium (Franc)					Floating rate	.0004347	.0004347	2300.00	2300.00
Commercial rate	.02540	.02558	39.35	39.08	Netherland (guilder)	.4715	.4743	2.1208	2.1080
Financial rate	.02530	.02546	39.52	39.27	New Zealand (dollar)	.6025	.6055	1.6597	1.6515
Brazil (cruzado)	1.0101	1.0101	.99000	.99000	Norway (krone)	.1478	.1484	6.7635	6.7365
Britain (pound)	1.7515	1.7575	.5709	.5689	Pakistan (rupee)	.05277	.05277	18.95	18.95
30-day forward	1.7464	1.7525	.5726	.5706	Peru (inti)	.0005903	.0005903	1694.00	1694.00
90-day forward	1.7367	1.7426	.5758	.5738	Phillippines (peso)	.048520	.048520	20.61	20.61
180-day forward	1.7253	1.7313	.5796	.5776	Portugal (escudo)	.006558	.006558	152.47	152.47
Canada (dollar)	.8442	.8463	1.1845	1.1815	Saudi Arabia (riyal)	.2667	.2667	3.7495	3.7495
30-day forward	.8430	.8453	1.1861	1.1830	Singapore (dollar)	.5175	.5170	1.9320	1.9340
90-day forward	.8403	.8425	1.1900	1.1869	South Africa (rand)				
180-day forward	.8363	.8385	1.1957	1.1925	Commercial rate	.4157	.4157	2.4055	2.4055
Chile (official rate)	.0040816	.0040816	245.00	245.00	Financial rate	.2551	.2551	3.9200	3.9200
China (yuan)	.268672	.268672	3.7220	3.7220	South Korea (won)	.0014705	.0014705	680.00	680.00
Colombia (peso)	.002915	.002915	343.00	343.00	Spain (peseta)	.0085506	.008643	116.95	115.70
Denmark (krone)	.1370	.1379	7.2990	7.2475	Sweden (krona)	.1572	.1577	6.3585	6.3390
Ecuador (sucre)					Switzerland (franc)	.6250	.6299	1.6000	1.5875
Floating rate	.0018587	.0018587	538.00	538.00	30-day forward	.6267	.6317	1.5956	1.5830
Finland (markka)	.2314	.2324	4.3205	4.3015	90-day forward	.6302	.6354	1.5866	1.5736
France (franc)	.1565	.1576	6.3875	6.3445	180-day forward	.6358	.6412	1.5726	1.5594
30-day forward	.1566	.1576	6.3855	6.3420	Taiwan (dollar)	.03616	.03616	27.65	27.65
90-day forward	.1566	.1578	6.3820	6.3365	Thailand (baht)	.039385	.039385	25.39	25.39
180-day forward	.1568	.1580	6.3740	6.3270	Turkey (lira)	.0005390	.0005390	1855.00	1855.00
Greece (drachma)	.006451	.006410	155.00	156.00	United Arab (dirham)	.2722	.2722	3.6725	3.6725
Hong Kong (dollar)	.128246	.128205	7.7975	7.8000	Uruguay (new peso)				
India (rupee)	.0659630	.0659630	15.16	15.16	Financial	.002150	.002150	465.00	465.00
Indonesia (rupiah)	.0005783	.005783	1729.00	1729.00	Venezuela (bolivar)				
Ireland (punt)	1.4316	1.4316	.6985	.6985	Floating rate	.02610	.02610	38.30	38.30
Israel (shekel)	.5503	.5503	1.8170	1.8170	W. Germany (mark)	.5321	.5357	1.8740	1.8665
Italy (lira)	.0007293	.0007331	1371.00	1364.00	30-day forward	.5335	.5372	1.8743	1.8615
Japan (yen)	.007671	.007704	130.35	129.80	90-day forward	.5363	.5401	1.8646	1.8514
30-day forward	.007701	.007733	129.85	129.30	180-day forward	.5404	.5444	1.8503	1.8366
90-day forward	.007761	.007794	128.84	128.29					
180-day forward	.007852	.007886	127.34	126.80	SDR*	1.31093	1.30880	0.762820	0.764061
Jordan (dinar)	2.0781	2.0781	.4812	.4812	ECU†	1.12004	1.11725	....	....
Kuwait (dinar)	3.4762	3.4762	.2876	.2876					

*Special drawing rights (SDR) are based on exchange rates for the U.S., West German, British, French, and Japanese currencies. Source: International Monetary Fund.
†European Currency Unit (ECU) is based on a basket of community currencies. Source: European Community Commission.
Source: *The Wall Street Journal*, February 1, 1989

trading at a discount when a currency's forward rate quotes are weaker than spot

market. If the forward DM quotations were lower than spot, they would be said to be **trading at a discount.**

So Many Yen, So Few Pounds

Look again at Figure 6–2, and you will see that it took about 130 yen to buy 1 US$, whereas less than 1 pound was enough for a dollar. Glancing up and down the column, you find that an Indonesian rupiah holder would need 1.729 rupiahs for US$1 and that a different number is required by holders of each of the other currencies quoted. It might seem that the fewer units of a currency required to buy a dollar, the harder or "better" that currency is compared to the others, but that is not necessarily correct.

As we have seen, the currencies of the world's major countries were set in value relative to the US$ at the end of World War II. Those exchange rates were the rates in the markets at that time; they were historical accidents. Since then, and particularly since 1973, the relative values of currencies, their convertibility, their hardness or softness, have been set by the supply and demand volumes of the foreign exchange markets. Those volumes are influenced by the policies of the various governments—their monetary and fiscal policies, their trade policies, and so on. Thus, the number of units of a currency per US$ on any given day does not indicate the relative strength of that currency. Many other factors must be examined to determine that.

The cost of a forward contract is the premium or discount required over the spot rate. Whether there is a premium or a discount and its size depend on the expectations of the world financial community, businesses, individuals, and governments about what the future will bring. These expectations factor in such considerations as supply and demand forecasts for the two currencies, relative inflation in the two countries, relative productivity and unit labor cost changes, expected election results or other political developments, and expected government fiscal, monetary, and currency exchange market actions.

Bid and asked prices.   When travelers or businesses contact a bank or an exchange agency to buy or sell a currency, they find a bid price and an asked price. The bid is the lower. The quotation for the French franc may be .16 bid and .17 asked. If the customer has francs to sell, the bank or agency is bidding—offering—16 cents (U.S. pennies) for each franc. If the customer wants to buy francs, the bank or agency is asking 17 cents, a higher price. The difference provides a margin—profit—for the bank or agency.

Commercial and financial rates.   In Figure 6–2, you will note two spot reports for Belgium and South Africa. They give commercial and financial rates. The commercial rate is for import/export transactions, and the financial rate is for all other transactions.

Fluctuating Exchange Rates Create Risk

When your activities involve more than one country, you must deal with more than one currency. For example, an American company exporting to France will, in most cases, want to receive US$s. If credit is involved, so that payment is not made when the goods are delivered, one of the parties will have a currency exchange risk. If the French importer agrees to pay French francs, then the American exporter bears a risk that the value of the French franc will fall and thus the French francs will buy fewer US$s when received than they would have at the earlier goods delivery date. On the other hand, if the French importer agrees to pay in US$ at a future time, then the importer bears that risk. (See Figure 6–3.)

The company financial manager is not without weapons for dealing with this type of risk. These are presented in Chapter 18. A greater potential hazard for the company is that a country in which the company has assets may institute exchange controls.

■ **FIGURE 6–3**
Currency Exchange Risk

February 1	Goods delivery date exchange rate	August 1	Payment date exchange rate
Suppose:	US$1 = Ff6		US$1 = Ff6
	Whichever party bore the currency exchange risk, neither gained nor lost.		
Suppose:	US$1 = Ff6		US$1 = Ff7
	Whichever party bore the currency exchange risk lost. It now requires Ff7 to buy the US$1, which could have been bought for Ff6 at the time the goods were delivered.		
Suppose:	US$1 = Ff6		US$1 = Ff5
	Whichever party bore the currency exchange risk gained. It now requires only Ff5 to buy the US$1, which would have cost Ff6 at the time the goods were delivered.		

CURRENCY EXCHANGE CONTROLS

currency exchange controls government controls that limit the legal uses of a currency in international transactions

Currency exchange controls limit or prohibit the legal use of a currency in international transactions. Typically, the value of the currency is arbitrarily fixed at a rate higher than its value in the free market, and it is decreed that all purchases or sales of other currencies be made through a government agency. A black market inevitably springs up, but it is of little use to the finance manager, who usually wants to avoid breaking the laws of a country in which the company is operating. In addition, the black market is rarely able to accommodate transactions of the size involved in a multinational business.

Thus, the company, along with all other holders of the controlled or blocked currency, must pay more than the free market rate if permission to buy foreign currency is granted by the government. If permission is not granted or if the cost of foreign currency is uneconomically high, the blocked currency can be used only within the country. This usually presents problems of finding suitable products to buy or investments to make within the country.

People will go to remarkable extremes to get blocked money out of exchange-controlled countries. A few years ago, in the west of France, an employee of a company operating in France strapped on a big money belt packed with large-denomination French franc bank notes. He then put on hang glider wings and glided into Switzerland, where he bought Swiss francs and deposited them in a Swiss bank account.

In New Delhi, the local manager of a major international airline gave a case of Scotch to a government official. Shortly thereafter, the agency for which that official worked granted the airline permission to use blocked rupees to buy almost US$20 million and transfer them to the airline's home country.

Those were extreme methods of converting blocked currencies to convertible currencies; the methods were, of course, also illegal. The great majority of finance managers do not resort to such methods, but they can take legal steps to protect the firm from the adverse effects of currency exchange controls. Those steps are considered in Chapter 18.

Table 6–1 shows the currency exchange control laws and regulations of several countries.* You can see that the controls differ greatly from country to

* The information in Table 6–1 comes from *Business International Money Report,* July 25, 1988, pp. 246–51. Many more countries are covered in that publication; we have presented only a few to give you an idea of the types of controls and how countries differ.

Country (Currency)	Regulatory Environment	Borrowing from Abroad	Incoming Direct Investment	Incoming Portfolio Investment
Argentina (austral, A)	Two FX* tiers since October; official rate for trade and foreign loans; free market rate for other transactions.	Terms must be fixed in advance, with minimum of 1 year.	Amounts under $5 million and equity injections under 30% of firm's capital freely permitted.	Freely permitted for listed shares of amounts under $2 million.
Chile (peso, $)	Ongoing liberalization; official FX rate set by Banco Central used for most transactions.	Registration and approval of loan required.	Investments over $5 million or in certain sectors require approval.	Freely permitted
China (renminbi, RmB)	Severe FX shortage; new foreign exchange centers offer minimal volume and high premiums.	A few local entities may borrow abroad, subject to restrictions.	Time-consuming approval process; minimum foreign equity, 25%.	No markets exist.
Egypt (pound, £E)	All transactions are at the free market rate, except basic commodity imports, traditional exports (e.g., cotton), and oil company transactions. These are at a rate of E0.7:US$1.	Permitted for new projects if within approved financing plan and for ongoing projects if they generate FX to service the debt.	Approval required; freely given in sectors needing foreign expertise or capital.	Approval required; foreign ownership limited in banking, insurance; priority given to export-oriented and import-substitution projects.
France (franc, F)	In the process of eliminating remaining controls.	Freely permitted	Freely permitted, but advance notification required so authorities can check source of funds.	Regulations gradually being relaxed.
Germany (deutsche mark, DM)	Extremely liberal	Freely permitted	No approval needed; stringent antitrust laws should be considered.	Freely permitted
Hong Kong (dollar, $)	All controls abolished in December 1972.	Freely permitted	Freely permitted; local business-registration procedures must be followed.	Freely permitted
India (rupee, Rs)	Strict controls; managed FX rate; parallel market exists, at 15–20% premium.	Approval required; borrowing usually limited to capital investments.	Approval required; maximum foreign equity; 40% in most cases.	Limited to authorized mutual funds.
Japan (yen, ¥)	Liberalization continuing; controls persist in certain areas (e.g., netting).	Freely permitted; must be reported to Ministry of Finance.	3 months' prior notice required.	Notification usually required.
Nigeria (naira, N)	Highly controlled; two different exchange rates—interbank rate and FEM rate. FEM rate determined at fortnightly auctions.	Subject to Finance Ministry approval.	Approval needed from Finance Ministry and Ministry of Internal Affairs; limits on foreign equity vary, 100% ownership not allowed.	Finance Ministry approval required.
Saudi Arabia (riyal, Sr)	No restrictions are placed on the inward or outward movement of funds.	Freely permitted	Freely permitted	Freely permitted
Switzerland (franc, SwF)	Controls usually avoided, but government has applied restrictions in the past.	Freely permitted	Freely permitted, except for a few public services.	Freely permitted for registered shares.
United Kingdom (pound sterling, £)	All controls have been removed.	Freely permitted	Freely permitted, although takeovers scrutinized by Department of Trade.	Freely permitted
United States (dollar, $)	Virtually no controls.	Freely permitted	Freely permitted in most sectors; some states have their own restrictions.	Freely permitted in most sectors.

*FX = Foreign exchange; †CB = National central bank; ‡FEM = Foreign Exchange Market.

Source: *Business International Money Report*, July 25, 1988. This table includes only a partial listing. For a more comprehensive list of countries and restrictions, see the *Business International Money Report*.

country and even within a country, depending on the type of transaction. As a generality, only the relatively rich industrialized countries have few or no currency exchange controls. They are a minority of the world's countries, and thus the great majority of the countries do impose exchange controls. The international businessperson must carefully study those laws and regulations both before and while doing business in any country. Even the industrialized countries may have some restrictions.

Remittance of Dividends and Profits	Remittance of Interest and Principal	Remittance of Royalties and Fees	Repatriation of Capital	Documentation for Remittances
Freely permitted at free market rate; heavy taxes on excess over 12% of capital base.	Freely permitted at commercial rate for approved loans.	Freely permitted at free market rate; fees must reflect market value.	Fully remittable 3 years after initial investment at free rate.	Authorization forms must be filed with the CB.†
Freely permitted	Freely permitted for registered loans.	Freely permitted for approved contracts.	Freely permitted for full amount after 3 years.	Requests must be filed with the CB.
FX income and expense must be balanced before remitting.	FX income and expense must be balanced before remitting.	Limited to 4% and 10-year period; low FX priority for fees.	Freely permitted, but FX shortage makes conversion difficult.	Onerous and complex requirements.
Approval required; 20% reserve required; firms without FX to cover remittance must apply to banks for FX allocation.	Freely permitted if the project generates sufficient FX to cover payment; if not, approval required.	Freely permitted if the project generates FX for payment; if not, approval required.	Allowed after 5 years, to be remitted in 5 equal annual payments; exceptions sometimes made.	Accountant's certificate of source of funds and proof of tax payment required.
No restrictions if minimum capital and reserve requirements met.	No restrictions on bonds or loans; prepayment requires approval.	No restrictions, but the CB requires the account number.	Freely permitted, if repatriated within 3 months of liquidation.	Notification needed; local bank must run transaction.
Freely permitted	Freely permitted	Freely permitted	Freely permitted	Notification required for statistical purposes.
Freely permitted	Freely permitted	Freely permitted	Freely permitted	No official requirements
Approval required; no ceiling on amount.	Freely permitted for approved loans.	Approval required; generally restricted to 4% of sales.	Approval required; amounts may be limited.	Onerous; FX must be obtained from authorized banks.
Freely permitted	Freely permitted for approved loans.	Freely permitted for approved contracts; tax authorities monitor rate changes.	Freely permitted	Handled by FX banks; mainly for reporting purposes.
Finance Ministry approval required; frequent delays. No ceilings if paid out of current-year after-tax profits.	Finance Ministry approval required.	Finance Ministry approval required; royalties limited to 1% of sales, fees to 2% of pretax profits.	Finance Ministry approval required, followed by authorized FX dealer's approval.	Onerous and complex requirements; transfers via authorized dealers only.
Freely permitted	Freely permitted	Freely permitted	Freely permitted	No official requirements
No restrictions, except for reserve requirements.	Freely permitted	Freely permitted	Freely permitted	Only that needed for ordinary bank transactions.
Freely permitted	Freely permitted	Freely permitted	Freely permitted	No official requirements
Freely permitted	Freely permitted	Freely permitted	Freely permitted	Foreign bank transaction records must be kept for 5 years.

BALANCE OF PAYMENTS

Balance of payments (BOP) was discussed in some detail in Chapter 5, but we would be remiss not to mention it as a major financial force. The state of a nation's BOP will tell observant management much of value. If the BOP is slipping into deficit, the government is probably considering one or more market or nonmarket measures to correct or suppress that deficit. Management should be alert for either currency devaluation or restrictive monetary or fiscal policies to induce deflation. Another possibility is that currency or trade controls may be coming. With foresight, the firm's management can adjust to the changing government policies or at least soften their impact.

On the export side, the company may start shopping for **export incentives—** government incentives to make its exports easier or more profitable. Lower-cost capital may be available if the company can demonstrate that exports will be boosted.

One of the most common export incentives is the financing of exports by a government agency that offers foreign buyers lower interest rates than they could get from other money sources. Sometimes the agency's loans are accompanied by an aid grant, which need not be repaid.

Countries that levy value-added taxes (see Chapter 11) are permitted by GATT rules to rebate them to exporters. This makes the exports less expensive and thus more competitive.

When firms are engaged in tough competition for major export contracts, their home governments may intervene to assist. Often, the potential customer is a government agency, and the intervention may be contact with the customer's decision makers by their counterparts in the home government.

> **export incentives** tax breaks, lower-cost financing, foreign aid, or other advantages that governments give to encourage businesses to export and foreign customers to buy goods and services

TARIFFS OR DUTIES

The words *tariffs* and *duties* are used interchangeably. These can be high or low, and it is of great importance to business to minimize them. They are discussed in the "Trade Restrictions" section of Chapter 3 and as one of the legal forces in Chapter 10, but they can certainly be classified as financial forces and therefore should be mentioned in this chapter.

The European Community (EC) and the other groupings of nations that we discussed in Chapter 4 have lowered or abolished tariffs on trade among member-countries. EC Project 1992 is an attempt to strip away all barriers to people, services, goods, and capital between the 12 member-countries. Such developments add new dimensions to the decision-making processes of companies located outside the groupings. For example, would the expenses and legal and personnel problems involved in establishing operations within a grouping be justified by tariff savings?

TAXATION

Inasmuch as most international business is conducted by corporations, we are concerned with tariffs paid by and taxes levied on corporations. The point may be made that corporations don't pay taxes; they only collect them. In the end, people pay taxes.[1] The taxes may be collected from customers in higher prices, from employees in lower wages, from stockholders in lower dividends or capital gains, or from suppliers in smaller orders. However, even though corporations act as tax collectors rather than bearing the ultimate burden, it is very much in their best interest to minimize taxes. If a corporation can achieve a lower tax burden than its competitors, it can lower prices to its customers or make higher profits with which to pay higher wages and dividends. The price

■ **FIGURE 6–4   Tax Revenues as Percent of GDP**

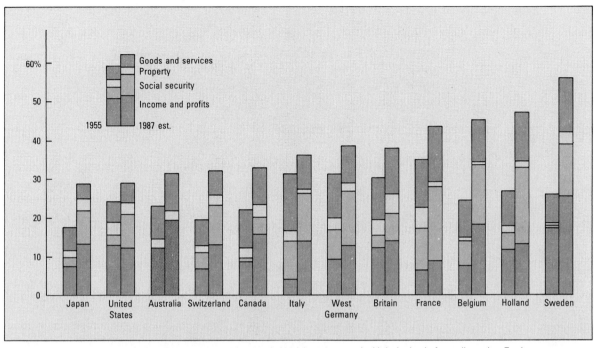

Over the past 30 years the role of the state has increased in every industrial country—and with it the level of overall taxation. Total tax revenues have gone up in America from 24% of GDP in 1955 to 29% of GDP in 1987; in Japan, from 17% to 29%; and in Britain, from 30% to 38%. Of the countries in the chart, Sweden has seen the biggest rise; its total tax revenues climbed from 26% of GDP in 1955 to 56% last year. The composition of taxation has changed too. In most countries, social security taxes have grown fastest. In America these took 3% of GDP in 1955, rising to 9% in 1987. Sweden's social security taxes have expanded from ½% of GDP to 13%. Generally, taxes on incomes and profits have risen by less. In America they have actually fallen, from 12½% of GDP in 1955 to 12% last year. Source: OECD.
Source: *The Economist*, October 8, 1988, p. 103.

of its stock tends to rise, and it can be a better customer for the components and raw materials it buys from others.

All of this is true for all corporations, but the multinational has more taxes—more countries—to consider, and therefore more risks. It also has more opportunities to save taxes.

Different Taxes in Different Countries

As you can see from Figure 6–4, tax rates and composition differ from country to country. They have also changed over time within each country.

Taxes rising as a percent of GDP. *   Also demonstrated in Figure 6–4 is the increasing role of the state in every industrial country over the past 30 years. Total tax revenues have gone up in America from 24 percent of GDP in 1955 to 29 percent in 1987; in Japan, from 17 percent to 29 percent; and in Britain, from 30 percent to 38 percent. Sweden has seen the biggest rise.

---

*   The GDP (gross domestic product) of a country is the gross national product minus net property invisible payments, such as dividends, interest, and royalty, paid to and received from other countries.

In Chapter 18, we shall see how financial managers can sometimes use different tax regimes and other measures to lower their taxes legitimately. Chapter 10 deals with taxes as legal forces.

The amount of taxes paid is affected by inflation. At one time, some thought that inflation was a problem limited to the LDCs and that the industrialized countries need not worry about it. Recent experience has shown how erroneous that view was, and so we shall examine inflation.

INFLATION

The phenomenon of increasing prices for almost everything over a period of time is familiar. Contagious inflation was probably the major cause of the end of the unprecedented world economic boom that lasted from the end of World War II until 1973. As prices of internationally traded goods rose due to a combination of rising demand and increased money supplies in all the DCs, inflation fever spread from one DC to the others.[2]

Inflation's Effects on Interest Rates

Inflation is clearly a financial force from outside the company but one with which finance managers must deal as best they can. As one indication of the effect of inflation on the cost of money raised by the company, see Table 6–2. Germany and Japan have the lowest inflation and interest rates, and the countries with higher inflation bear higher interest costs.

Monetary and Fiscal Policies Affect Inflation

Nations may conduct their monetary policies and fiscal policies in ways that cause inflation or cut it. *Monetary policy* is the control of the amount of money in circulation, whether it is growing and, if so, at what pace. *Fiscal policies* address the collecting and spending of money by governments. What kinds of taxes at what rates? On what and in what amounts does the government spend money?

Since World War II, several countries have been able to stop inflation and in some instances to keep it down. Policies that were adopted in 1948 in West Germany, in 1953 in the United States, and in 1958 in France succeeded in halting inflation. Those policies had two common denominators: (1) they removed artificial economic controls, such as wage and price controls, and (2) they applied fiscal and monetary restraint. The restraint included lower taxes and slower growth in the nation's money supply.[3]

Britain since 1979 and the United States since 1980 are two more recent examples of countries that have succeeded in lowering their inflation rates from around 20 percent per year to the 3–4 percent range. At the other extreme, many believe the infamous hyperinflation of the German mark in 1923 is the world's record. It is not. That dubious distinction belongs to the Hungarian pengo; inflation in Hungary in 1946 was a thousand times worse than the earlier German inflation. In 1939, one US$ bought 3.38 Hungarian pengos; in July 1946, the same dollar was worth

■ TABLE 6-2
1986 Inflation and
Interest Rates

	Inflation Rate	Prime Interest Rate	
		1986	1987
Canada (C$)	4.2%	9.75%	9.75%
France (Ff)	3.7	9.50	9.50
West Germany (DM)	1.0	3.50	2.50
Japan (¥)	1.2	3.00	2.50
United Kingdom (£)	4.0	11.00	8.50
United States (US$)	4.5	7.50	8.75

Source: OECD Main Economic Indicators, December 1988.

500,000,000,000,000,000,000 (500 million trillion) pengos. Never before or since has so much official money been worth so little.

Most Latin American countries have inflation troubles, although not as drastic as the Hungarian example. Two of the worst cases are Peru, where the 1988 inflation rate exceeded 1,700 percent,[4] and Brazil, where Brazilians over age 30 have seen their money's face value divided by a billion since they started spending it.[5]

Two Latin American countries have taken the tough fiscal and monetary steps needed to reduce inflation dramatically. In Bolivia, inflation ran at around 20,000 percent in 1985 but was cut to 11 percent in 1987 and 1988.[6] Chile succeeded in bringing its inflation rate from some 1,000 percent to 10 percent in 1987.[7]

Importance of Inflation to Business

Even within a single country, inflation is of concern to management. Should it raise capital at all and, if so, should this be done through equity or debt? High inflation rates encourage borrowing because the loan will be repaid with cheaper money. But high inflation rates bring high interest rates (see Tables 6-2 and 6-3) or may discourage lending. Potential lenders may fear that even with high interest rates, the amount repaid plus interest will be worth less than the amount lent. Instead of lending, the money holder may buy something that is expected to increase in value.

Lenders have begun to use variable interest rates, which rise or fall with inflation to shift the risk to the borrower. Of course, that risk requires the borrower to be much more careful about borrowing. The original rate and any future changes are based on a reference interest rate, such as the U.S. prime rate or the London Interbank Offer Rate (LIBOR).

High inflation rates make capital expenditure planning more difficult. Management may allocate $1 million for a plant and be forced to pay much more to complete construction.

Inflation and the multinational.   All of this also applies to international business, with the complication that inflation rates differ in different countries. For this reason, management of a multinational must try to forecast the rates for each of the countries in which the company is active. The comparative inflation rates will affect the comparative currency values as the currencies of high-inflation countries weaken vis-à-vis the currencies of the countries whose

Coping with treble-digit inflation

inflation rates are lower. Management will try to minimize holdings of the weaker currencies.

Higher inflation rates cause the prices of the goods and services produced or offered by a country to rise, and thus the goods and services become less competitive. The company's affiliate in that country finds it more difficult to sell its products in export, as do all other producers there. Such conditions tend to cause balance-of-payments (BOP) deficits, and management must be alert to changes in government policy to correct the deficit. Such changes could include more restrictive fiscal or monetary policies, currency controls, export incentives, and import obstacles.

Relative inflation rates affect where the multinational raises and invests capital. Interest rates tend to be higher where inflation is higher, and high inflation discourages new investment for all of the reasons we have seen.

Nominal and real interest rates.   Another important consideration for business, whether borrowing or lending, is the real rate of interest, and the inflation rate is one element in its computation. The nominal interest rate is the rate charged by the lender or the rate that a bond issue carries. From the nominal rate is subtracted the inflation rate, and the result is the real rate. When a lender charges, for example, 10 percent interest on a one-year loan and the inflation rate is 5 percent, the real rate of return for the lender is 5 percent, because the money is worth 5 percent less when it is repaid than it was worth when it was lent.

When money is lent for longer periods of time (5, 10, or 20 years), the lenders and borrowers must forecast—guess—what inflation will do over those longer periods. The longer the time, the more difficult the forecast, but the point here is that it is not only today's inflation rate that matters; it is also the lenders' and borrowers' forecasts that govern interest rates on loans or even whether loans will be made.

Table 6–3 illustrates computations of real interest rates for the US$ from

■ **TABLE 6–3**
Dollar Interest Rates and Inflation

	Three-Month Eurodollar Rate	U.S. Inflation	Real Interest Rate
1970	8.5%	5.9%	2.6%
1971	6.6	4.3	2.3
1972	5.4	3.3	2.1
1973	9.3	6.2	3.1
1974	11.0	11.0	0
1975	7.0	9.1	−2.1
1976	5.6	5.8	−0.2
1977	6.0	6.5	−0.5
1978	8.8	7.6	1.2
1979	12.0	11.3	0.9
1980	14.0	13.5	0.5
1981	16.8	10.4	6.4
1982	12.2	6.2	6.0
1983	9.6	3.2	6.4
1984	10.4	4.3	6.1
1985	8.1	3.5	4.6
1986	6.5	1.9	4.6
1987	6.9	3.7	3.2

Source: *Barclays Review,* 1984, 1987, and 1988.

■ **TABLE 6–4**
Real Interest Rates

	June 1985	January 1986	March 1986	July 1986	April 1987
United States	3.7%	3.9%	4.9%	4.8%	3.7%
Japan	3.6	5.4	4.5	4.2	5.0
West Germany	3.4	3.4	4.4	5.1	3.8
France	3.8	4.6	5.5	5.1	4.8
United Kingdom	5.5	7.3	7.5	7.2	5.4

Note: Three-month rates deflated by the annual change in consumer prices.
Source: *Barclays Review,* 1986, 1987, and 1988.

1970 through 1987. The "Three-Month Eurodollar Rate" is the nominal interest rate charged. The next column shows the inflation rate in the United States for the year, and subtracting that rate from the nominal rate, the table arrives at the real rate shown in the third column.

You will note that lenders lost money in the real interest rate sense in 1975, 1976, and 1977, when the real rate was negative. Another phenomenon to observe is the high real rate that began in 1981; even though U.S. inflation came down from its 1980 high, nominal interest rates went up. They came down in 1982 and 1983, but not enough to bring real rates below 6 percent, which historically is quite high. Probably the main reason for this is that lenders do not believe inflation will be kept in check; they are protecting themselves against higher future inflation, which they forecast.

Table 6–4 shows real interest rates in the five largest economies in 1985, 1986, and 1987. They have remained higher than they were in the 1970s and until 1981.

ACCOUNTING PRACTICES

Accounting practices vary widely from country to country and are financial forces with which multinational management must deal. Management must be prepared to use host country practices for subsidiaries operating in those countries. These results must then be translated into home country practices in order to be understood by home country investors, creditors, and government regulators. Accounting practices are financial forces, which is the reason for inclusion of the topic here. In Chapter 18, we shall examine some of management's solutions.

COUNTRIES WENT BUST

During the 1970s' lending binge by banks to developing countries (LDCs), the chairman of a major bank was quoted as saying, "Countries don't go bust." He was proved wrong, and a new and ominous financial force is now acting on international business. Contrary to many expectations, a number of developing countries found themselves unable to pay even the interest, much less the principal, on their debts. The sovereign debt crisis for Poland occurred in 1981; for Mexico, Brazil, Argentina, and others, it occurred in 1982 and thereafter.

We examined this matter in Chapter 4 from the point of view of the International Monetary Fund (IMF) and the Bank for International Settlements (BIS) because the IMF has been thrust into, and has taken the lead role in, trying to resolve these crises as they continue to arise, and the BIS has made bridge loans while the IMF was preparing to act.

Because these crises are so important and constitute a present and growing force on international business, we shall discuss some of the background in this chapter. Also, we can suggest some possible solutions.

Causes of Increasing LDC Indebtedness

The immediate causes of the growing debts were the jumps in oil prices (crude oil represents an average of 16 percent of the merchandise imports of the nonoil LDCs). In 1973–74, oil prices quadrupled; they then doubled in 1979–80, and that increase from a higher base represented an even larger increase in absolute terms than the 1973–74 rise.

Then, because the increased oil prices and their inflationary consequences led to a fall in economic activity in the developed world, another critical element of economic injury to the LDCs was a subsequent drop in the prices of primary nonoil commodities, which account for 45 percent of LDC (excluding Mexico and OPEC LDCs) exports. Mexico and the OPEC LDCs were hurt by the drops in oil prices beginning in 1981 as well as by uneconomic uses of the oil revenue and borrowed moneys they received during the 1970s and in the early 1980s.

Third, after the 1979–80 oil price jump, interest rates increased. That increase affected all new loans and the many existing loans that carried variable rather than fixed interest rates. Every 1 percent increase in US$

interest rates costs the LDCs some $2.5 billion per year more in interest payments.

Fourth, the US$ began to strengthen in value in the foreign exchange markets during 1980. It continued up into 1985 and gained over 80 percent on a trade-weighted basis by March 1985. LDCs borrow mainly in dollars but export in many currencies, so the rise in the value of the US$ created new burdens; they must earn that much more in deutsche marks, yen, francs, and so on to pay the US$ debts.

The US$ peaked in value in terms of the yen and West European currencies in February 1985. At that time, it began to move down in terms of those currencies, and by January 1988, it had fallen some 45 percent in terms of the yen and the deutsche mark and 30 percent against the British pound. However, the US$ weakened little or even continued to gain in exchange for currencies of Canada, Asian newly industrializing countries, and Mexico and other Latin American countries, all of which are important trading partners of the United States.

Debt Problem Solutions

The IMF, the BIS, national central banks, and commercial banks have been scrambling for solutions.

Short-term solutions.   The short-term answers have been rescheduling of debts that the debtor country was unable to pay as they came due. Table 6–5 shows the growth of the rescheduling process since 1983. But renegotiations are becoming more and more difficult. The BIS, the commercial banks, and the central banks are reluctant to come up with more money, and the IMF's resources are finite.

The debtor countries are balking at the stringent austerity programs being insisted on by the IMF. The LDCs' economic growth has halted as new money they receive from exports or loans must be used to repay debt rather than for productive investments. Social unrest, including rioting, has broken out in several countries, notably Venezuela, Argentina, and Brazil.

The debtor countries are in desperate straits, but the industrialized countries are also being damaged. As the debtor countries use money to repay debts, they do not buy goods and services from the developed countries. As a result, the developed countries have lost billions of dollars of export business and thousands of jobs.

The LDC debtor countries can reduce their debts only by exporting more than they import and thus running BOP surpluses. Some of the LDC debtor countries have been able to run BOP surpluses and make debt payments. However, these surpluses have been achieved as much by cutting imports as by expanding exports, and that has slowed or stopped economic development in the debtor countries and also hurt exports from countries that had been suppliers before the imports were curtailed.

Most of the LDC debtor countries have needed more money from private banks and international agencies and have been lent more. This has caused the debt burdens of these countries to increase at the same time that their economic development has been retarded, a process that cannot be sustained.

■ **TABLE 6-5**
Reschedulings of Latin American Countries' Debt from 1983 through 1988

Year	Billions of US$s*
1983	$ 36,676
1984	9,674
1985	66,891
1986	41,112
1987	122,292
1988	73,289

*Includes both commercial banks and official creditors.
Source: Barclays Group Economics Department estimates. Countries involved were Argentina, Bolivia, Brazil, Chile, Colombia, Ecuador, Mexico, Nicaragua, Panama, Peru, Uruguay, and Venezuela.

Longer-term solutions.   A number of cures have been suggested. We shall list a few.

1. Borrowing countries will have to pursue policies ensuring that new money they obtain is used for economic growth rather than for consumption, capital flight, or overambitious government schemes or armaments.

2. Borrowers should build up reserves in good years to enable them to withstand the fluctuations in commodity export prices that are inevitable even if no more oil price shocks occur.

3. The developed countries must strive for their own economic growth and open their markets to LDC exports even though that means competition with some DC industries.

4. The IMF and other creditors must not try to enforce too stringent austerity measures on debtors. Social unrest and trade contraction must be avoided or at least minimized.

5. The IMF, the World Bank, and other agencies that aid LDCs must be assured of sufficient funding so that they can take long-term views.

6. Parts of the huge LDC external debts must be changed in form to types of equity. These could be ownership interests in projects being developed or shares of export earnings. Other parts of the debts should be lengthened in maturity, with interest rate ceilings applied.

7. The LDCs must relax their restrictions on foreign investments and on repatriation of profits from existing investments. They must encourage new money from foreign private sources—nonbank sources—because the banks are now overcommitted with LDC loans and are not likely prospects for new, economic growth money.

8. Blame for the debt crises belongs to several parties. The LDCs borrowed more than they could productively invest, and much of the borrowed money was wasted at home or corruptly sent abroad for the personal accounts of political leaders. The lending banks were encouraged to lend by the governments of their countries because the governments were thus relieved to that extent of foreign aid demands by the LDCs. But the banks must also bear a share of the blame; they made limited inquiries regarding the uses of the borrowed money or the soundness of the projects in which the money would be invested. They failed to get collateral to secure the loans, and one reason they were so casual was that the loans were almost always to governments

or guaranteed by governments. One leading banker said, "Countries don't go bust"; he and his colleagues were proved wrong.

As a contribution to the solution of the debt crises, the banks should establish schedules to write down the loans on their books over a period of several years. Some European banks have already begun to sell off portions of these loans at discounts, and a market now exists for the discounted loans.

In May 1987, Citicorp added $3 billion to its loan loss reserves for foreign debt. Even though that caused a $2.5 billion second-quarter loss and a loss of $1 billion for the year, the move won positive reaction in U.S. financial markets. It was viewed as a realistic appraisal of the bank's chances of being repaid its loans to developing nations.

The Biggest "Debtor"? The United States

After 70 years as the world's leading creditor, the United States is now indebted to foreigners to the tune of some $600 billion and heading for a trillion by the early 1990s. This is deeply troubling for some, and unless the "debt" growth stops or reverses, there *will* be adverse effects for America. Before looking at some of those effects, we should define the "debt," see how it differs from the LDC debts, and put its growth into perspective with the growth rates of the other G7 countries.*

U.S. debt defined.   Conceptually, the U.S. foreign debt—what the Department of Commerce calls net negative international investment position—is the difference between the value of overseas assets owned by Americans and the value of United States assets owned by foreigners. These assets consist of commercial bank deposits, foreign exchange holdings, corporate securities, real estate, physical plant, and other direct investments. The value of all U.S. overseas assets at the end of 1986 was about $1.1 trillion, while the assets owned by non-Americans in the United States were valued at about $1.365 trillion. The difference between the two is the net U.S. foreign "debt" of some $265 billion. In 1982, there was a net "credit" of $171 billion.

Differences between U.S. and LDC debt.   First, over $300 billion of the U.S. foreign-owned assets are obligations of the U.S. Treasury or U.S. corporations that are traded daily in world financial markets. Their worth, unlike the face value of an LDC debt, is subject to constant change.

Second, U.S. foreign assets are often measured at book value, which results in an estimated undervaluation of up to $200 billion. Book value would be cost when bought, which may have been years ago, less depreciation. Inflation alone would result in prices much higher than book if the assets were sold today.

Third, U.S. assets abroad reportedly earn more in interest and dividend per dollar of investment than foreign holdings earn in America. Foreign-owned assets in the United States earned an estimated $67 billion in 1986, while the smaller U.S. balances abroad yielded $88 billion.

Fourth, although current U.S. net liabilities are immense in absolute terms, they are relatively small in terms of other economic indicators. Total U.S. debt

---

* G7 countries are Canada, France, Germany, Italy, Japan, the United Kingdom, and the United States.

in 1986 amounted to 6 percent of U.S. GNP—as compared to over 40 percent for Brazil, upward of 50 percent for Mexico, and over 60 percent for Venezuela. The annual service cost of the U.S. debt is less than 1 percent of U.S. exports of goods and services. The corresponding cost for the three developing countries mentioned above averages more than 32 percent.

Fifth, the most distinctive characteristic of the U.S. foreign debt is its denomination in US$s. In theory, at least, this implies that the United States could discharge its foreign obligations at any time by printing the needed number of US$s. The LDCs, whose debt is not denominated in their own currencies, do not have that power.

G7 debt growth.   During the 1973–87 period, the national debt growth rates of all G7 countries except the United Kingdom were faster than that of the United States. A legitimate complaint about using the 1973–87 period is that the American debt growth accelerated during the 1980s, when it more than doubled. But, even in the 1980–87 period, the debt growth rates of Canada, France, and Italy were faster than that of the United States; they were slower in Germany, Japan, and the United Kingdom. Thus the U.S. rate is about the same as the average for the other G7 countries.[8]

Adverse effects on America.   Having made the distinctions and comparisons, it cannot be denied that continuing growth of the U.S. net negative investment position will damage America. Financially, the interest cost of foreign debts is a drag on the balance of payments. Foreign creditors and suppliers may become reluctant to accept US$s. An increasing volume of world trade denominated in other currencies would cause losses for American companies and banks.

Politically, pressures could build up for protectionism, exchange controls, or restrictions on capital flows. A large debtor country could not remain a major reserve currency economic power for long, and America's power to affect world events would erode.

In sum, while the U.S. net foreign obligations may not create for the U.S. economy or policies the same problems that LDC debts present LDCs, these obligations are very real dangers for the American world position. It has been suggested that increasing the very low current rate of U.S. national savings would be an important step toward a solution. The U.S. savings rate is by far the lowest among the G7 countries.[9]

SUMMARY

The multinational's financial management must be aware of many financial forces that originate outside the company. Some of them, such as inflation, taxation, and fiscal and monetary policies of government, affect domestic as well as international business. But even for such forces, the concerns of the domestic manager are of a different magnitude than the concerns of the international manager because the domestic manager has to cope with only one country, whereas the international manager has to cope with two or more countries. The same may be said of accounting principles, which differ widely from country to country.

Fluctuating currency exchange rates, currency controls, and attendant risks are almost uniquely international problems. So are quotas and tariffs.

The balance of payments affects both domestic and international companies. It is, of course, related to inflation, taxation, fiscal and monetary policies, and such other factors as the competitiveness of a country's goods and services in the world markets.

The international debt crises have added new financial forces with which managers must cope. Many debtor countries must struggle to pay debts and thus have less money to pay for imports of goods or services. The

United States is now the world's biggest debtor, and although the U.S. and the LDC debt situations differ greatly and the growth of the U.S. debt is about average for the G7 countries, the U.S. debt will harm America if its growth is not reversed.

As suggested in the introduction, the financial manager is not without means for protecting and advancing the company. Those means are subjects of Chapter 18.

QUESTIONS

1. In an American financial paper, you see the quotation: "Norway (krone) . . . 1478." What does that mean?

2. On the same day, you see the quotation: "Norway (krone) . . . 6.7635." What does that mean?

3. In the world's currency-trading markets, why is the US$ the central currency through which almost all major trades go?

4. What is the difference between spot and forward currency markets?

5. What does it mean when a currency is said to be trading at a premium to the US$ in the forward market? Why would this happen?

6. If you agree to pay a certain amount of foreign currency to someone in six months, which of you bears the currency fluctuation risk? Explain.

7. What are currency controls? Why are they imposed?

8. What is the importance of the state of the BOP to private companies?

9. What are some ways in which inflation affects business decisions?

10. Have countries ever succeeded in stopping inflation? How?

11. What two other numbers must you know to compute real interest rates?

12. What is meant by currency translation?

13. To surmount the current debt crises, what are some things that must be done by (a) the LDCs, (b) the developed, creditor countries, and (c) the creditor banks?

14. What are some of the differences between the American and the LDCs' foreign debt situations?

15. Might the huge U.S. debt have adverse consequences for America? Explain.

MINICASE 6–1

Are the Socialists Coming?

You are the chief financial officer of Moulin S.A., a French manufacturing subsidiary of an American parent company. Moulin's product is sold in France and exported to countries within the EC, but the French market has received Moulin's major marketing attention.

The year is 1981, and the French presidential elections will be held in one month. One candidate is the incumbent, Giscard d'Estaing, heading a center/right coalition of political parties that has governed France since World War II. Everyone is familiar with the policies and personalities of

this coalition. Opposing it is a socialist/communist coalition headed by socialist François Mitterrand, and the opinion polls show Mitterrand's group holding a small lead.

Would you expect this situation to have any effect on the value of the French franc (Ff)? What effect? Why? If no effect, why not?

Would the situation cause you to recommend more or less emphasis on export marketing, or no change? Explain.

You have insisted on payment by your export customers in Ffs. Will you make any change in that policy? Explain.

MINICASE 6–2

Management Faces a BOP Deficit

You are the chief executive officer of a multinational's subsidiary in a developing host country. The sub has been in business for about eight years, making electric motors for the host country's domestic market with mediocre financial

results. Before you left the home country a month ago, you were told to make the sub profitable or to consider closing it.

After a month in the host country, you have discovered that it is running a worsening BOP deficit and that the government officials are very concerned about the situation. They are considering various measures to stanch or reverse the deficit flow.

What measures might be adopted? Can you think of some ways your company might profit from them, or at least minimize damage?

SUPPLEMENTARY READINGS

Bartlett, Bruce. "Supply Side Sparkplug." *Policy Review,* Summer 1986, pp. 42–47.

Bingham, T. R. G. "Financial Innovation and Monetary Policy." *OECD Observer,* January 1985, pp. 24–26.

Carbaugh, Robert J. *International Economics.* 2nd ed. Belmont, Calif.: Wadsworth Publishing, 1985.

Davidson, Paul. *International Money and the Real World.* New York: John Wiley & Sons, 1982.

DeSaint-Phalle, Thibaut. *Trade, Inflation and the Dollar.* New York: Oxford Univ. Press, 1981.

Emele, Bruno. "The Global Purchasing Power, Effects of Oil Price Changes." *Economic and Financial Prospects,* August–September 1986, pp. 1–4.

Ethier, Wilfred J. *Modern International Economics.* 2nd ed. New York: W. W. Norton, 1988.

Friedman, Milton, ed. *Studies in the Quantity Theory of Money.* Chicago: University of Chicago Press, 1956.

Harvey, Jack L. "Expected Growth in the Industrial Countries Revised Upward." (Federal Reserve Bank of Chicago) *International Letter,* June 1986.

Humphrey, Thomas N. *The Monetary Approach to the Balance of Payments, Exchange Rates and World Inflation.* New York: Praeger Publishers, 1982.

Kleitz, Anthony. "Tariff Preferences for the Developing Countries." *OECD Observer,* March 1983, pp. 38–41.

Krugman, Paul R., and Maurice Obstfeld. *International Economics.* Glenview, Ill.: Scott, Foresman, 1988.

Kvasnicka, Joseph G. "Restrictions on Imports: An Answer to U.S. Trade Problems?" (Federal Reserve Bank of Chicago) *International Letter,* April 1985.

Mayer, Martin. *The Fate of the Dollar.* New York: Times Books, 1980.

Michalski, Wolfgang; Henry Ergas; and Barrie Stevens. "Cost and Benefits of Protection." *OECD Observer,* May 1985, pp. 18–23.

Newman, Nigel. "Fiscal Expansion." *Barclays Review,* November 1985, pp. 69–80.

Ogi, Adolph. "World Free Trade in Danger." *Bulletin, Credit Suisse Magazine,* September 1985, pp. 14–16.

Owens, Jeffrey. "Tax Reform: Some European Ideas." *Europe,* September 1986, pp. 18–20.

Root, Franklin R. *International Trade and Investment.* 5th ed. Cincinnati: South-Western Publishing, 1984, chap. 5.

Salemi, Michael K. "The Efficiency of Forward Exchange Markets." *Economic and Financial Prospects,* August–September 1986, pp. 5–6.

Salvatore, Dominick. *International Economics.* 5th ed. New York: McGraw-Hill, 1984.

Tax News International, various issues, published by Ernst & Young.

Todd, Jonathan. "Battle Threatens over Tax on Multinationals." *Europe,* November–December 1983, pp. 22–23.

Winder, Robert. "Be Big and Bright." *Euromoney,* May 1986, pp. 184–202.

ENDNOTES

1. Discussed by Robert Z. Aliber, *The International Money Game,* 2nd. ed. (New York: Basic Books, 1976), pp. 189–90.

2. Samuel I. Katz, " 'Managed Floating' as an Interim International Exchange Rate Regime, 1973–1975," *New York University Bulletin,* 1975–3 (New York: Center for the Study of Financial Institutions, New York University, 1975), pp. 13–14.

3. Vermont Royster, "Thinking Things Over, 'A Thrice-Told Tale,' " *The Wall Street Journal,* May 10, 1978, p. 18.

4. Alan Riding, "Starting Over, the Ex-Peruvian Way," *The New York Times International,* January 21, 1989, p. 4.

5. "First, Divide by a Thousand," *The Economist,* January 21, 1989, p. 39.

6. "Bolivia Doing It by the Book," *The Economist,* May 28, 1988, pp. 74–75.

7. "Key Facts, Chile," *Financial Times,* September 28, 1988, sect. IV, p. Chile 2.

8. Mack Ott, "Growth Rates of National Debt in the G7, 1973–1987," October 1988 (Federal Reserve Bank of St. Louis), *International Economic Conditions,* p. 1.

9. Jahangir Amuzegar, "The U.S. External Debt in Perspective," *Finance & Development,* June 1988, pp. 18–19.

Chapter 7

Economic and Socioeconomic Forces

Profound thoughts about economic forecasting:

Forecasting is difficult, especially about the future.

Victor Borge

Economic forecasters have successfully predicted 14 of the last 5 recessions.

Anonymous

LEARNING OBJECTIVES

In this chapter, you will study:

1. The purpose of economic analyses.

2. The importance of monitoring interest rates in the firm's markets.

3. The limitations of GNP/capita as an economic indicator.

4. The importance of income distribution studies.

5. How a nation's consumption patterns change over time.

6. What factors cause changes in unit labor costs expressed in dollars.

7. The significance for businesspeople of the large foreign debts of some nations.

8. The reasons for the worldwide trend in birthrates and their implications for businesspeople.

9. Why declining birthrates are causing concern for European governments.

10. About national economic plans and their usefulness for businesspeople.

KEY WORDS AND CONCEPTS

- GDP (gross domestic product)
- Income distribution
- Disposable income
- Discretionary income
- Unit labor costs
- Vertically integrated
- Population density
- Population distribution
- Rural-to-urban shift
- Promotional mix
- National economic plans
- Indicative planning

BUSINESS INCIDENT

Pick a number, any number . . .

If ignorance is bliss, then the demographers, economists, marketing executives, and bureaucrats who study, forecast, sell in, and legislate for the European market must be the happiest people on earth. According to *International Management,* they are working "with some of the most bogus and out-of-date numbers available anywhere." Yet, economic statistics are an essential input to business and political decision making, and executives and politicians look forward to receiving them in order to make computer runs with the latest data. Governments oblige by publishing economic statistics dozens of times per week. Fortunes are made and lost in the stock market because of them, and decisions to invest millions of dollars in new projects are based on them. But, according to the deputy director of the division for statistical dissemination of Eurostat, the European Community's statistical office, "Nobody knows what the statistical scene across Europe is. It is a fact that statistical knowledge within Europe is bad."

One reason is that the degree of harmonization among the 12 member-states is low. For example, they have not yet agreed on how to classify activity within huge sections of industry, commerce, and government spending. This means it is often meaningless to compare Eurostat's data on interest rates, unemployment, and production for one country with that of another. However, the biggest obstacle to the free flow of data seems to be the great secrecy of European governments and companies in the dissemination of economic information that is readily available in other countries.

BUSINESS INCIDENT (concluded)

When analysts try to gather data on a specific industry, they find that the data published by the EC are missing or incomplete. The reason is that EC rules permit exceptions to reporting obligations by a member-state if either a company represents two thirds of an industry or the industry comprises three or fewer companies. Moreover, even when private economic consultants do a study for a company or an industry, the clients, unlike American companies, insist that the research be kept strictly private.

Source: Based on "Pick a Number, Any Number," *International Management*, May 1988, pp. 44–46; and "In a Maze of Numbers," *The Economist*, August 20, 1988, pp. 61–62.

Of all the uncontrollable forces with which businesses must contend, economic forces are undoubtedly the most significant. How the scarce resources of land, labor, and capital are being allocated to the production and distribution of goods and services and the manner in which they are consumed are of paramount importance to managers. To keep abreast of the latest developments and also to plan for the future, firms for many years have been assessing and forecasting the economic conditions at the local, state, and national levels.

Even though the data published by governments and international organizations, such as the World Bank and the IMF, are not as timely or as accurate as business economists would like, these are what they have and they must work with them. However, economists do not work solely with government-published data. Private economic consulting specialists—such as Data Resources, Inc., Chase Econometric Associates, Business International, the Economist Intelligence Unit, and Wharton Economic Forecasting Associates—provide economic forecasts (some do industry forecasts as well) to which many multinationals subscribe. Other sources are various industry associations, which generally provide industry-specific forecasts to their members.

In addition, economists and marketers use certain economic indicators that they have found to predict trends in their industry. Pitney Bowes' Data Documents division, for example, uses changes in the growth of the U.S. GNP to predict the sales of its business forms because its sales have for years generally lagged changes in GNP growth by six months.[1] We shall discuss the use of market indicators in Chapter 14, Market Assessment and Analysis.

The purpose of economic analyses is, first, to appraise the overall outlook of the economy and then to assess the impact of economic changes on the firm. To appreciate the extent to which a change in just one factor of the economy can affect all the major functional areas of the firm, let us examine Figure 7–1.

A forecast of an increase in employment would cause most marketing managers to revise upward their sales forecasts, which, in turn, would require production managers to augment production. This might be accomplished by adding another work shift, but if the plant is already operating 24 hours a day, new machinery will be needed. Either situation will require additional workers and raw materials, which will result in an extra workload for the personnel and purchasing managers. Should both the raw materials and labor markets be tight, the firm will probably have to pay prices and wage rates that are higher than normal. The financial manager may then have to negotiate with the banks

■ **FIGURE 7–1 Impact of Economic Forecast on Firm's Functional Areas**

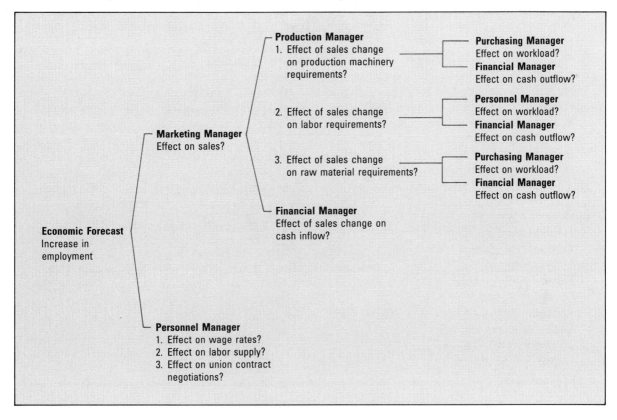

for a loan to enable the firm to handle the greater cash outflow until additional revenue is received from increased sales.

Note that all of this occurs because of a change in only *one factor*. Actually, of course, many economic factors are involved, and their relationships are complex. By means of an economic analysis, an attempt is made to isolate and assess the impact of those factors believed to affect the firm's operations.

INTERNATIONAL ECONOMIC ANALYSES

When the firm enters overseas markets, economic analyses become more complex because now managers must operate in two new environments: foreign and international. In the foreign environment, not only are there many economies instead of one, but they are also highly divergent. Because of these differences, policies designed for the economic conditions in one market may be totally unsuitable for the economic conditions in another market. For example, headquarters may have a policy requiring its subsidiaries to maintain the lowest inventories possible, and the chief financial officer may decree that they make only foreign currency-denominated loans because of more favorable interest rates. For nations whose annual inflation rates are low (0 to 15 percent), these policies usually work well. But what about countries such as Nicaragua—with an annual inflation rate of *10,205 percent*—or Peru—with

WORLDVIEW
Compiling EC Data: The Blind Leading the Blind

Indifference, inertia, and inefficiency among member governments are the biggest obstacles to compiling meaningful EC-wide data. Here's how EC statisticians rate the twelve:

Greece: "Too centralized. Athens has statistics only up to 1986, and only for basic industry."

Britain: "One of the worst. Their numbers are outdated and nearly always incomplete. The prevailing attitude in Britain is that statistics are the prerogative of government; if business wants them, let business collect them itself."

Luxembourg: "Very good."

Germany: "Worse than Britain, despite its reputation for orderly recordkeeping. Everything is decentralized. Each time we request something from Bonn, they have to rely on state governments to get it."

Holland: "Good, but no service-sector statistics."

Spain: "Fine for recent industry stats, but nothing on services—except hotels and transportation."

France: "Slow but generally delivers what we request. But then, they should: there are 40,000 employees in the country's statistical office."

Portugal: "Extremely understaffed. If the Commission doesn't pay for Portugal's upcoming agricultural survey— the country's first—then it won't get done. Figures for small business are based on the national business register, which is outdated. Many of the firms on the books no longer exist."

Denmark: "Everything we need including service statistics. They have a survey on almost every company— a statistician's dream."

Belgium: "Too many classification problems."

Italy: "We've had no headache at all with the Italians. They've simply not responded. They're too busy revising their GNP calculations each year."

Ireland: "Very bad. We offered to go there to help. They told us not to bother."

Source: *International Management,* May 1988, p. 46.

1,722 percent? The last thing headquarters wants is for the subsidiaries in these countries to have cash or foreign currency-denominated loans, so the policy for markets with high inflation rates will be just the reverse of what it is for countries with low rates of inflation. Table 7–1 illustrates that the chief financial officer has more than just Nicaragua and Peru to be concerned about.

Besides monitoring the foreign environments, economists must also keep abreast of the actions taken by components of the international environment, such as regional groupings (EC, EFTA) and international organizations (UN, IMF, World Bank). American firms are very attentive to the EC's progress in reaching its Europe 1992 goals and to the impact this will have on EC–U.S. trade relations. They are also following closely the UN's progress in developing world pollution standards, health standards, and so forth. Any of these actions can seriously affect the firm.[2]

International economic analyses should provide economic data on both actual and prospective markets. Also, as part of the competitive forces assessment, many companies monitor the economic conditions of nations where their major competitors are located, because changing conditions may strengthen or weaken their competitors' ability to compete in world markets.

Because of the importance of economic information to the control and planning functions at headquarters, the collection of data and the preparation of reports must be the responsibility of the home office. However, foreign-based personnel (subsidiaries and field representatives) will be expected to

■ **TABLE 7–1**
Annual Rates of Inflation for Selected Developing Countries

	1988	1987
All developing countries	58.3%	35.5%
Developing countries in Western Hemisphere	216.0	117.4
Nicaragua	10,205.0	911.1
Peru	1,722.0	1,222.1
Brazil	682.3	229.7
Argentina	343.0	131.3
Mexico	114.2	131.8
Ecuador	58.2	29.5
Chile	14.7	19.9
Asian developing countries	11.6	7.3
People's Republic of China	20.7	8.8
Sri Lanka	14.0	7.7

Note: Inflation rates for 1988 are not available for other developing nations.
Source: "Inflation up in 1988 in Developing Countries," *IMF Survey*, May 1, 1989, p. 140.

contribute heavily to studies concerning their markets. Data from areas where the firm has no local representation can usually be somewhat less detailed and are generally available in publications from national and international agencies.[3] An especially good source for economic information on a single country is the reports from central or international banks. A listing of these and other useful publications can be found in Appendix A at the end of this book.[4] Other possible sources are the American chambers of commerce located in most of the world's capitals, the commercial attachés in U.S. embassies, the United Nations, the World Bank, the International Monetary Fund, and the Organization for Economic Cooperation and Development.

Dimensions of the Economy

To estimate market potentials as well as to provide input to the other functional areas of the firm, managers require data on the size and the rates of change of a number of economic and socioeconomic factors. For an area to be a potential market, it must have sufficient people with the means to buy a firm's products. Socioeconomic data provide information on the number of people, and the economic factors tell us if they have purchasing power.

Economic dimensions.   Among the more important economic dimensions are GNP, distribution of income, personal consumption expenditures, personal ownership of goods, private investment, unit labor costs, exchange rates, inflation rates, and interest rates.

GNP.   Gross national product, the total of all final goods and services produced, and gross domestic product (GNP less net foreign factor incomes) are the values used to measure an economy's size. GNPs range from $4.5 trillion for the United States to $147 million for Guinea-Bissau (located on the western coast of Africa). What is the significance of GNP for the international businessperson? Is India, with a GNP of $239 billion, a more attractive market than Denmark, with $76.1 billion?

Imagine the reaction of managers who receive a report containing Figure 7–2, which shows a high *real* growth rate of **GDP (gross domestic product)**

GDP (gross domestic product) the total value of all goods and services produced domestically, not including (unlike GNP) net factor income from abroad

■ **FIGURE 7–2**
Five-Year Real Projected Growth in GDP
(Cumulative percentage change 1986–1990)

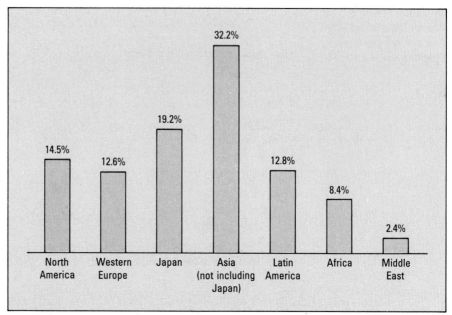

Source: Reprinted from page 4 of the January 9, 1989, issue of *Business International,* with the permission of the publisher, Business International Corporation (New York).

projected for Asia, at an annual rate of 7.2 percent. They will want to examine the data for individual countries in the area and compare growths with their subsidiaries' growths. The data might indicate that some markets where they have no operations need to be investigated. Of course, this is only the initial step. To compare the purchasing power of nations, managers also need to know among how many people this increase in GNP or GDP is divided.

GNP/capita.   The not altogether satisfactory method of employing GNP/capita to compare purchasing power reveals that Denmark is far ahead of India, with $14,390 versus $300. In other words, although India's pie is 3.1 times as big as Denmark's, there are 156 times as many people to eat it.

What can we learn from GNP/capita? As we saw in Chapter 3, we can generally assume that the higher its value, the more advanced the economy. Generally, however, the rate of growth is more important to the marketer because a high growth rate indicates a fast-growing market—for which they are always searching. Frequently, given the choice between investing in a nation with a higher GNP/capita but a low growth rate and a nation in which the conditions are reversed, management will choose the latter.

Although differences in GNP/capita do tell us something about the relative wealth of a nation's inhabitants, the information is somewhat misleading because few of them have the equal share indicated by what is an arithmetic mean. This first crude estimate of purchasing power must be refined by incorporating data on how the national income is actually distributed.

Income distribution.   Data on **income distribution** are gathered by the World Bank from a number of sources and published yearly in the *World Development Report.* Note that data in Table 7–2 refer to the distribution of

income distribution a measure of how a nation's income is apportioned among its people, commonly reported as the percentage of income received by population quintiles

■ TABLE 7-2
Percentage Share of Household Incomes by Percentile Group of Households

Country	Lowest 20 Percent	20–40 Percent	40–60 Percent	60–80 Percent	Highest 20 Percent	Highest 10 Percent
1. Argentina (70)	4.4%	9.7%	14.1%	21.5%	50.3%	35.2%
2. Australia (75–76)	5.4	10.0	15.0	22.5	47.1	30.5
3. Bangladesh (81–82)	6.6	10.7	15.3	22.1	45.3	29.5
4. Belgium (78–79)	7.9	13.7	18.6	23.8	36.0	21.5
5. Brazil (72)	2.0	5.0	9.4	17.0	66.6	50.6
6. Canada (81)	5.3	11.8	18.0	24.9	40.0	23.8
7. Costa Rica (71)	3.3	8.7	13.3	19.9	54.8	39.5
8. Denmark (81)	5.4	12.0	18.4	25.6	38.6	22.3
9. El Salvador (76–77)	5.5	10.0	14.8	22.4	47.3	29.5
10. Egypt (74)	5.8	10.7	14.7	20.8	48.0	33.2
11. Finland (81)	6.3	12.1	18.4	25.5	37.6	21.7
12. France (75)	5.3	11.1	16.0	21.8	45.8	26.4
13. West Germany (78)	7.9	12.5	17.0	23.1	39.5	24.0
14. Hong Kong (80)	5.4	10.8	15.2	21.6	47.0	31.3
15. Hungary (82)	6.9	13.6	19.2	24.5	35.8	20.5
16. India (75–76)	7.0	9.2	13.9	20.5	49.4	33.6
17. Indonesia (76)	6.6	7.8	12.6	23.6	49.4	34.0
18. Ireland (73)	7.2	13.1	16.6	23.7	39.4	25.1
19. Israel (79–80)	6.0	12.0	17.7	24.4	39.9	22.6
20. Italy (77)	6.2	11.3	15.9	22.7	43.9	28.1
21. Ivory Coast (85–86)	2.4	6.2	10.9	19.1	61.4	43.7
22. Japan (79)	8.7	13.2	17.5	23.1	37.5	22.4
23. Kenya (76)	2.6	6.3	11.5	19.2	60.4	45.8
24. Korea (76)	5.7	11.2	15.4	22.4	45.3	27.5
25. Malaysia (73)	3.5	7.7	12.4	20.3	56.1	39.8
26. Mauritius (80–81)	4.0	7.5	11.0	17.0	60.5	46.7
27. Mexico (77)	2.9	7.0	12.0	20.4	57.7	40.6
28. Nepal (76–77)	4.6	8.0	11.7	16.5	59.2	n.a.
29. Netherlands (81)	8.3	14.1	18.2	23.2	36.2	21.5
30. New Zealand (81–82)	5.1	10.8	16.2	23.2	44.7	28.7
31. Norway (82)	6.0	12.9	18.3	24.6	38.2	22.8
32. Panama (73)	2.0	5.2	11.0	20.0	61.8	44.2
33. Peru (72)	1.9	5.1	11.0	21.0	61.0	42.9
34. Philippines (85)	5.2	8.9	13.2	20.2	52.5	37.0
35. Portugal (73–74)	5.2	10.0	14.4	21.3	49.1	33.4
36. Spain (80–81)	6.9	12.5	17.3	23.2	40.0	24.0
37. Sri Lanka (80–81)	5.8	10.1	14.1	20.3	49.8	34.7
38. Sweden (81)	7.4	13.1	16.8	21.0	41.7	28.1
39. Switzerland (78)	6.6	13.5	18.5	23.4	38.0	23.7
40. Thailand (75–76)	5.6	9.6	13.9	21.1	49.8	34.1
41. Trinidad and Tobago (75–76)	4.2	9.1	13.9	22.8	50.0	31.8
42. Turkey (73)	3.5	8.0	12.5	19.5	56.5	40.7
43. United Kingdom (79)	7.3	12.4	17.7	23.4	39.2	23.4

■ **TABLE 7–2**
(concluded)

Country	Lowest 20 Percent	20–40 Percent	40–60 Percent	60–80 Percent	Highest 20 Percent	Highest 10 Percent
44. United States (80)	5.3	11.9	17.9	25.0	39.9	23.3
45. Venezuela (70)	3.0	7.3	12.9	22.8	54.0	35.7
46. Yugoslavia (78)	6.6	12.1	18.7	23.9	38.7	22.9
47. Zambia (76)	3.4	7.4	11.2	16.9	61.1	46.4
48. Zimbabwe (76)	3.4	7.4	11.2	16.9	61.1	n.a.

Notes:
1. Numbers in parentheses indicate year of study.
2. n.a. = Not available.
Source: Income Distribution, *World Development Report, 1988* (Washington, D.C.: World Bank, 1988), Table 26, pp. 272–73.

---

disposable income the amount of income remaining after taxes

the total **disposable income** of the entire household rather than *per capita* household income. This distinction is important to market analysts because households with low per capita income are frequently large households with a high *total* income while households with a lower total income are often smaller households with higher per capita income. Unfortunately, only a few countries gather data on the distribution of per capita income.

In spite of the difficulties associated with income distribution studies, such as inconsistent measuring practices and wide variations in the representativeness of samples, the data provide some useful insights for businesspeople:

1. They confirm the belief that, generally, income is more evenly distributed in the advanced nations, although there are important variations among *both* developed and developing nations.

2. From comparisons over time (not shown), it appears that income redistribution proceeds very slowly, so that older data are still useful.

3. These same comparisons indicate that income inequality increases in the early stages of development, with a reversal of this tendency in the later stages. This is true for developed, developing, and socialist nations. The fact that the middle quintiles are growing at the expense of the top and bottom 20 percent signifies an increase in middle-income families, which are especially significant to marketers.

Contingent on the type of product and the total population, either situation (relatively even or uneven income distribution) may represent a viable market segment. For example, although the Ivory Coast's total GNP is $8.2 billion, the fact that just 20 percent of the population receives over 60 percent of that income (10 percent gets 43.7 percent) indicates that there is a sizable group of people who are potential customers for low-volume, high-priced luxury products. On the other hand, the market is rather small (11.1 million population) for low-priced goods requiring a high sales volume.

This simple calculation based on GNP, total population, and income distribution may be all that is required to indicate that a particular country is not a good market; however, if the results look promising, the analyst will proceed to gather data on personal consumption.

Personal consumption.   One area of interest to marketers is the manner in which consumers allocate their disposable income (after-tax personal income) between purchases of essential and nonessential goods. Manufacturers of a

■ TABLE 7–3
Consumption Patterns for Selected Countries, 1986 (1979)

| Country | Private Consumption Expenditure/ Capita (US$) | | Percentage of Private Consumption Expenditures | | | | | |
			Food and Beverages		Clothing		Household Durables	
Switzerland	$13,738	($ 8,532)	27.3%	(28.3%)	4.9%	(5.0%)	6.0%	(6.0%)
United States	11,589	(6,214)	14.2	(16.3)	7.5	(6.8)	6.1	(7.2)
Japan	10,283	(4,694)	21.3	(25.5)	6.2	(7.1)	5.8	(6.2)
Denmark	9,745	(6,106)	23.8	(27.5)	5.7	(5.6)	6.6	(7.9)
West Germany	9,041	(5,767)	22.7	(26.5)	8.7	(9.5)	8.9	(11.4)
Norway	8,976	(5,081)	22.8	(27.9)	8.3	(8.9)	8.0	(8.7)
France	8,478	(5,470)	20.2	(23.1)	7.0	(7.0)	8.3	(9.7)
Canada	8,414	(4,984)	16.7	(20.8)	6.8	(7.6)	9.6	(8.4)
Sweden	8,393	(5,579)	21.8	(26.5)	8.1	(7.0)	6.9	(6.1)
Belgium	8,303	(6,093)	20.6	(25.4)	8.0	(6.7)	10.7	(14.5)
Netherlands	8,007	(5,547)	19.2	(22.2)	7.1	(8.7)	7.6	(9.8)
Italy	7,198	(2,908)	26.6	(32.8)	9.0	(8.6)	9.0	(6.2)
United Kingdom	6,153	(3,278)	18.9	(24.4)	8.3	(7.8)	7.5	(7.2)
Australia	6,144	(4,401)	22.4	(27.9)	7.4	(9.0)	8.8	(8.6)
Greece	2,660	(2,227)	38.6	(41.1)	7.8	(11.3)	7.5	(10.2)
South Korea	1,328	(802)	44.1	(54.5)	7.0	(9.3)	5.3	(4.1)
Venezuela	1,315	(1,570)	52.6	(39.3)	4.2	(6.3)	5.9	(8.8)
Jamaica	667	(797)	43.0	(45.3)	5.0	(n.a.)	6.3	(n.a.)
Sri Lanka	304	(125)	42.1	(65.8)	10.6	(7.4)	4.2	(4.4)
India	192	(125)	56.4	(58.2)	11.8	(8.7)	3.7	(3.7)

Note: n.a. = Not available.

Source: "Indicators of Market Size for 117 Countries," *Business International,* 1989, and "Indicators of Market Size for 131 Countries," *Business International,* 1980.

discretionary income the amount of income left after paying taxes and making essential purchases

certain class of essentials—household durables, for instance—will want to know the amounts spent in that category, whereas producers of nonessentials will be interested in the magnitude of **discretionary income** (disposable income less essential purchases), for this is the money available to be spent on their products. Fortunately, disposable incomes and the amounts spent on essential purchases are available from the *UN Statistical Yearbook,* and discretionary income may be obtained by subtracting the total of these items from disposable income. More detailed expenditure patterns can frequently be found in economic publications. Table 7–3, which reproduces data found in *Business International,* is an example.

Note how the consumption patterns have changed in just seven years. With the exception of Venezuela, consumers in all the countries shown have decreased the percentage spent on food as their total consumption expenditures have increased. As you would expect, a significantly higher percentage goes for food in the poorer nations, and less is spent on consumer durables. Interestingly, the clothing percentages do not vary much among nations—although would you expect the percentage spent on clothing in Italy to be 30 percent more than in France?

■ **TABLE 7–4   Per Capita Ownership or Consumption of Key Goods and Materials for Selected Countries**

Country	1986 Private Consumption Expenditure ($/capita)	1987 Passenger Cars/000 Population	1986 Telephones/ 000 Population*	1988 TV Sets/ 000 Population	1988 Steel Consumed (kilos/ capita)	1986 Percentage of U.S. Energy Consumption (capita)	1987 Cement Production (metric tons/ 000 population)	1986 Electricity (1,000 KWH/ capita)
Europe								
France	$ 8,478	387	416	394	266	40.9%	424	6.2
West Germany	9,041	445	423	377	477	59.8	413	6.7
Italy	7,198	383	304	255	411	33.8	623	3.3
Sweden	8,393	387	624	392	445	51.6	284	16.4
Switzerland	13,738	412	504	356	312	42.1	707	8.4
United Kingdom	6,153	350	380	328	264	56.5	252	8.7
Middle East								
Egypt	785	8	n.a.	n.a.	50	7.3	169	0.5
Israel	4,279	149	281	146	210	26.8	507	3.8
Kuwait	4,944	296	136	400	35	81.9	n.a.	9.6
Syria	1,111	8	8	59	27	12.6	400	0.7
Africa								
Ghana	356	4	3	13	n.a.	1.0	n.a.	0.3
Kenya	203	6	6	8	12	0.8	56	0.1
Mauritius	900	31	4	116	n.a.	4.4	n.a.	0.5
South Africa	1,093	91	73	78	175	29.3	181	3.8
Asia								
India	192	2	5	16	19	2.9	46	0.3
Japan	10,283	235	386	247	618	38.2	586	5.5
Pakistan	252	4	5	14	14	2.6	67	0.3
Philippines	403	6	7	113	25	2.6	68	0.4
South America								
Bolivia	636	5	24	65	6	3.5	n.a.	0.2
Brazil	1,391	75	52	250	104	8.0	180	1.5
Colombia	700*	20	58	183	42	8.2	199	0.9
Eastern Europe								
Romania	n.a.	11	n.a.	175	524	47.2	570	3.1
East Germany	n.a.	189	959	372	544	83.7	749	6.9
Poland	n.a.	108	66	292	476	49.5	486	3.7
Soviet Union	n.a.	42	n.a.	320	581	67.3	486	5.7
Yugoslavia	1,043	125	109	175	176	25.7	345	3.3
North America								
Canada	8,414	448	385	602	500	102.2	462	18.3
Mexico	732	65	45	114	78	16.9	269	1.2
United States	11,589	561	445	797	414	100.0	276	10.7

n.a. = Not available.
*Telephone access lines.
Source: "Indicators of Market Size for 117 Countries," *Business International*, 1989.

"Here's a leading economic
indication—my wallet is empty!"

From *The Wall Street Journal*, with permission of Cartoon
Features Syndicate.

Don't underestimate the importance of the small percentage differences
among nations. Marketers do not—each percentage point is worth a large sum
of money. To appreciate its value, try multiplying the total per capita
consumption expenditure times 0.01 times the population. If U.S. consumers
had spent 1 percent more on clothing in 1986, for example, this would have
amounted to $11,589 × 0.01 × 241.6 million, or $28.0 billion greater sales
for the clothing industry. For more detailed information on consumption
expenditures, see *World Development Indicators* published by the World
Bank, the UN's *Monthly Bulletin of Statistics*, the IMF's *International
Financial Statistics*, the UN's *Yearbook of National Accounts Statistics*, and
Eurostat's annual *Basic Statistics of the Community* for the EC.

Other indicators that add to our knowledge of personal consumption are
those concerned with the ownership of goods. In addition, the per capita values
for the consumption and production of strategic materials, such as steel,
cement, and energy, serve as measures of a nation's affluence and level of
development. As Table 7–4 illustrates, the more industrialized nations have
considerably higher values for these indicators than do the LDCs.

Private investment.   The amount of private investment (the part of national
income allocated to increasing a nation's productive capacity) is another factor
that contributes to the analysis of market size and growth. New investment
brings about increases in GNP and the level of employment, which are signals
to the analyst of a growing market. A history of continual investment growth
signifies, furthermore, that a propitious investment climate exists; that is, there
are numerous profitable investment opportunities, and the government enjoys
the confidence of the business community.

Table 7–5 shows the impact of the worldwide recession on the growth of
investment. In the table from which Table 7–5 was excerpted, 77 of the 93

■ **TABLE 7–5**
Average Annual Growth Rate of Consumption and Investment for Selected Countries (Percent)

Country	Public Consumption*		Private Consumption		Gross† Domestic Investment	
	1965–1980	1980–1987	1965–1980	1980–1987	1965–1980	1980–1987
Low-income countries						
Ethiopia	6.4%	5.6%	3.0%	1.3%	−0.1%	2.0%
Burundi	7.3	2.9	3.7	2.1	9.0	5.4
India	6.3	8.8	2.7	4.9	5.0	3.7
Central African Republic	−1.1	−3.1	4.2	1.6	−5.4	14.6
Lower-middle-income countries						
Philippines	7.7	−0.2	5.0	1.7	8.5	−14.6
Indonesia	11.4	4.1	5.9	4.9	16.1	4.1
El Salvador	7.0	3.2	4.1	−0.7	6.6	0.1
Paraguay	5.1	2.6	6.4	2.1	13.9	−4.3
Upper-middle-income countries						
Korea	7.7	5.5	7.8	5.5	15.9	10.0
Israel	8.8	−1.2	6.0	3.8	5.9	0.2
Mexico	8.5	3.2	5.8	−1.0	8.5	−7.9
Singapore	10.2	9.1	8.0	3.9	13.3	3.2
Industrial market economies						
United Kingdom	2.3	0.9	2.2	3.2	0.6	5.3
Japan	5.1	2.9	6.0	2.9	6.7	3.9
United States	1.2	3.6	3.1	4.1	2.6	5.0
Germany	3.5	1.4	4.0	1.2	1.7	0.5

*Includes all levels of government and defense spending.
†Includes changes in inventory levels.
Source: Adapted from *World Development Report, 1989* (Washington, D.C.: World Bank, 1989), pp. 178–79.

countries for which complete data are available suffered a smaller increase during the 1980–87 period, compared with the period 1965 to 1980. The industrialized nations fared considerably better than the rest of the world, with the rates of growth for the United Kingdom and the United States showing sizable increases over the previous period.

All nations reduced the growth rate of government spending except the United States and India, and, interestingly, only these two nations and the United Kingdom had increases in private consumption rates. See also how radically the investment climate changed in the Philippines as a result of the communist guerrilla attacks on the government and the overthrow of President Marcos. Cuts had to be made in government spending, and private consumption slowed dramatically. You can see the impact of the austerity measures that Mexico has had to take to service its huge foreign debt. In this environment of high inflation and reduced spending, investors were unwilling to invest in plants and inventories.

WORLDVIEW
If You Want to Get Ahead, Get a Telephone

What is the best gauge for measuring a country's level of development? Is it (1) per capita income, (2) state of the construction industry, (3) density of pollution, or (4) number of telephones? If you selected number four you are right, according to the International Telecommunications Union (ITU). In a recent report, the ITU observed that the total number of telephones installed in a country can often provide a better barometer of economic development than even per capita income.

The corollary is that nations with widespread and efficient telephone system also have highly developed economies and large disposable incomes. Conversely, countries with poor telephone service are often plagued with underdeveloped economies and low-income levels.

In using the number-of-telephones principle to assess a country's fortunes, it is interesting to look at the United States. Recent statistics show that there are 95 telephones for every 100 households; and Beverly Hills, California, and Washington, D.C., have more telephones than people.

In contrast, Asian Development Bank (ADB) data show that in Asian countries, the telephone density per 100 population is only 2 compared to 5.5 in Latin America and 0.8 in Africa. In Bangladesh and Nepal, there is less than one (0.1) telephone per 100 persons.

Most developing countries thus have a nagging communications problem. For example, an ADB report points out that in Pakistan the telephone density is 0.5 per 100 population. But in rural areas, the situation is even worse, with as little as one telephone per 1,000 people. In fact, out of Pakistan's 45,000 villages, only about 1,900 have access to telephone services. One reason for this is that less than 15,000 villages have electricity.

Moreover, the demand for telephone service continues unabated in Pakistan, where people sometimes have to wait 10 years to obtain a telephone. The quality of service also leaves much to be desired. A sample survey revealed that only 25 percent of local and 15 percent of international call attempts were successful.

Poor telecommunications services take their developmental toll. According to Yoshiro Takano, a telecommunications specialist of the ADB, there is evidence of significant losses in efficiency incurred in agriculture, transportation, commerce, banking, government, tourism, and other sectors due to the lack or inadequacy of telecommunications services. Telecommunications also contribute to the quality of life by facilitating communication with kin and friends as well as access to emergency services.

Source: Truman Becker, "If You Want to Get Ahead, Get a Telephone," *UN Development Forum,* November–December 1986, p. 7.

---

unit labor costs total direct labor costs divided by units produced

Unit labor costs.   One factor that contributes to a favorable investment opportunity is the ability to obtain **unit labor costs** (total direct labor costs/units produced) lower than those currently available to the firm. Foreign trends in these costs are closely monitored because each country experiences a different rate of increase.

Countries with slower-rising unit labor costs attract management's attention for two reasons. First, they are investment prospects for companies striving to lower production costs, as discussed in Chapter 2, and second, they may become sources of new competition in world markets if other firms in the same industry are already located there.

Relative changes in wage rates may also cause the multinational firm that obtains products or components from a number of subsidiaries to change its sources of supply.

General Motors, noting that costs were climbing in Germany, switched the source of supply of Opels sold in the United States to Japan in order to take advantage

■ **TABLE 7–6   Labor Compensation Rates, 1975–1987**

	Average Hourly Rate Including Fringe Benefits (US$)				Relative Index (US = 100)		Average Annual Exchange Rates (units local currency to $1)	
	1988	**1987**	**1980**	**1975**	**1988**	**1987**	**1988***	**1987**
Norway	$20.85	$17.58	$11.68	$6.60	149	120	6.2060	6.7375
Switzerland	18.47	17.06	11.04	6.24	132	123	1.4230	1.4912
Germany	18.38	16.83	12.33	6.35	131	124	1.7070	1.7974
Sweden	17.28	15.14	12.51	6.78	123	109	5.9300	6.3404
Belgium	16.32	15.08	13.15	6.07	116	116	37.3340	35.2300
Netherlands	16.27	15.11	12.06	6.60	116	108	1.9125	2.0257
Denmark	15.91	14.49	10.95	7.18	113	104	6.5330	6.8403
Finland	15.31	13.03	8.27	4.63	109	96	4.0480	4.3956
United States	14.03	13.46	9.80	6.33	100	100	—	—
Austria	14.02	12.82	8.56	4.70	100	95	11.9900	12.6430
Italy	13.46	12.33	8.00	4.65	96	93	1,266.0000	1,296.1000
Japan	13.37	11.34	5.61	3.05	95	85	125.7500	144.6400
France	13.33	12.36	9.12	4.33	95	92	5.7790	6.0107
United Kingdom	11.21	9.07	7.38	3.01	80	66	0.5373	0.6102
Ireland	10.01	9.13	5.88	3.27	71	67	0.6307	0.6720
Spain	9.09	7.82	5.96	2.55	65	58	112.7200	123.4800
Greece	5.47	4.69	3.73	1.40	39	36	136.7000	135.4300
Portugal	2.72	2.45	2.06	1.58	19	18	139.0000	140.8820
Korea	2.10	1.69	1.11	0.37	15	13	735.8000	822.5700

*Dollar conversions are at average annual exchange rates for 1975, 1980, and 1987, and at current rates (May 30, 1988) for 1988.

Source: *Business Europe,* January 28, 1983, p. 26, and May 30, 1988, p. 2.

of the relatively lower Japanese costs. Rollei, a German camera manufacturer, moved part of its production to Singapore for the same reason.

What are the reasons for the relative changes in labor costs? Three factors are responsible: (1) compensation, (2) productivity, and (3) exchange rates. Hourly compensation tends to vary more widely than wages because of the appreciable differences in the size of fringe benefits. Unit labor costs will not rise in unison with compensation rates if the gains in productivity outstrip the increases in hourly compensation. In fact, if productivity increases fast enough, the unit costs of labor will decrease even though the firm is required to pay more to the workers.

Table 7–6 illustrates the rapidity with which labor compensation costs change. In 1975, five nations had higher average hourly rates when expressed in dollars than did the United States. This number had increased to seven by 1980, but then dropped to zero in 1982. The United States had the highest hourly rate until 1986, when it was surpassed by Switzerland, West Germany, and Norway. Note that in 1988, the dollar bought fewer units of all currencies, and, as you would expect, the average labor cost expressed in dollars increased in all countries. However, the dollar cost did not increase at the same rate as

■ **TABLE 7–7**
The Latin American Debt Problem

Country	Total Debt, 1987 ($ billion)	Change in Debt since 1981 (percent)	Interest Payments as Percent of Export Revenue		Change in Real GNP/Capita (percent) 1981–87
			1981	1987	
Brazil	$106.1	+163%	31.9%	33.2%	+5.1%
Mexico	96.9	+182	28.2	38.4	−8.3
Argentina	50.3	+222	18.2	52.0	−9.9
Venezuela	32.7	+217	12.4	32.4	−12.0
Peru	13.9	+188	44.9	12.9	−5.6

Source: *World Tables,* 1988–89 ed. (Washington, D.C.: World Bank, 1989), pp. 96–467, and *The World Bank Atlas 1988,* pp. 6–9.

the exchange rate did. Why? Because an increase expressed in dollars may be due to one or both of the following: (1) a real increase in labor costs and (2) an appreciation of the local currency with respect to the dollar.

For example, the Norwegian average hourly rate in dollars rose from $17.58 in 1987 to $20.85 in 1988, a large rise of 18.6 percent. But did that increase result from real wage gains, or did it occur because the conversion to dollars in 1988 was made with more expensive Norwegian krone? To find out:

1. Convert the 1987 hourly rate to krone: $17.58 × 6.7375 = 118.45 krone.
2. Convert the 1988 hourly rate to krone: $20.85 × 6.2060 = 129.40 krone.
3. Percentage increase in krone = 9 percent (real wage gains).
4. Therefore, 52 percent [(18.6 − 9)/18.6] of the apparent increase in the hourly cost was due to a more expensive currency.[5]

If you wish to prepare a table of average wage costs for countries not included in Table 7–6, you will find a method for doing this in endnote 5 at the end of this chapter.

Other economic dimensions.   We have mentioned only a few of the many economic indicators that economists study, and you learned about the importance to businesspeople of interest rates, balances of payments, and inflation rates in Chapter 6, Financial Forces. Which of the economic measures the analyst chooses to study will depend on the industry and on the purpose of the study. Executives of an automobile manufacturer, for example, will want the economist's opinion as to where interest rates are headed and what is the rate of growth of a nation's GNP. GNP, as you saw earlier, is important to other producers of industrial products, such as Pitney Bowes.

The large international debts of a number of Latin American nations are causing multiple problems not only for their governments but also for multinational firms. Just look at the situation of the five countries listed in Table 7–7.

Is this a problem for international bankers only, or should it concern multinational managements as well? Is it significant to WWCs with subsidiaries in these countries that a high percentage of the countries' export earnings must go to service their foreign debts? If it is, then management will expect periodic reports on this situation from the economist. Let's examine the ramifications for a WWC of these large foreign debts.

If a large part of the foreign exchange the nation earns cannot be used to import components used in local products, then either local industries must begin their manufacture or the companies that import them must stop production. Either alternative can cause the multinational to lose sales if it has been selling to its subsidiary the parts made in one of its home country plants, a common occurrence because the WWC is usually more **vertically integrated** than its subsidiaries. A scarcity of foreign exchange can also make it difficult for the subsidiary to import raw materials and spare parts for its production equipment. If headquarters wants its affiliate to continue production, it may have to lend the foreign exchange and wait for repayment. Campbell Soup, Sears, Revlon, and Gerber closed their operations in Brazil because of this problem.[6] Other multinationals have resorted to barter or have begun to export their subsidiaries' products even though these actions have reduced exports or even local sales of their domestic plants.

Governments may impose price controls (which make it difficult for a subsidiary to earn a profit), cut government spending (which reduces company sales), and impose wage controls (which limit consumer purchasing power). The economic turmoil that follows can turn into a political crisis, such as occurred in Venezuela when rioting and looting resulted after the president tried to impose similar austerity measures.[7]

One aspect of debt reduction that has been of interest to some multinationals has been debt/equity swaps, which we discussed in Chapter 6. They have bought foreign debt for as little as 60 cents on a dollar and have used it to buy up local companies that the government has privatized. When Chile sold a government-owned insurance company, telephone system, and its national electricity grid, it permitted foreigners to pay with foreign debt they had purchased. Grupo Visa, a Mexican conglomerate, reduced its foreign debt from $1.7 billion to $400 million by giving foreign creditors a 40 percent share in the company.[8]

Scarcity of foreign exchange can affect even those firms that merely export to nations with high foreign debt because the governments will surely impose import restrictions. When Latin American debt increased rapidly from 1981 to 1983, that region's share of U.S. exports dropped by one third. To protect these export markets, firms had to extend long-term credit. From this you can see that WWC managements will expect to receive information on the status of the foreign debt in nations where it is high in addition to the other economic data we have been examining.

Socioeconomic dimensions.   A complete definition of market potential must also include detailed information about the population's physical attributes as measured by the socioeconomic dimensions. Just as we began with GNP in the study of purchasing power, we shall begin this section with an analysis of the total population.

Total population.   Total population, the most general indicator of potential market size, is the first characteristic of the population that the analysts will examine. They readily discover that there are immense differences in population sizes, which range from a billion inhabitants in China to less than

Rioting and looting greeted the attempts of Venezuela's new president, Carlos Andrés Pérez, to impose the austerity and price increases demanded by foreign creditors

Source: *Fortune,* April 24, 1989, p. 208

1 million each for 34 countries. The fact that many developed nations have less than 10 million inhabitants makes it apparent that population size alone is a poor indicator of economic strength and market potential. Switzerland, for example, with only 6.5 million people, is far more important economically than Bangladesh, with 106 million. Clearly, more information is needed; only for a few low-priced, mass-consumed products, such as soft drinks, cigarettes, and soap, does population size alone provide a basis for estimating consumption.

For products not in this category, large populations and populations that are increasing rapidly may not signify an immediate enlargement of the market; but if incomes grow over time, eventually at least a part of the population will become customers. Insight into the rapidity with which this is occurring may be obtained by comparing population and GNP growth rates (see Table 2–9, pp. 44–45). Where GNP increases faster than the population, there is probably an expanding market, whereas the converse situation is not only an indication of possible market contraction but may even point out a country as a potential area of political unrest. This possibility is strengthened if an analysis of the educational system discloses an accruement of technical and university graduates. These groups expect to be employed as and receive the wages of professionals, and when sufficient new jobs are not being created to absorb them, the government can be in serious trouble. Various developing nations already face this difficulty: Egypt and India are two notable examples.[9]

Age distribution.   Because few products are purchased by everyone, marketers must identify the segments of the population that are more apt to buy their goods. For some firms, age is a salient determinant of market size; but

■ **FIGURE 7–3   Population by Age and Sex—1975 and 2000 (Millions)**

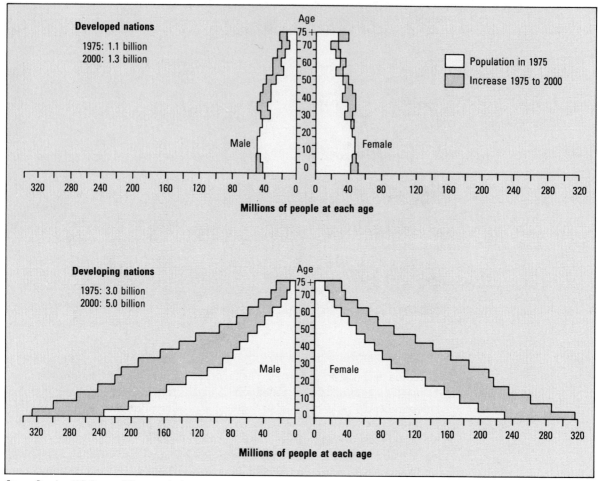

Source: Based on U.S. Bureau of Census projections.

unfortunately, the distribution of age groups within populations varies widely. Generally, because of higher birth and fertility rates, the developing countries have a more youthful population than the industrial countries. Figure 7–3 illustrates the tremendous difference in age distribution between developed and developing countries, which is the result of much higher birthrates in the developing nations. According to the World Bank, past and estimated average annual population percentage increases for nations grouped according to income are the following:

	1965–1980	1980–1987	1987–2000
Low-income economies	2.3%	2.0%	1.9%
Middle-income economies	2.4	2.2	1.9
Industrial market economies	0.9	0.7	0.5

Source: *World Development Report, 1989* (Washington, D.C.: World Bank, 1989), pp. 214–15.

■ FIGURE 7–4 Population Growth of Countries with over 100 Million Inhabitants in the Year 2000

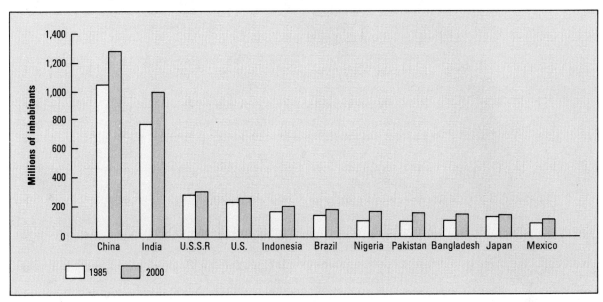

This situation is far from static, however, as decreasing birthrates are becoming a worldwide phenomenon. Of the 116 nations for which the United Nations provided information, only 11 experienced increases in their crude (born live) birthrates per thousand population over the 1965–87 period. Two were middle-income nations, and nine were low-income nations.[10]

The population of developing countries, which now account for about 75 percent of the world's population, will rise to 80 percent by the year 2000. Figure 7–4 shows you that of the 11 nations predicted to have over 100 million inhabitants by the year 2000, only 3 are industrialized; the rest are developing countries.

What does this signify for businesspeople? In the developed nations, there will be a decrease in the demand for products used in schools and for products bought by and for children, a smaller market for furniture and clothing, but an increased demand for medical care and related products, tourism, and financial services. Firms confronted by a decreasing demand for their products will have to look for sales increases in the developing economies, where the age distribution is reversed. The high growth rates in the developing nations will provide markets for transportation systems, higher-yield food grains, fertilizers, agricultural tools, appliances, and so forth.

Whirlpool, concerned about the decline in the number of householders aged 25 and under in the United States, has entered into a joint venture with the Dutch appliance maker, Philips. The new company will take over Philips' appliance operation, which markets in developing nations as well as in Europe. Whirlpool is also expanding on its own in the Third World. It has operations in Brazil and Mexico and is erecting a plant in India.[11]

Many forces are responsible for reductions in birthrates. Governments are supporting family planning programs, to be sure, but there is ample evidence that improved levels in health and education along with an enhanced status for women, a more even distribution of income, and a greater degree of urbanization are all acting to reduce the traditional family size. In Colombia, for example, 46 percent of the women with seven years or more of schooling use contraceptives, as compared with 14 percent of those who have not attended school. In Mexico, the percentages were 72 percent compared to 31 percent.[12]

While this is welcomed by governments in developing nations, the declining birthrate is causing concern in the governments of the industrialized countries. In Europe, for example, governments are preparing to lay off thousands of high school teachers, cut university subsidies, and extend the period that draftees serve in the NATO and Warsaw Pact armed forces. By the year 2000, when there will be fewer working taxpayers, they expect serious labor shortages and greatly increased retirement and medical costs.

In contrast to LDC governments that are offering incentives to lower birthrates, European governments are searching for ways to increase birthrates. In East Germany, for example, interest-free loans are given to young parents, and part of the debt is forgiven each time they have a baby. In France, all parents receive substantial payments and services to help with child rearing. Despite these efforts, the birthrate continues to fall. No one knows why, though many argue that a change in lifestyle is responsible. Many young women want careers to give them a better level of living. They perceive children as an expense rather than as an investment for support in old age.[13]

Company presidents in the developed nations are fearful that the discrepancy between developed and developing nations in the aging rate of the labor force will put their companies at a competitive disadvantage. Morale among younger workers in the developed countries may fall because the slowing of turnover in the higher-paying jobs requiring years of experience will keep them from advancing in their careers.

Also, the hospitalization costs for firms in the developed countries will be higher than those for firms in the LDCs and NICs because of a greater proportion of older workers. Similarly, pension costs are increasing because more employees live to full retirement age and then live longer after retirement. For example, the worker-to-retiree ratio, now 2.2 to 1 in Germany and 4.4 to 1 in Japan, is expected to fall to 1.1 to 1 and 1.6 to 1, respectively, by the year 2030. However, the demographic outlook for Great Britain is more optimistic because its dependency ratio will go from 3.3 to 1 to 2.1 to 1 in 2030. In the United States, the ratio, now 4.6 to 1, will reach only 2.4 to 1.[14] Due to relatively lower pension costs for American firms, economists are predicting that U.S. competitiveness in world markets will be enhanced.[15]

population density a measure of the number of inhabitants per area unit (inhabitants per square kilometer or square mile)

population distribution a measure of how the inhabitants are distributed over a nation's area

Population density and distribution.   Other aspects of population that concern management are **population density** and **population distribution.** Densely populated countries tend to make product distribution and communications simpler and less costly than they are where population density is low; thus you might expect Pakistan, with 129 inhabitants per square kilometer, to be an easier market to serve than Canada (2.6 inhabitants/square kilometer) or Brazil (16.6 inhabitants/square kilometer). The expectation, though, is another of those based on an arithmetic mean. We must know how these populations are distributed.

■ TABLE 7-8
The Most Populous Cities in the Year 2000 (Millions)

1975		2000	
1. New York–Northeastern New Jersey	19.8	1. Mexico City	31.0
2. Tokyo–Yokohama	17.7	2. São Paulo	25.8
3. Mexico City	11.9	3. Tokyo–Yokohama	24.2
4. Shanghai	11.6	4. New York–Northeastern New Jersey	22.8
5. Los Angeles–Long Beach	10.8	5. Shanghai	22.7
6. São Paulo	10.7	6. Beijing	19.9
7. London	10.4	7. Rio de Janeiro	19.0
8. Greater Bombay	9.3	8. Greater Bombay	17.1
9. Rhine–Ruhr	9.3	9. Calcutta	16.7
10. Paris	9.2	10. Djakarta	16.6

Note: Six of the largest urban centers will be in Asia, and none will be in Europe.

One needs only to compare the urban percentages of total population to learn that Canada and Brazil possess population concentrations that facilitate the marketing process. While only 31 percent of Pakistan's population is urban, the percentages for Brazil and Canada are 75 and 76 percent, respectively. The physical forces, as we shall see in Chapter 8, contribute heavily to the formation of these concentrations.[16]

rural-to-urban shift the movement of a nation's population from the rural areas to cities

An important phenomenon that is changing the population distribution is the **rural-to-urban shift,** which is occurring everywhere, especially in developing countries, as people move to cities in search of higher wages and more conveniences. This shift is significant to marketers because city dwellers, being less self-sufficient than persons living in rural areas, must enter the market economy. City governments also become customers for equipment that will expand municipal services to handle the population influx. Table 7–8 contains some good sales prospects.

An indicator of the extent of this movement is the change in the percentages of urban population. As Table 7–9 indicates, the greatest urban shifts are occurring in the low- and middle-income countries. In no country anywhere is there a net flow in the other direction. As you would expect, the percentage of the labor force in agriculture is also decreasing.

Other socioeconomic dimensions.   Other socioeconomic dimensions can provide useful information to management. The increase in the number of working women, for example, is highly significant to marketers because it may result in larger family incomes, a greater market for convenience goods, and a need to alter the **promotional mix.** Personnel managers are interested in this increase because it results in a larger labor supply. It also signifies that changes may be required in production processes, employee facilities, and personnel management policies.

promotional mix a blend of the promotional methods a firm uses to sell its products

Data on the country's divorce rate, when available, will alert the marketer to the formation of single-parent families and single-person households, whose product needs and buying habits differ in many respects from those of a two-parent family (see Figure 7–5). In many countries, important ethnic groups require special consideration by both marketing and personnel managers.

■ **TABLE 7–9**
Rural-to-Urban Shift

	Percentages of Population in Urban Areas		Percentage Increase	Percentage of Labor Force in Agriculture		Percentage Increase
	1965	1987		1965	1980	
Low-income countries	17%	30%	76%	77%	72%	−6.0%
Middle-income countries	42	57	36	56	43	−23.0
Industrialized countries	71	77	8	14	7	−50.0
Centrally planned economies	52	66	27	34	22	−35.0

Source: *World Development Report, 1988* (Washington, D.C.: World Bank, 1988), pp. 282–83, and *World Development Report, 1989,* pp. 224–25.

■ **FIGURE 7–5**
Changing Divorce Rates in Selected Countries

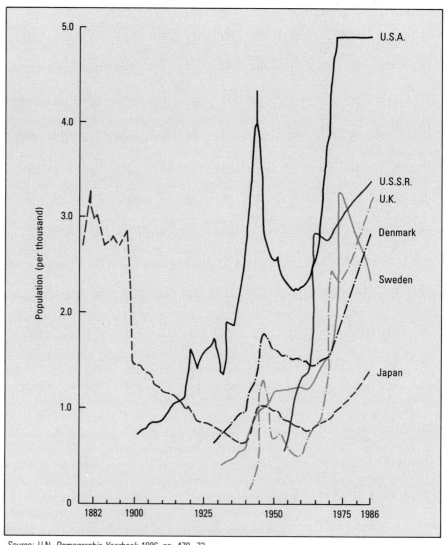

Source: U.N. *Demographic Yearbook 1986,* pp. 470–72.

The importance of the Chinese and Indian populations in Malaysia is emphasized by the fact that the Malaysian government has gone so far as to lay down specific targets for Malay representation in employment and ownership of business to enable the Malays to catch up with these groups. In Quebec, numerous policies have been adopted to "Frenchify" business.[17]

Which of these and other socioeconomic indicators are actually used will depend on a number of factors, such as the type of product, the target market, and the marketing strategy.

National Economic Plans

national economic plans plans prepared by governments stating their economic goals and means for reaching them, usuallly for periods of up to five years

One other source of economic data that may prove useful to the firm, especially for its marketers, is the **national economic plans** that many countries publish. These range from the annual and five-year plans (in reality, budgets) used as production control instruments by the communist countries to the "indicative" plans of some free market economies.

Prior to 1981, the five-year plans of the communist countries, with the exception of Yugoslavia, attempted to control all economic activity, including target quantities for domestic production, importation, and exportation. These were, in effect, marketing plans, and they were used as such by firms doing business with the Eastern-bloc nations. If the plans did not include the suppliers' products, the chances for their sale during the period were generally slim.

The 1981–85 plans, however, introduced a change in the planning concept. Because of the widespread failure to meet the goals of the previous five-year plans, a number of communist-bloc nations have taken a more flexible approach. They now look at the five-year plan as a long-term target that does not have to be attained by means of five one-year increments, as was the case previously. Moreover, because of Russia's drive for *perestroika* (economic reforms to boost productivity), which is also being accepted by other communist-bloc members, the plans are no longer considered fixed and unchangeable.[18]

Does this mean they are now of no use to Western suppliers? Not at all. The plans and the speeches that accompany them continue to be useful indicators of East European priorities and trends. For example, a high target rate for a sector is evidence that a high priority has been placed on it. This means it will now receive a greater part of the nation's resources, which should result in greater sales opportunities for the sector's suppliers.[19]

Planning as done by the Eastern-bloc nations, especially the German Democratic Republic, Hungary, and Czechoslovakia, is approaching the indicative planning of Western and Third World countries. Instead of setting production goals that are then passed down as orders to production units, under **indicative planning** the government merely establishes basic targets and issues some basic policy statements on how these will be achieved. It then attempts by means of the usual fiscal and monetary tools to create favorable conditions for business so that the targets may be attained. Although indicative plans do not have the same force as the five-year plans of the communist bloc, they do disclose the sectors favored by the government. This favoritism may be manifested in many ways, among which are special tax concessions to

indicative planning forecast made by government with industry collaboration of the direction the economy is expected to take

investors and foreign exchange allocations (when foreign exchange is controlled) to purchase imported capital equipment and raw materials.

Information about national development plans and budgets is regularly reported in such publications as *Business International* and *Business America.* Commercial attachés in American embassies and the overseas American chambers of commerce are additional sources of information.

In the *Highlights of Ninth Medium-Term Economic Development Plan for Taiwan (1986–1989),* for example, the government states that one policy is to "enhance energy efficiency." Then the strategy, called *supporting measure,* is to "develop mass transit systems, promote the production of oil-saving transport equipment, and establish efficiency standards for oil-consuming vehicles." What business opportunities are there in this strategy? It looks as though producers of subway systems, electric trolleys, and electric buses may have a chance to make some sales, but automobile manufacturers should find a way to provide input to the body responsible for the new standards, which could cause some expensive design changes.[20]

Industry Dimensions

Every firm is concerned about the general economic news because of its impact on consumer purchases, prices of raw materials, and investment decisions, but certain factors are more significant than others to a given industry or to a specific functional area of the firm. The size and growth trend of the automobile industry is of paramount importance to a tire manufacturer, for example, but is of no interest to an appliance manufacturer. Nor would the quantity of machine operators graduated by technical schools be useful to financial officers, although these data are of vital interest to human resources managers of manufacturing plants. Managers want data not only about the firm's industry but also about industries that supply and purchase from the company. Minicase 7–1 at the end of this chapter illustrates the use of both macroeconomic and industry-specific data.

Industry studies are generally made by the firm's economists or its trade association, but they can also be purchased from independent research organizations, such as Fantus (New York) and The Economist Intelligence Unit (London). Government agencies, chambers of commerce, and trade publications such as *Advertising Age* publish them as well. Many international banks publish free newsletters containing useful economic data. The Appendix at the end of the book lists some of these sources.

SUMMARY

To keep abreast of the latest economic developments and also to plan for the future, firms regularly assess and forecast economic conditions at the local, state, and national levels. When they enter international operations, the economic analysis increases in complexity because managers are operating in two new environments: foreign and international. There are more economies to study, and these economies are frequently highly divergent.

The various functional areas of the firm require data on the size and rates of change of a number of economic and socioeconomic factors. Among the more important economic dimensions are GNP, GNP/capita, distribution of income, personal consumption expenditures, private investment, unit labor costs, and financial data, such as exchange rates, inflation rates, interest rates, and the amount of a nation's foreign debt. The principal socioeconomic dimensions are total population, rates of growth, age distribution, population density, and population distribution.

Considerable information is available from publications put out by international agencies, governments, and banks and from business publications. National economic plans, for which no American counterpart exists, provide an insight as to government expectations. In the communist countries, national plans are often the equivalent of market studies. There is a tendency on the part of some communist governments to take a more flexible approach in their planning, however.

QUESTIONS

1. Management learns from the economic analysis of Country A that wage rates are expected to increase by 10 percent next year. Which functional areas of the firm will be concerned? Why are they concerned?

2. Check the *World Development Report* in the library to learn which country in each income group (low, middle, and industrial market economies) is the leader in the rate of GNP/capita growth over the last 10 to 15 years. In each case, is the rate of increase greater than the population growth? What can you deduce from that?

3. What common problem does the use of GNP/capita and population density values present?

4. Table 7–2 lists the income distribution for three poor nations. Could they be viable candidates for high-priced luxury goods when their GNP/capita, shown in Table 2–9, pp. 44–45, is so low? What is the approximate size of this segment? How can you use this information?

5. If the clothing industry association to which your firm's Swiss subsidiary belongs could mount a successful promotional program to cause the Swiss to increase their clothing expenditures by 1 percent annually, what would be the total increase in sales for the clothing industry?

6. In 1988, Switzerland had the second-highest average hourly compensation rate.

   a. What was the percentage increase in dollars?
   b. What was the percentage increase in the labor cost stated in Swiss francs?
   c. What percentage of the change when stated in dollars was due to changes in the franc–dollar exchange rate?

7. The staff economist has given to the chief financial officer a report on the foreign debt situation of Argentina, as shown in Table 7–7. What concerns might the chief financial officer have?

8. Declining birthrates appear to be a worldwide phenomenon.
   a. Why are they falling?
   b. What does this signify for businesspeople?

9. Of what use to businesspeople are the five-year plans of the communist bloc or the indicative plans of other countries?

10. What would be the concerns of the chief financial officer if he or she were to receive the information on annual inflation rates from Table 7–1?

11. What problems is the reduction in birthrates causing for European governments?

12. Choose a country and a product, and estimate the market potential of the product based on the economic and socioeconomic dimensions. What other environmental forces should you investigate?

MINICASE 7–1

International Drug Corporation

International Drug Corporation (IDC) is a multinational firm specializing in the production of ethical pharmaceuticals; that is, those available to the public from a pharmacist only on prescription. These products are characterized by a high degree of research effort and, because of the limited protection offered by patents, have a relatively short product life. IDC does make some over-the-counter products, but these are only about 20 percent of total company sales.

The vice president for the South American division needs to make a forecast for ethical drug sales, which he will use as a basis for setting quotas for the six countries that have manufacturing facilities in his division. These products produce about 75 percent of the total sales in each country. At present, IDC's market share and sales by category of drug (pediatric or geriatric and general) in each country are as follows:

	Market Share (percent)	Pediatric (0–14 years)	Geriatric and General (15 years and over)
Argentina	30%	32%	68%
Brazil	24	38	62
Chile	55	32	68
Paraguay	65	41	59
Peru	45	42	58
Uruguay	38	27	73

Total health care has grown faster than world population and world income since 1970. A conservative average of the total amount per capita spent on health care, both private and public, for pharmaceuticals in South America is 20 percent. This is considerably lower than in the United States and Europe; but in government clinics, medicine is generally offered without charge or at a substantial discount from the price charged in pharmacies. According to IDC's subsidiaries, the patients at the clinics probably pay, on average, 40 percent of the drugs' listed prices when those given at no charge are included. Obviously, the private drugstores that get only 40 percent off list (60 percent of the list price is their cost) cannot compete. IPC, however, still earns a 12 percent profit based on its selling prices when it sells to the governments at list less 50 percent because of the low marketing costs on such large volumes, as compared to an average of 20 percent of its selling prices on sales to private pharmacies.

Here are the data that the staff economist has just given to the vice president. Help him do his forecast. If you have to make any assumptions, please make a note of them. If marketing costs for government sales average 6 percent of IDC's selling price, while they average 11.7 percent of the selling price to private pharmacies, should the vice president try to change the present government–private pharmacy sales ratio that now prevails in any of the six markets? Should he have any other concerns based on these data?

	GDP (billions of dollars)			GDP/Capita			Foreign Debt (billions of dollars)			Percent Change from Previous Year		
	1982	1986	1988[a]	1982	1986	1988[a]	1983	1986	1988[a]	1983	1986	1988[a]
Argentina	$ 64.5	$ 69.8	$ 71.3	$2,271	$2,252	$2,241	$45.1	$ 51.4	$ 56.8	12.8%	4.5%	3.8%
Brazil	248.5	206.8	212.8	1,960	1,494	1,470	98.2	111.0	114.6	10.8	4.2	−5.5
Chile	24.1	16.8	18.9	2,096	1,377	1,492	18.0	20.7	19.1	7.6	4.7	−7.1
Paraguay	5.9	3.6	4.0	1,903	947	990	1.5	1.9	2.2	24.4	8.1	5.2
Peru	21.6	25.4	25.0	1,241	1,283	1,201	12.4	14.5	16.2	14.0	2.3	4.9
Uruguay	9.8	5.3	5.6	3,379	1,767	1,832	4.6	5.2	6.1	22.0	4.6	2.8

	Interest on Foreign Debt as Percentage of Export Receipts			Total Government Expenditures as Percentage of GDP			Percentage of Government Expenditures on Health Care			Private Consumption Expenditure (billions of dollars)			Annual Percentage of Private Consumption Spent on Medical Care
	1983	1986	1988[a]	1981	1986	1988	1982	1983	1986	1982	1983	1986	1980–1985
Argentina	58.4%	50.9%	40.4%	15%	12%	n.a.	1.1%	1.4%	1.3%	$38.7	$50.1	$53.7	4%
Brazil	43.5	41.4	29.7	n.a.	9[b]	n.a.	7.8	7.3	6.4	201.3	175.6	157.2	6
Chile	38.9	37.9	22.6	13	13	n.a.	6.8	6.0	6.0	18.6	14.5	11.6	5
Paraguay	14.3	18.5	11.6	7	7	n.a.	3.7	3.7	3.1	4.6	3.6	3.1	2
Peru	29.8	26.2	21.8	13	11	n.a.	5.3[c]	6.2[c]	n.a.	15.4	12.7	18.0	4
Uruguay	24.8	24.7	23.4	13	14	n.a.	3.3	6.5	4.8	7.3	3.5	3.9	6

	Population per Physician			Annual Inflation Rate			Population (millions)			Population Distribution 1985	
	1977	1980	1984	1983	1986	1988[a]	1982	1983	1987	0–14 Years	15 Years and Over
Argentina	530	430	370	444%	82%	372%	28.4	29.6	31.1	31%	69%
Brazil	1,700	1,200	1,080	179	58	816	126.8	129.7	141.4	39	61
Chile	1,930	1,930	1,230	24	17	11	11.5	11.7	12.5	31	69
Paraguay	2,190	1,310	1,460	14	24	17	3.1	3.2	3.9	41	59
Peru	1,530	1,390	1,040	125	63	1307	17.4	17.9	20.2	40	60
Uruguay	540	510	510	52	76	69	2.9	3.0	3.0	27	73

Note: n.a. = Not available.
[a]Estimate.
[b]1985.
[c]1981.
Sources: Various *World Development Reports* and Banco Nacional de Comercio Exterior *Comercio Exterior,* February and March 1989 issues.

MINICASE 7–2

Taiwan's Economic Development Plan, 1986–1989

Following are excerpts from Taiwan's Ninth Economic Development Plan that pertain to industry. The policies, priorities, and supporting measures that the government intends to take are listed. What business opportunities do there seem to be for local and foreign firms? What problems for foreign multinationals may occur in the future?

(II) INDUSTRY

An annual growth target of 6.1 percent has been set for the industrial sector during the plan period. Among subsectors, mining is targeted to grow 1.0 percent, manufacturing 6.3 percent, construction 5.7 percent, and public utilities 5.8 percent.

1. Basic policies.

1. Continue to intensify the development of strategic and important exporting industries and improve the industrial structure.
2. Speed up the development of technology-intensive industries and promote the export of capital goods and technology.
3. Continue to improve the domestic investment climate, promote the liberalization of investment, and encourage investment by domestic and foreign investors.

4. Facilitate coordinated development of private and public enterprises and technological exchanges between them.
5. Expand international cooperation in resource development and ensure a stable long-term supply of basic industrial materials.
6. According to the principles of international division of labor and comparative advantage, avoid any overexpansion of energy-intensive intermediate industries.
7. Assist existing labor-intensive industries to modernize machinery and equipment, to raise labor productivity and product quality, and to enhance their competitive position in international markets.

2. Development priorities.

(1) Strategic industries.

A. Machinery industry—Accelerate the transfer of technology and automation of production, plan for the standardization of parts and components, establish production and marketing order, and promote the exports of package plants.

B. Transportation equipment industry—Implement the "Automobile Industry Development Program" and the "Guidelines for the Financing of China Shipbuilding Corp.," formulate a "Motorcycle Industry Development Program" to enhance export competitiveness, and development of allied industries.

C. Electrical machinery industry—Strengthen research and development in new technology, promote computerized management, push forward with the manufacture of supplies and development of the heavy electrical machinery industry, encourage rationalization and standardization of production, and lower the degree of import dependency.

D. Electronics and information industries—

a. Speed up the development of digital electronic products and technologies for Very Large Scale Integrated Circuits (VLSI) and computers, recruit and cultivate manpower as needed, and set up market, technology, and parts-and-components information centers, and a marketing service network.

b. Vigorously develop microcomputers, digital electronic switching systems, and opto-electronic communications facilities; consolidate communications technology and machinery manufacturing to develop integrated products; study and develop an "Integrated Services Digital Network (ISDN)" to provide a combination of telephone, telegram, data, facsimile, TV, video telephone, and electronic mail services.

(2) Other industries.

A. Continue to encourage the modernization of equipment and facilities and the merger of manufacturers, and promote the automation and specialization of industrial production and the system of core-satellite plans with a view to improving production efficiency and product quality.

B. Encourage Chinese nationals and foreigners to invest in the manufacture of high value-added and high-technology industrial products, research and develop new products, and establish domestic manufacturers' own trademarks and marketing networks to lay a solid foundation for sustained industrial growth.

C. Devote greater efforts to controlling industrial pollution to protect public health and the ecological environment.

3. Supporting measures.

(1) Fiscal measures.

A. Modernize tax and customs administration, make timely adjustments in the structure of

taxes and import tariffs, expand the list of duty-free, basic raw materials, and promote the rationalization of industrial operations.

B. Implement the value-added tax and amend tax legislation to avoid double taxation.

C. Amend legislation relating to the income tax, land-value-increment tax, and other relevant taxes to spur the recovery of the building industry.

D. Continue to offer tax credit to industry as an incentive for investment.

E. Liberalize raw materials imports to eliminate abuses of the tariff-rebate system and reduce tariff-rebate costs.

(2) Financial measures.

A. Strengthen the roles of the Development Fund and all specialized banks in investment and financing and ease restrictions on bank financing of building and home construction.

B. Continue the promotion of international banking and the timely adjustment of the central bank rediscount rate and deposit-and-loan rates of the banking industry to accelerate the liberalization of interest rates.

C. Gradually relax restrictions on export-import foreign exchange collections and payments and ease foreign exchange control.

(3) Foreign trade.

A. Expand the role of the Export-Import Bank of China in export financing and the provision of export and exchange rate fluctuation insurance.

B. Streamline customs-clearance formalities and promote modernization of the customs reporting system.

(4) Assistance to small and medium enterprises.

A. Strengthen the role of the Medium Business Bank of Taiwan as a specialized bank and provide more medium- and long-term development credits to small- and medium-size enterprises.

B. Promote the modernization and automation of production and encourage the merger of small and medium business enterprises.

C. Assist small and medium enterprises in setting up a sound accounting system and provide them with commercial information to improve their operations and management.

(5) Assistance to industry.

A. Promote software technology of the information industry and upgrade the calibre of information software professionals.

B. Promote the development of industrial products with growth potential and cooperation with internationally recognized certification institutions, and establish a favorable international image for domestic brands.

C. Enforce "Good Manufacturing Practices (GMP)" and set up "Building and Equipment Standards for Food Processing Plants."

(6) Pollution prevention and control.

A. Provide credit assistance and tax and other incentives to encourage the purchase of pollution control equipment.

B. Tighten pollution control measures at existing plants and step up inspections at newly built plants.

C. Encourage pollution-producing plants to move to industrial estates where common pollution control measures may be taken, and promote the establishment of effective pollution detection and monitoring systems.

D. Tighten the controls of poisonous chemicals and noise in mining areas.

(7) Technology.

A. Step up international technological cooperation and transfer of key technologies, and encourage technological innovations and product development.

B. Promote the transfer and development of new technology to raise energy efficiency and prevent pollution.

C. Develop a basic ability to conduct research and development in materials science and technology, and establish an industrial technology information system.

(8) Promotion of investment.

A. Adopt the "negative list" approach and ease restrictions on investment to encourage the flow of capital into industry.

B. Continue to improve investment services, simplify administrative procedures, offer incentives to private investment, and promote the liberalization and rationalization of investment.

C. Relax restrictions on overseas investment by domestic concerns.

D. Amend the Labor Standards Law to take into account the interests of both labor and management.

(III) SERVICES

The service sector is targeted to grow 7.5 percent a year on average during the plan period, with transportation and communications targeted to grow 10.9 percent annually, commerce 7.5 percent, financing and insurance 10.0 percent, and other services 6.0 percent.

1. Basic policies.

1. Strengthen laws and regulations governing the service sector to improve commercial discipline and safeguard the interests of the entire economy and society.

2. Introduce modern managerial know-how and techniques to raise the productivity of the service sector.

3. Proceed gradually with financial and trade liberalization.

4. Upgrade the capacity and quality of the service sector, with a view to meeting the increasing needs of both agricultural and industrial producers and consumers.

2. Supporting measures.

1. Amend existing laws and regulations to strengthen commercial and financial administrative machinery, streamline regulatory and supervisory systems, create an environment for fair competition, and set up codes for conduct of business.

2. Improve the operation and management of the transportation and communications industries and promote the integrated development of various types of transport.

3. Promote a more rational rate structure for the transportation and communications industries and establish comprehensive transportation and communications services networks.

4 Strengthen modern business education, promote the concept of marketing-oriented business management, create marketing profits, and raise the productivity of commerce.

5. Ease restrictions on foreign investment in financing, insurance, and leasing operations; gradually liberalize import and export controls and bank interest rates; and promote the internationalization of the service sector.

6. Strengthen the protection of intellectual property rights, maintain discipline in trade, and establish a favorable international image for Taiwan's exports.

7. Develop an intelligent software industry and promote the sound development of professional services and family and personal services, such as health and medical care, sanitation, security, tourism, and entertainment.

VI. EXTERNAL SECTOR

In order to cope with changes in international economic conditions and to achieve an average annual economic growth target of 6.5 percent during the plan period, the following growth targets for goods-and-services imports and exports have been set:

- Goods-and-services exports are targeted to grow at a real annual rate of 7.3 percent (goods exports 7.0 percent, services exports 11.1 percent). Goods-and-services exports at 1985 prices will reach US$43.40 billion in 1989, up from US$32.76 billion in 1985. (Goods exports will climb to US$40.12 billion from US$30.61 billion.)

- Goods-and-services imports are targeted to grow at a real rate of 10.1 percent annually on average (goods imports 10.4 percent, services imports 8.5 percent). Goods-and-services imports at 1985 prices will approach US$36.96 billion in 1989, up from US$25.19 billion in 1985. (Goods imports will rise from US$20.10 billion to US$29.90 billion.)

(I) BASIC POLICIES

1. Actively promote trade liberalization, speed up the upgrading of industries, and enhance the competitiveness of exports.

2. Improve the environment for trade development, strengthen the capability of developing foreign trade, work for greater diversification of foreign markets, and promote balanced development of trade.

3. Strengthen trade discipline and establish a favorable international image for Taiwan's exports.

4. Raise administrative efficiency in trade and strengthen the role of trade administration.

(II) DEVELOPMENT PRIORITIES AND SUPPORTING MEASURES

1. Actively promote trade liberalization.

1. Continue to lower import tariffs and liberalize import control.

2. Reestablish a regulatory system for imports and exports with a "negative list."

3. Streamline procedures for customs clearance and reporting system.

4. Cut down the number of trade goods subject to inspection and establish an "Inspectors Licensing System."

2. Improve the composition of foreign trade.

1. Promote the development of strategic and technology-intensive industries, introduce key technologies, and push the export of new products.

2. Expand the exports of package plants.

3. Improve the domestic environment for investment and relax restrictions on investment overseas.

3. Take steps to counteract protectionism.

1. Promote trade ties with other nations, on the basis of equality and reciprocity.

2. Set up a specialized agency responsible for coordinating international trade negotiations.

3. Establish trade order and improve the international image of Taiwan-made products.

4. Set up a worldwide trade information network and assist local traders in developing counter- and triangular-trade relations.

4. Promote financial liberalization and internationalization.

1. Relax foreign exchange controls and permit business concerns to retain part of their foreign exchange proceeds.

2. Promote the internationalization of banking operations.

3. Set up a set of clear guidelines for Central Bank intervention in foreign exchange markets.

Source: Council for Economic Planning and Development, *Highlights of Ninth Medium-Term Economic Development Plan for Taiwan, Republic of China (1986–1989)*, January 1986.

SUPPLEMENTARY READINGS

Economics

"And Now, the Home-Brewed Forecast." *Fortune,* January 20, 1986, pp. 53–54.

"Indicators of Market Size for 117 Countries." *Business International,* June 1988.

"In a Maze of Numbers." *The Economist,* August 20, 1988, pp. 61–62.

"Norway Leaps Ahead in Labor Costs League." *Business Europe,* May 30, 1988, pp. 1–2.

OECD Economic Outlook. Paris: OECD, June 1988.

"The Hamburger Standard." *The Economist,* April 15, 1989, p. 86.

Foreign Debt

"A Latin Debt Plan that Might Work." *Fortune,* April 29, 1989, pp. 205–12.

"Can Third World Debtors Climb out of the Hole?" *U.S. News & World Report,* January 20, 1986, p. 12–15.

"Deals that Are Making a Dent in Third World Debt." *Business Week,* October 3, 1988, pp. 111–14.

"How the Debt Crisis Is Battering Multinationals." *Business Week,* July 25, 1983, p. 52–53.

"How to Make Sense of Italian Statistics." *Business Europe,* April 9, 1982, pp. 116–19.

Kim, Chongyoul. "Multinational Banks and the Third World's Debt: Are They in the Same Boat?" *Issues in International Business,* Summer/Fall 1985, pp. 13–20.

"Latin America's New Currency." *The Economist,* October 29, 1988, pp. 87–88.

"LDC Debt Conversions—A Survey." *Swiss Bank Prospects,* February/March 1989, pp. 1–5.

Inflation

"Brazil Back at the Brink." *The Economist,* January 7, 1989, pp. 18–19.

"Fear of Social Unrest Grows in Argentina as Economy Crumbles Ahead of Vote." *The Wall Street Journal,* April 29, 1989, p. A4.

Socioeconomic

"A Granny Crisis Is Coming." *The Economist,* May 14, 1984, pp. 59–62.

"Deutschland, Deutschland, älter alle." *The Economist,* January 7, 1989, pp. 39–40.

"Imported Youth." *The Economist,* December 3, 1988, p. 75.

"Population Policy: Country Experience." *Finance & Development,* September 1984, pp. 18–20.

"The World Population Heading for 6 Billion." *Weekly Bulletin.* Brussels: Kredeitbank, May 2, 1986, p. 1.

" 'White Goods' Makers Seek to Counter the Baby Bust." *The Wall Street Journal,* May 9, 1989, p. A23.

National Plans

Council for Economic Planning and Development. *Highlights of 1988 Economic Development Plan for Taiwan, Republic of China,* December 1987.

Peters, Tom. "A Case for Chaos." *U.S. News & World Report,* April 14, 1986, p. 54.

"Planning in a Market Economy." *Economic Review.* Taipei: Bank of China, January 1988, pp. 8–17.

Review of the Netherlands Economy. Amsterdam: Bank Mees & Hope NV, March/April 1988.

ENDNOTES

1. "And Now, the Home-Brewed Forecast," *Fortune,* January 20, 1986, pp. 53–54.

2. Many of these factors, of course, also affect the domestic firm, but the multinational firm is generally more vulnerable and usually must act more quickly.

3. If management for some reason is interested in a country as a possible site for investment, the same detailed information will be required as is required for an area where the firm is already involved.

4. An excellent bibliography, *International Bibliography, Information, Documentation (IBID),* is published quarterly by UNIPUB. Abstracts of publications and studies containing economic and demographic data are included.

5. You can make your own table for 34 countries by first getting the average hourly earnings in national currency from the U.S. Department of Labor, Bureau of Statistics, *Handbook of Labor Statistics.* However, the data in this publication lag considerably, so you then go to the latest issue of *International Financial Statistics,* published monthly by the IMF. Here, for each country listed in the *Handbook,* you can find a very recent index of average hourly costs. Multiplying a ratio of the IMF's index values by the latest value in national currency in the *Handbook,* you can derive more recent values in local currency. Then you go back to the IMF publication and select the average exchange rates for the years you are comparing and convert national currencies to dollars. You will find differences between *Business Europe's* figures and the results you obtain by this method. We're not sure why, but obviously *Business Europe* either used different exchange rates or obtained different values expressed in national currency (probably the exchange rates). This illustrates the problem in expressing any national statistic in dollars.

6. "How the Debt Crisis Is Battering Multinationals," *Businessweek,* July 25, 1983, p. 52.

7. "A Latin Debt Plan that Might Work," *Fortune,* April 29, 1989, p. 205.

8. "Latin America's New Currency," *The Economist,* October 29, 1988, p. 87.

9. Developed nations are not immune, either. France, the Netherlands, and Belgium have recently faced this problem.

10. *World Development Report, 1989* (Washington, D.C.: World Bank, 1989), pp. 216–17.

11. " 'White Goods' Makers Seek to Counter the Baby Bust," *The Wall Street Journal,* May 9, 1989, p. A23.

12. "Population Policy: Country Experience," *Finance & Development,* September 1984, pp. 18–19.

13. "Europe's Population Bomb," *Newsweek,* December 15, 1986, p. 52.

14. "Pensions after 2000," *The Economist,* May 19, 1984, pp. 59–62; and "The Case for More Immigrants," *U.S. News & World Report,* February 13, 1989, p. 29.

15. "The Economies of the 1990s," *Fortune,* February 2, 1987, p. 24.

16. *World Development Report, 1989,* Table 31, pp. 224–25.

17. "Ethnic Demands Abroad," *The Wall Street Journal,* December 18, 1978, p. 27.

18. "Eastern European Plans: 1981–85 Targets to Be Sober and Flexible," *Business International,* June 26, 1981, pp. 202–3; and "Perestrikeout," *Financial World,* November 29, 1988, pp. 20–21.

19. "Five-Year Plans: Guide to EE Sales Strategy?" *Business Eastern Europe,* May 15, 1981, pp. 153–54.

20. Council for Economic Planning and Development, *Highlights of Ninth Medium-Term Economic Development Plan for Taiwan, Republic of China (1986–1989),* January 1986, pp. 41–42.

Chapter 8
Physical Forces

If you do this . . .

Look at a map of the world, as large a map as possible. At first sight, it seems to be a maze of lines, colors, and unfamiliar names. Go on looking and studying until the mere mention of a town, country, or river enables it to be picked out immediately on the map. Those who are concerned with overseas marketing must, as a basis, know their export geography as well as the streets around their home.

Henry Deschampneufs, *Selling Overseas* (London: Business Publications, 1960), p. 46.

You won't be told this . . .

Middle East consultant, piqued by his clients' ignorance of the region, begins his briefings by saying, "Iraq isn't the past tense of Iran."

The Wall Street Journal, July 5, 1985, p. 32.

LEARNING OBJECTIVES

In this chapter, you will study:

1. The importance of a country's location in political and trade relationships.

2. How surface features contribute to economic, cultural, political, and social differences among nations and among regions of a single country.

3. The importance of inland waterways and outlets to the sea.

4. How climate exerts a broad influence on business.

5. Why managers must monitor changes in the discovery and use of mineral resources.

6. Why managers must be alert to changes in a nation's infrastructure.

7. The impact of industrial disasters, such as Bhopal and the Rhine River spill, on multinational firms.

KEY WORDS AND CONCEPTS

- Topography
- Canadian Shield
- Rhine waterway
- Landlocked
- Climate
- Natural resources
- Shale
- Polymetallic deposits

BUSINESS INCIDENT

Watches, lace, carvings, chocolate, cheese, precision machinery, pharmaceuticals—what do they have in common? All are produced in Switzerland, all have a high value per kilo, the Swiss versions are known for their quality, and the physical forces are primarily responsible for their being produced in Switzerland.

To appreciate why this so, review the following about the physical forces in Switzerland:

1. Switzerland is mostly mountainous; there is little level land.
2. Switzerland is close to the heavily populated lowlands of Western Europe.
3. Transportation across the mountains to these markets is relatively expensive.
4. Switzerland has practically no mineral resources.

One way to overcome the lack of local sources of raw materials and high transportation costs is to import small amounts of raw materials, add high value to them, and export a lightweight finished product. The Swiss have done precisely this with the manufacture of watches. They import small volumes of high-quality Swedish steel costing 40 cents per ounce that they then convert to watch movements selling for $60 per ounce. Because of their light weight, the cost of transporting these movements to market is minimal. Precision machinery and pharmaceuticals are other products that minimize the need for importing bulky raw materials. For all of these products, emphasis is placed on the value added by manufacturing, which is based on skill, care, and tradition.

Although the Swiss slopes do not support much agriculture, they are adequate for raising cattle and goats. Production of milk is no problem, but getting it to its major markets outside Switzerland is. Fluid milk is bulky in relation to its value and expensive to transport. The dairymen do to the milk what the watchmakers do to the steel—convert it to a concentrated, high-value product: cheese. Because Swiss cheesemakers have no advantage

223

BUSINESS INCIDENT (concluded)

over their counterparts in the lowland dairying areas nearer to the important markets, they have to compete on the basis of high quality and reputation, which they have carefully promoted.

The plentiful supply of milk is responsible for another product: milk chocolate. The Swiss import the raw chocolate and convert the milk into another high-value-per-kilo product. Certainly the Swiss manufacturer pays higher transportation costs to bring sugar and chocolate in and ship the finished product out than does Hershey in Pennsylvania. Again, their product must be perceived to be superior so that it will bring a higher price to offset the greater costs.

What about the lace and carvings? The physical forces are responsible for these also. The heavy snowfall and cold temperatures of the Swiss winter leave the dairymen and their wives with little to do. About the only work necessary is feeding the animals with stored hay. To help pass the time and earn some money, Swiss women make lace and embroidery while the men carve figures and cuckoo clocks.

Source: Adapted from Rhoads Murphey, *The Scope of Geography*, 2nd ed. (Skokie, Ill.: Rand McNally, 1973), pp. 65–67.

The Business Incident illustrates what one writer meant when he wrote that "the physical character of a nation is perhaps the principal and broadest determinant of both the society found there and the means by which that society undertakes to supply its needs."[1]

Strictly speaking, the physical elements are not forces because, except for natural disasters (such as earthquakes, floods, and hurricanes), they are passive. However, there are similarities between them and the uncontrollable forces we describe in this section: their effects are not constant, and although they have a profound impact on the way people organize their activities, the physical forces are only one set of the many factors that influence humanity. In fact, cultural, political, and economic factors may be more important than the physical factors in determining land use and the nature of the economy. How else can you explain the great differences between southeast China and the U.S. Southeast? Their physical environments are very similar, but they support different people with wide divergencies in their cultures and land use.

Probably the most important reason for considering the physical elements as uncontrollable forces is that they have many aspects of the foreign environmental forces we discussed in Chapter 1. Also, as we shall illustrate, managers must adjust their strategies to compensate for differences among markets of the physical forces just as they do for the other uncontrollable forces.

Although the scope of geography is extremely broad, it is possible to select some elements that are particularly significant for the businessperson: (1) location, (2) topography, (3) climate, and (4) natural resources.

LOCATION

Where a country is located, who its neighbors are, and what its capital and major cities are should be part of the general knowledge of all international businesspeople. Location is important because it is a factor in explaining a number of a nation's political and trade relationships, many of which directly affect a company's operations.

Political Relationships

Do you believe the Finnish government would expect a Finnish subsidiary of an American WWC to do business with Russia? Check the location of Finland on a map. You will note that Finland and Russia share a long common boundary—780 miles, to be precise. Now look at the country on its western border—Sweden, a nation with a long history of neutrality. Can you expect Finland's policy to be anything but one of strict neutrality? In fact, the Finns have worked so diligently to be neutral that when the country joined the European Free Trade Association (EFTA) to ensure duty-free entrance of its products to EFTA members, it joined as an associate, not as a full member. To appear strictly neutral, it also concluded a trading agreement with the Council for Mutual Economic Cooperation (COMECON), the Soviet bloc's economic organization.[2] Not until January 1986 did Finland become a full member of EFTA. However, when asked if his country would join the European Community, the Finnish minister of foreign trade was very emphatic in saying that its neutrality was incompatible with EC membership.[3]

Austria is another country whose location between the East and the West exerts an influence on its politics. As a politically neutral nation bounded on the west by Germany, Italy, and Switzerland and on the east by Czechoslovakia, Hungary, and Yugoslavia, Austria has become a popular location for multinationals' offices servicing Eastern European operations. Vienna, its capital, is considered more politically convenient than other European cities for visits by communist customers. However, apparently there are different levels of neutrality: Austria is considering EC membership.

Trade Relationships

Geographical proximity is often the major reason for trade between nations. As you saw in Chapter 2, the largest and the fourth-largest trading partners of the United States—Canada and Mexico—lie on its borders. Deliveries are faster, freight costs are lower, and it is less expensive for sellers to service their clients. This is also one of the reasons why so many American firms have plants on the Mexican side of the common border. Geographic proximity has always been a major factor in the formation of trading groups, such as the EC, EFTA, and now the agreement for the U.S.–Canada Free Trade Association, which was formed in 1989. There is considerable speculation that the other country on the U.S. border, Mexico, may eventually become a member.[4]

Nearness to the market is also the reason why Japan's sales to the Association of Southeast Asian Nations (ASEAN), the Southeast Asian trade group, are 40 percent higher than U.S. sales and 75 percent greater than sales of the European Community, a still more distant supplier.[5] Because it is closer to Japan, China has been able to take over part of the sales of soybeans and wheat formerly supplied by the United States.

Did you ever stop to think where the fresh grapes and raspberries that you eat in the dead of winter come from? Probably not, until cyanide poison was found in two grapes imported from Chile in 1989. Interestingly, Chile's sales of $700 million annually are possible for just the opposite reason that we have been discussing—its U.S. market is geographically distant.

WORLDVIEW
Dutch–Belgian Enclaves Are Giant Jigsaw

Baarle-Nassau-Hertog, Netherlands—Cross the road in this odd little town and the chances are you have passed from the Netherlands to Belgium, or perhaps the other way around.

Baarle-Nassau-Hertog, in the southern Dutch province of North Brabant near the border with Belgium, is a bewildering patchwork of intermingling Dutch and Belgian territories.

"We're the world's biggest jigsaw puzzle," joked Yvo Kortmann, mayor of eight Dutch areas that collectively form Baarle Nassau. His Belgian colleague, Dr. Jan van Leuven, controls about 20 parcels of land of varying sizes dotted between the Dutch parts and known as Baarle Hertog.

The two municipalities have separate police, churches, schools, and, most important for the local economy, shops.

Different Rules
Sunday in Baarle-Nassau-Hertog, as the 8,000 inhabitants call their town to help bemused outsiders, is rarely a day of rest because shops are open and Dutch consumers arrive in the thousands to buy cheap cigarettes and chocolate.

Sunday closing is the norm in the Netherlands, but the village is exempted because Belgium has different rules. The exemption is one of many that allow the town to flourish as a territorial oddity and tourist attraction.

It all started with disputes between nobility over land ownership in the 12th century, and the resulting puzzle remains to baffle officials and international lawyers today, even though the main Belgian–Dutch border was established in 1843.

House numbers are set on tiny metal national flags to give some indication where the borders run. Some houses have a border passing through them, and one has two different numbers because the front door is right on the border.

Border Bemusement
"Some people sleep in Belgium and eat in the Netherlands without even leaving the house," Kortmann said.

He and van Leuven, who lives across the proper border in the Belgian town of Turnhout, shuttle between The Hague and Brussels to work out the many local problems.

One of the most recent trips was to try to persuade Belgium that it was time to accept the two groups'

TOPOGRAPHY

topography the surface features of a region

Surface features such as mountains, plains, deserts, and bodies of water contribute to differences in economies, cultures, politics, and social structures, both among nations and among regions of a single country. Physical distribution is aided by some features but hindered by others. Differences in **topography** may require products to be altered. For example, the effects of altitude on food products begin to be seen at heights above 3,000 feet (producers of cake mixes must change their baking instructions); and internal combustion engines begin to noticeably lose power at 5,000 feet, which may require the manufacturer of gasoline-powered machinery to use larger engines.

Let us examine some of the principal surface features to give you an idea of what the businessperson should look for.

Mountains and Plains

Mountains are barriers that tend to separate and impede exchange and interaction, whereas level areas (plains and plateaus) facilitate them. The

garbage because it was cheaper than disposing of it in the Netherlands.

On a higher plane, both mayors are waiting for finance ministers to meet them to discuss value-added tax, which causes untold problems for village shopkeepers battling with the differing Belgian and Dutch rates.

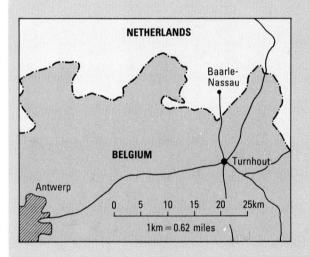

Lots of Confusion

Villagers naturally intermarry across the national divide, and this confuses matters further.

"My husband is Belgian, I'm Dutch. We live in Belgium and I work in the Netherlands. The tax men go crazy," one resident said.

The village's position is said to have attracted criminals keen to dart from one territory to the next to avoid arrest.

Unfortunately for them, it works the other way around, too.

In one celebrated case, a Dutch property consultant based in a Dutch part of town was wanted in the United States for involvement in a real estate swindle, but could not be extradited from his own country.

The lone Belgian policeman in Baarle Hertog obliged by arresting him as the man unwittingly crossed a border into a Belgian enclave. He was convicted in the United States and later returned to face trial in the Netherlands, too.

Source: Martin Nesirky, "Dutch–Belgian Enclaves Are Giant Jigsaw," *Los Angeles Times,* December 11, 1986, p. 28.

extent to which mountains serve as barriers depends on their height, breadth, length, ruggedness of terrain, and whether there are any transecting valleys.

An example of such a barrier is the Himalaya Mountains. Travel across them is so difficult that transportation between India and China has been by air or sea rather than overland. The contrast between the cultures of the Indo-Malayan people living to the south of the mountains and the Chinese living to the north is evidence of the Himalayas' effectiveness as a barrier. In similar fashion, the Alps, Carpathians, Balkans, and Pyrenees have long separated the Mediterranean cultures from those of northern Europe.

Mountains divide markets.   A greater problem for the businessperson is posed by those nations that are divided by mountain ranges into smaller regional markets, each with its own distinctive industries, climate, culture, dialect, and sometimes even language. Such is the case of Spain, where there are five separate regions. The cultural differences of two of them, Catalonia and the Basque country, are so great that they have separate languages, not dialects, and each has a sizable group that wishes to secede from Spain to form a separate nation. Although the Basques and the Catalonians can speak Spanish, when they are among themselves they use their own languages, which

■ **FIGURE 8–1**   **The Cantons and Major Language Areas of Switzerland**

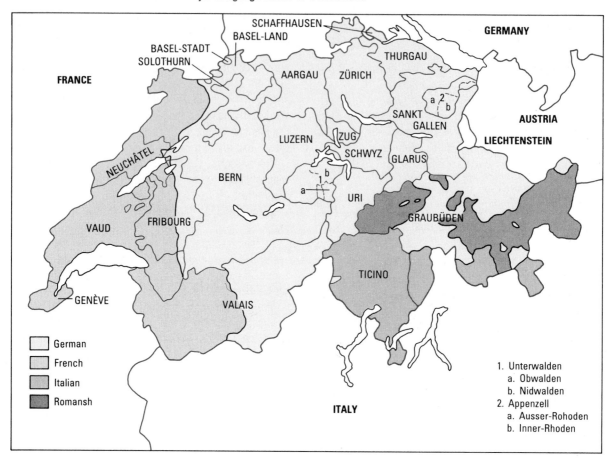

are completely unintelligible to other Spaniards in both commerce and the home. This creates the same kind of problems found wherever there are language differences: Spanish-speaking managers do not attain the empathy with their local employees that they do in other parts of Spain, and sales representatives who speak the local language are more effective.[6] Moreover, the language differences increase promotional costs if, to be more effective, Spanish companies choose to prepare their material in Basque, Catalonian, and Spanish.

Unrest is especially prevalent among the Basques, where—like the IRA in Ireland—terrorists frequently attack and kill government officials and the police. In 1979, a majority of Basque voters chose greater autonomy, but not total separation, from Spain, and for a while, the killings stopped. However, in 1989, a terrorist group known as the ETA renewed its terrorism.

Switzerland is another country that is separated into distinctive cultural regions by mountains. In a country one half the size of Maine, four different languages and 35 different dialects are spoken—Italian, French, German, and Romansh (see Figure 8–1). To the consternation of the advertising manager attempting to reach all regions of the country, each of the three major language groups has its own radio and television network, and the fourth, Romansh

■ **FIGURE 8–2**
Map of Colombia

Source: Reproduced by permission of the World Bank.

(Latin), is also used by the German stations. For a really confused cultural and political situation caused by mountains, see this chapter's Worldview.

Three ranges of the Andes divide Colombia from north to south into four separate markets, each with its own culture and dialect (see Figure 8–2). Depending on the product, this could require the creation of four distinctive promotional mixes.

Moreover, not only are the cultures different, but so are the climates. Because of its location near the equator, Colombia has no seasons but does experience a variety of climates due to the great differences in altitude. These range from hot and humid at sea level (mean average temperature of 82 degrees in Baranquilla) to cold and dry in the 10,000-feet-high snow-capped mountains (57 degrees in Bogota). Imagine the production and inventory problems that such differences occasion for the manufacturer that must supply a distinct product and package for each zone.[7]

Because these climatic conditions are not peculiar to Colombia, market analysts should examine topographical maps to see which tropical countries possess this combination of lowlands and mountains. If the firm's products will not function properly in such climatic extremes, either they must be redesigned or the company must bypass this market.[8]

Population concentration.   Mountains also create concentrations of population either because the climate is more pleasant at higher altitudes or because they are barriers to population movement. For example, nearly 80 percent of Colombia's population is located in the western highlands (only one third of the nation's area) because the climate there is moderate. Eighty percent of Brazil's 140 million people inhabit a 300-mile-wide coastal strip separated from the remainder of the country by a mountain range. Except in the tropics, the population density generally decreases as the elevation increases. If you were to place a population map over a topographic map, the blank areas on the population map would generally coincide with the areas of higher elevation. For example, 90 percent of Switzerland's population is located in a narrow belt at the base of the Alps. The reason for this is that dense population requires commerce, manufacturing, and agriculture, which all depend on the good transportation and ease of communication afforded by the plains.

Deserts and Tropical Forests

Deserts and tropical forests, like mountains, separate markets, increase the cost of transportation, and create concentrations of population.

Deserts.   Over one third of the earth's surface consists of arid and semiarid regions located either on the coasts where the winds blow away from the land or in the interior where mountains or long distances cause the winds to lose their moisture before reaching these regions. Every continent has them, and every west coast between 20 and 30 degrees north or south of the equator is dry. Since people, plants, and animals must have water to exist, the climatic and vegetational deserts are also the human deserts. Only where there is a major source of water, as in Egypt, is there a concentration of population.

Nowhere is the relationship between water supply and population concentration better illustrated than in Australia, a continent the size of the continental United States but with only 16 million inhabitants. Its surrounding coastline is humid and fertile, whereas the huge center of the country is mainly a desert closely resembling the Sahara (see Figure 8–3).

Because of its geography, the population has tended to concentrate (1) along the coastal areas in and around the state capitals, which are also major seaports and (2) in the southeastern fifth of the nation, where more than one half of the population lives. This gives Australia one of the highest percentages of urban population in the world. The 86 percent of the total population living in cities is surpassed only by Belgium (96 percent), Kuwait (92 percent), the

■ **FIGURE 8–3   Map of Australia**

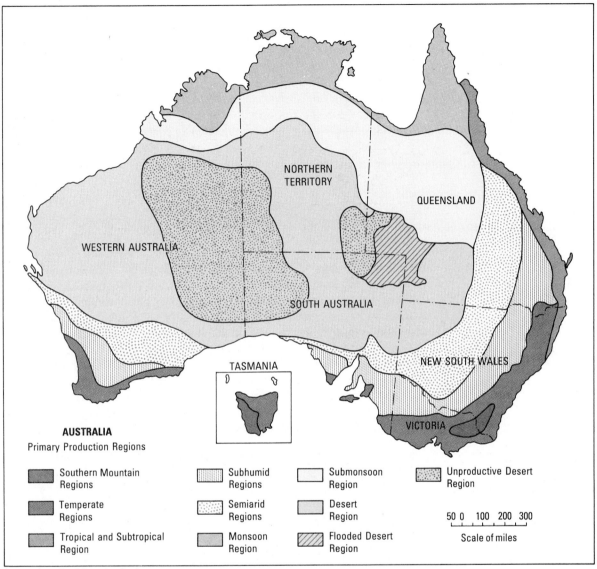

AUSTRALIA
Primary Production Regions

- Southern Mountain Regions
- Temperate Regions
- Tropical and Subtropical Region
- Subhumid Regions
- Semiarid Regions
- Monsoon Region
- Submonsoon Region
- Desert Region
- Flooded Desert Region
- Unproductive Desert Region

50 0   100   200 300
Scale of miles

Courtesy Australian Information Service.

United Kingdom (92 percent), Israel (90 percent), and the Netherlands (88 percent).[9]

The distances between these cities and the fact that they are seaports make coastal shipping preferred over road and rail transportation.[10] However, these long distances between major markets result in transportation accounting for as much as 30 percent of the final cost of the product, as compared with the more usual 10 percent in the United States and Europe.

The population distribution also has a profound impact on Australia's media. First of all, there are only three upper-socioeconomic-group newspapers and a few magazines that can be considered national media. All other media are concentrated in capital city areas. This requires advertisers to buy space or time on a state-by-state or city-by-city basis. Although most capital city areas have three commercial TV channels, there is little networking.[11]

Even though 70 percent of the country is arid or semiarid, some areas in the northern rim receive up to 100 inches of rainfall annually, much like the monsoon areas of India. Thus the firm entering the Australian market faces the same extreme differences of temperature and humidity encountered in Colombia.

Were it not for the uniform topography of Australia, the temperature differences would be even greater, as they are in countries with large, hot desert areas and irregular surfaces. Iran is such a nation. In the summer, temperatures may reach 130°F, whereas winter temperatures in high altitudes may drop to −18°F. From December to March, it is possible to ski just an hour-and-a-half's drive from Teheran, the capital. Like Australia, Iran's population distribution is heavily influenced by climate and topography. More than 70 percent of the country—consisting mostly of mountains and deserts—is uninhabited, and one half of the population lives in urban areas.

Tropical rain forests.   Vegetation can be an effective barrier to economic development and human settlement, especially when it is combined with harsh climate and poor soil. This occurs in the world's tropical rain forests located in the Amazon basin, Southeast Asia, and the Congo. Except in parts of West Africa and Java, they are thinly populated and little developed economically. For example, the greatest rain forest of them all—in the Brazilian Amazon— has been called one of the world's greatest deserts because of its low population density. Although it covers more than 1 million square miles (one fourth of the U.S. land area) and occupies one half of Brazil, it is inhabited by just 4 percent of the country's population. Only true deserts have a population density lower than the Amazon's one person per square mile.

Canadian Shield a massive area of bedrock covering one half of Canada's land mass

Canadian Shield.   Although the **Canadian Shield** is neither a desert nor a tropical forest, this massive area of bedrock covering one half of Canada's land mass has most of their characteristics—forbidding topography, poor soil, and harsh climate. The Shield is swept by polar air, which permits a frost-free growing season of only four months. During that time, residents are molested by swarms of black flies and mosquitoes. Like deserts and tropical forests, its population density is very low: only 10 percent of Canada's population inhabits the region.[12]

Relevance for businesspeople.   Managers know that in more densely populated nations, it costs less to market their products (population centers are closer, and communication systems are better), more people are available for employment, and so forth. Therefore, when they compare population densities like Canada's 2.6 inhabitants per square kilometer, Australia's 2.1, and Brazil's 16.3 with the Netherlands' 356 or Japan's 327, they may draw the wrong conclusions. However, if they are aware that the population in each of the first three countries is highly concentrated in a relatively small area for the reasons we have been examining, then a very different situation prevails. Notice in the next section how bodies of water also are responsible for concentrations of population.

Bodies of Water

This surface feature, unlike mountains, deserts, and tropical forests, attracts people and facilitates transportation. A world population map clearly shows that nearly all bodies of water have attracted more people than have the surrounding areas. Those densely populated regions that do not coincide with rivers or lakes are generally close to the sea. You would note from the map that populations cluster around the Amazon, the Congo, the Mississippi, the St. Lawrence, and the Great Lakes. In Europe, the plain of the Po (Italy) and the Rhine are easily recognizable. So are rivers that cross deserts, such as the Nile, the Indus (Pakistan), the Tigris-Euphrates (Iraq), and the Amu Darya in Russian Central Asia, although these are more important for the irrigation water and fertile soil they bring than for transportation.[13]

However, bodies of water that are significant because of their ability to provide inexpensive access to markets in the interior of various nations are the inland waterways.[14]

Inland waterways.   Before the construction of railways, water transport was the only economically practical carrier for bulk goods moving over long distances. Water transport has increased even after the building of railroads, although its importance relative to railroads has diminished everywhere with one exception—the Rhine waterway, the world's most important inland waterway system.

Rhine waterway a system of rivers and canals, the main transportation artery of Europe

Rhine waterway.   The **Rhine waterway**, the main transportation artery of Europe, carries a greater volume of goods than the combined railways that run parallel to it. As an illustration of the Rhine's significance, one half of Switzerland's exports and nearly three fourths of its imports pass through Basel, the Swiss inland port. This cargo is carried on the country's own 31-vessel ocean-going fleet via the Rhine to Rotterdam, 500 miles to the north (see Figure 8–4).

By means of the Rhine and its connecting waterways, shipments move between the Netherlands, Belgium, Germany, France, Austria, and Switzerland. When the Main–Danube connection is finished in 1992, the waterway will give access by means of 2,000-ton ships and two-unit push-barges (3,600 tons each) to 13 countries and the Black Sea. From there, shipments can continue to Moscow over the interconnected system of the Volga and Don rivers. While it is unlikely that many ships will undertake the entire 30-day voyage from Rotterdam to the Black Sea (3,500 kilometers), the completed waterway will stimulate shipping over shorter East–West routes, such as Nuremburg to Budapest or Vienna to Rotterdam.[15]

Other waterways.   In every continent except Australia, which has no inland waterways, extensive use is made of water transportation. In South America, the Amazon and its tributaries offer some 57,000 kilometers of navigable waterways during the flood season. Ocean-going vessels can reach Manaus, Brazil (1,600 kilometers upstream), and smaller river steamers can go all the way to Iquitos, Peru (3,600 kilometers from the Atlantic).

Based on economic value, the most important South American river system is the Parana. Ocean freighters travel from the Rio de la Plata near Buenos Aires to Santa Fe, Argentina (240 kilometers upstream), and riverboats bring

■ **FIGURE 8-4**
Europe's Major Inland Waterways

Source: Waterways map provided by the European Conference of Ministers of Transport, 1989.

cargo 1,360 kilometers to Asunción, the capital of the landlocked nation of Paraguay.

In Asia, the major waterways are the Yangtze (China), the Ganges (India), and the Indus (Pakistan). Rivers are especially important in China because water is the least expensive, and often only, means of moving industrial raw materials to the manufacturing centers. Ocean-going vessels can travel up the Yangtze as far as Wuhan, 1,000 kilometers from the sea. This river and its tributaries form the densest waterway system in the world, with over 30,000 kilometers usable by steamships, launches, or junks.

Rhine waterway

Courtesy of Photri

Although the United States possesses extensive rail and highway systems, it also depends heavily on two waterways. One, the Great Lakes–St. Lawrence, enables ocean freighters to travel 3,700 kilometers inland, thus transforming lake ports into ocean ports. The other waterway, the Mississippi, connects the Great Lakes to the Gulf of Mexico and is especially important for carrying bulky commodities, such as wheat, cotton, coal, timber, and iron ore.

Outlets to the sea.   Historically, navigable waterways with connections to the ocean have permitted the low-cost transportation of goods and people from a country's coast to its interior and even now are the only means of access from the coasts of numerous developing nations.

This has been a particularly troublesome problem for Africa, in which 14 of the world's 20 **landlocked** developing countries are located. Almost one third of all sub-Sahara countries are landlocked, and some are more than 1,000 kilometers from the sea by the shortest land route. The implications for these poor nations are obvious: they must construct costly, long truck routes and extensive feeder networks for relatively low volumes of traffic. Furthermore, governments in countries with coastlines through which the imports and exports of the landlocked nations must pass are in a position to exert considerable political influence. Small wonder that struggles for outlets to the sea still exist and are an important factor in the political as well as economic forces.

One outstanding example is the century-long struggle by Bolivia to regain from Chile an outlet to the Pacific Ocean. These countries have held

landlocked   when a nation is bordered on all of its frontiers by land

Port of Basel, Switzerland

Courtesy of H. Armstrong Roberts

discussions for decades, but no workable agreement has been reached. Until Bolivia has its own coastline, it must use Arica, the free port in northern Chile. The lack of a satisfactory solution continues to be a source of tension between the two governments.[16]

Farther south, two of the giants of South America, Brazil and Argentina, have been using Paraguay's need for an outlet to the Atlantic to further their ambitions to be the leader of South America. For years, Paraguay's only connection to the ocean was through the port of Buenos Aires. Brazil, observing that Paraguay was experiencing difficulty with the Argentine government over the right to use that nation's waterways, erected the Friendship Bridge on the Paraguay–Brazil border and completely paved a highway linking Paraguay with the Brazilian port of Paranagua. To further facilitate the movement of Paraguayan goods, the port was declared a free zone only for Paraguay. This has led to numerous cooperative ventures between the two countries, and it appears that Paraguay is now solidly in Brazil's area of influence. Important to international businesspeople is the knowledge that closer political ties bring closer economic ties, which alter traditional trading patterns. That certainly has been the case in this instance.[17]

CLIMATE

Climate (temperature and precipitation) is probably the most important aspect of the physical environment because it, more than any other factor, sets the limits on what people can do both physically and economically. When the

climate meteorological conditions, including temperature, precipitation, and wind, that prevail in a region

climate is harsh, there are few human settlements, but where it is permissive, generally there are great clusters of population. However, climate is not deterministic—it allows certain developments to occur, but it does not cause them. Nonclimatic factors, such as mineral deposits, accessibility to an area, economic and political organizations, cultural tradition, availability of capital, and the growth of technology, are more important than climate in the development of trade and manufacturing.[18]

Similar climates occur in similar latitudes and continental positions, and the more water-dominated an area, the more moderate its climate. Thus, the northwest United States and northwest Europe, which are at similar latitudes and are both influenced by the sea, have mild, moist climates. Southeast Australia, New Zealand, and part of South Africa are at the same latitude and are close to the sea. They too have mild, moist climates. At the other extreme, Kansas and Central Asia, which are both far from the sea and at the same latitude, are dry and have cold winters and hot summers.

Climate and Development

For centuries, writers have used climatic differences to explain differences in human and economic development. They have suggested that the greatest economic and intellectual development has occurred in the temperate climates of northern Europe and the United States because the less temperate climates limit human energy and mental powers.[19] The map in Figure 8–5 seems to support this thesis. However, marketers must not be taken in by this ethnocentric reasoning, which fails to explain why, for example, the northeastern United States, unlike northern Europe, was inhabited by Stone Age savages until the 1600s. Clearly there were other factors involved, such as the Industrial Revolution, population size, and location.

This is not to say that climate has not had some influence on economic development. Studies by the World Bank have shown that many of the factors responsible for the underdeveloped state of most tropical nations are present because of the tropical climate. Continuous heat and the lack of winter temperatures to constrain the reproduction and growth of weeds, insects, viruses, birds, and parasites result in destroyed crops, dead cattle, and people infected with debilitating diseases.[20]

As grim as this may sound, there is hope. The World Bank points out that techniques are becoming available to control pests and parasites. Once this is accomplished, the very characteristics that are now detrimental to tropical Africa will give it sizable advantages over the temperate zones in agriculture. The resulting income would create a market in tropical Africa that could easily surpass that of the Middle East at the time oil prices were at their highest.

Climatic Implications for Businesspeople

The differences in climatic conditions among a firm's markets can have a significant impact on its product mix. For example, internal combustion engines designed for temperate climates generally require extra cooling capacity and special lubrication to withstand the higher temperatures of the tropics. Goods that deteriorate in high humidity require special, more expensive packaging, machinery operating in dusty conditions needs special dust protection, and so forth.

■ **FIGURE 8–5   Impact of Climate on Economic Development**

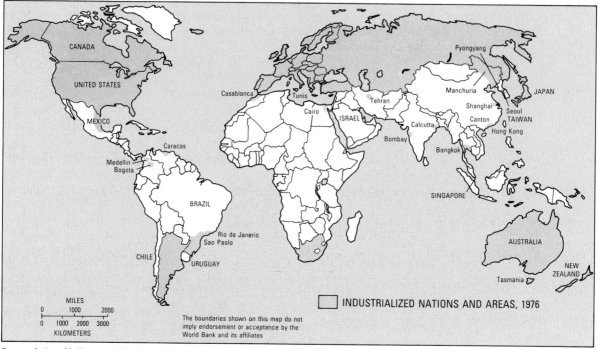

Source: Andrew M. Kamarack, *The Tropics and Economic Development* (Baltimore: Johns Hopkins University Press, 1976), pp. 6–7. Copyright © 1976 by the International Bank for Reconstruction and Development/The World Bank.

When climatic extremes exist in a single market and the product is temperature- or humidity-sensitive, the company may have to produce and stock two distinct versions to satisfy the entire market. Severe winters, such as those in Canada, or the heavy monsoon rains that fall in northern Australia and India can impede distribution. This may require the firm to carry extraordinarily large inventories in its major markets to compensate for delays in delivery from the factory. All of these conditions, of course, have an adverse effect on profitability.

NATURAL RESOURCES

natural resources anything supplied by nature on which people depend

What are **natural resources?** There is no commonly accepted definition among the professionals who work with them. One well-known economic geographer, Professor Joseph H. Butler, states, "To meet their economic needs— including the basic ecological requirements of water, food, clothing, and shelter—people undertake the production of goods and services by extracting *natural resources* from the environment." He adds that all three sectors of the natural environment provide raw materials: the solid portion of the earth, the water portion, and the atmosphere.[21] For our purposes, we can define natural resources as anything supplied by nature on which people depend.

Until fairly recently, business managers' and government officials' main concern about natural resources has been the supply of exhaustible minerals and mineral fuels, certainly an immediate and pressing problem. During the Arab–Israeli war in 1973, we saw how Arab exporters of petroleum used an oil embargo on some nations and the threat of an embargo on other nations to obtain political support from Western Europe. The realization by oil-importing nations that not only their industries but also their national defense depended on a substance that other nations could use as a political force initiated a worldwide campaign to conserve minerals and mineral fuels and to search for new energy sources.

Alternative Energy Sources

Oil sands and shale.   One potential energy source is the tar sands of Athabasca, Canada, which contain bitumen, a tarlike crude. Instead of being pumped from wells, bitumen is strip-mined and sent to a separation plant, where it is converted into a higher-quality synthetic crude oil. Although this crude is more costly to produce than conventional crude, after OPEC quadrupled its prices in 1974, a Sun Oil plant at Athabasca, which began production in 1967, suddenly became profitable.

The subsequent decline in world prices made the future of synthetic oil production uncertain, but the lack of discoveries of conventional crude to replace Canada's depleting reserves motivated the Canadian government to offer new tax incentives to bitumen producers. The Sun Oil plant now produces 49,000 barrels of synthetic crude daily, for example.[22] One fourth of Canada's total oil production already comes from this source. It is estimated that Canada has 70 billion barrels of recoverable oil in the form of bitumen, which is sufficient to meet its needs for the next 130 years.[23]

The United States has an equal amount of oil that is known to be recoverable from **shale** in Colorado, Utah, and Wyoming. However, the recovery process is also expensive, which makes the end product unable to compete with today's prices of conventional crude. In addition, there are environmental problems connected with the disposition of huge quantities of waste shale. So far, Union Oil is the only company to have built a recovery plant with a daily production of 5,000 barrels. The company is expanding the plant to double its daily output.[24] The total U.S. shale oil reserves are estimated to be 600 billion barrels—more than all of OPEC's total proven reserves.

Crude from coal.   A promising source of synthetic oil and gas is coal gasification. South Africa, concerned about being shut off from crude oil imports for political reasons, has built three Sasol plants; these supply a large portion of its oil and gas needs from low-grade coal, which is in plentiful supply. A coal gasification plant built in North Dakota with South Africa's help will produce enough gas to heat a quarter of a million homes. At present, a consortium operates a 1,000-ton-per-day plant in California.[25]

New finds.   Spurred by the high oil prices of the 1970s, which required oil-importing nations to divert huge sums of foreign exchange to pay for their oil imports, many governments opened their countries to oil exploration by foreign firms. In just a few years, new oil finds were made in the Middle East, Africa, Asia, and Latin America. Nations that are either approaching self-sufficiency in oil or have even begun to export it include Egypt, Syria, Oman, Tunisia, Malaysia, Zaire, Angola, Congo, Benin, Cameroon, India,

> **shale**   a fissile rock (capable of being split) composed of laminated layers of claylike, fine-grained sediment

Australia, Argentina, Peru, Brazil, and Colombia.[26] Colombia became an oil exporter in 1986, after Occidental Petroleum discovered a new field with a billion barrels of petroleum (the amount may reach 2 billion barrels as exploration continues). In 1984, when the field was discovered, oil imports cost Colombia $500 million. Government officials estimate that by 1990, Colombia will earn nearly $2 billion annually from oil exports. Another nation, Pakistan, may join the oil-exporting nations in three or four years. Its oil production already meets one third of its daily needs, and the new discoveries are causing its Oil and Gas Development Corporation to claim that it has billions of barrels of untapped reserves.[27] And still another country, Peru, made a major find in 1989 that should soon convert it to a net exporter.[28]

The increased oil production that has been supplanting OPEC imports has caused OPEC's members to lose revenue in two ways: (1) world oil prices have been driven down and (2) some OPEC nations have reduced their output to try to avoid price erosion.

How has this affected companies that depended heavily on OPEC members for sales in the 1970s? Because they have been obtaining less revenue from their oil sales, OPEC members have had to reduce their purchases. However, firms that keep abreast of this shift in crude oil production are able to compensate somewhat for their loss in sales to OPEC members by opening new markets in the non-OPEC nations that discover oil.

Nonfuel Minerals

Although much of the world's attention has centered on the discovery of new energy sources, Table 8–1 shows that there are also other mineral resources about which governments and industry are apprehensive. Nearly all of the world's chrome, manganese, platinum, and vanadium are produced by South Africa and the Soviet Union. Chrome and manganese are indispensable for hardening steel; platinum is a vital catalytic agent in the oil-refining process and is used in automotive catalytic converters; and vanadium is an ingredient in a steel alloy for metal-cutting tools. The United States depends on South Africa to supply 49 percent of its platinum, 55 percent of its chromium, 39 percent of its manganese, and 44 percent of its vanadium. Although South Africa has never threatened to stop the export of these strategic metals, government and industry leaders are well aware that should the South African source be lost, the major industrial societies in the West would be heavily dependent on the Soviet Union for their supply, in both wartime and peacetime.

Bleak situation?   The situation appears bleak, but remember that we are discussing *known reserves*. Do other sources exist? Consider this. Only relatively small areas, mostly in the traditional mining countries, have been adequately explored. For example, it is estimated that only 5 percent of the potential mineral-containing areas in Mexico and only 10 percent of those in Bolivia have been studied extensively.

Furthermore, a relatively new technology, satellite mapping, has enabled geologists to locate new sources. They now know that Brazil, for example, possesses extensive deposits of chrome, nickel, copper, lead, zinc, and manganese.

■ TABLE 8–1
Major World Sources of
Industrial Minerals That
the United States Must
Import

Mineral	Percentage of Consumption Imported	Distribution of Reserves (percent of world total)	Use
Aluminum	97%	Guinea (27), Australia (21), Brazil (11), Jamaica (9), India (5)	Aluminum products
Chromium	75	South Africa (78), USSR (12), Zimbabwe (2), Finland (2), Philippines (1)	Stainless steel
Cobalt	86	Zaire (38), Cuba (29), Zambia (10), New Caledonia (6), Indonesia (5)	Aerospace alloys
Columbium	100	Brazil (79), USSR (17), Canada (3), Nigeria (2), Zaire (1)	Aerospace alloys
Manganese	100	South Africa (41), USSR (36), Gabon (11), Australia (8), Brazil (2)	Electronics
Nickel	74	Cuba (34), Canada (14), USSR (13), Indonesia (7), South Africa (5)	Stainless steel
Platinum	88	South Africa (79), USSR (20)	Catalytic converters
Silver	57	USSR (16), Canada (15), Mexico (14), U.S. (12), Australia (10)	Photography, electronics
Tantalum	92	Thailand (27), USSR (17), Australia (17), Nigeria (12)	Electronics
Titanium	n.a.	Brazil (20), South Africa (14), India (12), Norway (14), Australia (9)	Aerospace alloys
Vanadium	96	USSR (60), South Africa (20), China (14), U.S. (4)	Aerospace alloys
Zinc	69	Canada (15), U.S. (13), Australia (11), South Africa (6), USSR (6)	Metal plating

Note: n.a. = Not available, but some U.S. production.
Source: *World Almanac* (New York: Newspaper Enterprise Association, 1986), p. 121; and 1989, p. 179.

Seabed mining—an untapped source.   The existence of metal deposits on the ocean floor was discovered in 1876, when a British explorer found a number of small, metal-containing nodules. Little attention was paid to them until the 1960s, when tests showed that these nodules were present in practically every sea and in some lakes, such as Lake Michigan. However, the nodules richest in metallic content are nearly all located on the ocean floor, at depths of from three to five miles. Although geologists are not sure how they are formed, they do know where they are most numerous and what their metallic content is. Analysis shows that all of the nodules contain some 30 metals but have an extremely high copper, nickel, manganese, and cobalt content. This last metal, all of which is now imported in the United States, is especially important, as it is widely used in military and vital civilian technologies. For example, 900 pounds of cobalt are needed to produce just one engine for the F16 fighter plane. Table 8–2 compares the metal content of seabed sources with that of land sources.

■ **TABLE 8–2**
Average Metal Content
(Percent)

	Copper	Cobalt	Nickel	Manganese
North Pacific	1.16%	0.23%	1.28%	24.6%
North Atlantic	0.15	0.34	0.30	14.2
South Atlantic	0.15	0.31	0.48	18.0
Indian Ocean	0.19	0.28	0.50	14.7
Continental reserves				
Minimum	0.50	0.07	0.40	40.0
Maximum	0.50	0.10	1.00	50.0

Source: "In Search of Metals on the Seabed," *Kredietbank Weekly Bulletin* (Brussels), June 13, 1980, p. 1.

polymetallic deposits
those which contain a number
of metals

Metal deposits are also found in the crust of chimneylike structures up to 100 feet in height that were formed when hot water rushed up from active volcano vents in the sea floor. The **polymetallic deposits** contain significant quantities of cobalt, manganese, nickel, and other metals.

Since 1974, 140 nations have been negotiating an agreement to put seabed mining under the control of the International Seabed Authority, a UN affiliate. In July 1982, the United States announced that it would not sign the Law of the Sea Convention because it objected to the seabed mining provisions. Instead, President Reagan proclaimed a U.S. Exclusive Economic Zone, which extends the jurisdiction of the United States to include all mineral resources within 200 nautical miles of the U.S. coast and the coast of U.S. island territories. Six international consortia, which include American companies, have already spent millions of dollars perfecting technologies to mine the seabed nodules. However, the combination of low mineral prices and the uncertainty of mining rights have kept the firms from proceeding on a commercial scale. In spite of these difficulties, seven communist countries formed a consortium in 1987 to mine cobalt, nickel, manganese, and copper from the sea floor at a depth of one mile.[29]

Changes Make Monitoring Necessary

Mineral resources.   You saw how crude oil prices spurred the discovery of oil by non-OPEC members as they sought to lessen their dependence on imported oil. New land-based sources of strategic nonfuel minerals have also been discovered, and we have learned that the seabeds contain vast amounts of these minerals in the form of nodules and seafloor crusts.

Concomitantly, important discoveries are being made that could lessen our need for these minerals. For example, in 1984 the U.S. Air Force in conjunction with Pratt and Whitney announced the development of two new *cobalt-free* superalloys for possible application in a new generation of fighter jet engines.

Probably the most fascinating discovery of all is a solar-powered technique to produce hydrogen from *water*. Instead of using gasoline for fuel, aircraft and automobiles might use hydrogen. In the 1950s, Lockheed flew a B-57 bomber that had one engine converted to burn hydrogen, and in 1988, a similarly converted Russian plane completed a test flight.[30] Hydrogen can also be used in conventional gasoline engines. South African engineering students have already built and driven an automobile that does so.[31]

WORLDVIEW
Undersea Ore Find in Pacific Ocean Said to Be Worth Millions

Scientists of the National Oceanic and Atmospheric Administration (NOAA) have discovered an immense undersea ore deposit worth billions of dollars in the eastern Pacific about 350 miles west of Ecuador. The rich lodes can be easily mined because they are on the surface around old volcanic vents. Although they are 8,500 feet below the ocean surface, the technology to get them already exists. Because of the depth and coldness, there is no life and no current. The area could be mined with virtually no damaging ecological effects. Using a deep-diving submersible, the scientists found a wide band of metallic sulfide deposits almost three fourths of a mile long. The ore body is 650 feet wide and 130 feet thick and is estimated to weigh 25 million tons.

The deposit is approximately 10 percent copper, worth $2 billion, and 10 percent iron. Other minerals include molybdenum, vanadium, zinc, cadmium, tin, and lead. The richness of the copper deposit (10 times that found in land mines) illustrates how the hot water shooting from the volcanic vents for 1,000 years has concentrated the minerals.

Similar volcanic areas have been found in the Gulf of California, off the coast of Oregon, and in the Pacific Ocean near the U.S. territories of Midway, Guam, and Samoa. A senior scientist at the Woods Hole Oceanographic Institution and a pioneer in seafloor exploration states, "A few years ago, we didn't know any of this existed. Now, after exploration of only a small sample of the seafloor, the whole picture has changed." He stresses that continued exploration is needed, but that we should not rush into large-scale mining because the "economics don't look favorable. . . . If shortages of metal develop, then we know where to go."

He notes that other countries are moving much faster. "France has a massive sulfide-exploitation program, and they're dead serious." A German firm working with Red Sea deposits for a group of nations that include Saudi Arabia and the Sudan has already brought up deposits to test a shipboard system for concentrating ore and refining metals. The Canadian Department of Mines estimates the recoverable amounts from Red Sea deposits at 1.7 million tons of zinc, 400,000 tons of copper, and 5,000 tons of silver.

Source: "Ocean Mining: Boom or Bust?" *Technology Review,* April 1984, pp. 55–66.

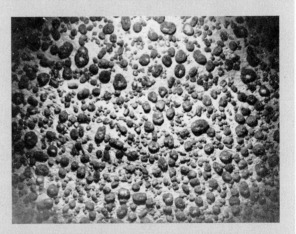

Potato-sized manganese nodules on the sea floor of the Central Pacific

What is the significance to businesspeople of these new discoveries? Obviously, sellers of commodities and products that are being threatened by the discoveries must monitor them and prepare for new competition. More important, *all* firms supplying goods and services to nations that depend on the traditional minerals for foreign exchange to pay for those goods and services must be aware of developments that can destroy old markets and create new ones. Imagine the loss of purchasing power in the Middle Eastern countries if lower-cost hydrogen available from water takes the place of gasoline! We have already seen cutbacks in the purchases of these countries because of lower crude oil prices, but what if petroleum were needed only by the petrochemical industry and not for transportation?

Other changing physical forces.   Mineral resources are not the only physical forces that change. Modifications of infrastructure, most of which are of great significance to businesspeople, are being made constantly. For example, new settlements and new industries are attracted to areas in which dams have been built to control flooding and to provide power and irrigation water. New highways and new railways reduce delivery times to present markets and thus enable firms to cut their distribution costs by reducing their inventories. For example, improved highways now permit regularly scheduled overland delivery service from London to cities as far east as Moscow. One Russian trucking firm now makes the London–Moscow run in just eight days, a trip that formerly took months by sea.

However, when the Brazilian government sought a World Bank loan to construct a paved highway to connect the mineral-rich but economically stagnant state of Acre to the rest of Brazil, American environmentalist groups complained, and the loan was postponed. Their concern was that the road would destroy the Amazon tropical forest, which they say converts carbon dioxide to oxygen and absorbs heat, thus reducing the greenhouse effect. Nevertheless, Brazil's foreign minister said, "Brazil isn't going to become the ecological reserve for the rest of the world. Our biggest commitment is with economic development."[32] Because Japanese firms want the lumber and other products that this road will carry to market, Japanese banks are making the loan.[33] Despite its cost, one of Latin America's major infrastructural achievements, the Trans-Andean Highway, has greatly increased trade and tourism between Argentina and Chile.

New infrastructure is responsible for economic development in developed nations also. The Channel Tunnel, which will connect England and Calais, France, by 1993, is already attracting heavy investment. Calais, for example, expects its population to double to 200,000, many of whom will be British citizens attracted by cheaper housing and the ability to live in France and commute daily to work in Great Britain. Distribution costs will be significantly lower because the trip by train from London to Paris will take only three and a half hours instead of the present seven hours.[34]

Another timesaver is the new Seto Ohashi Bridge in Japan, which links the island of Shikoku with the central island of Honshu. What was formerly a two-hour ferry ride is now a 10-minute drive. The sharp reduction in travel time is having a profound impact on agriculture. Faster delivery times for produce is calculated to result in a $30 million increase in farmers' income.[35]

Contamination of Resources

Historically, nations have paid relatively little attention to the contamination and destruction of the world's natural resources. Entire forests have been destroyed by people wanting to get firewood or to clear land and by contaminated air and water. Pollution control of air and water was considered a luxury that governments, anxious to attract new industry and to keep the industry they had, could ill afford to impose. As the secretary of mines and energy for the state of Bahia, Brazil, stated, "Brazil can't afford pollution control like Japan or the United States. It's cultural imperialism."

However, such tragedies as the Bhopal disaster and the horrendous Sandoz spill into the Rhine have forced officials to realize that the price for such negligence is too high.

Courtesy of Inter-American Development Bank

The Trans-Andean Highway

The Bhopal disaster. What is described as the world's worst manmade industrial disaster killed some 2,800 people and injured another 270,000. On December 3, 1984, the deadly gas methyl isocyanate, used in the production of pesticides, leaked from storage tanks at the Bhopal plant of Union Carbide (India), a joint venture of Union Carbide (50.9 percent) and Indian capital.

Although suits totaling $250 billion had been filed on behalf of Bhopal victims, in February 1989 the Indian Supreme Court reached an out-of-court settlement with Union Carbide (U.S.) under which the American company would pay $470 million to victims of the disaster.[36] Each victim will receive $14,460, about 50 times India's BNP/capita.[37] Although the Indian government had charged that the Bhopal plant was poorly designed and poorly maintained while Union Carbide insisted that the plant had been sabotaged, the court did not assign blame for the accident.

A key issue—whether the lawsuits seeking damages should be tried in American or Indian courts—had been decided earlier by an American court, which ruled that the case should be heard in India.

The Rhine spill. On November 1, 1986, a fire broke out in the Sandoz warehouse in Basel, Switzerland, where pesticides were stored. The building had neither automatic alarms nor a sprinkler system. By the time fire brigades arrived, the fire had spread throughout the building. The drainage system could not handle all of the water that was pumped into the flames, and soon chemicals mixed with water flowed into the Rhine nearby.

No one was harmed, and it was not until two days later that the first dead fish appeared. Soon, cities on the river turned off their river supplies of drinking water and closed floodgates to protect tributaries from contamination. In one part of the Upper Rhine, between Karlsruhe and Basel, almost every creature died. Experts claimed that a 120-mile section from Basel to Dusseldorf would be biologically dead for two to five years.

Critics of the manner in which the spill was handled compared the Swiss government's 24-hour delay in advising other governments to the Russian delay in informing the West about the Chernobyl disaster.[38] However, there is one noticeable difference between the two catastrophes: Russia refuses to pay any part of the $121 million damages claimed by German farmers as a result of the Chernobyl nuclear power plant explosion, whereas Sandoz has indicated it will pay claims.[39]

Alaskan oil spill.   Called America's Chernobyl, the worst oil spill in this country's history occurred near Valdez, Alaska, in 1989, when an Exxon tanker hit a reef and spilled 240,000 barrels of crude oil. The effects on the marine ecosystem will not be known for years, but already thousands of birds and mammals have died. Japanese buyers of herring have canceled orders, and fishermen believe the entire season of this multimillion-dollar industry will be lost.

Exxon vows it will pick up all the oil and leave the area as it was before the accident. Even if it does, the company will still be liable for damages exceeding $100 million if it is found to have been negligent.[40]

Consequences for multinationals.   Antipollution activism, already a potent force in Europe and North America, is spreading to other parts of the world. Local citizen groups have increased their impact on government policies and have worked to delay the projects of multinationals in newly industrializing countries, such as Brazil, India, Malaysia, Mexico, and Thailand. The notion of economic growth at any cost is being challenged, and many nations, developing as well as developed, are now requiring environmental impact assessments before approving new industrial plants. Multinational producers of hazardous materials are finding that these changes are resulting in higher costs and are making the locating of overseas plants more difficult.[41]

Multinationals in hazardous industries will resist the minority positions in joint ventures mandated by numerous governments when such positions cause them to lose control to the local majority on questions of equipment, plant safety, and environmental controls. Warren Anderson, chairman of Union Carbide at the time of the Bhopal disaster, voiced the concern of many multinational managements when he said, "India sued us on the novel theory that any multinational engaged in hazardous operations is totally liable for any mishap, regardless of what share it may own. Is the insistence by Third World countries on local content in goods manufactured for local markets always realistic? It was, for example, at India's insistence that Carbide started making, instead of just mixing, agricultural chemicals in the Bhopal plant."[42]

SUMMARY

The importance of a good knowledge of geography has perhaps not been given the emphasis it deserves. Because of the changes that have occurred, what was learned in grammar school geography will not suffice today. Businesspeople should be familiar with the locations of countries, their significant landforms, and their climates. These elements of the physical forces exert a powerful influence on the environmental forces. Mountain ranges, deserts, and tropical forests act as barriers to the movement of people, goods, and ideas, whereas bodies of water facilitate such movements.

Businesspeople must not be misled into believing that because the major industrialized nations are located in temperate climates, it follows that natives of the tropics are inherently inferior. Parasitic diseases and poor nutrition are responsible for their lower productivity.

Because of the rapid depletion of the known sources of natural resources, firms dependent on them for production have been forced to search for new supplies in previously unexplored regions. New discoveries are important to all firms, however, because they frequently create new markets. If substitutes are found that will decrease the need for a natural resource, a number of currently strong markets may diminish in importance.

Industrial accidents like the Bhopal disaster and the Rhine River spill have caused both the industrialized and the developing nations to be more concerned about the protection of national resources. The concept of growth at any cost is giving way to environmental considerations. Many nations, for example, now require environmental impact assessments before approving new industrial plants. WWC managements are reassessing the desirability of taking minority positions in joint ventures when they cannot control equipment choice, plant safety, and maintenance.

QUESTIONS

1. Go to the chalkboard and draw a map of South America. How many countries can you locate? Do you know their capitals?

2. Of the 25 nations listed by the United Nations as the least developed among the developed nations, 14 are landlocked. Is this a coincidence, or is the lack of a seacoast a contributing factor to their slower development?

3. Analyze the potential of oil shale and oil sands as future energy sources. What problems are involved in using these natural resources?

4. Assume you are a member of your company's long-range planning committee. You have heard that experiments have been successful in separating hydrogen from water and that the hydrogen is then combined with carbon to form hydrocarbons. It is said that the product may cost 20 percent less than crude oil obtained from wells. Discuss with your colleagues how this development may affect your marketing plans in the Middle East and in the oil-poor developing countries.

5. The manager of your Chilean manufacturing subsidiary in Antofagasta reports it is now possible to ship goods by train from Antofagasta to São Paulo, Brazil, via Santa Cruz, Bolivia, in about seven days. Check a map of South America, and speculate on what this means in terms of new business for the subsidiary.

6. The director of personnel in your firm's home office tells you, the plant manager home on leave from the Indonesian subsidiary, "The only reason we have an infirmary in our American plants is to take care of workers injured on the job. Why do you want to staff our infirmary in Indonesia with nutritionists and experts in parasitic diseases?" How would you answer that?

7. Your firm is planning to enter the markets in northern South America with electric motors. The vice president of marketing, who has had no experience in selling to this region, announces, "Our inventory requirements will be simple. Since the climate is moist and humid in these countries, we'll have to supply the higher-priced models that we market along the U.S. Gulf Coast, and we can forget about the less expensive motors we sell up North. Fortunately, our competitors will have to do the same thing because of the climate, so we won't have to worry much about price competition." You are the export manager. What is your reaction?

8. Explain how the physical forces of a country influence its sociocultural forces.

9. International businesspeople, unless they are in the business of refining minerals or petroleum, have no need to concern themselves with world developments in natural resources. True or false? Explain.

10. There are many critics of the U.S. policy of friendship with South Africa. Do you believe the physical

forces influence our policy? (Hint: Analyze Table 8–1, and check South Africa's location on a world map.)

11. What will be the consequences for multinational firms of such disasters as the Rhine spill and the Bhopal accident?

MINICASE 8–1

Planning for Mineral Shortages

The long-range planning committee of the James Metal Products Company is meeting to discuss the firm's dependence on imported raw minerals. The president, John Ashe, speaks:

Ashe:

Gentlemen, as you know, we are here to discuss what we can do to protect ourselves in case of a mineral shortage. You all remember that when rebel soldiers invaded Zaire, the price of cobalt shot up from $12 to $100 per kilo. No one knew how long supplies would be interrupted, and so everyone bid up the stocks that were available. We need a plan to reduce our vulnerability in the event of other shortages.

Stan Williams, technical manager:

John, wasn't the Zaire affair an oddity? That won't happen again, will it?

Ashe:

Well, Stan, the experts foresee the increasing use of strategic materials as political weapons to reach social, economic, or even ideological objectives. Don't forget that some 20 countries control the most important materials and that the top three producers often account for 50 to 90 percent of worldwide production.

Don Olsen, executive vice president:

Furthermore, Stan, the situation for some minerals is extremely delicate because most of these producers are Third World countries that have little domestic use for the materials they produce.

Roy Jackson, production manager:

Can someone tell me exactly what minerals we are talking about? I know what we use, but I don't know which ones are critical. Can you tell us, Pete?

Pete Jones, purchasing agent:

I am in about the same position you are, Roy. I found out that cobalt was critical when the price suddenly skyrocketed, but we haven't experienced serious problems with the others. We have been able to get what we want in the open market.

Olsen:

I read somewhere that the production of strategic materials in the Third World is often supervised by a single ministry or a state-owned company. That makes it pretty easy to use minerals as a bargaining tool for political favors or military support. You remember how some of the European governments acquiesced to political pressure from OPEC members during the oil shortage.

Ashe:

I don't believe, Don, that nonoil cartels are as threatening as OPEC has been, because there are more chances for substitution and recycling for minerals than there are for oil. Of course, if the African producers of chromium, nickel, or cobalt decided to join forces in a cartel, that could be serious.

Jackson:

John, I can see some substitution possibilities. Just the other day, a design engineer told me that instead of making a part from stainless steel, he was going to use plain carbon steel and then give it a coat of paint to protect it.

Olsen:

John, don't you think that it's up to governments to act to protect us against shortages? They can relax environmental laws and institute tax incentives to encourage domestic production. They might even extend the NATO concept to include protection of Japan, Brazil, Argentina, South Africa, Indonesia, and the Gulf states. They could have an international military force to occupy and operate important mineral fields when necessary. What I don't see is what we as a company can do.

Ashe:

Don, we've already touched on four major areas where we can take action to make us less vulnerable to supply disruptions. Let's review them.

What are the steps that James Metal Products can take?

Source: "How Dependent Are You on Strategic Minerals? Firms Should Take Stock," *Business International,* April 24, 1981, pp. 132–33; and "A Strategy for Coping with Mineral Shortages," *International Management,* April 1981, pp. 53–54.

MINICASE 8-2
Bhopal Fallout

Harry Johnson, CEO of International Chemical, called a meeting of the newly formed crisis management committee, which consists of the vice president of manufacturing; the vice president-legal; the vice president of health, safety, and environment; the chief financial officer; and the public relations officer. Johnson had formed the committee after Union Carbide's Bhopal disaster to examine International Chemical's contingency plans. Because the two companies have similar international organizations and produce similarly toxic products, he asked the members to review the information they had on the Bhopal disaster and make recommendations as to what each person's area would do should their company have a similar accident. Johnson also asked the vice president of health, safety, and environment to begin the meeting by giving the committee a synopsis of the series of events that occurred during the first days after the disaster.

He begins, "As you know, on the night of December 2, a series of runaway chemical reactions heated the interior of a partially buried tank holding 10,000 gallons of methyl isocyanate (MIC) used in the manufacture of Sevin and other pesticides. An escape valve opened, which released a lethal cloud over Bhopal. No one knows how it happened, but Union Carbide investigators say that, by accident or through sabotage, a large quantity of water had been poured into the tank, which then reacted with the MIC to produce heat and open the valve. A refrigeration unit that could have kept the tank temperature at a manageable level had broken down five months previously and had not been repaired. A temperature alarm that would have alerted workers was not properly set. Last of all, a scrubber designed to neutralize toxic vapors was not turned on until the reaction was out of control.

"Union Carbide headquarters in Connecticut first heard of the accident at 3 A.M. on December 3, when employees from Union Carbide in Bhopal called Lutz (chairman of UC Eastern, the division responsible for Asian operations) at his home. By 6 A.M., Lutz, Oldfield (president of the agricultural products division, which markets the insecticides produced at Bhopal), Browning (director of health, safety, and environment), and Van Den Ameele (manager of press relations) met at headquarters. Although they were skeptical about the accuracy of the growing estimate of the numbers of dead and injured, they agreed that a swift response was needed and that top management would need to make some decisions. By midmorning, they called UC's

president and went to a hastily called meeting of the senior management committee. When Carbide board chairman Warren Anderson, in bed with a bad cold, was informed by telephone of the problem, he organized a crisis committee of legal, finance, and public affairs people.

"Within 12 hours, the committee dispatched a medical and technical team to arrange relief for the victims, to investigate the incident, and to assist with the safe disposal of the remaining MIC supplies at the plant. They held a press conference even though they did not have all the answers for the press. The next day, as the death toll continued to mount, Anderson took the company jet to Bhopal. On arrival, he was arrested, held briefly, and then sent to New Delhi, the capital. There, Indian officials told him to leave for his own good. His offer of $1 million in aid and the use of the company guest house to shelter orphans of the victims was refused.

"Because Carbide managers did not know what had caused the leak, they stopped production of MIC in the United States and converted all of their stocks of MIC worldwide into pesticides. The crisis caused the price of Carbide stock to fall, so the team began to stress the company's financial soundness in press releases and briefings. To bolster employee morale, the UC president made a videotape for Carbide employees worldwide in which he assured them of the company's ability to handle any likely damage settlement. By the way, even though Carbide provided the specifications for the Indian plant, it was designed and built in India at the insistence of the Indian government, which has a 20 percent interest in the Indian company. Carbide has 50.9 percent, but it has been essentially an Indian operation. The other investors are Indian."

"Thanks for the rundown," said Johnson. "I don't need to tell you that managements of multinational producers all over the world are studying Union Carbide's situation very closely. I read that one executive said this accident could rewrite the whole book on how to operate in foreign countries and how one covers one's risks overseas. Who wants to start the discussion on (1) what we need to do now to avoid both an accident and risk to the company if there should be one and (2) what should our plan be in case—and I hope it never happens—we should have a similar accident?"

Source: Information on Bhopal disaster from "Union Carbide: Coping with Catastrophe," *Fortune*, January 7, 1985, pp. 50–53; "Anderson Reflects on Managing Bhopal," *Industry Week*, October 13, 1986, p. 21; "For Multinationals It Will Never Be the Same," *Businessweek*, December 24, 1984, p. 57, and "Bhopal Report," *C&EN*, February 11, 1985, pp. 14–52.

SUPPLEMENTARY READINGS

Climate, location, and topography

Basta, S. S., and A. Churchill. "Iron Deficiency Anemia and the Productivity of Adult Males in Indonesia." Staff Working Paper No. 174. Washington, D.C.: World Bank, 1974.

Butler, Joseph H. *Economic Geography.* New York: John Wiley & Sons, 1980.

"Doing Something about the Weather." *World Monitor,* December 1988, pp. 28–37.

"EC, EFTA to Prepare for 1992." *Europe,* November 1988, p. 39.

"Geography Defines Media Profile in Australia." *Advertising World,* July 1984, p. 14.

Hoyt, Joseph Bixby. *Man and the Earth.* Englewood Cliffs, N.J.: Prentice-Hall, 1967.

Kamarck, Andrew M. *The Tropics and Economic Development.* Washington, D.C.: World Bank, 1976.

Murphey, Rhoads. *The Scope of Geography.* 2nd ed. Skokie, Ill.: Rand McNally, 1973.

"North America into the Year 2000." *Business International,* October 3, 1988, pp. 301–12.

Price, L. W. *Mountains and Men.* Berkeley: University of California Press, 1981.

Robinson, H. *Geography for Business Studies.* 3rd ed. Estover: MacDonald and Evans, 1979.

"The Inconsistent Climate." *Geographical Magazine,* February 1989, pp. 26–29.

"U.S., EC Compete for Markets in ASEAN Countries." *Europe,* November/December 1985, pp. 24–25.

Wheeler, James O., and Peter O. Muller. *Economic Geography.* New York: John Wiley & Sons, 1981.

Natural resources

"A Back Door into the Amazon." *The Economist,* February 11, 1989, pp. 38–39.

Brewer, G. Daniel. "Hydrogen-Powered Aircraft." *ICAO Bulletin,* October 1980, pp. 8–10.

"Looking for Oil in India and Thailand." *OPEC Bulletin,* August 1988, p. 10.

"Metal Factories of the Deep." *Natural History,* 1/88, pp. 52–56.

"Ocean Mining: Boom or Bust?" *Technology Review,* April 1984, pp. 55–56.

"Polymetal Sulphides: More Riches from the Sea?" *DESI Facts 82/2.* New York: United Nations, March 1982.

"Sea Law: Highlights." *UN Chronicle* 19, no. 6 (June 1982), pp. 5–6.

"The Jigsaw Environment." *U.S. News & World Report,* December 26, 1989, pp. 92–93.

"The Mines of Aparthied." *Newsweek,* August 11, 1986, p. 30.

"U.S., Europe Eye Aerospace Planes." *Europe,* November/December 1985, pp. 22–23.

"U.S. Needs S. A. Minerals." *S. A. Digest,* February 13, 1987, pp. 5–7.

"Using Red Ink to Keep Tropical Forests Green." *U.S. News & World Report,* March 6, 1989, p. 48.

Pollution

"And Toxic Flows the Rhine." *World Health,* March 1987, pp. 24–26.

Bhargava, Ashok, and Suresh Desai. "Multinationals and Developing Countries: Impact of the Bhopal Disaster." *Issues in International Business,* Winter 1988, pp. 28–34.

"Bhopal Report." *C&EN,* February 1985, pp. 14–52.

"Bhopal Ruling to Affect Multinationals." *Business Insurance,* October 5, 1987, pp. 55–56.

"Changing Environmental Rules and Regulations at a Glance." *Business International,* September 12, 1988, pp. 280–81.

"How Green Is Your Company?" *International Management,* January 1989, pp. 24–27.

"Smothering the Waters." *Newsweek,* April 10, 1989, pp. 54–57.

"The Blotch on the Rhine." *Newsweek,* November 24, 1986, pp. 58–60.

"Union Carbide: Coping with Disaster." *Fortune,* January 7, 1985, pp. 50–52.

Transportation

"Bracing for the "Gold- Rush.' " *International Management,* December 1988, pp. 32–34.

"Europe's Great Waterway." *Standard Chartered Review,* February 1986, pp. 2–7.

"How the Channel Link Could Change Europe." *International Management,* January 1986, pp. 30–34.

"Moving the Third World." *OECD Observer,* June 6, 1988, pp. 9–10.

"Seto Ohashi Bridge." *Japan Update,* Winter 1989, pp. 10–11.

"The Honshu–Shikoku Bridge Is Redrawing the Industrial Map." *Japan Update,* Autumn 1987, pp. 1–2.

ENDNOTES

1. Robert Bartels, ed., *Comparative Marketing: Wholesaling in 15 Countries* (Homewood, Ill.: Richard D. Irwin, 1963), p. 4.

2. According to COMECON literature, Finland is an associate member of COMECON also. However, the commercial attaché at the Finnish embassy in Washington told us in a telephone call on February 5, 1988, that Finland is *not* an associate member of COMECON but does have a trading agreement with it. He also said that his government decided to become a full member of EFTA as of January 1, 1986, "to replace a void in EFTA caused by Portugal's leaving to join the EC." He felt a full membership in EFTA was no longer a political issue.

3. "EC, EFTA to Prepare for 1992," *Europe*, November 1988, p. 39.

4. "North America into the Year 2000," *Business International*, October 3, 1988, pp. 301–12.

5. "U.S., EC Compete for Markets in ASEAN Countries," *Europe*, November–December 1985, p. 24.

6. When a sales engineer from Madrid and one of the writers went to Barcelona, the Detroit of Spain, on a business trip, we were accompanied on our visits to customers by our salesman from Barcelona. Our meetings with customers always followed the same pattern. The Barcelona salesman would begin the meeting by telling the customer we were from Madrid and did not speak Catalan, the local language. The meeting would proceed in Spanish until either the customer or our local salesman, in searching for a word in Spanish, would use the more familiar (to him) in Catalan word. This would trigger the other to begin speaking in Catalan (completely unintelligible to anyone speaking only Spanish), and the sales engineer and the writer would be completely in the dark as to what was being discussed. After a moment, the local salesman and the customer would realize what they were doing and apologize. The discussions in Spanish would be resumed, and then the switch to Catalan would be repeated. If our local salesman had not been present to smooth over these lapses and provide the necessary empathy with the customer, these meetings would have been disastrous.

7. "Spain Still Battling Separatist Terrorism," *Insight*, June 6, 1988, p. 36.

8. A product with adequate cooling and lubrication for the temperate zone would function well in Bogota but might be woefully deficient in Barranquilla.

9. *World Development Report, 1988* (Washington, D.C.: World Bank, 1988), Table 32, "Urbanization," p. 285.

10. Australia has no north–south railway mainly because there is little population and economic activity in the center of the country to support one. There is an east–west coastal system in the more populous southern region that was completed partly because the federal government feared the western states might secede from the Australian union. The system, however, has the same problems as those of other large developing nations, such as India and Brazil. There are three different gauges along its length, with a few disconnected feeder lines going inland from the ports to mining and farm districts. Goods in transit between Sydney and Perth take 14 days when, because of the distance, they should take 5. Some unification has been done, but it is not complete. Goods and passengers still must be transferred at some state borders.

11. "Geography Defines Media Profile in Australia," *Advertising World*, July 1985, p. 14.

12. "The Canadian Shield," *The Royal Bank Letter*, November–December 1981, pp. 1–4.

13. Rhoads Murphey, *The Scope of Geography*, 2nd ed. (Skokie, Ill.: Rand McNally, 1973), pp. 188–89.

14. H. Robinson, *Geography for Business Studies*, 3rd ed. (Estover: MacDonald and Evans, 1979), pp. 451–55.

15. "Europe's Great Waterway," *Standard Chartered Review*, February 1986, pp. 2–7.

16. Until 1866, Bolivia possessed a 160-mile coastline, but a treaty with Chile that year reduced it by 60 miles. As a result of a war in 1879 primarily between Bolivia and Chile, although Peru also intervened, Bolivia lost its coastline to Chile. Peru also lost 160 miles of coastline but, in 1929, was able to regain 35 miles. Bolivia has been holding discussions with Chile ever since in an effort to obtain its outlet to the sea. In 1975, Chile proposed ceding a narrow strip to Bolivia but demanded what Bolivia considered excessive compensation. Peru offered an alternative solution in 1976 by which all three countries would share in the sovereignty of a port in northern Chile. Rumors were strong that there might be an armed confrontation between Peru and Chile. This crisis passed without a serious incident, and it looked as though Bolivia and Chile might reach an agreement based on a new Bolivian proposal made in 1987. However, the Chilean government rejected it.

    This dispute affects business transactions between the two countries. One of the writers, representing a Chilean subsidiary of an American multinational, called on a large government-owned mine in Bolivia to sell Chilean-made products. The purchasing agent asked how anyone could expect her, a Bolivian, to buy goods made in Chile. She appreciated the fact that the parent company was American, but as she said, "The products are still made in Chile."

17. One author claimed that Brazil has constructed highways, railroads, and bridges to connect its borders with those of its neighbors for the purpose of bringing them under Brazil's political and economic influence. See "Brasil: Potencia Emergente," *Vision*, August 1976, pp. 8–10.

18. Murphey, *Scope of Geography*, p. 115.

19. Ibid., p. 119.

20. Andrew M. Karmack, *The Tropics and Economic Development* (Washington, D.C.: World Bank, 1976), p. 5.

21. Joseph H. Butler, *Economic Geography* (New York: John Wiley & Sons, 1980), p. 108.

22. Sun Oil *Annual Report*, 1987.

23. "Canadian Oil Boom Is Seen in Unwieldy Crude," *The Wall Street Journal*, December 30, 1985, p. 6.

24. Union Oil *Annual Report*, 1987.

25. *1985 Annual Report* (Washington, D.C.: U.S. Synthetic Fuels Corporation).

26. "Discovery in Colombia Points up Big Change in World Oil Picture," *The Wall Street Journal*, May 13, 1985, p. 1.

27. "Exploring for Oil in Pakistan," *U.S. News & World Report*, July 15, 1985, p. 48.

28. "Major Oil Find in Peru," *San Francisco Chronicle*, January 23, 1989, p. B9.

29. "CMEA Countries Form Interozeanmetall," *Moscow Narodny Bank Press Bulletin*, August 19, 1987, p. 10.

30. "An Airplane Fuel That's Lighter than Air," *Business Week*, May 9, 1988, p. 107.

31. The engine output is altered by varying the amount of hydrogen, not the air, as in a conventional carburetor. From "Students Develop Unique Gas Car," *S. A. Digest*, April 27, 1984, p. 10. Mitsubishi, working with the Japanese government, is also trying to develop a hydrogen-powered car.

32. "Brazil Balks at International Pressure," *The Wall Street Journal*, February 13, 1989, p. A7B.

33. "A Back Door into the Amazon," *The Economist*, February 11, 1989, p. 38.

34. "Bracing for the 'Gold-Rush,'" *International Management*, December 1988, pp. 32–34.

35. "Seto Ohashi Bridge," *Japan Update*, Winter 1989, pp. 10–11.

36. "Union Carbide, India Reach $470 Million Settlement," *The Wall Street Journal*, February 15, 1989, p. A3.

37. "Bhopal Settlement," *Manteca Bulletin*, March 9, 1989, p. 13.

38. "The Blotch on the Rhine," *Newsweek*, November 24, 1986, pp. 58–60; and "Suddenly, a Deathwatch on the Rhine," *Business Week*, November 24, 1986, p. 52.

39. "Beyond the Spill on the Rhine," *World Press Review*, January 1987, p. 50.

40. "Smothering the Waters," *Newsweek*, April 10, 1989, pp. 54–77.

41. "What's in Store for MNCs as Concern for Environment Breeds Tougher Regulation," *Business International*, August 1987, pp. 250–54.

42. "Anderson Reflects on Managing Bhopal," *Industry Week*, October 13, 1986, p. 21.

Chapter 9

Sociocultural Forces

You can't understand a country's economy without also understanding its family structures, religions, and values.

M. L. Baba, professor of
anthropology and consultant to
General Motors

KEY WORDS AND CONCEPTS

- Culture
- Ethnocentricity
- Aesthetics
- Demonstration effect
- Protestant work ethic
- Confucian work ethic
- Caste system
- Islam
- Material culture
- Technological dualism
- Appropriate technology
- Boomerang effect
- Brain drain
- Lingua franca
- Unspoken language
- Bribes
- Extortion
- Extended family
- Associations

BUSINESS INCIDENT

Five Rules of Thumb

"Know your customer" is just as important anywhere in the world as it is at home, whether aiming to sell computers in Abidjan or soft drinks in Kuala Lumpur or hotel construction in Caracas. Foreign people are not inscrutable. Each culture has its logic, and within the logic of the culture are real, sensible reasons for the way foreigners do things. If the salesperson can figure out the fundamental pattern of the culture, he/she will be less frustrated and more effective interacting with foreign clients and colleagues.

The first rule of thumb is *be prepared.* Whether traveling abroad or selling from home, no one should approach a foreign market without doing his or her homework. A mentor is most desirable, complemented with endless reading which covers social and business etiquette, history and folklore, current affairs (including current relations between your two countries), the culture's values, geography, sources of pride (artists, musicians, novelists, sports, great achievements of the culture), religion, political structure, and practical matters such as currency, transportation, time zones, and hours of business. Mimi Murphy, an exporter who trades primarily in Indonesia, says, "Whenever I travel, the first thing I do in any town is read the newspaper, front to back. Then when I meet my customer, I can talk about the sports, or whatever the news of the day is. He knows that I am interested in the things he is interested in, and he will want to do business with me."

The second rule, for most Americans, is *slow down.* Americans are clock-watchers. Time is money. In many countries, we are seen to be in a rush, in other words, unfriendly, arrogant, and untrustworthy. Almost everywhere, we must learn to wait patiently.

BUSINESS INCIDENT (concluded)

The third rule: In many countries, American-style crisp business relationships will get the sales representative nowhere. Product quality, pricing, and clear contracts are not as important as the personal *relationship and trust* that is developed carefully and sincerely over time. The marketer must be established as simpatico, worthy of the business, and dependable *in the long run.*

Fourth: *Language* is extremely important. Obviously, copy must be translated by a professional who speaks both languages fluently, with a vocabulary sensitive to nuance and connotation in each culture, as well as talent with idiom and imagery in each culture. An interpreter is often critical and may be helpful even where one of the parties speaks the other's language.

The fifth rule is to *respect the culture.* Manners are important. The traveling sales representative is a guest in the country and must respect the hosts' rules. As a Saudi Arabian official states in one of the *Going International* films, "Americans in foreign countries have a tendency to treat the natives as foreigners and they forget that actually it is *they* who are the foreigners themselves!"

Source: U.S. Department of Commerce, *Business America,* June 25, 1984, p. 7.

The Business Incident emphasizes some of the differences among business cultures that businesspeople should be aware of when they leave their home country to work in other cultures. Of course, even without leaving the country, we all find it necessary to increase our cultural knowledge as we mature, take business courses in a college or university, and then obtain employment. You may not consciously appreciate that you have acquired knowledge about three dimensions of our culture: general, business, and corporate. Yet, when you analyze what you have learned, you realize that each succeeding dimension going from general to corporate is increasingly specific and constrained by the one preceding it.[1]

For instance, you learn early in life about the spirit of fair play and what is acceptable conduct, but in college, you learn more specifically about the conduct that businesses expect from their employees. When you go to work, you learn about the values and norms governing acceptable behavior in that company. If you change jobs, you probably shall find a different emphasis in another firm.

At Procter & Gamble, you would soon learn that new managers are judged on their ability to increase sales volume and profits; but at J. C. Penney, the dominant cultural values are customer satisfaction and employee satisfaction. However, don't use the term *employees*—at Penney's, they're *associates.* Part of your cultural training is learning the corporate language.[2]

After the extensive international bribery scandals of the 1970s (discussed in this chapter and in Chapter 10), companies operating worldwide were quick to formulate and publish codes of conduct for their employees. Let's compare the published statements of two of them. Most points are covered in both, but the emphasis seems different. Following are the major headings of each and the order in which they are written.

Caterpillar's *Code of Worldwide Business Conduct*	Union Carbide's *International Responsibilities of a Multinational Corporation*
1. Ownership and investment	1. To recognize that our people shape our future
2. Corporate facilities	2. To honor mutual rights and obligations
3. Relationships with employees	3. To let the market set the price
4. Product quality	4. To spread the benefits of research
5. Technology	5. To protect, to preserve, to improve our responsibility to the environment
6. Finance	6. To invest wisely, competitively, and for the long term
7. Intercompany pricing	7. To manage well for the best results
8. Differing business practices	8. To build for economic growth
9. Competitive conduct	9. To safeguard currency holdings
10. Observance of local laws	
11. Business ethics	
12. Public responsibility	
13. International business	

Sources: *A Code of Worldwide Business Conduct* (Peoria, Ill.: Caterpillar Tractor Company, no date); and *The International Responsibilities of a Multinational Corporation* (New York: Union Carbide Corporation, no date).

The topics seem to reflect the concerns of top management. Can it be that their order indicates management's priorities?

WHAT IS CULTURE?

culture sum totals of beliefs, rules, techniques, institutions, and artifacts that characterize human populations

Although there are almost as many definitions of culture as there are anthropologists, most anthropologists view **culture** as the *sum total of the beliefs, rules, techniques, institutions, and artifacts that characterize human populations.*[3] In other words, culture consists of the learned patterns of behavior common to members of a given society—the unique lifestyle of a particular group of people.[4] Most anthropologists also agree that (1) culture is *learned,* not innate, (2) the various aspects of culture are *interrelated,* (3) culture is *shared,* and (4) culture *defines the boundaries* of different groups.[5]

Because society is composed of people and their culture, it is virtually impossible to speak of one without relating to the other. Anthropologists often use the terms interchangeably or combine them into one word—*sociocultural.*[6] This is the term we shall use, because the variables in which businesspeople are interested are both social and cultural.

SIGNIFICANCE OF CULTURE FOR INTERNATIONAL BUSINESS

When people work in societies and cultures that differ from their own, the problems they encounter in dealing with a single set of cultures are multiplied by the number of cultural sets they find in each of their foreign markets.

All too often, unfortunately, people who are familiar with only one cultural pattern may believe they have an awareness of cultural differences elsewhere, when in reality they do not. Unless they have had occasion to make comparisons with other cultures, they are probably not even aware of the

ethnocentricity belief in the superiority of one's own ethnic group

important features of their own. They are probably also oblivious to the fact that each society considers its culture superior to all others (**ethnocentricity**) and that their attempts to introduce the "German way" or the "American way" may be met with stubborn resistance.

How do international businesspeople learn to live with other cultures? The first step is a realization that there are cultures different than their own. Then they must go on to learn the characteristics of those cultures so that they may adapt to them. E. T. Hall, a famous anthropologist, claims this can be accomplished in only two ways: (1) spend a lifetime in a country or (2) undergo an extensive, highly sophisticated training program that covers the main characteristics of culture, including the language. The program he mentions is more than an area orientation in which participants are briefed on a country's customs. What Hall refers to is a study of what culture is and what it does and the acquisition of some knowledge of the various ways in which human behavior has been institutionalized.[7]

Culture Impacts All Business Functions

Marketing.   In marketing, for example, the wide variation in attitudes and values prevents many firms from using the same marketing mix in all markets.

> In Japan, Procter & Gamble (P&G) used an advertisement for Camay soap in which a man meeting a woman for the first time compared her skin to that of a fine porcelain doll. Although the ad had worked well in South America and Europe, it insulted the Japanese. "For a Japanese man to say something like that to a Japanese woman means he's either unsophisticated or rude," said an advertising man who worked on the account. Interestingly, P&G used the ad despite the warning from the advertising agency.
>
> P&G also erred because it lacked knowledge of the business culture. The company introduced Cheer detergent by discounting its price, but this lowered the soap's reputation. Said a competitor, "Unlike in Europe and the United States, once you discount your product here, it's hard to raise the price again." Wholesalers were alienated because they made less money due to lower margins. Moreover, apparently P&G didn't realize that Japanese housewives do not have a family car to carry groceries, so they shop in the neighborhood mom-and-pop stores close to home. These small retailers, who sell 30 percent of all the detergent sold in Japan, have limited shelf space and thus do not like to carry discounted products because of the lower profit earned. P&G is estimated to have lost a quarter of a billion dollars since entering the Japanese market. As a bitter Japanese ex-P&G employee put it, "They didn't listen to anybody." Evidently P&G has learned from its costly mistakes: its latest detergent is formulated for Japanese washing habits—short cycles, cold water, and small machines.[8]

Unlike P&G, apparently Walt Disney has the ideal global product. According to the *Tokyo Disneyland Guidebook*, it is similar to the theme parks in California and Florida. Euro Disneyland, which is being built 20 miles east of Paris, will also be similar, according to a recent press release that states, "Euro Disneyland will offer visitors a Magic Kingdom similar to those in California, Florida, and Tokyo."

Human resource management.   The national culture is also a key determinant for the evaluation of managers. In the United States, results are generally the criteria for the selection and promotion of executives; but in Great Britain, an American general manager complained that people were promoted because of the school they attended and their family background but not for their accomplishments. School ties are important in France, too. IBM would hire an Italian who fits within the IBM way of doing things, but Olivetti, whose corporate culture is informal and nonstructured with little discipline, looks for strong personalities and not "too good grades."[9] You can get Olivetti's address from the nearest AT&T office.

Production and finance.   Personnel problems can result from differences in attitudes toward authority, another sociocultural variable. Latin Americans have traditionally regarded the manager as the *patron* (master), an authoritarian figure responsible for their welfare. When American managers accustomed to a participative leadership style are transferred to Latin America, they must become more authoritarian, or their employees will consider them weak and incompetent and they will encounter serious difficulties in having their orders carried out.

> A production manager who had been sent to Peru from the United States was convinced that he could motivate the workers to higher productivity by instituting a more democratic decision-making style. He brought in trainers from the home office to teach the supervisors how to solicit suggestions and feedback from the workers.
>
> Shortly after the new management style was introduced, the workers began quitting their jobs. When asked why, they replied that the new production manager and his supervisors apparently didn't know what to do and were therefore asking the workers for advice. Obviously, the company wouldn't last long with that kind of management, and they wanted to quit before the collapse, because then everyone would be hunting for a job at the same time.

Production managers have found that attitudes toward change can seriously influence the acceptance of new production methods, and even treasurers come to realize the strength of the sociocultural forces when, armed with excellent balance sheets, they approach local banks, only to find that the banks attach far more importance to who they are than to how strong their companies are.[10] These are just a few examples to show that sociocultural differences do affect all of the business functions. As we examine the components of the sociocultural forces, we shall mention others.

SOCIOCULTURAL COMPONENTS

From the foregoing, it should be apparent that to be successful in their relationships with people in other countries, international businesspeople must be students of culture. They must have factual knowledge, which is relatively easy to obtain, but they must also become sensitive to cultural differences, and this is more difficult. Hall, as we saw, recommended spending a lifetime in a country or, in lieu of this, undergoing an extensive program to study what the culture is and what it does. But most newcomers to international business do not even have the opportunity for area orientation. They can, however, take the important first step of realizing that there are other cultures. In this short chapter, we cannot do more than point out some of the important sociocultural differences as they concern businesspeople, in the hope that the readers will become more aware of the need to be culturally sensitive—to know that there are cultural differences for which they must be on the lookout. Remember that the more you know about another's culture, the better will be your predictions of that person's behavior.

The concept of culture is so broad that even the ethnologists (cultural anthropologists) have to break it down into topics to facilitate its study. A listing of such topics will give us a better understanding of what culture is and may also serve as a guide to the international manager when he or she is analyzing a particular problem from the sociocultural viewpoint.

As you can imagine, experts vary considerably as to the components of culture, but the following list is representative of their thinking : (1) aesthetics, (2) attitudes and beliefs, (3) religion, (4) material culture, (5) education, (6) language, (7) societal organization, (8) legal characteristics, and (9) political structures.[11] We shall examine the first seven components in this chapter and leave the legal characteristics and political structures for later chapters.

Aesthetics

aesthetics   a culture's sense of beauty and good taste

Aesthetics pertains to a culture's sense of beauty and good taste and is expressed in its art, drama, music, folklore, and dances.

Art.   Of particular interest to international businesspeople are the formal aspects of art, color, and form, because of the symbolic meanings they convey. Colors, especially, can be deceptive because they mean different things to different cultures. The color of mourning is black in the United States, white in the Far East, purple in Brazil, and yellow in Mexico. Because green is a propitious color in Islam, any ad or package featuring green is looked at favorably in the Islamic world. However, it is repugnant in parts of Asia, where it connotes the illness and death of the jungle. While in the United States mints are packaged in blue or green paper, in Africa the wrapper is red. These examples illustrate that marketers must be careful to check if colors have any special meanings before using them for products, packages, or advertisements.

Be careful of symbols, too. Seven signifies good luck in the United States but just the opposite in Singapore, Ghana, and Kenya. In Japan, the number 4 is unlucky. In general, the marketer should avoid using a nation's flag or any symbols connected with religion.

> Saudi religious leaders were enraged when a Taiwanese firm sold "blasphemous" shoes in their country. How could they walk on the sacred name, Allah, which was molded into the sole?[12]

It is also important to learn whether there are local aesthetic preferences for form that could affect the design of the product, the package, or even the building in which the firm is located. The American style of steel and glass in the midst of oriental architecture will be a constant reminder to the local population of the outsider's presence.

Music and Folklore.   Musical commercials are generally popular worldwide, but the marketer must know what kind of music each market prefers, because tastes vary. Thus, the commercial that used a ballad in the United States might be better received to the tune of a bolero in Mexico or a samba in Brazil. However, if the advertiser is looking to the youth market with a product patently American, then American music will help reinforce its image.

Those who wish to steep themselves in a culture find it useful to study its folklore, which can disclose much about a society's way of life. Although this is usually more than the foreign businessperson has time for, the incorrect use of folklore can sometimes cost the firm a share of the market. For example, associating a product with the cowboy would not obtain the same results in Chile or Argentina as it does in the United States, because in these countries the cowboy is a far less romantic figure—it's just a job. In another instance, a U.S. company may be paying handsome royalties to use American cartoon characters in its promotion, only to find they are considerably less important in foreign markets. In Mexico, songs of the "Singing Cricket" are known to all youngsters and their mothers, and a commercial tie-in with that character would be as advantageous to the firm as its use of Peanuts or Mickey Mouse. In many areas, especially where nationalistic feeling is strong, local firms have been able to compete successfully with foreign affiliates by making use of indigenous folklore in the form of slogans and proverbs. As Herskovits states, tales of folklore are valuable in maintaining a sense of group unity.[13] Knowing them is an indication that one belongs to the group, which recognizes that the outsider is unfamiliar with its folklore.

Attitudes and Beliefs

Every culture has a set of attitudes and beliefs that influence nearly all aspects of human behavior and help bring order to a society and its individuals. The more managers can learn about certain key attitudes, the better prepared they will be to understand why people behave as they do, especially when their reactions differ from those that the managers have learned to expect in dealing with their own people.

Among the wide variety of subjects covered by attitudes and beliefs, some are of prime importance to the businessperson. These include attitudes toward time, toward achievement and work, and toward change.

Attitudes toward time.   This cultural characteristic probably presents more adaptation problems for Americans overseas than any other. Time is important in the United States, and much emphasis is placed on it. If we must wait past the appointed hour to see an individual, we feel insulted. This person is not giving our meeting the importance it deserves. Yet the wait could mean just the opposite elsewhere. Latin American or Middle Eastern executives may be taking care of the minor details of their business so that they can attend their important visitor without interruption.

> An American who has worked in the Middle East for 20 years explains the Middle Eastern concept of time this way: "A lot of the misunderstandings between Middle Easterners and foreigners are due to their different concepts of time and space. At worst, there is no concept at all of time in the Middle East. At best, there is a sort of open-ended concept." The head of Egypt's Industrial Design Center, an Egyptian, states, "The simple wristwatch is, in some respects, much too sophisticated an instrument for the Middle East. One of the first things a foreigner should learn in Egypt is to ignore the second hand. The minute hand can also be an obstacle if he expects Egyptians to be as conscious as he of time ticking away.[14]

Probably even more critical than short-term patience is long-term patience. American preoccupation with monthly profit and loss statements is a formidable barrier to the establishment of successful business relationships with Asian and Middle Eastern executives, especially during the development of joint ventures and other business relationships that have good potential in the long run—precisely the factors in which these people are most interested.[15]

Americans, be prompt.   Few cultures give the same importance to time that Americans and Europeans do. If any appointment is made with a group of Germans to see them at 12 noon, we can be sure they will be there; but to get the same response from a Brazilian, we must say noon English hour. If not, the Brazilian may show up anytime between noon and 2 o'clock. Compare this with Japan, where a description of an apartment in the rental contract includes the time in minutes required to walk to the nearest train station![16]

Should Americans follow the local custom or be prompt? It depends. In Spain, a general rule is to never be punctual. If you are, you will be considered early.[17] However, in the Middle East, the American penchant for punctuality is well known, and lateness from Americans is considered impolite. The Arabian executives, nonetheless, will usually not arrive at the appointed hour; why should they change their lifetime habits just for a stranger?[18]

Mañana.   Probably one of the most vexing problems for the newcomer to Latin America is the *mañana* attitude. Ask the maintenance man when the machine will be ready, and he responds *mañana*. The American assumes this means "tomorrow," the literal translation, but the maintenance man means "some time in the near future," and if he is reprimanded for not having the machine ready the next day, he is angry and bewildered. He reasons that everyone knows *mañana* means "in the next few days."

This example illustrates that the ability to speak the local language is only half the task of communicating. A manager of an American subsidiary in Saudi Arabia says, "You can be talking the same language with someone, but are you talking on the same wavelength?" He states that he has met few Japanese or Koreans fluent in Arabic, yet they are able to understand and adapt to local conditions much better than Westerners can because they seem to be more sensitive to the Middle Easterner's mentality.[19]

Directness and drive.   The American pride in directness and drive is interpreted by many foreigners as being brash and rude. Although we believe it expedient to get to the point in a discussion, this attitude often irritates others. Time-honored formalities are a vital part of doing business, and help to establish amicable relations, considered by people in many countries to be a necessary prerequisite to business discussions.[20] Any attempt to move the negotiations along by ignoring some of the accepted courtesies invites disaster.

Deadlines.   Our emphasis on speed and deadlines is often used against us in business dealings abroad. In Far Eastern countries such as Japan, the American may be asked how long he or she plans to stay at the first meeting. Then negotiations are purposely not finalized until a few hours before the American's departure, when the Japanese know they can wring extra concessions from the foreigner because of his or her haste to finish and return home on schedule.

Three Americans, none of whom had ever been to Japan, went to sell tractors to Japanese buyers. They thought the discussions had gone well and prepared to wrap up the deal. However, there was no reaction from the Japanese. The silence became disquieting, and so the Americans lowered the price. Because there was still no reaction, they again lowered the price. This went on until there price was far lower than they had planned. What they didn't know was that the Japanese had become silent not to indicate rejection of the proposition, but merely to think it over, a customary Japanese motivating practice.[21]

Russian negotiators reportedly employ a similar strategy.

Attitudes toward achievement and work.   There is a saying in Mexico, "Americans live to work, but we work to live." This is an example of the extreme contrasts among cultural attitudes toward work. Where work is considered necessary to obtain the essentials for survival, once these have been obtained, people may stop working. They do not make the accomplishment of a task an end in itself. This attitude is in sharp contrast to the belief in many industrial societies that work is a moral, and even a religious, virtue.

To the consternation of the production manager with a huge back order, the promise of overtime often fails to keep the workers on the job. In fact, raising employees' salaries frequently results in their working less (economists call this effect the backward-bending labor supply curve).

It is important, however, to note that an additional change has occurred repeatedly in many developing countries as more consumer goods have become available. The **demonstration effect** (seeing others with these goods) and improvements in infrastructure (roads to bring the products to them and electric power to operate them) cause workers to realize they can have greater prestige and pleasure by owning more goods. Thus, their attitude toward work changes, not because of any alteration of their moral or religious values, but because they now want what only money can buy.

> A Mexican distributor came to one of the writers to complain that a number of his salesmen were producing well for the first week or two of the month but were then slacking off. Investigation showed that the commissions plus salary earned during the periods of high production were about the same each time. It was apparent that the salesmen had earned what they required to live so that they could loaf the rest of the month. By instituting contests and informing the salesmen's wives about the prizes to be won, considerable improvement was obtained.

In the industrialized nations, the opposite trend is being observed. A feeling of prosperity is causing a tendency toward longer vacations (a month in Europe), shorter workweeks, and a greater emphasis on leisure activities. The same is true of Japan. In 1987, the Japanese workweek was pared from 48 to 46 hours, and it will drop to 40 hours by 1993.[22]

Religion and achievement.   Researchers have found differences among cultures with respect to achievement motivation, and attempts have been made to explain these differences on the basis of religion, as we will see in the next section. Although religion is not the only explanatory variable, and may not be the principal explanatory variable, the correlation between the predominant religion and a nation's per capita income is too high to disregard the influence of religion on past economic growth.[23]

Prestigious jobs.   Another aspect of the attitude toward work is the prestige associated with certain kinds of employment. In this country, some types of work are considered more prestigious than others, but there is nowhere near the disdain for physical labor here that there is in many developing countries.

demonstration effect result of having seen others with desirable goods

The result is an overabundance of attorneys and economists and a lack of toolmakers and welders even when the wages are higher for the latter. The distinction between blue-collar workers and office employees is especially great, as typified by the use of two words in Spanish for the worker—*obrero* (one who labors) signifies a blue-collar worker, whereas *empleado* (employee) signifies an office worker.[24]

Source of recruits.   The lesson to be learned from this discussion is that there are generally sharper differences in the attitudes toward work and achievement among other cultures than American managers find in their own culture. When these managers go abroad, their problem is to recruit subordinates with a need to progress, whatever the underlying motive. Many firms have been successful in locating such persons among relatively well-educated members of the lower social class who view work as a route to the prestige and social acceptance that have been denied them because of their birth.

Attitudes toward change.   The American firm, accustomed to the rapid acceptance by Americans of something new, is frequently surprised to find that new does not carry that kind of magic in markets where something tried and proven is preferred to the unknown. Europeans are fond of reminding Americans that they are a young nation lacking traditions. The near reverence for traditional methods makes it more difficult for the production manager to install a new process, for the marketer to introduce a new product, or for the treasurer to change the accounting system.

The new idea.   Yet, undeniably, international firms are agents of change, and their personnel must be able to counter resistance to it. The new idea will be more readily acceptable the closer it can be related to the traditional one while at the same time being made to show its relative advantage. In other words, the more consistent a new idea is with a society's attitudes and experiences, the more quickly it will be adopted.

Economic motivation.   In these times of rising expectations, economic motives can be a strong influence for accepting change. Thus, if factory workers can be shown that their income will increase with the new machine or housewives can be convinced that the new frozen food will enable them to work and still provide satisfactory meals for their families, they can be persuaded by the gain in their economic welfare to accept ideas that they might otherwise oppose.

Religion

Religion, an important component of culture, is responsible for many of the attitudes and beliefs affecting human behavior. A knowledge of the basic tenets of some of the more popular religions will contribute to a better understanding of why people's attitudes vary so greatly from country to country.

Protestant ethic.   We have already mentioned the marked differences in the attitudes toward work and achievement. Europeans and Americans generally view work as a moral virtue and look unfavorably on the idle. This view stems in part from the **Protestant work ethic** as expressed by Luther and Calvin, who believed it was the duty of Christians to glorify God by hard work and the practice of thrift.

Protestant work ethic
Christian duty to glorify God by hard work and the practice of thrift

---

The new idea

Courtesy McDonald's Corporation

Confucian work ethic
same as Protestant work
ethic

In Asian countries where Confucianism is strong, this same attitude toward work is called the **Confucian work ethic**, and in Japan, it's called the Shinto work ethic after the principal religion of that nation.[25] Interestingly, because of other factors—such as a growing feeling of prosperity and a shift to a five-day workweek (with two days off, workers develop new interests)—Japanese employers are finding that the younger workers no longer have the same dedication to their jobs that their predecessors had. Workers rarely show up early to warm the oil in their machines before their shifts start, and some management trainees are actually taking all of their 15 days' vacation time. A representative of the Employers Association states, "Our universities are leisure centers." A recent college graduate claims, "Students ski in the winter and play tennis in the summer. What the companies sometimes find out is that they like skiing better than working."[26]

"The Protestant work ethic isn't cutting it, so we're switching to Shinto."

From *The Wall Street Journal*, with permission of Cartoon Features Syndicate.

Asian religions. People from the Western world will encounter some very different notions about God, Man, and Reality in Asian religions. In the Judeo-Christian tradition, this world is real and significant because it was created by God. Human beings are likewise significant, and so is time, because it began with God's creation and will end when His will has been fulfilled. Each human being has only one lifetime to heed God's word and achieve everlasting life.

In Asian religions, especially in the religions of India, the ideas of reality are different. There is a notion that this world is an illusion because nothing is permanent. Time is cyclical, so all living things, including humans, are in a constant process of birth, death, and reincarnation. The goal of salvation is to escape from the cycle and move into a state of eternal bliss (*nirvana*). The notion of *karma* (moral retribution) holds that evil committed in one lifetime will be punished in the next. Thus, *karma* is a powerful impetus to do good so as to achieve a higher spiritual status in the next life. Asians who hold these views cannot imagine that they have not had past lives when they may have been plants, animals, or human beings. Of the seven best-known religions that originated in Asia, four came from India (Hinduism, Buddhism, Jainism, and Sikhism), two from China (Confucianism and Taoism), and one from Japan (Shintoism).[27]

Hinduism. This is a conglomeration of religions, without a single founder or a central authority, that is practiced by more than 80 percent of India's population. Although there is great diversity among regions and social classes, Hinduism has certain characteristic features. Most Hindus believe that everything in the world is subject to an eternal process of death and rebirth (*samsura*) and that individual souls (*atmans*) migrate from one body to another. They believe one can be liberated from the *samsura* cycle and achieve that state of eternal bliss (*nirvana*) by (1) yoga (purification of mind and body), (2) devout worship of the gods, or (3) good works and obedience to the laws and customs (*dharmas*) of one's caste.

A knowledge of the **caste system** is important to managers because the castes are the basis of the social division of labor. The highest caste, the Brahmins or priesthood, is followed by the warriors (politicians, landowners),

caste system an aspect of Hinduism by which the entire society is divided into four groups (plus the outcasts) and each is assigned a certain class of work

Courtesy of Paul Chesley Photographers/Aspen

Generational differences show up in this unposed photo at Kawasaki Steel. Older workers grind away while younger ones share a laugh.

the merchants, the peasants, and the untouchables. An individual's position in a caste is inherited, as is that person's job within the caste, and movement to a higher caste can be made only in subsequent lives. If the gods choose to punish a person, his or her next life will be at a lower caste level. Although the government of India has officially outlawed discrimination based on the caste system, and in fact has worked to improve the situation of those in the lower castes, such discrimination still exists. The manager who places a member of a lower caste in charge of a group of people from a higher one does so at a considerable risk of employee dissatisfaction.[28]

Buddhism.   This religion began in India as a reform movement of Hinduism. At the age of 29, Prince Gautama rejected his wife, son, and wealth and set out to solve the mysteries of misery, old age, and death. After six years of experimenting with yoga, which brought no enlightenment, he suddenly understood how to break the laws of *karma* and the endless cycle of rebirth (*samsura*). Gautama emerged as the Buddha (the Enlightened One).

He renounced the austere self-discipline of the Hindus as well as the extremes of self-indulgence, both of which depended on a craving that locked people into the endless cycle of rebirth. Gautama taught that by extinguishing desire, his followers could attain enlightenment and escape the cycle of existence into *nirvana*. By opening his teaching to everyone, he opposed the caste system.

Because Buddhist monks are involved in politics in the areas where their religion is prevalent and because they are a mobilizing force for political and social action, managers working in these areas need to be aware of what these religious leaders are doing. Even American public opinion was influenced by pictures of Buddhist monks who had set themselves on fire to protest American participation in the Vietnam War.

The Buddhist teaching that if the followers of Buddha have no desires, they will not suffer is also important, because if they have no desires, Buddhists and Hindus have little motive for achievement and for the acquisition of material goods.

Jainism.   This religion was founded by Mahavira, a contemporary of Buddha. The Jain doctrine teaches that there is no creator, no god, and no absolute principle. Through right faith, correct conduct, and right knowledge of the soul, Jains can purify themselves, become free of *samsura*, and achieve *nirvana*. Although relatively few in number, Jains are influential leaders in commerce and scholarship. Their greatest impact on Indian culture is manifested in the widespread acceptance of their nonviolence doctrine, which prohibits animal slaughter, war, and even violent thoughts.

Sikhism.   This is the religion of an Indian ethnic group, a military brotherhood,* and a political movement that was founded by Nanek, who sought a bridge between Hinduism and Islam. Sikhs believe there is a single god, but they also accept the Hindu concept of *samsura, karma,* and spiritual liberation. The Sikh's holiest temple was partly destroyed by Indian troops who suppressed their movement for self-government. More than 80 percent of all Sikhs live in the Indian state of Punjab, which they hope to make an autonomous state.

Confucianism.   The name of Confucius is inseparable from Chinese culture and civilization, which were already well developed when he set out to master ancient traditions and transform them into a rational system capable of guiding his people's personal and social behavior. Confucianism may be considered a religion inasmuch as Confucius built a philosophy on the notion that all reality is subject to an eternal mandate from heaven; however, he refused to speculate on the existence of Chinese folk deities and was agnostic on the question of life after death. Essentially, Confucianism is a humanism that elaborates the moral ideals governing human relations.

Confucius taught that each person bears within himself the principle of unselfish love for others, *jen,* the cultivation of which is its own reward. A second principle, *li,* prescribes a gentle decorum in all actions and accounts for the Chinese emphasis on politeness, deference to elders, and ritual courtesies such as bowing.

Taoism.   This is a mystical philosophy founded by Lao-tzu, a contemporary of Confucius. Taoism, which means "philosophy of the way," holds that each of us mirrors the same forces, the male and the female energies (yin and yang) that govern the cosmos. The aim of Taoist meditation and rituals is to free the self from distractions and become empty so as to allow the cosmic forces to act. There should be a unity of the person with nature, so that good acts become spontaneous.

Shintoism.   This is the indigenous religion of Japan. It has no founder or bible. Shinto legends define the founding of the Japanese empire as a cosmic act, and the emperor was believed to have divine status. As a part of the World War II settlement, the emperor was forced to renounce such a claim. Shintoism

---

*Baptism into the Sikh brotherhood requires all members to take Singh as a second name.

has no elaborate theology or even an organized weekly worship. Its followers come to the thousands of Shinto shrines when they feel moved to do so.

Islam.   About 850 million followers make this youngest universal faith the second largest after Christianity (which has 1.4 billion adherents). Islam means "to submit" in Arabic; and Muslim, meaning "submitting," is the present participle of the same verb. This faith accepts as God's eternal word the Koran, a collection of Allah's (God's) revelations to Muhammad, the founder of Islam. Unlike the founders of the other major religions, the prophet Muhammad was not only the spokesman of Allah but also the founder of what became a vast temporal and ecclesiastical empire; in other words, he was a head of state as well as a prophet of God. In Muslim nations, there is no separation of church and state.

The basic spiritual duties of all Muslims consist of the five pillars of faith: (1) accepting the confession of faith ("There is no God but God, and Muhammad is the Messenger of God"); (2) making the five daily prayers while facing Mecca (Muhammad's birthplace, where he was inspired to preach God's word in the year A.D. 610); (3) giving charity; (4) fasting during the daylight hours of Ramadan, a 29- or 30-day month in Islam's lunar calendar; and (5) making a pilgrimage to Mecca at least once in their lifetime. Some Muslims claim there is a sixth duty, *jihad*, which refers to the various forms of striving for the faith, such as the inner struggle for purification. However, this term is often translated as "the holy war."

The split that occurred between the Sunnis and the Shiites over the succession to Muhammad's authority is as important as the division that took place in Christendom with the Reformation. Muhammad's survivors decided that his successors (called caliphs) should be elected by members of the Islamic community, and they were—four times. But after the fourth successor, Ali (Muhammad's cousin) was murdered and the caliphate passed to the monarchical house of Ummaya. Ali's son, Hussayn, claimed the caliphate was his, as Muhammad's heir, and he started a rebellion to confirm his claim. Hussayn was killed in a battle by a Sunni caliph.

This split the Muslim world between the Sunnis (followers of the Prophet's Path) and the Shiites (Party of Ali). After their defeat, the Shiites, feeling that they had been wronged, became dissenters within the Arab empire who were given to violence against authority. Although the Shiites and the Sunnis agree on the fundamentals of Islam, they differ in other respects. The Sunnis are an austere sect that is less authoritarian and more rational than the Shiites. In their view, as long as Muslims accept Allah, they are free to interpret their religion as they like. The Shiites, on the other hand, insist that those claiming to be Muslim must put themselves under the authority of a holy man (*ayatollah*). This has created a clergy that wields enormous temporal and spiritual power. It was the Iranian Shia clergy who brought down the shah of Iran.[29]

Another example of the Shiites's political power occurred in early 1989, when a book, *The Satanic Verses*, precipitated what some Islamic experts regard as the most incendiary literary fight in Islamic history. Although Salman Rushdie, the author, denied that his novel was antireligious, nearly all Muslims considered it blasphemous. The first Muslim protests occurred in Great Britain and were orderly but passionate. However, people were killed in the second round of demonstrations in Pakistan, India, and Bangladesh. On February 14,

Ayatollah Khomeini, Iran's spiritual ruler, announced that the author must die for the sin of insulting Islam and promised martyrdom for anyone who killed him. Another cleric announced that a bounty of $2.6 million had been offered. The following day, the bounty was doubled.[30]

Critics claim that the ayatollah had noticed a sharp decline in revolutionary fervor among his followers and used the book as a tool to mobilize his constituency. Marvin Zonis, a political scientist at the University of Chicago, said, "It's a way to make domestic capital out of foreign adventure." But Georges Sabagh, director of UCLA's Near East Studies Center, stated, "If the man is struck by a thunderbolt, all the better."[31] Later, Iran's president remarked that Rushdie's death threat might be withdrawn if he would apologize to Muslims and to Khomeini. A day later, Rushdie apologized.

Businesspeople doing business with Muslim countries should understand the Sunni–Shia conflict, because much of what occurs in these countries is the result of this conflict. Although most Muslim countries are Sunni governed, many of them, such as Kuwait, the emirates, Bahrain, and other small states in the Gulf, have substantial Shia populations. Furthermore, small Shia minorities can cause trouble for the government. For example, Saudi Arabia's Shia population is very small—only 250,000—it is concentrated in the eastern oil fields. Iran's Shia government continually broadcasts appeals to the Saudi Shiites to overthrow the regime. In Iraq, 52 percent of the population is Shiite, and, as you can imagine, this division has given rise to violent clashes between religious dissidents and the government's all-Sunni army. Syria, on the other hand, is predominantly Sunni, but its government is controlled by secular pro-Soviet Baathist socialists who belong to a Shia sect (Alawi).[32]

Even where the Sunni–Shia conflict is not a problem, two of the five pillars of faith can be bothersome to Western managers. The dawn-to-dusk fasting during the month of Ramadan causes workers' output to drop sharply, and the requirement to pray five times daily also affects output, because when they hear the call to prayer, Muslim workers stop whatever they are doing to pray where they are.

> An American manager in Pakistan for the purpose of getting a new factory into production came to the plant the first day, saw that production had started as it should, and went into his office to do some work. Suddenly, all of the machinery stopped. He rushed out, expecting to find a power failure. Instead, he found workers on their prayer rugs. The manager returned to his office and lowered his production estimates.

Animism.   In a number of African and Latin American countries, animism, a kind of spirit worship that includes magic and witchcraft, is a major religion. It is often combined with Catholicism to present a strange mixture of mysticism, taboos, and fatalism. Animists believe their dead relatives are ever present and will be pleased if the living act in the same way as their ancestors. The resultant strong tendency to perpetuate traditions makes it extremely difficult for marketers and production managers to initiate changes. To be accepted, these changes must relate to the animists' beliefs. The foreign manager must also be cognizant of the proper religious protocols in situations such as factory and store dedications. Note the photograph of the aircraft dedication by the High Lama in Bhutan. If the evil spirits are not properly exorcised, they will remain to cause all sorts of problems, such as worker injuries, machinery breakdowns, and defective products.

The High Lama and 40 Bud-dhist Lamas conducting reli-gious ceremonies for the con-secration of a new commercial airplane

Courtesy ICAO Bulletin and Rolf Christ

Evil spirits wreaked havoc in an American-owned semiconductor factory in Kuala Lumpur, Malaysia. The plant consists of an enormous room filled with hundreds of women looking into microscopes and television monitors.

One afternoon, a girl claimed she saw an ugly woman in her microscope. The operator was pulled screaming to the first-aid room. The manager admitted that was a mistake: "Before I knew it, we had girls all over being held down by super-visors. It was like a battlefield."

The factory was evacuated, but when the night crew arrived, the spirit returned. "Word had gone out that evil spirits were loose in the factory because of a dance we had the previous weekend. At night, it was worse. All we could do was hold them down, carry them out to the buses, and send them home."

The next morning, a licensed healer was brought in. His recommendation—sacrifice a goat. That afternoon, a goat was killed and its blood was sprinkled on the factory floor. It was cooked in the cafeteria and eaten by the workers.

"Next morning, we started up, and everything was fine."[33]

Table 9–1 lists the religious populations of the world.

The importance of religion to management.   You have seen that religions have a pervasive influence on business. How effective can offers to pay time and a half for overtime and bonuses based on productivity be in a company whose workers are mainly Buddhists or Hindus? Strict adherents to these religions attempt to rid themselves of desires, and thus they have little need for an income beyond that which permits them to attain the basic necessities of life. When their incomes begin to rise, they have a tendency to reduce their efforts so that personal incomes remain unchanged.

Religious holidays and rituals can affect employee performance and work scheduling. When members of different religious groups work together, there may even be strife, division, and instability within the work force. Managers must respect the religious beliefs of others and adapt business practices to the religious constraints present in other cultures.[34] Of course, to be able to do this, they must first know what those beliefs and constraints are.

■ TABLE 9–1   Estimated Religious Population of the World

Religionists	Africa	East Asia	Europe	Latin America	Northern America	Oceania	South Asia	U.S.S.R.	World	Percent
Christians	271,035,700	78,100,000	413,920,700	399,554,500	232,048,400	21,287,100	129,076,700	103,373,400	1,644,396,500	32.9%
Roman Catholics	102,552,200	9,204,000	257,155,000	371,863,600	91,209,800	7,434,000	81,694,100	5,111,900	926,194,600	18.5
Protestants	71,883,000	32,100,000	76,652,000	13,960,000	94,965,500	7,510,000	26,142,100	8,803,800	332,016,400	6.6
Orthodox	24,746,700	81,000	35,606,100	570,000	5,910,000	507,400	3,200,000	89,442,300	160,063,500	3.2
Anglicans	22,389,900	334,000	32,886,200	1,210,000	7,511,000	5,350,000	290,000	400	69,971,500	1.4
Other	49,493,900	36,381,000	11,621,400	7,950,900	32,452,100	485,700	17,750,500	15,000	156,150,500	3.1
Muslims	245,110,500	23,795,000	8,901,500	645,000	2,682,600	96,000	547,350,500	31,807,200	860,388,300	17.2
Nonreligious	1,495,000	641,756,600	50,923,940	13,237,000	21,047,700	2,884,400	20,651,100	84,332,030	836,327,770	16.7
Hindus	1,410,000	10,100	590,000	660,000	810,000	295,000	651,918,900	1,200	655,695,200	13.1
Buddhists	12,800	154,796,300	216,000	490,000	190,000	16,000	153,585,000	320,000	309,626,100	6.2
Atheists	240,000	136,886,000	17,803,000	2,538,000	1,073,000	512,000	5,300,000	60,774,500	225,126,500	4.5
Chinese folk religionists	9,500	179,103,100	49,000	60,000	110,000	16,000	8,169,400	100	187,517,100	3.7
New Religionists	13,000	42,217,200	34,000	370,000	1,075,600	6,100	66,990,000	200	110,706,100	2.2
Tribal religionists	68,219,450	730,000	100	1,160,000	60,000	81,000	24,508,200	0	94,758,750	1.9
Jews	257,000	1,800	1,483,600	990,000	8,084,000	86,000	4,050,000	3,123,000	18,075,400	0.4
Sikhs	26,000	1,000	215,000	6,000	9,500	6,600	16,340,000	50	16,604,150	0.3
Shamanists	1,000	12,500,000	400	400	200	200	10,000	250,000	12,762,200	0.2
Confucians	500	5,900,000	1,000	500	10,000	200	2,000	200	5,914,400	0.1
Baha'is	1,265,000	48,400	70,500	570,000	310,000	59,000	2,300,000	5,000	4,627,900	0.1
Jains	47,500	500	9,900	2,000	2,000	900	3,400,000	20	3,462,820	0.1
Shintoists	50	3,400,000	360	800	1,000	500	200	100	3,403,010	0.1
Other religionists	65,000	62,000	310,000	6,768,800	750,000	25,000	230,000	6,000	6,216,800	0.2
World Population	589,208,000	1,279,308,000	494,529,000	423,053,000	268,264,000	25,372,000	1,633,882,000	283,993,000	4,997,609,000	100.0

Source: *World Almanac 1989,* p. 591.

Material Culture

material culture all man-made objects; concerned with *how* people make things (technology) and *who* makes *what* and *why* (economics)

Material culture refers to all man-made objects and is concerned with *how* people make things (technology) and *who* makes *what* and *why* (economics).

Technology.   The technology of a society is the mix of the usable knowledge that the society applies and directs toward the attainment of cultural and economic objectives; it exists in some form in every cultural organization.[35] It is significant in the efforts of developing nations to improve their level of living and a vital factor in the competitive strategies of multinational firms.

Technological superiority is the goal of most companies, of course, but it is especially important to worldwide corporations because:

1. It enables a firm to be competitive or even attain leadership in world markets.

   At one time, Procter & Gamble and Unilever were competing worldwide for the laundry detergent market, but then P&G introduced Tide, a synthetic detergent with superior cleaning power. Its sales took off and left Unilever far behind. Finally, Unilever introduced its own synthetic detergent, but P&G had stolen the lead.[36]

2. It can be sold (licensing or management contract), or it can be embodied in the company's products.

3. It can give a firm confidence to enter a foreign market even when other companies are already established there.

4. It can enable the firm to obtain better-than-usual conditions for a foreign market investment because the host government wants the technology that only the firm has (for example, permission for a wholly owned subsidiary in a country where the government normally insists on joint ventures with a local majority).

   IBM, confident of its superior technology, insisted on and obtained permission from the Mexican government to set up a wholly owned subsidiary when other computer manufacturers were forced to accept local partners.

5. It can enable a company with only a minority equity position to control a joint venture and preserve it as a captive market for semi-processed inputs that it—but not the joint venture—produces.

7. It can change the international division of labor. Firms that had moved production overseas where labor was cheaper have now returned to their home countries because automation has drastically reduced the direct labor content of their products.

8. It is causing major firms to form competitive alliances in which each partner shares the high costs of research and development.

9. It is a major reason why communist-bloc nations, anxious to obtain superior technology, have permitted joint ventures with Western partners.

Cultural aspects of technology.   Technology includes not only the application of science to production, but also skill in marketing, finance, and management. Its cultural aspects concern governments because their people may not be ready to accept the cultural changes that a new technology may bring.[37] Some say the Shah of Iran's overthrow resulted in part from his trying to introduce new technology at a too rapid rate.

Technology's cultural aspects are certainly important to international managers, because new production methods and new products often require people to change their beliefs and ways of living. The self-employed farmer frequently finds the discipline required to become a factory worker excessively demanding. If workers have been accustomed to the production conditions of cottage industries in which each individual performs all of the production operations, they find it difficult to adjust to the monotony of tightening a single bolt. The "throw away instead of repair" philosophy behind the design of so many new products necessitates a change in the use habits of people who have been accustomed to repairing something to keep it operating until it is thoroughly worn out. *Generally, the greater the difference between the old and new method or product, the more difficult it is for the firm to institute a change.*

High GNP—High level of technology.   The differences in levels of technology among nations are used as a basis for judging whether nations are developed or developing. Generally, a nation with a higher GNP per capita utilizes a higher level of technology than one whose per capita income is smaller. Because of technological dualism, however, analysts must be wary of assuming that just because the general technological level is low, the particular industry they are examining is employing a simple technology.

technological dualism the side-by-side presence of technologically advanced and technologically primitive production systems

Technological dualism.   **Technological dualism** is a prominent feature of many LDCs. In the same country, one sector may be technologically advanced, with high productivity, while the production techniques of another sector may be old and labor intensive. This condition may be the result of the host government's insistence that foreign investors import only the most modern machinery rather than used-but-serviceable equipment that would be less costly and could create more employment.

Sometimes the preferences are reversed, with the host government beset by high unemployment arguing for labor-intensive processes, while the foreign firm prefers automated production, both because it is the kind with which the home office is most familiar and because its use lessens the need for skilled labor, which is usually in short supply. To understand which policy the host government is following, management must study its laws and regulations and talk with host country officials.

appropriate technology the technology (advanced, intermediate, or primitive) that most closely fits the society using it

Appropriate technology.   Rather than choosing between labor-intensive and capital-intensive processes, many experts in economic development are recommending **appropriate technology**, which can be labor intensive, intermediate, or capital intensive. The idea is to choose the technology that most closely fits the society using it. For example, in Africa, bricks are usually made in large-city factories using modern technology or locally in hand-poured, individual molds. In Botswana, an American group, AT International, designed an inexpensive small press with which four people can produce 1,500 bricks a day.[38] This is an intermediate technology that is also an appropriate technology.

In India, a small manufacturer, Patel, has taken three fourths of the detergent market from Lever, the giant multinational, by using labor-intensive technology. Lever's Surf brand dominated the market until Patel, realizing that a high-quality, high-priced product was not appropriate for a poor country, set up a chain of shops in which people mixed the ingredients by hand. This primitive method is tailored to Indian conditions and now enables the company to outsell Lever on the basis of price. Its annual sales exceed $250 million.[39]

Technology transfer's impact on politics.   Technological superiority is also active in international politics. You may not realize that the need for American technology is driving neutral countries to cooperate politically with the United States. Of continuing concern to the U.S. government is (1) technology that had been sold to neutral nations will then be passed to the communist bloc and (2) sensitive products exported to them or passing through their free ports and duty-free zones, although ostensibly destined to be delivered to an American ally, will be diverted to the communists.

Despite repeated requests, governments of these countries exercised little vigilance to stop these leaks of American technology until the United States charged two multinationals belonging to the Swedish industrialist Wallenberg with illegally transferring U.S. technology to the communist bloc. Although Wallenberg paid a $3.1 million fine, he avoided a denial of export privileges, which would have prevented his firms from importing U.S. components for their products, marketed worldwide.

Moreover, Wallenberg influenced the Swedish government to pass an ordinance extending U.S. controls to American products imported by Swedish nationals as well as locally produced products when they have components of U.S. origin. Two other neutral nations, Austria and Switzerland, have also passed tougher in-transit laws, and all the neutral European nations as well as most major Asian buyers of U.S. technology protect it from being transferred. In addition, the United States has even persuaded a number of governments not to sell to the Soviet bloc the high-tech products that they themselves manufacture.[40] Perhaps you remember the scandal in Japan and the United States caused by Toshiba's sale to the Soviets of equipment for producing quieter-running propellers.

Yet Japanese firms have become less willing to sell their technology to NICs, such as Korea. What they fear is the **boomerang effect**—by giving Korea their technology today, they make Korea a tougher competitor tomorrow. As a result, Korea is turning more to the United States for technical assistance. This suggests why Korean–American ties of all kinds are strengthening. As an official from the Korean Ministry of Science and Technology said on a visit to the United States, "If America and Korea join together, we can overcome Japan."[41] Interestingly, fear of the boomerang effect has caused some American firms to restrict the sale of their technology to the Japanese.

Government controls.   The influence of technology is very great because the level of technology used affects the size of the foreign investment, the quality and number of workers employed, and even what a particular country can produce.[42] For these reasons, plus what many LDC governments consider abuses in the sale of technology by the multinationals, many LDCs have enacted strong laws controlling the purchase of technical assistance. Some have laws that limit the amount of royalties paid and prohibit many of the restrictions regularly used by the multinationals, such as those that oblige licensees to purchase raw materials from the licensor, prohibit licensees from exporting, and require licensees to transfer to licensors any improvements they

boomerang effect technology sold to companies in another nation may be used to produce goods that will then compete with those of the seller of the technology

have made in the technology. This worldwide trend among developing nations toward a severe limitation on the after-sale control that a WWC has over its own technology has caused many firms not only to cut back on licensing but also to reduce new foreign investments.[43]

The LDCs' reaction.   Because of complaints from developing nations that technology from the industrialized countries was excessively capital-intensive as well as expensive, the United Nations Industrial Development Organization (UNIDO) established an Industrial and Technological Bank (INTIB) in 1977 to facilitate the exchange of technologies that are simpler, less expensive, or more appropriate than those obtainable from developed nations. In addition, a Technological Information Exchange System was created to permit the exchange of information concerning the terms and conditions of the technology contracts approved by government technology regulatory agencies. Another INTIB activity is a Joint Patents Program with the World Intellectual Property Organization. Valuable information is obtained from patent documents, cataloged, and made available to firms in developing nations.

Apparently, the activities of INTIB will reduce the profitability in sales of technology by the WWCs. Because all governments will have access to the terms of licensing contracts, charging one client more than another for the same technology will be difficult. The inclusion of technology as part of a package deal will be less lucrative because information furnished by INTIB will improve the ability of an LDC regulatory body to separate the cost of know-how from that of hardware and engineering. Finally, some technology that firms in LDCs would have heretofore had to purchase from multinationals will be available free of charge.

Economics.   The decision the WWC headquarters makes as to the kind of technology to be used by a subsidiary will, within any constraints imposed by the host government, depend on various measurements of the material culture. Economic yardsticks such as power generated per capita and number of high school graduates can uncover possible problems in the distribution and promotion of the product, help determine market size, and provide information on the availability of such resources as raw materials, skilled and unskilled labor, capital equipment, economic infrastructure (communications, financial system), and management talent. You studied these in Chapter 7.

Education

Although education in its widest sense can be thought of as any part of the learning process that equips an individual to take his or her place in the adult society, nearly everyone in the Euroamerican culture equates education with formal schooling.

Education yardsticks.   The firm contemplating foreign investment has no indicators of the educational level of a country's inhabitants except the usual yardsticks of formal education: literacy rate, kinds of schools, quantity of schools and their enrollments, and possibly the amount per capita spent on education. Such data underestimate the size of the vocationally trained group in the many developing countries where people learn a trade through apprenticeships starting at a very early age (12 to 13 years). Like other international statistics, the published literacy rate must be suspect. The literacy

■ **TABLE 9–2**
Percentage of Adults, Ages 20 to 24, in Post-High School Education

Economics	1965	1985
Low income	1%	5%
Lower-middle income	4	13
Upper-middle income	7	16
High income oil-exporting	1	11
Industrial market	21	39
Nonreporting (communist)	27	21

Source: *World Development Report, 1988* (New York: World Development Bank, 1983), pp. 280–81.

census often consists of asking respondents whether they can read and write, and the signing of their names is taken as proof of their literacy. Nonetheless, these data do provide some assistance. Marketers are interested in the literacy rate because it helps them decide what type of media to employ and at what level they should prepare advertisements, labels, point-of-purchase displays, and owner's manuals. The personnel manager will use the literacy rate as a guide in estimating what kinds of people will be available for staffing the operation.

As with most kinds of data, the trends in education should be studied. It is important to realize that the general level of education is rising throughout the world, except for a few communist nations. Table 9–2 illustrates the extent of this increase.

Note that in 20 years, the percentage has quintupled in the low-income nations, increased by 11 times in the high-income oil-exporting countries, and doubled in the industrial nations. Only in the communist nations taken as a whole has the percentage declined, although it has increased in some Eastern-bloc countries. The implication for international businesspeople is that they must prepare to meet the needs of more sophisticated and better-educated consumers. They also can expect a better-educated work force.

While these data are indicative of the general level of education, unfortunately they tell us nothing about the quality of education, nor do they indicate how well the supply of graduates meets the demand.

Educational mix. Until the 1970s, management education in Europe lagged far behind what was available in the United States. There was a feeling that managers were born, not made, and that they could be trained only on the job. Thus, there was little demand for formal business education.

However, a combination of factors has caused a proliferation of European business schools patterned on the American model:

1. Increased competition in the European Community, resulting in a demand for better-trained managers.
2. The return to Europe of American business school graduates.
3. The establishment of American-type schools with American faculty and frequently with the assistance of American universities.[44]

This trend has been much slower in developing countries, where, historically, higher education has emphasized the study of the humanities, law, and medicine. Engineering has not been popular because, with the exception of architecture and civil engineering, there have been few engineering job opportunities in these preindustrial societies. Business education has been less popular than other fields because a business career lacked prestige.

In Chile, one of the writers was given an engineer to train as a V-belt technician. When he began using engineering terms, he noticed that the engineer could not comprehend him, and so he asked the man what kind of engineer he was. To his surprise, the answer was *commercial engineer*. In a land of professional titles, apparently the government thought this was the best way to give professional recognition to business graduates. In Latin America, a person is commonly addressed by his professional title—*Ingeniero* Garcia (engineer) or *Licenciado* Lopez (economist or attorney). A similar practice is followed in Germany and in most communist countries.

As developing nations industrialize, there is a greater competition in the marketplace and the job opportunities for engineers and business school graduates increase. Not only do the multinationals recruit such personnel, but the local firms do too when they find that the new competition forces them to improve the efficiency of their operations.

Brain drain.   Most developing nations are convinced that economic development is impossible without the development of human resources, and for the last two decades especially, governments have probably overinvested in higher education in relation to the demand for students. The result has been rising unemployment among the educated, which has led to a **brain drain**—the emigration of professionals to the industrialized nations. A study done by UNCTAD estimated that about 500,000 professionals had left Third World countries since World War II. However, the incidence of brain drain varied enormously because most come from a limited number of countries in Asia, such as India, Pakistan, Egypt, and Korea.[45]

The International Labor Organization estimates that each emigrant signifies a loss of $20,000 to that country; on that basis, the cost of the brain drain to the developing nations would be over $6 billion.[46]

Brain drain facts:

1. Each year, 6,000 Taiwanese come to study in the United States, but only 20 percent return home.
2. There are 8,000 Israeli engineers in the United States, which Israel says has created a severe bottleneck in its own development of sophisticated industry.
3. About one half of the 1,000 students who graduate annually from the 27 Philippine medicine schools go abroad.
4. The United States alone has 4,000 Greek research scientists, compared with just 5,000 living in Greece. There are also 1,200 Greek business professors working in the United States, but there is no university M.B.A. program in Greece and there is an acute shortage of skilled managers.
5. In U.S. graduate schools of engineering, half of the assistant professors under age 35 are foreign.
6. At IBM's research headquarters, 27 percent of the researchers are foreign.[47]

The prime minister of Jamaica made an interesting observation. During the 1977–80 period, over 8,000 top professionals, 50 percent of the country's

brain drain the emigration of highly educated professionals to another country

most highly trained citizens, emigrated, primarily to the United States. He estimated that the education of these people cost his nation $168.5 million. During that same period, U.S. aid to Jamaica totaled only $116.3 million.[48]

Developing countries are now demanding that the industrial nations pay compensation for the loss of revenue due to the outflow of skilled people. In rebuttal, a U.S. State Department economist told a UN conference that "the proposal tends to ignore the fact that people are people. They aren't commodities, and they aren't traded."[49] Obviously, he knew nothing about professional baseball.

Government authorities are deeply concerned about the loss of skills and have come to realize that there must be faster new job creation, not only to stop the costly loss but also to avoid serious political repercussions. To provide more jobs, they are adopting developmental plans that encourage labor-intensive exports and discourage the introduction of labor-saving processes. The pressure of the unemployed educated is also forcing officials in many areas to soften the terms for foreign investment.

Reverse brain drain. A "reverse brain drain" is preoccupying American educators and businesspeople. After suffering a severe brain drain for over 30 years, Korea and Taiwan are luring home those Korean and Taiwanese engineers and scientists with American doctorates and 10 or more years' experience in American high-tech firms. More money and the opportunity to start businesses in these industrializing countries are the attractions.[50] The returnees are having a visible effect on their countries' competitiveness. A vice president at TRW, which employs many scientists and engineers, calls the reverse brain drain "the largest technology transfer program in the history of the world."[51]

The director of the Commission on Professionals in Science and Technology said, "We've been counting on foreign graduates to stay here and fill our needs because we haven't been filling our own needs for a long time. There's nobody to replace them." According to the Council on Competitiveness, between 1,300 and 1,800 jobs for engineering professors are unfilled, and the shortage is expected to grow as many American professors are approaching retirement age.[52]

Adult literacy. Many governments are also questioning the wisdom of spending funds to highly educate a few and are now giving priority to primary educators as a means of achieving universal *literacy*. The success of these programs and of the programs to reduce adult illiteracy is evidenced by the fact that from 1960 to 1980, world adult literacy was reduced from 42 percent of the adult population to 31 percent.

However, 1987 data show that the literacy rate was still below the world average in at least 70 nations. Only Norway claimed 100% adult literacy, and in Saudi Arabia and Togo, only the male literacy rate was mentioned. Figure 9–1 lists the nations with literacy rates of less than 20 percent.

Inasmuch as the results of an adult literacy program are immediate, whereas it takes 10 to 20 years for the primary school generation to be productive, more attention is being given to adult education, an important trend for WWC managements to note. For example, in only four years, Brazil was able to reduce the illiteracy rate for adult Brazilians by one third, and the cost, allowing for dropouts, was only $11 per student. The program's annual budget

■ **FIGURE 9–1**
Nations Whose Adult Literacy Rate Is Less than 20 Percent

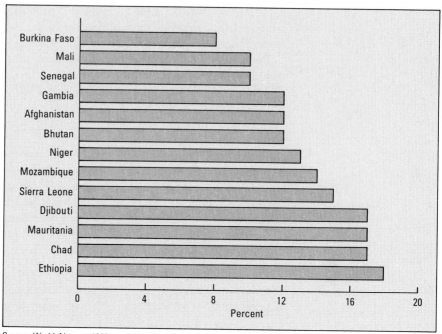

Source: *World Almanac 1989*, pp. 647–737.

was $26 million, which is less than New York City spends just to repair and maintain its school buildings.[53]

Women's education.   Another important trend is the fall in the illiteracy rate for women. The literacy differences between older and younger female age groups is striking. In Africa, which has the world's highest illiteracy rate, the percentage of women who could read and write grew from 18 percent to 27 percent between 1970 and 1980, and was expected to rise to 40 percent by 1990.

Nearly every government now has a goal, if not an actual policy, of providing free and compulsory education for both genders. Notice in Table 9–3 the improvement from 1965 to 1986.

Many more women are enrolling in universities worldwide. As you can see in Table 9–4, the percentage of women of university age attending universities in Africa and the Arab states has tripled in just 25 years.

These statistics are significant to businesspeople because in almost every country, educated women have fewer, healthier, and better-educated children than do uneducated women. They achieve higher labor force participation rates and higher earnings. Undoubtedly, this is leading to an increased role for women in the family's decision making, which will require marketers to redo their promotional programs to take advantage of this consequential trend.

Language

Probably the most apparent cultural distinction that the newcomer to international business perceives is in the means of communication. Differences in the spoken language are readily discernible, and after a short period in the

■ **TABLE 9-3**
Percentage of School-Age Population in Primary Schools

	Male		Female	
Economies	1965	1986	1965	1986
Low income	60%	83%	37%	68%
Lower-middle income	96	108*	81	100
Upper-middle income	97	104	102	107
High income oil-exporting	78	114	59	105
Industrial market	107	103	106	102

*Percentages may exceed 100 percent because some pupils are younger or older than the country's standard primary school age.

Source: *World Development Report, 1989*, (New York: World Bank, 1989), pp. 220–21.

■ **TABLE 9-4**
Percentage of University-Age Women Enrolled in Universities

	1960	1985
World	38%	50%
Developed nations	64	76
Developing nations	28	44
Africa	14	42
North American	39	66
Arab states	16	46
Asia	31	43
Oceania	61	67

Source: *UNESCO Statistical Yearbook 1987* (New York), pp. 2–32, 2–33.

new culture it becomes apparent that there are variations in the unspoken language (manners and customs) as well.

Spoken language.   Language is the key to culture, and without it, people find themselves locked out of all but a culture's perimeter. At the same time, there is no way to learn a language so that the nuances, double meanings of words, and slang are understood unless one also learns the other aspects of the culture. Fortunately, the learning of both goes hand in hand; a certain feel for a people and their attitudes naturally develops with a growing mastery of their language.

Languages delineate cultures.   Spoken languages demarcate cultures, just as physical barriers do. In fact, nothing equals the spoken language for distinguishing one culture from another. If two languages are spoken in a country, there will be two separate cultures (Belgium); if four languages are spoken, there will be four cultures (Switzerland); and so forth.[54]

A poll taken of the German-speaking and French-speaking cultures in Switzerland illustrates how deeply opinions on crucial issues diverge even in a small country.[55] For example, 83.3 percent of the German Swiss regard environmental protection as one of Switzerland's five major problems, compared to 45.1 percent of the French Swiss. Note in Figure 9–2 how each culture rates the importance of various domestic issues.

What is occurring in Canada because of the sharp divisions between the English- and French-speaking regions is ample evidence of the force of

■ **FIGURE 9–2**   **Differences between German-speaking and French-speaking Switzerland (Percent)***

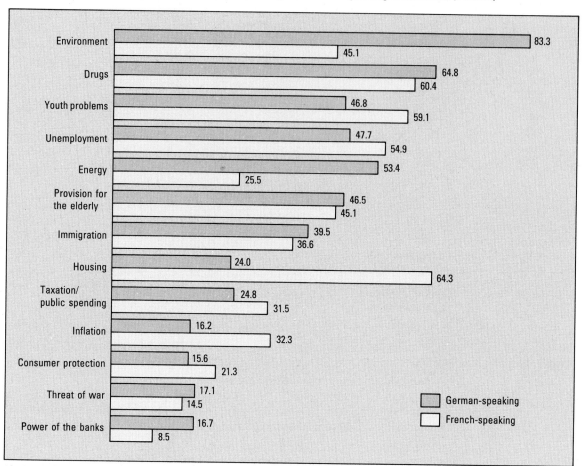

*Carried out by Isopublic on a representative sample of respondents from all sections of the population between May 4 and July 8, 1988.
Source: "What's Worrying the Swiss?" *Bulletin* (Zurich: Crédit Suisse, April 1988), p. 4.

languages in delineating cultures. The differences among the Basques, Catalonians, and Spaniards and the differences between the French and Flemish of Belgium are other notable examples of the sharp cultural and often political differences between language groups. However, it does *not* follow from this generalization that cultures are the same wherever the same language is spoken. As a result of Spain's colonization, Spanish is the principal language of 21 Latin American nations, but no one should believe that Chile and Mexico are culturally similar. Moreover, generally because of cultural differences, many words in both the written and spoken languages of these countries are completely different. Even within a country, words vary from one region to another, also due in part to cultural differences.

Foreign language.   Where many spoken languages exist in a single country (India and many African nations), one foreign language usually serves as the principal vehicle for communication across cultures. Nations that were formerly colonies generally use the language of their ex-rulers; thus French is

Evidence of the language division in Belgium. Where to go? North or South?

lingua franca a foreign language used to communicate among a nation's diverse cultures that have diverse languages

the **lingua franca** or "link" language of the former French and Belgian colonies in Africa, English in India, and Portuguese in Angola.[56] Although they serve as a national language, these foreign substitutes are not the first language of anyone and, consequently, are less effective than the native tongues for reaching mass markets or for day-to-day conversations between managers and workers. Even in countries with only one principal language, such as Germany and France, there are problems of communication because of the large numbers of Greeks, Turks, Spaniards, and others who were recruited to ease labor shortages. A German supervisor may have workers from three or four countries and be unable to speak directly with any of them. To ameliorate this situation, managements try to separate the work force according to origin; that is, all Turks are placed in the paint shop, all Greeks on the assembly line, and so on, but the preferred solution is to teach managers the language of their workers. Invariably, such training has resulted in an increase in production, fewer product defects, and higher worker morale.

> General Tire-Chile sponsored a reverse language training program in which every employee could take free English courses given on the premises after work. Not only managers but also supervisors and even workers attended classes. The program was an excellent morale builder.

English, the link language of business.   When a Swedish businessperson talks with a Japanese businessperson, the conversation generally will be in English. The use of the English as a business *lingua franca* is spreading in Europe so rapidly that it is replacing French and German as the most widely spoken language among Europeans. Satellite television is credited for bringing it to

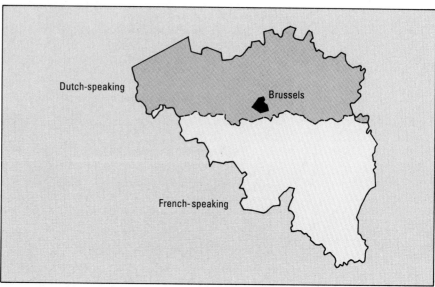

Belgium divided

Courtesy of European Community

millions of homes where English was previously not spoken. Already 10 million homes receive English news broadcasts from the Super Channel in England, and this number is expected to rise to 45 million homes by 1996. In Norway, for example, learning English is compulsory; in the Soviet Union, where language study is compulsory, the majority study English.[57] Even in France, where officials scoff at *la langue de Coca-Cola*, over 80 percent of the secondary school students take four years of English.[58] A number of European multinationals—such as Philips, the Dutch electronics manufacturer ($26 billion annual sales), and SKF, the Swedish producer of ball bearings ($3 billion annual sales)—have adopted English as their house language.

Must speak the local language.   Even though more and more businesspeople are speaking English, when they buy, they insist on doing business in their own language. The seller who speaks it has a competitive edge. Moreover, knowing the language of the area indicates respect for its culture and the area's people.

In many countries, it is a social blunder to begin a business conversation by talking business. Most foreigners expect to establish a social relationship first, and the casual, exploratory conversation that precedes business talks may take from 15 minutes to several meetings, depending on the importance of the meetings. Obviously, a better rapport can be established in a one-on-one conversation than through an interpreter. Look at the trouble this person would have avoided if he had spoken Spanish.

A German engineer, in Colombia to work on a pipeline, arrived at a hotel in the interior, where he tried to explain to the desk clerk that he had a suitcase full of cash that he wanted the hotel to keep. Because he knew no Spanish, he was having difficulty making himself understood. During the conversation, the desk clerk opened the suitcase in front of everyone in the lobby. A week later, the engineer was kidnapped by a guerrilla group and held for a month.[59]

Translation.   The ability to speak the language well does not eliminate the need for translators. The smallest of markets requires technical manuals, catalogs, and good advertising ideas, and a lack of local talent to do the work does not mean that the organization must do without these valuable sales aids. The solution, even when the parent firm does not insist on international standardization, is to obtain this material from headquarters and have it translated if the costs are not prohibitive and suitable reproduction facilities are available locally. If the catalog or manual cannot be reproduced locally, the translation can be made and sent to the home office for reproduction. The home office already has the artwork, so the only additional cost is setting the type for the translations. Remember, though, that a French or Spanish translation will be up to 25 percent longer.

Allowing headquarters to translate can be extremely risky because words from the same language frequently vary in meaning from one country to another or even from one region to another, as was mentioned earlier. A famous example that illustrated how only a single word incorrectly translated can ruin an otherwise good translation occurred in Mexico. The American headquarters of a deodorant manufacturer sent a Spanish translation of the manufacturer's international theme, "If you use our deodorant, you won't be embarrassed in public." Unfortunately, the translator used the word *embarazada* for embarrassed, which in Mexico Spanish means pregnant. Imagine the time that the Mexican subsidiary had with that one.[60]

Use two translations.   To avoid translation errors, the experience marketer will prefer what are really two translations. The first will be made by a bilingual native, whose work will then be translated back to a bilingual foreigner to see how it compares with the original. This work should preferably be done in the market where the material is to be used. No method is foolproof, but the double-translation approach is the safest way devised so far.

Some problems with translations:

1. "Hydraulic ram" was translated from English to Italian as "wet sheep."
2. A sign in a Moscow hotel—"If this is your first visit to the U.S.S.R., you are welcome to it."
3. A hotel sign in Czechoslovokia—"Take one of our horse-driven city tours. We guarantee no miscarriages."
4. Sign in an Italian shop—"Dresses for streetwalking."
5. Probably the best translation was found on an elevator door of a Romanian hotel—"The lift is being fixed for the next few days. During that time, we regret that you will be unbearable."

Technical words.   The usual run of translators have a problem with technical terms that do not exist in a language and with common words that have a special meaning for a certain industry. Portuguese, for example, is rich in fishing and marine terms, a reflection of Portugal's material culture; but unlike English, it is exceedingly limited with respect to technical terms for the newer industries. The only solution is to employ the English word or fabricate a new word in Portuguese. Unless translators have a special knowledge of the

"First, le coca cola. Now peanut butter. Who will save La Belle Langue Française?"

Pearson, *Knickerbocker News,* Albany, New York

industry, they will go to the dictionary for a literal translation that frequently makes no sense or is erroneous.

Resolving such problems by using English words may not be a satisfactory solution even if the public understands them, especially in France or Spain, which have national academies to keep the language "pure." The French have gone so far as to ban by law over 300 anglicisms, and have even fined a fast-food chain $300 for advertising hamburger instead of *steak haché.*

Although the French government has admitted defeat in its efforts to get rid of the old standbys, such as *le weekend, le parking,* and *le jogging,* it has drawn the line on the scientific use of such American computer terms as *le hardware,* and *le databank.* The French Computer Terminology Commission has been asked to create French substitutes.[61]

At first thought this may seem to be another bureaucratic boondoggle akin to studying the love life of a gnat; but on further reflection, one comprehends that these countries have good economic reasons for keeping their languages pure as part of their global campaign to teach it to foreigners. Those learning French are not only potential tourists but also become more empathetic toward anything French. The Argentine engineer who reads French and not English will turn to French technical manuals and catalogs before specifying the supplier for the new power plant he is designing. However, if he constantly finds English technical terms in the French text, which forces him to go to his Spanish–English dictionary, he may decide to learn English and read American manuals and catalogs.

In Japan, the reverse situation exists, probably because for decades the country coveted foreign products while it struggled to overtake the more advanced West. Even now, most Japanese cars sold in the domestic market

Politeness at a Japanese department store

have almost nothing but English on them. A Nissan official explains that English is thought to be more attractive to the eye. Perhaps this is why people quench their thirst with a best-selling soft drink called "Pocari Sweat" and order from menus announcing "sand witches" and "miss Gorilla" (mixed grill). They also puff away on a cigarette called Hope.[62]

No unpleasantness.   One last aspect of the spoken language worthy of mention is the reluctance in many areas to say anything disagreeable to the listener. The politeness of the Japanese and their consideration for others make *no* a little-used word even when there are disagreements. The American executive, pleased that her Japanese counterpart is nodding and saying yes to all of her proposals, may be shaken later to learn that all the time the listener was saying yes (I hear you) and not yes (I agree). Western managers who ask their Brazilian assistants whether something can be done may receive the answer *meio difícil* (somewhat difficult). If managers take this answer literally, they will probably tell the assistants to do it anyway. The assistants will then elaborate on the difficulties until, hopefully, it will finally dawn on the executives that what they ask is impossible, but the Brazilians just don't want to give them the bad news.

unspoken language nonverbal communication, such as gestures and body language

Unspoken language.   Nonverbal communication, or the **unspoken language,** can often tell businesspeople something that the spoken language does not—if they understand it. Unfortunately, the differences in customs among cultures may cause misinterpretations of the communication.

Gestures.   Although gestures are a common form of cross-cultural communication, the language of gestures varies from one region to another. For instance, Americans and most Europeans understand the thumbs-up gesture to mean "all right," but in southern Italy and Greece, it transmits the message for which we reserve the middle finger. Making a circle with the thumb and the forefinger is friendly in the United States, but it means "you're worth zero" in France and Belgium and is a vulgar sexual invitation in Greece and Turkey.[63] The best advice for the foreign traveler is to leave gestures at home.

Closed doors.   Americans know that one of the prequisites of an important executive is a large office with a door that can be closed. Normally, the door is open as a signal that the occupant is ready to receive others, but when it is closed, something of importance is going on. Contrary to the American open-door policy, Germans regularly keep their doors closed. Hall says that the closed door does not mean that the person behind it wants no visitors but only that he or she considers open doors sloppy and disorderly.[64]

Office size.   Although office size is an indicator of a person's importance, it means different things to different cultures. In the United States, the higher the executive, the larger and more secluded the office; but in the Arab world, the president may be in what for us is a small, crowded office. In Japan, the top floor of a department store is reserved for the "bargain basement" (bargain penthouse?) and not for top management. The French prefer to locate important department heads in the center of activities, with their assistants located outward on radii from this center. To be safe, never gauge people's importance by the size and location of their offices.

Conversational distance.   Anthropologists report that conversational distances are smaller in the Middle East and Latin America, though our personal experience in Latin America has not shown this to be the case.[65] Whether this generality is true or false, we must remember that generalities are like arithmetic means; perhaps more people do than do not act in a certain way in a culture, but the businessperson will be dealing with just a few nationals at a time. Luck may have it that he or she will meet exceptions to the stereotype.

The language of gift giving.   Gift giving is an important aspect of every businessperson's life both here and overseas. Entertainment outside office hours and the exchange of gifts are part of the process of getting better acquainted. However, the etiquette or language of gift giving varies among cultures, just as the spoken language does, and although foreigners will usually be forgiven for not knowing the language, certainly they and their gifts will be better received if they follow local customs.

Acceptable gifts.   In Japan, for example, one never gives an unwrapped gift or visits a Japanese home empty-handed. A gift is presented with the comment that it is only a trifle, which implies that the humble social position of the giver does not permit giving a gift in keeping with the high status of the recipient. He in turn will not open the gift in front of the giver because he knows better than to embarrass him by exposing the trifle in the giver's presence.

The Japanese use gift-giving to convey one's thoughtfulness and consideration for the receiver, who over time builds up trust and confidence in the giver. Japanese never give four of anything or an item with four in the name because the word sounds like the one for death. White and yellow flowers are not good choices for gifts because in many areas they connote death. In Germany, red roses to a woman indicate strong feelings for her, and if you give cutlery, always ask for a coin in payment so that the gift will not cut your friendship. Cutlery is a friendship cutter for the Russians and French also. Traditions vary greatly throughout the world, but generally safe gifts everywhere are chocolates, red roses, and a good Scotch whiskey (not in the Arab world, however—instead, bring a good book or something useful for the office).[66]

Gifts or bribes?   The questionable payments scandals (called bribery scandals by the press) exposed the practice of giving very expensive gifts and money to well-placed government officials in return for special favors, large orders, and protection. Some payments were **bribes;** that is, payments were made to induce the payee to do something for the payer that is illegal. But others were **extortion** made to keep the payee from harming the payer is some way. Still others were tips to induce government officials to do their jobs.[67]

All three are payments for services, and usually they are combinations of two or possibly all three types. To distinguish among them, look at this example. If you tip the head waiter to get a good table, that is a bribe; but if you tip him because you know that without it, he'll put you near the kitchen, that's extortion. If you tip him for good service after eating, that is a tip. Part of the problem of adhering to American laws is the difficulty in making this distinction.[68]

Although the media exposure about questionable payments is fairly recent, for a long time it has been common knowledge in the international business community that gifts or money payments are necessary to obtain favorable action from government officials, whether to obtain a large order, avoid having a plant shut down, or receive faster service from customs agents. Their pervasiveness worldwide is illustrated by the variety of names for bribes— *morbida* (bite in Latin America), *dash* (West Africa), *pot de vin* (jug of wine—France), *la bustarella* (envelope left on Italian bureaucrat's desk), or *grease* (United States). Even the Russians are not exempt according to a *Business International* study of WWC managers, who declared that representatives of the Russian state trading organization permit gifts to be deposited in their Swiss back accounts.

According to Radio Moscow, one man who was arrested for taking bribes had in his possession 12 cars, 47 tape recorders and color TVs, 79 suits, and 149 pairs of shoes. Another had 735,000 rubles ($970,000 in cash), 450 gold coins, and 398 gold watches.[69]

Questionable payments.   These come in all forms and sizes from the petty "expediting" payments that have been necessary to get poorly paid government officials to do their normal duties to huge sums to win large orders.

> One of the writers was able to reduce by one half the average age of receivables from a major governmental customer by the payment of $4 a month to a clerk whose sole job was to arrange suppliers' invoices according to their dates, so that the oldest were on top and would be paid first. His company's invoices were placed on top regardless of their date and were paid promptly.

Included by the Securities and Exchange Commission (SEC) as questionable payments are contributions to foreign political parties and the payment of agents' commissions, even when these actions are not illegal in the country where they are made.[70] The United States, in effect, is requiring American firms to operate elsewhere according to this country's laws, which frequently places these firms at a competitive disadvantage.* Many managements have responded by issuing strict orders not to make any questionable payments, legal or illegal, and some have been surprised to find that their business has not fallen off as they expected. Their action has been reinforced by a number of

_____

* This subject is discussed further in Chapter 10.

bribes gifts or payments to induce the receiver to do something illegal for the giver

extortions payments to keep the receiver from causing harm to the payer

governments that have either passed stricter laws or begun to enforce those they already have. Given the combination of low salaries of foreign officials and the intense competition for business, one should not be too sanguine about the prospects for completely eliminating this practice.

Societal Organization

Every society has a structure or an organization that is the patterned arrangement of relationships defining and regulating the manner by which its members interface with one another. Anthropologists generally study this important aspect of culture by breaking down its parts into two classes of institutions—those based on *kinship* and those based on the *free association* of individuals.

Kinship.   The family is the basic unit of institutions based on kinship. Unlike the American family, which is generally composed of the parents and their children, families in many nations—especially in the developing ones—are extended to include all relatives by blood and by marriage.

extended family includes relatives beyond the parents and children

Extended family.   The impact of the **extended family** on the foreign firm derives from the fact that it is a source of employees and business connections. The trust that people place in their relatives, however distant, may motivate them to buy from a supplier owned by their cousin's cousin even though the price is higher. Local personnel managers are prone to fill the best jobs with family members, regardless of their qualifications.

Member's responsibility.   Although the extended family is large, each member's feeling of responsibility to it is strong. An individual's initiative to work is discouraged when he or she may be asked to share personal earnings with unemployed extended family members, no matter what the kinship is. Responsibility to the family is frequently a cause of high absenteeism in developing countries where the worker is called home to help with the harvest. Managements have spent large sums to provide comfortable housing for workers and their immediate families only to find them living in crowded conditions when members of the extended family have moved in.

Pedro Diaz Marin.   In Latin America, where the extended family form is common, individuals use the maternal surname (Marin) as well as the paternal (Diaz) to indicate both branches of the family. It is a common sight to find two businesspeople or a businessperson and a government official, when meeting for the first time, exploring each other's family tree to see whether they have common relatives. If they find any kinship at all, the meeting goes much more smoothly—after all, they're relatives.

associations social units based on age, gender, or common interest, not on kinship

Associations.   Social units not based on kinship, known as **associations** by the anthropologists, may be formed by age, gender, or common interest.[71]

Age.   Manufacturers of consumer goods are well aware of the importance of segmenting a market by age groups, which often cut across cultures. This fact has enabled marketers to succeed in selling such products as clothing and records to the youth market in both developed and developing nations. However, international marketers may go too far if they assume young people everywhere exert the same buying influence on their parents as they do here. Kellogg's attempt to sell cereals in Great Britain through children was not successful because English mothers are less influenced by their children with respect to product choice than are American mothers. The senior citizen segment is an important separate group in the United States, where older people live apart from their children; but where the extended family concept is prevalent, older people continue to live with and exert a powerful influence on younger members of the family.

Gender.   Generally, the less developed the country, the less equal are the genders with respect to job opportunities and education. Even today, the Chinese offer congratulations only on the birth of a son; the birth of a daughter draws condolences.[72]

As nations industrialize, more women enter the job market and thus assume greater importance in the economy. This trend is receiving further impetus as the women's movement for equality of the sexes spreads to the traditionally male-dominated societies of less developed countries. Among the industrialized nations, the United States has the greatest percentage of women in upper management. Although women in Germany, Great Britain, Denmark, and France make up 40 percent of the work force, only 4 percent are in executive positions.[73] According to a United Nations report, women do two thirds of the world's work, receive a tenth of its income, and own a hundredth of its property.[74]

A word of caution, however, must be given to those who, noting the apparently sequestered life of women in some areas, conclude that they have little voice in what the family buys or how it acts. Despite the outward appearance of male domination, women exert a far more powerful influence behind closed doors than the unknowing outsider might suspect.

Common interest.   The common interest groups are composed of people who are joined together by a common bond, which can be political, occupational, recreational, or religious.[75] Even before entering a country, management should identify such groups and assess their political and economic power. As we will see in later chapters, consumer organizations have forced firms to change their product, promotion, and prices, and investments have been supported or opposed by labor unions, which are often a powerful political force.

Class mobility.   In most countries, the ease of moving from one social class to another lies on a continuum from the rigid caste system of India to the relatively flexible social structure of the United States. Less developed countries tend to be located nearer the position of India, whereas the industrial nations are closer to the U.S. position. As industrialization progresses, barriers to mobility become weaker. Mobility between classes must be assessed by management because interclass rigidity, especially when it is accompanied by low social status for business, can make it extremely difficult for the firm to obtain good management personnel locally.

SUMMARY

Culture, the sum total of the beliefs, rules, techniques, institutions, and artifacts that characterize the human population, is of interest to anyone who does business in other countries because of its pervasive influence on all the functions of the firm. To be successful in their relationships overseas, international businesspeople must be students of culture. They must not only obtain factual knowledge, they must also become culturally sensitive.

Because society is composed of people and their cultures, we have followed the practice of many anthropologists in calling the variables *sociocultural*. Although the experts differ considerably as to the relevant components of culture, the following list is representative of their thinking: (1) aesthetics, (2) attitudes and beliefs, (3) religion, (4) material culture, (5) education, (6) language, (7) societal organization, (8) legal characteristics, and (9) political structure.

Aesthetics is concerned with a culture's sense of beauty and good taste and is expressed in the arts, drama, music, folklore, and dances. Examples have been given to illustrate their importance in business. Attitudes and beliefs, especially those concerned with time, achievement, work, and change, can be radically different than those to which the businessperson is accustomed. Being aware of the differences can often decide the outcome of a business venture. A knowledge of the basic tenets of other religions will contribute to a better understanding of their followers' attitudes.

Material culture, especially technology, is of great importance to managements contemplating overseas investments. Foreign governments are becoming increasingly involved in the sale and control of technical assistance. The educational level will not only determine the kinds of people available to staff foreign operations but will also exert an important influence on the affiliate's marketing mix.

Language is the key to culture and must be learned if a person is to understand the people of a culture. Generally, there will be as many cultures in a country as there are languages. Students of culture should learn both the spoken and unspoken language. A knowledge of how a society is organized is useful because the societal organization defines and regulates the manner in which its members interface with one another. The extended family and the responsibility of each member to it are especially significant.

The nine cultural components mentioned in this chapter will serve as a helpful checklist to managers who must make cultural assessments.

QUESTIONS

1. How do attitudes toward time, attitudes toward change, and attitudes toward achievement and work affect the various functional areas of international business (personnel, marketing, and so forth)?

2. Why are international firms called agents of change? Give some examples.

3. John Adams, with 20 years' experience as a general foreman in an American firm, is sent as production superintendent to the company's newest plant in Cali, Colombia. He was chosen because of his outstanding success in handling workers. Adams uses the participative leadership style. Can you foresee his having any problems in this new job?

4. The governments of developing nations should impose restrictions forcing U.S.-trained engineers and scientists to return home after graduation. Agree or disagree? What is the basis of your opinion?

5. How can the international firm get people to accept a new idea?

6. Is there a relationship between religion and the attitude toward achievement?

7. What is the relationship between religion and business in the Middle East?

8. What is occurring in the LDCs that makes licensing agreements less attractive for the international firm?

9. What is probably the most foolproof way to avoid translation errors?

10. Gift-giving in other countries seems very involved. How can traveling business executives keep track of all the rules?

11. The competition is giving bribes—shouldn't we? Discuss.

12. What is the significance of the extended family for the international manager?

MINICASE 9–1

Be Attuned to Business Etiquette

The proverb, "When in Rome, do as the Romans do," applies to the business representative as well as the tourist. Being attuned to a country's business etiquette can make or break a sale, particularly in countries where thousand-year-old traditions can dictate the rules for proper behavior.

Some of the considerations anyone interested in being a successful marketer should be aware of include:

Local customer, etiquette, and protocol. (An exporter's behavior in a foreign country can reflect favorably or unfavorably on the exporter, the company, and even the sales potential for the product.)

Body language and facial expressions. (Often, actions do speak louder than words.)

Expressions of appreciation. (Giving and receiving gifts can be a touchy subject in many countries. Doing it badly may be worse than not doing it at all.)

Choices of words. (Knowing when and if to use slang, tell a joke, or just keep silent is important.)

The following informal test will help exporters rate their business etiquette. See how many of the following you can answer correctly. (Answers follow the last question.)

1. You are in a business meeting in an Arabian Gulf country. You are offered a small cup of bitter cardamom coffee. After your cup has been refilled several times, you decide you would rather not have any more. How do you decline the next cup offered to you?
   a. Place your palm over the top of the cup when the coffee pot is passed.
   b. Turn your empty cup upside down on the table.
   c. Hold the cup and twist your wrist from side to side.

2. In which of the following countries are you expected to be punctual for business meetings?
   a. Peru.
   b. Hong Kong.
   c. Japan.
   d. China.
   e. Morocco.

3. Gift giving is prevalent in Japanese society. A business acquaintance presents you with a small wrapped package. Do you:
   a. Open the present immediately and thank the giver?
   b. Thank the giver and open the present later?
   c. Suggest that the giver open the present for you?

4. In which of the following countries is tipping considered an insult?
   a. Great Britain.
   b. Iceland.
   c. Canada.

5. What is the normal workweek in Saudi Arabia?
   a. Monday through Friday.
   b. Friday through Tuesday.
   c. Saturday through Wednesday.

6. You are in a business meeting is Seoul. Your Korean business associate hands you his calling card, which states his name in the traditional Korean order: Park Chul Su. How do you address him?
   a. Mr. Park.
   b. Mr. Chul.
   c. Mr. Su.

7. In general, which of the following would be good topics of conversation in Latin American countries?
   a. Sports.
   b. Religion.
   c. Local Politics.
   d. The Weather.
   e. Travel.

8. In many countries, visitors often are entertained in the homes of clients. Taking flowers as a gift to the hostess is usually a safe way to express thanks for the hospitality. However, both the type and color of the flower can have an amorous, negative, or even ominous implications. Match the country where presenting them would be a social *faux pas.*
   a. Brazil.   1. Red roses.
   b. France.   2. Purple flowers.
   c. Switzerland.   3. Chrysanthemums.

9. In Middle Eastern countries, which hand does one use to accept or pass food?
   a. Right hand.
   b. Left hand.
   c. Either hand.

10. Body language is just as important as the spoken word in many countries. For example, in most countries, the thumbs-up sign means "OK." But in which of the following countries is the sign considered a rude gesture?
   a. Germany.
   b. Italy.
   c. Australia.

Answers: 1—*c.* It is also appropriate to leave the cup full. 2—*a, b, c, d,* and *e.* Even in countries where local custom does not stress promptness, overseas visitors should be prompt. 3—*b.* 4—*b.* 5—*c.* 6—*a.* The traditional Korean pattern is surname, followed by two given names. 7—*a, d* and *e.* 8—*a* and 2. Purple flowers are a sign of death in Brazil, as are chrysanthemums in France (*b* and 3). In Switzerland (*c* and 1), as well as in many other north European countries, red roses suggest romantic intentions. 9—*a.* Using the left hand would be a social gaffe. 10—*b.*

How's Your Business Etiquette?

8–10 Congratulations—you have obviously done your homework when it comes to doing business overseas.

5–7 While you have some sensitivity to the nuances of other cultures, you still might make some social errors that could cost you sales abroad.

1–4 Look out—you could be headed for trouble if you leave home without consulting the experts.

Where to Turn for Help

Whether you struck out completely in the business etiquette department of just want to polish your skills, there are several sources you can turn to for help.

Books. While two years ago business etiquette information may have been difficult to locate, most good bookstores today carry a variety of resource materials to help the traveling business representative.

Workshops and seminars. Many private business organizations and universities sponsor training sessions for the exporter interested in unraveling the mysteries of doing business abroad.

State marketing specialists. In some states, your first contact should be your state agriculture department, where international specialists there can pass on their expertise or put you in touch with someone who can.

Source: *Foreign Agriculture*, U.S. Department of Agriculture, February 1987, pp. 18–19.

MINICASE 9–2

Is It a Bribe?

Nick Brown, the sales manager of the Johnson Rubber subsidiary in El Pais, has been selling about a half-million dollars a year in industrial rubber products (rotary drilling hose, oil suction and discharge hose) to the government-owned oil monopoly. He faces stiff competition from the local subsidiary of another multinational rubber manufacturer, which is trying to increase its share of the business. The principal reason for his success is his personal friendship with Captain Corona, the buyer. Brown has never bought anything for Corona except an occasional lunch and a reasonably priced ($50) Christmas gift.

One day in December, he received a call from Captain Corona, who said that just as he was leaving the house, his wife complained that she needed a new refrigerator. Corona was calling Brown because he knew that the marketing manager of a refrigerator manufacturer was Brown's close friend and he wondered whether Brown could arrange for a discount through his friend. Brown told Captain Corona that he would call his friend to see whether the friend could get Corona the discount.

After the call, Brown began thinking about his conversation with Corona. The man was responsible for his receiving a half-million dollars in orders every year. This was three times the business his competitor was obtaining, even though the product quality and prices were similar. Every year, he gave the captain a Christmas present worth about $50. The refrigerator would cost $250. Never had the captain asked him for anything. Johnson Rubber had no rules regarding restricting the value of gifts, but employees were expected to exercise good judgment. Could this be the beginning of a series of requests for expensive gifts, or was Captain Corona only interested in getting the best price possible?

What would you do if you were Nick Brown?

MINICASE 9–3

Evans Machinery–France

Evans Machinery–France is the French subsidiary of Evans Machinery, headquartered in Chicago. The firm specializes in the production of highly sophisticated materials-handling equipment, most of which must be specially designed for the job. There are few competitors in France or in any other part of the European Community

Business has been excellent, though recently the company lost two sizable orders to a French competitor. One customer was the government-owned automobile factory, Renault, and the other was a French-owned textile factory. Both customers had made various purchases from Evans Machinery in the past.

Frank Bowen, the subsidiary's managing director, sat in his office reviewing the two lost sales. He knew that the French competitor did not have Evans's technical capability, and he was confident that the competitor's price could not have been significantly lower. Bowen walked to the window overlooking the front of the building. He was proud of that plant. The lawn was well kept. There was a flagpole with the American flag flying, just as in Chicago. Bowen was thinking that he had a good chance for the executive vice president's job that was coming up soon back at headquar-

ters if Evans Machinery–France continued to do as well as it had done for the last three years under his management. The loss of two sizable orders wouldn't help his record, though. What was the reason? An idea came to him. He called his friend Henri in Renault's technical department. Bowen liked Henri, who had been educated in the United States and spoke English like an American. He explained to Henri that he was concerned about having lost Renault's order. Did Henri know why this had happened? After a pause, Henri said, "Frank, my friend, the boom years in France are over, and the government is concerned. The order was earmarked for a French company."

What can Frank Bowen do to stop this loss of orders?

SUPPLEMENTARY READINGS

Brain drain

"A Reverse Brain Drain That's Pumping up East Asian Economies." *International Management*, April 1986, pp. 22–23.

"Brain Drain." *The Wall Street Journal*, October 21, 1983, p. 1

"Brain Drain in Reverse." *Forbes*, April 17, 1989, pp. 114–15.

"Brain Drain Slows Mexico's Development." *The Wall Street Journal*, May 5, 1989, p. A10.

"China Chicken Feed." *The Economist*, November 26, 1988, p. 36.

"China Weighs Shifts in Overseas Studies: Brain Drain Feared." *The Chronicle of Higher Education*, May 11, 1988, p. A1.

"Costly Export." *The Wall Street Journal*, April 18, 1989, p. A1.

"Let Open Doors Swing Both Ways." *The Wall Street Journal*, June 15, 1988, p. 22.

"The Brain Drain." *Kredietbank Weekly Bulletin*, March 6, 1987, p. 1.

"The Exodus of the Elite." *International Management*, February 1988, pp. 54–56.

Bribes, extortion

"All in Favor of Bribery, Please Stand Up." *Across the Board*, June 1984, pp. 3–5.

Beeman, Don R., and Sherman A. Timmons. "Who Are the Villains in International Business?" *Business Horizons*, September/October 1982, pp. 7–10.

"Bribery around the World." *Business International*, January 16, 1981, pp. 20–21.

"Corruption: How Firms Cope in Korea." *Business Asia*, November 26, 1982, pp. 337–78.

"Dingell Says Northrup Raised $6 Million to Bribe Koreans." *Aviation Week & Space Technology*, October 3, 1988, p. 21.

"Indonesia's Struggle to Wean Itself from Oil." *International Management*, September 1985, pp. 113–15.

Jacoby, Neil H., Peter Nehemkis, and Richard Eells. *Bribery and Extortion in World Business*. New York: Macmillan, 1977.

"Some Guidelines on Dealing with Graft in Korean Operations." *Business International*, February 25, 1983, p. 62.

Culture in business

"Blunders Abroad." *Nation's Business*, March 1989, pp. 54–55.

"Capitalist Chic." *The Wall Street Journal*, June 10, 1988, p. A1.

Copeland, Lennie, and Lewis Griggs. *Going International*. New York: Random House, 1985.

"Enjoy, Enjoy." *Forbes*, December 12, 1988, pp. 144–50.

Harris, Phillip R., and Robert T. Moran. *Managing Cultural Differences*. 2nd ed. Houston: Gulf Publishing, 1987.

"In Japan, It's 'Learn the Hard Way,'" *Advertising Age*, August 20, 1987, p. 144.

Kim, W. Chan, and R. A. Mauborgne. "Cross-Cultural Strategies." *The Journal of Business Strategy*, Spring 1987, pp. 28–35.

Knotts, Rose. "Cross-Cultural Management: Transformations and Adaptations." *Business Horizons*, January–February 1989, pp. 29–33.

Lee, James A. "Cultural Analysis in Overseas Operations." *Harvard Business Review*, March–April 1966, pp. 106–14.

"Regulations Direct Ad Traffic Differently around the World." *Advertising World*, April–May 1988, pp. 39–40

Terpstra, Vern, and Kenneth David. *The Cultural Environment of International Business*. 2nd ed. Cincinnati: South-Western Publishing, 1985.

"Tradition." *The Wall Street Journal*, September 15, 1986, p. 20.

Education

"A People Problem." *The Economist*, November 26, 1988, pp. 49–50.

"Chinese M.B.A. Holders Find a Degree Earned in the West Doesn't Go Far at Home." *The Wall Street Journal*, June 2, 1988, p. 8.

"Degrees of Confusion." *International Management*, January 1988, pp. 34–38.

The European Community and Education. Brussels: Commission of the European Community, 1985.

Gifts

Fadiman, Jeffrey A. "A Traveler's Guide to Gifts and Bribes." *Harvard Business Review*, July–August 1986, pp. 122–36.

"How to Succeed in Business by Polishing Your Manners." *U.S. News & World Report*, October 25, 1985, p. 45.

Reardon, Kathleen. *International Business and Gift-Giving Customs.* Janesville, Wis.: Parker Pen, 1981.

Reeder, John A. "When West Meets East: Cultural Aspects of Doing Business in Asia." *Business Horizons*, January–February 1987, pp. 69–74.

"Venturing through China's 'Open Door.'" *Business Marketing*, February 1988, pp. 63–66.

Language

"A Linguistic Problem." *Europe*, September 1986, pp. 3–4.

"Computers Threaten Another Tradition: The Glory of France." *The Wall Street Journal*, October 10, 1985, p. 1.

"English: The Common Language of Europeans?" *International Management*, February 1988, pp. 59–61.

"English Out to Conquer the World." *U.S. News & World Report*, February 18, 1985, pp. 49–52.

"The International Language of Gestures." *Psychology Journal*, May 1984, pp. 64–67.

"Why Speaking English Is No Longer Enough." *International Management*, November 1986, pp. 39–42.

Religion

"Central Asia: The Rise of the Moslems." *U.S. News & World Report*, April 3, 1989, pp. 48–49.

"Hunted by an Angry Faith." *Time*, February 27, 1989, pp. 28–33.

"Islam for Beginners." *The Economist*, March 18, 1989, pp. 95–96.

"Islamic Fundamentalism: Friend or Foe?" *Business International*, December 20, 1985, pp. 401–02.

"Islam: Seeking the Future in the Past." *U.S. News & World Report*, July 6, 1987, pp. 33–41.

"Religions of Asia." *Modern Maturity*, December 1984/January 1985, pp. 72–78.

"Rising Islamic Fervor Challenges the West, Every Moslem Ruler." *The Wall Street Journal*, August 7, 1987, p. 1.

Technology

"A Maverick Man and His Steam Machine." *Far Eastern Economic Review*, June 9, 1988, p. 85.

Fatemi, Khosrow. "Multinational Corporations, Developing Countries, and Transfer of Technology: A Cultural Perspective." *Issues in International Business*, Summer/Fall 1985, pp. 1–6.

"Global Reach." *The Wall Street Journal*, Aptil 29, 1985, p. 1.

"How to Sell Soap in India." *The Economist*, September 10, 1988, p. 82.

"Reaching Out." *The Wall Street Journal*, January 7, 1986, p. 1.

Reddy, Allan C., and C. P. Rao. "Technology Transfer from Developed to Developing Countries: Needs, Problems, and Suggestions." *Issues in International Business*, Summer/Fall 1985, pp. 7–12.

"Secrets Police." *The Wall Street Journal*, November 15, 1987, p. 1.

"They Didn't Listen to Anybody." *Forbes*, December 15, 1986, pp. 168–69.

"Where Technology Is the Appropriate Word." *The Economist*, April 18, 1987, pp. 83–84.

Women

"Equality of the Sexes Threatens Cultural Ecology." *Liberal Star*, October 10, 1988, pp. 6–7.

"Europe's Women Unite to Throw Off Their Chains." *International Management*, July/August 1987, pp. 42–49.

"Japan's Secret Economic Weapon: Exploited Women." *Business Week*, March 4, 1985, pp. 54–55.

"Look Whose Sun Is Rising Now: Career Women." *Business Week*, August 25, 1986, p. 50.

"More and More Women at Work." *Deutsche Bank Bulletin*, December 1986, pp. 9–12.

"The Old Sexism in the New China." *U.S. News & World Report*, April 24, 1989, pp. 36–38.

"The Triumphant Spirit of Nairobi." *Time*, August 5, 1985, pp. 38–40.

"Women Managers and Turkey's Sexist Society." *The Wall Street Journal*, May 15, 1985, p. 38.

ENDNOTES

1. P. Harris and R. Moran, *Managing Cultural Differences* (Houston: Gulf Publishing, 1987), p. 13.
2. Richard L. Daft, *Management* (Hinsdale, Ill: Dryden Press, 1988), p. 492.
3. I. Brady and B. Isaac, *A Reader in Cultural Change*, vol. 1 (Cambridge, Mass.: Schenkman Publishing, 1975), p. x.
4. V. Barnouw, *An Introduction to Anthropology* (Homewood, Ill: Dorsey Press, 1975), p. 5.

5. E. T. Hall, *Beyond Culture* (Garden City, N.Y.: Double-day, 1977), p. 16.

6. G. Foster, *Traditional Societies and Technological Change* (New York: Harper & Row, 1973), p. 11; and Vern Terpstra and K. David, *The Cultural Environment of International Business* (Cincinnati: South-Western Publishing, 1985), p. 7.

7. Hall, *Beyond Culture*, p. 54.

8. "They Didn't Listen to Anybody," *Forbes*, December 15, 1986, pp. 168–69.

9. "National versus Corporate Culture: Implications for Human Resource Management," *Human Resource Management*, Summer 1988, pp. 232–45.

10. One of the writers installed in a Spanish factory new production equipment that was to replace old but still serviceable machinery. Before leaving for a week's work in Madrid, he tested the equipment, trained some workers to use it, and advised the supervisor that it was ready. On his return, he was surprised to find that the new equipment was not being utilized. The supervisor explained that the old machinery was working well and he didn't want to "disrupt production." Actually, the new equipment was easier to use and would greatly increase output. Realizing that drastic action was called for, the writer grabbed a sledge hammer and made a token effort to destroy the old equipment. Only then did the supervisor get the message. Admittedly, the action was unorthodox, but it did bring immediate results. Not wanting to replace a still serviceable object with a new object, even when the new object is superior, is a quite common attitude in many countries.

11. This classification depends in part on M. J. Herskovits, *Man and His Works* (New York: Alfred A. Knopf, 1952), p. 634. It was embellished by anthropologists at the University of South Alabama.

12. L. Copeland and Lewis Griggs, *Going International* (New York: Random House, 1985), pp. 63–64.

13. Herskovits, *Man and His Works*, p. 414.

14. "The Middle East Mirage," *International Management*, April 1979, p. 21.

15. John A. Reeder, "When West Meets East: Cultural Aspects of Doing Business with Asia," *Business Horizons*, January–February 1987, pp. 18–22.

16. "Tokyo Pedestrians Run on Time," *The Wall Street Journal*, November 19, 1983, p. 2.

17. "European Etiquette," *European Community*, May 1975, p. 17.

18. "Bridging that Other Gulf," *Vision*, May 1975, p. 50.

19. "Middle East Mirage," p. 23.

20. Rose Knotts, "Cross-Cultural Management: Transformations and Adaptions," *Business Horizons*, January–February 1989, p. 30.

21. "Blunders Abroad," *Nation's Business*, March 1989, p. 54.

22. "Enjoy, Enjoy," *Forbes*, December 12, 1988, p. 144.

23. Benjamin Higgins, *Economic Development* (New York: W. W. Norton, 1968), pp. 241–44.

24. It is difficult to adequately translate the connotations of the two words. No one proudly says he is an *obrero* even if he earns more than the *empleado* who is a file clerk.

25. "What Is Culture's Role in Economic Policy?" *The Wall Street Journal*, December 22, 1986, p. 1.

26. "Cracks in the Japanese Work Ethic," *Fortune*, May 14, 1984, pp. 162–68.

27. Kenneth L. Woodward, "Religions in Asia," *Modern Maturity*, December 1984/January 1985, pp. 72–74.

28. V. Terpstra and K. David, *The Cultural Environment of International Business*, 2nd ed. (Cincinnati: South-Western Publishing, 1985), p. 89.

29. Woodward, "Religions in Asia," pp. 75–78; and "Islam: Seeking the Future in the Past," *U.S. World News & World Report*, July 6, 1987, pp. 33–36.

30. "Hunted by an Angry Faith," *Time*, February 27, 1989, pp. 28–33; and "Islams Arrow of Death," *The Economist*, March 11, 1989, p. 41.

31. "Hunted by an Angry Faith," p. 32.

32. "Sunnis? Shiites? What's That Got To Do with the Price of Oil?" *Forbes*, April 12, 1982, pp. 88–92; and "Mosque and State," *The Wall Street Journal*, August 7, 1987, p. 1.

33. "Malaysian Malady: When the Spirit Hits, a Scapegoat Suffers," *The Wall Street Journal*, March 3, 1980, p. 1.

34. "Cross-Cultural Strategies," *The Journal of Business Strategy*, Spring 1987, p. 32.

35. Daniel D. Roman and Joseph F. Puett, Jr., *International Business and Technological Innovation* (New York: North-Holland, 1983), p. *xxi*.

36. "Sensing Your Way up the 'S-Curve,'" *International Management*, October 1986, p. 72.

37. Khosrow Fatemi, "Multinational Corporations, Developing Countries, and Transfer of Technology: A Cultural Perspective," *Issues in International Business*, Summer/Fall 1985, p. 1.

38. "Where Technology Is the Appropriate Word," *The Economist*, April 18, 1987, p. 83.

39. "How to Sell Soap in India," *The Economist*, September 1988, p. 82.

40. "Neutral Nations Guard American Technology to Gain Import Rights," *The Wall Street Journal*, November 15, 1987, p. 1.

41. "Weak in Technology, South Korea Seeks Help from Overseas," *The Wall Street Journal*, January 7, 1986, p. 1.

42. Exports and foreign exchange earnings can be affected if the product cannot compete in the world market because of excessive manufacturing costs, inferior quality, or an obsolete design.

43. The reason is that multinationals will generally make licensing agreements even with wholly owned foreign subsidiaries to establish a legal basis for requiring royalty payments and service fees.

44. "Europe's Best Business Schools," *Fortune*, May 23, 1988, pp. 106–10.

45. "Let Open Doors Swing Both Ways," *The Wall Street Journal*, June 15, 1988, p. 22.

46. "Migracion de Profesionales," *Comercio Exterior* (Mexico City: Banco Nacional de Comercio Exterior, May 1978), p. 581.

47. "Costly Export," *The Wall Street Journal*, April 18, 1989, p. A1.

48. "Costly Brain Drain," *Development Forum* (Geneva: United Nations, March 1982), p. 12.

49. "Developing Nations Demand Compensation for Loss of Skilled People to Industrial Nations," *The Wall Street Journal*, September 3, 1982, p. 30.

50. "Brain Drain in Reverse," *Forbes*, April 17, 1989, pp. 114–15.

51. "Costly Export," p. A1.

52. Ibid., p. A20.

53. "Brazil's Amazing Literacy Plan," *The Wall Street Journal*, December 3, 1974, p. 28.

54. Africa has an unparalleled mixture of cultures and languages. Kenya, for example, has 22 distinct languages, and Nigeria has 125.

55. "What's Worrying the Swiss?" *Bulletin* (Zurich: Crédit Suisse, April 1988), pp. 4–5.

56. To avoid using English as the link language in India, Hindi was declared the official language. As late as 1986, Tamil-speaking students from the south were rioting against the imposition of Hindi, which was spoken by 30 percent of the population, mainly in the north. The students wanted English to be the link language. From *Los Angeles Times*, December 11, 1986, part I, p. 5.

57. "English: The Common Language of Europeans?" *International Management*, February 1988, pp. 59–61.

58. "English Out to Conquer the World," *U.S. News & World Report*, February 18, 1985, p. 51.

59. "Why Speaking English Is No Longer Enough," *International Management*, November 1986, p. 42.

60. This mistake was caught before it was published locally, but an incident happened to one of the writers, newly arrived in Brazil, that did go all over the country. The ad manager, a Brazilian, brought him a campaign emphasizing that car owners should maintain 24 pounds per square inch in their tires to get maximum wear. To really get the point across, life-size figures of a tire company salesman were made up, with the name of the company and a large "24" printed across his chest. Care was taken to get these figures out to the dealers, who were to set them up on a "D day." The writer, sitting in his São Paulo office, proud of the unusually good coordination of the campaign, began receiving calls from competitors asking what type of people worked in his company. Over the laughter came the message—24 in Brazilian Portuguese means homosexual!

61. "Computers Threaten Another Tradition: The Glory of France," *The Wall Street Journal*, October 10, 1985, p. 1.

62. "In Japan, They Demand English—Even If It's Bad," *Modesto Bee*, July 10, 1983, p. E–6.

63. "The International Language of Gestures," *Psychology Today*, May 1984, p. 64–67.

64. E. T. Hall, *The Hidden Dimension* (Garden City, N.Y.: Doubleday, 1969), pp. 134–35.

65. One of the writers, who lived in Latin America for 15 years, was surprised to read this statement in *The Silent Language in Overseas Business* by E. T. Hall. His Mexican wife, who had lived on both sides of the border, absolutely refuted it, so when he went to Ecuador recently as a consultant, he was careful to observe conversational distances. In no instance did he note any appreciable difference.

66. Kathleen Reardon, *International Business Gift-Giving Customs* (Janesville, Wis.: Parker Pen, 1981).

67. Neil H. Jacoby, Peter Nehemkis, and Richard Eells, *Bribery and Extortion in World Business* (New York: MacMillan, 1977), pp. 174–75.

68. "Bribes versus Gifts: Soviet Interpretation Unclear," *Business Eastern Europe*, February 10, 1986, p. 45; and "Ethical Codes in Industry: Dealing with the FCPA and with Ambiguity" (Lubin School of Business) *Letter*, February/March 1988, pp. 10–12.

69. "On the Take," *Parade Magazine*, March 1977, p. 8.

70. Interestingly, the Foreign Corrupt Practices Act of 1977 permits *grease* to be paid when its sole purpose is to expedite nondiscretionary official actions.

71. Herskovits, *Man and His Works*, p. 303.

72. "The Old Sexism in the New China," *U.S. News & World Report*, April 24, 1989, p. 37.

73. "Europe's Women Unite to Throw Off Their Chains," *International Management*, July/August 1987, pp. 42–49.

74. "Sexes' Equality a Myth," *U.S. News & World Report*, July 8, 1985, p. 40.

75. V. Terpstra, *International Marketing* (Hinsdale, Ill.: Dryden Press, 1986), p. 106.

Chapter 10
Political Forces

Politics have no relation to morals.

Niccoló Machiavelli

Man's capacity for justice makes democracy possible, but man's inclination to injustice makes democracy necessary.

Reinhold Niebuhr,
American theologian

LEARNING OBJECTIVES

In this chapter, you will study:

1. The ideological forces that affect business, and how they affect it.

2. The importance of government-owned business even in countries that refer to themselves as capitalist.

3. Nationalism as a powerful emotional force with political repercussions on business.

4. The necessity for adequate government protection of business and its personnel from terrorism and invasion.

5. How government instability and sudden changes in government policy affect business.

6. The effects on business of traditional hostilities between peoples and nations.

7. The political power of international organizations.

8. Labor as a political force.

9. WWCs' abilities to influence political decisions.

KEY WORDS AND CONCEPTS

- Communism
- Expropriation
- Confiscation
- Capitalism
- Socialism
- Conservative
- Right wing
- Liberal
- Left wing
- Privatization
- Nationalism
- Terrorism
- Stability
- Instability
- Traditional hostilities
- Country risk assessment

BUSINESS INCIDENT

Governments sometimes take over privately owned businesses, expropriate them, and pay the previous owners some compensation. But frequently it goes the other direction, and governments sell businesses to private buyers.

In 1982, the British government sold National Freight Corporation (NFC), Britain's largest freight handler, to its 12,000 workers. They paid the equivalent of $1.50 per share, and by August 1983, the shares were valued at about $5.10.

The worker-owners say they now turn off unnecessary lights and take better care of trucks and other equipment than they did before. Sales and profits rose, in part because of the boost in workers' drive and motivation.

This story has a happy ending. In 1988, NFC's profits were almost $105 million on turnover of over $2 billion, up from profits of about $20 million and turnover of some $838 million five years earlier. Also in that year, the NFC employee-owners voted to list the company shares of stock on the London stock exchange, which made instant millionaires of many of those owners—who are trying to have their cake and eat it too. They will attempt to maintain control of NFC against purchasers of new shares on the stock exchange by allowing employee-shareholders to have double voting powers in the event of a takeover bid.

Source: John Marcom, Jr., *The Wall Street Journal,* August 30, 1983, p. 30; and Kevin Brown, *Financial Times,* February 22, 1988, p. 6.

C hapter 11 deals with the legal forces affecting international business. Of course, laws and their interpretation and enforcement reflect political ideologies and outlooks as well as government stability and continuity. Therefore, this chapter is intended as background for and a companion to Chapter 11.

In a number of ways, the political climate of the country in which a business operates is as important as the country's topography, its natural resources, and its climate in the sense of weather. Indeed, we shall see examples in which a hospitable, stable government can encourage business investment and growth despite geographic or weather obstacles and scarcity of natural resources. The opposite is equally true. Some areas of the world that are relatively blessed with natural resources and with not too difficult topography and weather have been very little developed because of government instability. Occasionally, the government of a country is hostile to investment in its territory by foreign companies even though they might provide capital, technology, and training for development of the country's resources and people.

Many of the political forces with which business must cope have ideological sources, but there are a large number of other sources. These include nationalism, terrorism, traditional hostilities, unstable governments, international organizations, and government-owned business.

It should be pointed out that the WWC itself can be a political force. Some firms have budgets or sales larger than the GNP of some of the countries with which they negotiate. Although budgets and GNPs do not translate directly or necessarily into power, it should be clear that companies with bigger budgets and countries with bigger GNPs possess more assets and facilities with which to negotiate. Refer to Table 1-1 (pp. 10-11) for some examples.

This chapter will provide an indication of the types of risks to private business posed by political forces. As we shall see, some of the risks can stem from more than one political force.

IDEOLOGICAL FORCES

Such names as communism, socialism, capitalism, liberal, conservative, left wing, and right wing are used to describe governments, political parties, and people. These names indicate ideological beliefs.

Communism

In communist countries, the government owns all the major factors of production. With minor exceptions, all production in these countries is by state-owned factories and farms. Labor unions are government controlled.

communism Marx's theory of a classless society, developed by his successors into control of society by the Communist party and the attempted worldwide spread of communism

Communism as conceived by Karl Marx was a theory of social change directed to the ideal of a classless society. As developed by Lenin and others, communism advocates the seizure of power by a conspiratorial political party, the maintenance of power by stern suppression of internal opposition, and commitment to the ultimate goal of a worldwide communist state.

Although private companies from noncommunist countries usually cannot own plants in a communist country, they can do business with it. We shall discuss how this is done in Chapter 17. But before we get there, we should point out that recent developments in the People's Republic of China and in Eastern Europe may be opening opportunities for foreign investment.

Communist government takeover of a previously noncommunist country. This business risk is not dealt with in Chapter 17. Given one of communism's basic tenets—state ownership of all the productive factors—private business will be taken over by the government. This occurred in Russia after the 1917 Bolshevik Revolution, and it has been repeated after each communist takeover of a country.

Compensation of expropriated property. To date, none of the new communist governments has compensated the foreign former owners directly. A few of the owners have gotten some reimbursement indirectly out of assets of the communist government seized abroad after the communist government confiscated foreign private property within its country. For example, the U.S. government seized assets of the Soviet Union in the United States after American property in the USSR was confiscated. American firms or individuals whose property had been confiscated in the USSR could file claims with a U.S. government agency, and if they could substantiate their loss, a percentage of it was paid.

Expropriation and confiscation. The rules of traditional international law recognize a country's right to expropriate the property of foreigners within its jurisdiction. But those rules require the country to compensate the foreign owners, and *in the absence of compensation,* **expropriation** *becomes* **confiscation.**

Capitalism

The capitalist, free enterprise ideal is that all the factors of production should be privately owned. Under ideal **capitalism,** government would be restricted to those functions that the private sector cannot perform—national defense; police, fire, and other public services; and government-to-government international relations. No such government exists.

Reality in so-called capitalist countries is quite complex. The governments of such countries typically regulate privately owned businesses quite closely, and frequently these governments own businesses.

Regulations and red tape. All businesses are subject to countless government laws, regulations, and red tape in their activities in the United States and all other capitalist countries. Special government approval is required to practice the professions, such as law or medicine. Tailored sets of laws and regulations govern banking, insurance, transportation, and utilities. States and local governments require business licenses and impose use restrictions on buildings and areas.

Complying with all the laws and regulations and coping with the red tape require expertise, time, and of course, expense. Risk is always present that a business may be found in noncompliance, which can result in fines or even in the imprisonment of its management.

expropriation government seizure of the property within its borders owned by foreigners, followed by prompt, adequate, and effective compensation paid to the former owners

confiscation government seizure of the property within its borders owned by foreigners without payment to them

capitalism an economic system in which the means of production and distribution are for the most part privately owned and operated for private profit

Socialism

socialism public, collective ownership of the basic means of production and distribution, operating for use rather than for profit

Socialism advocates government ownership or control of the basic means of production, distribution, and exchange. Profit is not an aim.

In practice, so-called socialist governments have frequently performed in ways not consistent with the doctrine. One of the most startling examples of this is Singapore, which professes to be a socialist state but in reality is aggressively capitalistic.[1]

European socialism.   In Europe, socialist parties have been in power in several countries, including Great Britain, France, Spain, Greece, and West Germany. In Britain, the Labour party—as the socialists there call their political party—has nationalized some basic industries, such as steel, shipbuilding, coal mining, and the railroads, but has not gone much further in that direction. A vocal left wing of the Labour party advocates nationalizing all major British business, banks, and insurance companies.

Social Democrats is the name the West Germans use for their socialist political party. During the several years that this party was in power before it lost to the Christian Democrats in 1982, it nationalized nothing and, in action and word, seemed more capitalist than socialist. The socialist governments of France and Spain have embarked on programs to privatize government-owned businesses; such programs do not conform to pure socialist doctrine.

LDC socialism.   The less developed countries (LDCs) often profess and practice some degree of socialism. The government typically owns and controls most of the factors of production. Among the characteristics of an LDC are shortages of capital, technology, and skilled management and labor. Aid from DCs or from international organizations usually comes to (and hopefully through) the LDC government. Many of the educated citizens tend to be in or connected with the LDC government. It follows that the major factories and farms would be owned or controlled by the government.

Unless the LDC government is communist, it will make occasional exceptions and permit capital investment. This happens when the LDC perceives advantages that would not be possible without the private capital. The advantages could be more jobs for its people, new technology, skilled managers or technicians, and export opportunities.

Risks for businesses dealing with socialist countries.   As you can see, there is an extremely wide range of practice among the countries that profess socialism. At the extreme illustrated by Singapore, one must be careful to comply with all the applicable laws and regulations, as in any capitalist country. At the other extreme, such as an LDC, where most or all of the major production factors are government owned, one must do business much as it is done in a communist country.

Conservative or Liberal

conservative a person who wishes to minimize government activities and maximize private ownership and business

We should not leave the subject of ideology without mention of these words as they have come to be used in the mid- and late 20th century. Politically, the word **conservative** connotes a person, group, or party that wishes to minimize government activity and to maximize the activities of private businesses and

WORLDVIEW
Right and Left—What Do These Terms Mean?

After the French Revolution, an assembly was chosen, and it settled down to face the problems of reform. The radicals sat on the president's left and the conservatives on his right. This disposition provided thereafter—in other countries as well as France—a useful addition to the terminology of politics.

A former member of the British Parliament made some interesting points on this subject. He found the Far Left similar to the Far Right.

> The terms "Right" and "Left" are losing their purchase. Under conventions established earlier in our century, people on the Far Right are seen as "Fascists" and people on the Far Left as "Communists," so that on the Left–Right axis, the two are supposed to be opposites, or at least at opposite extremes as far away from each other as it is possible to get. But a majority of observers seem to agree that the kinds of society they establish when they get into power have fundamental features of a striking nature in common—and are a good deal more like each other than either of them is like Liberal Democracy, which is supposed to separate them in the middle, halfway between them.

Source: *Forbes,* May 23, 1983, p. 20.

---

right wing a more extreme conservative

liberal in the 20th-century United States, a person who urges greater government involvement in most aspects of human activities.

left wing a more extreme liberal

individuals. Conservative is used to mean something similar to **right wing,** but in the United States and the United Kingdom, the latter is more extreme. For instance, the Conservative party, one of the major political parties in the United Kingdom, is said to have a right-wing minority.

Politically, in the United States in the 20th century, the word **liberal** has come to mean the opposite of what it meant in the 19th century. It has come to connote a person, group, or party that urges greater government participation in the economy and regulation or ownership of business. Liberal and **left wing** are similar, but the latter generally indicates more extreme positions closer to socialism or communism.

Unique to the United States.   This usage has not spread outside the United States.

> A conversation one of the authors had with an Italian lawyer at lunch in Rome turned to politics. The Italian identified himself as a liberal, and the author understood it in the American meaning. As the conversation proceeded, the author learned that he had been wrong. The lawyer meant it in the Italian sense; he was a member of the Liberal party, a political party near the right end of the Italian political spectrum.

There are other Liberal parties in Europe. They are not liberal in the American sense.

We do not want to overemphasize the importance of the labels *conservative, liberal, right wing,* and *left wing.* For one thing, individuals and organizations may change over time or may change as they perceive shifts in the moods of voters. Some feel that these labels are too simplistic or even naive and that reality is more complex. Nevertheless, we wanted to bring them to your attention because they are much used in media and other discussions of international events and because different political forces flow from, for example, a right-wing government than from a left-wing one.

GOVERNMENT OWNERSHIP OF BUSINESS

One might reasonably assume that government ownership of the factors of production is found only in communist or socialist countries, but that assumption is not correct. Large segments of business are owned by the governments of numerous countries that do not consider themselves either communist or socialist. From country to country, there are wide differences in the industries that are government owned and in the extent of government ownership (see Figure 10–1).

Why Firms Are Nationalized

There are a number of reasons, sometimes overlapping, why governments put their hands on firms. Some of them are (1) to extract more money from the firms—the government suspects that the firms are concealing profits; (2) an extension of (1)—the government believes it could run the firms more efficiently and make more money; (3) ideological—when left-wing governments are elected, they sometimes nationalize industries, as has occurred in Britain, France, and Canada; (4) to catch votes as politicians save jobs by putting dying industries on life-support systems, which can be disconnected after the election; (5) because the government has pumped money into a firm or an industry, and control usually follows money; and (6) happenstance, as with the nationalization after WW II of German-owned firms in Europe.

All governments are in business to some degree, but outside the communist nations or LDCs, none is so far into business as Italy.

Italy.   The Italian government-owned Institute for Industrial Reconstruction (IRI) has been called an "industrial octopus."[2] In 1978, IRI was a leader in one category: it lost more money—$970 million—than any other company. (The number 2 loser was another state-owned company, British Steel, which lost $798 million.) The Italian government owns companies in many industries, including salt, tobacco, matches, mining, railways, airlines, auto manufacturing, steel, telephone, power plants, banking, restaurants, chocolate and ice cream production, radio and television stations, and refineries.

The IRI's losses continued, and by the end of 1986, its accumulated losses since 1979 were about $12 billion. In late 1984, however, a new chairman took over and began the gigantic job of turning IRI around. He is Ramano Prodi, a highly respected industrial economist whose strategy is to get IRI out of doing things that the private sector can do better. Prodi may have some difficulty selling off parts of IRI because the socialist premier, Bettino Craxi, was opposed to doing so. In 1987, Craxi was succeeded by a Christian Democrat as premier, but the socialists remained a part of the ruling coalition.

IRI's losses fell in 1985 and 1986, and cash flow increased as some of the managers brought in by Prodi to run IRI companies turned losers to winners.

Another Italian state-owned company that had been turned around to profit by 1987 is Ente Nazionale Idrocarburi (ENI), the energy and chemicals group. Having named British Steel as a loser, that story should be brought up to date: by 1989, it had become the world's most profitable integrated steel company and is being privatized. Privatization is discussed later in this chapter.

United States.   Historically, the United States has been opposed to nationalizing industries, but it took a large step in that direction when it set up the

FIGURE 10–1 Government/Private Ownership of Business

Privately owned: ◯ all or nearly all

Publicly owned:

◔ 25% ◑ 50% ◕ 75% ● all or nearly all

	Mail Posts	Telecommunications	Electricity	Gas	Oil production	Coal	Railways	Airlines	Motor industry	Steel	Shipbuilding	
Australia	●	●	●	●	○	○	●	◔	○	○	na	Australia
Austria	●	●	●	●	●	○	●	●	●	●	na	Austria
Belgium	●	●	◔	◔	na	○	●	●	○	◔	○	Belgium
Brazil	●	●	●	●	●	●	●	◕	○	◕	○	Brazil
Britain	●	●	●	●	◔	●	●	◕	◑	◕	●	Britain
Canada	●	◕	●	○	○	○	◑	◑	○	○	○	Canada
France	●	●	●	●	na	●	●	◕	◑	◕	○	France
West Germany	●	●	◔	◑	◔	◑	●	●	◔	○	◔	West Germany
Holland	●	●	◕	◕	na	na	●	◕	◑	◕	○	Holland
India	●	●	●	●	●	●	●	●	○	◕	●	India
Italy	●	●	◔	●	na	na	●	●	◕	◕	◕	Italy
Japan	●	●	○	○	na	○	◔	◔	○	○	○	Japan
Mexico	●	●	●	●	●	●	●	◑	◕	◕	●	Mexico
South Korea	●	●	◔	○	na	◕	●	●	○	◕	○	South Korea
Spain	●	◑	○	◔	na	◑	●	●	○	◑	◕	Spain
Sweden	●	●	◑	●	na	na	●	◑	○	◕	◕	Sweden
Switzerland	●	●	●	●	na	na	●	◔	○	○	na	Switzerland
United States	●	○	◔	○	○	○	◔*	○	○	○	○	United States

na - not applicable or negligible production *including Conrail

Source: *The Economist,* December 21, 1985, p. 72.

Consolidated Rail Corporation (Conrail) in 1976. Conrail took over six bankrupt railroads in the northeastern United States. Ten years later, the U.S. government was taking steps to sell Conrail; one proposal was to sell it to a private rail company, but this evoked opposition from Conrail's managers and employees as well as from competing railroads. Instead, its stock was sold publicly to private buyers who included many Conrail workers and managers.

France. The French government has been in business for centuries. When Louis XIV began building the magnificent Versailles Palace, the plans included thousands of mirrors and crystal chandeliers. The Venetians were the dominant glassmakers of the world at that time, and Louis's finance minister, Colbert, did not like the thought of paying them for all of those mirrors and chandeliers. Colbert set up the company now known as Saint-Gobain, and Louis insisted on owning the company himself, rather than allowing noble and idle courtiers to own it. Louis feared that if they owned the company, they would become rich and powerful and possible rivals to his rule.

Likewise, socialists did not nationalize the Renault automobile company. Charles de Gaulle's post-WW II government did so to avenge its founder's collaboration with the occupying Germans. Renault has drawn money from the French government for investments and has made occasional profits in the years since.

In 1981, the socialists under François Mitterrand won French elections and promptly nationalized six big industrial groups and 36 private banks and bought controlling stakes in three other companies. That proved to be expensive. Only one of the companies taken over, Compagnie Générale d'Electricité, was profitable in 1982, and several were nearly broke when the Mitterrand government seized them. A French banker remarked, "Perhaps that is why we have not seen a single case of shareholders contesting their compensation," when the government paid for the seized shares. In 1983, it cost over 60 billion French francs (about $7.5 billion) for the French government to keep its nationalized industries in business. This was nearly double their 1980 cost.

Between 1981 and 1986, the French government invested over $5 billion in the industries it nationalized—20 times more than private shareholders had invested over a 20-year period. At least partly as a result of that investment, many nationalized firms have been bought back to profit (exceptions are the steelmakers Sacilor and Usinor and the automaker Renault).

Unfair Competition?

Where government-owned companies compete with privately owned companies, the private companies sometimes complain that the government companies have unfair advantages. Some of the complaints are (1) government-owned companies can cut prices unfairly because they do not have to make profits; (2) they get cheaper financing; (3) they get government contracts; (4) they get export assistance; and (5) they can hold down wages with government assistance.[3]

Government–Private Collaboration Difficult

The objectives of private firms and those of government agencies and operations usually differ. Figure 10–2 illustrates some of the differences.

■ **FIGURE 10–2   Planners and Business Investors—Why Can't They Collaborate?**

Raise return · Long-range planning · Risk reduction · High resource productivity · Competitive advantage · Local technology · Short payback period · **Firm objectives** · Market penetration · Service to community (market) · Lower costs or taxes · Regional economic impact · Short-range goals · Planning resources use · Job creation · Increase tax base · **Agency objectives** · Political goals · Raise domestic incomes

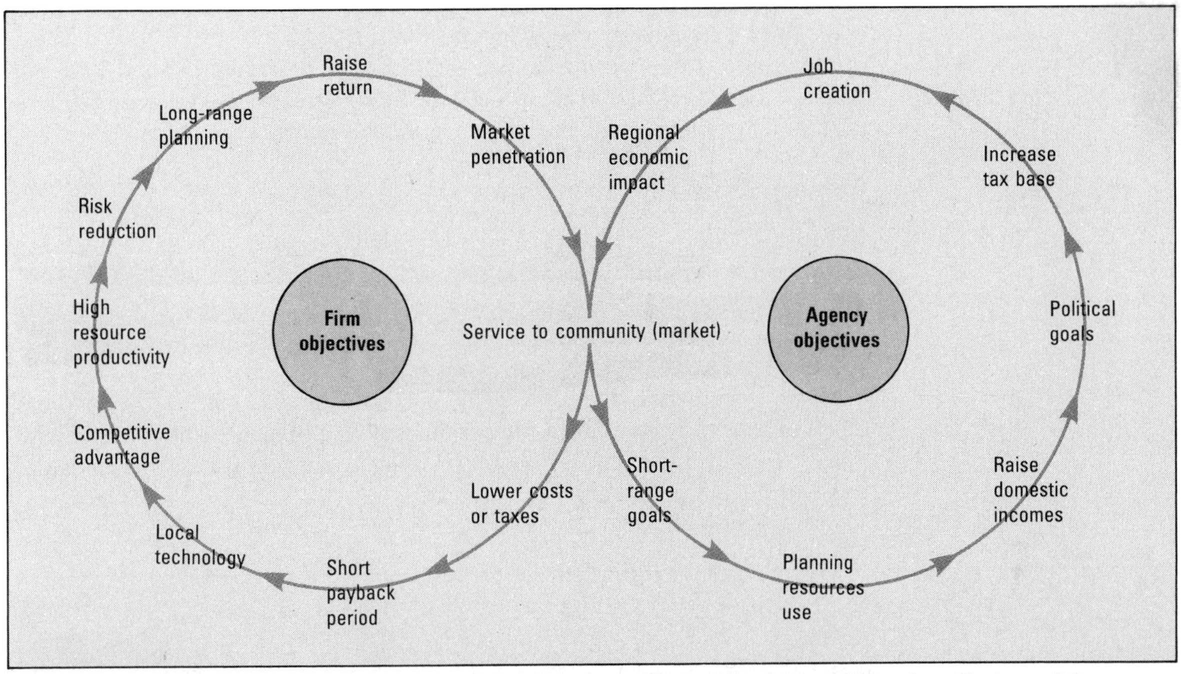

Source: Robert P. Vichas and Kimon Consias, "Public Planners and Business Investors—Why Can't They Collaborate?" *Long Range Planning*, no. 3 (Pergamon Press, Ltd., 1981), p. 83.

PRIVATIZATION

The tide turned during the early 1980s, and by 1989, the selling of state assets—from airlines to telephone companies—had captivated politicians everywhere, even in socialist Spain and communist China. Given the American devotion to private enterprise, it is odd but accurate to report that the United States is lagging behind other countries in selling its assets.

privatization the transfer of public-sector assets to the private sector, the transfer of management of state activities through contracts and leases, and the contracting out of activities previously conducted by the state

Countries involved in the **privatization** movement include Canada, the United States, Mexico, Chile, Brazil, Britain, France, Spain, Italy, Holland, West Germany, Turkey, Thailand, Singapore, Japan, the Philippines, and Malaysia. Britain, under Margaret Thatcher, is the acknowledged leader of the movement.

Perhaps surprisingly, among the services and assets being privatized are social security, public housing, highways, and bus service.

Private Sector More Efficient Than State?

Proof beyond all doubt may be impossible to obtain. Academics nonetheless try. One study found that it cost the New York Department of Sanitation $40 (of which $32 was for labor) to deal with a ton of rubbish. It cost private collectors only $17 (of which $10 was for labor).

Research in Australia found the private airline, Ansett, considerably more productive than the public sector's Trans Australian Airline. Interviews with managers moving from the public to the private system show a large majority who say that privatization has improved their performance. They cite the demoralizing effects of political interference and bureaucratic delay when their companies were government owned.

However, as pointed out above, the Italian state-owned IRI and ENI and British Steel—which is in the process of being privatized—were turned into profitable operations while still in government hands.

Other Forms of Privatization

Privatization does not always involve ownership transfer from government to private entities. For example, activities previously conducted by the state may be contracted out, as Indonesia has contracted a Swiss firm to run its customs administration and Thailand has private companies operating some of the passenger lines on its state-owned railroad.

Governments may lease state-owned plants to private entities, as Togo has done, or they may combine a joint venture with a management contract with a private group to run a previously government-owned business. Rwanda did this with its match factory.[4]

NATIONALISM

nationalism a devotion to one's own nation, its political and economic interests or aspirations, and its social and cultural traditions

Nationalism has been called the "secular religion of our time." In most of the older countries, loyalty to one's country and pride in it were based on such shared common features as race, language, religion, or ideology. Many of the newer countries, notably in Africa, have accidental boundaries resulting from their colonial past, and within these countries, there are several tribes and languages. This has resulted in civil wars, as in Nigeria and Angola, but it has not prevented these new countries from developing instant and fierce nationalism.

Nationalism is an emotion that can cloud or even prevent rational dealings with foreigners. The ills of a society can be blamed on foreign companies, which is what the chief of the joint staffs of the Peruvian military did when the military forces took charge in Peru.

Some of the effects of nationalism on WWCs are (1) requirements for minimum local ownership or local product assembly or manufacture; (2) reservation of certain industries for local companies; (3) preference of local suppliers for government contracts; (4) limitations on the number and types of foreign employees; (5) protectionism, using tariffs, quotas, or other devices; (6) seeking a "French solution"* instead of a foreign takeover of a local firm;[5] and (7) in the most extreme cases, expropriation or confiscation.[6]

GOVERNMENT PROTECTION

A historic function of government, whatever its ideology, has been the protection of the economic activities—farming, mining, manufacturing, etc.—within its geographic area of control. These must be protected from

---

*The French solution is to make every effort to find a French company rather than a foreign one to take over the French firm.

attacks and destruction or robbery by terrorists, bandits, revolutionaries, and foreign invaders. The mines of Shaba were not so protected.

Economically Targeted Invasion

The mineral production of the Shaba Province of Zaire accounts for some 75 percent of Zaire's total export earnings.[7] Military forces, apparently armed and trained in Angola, invaded Shaba twice during the 1970s, and Zaire's military was unable to protect Shaba.

The output of the Shaban mines was virtually halted, at least temporarily, and that seems to have been the intent of the invaders. They retreated without attempting to establish control over the area as soon as rescue forces arrived from France and Belgium; but before retreating, they massacred several hundred Europeans who played a major role in the production of Zaire's wealth. The invaders also killed many of the native workers, but not indiscriminately as with the Europeans. The natives were murdered selectively, and those chosen were, in large part, the skilled workers, technicians, and executives of the mines.[8]

Terrorism

Since the 1970s, the world has been plagued by various groups that have hijacked airplanes, shot and kidnapped people, and bombed people and objects. A common denominator of these terrorist groups has been hatred of the social, economic, and political orders that they find in the world. Another characteristic is their confusion as to what sort of order they would substitute if they had the chance.

Acts of **terrorism** have occurred worldwide outside the communist countries. We shall look at the Italian experience to observe some results of terrorism and of the countermeasures taken against it. Italy was chosen because it has been so hard hit.

terrorism unlawful acts of violence committed for a wide variety of reasons, including to overthrow a government, gain release of imprisoned colleagues, exact revenge for real or imagined wrongs, or punish nonbelievers of the terrorists' religion

Terrorism against politicians.   There have been many politically inspired shootings of politicians, judges, and police. A typical method is to shoot at the knees, but some targets have been killed, as was Aldo Moro in 1978. Moro had been premier of Italy, and at the time of his kidnapping and murder, he was a leader of a political party.

Violence against business, too.   Politicians are not the only targets of terrorist violence. Fiat S.P.A., Italy's largest private enterprise, says that acts of insubordination and violence cut its output more than 12 percent in 1979 and sharply increased costs.

In addition to the more commonly known costs of terrorist activity (property damage, ransom payments, and expenditures for security), terrorism has detrimental effects on companies' productivity. U.S. manufacturers in El Salvador offer prime examples. With travel of trained technicians to plants in the country largely embargoed, machinery that breaks down remains idle, distribution of products comes to a standstill, and some firms are forced to ship machinery back to the United States for overhauls.

Labor-intensive operations can respond more flexibly to terrorism. They can suspend operations temporarily or pull out permanently—with little or no loss of investment in equipment.

Kidnapping for ransom.   Kidnapping is another weapon used by terrorists. The victims are held for ransom, frequently very large amounts, which provides an important source of funds for the terrorists. Italian industry is not alone in being subjected to terrorism and kidnapping for ransom. For example, it is said that industry in Argentina has paid ransom of several hundred million dollars for the release of kidnapped business executives.[9]

By 1986, Colombia and Peru had become the most dangerous places for American executives, and a long stay by a high-ranking American executive in either country is risky. Brief visits are usually fairly safe because kidnappings take a while to plan, so top executives from the United States practice what is called commando management. They arrive in Bogota or Lima as secretly as possible, meet for a few days with local employees, and fly off before kidnappers learn of their presence.[10]

Countermeasures by the government.   The Italian government issued a series of antiterrorist decrees and created a special antiterrorist squad, some 25,000 strong, with new powers to arrest and question suspects. Between 1975 and 1982, terrorist groups almost shattered Italy's faith in its ability to govern itself without resorting to a communist- or fascist-style police state. Over 3,000 suspected or convicted terrorists had been jailed or sentenced to prison, and in January 1983, 32 people were sentenced to life imprisonment for Moro's kidnapping and murder. Among the encouraging signs were the increase in the numbers of penitents and defectors and the terrorists' difficulty in recruiting as their charisma among Italian youth faded.

Remaining terrorists find new allies.   As their original source of recruits—educated, idealistic young Italians—became disenchanted, the remaining terrorist leaders turned to crime. They cooperated with Mafia groups in kidnapping for ransom. They cooperated with the Soviet, Libyan, and Syrian secret services in running heroin and guns from Turkey and Eastern Europe to the West, and although they call themselves communist revolutionaries, much of the money and guns they got was supplied to neofascist terrorists.[11]

Arrests made in 1988 by Italian police were disturbing because the people arrested had no past criminal records or known terrorist associations. They had blended anonymously into the big-city life of Milan but were members of the Fighting Communist party, and in the raided apartment, police found machine guns, pistols, $47,000 in cash, and considerable propaganda material. Leaflets in the apartment claimed credit for three assassinations, including that of Senator Roberto Ruffilli, a Christian Democrat, in April 1988.[12]

Government-sponsored terrorism; acts of war.   During the 1980s, evidence began to mount that many terrorists were trained, financed, and directed by governments—for example, the Soviet Union, Iran, Syria, and Libya. The U.S. Navy and Air Force bombed Tripoli, the Libyan capital, in spring 1986 because the U.S. government was convinced that the Libyan government had sponsored terrorism that had cost American lives. In fall 1986, a British court convicted a Palestinian of trying to smuggle explosives (concealed in the baggage of his pregnant girlfriend) aboard an El Al Israel 747 aircraft. The flight from London to Tel Aviv would have been blown up over Austria. It was developed at the trial that the material for the explosives had been brought into London in Syrian diplomatic pouches aboard the Syrian government airline and that the Syrian ambassador had sanctioned or even directed the operation. In international law, government action to damage or kill in another country is an act of war.

More female terrorists. A Rand study found a high percentage of female terrorists. Profiles of German and Italian female terrorists show that they have generally proven more ruthless and dangerous than their male counterparts. They are tougher and crueler, and men in groups dominated by women are more brutal and competitive than men in other groups.[13]

Countermeasures by industry. Fiat fired several hundred workers for insubordination and violence. An Italian labor court upheld Fiat when the workers sued to retrieve their jobs. Perhaps more surprising, an important part of Italy's Communist party leadership agreed with Fiat management that the firings were reasonable and proper.

As kidnapping and extortion directed against businesses and governments have become common fund-raising and political techniques for terrorists, insurance against such acts has grown into a multimillion-dollar business. The world's largest kidnapping and extortion underwriting firm is located in London. The firm, Cassidy and Davis, underwrites for Lloyd's of London and says that it covers some 9,000 companies. Cassidy and Davis does not sit back and wait for claims to be filed. It runs antiterrorism training courses for executives, in which the subjects covered range from defensive driving techniques—escape tactics and battering through blockades—to crisis management. Country-by-country risk analyses are instantly available on international computer hookups.

Cassidy and Davis works closely with Control Risk, Ltd., a London-based security service company. Control Risk works behind the scenes to advise companies or families in negotiations with kidnappers.

Cassidy and Davis encourages its clients to use Control Risk services. The premiums for the insurance underwritten by Cassidy and Davis range from some $3,000 a year for $1.5 million of coverage in low-risk England to $60,000 a year for the same coverage in high-risk Peru.[14]

GOVERNMENT STABILITY

stability a government can be said to be stable if it maintains itself in power and when its fiscal, monetary, and political policies are predictable and not subject to sudden, radical changes

Government **stability** can be approached from two directions. One can speak of either a government's simple ability to maintain itself in power or the stability or permanence of a government's policies. It is safe to generalize that business (indeed almost all agricultural, commercial, and financial activities) prospers most when there is a stable government with permanent—or at most, gradually changing—policies.

Stability and Instability: Examples and Results

instability an unstable government is the opposite of a stable one. It cannot maintain itself in power or makes sudden, unpredictable, and/or radical policy changes

Instability in Lebanon. Here is a classic example of the impact of a change from order to chaos—from stability to **instability**—on the business and finance of a prosperous country. Until 1974, Lebanon prospered as the trading, banking, international company regional headquarters, business services (that is, accounting, legal, and financial services), transportation, and tourist center of the Middle East. The country achieved this prosperity with virtually no natural resources; its land is mostly arid desert or mountains. Its prosperity was the work of an industrious people given political stability.

Then civil war broke out in Lebanon. The details of that civil war are beyond the scope of this book, but its reasons included ideological and religious differences. The results were catastrophic.

Homes, offices, banks, stores, transportation, communications, and sanitary facilities were destroyed. The people fled the country or fought and survived as best they could. Almost all of the previous commercial activities ended.

Stability in Bolivia?   In 152 years of independence from Spain, Bolivia had 187 governments. Then, in 1972, a government seized power and by 1976 had established the durability record for any Bolivian government in the 20th century. The economic results were startling and encouraging.

Bolivia's GNP grew by 7.3 percent in 1975 and 7 percent in 1976, and its inflation rate was about 12 percent. At the same time, such neighbors as Argentina, Chile, and Peru were experiencing varying types of political unrest, were growing more slowly or not at all, and were suffering much higher rates of inflation.

Hector Ormachea, the Bolivian government official in charge of negotiating development loans abroad, spoke of "projects, not politics." And projects resulted—more than 300 by 1977. They ranged from roads into areas previously accessible only by air, to oil exploration, mining ventures, and agricultural and industrial development.

Unused wealth.   Bolivia is potentially a rich country. Its resources include tin, zinc, antimony, copper, gold, tungsten, and bismuth, and it is more than self-sufficient in oil despite very little recent exploration or drilling.

The country's resources have scarcely been touched, at least in part because of Bolivia's previous political instability. Past governments had been quick to nationalize foreign mines. Given the mid-1970s stability, European, Japanese, and U.S. firms negotiated to explore for and extract the resources.[15]

Renewed foreign confidence.   Another sign of renewed foreign confidence in Bolivia was given in 1977. Underwriters led by the Arab Finance Corporation and Merrill Lynch International handled the sale in Europe of Bolivian debt securities. Although the amount was a relatively small $15 million, it was the first offering to foreign investors in about 50 years. Until Bolivia had achieved political stability, it would have been fruitless to try to borrow money abroad; no one would have lent it.[16]

Perils of Pauline.   By 1979, there was further political turmoil in Bolivia; between then and 1985, there were 12 Bolivian governments—most of them military. Inflation soared to about 25,000 percent in 1985, and in that year over half of Bolivia's export earnings—some $600 million—came from sales of cocaine; less than $500 million came from sales of minerals, oil, gas, and agricultural products. While the few cocaine traffickers got rich, the great bulk of the Bolivian population—growing at 2.6 percent a year—sank more deeply into poverty. Domestic investment declined and production collapsed.

*Miracle of La Paz?** In 1985, a new Bolivian president, Victor Paz Estenssero, was democratically elected. Estenssero immediately froze salaries in the state sector (which accounted for roughly 40 percent of the economy), removed price controls, stopped subsidies, slashed many import tariffs, floated the peso, and liberalized labor laws to allow easy firing and hiring. He told state enterprises to cover their costs or close, put new taxes on cars and houses, and offered a back tax amnesty.

Inflation plunged to near zero, foreign development aid is being restored, local investments have been starting up, and an attack has begun on the big drug traffickers. Both the World Bank and the International Monetary Fund have provided millions to finance Bolivia's agricultural and industrial recovery and to compensate it for the collapse of international tin prices (tin was once Bolivia's main export).[17]

By 1988, inflation was holding at 11 percent, GDP had begun to grow, and Bolivia's 54 commercial bank creditors, led by Bank of America, had allowed the government to buy back as much of its debt as it could afford. Bolivia bought 48 percent of its $670 million debt at 11 cents on the dollar. The IMF and the IDA arm of the World Bank were providing new money, and some of the private capital that had fled the country was flowing back as long-battered confidence started to revive.[18] The winner of the May 1989, presidential election pledged to continue the policies that were permitting Bolivia to recover.

TRADITIONAL HOSTILITIES

traditional hostilities long-standing enmities between tribes, races, religions, ideologies, or countries

One need mention only a few of the **traditional hostilities** to illustrate their powerful impact on business and trade.

Arab Countries – Israel

Israel is surrounded on three sides by Arab countries, but until the peace efforts initiated by the Egyptian Anwar Sadat, the Arab countries would not trade or have other peaceful dealings with it. Indeed, some Arab countries still boycott companies that trade with Israel, and because some of the Arab countries are extremely rich OPEC members, the boycott can be financially painful.[†]

Vietnam – Cambodia

The people of these two countries have been hostile to each other for centuries. After American involvement in Vietnam ended, the Vietnamese army invaded Cambodia. Vietnamese forces left the country in September 1989, leaving behind a puppet Cambodian government they had supported. The Vietnamese do not want the brutal Khmer Rouge faction to resume control of the country, but the Khmer Rouge are supported by China and are well armed. The Vietnamese may return. Cambodia has been closed to outside business or

---

*La Paz is the capital of Bolivia.
†See Chapter 11 for a discussion of U.S. law dealing with this boycott.

investment, although the Thai president, who assumed office in 1988, is making efforts to renew trade and other commercial contacts in the area.

North Atlantic Treaty Organization (NATO)–Warsaw Pact

For years after WW II, during the so-called Cold War, the NATO nations (Canada, the United States, and Western Europe plus Greece and Turkey) embargoed goods considered to have strategic military value to the Warsaw Pact (most of the communist countries led by the Soviet Union). As ideas of détente pervaded NATO, the embargo was considerably relaxed. Then, with Soviet-backed Cuban troops marching about Africa, and Soviet troops invading Afghanistan, the embargo was stiffened. In 1989, Soviet troops retreated from Afghanistan, but the Soviet government continued to support the Afghan government it had installed. Also in 1989, Cuba agreed to begin pulling its armies out of Angola—the withdrawal to be completed by 1991—in return for South Africa's agreement to stop supporting Angolan rebels and to withdraw from neighboring Namibia. But stiff or relaxed, the NATO embargo has been in effect for years and is a political force acting on international trade.

South African Apartheid

This racially based system is universally condemned outside South Africa. Some countries have asked their companies not to trade with or invest in South Africa and to pull out existing investments—that is, to disinvest.

Many people, including black and white South Africans, protested saying the departure of foreign firms would damage the very people it was supposed to help, the black South African workers and their families. Others argued it was necessary to make a moral statement with economic muscle.

The U.S. Congress took the latter point of view and passed laws that made it very expensive for American companies to keep South African investments. Some of the results are presented in the Worldview on pages 318–19.

INTERNATIONAL ORGANIZATIONS

As discussed above, nationalism is a powerful political force that has grown greatly during the mid- and late 20th century. There are also international political forces with which business must contend. Here we shall cover briefly the political impact of some of the international organizations introduced in Chapter 4.

United Nations (UN)

The UN is highly politicized. The member-countries vote as blocs formed because of ideology or perceived similar objectives. There are the communist and noncommunist groupings and the developed countries versus the less developed countries.

United Nations personnel advise UN members on such matters as tax, monetary, and fiscal policies. The UN is active in the harmonization of laws affecting international trade. It had a hand in drafting an international commercial arbitration convention. It has drafted a code of conduct for multinational business. Any of the political ideologies we have discussed can be reflected in the content and spirit of tax, trade, and arbitration laws; conduct codes; and fiscal or monetary policies.

UNCTAD is credited with having influenced the IMF to ease its restrictions on loans to LDCs. This is important to banks lending to and suppliers selling to LDCs.

Virtually all of the specialized UN agencies are now actively advising LDCs about what to buy for their agriculture, industry, airlines, health programs, weather stations, and so forth. These are huge markets for business.

World Bank Group

One or another member of the World Bank Group finances large parts of the purchases made by LDCs. Although the bank's charter bans political activity by its officers and employees, it is reported that its president was involved in campaign-planning strategy for one of the U.S. presidential candidates in 1980.[19]

IMF, GATT, and OPEC

The IMF can have great influence on the fiscal and monetary policies of the nations that it assists, and, as reported in Chapter 4, many believe its power is growing.

Although GATT has in general striven to lower barriers to trade, it has condoned their erection by LCDs in some cases. Import barriers are, of course, an important political force affecting multinational business operations.

The political power of OPEC was discussed in Chapter 4. We mention it here again to remind you that petroleum is now as much a political force as it is a commodity.

EC

Slowly but surely, the member-nations of the EC are surrendering parts of their sovereign powers to the Brussels headquarters. One need mention only a few areas to realize the extent of the EC's influence on business. Among other things, the EC is working to harmonize laws dealing with taxes, patents, labor conditions, competition, insurance, banking, and capital markets.

Harmonization of differing national laws is one matter, but the EC has now gone a step beyond that—to lawmaking. This is occurring in such fields as company law, antitrust, and consumer and environmental protection.[20]

Now the EC is embarked on Project 1992, and the objective of some Europeans is to create a political—as well as an economic—power to rival America, Japan, and the Soviet Union. Almost no one believes that can be achieved by 1992, but almost everyone believes a process moving in that direction is under way. The EC Project 1992 was discussed in Chapter 4.

Organization for Economic Cooperation and Development (OECD)

This 24-member organization of industrialized countries has issued "Guidelines for Multinational Enterprises." One writer states that rather than being a stifling set of legal do's and don'ts, the guidelines create a voluntary set of principles upon which to build sound international economic relations.[21]

WORLDVIEW
Some Very Odd Results from Disinvestment in South Africa

At the end of 1987, South African businessmen left their steaming cities and headed for the beaches, secure in the belief that disinvestment, after convulsively reshaping the country's industrial sector, had kicked up as much dust as it was going to.

No one expected Representative Charles B. Rangel's amendment to the deficit-reduction bill, signed by President Reagan close to midnight on December 22. The effect of the amendment was to push up tax rates on American companies' South African earnings from 57.5 percent to 72 percent. The 160-odd American corporations that were affected faced the unpleasant choice of either paying up or piling out—and many of them are expected to opt for the latter.

For many acquisition-hungry South African businessmen and conglomerates, whose money is locked into the country by exchange-control laws, the new legislation was practically a gift. By intensifying the pressure on American corporations to shed their South African subsidiaries, it effectively reduces the market values of such businesses. Locals can pick them up for a pittance.

Indeed, American companies, faced with political demands to cut ties to South Africa, have been selling out at distress-sale prices since disinvestment began in earnest in 1985. Ford Motor Company, for example, donated to the unions most of its 42 percent stake in the South African Motor Corporation (Samcor), and sold the rest to Anglo American Corporation, the country's largest mining company, for a total of one dollar. On top of that, the company agreed to pump $4 million into community

development trusts. Subsequently, Ford coughed up $61 million in debt liquidation to prevent Anglo American from closing down Samcor, a move that would have cost the jobs of 4,900 workers, 70 percent of them black.

The fact is that neither trade sanctions nor disinvestment has managed to bring South Africa to her knees economically, nor, unfortunately, has either forced Pretoria to end apartheid. True, the outflow of capital has been uncomfortable for the government, and the country is bound to suffer from the loss of access to foreign capital, skilled manpower, and technology. But South Africans have proved that they can take over abandoned companies and run them just as well as the previous owners did, if not better.

The surprising health of the South African business community has caused critics of sanctions and disinvestment—including some black leaders—to complain. They say that these policies, instead of exerting pressure on the government, have served only to concentrate wealth and economic power further in the hands of white South African beneficiaries. According to a report in the *Journal of Defense & Diplomacy,* published in McLean, Virginia, disinvestment by U.S. companies alone created 168 new South African millionaires in the first 12 months in which sanctions were in effect. More than a few of the newly rich were executives of former subsidiaries, who acquired their companies through leveraged buy-outs.

Almost none of the money has gone into the pockets of black businessmen. The Soweto Investment Trust Company recently bought Pepsi-Cola's South African

Nevertheless, these ostensibly voluntary guidelines can have a significant impact.

> When Badger, Raytheon's subsidiary in Belgium, closed shop, it did not have enough money to meet its labor termination obligations. The Belgian government and labor unions used the pressure of the OECD "voluntary" guidelines to require Raytheon to pay Badger's obligations.[22]

LABOR

Workers and labor unions are the subject of Chapter 12, but we would be remiss if we did not mention them in connection with the political forces bearing on business. The European labor unions are ideologically oriented,

subsidiary, but few other black-owned companies have acquired any real slices of the disinvestment cake. And the acquisition could turn out to be more of a liability than an asset, since Pepsi's share of the soft-drink market is reported to have fallen to 5 percent.

Aside from altered signs and letterheads, the changes brought on by new ownership are rarely noticeable to customers or even employees. One reason is that most foreign subsidiaries have long been staffed and managed almost entirely by South Africans.

For example, the chief executive of First National Bank, formerly a subsidiary of Barclays, has, since the late 1960s, reported to a board of directors made up primarily of local businessmen with a sprinkling of executives from the parent bank's headquarters in London. Barclays has now departed the country, but Chris Ball, managing director of First National, says that "nothing has really changed other than that Barclays representatives no longer sit on our board. I think we've actually grown in stature," Ball says. "We're not beholden to anyone other than our South African shareholders, so our people feel bigger and more independent."

For some South African businessmen, the introduction of sanctions and the reality of disinvestment have come as a welcome relief. Living and working with threat and uncertainty was bad for business. "Disinvestment and South Africanization have resulted in increased consumer confidence," says Clive Jandrell, managing director of Xeratech, formerly Rank Xerox South Africa, which was acquired last May by a South African electronics company, Altron. "The company had been in a state of threatened disinvestment for more than a year," Jandrell says. "Customers and staff felt insecure. Now they've settled down, and this has led to higher productivity and more positive output."

In fact, as far as Jandrell is concerned, there have been distinct advantages to becoming part of a large South African group. "Growth was restrained before because of pressures that would have been brought to bear on our parent," he says. "Now we see opportunities and can go for them. There is also greater commitment by managers, greater attention to detail and greater involvement by the holding company, and we've started running a tighter ship."

Executives who were given the opportunity to buy out their old employers have been some of the biggest winners from disinvestment. Take, for example, Paul Edwards, who became managing director of Information Trust Corporation last year, after the parent company, Dun & Bradstreet Corporation, pulled out and left its shares to the staff of roughly 350 people. "It wasn't a difficult transition, just a case of replacing our American managing director," says Edwards. "At one stage there were 50 directors and managers. Today there are 26."

"The whole team is much leaner, but there's a high degree of productivity and initiative," Edwards says. "We've had a dramatic increase in profitability. This shows that you can take the same team, give them a stake in the company and get entirely different results. Now it's our business, and we want to see it succeed."

Source: Carolyn Raphaely, *Business Month*, April 1988, pp. 18–19.

usually toward the left. The American unions are said to be more pragmatic, but in practice they are extremely active politically. They supply large amounts of money and political workers to support the political candidates they favor.

In Europe, the United States, and, increasingly, in Japan, labor makes its political force felt not only at the polls but also in the legislatures. The unions lobby for or against laws as these are perceived to be for or against the interests of labor.

WORLDWIDE COMPANIES (WWCs)

International business is not merely a passive victim of political forces. It can be a powerful force in the world political arena.[23]

Forty Percent of World's Top Economic Units Are Firms, Not Nations

A WWC negotiating with a country may be bigger than the country. According to rankings in 1987, General Motors' sales of $102 billion made it the 19th largest economic unit. Its sales were larger than the $97.9 billion GNP of Denmark. Exxon's sales of $76.4 billion made it the 25th largest economic unit, surpassing Argentina. Of course, the GNP of the great majority of other countries is even smaller.[24]

Such financial size carries power. However, the WWC's power need not rest solely on size. It can come from the possession of scarce capital, technology, and management plus the capability to deploy those resources around the world. The WWC may have the processing, productive, distributive, and marketing abilities necessary for the successful exploitation of raw materials or for the manufacture, distribution, and marketing of certain products. Those abilities are frequently not available in LDCs. Recognition of the desirability of WWC investments is growing.[25]

COUNTRY RISK ASSESSMENT (CRA)

country risk assessment (CRA)   a bank or business having an asset in or payable from a foreign country, or considering a loan or an investment there, evaluates that country's economic situation and policies and its politics to determine how much risk exists of losing the asset or of not being paid

It is arbitrary to place this subject in a chapter on political forces because **country risk assessment (CRA)** involves many risks other than political risks. It is probably important enough to warrant a separate chapter, but one of our objectives is to avoid an overlong book. We shall introduce our readers to CRA here; there is a growing literature about it, and those who are interested can find much material.[26]

Although it is arbitrary to put CRA in this chapter, it is not unreasonable, because the political events of recent years have concentrated much more attention on the subject. Firms that had already done CRA updated and strengthened the function, and many other companies began CRA.

Types of Country Risks

Country risks are increasingly political in nature, caused or influenced by political developments. There are wars, revolutions, and coups. Less dramatic, but nevertheless important for businesses, are government changes by election of a socialist or nationalist government, which may be hostile to private business and particularly to foreign-owned business.

The risks may be economic or financial. There may be persistent balance-of-payments deficits or high inflation rates. Repayment of loans may be questionable.

Labor conditions may cause investors to pause. Labor productivity may be low, or labor unions may be militant.

Laws may be changed about such subjects as taxes, currency convertibility, tariffs, quotas, or labor permits. The chances for a fair trial in local courts must be assessed.

Terrorism may be present. If it is, can the company protect its personnel and property?

Information Content for CRA

The types of information that a firm will need to judge country risks will vary according to the nature of its business and the length of time required for the investment, loan, or other involvement to yield a satisfactory return.

Nature of business.   Consider, for example, the needs of a hotel company compared with those of heavy-equipment manufacturers or manufacturers of personal hygiene products or mining companies. Banks have their own sets of problems and information needs. Sometimes there are variations between firms in the same industry or on a project-to-project basis. The nationality—home country—of the company may be a factor; does the host country bear a particular animus, or friendly attitude, toward the home country?

Length of time required.   Export financing usually involves the shortest time period of exposure. Typically, payments are made within 180 days—usually less—and exporters can get insurance or bank protection.

Bank loans can be short, medium, or long term. However, when the business includes host country assembly, mixing, manufacture, or extraction (oil or minerals), long-term commitments are necessary.

With long-term investment or loan commitments, there are inherent problems with risk analysis that cannot be resolved. Most such investment opportunities require 5, 10, or more years to pay off. But the utility of risk analyses of social, political, and economic factors decreases precipitously over longer time spans.

Who Does Country Risk Assessing?

General or specific analyses, macro or micro analyses, and political, social, and economic analyses have been conducted—perhaps under different names—for years. The Conference Board located bits and pieces of CRA being performed in various company departments—for example, the international division and public affairs, finance, legal, economics, planning, as well as product-producing departments. Sometimes the efforts were duplicative, and the people in one department were unaware that others in the company were similarly involved.

Efforts are now being made to concentrate CRA and to maximize its effectiveness for the company. These efforts include guidelines about the participation of top management.

Another source of country risk analysis is the outside consulting and publishing firm. As CRA has mushroomed in perceived importance, a number of such firms have been formed or have expanded.

Instead of or in addition to the outside consultants, a number of firms have buttressed their internal risk analysis staffs by hiring such experts as international business or political science professors or retired State Department, CIA, or military people.

CRA Procedure

There are a multitude of possible approaches to CRA. One set of steps, suggested by the Swiss bank Crédit Suisse, is illustrated in Table 10–1.

One of the steps suggested in Table 10–1 is arrow diagrams, and Figure 10–3 provides an illustrative arrow diagram of the domestic stability of Saudi

■ **TABLE 10–1**
Major Methodological Steps Used in Political Risk Analysis

Determining the situation: Where do we stand?

1. Collecting information on countries and events
2. Compiling data
3. Creating and running a documentation service
4. Setting up a data base
5. Evaluation of periodical information services
6. Application of simple indicators
7. Composite indicators (indexes)
8. Scaling
9. Construction of typologies
10. Classification
11. Multidimensional scaling

Explanation: Why are things as they are?

12. Arrow diagrams
13. Cognitive mapping: analysis of motives and intentions
14. Utilization of theoretical findings
15. Systematic evaluation of the professional literature
16. Systems analysis
17. Correlations analysis
18. Regression analysis
19. Analysis of nonlinear relationships
20. Partial and multiple correlations analysis
21. Multiple regression analysis
22. Path analysis
23. Historical analogies

Preview: What's ahead?

24. General analogies
25. Systematic expert judgment
26. Delphi analysis
27. Bayesian inference
28. Cross-impact analysis
29. Early warning indicators
30. Extrapolation with moving averages
31. Trend analysis
32. Time series analysis
33. Spectral analysis
34. Combined time series and trend analysis
35. Analysis of changing trends

Preparing decisions: What can we do?

36. Decision tree in problem analysis
37. Game theory approach to problem analysis
38. Scenario writing
39. Application of morphological approaches
40. Gaming
41. Computer simulation
42. Econometric models
43. Global models

Deciding: What will we do?

44. Decision tree
45. Decision matrix
46. Decision tree with incomplete information (linear partial information analysis)

Source: *Bulletin*, Crédit Suisse, Autumn 1983, p. 6.

Arabia. Note that this diagram starts with the world economy; it does not consider the Iran-Iraq war and other Middle East unrest.

Country risk monitor. Figure 10–4 is the Country Risk Monitor of Swiss Bank Corporation for an unnamed country. The country's identity is confidential "because it is a way of saying thank you for the open discussion."

Lessons of the International Debt Crisis

There are at least five lessons that CRA analysts should have learned. First, many developing countries are vulnerable to external shocks. One thing that has become apparent is the importance of a country's export and import structure in weathering an external economic shock. For example, the newly industrialized countries of Asia with their diversified export structures have been in a much better position to deal with the collapse of commodity prices and the erection of protectionist barriers than have been other countries with

■ **FIGURE 10–3** **Domestic Political Stability in Saudi Arabia**

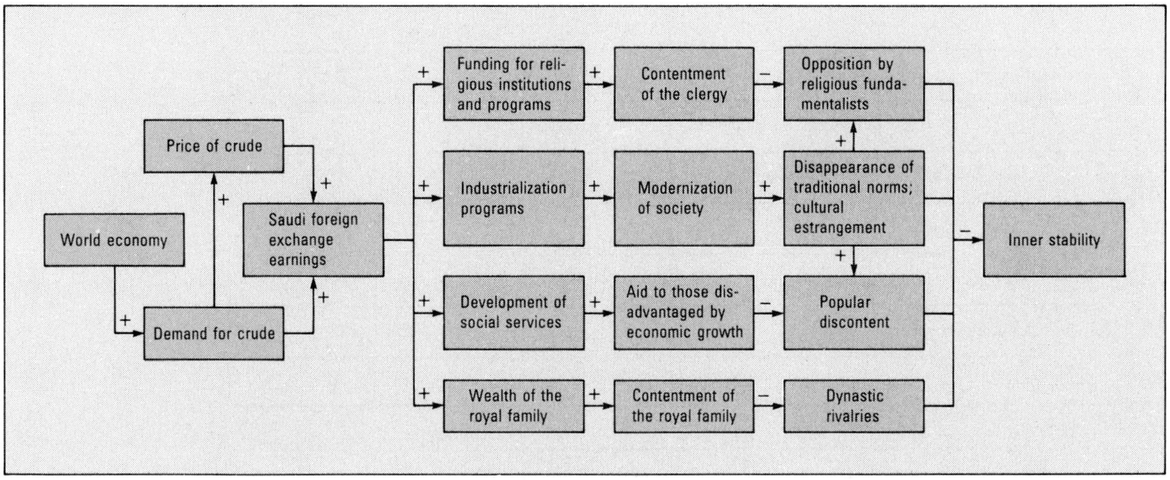

Source: *Bulletin,* Crédit Suisse, Autumn 1983, p. 6.

a comparable level of development but lopsided export structures (such as Indonesia and Mexico).

Second, the development of the debt crisis has shown clearly that the economic policies of debtor countries have a decisive impact on default risk. The countries that have become most deeply mired in the crisis are the ones that adopted expansionary fiscal and monetary policies. The results were inflation, current account deficits, loss of international competitiveness, and capital flight. Such has been the fate of the Philippines and the high-debt countries of Latin America.

By contrast, those countries that allowed the altered world market prices and demand conditions to take effect on their economies and adapted their economic policies to accommodate changed conditions have fared much better. Restrictive fiscal and monetary policies damped inflation, while occasional devaluations of their currencies kept trade balances under control. South Korea withstood the debt crisis through skillful economic policies.

Third, sustained economic growth is a major requirement for high-debt countries to service their debt and reduce its burden. Austerity alone cannot be a solution—economically, politically, or socially.

Fourth, the social and potential political costs of overindebtedness combined with austerity are proving high. In Latin America, real imports fell by about 30 percent, and real per capita income by some 7 percent, between 1981 and 1985. Social and political tensions have risen sharply and threaten the survival of several democratically elected governments. That, in turn, greatly increases the danger of a debt moratorium.

The fifth lesson from the debt crisis for CRA analysts is the global ripple effect of seemingly independent risks or economic shocks. For example, the oil price collapse at the beginning of 1986 jacked up oil-exporting countries' default risk while lessening that risk for oil importers, thus affecting international interest and exchange rates and triggering a whole series of fiscal and monetary policy responses.

■ **FIGURE 10–4**   **Swiss Bank Corporation Country Risk Monitor**

	Indicators		1984	1985	1986	1987	Estimate 1988	Outlook 1989
Domestic Economy	1. Real GDP growth	%	5.2	3.1	1.2	−4.5	−3.2	1.5
	2. Investment / GDP international average = 25%		25.6	24.9	24.1	18.5	14.7	↗
	3. Investment efficiency (1:2) Critical level ≤ 0.2		0.23	0.19	0.13	−0.02	−0.11	→
	4. Inflation (period average)	%	18.5	22.3	24.9	52.6	18.2*	↗
	5. Money supply growth (end of period)	%	22.8	18.5	19.6	6.9	9.8*	→
	6. Real domestic credit creation	%	16.8	27.9	37.2	−15.0	−9.4*	up
	7. Fiscal balance / GDP	%	−3.5	−5.1	−2.5	−1.8	−1.7	↘
External Economy	8. Competitiveness (real exchange rate) index 1980 = 100		109.5	105.4	85.6	84.0	80.0	↗
	9. Trade balance (goods)	US $ bn	−1.84	−2.95	−3.94	−2.40	−0.80	↗
	10. Exports (goods + services)	US $ bn	8.60	8.10	8.15	8.30	9.10	↗
	11. Imports (goods + services)	US $ bn	10.81	11.95	12.54	11.40	10.30	up
	12. Current account balance	US $ bn	−1.95	−3.55	−4.12	−2.60	−0.90	↗
	13. Exports / GDP	%	23.0	20.7	23.5	21.5	23.0	→
	14. Export concentration (high = critical)†	%	33.4	35.2	36.7	35.6	35.0	→
	15. Imports from Switzerland	SFr. m	104.2	110.3	117.9	106.2	105.0	↗
Debt	16. Total external debt (public + private)	US $ bn	16.8	20.9	25.1	27.3	28.0	↘
	17. International reserves (excluding gold)	US $ bn	3.12	1.94	0.95	0.81	1.00	↗
	18. External debt service	US $ bn	2.45	2.71	2.96	2.82	3.40	↘
	19. External debt / Exports critical level ≥ 150%		195	258	308	329	308	↗
	20. External debt service / Exports critical level ≥ 25%		28.5	33.4	36.3	34.0	37.3	↗
	21. Interest-adjusted current account / Interest payments	%	−25	−67	−84	−13	67	↗
	22. International reserves / Imports critical level ≤ 3 mths		3.5	1.9	0.9	0.9	1.2	↗
	23. Political risk points 1 ⎯ 10		7	7	7	6	6	→
	24. Recorded unemployment rate	%	11.2	10.5	11.0	13.4	13.5	→
	25. Per capita GDP growth	%	2.8	0.7	−1.1	−6.8	−5.5	−0.8

Remarks: ▢ : Figure beyond critical level   ▢ : Figure in critical change vs. previous year   ▢ : Figure in critical change and beyond critical level

*January 1988.

†Sales to United States as percentage of merchandise exports.

Source: Swiss Bank Corporation, *Economic and Financial Prospects,* Supplement to No. 1/1988, February 5, 1988.

The 1987 stock market crash caused worldwide economic reverberations. Other events that would have global effects if they were to occur include sustained changes in world interest rates, recession in major market countries, creation of debtor-country cartels, or the banking system's loss of confidence in an entire region.

SUMMARY

Ideologies are defined in dictionaries and textbooks. Countries and political parties use names with ideological meanings to describe themselves, but you must view these names cautiously because the political and economic actions of countries and parties may not be what you would expect from their names.

Until recently that was not true for the communist countries, whose political and economic actions followed true to form, including ownership or control of all important factors of production. Some changes are now taking place in communist countries, such as possibilities for private ownership or operation of farms and businesses and for foreign private companies to own or joint venture businesses. These changes began in the People's Republic of China and have spread to the Soviet Union and some—but not all—Soviet satellite countries. This topic will be discussed in Chapter 17.

The problem in capitalist countries is to abide by the many laws and regulations that affect business. In addition, several governments of capitalist countries own companies that operate both domestically and internationally, sometimes in competition with privately owned companies. As in the case of Great Britain, countries sometimes denationalize or privatize government-owned companies by selling them to private investors who are, in some instances, the company's employees.

Nationalism is an emotional force with political effects. If foreign companies wish to operate in a country, they must deal with nationalism, and there are quite a few ways to do so.

Some governments are unable, to a greater or lesser degree, to protect business and its managers from terrorism or other forms of attack. Countermeasures being taken against terrorism promise to reduce its frequency and success. Terrorism seems to be becoming less idealistic and more brutal as it turns to collaboration with the Mafia and the Soviet and other secret services as well as with fascist groups and profits from sales of guns and drugs.

Another new development in the terrorist tale is the increasing evidence that nations are training and financing terrorists and directing terrorist attacks in other countries. Evidence has implicated Syria, the Soviet Union, Iran, and Libya. In international law, such state activities are acts of war.

Gradual changes of government policies toward business are expected by business and can be coped with. However, sudden changes of such government policies or sudden changes of government are unsettling or alarming to business. When confronted by such changes, it tends to go away or stay away.

Traditional hostilities between world groups cause problems for business. One of these groups may boycott a company if it deals with the other. The UN or other groups of nations may embargo trade with some country or other group.

International organizations such as the UN and the EC are becoming more politicized and are gaining more political powers. Their influence on international business is growing.

Labor is a major political force. Even where it does not control important political parties, it can dispose of large amounts of money and personnel to affect elections and influence governments.

The WWC has political power. Some WWCs have more resources than the nations with which they deal. In addition, WWCs can use technology, distribution, management, capital sources, and other strengths in their negotiations with host countries.

Increasing world unrest, which stems from many causes, has made systematic country risk assessment necessary for banks and businesses operating internationally. They can seek help for such assessments from a number of internal and external sources. CRA must now be more global and should not be limited to one country alone; this is one of the lessons CRA analysts should have learned from the debt crisis.

QUESTIONS

1. *a.* What is ideology?
   b. Why is it important to international business?
2. *a.* What is the capitalist, free enterprise ideal?
   b. What is the actual situation in capitalist countries?
3. How and why do socialist LDCs and privately owned WWCs cooperate to their mutual profit?
4. What are some reasons why "capitalist" governments nationalize private businesses?
5. *a.* What is nationalism?
   b. What are some effects it can have on foreign business?
6. What impact can terrorism have on business?
7. Why does business fear sudden changes in government policies?
8. How can traditional hostilities affect business?
9. Give some examples of international organization activities that affect business.
10. Why do labor organizations have political power?
11. How can WWCs use their strengths to influence government policies?
12. What is country risk assessment as practiced by WWCs? Why is it a growing project?
13. Is country risk assessment an exact science? Explain.
14. *a.* In terms of exposure to political risk (for example, expropriation), which of the following businesses would you consider the most and least vulnerable?

banks	cosmetics manufacturers
mines	manufacturers of personal hygiene products
oil fields	
oil refineries	hotels
heavy-equipment manufacturers	automobile manufacturers

   b. Are the most vulnerable businesses high profile or low profile? What are some ways to change the profile of a company in a foreign country?
15. Discuss the lessons CRA analysts should have learned from the world debt crisis.

MINICASE 10–1

Company Privatization

You are the chief executive officer of a company that the government has just denationalized by selling the company's stock to the company's employees. In the past, any major decision about company policy required approval by a government agency, which was time consuming. Wages and salaries had been established by reference to civil service "equivalents," and incentive payments were unheard of.

Maintenance of the plant and equipment was lax, breakdowns were frequent and expensive, and utility expenses were high.

You want the newly privatized company to be a success. Suggest some programs that you would institute to improve its chances of success.

SUPPLEMENTARY READINGS

Aitken, Thomas. "Assessing the Political Environment: An Emerging Function in International Companies." New York: Conference Board, 1980.

Ball, Donald A., and Wendell H. McCulloch, Jr. "Country Risk Analysis: Fad or Business Investment?" *Collegiate Forum,* Spring 1982, p. 12.

Haner, F. T., and J. S. Ewing. *Country Risk Assessment Theory and Worldwide Practice.* New York: Praeger Special Studies, 1985.

Parry, Thomas G. *The Multinational Enterprise: International Investment and Host-Country Impacts.* Greenwich, Conn.: JAI Press, 1980.

Pirie, Madsen. *Dismantling the State: The Theory and Practice of Privatization.* Dallas: National Center for Policy Analysis, 1985.

Rogers, Jerry, ed. *Global Risk Assessments: Issues, Concepts, and Applications.* Riverside, Calif.: Global Risk Assessments, 1986.

Sachs, J. D. "The Current Account and the Macroeconomic Adjustment in the 1970s." Washington, D.C.: Brookings Papers on Economic Activity, no. 1, 1981.

_____. "External Debt and Macroeconomic Performance in Latin America and East Asia." Washington, D.C.: Brookings Papers on Economic Activity, no. 2, 1985.

Streeten, Paul. *Development Perspectives.* New York: St. Martin's Press, 1981.

Vernon, Raymond, ed. *The Promise of Privatization.* New York: Council on Foreign Relations, 1988.

ENDNOTES

1. Keyes Beech, "Singapore Reeks with Riches and the Good Life," *Los Angeles Times,* April 21, 1980, part 4, p. 1.

2. Murray Seeger, "Italy Takes Prize for Its Corporate Octopus," *Los Angeles Times,* November 1, 1979, part 1, p. 12.

3. Charles C. Tillinghast, Jr., "Competing against State-Owned Companies," paper presented at the Academy of International Business Annual Meeting, 1979.

4. Mary Shirley, "The Experience with Privatization," *Finance & Development,* September 1988, p. 34–35.

5. Felix Kessler, "France's Erratic Policies on Investment by Foreigners Confuse Many U.S. Firms," *The Wall Street Journal,* April 7, 1980, p. 24.

6. For a good discussion of nationalism, see Richard N. Farmer and Barry M. Richman, "Behavioral Problems in International Business," in *International Business,* 3rd ed. (Bloomington, Ind.: Cedarwood Press, 1980), chap. 5, pp. 165–81.

7. *The Economist,* May 27, 1978, p. 61.

8. Ibid.

9. David G. Hubbard, "Lilliput Revisited: A Data-Based Critique of Corporate Captivity in Connection with Kidnapping and Terrorist Threat," in *The International Essays for Business Decision Makers,* vol. 4, ed. Mark B. Winchester (Dallas: Center for International Business, 1979), pp. 19–31.

10. Brian O'Reilly, "Business Copes with Terrorism," *Fortune,* January 6, 1986, pp. 47–55.

11. Claire Sterling, "The Red Brigades Have Strange Partners in Crime," *The Wall Street Journal,* August 18, 1982, p. 27.

12. William D. Montalbano, "New Breed of Terrorists Emerges in Italy, Police Say," *Los Angeles Times,* June 21, 1988, p. 6.

13. "Terrorism and Beyond: An International Conference on Terrorism and Low-Level Conflict," Brian M. Jenkins, conference director, R–2714-DOE/DOJ/DOS/RC, December 1982.

14. Peter Almond with Bill Whalen, "Insurance against Terrorists an Emerging Growth Industry," *Insight,* March 17, 1986, pp. 52–54.

15. Everett G. Martin, "Playing It Cool in Bolivia," *The Wall Street Journal,* June 3, 1976, p. 14.

16. *The Wall Street Journal,* April 11, 1977, p. 12.

17. *The Economist,* May 24, 1987, p. 76; and Eric Morgenhaler, "Clamping Down," *The Wall Street Journal,* August 13, 1986, p. 1.

18. "Bolivia Doing It by the Book," *The Economist,* May 28, 1988, p. 7; and see Robert Graham, "Bolivia Comes Down to Earth with a Bump," *Financial Times,* July 23, 1987, p. 14.

19. Shirley Hobbs Scheibla, "McNamara's Band Sour," *Barron's,* December 3, 1979, pp. 9, 26, 27.

20. *Business International,* January 21, 1983, pp. 17–19.

21. Lee L. Morgan, "Opportunities for Mutual Action by Government and Business Leaders in 1977," in *Contemporary Perspectives in International Business,* ed. Harold W. Berkman and Ivan R. Vernon (Skokie, Ill.: Rand McNally, 1979), p. 284.

22. William J. Barton, "International Government Relations: A Required Management Function for International Business," in *The International Essays for Business Decision Makers,* vol. 3, ed. Mark B. Winchester (New York: AMACOM, 1978), pp. 218–19.

23. For a good discussion of the powers that an MNE can use, see Stefan H. Robock and Kenneth Simmonds, *International Business and Multinational Enterprises* (Homewood, Ill.: Richard D. Irwin, 1989), chap. 15.

24. See Table 1–1 on pages 10–11.

25. "Come Back Multinationals," *The Economist,* November 26, 1988, p. 73.

26. For several good discussions of various aspects of CRA, see Jerry Rogers, ed., *Global Risk Assessments: Issues, Concepts, and Applications,* book 2 (Riverside, Calif.: Global Risk Assessments, 1986); also see the supplementary readings dealing with CRA.

Chapter 11
Legal Forces

After 35 years, I have finished a comprehensive study of European comparative law. In Germany, under the law, everything is prohibited, except that which is permitted. In France, under the law, everything is permitted, except that which is prohibited. In the Soviet Union, under the law, everything is prohibited, including that which is permitted. And in Italy, under the law, everything is permitted, especially that which is prohibited.

Newton Minow, former chairman of the U.S. Federal Communications Commission, in a speech to the Association of American Law Schools

LEARNING OBJECTIVES

In this chapter, you will study:

1. The complexity—due to their many sources (e.g., national laws, treaties, international organizations, private international law)—of the legal forces that may confront you.

2. Taxes, which frequently have purposes other than the raising of revenue.

3. U.S. antitrust laws and their enforcement.

4. Industrial espionage, which in some countries is a crime punished by fines or imprisonment.

5. The concept of sovereign immunity, which can protect a government from being sued or prevent a court from having jurisdiction over it.

6. Contract devices, and institutions that assist in interpreting or arbitrating international contracts.

7. The need to examine the law of each country where you do business to ensure protection of your intellectual properties such as patents, trademarks, trade names, copyrights, and trade secrets.

8. Why tariffs, quotas, and other trade obstacles of each country into which you wish to import a product are important.

9. The possibility that your property in a foreign country may be seized by the government or that you may be forced to give up control of it.

10. The risk of monetary damages or imprisonment if your company manufactures/sells a faulty or dangerous product, or if an employee fails to observe host country law or falls afoul of corrupt officials.

11. The need to comply with wage and price controls and with currency exchange controls.

12. The numerous difficulties and burdens placed by U.S. laws and practices on American WWCs, which no other industrialized country imposes on its WWCs.

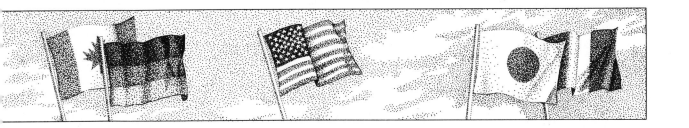

KEY WORDS AND CONCEPTS

- Nonrevenue tax purposes
- Foreign tax credit
- Tax treaties
- Antitrust laws
- Restrictive trade practice
- Extraterritorial applications of laws
- Tariffs
- Quotas
- Domestication
- Product liability
- Price and wage controls
- Sovereign immunity
- Arbitration
- Industrial espionage
- National tax jurisdiction
- Territorial tax jurisdiction
- Questionable or dubious payments

BUSINESS INCIDENT

Kenny International Corporation is a stamp-distributing company owned by two New Yorkers, Finbar B. Kenny and his wife, Marianne. Kenny had the exclusive rights to distribute the stamps of the Cook Islands. Most of the stamps are sold to collectors, and such sales totaled $1.5 million in 1978. Domestic sales, for actual postage, were only about $20,000 in 1978. Kenny split the $1.5 million with the Cook Islands.

In March 1978, there was a general election in the Cook Islands. According to the U.S. Justice Department, in an effort to protect its valuable franchise, Kenny agreed to help reelect the then premier, Sir Albert Henry, and his political party. To that end, Kenny used $337,000 out of the Cook Island account to charter jet passenger planes. The planes flew some 450 Cook Islanders in from New Zealand, and their votes provided the margin of victory that secured Sir Albert's reelection. In July 1978, however, the Cook Islands High Court disallowed those votes as "tainted by bribery" and threw Sir Albert out of office.

Kenny pleaded guilty to breaking Cook Island law and repaid the $337,000. But American law? It was also broken, said the U.S. Justice Department, and the Kennys pleaded guilty in a U.S. federal district court in Washington. Their company was fined $50,000.

The U.S. law that was broken was the Foreign Corrupt Practices Act of 1977. The Kenny case was the first criminal action brought under it.

Source: From *The Wall Street Journal*, August 3, 1979, p. 29. Reprinted with permission. © Dow Jones & Company, Inc. 1979. All rights reserved.

Any attempt to teach a course on "The Legal Forces That Affect International Business" would be overwhelmed or bogged down by the immensity and variety of those forces. International business is affected by countless thousands of laws and regulations on hundreds of subjects that have been issued by states, nations, and international organizations.

Nevertheless, this text, which is an introduction to international business, would be incomplete if it did not inform students or businesspersons that many legal forces do affect international business and if it did not give them an idea of what some of the most important are. We shall examine first several national legal forces, with brief comments, and then we shall discuss some international legal forces.

Although many U.S. laws and regulations affect the activities of multinational firms, there has been no successful effort to coordinate them. Some of them are at cross-purposes, and some diminish the competitiveness of American business as it attempts to compete with foreign companies. We shall close this chapter with a brief examination of some of these laws and regulations. The business incident about Kenny International's legal difficulties illustrates the application of one such law.

We shall now proceed to deal with specific legal forces. (They are not presented in any particular order.) Some of them, such as taxation, concern every business and businessperson, whereas others, such as antitrust, involve fewer firms.

SOME SPECIFIC NATIONAL LEGAL FORCES

Taxation

nonrevenue tax purposes include redistributing income, discouraging consumption of some product, such as tobacco or alcohol; or encouraging purchase of domestic rather than imported products

Purposes.   The primary purpose of certain taxes is not necessarily to raise revenue for the government. That fact may surprise the reader who has not had occasion to study taxation. Some of the many **nonrevenue tax purposes** are to redistribute income, to discourage consumption of such products as alcohol or tobacco, to encourage consumption of domestic rather than imported goods, to discourage investment abroad, to achieve equality of the tax amounts paid by taxpayers earning comparable amounts, and to grant reciprocity to resident foreigners under a tax treaty.

Even this short list of purposes (there are many more) suggests the economic and political pressures brought to bear on government officials who are responsible for tax legislation and collection. Powerful groups in every country push for tax policies that favor their interests. These groups and interests differ from country to country and frequently conflict, which accounts, in part, for the complexity of the tax practices that affect multinationals.

National differences of approach.   Among the many nations of the world, there are numerous differences in tax systems.

Tax levels.   For one thing, tax levels range from relatively high (up to 100 percent in some instances) in some West European countries to zero in tax havens.* Some countries have capital gains taxes,† and some do not. Those

---

* A tax haven is a country in which income of defined types incurs no tax liability.
† Capital gain is realized when as asset is sold for an amount greater than its cost.

that have them tax capital gains at different levels. Incidentally, the United States levies the highest long-term capital gains tax. Capital gains tax rates of the world's major industrial nations are as follows:

Capital Gains Tax Rates

Country	Maximum Long-Term Rate	Maximum Short-Term Rate
United States	33%	33%
United Kingdom	30	30
Sweden	18	45
Canada	17.5	17.5
France	16	16
Germany	Exempt	56
Belgium	Exempt	Exempt
Italy	Exempt	Exempt
Japan	Exempt	Exempt
Netherlands	Exempt	Exempt
Hong Kong	Exempt	Exempt
Singapore	Exempt	Exempt
South Korea	Exempt	Exempt
Republic of China	Exempt	Exempt

Tax types.   There are different types of taxes. We have just introduced one, the capital gains tax. Although the United States levies a relatively high capital gains tax, it relies for most of its revenue on the income tax. As indicated by the name, this tax is levied on the income of individuals and businesses. A generality, subject to exceptions, is that the higher the income, the higher the income tax. In the 1970s and 1980s, much discontent developed among Americans over the impact of the income and other taxes. Possibly as a result of that, there has been growing support for a *value-added tax (VAT)* in the U.S. Congress and Treasury.

Suggestions are that the U.S. VAT be similar to the VATs in effect in all European Community countries, for which the VAT is a main source of revenue. A simplified example of how the VAT works on a loaf of bread can be seen in Table 11–1. We shall assume a VAT of 10 percent. The wheat farmer sells to the miller for 30 cents the part of the wheat that eventually becomes the loaf. So far, the farmer has added 30 cents of value by planting, growing, and harvesting the wheat. The farmer sets aside 3 cents (10 percent of 30 cents) to pay VAT. The miller makes loaves of bread out of the wheat and sells them to the wholesaler for 50 cents each. Thus, the miller has added 20 cents of value (50 cents − 30 cents) and must pay a VAT of 2 cents (10 percent of 20 cents). The wholesaler now advertises and distributes the loaves, selling them to retailers at 70 cents. The wholesaler has added 20 cents of value and owes 2 cents VAT. Finally, the retailer adds 40 cents by its display, advertising, and sales efforts and owes 4 cents of VAT. The loaf of bread is sold for $1.10 retail and has borne a cumulative VAT of 11 cents, 10 percent of $1.10.

Stage of Production	Selling Price	Value Added	VAT at 10 percent	Cumulative VAT
Farmer	30¢	30¢	3¢	3¢
Miller	50¢	20¢	2¢	5¢
Wholesaler	70¢	20¢	2¢	7¢
Retailer	$1.10	40¢	4¢	11¢

The VAT has proponents and opponents.[1] You can read the footnote and other material for details, but in general they are as follows: The proponents say the VAT is relatively simple and can be raised or lowered easily to balance desired income with the burden. The opponents argue that it is a consumption-type tax that bears most heavily on the poor.

Another argument of VAT proponents in the United States is that the present situation, in which the major European countries rely heavily on the value-added tax, is unfair to the United States because of GATT* regulations. GATT permits the rebate of VAT when a product is exported from a country but does not permit rebate of income taxes. The rebates permit lower-priced, more competitive goods, and VAT proponents want the United States to inaugurate the VAT and lower income taxes to take advantage of those GATT rules.

Complexity of tax laws and regulations. From country to country, the complexity of tax systems differs. Many consider that of the United States to be the most complex; the Internal Revenue Code runs over 5,000 pages, and official interpretations add more than 10,000 to that number. In addition to the code and Treasury interpretations, there are countless thousands of pages of judicial rulings.

Who obeys the law? Compliance with tax laws and their enforcement vary widely. Some countries, such as Germany and the United States, are strict. Others, such as Italy and Spain, are relatively lax, the Italian practice being for the taxpayer to declare a very low taxable income amount to which the government counters with a very high amount. They then negotiate to a compromise figure.

> One of the authors remembers the shock and horror that greeted his suggestion to Italian tax advisors that a new Italian subsidiary of an American WWC declare its true income to the Italian authorities. As the advisers forcefully pointed out, no one would believe us.

foreign tax credit U.S. citizens who reside and pay income taxes in another country can credit those taxes against U.S. income tax

Other differences. There are many other differences, too numerous even to list here, but a few are tax incentives to invest in certain areas, exemptions, costs, depreciation allowances, **foreign tax credits,** timing, and double corporate taxation—that is, taxation of the profits of a corporation and then of dividends paid to its stockholders.

tax treaties treaties between countries that bind the governments to share information about taxpayers and to cooperate in tax law enforcement

Tax conventions (treaties). Because of the innumerable differences among the nations' tax practices, many of them have signed **tax treaties** with each

* See Chapter 4 for discussion of the General Agreement on Tariffs and Trade.

other. Typically, a tax treaty defines such terms as income, source, residency, and what constitutes taxable activities in each country. It also reduces taxation by each country of income going to residents who are nationals of the other and deals with taxation by each country of nationals of the other living or working in the country. All of these treaties contain provisions for the exchange of information between the tax authorities of the two countries.

Antitrust and Restrictive Trade Practices Legislation

In the tax area, it is the taxpayers (we are dealing with international business taxpayers) against the tax collectors (the governments). In antitrust, it is business versus government and, increasingly, government versus government.

U.S. laws and attitudes are different.   The U.S. **antitrust laws** are stricter and more vigorously enforced than those of any other country. However, other countries, as well as the EC, are becoming more active in the antitrust field. In the EC, these laws are referred to as **restrictive trade practices laws.**

antitrust laws American laws to prevent price-fixing, market sharing, and business monopolies

The West German antitrust laws are the toughest after those of the United States, and, during 1986, the German Federal Cartel Office was tightening its grip—literally, in some cases. Wolfgang Kartte, president of the Cartel Office, tells the story of a raid his investigators made on the office of a heating equipment supplier. One of the supplier's managers stuffed a memo in his mouth and tried to swallow it, but a quick-thinking investigator grabbed the man by the throat and forced him to spit out the memo. Half-chewed but still legible, it provided valuable evidence of illegal price-fixing.

restrictive trade practices laws the European phrase for what are called antitrust laws in the United States

The EC Commission was also stepping up its restrictive trade practices activities. In December 1988, a group of 23 West European chemical companies was fined a record ECU 60 million ($66 million) for illicit price-fixing and production sharing. They were found guilty of contravening Article 85 of the Treaty of Rome, the EC's constitution, which outlaws any agreement designed to rig markets or otherwise distort competition, as well as Article 86, which bans abuses of a dominant position.[2]

A number of important differences in antitrust laws, regulations, and practices exist between the United States, other nations, and the EC. One difference is the effort of the United States to apply its laws, extraterritorially (outside the United States). We deal with that later in this chapter. Another difference is the per se concept of the U.S. law.

Under the U.S. laws, certain activities, such as price-fixing, are said to be illegal per se. This means that they are illegal even though no injury or damage results from them.

The Treaty of Rome articles dealing with restrictive trade practices do not contain the per se illegality concept of U.S. antitrust law. For example, a cartel that allows consumers a fair share of the benefits is legally acceptable in the EC. Also, the treaty is not violated by market dominance—only by misuse of that dominance to damage competitors or consumers.

The EC versus Hoffman-La Roche.   As indicated above, EC antitrust enforcement is not toothless. In 1979, the EC Court of Justice upheld the EC Commission's decision that the giant Swiss drug company Hoffman-La Roche was guilty of abusing its dominant position. Hoffman was fined DM732,000.[3]

There was at least one bizarre element in the Hoffman case. Stanley Adams, a British subject, was an employee at the company's head office in Basel,

Switzerland. He took some confidential documents about Hoffman's pricing and marketing practices and made them available to the EC antitrust regulators, who were already investigating the company. The company and the Swiss government reacted furiously, and when Adams, who was in Italy when the loss of the documents was discovered, returned to Switzerland, he was arrested and convicted under Swiss laws against industrial espionage. He was sent to prison, and his wife committed suicide on being told that he would be in prison at least 20 years. Finally, the EC bailed him out of the Swiss prison and he left the country.

Although Adams had his freedom, his troubles were not over. He was unable to get credit or employment, and he lost a farm he tried to operate in Italy. He then moved to England and sued the EC Commission for £500,000 damages for revealing his identity to Hoffman and for not warning him of the dangers he faced if he returned to Switzerland. In 1985, Adams won his case in the European Court of Justice.[4]

The Swiss government versus the EC.   The Hoffman-La Roche case caused government-versus-government friction. The EC complained to the Swiss that Adams should not be prosecuted under Swiss law, because all he had done was cooperate with the EC Commission's efforts to enforce the law. The Swiss prosecuted and convicted him, notwithstanding the EC's complaints, because he had violated Swiss law in Switzerland.

The U.S. government versus other governments.   A more common example of government-versus-government conflict is pitting the U.S. government against various other governments as the United States attempts to enforce its antitrust laws outside the U.S. borders. This is referred to as **extraterritorial application of the law.** In 1979, a grand jury in Washington, D.C., indicted three foreign-owned ocean-shipping groups on charges of fixing prices without getting approval from the U.S. Federal Maritime Commission. The other governments, European and Japanese, protested bitterly, arguing (1) that shipping is international by definition, so the United States has no right to act unilaterally and (2) that the alleged offenses were both legal and ethical practices outside the United States.[5]

Sir Freddie Laker's airline, a low-price transatlantic service, ceased operations on February 5, 1982. Shortly thereafter, its liquidators commenced a private antitrust suit in an American court, alleging that some other airlines had conspired to put Laker out of business. They asked over $1 billion in damages, and two other British airlines were among the defendants.

The private suits irked the British government, but what disturbed it most was the U.S. Justice Department's move in spring 1983 to begin a criminal grand jury investigation of essentially the same allegations. It was another example of the U.S. government's efforts to apply its law extraterritorially.

Other governments versus the U.S. government.   In 1977, the United States tried to force seven executives of the British company Rio Tinto-Zinc to testify in connection with an antitrust action in the United States. In that instance, Britain's highest court, the House of Lords, turned down the U.S. demands on the grounds that they were an infringement of British jurisdiction and

extraterritorial application of the law   when a country attempts to apply its laws to foreigners or nonresidents and to acts and activities that took place outside its borders

sovereignty and that the United States was trying to investigate the activities of companies not subject to U.S. jurisdiction.[6]

A number of countries have passed statutes to prevent persons within their territories from cooperating with the United States and have established criminal sanctions for those who comply with U.S. law in violation of those statutes. Among these countries are Australia, Canada, Britain, the Netherlands, and West Germany. Thus, persons or companies can find themselves in the position of being forced to break the law of either the United States or of a country with this type of statute.

U.S. labor versus OPEC.   One of the oddest attempts to use U.S. antitrust laws to achieve results internationally was the lawsuit filed in December 1978 by the International Association of Machinists and Aerospace Workers (IAM) against OPEC. The IAM charged price-fixing that had caused severe damage to the U.S. economy.

OPEC, as a group of nations, claims sovereign immunity, which would prevent its being sued in the courts of a non-OPEC nation. In 1976, however, the United States adopted the Foreign Sovereign Immunities Act, which strips immunity from a government when it engages in commercial activities. The IAM argued that producing and selling petroleum was a commercial activity—OPEC had nationalized and was operating assets previously owned and operated by private oil companies in OPEC territories. The IAM's position was that because those private American oil companies would clearly be subject to U.S. antitrust prosecution for price-fixing, the new OPEC owners should also be liable and should not be permitted to rely on sovereign immunity.

West Germany, the country second to the United States in aggressive antitrust policy, decided not to take on the oil cartel. "They were just too big for us," said one Berlin* official, and he was talking about the oil companies, not OPEC.[7] It remains to be seen what will flow (more or less oil?) from the IAM action, though the issue was probably settled in 1981, when a federal court of appeals ruled that it had no jurisdiction over OPEC oil pricing. The IAM did not appeal that ruling.

Tariffs, Quotas, and Other Trade Obstacles

tariffs taxes on imported goods

Every country has laws on one or more of these subjects. The purposes of **tariffs** are to raise revenue for the government and to protect domestic producers. Tariffs are either ad valorem, which means they are a percentage of the value of the imports, or they are specific. The specific tariff is based on the weight or number of items imported. **Quotas,** which limit the number or amount of imports, are for protection.

quotas limits on the number of an item that may be imported

There are many other forms of protection or obstacles to trade in national laws. Some are health or packaging requirements. Others deal with language, such as the mandatory use of French on labels and in advertising, manuals, warranties, and so forth for goods sold in France.[8]

The following list is a sampling of U.S. export products, export destinations, and the trade barriers encountered at the destinations.

* Berlin is the site of the West German cartel office.

Product	Destination	Barrier
Carbon steel	EC	Imports limited to 8 percent of market
Pesticides	Canada	Residue standards bar some U.S. chemicals
Machine tools	Japan	Government subsidizes domestic industry
Machine tools	Argentina	Money from sales must remain in Argentina for months
Paperboard	Japan	Specifications require smoother board than is produced in the United States

In other countries, U.S. exports may encounter weak patent or trademark protection, very high tariffs, zero quotas, quarantine periods, or a variety of other obstacles.

Of course, the United States imposes barriers against the import of a number of products. It sometimes uses tariffs, sometimes quotas, and often a more modern form of quota called by some "voluntary" restraints agreements (VRAs) and by others "voluntary" export restraints (VERs). "Voluntary" is in quotes because these barriers are imposed by the U.S. government on the exporting countries. The inevitable result is higher costs to American consumers as exporters send only the higher-priced, top of their lines and importers charge more for scarcer products.[9] Table 11–2 shows one researcher's estimate of the price increase percentage and annual additional cost to consumers.

One justification of protectionism is that it saves domestic jobs. One estimate of the cost to the American consumer to save one job in the U.S. car industry was $250,000.[10]

It should be understood that the United States is not the only country that imposes VRAs and VERs on its trading partners. Far from it; Japan, Canada, the EC countries, and many others require countries exporting to them to "voluntarily" limit the number or value of goods exported.

In 1982, the French came up with a novel protectionist device. Japanese videotape recorders were one of the French imports causing a large balance-of-payments deficit with Japan. The recorders normally entered France through the major port of Le Harve, which had a large detachment of customs officers to process imports. Then the French government issued a decree requiring all of the recorders to enter France through Poitiers, which had a tiny customs post. The result was long delays that reduced the number of recorders entering France. Japan then "voluntarily" agreed to limit the number of recorders it exported to France.

Expropriation or Confiscation

Governments frequently pass laws under which they expropriate or confiscate foreign-owned property. OPEC members have seized foreign-owned assets within their borders, particularly natural resource assets.

Domestication

domestication a host of government takes—by law or persuasion—a share of ownership (usually less than 100 percent but more than 50 percent) of a foreign-owned company operating in the host country

Domestication is a less drastic takeover of foreign assets. Here the host government uses various forms of pressure to "persuade" foreign owners to sell some significant percentage, usually enough to enable the host government or local shareholders to gain control of the foreign-owned company.[11] A

■ TABLE 11–2
The Cost of
Protectionism

Georgetown University Professor Gary Hufbauer researched the costs of special protection legislation in a 1986 book published by the Institute for International Economics. Some of his results are shown in the following table. Where an asterisk follows a date of enactment, it means that the current program replaced some previous form of protection. The price increase column represents Hufbauer's estimate of the percentage boost in U.S. prices caused by protection. The consumer cost is that increase applied to total U.S. consumption of the products protected. VRA is Voluntary Restraint Agreement.

Industry	Type of Restraint	Dates From	Price Increase	Annual Consumer Cost ($ millions)
Maritime	Restricted	1789	60.0%	$3,000
Book publishing	Quota	1891	12.0	500
Glassware	Tariff	1922	4.5	200
Rubber footwear	Tariff	1930	21.0	230
Ceramic articles	Tariff	1930	7.0	95
Ceramic tiles	Tariff	1930	17.3	116
Orange juice	Tariff	1930	35.0	525
Canned tuna	Tariff	1951	10.0	91
Textiles, apparel	Tariff, quota	1982*	22.0	27,000
Steel	VRA	1982*	12.0	6,800
Specialty steel	VRA	1986*	15.0	520
Automobiles	VRA	1981	4.4	5,800
Semiconductors	VRA	1986	15.0	3,000
Machine tools	VRA	1986	10.0	500
Softwood lumber	Tariff	1986	20.0	1,000
Sugar	Quota	1982*	30.0	930
Dairy products	Restricted	1953	40.0	5,500
Peanuts	Restricted	1953	28.0	170
Meat	Restricted	1965	7.0	1,800
Fish	Quota, Restricted	1977	10.0	560

Source: *Barron's,* June 27, 1988, p. 70.

number of countries, including the Andean Pact nations, Brazil, India, Mexico, and Nigeria, have enacted laws or enforced policies to require or encourage foreign-owned companies to sell part ownership to the host government or to local shareholders. This is referred to as "Mexicanization" if it occurs in Mexico, "Brazilianization" if it occurs in Brazil, and so forth.

Product Liability, Civil and Criminal*

product liability holding a company and its officers and directors liable and possibly subject to fines or imprisonment when their product causes death, injury, or damage

Manufacturers' liability for faulty or dangerous products was a boom growth area for the American legal profession in the 1960s and 70s. Liability insurance premiums have soared, and there are concerns that smaller, weaker manufacturing companies cannot survive.

Now that boom is spreading in Europe, where the EC Commission and the Council of Europe are pushing new **product liability** laws. Those laws would standardize and toughen the present tangle of national laws.[12]

---

* Civil liability calls for payment of money damages. Criminal liability results in fines or imprisonment.

"Excuse me, sir... Want to sue a multinational?"

© 1987, Cartoonists & Writers Syndicate.

Another new development in Europe is causing what the president of one U.S.-controlled company in France called a "fear psychosis." This development is criminal liability of management for workers' death or injuries. In France, managers have been found guilty of involuntary homicide* and criminal responsibility after accidents caused workers' deaths.

In Britain, a 1976 Health and Safety Act gave inspectors the right to haul accused managers into courts that have the power to impose prison terms.

Pressures that could result in stiffer product safety standards are coming from numerous directions. One of them is the UN Economic and Social Council, and another is the International Organization of Consumers Unions.[13]

The European Parliament and many other groups have expressed concern that too sweeping government involvement in product safety and too heavy liability burdens on industry will stifle product innovation and hit small producers, which would be less able to either afford higher insurance premiums or pass on higher self-insurance costs. The British government has also expressed that point of view.

The British dissented from a July 1985 EC Council of Ministers directive to the effect that plaintiffs could seek redress for damages without having to prove negligence on the part of the manufacturers. The British position is that manufacturers should not be liable for product defects that—given the state of

---

* This means causing the death of some person or persons, and it is a crime even though it was "involuntary"—that is, unintentional.

THE WALL STREET JOURNAL

"He's in jail. May I take a message?"

From *The Wall Street Journal*, with permission of Cartoon Features Syndicate.

scientific and technological knowledge—could not have been detected when the product was made. This is called a "state-of-the-art" or "development risks" defense. In 1988, a new German law agreed with the British position that companies should have the development risks defense, but the same law extended companies' responsibility by permitting them to be liable for damages from faulty products without plaintiffs having to prove negligence.[14]

Nevertheless, the costs of liability insurance have risen and the availability of liability insurance has shrunk in all European countries. Product liability laws varied among EC countries in 1987, but an EC directive required all countries to introduce new legislation by July 1988. One important difference between European and American law in this field is that punitive damages,* which have played a large part in high U.S. awards, are not permitted in EC countries. Another difference is that European lawyers cannot take cases on a contingency fee basis†; American lawyers commonly do so.[15]

In a survey of more than 500 chief executives by the Conference Board, more than one fifth believe strict American product liability laws have caused their companies to lose business to foreign competitors.[16] But, as foreign firms buy or build U.S. plants, they are being hit by the same liability and insurance problems long faced by American companies.[17]

One of the worst product disaster incidents was the 1984 explosion at a Union Carbide chemical plant in Bhopal, India; thousands were killed, and many more were injured. In 1988, the lawsuits rising out of that accident—Union Carbide claimed it was caused by sabotage—were settled, but India passed a new law that would make top management responsible for any future mishaps. This could lead to all directors—including foreigners not involved in day-to-day management—being held responsible for mishaps. Penalties include fines and up to five years' imprisonment.[18]

---

* Punitive damages are in addition to the actual damages proven and are awarded to punish the manufacturer of a faulty product.

† Contingency fees are lawyers' fees paid only if the plaintiff's case is won or is settled by agreement of the defendant to make a payment.

Price and Wage Controls

Some countries that have **price and wage control laws** call them "voluntary," but the governments can bring pressures to bear on companies or labor unions that raise prices or demand wage increases above established percentages. The U.S. government, for example, has withheld government business from companies that violate its guidelines. This has resulted in lawsuits by labor unions challenging the legality of such punishment by the government because wage increases exceeded "voluntary" guidelines.

Communist countries, of course, just set prices and wages. There are no significant free markets and no effective labor unions that are not government agencies. Most noncommunist countries also have some price and wage control laws. As inflation spreads and grows in the world, **price and wage controls** can be expected to become more widespread and more restrictive.

---

price and wage controls prohibitions or limits on upward movements of prices or wages that are imposed by governments to combat inflation when the government has been unable or unwilling to slow or halt it by fiscal or monetary measures

---

Labor Laws

Virtually every country has laws governing working conditions and wages for its labor force. Even though hourly wages may be low in a country, the employers must beware, because fringe benefits can greatly increase labor costs. Fringe benefits can include profit sharing, health or dental benefits, retirement funds, and more. Some labor laws make the firing of a worker almost impossible or at least very expensive. This subject is considered more extensively in Chapter 12.

Currency Exchange Controls

Almost every country has currency exchange controls—laws dealing with the purchase and sale of foreign currencies. Most countries, including the LDCs and the communist countries, have too little hard foreign currency.* There is the rare case, such as Switzerland, that sometimes feels it has too much.

Exchange control generalities. The law of each country must be examined, but some generalities can be made. In those countries where hard foreign currency is scarce, it is allocated by a government agency. Typically, an importer of productive capital equipment would be given priority over an importer of luxury goods.

People entering such a country must declare how much currency of any kind they are bringing in. On departure, they must declare how much they are taking out. One side of the intent is to discourage bringing in the national currency that the traveler may have brought abroad at a better exchange rate than the traveler can get inside the country. The other side is to encourage the bringing in of hard foreign currency.

Switzerland—A special case. Switzerland is a special case because its government has imposed controls to keep foreign currencies out rather that in. Switzerland enjoyed relatively low inflation during the 1970s and into the 1980s, and its Swiss franc has remained one of the hardest of the hard currencies. As a result, people from all over the world have wanted to get their money into Switzerland, and the Swiss have felt the need to defend against being inundated by too much currency, which would cause their inflation to

---

* A hard currency is readily exchangeable for any other currency in the world.

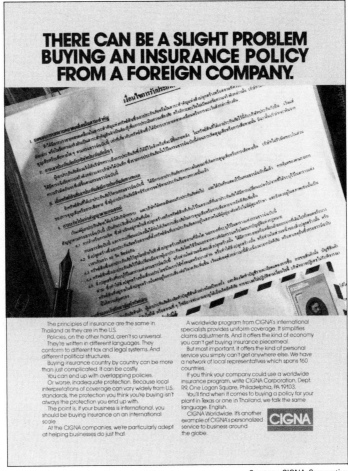

Courtesy CIGNA Corporation

escalate. They have used several devices to discourage the inflow of foreign money. Among these devices are low interest rates and even a negative interest rate on some kinds of deposits. Limitations have been placed on the sale to foreigners of bonds denominated in Swiss francs.

Miscellaneous Laws

Individuals working abroad must be alert to avoid falling afoul of local laws and of corrupt police, army, or government officials. Some examples may serve to make the point.

A Plessey employee, a British subject, is serving a life sentence in Libya for "jeopardizing the revolution by giving information to a foreign company." In the summer of 1986, two Australians were executed in Malaysia for possession of 15 grams or more of hard drugs. Saudi Arabia and other Muslim countries strictly enforce sanctions against importing or drinking alcohol or wearing revealing clothing. Foreigners in Japan who walk out of their homes without their alien registration card can be arrested, as was one man caught without his card while he was carrying out the garbage. In Thailand, you can be jailed for mutilating paper money or for damaging coins that bear the picture or image of the royal prince, as was one foreigner who stopped a rolling coin with his foot. Neither *Playboy* nor *Penthouse* can be brought into Singapore.

INTERNATIONAL FORCES

Contract Enforcement

Increasingly, businesses find themselves contracting with governments or government-owned companies. This is a common occurrence now; in communist countries, all commercial activities of any importance are conducted by government agencies. To buy from or sell to such countries, one must contract with those agencies only. The same is true of many LDCs, and there are numerous government-owned companies in Western Europe. Contract enforcement problems of different natures can arise when one of the contract parties is a government.

A communist government.   An example involving a communist country arose in 1977, when Rolimpex, the Polish state export agency, reneged on a contract it had made in 1974 to sell and deliver sugar to a British company. By 1977, sugar prices were much higher than they had been in 1974, and Poland faced a sugar shortage due to bad harvests. The British company sued Rolimpex in an English court, where Rolimpex lawyers argued that the Polish government had forbidden Rolimpex to perform the contract, which constituted "government intervention beyond seller's control." The lawyers of the British company countered that in a communist country, the government is the sole seller of goods, so Rolimpex and the Polish state should be considered identical. They argued that to forbid yourself to perform a contract is not a legal defense when you breach it by nonperformance.

   The British trial court found for Rolimpex. There has been considerable discussion of the possible long-term damage that the court's decision may do Poland if potential foreign contract parties refuse to do business with Polish agencies or charge higher prices because of the risk that the Polish contract party, always a government agency, can breach the contract with impunity.

sovereign immunity government is sovereign—it has power—over the area and people under its control; an extension of that power is the government's immunity to being sued unless it consents to be sued

An LDC government.   An LDC that has used the **sovereign immunity** defense is Nigeria. In 1975, Nigeria ordered far too much cement from international suppliers and then tried to cancel as many contracts as possible. When Nigeria was sued by the suppliers, it argued that as a government it could not be sued. The lawsuits were settled before a court decided the legality of Nigeria's argument.

Other international contract problems.   Even if governments are not parties to international contacts, problems of jurisdiction, interpretation, and enforcement arise. When the two contracting parties are in one country, the courts of that country have jurisdiction, interpretation is under that country's laws, and a court judgment can be enforced through the procedures of that country. When residents of two or more countries contract, those easy answers are not available.

   It is to the credit of international business, including government agencies doing business, that world trade goes smoothly as a rule and has grown tremendously in volume.

World trade grew at an average annual rate of 8.5 percent from 1963 to 1973 and 4.25 percent from 1973 to 1979. In 1980, the dollar value of world trade reached a peak of $2 trillion.[19] World trade fell more than 11 percent during the recession-hit years between 1980 and 1983 and was down to about $1.666 trillion in 1983. Trade activity then began to expand again, reaching $1.763 trillion in 1984 and $1.785 trillion in 1985, for a two-year gain exceeding 7 percent. The growth continued, reaching $2.4 trillion in 1987, and growth for 1988 is estimated to have been about 4.3 percent.[20]

The point we mean to make is that although recession may temporarily depress trade, the growth of trade over many years and the resumption of that growth after recession give evidence that most international contracts are performed fairly satisfactorily in spite of legal uncertainties.

Solutions to Jurisdiction, Interpretation, and Enforcement Problems

Devices used in attempts to solve the jurisdiction, interpretation, and enforcement problems in international contracts include contractual clauses agreeing (1) what law shall be applicable (for example, the law of France or the law of New York) in the interpretation of such contracts; (2) which language (where two or more are involved) shall govern ambiguities or contradictions of translations; (3) to submit to the jurisdiction of a specified court (for example, that of the Canton of Geneva or that of the Argentine court in Buenos Aires); and, increasingly popular, (4) to submit to arbitration (for example, by the International Chamber of Commerce in Paris or by an arbitration panel in London, where many international grain contract disputes are settled).

arbitration parties to disputes agree not to sue each other in a court but rather to appoint—or have appointed by a neutral person—an arbitrator to hear both sides and make a decision by which both parties agree to be bound

Among the advantages of **arbitration** as compared to court proceedings are speed and informality. The courts in many countries have backlogs of cases, and it can be months or years between the time a lawsuit is filed and the time it comes to trial. In business, such delays and their accompanying uncertainties are expensive. The courts of all countries have numerous formalities and procedures that have been built up over the years, and these can make it slow, difficult, or impossible to introduce evidence that the parties feel relevant and important.

Arbitration can solve both problems. The parties can choose their arbitrators and get into arbitration immediately. In addition, arbitrators are not bound by court procedures. They can admit and consider any evidence they believe relevant and important. A further advantage of arbitration is that the parties can waive any right to appeal from the arbitrators' award, whereas in court the loser in the first court to hear the case can almost always appeal to a higher court. Appellate procedures can consume further months or years, thus extending the uncertainties as to final results. As we have said, uncertainties are costly to business.

Arbitration by the International Chamber of Commerce was mentioned. It should be added that the American Arbitration Association and arbitral groups in Switzerland are frequently used to arbitrate international contract disputes.

Enforcement of foreign arbitration awards can pose problems. An attempted solution is the UN Convention on the Recognition and Enforcement of Foreign Arbitral Awards. The United States has adhered to this convention, and adherence binds a nation to compel arbitration when the parties have so agreed and to enforce awards.[21]

In instances where the contract in dispute involves investment in a country from abroad, another arbitration tribunal is available. This is the International Center for Settlement of Investment Disputes, sponsored by the World Bank. Investors were encouraged in 1986 when Indonesia proved willing to abide by a decision of the center even though an adverse opinion could have cost the country several million dollars.

On January 1, 1988, a new body of law governing contracts for the international sale of goods between merchants came into effect for the 11 countries, including the United States, that had ratified the UN Convention on the International Sale of Goods. It has been estimated that as many as 40 countries will sign on in the near future; and from the beginning, such important American sales partners as France, Italy, the People's Republic of China, and Egypt have ratified. The new code is an attempt to create a single body of sales law.[22]

Other organizations are working toward a worldwide business law. The Incoterms of the International Chamber of Commerce and its Uniform Rules and Practice on Documentary Credits now enjoy almost universal acceptance. The UN Commission on International Trade Law and the International Institute for the Unification of Private Law are doing much useful work. The Hague-Vishy Rules on Bills of Lading sponsored by the International Law Association have been adopted by a number of countries.[23]

Patents, Trademarks, Trade Names, Copyrights, and Trade Secrets

A patent is a government grant to the inventor of a product or process of the exclusive right of manufacturing, exploiting, using, and selling the invention or process. Trademarks and trade names are designs and names, often officially registered, by which merchants or manufacturers designate and differentiate their products. Copyrights are exclusive legal rights of authors, composers, playwrights, artists, and publishers to publish and dispose of their works. Trade secrets are any information that a business wishes to hold confidential.

Trade secrets can be of great value, but each country deals with and protects them in its own fashion. The duration of protection differs, as do the products that may or may not be protected. Some countries permit the production process to be protected but not the product. Therefore, international business must study and comply with the laws of each country where it might want to manufacture, create, or sell a product.

Patents.   In the field of patents, some degree of standardization is provided by the International Convention for the Protection of Industrial Property, sometimes referred to as the Paris Union. Some 90 countries, including the major industrial nations, have adhered to this convention.

Most Latin American nations and the United States are members of the Inter-American Convention. The protection it provides is similar to that afforded by the Paris Union.

A major step toward the harmonization of patent treatment is the European Patent Organization (EPO). Members are the EC countries plus Austria, Sweden, and Switzerland. Through EPO, an applicant for a patent need file only one application in English, French, or German to be granted patent protection in all member-countries. Prior to EPO, an applicant had to file in each country in the language of that country. This is still necessary in every country that is not a member of EPO.

At the UN, representatives of the developing nations have been mounting attacks on the exclusivity and length of patent protection. They want to shorten the protection periods from the current 15 to 20 years down to 5 years or even 30 months. The companies in the industrialized countries, which are responsible for the new technology eligible for patents, are resisting the changes. They point out that the only incentives they have to spend the huge amounts required to develop the technology are periods of patent protection long enough to recoup their costs and make profits.[24]

Trademarks.   Trademark protection varies from country to country, as does its duration, which may last from 10 to 20 years. Such protection is covered by the Madrid Agreement of 1891 for most of the world, though there is also the General American Convention for Trademark and Commercial Protection for the Western Hemisphere. In addition, protection may be provided on a bilateral basis in friendship, commerce, and navigation treaties.

An important step in harmonizing the rules on trademarks was taken in 1988 when regulations for a European Community trademark were drafted. A single European Trade Mark Office will be responsible for the recognition and protection of proprietary marks in all EC countries—including trademarks belonging to companies based in non-EC member-countries.

Trade names.   Trade names are protected in all countries adhering to the Industrial Property Convention, which was mentioned above in connection with patents. Goods bearing illegal trademarks or trade names or false statements on their origin are subject to seizure at importation into these countries.

> Two thirds of Kenya's 1979 coffee crop was lost after treatment with a worthless powder packaged to look like an effective, popular fungicide. More than 357 heart pumps were recalled from U.S. hospitals in 1978 because it was feared that some of the $20,000 devices contained bogus parts imported at $8 each.

Goods counterfeiting was once confined to such items as designer jeans, jewelry, tape recordings, and sporting goods. As the above examples indicate, commercial counterfeiting has now reached a point where it jeopardizes the health and safety of consumers, not just their pocketbooks.[25]

Copyrights.   Copyrights get protection under the Berne Convention of 1886, which is adhered to by 55 countries, and the Universal Copyright Convention of 1954, which has been adopted by some 50 countries. The United States did not ratify the Berne Convention until 1988, by which time it was driven to do so by the need for greater protection against pirating of computer software.

Trade secrets.   Trade secrets are protected by laws in most nations. Employers everywhere use employee secrecy agreements, which in some countries are rigorously enforced.*

Industrial espionage among companies that develop and use high technology is not unusual, but 1983 saw the end of an extraordinary example of

---

industrial espionage the effort of one company to steal another company's trade secrets by, for example, attempting to bribe an employee, eavesdropping electronically on internal communications, or hacking into the target company's computer data

---

* Remember the unfortunate Mr. Adams, who was imprisoned by the Swiss for giving Hoffman-LaRoche secrets to the EC, and the even more unfortunate Mrs. Adams, who committed suicide after being told that her husband would be in prison 20 years.

Cheap copies of a Cartier Vermeil watch—more than 4,000 of them—are destroyed by a 12-ton roller

Courtesy Larry Besselp/Los Angeles Times

corporate warfare between two of the world's mightiest and most technologically advanced corporations. Hitachi tried to obtain trade secrets of IBM, and in June 1982, two Hitachi employees were arrested by the FBI. IBM and the FBI had cooperated in what *Fortune* called a "superbly executed sting." In February 1983, Hitachi and two of its employees pleaded guilty to an indictment of conspiring to transport stolen IBM property from the United States to Japan.

Costly intellectual property rip-offs.   Patents, trademarks, trade names, copyrights, and trade secrets are collectively referred to as intellectual property, and the U.S. International Trade Commission says unauthorized use abroad of American-owned intellectual property costs the United States more than $40 billion a year. That is the amount of lost exports, domestic sales, and royalties.

U.S. industry and the government are trying to combat this. Among other means, several companies have gathered evidence of pirating in countries that have laws against such activities but whose police are unwilling or unable to actively enforce them. On being presented with evidence of illegal practices, they have no excuse not to do their duty.

The government is using bilateral aid and trade pressures to push other countries—including Japan, Taiwan, South Korea, Thailand, and Indonesia—to pass and enforce intellectual property protection laws.

The U.S. government is also trying to have GATT's Uruguay Round deal effectively with intellectual property piracy. It is having some success, but strong opposition is being led by Brazil and India.[26]

INTERNATIONAL STANDARDIZING FORCES

Several international standardizing forces have already been discussed. In the tax area, there are tax conventions (treaties) among nations. Each country tries to make each such treaty as nearly as possible like the others, so that patterns and common provisions may be found among them.

In antitrust, the EC member-countries operate under Articles 85 and 86 of the Treaty of Rome. In an unusual bilateral move, West Germany and the United States signed an executive agreement on antitrust cooperation. This was the first attempt by national governments to cooperate on antitrust matters concerning firms operating in both countries.

In the field of commercial contract arbitration, we mentioned the UN Convention. If the disputed contract involves investment from one country into another, it can be submitted for arbitration by the International Center for Settlement of Investment Disputes at the World Bank and, in 1988, the UN Convention on the International Sale of Goods came into effect.

Several international patent and other agreements were pointed out. Chapter 4 covered a number of UN-related organizations and other worldwide associations. Each of them has some harmonizing or standardizing effect. The same can be said of the regional international groupings and organizations dealt with in Chapter 4.

Two standardizing organizations that American industry will ignore at its peril are the International Organization for Standardization (IOS) and the International Electrotechnical Commission (IEC). The IEC promotes standardization of measurement, materials, and equipment in almost every sphere of electrotechnology. The IOS recommends standards in other fields of technology. Most government and private procurement around the world demands products that meet IEC or IOS specifications, and therein lies the danger for American companies. All IEC and IOS measurements are in the metric system, which has not been adopted in the United States, thereby imposing an additional burden on American firms trying to export American-made products.

U.S. LAWS THAT AFFECT THE INTERNATIONAL BUSINESS OF U.S. FIRMS

Although every law relating to business arguably has some effect on international activities, some laws warrant special notice. We will look briefly at U.S. antitrust and taxation laws, the Foreign Corrupt Practices Act, and the antiboycott act.

Antitrust

Earlier in this chapter, we mentioned the hostility aroused among foreign governments by the aggressive enforcement abroad of U.S. antitrust laws.

The laws impede U.S. exports.   An aspect of U.S. antitrust that impedes exports is the rules preventing American companies from teaming up to bid on major products abroad. For example, General Electric and Westinghouse had to compete against each other for pieces of the $450 million Brazilian Itaipu

Dam generator and turbine contracts. The contracts went to a huge European group led by Siemens of Germany and Brown Boveri of Switzerland. The European governments actively supported their companies. The U.S. government, however, would not let GE and Westinghouse cooperate and did nothing to support their efforts.[27]

Such restrictions on cooperation abroad were cited as the worst obstacle to exports caused by the U.S. antitrust regulations and enforcement procedures in a study by the National Association of Manufacturers (NAM). About 70 percent of the over 100 companies that responded to the NAM questionnaire said U.S. antitrust laws and practices caused a decline in their international competitiveness.

Export trading companies (ETCs).   In October 1982, the Export Trading Company Act of 1982 was signed into law by President Reagan. The centerpiece of the ETC Act is its limitation of the applicability of antitrust law to foreign trade. There are many ambiguities in the act, but it does make some important changes in antitrust law.

Companies wishing to establish ETCs apply to the U.S. government for a certificate of antitrust immunity. The certificate safeguards the ETC from government prosecution—assuming the ETC performs as indicated in the certificate of application—but does not immunize the ETC against private party antitrust suits. However, any damages awarded in such suits are limited to actual damages rather than the treble damages awarded in other such private actions.*

The ETC Act also permits American banks to own shares of ETCs. Some of the larger banks are moving aggressively into the ETC field, offering financing and even countertrade† services to ETC shareholders. Smaller banks are feeling competitive pressures to get involved in ETCs for fear that larger banks will take their export company customers.[28]

Despite passage of the ETC Act, there is strong feeling both in and out of government that the antitrust laws constitute severe burdens on the ability of American companies to compete at home or abroad with foreign competitors. The late Malcolm Baldrige, secretary of commerce in the Reagan administration, made several points. The U.S. antitrust laws were largely written in the early 1900s, and they followed the economic theory of that time: "Big is bad; small is good." That theory was proper when other countries could not compete with America, and U.S. companies did not need to export to grow. But now, more than 70 years later, U.S. goods face severe competition, and the range and variety of that competition are increasing. The world economy has changed, trade patterns have changed, but the antitrust laws have not.

Baldrige and others would like Congress to repeal Section 7 of the Clayton Act, which prohibits mergers and acquisitions that *may* reduce competition or *tend* to create a monopoly. Baldrige made this comment on the italicized words: "No one can live in an environment where the antitrust enforcers try

---

* The possibility of treble damages against British Airways is one of the worries of the U.K. government because of the private antitrust action being brought against BA and other airlines by the Laker Airways liquidator.

† *Countertrade* is a generic term for the many methods of trading when the customer does not have enough hard currency to buy what it wants from other countries. This subject is discussed in Chapter 17.

to read your mind and then can arrest you for their idea of what you might be thinking."[29]

Taxation

As we have remarked, the U.S. tax system is considered by many to be the world's most complicated. That in itself makes doing business more complicated and, therefore, more expensive for a U.S. company than for companies based elsewhere. There is, however, one tax incentive for exports worthy of mention.

Export incentive.   In 1971, the U.S. Congress amended the Internal Revenue Code (IRC) to permit the Domestic International Sales Corporation (DISC) as an encouragement for American companies to export. This gave a tax break to companies that manufactured in the United States with American labor and exported the product.

It worked. The U.S. Treasury estimated that in the fiscal year ended June 30, 1976, DISC operations boosted U.S. exports to an amount some $2.9 billion higher than they would have been without DISCs.[30] In spite of that and in the face of continuing and growing U.S. BOP deficits, the Carter administration recommended abolishing the DISC.[31] U.S. labor unions favor its abolition on the basis that it favors big business, even though exports mean jobs. Congress did not abolish the DISC, but it did cut back the tax benefit originally provided.

The Tax Reform Act of 1984 largely replaced the DISC with the new Foreign Sales Corporation (FSC). From the point of view of exporters, a major advantage of the FSC over the DISC is that the tax exemption is permanent—there is no recapture of the benefit in future years if dividends are paid or if the FSC no longer satisfies qualification requirements. Another break given exporters by the 1984 law is permanent forgiveness of taxes deferred under DISC provisions.

national tax jurisdiction a tax system for expatriate citizens of a country whereby the country taxes them on the basis of nationality, even though they live and work abroad

Taxing Americans who work abroad.   Observing a so-called **national tax jurisdiction,** rather than a **territorial tax jurisdiction,** the United States is almost alone among countries in taxing its people according to nationality rather than on the basis of where they live and work. As a result, Americans living or working in another country must pay taxes there and to the United States. In addition to higher tax payments, this requires the time and expense of completing two sets of complicated tax returns. In 1981, the sections of the IRC dealing with this subject were again amended. Although the burden of completing two tax returns was not lifted, the new law gave relief, starting in 1982, in the amount of American taxes to be paid by exempting the first $85,000 of earned income.*

territorial tax jurisdiction expatriate citizens who neither live nor work in the country—and therefore receive none of the services for which taxes pay—are exempt from the country's taxes

When American taxes are anti-American.   Suppose an American multinational wants to open a new factory, store, warehouse, or office building in the United States. That would create new jobs for Americans, along with all the benefits that flow from new jobs.

---

* Earned income includes salaries, bonuses, and commissions. Interest, dividend, and royalty income is called unearned income.

But when the company's executives look at the new U.S. tax law, they hesitate because of the section dealing with allocation of interest expense. When an American company with subsidiaries in many countries borrows money to finance a U.S. business, the interest is treated as if it were paid in part to finance foreign operations. That results in a partial loss of the tax deduction and, thus, higher after-tax interest cost.

Foreign companies—including foreign-based multinationals—have no such requirement and can deduct 100 percent of interest on borrowings to finance a U.S. operation. Therefore, they have lower after-tax interest costs and, to that extent, can be more competitive in the United States than many U.S. companies.

Foreign Corrupt Practices Act (FCPA)

questionable or dubious payments bribes paid to government officials by companies seeking purchase contracts from those governments

During the 1970s, revelations of **questionable or dubious payments** by American companies to foreign officials rocked governments in the Netherlands and Japan. Congress considered corporate bribery "bad business" and "unnecessary," and President Carter found it "ethically repugnant." As a result, the Foreign Corrupt Practices Act (FCPA) was passed and signed.

Uncertainties.   There were a number of uncertainties about terms used in the FCPA. An interesting one involves *grease.* According to the FCPAs drafters, the act does not outlaw grease, or facilitating payments made solely to expedite nondiscretionary official actions. Such actions as customs clearance or transatlantic telephone calls have been cited. There is no clear distinction between supposedly legal grease payments and illegal bribes. To confuse matters further, U.S. Justice Department officials have suggested that they may prosecute some grease payments anyway under earlier antibribery laws that were written to get at corruption in the United States.[32]

Other doubts raised by the FCPA concerned the accounting standards it requires for compliance. That matter is connected to questions about how far management must go to learn whether any employees, subsidiaries, or agents may have violated the act; even if management were unaware of an illegal payment, it could be in violation if it "had reason to know" that some portion of a payment abroad might by used as a bribe.[33]

*Other countries' reactions to bribes.**   Attitudes of business and government officials in Europe toward the FCPA range from amusement to incredulity, and no other government has taken a position similar to that represented by the FCPA—quite the opposite.[34] West Germany tax collectors, for example, permit resident companies to deduct foreign bribes, which are called *sounderpesen,* or special expenses. In Britain, corrupt payments, even to British government officials, qualify for tax deductions. Even the government-owned British Leyland (BL) was found to have been paying bribes overseas to obtain orders for its Range Rovers.

> One comical aspect of the BL story was that its factories were unable to produce enough Rover vehicles to meet the very large demand for them in the export market. The bribes for new orders were being paid at a time when BL already had more orders than it could fill.

* Other words with similar connotations are *dash, squeeze, mordida, cumshaw,* and *baksheesh.* Bribes and questionable payments were mentioned in connection with sociocultural forces in Chapter 9.

Another interesting, and possibly embarrassing, facet of the BL story is that it was published in British newspapers only two weeks after the British prime minister, James Callaghan, had promised to eliminate "irregular practices and improper conduct" in international business. The promise was made to President Carter, who wanted other countries to cooperate with the United States in stopping such practices and conduct.

Just how pervasive these practices are was disclosed by Lloyd N. Cutler, a Washington attorney who did a study of the subject for the Northrop Corporation. Cutler was quoted as saying, "Almost all European and Japanese export sales of the type that generate corrupt payments are arranged with government export financing or other government support."[35] So far, no other industrialized nation has a law resembling the FCPA, and an anticommercial bribery treaty proposed by the United States is languishing in an inactive committee of the United Nations.

In 1985, Dancare Corporation, a Danish company, got in trouble because of $730,000 in bribes that it had paid to Saudi Arabia. The trouble was not that it had paid the bribes, but that the bribes were not clearly indicated as such in the company's tax records. The Danish tax chief now advises Danish firms to book illicit payments openly under "bribes." Whether the bribes are in the form of cash, sexual favors, or luxury goods doesn't matter, as long as their value is noted on the tax records. Receipts are desirable but not essential.[36]

Bribes paid in Denmark are illegal; bribes paid abroad to secure export business are both legal and a tax-deductible expense. In the contest for the Saudi Arabian business, the Dancare Corporation bid was more than $730,000 above potential American competitors. Of course, they would have been in violation of the FCPA if they paid a bribe to get the contract and certainly would have been unable to deduct the payment from American taxes.

Is America losing?   Is the FCPA causing American exporters to lose business? Yes, answer a number of companies, several of which are in the construction business. The United States, which in 1976 ranked first in the overseas construction market, dropped to fifth in 1987, falling behind Japan, Korea, West Germany, and Italy.

A White House task force on export disincentives studied the FCPA, among other disincentives. Its estimate of exports lost to American business as a result of the FCPA is $1 billion per year.[37]

The view that the FCPA is causing American companies to lose export business is not unanimous. In 1976, the Securities and Exchange Commission (SEC) forecast that cessation of the payment of foreign bribes would not seriously affect the ability of American business to compete in world markets.[38]

A study made by Professor Richman in 1977–78 indicated that it was unwise and unsound, on both ethical and economic grounds, for U.S. corporations to engage in questionable foreign payments and practices. Professor Richman's study covered 65 U.S. corporations and agreed with the SEC conclusions.[39]

The consensus now is that America's unilateral approach to payoffs is very costly in terms of export business lost to foreign competitors. They can pay to get it.

Billions lost overseas.   There are estimates of losses in the billions of dollars. Critics have cited the ambiguities in the FCPA as one of the possible causes of

U.S. business foregoing legitimate overseas opportunities. It cannot operate comfortably in an environment in which management is unsure of the FCPA's interpretation and application.

In response to the negative feedback about the FCPA's effect, the General Accounting Office completed a survey in 1981. It randomly selected 250 companies from Fortune's list of the 1,000 largest industrial firms. About one third of the respondents stated they had lost overseas business as a result of the FCPA. Over 60 percent were of the opinion that, all other things being equal, U.S. multinationals could not profitably compete against foreign companies that could legally bribe to make sales.[40]

Antiboycott Law

As a part of the hostility and wars between the Arab countries and Israel, several of the Arab countries boycott foreign companies that do business with Israel. They will not buy from such companies. Inasmuch as several Arab countries are extremely rich oil producers, they are very large potential markets from which sellers do not like to be excluded. In 1977, however, the United States passed an act forbidding American companies to comply with any Arab boycott law or regulation.

Contrast American and British attitudes.   As in the case of the FCPA, no other country has any such antiboycott law. A British House of Lords select committee studying similar legislation for Britain found 2.7 billion reasons to bury it in 1978. During 1977, British exports to Arab markets totaled £2.7 billion.[41]

Action under the antiboycott law.   Some complained that the antiboycott law was laxly enforced in the early years of its existence; fines ran around $500 to $600 for each violation. Then, in 1982, the Department of Commerce, which enforces the law, became more aggressive; more companies were charged with boycott-related offenses, and the fines imposed were in larger amounts.[42] The largest so far is a $995,000 fine levied against Safeway Stores. As the Department of Commerce continued to tighten enforcement, it collected $1.4 million in fines in 1984, up from $520,000 the previous year; in 1988 it levied fines of $3.9 million.[43]

The regulations that implement the antiboycott legislation forbid response to any Arab question or questionnaire that deals with Israel. As a condition of bidding on a contract with an Arab country, your company may be asked whether any components to be supplied under the proposed contract will be sourced in Israel. Even though your company has no Israeli suppliers and no intentions of using any, it would be in violation of the antiboycott law and regulations to so inform the Arab country.

Are export contracts being lost?   Is the antiboycott law causing American exporters to lose business? Yes, according to Chase Manhattan Bank, especially in the relatively hard-line Arab countries, such as Iraq, Libya, and Syria. Even in other Arab countries friendlier to the United States, the law causes difficulties and burdens not faced or borne by non-American competitors.[44] Commenting on the law and the government's tough enforcement of it, Philip Hinson, Middle East affairs director of the U.S. Chamber of Commerce, says, "They've had a randomly harmful effect on U.S. exports."

Another complaint by American companies about the law is the cost of compliance. Joseph Komalick, editor of the *Boycott Law Bulletin*, says that some U.S. multinationals have as many as 20 lawyers check the legality of Middle East contracts to make sure they don't violate the law.[45]

One argument against the boycott legislation is that it hurts American business but does no harm to the Arab countries. They can buy whatever they want—or adequate substitutes—from Europe or Japan.[46]

1988 Trade Law

Frustrated by years of presidential unwillingness to identify countries that maintain "unfair" trade policies, Congress passed new trade legislation that it thought would force the administration to take a hard line against U.S. trade partners. Harold B. Malmgren, a former Democratic trade official, calls the law a "Frankenstein monster" that will only tie U.S. trade policy in knots, divert attention from GATT and other international trade talks, and make policymaking more difficult.

Bush administration officials fear that the only exports created by the 1988 law will be red tape. It requires voluminous reports to Congress from the administration on short deadlines, plus time-consuming testimony to congressional committees by administration officials—notably by Carla A. Hills, the U.S. trade representative. One trade official said, "These days we're spending more time negotiating with Congress than with other countries."[47]

Some Laws and Agencies Aid U.S. Exports and Investment

We do not mean to give the impression that all U.S. laws and government agencies pose obstacles to the international business of U.S. companies. The U.S. Department of Commerce actively encourages exports by American companies. U.S. embassies and consular offices can be helpful with information and introductions for Americans who wish to export to or invest in foreign countries. The FSC provides some tax incentives for U.S. exporters.

COMMON LAW OR CIVIL LAW?

Historically, there has been a clear distinction between common law, which developed in England and spread to the English colonies, and civil law, which originated on the continent of Europe. Courts made common law as they decided individual cases; civil law was made by kings, princes, or legislatures issuing decrees or passing bills.

As time has passed, legislatures and government agencies in the United States have made more and more laws and regulations. The courts, in turn, have interpreted these laws and regulations as parties have argued about what they mean. That is the sort of procedure one finds in Europe, but vast differences in practices have developed that have less to do with the traditional common–civil law approaches than with historic government–citizen (or subject) relationships and attitudes.

European Practice

Europe has a history of thousands of years of tyranny, which recently has been covered with a veneer of democracy. People have greater reason to fear their governments in Europe than in the United States, and government service has more prestige. Before a new law is presented to the legislature (which, unlike

WORLDVIEW
European Parliament, U.S. Congress Compared

Palais de l'Europe in Strasborg   Courtesy Photri

Capitol of the United States   Courtesy Photri

European Parliament

Legislative roles. Advisory, and may amend commission proposals before their consideration by the council. Approves budget.

Relation to executive. Reacts to specific commission proposals, but provides public forum for EC issues. Can remove entire commission but not replace it. Can force some changes in budget. Questions commissioners in plenary.

Election, chambers, sessions. Elected for five-year term by direct vote, but under national electoral laws. Single chamber meets one week in plenary, two weeks in committee, and one week in political groups each month.

Jurisdictions. Community laws, regulations, and budget (in part), which cover areas defined by the Treaty of Rome creating the EC. Defense excluded.

U.S. Congress

Legislative roles. Exclusive authority to introduce legislation. Two houses consider, amend, and move draft laws to the other for final vote: bills passed proceed to president for action.

Relation to executive. Legislative coresponsibility. Consents to treaties and appointments (Senate). Has own investigative and budget arms to check on executive. Committees both authorize and allot funds and oversee expenditure. Questions executive officials in committee.

Election, chambers, sessions. Two chambers: House elected for two years by equal populations districts; Senate elected for six years by states; generally equal roles in legislation. House and Senate together set a calendar of sessions, which average 180–200 days a year.

Jurisdictions. Entire federal structure, which, under the Constitution, extends to almost every aspect of country except local and state taxing, police, and education functions.

European Parliament

Staffs. Entrance exam into civil service for secretarial; free hire for political groups. Very small personal staff.

Committee structure. *Substantive* (12): Political Affairs; Agriculture; Economics & Monetary; Energy, Research & Technology; External Economic Relations; Social Affairs & Unemployment; Regional Policy & Planning; Transport; Environment, Public Health & Consumer Protection; Youth, Culture, Education, Information & Sport; Development & Cooperation. *Budgetary:* Budget; Budgetary Control. *Institutional:* Rules of Procedure & Petitions; Verification of Credentials; Institutional Affairs.

Leadership. President and 12 vice presidents represent national and party balance in plenary vote; they form Bureau for general direction of Parliament. Seven political group chairmen are added to form Enlarged Bureau, which handles most important matters involving political management. Five questors serve as ombudsmen for many administrative matters. Rapporteurs, selected by committee members, draft and defend reports. Committee chairmen function as

Role of parties. Committee assignments, chairmenships, and interparliamentary delegations determined by relative size of each of seven political groups. Discipline varies depending on ideological breadth of groups, but generally is much greater than in U.S. Congress. Group chairmen elected for one half of five-year term of Parliament but may be reelected. Parties tried to run Community-wide electoral campaigns in first direct election in 1979, with varying success. Most members elected on party-list system, which requires them to keep active role in national parties.

U.S. Congress

Staffs. Generally meritocratic entrance to committee staff. Political appointment for some housekeeping jobs. Large personal staffs.

Committee structure. *Substantive* (17) (House used as example, but Senate is similar): Agriculture; Armed Services; Banking, Finance & Urban Affairs; Education & Labor; Energy & Commerce; Foreign Affairs, Intelligence; Interior & Insular Affairs; Judiciary; Merchant Marine & Fisheries; Post Office & Civil Service; Public Works & Transportation; Science & Technology; Small Business; Veterans; Ways & Means. *Budgetary:* Appropriations; Budget. *Institutional:* Administration; Rules; Standards of Conduct. *Investigative:* Government Operations.

Leadership. *House:* Speaker elected by majority party and speaks for it, but his function, partly, is to represent House in broad nonpartisan way; majority and minority parties each name leader and whip. These five form leadership for the management of 435-member House. *Senate:* Vice president is constitutionally presiding officer, but this is largely a ceremonial function; majority and minority leaders, and their whips, manage 100-member Senate on collegial basis. *Both:* Committee chairmen and (in last decade) subcommmittee chairmen play major role in writing legislation and managing it on floor.

Role of parties. Only two major parties. Decisions taken by each house on organization generally follow party votes. Substantive issues bring more diversity, although speaker and president can have effects in organizing party positions. National parties very weak and have have almost no effects on Congress, which runs own campaign committees, by party, in each house. No effective means of disciplining errant members. Committee assignments and chairmanships depend on party caucus votes. Seniority plays presumptive role in these votes.

legislatures in the United States, is always controlled by the same political party that controls the executive branch), consensus is achieved among most of the people, businesses, and government agencies that will be affected.

In contrast to American practices, European legislation is rarely amended, and regulations are rarely revised. Courts are not as often asked to give their interpretations, and if they are, the decisions are rarely appealed. Once a consensus has been reached, it is considered very bad form to open the subject again, and those who do may find themselves left out of the consultations the next time around.

American Practice

In contrast to European custom, Americans have a weaker tradition of obeying their governments and have had very little fear of them. Americans are much more likely than Europeans to challenge laws in the courts, in the streets, or by disobedience. Legislation in America is a product of an ongoing adversarial proceeding, not of consensus; law is written by one independent branch of government for implementation by a second and for interpretation by yet a third. Different political parties or people with conflicting philosophies frequently control the three different branches of government.

Laws and regulations are constantly being amended or revised by the legislatures and the agencies. Courts interpret laws in ways that are sometimes surprising, and courts may strike laws down as being unconstitutional.

In the United States, the legislative body is now called Congress, and it convened as representatives of the several English colonies even before the United States become a country. In Europe, the legislative body of the European Community is called the European Parliament. It was brought into being by the Treaty of Rome, which was signed in 1957. The Worldview contains an interesting comparison of those two legislatures. Bear in mind that the European Parliament will probably gain power as a result of EC Project 1992, and this gain can be expected to continue.

SUMMARY

We have seen that taxes can have many purposes, and raising revenue for the government is only one of them. Other purposes are the encouragement of activities deemed desirable by the government and the discouragement of others. Taxes are used to redistribute income, to protect certain industries, and to accomplish many other goals.

Taxes differ greatly from country to country. Some countries have high taxes, others low or no taxes. Most countries have some sort of income tax, but many rely more on the value-added tax (VAT). Enforcement of tax laws is strict in the United States and some other countries but relatively lax elsewhere.

The United States has the most comprehensive antitrust laws, and it tries to apply and enforce them extraterritorially. Other countries resent what they perceive as intrusion into their sovereignty as the United States attempts to bring their citizens and companies under U.S. law for acts performed outside the United States. Other countries and the European Community have antitrust-type laws, which are frequently called restrictive trade practices laws, but none of them is as vigorously enforced as are the U.S. antitrust laws.

Nations try to protect or favor their own business by putting obstacles in the way of imports. The obstacles can be tariffs, quotas, packaging requirements, health requirements, or any of hundreds of other requirements that foreign goods must satisfy before they are permitted into the country.

Nations sometimes seize foreign-owned property. If they don't take 100 percent of the property, they may "domesticate" it by taking enough—for example, 51 percent ownership—to control it.

Executives of companies in Europe are discovering

that their companies—and even they personally—can be liable to workers or to the public if one of their products causes injury or death. The liability can be civil or criminal.

Price and wage control laws are found in most countries. As inflation continues, these laws can be expected to be expanded.

Labor laws exist everywhere and must be studied. They can greatly increase labor costs above the hourly wage paid to employees.

Although money (currency) flows relatively freely among the industrialized countries, they are the minority. Almost all LDCs and communist countries have currency control laws, and some of them enforce these laws very harshly.

Contracts between parties in different countries can cause problems that are not present when the parties to contracts are citizens of only one country, in situations where one of the parties fails to perform satisfactorily. However, many solutions have been found, such as agreements in the contracts as to applicable law or language or as to arbitrating differences before a named body, such as the International Chamber of Commerce.

Intellectual property, such as patents, is protected by a number of multinational conventions (treaties) and by bilateral treaties. The protection of trade secrets took a step forward in 1980, when the United States got the first criminal conviction under an industrial espionage law. Other countries enforce similar laws.

There is a growing complaint by American business that U.S. laws and their enforcement by the government are lessening the competitiveness of U.S. companies as compared to foreign companies. Cited are the antitrust and tax laws, the Foreign Corrupt Practices Act, and the antiboycott law.

QUESTIONS

1. What are some purposes of taxes other than to raise revenues?

2. Why do some people feel that a VAT should replace some or all of the U.S. income tax?

3. What is a national tax system?

4. What objections have other countries to extraterritorial application by the United States of its antitrust laws?

5. What was the chief legal argument made on behalf of OPEC in the antitrust suit against it by the IAM?

6. What are some advantages that arbitrating contract disputes may have as compared to using the courts?

7. Are tariffs the only type of obstacle to international trade? If not, name some others.

8. Can product liability be criminal? If so, in what sort of situations?

9. Why do most countries impose currency exchange controls?

10. How might the ETC Act limit U.S. antitrust activity abroad?

11. *a.* Does the Foreign Corrupt Practices Act forbid all bribes? Explain.

   b. Does the antiboycott law permit U.S. exporters to Arab countries to certify that the products are not of Israeli origin if that is true?

   c. Do countries such as Britain, France, Germany, and Japan, whose companies compete with American companies, have such laws as the FCPA and the antiboycott statute?

12. *a.* Comparing the United States with Western Europe, what are the differences in practices as to making, amending, and interpreting laws?

   b. What are the reasons for those differences?

MINICASE 11–1

American Law

Your company manufactures specialty motors in the United States. Business in the United States has been slack, and you have embarked on an export drive using facilities of the Department of Commerce as well as a private export sales agency.

You know that Saudi Arabia is an excellent potential market for your motors as it rapidly expands factories, ports, hospitals, and many other facilities. Therefore, you are delighted when your sales agency phones you one day to inform you that your motors are perfect for a new Saudi refinery for which procurement is beginning. The agent has the Saudi invitation to bid for the contract and is sending it by express to you today.

The invitation is received the next day. The agent was

right. Your motors precisely match the specifications, you know the competition, and you feel confident that you can win this big, market-entry order.

Accompanying the invitation is a questionnaire for new bidders for Saudi business. The questions are about your company—how long in business, the identity of its customers and suppliers, its financial strength, and the identity of its officers, directors, and major shareholders. The company is well established and has many satisfied customers and dependable suppliers, all in the United States. There is no single, dominant stockholder, and all of the directors and officers are experienced, reputable Americans.

Should the above facts alert you to any possible American law problems?

MINICASE 11–2

Italian Law

A California-based company is expanding very well and has just made its first export sale. All of its sales and procurement contracts up to now have contained a clause providing that if any disputes should arise under the contract, they would be settled under California law and that any litigation would be in California courts.

The new foreign customer, which is Italian, objects to these all-California solutions. It says it is buying and paying for your products, so Italian law and courts should govern and handle any disputes.

You are the CEO of the California company, and you very much want this order. You are pleased with the service your law firm has given, but you know it has no international experience. What sort of solutions would you suggest that your lawyers research as possible compromises between your usual all-Californian clause and the customer's wish to go all-Italian?

SUPPLEMENTARY READINGS

Aaron, Henry J., ed. *The Value-Added Tax: Lessons from Europe.* Washington, D.C.: Brookings Institution, 1981.

Cateora, Phillip R. *International Marketing.* 5th ed. Homewood, Ill: Richard D. Irwin, 1983, chap. 7.

Crosswick, Stanley A. "U.S. Protectionism as Seen from Europe," *Europe,* January/February 1986, pp. 8–10.

de Jantscher, Milka Casanegra, "Tax Havens Explained." In *Contemporary Perspectives in International Business,* ed. Harold W. Berkman and Ivan R. Vernon, Skokie, Ill.: Rand McNally, 1979, pp. 83–92.

Ernst & Young, ed. *Tax News International.* London: Quarterly.

_____. *Tax Reform around the World.* London: 1988.

"Foreign Patent Protection for Exporters." *Business American,* August 27, 1979, pp. 3–14.

Greanias, George C. *The FCPA: Anatomy of a Statute.*

Lexington, Mass.: Lexington Books, 1982.

Lewis, P. "Taxing Americans Abroad: New U.S. Tax Law May Affect Business in Europe." In *Contemporary Perspectives in International Business,* ed. Harold W. Berkman and Ivan R. Vernon. Skokie, Ill.: Rand McNally, 1979, pp. 77–82.

Pletka, Danielle. "Boycott Squeezes U.S. Firms, Israel," *Insight,* September 19, 1988, p. 44.

Robock, Stefan H., and Kenneth Simmonds. *International Business and Multinational Enterprises.* Homewood, Ill.: Richard D. Irwin, 1989, chaps. 8 and 12.

Root, Franklin R. *International Trade and Investment.* Cincinnati: South-Western Publishing, 1984, chaps. 8, 15, 23.

Schmitthoff, Clive M., and Chia-Jui Cheng, ed. *Select Essays on International Trade Law.* London: Martinus, Nijhoff, Graham & Trotman, 1988.

ENDNOTES

1. Dan Throop Smith, "Value-Added Tax: The Case For," *Harvard Business Review,* November–December 1970, pp. 77–85; and Stanley S. Surrey, "Value-Added Tax: The Case Against," *Harvard Business Review,* November–December 1970, pp. 86–94.

2. William Dawkins, "Brussels Fines 23 Chemical Groups for Fixing Prices," *Financial Times,* December 22, 1988, p. 1.

3. *The Economist,* February 17, 1979, pp. 58–59.

4. Raymond Hughes, law courts correspondent, "Partial Victory for Adams in Commission Case," *Financial Times of London,* July 12, 1985, p. 2.

5. *The Economist,* June 9, 1979, pp. 91–92.

6. *The Economist,* December 10, 1977, pp. 77–78.

7. *The Economist,* June 30, 1979, p. 80.

8. "France Issues Regulations on Language Requirements," *Commerce America*, June 6, 1977, p. 21.

9. Thomas G. Donlan, "Not So Free Trade: U.S. Preaches What It Doesn't Always Practice," *Barron's*, June 27, 1988, pp. 70–71.

10. "The American Car Industry's Own Goal," *The Economist*, February 6, 1988, p. 69. For a good discussion of protectionism, see Robert Z. Lawrence and Robert E. Litan, "Why Protectionism Doesn't Pay," *Harvard Business Review*, May–June 1987, pp. 60–67.

11. "Brazil: Even Components Must Be Brazilianized," *Business Week*, January 24, 1977, p. 34.

12. *The Economist*, July 30, 1977, pp. 64–65.

13. *Business International*, April 22, 1983, pp. 123–24.

14. "New Law Extends Company Responsibility," *Business Europe*, May 2, 1988, p. 7.

15. Michael Skapinker, "Why the Product Liability Plague Is No Longer Just a U.S. Malady," *International Management*, July 1986, pp. 27–34.

16. Carolyn Lochhead, "Strict Liability Causing Firms to Give up on Promising Ideas," *The Washington Times*, August 22, 1988, p. B5.

17. Steven P. Galante, "American Insurance Crisis Begins to Hurt European Firms with Operations Here," *The Wall Street Journal*, December 29, 1985, p. 12.

18. "New Corporate Liability Rules Raise Costs for Investors in India's Chemical Sector," *Business Asia*, September 19, 1988, p. 305.

19. *International Letter*, Federal Reserve Bank of Chicago, March 11, 1983.

20. "World Economic Survey," *IMF Survey*, July 25, 1988, pp. 250–51.

21. Cecilian E. Cosca and Joseph J. Zimmerer, "Judicial Interpretations of Foreign Arbitral Awards under the UN Convention," *Law and Policy in International Business*, Summer 1976, p. 737.

22. Lawrence W. Newman, "UN Sales Pact Will Simplify Contract Disputes," *Northeast International Business*, June 1988, p. 34.

23. A. H. Herman, "Growth in International Trade Law," *Financial Times*, March 30, 1989, p. 10.

24. "Pooh-Poohing Patent Protection," *Business International*, July 22, 1983, p. 228; and "At the UN, a Mounting War on Patents," *Backgrounder*, Heritage Foundation, October 4, 1982. For a good reading about different national approaches to patent protection, see Thomas J. Maronick, "European Patent Laws and Decisions. . . ," *International Marketing Review*, Summer 1988, pp. 31–40.

25. Karen Tumulty, "Witnesses Warn of Commercial Counterfeiting," *Los Angeles Times*, August 3, 1983, part 1, p. 1.

26. Eduardo Lachica, "Trade Thievery," *The Wall Street Journal*, March 16, 1989, pp. AL, 10.

27. *Business Week*, April 10, 1978, p. 60.

28. "Trading Company Act—I: A Look at What It Does in Antitrust Area," *Business International*, November 12, 1982, pp. 361–63; "Trading Company Act—II: Opening for Bankers Is Wide but Complex," *Business International*, November 26, 1982, pp. 379 and 382; "Trading Company Act—III: Allowable Scope of Action Poses Real Dilemmas for ETCs," *Business International*, December 17, 1982, pp. 401–3; "Trading Company Act—IV: Conflicting Interests and Goals Key Concerns of Banks, MNCs," *Business International*, December 31, 1982, pp. 409–11. For a look at perceived flaws in the ETC Act, see "Export Trading Companies: Current Legislation, Regulation, and Commercial Bank Involvement," *Columbia Journal of World Business*, Winter 1981, pp. 42–47; and "Drawback Seen in Liberal Export Trading Company Regs from FRB," *Peat, Marwick Executive Newsletter*, June 16, 1983, p. 4.

29. Malcolm Baldrige, "Rx for Export Woes: Antitrust Relief," *The Wall Street Journal*, October 15, 1985, p. 32.

30. *The Wall Street Journal*, April 14, 1978, p. 14.

31. Ibid.

32. John S. Estey and David W. Marston, "Pitfalls (and Loopholes) in the Foreign Bribery Law," *Fortune*, October 9, 1978, pp. 182–88.

33. Barbara Crutchfield George and Mary Jane Dundas, "Responsibilities of Domestic Corporate Management under the Foreign Corrupt Practices Act," *Syracuse Law Review* 31, no. 4, 1980, pp. 866–905; and "Some Guidelines on Dealing with Graft," *Business International*, February 25, 1983, p. 62.

34. Wendell H. McCulloch, Jr., interviews conducted in Europe during July and August 1979.

35. Jerry Landauer, "Proposed Treaty against Business Bribes Gets Poor Reception Overseas, U.S. Finds," *The Wall Street Journal*, March 28, 1977, p. 26.

36. *The Wall Street Journal*, October 31, 1985, p. 32.

37. *International Herald Tribune*, August 3, 1979, p. 11.

38. Report of the Securities and Exchange Commission on Questionable and Illegal Corporate Payments and Practices, May 1976.

39. Barry Richman, "Can We Prevent Questionable Foreign Payments?" *Business Horizons*, June 1979, pp. 14–19.

40. Barbara Crutchfield George, "The U.S. Foreign Corrupt Practices Act: The Price Business Is Paying for the Unilateral Criminalization of Bribery," *International Journal of Management*, September 1987, pp. 391–402.

41. *The Economist*, September 2, 1978, p. 101.

42. Laurie McGinley, "Boycott Law Enforcement Is Toughened," *The Wall Street Journal*, December 9, 1982, p. 33.

43. Victor Mallet, "Dodging the Arab Blacklist," *Financial Times*, July 27, 1989, p. 15.

44. *The Wall Street Journal*, April 3, 1978, p. 6.

45. Eduardo Lochia, "U.S. Law Successfully Blocks Arab Bid to Keep American, Israeli Firms Apart," *The Wall Street Journal*, July 14, 1984, p. 28.

46. David Ignatius, "Catch 22: Trading with Iraq," *The Wall Street Journal*, March 25, 1982, p. 22.

47. Art Pino, "New Trade Law Has the Makings of a Monster," *Los Angeles Times*, March 26, 1989, pp. 1, 1G.

Chapter 12
Labor Forces

Moves of unions to join a board of directors offer little to American unions. We do not want to blur in any way the distinctions between the respective roles of management and labor in the plant. If unions were to become a partner in management, they would be most likely the junior partner in success and the senior partner in failure.

> Thomas R. Donahue, executive assistant to the president, AFL–CIO

To stay competitive, U.S. manufacturers must redesign their products to be assembled by robots that act like machines, not humans.

> *Technology Review*

LEARNING OBJECTIVES

In this chapter, you will study:

1. Forces beyond management control that affect the availability of labor.

2. Political or economic repression, which causes people to flee. As many leave as can get out, regardless of age, skills, gender, or state of health.

3. Why refugees are a source of labor yet a burden for the countries to which they flee.

4. Guest workers, who go to countries to fill specific jobs for which they have the requisite skills.

5. The composition of a nation's labor force, which affects productivity.

6. Other forces that affect productivity.

7. Why a foreign employer's failure to take into account the social status, gender, race, traditional society, or minorities attitudes of the host country can be costly.

8. How labor union strengths and philosophies differ mightily from area to area.

9. Why labor is getting a voice in management in important parts of the industrial world.

KEY WORDS AND CONCEPTS

- Labor quality
- Labor quantity
- Labor mobility
- Labor force composition
- Labor productivity
- Unit labor cost
- Traditional society
- Minorities
- Labor market
- Labor unions
- Codetermination

BUSINESS INCIDENT

"Responsibility follows power" is a law of politics. If it is disregarded—as it was by the union members on the board of Volkswagen, who delayed the company's plan to build a plant in the United States because it would have meant "exporting German workers' jobs"—the result is serious damage. In V W's case, the share of the American automobile market fell from 8 percent in 1969 to less than 1 percent now. As a result, the survival of the whole operation is threatened, including the jobs of many German workers.

The threat reported in *The Wall Street Journal* article was real. By 1987, the last V W had rolled off the production line of the Pennsylvania plant in which the company had invested millions of dollars.

Source: *The Wall Street Journal,* September 22, 1982, p. 28, and February 8, 1989, p. A4.

The quality, quantity, and composition of the available labor force are considerations of great importance to an employer. This is particularly true if the employer is required to be efficient, competitive, and profitable. As we have indicated, there are government-owned plants whose objectives are to provide employment or essential services, and in these plants profitability and competitiveness are secondary.

labor quality the skills, education, and attitudes of available employees

Labor quality refers to the attitudes, education, and skills of available employees. **Labor quantity** refers to whether there are enough available employees with the skills and so forth required to meet your business needs. Circumstances can arise in which there are too many available workers, and this can be good or bad for the business.

labor quantity whether there are enough available employees with the skills required to meet an employer's business needs

If there are more qualified people than you can economically employ, your bargaining position as an employer is strengthened; you can choose the best at relatively low wages. On the other hand, high unemployment can cause and precede social and political unrest, which is usually not conducive to profitable business.

Many of the labor conditions in an area are determined by the social, cultural, religious, attitudinal, class distinction, and other forces we have already discussed. Other determinants of labor conditions are political and legal forces, and here we shall enlarge somewhat on those that were introduced in Chapters 10 and 11. A number of steps that management can take to avoid or minimize labor problems or maximize labor strengths are presented in Chapters 20 and 22, which deal with personnel and staffing.

Here we shall look at such subjects as labor availability, the reasons for its availability or scarcity, the types of labor that are likely to be available or scarce under different circumstances, productivity, and employer–employee relationships. These relationships are affected by employee organizations, such as labor unions. One cannot generalize about unions because they differ so greatly from country to country or even within one country.

Management of private business in capitalist societies has been thought of as representing the shareholders/owners and bondholders/lenders who put up the money that enabled the business to start and run. The shareholders and bondholders could call the tunes. Some new and different music is now being heard by management in several countries where labor is getting seats on the boards of directors. Management has been reluctant to see that happen, and one of the reasons for that reluctance is illustrated in the business incident.

LABOR MOBILITY

Classical economists assumed the immobility of labor, one of the factors of production. Undoubtedly, labor is imperfectly mobile; leaving aside political and economic obstacles, more complications are involved in moving people than in moving capital or most goods.

labor mobility people do move from country to country or area to area to get jobs

But however imperfect the mobility of labor, **labor mobility** does exist. At least 60 million people left Europe to work and live overseas between 1850 and 1970. Between the end of World War II and the mid-1970s, some 30 million workers from southern Europe and North Africa flowed into eight northern European countries where they were needed due to the economic boom enjoyed by most of the world during those years. This movement is slowing or even reversing now.[1] These "guest workers" are discussed further later in this chapter.

Another huge worker migration began during the 1970s as the sparsely populated Arab OPEC countries needed labor not only in their oil fields but also for the burgeoning construction projects and services being sought by the newly very rich host countries. Countries supplying most of these workers were Egypt, Algeria, Morocco, Pakistan, and India.

There are probably 9 million Mexicans at work in the United States (most illegally), and the number is growing. In addition, there are many Cubans, Haitians, Central Americans, Southeast Asians, and others in the U.S. work force. The causes of these migrations were and are combinations of problems, economic or political, at their sources and perceived opportunities at their destinations.

Refugees: Political and Economic

Throughout history, there have been flights of people from oppression. During the decades of the 1960s and 70s, millions fled from East to West Germany, from the People's Republic of China to Hong Kong and elsewhere, from North to South Vietnam and then as "boat people" from Vietnam to wherever they could land and hope to be accepted. In 1980, the flight of people from Cuba resumed. These were and are political refugees. Those going from Mexico to the United States and from southern Europe to northern Europe go for primarily economic reasons: better jobs and pay.

Population pressures.   The most important pressure creating both political and economic refugees is the booming population growth taking place primarily in the poor LDCs. Some 95 percent of the projected increase in the world's population from 5 billion in 1989 to over 6 billion by the year 2000 will be in those areas.[2]

Women bear the brunt and most of the burdens of the multiple baby boom, as is graphically illustrated by the photograph that follows. In addition, the closely spaced pregnancies plus the resulting constant child-care responsibilities are resulting in a growing number of female illiterates and the deterioration of female health.

These are human tragedies first and foremost. In terms of labor force efficiency and productivity, the women and children victims of these developments will be negative forces.

25 million migrants.   Around the world, there are estimated to be at least 25 million people who have migrated to another country. Several million Afghan refugees in Pakistan and Iran are awaiting reestablishment of peace in their country now that the Soviet army has left. Colombians move into the Venezuelan oil country, though that migration slowed as oil prices slid during the late 1980s. The drop in oil prices made Nigeria a less attractive destination, and the strong Ivory Coast economy has made it the new magnet country in central Africa. More than 200,000 men trek into South Africa each year from black African states to work that country's mines. Oil-producing and industrializing Malaysia is estimated to have more than a million illegal aliens, most of whom are from overcrowded Indonesia. Because most Argentineans are urbanites, much fertile land is not being farmed, and that draws immigrants from Chile, Bolivia, Paraguay, and Uruguay.

*Will these women have time
for other work?*

Source: Ric Ergenbright Photography

Refugees welcome?   Refugees are not welcome in most countries. The few
countries willing to accept some refugees will take only limited numbers. Their
reasons differ. Countries near Vietnam and Cambodia, from which refugees
flow, are poor and have difficulty feeding their own people. Most of the richer
countries, such as Japan and the countries of Western Europe, are not racially
diverse and are reluctant to bring in large numbers of alien races. European
countries with guest workers (see below) are experiencing some race relations
problems. Even in such a relatively rich and racially diverse country as the
United States, which is accepting—or getting—millions of refugees, there are
difficulties. One of them is finding work for all of the new people, and another
is educating their children.

Packing up.   When oil prices were high, the Middle East's fastest-growing
export was labor. For such countries as Egypt, Jordan, Pakistan, and North
and South Yemen, workers' remittances were bigger than total merchandise

exports. As tumbling oil prices pushed the area's oil producers into recession, the expatriates who flocked to jobs there in the 1970s and early 1980s were packing their bags and going home. The home countries will sorely miss the income; but on the bright side, the returning workers will bring home the skills they learned and the capital they earned abroad.

LABOR SHORTAGES AND GUEST WORKERS

Countries that receive many refugees or have high birthrates may have too many people for the available jobs, but there are also countries that have too few people. France, Germany, the Scandinavian countries, and Switzerland fall into the latter category. Those countries have few refugees and low birthrates. To them have come the so-called guest workers, who are in the country legally to perform certain types of jobs, usually in service, factory, or construction work.

In 1988, there were 4.3 million immigrants in France who did not qualify for French nationality, including 1.4 million Arabs and 106,000 people from black Africa. West Germany had 4.6 million foreigners, of whom 1.7 million are Turks. England, Switzerland, and the Scandinavian countries also had large numbers of foreign workers and their families. Most of the guest workers are from southern Europe, North Africa, and Turkey.

Guest Worker Problems

Economic.   The guest workers provide the labor needed by the host countries, which is desirable as long as the economies are growing. But when the economies slow, as they did during the mid-1970s and again in the early 1980s, fewer workers are needed and problems appear. Unemployment increases among the native workers, who then want the jobs held by guest workers. It is conveniently forgotten that the guest workers took jobs that the natives would not do when times were good. To appease their citizens, some countries refused to renew the guest workers' permits. In other countries, where the work was seasonal, the guest workers were deported at the end of the season instead of being permitted to stay and take other work. The French, for example, paid surplus foreign workers 10,000 francs (about $1,500) as a "go home" bonus;[3] and Germany offered "repatriation assistance" — equivalent to about $4,000, plus a lesser amount per child—for certain unemployed foreign workers to leave.[4]

Racial.   The introduction of large numbers of foreigners into host countries caused some racial frictions even while the economies were healthy. In France, for instance, Algerian workers claim that 80 countrymen were killed in racial conflicts between 1975 and 1979. French workers often refuse to share low-cost housing projects with outsiders, especially Arabs and Africans.

The Swiss complain about "overforeignization," and a proposal to drastically cut the number of foreigners was only narrowly defeated in a national referendum.

In Germany, there is concern about the foreigners—workers and their families—who show no signs of wanting to leave. The worst relations are with the Turks, who form the largest alien group.

WORLDVIEW
The Door Creaks Open

Japan's obsession with racial purity has always made foreign workers unwelcome, but a labour shortage and global business pressure are forcing a gradual change.

Thousands of dark, ramshackle buildings crowd the lowlands near Tokyo's Arakawa River. The odourous sprawl is a cluster of small factories typical of those that once formed the backbone of Japan's industrial economy. Few Japanese are willing to work in these unpleasant and smelly tanning and metalworking plants, but destitute foreigners—many of them illegal itinerant workers—are eager to oblige. The cheap labour of young South and Southeast Asians is helping to keep many of these small-scale industries afloat.

Japan has become the salvation for young unemployed men and women from other Asian countries, willing to work for lower-than-average wages despite hardship and the risk of being caught and deported. The growing flood of illegal foreign labourers embarrasses the government. Mindful of the "guest worker" situation in Europe, Japanese officials say they want to avoid developing what could become a permanent "underclass" of unskilled foreign labourers. At the same time, Japan is anxious to attract highly educated foreign professionals, in part to demonstrate progress in "internationalizing" its closed society.

But the growing presence of illegal workers, mostly from the Philippines, Bangladesh, and Pakistan, has provoked a hot debate in Japan over whether Asians from developing countries, lured by the yen's strength, should be allowed to fill jobs Japanese apparently do not want.

In the absence of adequate controls, foreign manual labourers like "Shak," a young sturdy man from Bangladesh, keep coming. The Justice Ministry reports that 11,307 foreigners were arrested and deported for working illegally in Japan in 1987; almost twice as many as in 1986. Officials admit the vast majority are not caught, and that as many as 50,000 foreigners are employed in factories, at construction sites and ports, and in the bars and massage parlours of Japan's ubiquitous "entertainment" industry.

Shak's work in a metal parts factory along the Arakawa River is unpleasant, but he says it pays about 20 times what he would make at home. These workers are welcome in Japan's "second economy," a world of day labour and temporary work in small factories that contrasts sharply with Japan's conventional image of clean, modern efficiency.

Government and industry leaders oppose allowing foreign labourers to work legally in Japan on the grounds that their presence will lower average wages and working conditions, says Eri Aoki, head of the Labour Ministry's employment policy section.

Most business leaders agree. A delegation of the Japan Chamber of Commerce and Industry recently visited Sweden, West Germany, France, and Italy to investigate the situation of foreign workers in Europe. They had hoped to gain some insight into how Japan could deal with migrant labour, but found mostly "cases of failure," says JCCI Chairman Rokuro Ishikawa.

"Many social problems could arise as Japan becomes wealthy and more workers come here from developing countries to do the dirty work," Ishikawa says.

Pointing to social problems faced by migrant workers and their dependents in Germany and other European countries, Aoki says foreign workers could deprive Japanese citizens of jobs during times of economic hardship and eventually overburden the social welfare system.

The alien workers and their families are frequently crowded into older, substandard housing. They have created slum neighborhoods in the midst of wealthy Western Europe, and with higher birthrates they are growing in numbers more rapidly than the natives, whose birthrates are among the world's lowest.

A potentially more acute foreign labor problem exists in the Arab Gulf countries. The rapid infrastructural development of the 1970s and early 1980s created huge demands for foreign workers. With lowered oil revenues and

"It's natural for unemployed, poor labourers to leave their homes when there are higher-paying jobs overseas. That's how the labour market works," Aoki says. "But it's absolutely unacceptable to have an underclass of foreigners in the least desirable, most dangerous jobs. Tens of thousands of people are working illegally, and we feel it's a serious problem."

In Japan, where uniformity is a deeply ingrained value, workers from less affluent countries are viewed as potential troublemakers. Officials cite an alarming rise in the number of non-Japanese apprehended for theft. Illegal foreign workers, of course, evade Japan's strict residential registration system, which keeps track of household members and where they work. The system is one reason Japan's crime rate is so low. "We saw there was a very undesirable gap between the Turkish migrant workers and Germans, who have very different cultures and lifestyles," says Munechika Goh, who headed the JCCI study mission to Europe. "And due to language problems, even if they wanted to have the same labour conditions, it's impossible."

Most illegal workers travel to Japan with tourist visas, often on false passports, find jobs and stay. The lack of a visa requirement for citizens of Bangladesh and Pakistan makes it particularly easy for "sightseers," who are allowed to stay legally in Japan for 90 to 180 days, to come with the purpose of finding work.

No one knows exactly how many firms have hired illegal workers, but a construction boom and the powerful recovery from last year's economic slump have generated a huge demand for workers. Companies unable to find skilled Japanese labourers are hiring and training foreigners to fill the jobs.

A few industrial leaders have spoken out in favour of hiring foreign workers. Nobuo Ishibashi, chairman of the Japan Prefabricated Construction Suppliers and Manufacturers Association, says he plans to campaign to persuade the government to permit employment of foreign labourers. "We are now suffering from a severe shortage of workers for assembly and paint jobs," Ishibashi told a local newspaper.

Just as European contractors did in the 1970s, Japan's smaller manufacturers have begun to depend on cheap foreign labour to cut rising costs associated with the yen's appreciation, says labour economist Eiko Shinotsuka of Ochanomizu University in Tokyo.

The experiences of clandestine workers in Japan parallel those of illegal migrants in other countries. Fearing detection, most refuse to be identified by their real names. Like "Shak," they share cramped (2.5 square metre) rooms with three or four other illegal workers.

A recent Labour Ministry survey of 43 companies employing 154 foreign labourers showed that on average they earn less than half the wages of their Japanese co-workers. Firms save even more on labour costs because clandestine workers do not receive the insurance or other benefits usually demanded by Japanese employees.

Those non-Japanese labourers work an average 60 to 70 hours a week as boiler inspectors, tanners, in small factories, and in the fast-food industry. Sometimes recruited overseas, they often find themselves entangled with Japan's underworld, says Father Joseph Wellens, a Catholic priest who assists Filipinos staying illegally in Japan. The involvement of Japanese gangs in hiring day labourers puts illegal workers at the mercy of gang members. It also inhibits enforcement of laws against hiring foreign workers because police find it convenient to look the other way.

The law only prohibits migrant labourers from working in Japan. It does not prohibit employers from hiring them. So clandestine workers in Japan have no legal rights.

(continued)

infrastructure* largely completed, there is a surplus of foreign workers; many of them are not legally in the host countries but are reluctant to go home.

Some percentages illustrate the gravity of the problems. In the United Arab Emirates (UAE), 80 percent of the workers are foreign (mostly Asian), and in Kuwait, only about 25 percent of the workers are Arab.[5] An even smaller

---

* A nation's infrastructure consists of its social and economic foundations—schools, hospitals, power plants, railroads, highways, ports, communications, airfields, and so forth.

WORLDVIEW
(concluded)

They cannot force employers to pay fair wages or appeal to the police for protection. "The government and police view these people as lawbreakers, so it doesn't matter to them if the employers refuse to pay their wages or make them work under dangerous conditions," says Yaeko Takeoka, a lawyer active in Japan's human rights movement.

The situation is particularly dangerous for young women employed in Japan's hostess bars, nightclubs, and massage parlours. "These young women come to Japan expecting to work as waitresses and hotel clerks. But once they are here, their passports are taken away and the girls are sometimes forced to work as prostitutes in order to pay the fees demanded by the brokers who brought them to Japan," Takeoka says.

"The government and police have not yet recognized that the people bringing these people to Japan and hiring them are breaking the law by depriving them of basic human rights," she says. But officials agree that the ban on foreign manual labour cannot be enforced unless employers face severe punishment for hiring illegally.

Japan historically has relied heavily on foreign workers to fill labour shortages, but it is far from a melting pot. Thousands of Koreans and Chinese were forcibly recruited during World War II to work in factories and mines. Most of the 656,000 people of Korean and Chinese ancestry are virtually indistinguishable from their Japanese neighbours. But they are still consid-

ered "resident aliens" and must carry alien registration cards.

Today, Tokyo is going all out to attract more non-Japanese with special expertise to Japan. Proposals now under consideration would allow a broader range of foreigners, including those with managerial skills, doctors, nurses, guides, language teachers, engineers, and foreigners who graduate from Japanese universities, to work legally in Japan.

The push comes from trading partners and from major Japanese corporations that are actively recruiting foreign professionals for their growing international operations. NEC Corp., Hitachi Lt., Matsushita Electric Industrial Co., Nippon Telegraph and Telephone Corp., (NTT) and Kobe Steel are particularly active in the hiring of non-Japanese.

Japanese companies with international operations that once hired non-Japanese just for their foreign language ability are increasingly turning to foreign professionals for their understanding of overseas markets, their business ties, and experience. "People are no longer being hired just for their English ability. They have to at least speak Japanese and have experience and professional connections," says Charlotte Takahashi-Kennedy, director of Oak Associates, a company that recruits foreigners for placement in 150 Japanese firms.

Takuya Maruiwa, a board director at computer maker Fujitsu Ltd., says his company recently employed 10 foreigners from the United States, Britain, Taiwan, and

percentage are Kuwaitis, and there is some worry in the area about the large numbers of Egyptians, Lebanese, and Palestinians in important positions.

COMPOSITION OF THE LABOR FORCE

Political or Economic Refugees and Guest Workers

When people flow into a country as refugees, the resulting growth of the labor force includes whatever ages, genders, and skills are able to get in. They are not coming for specific jobs; they are fleeing oppression or poverty. At the outset, they cause problems for the host country, which must try to feed, clothe, educate, and find work for the newcomers.

Some, for various reasons, remain burdens on the host country or on

South Korea and plans to hire more engineers, managers, and researchers.

"We are hiring foreign specialists because we need to suit our products to overseas markets and need employees who understand how things like satellite communication systems work overseas," Maruiwa says.

A shortage of qualified scientists and engineers to keep Japan's high-tech boom rolling is another factor prompting Japanese firms to hire foreign specialists. Ricoh Co., a copier and office machines firm, has hired 17 Irish engineering graduates and plans to employ 12 more. The foreign scientists work in Ricoh's computer technology development labs.

Cross-cultural employment presents a challenge both to the foreigners working in an unfamiliar environment and to firms integrating individualistic non-Japanese into an organization where promotion and authority depend on demonstrated commitment to the company.

"I've had emergency phone calls from foreigners who have worked in Japanese companies for three to five years who have a tremendous sense of isolation," says Kennedy-Takahashi. But she views the experience, however difficult, as very valuable.

"I think young foreigners can really benefit from the discipline of a Japanese company," she says. "When counseling people, I tell them. 'Think of what you'll learn. The isolation and culture shock will make you a stronger professional.'"

Gary Tsuchida, 33, an American who has worked for Kobe Steel for seven years, says he enjoys the sense of responsibility his job provides, although "every day is not a bed of roses."

Kobe has found that its 25 foreign employees play an important role in acquainting Japanese employees to the ways of foreigners. "Aside from the benefit of raising their linguistic abilities, having foreigners working in the company lets Japanese know how they behave," Tsuchida says. "That way, when they go overseas, they make fewer mistakes."

However, even companies anxious to recruit more foreigners are generally not interested in altering practices to accommodate their non-Japanese employees. "We have no plans to change our business style to something like in the United States," says Fujitsu's Maruiwa. "This is Japan, and our management style is suited to Japanese society," he says.

Due to the limits imposed by cultural and linguistic differences, foreigners will probably remain in the margins of Japanese companies, as in the society as a whole. They are needed to do jobs that Japanese workers cannot or will not take but are usually not fully integrated into the corporate structure.

Source: Elaine Kurtenbach, "The Door Creaks Open," *International Management,* September 1988, pp. 49, 52–53.

international refugee relief agencies. So it has been for many of the Palestinians who fled from Israel. This is not to suggest that the Palestinians are less intelligent or industrious than other groups. Their problems and difficulties have been tremendously increased by the wars and political upheavals in the Middle East.

Others find more peaceful surroundings, adapt relatively quickly, and become upwardly mobile in their new society. This holds true for many of the Cuban refugees in the United States. Many believe the rehabilitation and growth of downtown Miami owes much to the Cubans' influence and work.[6]

Quite different is the type of worker involved in the movement from southern to northern Europe. There, specific types of workers and skills were needed, and only persons who fit the needs were given work permits. They often did not or could not bring their families. They tended to be immediate benefits rather than burdens to the host economy.

The status of the Mexicans in the United States falls between that of the guest worker and that of the political refugee. For one thing, the great majority of guest workers are legally in the host country; the opposite is true for the Mexicans in the United States. For the most part, the Mexicans are economic, not political, refugees, but they bring their families when possible, thus creating more social burdens than do guest workers. Although the Mexicans usually come to work, they do not necessarily come prepared for specific jobs that are available in the host country.

Labor Force Composition and Comparative Productivity

labor force composition
the mix of people available to work, their age, skill, gender, race, and religion

Another change in **labor force composition** in the United States began in the mid-1970s. The percentage of adult women in the American labor force increased by some 10 percent during the decade of the 1970s.[7] By 1988, 62 percent of all American women aged 18 to 64 worked at least part time. In that year, 52 percent of all women over the age of 16 were in the labor force, up from 43 percent in 1970 and less than 34 percent in 1950.[8] In addition, women have been making inroads in fields formerly viewed as the exclusive domain of men.

Yet another change was the influx of more young workers. Both the end of the American involvement in the Vietnam War and some questioning about the value of a university education resulted in a smaller proportion of young people continuing school and a large proportion entering the job market. The inexperience of many new workers has been given as a cause of slower productivity growth.

To accommodate these new workers, the United States created more new jobs between 1973 and 1978 than any other industrial country, and that process continued through 1989. This was a great humanitarian and economic achievement, but relative productivity suffered, in part because so many less experienced workers entered the work force at the same time. The newly working women were joined by the refugees from Mexico and elsewhere and by young men and women who were demobilized after the Vietnam War. No other industrialized country was involved in that war to the extent that the United States was.

The size of the U.S. labor force increased by 28.4 million workers between 1974 and 1987, a gain of over 30 percent. The number of female workers grew by 18 million, a growth of 50 percent. A unique feature of U.S. labor force growth—female and male—is that many of the new workers are political or economic refugees who speak little, if any, English in addition to being unskilled.

labor productivity measures how many acceptable units of a product are produced by a worker during a given time and the cost per unit

The American labor force grew much more rapidly than did the labor force of any other industrial country. The increase in the number of working women was a major component of that growth, and refugee immigrants added many more. Figure 12–1 describes the labor force of male and female workers in a number of countries.

Partly as a result of all the new—many non-English–speaking—workers, **labor productivity** grew more slowly in the United States than in most other industrial nations until 1984. Table 12–1 illustrates this.

unit labor cost the cost in labor to produce one unit of output

Comparative **unit labor cost** figures offer some hope that America's decline in competitiveness may be ending. Unit labor cost is the cost in labor to

■ **FIGURE 12–1   Women at Work**

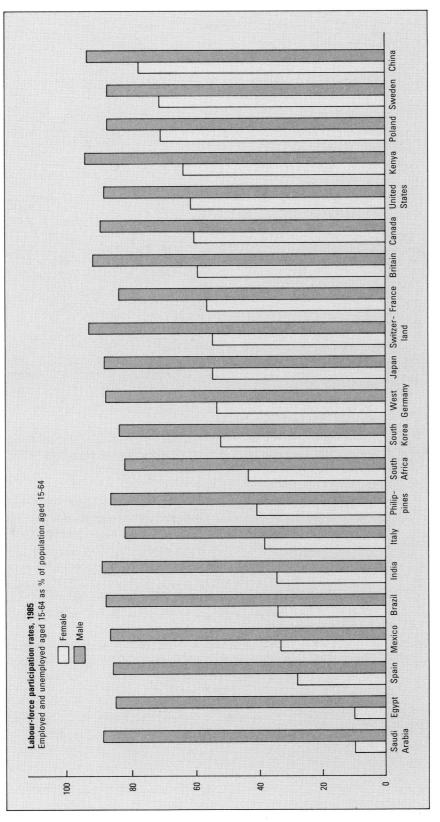

Labour-force participation rates, 1985
Employed and unemployed aged 15-64 as % of population aged 15-64

☐ Female
▨ Male

How well do different countries make use of the sex that makes up half their populations? The International Labour Office has had a look. In most industrial countries, between 40 percent and 70 percent of women aged between 15 and 64 work; Spain is at the bottom of the list, Sweden at the top (as are other Scandinavian countries, partly because they all have generous child-minding arrangements). Saudi Arabia's yashmak-wearing, nondriving women have the lowest participation rate in the figures, —closely followed by Egypt. In the Third World, the figures are distorted by the form agriculture takes in the economy. In countries where women work smallholdings (for example, India), many elude the statisticians; in China, with its ex-communes, the figure, at 76 percent, is the highest.

Source: *The Economist*, July 30, 1988, p. 97. © 1988 by The Economist Newspaper Ltd.

■ **TABLE 12–1**
Growth of Productivity in Selected Industrial Countries (Output per hour; 1977 = 100)

	1982	1983	1984	1985	1986	1987
United States	105	112	121	114	115	120
Japan	135	142	117	119	119	123
West Germany	112	119	100	103	105	105
France	123	129	99	100	100	102
United Kingdom	112	121	103	107	110	114
Canada	101	107	111	116	118	122

Source: *OECD Main Economic Indicators*, December 1988, p. 40.

■ **TABLE 12–2**
Unit Labor Costs in Selected Industrial Countries (1977 = 100)

	1982	1983	1984	1985	1986 (1st quarter)
United States	115	111	109	111	111
Japan	112	113	108	109	113
France	132	146	158	167	170
West Germany	109	108	107	107	110
United Kingdom	114	116	120	128	134
Canada	126	125	128	130	132

Source: *OECD Main Economic Indicators*, August 1986.

produce one unit of output. Table 12–2 illustrates the improvement of America's comparative position.

Later figures, however, indicate a slowing of U.S. improvement in this regard. Figure 12–2 shows America near the higher end of the scale in terms of increasing unit labor costs. Japan and several European countries were doing better for 1989 and 1990.

One study showed that as of 1986, each American manufacturing worker produced more per hour than a worker in any other industrial country. The Japanese worker was closest, and manufacturing productivity in Japan has grown more rapidly than in the other countries. With the U.S. productivity level at 100, the other industrial countries (in declining order) were Japan, 93.3; Germany, 90.4; Canada, 85.7; Italy, 84.1; France, 81.3; and the United Kingdom, 59.3.[9] It is the opinion of at least one economist that productivity levels in all countries eventually will converge as capital and technology spread throughout the world.[10]

In addition to the relative skill of labor forces, there are other causes for rapidity or slowness of productivity growth. These causes are interlocking, and we shall look briefly at some of them.

Research and development (R&D).   More efficient tools and machines result from more extensive and effective R&D. The R&D that a company can do depends on its management policies but also on how many after-tax dollars are available and on whether R&D can be deducted as a pre-tax expense. Governments do a great deal of R&D, which can also boost productivity.[11]

Tax policies.   As indicated, a nation's tax policies can influence how much money is available to private business for R&D. They can also make immense

■ **FIGURE 12–2   Labour Costs**

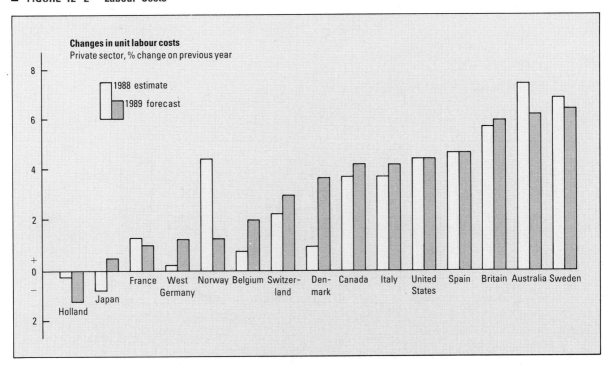

Unit labour costs in the private sector rose by 3.25 percent on average in OECD countries in 1988 and are forecast to increase by a further 3.75 percent in 1989. Labour costs are rising fastest in Australia, Sweden, and Britain. In all three countries, nominal wages grew rapidly in 1988. In Sweden, employers' social security contributions were increased, too. America had faster productivity growth last year, but not fast enough to offset wage increases. Moderate wage rises meant that unit labour costs increased modestly in most continental European countries. Norway experienced rapid wage growth; it is forecast to slow in 1989. Unit labour costs fell .75 percent in Japan and .25 percent in Holland in 1988. The OECD forecasts that they will fall 1.25 percent in Holland this year but rise by .5 percent in Japan.

Source: *The Economist*, February 11, 1989, p. 97. © 1989 by The Economist Newspaper Ltd.

differences in the amount available to private business to buy new plant, tools, and machines. They can do this through higher or lower tax rates.

Policies on depreciation are also important. Present U.S. tax policy permits depreciation only of the historic cost of plant, tools, and machines. With inflation, however, the replacement cost will be higher than the historic cost. If business could depreciate the current or replacement cost, the result would be lower taxes and more money left to the company for R&D, reinvestment, or other uses. See Chapter 6 for more on this.

Savings rates.   If people save a large percentage of their income (as opposed to spending it on current consumption), there is a larger pool of money available with which to buy company stocks or lend to business. People save for such reasons as creating a nest egg against hard times and because they have confidence in their currencies. A number of countries give tax breaks to interest or dividends earned on savings, and some countries have involuntary savings plans. Most OECD countries have savings rates higher than those of the United States and have higher economic and productivity growth rates.[12] Figure 12–3 shows the relative savings ratios.

■ FIGURE 12–3   Savings Ratios

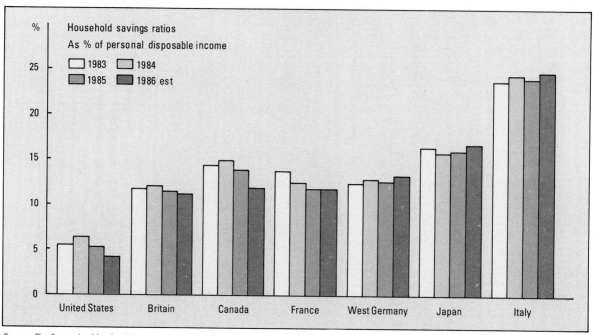

Source: *The Economist,* May 9, 1987, p. 99. © 1987 by The Economist Newspaper Ltd.

The average Italian household saved 25 percent of its disposable income in 1986; the average Japanese family, 17 percent. Americans saved only 4 percent of their income. Why are some nations so much thriftier than others? One of the biggest factors is age. Savings behavior varies over a lifetime: the young worker saves to buy a house, his retired grandparents run down their savings. So a country like Japan, with a low proportion of retired people, will have a higher savings ratio. As Japan's population ages, so its savings rate will fall. In countries with high inflation, such as Italy, households need to save a bigger chunk of their income to maintain the real value of their financial assets.

The pessimist—realist?   Dr. Paul W. McCracken, an eminent economist who is now professor emeritus, University of Michigan, says the United States must improve its productivity performance. He says that if the trends of the 1980s continue through the 1990s for the Big Seven of the industrial world, Japan's per capita output will exceed that of the United States by nearly 40 percent. Real incomes in France and Germany will also be well above those here; Italy and Britain would still be lower than the United States but would be closing the gap.

Dr. McCracken says the Bush administration and Congress must severely restrain the stampede to launch new programs and sweeten old ones. Most economies of the industrial world delivered stronger gains in productivity than the United States during the 1980s, and the United States must learn how they did it.

An economy's rate of productivity gain is closely related to the amount of capital in place per worker, and the reduced rate of improvement in U.S. productivity parallels a comparable slowdown in the rate of increase in U.S. capital stock per worker.

The cost of capital confronting U.S. companies is higher than it is for their international competitors, and more U.S. capital has been devoted to objectives not included in output (for example, cleaner air and water and other social objectives).

Dr. McCracken also points out that the American education system has been sending employers less well-educated workers than is the case in some other countries. He calls on national, state, and local governments and business to cooperate in solving these problems.[13]

SOCIAL STATUS, GENDER, RACE, TRADITIONAL SOCIETY, OR MINORITIES: CONSIDERATIONS IN EMPLOYMENT POLICIES

Social Status

There are societies in which a person's social status is established by the caste or social group into which the person is born. India presents an extreme example of the caste system, and intercaste battles that cause fatalities and home burnings still occur between upper-caste Hindus and the untouchables, whom Mahatma Gandhi called *harijans,* the children of God.[14] Obviously, a would-be employer must tread carefully when both upper-caste Hindus and harijans are in the employee pool.

Some say that the class system in Great Britain is eroding, but people there are still classified by the accents they acquire at home and school. When Margaret Thatcher was elected prime minister, commentators saw fit to point out that she was "only" the daughter of a small-store owner even though her accent was "upper class," apparently acquired at Oxford University. Although class differences do not cause riots in Britain, as caste differences do in India, a foreign employer should, nevertheless, be conscious of the possibilities for friction arising from those differences.

In Japan, there remains an odd caste holdover from the 17th century, when the feudal Togugawa regime imposed a rigid social pecking order on the country. The warrior-administrator samurai were at the top. Below them were farmers and artisans, then merchants, and at the very bottom, those with occupations considered dirty and distasteful, such as slaughterers, butchers, and tanners.

As in India, where discrimination against untouchables is illegal, all natives of Japan are legally equal. However, the descendants of the lowest Japanese class remain trapped in their ghettos, working in small family firms that produce knitted garments, bamboo wares, fur and leather goods, shoes, and sandals. They call themselves *burakumin* (ghetto people), and they claim that they number about 3 million people living in some 6,000 ghettos. Their average income is far below that of other Japanese.

Gender

Degrees of women's liberation and of women's acceptability in the work force range from fairly advanced in the United States to virtually nil in many countries. Even where women have made some strides out of their traditional roles, their progress is not necessarily secure, as witness the women's marches in Iran when the Islamic government that succeeded the shah ordered women back to their traditional dress and roles.

The employer must consider the sexist attitudes of the host society. In a country such as the United States, which has seen large strides in the status and acceptability of women in business and the professions, the hiring and promotion of women can be a business advantage. It can also be a legal advantage, because it complies with "affirmative action" laws and regulations of the U.S. and state governments. These laws encourage the hiring and promotion of women and minorities. But there are many countries in which customs, attitudes, or religion are hostile to women in the professions or business.

> Think like a man, act like a lady, work like a dog.
> That is the formula for the success of a woman working in the man's world of Japanese business.*

One of the quotations at the beginning of Chapter 22 indicates the scarcity of females in Japanese management. Women make up only 6.7 percent of the executive roster of the country, which is far below the American or Swedish rates. One reason is tradition, which is a burden for women executives in most countries.

A second reason is after-hours drinking sessions, which are common in many countries but more prevalent in Japan. Much of Japanese consensus decision making is accomplished during such sessions. Female managers tend to consider these a waste of time and to be somewhat uncomfortable at the freewheeling exchanges among the men as inhibitions fall away. The drinking is often very heavy, and drunkenness is not a disgrace; overimbibers are delivered carefully home.

The discomfort goes both ways. One computer salesman, talking about after-hours drinking sessions with his female section chief, complained, "I don't know what to talk about with her. She's not married, so I must avoid any remarks with sexual connotations. With a man, I could have a drink and talk about anything."

Other countries hinder women.   Japan is not the only country where women are encountering problems in making or retaining progress. We spoke of the setback for women in Iran, and women have been having troubles in other Moslem countries also.

One step forward in Pakistan has been accompanied by several steps backward. The forward step was a decision by the federal court that women could serve as judges. Two of the backward steps are banning women from taking part in public sporting events and changing the law of evidence to make the word of one male witness equal to that of two women. When women in Lahore protested against this devaluation of their legal personalities, they were set upon by the police, who injured 13 of the protestors.

Other backward steps in Pakistan are proposals to deny women the vote, to deny them the right to drive a car (as in Saudi Arabia), to halve the blood money paid for a female victim as compared with a male victim, and to impose the death penalty for prostitution—but only for the woman and not for her customer. Segregated schools for women only are being established. Women cannot attend men's schools in Saudi Arabia, and that country, which gives much financial aid to Pakistan, is thought to be a strong influence on its policies. A pointer to what the segregated female schools may teach is provided by one college, which has banned women from physics and mathematics and channeled them instead into a new course called household accounts.

* "Japan's Women Executives Finding Progress Painful," *Asian Wall Street Journal,* December 13, 1982, p. 11.

Some succeed. Despite hazards and difficulties for women in Pakistan and India, some achieve success as physicians, in business, and in politics. Indeed, in India, Indira Gandhi succeeded her father as head of state, and the current Pakistani prime minister is Ms. Benazir Bhutto, whose father held the same office several years before. And in Eritrea, which is fighting for its independence from Ethiopia, women fight in the front ranks of the army. One correspondent says there is probably greater sexual equality in Eritrea than in just about any other place in the world.[15]

Soviet women. In 1982, a Soviet feminist was sentenced to four years in jail to be followed by two years of internal exile for the offense of challenging the state doctrine that the female sex has been fully liberated since the 1917 Bolshevik Revolution. Women are equal at law, but life contradicts the law.

In 1980, Julia Voznesenskaya, the daughter of a high-ranking Soviet army officer, was exiled after writing a firsthand account of a women's work camp for *Almanac: Women and Russia,* the USSR's first feminist underground journal. In exile in Munich, Voznesenskaya wrote a book from which the following grim depiction of the current state of Soviet sisterhood is taken.

> In Mother Russia, women are still the second sex. Their working hours are spent as all-purpose workhorses, breeders, sex objects, rape victims. Their dreams are modest; not of women's liberation, but merely of a more civilized version of patriarchy and the status quo.[16]

Race

Unfortunately, examples of racial conflicts and discrimination are found worldwide. There have been black-versus-white conflicts in such places as the United States, South Africa, and Great Britain, and Arab-, Indian-, or Pakistani-versus-black conflicts in Africa. Earlier in this chapter, we discussed racial friction caused by guest workers in Europe, and there has been bloody conflict in Sri Lanka between Tamils and Sinhalese. Some say the Chinese have an attitude of superiority toward blacks, and in 1988, antiblack riots erupted at several Chinese universities.[17]

The South African separate-races system, called apartheid, has been denounced in North America and Western Europe as well as in South Africa. Powerful pressures were put on American and European companies to disinvest from—take their money and presences out of—South Africa. Some felt that disinvestment would cause the South African government to end apartheid.

Others disagreed, including some prominent black South Africans and white business and political leaders opposed to apartheid. One black leader, the Zulu* chief Buthelezi, argued that disinvestment would rob blacks of needed jobs. Another, Lucy Mvubelo, head of the black National Union of Clothing Workers, felt that foreign investment offered the best hope of economic progress for South African blacks.[18]

Helen Suzman, a white political opposition leader in the South African Parliament, has been an unrelenting foe of the government's apartheid policies. She had this to say about sanctions by the U.S. government: "But, should the U.S. Congress impose sanctions, the results would be disastrous for those the

---

* The Zulu tribe is the largest in South Africa.

United States most wants to help." She referred to sanctions as "a moral free lunch."[19]

Congress, nevertheless, enacted sanctions, and American as well as European companies disinvested from South Africa. In the companies' cases, disinvestment was, by their own statements, motivated at least in part by economic considerations; the South African operations had become unprofitable, and they feared further economic deterioration as well as social and political unrest.

The immediate results of sanctions and disinvestment have included the toughening of apartheid enforcement practices by the government, the loss of jobs held by blacks, and anger of blacks and the South African government at U.S. government and companies. It remains to be seen whether the longer-term results will weaken apartheid and assist the majority black population. From both the business and political points of view, the disinvestments and sanctions are unprecedented or unusual, so the outcomes are difficult to predict.

In another part of the world, Japan has come under increasing criticism for its laws denying Japanese citizenship to anyone not of the Japanese race. The largest "alien" group affected is the Koreans, many of whom were brought to Japan as workers when Japan occupied Korea. Now the second- and third-generation descendants of those Koreans, all of whom were born in Japan, with Japanese as their native tongue, are still "aliens" and not granted the rights and privileges of Japanese citizenship. The relatively few Vietnamese refugees permitted into Japan are beginning to feel the same racial discrimination.

In the interest of balance, it should be pointed out that blacks have been known to discriminate against other races. Probably the best-known instance occurred in Uganda when the black-run government seized the property, shops, and land of people of Indian or Pakistani heritage, drove them out, and turned the seized assets over to black Ugandan citizens.

Traditional Society

A number of LDCs have barely begun to modernize, and many of their people are still relatively primitive. They may be organized in tribal groups with a chief, in feudal organizations with a patron or landowner at the head, or in some other paternalistic arrangement. Here the foreign employer may be forced to assume the paternal position and become the protector and master rather than the employer in the usual sense. Workers sometimes come to the company with personal problems and family problems, and the manager should not turn them away. There may be problems with a wife or husband, with a child's education, or with the family's health.

traditional society the tribal, nomadic state of a people before they turn to organized agriculture or industry

In the ambience of a **traditional society**, the employer must keep in mind tribal and family loyalties. Nepotism may be the rule rather than the exception.

Minorities

Traditional societies combined with racial attitudes sometimes present opportunities combined with problems for employers. There are societies in which merchants, businesspeople, and bankers are looked down on, and the people prefer to follow political, religious, military, professional, or agricultural careers. In such societies, outsiders may dominate commercial and banking activities. Some examples are the Indians and Pakistanis in East Africa, the Chinese in southeast Asia, and the Greeks in Turkey.

An advantage for a foreign employer moving into these societies is that such **minorities** may be immediately available, bringing financial and managerial skills to the employer. They speak the local language and usually one or more others, and they are less nationalistic and more likely to be aggressive.

A disadvantage is that such people are often unpopular with the majority local population. The foreign employers can easily become too dependent on minority employees, thus becoming isolated and insulated from the real world of the majority.[20]

minorities usually a relatively smaller number of people identified by race, religion, and/or national origin who live among a larger number of different people

EMPLOYER–EMPLOYEE RELATIONSHIPS

labor market the availability, skills, and attitudes of potential employees within commuting distance from an employer

When a foreign employer arrives in a **labor market,** it must take what it finds. Of course, a prudent company will have included the labor market among its measurements when considering whether to invest in a country. A company does not even have to travel to a prospective host country to gain information about its labor force. In addition to *Foreign Labor Trends* released by the Bureau of International Labor Affairs of the U.S. Department of Labor, two good information sources are the *Handbook of Labor Statistics* (available from the Bureau of Labor Statistics of the U.S. Department of Labor in Washington, D.C.) and the *Yearbook of Labor Statistics* (published by the United Nation's International Labor Office in Geneva, Switzerland).

In these sources, you will find information for most countries of the world on several subjects. There will be the number of labor strikes—or work stoppages, as they are sometimes called—per year. The number of workers who went on strike is indicated, as is the number of working days lost. Last, but perhaps most informative, for each country the days lost per thousand employees in nonagricultural industries is reported.

The countries about which those labor figures are reported vary greatly in size, culture, labor laws, and militancy of labor unions. Thus, the days lost per thousand is the only direct comparison among the countries. But these statistics are all raw numbers, and the potential employer should investigate more deeply when considering a labor market.

Here are some other questions that the planner should look into: (1) Was the period abnormal for any of the countries? (2) Were the strikes peaceful, or were they accompanied by violence, destruction, or death? (3) Were the strikes industrywide, or were they only against selected employers? (4) Were the strikes wildcat (unannounced), or was there usually warning that they were coming? and (5) Do the unions and the workers abide by labor agreements, and if not, what can the employer do?

The company planning investment in the traditional-society LDCs will examine the cultural, religious, tribal, and other factors discussed elsewhere. Of course, religious, racial, and linguistic schisms are not confined to LDCs. Among the developed countries where such problems exist are Belgium, Canada, Ireland, and Spain, and the United States is not free of racial disturbances. In addition to these matters, a would-be employer will study the organizations of laborers.

Labor Unions: European, American, and Japanese

European **labor unions** are usually identified with political parties and socialist ideology. A sense of worker identity is common in these unions, probably because European labor gained freedom from feudalism as well as various rights and powers through collective action.

In the United States, on the other hand, many civil rights, including the vote, were already possessed by laborers by the time unions became important. As a result, unionism in the United States has been more pragmatic than political and more concerned with the immediate needs of the workers.[21]

Labor legislation in the United States mostly confined itself to the framework of collective bargaining. In Europe, government's role is more active, with wages and working conditions frequently legislated. Many Latin American governments are very active in employer–employee relationships, frequently because the unions are weak and the union leaders are inexperienced or uneducated.

There has been so much discussion and writing about Japanese labor and labor policies that we should comment at least briefly about them. Already mentioned have been the growing productivity of Japanese labor and the low number of days lost to strikes.

The better productivity is probably the result of greater savings being invested in capital equipment and may be due in part to the loyalty of labor to the employer. Some say that traditional loyalty to the family or the emperor has been transferred to the employer. The practice of lifetime employment by much of Japan's larger industry would reinforce the loyalty and reduce the tendency to strike.[22]

In 1989, Japan's two labor federations united. The 4.5-million-member General Council of Trade Unions of Japan, which was known as Sohyo and represented mostly public-sector employees, saw its power eroded by rising prosperity, declining unionization, and increased use of part-timers. Therefore, Sohyo was merged into the 5.4-million-member Japanese Private Sector Trade Union Confederation, called Rengo.

The merger isn't expected to have much impact on the usually cooperative relations between companies and their employees. If anything, relations could be even more cordial, because the socialist-inclined Sohyo was more likely to have been confrontational than was Rengo.[23]

In West Germany and France, the influences of law and government administrative actions are more extensive and evident. Negotiations are conducted on national or at least regional levels, and in France, government representatives take part.

Multinational Labor Activities

The internationalization of business has been under way for many years, and multinational companies have expanded rapidly since the 1950s. National unions have begun to perceive opportunities of companies to escape the organizing reach of unions by the relatively simple step of transferring to or commencing production in another country. The companies' opportunities are seen as dangers to the unions.

To combat those dangers, national unions have begun to (1) collect and disseminate information about companies, (2) consult with unions in other countries, (3) coordinate with those unions' policies and tactics in dealing with some specific companies, and (4) encourage international companies' codes of conduct. Such multinational labor activity is likely to increase, although unions are divided by ideological differences and are frequently strongly nationalistic. Vastly more effort and money have been spent on lobbying for protection of national industries than on cooperating with unions in other countries.

Some developments that occurred in 1980 demonstrate, however, that cooperation is possible. The Geneva-based International Union of Food and Allied Workers Association coordinated a boycott of Coca-Cola in Sweden, Spain, Mexico, and Finland. The cause of the boycott was alleged "antilabor practices" by the Coca-Cola franchise holder in Guatemala.

The International Metalworkers Federation asked West European governments to use their economic power against International Telephone & Telegraph Corporation (ITT) because it wanted changes in ITT's "personnel and social policies."

The first important arena in which successful multinational unionism may develop is the European Community (EC). The 12 EC member-countries are steadily eliminating or harmonizing their tariffs, taxes, monetary systems, laws, and much more. The resulting atmosphere will be more hospitable for the cooperation of national unions.

A number of national unions have affiliated themselves with international trade secretariats (ITSs), which usually make Geneva their headquarters. The UN's International Labor Organization (ILO) is also located in Geneva. There are 19 operational ITSs, but only 4 have made themselves felt by multinational business: the International Metalworkers Federation; the International Federation of Chemical, Energy, and General Workers' Unions; the International Federation of Commercial, Clerical, Professional, and Technical Employees; and the International Union of Food and Allied Workers Association.[24] The other 14 have small staffs and limited functions in specialized fields.[25]

The American union federation, the AFL–CIO, cooperates with LDC labor in three organizations: the African-American Labor Center; the American Institute for Free Labor Development for Latin America; and the Asian-American Free Labor Institute.

However, in one highly competitive field—automobiles—the internationalization of the industry is emphasizing differences rather than cooperation among national unions. The managements of car companies have long since stopped being as alarmed by threats of international action as they were when the unions first made them. Natural nationalism is made worse in some countries by multiunion industries, and when political differences are added, unions frequently find themselves competing rather than cooperating with one another.[26]

Codetermination

Europe, particularly West Germany, is in the vanguard of another labor development, which, at first sight, horrified many business managers and owners. Laws were adopted that required employees to be given seats on the employer board of directors.

codetermination participation by workers in a company's management

It began in Germany.   Worker participation in management, frequently called **codetermination,** began in the German coal and steel industries in 1951.

The law gave worker and shareholder representatives each 50 percent of the directorships. A neutral board member selected by both sides breaks any deadlocks, but that vote has rarely been needed, as labor and shareholder representatives usually resolve their differences.

The 50–50 system was extended to all large German industry by a 1976 law that was challenged in court by German employers but upheld by the West German high court in March 1979.[27]

It has spread.   Other European countries and Japan either have or are seriously discussing codetermination-type legislation or practices. In the United States, neither business nor labor showed much enthusiasm for codetermination until the late 1970s. However, things are changing in the United States, where the terms *industrial democracy* and *worker participation* are sometimes used.

Developments in the United States.   During the late 1970s and into the 1980s, the concept of industrial democracy spread in America. Both Chrysler Corporation and American Motors have had United Automobile Workers (UAW) officers as members of their boards of directors. Workers at General Motors get together in "quality circles" to help make decisions about their jobs and production quality. The Communications Workers of America signed a contract in August 1980 with American Telephone & Telegraph that included worker participation concepts. New Labor contracts in the steel, rubber, oil, paper, glass, aerospace, food processing, and electrical products industries contain similar concepts. In addition, hundreds of large and small nonunion employers have adopted their own versions of industrial democracy; among these are IBM and Texas Instruments.[28]

Not everyone in the United States is pleased with worker participation (see the first quotation at the beginning of this chapter). When Douglas Fraser, the UAW president, was elected to Chrysler's board in 1980, there were fears in labor and management that the conflicts between the two jobs were too great.

In his efforts to sell a new Chrysler contract to the UAW rank and file, Fraser reversed the typical charge of labor leaders—that management is bargaining in bad faith when it claims that it cannot afford fatter wage and benefit offers. Fraser took just the opposite tack and chided the Chrysler chairman for painting too rosy a picture of Chrysler's finances. He even said that Chrysler's reported profits were based in part on financial "manipulations."

As a result, neither the UAW nor Chrysler management was happy with Fraser. Some union members felt he had not squeezed the company hard enough; management feared his talk of financial weakness and manipulation would hurt the company's reputation with its bankers and the investment community.[29] When Fraser resigned in 1986, he was not replaced by a UAW officer.

Workers of the World

Some comparisons are interesting as to how long workers work and how much they are paid in cities around the world.

Hours they work.   These are 1987 real annual working hours of production workers in manufacturing industries. They are working hours per year

■ **TABLE 12-3 Pay for the World's Workers**

City	Production Department Head			Primary School Teacher			Secretary		
	Gross Pay	Net Pay	Buying Power	Gross Pay	Net Pay	Buying Power	Gross Pay	Net Pay	Buying Power
Luxembourg	$55,236	$39,100	$46,615	$35,900	$27,301	$32,547	$24,701	$18,200	$21,697
Hong Kong	33,399	27,901	38,861	13,901	13,199	18,385	9,200	8,599	11,978
Geneva	67,200	45,300	35,789	57,301	41,899	33,103	31,300	26,199	20,699
New York	58,199	35,500	35,500	26,001	20,300	20,300	20,300	14,400	14,400
Brussels	64,600	31,900	34,933	21,299	14,300	15,659	22,800	14,300	15,659
Copenhagen	77,099	41,199	32,259	28,300	16,501	12,919	29,100	17,000	13,311
Dusseldorf	55,400	30,700	32,081	27,199	21,701	22,677	25,301	16,000	16,720
Amsterdam	44,000	26,100	30,503	25,700	17,801	20,804	20,200	12,100	14,142
Sydney	39,001	23,800	28,437	22,701	15,700	18,758	16,400	12,199	14,577
Vienna	46,700	27,700	27,864	18,801	13,100	13,177	19,900	13,400	13,479
Tokyo	73,000	54,599	27,645	44,199	36,200	18,329	20,600	17,501	8,861
Toronto	34,900	22,800	26,148	33,699	21,500	24,656	18,801	13,700	15,711
London	37,600	25,800	25,706	20,900	15,300	15,245	21,401	14,901	14,847
Singapore	30,600	20,600	24,752	8,100	5,900	7,089	11,700	8,299	9,973
Dublin	44,400	24,899	24,717	22,900	16,799	16,678	13,799	9,400	9,333
Paris	29,100	22,401	23,489	17,300	14,300	14,995	18,399	13,400	14,050
Milan	28,199	19,000	21,375	17,300	13,700	15,413	16,501	11,800	13,275
Helsinki	47,201	27,301	19,745	26,001	16,700	12,078	19,300	13,400	9,691
Stockholm	48,600	23,900	18,357	22,800	14,799	11,367	19,200	12,901	9,909
Oslo	39,299	14,799	10,264	22,500	10,800	7,491	21,600	9,800	6,797
Madrid	11,800	9,400	9,717	17,000	13,100	13,542	9,700	7,900	8,167
Lisbon	7,599	5,999	8,629	7,900	6,401	9,207	6,900	5,600	8,054

Source: *Financial Times*, November 23, 1988, p. 13.

stipulated in labor contracts minus vacation and absent days, plus overtime hours.[30]

Japan 2.150
United States 1.950
United Kingdom 1.934
West Germany 1.633

Money they earn. The Union Bank of Switzerland with the help of its international branches and associates made a study of pay and living costs in 52 cities around the world. The study covered a dozen different types of jobs, three of which are included in Table 12-3.

In each case, the table starts with the jobholder's gross pay received in money, including bonuses and the like as well as salary. Next comes the net pay after deductions for taxes, retirement, and whatever is applicable for the type of person in the city of work.

The third column is what the net pay will buy in terms of a "basket" of commonly required goods and services, excluding housing. This is an application of purchasing power parity, which was introduced in Chapter 5.

We have chosen 3 of the 12 jobs reported on by Union Bank. First is a production department head with a staff of at least 100 employees. The other two are a primary school teacher and a secretary. In most cases, the production department head is the best paid of the 12 positions. The exceptions are in Madrid and Lisbon, where school teachers take home more pay.

SUMMARY

Before investing in a country or an area, a company's management will examine the potential employee pool— its composition, skills, and attitudes. These are elements over which management has no control before it invests and which may change for reasons beyond its control after investments have been made. It is the purpose of this chapter to bring at least some of these elements to your attention.

Management may find itself dealing with a labor force that consists of local citizens or foreigners. If the workers are foreign to the host country, they may be guest workers who are legally in the country to perform certain tasks that the natives do not want to do. Foreign workers may also be refugees, legally or illegally in the host country, who came primarily to escape something and not primarily to perform specific work.

Foreign workers sometimes cause problems. When the economy slows, the local citizens want the jobs held by them. Even in prosperity, there are racial conflicts between foreign workers and the natives.

The composition of the labor force affects labor productivity, and when the labor force grows rapidly due to an influx of unskilled workers, productivity suffers.

Another influence on productivity is the capital equipment available to the labor force. The amount of capital equipment is affected by (1) research and development and (2) savings rates, both of which can be encouraged or discouraged by tax policies.

Management moving into a different country should also consider, as they affect employment policies, the local attitudes toward social status, gender, race, religion, and minorities. Management would have to perform differently in a traditional society than in a more-developed, industrialized country.

A company management weighing investment in a country should study the labor unions and the strike records. Labor laws and government intervention in employer–employee relationships should be examined.

Labor unions have begun to be active internationally and to coordinate studies and labor action. Such coordination has been growing in Europe, and it was in Europe—first in Germany—that codetermination began. Some sort of worker participation in management can now be found in several European countries, Japan, and the United States.

QUESTIONS

1. *a.* How could an excess of qualified employees be beneficial for an employer?
   b. How could it be detrimental?
2. Classical economists assumed the labor factor of production to be immobile. Is this assumption correct in the modern world?
3. What are some differences between labor that moves as do the European guest workers and labor that moves as do political or economic refugees?
4. What is the effect on productivity of the influx into the work force of inexperienced, unskilled workers?
5. How could a caste system affect employment decisions?
6. What is a typical response of an American firm to demands that it close its South African subsidiaries?
7. In several Southeast Asian and South Pacific countries, the Chinese minority is prominent in banking, finance, and business. What are the dangers for a foreign employer staffing the local company primarily with such a minority?
8. What is a major difference between European and American unions?
9. What are the prospects for effective multinational union collaboration? Discuss.
10. *a.* What is codetermination?
    b. Has codetermination worked well? Discuss.
11. What are some arguments against codetermination?
12. In Soviet law, women are equal with men. How does Soviet life reflect Soviet law in this respect?

MINICASE 12–1

Codetermination—Deutsche Stevens*

"Have you been following the problems that Opel has been having because of Mitbestimmung (codetermination)?"[†] Mat Burns, the president of Deutsche Stevens, a wholly owned subsidiary of Houston-based Stevens Industries, was talking to his management committee. "The worker representatives on the board of directors have become very militant. They are bringing up a lot of issues in board meetings that ought to be settled by labor negotiations."

"What kinds of issues, Mat?" asked Ned Webster, vice president for production.

Burns:

Things like the right to name the new personnel director, improve retirement benefits, and even plant ventilation. This militancy is also being felt in the legitimate issues that the board ought to discuss. It used to be that management presented the worker representatives with investment decisions after they were made, but now, I'm told, they want to review them one at a time very carefully. They say it is as important to use funds to improve working conditions as it is to spend them for increased production capacity and product development.

Jim Perrin, vice president for personnel:

Mat, do you know the cause of this increased militancy?

Burns:

I've been told there are a number of causes. One is the rapid growth of the work force. Since 1975, it has grown from 33,000 to 43,000 employees. The newest workers are younger and, of course, do not have the loyalty to Opel that the old-time employees have.

Perrin:

Do you think that's the only reason?

Burns:

No, I've been told there are others. The plant is running at full capacity and is crowded and uncomfortable. Part of the plant dates from the 1930s. The head of the works council claims that the workers are under pressure to produce every second, as he puts it, and that conditions are very severe.[‡]

Webster:

Sounds bad, Mat, but we don't have these problems; not yet, anyway.

Burns:

That's true, but remember, we have less than 2,000 employees, so only a third of our board of directors consists of workers' representatives. However, as you know, we are getting close to that figure. Marketing wants to add a whole new product line, and this will require us to add at least 400 new employees, which will put over the 2,000 level. That means we shall have an equal representation of labor and management on the board. In the event of a tie, I can still cast the deciding vote for management. However, every time I have to do that, the labor representatives are going to feel frustrated, and it's going to show up on the production line.

Ludwig Schmidt, company attorney:

Mat, maybe there's another way to do it.

Burns:

How's that, Ludwig?

Schmidt:

Well, ITT's subsidiary, Standard Elektrik Lorenz, has changed two of its companies to limited partnerships, which makes them exempt from the law. Other companies are spinning off operations into separate companies so that no one company has more than 2,000 employees. They still must have one-third worker representation on the board, as we do now, but that's better than a 50–50 split.[¶]

Burns:

That seems like a good idea, Ludwig—the forming of another company, I mean. Will you get together with Don here [Don Jones, vice president for marketing] and see if we should form a new company? You'll want to be in on these discussions, too, Ned. Also, Ned, I wish you and Jim would review our working conditions to see if we have any potential problem areas similar to Opel's. Parts of our plant are rather old, and we have been push-

---

* "West Germany, the Worker Dissidents in Opel's Boardroom," *Business Week,* July 23, 1979, p. 79.

† Opel is General Motors' German subsidiary.

‡ The works council is a body composed of employees elected by all the employees of the plant. It monitors the carrying out of labor agreements and is involved in grievance proceedings.

¶ "Companies in Germany Confront Codetermination Practice," *Business Europe,* January 20, 1978, p. 22.

ing the workers pretty hard to get the production out, haven't we?

1. What would you suggest if you were either the attorney or the marketing manager? Are there any problems involved if a separate company is formed to han-

dle the new product line?

2. What should the vice president for production and the vice president for personnel consider?

3. Do any large American companies have worker representatives on their boards of directors?

MINICASE 12–2

Racism

Your company, an American WWC, has decided to expand aggressively in Asia. It plans to source much of its raw material and subcontracting there and manufacture and market throughout Asia, from Japan in the north through New Zealand in the south.

You were appointed to organize and direct this major new effort, and one question was where to locate the regional headquarters for the Asian Division. After considerable study, you selected the island nation of Luau.

Luau's advantages are several. It is about equidistant between New Zealand and Japan. It was a British colony, so the main language is English. It has a relatively efficient telephone and telegraph system and good air service to all the major Asian destinations in which you are interested and to the United States.

Not least important, the Luau government is delighted to have your company locate and invest there. It has made very attractive tax concessions to the company and to its personnel who will move there.

The company moves in, leases one large building, and puts out invitations to bid on the construction of a larger building, which will be its permanent headquarters. Now, as you begin to work much more with the private banking and businesspeople of Luau and less with government officials, you begin to be more aware of a Luau characteristic about which you had not thought much previously. Almost all of the middle- and upper-management personnel in the business and finance sector are of Chinese extraction. The native population of Luau, which is the great majority, is a Micronesian race.

On inquiring why the Chinese are dominant in banking and business while the Micronesians stay with farming, fishing, government, and manual labor, you are told that this is the way it developed historically. The Chinese enjoy and are good at banking and business, while the native Luauans do not like those activities and have stayed with their traditional pastimes. The two groups buy and sell from and to each other, but there are almost no social relations and very little business or professional overlap between the groups. Occasionally, some of the Micronesians study abroad, and some work abroad for periods; when they return, they frequently go to work in a bank or business or take a government position.

You must staff your headquarters with middle- and lower-management people and with clerical help. You find that the only applicants for the jobs are Chinese, and you select the best available. They are quite satisfactory, and the operation gets off to a good start.

Then, as the months pass, you notice a gradual change of attitude toward you and the company among the government officials and among the people in general. They have become less friendly, more evasive, and less cooperative. You ask your Chinese staff about it, but they have noticed nothing unusual.

What could be happening? Why might the Chinese staff not notice it? What might you do to improve government and public relations?

SUPPLEMENTARY READINGS

Adams, Walter, ed. *The Brain Drain.* New York: Macmillan, 1979.

Aggarwal, R., and I. Khera. "Exporting Labor: The Impact of Expatriate Workers on the Home Country." *International Migration* 25, no. 4 (1987), pp. 415–24.

Bain, Trevor, "German Codetermination and Employment Adjustments in the Steel and Auto Industries." *Columbia Journal of World Business,* Summer 1983, pp. 40–47.

Bairstow, Frances. "The Trend toward Centralized Bargaining—A Patchwork Quilt of International Diversity." *Columbia Journal of World Business,* Spring 1985, pp. 75–83.

Banks, Robert, and Jack Stieber, ed. *Multinationals, Unions, and Labor Relations in Industrialized Countries.* Ithaca: New York State School of Industrial and Labor Relations, Cornell University, 1977.

Benelli, Giuseppe; Claudio Loderer; and Thomas Lys. "Labor

Participation in Corporate Policymaking Decisions: West Germany's Experience with Codetermination." *Journal of Business.* October 1987, pp. 553–75.

Blanpain, Roger, *The Badger Case and the OECD Guidelines for Multinational Enterprises.* Translated by Michael Jones. Deventer, Netherlands: Kluwer, 1977.

Blum, Alfred, ed. *International Handbook of Industrial Relations: Contemporary Developments and Research.* Westport, Conn.: Greenwood Press, 1981.

Brooke, Michael Z. *International Management.* London: Hutchinson, 1986.

Enderwick, Peter. *Multinational Business and Labor.* New York: St. Martin's Press, 1985.

Kao, Charles. *Brain Drain.* Hong Kong: Mei Ya China International Specie Bank, 1980.

King, Charles, and Mark van de Vall. *Models of Industrial Democracy: Consultation, Codetermination, and Workers*

Management. New York: Mouton, 1978.

Liebhaberg, Bruno. *Industrial Relations and Multinational Corporations in Europe.* New York: Praeger Publishers, 1981.

Lindert, Peter. *International Economics.* Homewood, Ill.: Richard D. Irwin, 1986.

Morgan, Alun, and Roger Blanpain. *The Industrial Relations and Employment Impacts of Multinational Enterprises: An Inquiry into the Issues.* Paris: Organization for Economic Cooperation and Development, 1977.

Scholl, Wolfgang. "Codetermination and the Ability of Firms to Act in the Federal Republic of Germany." *International Studies of Management and Organization,* Summer 1987, pp. 27–37.

Thim, Alfred L. "How Far Should German Codetermination Go?" *Challenge,* July 1981, p. 13.

ENDNOTES

1. Barry Newman, "Unwelcome Guests," *The Wall Street Journal,* May 9, 1983, pp. 1, 22.

2. Carl Wahren, "The Impact of Population Growth," *OECD Observer,* December 1988/January 1989, pp. 8–11.

3. *The Economist,* May 21, 1977, pp. 85–86.

4. *The Economist,* August 6, 1983, p. 39.

5. *Business International,* August 19, 1983, pp. 257, 261.

6. Anthony Ramirez, "Making It," *The Wall Street Journal,* May 20, 1980, pp. 1, 27.

7. *The Economist,* April 14, 1979, p. 80.

8. *Equal Employment Opportunity for Women: U.S. Policies* (Washington, D.C.: Women's Bureau, U.S. Department of Labor, 1982), Table 2.

9. Molly McUsic, "U.S. Manufacturing: Any Cause for Alarm?" (Federal Reserve Bank of Boston) *New England Economic Review,* January/February 1987, p. 10.

10. William J. Baumol, "A Modest Decline Isn't All that Bad," *The New York Times,* February 15, 1987, p. 14.

11. Paul W. McCracken, "Congress and the Budget Beanstalk," *The Wall Street Journal,* February 29, 1980, p. 22.

12. June Kronholz, "The Super-Savers: Europe's Saving Rate Far Outstripping U.S., Aids Economic Growth," *The Wall Street Journal,* October 5, 1979, pp. 1, 33.

13. Paul W. McCracken, "Lick the American Disease before It's an Epidemic," *The Wall Street Journal,* January 16, 1989, p. A8.

14. *Los Angeles Times,* February 27, 1980, part 1, p. 2; see also "The Cost of Caste," *The Economist,* February 16, 1980, pp. 46–47.

15. Peter Worthington, "Eritrean Wins Put Mengistu on Defensive," *The Wall Street Journal,* May 24, 1988, p. 14.

16. Julia Voznesenskaya, *The Women's Decameron* (New York: Atlantic Monthly Press, 1986); also see Maska Hamilton, "Soviet Super-Moms Want Changes," *Los Angeles Times,* March 6, 1989, part I, pp. 10–11.

17. Daniel Wattenberg, "Internationalism Turns Ugly with Attacks on Africans," *Insight,* January 30, 1989, pp. 28–30.

18. William Raspberry, "Black South African Pleads for U.S. Investment," *Los Angeles Times,* October 24, 1979, part 2, p. 7.

19. Miles Cunningham, "Government Member, Not Friend," *Insight,* September 1, 1986, p. 31.

20. See the discussion of employee attitudes and motivation in Sincha Ronen, *Comparative and Multinational Management* (New York: John Wiley & Sons, 1986), chap 5.

21. Everett M. Kassalow, *Trade Unions and Industrial Relations: An International Comparison* (New York: Random House, 1969).

22. There are countless books and articles about Japanese labor and management practices. A few are Yoshi Tsurumi, *The Japanese Are Coming* (Cambridge, Mass.: Ballinger Publishing, 1976); Robert H. Hayes, "Why Japanese Factories Work," *McKinsey Quarterly,* Autumn 1982, pp. 32–48; and Hugh Sandeman, "The Best at the Game," *The Economist,* July 18, 1981, a survey of Japanese industry.

23. Masayoshi Kanabayashi, "Union Union," *The Wall Street Journal,* March 14, 1989, p. A1.

24. Roy B. Helfgott, "American Unions and Multinational Companies: A Case of Misplaced Emphasis," *Columbia Journal of World Business,* Summer 1983, p. 82.

25. Adolf Sturmthal, "Union Differences," *Europe,* May–June 1983, pp. 35–36.

26. *The Economist,* March 15, 1986, pp. 69–70.

27. *The Wall Street Journal,* March 12, 1979, p. 18.

28. Harry Bernstein, "Democracy Moves into Workplace," *Los Angeles Times,* October 23, 1980, pt. 1, pp. 1, 14–15.

29. "Doug Fraser's Conflicts," *The Wall Street Journal,* September 22, 1982, p. 28.

30. Sam Jameson, "Japanese Government to Its People: Work Less, Be Happy," *Los Angeles Times,* February 13, 1989, part 4, p. 3.

Chapter 13

Competitive and Distributive Forces

If there is a single great fact of our era, it is the emergence of the first truly international marketplace and the struggle between the leading trading nations and blocs: the United States, Western Europe, Japan, Singapore–Taiwan– Hong Kong–Korea, Mexico–Brazil, and, potentially, China.

Paraphrased from H. Lewis and D. Allison, *The Real War: The Coming Battle for the New Global Economy and Why We Are in Danger of Losing*

LEARNING OBJECTIVES

In this chapter, you will study:

1. The reasons why international competition has increased among the United States, Japan, the EC, and the newly industrializing nations.

2. The responsibilities of government, management, labor, and consumers in returning the United States to international competitiveness.

3. The changes in the EC that are the basis of Europe 1992.

4. The magnitude of product counterfeiting.

5. Competitive analysis.

6. The sources of competitive information.

7. The channel members available to those who export indirectly or directly or manufacture overseas.

8. Structural trends in wholesaling and retailing.

9. Parallel importing.

10. The factors influencing channel selection.

11. The bases on which management compares channel alternatives.

KEY WORDS AND CONCEPTS

- Generalized System of Preferences (GSP)
- National competitiveness
- Hit list (super 301)
- Industrial targeting
- Reverse imports
- European Economic Zone
- Lomé Convention
- Hollowing out
- Counterfeiting
- Reverse engineering
- Industrial espionage
- Competitive analysis
- Competitor Intelligence System (CIS)
- Sogo shosha
- Export trading company (ETC)
- Certificate of review
- Cooperative exporters
- Manufacturer's agent
- Distributors
- Trading companies
- Parallel importing
- Gray market
- Hypermarkets
- Superstores

BUSINESS INCIDENT

THIS IS WAR! At least it is according to William Peacock, former assistant secretary of the U.S. Army and a colonel in the Marine Corps Reserve. He says that although society sets up rules to prevent unfair practices, and the objective is not to destroy your competitors, business and war have much in common. Executives should apply the nine principles of war (MOOSEMUSS) that have always brought victorious military campaigns:

1. *Mass*—concentrate your strength at the enemy's weak point.
2. *Objective*—you must be clear as to what you want to accomplish.
3. *Offense*—few competitions are won by passivity.
4. *Simplicity*—make your own strategy simple and clear for your employees.
5. *Economy of force*—the fewest resources possible to keep the operation functioning.
6. *Maneuver or strategy used*—frontal, flanking, or rear assault.
7. *Unity of command*—clear assignments of responsibility.
8. *Surprise*—timing of battle.
9. *Security*—keep your strategy secret.

It is apparent that many chief executives, a number of whom have military training, are following these concepts. Companies go to great lengths to keep their plans secret: IBM, for example, has a sign posted in its offices that shows two people at a lunch table and a warning, "Be careful in casual conversation. Keep security in mind." And, like the military, many have installed intelligence systems. Motorola, seeking a full-scale intelligence effort, hired a former CIA agent to organize its program. Its intelligence efforts paid off.

The company's top managers, in a meeting with the corporate intelligence people and European managers, raised the question, "Are you concerned about Japanese semiconductor makers?" One European manager said,

BUSINESS INCIDENT (concluded)

"We see the Japanese—they have operations in Europe. But they're not aggressive." This prompted the intelligence staff to wonder why the Japanese weren't as aggressive with semiconductors as they were with VCRs and TVs. Motorola sent one of its intelligence staff, fluent in Japanese, to Tokyo. By visiting the U.S. embassy and various government offices, he learned that Japanese electronic manufacturers did plan within the next two years to double their capital investment in Europe for semiconductor plants, not for more VCR and TV plants. With this information, Motorola changed its strategy and began to work more closely with European manufacturers and customers and to compete vigorously with the Japanese for more partnerships in Europe. As a result, the company increased its market share even though the Japanese had begun their European assault.

Sources: William Peacock, *Corporate Combat* (Berkeley, Calif.: Berkeley Publishing, 1987), pp. 1–12; P. Kotler and G. Armstrong, *Principles of Marketing*, 4th ed. (Englewood Cliffs, N.J.: Prentice-Hall, 1989), p. 93; "Competitive Intelligence Efforts on the Rise," *Marketing Communications*, January 20, 1987, p. 5; and "Corporate Spies Stoop to Conquer," *Fortune*, November 7, 1988, p. 76.

F or a number of reasons, many of which were discussed in Chapter 2, world competition has intensified, and a total of four nations and distinguishable groups of nations whose firms are in worldwide competition with each other have emerged: (1) the United States, (2) the European Community, (3) Japan, and (4) the newly industrializing countries (NICs), especially South Korea, Taiwan, Hong Kong, and Singapore (see the quotation at the beginning of this chapter).

Generalized System of Preferences (GSP) an agreement under the auspices of GATT, under which many products of developing nations are provided duty-free access to most developed nations.

When the U.S. trade deficit with the Asian NICs reached $37 billion (22 percent of the total U.S. trade deficit) in 1987, the United States decided to remove them from the trade program for developing nations, the **Generalized System of Preferences (GSP)**, beginning in 1989. Under the GSP, products from 140 nations not given preferential treatment under any other agreement are provided duty-free access to most developed nations. During the Uruguay Round, other GATT members also recognized that these four nations had "graduated."

Let us examine these four groups, first at the national (macro) level and then at the industry (micro) level.

COMPETITION AT THE MACRO LEVEL (NATIONAL COMPETITIVENESS)

A new concern for the ability of a nation to compete has arisen in the United States, the European Community, and, more recently, in Japan. Nations, of course, do not compete against each other; their companies do. However, because most economic and social conditions as well as political actions affect the ability of all of a nation's firms to compete in world markets, it is convenient to speak of **national competitiveness.**

national (macro) competition ability of a nation's producers to compete successfully in world markets and with imports in their own domestic markets.

United States

Although the lag in national competitiveness did not become apparent until the 1980s, it began in the 1970s. During that time, imports were getting a bigger share of the market, but they were offset by a growing share of the export market achieved with a dollar whose value was dropping relative to other major currencies at an average annual rate of 2.5 percent. However, when the dollar's value rose at the beginning of the 1980s, American unit labor costs mounted, causing imports to increase and U.S. exports to decrease, and, not until 1985 — when the dollar's value again declined — did labor costs begin to fall and American exports become more price competitive.[1]

During these years, American firms first experienced growing competition in this country from European and Japanese firms that were buying U.S. firms because the cheap dollar made them inexpensive in those currencies. Moreover, the size of the market, and the availability of raw materials, the developed capital markets, and the political stability combined to attract massive foreign investment, which created new competitors and strengthened old ones.

As the value of the dollar rose and U.S. firms experienced difficulty competing in both the U.S. and overseas markets, protectionist sentiment grew in this country, which provided additional impetus for foreign investors to set up U.S.-based operations. Of course, when the dollar again fell in the late 1980s, foreign firms that were still supplying this market with exports found it difficult to compete pricewise with domestic products, and thus they too established production in the United States. Those that did not lost either sales or profits if they cut prices to remain competitive. Japanese exporters of high-technology items, including automobiles, electronics, and computers, lost over 40 percent of their profits as they tried to meet U.S. prices in face of a yen that rose from 260 per dollar to 123 in just two years.[2]

Although the overvalued dollar was one of the principal reasons for the decrease in American competitiveness, it was not the only one. A number of nonprice factors, such as quality, delivery, time, after-sales service, reliability of supply, and trade barriers to U.S. exports, were also responsible. It was obvious that to increase American exports, corrective measures had to be taken by government, management, and labor.

Government.   Government officials have for some time been pressuring other governments to lower their trade barriers and stimulate their economies to increase demand for American exports. As a result of American insistence, Germany lowered its discount rate, and Japan adopted several fiscal and monetary measures to encourage consumption. The U.S. government is also using the threat of retaliation more effectively. This caused Japan to stop dumping semiconductors into third markets and to open up its telecommunications market to American firms. The threat of retaliation has worked even better in Taiwan and Korea because they are more dependent on the American market than is Japan. Both have eliminated some trade barriers and have enacted new laws to protect American patents, which is important because of the illegal copying of U.S. goods.

Hit list.   Acting under Section 301 of the 1988 Trade Act, nicknamed "super 301," Carla Hills, U.S. trade representative, placed Japan, India, and Brazil on the unfair trading partner **hit list** in May 1989. Japan was designated specifically for unfairly resisting imports of satellites, supercomputers, and forest products; Brazil for requiring import licenses (to protect local industry, it refuses 90 percent of the applications for importing capital goods); and India for its barriers to foreign investment and foreign insurance companies. The law requires the government to negotiate with these countries on these specific

hit list (super 301) Section 301 of the U.S. 1988 Trade Act, which requires U.S. trade representative to prepare a list of countries that systematically restrict access of American products to their markets

points and, if they are not resolved, to impose trade sanctions. As evidence of the new trade law's potential for opening markets, officials note that Korea and Taiwan made recent concessions to remain off the list. The administration placed 8 nations (including Brazil, for other trade practices) on a priority watch list, which will be reviewed in eight months, and another 25 on a watch list. Europe was on the list originally but was dropped, some people say, for political reasons.[3]

Complaints against the United States.   The United States has also come under attack from its trading partners for ignoring GATT rules while insisting that GATT's dispute procedure be strengthened. In 1988, a GATT panel agreed with a complaint from the EC that Section 337 of the 1988 Trade Act discriminates against non-American patent holders. At four subsequent GATT meetings, American representatives have blocked adoption of the report.[4] A number of governments also complain about U.S. restrictions on the imports of automobiles, textiles, and steel.

Other efforts of the government to improve U.S. competitiveness include (1) stricter enforcement of dumping laws, (2) focusing on improvement of the nation's educational system, and (3) working to complete deregulation of industry (as an example from the trucking industry, a Dallas retailer pays *less* transportation costs to import a pair of jeans from Taiwan than it does to bring them in from Texas manufacturers in El Paso).

Government must do more.   Critics, nonetheless, point out that more must be done. Some economists believe the most significant action the government can take to reduce the trade deficit is to lower the federal budget deficit, thereby decreasing the amount of savings consumed by the government.[5] But others claim that the trade deficit exists because the strong U.S. economy has created a demand for imports that is greater than the volume of American exports that the less robust foreign economies can buy. In fact, it has been estimated that if economic activity outside the United States grew by 1 percent, the U.S. trade balance would improve by $10 billion annually.

Another measure suggested is to eliminate the double taxation of company profits. If shareholder's dividends aren't taxed, proponents say, more will be invested in America's industries. They want capital gains taxes brought back for the same reason. Some say the United States must have a national economic plan, but others compare this country's economic preference with that of countries having plans and say the less government involvement, the better. Legal experts recommend changes in U.S. antitrust laws to permit firms to finance, construct, and operate expensive high-tech production facilities jointly without fear of an antitrust suit. Such arrangements are becoming commonplace in Europe and Japan.

Research consortia are permitted in the United States, however, and in fact, the government is encouraging their formation. Recently, AT&T, IBM, and MIT announced the formation of the Consortium for Superconducting Electronics, which will compete with the Japanese in the commercialization of high-temperature superconductivity. More than 100 research consortia have been formed by U.S. firms to foster development of products ranging from computers to light bulbs. The government is urging industry to organize a consortium to develop high-definition television, a field in which Japanese industry has already made considerable progress.[6]

industrial targeting   government practice of assisting selected industries to grow

Industrial targeting.   The government can also do more to support American companies that face competition from targeted industries. **Industrial targeting,** the practice of government assisting selected industries to grow by a variety of means, is becoming common in Europe and Japan. France, for example, modernized its railroad industry by modernizing its rail system. Equipment contracts were given only to French suppliers. By building a strong home base first, French suppliers were ready for the export market. Increasingly, the U.S. mass transit market is being dominated by the French and the Japanese, both of whose governments support target industries. Another industry targeted by European nations is the manufacture of aircraft built around the Airbus, which is estimated to have received $6 billion in subsidies since the 1970s. A Boeing official states that the "Airbus was allowed to start a program without a sufficient order base and at production rates that would force a U.S. manufacturer to shut down."[7]

Accusations that Japan has targeted its aviation industry for world status arose when General Dynamics announced a plan to collaborate with Mitsubishi Heavy Industries to design and produce the FSX, an improved version of the F-16, a U.S. jet fighter plane. Instead of buying the F-16 from General Dynamics, as opponents of the arrangement argue it should, the Japanese government wants joint Japanese-American development of a new plane. It has guaranteed that the U.S. partner will get 40 percent of the aircraft's production as well as 40 percent of its research and development. Mitsubishi will also provide advanced radar and electronic warfare systems not currently available in the United States. Furthermore, it will not gain access to the F-16's computer software, which controls the plane's flight and weapons systems. General Dynamics expects to earn $480 million from the new plane's development and $2 billion from production of the 130 fighter planes. Although some representatives from Congress objected that the United States was giving away its technology, President Bush approved the project.[8]

As you can see, the role of the government in improving the competitive position of American industry is significant; however, there is much that management, labor, and the consumers can do.

Management.   Company presidents must make product quality and increased productivity their top priorities. They must also prepare long-range strategic plans and be willing to invest long-term instead of expecting an immediate return, and they must be more aggressive against foreign competition. More companies should emulate 3M (see Worldview).

It appears that there has been a marked change in how American executives assess the blame for the U.S. decline in competitiveness. A poll of Fortune 500 CEOs showed that nearly all believed it was their fault.[9] When asked what were the most important steps U.S. industry can take to improve its world competitiveness, 30 percent responded, "Improve quality"; 29 percent answered, "Improve productivity"; and 21 percent replied, "Increase R&D and modernize plants." One executive commented, "We make too many excuses rather than tailor our products to serve foreign markets." He agreed with Tom Peters (*A Passion for Excellence*) that American firms don't extend themselves to meet Japan's needs and gave as an example the reason for U.S. automobile manufacturers' failure to sell many cars in Japan: they refuse to put steering wheels on the right side (Japanese drive on the right side of the road)

WORLDVIEW
3M Positions Itself for Long-Term Growth

Minnesota Mining & Manufacturing Co. (3M) makes 60,000 products, which generated revenues in 1988 of $10.6 billion, an increase of 12 percent over 1987. Operations in 50 other countries account for 40 percent of these sales and 41 percent of its profits. In *Fortune's* annual survey, it ranked 6th out of 306 entries as the most admired company. It is often cited for its product innovation. In fact, researchers are encouraged to spend 15 percent of their time pursuing pet projects that might not pay off for a long time. Another encouragement to innovation is that 25 percent of each division's annual sales are expected to come from products developed in the previous five years. Besides bringing out new products, researchers are required to protect and extend the product line to keep ahead of competitors.

It was not always this way. In 1970, 3M had 30 percent of the market for magnetic recording tape, which it had developed. Yet in only five years, Japanese producers such as Maxell and TDK had taken most of that market.

Now 3M is in another war with the Japanese—videotape. The company believes the Japanese thought they could drive it out of tapes again by slashing prices, but this time 3M has matched their prices. The company is spending heavily to improve the quality and production efficiency of its tapes and floppy disks—22 percent of its total capital budget. It is also spending heavily on packaging, advertising, and sales promotion. Says the sales director of TDK's American subsidiary, "I have never seen an effort of this magnitude."

The company appears to be winning its battle, as it is now the leading brand produced in the United States, with a 19 percent market share. It has 13 percent of the world market. One dramatic change is 3M's departure from its practice of refusing to fund ventures that do not measure up to its ROI standards. The group vice president in charge of these products insists that 3M will not give in: "We are positioning everything with the long term in mind." An industry analyst adds, "For one of the first times, the company is looking longer than just one quarter."

Sources: "Keeping the Fires Lit Under the Innovators," *Fortune,* May 1988, p. 22; and "How 3M Is Trying to Out-Japanese the Japanese," *Business Week,* August 26, 1985, p. 65.

---

and then assume the Japanese won't buy American cars because they don't like them.[10]

Marketing myths.   However, according to one writer, the "steering wheel on the wrong side" is a marketing myth. The reality, he claims, is that most Japanese who buy a Mercedes or a BMW prefer having the steering wheel on the left side. Apparently, it's a status symbol. If you were given a Rolls Royce, would you put up with the inconvenience of a steering wheel on the right side? Honda quickly sold out the U.S.-made Accords it recently brought to Japan because, according to a Japanese writer, "This automobile captured the hearts of young people with its left-hand steering wheel and luxury interior, because it was 'unlike other cars found in Japan.' "[11] This is just one of a growing number of Japanese **reverse imports.**

reverse imports products made by a multinational's overseas subsidiaries that are exported to the home country

This myth is like another that has been told for many years. As the story goes, Chevrolet couldn't sell Novas in _____ (the storyteller picks a Spanish-speaking country) because Nova means *no va* (doesn't go) in Spanish. What the person doesn't realize is that the two are pronounced differently—Nova has the accent over the first syllable, whereas the accent for *no va* falls on the *va.* Therefore, to someone speaking Spanish, the words are pronounced

Shoppers examine a Chevrolet Camaro in a Tokyo showroom

Source: *Time*, June 5, 1989, p. 55

very differently and have very different meanings. You may be surprised to learn that Pemex, the government-owned oil monopoly that is the exclusive refiner and retailer of gasoline in Mexico, has named its no-lead gasoline *Nova*.[12]

Labor.   Labor must also take the long-term view, and unions have done so in recent years. There has been a marked increase in their willingness to work with management instead of maintaining the traditional adversarial role. An example is the looser work rules. Workers can be transferred to another work station when needed and can perform a simple maintenance job instead of calling a maintenance worker to do it while they wait and do nothing. Managers' efforts to share profits and to involve workers in decision making by means of quality circles and shop floor meetings have contributed to this change in attitude.

Consumers.   The role of the consumer is crucial in American industry's drive to improve its competitiveness. Although U.S. automobiles cost less than comparable foreign models, American buyers seem to ignore the price advantage. As a result, the market share of GM, Ford, and Chrysler has continued to decline to less than 70 percent at present. People buy a Toyota Camry with a four-cylinder motor, air conditioning, cruise control, and AM/FM stereo for $16,562 when they could have a Pontiac Bonneville LE, a bigger car with a V-6 engine, automatic transmission, and power windows in addition to the equipment on the Toyota, for $16,429. When asked why, one buyer responded, "I have a 1982 Toyota. It's been seven years and 93,000 miles, just minimum maintenance. I love 'em." Foreign car buyers apparently don't realize that all U.S. automakers have gotten the message on quality. One Olds dealer says, "Our quality is good now. We've laid off mechanics because

■ **FIGURE 13–1   Many American Products Command a Major Share of the Japanese Market**

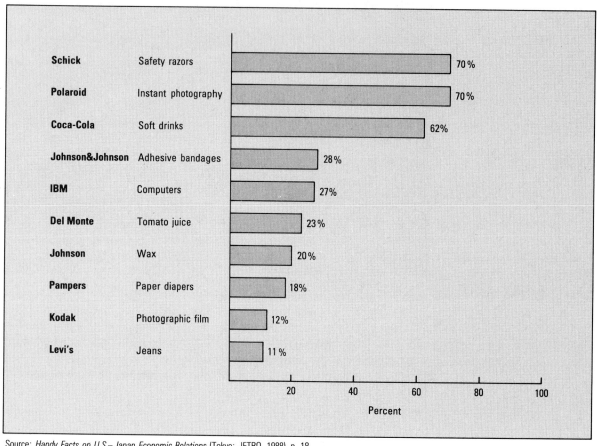

Source: *Handy Facts on U.S.–Japan Economic Relations* (Tokyo: JETRO, 1988), p. 18.

the warranty business is not there. But a few years ago, customers were lined up to get in for repairs."[13]

But it isn't only the American automakers that have the problem of convincing American consumers to buy their products. How about this example of schizophrenia? A secretary in Chicago said, "I resent foreigners coming in and taking over our country." But she recently bought a Mitsubishi color television and video recorder.[14] Meanwhile, Matsushita exports U.S.-made TV sets to Japan.

For the most part, Japanese manufacturers don't have this problem. Although the younger Japanese are avid purchasers of imports, consumers generally seem to have a bias against foreign goods, as the Japanese premier found when he tried to exhort them to buy American imports to reduce the Japanese trade surplus with the United States. In Tokyo, a 50-year-old was looking at a CD player made in Korea whose price was less than half of what he would have to pay for a Japanese equivalent. He shrugged and put it back. "No," he said, "I'm afraid it might break."[15] As Figure 13–1 illustrates, there seems to be much less reluctance toward buying locally made products from American affiliates.

European Community

With the formation of the European Community, one market was created out of six. Not only did the larger market attract new competitors from outside Europe, it also gave firms that had heretofore been selling in only one member-country easy access to five additional markets. Competition increased with the admission of Greece in 1981 and was heightened when Spain and Portugal entered in 1986. In addition, producers of industrial—but not agricultural—products were confronted with competition from EFTA member-countries when the **European Economic Zone,** combining the EFTA and EC nations, was formed in 1984 (see Figure 13–2).

A preferential arrangement, known as the **Lomé Convention,** which is similar to the GSP, was begun in 1974 and is a source of LDC competition for some European producers. This is an aid, trade, and investment treaty between 66 African, Caribbean, and Pacific states (ACP) and the EC that is renewed every five years. Virtually all ACP exports enter the EC duty free and are not subject to quotas (see Figure 13–3).[16]

Competition from Japan.   European industry was also getting competition from outside the EC. Japanese automakers, which had sold few cars in Europe in the 1970s, began increasing their market share wherever EC member-nations' import quotas permitted. In countries where they have relatively free access, such as Ireland, the Netherlands, and West Germany, they are formidable competitors. In Ireland, for example, they have 43 percent of the market; but in Italy, which has an agreement with Japan to limit car imports, Japanese imports have only 0.5 percent. France permits only 3 percent; Great Britain, 10 percent; and Spain, 1 percent. Ironically, the treaty with Japan was designed to prevent *Italian* cars from flooding *Japanese* markets shortly after WW II.[17] Despite the restrictions, Japan is selling over 1 million cars in the EC annually, and its total market share is already 11 percent.[18] Europe has become Japan's prime export target, the Europeans say, because the U.S. Voluntary Restraint Agreement limits car exports to the U.S. market.

As you know, many Japanese firms have established production facilities in the United States because of the threat of protectionism, and about 400 have also begun to produce within the EC. Interestingly, although there are indicators that all the Japanese automakers are planning production facilities in Europe, only Nissan has one, a plant located in England. In contrast, General Motors and Ford have had a number of plants in Europe for years (GM started in Denmark in 1923 and Ford in England in 1911).[19]

Not only automobiles.   Automobiles are only one facet of the Japanese onslaught in Europe. As in the United States, Japanese imports have nearly eliminated the European motorcycle industry. Japanese cameras and watches are market leaders, and every small color TV tube used in Europe is made by Japanese electronic companies with local production facilities.

Since 1982, Japanese exports to Europe have doubled—from $17 billion to over $40 billion. European firms have reacted by initiating a wave of dumping complaints to force the European Community to raise antidumping duties, but even more worrisome to Japanese exporters is the threat to include an "anti-screwdriver" provision in EC import regulations. European and also American officials complain that Japanese companies are avoiding dumping penalties by

---

European Economic Zone the European Free Trade Zone, consisting of the EC and EFTA

Lomé Convention an agreement between 66 African, Caribbean, and Pacific states (ACP) and the EC by which 99.2 percent of the ACP's exports are admitted duty free to the EC

■ **FIGURE 13–2   The European Economic Space (EC and EFTA) Takes in Some 350 Million Consumers**

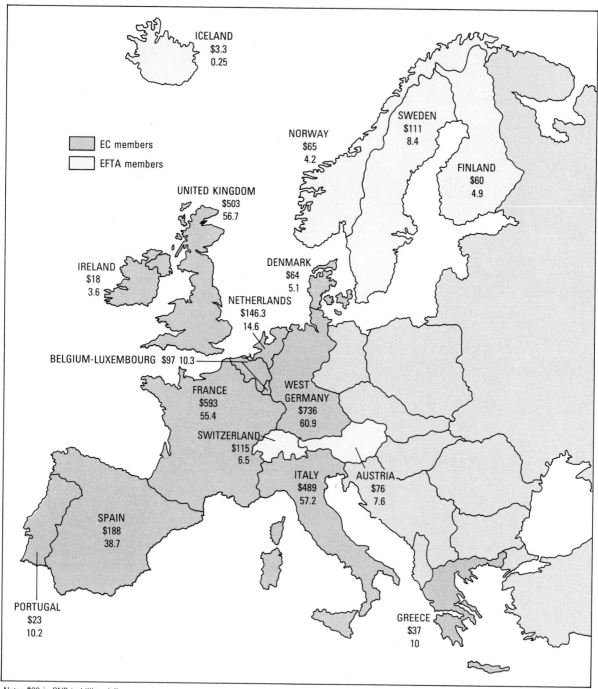

ICELAND
$3.3
0.25

EC members
EFTA members

NORWAY
$65
4.2

SWEDEN
$111
8.4

FINLAND
$60
4.9

UNITED KINGDOM
$503
56.7

IRELAND
$18
3.6

DENMARK
$64
5.1

NETHERLANDS
$146.3
14.6

BELGIUM-LUXEMBOURG $97 10.3

FRANCE
$593
55.4

WEST
GERMANY
$736
60.9

SWITZERLAND
$115
6.5

ITALY
$489
57.2

AUSTRIA
$76
7.6

SPAIN
$188
38.7

PORTUGAL
$23
10.2

GREECE
$37
10

Note: $00 is GNP in billion dollars.
      00.0 is population in millions.
Source: Data from *World Development Report, 1988* (New York: World Bank, 1988), p. 223.

■ **FIGURE 13-3   Countries Linked to the EC in the Lomé Convention Trade-and-Aid Treaty**

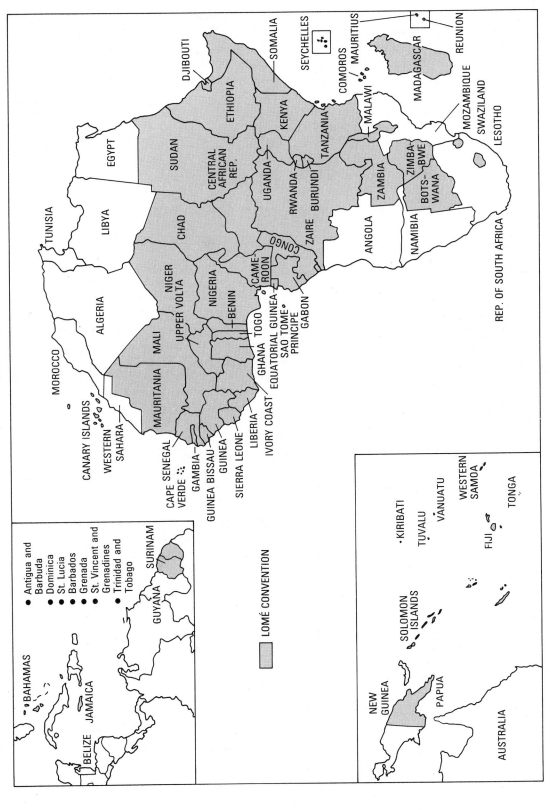

importing products in pieces involved at lower prices and assembling them with no more capital equipment than a screwdriver. Requiring higher local content would halt this practice, but it would also accelerate local investment by Japanese parts manufacturers, thus reducing the benefits that European firms could expect to receive from this provision. In fact, Common Market rules state that any car must have a minimum of 60 percent European content to be treated as European-made and therefore exempt from quotas. However, French and Italian producers are pressing for 80 percent because at that level, they believe Nissan will have difficulty maintaining an advantage over European manufacturers in cost and quality. What about automobiles made in the United States by Japanese companies? Fiat chairman Agnelli replies, "American car exports are welcome in Europe—provided they are American products, not Japanese cars made in the United States." In other words, U.S.-made Japanese cars will have to increase their American content from the present 55 percent average to be considered American exports in Europe.[20]

Competition from the United States.   European firms face competition from American exports like they do from Japan, but, unlike Japan, U.S. companies have had European-based manufacturing facilities for a long time. European-produced GM and Ford cars compete in the automobile market; brands such as Heinz, Kodak, and Coca-Cola are household names (the English "hoover" their rugs instead of vacuuming them); and computer manufacturers IBM and Digital Equipment dominate the market. Probably because of the long-term political and cultural ties plus the fact that European multinationals have been free to invest in the United States with minimum hindrance, American companies have generally been well accepted in Europe. The occasional EC–U.S. "chicken," "pasta," and "citrus" wars have not had a serious impact on the European subsidiaries of American WWCs.

Yet, European governments are working to defend certain national companies from American competition. They have helped Airbus in its battle against Boeing and have funded the Joint European Submicron Silicon (JESSI), a semiconductor consortium, to help European companies compete against American and Japanese chipmakers. IBM, which makes 35 percent of its chips in Europe, wants to join, but JESSI is resisting because Sematech—a U.S. consortium composed of Texas Instruments, IBM, Motorola, Intel, LSI Logic, and AT&T—refuses to admit foreigners.[21] However, and most important of all for American firms, the European Community is preparing for Europe 1992.

Europe 1992.   Three changes that have taken place are the basis of Europe 1992:

1. Europeans have come to realize that they cannot compete with the United States and Japan as long as EC markets are fragmented.
2. EC nations have agreed to trust each other sufficiently to reach a decision by majority vote rather than by unanimity, as was previously required.
3. They have recognized that the 12 member-nations could only become a single market by harmonizing safety, health, and other standards.[22]

One of the few generalizations that can be made about post-Europe 1992 is that competition is going to be much greater and that it will come from (1)

European firms made stronger by mergers, alliances, and acquisitions and (2) American and Japanese firms that are rushing to become established within the EC. Despite EC assurances to the contrary, many believe "fortress Europe" is a realistic threat because the whole object of Europe 1992 is to make the EC a true economic superpower. As a representative of British International Computers put it, "We shall buy from European sources whenever we can. We want to create a third force, like the United States and Japan, and frankly, we're going to use the same methods they've used for years.[23]

A counselor at the EC Delegation offices in Tokyo made a statement that troubles many Japanese firms: "We may well have to create a Community regime for very specific sectors which are still sensitive, where we cannot afford, in a period of high unemployment, to see an industry go under to the kind of laser beam torrential exports which we have suffered, only too painfully, in the past." This is something the Japanese understood, because they have protected various industries from foreign competition until they became world competitors. Fortunately for U.S. and Canadian WWCs, the U.S.–Canada Free Trade Agreement will give these nations more strength in dealing with the new EC.[24]

Competition from the Asian newly industrializing countries. Much as Japanese firms have done, the Asian NICs have increased their exports—especially of electronics, textiles, and shoes—to Europe in the face of increasing U.S. pressure to lower their trade surpluses with the United States. Korea's efforts to diversify its export markets, for example, have expanded the European share of its total exports at an average annual rate of 23 percent since 1983. In 1987, Korean firms sold 1.7 million microwave ovens, more than were produced in all of the EC. Taiwan, Hong Kong, and Singapore have made large export gains as well. Low labor costs and favorable exchange rates have enabled manufacturers from all of these countries to sell at prices at which European producers cannot compete. The European Commission found that Korean shoe manufacturers were underselling French firms by 70 percent, enabling them to sell 23 million pairs in 1987. It put antidumping duties of almost 30 percent on VCRs made by Samsung, Daewoo, and Goldstar. Because the EC is fighting their predatory pricing, Korean firms are following the Japanese example of setting up plants inside the EC.[25] Thailand, who many believe is going to be the next Asian NIC, and India are also increasing their exports to Europe. Interestingly, some Korean firms are now moving part of their operations to Thailand because of the educated work force and lower labor costs.

Japan

Thirty-eight percent of the textile manufacturers have shut down, and textile employment has halved. Cheap imports and a strong currency make it impossible for them to compete. They're accusing developing nations of dumping. And it is not only textiles—electrical appliances and cameras are also suffering. Walk into any mass marketer like K mart and you no longer see foreign-made products with national brand names. Now those foreign manufacturers are putting their own brands on them.

Trying to remain competitive, national manufacturers are cutting prices (and their profits) and cutting costs by laying off workers and moving many operations overseas, where labor costs are lower. They've closed production facilities and slashed salaries and overtime pay. Unemployment is record high, and so are business failures. There are complaints that key industries are **hollowing out,** that is, closing their local production facilities and becoming marketing organizations for other, mostly foreign, producers. Complaints are being heard that the nation is becoming a service economy.[26]

hollowing out firms closing their production facilities and becoming marketing organizations for other, mostly foreign, producers

Japan is facing increased competition, too.   Is this the United States? No, this is Japan whose industry is facing increasing competition in foreign markets as well as at home. Much of it has been caused by the strong yen, of course, but pressure from Japan's trading partners to relax the legal and administrative barriers to imports and foreign investment is also a contributing factor. Japan has responded with tariff reductions (it now has the lowest average import duty rates of the developed nations), changes in the law that permit wholly owned subsidiaries, and a general streamlining of government administrative procedures.

These activities have resulted in a stepped-up involvement of foreign firms in the Japanese economy.[27] In data processing, for example, six American multinationals compete with Japanese producers for a share of the world's second-largest market. IBM once held first place in this market but slipped to third place behind Japan's Fujitsu and NEC. After making numerous changes in its marketing strategy, its sales rose in 1988 to tie with NEC's, and its 27 percent market share approached the 29 percent of Fujitsu. IBM also won a copyright battle with Fujitsu, who agreed to pay $833.2 million to obtain immunity against IBM's claims that it illegally copied IBM's mainframe operating system. Hitachi, the fourth-ranked competitor, settled a similar case in 1983.[28]

Another area of business in which the American WWCs have achieved significant market penetration is the restaurant industry. Fast-food chains, such as McDonald's, Kentucky Fried Chicken, and Denny's, have been so successful in what is described as a $34 billion market that they have appreciably altered Japanese dining habits. Such WWCs as Avon, PepsiCo, Exxon, Nestlé, and Coca-Cola have shown that the Japanese market is penetrable when time and money are spent first to investigate the market and then to make a long-term commitment to develop it. U.S. companies are represented in over 85 percent of Japan's 126 industrial sectors, and 12 American companies hold the top market position in their fields.[29]

Expensive yen causes export problems.   As you saw in the beginning of this section, it is in the export market that Japanese manufacturers are finding their greatest challenge. The appreciation of the yen from 260 per dollar in 1985 to 123 per dollar in 1988 caused exporters' profits to decrease by more than 60 percent. Export volume has dropped, though the results have been masked by the fact that Japanese trade statistics are reported in dollars. Because the yen has appreciated against the dollar faster than exports valued in yen have fallen, Japan's export performance appears better than it really is.

The newly industrializing countries whose currencies have not risen appreciably against the dollar are making serious inroads into Japanese export markets, especially the United States. South Korea has greatly increased its U.S. and Japanese market share of television sets, steel, and VCRs.

■ TABLE 13–1
Increases in
Merchandise Exports for
Selected Countries,
1965–1987 (Dollars in
billions)

| | Percentage Increase | | |
	1980–87	1965–80	Value in 1987
Turkey	17.1%	5.5%	$ 10.19
South Korea	14.3	27.2	47.17
Taiwan	13.5	19.0	50.8
China	11.7	5.5	39.5
Hong Kong	11.4	9.5	48.5
Thailand	10.2	8.5	11.7
Malaysia	9.7	4.4	17.9
Mexico	6.6	7.6	20.9
Canada	6.3	5.4	92.9
Singapore	6.1	4.7	28.6
Japan	5.8	11.4	229.1
Brazil	5.6	9.3	26.2
West Germany	4.7	7.2	293.8
United States	−0.5	6.4	252.6
EC (12)	7.8	2.1	1,094.1

Source: *World Development Report 1989* (Washington, D.C.: World Bank, 1989), Table 14, pp. 190–91.

In response to this competition, Japanese firms have attempted to maintain export market share by passing through only part of the yen's appreciation to foreign customers. For example, Toyota raised its U.S. prices in 1986 just three times, for a total of 10 percent, although the yen appreciated more than 30 percent. In addition, Japanese firms are trying to avoid direct competition from the NICs by hurriedly bringing out sophisticated new products that will justify higher prices, such as luxury automobiles and large-screen TVs. They are also building plants in countries where labor costs are lower, and they are increasing their investments in the United States and Europe to protect themselves from the appreciated yen.

Japan was facing unprecedented rates of unemployment and company failures by 1987, and the government had come to realize that to sustain economic growth, the country must reduce its current high dependence on exports and enlarge the domestic market. The increase in government spending and the tax-revision plan are indications that it is moving in this direction.

Developing Nations

Not only have the Asian NICs greatly increased their merchandise exports, but certain developing nations have done so as well, as Table 13–1 illustrates.

Although the export growth of the Asian NICs should be no surprise, you might not have been aware that nations such as Turkey, Brazil, Thailand, Mexico, and China had made such sizable gains. You can also see from Table 13–1 why the rest of the world is following the development of Europe 1992, already the world's largest trading bloc. Turkey is industrializing and should become the next EC member if Austria decides not to join first. Brazil has an especially diverse export mix, and much of the $10 billion in manufactured

From fake dolls to . . .

Source: © 1984, Walt Disney Productions

products exports goes to developing nations (42 percent). They are especially strong in Africa because of geographic proximity and similarities of race, culture, and climate. Brazil sells such products as automobiles, trucks, armored vehicles (it is the largest exporter in the world after the USSR), airplanes, shoes, and heavy construction equipment.

Counterfeiting.   A special kind of competition confronted by WWCs in developing and developed nations is **counterfeiting.** The use of manufacturers' names on products that are copies of the genuine products is estimated to cost the legitimate owners over $70 billion annually and is especially prevalent in countries such as Korea, Hong Kong, Thailand, and Indonesia. Until recently, Taiwan was one of the major sources of counterfeit products; shoppers couldn't tell Oranges and Pineapples from Apples. But after four years and more than 100 lawsuits against the product pirates, Apple has stopped the illegal copying of its computers.

Although Apple used a former narcotics agent and attorneys to locate and prosecute counterfeiters and their dealers, the company gives the Taiwanese government much of the credit for its success, as does General Motors, who says Taiwan's police have closed shops making fake GM parts.[30] A new law levies a $3,750 fine or a sentence of up to five years in jail for violators.

Counterfeit products can be dangerous.   Is your Polo shirt or Gucci handbag real? Easy-to-copy products with high markups, such as luxury goods (Gucci, Vuitton, and Cartier) have long been counterfeited, but products now routinely copied include pesticides, fertilizers, drugs, toys, car and airplane parts, and electronic items. Besides causing legitimate manufacturers to lose sales, these fakes sometimes bring tragedy to users when, as is frequent, they fail to perform as well as the original. Farmers in Zaire and Kenya bought what they thought was Chevron's top-quality pesticide, which turned out to be a fake made of chalk. The two countries lost two thirds of their cash crops for

counterfeiting   illegal use of a well-known manufacturer's brand name on copies of the firm's merchandise

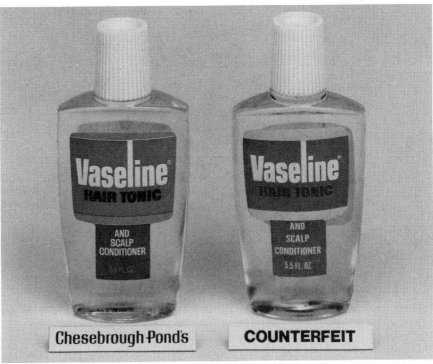

Fake hair tonic

that year. Bell Helicopter found counterfeit parts in 600 helicopters sold to civilians and the military; it said some of them may have caused crashes. One or more tragedies were avoided when the Food and Drug Administration recalled 350 pumps used to keep people alive during open-heart surgery. It found an $8 counterfeit part in a $20,000 pump that threatened to stall.[31] Even bolts are counterfeited. Army investigators checking for Japanese counterfeit bolts were told by a tank commander, "If you want to collect samples of bad bolts, just follow my tanks down the road." At Fort Ord, California, a battalion officer became so frustrated with bolt problems on his troops' vehicles that he bought legitimate bolts from a local hardware store with his own money.[32]

Combating imitations.   Levi Strauss has probably gone further than most firms to rid the market of imitations. The company has a corporate security organization with an annual million-dollar budget to stop this unfair competition. Levi Strauss was also instrumental in forming the International Anticounterfeiting Coalition (IAC), which now has 60 member-firms from 11 countries. Member-firms exchange information on problems they are encountering in certain markets and how they are handling them. The coalition lobbies in the United States and other countries to increase the penalties for commercial counterfeiting. Because of these efforts, U.S. Customs is now empowered to seize and destroy counterfeit goods when they are discovered at a point of entry.

In addition to the ICA, other industry groups are working to stop product counterfeiting. One is the Intellectual Property Committee comprising 13 of

Vrai (true) and Faux (false)

Courtesy of les must de Cartier

the largest U.S. patentholders, such as IBM, General Electric, and Pfizer (the pharmaceutical industry is one of the biggest victims of international piracy). Another group, the International Intellectual Property Alliance, represents 1,600 firms in the software, motion picture, computer, and book and music publishing industries. A third, Business Software Association, claims that illegal copies in such countries as Brazil, Taiwan, Mexico, India, and Korea cost its members $4.1 billion in lost sales annually.[33] Industry pressure was a significant factor in motivating the U.S. government to negotiate a worldwide agreement to protect intellectual property rights at the ongoing GATT meeting in Uruguay.

Industrial espionage.   Usually, a counterfeiter can copy a patented design by **reverse engineering** (taking the finished article apart), but when that is not feasible, the copier may obtain blueprints or process information by means of **industrial espionage.**

For years, companies have been acquiring information about each other by hiring competitors' employees, talking to competitors' customers, and so forth. More recently, however, intensified competition has motivated firms to become more sophisticated in this endeavor, even to the point of committing illegal acts. Mitsubishi, for example, was indicted on charges of stealing industrial secrets from Celanese, and Hitachi pleaded guilty to conspiring to transport stolen IBM technical documents to Japan.

The Soviet Union has a massive program to steal technology from American firms, especially those in the aircraft and computer industries. West Germans employed by Russia successfully moved semiconductor equipment from Silicon Valley through Western Europe to the USSR. Only 16 months after Boeing had flown its first short takeoff and landing plane (STOL), the Russians flew an exact copy with all of Boeing's breakthroughs in aerodynamic design.[34] Industrial espionage by foreign companies and governments is estimated to cost American industry $20 billion annually.

---

reverse engineering (benchmarking) dismantling a competitor's product to learn everything possible about it

---

industrial espionage spying on a competitor to learn its trade and production secrets

---

COMPETITION AT THE INDUSTRY LEVEL

When we discussed national competitiveness, we had to look at competitiveness between industries in the four trading groups and even at competition within an industry because all of this is part of competition at the macro level. However, when you study the histories of the major industries, such as steel, chemicals, pharmaceuticals, or electronics, you find a similar set of factors concerning competition. As you read about the steel industry, think about similar situations you have already encountered in this chapter.

Steel Industry

After WW II, the U.S. steel industry possessed technological superiority over its international competitors. By 1955, the United States supplied 40 percent of the world's steel needs and imported only 1 percent of its domestic consumption. Thirty years later, however, the U.S. steel industry accounted for just 11 percent of the world's production, and over 25 percent of U.S. consumption was imported.[35] What caused this change?

Reasons for the decline in U.S. competitiveness.   First, many producers misjudged their demand prospects. Because the demand for steel is a derived demand (that is, sales depend on the demand for products using steel), managements failed to appreciate that the major growth industries, such as telecommunications, energy, aerospace, computers, and electronics, unlike the leading industries prior to 1950, were not intensive users of steel. They also failed to foresee the impact that the large increases in energy prices would have on the automotive industry, one of their largest customers. Lighter-weight and more corrosion-resistant materials, such as aluminum, plastics, and fiberglass, took a large share of their market. The amount of steel required to produce $1 of GDP in the United States fell by 4 percent annually from 1973 to 1984.

Second, during the 1970s and 80s, the LDCs more than doubled their steel output, which not only resulted in a loss of export markets for steelmakers in the United States and other industrialized nations but also gave them more competition in their home markets. Tables 13–2 and 13–3 illustrate what occurred.[36]

Other reasons for the decline in U.S. competitiveness in the steel industry are excessive wage settlements, inadequate investment in new technology, low R&D expenditures, burdensome environmental and other governmental regulations, unfair competition, and unfavorable exchange rates. For example, a major technological innovation during the 1970s was the continuous-casting process, which reduces wastage of molten steel, lowers energy used, and produces more uniform quality. By 1984, only 40 percent of the U.S. steelmaking capacity used continuous casting, compared with 89 percent in Japan and 65 percent in the EC.[37]

Japan's steel industry.   How has Japan's steel industry fared? In the late 1970s, Nippon Steel, the most modern steel company in Japan, spent $5 billion to erect a big integrated plant. But Nippon, like other Japanese steel producers, knows it will be difficult to compete with low-cost producers of common steel from low-cost countries, such as Korea, Brazil, and Taiwan. Consequently, it is upgrading its product mix to include more sophisticated products. Like other

■ **TABLE 13–2**
World Production of Raw Steel (Percentage share)

	United States	EC	Japan	Other Industrial Countries	LDCs	Communist Nations
1950	47%	26%	3%	4%	2%	19%
1960	26	28	6	5	3	31
1970	20	23	16	6	5	30
1980	14	18	16	7	10	36
1985	11	17	15	6	12	38

Source: "The Decline of the U.S. Steel Industry," *Finance & Development,* December 1987, p. 31.

■ **TABLE 13–3**
Share of U.S. Imports (Percent of apparent U.S. supply)

	Total	Japan	EC	LDCs	Other*
1955	1.2%	0.1%	0.8%	—	0.3%
1965	10.4	4.4	4.9	0.2%	0.9
1975	13.5	6.6	4.6	0.6	1.7
1985	25.2	6.2	7.2	5.3	6.0

*Includes industrial countries other than Japan and the EC, plus communist countries.
Source: "The Decline of the U.S. Steel Industry," *Finance & Development,* December 1987, p. 31.

Japanese industries, the steel companies are buying into their American counterparts and investing in Third World countries.[38]

Recipe for survival.   To survive, steel producers in the industrialized nations know they must restructure their operations. In the United States, the industry has reduced production capacity by 27 percent, reduced employment by half, and invested $11 billion to make it the world's most productive.[39] Bethlehem Steel is an example: it has slashed jobs, closed old mills, and invested billions of dollars in upgrading those mills that remain. Management has formed teams of hourly and salaried employees who get customer input so they can solve quality problems. With pay incentives tied to profits, workers now monitor production lines to prevent errors instead of waiting to reject bad steel after it is made. These changes have reduced the percentage of steel rejected by Ford from 8 percent in 1982 to 0.8 percent in 1989. Bethlehem's CEO says, "We will not be satisfied until it's zero."

Japanese steel executives who boasted that their more modern plants would bury Bethlehem are impressed that it makes steel in only 2.8 hours, a record their plants have not yet matched. Said one executive to a Japanese newspaper after he had visited Bethlehem, "We have to be more humble."[40]

ANALYSIS OF THE COMPETITIVE FORCES

"The biggest single problem in international planning is the lack of efficient and good competitive information."[41] This is the conclusion of *Business International's* study of 90 worldwide companies. The study also found that many companies have no organized approach to global competitive assessment; whatever is done is diffused among the various parts of the company. The Conference Board found, however, that more companies are establishing systematic methods for tracking competitive activity, and, according to the

Society of Competitor Intelligence Professionals, 80 percent of the Fortune 1,000 maintain in-house competitor analysts.[42]

Is Competitive Assessment New?

Sales and marketing managers have always needed information about their competitors' products, prices, channels of distribution, and promotional strategies to plan their own marketing strategies. Sales representatives are expected to submit information on competitors' activities in their territories as part of their regular reports to headquarters. It also has been common practice to talk to competitors' customers and distributors, test competitors' products, and stop at competitors' exhibits at trade shows. Larger firms maintain company libraries whose librarians regularly scan publications and report their findings to the functional area they believe would have an interest in the information.

> One of the writers was working at Goodyear when a librarian reported reading about a patent application for vulcanizing hose that Dunlop, a competitor, had filed in South Africa. The process, although new, had already been patented elsewhere. She reasoned correctly that this new application in South Africa indicated Dunlop was preparing to use the process, which would enable it to produce a better-quality product at a lower price in its South African plant.
>
> Inasmuch as the Goodyear-South Africa facility had nothing to equal it, the process would give Dunlop a strong competitive advantage. Headquarters immediately notified the South African affiliate, which hurriedly modernized its vulcanization process. By the time Dunlop installed its new process, the local Goodyear plant was ready. Thanks to an alert librarian, Dunlop failed to gain the competitive advantage it had expected.

competitive analysis principal competitors are identified, and their objectives, strengths, weaknesses, and product lines are assessed

Gathering information about the competition has been going on for so long, what is different about present-day **competitive analysis**? Essentially, the difference lies in top management's recognition that (1) increased competition has created a need for a broader and more in-depth knowledge of competitors' activities and (2) the firm should have a **competitor intelligence system (CIS)** for gathering, analyzing, and disseminating information to everyone in the firm who needs it. Moreover, many firms hire consultants or firms specializing in competitive analysis to provide information, and others send employees to seminars to learn how to do it themselves. Some even employ former CIA agents or investigators to handle data gathering and analysis (recall Motorola in the business incident).

competitor intelligence system (CIS) procedure for gathering, analyzing, and disseminating information about a firm's competitors

Sources of Information

There are five sources of information about the strengths, weaknesses, and threats of a firm's competitors: (1) within the firm, (2) published material, (3) customers, (4) competitors' employees, and (5) direct observation or analyzing physical evidence of their activities.[43] These sources are all used in the United States and other industrialized countries, but they can be especially helpful in developing nations, which usually have a paucity of published information.

Within the firm.   As we mentioned previously, a firm's sales representatives are the best source of this kind of information. Librarians, when firms have them, can also provide input to the CIS. Another source is the technical and

R&D people, who, while attending professional meetings or reading their professional journals, frequently learn of developments before they are general knowledge. Incidentally, government intelligence agencies from all countries subscribe to and analyze other nations' technical journals.

Published material.   We mentioned technical journals, but other types of published material can also provide valuable information. Business data bases provide information from SEC reports, annual reports, patent information, balance sheets, and so forth. England's Economist Intelligence Unit and the U.S.'s Predicast publish useful industry reports; and under the Freedom of Information Act, American firms and their foreign competitors can get information about companies from public documents. Aerial photographs of competitors' facilities are often available from the EPA or the U.S. Geological Survey if the company is near a waterway or has done an environmental impact study. The photos may reveal an expansion or the layout of the competitor's production facilities. Be careful not to take unauthorized aerial photographs—this is trespassing and is illegal.

Customers.   Companies frequently tell their customers in advance about new products to keep them from buying elsewhere, but often the customer passes this information on to competitors. For example, Gillette told a Canadian distributor when it planned to sell its new disposable razor in the United States. The distributor called BIC, who hurried its development and was able to begin selling its own razor shortly after Gillette did.[44]

A company's purchasing agent can ask its suppliers how much they are producing or what they planning to produce in the way of new products. Because buyers know how much their company buys, any added capacity or new products may be for the firm's competitors. They can also allege that they are considering giving a supplier new business if the sales representative can prove the firm has the capacity to handle it. Salespeople often are so eager for the new business that they divulge their firm's total capacity and the competitor's purchases to prove they can handle the order.

Competitors' employees.   Competitors' employees, actual or past, can provide information. Experienced human relations people pay special attention to job applicants, especially recent graduates, who reveal they have worked as interns or in summer jobs with competitors. They sometimes reveal proprietary information unknowingly. Companies also hire people away from competitors, and unscrupulous ones even advertise and hold interviews for jobs they don't have to get information from competitors' employees.

Direct observation or analyzing physical evidence.   Companies sometimes have their technical people join a competitor's plant tour to get details of the production processes. A crayon company sent employees to tour a competitor's plants under assumed names. Posing as potential customers, they easily gained access and obtained valuable information about the competitor's processes; admittedly, this was unethical, although standing outside a plant to count employees and learn the number of shifts a competitor is working is not considered unethical.

We have already mentioned the common practice of reverse engineering, which is an example of analyzing physical evidence, but intelligence analysts even buy competitors' garbage. It is illegal to enter a competitor's premises to collect it, but it is permissible to obtain refuse from a trash hauler once the material has left the competitor's premises. Another interesting analysis was done by a Japanese company that sent employees to measure the thickness of rust on train tracks leaving an American competitor's plant. They used the results to calculate the plant's output.[45]

You have noticed that we have pointed out when an act is legal or illegal and have also commented on whether, in our opinion, it was ethical. Certainly, businesspeople have a responsibility to use all ethical means to gather information about their competitors. The Japanese owe much of their rapid progress in high technology to their ability to gather information. Mitsubishi occupies two floors of a New York office building in which dozens of people screen technical journals and contact companies for brochures and other materials. Mitsubishi and other large Japanese firms do their own micro-filming, which they send to their Tokyo headquarters for analysis.[46]

DISTRIBUTIVE FORCES

The channels of distribution—systems of agencies through which a product and its title pass from the producer to the user—are both a controllable and an uncontrollable variable. They are controllable to the extent that the channel captains are free to choose from the available channels those that will enable them to reach their target markets, perform the functions they require at a reasonable cost, and permit them the amount of control they desire.* If the established channels are considered inadequate, they may assemble different networks.

> Coca-Cola, dissatisfied with the complex Japanese system of distributing through layers of wholesalers, created its own system in which 17 bottlers sell directly to over 1 million retailers. The dramatic reduction in distributive costs coupled with the fact that each bottler was well versed in its own market enabled Coca-Cola to obtain 60 percent of the Japanese market. Note, however, that although a new system was created, new agencies were not.

The distributive *structure*, the agencies themselves, is generally beyond the marketer's control, so it must use those that are available. Yet new agencies are occasionally created when the established institutions do not fulfill the channel captain's requirements.

> UK automaker Austin Rover, long established in Germany, had lost 60 percent of its dealers because of a low-quality image. Although its new models had achieved European-wide success, its German dealers managed to sell only 0.15 percent of the market. Searching for a novel approach, Austin Rover concluded a deal with Massa, Germany's largest retailer and owner of 27 hypermarkets (huge combina-tion supermarkets/discount stores), under which Massa was to build showrooms and service departments at each of its store sites. The enormous advertising power obtained through Massa's newspapers, delivered to 5.5 million households, coupled with Massa's reputation for quality enabled the chain to sell 800 cars the first month. Rover expects Massa to sell more cars than all of its 200 traditional dealers.[47]

---

* The *channel captain* is the dominant and controlling member of a channel of distribution.

■ **FIGURE 13–4   International Channels of Distribution**

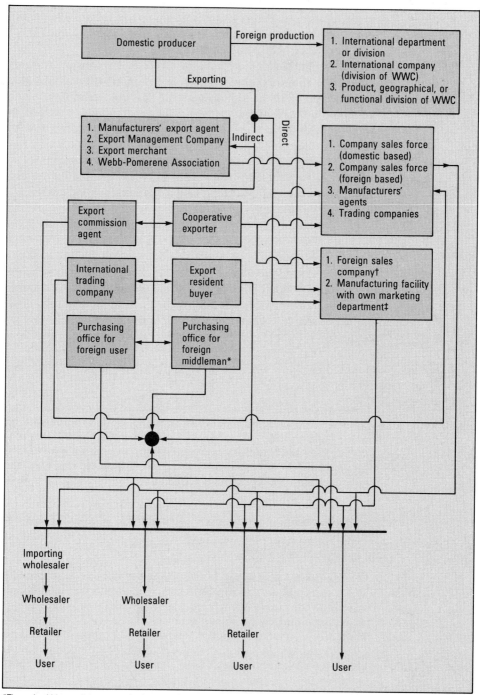

*There should be no direct connection between this category and the user. For simplification, a separate line to eliminate the user is not shown.
†Can be wholly owned or a joint venture. The foreign sales company may sell imports as well as local production from licensee, contract manufacturer, or joint venture.
‡Can be wholly owned, joint venture, or a licensee.

INTERNATIONAL CHANNEL OF DISTRIBUTION MEMBERS

The selection of channel of distribution members to link the producer with the foreign user will depend first of all on the method of entry into the market. In Chapter 2, you learned that to do business overseas, a firm must either export to a foreign country or manufacture in it. If the decision is to export, the firm may do so *directly* or *indirectly*. Figure 13–4 shows that management has considerable latitude in forming the channels.

Indirect Exporting

For indirect exporting, a number of U.S.-based exporters (A) sell for the manufacturer, (B) buy for their overseas customers, (C) buy and sell for their own account, or (D) purchase on behalf of foreign middlemen or users. Although each type of exporter usually operates in the following manner, any given company may actually perform one or more of these functions.

A. Exporters that sell for the manufacturer.
  1. *Manufacturers' export agents* act as the international representatives for various noncompeting domestic manufacturers. They usually direct promotion, consummate sales, invoice, ship, and handle the financing. They are commonly paid a commission for carrying out these functions in the name of the manufacturer.
  2. *Export management companies* (EMCs), formerly known as combination export managers (CEMs), act as the export department for several noncompeting manufacturers. They will also transact business in the name of the manufacturer and handle the routine details of shipping and promotion. When the EMC works on a commission basis, the manufacturer invoices the customer directly and carries any financing required by the foreign buyer. However, most EMCs work on a buy-and-sell arrangement under which they pay the manufacturer, resell the product abroad, and invoice the customer directly. Depending on the arrangement, the EMC may act in the name of the firm it represents or in its own name.
  3. *International trading companies* are similar to EMCs in that they also act as agents for some companies and as merchant wholesalers for others. This, however, is only part of their activities. They frequently export as well as import, own their own transportation facilities, and provide financing. W. R. Grace was at one time a major trading company that operated on the Pacific coast of South America. It owned sugar mills, large import houses, various manufacturing plants, a steamship company, and an airline. Although there have been a number of European and American international trading companies in operation for centuries, certainly the most diversified and the largest are the Japanese **sogo shosha** (general trading companies).
    a. *Sogo Shosha.* The general trading companies were originally established by the *zaibatsu*—centralized, family-dominated economic groups, such as Mitsui, Mitsubishi, and Sumitomo—to be the heart of their commercial operations. The head of Mitsui, for example, established a general trading company, Mitsui Bussan, at the same time (1870s) that he created the Mitsui Bank. Both institutions served as the nucleus for the rest of the

sogo shosha the largest of the Japanese general trading companies

Mitsui empire. The general trading companies obtained export markets, raw materials, and technical assistance for other companies of the zaibatsu and also imported goods for resale. Included in the zaibatsu in addition to banks and general trading companies were transportation, insurance, and real estate companies and various manufacturing firms. In 1933, 6.2 percent of Japan's social overhead capital belonged to four major zaibatsu—Mitsui, Mitsubishi, Yasuda, and Sumitomo. Although the zaibatsu were forced to dissolve after WW II, the companies that had been their major components survived.

The largest general trading company is Mitsui & Co. This sogo shosha has $150 billion in sales and employs 12,000 persons throughout the world. It also has equity investments in more than 620 companies in Japan and 320 overseas.[48] Although Mitsui & Co. is huge, it is only one company in the Mitsui Group (formerly the Mitsui zaibatsu), which consists of several hundred companies whose activities range from steelmaking and shipbuilding to banking and insurance, from paper to electronics, and from petroleum to warehousing, tourism, and nuclear energy. The Mitsui Group is not a legal entity but exists as an informal organization of major enterprises that have related interests and related financial structures. They cooperate in promoting the economic interests of group members. To ensure cooperation, the top executives of the 68 major components of the former Mitsui zaibatsu meet for a weekly luncheon meeting.[49] Interestingly, the American subsidiaries of Mitsubishi and Mitsui together account for 10 percent of *all* U.S. exports.

b. *Export trading company.* In 1982, the Reagan administration, impressed by the success of the Japanese, Taiwanese, and Korean general trading companies, worked closely with Congress to obtain the passage of the Export Trading Company Act. The measure provides the mechanism for creating a new indirect export channel, the **export trading company (ETC)**. For the first time in U.S. history, businesses were permitted to join together to export goods and services or offer export-facilitating services without fear of violating antitrust legislation. Bank holding companies may also participate in ETCs. This not only increases the ability of trading companies to finance export transactions but also gives them access to the banks' extensive international information systems. Furthermore, because ETCs can import as well as export, they can engage in countertrade by selling their customers' products in other markets.[50]

Any potential exporter may apply to the Department of Commerce for a **certificate of review**, a legal document that provides immunity from state and federal antitrust prosecution and significant protection from certain private antitrust lawsuits. The certificate allows firms and associations to engage in joint price setting and joint bidding and gives them the freedom to divide up export markets among companies and jointly own warranty, service, and training centers in various overseas markets. Note that the benefits of the ETC Act are available to *all exporters*, not just export trading companies.[51]

The Commerce Department has issued 107 certificates covering 4,400 companies. Most companies that have received certificates are export intermediaries for two or more firms from the

export trading company a firm established principally to export domestic goods and services and to assist unrelated companies to export their products

certificate of review a legal document issued by the U.S. Department of Commerce that grants immunity from state and federal antitrust prosecution to export trading companies

Colonel Sanders in Japan (a joint venture with Mitsubishi, a sogo shosha)

Courtesy of R. J. Reynolds, 1982 Annual Report

same industry, although now the majority of the certificates are being issued to groups of companies. For example, the National Tooling and Machining Association, a national trade association with 3,150 members, received a certificate in 1988. The American Film Marketing Association (67 members) is another example.[52]

B. Exporters that buy for their overseas customers.

Export commission agents represent overseas purchasers, such as import firms and large industrial users. They are paid a commission by the purchaser for acting as resident buyers in industrialized nations.

C. Exporters that buy and sell for their own account.

1. *Export merchants* purchase products directly from the manufacturer and then sell, invoice, and ship them in their own names so that foreign customers have no direct dealing with the manufacturer, as they do in the case of the export agent. If export merchants have an exclusive right to sell the manufacturer's products in an overseas territory, they are generally called *export distributors*. Some EMCs may actually be export distributors for a number of their clients.

cooperative exporters established international manufacturers who export other manufacturers' goods as well as their own

2. Sometimes called piggyback or mother hen exporters, **cooperative exporters** are established international manufacturers that sell the products of other companies in foreign markets along with their own. Carriers (exporters) may purchase and resell in their own name, or they may work on a commission basis. Carriers, like EMCs, serve as the export departments for the firms they represent. Large companies, such as General Electric and Borg-Warner have been acting as piggyback exporters for years. A single carrier usually represents between 10 and 20 suppliers, though there is one large manufacturer of industrial machinery that has more than 1,000!

3. *Webb-Pomerene Associations* are organizations of competing firms that have joined together for the sole purpose of export trade. The Export Trade Act of 1918 provides for the formulation of such groups and generally exempts them from antitrust laws. They are permitted to buy from the members and sell abroad, set export prices, or simply direct the promotional activities that are destined for overseas markets. At this time, there are only 30 associations, of which those in phosphate rock, wood pulp, movies, and sulfur are the most active. The Webb-Pomerene Associations failed to become an important export channel because (1) the antitrust exemption was very vague and (2) the exporting of services was not included. The intent of the Export Trading Act is to remedy these deficiencies.

D. Exporters that purchase for foreign users and middlemen.
   1. Large foreign users, such as mining, petroleum, and international construction companies, buy for their own use overseas. The purchasing departments of all the worldwide companies are continually buying for their foreign affiliates, and both foreign governments and foreign firms maintain purchasing offices in industrialized countries.
   2. *Export resident buyers* perform essentially the same functions as export commission agents. However, they are generally more closely associated with a foreign firm. They may be appointed as the official buying representatives and paid a retainer, or they may even be employees. This is in contrast to the export commission agent, who usually represents a number of overseas buyers and works on a transaction-by-transaction basis.

Direct Exporting

If the firm chooses to do its own exporting, it has four basic types of overseas middlemen from which to choose: (A) manufacturers' agents, (B) distributors, (C) retailers, and (D) trading companies. These may be serviced by sales personnel who either travel to the market or are based in it. If the sales volume is sufficient, a foreign sales company may be established to take the place of the wholesale importer. The manufacturing affiliates of most worldwide companies also import from home country plants or from other subsidiaries products that they themselves do not produce.

manufacturers' agents independent sales representatives of various noncompeting suppliers

A. *Manufacturers' agents* are residents of the country or region in which they are conducting business for the firm. They represent various noncompeting foreign suppliers, and they take orders in these firms' names. **Manufacturers' agents** usually work on a commission basis, pay their own expenses, and do not assume any financial responsibility. They often stock the products of some of their suppliers, thus combining the functions of agent and wholesale distributor.

B. *Distributors* or wholesale importers are independent merchants that buy for their own account. They import and stock for resale. **Distributors** are usually specialists in a particular field, such as farm equipment or pharmaceuticals. They may be given exclusive representation and, in return, agree not to handle competing brands. Distributors may buy through manufacturers' agents when the exporter employs them, or they may send their orders directly to the exporting firm. Instead of manufacturers' agents, exporters may employ their own salespeople to cover the territory and to assist the distributors. For years, worldwide companies such as Caterpillar, Goodyear, and Goodrich have utilized field representatives in export territories.

C. *Retailers,* especially of consumer products requiring little after-sales servicing, are frequently direct importers. Contact on behalf of the exporter is maintained either by a manufacturers' agent or by the exporter's sales representative based in the territory or traveling from the home office.

D. *Trading companies* are relatively unknown in the United States but are extremely important importers in other parts of the world. In a number of African nations, **trading companies** are not only the principal importers of goods ranging from consumer products to capital equipment, but they also export such raw materials as ore, palm oil, and coffee. In addition, they operate department stores, grocery stores, and agencies for automobiles and farm machinery. Although many trading companies are large, they are in no way comparable in either size or diversification (products and functions performed) to the sogo shosha.

Trading companies in Brazil, Korea, Taiwan, and Malaysia are a recent development. They are of little use to exporters to these countries, inasmuch as their primary function is to promote their own country's exports. On the other hand, the English *importer/factor,* which performs some of the functions of a trading company, is of value to exporters. It will, on behalf of foreign manufacturers, warehouse goods, price them for the local market, deliver anywhere in the country, and factor (buy the seller's accounts receivable). The exporter must still develop the sales, however.

Another form of trading company is owned by the state. State trading companies handle all exports and imports in the communist bloc, and in noncommunist nations where an industry is a government monopoly, such as tobacco in Spain or petroleum in Mexico, exporters or their agents must deal with these government-owned entities.

Foreign Production

When the firm is selling products produced in the local market, whether manufactured by a wholly owned subsidiary, a joint venture, or a contract manufacturer, management's concern is with the internal channels. Generally, the same types of middlemen are available, although the established channels and their manner of operating may differ appreciably from that to which management is accustomed. Differences between the foreign and domestic environmental forces are responsible.

distributors independent importers that buy for their own account for resale

trading companies firms that develop international trade and serve as intermediaries between foreign buyers and domestic sellers and vice versa

Wholesale institutions.   In other developed nations, as in the United States, the marketer will be able to select wholesalers that take title to the goods (merchant wholesalers, rack jobbers, drop shippers, cash-and-carry wholesalers, truck jobbers) and those that do not (agents, brokers). However, just as in the United States, as retailers have become larger, they have sought to bypass wholesalers to purchase directly from local manufacturers and foreign suppliers. Direct imports accounted for 10 percent of 1988 sales at Daiei, Japan's largest store chain, and they are rising 30 percent annually.[53] They accounted for an even higher percentage—16 percent—for Japan's 1,600 largest department stores and supermarkets, who either import directly or buy from an importer. In contrast, few foreign products are stocked by small retailers (four clerks or less), who compose 75 percent of the Japanese retailers and are supplied by the usual chain of primary to secondary to tertiary wholesalers.

Such pressure in Japan and other industrialized nations forced many smaller wholesalers out of business, with the result that wholesalers were becoming fewer in number but greater in size. To remain competitive, wholesalers have specialized, and there seems to be a tendency for more and smaller wholesalers as nations industrialize.[54]

Diversity of wholesaling structures.   The diversity of the wholesaling structures among nations may be seen in Table 13–4. Generally, you will find that the structure varies with the stage of economic development. In the less developed countries that depend on imports to supply the market, the importing wholesalers are large and few in number, and the channels are long. Historically, many of the importers were trading companies formed by the WWCs to import the machinery and supplies required by their local operation and to export raw materials for use in the home country plants. To obtain distributor prices, they were required by their suppliers to sell to other customers as well. Some of these operations became extremely diversified, owning automobile and industrial machinery agencies, grocery stores, and department stores. They literally could and did supply a complete city and an industry with all of its requirements.

As colonies became nations, the new governments began applying pressure to convert these trading companies to local ownership. Furthermore, these countries were industrializing, which meant more goods were being produced locally and fewer goods were being imported. Many of the local manufacturers were able to take control of the channels from the import jobber. To obtain more extensive market coverage, they canceled the importing wholesaler's exclusivity and gave their product lines to new wholesalers, many of which were formed by ex-employees of the importer. As economic development continued, markets broadened, permitting greater specialization by more and smaller wholesalers. The small sample in Table 13–4 hints at this cycle. Compare the few large wholesalers in Chile, El Salvador, and Swaziland (employees per wholesaler and population per wholesaler) with the smaller and more numerous wholesalers in the United States and Austria. By comparing the Japanese and American ratios of population to wholesalers and noting that the number of wholesalers are the same in both countries, you can understand foreigners' complaints about the complexity of Japan's distribution system. Note the similarity among the population-per-wholesaler ratios of the United States, Austria, the United Kingdom, Italy, and France, although the

TABLE 13-4   Wholesaling and Retailing in Selected Countries

Country	Number of Wholesalers	Employees per Wholesaler	Population per Wholesaler	Number of Retailers	Employees per Retailer	Population per Retailer	Ratio of Retailers to Wholesalers
United States (1985)	416,000	12.0	557	1,410,000	11.4	170	3.4
Austria (1983)	12,890	11.5	590	37,524	6.0	203	2.9
Brazil (1980)	46,000	9.6	2,630	885,600	2.2	143	19.3
Chile (1983)	561	28.3	20,600	1,125	21.2	10,300	2.0
El Salvador (1983)	396	16.9	131,300	1,416	8.5	3,672	3.6
Finland (1983)	5,400	14.5	888	35,800	5.1	134	6.6
France (1984)	79,700	4.0	689	608,600	1.9	90	7.6
Greece (1983)	24,400	2.0	406	164,400	1.8	60	6.7
Hungary (1982)	17,500	11.4	611	55,400	6.0	193	3.2
Italy (1983)	113,600	4.6	500	1,266,000	n.a.	45	11.1
Japan (1985)	413,000	9.7	292	1,629,000	3.9	74	3.9
Korea (1982)	45,568	3.8	862	542,458	1.7	72	11.9
Norway (1984)	16,429	6.3	250	34,784	3.6	118	2.1
Philippines (1981)	20,642	7.6	2,403	280,000	2.5	173	13.6
Portugal (1981)	6,600	21.0	1,506	14,800	8.2	672	2.2
Spain (1982)	35,700	9.1	1,061	371,800	3.3	102	10.4
Sweden (1984)	31,960	6.2	260	83,640	3.6	99	2.6
Swaziland (1983)	79	15.2	9,240	646	7.6	1,130	8.2
United Kingdom (1984)	70,600	12.4	718	337,700	6.5	167	4.3
USSR (1980)	140,000	16.5	1,900	695,200	6.7	383	5.0

employee-per-wholesaler ratios indicate that French and Italian wholesalers are much smaller.

Japan's multilayered system.   Characterized as a formidable trade barrier by foreign firms attempting to enter the market, the maze of wholesalers and retailers employed to reach the Japanese consumer has been severely criticized for its inefficiency. Figure 13–5 illustrates that channels for automobiles are certainly complex; but even simple products like soap may move through a "sales agent" (primary wholesaler) named by the manufacturer to sell to the rest of the wholesalers, two or three wholesalers, and a retailer in going from the manufacturer to the final consumer. Note the presence of the parallel importer.

Parallel importers and gray market goods.   **Parallel importers** are either wholesalers that import products independently of the authorized (by the manufacturer) importer or that buy products for export and then sell them in the domestic market. Four transactions are possible:

1. Importer buys from an overseas dealer in the home country. This occurs when authorized dealers charge more for the import than do home country dealers. When the strong dollar lowered the dollar price of Mercedes automobiles and the American authorized dealers did not

parallel importers wholesalers that import products independently of manufacturer-authorized importers or buy goods for export and divert them to the domestic market

■ **FIGURE 13–5** **Passenger Car Distribution Channels in Japan**

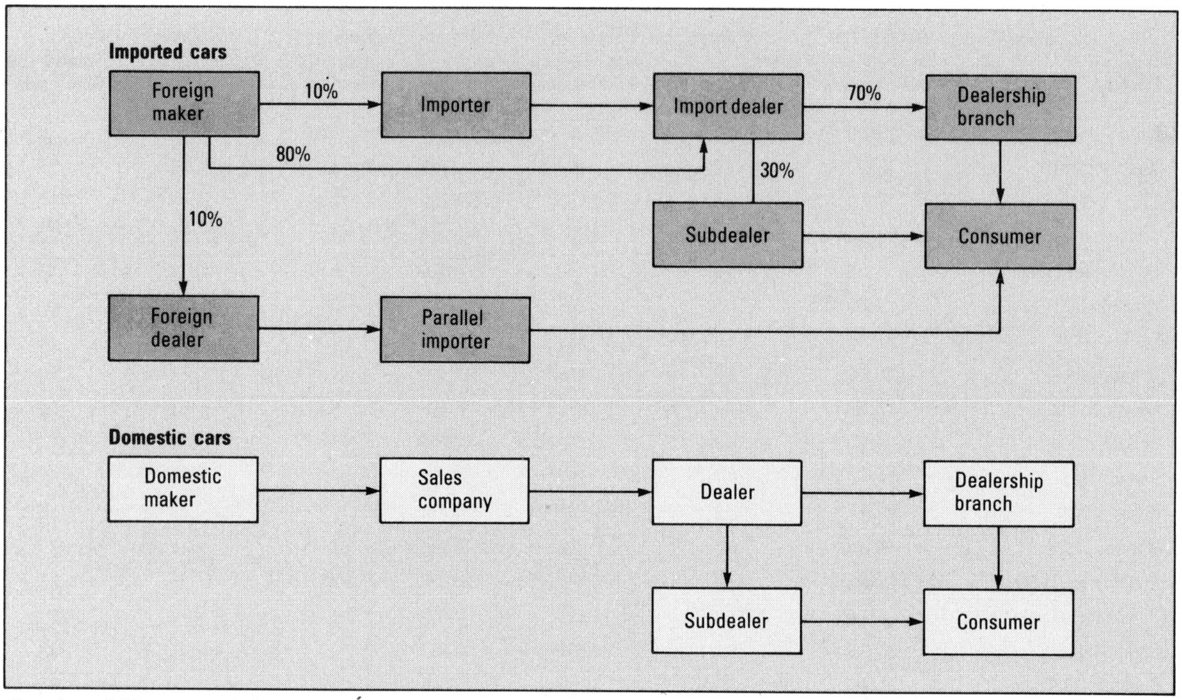

Note: A parallel importer acts independently of the foreign manufacturer and its authorized importer by obtaining the product from another source. It is a competitor of the authorized importer.

lower their prices, a parallel importer could make money by selling a Mercedes 500 SEL with American pollution-control equipment for $8,000 less than the authorized dealer would. French Opium perfume was sold at a profit for $75 an ounce, compared to the $165 price that retailers buying from the authorized importer were asking.[55]

2. Unauthorized dealer imports from foreign subsidiary and competes in home country against locally made products. Caterpillar dealers of U.S.-made excavators and loaders were competing against unauthorized dealers selling the same products made in Scotland, Belgium, and Japan for 15 percent less.[56] Again, this occurred when the dollar was strong. Recall reading previously in this chapter that Honda and other Japanese manufacturers are legitimately reverse exporting—exporting American-made products to Japan.

3. Unauthorized importer buys products overseas from the home office and competes with the local subsidiary. Most WWCs can price lower for the export market than for the domestic market because they have less promotional expense. The subsidiary's price can be higher than that of the home country because of production volume, higher distribution costs, and so forth.

4. Goods are bought for export but are sold on the domestic market instead. This can occur when a manufacturer's export prices are lower than its domestic prices. Quality King Distributors in New York annually sells millions of dollars' worth of Pampers, Tylenol, and Johnson & Johnson toothbrushes to dealers at prices 30 percent lower than domestic wholesalers can. The firm buys such products from

exporters who sell to it rather than export them. A number of Japanese exports actually make a round trip from Japan to New York and back again. Unauthorized Japanese dealers can buy a Sony Walkman in New York for $90 and retail it in Tokyo for $165, the price that Japanese retailers normally ask.[57]

Although American manufacturers have gone to court trying to stop these **gray market** operations, they have had little success. U.S. gray market sales are estimated to total $10 billion annually.[58]

Retail institutions.   The variation in size and number is even greater for retailers than for wholesalers. In Table 13–4 compare Chile, Austria, Japan, and France, for example. Generally, *the less developed the country, the more numerous, the more specialized, and the smaller the retailers.* France, Japan, and Italy are exceptions because the situation of many small retailers has been maintained by stringent laws that have kept the expansion of supermarkets and mass merchandisers at a much lower rate than that of similarly developed countries. Obviously, Chile's ambulatory peddlers, common in all LDCs, are not included in its retailer count, even though from the manufacturers' standpoint, these retailers can be responsible for considerable sales volume. In Africa, the market "mammy" who walks the street selling to passersby from a pan on the top of her head is a major outlet for small-unit goods, such as soap, cigarettes, and candy. Although the system seems primitive and ineffective to a Westerner, the market mammy is a powerful force, and associations of these women act as banks, back wholesalers, and even influence politicians.

When retailing methods in the developed and developing nations are compared, the following generalizations are notable: *in going up the scale from LDCs to developed countries, one encounters more mass merchandising; more self-service, large-sized retail units; and a trend toward retailer concentration* (see Figure 13–6).

Typical of this trend is the emergence of the European **hypermarket**—a huge combination supermarket/discount house with five or six acres of floor space where both soft goods and hard goods are sold. A similar type of outlet in Japan, the **superstore,** is a recent phenomenon that now accounts for over 10 percent of all retail sales. In Scandinavia and Switzerland, there is also a marked trend toward retailer concentration, but it is occurring for the most part through retailer-controlled voluntary chains and consumer cooperatives rather than through company-owned chains (see Tables 13–5 and 13–6).

Channel Selection

Direct or indirect marketing.   The first decision that management must make is whether to use middlemen, because it frequently has the option of marketing directly to the final user. Sales to original equipment manufacturers (OEMs)* and governments are, for the most part, made directly, as are the sales of high-priced industrial products like turbines and locomotives, because the firm is dealing with the relatively few customers and transactions but with large dollar volume. Even in these cases, export sales may be consummated by local agents if (1) management believes this is politically expedient or (2) the country's laws demand it.

---

* Original equipment manufacturers buy components that are incorporated into the products they produce (for example, spark plugs to an automobile manufacturer).

---

gray market the sale of goods that are either legal-but-unauthorized imports bearing domestic manufacturers' trade names, or exports that have been diverted to the domestic market

hypermarkets huge combination supermarkets/discount stores where soft and hard goods are sold

superstores name given to hypermarkets in Japan, some parts of Europe, and the United States

■ FIGURE 13–6
**Food Distribution
Methods at Various
Levels of Development**

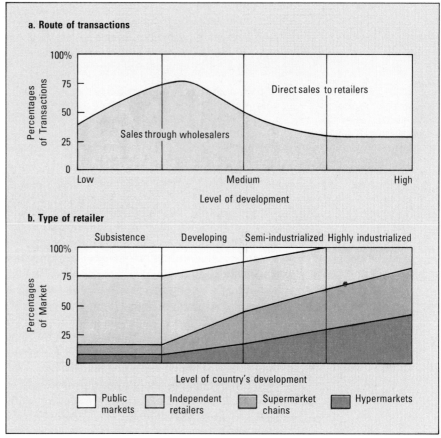

Source: L. Solis and A. Montemayor, "Modernización Commercial y Desarollo Economico," *Comercio y Desarroll*, November–December 1977, p. 7.

■ TABLE 13–5
**European Food
Distribution by Type of
Organization (Percent of
market)**

	Co-ops	Chains	Retailer-Controlled Voluntary Associations	Independents	Other*
Austria	21%	28%	42%	—	9%
Belgium	1	63	8	12%	16
Finland	22	45	30	—	3
France	8	44	39	—	9
Ireland	1	64	21	—	14
Italy	5	9	25	59	2
Netherlands	1	59	26	12	2
Norway	24	21	43	—	12
Portugal	1	8	—	86	5
Sweden	28	17	43	—	12
Switzerland	41	12	16	13	18
United Kingdom	8	54	7	5	26
West Germany	9	36	42	10	3

*Other refers to specialty shops and department stores.
Source: *European Marketing Data & Statistics, 1988* (London: Euromonitor, 1988), p. 285.

■ TABLE 13–6
European Hypermarkets
and Superstores
(Quantity)

	1980	1983	1986
Austria	51	53	60
Belgium	79	82	91
Denmark	29	38	45
Finland	27	30	35
France	421	515	629
Greece	—	2	6
Ireland	—	—	35*
Italy	14	20	22
Luxembourg	3	4	5
Netherlands	37	35	34
Norway	67	73	80
Portugal	—	—	21*
Spain	34	58	75
Sweden	65	73	75
Switzerland	81	82	85
United Kingdom	201	287	416
West Germany	813	880	952*

*Estimated.
Source: *European Marketing Data & Statistics, 1988* (London: Euromonitor, 1988), p. 273.

Other types of industrial products and consumer goods are marketed indirectly. The channel members are selected on the basis of their market coverage, their cost, and their susceptibility to company control. They must also, of course, perform the functions required by management.

Factors influencing channel selection.   The factors that influence the selection of market channels may be classified as the characteristics of the market, the product, the company, and the middlemen.

Market characteristics.   Inasmuch as the reason for using channels is to enable the manufacturer to reach its target markets, the obvious place to start in channel selection is at those markets. Which of the available alternatives offer the most adequate coverage? Because of the variance in the target markets, the firm will most likely require multiple channels. Large retailers, governments, and OEMs may be handled by the company sales force or manufacturers' agents, whereas smaller retailers are supplied through wholesalers.

Product characteristics.   A low-cost product sold in small quantities per transaction generally requires long channels, but if the goods are perishable, short channels are preferable. If the product is highly technical, it may be impossible to obtain knowledgeable middlemen, and the manufacturer will be forced either to sell directly through company-owned distributors or to train independent middlemen. Caterpillar has enjoyed tremendous success in choosing this second alternative.

Company characteristics.   A firm that has adequate financial and managerial resources is in a much better position to employ its own sales force or agents than one that is lacking in these areas. A financially weak company must use middlemen that take title to and pay for the goods. If management is inexperienced in selling to certain markets, it must employ middlemen who have that experience.

Middlemen's characteristics.   Most industrial equipment, large household appliances, and automobiles require considerable after-sales servicing, and much of the firm's success in marketing depends on it. If the firm is not prepared to provide this service, it cannot use agents. The same is true for warehousing and promotion to the final user. If the firm is unable to perform these functions or perceives a cost advantage in not performing them, then it must select middlemen that will service, warehouse, and promote its products.

It may be that no channel members are available to reach the firm's target markets and perform the desired functions. If there are none, management must decide to (1) desist from entering the market, (2) select other target markets, or (3) create a new channel. For example, if a frozen-food processor, after studying the available channels, finds that wholesale and retailer cold-storage facilities are nonexistent, it can either abandon the market or persuade middlemen to acquire the facilities. In a number of overseas markets, firms have purchased the equipment and either rented, leased, or sold it on easy terms to distributors and retailers.

> An Italian cheese producer in Brazil not only supplied cold-storage equipment but also established gathering facilities for the dairy farmers. The company provides veterinarians and dairy experts to teach the dairy farmers how to maintain their herds and increase output. Nestlé has similar programs throughout its LDC markets.

Legal requirements.   Because the legal requirements for terminating middlemen vary from country to country, the time to think about how to terminate an agreement is before it is made. Although most countries have no special laws penalizing or precluding the termination of an agreement between the manufacturer and middlemen, some do. In Venezuela, for example, unjustly discharged agents may be entitled to the same severance benefits as discharged employees. In other countries, laws specify high termination compensation related to an agent's longevity, past earnings, goodwill, or "investment" in the product line. Countries with laws making it difficult to terminate agreements include Belgium, Costa Rica, the Netherlands, Norway, and Sweden. Evidently, before preparing a contract, management must consult local attorneys or local correspondents of international law firms.[59]

Information Sources

Various sources will provide information about channels of distribution. The U.S. Department of Commerce, banks, credit agencies, and American chambers of commerce in foreign cities are all good. If the names of other companies whose products are being handled by prospective channel members are known, these companies should be contacted. We will discuss the information sources at greater length in the chapter on exporting (Chapter 16).

SUMMARY

World competition has intensified, and there are four nations and groups of nations whose firms are in worldwide competition with each other—the United States, Japan, the EC, and the NICs. Nations do not compete with each other—their firms do; but most economic and social conditions, as well as political actions, affect the ability of all of a nation's firms to compete. Using the term **national competitiveness** is a convenience.

As the dollar's value rose, American companies experienced difficulty competing in world markets, but the dollar's high value was only one of the reasons. Various nonprice factors were also responsible. The government, industry, labor, and consumers can contribute to the return of American competitiveness. Industry in the European Community has problems similar to those of the United States. By 1992, competition among European firms and from companies of other nations will

be greater. Japan is beginning to face the same competitive problems that the United States and Europe have been facing. Counterfeiting and industrial espionage are also competitive problems Although competitive assessment is not new, its use is increasing, and companies are establishing competitor intelligence systems.

Channels of distribution are both controllable and uncontrollable variables. To assist a firm to export indirectly or directly or to distribute in a foreign market, various kinds of channel members are available. The wholesaling and retailing structures vary among nations. An unauthorized wholesaler, the parallel importer, costs authorized importers billions of dollars in lost sales annually.

When selecting channels of distribution, management must consider the characteristics of the market, the product, the company, and the intermediaries available.

QUESTIONS

1. If firms, not nations, compete worldwide, how can we speak of national competitiveness?
2. How can the U.S. government help American industry increase its competitiveness? What can industry and labor do? Do consumers have a role to play?
3. What similarities do you see in the sequence of events concerning the export performances of the United States and Japan? Can they occur in the Asian NICs?
4. What changes that took place in the EC are bringing about Europe 1992?
5. Do American firms have anything to fear from Europe 1992? How about Japanese firms?
6. Define *counterfeiting* in the sense used in the text. Why is counterfeiting a problem for legitimate trademark owners? For consumers? How can the legitimate owners protect themselves?
7. Did the American steel industry lose competitiveness due to special problems that other industries have

not had? If so, what were these problems?
8. Is competitive assessment new? Compare present-day competitive analysis with what used to be done.
9. What are some sources of information for firms to know more about their competitors? What are some of the ethical issues involved in using these sources?
10. Name and discuss the four basic types of U.S.-based exporters available to firms that prefer to export directly.
11. What can you learn from Table 13–4, Wholesaling and Retailing in Selected Countries?
12. How do you define *parallel importers?* What is the gray market?
13. Discuss the five factors affecting the selection of marketing intermediaries.
14. What are the sogo shosha? How do they differ from their American counterpart?

MINICASE 13–1

Aikens-Malaysia and the Parallel Importer

Jim Hutton, managing director of Aikens-Malaysia, is discussing the latest competitive threat with Irene Olson, the marketing manager.

Hutton:

So you say that product from the home plant in Cleveland is being imported and sold here in competition with our locally made product?

Olson:

That's right, Jim. There's a parallel importer that buys in the United States and ships the product here. I wonder how he can compete pricewise when he has to pay those transportation costs. In fact, he and his wholesalers are making more than our wholesalers because they sell to the public at a higher price. My wholesalers tell me that the Malaysians will pay more for the imported product. There isn't any difference in quality, is there, Jim?

Hutton:

No. On the contrary, we're following Cleveland specs to the letter. The people here can get the same high-quality product made locally, and they're supporting a local industry that hires 500 Malaysian workers. As to the costs, remember, Irene, that our production costs are higher here. Our plant is newer and is being depreciated rather heavily. Furthermore, our production runs are much smaller, and that also makes our costs higher. We just don't have the economies of scale that Cleveland has. The lower wages here just can't compensate for this big difference. There's another angle, though. What about the import duties on the Cleveland product?

Olson:

They're rather low, although they're higher than the duties on the raw materials we import.

Hutton:

But the differences in duties is not high enough to compensate for our higher production costs, right?

Olson:

That's about it, Jim. There's also another aspect to consider.

Hutton:

What's that?

Olson:

As you know, the Malaysian ringit fluctuates with respect to the dollar. My wholesalers tell me that the importer watches the fluctuation closely, and when the ringit is low, he places a large order. At times, he can gain as much as a 20 percent advantage. Jim, do we take advantage of these currency fluctuations when we buy imported raw materials?

Hutton:

We try to, but since we have to order them months in advance, we're not able to respond very quickly to changes in the currency values.

Olson:

You know, Jim, the importer has another advantage. He gets a free ride from our advertising. We do all the promoting, and he reaps the benefits. He doesn't need to advertise.

Hutton:

Irene, I've just thought of something. How does this guy get our American product in the first place?

Olson:

I understand that he just places orders with our export department in Cleveland.

Hutton:

Don't these people know what the final destination is?

Olson:

Sure they do. He has to tell them when he places the order. By U.S. law, the destination has to be on the U.S. invoice. Cleveland knows he is not an American distributor. In fact, he gets an extra 10 percent because he does buy for export. Cleveland figures that exports should not have to pay any part of the domestic marketing costs.

Hutton:

This is a tough one, Irene. I have an idea. Didn't we and not Cleveland register our trademark here in Malaysia?

Olson:

Yes, Aikens-Malaysia is the owner of the trademark.

Hutton:

It seems to me, Irene, that there are a number of things we can do to reduce and possibly eliminate competition from this parallel importer. Will you draw up a plan for us?

Assume you are Irene Olson. Draw up a plan for Jim Hutton.

MINICASE 13–2

Reciprocal Market Penetration*

Kenichi Ohmae of McKinsey & Co. (a U.S. multinational consulting firm) has put forward the concept of reciprocal market penetration. He calculates that in 1984, Japanese imports from the United States were $25.6 billion, while goods produced in Japan by American subsidiaries totaled $43.9 billion, making the total American penetration in the

* Source: "Toward a True Internationalism," *Speaking of Japan,* January 1987, p. 25.

Japanese market $69.5 billion. In the same year, Americans purchased $56.8 billion of Japanese imports and another $12.8 billion in goods produced and sold in the United States by Japanese firms, for a total penetration of $69.6 billion. Ohmae believes this reveals an overall parity that is more than a coincidence. Because Japan's population is about one half that of the United States, these figures also suggest that the Japanese spend twice as much per capita on American products as Americans spend on Japanese products.

The vice chairman of Mitsubishi Motors claims that "these figures reflect a fundamental structural difference in the way that the economies of the United States and Japan have developed over the past several decades. For the most part, Japanese companies have stayed home and entered overseas markets through exports, while American companies were much more aggressive about setting up production in overseas markets. Quite a few major American companies have achieved prodigious successes in the Japanese market, but for obvious reasons, they have not gone out of their way to tell the world about it.

1. The Mitsubishi executive states that Japan is moving in the right direction to change the mix of exports to the United States and the goods produced by Japanese subsidiaries in the United States. What is his basis for making this statement?

2. Assuming Ohmae's figures are correct, what will be the impact on jobs, profits, and the economy as a whole in each country as the Japanese mix between exports to and production in the United States approaches the U.S. mix for its exports to and its production in Japan?

3. What does the concept of market penetration do to the U.S. argument that Japanese–American trade greatly favors Japan?

SUPPLEMENTARY READINGS

Competition and the Europeans

"Car Wars: Europe's Industry Gears Up." *Europe,* September 1987, pp. 24–28.

"EC, EFTA Meet to Prepare for 1992." *Europe,* November 1988, pp. 38–39.

"EEC and Japan." *The Economist,* February 18, 1989, p. 52.

"Europe Goes Wild for Yankee PCs." *Fortune,* June 5, 1989, pp. 257–60.

Europe without Frontiers—Completing the Internal Market. Luxembourg: European Communities, 1987.

"Europeans Start to Play a Little Rough." *Business Week,* February 9, 1987, p. 47.

"Fortress Europe." *International Management,* December 1988, pp. 24–30.

"Gianni Agnelli's Days in the Sun." *Forbes,* November 14, 1988, pp. 130–36.

"How the Member-States Are Preparing for 1992." *Business International,* June 27, 1988, pp. 200–202.

"1992: A Tremendous Challenge for EFTA." *EFTA Bulletin,* 1/89, pp. 6–15.

"1992: The Bad News." *International Management,* September 1988, pp. 22–26.

"Scrambling for 1992." *Business Marketing,* February 1989, pp. 49–59.

"The Coming Superpower." *Traffic Management,* April 1989, pp. 97A–102A.

"The Rise and Rise of European Takeovers." *International Management,* November 1988, pp. 24–28.

"U.S. Business Should Prepare Now for EC 1992." *Business America,* October 24, 1988, pp. 12–16.

Competition and the Japanese

"Can Asia's Four Tigers Be Tamed?" *Business Week,* February 15, 1988, pp. 46–50.

"Damn the Dollar, Full Speed Ahead." *U.S. News & World Report,* December 4, 1987, pp. 50–51.

"Fear and Trembling in the Colossus." *Fortune,* March 30, 1987, pp. 32–46.

"How Japanese MNCs Are Responding to the Strong Yen." *Business Asia,* June 29, 1987, pp. 202–3.

"How to Mix Sake and Tequila." *Forbes,* March 23, 1987, pp. 48–51.

"Ideal State." *The Wall Street Journal,* August 19, 1988, p. A1.

"Japan and Europe: What Next?" *International Management,* December 1988, pp. 35–52.

"Japanese Managers Alarmed in Land of the Rising Yen." *International Management,* December 1986, pp. 58–66.

"Japan's Latest Trade War Is with Its Own Customers." *Business Month,* December 1988, p. 21.

"Japan's Troubled Future." *Fortune,* March 30, 1987, pp. 21–28.

"Now It's Japan's Turn to Sweat a Bit." *U.S. News & World Report,* March 9, 1987, pp. 42–43.

"Trade Liberation." *Japan Update,* Spring 1989, pp. 3–7.

"Trade Switch." *The Wall Street Journal,* July 20, 1988, p. A1.

Competition and the United States

"A Humbler IBM Switches Its Marketing Strategies to Win back Japanese Buyers." *The Asian Wall Street Journal,* April 11, 1988, p. 14.

"America's Competitive Revival." *Fortune,* January 4, 1988, pp. 44–52.

"Can Consortiums Defeat Japan?" *Fortune,* June 5, 1989, pp. 245–54.

"CEOs Grid for Global Battle." *Fortune,* April 24, 1989, pp. 65–66.

"Competitiveness: Getting It Back." *Fortune,* April 27, 1987, pp. 217–23.

"Designation of Japan as Unfair Trader Holds Promise but Much Risk." *The Wall Street Journal,* May 26, 1989, p. A1.

Dertouzos, Michael L.; Richard K. Lester; and Robert M. Solow. *Made in America.* Cambridge, Mass.: MIT Press, 1989.

"Fitting into a Global Economy." *U.S. News & World Report,* January 2, 1989, pp. 80–82.

"GATT Bashing America." *The Economist,* May 20, 1989, p. 79–80.

"Getting Tough with Tokyo." *Time,* June 5, 1989, pp. 50–52.

"Going for the Lion's Share." *Business Week,* July 18, 1988, pp. 70–72.

"Habit Dies Hard." *Forbes,* May 29, 1989, pp. 264–66.

"How to Beat the Japanese." *U.S. News & World Report,* August 24, 1987, pp. 38–43.

"How to Deal with Japan." *Fortune,* July 6, 1988, pp. 107–18.

"IBM's Vexing Slide in Japan." *Fortune,* March 28, 1988, pp. 73–77.

"Made in the USA." *Business Week,* February 29, 1988, pp. 60–66.

"The FSX—Done Deal at Last." *The Economist,* May 20, 1989, pp. 32–33.

"The U.S. Gets Back in Fighting Shape." *Fortune,* April 24, 1989, pp. 42–48.

"U.S. Exporters That Aren't American." *Business Week,* February 29, 1988, pp. 70–71.

Whitehill, Arthur M. "America's Trade Deficit: The Human Problems." *Business Horizons,* January–February 1988, pp. 18–23.

"Why Americans Aren't Likely to Start Buying American." *Business Week,* November 23, 1987, p. 34.

"Why Made-in-America Is Back in Style." *Business Week,* November 7, 1988, pp. 116–20.

Competitor intelligence systems and industrial espionage

"Corporate Spies Snoop to Conquer." *Fortune,* November 7, 1988, pp. 68–76.

"George Smiley Joins the Firm." *Newsweek,* May 2, 1988, pp. 46–47.

"How to Snoop on Your Competitors." *Fortune,* May 14, 1984, pp. 28–33.

Peacock, William E. *Corporate Combat.* Berkeley, Calif.: Berkeley Publishing, 1987.

"Tackling the Technobandit." *U.S. News & World Report,* February 1, 1988, p. 36.

"The Battle Raging over Intellectual Property." *Business Week,* May 22, 1989, pp. 78–88.

"What Motorola Learns from Japan." *Fortune,* April 24, 1989, pp. 157–68.

Counterfeiting

"Asia's Export Upstarts Face High Winds from Washington." *Business Week,* November 7, 1988, pp. 52–53.

"Busting the Software Pirates." *Business Week,* June 17, 1985, p. 56.

"Companies Are Knocking off the Knock-off Outfits." *Business Week,* September 26, 1988, pp. 86–87.

"How High Tech Foils the Counterfeiters." *Business Week,* May 20, 1985, p. 119.

"How Taiwan Got the Goods on Product Counterfeiters." *International Management,* October 1985, pp. 89–92.

"That's the $60 Billion Question." *Forbes,* November 17, 1986, pp. 40–41.

"The Cost of Counterfeit Products." *Consumers' Research,* May 1986, pp. 33–35.

"The Counterfeit Trade." *Business Week,* December 16, 1985, pp. 64–72.

"The Hidden Threat to Air Safety." *Fortune,* April 13, 1987, pp. 81–84.

"The High Cost of Bolts." *Forbes,* June 13, 1988, pp. 56–57.

"Tips on How to Spot Counterfeit Goods." *U.S. News & World Report,* February 10, 1986, pp. 52.

Distributive forces

"A Land of Papa-Mama Shops." *U.S. News & World Report,* April 24, 1989, pp. 47–48.

Anderson, Erin, and Anne T. Coughlan. "International Market Entry and Expansion via Independent or Integrated Channels of Distribution." *Journal of Marketing,* January 1987, pp. 71–82.

"Austin Rover Links with Retailer to Break open German Market." *Business Europe,* January 18, 1985, pp. 17–18.

"Automation and Information Strengthen Retailer Power." *Business Europe,* March 8, 1985, pp. 73–75.

"Cheaper Shopping in Japan." *The Economist,* January 28, 1989, p. 15.

"Consumer/Drug MNC Offers Thailand Distribution Tips." *Business Asia,* February 6, 1989, pp. 44–45.

"Corporate Strategies: Differences in American and Japanese Approaches." *Pacific Northwest Executive,* July 1988, pp. 23–25.

"Drug on the Market." *The Economist,* December 1988, p. 70.

"Foreign Business in Japan." *The Economist,* November 12, 1988, pp. 76–77.

"How Amstrad Successfully Set up a Distribution Channel in Spain." *BI/Ideas in Action,* March 14, 1988, pp. 4–6.

"How Texas Instruments Is Improving Distributor Performance." *BI/Ideas in Action,* August 31, 1987, pp. 2–4.

"How to Avoid Pitfalls with LA Distributor and Agent Agreements." *Business Latin America,* June 13, 1988, pp. 187–91.

"Japan's Three-Tiered Distribution." *Industrial Distribution,* July 1986, pp. 53–57.

"Managing Distribution in Australia." *National Australia Bank Monthly Summary,* January 1986, pp. 12–15.

"Marketing in Korea: Look beyond Income Stats, Beware Distribution Pitfalls." *Business Asia,* July 11, 1988, pp. 222–23.

"OPEC Nations Move to Market Gasoline Directly to Consumers." *The Wall Street Journal,* April 20, 1988, p. A1.

"The Hungry Frenchman's Recipe for Europe." *International Management,* April 1988, pp. 20–27.

"They Have Names Too." *The Economist,* December 24, 1988, pp. 98–99.

"Too Many Shopkeepers." *The Economist,* January 1989, pp. 70–71.

"Using Overseas Trade Fairs to Locate Agents and Distributors." *Business America,* July 18, 1988, pp. 3–4.

"What the Worst Laws Say." *Business International,* July 12, 1988, p. 218.

Export trading companies

"Commerce Certificate Gives Antitrust Protection for Export Ventures of 3,150 Tooling and Machining Firms." *Business America,* November 7, 1988, p. 14.

"Export Trading Companies." *Business America,* October 12, 1987, pp. 2–9.

Howard, Donald G. "Export Management Companies?" *International Marketing Review,* Winter 1988, pp. 4–10.

Lenberg, Robert A., and Thomas H. Becker. "A New International Marketing Era for U.S. Small & Medium-Size Business?" Paper presented at the Western Marketing Educators' Conference, April 21–23, 1983.

"The Export Trading Company Act Is Alive, Healthy, and Promoting U.S. Exports." *Business America,* February 16, 1987, pp. 19–21.

Visvabharathy, Ganesan. "Trading Companies as Vehicles for Export Promotion." *Asia Pacific Journal of Management,* January 1984, pp. 120–32.

"Yarn Producers Boost Foreign Sales with an Export Trading Company." *Business America,* February 13, 1989, p. 15.

Zurawicki, Leon. "Brazilian Trading Companies." *Issues in International Business,* Winter–Spring 1986, pp. 25–30.

Parallel importing

"Gray Market Update: Destined to Get Darker before Getting Better?" *Business International,* June 2, 1986, pp. 171–74.

"Now, Japan Is Feeling the Heat from the Gray Market." *Business Week,* March 14, 1988, pp. 50–51.

"Owners of U.S. Trademarks Fight Treasury Department over 'Gray Market' Imports." *Business International,* April 12, 1985, pp. 113–14.

"See the Nice, Gray Cat." *Forbes,* May 6, 1985, p. 31.

"The Opening of Japan." *The Economist,* December 17, 1988, pp. 69–70.

"There's Nothing Black-and-White about the Gray Market." *Business Week,* November 7, 1988, pp. 172–80.

"The $7 Billion Gray Market: Where It Stops, Nobody Knows." *Business Week,* April 15, 1985, pp. 86–87.

Steel industry

Ballance, Robert H. *International Industry and Business.* London: Allen & Unwin, 1987.

"Forging the New Bethlehem." *Business Week,* June 5, 1989, pp. 108–9.

"The Decline of the U.S. Steel Industry." *Finance & Development,* December 1987, pp. 30–33.

"The Quotas That Saved Steel Are Backfiring on Buyers." *Business Week,* September 26, 1988, p. 49.

ENDNOTES

1. "Competitiveness: Getting It Back," *Fortune,* April 27, 1987, pp. 217–23.

2. "Waiting for the Yen to Stop Pummeling Profits," *Business Week,* June 1, 1987, pp. 58–59.

3. Priority watch list—Brazil, India, South Korea, Taiwan (all for other practices), Mexico, China, Saudi Arabia, Thailand. From "Singled Out," *The Wall Street Journal,* May 26, 1989, p. A1.

4. "Bashing America," *The Economist,* May 20, 1989, p. 79–80.

5. "Dollar Signs," *The Wall Street Journal,* January 26, 1987, p. 1.

6. "Love Thy Competitor as Thyself," *U.S. News & World Report,* June 5, 1989, p. 12.

7. "America's Hidden Problem," *Business Week,* August 29, 1983, pp. 50–54.

8. "The FSX—Done Deal at Last," *The Economist,* May 20, 1989, pp. 32–33.

9. "CEOs Gird for Global Battle," *Fortune,* April 29, 1989, pp. 65–66.

10. Tom Peters, "Closed Minds Can't Open Markets," *U.S. News & World Report,* March 3, 1986, p. 59.

11. "Myth and Marketing in Japan," *The Wall Street Journal,* April 6, 1989, p. B2; and "The High Yen: Signs of Growth and Change," *The Wheel Extended* (Tokyo: Toyota Motor Corporation, no. 1, 1988), p. 4.

12. Most native Spanish-speaking people connect *nova* with the star or with *nuevo* (new), which is probably what General Motors had in mind.

13. "Habit Dies Hard," *Forbes,* May 29, 1989, pp. 264–66.

14. "Why Americans Aren't Likely to Start Buying American," *Business Week,* November 27, 1987, p. 34.

15. "Still Only a Half-Open Door," *Newsweek,* February 13, 1989, pp. 48–50.

16. "EC, Lomé Negotiate Trade-and-Aid Agreement," *Europe,* March 1989, pp. 29–30.

17. "Car Wars," *Europe,* September 1987, p. 26.

18. "Japan's Carmakers Take on the World," *Fortune,* June 20, 1988, pp. 67–76.

19. Telephone conversations with both companies on June 1, 1989.

20. "Gianni Agnelli's Days in the Sun," *Forbes,* November 14, 1988, pp. 130–40.

21. "Can Consortiums Defeat Japan?" *Fortune,* June 5, 1989, p. 248.

22. "U.S. Business Should Prepare Now for EC 1992," *Business America,* October 24, 1988, pp. 12–16.

23. "United Front," *The Wall Street Journal,* December 29, 1988, p. A1.

24. "North America's New Trade Punch," *Fortune,* May 22, 1989, pp. 123–27.

25. "Dragons against the Fortress," *International Management,* October 1988, pp. 59–63.

26. "Japanese Managers Alarmed in Land of Rising Yen," *International Management,* December 1986, pp. 58–64; "Trade Switch," *The Wall Street Journal,* July 20, 1988, p. A1; and "The Rampaging Yen Is Leaving a Trail of Misery," *Business Week,* February 16, 1987, p. 46.

27. "Radical Revisions," *The Asian Wall Street Journal Weekly,* April 11, 1988, p. 14.

28. "Fujitsu Can Legally Clone IBM Software," *The Wall Street Journal,* December 1, 1988, p. B1.

29. Vernon R. Alden, "Who Says You Can't Crack Japanese Markets?" *Harvard Business Review,* January–February 1987, p. 52.

30. "Trade Thievery," *The Wall Street Journal,* March 16, 1989, p. A1.

31. "The Counterfeit Trade," *Business Week,* December 16, 1985, pp. 64–72.

32. "The High Cost of Cheap Bolts," *Forbes,* June 13, 1988, p. 57.

33. "Computing Manufacturers Combat Third World Pirates," *Personal Computing,* November 1988, p. 40.

34. "Cutting Russia's Harvest of U.S. Technology," *Fortune,* May 30, 1983, p. 103.

35. "The Decline of the U.S. Steel Industry," *Finance & Industry,* December 1987, pp. 30–33.

36. Robert H. Ballance, *International Industry and Business* (London: Allen & Unwin, 1987), p. 215.

37. "Decline of the U.S. Steel Industry," p. 32.

38. "The Worldwide Steel Industry: Reshaping to Survive," *Business Week,* August 20, 1984, pp. 150–53.

39. "The Quotas that Saved Steel Are Backfiring on Buyers," *Business Week,* September 26, 1988, p. 449.

40. "Forging the New Bethlehem," *Business Week,* June 5, 1989, pp. 108–10.

41. *Business International* proposal describing multiclient study on the practice and application of assessing competitors internationally.

42. "George Smiley Joins the Firm," *Newsweek,* May 2, 1988, pp. 46–47.

43. Adapted from "How to Snoop on Your Competitors," *Fortune,* May 14, 1984, pp. 28–33.

44. Ibid., p. 31.

45. "George Smiley Joins the Firm," p. 47.

46. "The Business Intelligence Beehive," *Business Week,* December 14, 1981, p. 52.

47. "Austin Rover Links with Retailer to Break open German Market," *Business Europe,* January 18, 1985, pp. 17–18.

48. *Mitsui Trade News* (Tokyo: Mitsui & Co., March/April 1988), p. 2.

49. Actually, major companies within the zaibatsu were split up and made independent organizations. The present Mitsui sogo shosha, Mitsui & Co., was started in 1947. See *Mitsui Group,* rev. ed. (Tokyo: Mainichi Newspapers, 1982), pp. 30–31.

50. *The Export Trading Company Act of 1982* (Washington, D.C.: Chamber of Commerce of the United States of America, January 1983).

51. "The Exports Trading Company Act Is Alive, Healthy, and Promoting U.S. Exports," *Business America,* February 16, 1987, p. 19.

52. Telephone conversation with Vanessa Bachman, Department of Commerce, June 6, 1989.

53. "A Land of Papa-Mama Shops," *U.S. News & World Report,* April 24, 1989, p. 48.

54. You can see this trend by comparing data form Table 176, *U.N. Statistical Yearbook, 1981,* and Table 138, *U.N. Statistical Yearbook, 1985/1986.*

55. "The Assault on the Right to Buy Cheap Imports," *Fortune,* January 7, 1985, p. 89.

56. "See the Nice, Gray Cat," *Forbes,* May 6, 1985, p. 31.

57. "Now, Japan Is Feeling the Heat from the Gray Market," *Business Week,* March 14, 1988, p. 50.

58. "A Red-Letter Date for Gray Marketers," *Business Week,* June 13, 1988, p. 30.

59. "What the Worst Laws Say," *Business International,* July 12, 1985, p. 218.

Section Four

How Management Deals with Environmental Forces

Section One introduced you to international business, trade, investment, and economic development. Section Two presented the framework of international organizations and the monetary system within which international business functions. Section Three discussed a number of the forces affecting international business with which its management must cope.

Section Four will give you a number of the management responses and solutions to problems caused or magnified by the foreign and international environments. The reader should bear in mind that this book is intended to be only an introduction to international business.

The student or businessperson who wishes to delve more deeply into specific areas should look to textbooks specializing in those areas. Fortunately, some business and law schools are offering more internationally oriented courses.

Chapters 14 and 15 deal with assessing and analyzing markets and with international marketing as it differs from domestic marketing. Chapter 16, on export practices and procedures, logically follows international marketing. Chapter 17 covers trade and relations between the communist and noncommunist worlds.

Chapters 18 through 22 present management solutions to or methods of dealing with the environmental forces discussed in Section Three. Chapter 18 covers financial management, while Chapter 19 deals with production systems. Chapter 20 presents material on labor relations' policies as they relate to nonexecutive, technical, or sales employees. Chapters 21 and 22 are intended to cap the solutions and methods material dealing with planning, organization, political risks, control, and executive personnel policies. The final chapter, Chapter 23, presents our thoughts on what the future holds for international business.

Chapter 14

Market Assessment and Analysis

The worst enemy of good research is the client who appears with a standard sampling technique and questionnaire and tells us to administer it across four or five countries. In some countries, high consumption of alcohol is seen as a macho attribute; but in others, where driving after only one drink can land you in jail, it is not surprising that people underclaim consumption.

Dawn Mitchell, managing
director of RSL/Burke, English
advertising research firm

LEARNING OBJECTIVES

In this chapter you will study:

1. Environmental analysis and a modified version, market screening, used for market assessment and analysis.

2. Market indicators and market factors.

3. Statistical techniques for estimating market demand and grouping similar markets.

4. The value to businesspeople of trade missions and trade fairs.

5. Some of the problems market researchers encounter in foreign markets.

6. The purpose of an international management information system (IMIS).

7. Sources of information for the screening process.

KEY WORDS AND CONCEPTS

- Environmental scanning
- Market screening
- Market indicators
- Market factors
- Estimation by analogy
- Regression analysis
- Trend analysis
- Cluster analysis
- Trade mission
- Trade fair
- International management information system (IMIS)

BUSINESS INCIDENT

To learn to what extent American multinationals are doing environmental scanning, a study was made of large American firms operating in at least three foreign countries. These are the results:

1. Over half of the respondents were conducting continuous international environmental scanning, another 14 percent used consultants and subscription services to continuously track changing conditions, and 27 percent used scanning when needed.
2. Over 60 percent of those responding relied more on internal capabilities for collecting environmental information than they relied on external sources.
3. About 70 percent used publications and reports. *The Wall Street Journal* and *Business Week* were the business publications cited most often: Business International, Data Resources International, Frost & Sullivan, and Business Environment Risk Information were the subscription services most often used.
4. The respondents ranked these six environmental components in order of importance: economic, competitive, political, legal, technological, and cultural.

environmental scanning a procedure in which a firm scans the world for changes in the environmental forces that might affect it

market screening a version of environmental scanning in which the firm identifies desirable markets by using the environmental forces to eliminate the less desirable markets

C ompared to the results of earlier studies, more multinational firms are now involved in environmental scanning, and various studies indicate those that scan outperform those that do not. In a related study, conducted by the Conference Board in 1988, 71 percent of the respondents expected to increase their monitoring efforts.[1] As you can imagine, greater worldwide competition from Europe 1992, Japan, and the NICs, which we examined in Chapter 13, is contributing to this increase.

Environmental scanning, the object of the business incident, is a systematic means of monitoring the foreign and international environmental forces. It is used as part of the planning process to provide information to top management about worldwide threats and opportunities. In addition, a modified version, **market screening,** will assist firms in two situations: (1) management of a company selling exclusively in the domestic market believes sales could be increased by expanding into overseas markets and (2) a firm that is already a multinational wishes to be certain that changing conditions are not creating markets of which its management is unaware. In both instances, managers require an ordered, relatively fast method of analyzing and assessing the nearly 200 countries to pinpoint the most suitable prospects.

MARKET SCREENING

Market screening is a method of market analysis and assessment that permits management to identify a small number of desirable markets by eliminating those judged to be less attractive. This is accomplished by subjecting the countries to a series of screenings based on the environmental forces examined in Section Three. Although these forces may be placed in any order, the arrangement suggested in Figure 14–1 is designed to progress from the least to the most difficult analysis based on the accessibility and subjectivity of the data. In this way, the least number of candidates is left for the final, most difficult screening.[2]

Initial Screening

Basic need potential.   An initial screening based on the basic need potential is a logical first step, because if the need is lacking, no reasonable expenditure of effort and money will enable the firm to market its goods or services. For example, the basic need potential of certain goods is dependent on various physical forces, such as climate, topography, or natural resources. If the firm produces air conditioners, the analyst will look for countries with warm climates. Manufacturers of large farm tractors would not consider Switzerland a likely prospect, because of its mountainous terrain, and only countries known to possess gold deposits would be potential customers for gold-dredging equipment.

Generally, producers of specialized industrial materials or equipment experience little difficulty in assessing their basic need potential. The builder of cement kilns, for example, can obtain the names and addresses of cement plants worldwide merely by contacting the Portland Cement Association in Chicago. A list of firms in an industry, often on a worldwide basis, is available either from the industry association or from specialized trade journals.

**■ FIGURE 14–1
Selection of Foreign
Markets**

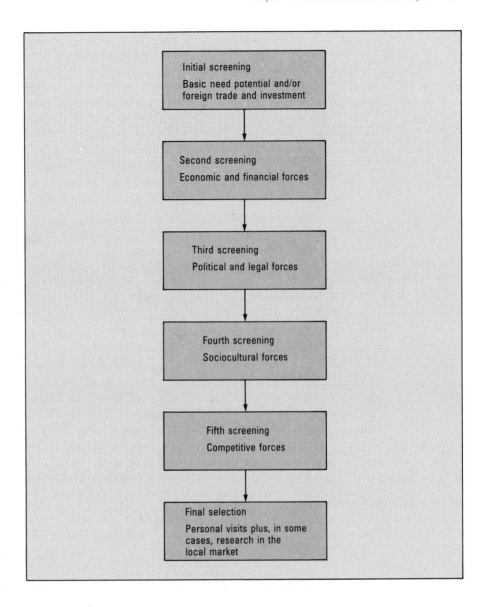

This is certainly straightforward, but what about the less specialized products of more widespread consumption?

Foreign trade and investment.   If the nature of the good or service is such that a definite basic need potential cannot be readily established, an analyst can learn if other American competitors are already exporting its products and if so, where. The U.S. Department of Commerce *Foreign Trade Report, FT 410* (Superintendent of Documents No. C 3.164:410) is available in most public and university libraries and Department of Commerce district offices. Minicase 14–1 shows part of a page from the *FT 410*. Note that both the quantity and the export value are given, from which you can calculate the export selling price per unit. Not all categories provide the units, however, and often the product categories are too aggregated to be helpful.

Analysts can obtain from the nearest Department of Commerce field office numerous studies prepared by U.S. embassies to help their search for markets. *Annual Worldwide Industry Reviews* and *International Market Research Reports* indicate major markets for many products. The *Country Market Surveys* indicate products for which there is a good market in a given country. We shall discuss these publications in greater detail in Chapter 16.

Other countries publish similar data. For example, the data office of the European Community, Eurostat, publishes an annual, *External Trade.* Additional information is available from *The Economist, Business International,* and other business publications listed in the appendix to this chapter. Many trade associations also publish export data.

Imports don't completely measure market potential.   Even for the situation where a basic need is clearly indicated, most experienced researchers will still investigate the trade flows to have an idea of the magnitude of present sales.

Management is aware, of course, that imports alone are rarely a measure of the full market potential. Myriad reasons are responsible, among which are lack of foreign exchange, high prices (duties and markups), and political pressures.

Moreover, import data indicate only that a country has been buying certain products from abroad and are no guarantee that it will continue to do so. Managements know that a competitor may decide to produce locally, which in many markets will cause imports to cease. Change in a country's political structure may stop imports also, as we saw in the case of Iran, where orders worth billions of dollars were suddenly canceled. Nevertheless, when there is no local production, import data do enable the firm to know how much is currently being purchased and do provide management with an estimate, though conservative, of the immediate market potential at the going price. If local production is being considered and calculations show that goods produced in the country could be sold at a lower price, even without knowing the price elasticity of demand, the firm can reasonably expect to sell more than the quantity being imported.

Companies wanting to know about the amounts and geographic areas of U.S. foreign investment can obtain information at the industry level from certain issues of the *Survey of Current Business,* which also publishes similar information about foreign investors in the United States.

Second Screening—Financial and Economic Forces

After the initial screening, the analyst will have a much smaller list of prospects. This list may be further reduced by a second screening based on the financial and economic forces. Trends in the rates of inflation, of exchange, and of interest are among the major financial points of concern. Credit availability, paying habits of customers, and rates of return on similar investments are still other financial factors that should be considered. It should be noted that this screening is not a complete financial analysis. This will come later if the market analysis and assessment disclose that a country has sufficient potential for capital investment.

Economic data may be employed in a number of ways, but two measures of market demand based on them are especially useful. These are *market indicators* and *market factors.* Other methods for estimating demand that depend on economic data are regression analysis, trend analysis, and cluster analysis.

Market indicators.   **Market indicators** are economic data that serve as yardsticks for measuring the relative market strengths of various geographic areas. A well-known American example is the Buying Power Index published in the annual "Survey of Buying Power" by *Sales & Marketing Management*. The purpose of this index is to enable marketers to compare the relative buying power of countries and cities in the United States.

A somewhat similar index on a worldwide scale is published by *Business International*. This index employs 40 indicators for 117 nations. The indicators include population, GDP, various categories of private consumption expenditures, and the production or consumption of steel, cement, electricity, and energy. These indicators are weighted and combined to form composite indexes of (1) market size, (2) market intensity, and (3) market growth.

> market indicators economic data used to measure relative market strengths of countries or geographic areas

1. *Market size* shows the relative size of each market as a percentage of the total world market. The percentages for each market are obtained by averaging data on population (given double weight), urban population, private consumption expenditures, steel consumption, cement and electricity production, and ownership of telephones, cars, and television sets.

2. *Market intensity* measures "the richness of the market" or the degree of concentrated purchasing power as compared to the world intensity of 1.00. The intensity for each market is calculated by averaging per capita consumption of energy, ownership of passenger cars, and telephone access lines. Double weight is given to overall private consumption expenditures. The proportion of urban population is also included and double-weighted because in many developing countries, much of the rural population does not actually participate in the money economy.

3. *Market growth* is an average of the percentage growth of the following indicators over the past five years: population; steel consumption; electricity production; ownership of cars, trucks, buses, and television sets; private consumption expenditure; and real GNP.

An analysis of these three indexes will show the international sales manager which major regions and major markets were the fastest growing, what their growth rates were, and which have the highest degree of concentrated purchasing power. Table 14–1 presents these indexes, which show that from 1978 to 1986, the EC, Eastern Europe, Middle East, Australasia, Latin America, and Africa increased their market size measured as a percentage of the world market. However, of these areas, the market intensity indexes of the Middle East, Latin America, and Africa are below the world average. Looking at the 10 major markets, you find that all nations except the United States, West Germany, and the United Kingdom increased their market size, though only Japan, the United Kingdom, and Italy increased their "richness."

By comparing the values of the indexes with the sales results of the company's subsidiaries, management can quickly judge their performance. Other uses of the indexes are to set sales targets and to serve as a basis for allocating the promotional budget. Although Euromonitor does not calculate indexes, it does publish two annuals, *European Marketing Data & Statistics*

■ **TABLE 14–1**
World Market Intensity Index, 1978 versus 1986

	Market Size (percent of world market)		Market Intensity (world = 1.00)		Five-Year Market Growth (percent)	
	1978	1986	1978	1986	1978–83	1981–86
Major Regions						
Western Europe	23.60%	24.05%	2.09%	2.20%	−7.31%	8.44%
EC*	(17.04)	(19.60)	(3.46)	(2.40)	(4.23)	(6.87)
EFTA	(2.70)	(2.63)	(2.38)	(2.50)	(10.89)	(9.98)
Eastern Europe	16.51	17.49	1.38	1.40	12.82	10.48
Middle East	2.14	2.92	0.50	0.60	44.19	32.91
Africa	4.32	5.01	0.22	0.20	37.03	15.93
Asia (market economies)	20.07	16.31	0.37	0.50	20.90	18.90
Australasia	1.24	1.31	2.71	2.90	13.17	11.01
North America	24.75	21.93	3.84	3.50	0.89	8.84
Latin America	7.74	9.33	0.69	0.70	22.23	11.89
LAIA	(6.93)	(8.34)	(0.75)	(0.90)	(20.69)	(15.75)
World (total or average)	100.00	100.00	1.00	1.00	10.38	151.00
Major Markets						
United States	22.49	20.80	3.87	3.70	1.10	8.84
USSR	11.89	12.24	1.41	1.40	15.15	11.35
Japan	7.79	8.07	2.43	2.70	8.48	12.27
West Germany	4.67	4.41	2.90	2.80	6.25	5.26
United Kingdom	3.38	3.29	2.19	2.40	1.64	−6.61
France	3.59	3.84	2.60	2.60	2.77	9.16
Italy	3.27	3.36	2.11	2.20	12.86	7.09
Brazil	2.80	3.60	0.75	0.70	15.20	24.32
Canada	2.26	2.30	3.50	3.50	2.12	9.76
Spain	1.76	1.87	1.70	1.60	23.70	11.79

*Spain and Portugal are included in 1986 figures.

Source: BI/DATA. Reprinted from "Indicators of Market Size for 117 Countries, June 1988," with the permission of the publisher, Business International Corporation (New York).

and *International Data & Statistics*, which provide valuable data, some of which you saw in Chapter 13.

Market factors.   **Market factors** are similar to market indicators, except they tend to correlate highly with the market demand for a given product. If the analyst of a foreign market has no factor for that market, he or she can usually use one from the domestic market to get a reasonable approximation. Moreover, an analyst who works for a multinational firm may be able to obtain market factors developed by comparable subsidiaries. To be able to transfer these relationships to the country under study, the analyst must assume that the underlying conditions affecting demands are similar in that market.

The transfer process, **estimation by analogy,** works like this: If car registration × 1.6 is used to estimate annual tire purchases in the United States,

---

market factors economic data that correlate highly with market demand for a product

---

estimation by analogy using a market factor that is successful in one market to estimate demand in a similar market the forecaster who has no market factor for the country under study can use the same 1.6 for that market. The constant in the country under study may be somewhat different (it usually is); but with this approach, the estimates will be in the right ballpark. Many such factors exist, and generally research personnel, either in the domestic operation or in foreign subsidiaries, are familiar with them.

regression analysis statistical technique utilizing a linear model to establish relationships between independent variables and the dependent variable

Regression analysis.   In **regression analysis,** instead of one economic variable (such as car registration), the domestic division may be utilizing several in a linear regression model of the form $MP = a + bx_1 + \ldots zx_n$, where MP = market potential and the xs are independent economic variables, such as GNP, number of telephones, or births. Again, the analyst has the choice of employing the same model or, when sufficient historical data are obtainable locally, constructing a new one by means of regression analysis.[3]

Trend analysis.   When the historic growth rates of either the pertinent economic variables or imports are known, future growth can be forecast by means of **trend analysis.** A time series may be constructed, or the arithmetic mean of past growth rates may be applied to historical data. Caution is advised when using this second method because if the average annual growth rate is applied mechanically, in just a few years the dependent variable may reach an incredible size. For example, a 5 percent growth rate compounded annually will result in a doubling of the original value in only 15 years.

trend analysis statistical technique by which successive observations of a variable at regular time intervals are analyzed to establish regular patterns that are used for establishing future values

Inasmuch as trend analysis is based on the assumption that past conditions affecting the dependent variable will remain constant, the analyst will generally modify the outcome to take into account any changes that can be foreseen. Often there are obvious constraints that will limit upward growth, one of which is the near certainty that competitors will enter the market if large increases in demand continue for very long.

cluster analysis statistical technique that divides objects into groups so that the objects within each group are similar

Cluster analysis and other multivariate techniques.   As multinationals extend their presence to more markets, managers in all functional areas are searching for ways to group countries and geographic regions by common characteristics to simplify their control. **Cluster analysis,** for which various computer programs are available, divides objects (market areas, individuals, customers, and other variables) into groups so that the variables within each group are similar. Marketers, for example, use cluster analysis to identify a group of markets where a single promotional approach can be employed; attorneys can use it to group nations according to similarities in certain types of laws; and so forth. Multidimensional scaling, factor analysis, and conjoint analysis are other techniques for examining differences and similarities among markets.[4]

Periodic updating.   If the estimates are altered appreciably in the periodic updatings that all long-term forecasts undergo, management may change the extent of the firm's involvement to be in line with the new estimates. Fortunately, the alternative forms of participation in a market permit the firm to become progressively more involved, with corresponding increases in investment. Most companies can enter a market in stages, perhaps in this sequence: exporting, establishment of a foreign sales company, local assembly, and, finally, manufacturing. Even when the decision is whether to produce overseas, management may plan to assemble a combination of imported and domestically produced parts initially and then progressively to manufacture more components locally as demand rises. Automobile manufacturers have begun a number of foreign operations employing this strategy.

Third Screening—Political and Legal Forces

The elements of the political and legal forces that can eliminate a nation from further consideration are numerous.

Entry barriers.   Import restrictions can be positive or negative, depending on whether management is considering exporting (can the firm's products enter the country?) or setting up a foreign plant (will competitive imports be kept out?). If one of management's objectives is 100 percent ownership, will the nation's laws permit it, or is some local participation required? Will the government accept a minority local ownership, or must a minimum of 51 percent of the subsidiary be in the hands of nationals? Are there laws that reserve certain industries for either the government or its citizens?[5] Depending on management's preferences, any one of these conditions may be sufficient cause for eliminating a nation from further consideration. For example, in the business incident study, foreign equity restriction was ranked second in the respondents' concerns. Only repatriation of profits was greater.[6]

Profit remittance barriers.   When there are no objectionable requisites for entry, a nation may still be excluded if there are what management believes to be undue restrictions on the repatriation of earnings. Limits linked to the amount of foreign investment or other criteria may be set, or the nation may have a history of inability to provide foreign exchange for profit remittances.

> Decision 24 of the Andean Group has for years limited remittances to 14 percent of the foreign investment and automatic reinvestment of profits to 5 percent.
> Now these restraints have been loosened to 20 and 70 percent, respectively, in an effort to make foreign investment more attractive.

Other factors.   Another factor of serious import is the stability of the government, which is more important than its form. Business can adapt to form and thrive as long as the conditions are stable. Instability creates uncertainty, and this complicates planning. An often heard complaint of businesspeople is that "they've changed the rules again."

Other concerns of management are tax laws, safety standards, price controls, and the many other factors we examined in the chapters on the political and legal forces. No matter how large a nation's potential market is, if its legal and political constraints are unacceptable to management, that nation must be eliminated from further consideration.

Some excellent sources of this kind of information may be found in *Financing Foreign Operations*, published by Business International; *Overseas Business Reports*, obtainable from the U.S. Department of Commerce; the *Ernst & Young International Series;* and *Digest of Commercial Laws of the World,* published by Oceana.

Fourth Screening—Sociocultural Forces

A screening of the remaining candidates on the basis of sociocultural factors is arduous because these "facts" are highly subjective. The analyst, unless he or she is a specialist in the country, must rely on the opinions of others. It is possible to hire consultants, but they are expensive. U.S. Department of

Commerce specialists can provide some assistance, and professional organizations and universities frequently hold seminars at which the sociocultural aspects of doing business in a particular area or country are explained. Reading *Overseas Business Reports* (U.S. Department of Commerce), international business publications *(Business International* and *The Economist),* and specialized books will augment the analyst's sociocultural knowledge. The use of a checklist of the principal socioeconomic components as explained in Chapter 9 will serve as a reminder of the many factors that must be considered in this screening.

After the fourth screening, the analyst should have a list of countries for which an industry demand appears to exist. However, what management really wants to know is which of these countries seem to be the best prospects for the *firm's* products. A fifth screening based on the competitive forces will help to provide this information.

Fifth Screening—Competitive Forces

In this screening, markets are examined on the basis of such elements of the competitive forces as:

1. The number, size, and financial strength of the competitors.
2. Their market shares.
3. Their apparent marketing strategies.
4. The apparent effectiveness of their promotional programs.
5. The quality levels of their product lines.
6. The source of their products—imported or locally produced.
7. Their pricing policies.
8. The levels of their after-sales service.
9. Their distribution channels.
10. Their coverage of the market. (Could market segmentation produce niches that are currently poorly attended?)

Countries in which management believes strong competitors make a profitable operation difficult to attain are eliminated unless management (1) is following a strategy of being present wherever its worldwide competitors are or (2) believes entering a competitor's home market will distract the competitor's attention from its home market, a reason for foreign investment we discussed in Chapter 3 (cross investment).

Final Selection of New Markets

Those countries that still appear to be good prospects should be visited by an executive of the firm. Before leaving, this person will review the data from the various screenings along with any new information that the researcher can supply. Based on this review and on experience in making similar domestic decisions, the executive will prepare a list of points on which information must be obtained on arrival. Management will want the facts uncovered by the desk study (the five screenings) to be corroborated and will expect a firsthand report on the market, which will include information on competitive activity and appraisal of the suitability of the firm's present marketing mix and the availability of ancillary facilities (warehousing, service agencies, media, credit, and so forth).

Field trip.   The field trip should not be hurried; as much time should be allotted to this part of the study as would be spent on a similar domestic field trip. Often time can be saved if the executive can join a government-sponsored trade mission or visit a trade fair, because such events attract the kinds of people this person will want to interview.

Government-sponsored trade missions and trade fairs.   An important mission of foreign diplomatic ministries, such as the U.S. Department of State and the government department representing industry (the Department of Commerce in the United States), is to promote a nation's foreign trade. This is why commercial officers stationed in U.S. embassies report to both State and Commerce. One of the many means of assisting American firms is to sponsor **trade missions.**

When U.S. Department of Commerce trade specialists perceive an overseas market opportunity for an industry, they will organize a trade mission whose purpose is to send a group of executives from firms in the industry to a country or group of countries. Company representatives will learn firsthand about the market, meet importance customers face to face, and make contacts with people interested in taking on representation of their products. Because of discounted air fares, hotels, and so forth, the cost to the firm is less than what it would pay if it went on its own. Moreover, the impact of a group visit is greater than it is for an individual. Before the mission's arrival, consular or embassy officials will have publicized the visit and will have made contact with local companies they believe are interested. Most governments organize trade missions.

Probably every nation in the world holds a **trade fair** periodically. Usually, each nation has a specifically marked area where its exhibitors have their own booths staffed by company representatives. Although trade fairs are open to the general public, at certain hours (generally mornings), entrance is limited to businesspeople interested in doing business with the exhibitors. Fairs are especially important in communist countries (as we mention in Chapter 17, East–West Relations) because they are often the only means for sellers from Western nations to meet the actual users of their products.

Sometimes local research is required.   For many situations, the executive's report will be the final input to the information on which the decision is based. However, occasionally the proposed human and financial resource commitments are so great that management will insist on gathering data in the proposed market rather than depending solely on the desk and field reports.[7] This would undoubtedly be the position of a consumer products manufacturer that envisions entering a large competitive market of an industrialized country. It might also be the recommendation of the executive making the field trip if he or she discovered that market conditions were substantially different from those to which the firm was accustomed. Often, in face-to-face interviews, information is revealed that would never be written. In these situations, research in the local market will not only supply information on market definition and projection but will also assist in the formulation of an effective marketing mix.

Research in the local market.   When the firm's research personnel have had no experience in the country, it is advisable to hire a local research group to do the work unless there is a subsidiary in a neighboring country from which a research team may be borrowed. Generally, home country research techniques

---

trade mission group of businesspeople and/or government officials (state or federal) that visits a market in search of business opportunities

trade fair a large exhibition, generally held at the same place and same time periodically, at which companies maintain booths to promote the sale of their products

may be used, though they may need to be adapted to local conditions. It is imperative, therefore, that the person in charge of the project have experience either in that country or in one that is culturally similar and preferably in the same geographic area.

Just as at home, the researchers will first try to obtain secondary data, but they frequently find that, except in developed nations, they either cannot find what they need or what they encounter is suspect. Fortunately, international agencies, such as the United Nations and the IMF, regularly hold seminars to train government officials in data collection, so that the recency and quality of secondary data in some countries are improving.

If secondary data are unavailable, the researchers must collect primary data, and here they face other complications caused by *cultural problems* and *technical difficulties*.

Cultural problems.   If the researchers are from one culture and are working in another, they may encounter some cultural problems. When they are not proficient in the local language or dialect, the research instrument or the respondents' answers must be translated. As we learned in the chapter on sociocultural factors, a number of languages may be spoken in a country, and even in countries where only one language is used, the meaning of some words changes from one region to another.

Cultural problems continue to plague the researchers as they try to collect data. The low level of literacy in many developing nations makes the use of mail questionnaires virtually impossible. If a housewife is interviewed in a country where the husband makes the buying decisions, the data obtained from her are worthless. Respondents sometimes refuse to answer questions because of their general distrust of strangers. In other instances, however, the custom of politeness toward everyone will cause respondents to give answers calculated to please the interviewer.

Often there is a practical reason for not wanting to be interviewed. In some countries, income taxes are based on the apparent worth of individuals as measured by their tangible assets. In such countries, when an interviewer asks a respondent if there is a stereo or TV in the household, the interviewer is suspected of being a tax assessor and the respondent refuses to answer. To overcome this problem, experienced researchers often hire college students as interviewers because their manner of speech and dress correctly identify them for what they are.

Technical difficulties.   As if the cultural problems were not enough, the researcher may also encounter technical difficulties. First, up-to-date maps are often unavailable. Streets chosen to be sampled may have three or four different names along their length, and the houses may not be numbered. Telephone surveys can be a formidable undertaking, because in many countries, only the wealthy have telephones and the telephone directories are frequently out of date. In such countries as Brazil and Mexico, researchers often have problems in using their own phones because overloaded circuits make it next to impossible to get a line.[8] Should they consider using a mail survey, they might change their minds when they learn that mail deliveries within a city may take weeks or are sometimes not even made.

> The postal service in Italy has been so slow (two weeks for a letter to go from Rome to Milan) that Italian firms have used private couriers to go to Switzerland to dispatch their foreign mail.

WORLDVIEW

Monitoring Competition: Do You Know What's Happening in the Outside World?

Change is the only certainty in tomorrow's world. Only companies and executives who can adapt to change are likely to survive in the new technological age.

How well do you monitor the outside world? Answering these questions will help you to find out.

1. **Would you form a quality circle to**

   (a) Select employees for senior management jobs? ☐
   (b) Encourage employees to generate ideas for improvements? ☐
   (c) Assist you in determining long-range strategies? ☐

2. **What is the "Boston effect"?**

   (a) A personality test that measures resistance to stress. ☐
   (b) A method of categorizing products and services. ☐
   (c) A statistical technique used in inventory control. ☐

3. **How would you use "positive reinforcement"?**

   (a) Allocating more resources to high-growth activities. ☐
   (b) Improving the organization's public image. ☐
   (c) Recognizing good performance by individuals or groups. ☐

4. **What is "synectics"?**

   (a) A creative problem-solving technique. ☐
   (b) A branch of laser technology used in glass manufacture. ☐

   (c) A method of forecasting retail sales. ☐

5. **Who wrote the best-selling book *Quality Is Free*?**

   (a) Peter Drucker. ☐
   (b) Philip Crosby. ☐
   (c) Yukio Mishima. ☐

6. **Which computer is likely to have had the highest sales growth during the 1980s?**

   (a) General-purpose computers. ☐
   (b) Minicomputers. ☐
   (c) Desktop computers. ☐

7. **Which computer language would you be most likely to learn in order to programme your personal computer?**

   (a) PL/1. ☐
   (b) Basic. ☐
   (c) Fortran. ☐

8. **What is the no. 1 objective of most large Japanese companies?**

   (a) High market share. ☐
   (b) Maximum profit. ☐
   (c) Excellent employee relations. ☐

9. **The book *The Third Wave* describes the kind of society that will result from the influence of new technologies. Who wrote it?**

   (a) Herman Kahn. ☐
   (b) Alvin Toffler. ☐
   (c) E. F. Schumacher. ☐

Mail questionnaires are not well received in Chile, where the recipient is required to pay the postman for each letter delivered. The response to a mail survey is often low by American standards in countries where the respondent must go to the post office to mail a letter—for example, Brazil. To increase returns, firms often offer such premiums as lottery tickets or product samples to persons who complete a mail questionnaire.

Research as practiced.   The fact that hindrances to marketing research exist does not mean it is not carried out in foreign markets. As you might surmise from the discussion of the availability of secondary data, marketing research is highly developed in industrialized nations, where markets are large and incorrect decisions are costly. Problems like those we have mentioned are

10. **How would you use "transactional analysis"?**

(*a*) Forecasting potential bad debts. ☐
(*b*) Improving communication and personal relationship. ☐
(*c*) Identifying companies as possible acquisition prospects. ☐

11. **Which of the following types of work is likely to provide the greatest opportunities for the use of industrial robots?**

(*a*) Assembly work. ☐
(*b*) Handling soft goods, e.g., the garment and shoe industries. ☐
(*c*) Packaging and package distribution. ☐

12. **What is the most important capability which the more advanced robots of the future will need?**

(*a*) Improved sense of vision. ☐
(*b*) Better tactile sensing. ☐
(*c*) Greater mobility. ☐

13. **Who was the famous writer who devised "the three laws of robotics"?**

(*a*) Kurt Vonnegut. ☐
(*b*) Erich von Daniken. ☐
(*c*) Isaac Asimov. ☐

14. **What is "Scimitar"?**

(*a*) A systematic approach to new-product development. ☐
(*b*) A computerized production system. ☐
(*c*) A linear programming technique used by Japanese companies for controlling suppliers. ☐

15. **What do you plan to do to fill any gaps in your knowledge revealed by this test?**

(*a*) I'll hire a top-flight consultant for advice. ☐
(*b*) Nothing—I'll wait until I'm sure I know what I need. ☐
(*c*) As a first step I'll read some books on each subject. ☐

Rate yourself by checking your score below.

How you rate in adapting to change
(5 marks for each correct answer)

1. (b)	6. (c)	11. (a)
2. (b)	7. (b)	12. (a)
3. (c)	8. (a)	13. (c)
4. (a)	9. (b)	14. (a)
5. (b)	10. (b)	15. (c)

60–75 *You actively manage your own development. For you, change is welcome and exciting.*

40–55 *You have a positive attitude to change but could push yourself a little harder to keep up with new developments.*

20–35 *You are in danger of becoming out of date. Act now and set yourself some really challenging goals.*

0–15 *You have a great deal of catching-up to do.*

Source: *International Management,* March 1984, pp. 29–30.

prevalent in the less developed nations, but they are well known to those who live there. It does not take long for the newcomer to become aware of them either, because longtime residents are quick to point them out.

There is a tendency in these nations to do less research and use simpler techniques, because often a firm is in a seller's market, which means everything produced can be sold with a minimum marketing effort. Bigger headaches, such as a constant lack of foreign exchange for importing raw materials or the necessity of operating in an economy suffering from hyperinflation, require top management to concentrate its efforts in areas other than marketing. Competition is generally less intense because there are fewer competitors and because their managements are grappling with the same problems, which keep them from devoting more time to the marketing function. Although the situation is changing, the most common technique still seems to be a combination of trend analysis and the querying of knowledgeable persons (salespeople, channel members, and customers), whose findings are then adjusted on the basis of the subjective considerations of the researchers.[9]

RECAPITULATION OF THE SCREENING PROCESS

Although the screening process we have described may appear time consuming, it does assure management that the principal factors have not been overlooked. Because most market-entry decisions can be implemented in stages, the firm can usually make adjustments in time to avoid significant losses when conditions change or if additional information indicates the initial decision was incorrect.

Where do you find this information? You may believe data are difficult to find, but the list in the appendix at the end of this chapter will show you there are many sources. The difficulty lies in converting all of these data into information that managers can utilize. For this, the firm needs an international management information system.

INTERNATIONAL MANAGEMENT INFORMATION SYSTEM (IMIS)

international management information system (IMIS) organized process of gathering, storing, processing, and disseminating information to managers to assist them in making business decisions

The **international management information system (IMIS)** is an organized, continuous process of gathering, storing, processing, and disseminating information for the purpose of making business decisions. The system's size and complexity can range from a simple filing cabinet in a small firm to a system employing computers to process and store data, as is found in large firms. The means are less important than the end, which is to enable marketing and other managers to use all the sources of information at their disposal. These are:

1. *Internal sources*—market analyses, special research reports, and data from company sales, production, financial, and accounting records as reported by foreign subsidiaries, sales representatives, customers, and channel of distribution members.

2. *External sources*—reports from governments, trade associations, banks, consultants, customers, and data bases.

Both types of sources can provide data concerning the changes and trends in the uncontrollable environmental variables as well as feedback on the performance of the firm's controllable variables. There is a trend now toward decision support systems, which permit managers to make inquiries and receive specific answers not only from the firm's data base, but from external, on-line data bases as well.

SUMMARY

A complete market analysis and assessment as described in this chapter would be made by a firm that either is contemplating entering the foreign market for the first time or is already a multinational but wants to monitor world markets systematically to avoid overlooking marketing opportunities and threats. Many of the data requirements for a foreign decision are the same as those required for a similar domestic decision, though it is likely that additional information about some of the international and foreign environmental forces will be needed.

Essentially, the screening process consists of examining the various forces in succession and eliminating countries at each step. The sequence of screening based on (1) basic need potential, (2) economic and financial forces, (3) political and legal forces, (4) sociocultural forces, (5) competitive forces, and (6) personal visits is ordered so as to have a successively smaller number of prospects to consider at each of the succeedingly more difficult and expensive stages.

When the proposed commitment of the financial and human resources is large, managements may be reluctant to make a decision based solely on the desk study and will require that research be undertaken in the market. If the researchers cannot obtain satisfactory secondary data, they will need to collect primary data.

Cultural problems, such as a low level of literacy and distrust of strangers, complicate the data-gathering process, as do technical difficulties, such as a lack of maps, telephone directories, and adequate mail service. These hindrances to marketing research do not prevent the work from being done. There is a tendency in many markets, however, to do less research and use simpler techniques.

To provide continuing information on changes in the uncontrollable variables as well as feedback on the performance of the firm's controllable variables, many companies have set up an international management information system to gather, store, and use information in an organized manner.

QUESTIONS

1. Select a country and a product that you believe your firm can market there. Prepare a study based on the information obtained from the first four screenings for your firm's executive committee, which will decide whether to proceed with your recommendations.

2. What is the basis for the order of screenings presented in the text?

3. If import data for a country are unobtainable, what readily available data might serve as a substitute?

4. Do a country's imports completely measure the market potential for a product? Why or why not?

5. What are some barriers related to the political and legal forces that may eliminate a country from further consideration?

6. What is the reason for making personal visits to markets that survive the first five screenings?

7. Why should a firm's management consider going on a trade mission or exhibiting in a trade fair?

8. What are the two principal kinds of complications that researchers face when they collect primary data in a foreign market?

9. Is there any connection between Europe 1992 and an increase in the use of clustering analysis and similar statistical techniques?

10. What is an international management information system? What is the minimum recommended computer size?

MINICASE 14–1

Rapid Research—Universal Tire Company

Sam Johnson, president of Universal Tire International, calls June Ashton, head of marketing research:

Johnson:

    June, you may have heard that I've been talking with Dates Rubber about giving us a license to make fan belts in our Spanish factory.

Ashton:

    I was surprised to hear that, Sam. We don't make fan belts in any of our factories now. Why are we interested in Spain?

Johnson:

    It's because one of the large automobile manufacturers there told our Spanish plant that if it can make a belt of American quality for them, they'll give it the major share of their tire business. This company is tired of having fan belt problems.

Ashton:

    You feel, then, that our plant can make a satisfactory belt with Dates technology. Is it expensive?

Johnson:

Who cares? With the size of that OEM business in tires, we could give the belts away. Look, the reason I'm calling you is that the Dates attorney called to say that they've agreed to our conditions for the Spanish contract and are ready to sign. However, he also asked if we want the rights to produce the belts in any of our other overseas plants. The reason he's asking is that one of our competitors has approached them for licenses, but he wants to give us first chance because we began talking with them first. The countries we don't want will be open to our competitor. June, do you have any way to run a quick check to see which, if any, of our other plants we should include in the agreement? It seems, offhand, as though Colombia might be a good prospect, perhaps Venezuela, and possibly Ecuador. Mexico is out, I imagine, because Goodrich and Goodyear already have local production. I have to call them back today.

Ashton:

What about our French or German plants?

Johnson:

Oh, I wouldn't think so. A number of companies produce belts in France. In fact, somebody is producing belts in every EC country. I'll bet the United States doesn't export a single belt to Europe.

Ashton:

What are we talking about with respect to market size? How many belts do we need to make a year for this operation to be viable?

Johnson:

The Dates president told me that we won't need much new equipment because the same machinery that prepares the inputs for tires can be used for belts. We can buy some used production machinery, also. He says we shouldn't have to spend more than $200,000 per plant on machinery. Training costs for labor are low because an experienced tire builder can be trained in a matter of days to build belts. According to Dates, if we can sell 150,000 belts a year at about $2 per belt, their average export price for automobile and truck belts, we can make money.

Ashton:

We're talking about a minimum of $300,000 gross revenue per country.

Johnson:

That's right, and we don't have to start production immediately in all the countries we name in the contract. It's really more of an option that we are getting. What we're doing is staking out the territory in which we want to build belts within the next three to four years.

Ashton:

If we don't ask for all the countries where we have tire plants now, can we go back to Dates later for those?

Johnson:

Only if our competitor hasn't taken them.

Ashton:

Let's ask for all of them now, then.

Johnson:

It may be that we won't want to put up belt plants in all the places where we have tire plants. If we ask for the right to produce in a market, Dates will expect us to go through with it—not all at once, because we don't have the supervisors and engineers available to do that. I believe they'll give us three, possibly four, years. Anything else I can tell you?

Ashton:

Let's see. I don't have time to get import figures from any of the countries, so I'll have to go with the *FT 466* or *FT 410*. Both reports will show the major markets for U.S. exports, but, of course, they won't give us total imports of any market. I've got the automobile and truck registrations because we use them for forecasting tire sales. Can I call Dates for market help?

Johnson:

No, unfortunately. They said specifically that the license excluded their marketing know-how. They won't give that to anyone.

Ashton:

Did you by any chance find out how long their belts were lasting?

Johnson:

Yes, I remember that when we were talking about product quality, he bragged that their belts had an average life of four years, which he said was good, considering that this included older cars with worn pulleys as well as new cars. He also said that Dates makes fan belts for more kinds of cars and trucks than any other manufacturer anywhere. That's all he'd tell me. I know it's not much to go on, but will you take a look at the markets where our plants are and choose which ones we ought to enter within the next five years? It would be helpful if you would rank them and give me your reasons why you ranked them as you did.

Ashton:

One last question. What about the number of fan belts per car? Most European cars don't have air conditioning. Can I safely assume one belt per car?

Johnson:

That will probably be a little conservative, but use the

one-belt-per-car figure for this study. When we get to the point of designing a plant, we'll get more data on the actual belts per make and model.

Ashton:

Let me have a couple of hours, and I'll get back to you.

For which of the countries where Universal now has tire factories do you believe Ashton will recommend fan belt production? How will she rank them? Why will she rank them in this manner? (Note: All of the information that Ashton has on hand is contained in the following table.)

Ashton's Data

Country*	1986 Auto Registration	Percent Cumulative Increase (over past 5 years)	1986 Truck Registration	Percent Cumulative Increase (over past 5 years)
1. Colombia	591,000	27.4%	599,000	201.0%
2. Venezuela	1,564,000	6.4	916,000	8.8
3. Ecuador	77,000	0.0	178,000	2.3
4. Saudi Arabia	1,300,000	21.7	1,450,000	8.3
5. South Korea	664,000	20.0	645,000	17.0
6. Kuwait	555,000	18.3	204,000	2.5
7. Nigeria	786,000	23.6	619,000	8.0
8. Spain	9,274,000	11.0	1,610,000	6.9
9. France	20,940,000	3.2	3,426,000	27.4
10. Mexico	5,157,000	12.3	2,254,000	18.8

*The countries shown are those where Universal Tire plants are located.

Country of Destination	Schedule E Commodity Number, Description, and Unit of Quantity			
	Current Month		Cumulative, January to Date	
	Net Quantity	Value (000 dollars)	Net Quantity	Value (000 dollars)
891C240 Motor vehicle belts and belting of rubber or plastics				
Canada	—	$425	—	$5,844
Mexico	—	364	—	1,941
Panama	—	2	—	232
Colomb	—	12	—	145
Venez	—	137	—	548
Ecuador	—	6	—	107
Chile	—	—	—	77
Brazil	—	15	—	154
Argent	—	2	—	159
U King	—	2	—	272
Belgium	—	58	—	888
France	—	364	—	4,001
FR Germ	—	15	—	425
Israel	—	39	—	104
Kuwait	—	11	—	116
S Arab	—	—	—	432
Thailnd	—	—	—	115
Singapr	—	—	—	175

(continued)

| Country of Destination | Schedule E Commodity Number, Description, and Unit of Quantity (concluded) | | | |
| | Current Month | | Cumulative, January to Date | |
	Net Quantity	Value (000 dollars)	Net Quantity	Value (000 dollars)
891C240 Motor vehicle belts and belting of rubber or plastics				
Phil R	—	8	—	95
Kor Rep	—	9	—	1,460
China T	—	12	—	122
Japan	—	10	—	82
Austral	—	189	—	2,444
N Zeal	—	10	—	199
Egypt	—	0 ·	—	562
Oth Cty	—	58	—	782
Total	—	1,745	—	21,482

Source: U.S. Department of Commerce, *FT 410,* December 1986, p. 2–439.

MINICASE 14–2

Benton Products

Benton Products is a multinational firm producing kitchen appliances (washers, dryers, electric ranges, refrigerators, and dishwashers). They have wholly owned production facilities in the United States, Canada, Japan, five EC countries, Brazil, and Mexico. The complete product line is manufactured only in the United States and Brazil. Although no single plant in the EC produces all the company's products, the five taken together do produce the complete product line. Joint ventures are manufacturing some products in India and Indonesia; and in South Korea and Australia, certain products are obtained from contract manufacturers who supply them with the Benton brand name. Benton markets in South Korea and Australia through wholly owned sales companies.

Bill Easton, vice president of marketing, has just finished reading an article on *Business International*'s market indexes and is wondering if they could be useful in analyzing Benton's sales. Easton calls in Lianne Ball, head of marketing research, and asks her to study the article, which contains the indexes for 33 major countries, and give him her recommendations. Later that day, she gives him the following note:

To Bill Easton

From the desk of L. Ball

Bill, I gave the article a "quick read" as you requested, and it has possibilities. I converted the BI world market size index to a "Benton world" market size index, which I believe we can use. See the following tables. If you agree, I can do a detailed analysis after I finish the rush job I am on now.

Business International's Market Indicators for Benton Countries

Country	BI Market Size (percent)	Benton Market Size (percent)	Market Intensity Index	Five-Year Market Growth (percent)
United States	19.12%	34.1%	3.9	8.84%
Japan	7.16	12.8	2.7	12.27
India	5.22	9.3	0.1	40.90
West Germany	3.95	7.1	2.8	5.26

(continued)

Business International's Market Indicators for Benton Countries (concluded)

Country	BI Market Size (percent)	Benton Market Size (percent)	Market Intensity Index	Five-Year Market Growth (percent)
France	3.49	6.2	2.7	9.16
United Kingdom	2.96	5.3	2.5	6.61
Italy	2.96	5.3	2.3	7.09
Brazil	2.30	4.1	0.8	24.32
Canada	2.09	3.7	3.7	9.76
Spain	1.63	2.9	1.7	6.61
Mexico	1.54	2.8	0.7	10.18
South Korea	1.26	2.3	1.2	41.59
Indonesia	1.25	2.2	0.1	31.13
Australia	1.07	1.9	2.9	11.79
Total	56.00%	100.0%		

Benton Products Sales by Country

Country	1986 Sales ($ millions)	Five-Year Market Growth (percent)
United States	$299	9.1%
Japan	97	13.1
India	65	22.8
West Germany	69	8.4
France	55	11.1
United Kingdom	46	6.7
Italy	50	6.8
Brazil	27	18.1
Canada	32	9.6
Spain	22	7.8
Mexico	19	10.7
South Korea	17	29.3
Indonesia	15	32.1
Australia	17	11.5
Total	$830.0	

Easton looks her note over and decides to call in Jim Allen, marketing manager for international sales.

Easton:

Good morning, Jim. Do you know anything about the market indexes that *Business International* publishes?

Allen:

I've heard of them, but I haven't used them. They try to do for the world what the Buying Power Index of *Sales & Marketing Management* does for the United States.

Easton:

Something like that. You know, I'm wondering if the sales of our foreign subsidiaries are keeping up with the growth in their markets. I notice that many countries' GNPs are growing, levels of living are rising—it seems to me that more people are becoming able to buy our products.

Allen:

Yes, Bill, sales are rising everywhere. Look at these sales in India—a 23 percent growth over the past five years; Korea, 29 percent; Indonesia, 32 percent; Brazil, 18 percent. You don't see that kind of increase in this country, do you? I tell you, Bill, everything's just fine. Our people are really on the ball.

Easton:

Don't be so sure. I made a calculation off the top of my head for India with Lianne's index, and I'm not so certain as you seem to be. Look at the following table:

(1) Benton-India Sales	(2) Lianne's Index	(3) Sales Should Be	(4) India Sales / Total Sales	(5) Column (4) / Column (2)
$65 million	9.3%	$77.2 million	$65 m./$830 m. = 7.80%	0.839

Allen:

How did you calculate what India's sales should be in column (3)?

Easton:

I multiplied Lianne's market size percentage by the total company sales of $830 million.

Allen:

What does column (5) indicate?

Easton:

I was trying to come up with a single number to measure how each market is doing compared to what it should do based on Lianne's index; in other words, in spite of India's remarkable sales increase, its sales are still not what they should be according to the index. According to *Business International,* they should be doing considerably more.

Allen:

This may have possibilities. Let me work with it. By the way, do you know how *BI* arrives at this market size index?

Easton:

Yes, here are their calculations in the article.

$$Size(\%) = \frac{2(POP) + POPU + PCE + KWH + STL + CEM + TEL + CAR + TV}{2(POPR) + POPUR + PCER + KWHR + STLR + CEMR + TELR + CARR + TVR} \times 100$$

where:

POP	=	Total population
POPU	=	Urban population
PCE	=	Private final consumption in U.S. dollars
KWH	=	Electricity production
STL	=	Apparent crude steel consumption
CEM	=	Cement production
TEL	=	Telephones in use
CAR	=	Passenger cars in use
TV	=	Television sets in use

A variable ending in R stands for regional or world total.

Allen:

Well, these aren't the market factors we use. We look at housing starts, size of households, marriages, population, and private consumer expenditures. In some countries, we can even get data on expenditures for household appliances.

Easton:

Do you combine them in any way?

Allen:

Yes, we use a regression equation that includes these variables.

Easton:

So, if each market's sales increase is in the line with the increases in these variables, you feel that we're doing a decent job in that market?

Allen:

At least this indicates we're holding our own, and, of course, we're always trying to increase market share. Another calculation we make is sales dollars per household in each market. We divide our sales in Germany, for example, by the number of households in Germany. We do that for each market and compare them. I learned that from our domestic manager.

Easton:

Yes, I know about that one. Tell you what, Jim. Why don't you take Lianne's index and the rest of the *BI* data and make some comparisons. Look at the "richness" index, they call it Market Intensity Index, and compare their market growth rates with ours. Let's look over your calculations together when you're ready.

Allen:

Give me a couple of days, Jim.

Make your calculations and point out which subsidiaries are doing well and which should be able to improve.

SUPPLEMENTARY READINGS

"A European Researcher's View of European Business Marketing." *Business Marketing,* April 1984, pp. 72–76.

"Attitude Research Assesses Global Market Potential." *Marketing News,* August 1, 1988, p. 10.

Douglas, Susan P., and C. Samuel Craig. *International Marketing Research.* Englewood Cliffs, N.J.: Prentice-Hall, 1983.

"Euronet." *Europe,* July–August 1982, p. 7.

"Eyeing the Consumer." *The Economist,* April 22, 1989, pp. 63–66.

"First Worldwide Survey of Leading Researchers." *Advertising Age,* July 18, 1983, p. 3.

"From Market Research to Business Research." *McKinsey Quarterly,* Autumn 1984, pp. 50–62.

Johansson, Johny K., and Ikujiro Nonaka. "Market Research the Japanese Way." *Harvard Business Review,* May–June 1987, pp. 16–18.

"Making MkIS Work for You." *Business Marketing,* October 1987, pp. 71–73.

Malhotra, Naresh K. "A Methodology for Measuring Consumer Preferences in Developing Countries." *International Marketing Review,* Autumn 1988, pp. 52–65.

"Marketing Research Wins Fans in India." *Advertising Age,* January 26, 1987, p. 57.

Ofir, Chezy, and Donald R. Lehman. "Measuring Images of Foreign Products." *Columbia Journal of World Business,* Summer 1986, pp. 105–08.

"Overcoming the Obstacles to International Research." *Marketing News,* August 29, 1988, p. 12.

"Probing Japanese Buyers' Minds." *Business Marketing,* November 1987, pp. 85–90.

"The Importance of Market Research." *Japan Update,* Autumn 1988, pp. 12–15.

"Third World Research Is Difficult, but It's Possible." *Marketing News,* August 26, 1987, pp. 50–51.

"Why Re-Invent the Wheel?" *Business America,* February 15, 1988, pp. 8–9.

ENDNOTES

1. J. F. Preble, P. A. Rau, and A. Reichel, "The Environmental Scanning Practices of U.S. Multinationals in the Late 1980s," *Management International Reports,* April 1988, pp. 4–13; and *Competitive Intelligence* (New York: The Conference Board, 1988), p. 7. Sixty-eight percent of the respondents said monitoring competitors' activities is important, but only 9 percent believed they have an effective system now.

2. Richard D. Robinson recommends a similar methodology, which he calls filtering, in *International Business Management,* 2nd ed. (Hinsdale, Ill: Dryden Press, 1978), pp. 52–55. Also see F. T. Haner, *Multinational Management* (Columbus, Ohio: Charles E. Merrill Publishing, 1973), pp. 20–25; and R. W. Walvoord, "Export Market Research," *American Export Bulletin,* May 1980, pp. 82–91.

3. Regression analysis is a statistical technique employing the least squares criterion to determine the relationship between the dependent variable and one or more independent variables. In the text, *MP* is the dependent variable, and x_1 through x_n are the independent variables. The analyst wants to solve for the constants *a* through *z.* For an in-depth explanation of regression analysis, see any statistics text.

4. Susan P. Douglas and C. Samuel Craig, *International Marketing Research* (Englewood Cliffs, N.J.: Prentice-Hall, 1983), pp. 259–73.

5. Commonly, public utilities, mineral extraction, banking, and communications are reserved either for the government or its citizens. Many of the LDCs tend to limit foreign participation to 49 percent generally and even less in certain industries.

6. Preble et al., "Environmental Scanning Practices," p. 12.

7. Secondary data and some primary data will be gathered on the field trip, but the visitor rarely has the time or the ability to conduct a complete research study.

8. While in São Paulo, one of the writers wanted to call Santos (an hour's drive away). The assistant to his secretary, whose principal job was to dial for an outside line, had tried to place the call all morning. Finally, at noon, he drove to Santos, completed his business, and returned to find the assistant still dialing.

9. "Market Research Wins Fans in India," *Advertising Age,* January 26, 1987, p. 57; and "Third World Research Is Difficult, but It's Possible," *Marketing News,* August 26, 1987, pp. 50–51.

APPENDIX

Sources of Information Used in Screening

I.–II. First and second screening (basic need potential, economic and financial forces).

    A. GATT *Yearbook*.

    B. IMF *Direction of Trade* and other publications.

    C. OECD *Economic Outlook* and other publications.

    D. United Nations.

       1. Statistical Yearbook.

       2. *Demographic Yearbook.*

       3. Contact UN for catalog of publications.

    E. Eurostat publishes much data on EC trade. Ask EC office in New York City.

    F. World Bank–*World Development Report* (annual)—also available on computer disk. Ask for catalog of publications.

    G. Asian Development Bank—*Annual Report* and newsletter.

    H. InterAmerican Development Bank—*Annual Report* and newsletter.

    I. Small Business Administration—*Export Information System Data Reports.*

    J. U.S. Department of Commerce.

       1. *FT 410, FT 450, FT 990,* and other foreign trade reports.

       2. *Foreign Trade Highlights.*

       3. *Annual Worldwide Industry Reviews.*

       4. *Country Trade Statistics* and many others. See *A Basic Guide to Exporting* ($8.50 from the Government Printing Office) for a complete list or request information from nearest Department of Commerce field office. Additional Commerce publications are listed in Chapter 16.

    K. *Business International* "Indicators of Market Size for 117 Countries" (annual).

    L. Monitor, London, England.

       1. *Europe Marketing Data & Statistics* (annual).

       2. *International Marketing Data & Statistics* (annual).

    M. Commercial officers of foreign embassies in Washington, D.C.

    N. Trade associations.

    O. Banks with international departments.

    P. Chambers of commerce, such as the German-American Chamber of Commerce in New York City or the Mexican-American Chamber of Commerce in Mexico City.

    Q. Professional data bases, such as Predicasts in Cleveland, Ohio, and The Economist Intelligence Unit in London, England.

    R. Write to commercial officers in American embassies.

    S. Your company's suppliers and customers have data they might share.

    T. Big 8 accounting firms sell studies that they conduct, and some publish newsletters.

III. Political and legal forces.

    A. *Business International—Country Assessment Service.*

    B. *Business Environment Risk Index.*

    C. Frost and Sullivan—*Political Risk Country Reports.*

    D. European Community—*Europe.*

    E. Oceana Publishers, Dobbs Ferry, New York—publications on various law categories.

    F. International Chamber of Commerce—various publications.

    G. Association newsletters.

    H. Major city newspapers.

    I. Business magazines.

IV. Cultural forces.

    A. Brigham Young University—*Culturegrams.*

    B. Business magazines.

       1. *Business Week.*

       2. *The Economist.*

       3. *Fortune.*

       4. *Forbes.*

    C. Major city newspapers.

V. Competitive forces.

    A. Most of the sources listed in Part I.

    B. Talk with knowledgeable people, but be careful! You may be given misinformation on purpose.

Chapter 15

Marketing Internationally

Over the last several years, the needs and preferences of consumers in free nations on every continent have been evolving into a commonality that transcends national borders and centers around quality, competitive pricing and uniqueness of performance characteristics—all factors that make up perception of value.

Robert Mercer, chairman of the board, Goodyear Tire & Rubber

LEARNING OBJECTIVES

In this chapter, you will study:

1. The reasons for differences between marketing domestically and marketing internationally.

2. The reasons why multinational managers wish to standardize the marketing mix.

3. Why it is often impossible to standardize the marketing mix worldwide.

4. The importance of distinguishing between the total product and the physical product.

5. Why consumer products generally require greater modification than industrial products and services.

6. The importance of the environmental forces on the marketing mix.

7. The product strategies that can be formed from three product alternatives and three kinds of promotional messages.

8. The programmed-management approach to advertising programs.

9. The intricacies of transfer pricing.

KEY WORDS AND CONCEPTS

- Total product
- Promotion
- Advertising
- Programmed-management approach
- Sales promotion
- Public relations
- Foreign national pricing
- Transfer price

BUSINESS INCIDENT

Procter & Gamble, an evolving global corporation . . . .

There have been some false starts and even some failures, but now Procter & Gamble's global marketing efforts are starting to bring results. The company, ranked number 42 in Fortune's "The World's 50 Biggest Industrial Corporations," obtained $5.5 billion (33 percent of its total sales) from its non-U.S. operations, according to the latest report.

This is all the more notable inasmuch as P&G faces more pressures in most foreign markets than it does in the United States. Many foreign countries have price controls, and there are more competitors in Europe because of the ease of shipping products across borders. For example, in France, P&G competes against Swedish, Danish, and Italian firms in many of its product categories. Commercial TV time, the most efficient way to introduce new products quickly, is limited and in many countries, such as Belgium, Germany, Italy, and Japan, the use of premiums and gifts for promotion are either banned or severely restricted.

In the 1940s, P&G's strategy was to export its core products to build demand and then establish local sales companies or production facilities. Whether the products were exported or produced locally, they were marketed similarly everywhere. Although those products were not launched with global distribution in mind, new products are. According to Edwin Artzt, the president of P&G International, "If P&G were introducing Pampers today, it would plan to get the product into world markets in five years or less." It took the company 15 years to get them into 70 countries. Now the company tries to introduce products on a worldwide scale early in their development, not after they are established in one market, which gives competitors time to react in all other markets.

Sometimes P&G approaches foreign markets more as a regional market than as a global one; many of its products are changed to suit the local markets, for example.

BUSINESS INCIDENT (concluded)

Camay's smell, Crest's flavor, and Head & Shoulders' formula vary from one region to another, as does the company's marketing strategy. "The idea of moving quickly by taking a piece of technology and implementing it to fit the habits of local markets has taken hold and is leading our operation," says Artzt. "[But] there is a reluctance to fix something that isn't broke—i.e., alter a product or a marketing strategy that is successful in one market just because it doesn't fit the global pattern."

For many years, P&G had a philosophy of employing overseas the same policies and procedures that had been successful in the United States, but this practice gave the company problems. Based on Liquid Tide, the company rolled out Vizir in Europe in the 1980s. What the marketers failed to realize was the European washing machines were not equipped to accept liquid detergents. When Vizir was added to a powder dispenser, 20 percent was lost in the bottom of the washer. P&G developed a plastic dispenser that fit into powder dispensers and offered it free to consumers. One small problem—European washing machines are bolted to the wall. "When we called these women and said we wanted to mail you a liquid dispenser free, just tell us the washer model number, they said, 'I don't know, the washer is bolted to the wall and I can't see it,'" explained Artzt. The company

finally solved the problem by inventing a reusable ball that sits on top of the clothes and dispenses the liquid. Vizir is now the third-largest-selling detergent in France and has been relaunched in other European countries. Artzt claims, "I think this will go down in history as one of the great all-time rescue jobs."

To avoid this kind of problem, Procter & Gamble's strategy is to make global plans, then replan for each region and execute the plan locally. It uses autonomous "core teams" composed of representatives of each country in a region to plan a testing program or a development program for new products and product improvement. They recommend products and marketing strategies for the core products (product lines)—soap, toothpaste, diapers, and shampoo. P&G core teams are working on the smell and concentration levels of fabric softeners for different parts of the world, for example.

Even the core team concept is evolving; a new one for disposables and beverages has been organized globally rather than regionally, as the first four teams were.

Sources: "The World's 50 Biggest Industrial Corporations," *Fortune*, August 1, 1988, p. D4; "The 100 Largest U.S. Multinationals," *Forbes*, July 25, 1988, p. 152; J. Boddewynn, *Premiums, Gifts, Competitions and Other Sales Promotions* (New York: International Advertising Association, 1988), pp. 15–19; and "A Global Comeback," *Advertising Age*, August 20, 1987, pp. 144ff.

If the marketing concepts and techniques that are learned and practiced in the United States can be applied in overseas markets as the business incident illustrates, why distinguish between marketing domestically and marketing internationally? Isn't it true that marketers anywhere must (1) know their markets, (2) develop products or services to satisfy customers' needs, (3) price the products or services so that they are readily acceptable in the market, (4) make them available to the buyers, and (5) inform potential customers and persuade them to buy?

ADDED COMPLEXITIES OF INTERNATIONAL MARKETING

Although the basic functions of domestic and international marketing are the same, the distinction lies in the fact that the international markets served differ widely because of the great variations in the uncontrollable environmental forces that we examined in Section Three. Moreover, even the forces we think of as controllable vary among wide limits: distribution channels to which the marketer is accustomed are unavailable, certain aspects of the product may be different, the promotional mixes are often dissimilar and distinct cost structures may require different prices to be set. The increased complexity of the international marketing manager's task is readily perceived when one realizes that they frequently must plan and control a variety of marketing strategies rather than one, and then they must coordinate and integrate those strategies into a single marketing program.

Even those who utilize a single, worldwide strategy must know enough about the uncontrollable variables to be able to make changes in its implementation when necessary.

International marketers, like their domestic counterparts, must develop marketing strategies by assessing the firm's potential foreign markets and analyzing the many alternative marketing mixes. Their aim is to select target markets that the firm can serve at a profit and to formulate combinations of tactics for product, price, promotion, and distribution channels that will best serve those markets. In the previous chapter, we examined the market assessment and selection process; in this chapter, we shall study the formulation of the marketing mix.

THE MARKETING MIX (WHAT AND HOW TO SELL)

As we indicated above, the marketing mix consists of a set of strategy decisions made in the areas of product, promotion, pricing, and distribution for the purpose of satisfying the customers in a target market. The number of variables included in these four areas is extremely large, making possible hundreds of combinations. Often the domestic operation has already established a successful marketing mix, and the temptation to follow the same procedures overseas is strong. Yet, as we have seen, important differences between the domestic and foreign environments may make a wholesale transfer of the mix impossible. The question that the international marketing manager must resolve is, "Can we standardize worldwide, must we make some changes, or must we formulate a completely different marketing mix?"

Standardization, Adaptation, or Completely Different?

Management would prefer global standardization of the marketing mix—that is, it would prefer to employ the same marketing mix in all of the firm's operations because standardization can produce significant cost savings. If the same product that is sold in the domestic market can be exported, there can be longer production runs that lower manufacturing costs. Even when the standard product is manufactured overseas, production costs will be less because the extra research and design expense of either adapting domestic products or designing new ones for foreign sales will be avoided. Just the task of keeping many sets of specifications current requires additional, highly paid personnel in the home office.[1] For the many products, both consumer and industrial, that require spare parts for after-sales servicing, standardization greatly simplifies logistics and acquisition.

If advertising campaigns, promotional materials (catalogs, point-of-purchase displays), and sales training programs can be standardized, the expensive creative work and artwork need be done only once. Standardized pricing strategies for multinational firms that source markets from several different plants avoid the embarrassment of having an important customer receive two distinct quotations for the same product. Although economies of scale are not as readily attainable for standardizing channels of distribution as for the other elements of the marketing mix, there is some gain in efficiency when the international marketing manager can use the same strategy in all markets. In summary, the benefits from standardization of the marketing mix are (1) lower costs, (2) easier control and coordination from headquarters, and (3) reduction of the time consumed in preparing the marketing plan.

In spite of the advantages of standardization, many firms find it necessary to either modify the present mix or develop a new one. The extent of the changes depend on the type of product (consumer or industrial), the environmental forces, and the degree of market penetration desired by management.

Product Strategies

The product is the central focus of the marketing mix. If it fails to satisfy the needs of consumers, no amount of promotion, price cutting, or distribution will persuade them to buy. The housewife will not repurchase a detergent if the clothes do not come out as clean as the TV commercials say they will. She will not be deceived by advertisements announcing friendly service when her experience demonstrates otherwise.

total product what the customer buys, including the physical product, brand name, after-sales service, warranty, instructions for use, company image, and package

In formulating product strategies, it is especially important that the international marketing manager never overlook the fact that the product is more than a physical object. The **total product,** which is what the customer buys, also includes the package, the brand name, accessories, after-sales service, warranty, and instructions for use. The fact that the total product is purchased often makes it less expensive and easier for the worldwide company to adapt the present product or even create a new one without altering its physical characteristics. Different package sizes and promotional messages, for example, can create a new total product for a distinct market. The relative ease of creating a new total product without changing the manufacturing process is an important reason why there is more physical product standardization internationally than one might expect.

Total and physical product. Much of the confusion in the ongoing discussion about whether a global firm can have global products is due to the fact that the discussants do not differentiate between the *total* and the *physical* products. For example, Coca-Cola is always offered as an example of a global product and the total product is global. However, the physical product is multinational; its sweetness varies according to local tastes, even in the United States.

Consider two products that Cadbury-Schweppes, the British-based food and soft drink WWC, produces—tonic water and chocolate. The tonic water is a global product physically, but, as a total product, it is multinational because people buy it for different reasons. The French drink it straight, and the English mix it with alcohol. Chocolate is neither a global physical product nor a global total product; it is eaten as a snack in some places, put in sandwiches in some places, and eaten as a dessert in others. Because of strong local preferences, it also varies greatly in taste.[2] So does Nestlé instant coffee, which is produced in 200 different blends globally, all of which are sold under the brand name Nescafe.[3]

WORLDVIEW
On Global Marketing

"The globalization of markets is at hand. With that, the multinational commercial world nears its end and so does the multinational corporation. Different cultural preferences, national tastes and standards, and business institutions are vestiges of the past." So says Theodore Levitt, a Harvard business professor. The world has been homogenized, and the smart firms sell standardized products using standardized promotion methods. Levitt cites such examples as Coca-Cola, Pepsi-Cola, McDonald's, and Revlon.

But Coca-Cola's own advertising director replies, "What looks good as a generalization sometimes doesn't follow. The world is certainly becoming more globalized, but the global village is certainly not here, not will it ever be." Coke's marketing manager noted that "Diet Coke clearly in many ways isn't appropriate for some undeveloped worlds." PepsiCo lets its overseas offices choose and reedit commercials it makes in the United States and makes local soft drinks like Shani, a currant-and-blackberry soda popular in the Mideast during Ramadan, the Moslem holy month. McDonald's, another company cited by Levitt, says it isn't an advocate of global marketing; it sells beer in Germany, wine in France, pot pie in Australia, and noodles in the Philippines. "We rely on the people native to the country to develop marketing programs," says the marketing vice president. Interestingly, McDonald's retains 74 different ad agencies in the United States to customize its promotion for local markets. Campbell Soup split the country into 22 different regions, each with different marketing strategies.

Is global marketing a nice fad, as a member of Booz, Allen & Hamilton, a well-known consulting firm, says it is? Is it a new idea? No, to both questions. Timken has made the same product and promoted it the same way for decades; its ad in this chapter is more than 15 years old. Thirty years ago, Goodyear's Hi-Miler truck tire was being produced in Akron and its overseas plants and sold under translated names such as *Tragaleguas* (league-eater) for Spanish-speaking markets.

What is new is that companies are first studying their global markets and then, where possible, making a single product for all of them instead of making the product for the domestic market and adapting it to foreign markets. They search for global themes and adapt the promotion of them to fit the local markets. Products that are not culturally sensitive, such as nearly all industrial products and most consumer durables, clothing, and toilet articles, lend themselves to a single, worldwide theme and message; food products require much more adaptation to the local culture. For example, Colgate-Palmolive's Oral Care promotional program (for toothpaste) was successful worldwide.

To sum up, the success of global marketing depends on the kind of product and knowing when product and/or promotional adaptations are necessary.

Sources: Theodore Levitt, "The Globalization of Markets," *Harvard Business Review,* May–June 1983, pp. 92 and 96; and "Ad Fad," *The Wall Street Journal,* May 12, 1988, pp. 1 and 17.

Type of product.   One important factor that influences the amount of change to be made in a product is its classification as a consumer or industrial product or service. Generally, consumer products require greater adaptation than industrial products to meet the demands of the world market. If the consumer products are high style or the result of a fad, they are especially likely to require changes. We can think of these product types as being on a continuum ranging from insensitive to the foreign environment to highly sensitive, as shown in Figure 15–1.

Industrial products.   As one would gather from Figure 15–1, many highly technical industrial products can be sold unchanged worldwide. Transistors, for example, are used wherever radios are manufactured. Timken advertises that its bearing are interchangeable no matter where they are produced (see Figure 15–2).

■ **FIGURE 15–1**
Continuum of Sensitivity to the Foreign Environment

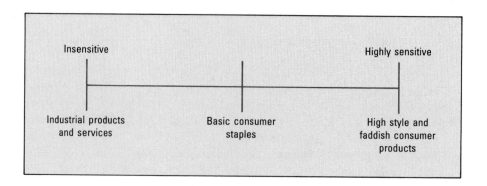

If product changes are required, they may be only cosmetic, such as converting gauges to read in the metric system by pasting a new face on a dial or printing instruction plates in another language. Relatively simple adaptations, such as lengthening pedals or changing seat positions, are frequently sufficient to compensate for the physical differences of foreign operators.

Somewhat more drastic modifications in the physical product may be necessary because of two problems that are especially prevalent in the developing countries—a tendency to *overload equipment* and to *slight maintenance*. These problems are comprehensible to anyone familiar with the cultural and economic forces in the foreign environment. Unlike American children, who grow up owning automobiles and working with tools, the mechanics and operators in many foreign countries rarely have such experience until they enter a training program, which is often on the job.[4]

A bulldozer operator learns that if he pulls a lever and steps on a pedal, his machines will push whatever is in front of it. It is not uncommon to see a bulldozer pushing on some immovable object until the engine fails or a part breaks from the overload. The extraordinary noise coming from the engine makes no impression on the operator. Despite the careful instructions concerning cleanliness that ball bearing manufacturers include in the package, one can find a mechanic removing the protective oiled paper to leave the bearing exposed to dust and grime before using it (he probably can't read). A very low-paid, uneducated man may be given the responsibility of lubricating equipment worth millions of dollars. He may overgrease or miss half of the fittings, and the equipment is destroyed.

To overcome these difficulties, such manufacturers as Caterpillar and Allis-Chalmers have established very thorough training programs wherever their products are sold. Many manufacturers have prepared simple instructions with plenty of pictures to get their message across to persons with limited reading ability. The other alternative is to modify the equipment, perhaps using a simpler bearing system that requires little maintenance. The machine may make more noise and be less efficient, but it runs longer with less maintenance.

Where the technology of even that adapted product is too advanced for their customers, manufacturers may market an entirely different product to accomplish the same purpose. A firm that produces electric cash registers in the United States, for example, may be able to earn good profits by marketing a hand-operated model in areas where electricity is unavailable. Products considered obsolete in advanced countries are frequently what the developing

■ FIGURE 15–2
Timken Ad

Courtesy The Timken Company

countries need.[5] Also, foreign subsidiaries sometimes find market opportunities for product lines not manufactured by the parent company.

> Marketing managers in General Tire's affiliates saw the profit possibilities in selling batteries to their tire customers. Although the domestic company did not produce them, management obtained the technology for their subsidiaries through licensing agreements, so that this totally new product was manufactured in a number of foreign plants.

Occasionally, adaptations are necessary to meet local legal requirements, such as those that govern noise, safety, or exhaust emissions. To avoid changing the product, some manufacturers follow the practice of designing it to meet the most stringent laws even though this means it will be overdesigned for the rest of the markets. A number of foreign car manufacturers, for example, produce a model for the entire U.S. market that meets the California emission requirements (the most demanding in the United States).

In some instances, governments have passed very strict laws to protect a local manufacturer from imports. When this occurs, it may be preferable to design the product to the next most stringent laws and stay out of the first market. Of course, this is what the government had in mind when it passed the laws. However, a word of caution for the company in this situation—test the local manufacturer's product before giving up on the market. On occasion, the local product also has failed to meet the specifications. When confronted with this evidence, the government has had to change the laws.

Consumer products.   Although consumer products generally require greater modification to meet local market requirements than do industrial products, some of them can be sold unchanged to certain market segments. Consumer products of this kind include a number of luxury items, such as large automobiles, sporting equipment, and perfumes. This is because every country of the free world contains a market segment that is more similar to the same segment in other free world countries with respect to economic status, buyer behavior, tastes, and preferences than it is to the rest of the segments in the same country. This market segment includes the "jet-set," foreign-educated and well-traveled citizens, and expatriates. Many products and services foreign to local tastes and preferences have been successfully introduced by first being marketed to this group. Gradually, members of other market segments have purchased these products and services until consumption has become widespread.

> Before McDonald's and other American fast-food franchisors went abroad, a common complaint among U.S. expatriates was that they couldn't get a good hamburger. A Brazilian returned from college in the United States and opened a drive-in similar to Dairy Queen in Rio de Janeiro. The first customers were Americans and members of the international set, but before long, word spread and Brazilians became customers. Thirty years ago, there was only one A&W root beer stand and one Dairy Queen in Mexico City. American expatriates and tourists were the principal customers. Today, many of the American fast-food franchisors are in such cities as Mexico City, Guadalajara, and Monterrey. When you arrive in Acapulco, the signs of Ponderosa, Kentucky Fried Chicken, and so forth make you think you never left home.

In introducing new products, especially when the goal is immediate market penetration, the marketer must be aware that *generally, as you go down the economic and social strata in each country, you tend to find greater dissimilarities among countries with respect to social and cultural values*. It follows from this that in general, the deeper the immediate market penetration desired, the greater must be the product modification. This does not necessarily mean the physical product must be changed. Perhaps a modification of one of the other elements of the total product is sufficient—a different size or color of the package, a change in the brand name, or a new positioning if the product is consumed differently.

> Mars faced a drop in Bahrain's imports of candy when it was ready to launch M&Ms. Fortunately, its marketing research discovered that Bahrainis consider the peanut to be a health food, so Mars repositioned its peanut M&Ms. The company was able to turn the hot Gulf climate to its advantage by emphasizing its traditional slogan, "M&Ms melt in your mouth, not in your hand." As you will see later in this chapter, Mars followed promotional strategy number 2: same product—different message, although part of the message (slogan) remained the same.[6]

Detergent manufacturers were able to achieve deeper market penetration by offering consumers with limited purchasing power the small packages that we find only in American laundromats. In humid climates, cookies and crackers are packed in metal boxes to preserve both the package and the product.

Services.   The marketing of services, sometimes called *intangibles,* is similar to the marketing of industrial products in that these products are generally easier to market globally than consumer products are. Consultant McKinsey & Bain's professional staff of 1,750 people offer worldwide the same kinds of expertise in business strategy that they sell to American clients. It is true that laws and customs sometimes force providers to alter their products. There are some markets that Manpower cannot operate in, for example, because in these countries, private employment agencies are against the law. Accounting laws vary substantially between nations, but Big Eight accounting firms operate globally. Ernst & Young, for instance, has 400 offices in 80 countries, and over half of its 32,000 employees work overseas. There are worldwide subscribers to Nexis, Mead Corporation's data base, one aspect of the fast-growing international computer and data processing industry. Service Master, American Express, and Visa—which now has an international payment card even in the Soviet Union—are other examples of successful firms in global markets. The physical product may vary slightly because of the local environmental forces, but the total product remains the same.

Foreign environmental forces.   In Section Three, we examined the foreign environmental forces rather extensively, so here we will limit our discussion to a few concrete examples of how some of these forces affect product offerings.

Sociocultural forces.   Dissimilar cultural patterns generally necessitate changes in food and other consumer goods. The worldwide variation in the mundane chore of clothes washing certainly has caused problems for Procter & Gamble, as you read in the business incident, but it is also troublesome for appliance makers. Because the French want to load their washing machines from the top, the British want front loading, the Germans insist on high-speed machines that remove most of the moisture in the spin-dry process, but the Italians prefer slower spin speeds because they let the warm sun do the drying, Whirlpool must produce a variety of models. *And this is only in the EC![7]* The company must make still other models for other parts of the world.

Although some multinational firms, such as Kodak and Campbell, have been extremely successful in employing the same brand name, label, and colors worldwide, other firms are sometimes surprised to learn they must change to other names, labels, or colors because of cultural differences. Green packages are taboo in the Far East because they remind the public of the dangers and illnesses of the jungle, but gold appears frequently on packages in Latin America because Latin Americans view it as a symbol of quality and prestige. In the Netherlands, blue is considered warm and feminine, but the Swedes consider it masculine and cold.

Procter & Gamble found out that a gold package has value in Europe too after it launched its Crest Tarter Control Formula in the United Kingdom in a silver box, which was followed two months later by Colgate's equivalent in a gold box. Sheepish P&G officials, agreeing that Colgate's choice of gold was better than their silver, explained that silver was required because that was how the product was packaged in the United States.[8]

Even if the colors can remain the same, instructions on labels, of course, must be translated into the language of the market. Firms selling in areas where two or more languages are spoken, such as Canada or Switzerland, may use multilingual labels. Where instructions are not required, as in the case of some consumer or industrial products whose use is well known, there is an advantage to printing the label in the language of the country best known for the product. French labels on perfumes and English labels on industrial goods help to strengthen the product's image.

> A Mexican firm in which one of the writers had an interest copied an American brand of penetrating oil that was the best-selling import, even to the blue color. It put a label in English on the can. Then, to comply with the law, a gummed sticker saying *Envasado in Mexico* (Can filled in Mexico) was placed over part of the label. The Mexican product, unlike most locally made industrial products, had excellent acceptance from the start.

A perfectly good brand name may have to be scrapped because of its unfavorable connotations in another language. An American product failed to make it in Sweden because its name translated to "enema." In Latin America, a product had to be taken off the market when the manufacturer found that the name meant "jackass oil." Of course, this problem occurs in both directions, as a Finnish brewery found when it was about to introduce "Koff" beer and "Siff" soft drinks to this country. Incidentally, an economic constraint to the international standardization of brand names is the refusal of some firms to let a subsidiary put their brand on a locally made product if it fails to meet their quality standards because of the inability to import the necessary raw materials or because the required production equipment in unavailable.

An important difference in the social forces to which American marketers are not accustomed is the housewife's preference in other nations, both developed and developing, for making daily visits to the small neighborhood specialty shops and the large, open markets where she can socialize while shopping. More frequent buying permits smaller packages, which is especially important to the shopper who has no automobile in which to carry her purchases. However, this custom is changing in Europe, where a growing sophistication of consumption patterns is demanding the kinds of assortments that only a large store can offer. Shopping frequency is also slowing as the European housewife, especially if she is employed, is finding that she does not have as much free time as she previously had. One can easily draw a parallel in this situation to that which began in the 1940s in the United States. The same conditions of rising incomes, a growing middle class, and an increasing number of working wives have combined to put a premium on the shopper's time, and just as occurred in the United States, supermarkets, mass merchandising, and catalog selling have moved in to fill this need.

Legal forces. Legal forces can be a formidable constraint in the design of product strategies because if the firm fails to adhere to a country's laws governing the product, it will be unable to do business in that country. Laws concerning pollution, consumer protection, and operator safety are being enacted rapidly in many parts of the world and are severely affecting the marketer's freedom to standardize the product mix internationally. For example, American machinery manufacturers exporting to Sweden have found their operator safety requirements to be even stricter than those required by OSHA, so that if they wish to market in Sweden, they must produce a special model. Similarly, the stricter American emission-control laws force producers of foreign automobiles to make significant model changes to sell in the United States.

Laws prohibiting certain classes of imports are extremely common everywhere, as potential exporters learn when they research the world for markets. We know that products considered luxuries as well as products already being manufactured are among the first to be excluded from importation, but such laws also affect local production. As we saw in the previous section, prohibition of essential raw material imports can require a subsidiary to manufacture a product substantially different than what the parent company produces.

Foods and pharmaceuticals are especially influenced by laws concerning purity and labeling. Food products sold in Canada, whether imported or produced locally, are subject to strict rules that require both English and French on the labels as well as metric and inch-pound units. The law even dictates the space permitted between the number and the unit—16 oz. is correct, but 16oz. is not. The Venezuelan government, in an effort to protect the consumer from being overcharged for pharmaceuticals, has decreed that the manufacturer or the importer must affix to the package the maximum retail price at which the product can be sold.[9] Because of the Saudi Arabians' preoccupation with avoiding food containing pork, the label of any product containing animal fat or meat that is sold in Saudi Arabia must state the kind of animal used or must state that no swine products were used.

Legal forces may also prevent a worldwide firm from employing its brand name in all of its overseas markets. Managements accustomed to the American law, which establishes the right to a brand name by priority in use, are surprised to learn that in code law countries, a brand belongs to the person registering it first. Thus, the marketer may go into foreign markets expecting to use the company's long-established brand name only to find that someone else owns it. The name may have been registered by someone who is employing it legitimately for his own products, or it may have been pirated—that is, registered by someone who hopes to profit by selling the name back to the originating firm.

Both reasons stopped Ford from marketing its automobiles under established names in Mexico and Germany. In the case of Mexico, the reason was brand piracy. Ford refused to pay the high price that the registrant wanted for the name, so for years the Falcon was known as the Ford 200. The use of the name Mustang by a bicycle manufacturer in Germany was legitimate. The firm was producing under that name when Ford entered the market.

To avoid Ford's predicament, the firm must register its brand names in every country where it wants to use them or where it might use them at a future date. And this must be done rapidly. The Paris Convention grants a firm that has registered a name in one country only six months' priority in registering it elsewhere. Unilever, the English-Dutch manufacturer of personal care products, has over 100,000 registered trademarks registered throughout the world, most of which are not in use but are kept in reserve.

Economic forces.   The great disparity among the world markets with respect to income is an important obstacle to worldwide product standardization. Many products from the industrialized countries are simply too expensive for consumers in the developing countries, so if the firm wishes to achieve market penetration, it must either simplify the product or produce a different, less costly one.

When Gillette discovered that only 8 percent of Mexican men used shaving cream (the rest use soapy water), it introduced a plastic tube of shaving cream at half the price of its aerosol can. Now more than twice that percentage use the less expensive package, and Gillette plans to sell the tube in other parts of Latin America. Because many Latin American customers can't afford to buy American-sized packages, the company sells packages of single razor blades and half-ounce packages of Silkience shampoo. Use of the plastic squeeze bottle, "the poor man's aerosol," is common where incomes are low.[10]

Similarly, Hoover saw an opportunity to sell a simple washing machine to Mexicans who could not afford the high-priced American-type machine. Although Hoover had no American model to simplify, it was able to copy its inexpensive English washer, which became an overnight success.

Economic forces affect product standardization in still another way. Poor economies signify poor infrastructure—bad roads, lack of sufficient electric power, and so on. Driving conditions in Mexico required Goodrich to design a tire for cut and bruise resistance rather than for high speed, as in the United States. The tire was so successful that residents in U.S. border towns preferred it to the U.S. product even though its price was higher.

The lack of a constant supply of electricity, another characteristic of many poorer countries, has compelled refrigerator manufacturers to supply a gasoline-driven product and office equipment firms to manufacture hand-operated machines. As one would expect, this condition has also provided the producers of small diesel standby generators with a ready market. Any users requiring a steady source of power, such as hospitals and theaters, are potential customers.

Market size influences the product mix, and, in the poorer countries, the populations are not only frequently smaller but also contain a large number of economic zeros (people who have no means to purchase anything but the bare necessities of life), thereby making the already small market even smaller. This means that normally the foreign subsidiary cannot afford to produce as complete a product mix as does the parent. Most automobile manufacturers assemble only the least expensive line and broaden the local product mix by importing, when permitted, the luxury cars. This marketing technique is practiced by all WWCs whenever possible because a captive foreign sales organization is available to promote the sales of the home organization's exports and because the revenue derived helps pay the subsidiary's overhead. Philips, the Dutch electrical products giant, owns a light-bulb plant in Chile that supplements its revenue by importing various small domestic appliances from its parent. Some foreign manufacturing subsidiaries carry this practice one step further by selling imports from other firms when these products are suited to their present distribution channels and marketing expertise.

Physical forces.   Elements of the physical forces, such as climate and terrain, also mitigate against international product standardization. Where the heat is intense, gasoline-driven machinery and automobiles must be fitted with larger radiators for extra cooling capacity. Gasoline must have a higher flash point to prevent vapor locks and stalling. As we noted in the chapter on the physical forces, insects proliferate when the winters are not cold enough to kill them. The problems this causes the agricultural industry are obvious, but even some consumer products are affected. In Brazil, the combination of intense heat and wooden floors forced the floor wax manufacturers to add a flea killer to their formulations.[11]

The heat and high humidity in many parts of the tropics require electrical equipment to be built with extraheavy insulation. Consumer goods that are affected by moisture must be specially packaged to resist its penetration. Thus, one finds pills wrapped individually in foil and baked goods packaged in tin boxes to prevent their degradation by moisture.

High altitudes frequently require product alteration. Food manufacturers have found that they must change their cooking instructions for people who live at high altitudes because at such altitudes it takes much longer to cook and bake. The thinner atmosphere requires producers of cake mixes to include less yeast. Gasoline and diesel motors generate less power at high altitudes, so the manufacturer must often supply a larger engine.

Mountainous terrain implies high-cost highways, so in the poorer countries, roads of the quality we know are nonexistent. Trucks traveling poorer-quality roads need tires with thicker treads and heavy-duty suspensions. Because of the rough ride, packaging must be stronger than that used in the United States. From these examples, we can appreciate that even though an unchanged product may be culturally and economically acceptable in a market, the effect of the physical forces alone may be strong enough to require some product modification.

Boeing's 737 has become the best-selling commercial jet in history partly because its engineers redesigned it for Third World aviation after its initial sales to developed nations dropped off. The runways in developing countries were too short for the original design and, being made of less expensive asphalt rather than concrete, were also too soft. By redesigning the wings to allow shorter takeoffs and landings and by selling 1 or 2 at a time instead of batches of 20 or 30, which airlines in the developed nations order, Boeing built a reputation with developing countries airlines, which, as they grew, began to buy Boeing's larger planes.[12]

Due to space limitations, it is impossible to examine the influence of every environmental force on foreign product strategies. We believe sufficient practical examples have been offered so that these, together with the information contained in the chapters on these forces, will give the reader an idea of their pervasiveness not only in the formulation of the product strategies but also in the design of the entire marketing mix. In fact, as we will show at the end of this chapter, a useful guide in the marketing mix preparation is a matrix in which the marketing mix variables are tabulated against the environmental forces.

Promotional Strategies

promotion all forms of communication between a firm and its publics

Promotion, one of the basic elements of the marketing mix, is communication that secures understanding between a firm and its publics to bring about a favorable buying action and achieve a long-lasting confidence in the firm and the product or service it provides. Note that this definition employs the plural, publics, because the seller's promotional efforts must be directed to more than just the ultimate consumers and the channel of distribution members. Far too often, the other publics have been ignored by business not only in the United States but in other markets as well. Managements have awakened to the fact that the old advice of always maintaining a low profile in a foreign country is not necessarily the best course of action. Many companies have changed this strategy and are now making the general public and governments aware of their public-service activities.

Because promotion both influences and is influenced by the other marketing mix variables, it is possible to formulate nine distinct strategies by combining the three alternatives of (1) marketing the same physical product everywhere, (2) adapting the physical product for foreign markets, and (3) designing a different physical product with (*a*) the same, (*b*) adapted, or (*c*) different messages.[13] Let us examine the six strategies most commonly used.

1. *Same product—same message*. When marketers find that target markets vary little with respect to product use and consumer attitudes, they can offer the same product and use the same promotional appeals in all markets. Avon, Maidenform, and A.T. Cross follow this strategy. See Figure 15–3, which uses exactly the same message.

2. *Same product—different message*. The same product may satisfy a different need or be used differently elsewhere. This means the product may be left unchanged, but a different message is required. Honda's campaign, "You meet the nicest people on a Honda" appeals to Americans who use their motorcycles as a pleasure vehicle, but in Brazil, Honda stresses economy as it tries to make its product a means of basic transportation.

3. *Product adaptation—same message*. In cases where the product serves the same function but must be adapted to different conditions, the same message is employed with a changed product. A number of product alterations have been cited in the section on product strategies.

4. *Product adaptation—message adaptation*. When both product use and buying habits are unlike those of the home country, both the message and the product must be modified. In Chile, greeting cards carry no message and are sufficiently general in design so that they may be used for a number of occasions. The Starlight Tissue Company of West Germany is turning out rolls of toilet paper with English lessons printed on them. The course consists of 26 lessons, with each roll bearing one lesson that is repeated on every sixth square of paper. The promotion states that the idea is for Germans who say they have always wanted to learn English but have never had the time.

5. *Different product—same message*. As we pointed out in our discussion of the economic forces' influence on product strategies, the potential customers in many markets cannot afford the product as manufactured in the firm's home country. The product may also be too technologically advanced to gain widespread acceptance. To overcome these obstacles, companies have frequently produced a very distinct product for these markets. The previously mentioned low-cost plastic squeeze bottle and inexpensive manually operated washing machines are two examples. The promotional message, however, can be very similar to what is used in the developed countries if the product performs the same functions.

■ **FIGURE 15–3**
Advertisements for the Identical Luxury Product with a Very Literal Translation

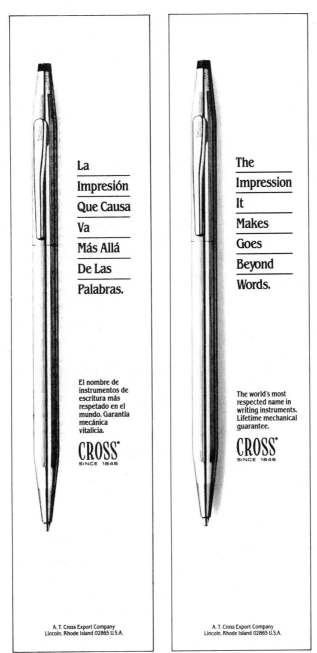

La Impresión Que Causa Va Más Allá De Las Palabras.

El nombre de instrumentos de escritura más respetado en el mundo. Garantía mecánica vitalicia.

CROSS°
SINCE 1846

A. T. Cross Export Company
Lincoln, Rhode Island 02865 U.S.A.

The Impression It Makes Goes Beyond Words.

The world's most respected name in writing instruments. Lifetime mechanical guarantee.

CROSS°
SINCE 1846

A. T. Cross Export Company
Lincoln, Rhode Island 02865 U.S.A.

Courtesy of A.T. Cross

6. *Different product for the same use—different message.* Frequently, the different product requires a different message as well. Welding torches rather than automatic welding machines would be sold on the basis of low acquisition cost rather than high output per labor-hour. LDC governments faced with high unemployment would be persuaded by a message emphasizing the job-creating possibilities of labor-intensive processes rather than the labor saving of highly automated machinery.

The tools for communicating these messages—the promotional mix—are advertising, personal selling, sales promotion, public relations, and publicity. No one of these tools is inherently superior to the others, though circumstances in a given situation may dictate that one of them should be emphasized more than the others. Just as in the determination of the product strategies, the composition of the promotional mix will depend on the type of product, the environmental forces, and the amount of market penetration desired.

advertising paid, nonpersonal presentation of ideas, goods, or services by an identified sponsor

Advertising.   Of all the promotional mix elements, **advertising** is the one with the greatest similarities worldwide. The reason for this is that most advertising everywhere is based on American practices. U.S. ad agencies have greatly aided the global propagation of American techniques as they have followed their domestic customers overseas. Today the major American agencies are all multinational, with wholly owned subsidiaries, joint ventures, and working agreements with local agencies. The latest annual worldwide ranking of the top advertising agencies by revenue illustrates the American dominance. Although a Japanese agency, Dentsu, helped by the strong yen in the translation of its billings, was the largest, 27 of the top 50 were American. Twelve other Japanese agencies and numerous English and French agencies, also aided by their strong currencies, were ranked, many for the first time. Only one other country, Korea, had an agency on the list.[14]

The trend toward global marketing and the economies of scale have prompted many firms to stress the standardization of advertising procedures. Coca-Cola, for example, estimates that it saves more than $8 million annually in the cost of thinking up new imagery by repeating the same theme everywhere. Texas Instruments, which used to have four different creative approaches in Scandinavia (one for each country), now runs similar ads in all four countries at a savings of $30,000 a commercial.

The multinational advertising agencies obviously argue for international standardization because their presence in various world markets gives them a sales advantage over the local agency. This approach often appeals as well to top managements, which want their firms to present a single, unified image and logo in all markets.

Even when the advertising campaigns are standardized worldwide, international advertisers have generally preferred national media to reach mass audiences. One exception to this generalization, however, is the situation in which the advertisements are shown on a TV station that is also viewed in neighboring countries or are placed in internationally distributed publications such as *Reader's Digest, Time, The Wall Street Journal, Business Week,* and *Fortune.*

The international advertising manager must be prepared to hear arguments against standardization from personnel in the foreign subsidiaries. "Our market is unique," they will argue, "and so we can't use what the home office sends us." The manager's task is to weigh the pros and cons of standardization, taking into consideration the cost of lower morale that it might bring and then choosing the approach that will produce the greatest sales at the least cost. When making this decision, he or she needs to realize that certain factors may at times be decisive, such as the type of product, media availability, and the foreign environmental forces.

■ **FIGURE 15-4   Esso Tiger Ad**

| Belgium | Finland | Italy | Austria |

Source: Reproduced with permission of Exxon Corporation.

Type of product.   Buyers of industrial goods and luxury products usually act on the same motives the world over, and thus these products lend themselves to the standardized approach. This enables manufacturers of capital goods, such as NCR and Westinghouse, to prepare international campaigns that require very little modification in the various markets. Certain consumer goods markets are similar too. When the product is low priced, is consumed in the same way, and is bought for the same reasons, then generally the same appeals and advertising campaigns can be employed. Examples of such products are gasoline, soft drinks, detergents, cosmetics, and airline services.

Firms such as Esso (now Exxon), Coca-Cola, Avon, and Levi Strauss have for years used the international approach successfully. Generally, the only changes they have made are a translation into the local language and the use of natives as models. Figure 15–4 illustrates how Esso's highly successful "tiger in the tank" campaign looked in several languages.

Availability of media.   Even when the message is standardized, advertisers will find that they cannot always use the same media mix from country to country because the media are not equally available in all markets. Historically, radio and TV have been highly government regulated, and many stations did not accept advertising. This, until recently, was the case in most EC and EFTA nations. However, the advent of Sky Channel and Super Channel (satellite TV broadcasters from England that transmit to local cable TV networks) and of other local cable networks with their own programming made it impossible for governments to keep out commercial television.

The competition from American programs, which all of these systems buy, forced the English, French, and most other European governments to relax their ban on commercial television. They simply did not have the money or the production capacity to compete with American firms (the three major TV networks, the motion picture industry) and Japanese producers. Disney, for example, sells TV shows for profit and also uses them to promote its Euro-Disneyland theme park near Paris. Likewise, American professional sports leagues send their teams to play exhibition games in Europe not only to earn money, but also to promote the sales of broadcast rights to regular games they play in the United States. In 1989, British, French, and Italian networks relayed the Super Bowl game to national audiences.[15]

At present, 70 percent of European programming consists of fictional series from the United States, about 15 percent in advertising, some American and Japanese animated series, and a minimum amount of European production and national news programs. But even this last category is losing out to television news shows produced by Ted Turner and the Anglo-American communications company owned by Rupert Murdoch.[16]

Sweden and Norway are now the only nations without any commercial TV or radio stations, but they are expected to remove these restrictions by the early 1990s. Sky Channel already has a 25 percent share of the Scandinavian adult viewing audience and 44 percent of the 16- to 24-year-olds, who would rather watch "Dallas" than the boring fare on local TV. As an American who sells U.S. programs to Scandinavia put it, "During prime time in Sweden, you might get a documentary on pig farming in Jutland, followed by a debate on pig farming in Jutland."[17]

There are still national government restrictions on EC advertisers: in West Germany, commercials are illegal on Sunday; in France, TV ads for margarine are not permitted any time.[18] But such rules are being relaxed and should be unified when an EC proposal for a single broadcast area is passed as part of its Europe 1992 program.[19] By then, Europe is expected to have double the 50 TV stations it has now.[20]

Pan-European media availability is enabling companies to take a regional approach to promotion. Gillette used to market a razor under different brand names—Desechable ("throw-away") in Spain, Radi & Getta in Italy, and Blue II in England—but changed to a uniform Blue II across Europe. It then ran a uniform spot dubbed in 10 languages on a Europeanwide network that invited shavers "to step into the blue."[21] Coca-Cola has no name problem and is using Sky Channel to reach the youth market in all Europe with a clone of "American Bandstand." That Sky Channel's programming is in English is no handicap, because it is precisely the younger population that has the largest percentage of people who already speak English or who want to learn.[22]

Africa is marked by a scarcity of all media. Only 163 radio stations serve an area twice the size of the United States, and although there are 84 TV stations in all, one third of them are located in just two countries. (Nigeria—18 and Ivory Coast—10). Ten countries have no TV. Even these numbers are misleading, because in many countries the stations are government owned and noncommercial. Although there are 168 daily newspapers in the 51 African countries, 86 of them are located in only 6 countries. Nine countries have no daily paper, and 13 have only one.[23] In this seller's market, an advertiser may find that the newspaper has accepted too many ads for the available space. Some newspapers' solution is a raffle to decide which ads will be published!

In Latin America and the Middle East, the opposite situation exists: there are too many newspapers and magazines. The problem in those regions is choosing the right ones for the firm's target market. In which of the 900 newspapers in Brazil or the 400 in Turkey should the ad be placed? Circulation figures are greatly exaggerated, and the advertisers must also be careful of the publication's political position to avoid associating their firms with the

■ **TABLE 15–1   Advertising Expenditures in Selected Countries, 1987**

| Rank | Country | Total Expenditures ($ millions) | Percent of Total | | | | | Advertising Expenditures as percentage of GNP |
			Print	Cinema	Radio	TV	Direct Advertising	
1	United States	$109,650	34.3%	n.a.	6.6%	21.8%	17.4 %	2.4%
2	Japan	27,273	33.7	n.a.	4.4	30.0	10.0	1.4
3	United Kingdom	10,266	56.8	0.4 %	1.8	29.9	7.7	1.7
4	West Germany	9,985	72.0	0.9	3.5	9.0	11.5	1.1
5	France	6,723	50.6	0.9	6.6	19.4	10.7	0.9
6	Canada	5,480	42.6	n.a.	9.0	16.2	23.4	1.4
7	Italy*	4,380	42.6	0.3	3.5	48.5	n.a.	0.7
8	Spain	4,373	39.0	0.5	9.2	24.1	11.3	1.9
9	Netherlands	3,193	46.2	0.2	1.1	8.9	28.3	1.8
10	Australia	3,033	42.9	1.3	8.2	30.8	10.3	1.7
13	Brazil	1,991	22.0	0.2	4.6	45.3	n.a.	0.6
16	South Korea	1,182	39.7	1.7	4.9	36.3	3.0	1.0
20	India	802	58.5	1.1	2.7	13.5	n.a.	0.3
26	Mexico	508	16.0	0.1	10.9	54.8	n.a.	0.3
50	Nigeria	46	20.7	1.5	15.3	18.5	n.a.	0.1

*As an illustration of how commercial TV availability affects promotional expenditures, in 1981, when freedom of TV advertising in Italy was just beginning, only 15.2% of total advertising expenditures was spent on TV. With no commercial TV and radio, Sweden and Norway use print (96% and 97%), outdoor transit, and cinema.

n.a.=Data not available.

Source: *World Advertising Expenditures,* Starch, INRA, Hooper & LAA 1988, pp. 42–43.

"wrong-side"—the one contrary to what the majority of their potential customers believe in.

These problems and the high illiteracy rate in some nations have forced advertisers to go to other media to reach their markets. Cinema advertising is heavily used in many parts of the world, as are billboards. In the Middle East, where media options are limited, videotape ads are rapidly becoming an integral part of the media mix. Advertisers penetrate this lucrative market by buying spots on popular video tapes. Three or four breaks with six or seven spots each are created at the beginning, middle, and end of the film. Three quarters of the households in the United Arab Emirates, Saudi Arabia, and Kuwait have videocassette recorders, and in the first three months after release, a well-received video tape can draw an audience of 1 million viewers in Saudi Arabia alone.[24] In a number of less developed countries, automobiles equipped with loudspeakers circulate through the cities announcing products, and street signs are furnished by advertisers that hang their messages on them. Homeowners can get a free coat of paint by permitting advertisers to put ads on their walls. Where mail delivery is reliable, direct mail is a powerful medium, as are trade fairs. Probably one of the most ingenious campaigns ever was that of a tea company that gave away thousands of printed prayers with a tea commercial on the other side to pilgrims bound for Mecca. Table 15–1

Sales promotion in Spain

Source: R.J. Reynolds Annual Report

and its footnotes illustrate how the constraints we have discussed affect the distribution of advertising expenditures.

The point is that media of some kind are available in every country, and the local managers and ad agencies are familiar with the advantages of each kind. Media selection is extremely difficult for international advertising managers who try to standardize their media mix from the home office. We have mentioned only some of the problems, but from these the reader can appreciate that the variation in media availability is a strong reason for leaving this part of the advertising program to the local organization.

Foreign environmental forces.   Like variations in media availability, the foreign environmental forces act as deterrents to the international standardization of advertising, and, as you would expect, among the most influential of these forces are the *sociocultural* forces, which we examined in Chapter 9.

A basic cultural decision for the marketer is whether to position the product as foreign or local, and which way to go seems to depend on the country, the product type, and the target market. In Germany, for example, consumers are not at all impressed by the carmaker that announces it has American know-how. "After all," reason the Germans, "if so many Americans prefer

The typical exterior design of McDonald's restaurants in Japan

Courtesy of Ric Ergenbright Photography

Volkswagen and Mercedes over U.S. cars, why shouldn't we?" At the same time, such purely American products as bourbon, fast-food restaurants, and blue jeans have made tremendous inroads not only in Germany but in the rest of Europe. McDonald's introduced the Big Mac in London by advertising "For 48 pence, the United States of America."

Similarly in Japan, American identity for consumer products enhances their image. The young and the status conscious prefer the casual American look in clothing and seek the American label that identifies the wearer as belonging to the "in group." The influence of the American-style fast-food restaurants on Japanese youth was emphasized in a survey taken by the Japanese Ministry of Agriculture, which found that more than 50 percent of the country's teenagers would rather eat occidental foods than the traditional dishes. These restaurants are now grossing over $2 billion, with U.S.-based ventures such as McDonald's (already the second-largest Japanese restaurant business), Dairy Queen, Mister Donut, and Kentucky Fried Chicken accounting for over 50 percent of that amount.[25] The experience of the suppliers to the youth market already indicates that this too is essentially an international market segment, much like the market for luxury goods. What this means for marketers is that they can formulate global advertising campaigns for these consumers that will require little more than a translation into the local language. Before making the decision concerning local versus foreign identity, however, management is advised once again to check with local personnel on a country-by-country basis.

Inasmuch as communication, the reason for advertising, is impossible if the language is not understood, translations must be made into the language of the consumers. Unfortunately for the advertiser, almost every language varies from one country to another. The same word may be perfectly apt in one country while signifying something completely different or even vulgar in another, as was illustrated in Chapter 9. To avoid translation errors, the experienced advertising manager will use (1) a double translation and (2) plenty of illustrations with short copy.

Because a nation's laws generally reflect public opinion, closely allied to the cultural forces are the legal forces, which exert an extremely pervasive influence on advertising. We have seen how laws affect media availability, but they also restrict the kinds of products that can be advertised and even the copy employed in the advertisements.

Goodyear found that it could not use its multinational campaign claiming the nylon tire cord was stronger than steel in Germany, because doing so would violate a law against comparing products. Coca-Cola thought that Malaysia also had such a ban. Consequently, when Pepsi-Cola mounted a half-million-dollar taste test campaign on TV, Coke's ad agency protested. However, Pepsi had followed the rules in not naming the competitor's products. It merely showed side-by-side taste tests of two different products in unmarked bottles. The government body that regulated advertising stated that it had no objection to the taste tests, and the commercials resumed.

Until 1986, many products were banned from French TV: jewelry, margarine (to protect milk producers), airlines (to protect Air France), publications, films, concerts, records, retailers, and alcoholic drinks. But many changes occurred when La 5, France's first all-commercial network, began operation in 1986. First, the programs are livelier, and even more important for advertisers, commercial breaks during programs are permitted. Also, companies can advertise such products as books, wine, beer, and margarine, all of which are banned from government-owned stations. However, the ban still exists for child models in ads and for the use of non-French words when there is a French equivalent. Announcers cannot get friendly with the audience either—the formal *vous* must always be employed.[26]

Advertisers in the Islamic nations have had to be resourceful to avoid censorship. The use of women's photos in advertisements is forbidden unless the models are clearly Western—preferably blondes or redheads. "Erotic" sound effects are not permitted: a TV soft-drink commercial with a girl licking her lips to show she liked the taste was declared "obscene." In Pakistan, the government decreed that women models could advertise only women's products on TV. They cannot advertise cars or men's cologne, for example. Imagine Ford trying to sell its Mercury with a slinky male posed seductively behind the wheel, or how about an all-male Old Spice commercial?[27]

Just as in the United States, there is a strong tendency for governments elsewhere to control advertising even more as government leaders, urged on by consumer groups, enact stricter laws. In Sweden, consumer ombudsmen (government officials) can require companies to provide total disclosure in advertising. If they wish, these ombudsmen can force a manufacturer of cameras to state not only the cost of the camera but also what the film and processing will cost the buyer. Products that do not live up to their claims can be forced off the market. Mexico's law on consumer protection gives major emphasis to advertising. Dealers as well as suppliers are obligated to make good any guarantees or offers announced to the public and must even obtain governmental approval before announcing a sale or a special offer.

In some governments, a strong bias against advertising in general or against certain media is reflected in advertising taxes. The result of variations in the taxation of advertising media is to limit the advertisers' choice among media and to cause them to employ more of the other promotional mix elements than they might normally use. All national governments in Europe except Switzerland apply a value-added tax to advertising, though France, Ireland, the Netherlands, Norway, the United Kingdom, and West Germany exempt foreign-based companies that place advertising from the home country. Some of these countries also place additional taxes on advertising. Greece is notorious for extra taxes that are really punitive—47 percent on TV, 20 percent on newspapers and radio, and 16 percent on magazines. Advertisers using billboards pay as much as 50 percent extra when municipal taxes are included. It is important to know whether local taxes are levied, because they can be very discriminatory. Outdoor advertising is subject to an additional local tax in Italy, as is outdoor and cinema advertising in Portugal. Furthermore, in many countries such taxes vary among municipalities.[28] One of Europe 1992's objectives is to standardize all value-added taxes.

Programmed-management approach.   With so many obstacles to international standardization, what should be the approach of the international advertising manager? The opinion of some experts seems to be that good ideas and good promotions can cross international borders. Robert Trebus, an ad agency executive, believes that far too often businesspeople ask how the product can be sold in Germany without first asking how the firm did it successfully in Sweden. Trebus stated back in the 1970s that "rarely will a campaign be a success in Sweden without having registered a like success in Greece." He believes too many managers are convinced that to be successful in different markets, they must approach each market differently.[29] This school of thought looks for similarities across segments and countries so as to capitalize on them by providing promotional themes with worldwide appeal, the strategy now followed by global corporations.

A second school of thought believes that even though human nature is the same everywhere, it is also true that a Spaniard will remain a Spaniard and a Belgian a Belgian. Thus, it is preferable to develop separate appeals to take advantage of the differences among customers in different cultures and countries.

The results of a study made by *International Advertiser* confirms a previous discussion. It showed that the primary result (50 percent of the respondents) for global standardization was cost reduction in planning and control. International brand and corporate image was second (38 percent), and simplification of coordination and control was third (31 percent). The primary reasons against standardization were insufficient consideration of local peculiarities (53 percent), the heterogeneous media scene (25 percent), and differences in the stage of the product life cycle (19 percent). The survey indicated that the extent of actual standardization of advertising decisions was generally higher than the judgment on the possibility of standardization. This means that the reasons in favor of standardization influence the basic objective of the international firm more than do the obvious differences among nations.[30]

programmed-management approach a middle-ground advertising strategy between globally standardized and entirely local programs

From the previous discussion, you have probably already gathered that neither the entirely standardized nor the entirely local campaign is the best way to handle international advertising. There is a middle ground, called by some the **programmed-management approach,** in which the home office and the foreign subsidiaries agree on marketing objectives, after which each puts together a tentative advertising campaign. This is submitted to the home office for review and suggestions. The campaign is then market tested locally, and the results are submitted to the home office, which reviews them and offers comments. The subsidiary then submits a complete campaign to the home office for review. When the home office is satisfied, the budget is approved and the subsidiary begins implementing the campaign. The result may be a highly standardized campaign for all markets or one that has been individualized to the extent necessary to cope with local market conditions. The programmed-management approach gives the home office a chance to standardize those parts of the campaign that may be standardized but still permits flexibility in responding to different marketing conditions.[31]

Instead of having 43 different versions of ads running worldwide, as in the past, Playtex asked its ad agency, Grey, a huge multinational with affiliates in 33 major cities overseas, to develop a global campaign for TV that would work in every market. Grey's main office in New York prepared the boards (a series of still pictures with suggested dialogue depicting the commercial) and sent them to its overseas affiliates with instructions to look for things that would not work in their markets. The agency also showed Playtex foreign managers videotapes of potential models. Dozens were rejected until they all agreed on three that were deemed to have universal appeal.

Although the cross-your-heart message was the same everywhere, there were some local differences that had to be taken into account. One was the brassiere style. The French like lacy bras, whereas Germans and Americans prefer the plainer types. Also, European TV permits live models, whereas South African and U.S. TV do not (U.S. networks changed this rule in 1987). To accommodate these differences, shots were made both ways then spliced into the ads for each market. To comply with Australian law, the Australian ads had to be shot locally.

Names for the bras had to be found for different languages because WOW (without wires) could not be translated literally. Traumbugel (dream wire) was used in Germany, Alas (wings) in Spain, and Armagique (contraction for structure and magic) was chosen for France. Interestingly, even the packaging is different. Bras are put on hangers in the UK and the United States but are packaged in boxes elsewhere.

Global advertising permitted Playtex to present one unified message in all markets and also to save money. Grey claims it was able to produce the WOW ad for a dozen countries at a cost of only $250,000. The average cost of producing a single U.S. ad is $100,000.

Personal selling. Along with advertising, personal selling constitutes a principal component of the promotional mix. The importance of this promotional tool as compared to advertising depends to a great extent on the relative costs, the funds available, media availability, and the type of product sold.

Just as in the United States, manufacturers of industrial products rely more on personal selling than advertising to communicate with their overseas markets. However, producers of consumer products may also emphasize personal selling overseas, especially in the developing countries, because salespeople in these countries will often work for less compensation than would be demanded in the home country. A newcomer to marketing must be careful, nonetheless, to consider all of the expenses in maintaining a salesperson, as expense items like automobiles and their maintenance (rough treatment on bad roads) frequently may be three or four times the U.S. cost. Fringe benefits are commonly stipulated by law, and these too often comprise a higher percentage of the base wage in other countries.

Marketing managers will also give greater emphasis to personal selling where commercial TV and radio are unavailable or where the market is too small to support an advertising campaign.

International standardization. By and large, the organization of the overseas sales force, sales presentation, and training methods are very similar to those employed in the home country.

> Avon follows the same plan of person-to-person selling in Venezuela or the Far East as it does in this country and is extremely successful with it. When Avon entered Mexico, many of the local experts predicted that its plan would fail. The Mexican middle-class housewife would be out of the home shopping and playing bridge. The wall around the house would keep the Avon lady from reaching the front door, and when she rang the bell, the maid, as she did with all peddlers, would not let her in. Other American firms had used this approach and had failed for these reasons. However, Avon made small but important changes. For one thing, it mounted a massive advertising campaign to educate the Mexicans as to what they could expect from the visits before sending its salespeople out. Although the advertisements were the same as those in the United States, the advertising campaign was more extensive because the Mexican housewife had to be taught a new concept. This was not the common door-to-door salesperson whom she knew but a professional trained to help her look beautiful. Avon recruited educated middle-class women as representatives and trained them well. They were encouraged to visit their friends, much as Tupperware representatives do. What was essentially an American plan, with slight changes for cultural differences, made Avon's entry into the Mexican market an unqualified success.
>
> Avon still follows this strategy, with one exception—China. However, the company informed one of the writers that selling in foreign-currency stores is only temporary while the company learns more about the market and builds up a customer base.[32]

Other firms also follow their home country approach. Missionary salespeople from pharmaceutical manufacturers, such as Pfizer and Upjohn, introduce their products to physicians, just as they do in the United States. Sales engineers from General Electric and Westinghouse supply their customers with the same kind of information required in this country. Salespeople calling on channel members perform the same tasks of informing middlemen, setting up point-of-purchase displays, and fighting for shelf space as do their American counterparts.

Because of the high costs of a sales call, many firms are using telemarketing and direct mail to qualify prospects and make appointments for the sales representatives. As you can imagine, European subsidiaries of American firms, such as Ford, Digital Equipment, and IBM, having learned the advantages of telemarketing from their American parents, are using the technique to increase sales. Barbie Doll sends her French fans messages in special ink that can only be read under special lights in toy stores.

■ **FIGURE 15–5   Cost of a Sales Call**

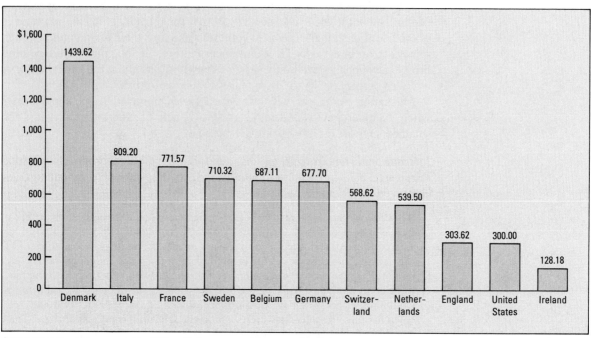

Source: *International Management,* May 1988, p. 15. Average cost of European call is $640.13.

Now, European-based companies are also using telemarketing. Peugeot, the French car manufacturer, regularly sends personalized letters to its customers all over Europe, telling them when they need service calls, where to get the best deal on tires, and how to buy special-offer accessories. Its marketing manager says, "Its a far more scientific way of getting to people likely to want our products than straightforward advertising." Still, over half the 465 firms polled by European postal services replied that direct marketing would tarnish their image.

> Direct mail and telemarketing are only beginning in Japan. There are no bulk postal rates, and 800 numbers did not become available until 1986. Dentsu, the Japanese ad agency, has formed a telemarketing joint venture with the American firm of Young & Rubicam and is already selling computers successfully by mail. In the opinion of a director of a London ad agency, "The Japanese have discovered it now, and once they start to use it effectively, it will be a frightening experience."[33]

Computerized prospecting, or using computers to analyze customer call patterns to plan customer visits, are another American sales tool adopted by Europeans to reduce the cost of a sales call. Obviously, it's needed. See in Figure 15–5 what it costs to make a sales call in Europe compared to the United States.

Recruitment.   Recruiting salespeople in foreign countries is at times more difficult than recruiting them in the home country because sales managers frequently have to cope with the stigma attached to selling that exists in some areas (cultural forces). To help overcome this obstacle, salespeople are given titles that are essentially translations of American titles designed for the same purpose (territory or zone manager).

Another instance of the influence of cultural forces on recruiting is the need to hire salespeople who are culturally acceptable to customers and channel members. This can be difficult and costly in an already small market that is further subdivided into several distinct cultures with different customs and even languages, as we saw in the chapter on physical forces. If a cultural pocket will support a salesperson at all, the experienced sales manager will make every effort to recruit a person indigenous to the region.

American firms are aided in recruitment by their reputation for having excellent training programs. These generally come from the home office and are adapted, if necessary, to local conditions. When the product is highly technical, the new employees are often sent to the home office for training. Of course, the opportunity to take such a trip is also an effective recruiting tool.

sales promotion selling aids, including displays, premiums, contests, and gifts

Sales promotion.   **Sales promotion** provides the selling aids for the marketing function and includes such activities as the preparation of point-of-purchase displays, contests, premiums, and trade show exhibits. If no separate department exists for these activities, they will be performed in either the advertising or sales department.

The international standardization of the sales promotion function is not difficult, because the experience has shown that what is successful in the United States generally proves effective overseas. Some cultural and legal constraints must be considered, nonetheless, when sales promotion techniques are transferred to other countries.

Legal constraints.   Laws concerning sales promotions tend to be more restrictive in other countries than they are in the United States or Great Britain. The Belgian, German, and Scandinavian governments are rather negative toward premiums, for example, because they believe premiums detract consumers from considering just the merits of the product. "Two-for-one" offers are prohibited in Sweden and Norway, and, although free samples are permitted everywhere, some governments limit their size.[34] Mexico requires special offers and cents-off deals to be approved by a government agency before they can be used. Although these legal restrictions are bothersome, they have not stopped the use of sales promotions.

Sociocultural and economic constraints.   The cultural and economic constraints are more consequential than the legal constraints and do make some sales promotions difficult to use. If a premium is to fulfill the objective of being a sales aid for the product, it must be meaningful to the purchaser. A gadget to be used in the kitchen will be valued by the American housewife but will not be particularly attractive to a Latin American housewife if she has two maids to do the housework. Firms that attach premiums to the outside of packages in the less developed countries usually do this just once. Less than a week after the packages are on the shelf, the detached premiums are already being sold in the streets. Putting the prize inside the package is also no guarantee that it will be there when the purchaser takes the package home.

While living in Mexico, one of the writers bought a product for the plastic toy it contained. When he opened the package at home, there was no toy for the children. Examining the package closely, he found that a small slot had been made in the top. Where labor costs and store revenues are low, the income from the sales of these premiums is extra profit for the retailer.

Contests, raffles, and games, however, have been extremely successful in countries where people love to play the odds. If Latin Americans or the Irish will buy a lottery ticket week after week, hoping to win the grand prize playing against the odds of 500,000 to 1, why shouldn't they participate in a contest that costs them nothing to enter? Point-of-purchase displays are well accepted by retailers, though many establishments are so small that there is simply no place to put all of the displays that are offered to them. Sales promotion is generally not as sophisticated overseas as it is in the United States, and our experience indicates that even American subsidiaries do not make sufficient use of the ideas coming from headquarters. The marketing manager who prepares a well-planned program after studying the constraints of the local markets can expect excellent results from the time and money invested.

public relations various methods of communicating with the firm's publics to secure a favorable impression

Public relations.   **Public relations** is the firm's communications and relationships with its various publics, including the governments where it operates, or, as one writer has put it, "Public relations is the marketing of the firm." Although American WWCs have had organized public relations programs for many years in the United States, they have paid much less attention to this important function elsewhere.

Ironically, it is on the whole not true that they have neglected public-service activities through their foreign subsidiaries—only that they have failed to inform their publics of what they are doing. Exxon has for years sponsored the study of foreign art students in the United States, and the ITT International Fellowship Program, started in 1973, has already enabled more than 750 students from 54 countries to pursue advanced degrees in the United States and abroad. The foreign subsidiary that does not participate in local charitable and cultural activities is exceedingly rare, but far too often only the recipients know about it.

The rising wave of nationalism and antimultinational feeling in many countries has made it imperative for companies with international operations to improve their communications to their nonbusiness publics with more effective public relations programs.

An example of a successful public relations program was the one launched by Nestlé in response to an attack by the International Baby Food Action Network (IBFAN). This consumers' organization accused the company of persuading mothers in LDCs to bottle-feed their babies with formula rather then breast-feed. The IBFAN and various church groups that advocated breast-feeding charged that contaminated water in the formula was contributing to infant mortality. This was the same water, of course, that had always been mixed with homemade baby food. Although 17 WWCs sold infant formula. Nestlé was singled out for attack, according to the boycott director, "Because it has the largest market share."[35]

The company responded to the attack by implementing the 1981 World Health Organization's code on the marketing of breast-milk substitutes. It also created a semi-independent review panel to examine its marketing practices and its adherence to the code. This unprecedented action slowed the attack of its critics, who finally called the boycott off. However, five years later, another group, Action for Corporate Accountability, began to boycott the company for the same reasons. Although Nestlé claims it complies fully with the World Health Organization's code, it did hire the publication relations unit of Ogilvy & Mather's ad agency to help it respond to this latest attack.[36]

Other consumer activist groups that appear to be in a position to inflict significant public relations damage on WWCs are the (1) Pesticide Action Network, (2) Health Action International for pharmaceuticals, and (3) World Council of Churches, which is concerned with such issues as the nature of Third World poverty and Western support for "racist, authoritarian" regimes.

One of the firms' most vexing problems is how to deal with such critics. Some try to defuse criticism before it becomes a full-scale attack by holding regularly scheduled meetings at which topics of interest are debated. Others prefer to meet with critics privately, though they might find themselves caught in a never-ending relationship in which the critics continually escalate their demands. This is especially true of single-issue groups, whose existence depends on the continuance of the issue.

A successful strategy employed by some firms has been to address the issue without dealing directly with the critics. Instead, they work with international or governmental agencies. Another alternative is to do nothing. If the criticism receives no publicity, it may die from lack of interest. However, bad handling of a situation can have serious repercussions for a firm. Union Carbide's bungling of the Bhopal accident is an example. An example of a firm that uses public relations effectively is IBM. Its strong lobbying effort with EC commissioners has convinced them that the highly regulated state-owned telephone and postal organizations are responsible for costly, inefficient phone systems. Partly because of IBM's efforts, one of the EC's main objectives for Europe 1992 is to standardize and liberalize telecommunications.[37]

Pricing Strategies

Pricing, the third element of the marketing mix, is an important and complex consideration in formulating the marketing strategy. Pricing decisions affect other corporate functions, directly determine the firm's gross revenue, and are a major determinant of profits.

Pricing, a controllable variable.   Marketers, especially Americans, have become increasingly cognizant that effective price setting consists of more than mechanically adding a standard markup to a cost. To obtain the maximum benefits from pricing, management must regard it in the same manner as it regards other controllable variables; that is, pricing is one of the marketing mix elements that can be varied to achieve the marketing objective of the firm.

For instance, if the marketer wishes to position a product as a high-quality item, setting a relatively high price will reinforce promotion that emphasizes quality. However, combining a recognizably low price with a promotional emphasis on quality could result in an incongruous pairing that would adversely affect its credibility with the consumer—the low price might be interpreted as the correct price for an inferior product. Pricing can also be a determinant in the choice of middlemen, because if the firm requires a wholesaler to take title, stock, promote, and deliver the merchandise, it must give the wholesaler a much larger trade discount than would be demanded by a broker, whose services are much more limited.

These examples illustrate one of the reasons for the complexity of price setting—the interaction of pricing with the other elements of the marketing mix. In addition, two other sets of forces influence this variable: (1) interaction between marketing and the other functional areas of the firm and (2) environmental forces.

Interaction between marketing and the other functional areas.   To illustrate this point, look at the following:

1. The finance people want prices that are both profitable and conducive to a steady cash flow.
2. Production supervisors want prices that create large sales volumes, which permit long production runs.
3. The legal department worries about possible antitrust violations when different prices are set according to type of customer.
4. The tax people are concerned with the effects of prices on tax loads.
5. The domestic sales manager wants export prices to be high enough to avoid having to compete with company products that are purchased for export and then diverted to the domestic market (one aspect of parallel importing).

The marketer must address all of these concerns and also consider the impact of the legal and other environmental forces that we examined in Section Three. Table 15–3 at the end of this chapter examines this aspect of pricing in greater detail.

International standardization.   Companies that pursue a policy of unifying corporate pricing procedures worldwide know that pricing is acted on by the same forces that militate against the international standardization of the other marketing mix components. Pricing for the overseas markets is more complex because managements must be concerned with two kinds of pricing: (1) **foreign national pricing**, which is domestic pricing in another country, and (2) **international pricing** for exports.

Foreign national pricing.   Many foreign governments in their fight against inflation have instituted price controls, and the range of the products affected varies immensely from country to country. Some governments attempt to fix prices on just about everything, while others are concerned only with essential goods. Unfortunately, no agreement exists on what is essential, so in one market the prices of gasoline, food products, tires, and even wearing apparel may be controlled, while in another market only the prices of staple foods may be fixed. In nations with laws on unfair competition, the minimum sales price may be controlled rather than the maximum. The German law is so comprehensive that under certain conditions, even premiums and cents-off coupons may be prohibited because they are considered to violate the minimum price requirements. The international marketer must be watchful of a recent tendency of many nations, especially EC members, to open up their markets to price competition by weakening and even abolishing retail price maintenance laws.

Prices can vary because of appreciable cost differentials on opposite sides of a border. One government may levy higher import duties on imported raw materials or may subsidize public utilities, while another may not. Differences

---

foreign national pricing
local pricing in another country

in labor legislation will cause labor costs to vary. Competition among local suppliers may be intense in one market, permitting the affiliate to buy inputs at better prices than those paid by an affiliate in another market, which must purchase raw materials from a single supplier, possibly a government monopoly.

Competition on the selling side is also diverse. Frequently, an affiliate in one market will face heavy local competition and be severely limited in the price it can charge, while in a neighboring market, a lack of competitors will allow another affiliate to charge a much higher price. As regional economic groupings reduce trade barriers among members, such opportunities are becoming fewer because firms must then meet regional as well as local competition.

Because the firm, for a number of reasons, does not introduce a new product simultaneously in all markets, the same product will not be in the same stage of the product life cycle everywhere. In markets where it is in the introductory stage, there is an opportunity to charge a high "skimming" price or a low "penetration" price, depending on such factors as market objectives, patent protection, price elasticity of demand, and competition. As the product reaches the maturity or decline stage, the price may be lowered, if doing so permits a satisfactory return. Because life cycles vary among markets, prices too will be different.

International pricing.   International pricing involves the setting of prices for goods produced in one country and sold in another. The pricing of exports to unrelated customers falls in this category and will be treated separately in the chapter on exporting. A special kind of exporting, *intracorporate sales,* is exceedingly common among worldwide companies as they attempt to rationalize production by requiring subsidiaries to specialize in the manufacture of some products while importing others. Their imports may consist of components that are assembled into the end product, such as engines made in one country that are mounted in car bodies built in another, or they may be finished products imported to complement the product mix of an affiliate. No matter what the end use is, problems exist in setting an intracorporate price (**transfer price**).

transfer price intracorporate price, or the price of a good or service sold by one affiliate to another, the home office to an affiliate, or vice versa

Because it is possible for the firm as a whole to gain while both the buying and selling subsidiaries "lose" (receive prices that are lower than would be obtained through an outside transaction), the tendency is for transfer prices to be set at headquarters. The reason for this apparent anomaly is that the company obtains a profit from *both* the seller and the buyer.

The selling affiliate would like to charge other subsidiaries the same price that it charges all customers, but, when combined with transportation costs and import duties, such a price may make it impossible for the importing subsidiary to compete in its market. If headquarters dictates that a lower-than-market transfer price be charged, the seller will be unhappy because its profit-and-loss statement suffers. This can be a very real headache to personnel whose promotion bonuses depend on the bottom line. In Chapter 22, we will see how home office management deals with this problem.

Both foreign governments and the U.S. government are also interested in profits and the part transfer prices play in their realization, because of the influence of profits on the amount of taxes paid. Foreign tax agents and the IRS have become very much aware that because of differences in tax structures, a firm can obtain meaningful profits by ordering a subsidiary in a country with high corporate taxes to sell at cost to a subsidiary in a country where corporate taxes are lower. The profit is earned where less income tax is paid, and the company clearly gains.

Transfer prices may also be employed to circumvent currency restrictions. When a country is suffering from a lack of foreign exchange, it may impose controls that totally prohibit, or at least place a low limit on, the amount of profit that can be repatriated. Suppose Country A, lacking dollars, places severe controls on all dollar transactions. There is trade with Country B, which does have dollars or another convertible currency. The home office could order its subsidiary in A to buy from the B affiliate at a price well over cost, which would transfer A's profit to B. Once in B, the profits could be sent home. The same strategy could be followed in any situation where it appeared necessary to either reduce A's profits or take them out of the country, such as:

1. Imminent currency devaluation.
2. Government pressure to reduce prices because of excessive profits.
3. Labor's clamor for higher wages based on high profits earned.

The manipulation of transfer prices for the reduction of income taxes and import duties or the avoidance of exchange controls has caused many governments to insist on arm's-length prices—the prices charged to unrelated customers. Under Section 482 of the Internal Revenue Code, U.S. tax authorities are empowered to reconstruct an intracorporate transfer price and tax the calculated profits whenever there is reason to suspect that low prices were set for tax evasion. Customs authorities in a number of European countries have increased the invoice price of imports by as much as 125 percent, forcing the importing subsidiary to pay a much higher than normal duty.

Despite the advantages of price manipulation, a recent study found that many large American companies most often used the market price as the transfer price.[38] One imposing reason is government intervention, especially under Section 482 of the tax code; in addition, it is much easier to monitor and evaluate foreign managers' performance when the market price is the transfer price.

Distribution Strategies

The development of distribution strategies is a difficult task in the home country, but it is even more so internationally, where marketing managers must concern themselves with two functions rather than one: (1) getting the products *to* foreign markets (exporting) and (2) distributing the products *within* each market (foreign distribution). In this section, we will examine foreign distribution only, leaving the export channels for the next chapter.

Interdependence of distribution decisions.   When making decisions on distribution, care must be taken to analyze their interdependence with the other marketing mix variables. For example, if the product requires considerable after-sales servicing, the firm will want to sell through dealers that have the facilities, personnel, and capital to purchase equipment and spare parts and to train servicepeople. This will necessitate using a merchant wholesaler, which will demand a larger trade discount than would an agent, because an agent does not perform these functions. Channel decisions are critical because they are *long-term* decisions; once established, they are far less easy to change then those made for price, product, and promotion.

International standardization.   Although management would prefer to standardize distribution patterns internationally, there are two fundamental constraints on its doing so: (1) the variation in the availability of channel members among the firm's markets and (2) the inconsistency of the influence of the environmental forces. Because of these constraints, international managers have found it best to establish a basic but flexible overall policy. This policy is then implemented by the subsidiaries, which design channel strategies to meet local conditions.

Availability of channel members.   As a starting point in their channel design, local managers have the successful distribution system used in the domestic operation. Headquarters' support for a policy of employing the same channels worldwide will be especially strong when the entire marketing mix has been built around a particular channel type, such as direct sales force or franchised operators. Avon, Encyclopaedia Britannica, and McDonald's are examples of firms that consider their distribution systems inviolate, so locally there is little latitude in planning channel strategies. However, companies utilizing the more common types of middlemen are usually more inclined to grant the local organization greater freedom in channel member selection.

Although a general rule for any firm entering a foreign market is to adapt to the available channels rather than create new ones, a number of companies have successfully avoided the traditional channels because of their appalling inefficiencies. Coca-Cola did this in Japan, as we mentioned in Chapter 13.

Experienced marketers know they cannot get their products to the consumer by the same retail channel in every country, and even in Europe the differences are substantial. What is the best way to sell toys in France? A sure outlet is the hypermarket, which sells 36 percent of all toys purchased in France. In Germany, however, the hypermarket accounts for only 15 percent of toy sales (see Table 15–2). The most important kind of outlet for toys in Germany is independent retailers, which are organized into buying groups. Table 15–2 also indicates the differences in the way shoes are sold in these two neighboring countries.

Foreign environmental forces.   Environmental differences among markets add to the difficulty in standardizing distribution channels. Changes caused by the cultural forces generally occur over time, but those caused by the legal forces can be radical and quick and can dramatically slow trends responding to cultural demands.

To illustrate, hypermarkets, which are changing distribution patterns in Europe and particularly in France, a nation of small shopkeepers, numbered only 11 in that country in 1972. The combination of lower prices and one-stop shopping caught on with the French consumer, and 51 hypermarkets were opened in 1973. Manufacturers that saw a quick end to small shopkeepers failed to appreciate their political power. The Royer Law, passed in 1973, gave local urban commissions, often dominated by small merchants, the power to refuse construction permits for supermarkets and hypermarkets. After the law

■ **TABLE 15–2   Percentage of Total Sales by Type of Outlet**

Shoes	Percent of Total Sales	Toys	Percent of Total Sales
Germany		*Germany*	
Organized independents (buying groups)	35%	Organized independent toy stores (buying groups)	37%
Major shoe chains	29	Department stores	27
Mail	7	Hypermarkets	15
Department stores	6	Mail	8
Hypermarkets	6	Independent toy stores	4
Discount stores	6	Other retailers	9
Independent shoe stores	4		100%
Other retailers	7		
	100%		
France		*France*	
Independent shoe stores	56%	Hypermarkets/supermarkets	36%
Direct sales	14	Toy stores	22
Clothing stores	2	Department and variety stores	14
Department stores	2	Mail	8
Variety stores	1	Other retailers	20
Other retailers	25		100%
	100%		

Source: *Retail International* (London: Euromonitor, 1988), pp. 162, 171, 480, 489.

took effect, only 40 percent of the large-store applications were approved, with the result that just 14 hypermarkets were opened in 1975.

Although the trend toward more giant stores has not been stopped by the law (there were 629 French hypermarkets in 1986), it has certainly been slowed. The president of Carrefour, France's largest hypermarket chain, says, "It is becoming increasingly hard to find a site where we can get a building permit. Opposition of small shopkeepers is the only thing keeping us from growing more rapidly." Japan's Large-Scale Retailers Law, very similar to France's Royer Law, also has slowed but not stopped the opening of large retailers. Moreover, the Japanese government and public are recognizing the need for reforming the country's distribution system. In fact, the prime minister promised to deregulate it at the Toronto economic summit meeting in 1987. Italy and Belgium also have Royer-type laws.

Manufacturers in the EC that have tried to prevent distributors from selling across national borders have been prohibited from doing so by the Commission through the EC's antitrust laws. Exclusive distributorships have been permitted, but every time the manufacturer has included a clause prohibiting the distributor from exporting to another EC country, the clause has been stricken from the contract. In effect, the firm that has two factories in the EC with different costs, and thus distinct prices, is practically powerless to prevent products from the lower-cost affiliate from competing with higher-cost products from the other affiliate.

Economic differences also make international standardization difficult, although marketers can adapt to economic changes. In 1960, very little frozen food was sold in France because of the consumer's preference for fresh food. However, tight economic conditions forced many housewives too seek employment, and with less time to spend preparing meals, they turned to frozen food. An added attraction of frozen food items was the fact that their prices did not rise as fast as those of fresh foods. The result has been sales increases of 10 percent or more a year since 1973.

In Japan, high prices have also forced women to find jobs, and they no longer have time to shop and prepare the traditional Japanese foods. They fill their needs by purchasing more convenience foods advertised on TV with home delivery or by going to the more than 50 chains of convenience stores. The largest, 7-Eleven, has over 3,200 licensees, most of whom are former small shopkeepers.[39] Its point-of-sale computer network is eliminating the need for small-scale wholesalers, whose number is already declining all over Japan.[40] Worldwide, marketers are seeing cultural barriers fall as economic conditions force housewives to obtain employment to supplement household income. The premium that outside employment places on their time is leading them to prefer one-stop shopping, laborsaving devices, and convenience foods. The result is an upheaval in the way goods are distributed, but American marketers that have U.S. experience as a guide are in a position to make inroads on their foreign competitors, for which this is a new phenomenon.

Can retailing be globalized? Retailers like France's Carrefour, with stores in France, Spain, Brazil, Argentina and the United States, think it can. So do Safeway supermarkets, Gucci, Cartier, Benetton, and Toys "R" Us, which has made aggressive penetration in Germany and Great Britain. Kaufhof, the German retailing giant, has 100 shoe stores located in Austria, France, Switzerland, and Germany and is also the leading mail-order shoe retailer in Europe. As Peter Drucker said in 1987, "To maintain a leadership position in any one developed country, a business—whether large or small—increasingly has to attain and hold leadership positions in all developed markets worldwide."[41]

Foreign Environmental Forces and Marketing Mix Matrix

The matrix[42] shown in Table 15–3 summarizes many of the constraints on the internationalization of the marketing mix that have been discussed in this chapter and in Section Three. Table 15–3 will serve as a reminder of the many factors that marketing managers should consider when they are contemplating the standardization of one or more marketing mix elements.

SUMMARY

Although the basic marketing functions are the same for both domestic and international marketing, the markets served can be very dissimilar because of differences in the environmental forces. The work of the international marketing manager has an added complexity caused by the necessity of planning and controlling marketing strategies in a number of countries instead of just one. Most worldwide companies would prefer to standardize the marketing mix components internationally to lower their costs and simplify their control, but market differences caused by varying environmental forces militate against standardization.

Much of the confusion about whether a global firm can have global products is due to the fact that the discussants do not differentiate between the physical and total products. A total product is easier than a physical product to standardize. Industrial products and services generally can be marketed globally with less change than can consumer products. As you go down the economic and social strata in a country, you tend to find greater dissimilarities among countries' social and cultural values.

Six commonly used promotional strategies can be formulated by combining the three alternatives of mar-

■ **TABLE 15–3   Foreign Environment Constraints to International Standardization of Marketing Mix**

Factors Limiting Standardization	Product	Price	Distribution	Sales Force	Promotion
1. Physical forces	1. Varying climatic conditions—special packaging, extra insulation, mildew protection, extra cooling capacity, special lubricants, dust protection, special instructions 2. Difficult terrain—stronger parts, larger engines, stronger packing	1. Special product requirements add to costs 2. Difficult terrain—extra transportation costs, higher sales expense (car maintenance, longer travel time)	1. Difficult terrain—less customer mobility, necessitating more outlets, each with larger stock 2. Varied climatic conditions—more stock needed when distinct products are required for different climates	1. Dispersion of customers 2. Difficult terrain—high traveling expense 3. Separate cultures created by barriers—salespeople from each culture necessary	1. Cultural pockets created by barriers—separate advertisements for different languages, dialects, words, customs 2. Different climates—distinct advertising themes
2. Sociocultural forces	1. Attitudes toward products 2. Colors—varying significance 3. Languages—labels, packaging 4. Religion—consumption patterns 5. Attitudes toward time—differences in acceptance of timesaving products 6. Attitudes toward change—acceptance of new products 7. Educational levels—varying comprehension of instructions, varying ability to use product 8. Tastes and customs 9. Different shopping habits	1. Cultural objections to product—lower prices for market penetration 2. Lower educational level, lower incomes—lower prices for mass market acceptance 3. Attitudes toward bargaining	1. More, perhaps smaller, firms to handle various subcultures 2. Positive attitudes toward bargaining—small retailers 3. Attitudes toward change—varying acceptance of new kinds of outlets 4. Different shopping habits—different outlets	1. Separate salespeople for subcultures 2. Attitudes toward work, time, achievement, and wealth vary among cultures—difficult to motivate and control sales force 3. Different buying behavior—different kinds of sales forces	1. Language—special labels, instructions, advertisements; unfavorable connotations 2. Literacy, low—simple labels, instructions, advertisements with plenty of graphics 3. Symbolism—responses differ 4. Different significances of colors 5. Attitudes toward advertising 6. Male or female buying influence 7. Cultural pockets—different promotions 8. Religion—varying taboos and restrictions 9. Attitudes toward foreign products and companies
3. Legal-political forces	1. Some products prohibited 2. Certain features required or prohibited	1. Retail price maintenance 2. Markups controlled 3. Antitrust laws	1. Some kinds of middlemen outlawed 2. Markups controlled	1. Selling practices regulated 2. Employment laws	1. Use of languages 2. Legal limits to expenditures

■ **TABLE 15–3**   (concluded)

Factors Limiting Standardization	Product	Price	Distribution	Sales Force	Promotion
	3. Label and packaging requirements 4. Product standards 5. Patent laws 6. Tax laws 7. Import duties and restrictions 8. Local production required of all or part of product 9. Requirements to use local inputs	4. Import duties 5. Tax laws 6. Transfer pricing controls	3. Retail price maintenance 4. Turnover taxes 5. Restrictions on middlemen— number and kinds of lines handled, licenses for each line 6. Ease of changing middlemen		3. Taxes on advertising 4. Prohibition of promotion for some products 5. Special requirements for promotion of some products (cigarettes, pharmaceuticals) 6. Media availability 7. Trademark laws
4. Economic forces	1. Purchasing power—package size, product sophistication, quality levels 2. Wages—varying requirements for laborsaving products 3. Condition of infrastructure— heavier products, hand instead of power operated 4. Market size— varying width of product mix	1. Different prices	1. Availability of outlets 2. Size of inventory 3. Size of outlets 4. Dispersion of outlets 5. Extent of self-service 6. Length of channels	1. Sales force expense 2. Availability of workers	1. Media availability 2. Funds available 3. Emphasis on saving time 4. Experience with products
5. Competitive forces	1. Rate of new product introduction 2. Rate of product improvement 3. Quality levels 4. Package size	1. Competitors' prices 2. Number of competitors 3. Degree of importance of price in marketing mix	1. Competition's control of middlemen 2. Competition's margins to middlemen 3. Competition's choice of middlemen	1. Competitors' sales force— number and ability 2. Competitors' emphasis on personal selling in promotional mix 3. Competitors' rates and methods of compensation	1. Competitors' promotional expenditures 2. Competitors' promotional mix 3. Competitors' choice of media
6. Distribution forces	1. Service requirements 2. Package size 3. Branding— dealers' brands	1. Margins required	1. Availability of middlemen 2. Number of company distribution centers	1. Size of sales force 2. Kind and quality of sales force	1. Kinds of promotion 2. Amounts of promotion

keting the same product everywhere, adapting it, or designing a new product with the same, adapted, or different message.

Advertising is the promotional mix element with the greatest global similarities. The advertiser is constrained in standardizing the advertising campaign by type of product, media availability, and the environmental forces. The programmed-management approach assists in the standardization. Many companies standardize the personal-selling function. Telemarketing and computer-ized prospecting are helping to reduce sales call costs. Legal constraints and the other environmental forces often require the manager to adapt the global promotion program to local conditions.

Marketers must be concerned with foreign national, export, and transfer pricing. The availability of channel members and the variability of the environmental forces are responsible for deviations from a global distribution policy.

QUESTIONS

1. "Consumers are not standardized globally; therefore, with global brands, you either get lowest common denominator advertising or you get advertising that's right somewhere, but wrong elsewhere." This is an actual statement of a CEO of an international advertising agency. What's your opinion?

2. If the basic functions of domestic and international marketing are the same, why distinguish between them?

3. Are there any advantages to standardizing the marketing mix worldwide?

4. On what does the extent of changes in the marketing mix among markets depend?

5. What classes of products best lend themselves to global marketing? What products least lend themselves?

6. What is a generality about similarities of social and cultural values in a country?

7. Why is food retailing changing in Europe and Japan?

8. Why must a marketer consider the economic forces when formulating a product strategy? Give some examples.

9. Discuss the six distinct strategies that can be formulated by combining the three alternatives of selling the same product everywhere, adapting it to foreign markets, or designing a completely different product with the same, adapted, or different message.

10. Why might the advertising manager in the global corporation's home office not be able to standardize the firm's advertising campaigns?

11. Which product classes are the easiest to standardize globally?

12. What does the programmed-management approach accomplish?

13. Personal sales calls are expensive. Why would a company use personal selling instead of TV and print media?

14. What are firms doing to improve the effectiveness of their sales forces? Have these techniques arrived in the United States from Japan yet?

15. At least sales promotion techniques can be standardized. True or false?

16. How should firms deal with critics' attacks?

17. If manipulation of transfer pricing is so advantageous, why do so many companies use the market price as the transfer price?

18. Can manufacturers in the EC prevent their distributors from selling across national borders?

MINICASE 15–1

U.S. Pharmaceutical of Korea*

U.S. Pharmaceutical of Korea (USPK) was formed in 1969. Its one manufacturing plant is located just outside Seoul, the capital. Although the company distributes its products throughout South Korea, 40 percent of its total sales of $5 million were made in the capital last year.

There are no governmental restrictions on whom the company can sell to. The only requirement is that the wholesaler, retailer, or end user have a business license and a taxation number. Of the 400 wholesalers in the country, 130 are customers of USPK, accounting for 46 percent of the

* Based on an actual situation in Korea.

company's total sales. The company also sells directly to 2,100 of the country's 10,000 retailers; these account for 45 percent of total sales. The remaining sales are made directly to high-volume end users, such as hospitals and clinics.

Tom Sloane, marketing manager of USPK, would prefer to make about 90 percent of the company's sales directly to retailers and the remaining 10 percent directly to high-volume users. He believes, however, that this strategy is not possible because there are so many small retailers. Not only is the sales volume per retailer small, but there is also a risk involved in extending them credit. USPK tends to deal directly with large urban retailers and leaves most of the nonurban retailers to the wholesalers.

However, the use of wholesalers bothers Sloane for two reasons: (1) he has to give them larger discounts than he gives retailers that buy directly from the firm and (2) because of the intense competition (300 pharmaceutical manufacturers in Korea), his wholesalers frequently demand larger discounts as the price for remaining loyal to USPK.

This intense competition affects another aspect of USPK's operations—collecting receivables. USPK has found that many wholesalers collect quickly from retailers but delay paying it. Instead, they invest in ventures that offer high short-term returns. For example, lending to individuals can bring them interest rates of up to 3 percent a month. The company's receivables, meanwhile, range from 75 to 130 days. Wholesalers are also the cause of another problem. Many are understaffed and have to rely on "drug peddlers" for sales. The drug peddler (there are perhaps 4,000 just in Seoul) make most of their money either by cutting the wholesalers' margins (selling at lower than recommended prices) or by bartering USPK's products for other pharmaceuticals. They do this by finding retail outlets where products are sold for less than the printed price. They exchange USPK's products at a discount for other drugs, which they sell to other retail outlets at a profit. As a result, USPK's products end up on retailers' shelves at prices lower than those that the company and its reputable wholesalers are selling them for.

The pharmaceutical industry has made some progress in persuading wholesalers and retailers to adhere to company price lists, but nonadherence is still a serious problem. One issue that manufacturers have not been able to resolve as yet is the manner in which demands from hospitals and physicians for gifts should be handled.

Sloane believes the industry can do much to solve these problems, although intense competition has thus far kept the pharmaceutical manufacturers from joining together to map out a solution.

1. What should Tom Sloane and U.S. Pharmaceutical of Korea do to improve collections from wholesalers?

2. How would you handle the distribution problem?

3. Can anything be done through firms in the industry to improve the situation?

4. How would you handle the demands for gifts?

MINICASE 15–2

Marketing a Potentially Harmful Product*

The Swiss pharmaceutical global corporation Hoffman-La Roche has made a major breakthrough in the relief of a serious disabling disease that affects 3 percent of the world's population. Their new product, Tigason, is the first product that effectively controls severe cases of psoriasis and dyskeratoses, skin disorders that cause severe flaking of the skin. Sufferers from this disease frequently retreat from society because of fear of rejection, thus losing their families and jobs. Tigason does not cure the disease, but it causes the symptoms to disappear.

There is one potential problem. Because of the risk of damage to unborn babies, women should not take the drug for one year before conception or during pregnancy. Hoffman-La Roche is well aware of the potential for harm to the company if the product is misused. It has seen the problems of another Swiss firm, Nestlé. After much discussion, the company has decided the product is too important to keep off the market. It is, after all, the product that gives the greatest relief to sufferers.

The marketing department is asked to formulate a strategy for disseminating product information and controlling Tigason's use.

As marketing manager, what do you recommend?

* This is an actual situation.

MINICASE 15–3

Cigarette Marketing Strategy in Brazil*

In an effort to take market share from one another in a shrinking market, Brazil's top three cigarette manufacturers are launching inexpensive brands. This is in response to the trading down by Brazil's smokers because of difficult economic conditions. The trend is to buy more low-priced cigarettes, those priced at the bottom of the country's 11-tier cigarette price structure, which is labeled A through K. Prices range from US$0.25 for the A class to US$0.63 for the K class.

The current battle is in the C class, priced at US$0.29 per pack. As an example of the downtrading that has taken place, the C class now holds 21 percent of the market share, whereas its share was 1 percent only a year ago. A new factor that is expected to both accelerate the downtrading and increase the overall drop in consumption, which amounted to over 2 percent last year, is the new government-controlled 50 percent price increase for all brands.

The three major companies and their overall brand shares are British American Tobacco (BAT) (79 percent), Philip Morris (11 percent), and R. J. Reynolds (nearly 9 percent).

In the intensified competition for market share of the lower-priced cigarettes, British American Tobacco's new C brand, Belmont, has taken 15 percent of Brazil's cigarette market in only seven months. R. J. Reynolds' Mustang (Class B—US$0.27) has become that company's best-selling brand, with a 5 percent market share. Incidentally, Belmont was launched in the B class but was moved up to C because BAT was not earning any money at the B price. Philip Morris now obtains 19 percent of its volume from two resurrected Liggett & Myers brands, Mistura Fina and Master, both in the C category.

The current marketing strategy has two new C brands, which are poised to strike at each other from the test market. Four months ago, BAT started testing its Montreal brand, apparently to counter Reynolds' Monaco brand. According to a Reynolds executive, "We put Monaco in test marketing as a warning, saying 'We're ready to roll another C brand out if you do.'"

As recently as one year ago, cigarette sales were evenly divided between the H–K upper-level brands and the A–G lower-level brands. Then BAT started the downtrading by expensive launches of Plaza in the E class and Cassino in the D. Now the cheaper brands account for 59 percent of the market. The very cheapest brands (A,B,C) increased their market share from 6.5 percent to 26 percent in a year. For example, BAT's best-selling Hollywood brand fell from 30 percent to 25 percent of its total sales as Belmont became its best-selling brand.

Because C brands are just marginally profitable, there is little money to spend on advertising other than a minimal use of radio and billboards. Instead, they are being pushed to cigarette retailers and wholesalers in a fierce giveaway war. The three manufacturers are loading up these middlemen with free gifts ranging from calculators to dominoes.

As a result of the increased popularity of cheaper brands with low margins and a shrinking market, spending for ads in the media dropped about 30 percent last year for all manufacturers. R. J. Reynolds' cut was more severe—its marketing and ad spending were reduced by half.

Says one cigarette marketing executive, "Cooperatively, we've succeeded in screwing up our product mixes."

1. How would you describe the companies' marketing strategies up to this point?
2. Do their American operations follow the same strategy?
3. If the home offices question the Brazilian subsidiaries about the appropriateness of their strategies, what do you believe the marketing managers of the subsidiaries would reply?
4. What do you believe the subsidiaries should do to improve their profitability?

* In Brazil, there are 11 price levels of cigarettes. Most manufacturers have a brand for each category.

SUPPLEMENTARY READINGS

Advertising

"African Advertising Expands." *World Press Review,* February 1984, p. 48.

"Agencies Brace for New Europe." *Advertising Age,* June 5, 1989, p. 42.

"Centralized International Advertising." *International Advertiser,* September 1986, pp. 35–36.

"Europe's Priorities." *The Economist,* December 20, 1986, pp. 16–18.

"Fulfilling an Eastern Fantasy." *Advertising Age,* May 8, 1989, p. 40.

"How to Do Multinational Advertising Internationally." *Advertising World,* June 1985, pp. 6–30.

"No Women, No Alcohol; Learn Saudi Taboos before Placing Ads." *International Advertiser,* February 1986, pp. 11–12.

"No. 1 Dentsu Hits Lofty $1.2 Billion in Gross Income." *Advertising Age,* March 29, 1989, pp. 1–70.

"Saatchi Leads Top 11 Mega-Groups." *Advertising Age,* March 29, 1989, p. 80.

"Similarity of Cultures Simplifies Advertising to the Pan-Arab World." *International Advertiser,* February 1986, pp. 6–10.

"Solving the Cost Crunch in Foreign Advertising." *Business Marketing,* January 1985, pp. 62–64.

"Tube Wars." *Business Month,* December 1988, pp. 61–62.

Global versus Multinational

"A Global Comeback." *Advertising Age,* August 20, 1987, pp. 142–214.

"Creative Ad Ventures." *World,* January–February 1986, pp. 8–20.

"Differences, Confusion Slow Global Marketing Bandwagon." *Marketing News,* January 16, 1987, p. 1.

"Global Advertising: Multinational versus International Pros and Cons." *International Advertiser,* February 1986, pp. 34–37.

"Global Competitors: Some Criteria for Success." *Business Horizons,* January–February 1988, pp. 34–41.

"Global Marketing Campaign with a Local Touch." *Business International,* July 4, 1988, pp. 205–10.

"Global versus Local Advertising." *Management Review,* June 1986, pp. 27–31.

"How Countries Compare in Their Efforts to Think Internationally." *International Management,* November 1986, pp. 24–31.

Keegan, Warren. "Global Competition: Strategic Alternatives." Paper for Lubin Graduate School of Business, Pace University, January 1989.

Levitt, Theodore. "The Globalization of Markets." *The McKinsey Quarterly,* Summer 1984, pp. 2–20.

"Penmanship with a Flourish." *Forbes,* April 3, 1989, pp. 152–54.

Quelch, John A., and Edward J. Hoff. "Customizing Global Marketing." *Harvard Business Review,* May–June 1986, pp. 59–68.

"The Ad Biz Gloms onto 'Global.'" *Fortune,* November 12, 1984, pp. 77–80.

Personal Selling

"Cut Bureaucracy with Shared Salesmen." *Business Europe,* June 21, 1985, pp. 193–97.

"Direct Marketing Wins High-Value Sales." *Business Europe,* April 26, 1985, pp. 132–33.

"Electrolux Brings Direct Sales Techniques to Asia's Front Door." *Business Asia,* November 1, 1985, pp. 349–52.

"Getting Maximum Results from Computerized Prospecting." *Business International Ideas in Action,* August 4, 1986, pp. 2–4.

"How Rank Xerox Profits from In-House Telephone Sales." *Business Europe,* February 15, 1985, pp. 49–50.

"Meeting the Competition: Burroughs Taps New Channel for Sales to Tough Markets." *Business International,* July 26, 1985, pp. 233–34.

"Organizing for Sales Force Effectiveness." *Business International Ideas in Action,* June 8, 1987, pp. 2–6.

"Why Direct Selling Is Now a Crucial Tool for Big Business." *International Management,* March 1986, pp. 38–46.

Pricing

Adelberg, Arthur. "Resolving Conflicts in Intracompany Transfer Pricing." *Accountancy,* November 1986, pp. 86–89.

"Avon's Close-In Pricing: Four Steps toward Implementing the Strategy." *Business International Money Report,* February 10, 1986, pp. 42–43.

"Close-In Pricing System Protects Avon's Margins in Hyperinflationary Nations." *Business International Money Report,* February 3, 1986, pp. 33–34.

"Do You Want to Avoid a Government Review of Your Transfer Pricing?" *Business International Money Report,* May 2, 1988, pp. 147–51.

"Firms Use EEC Law to Fight Price Controls." *Business Europe,* September 7, 1987, pp. 1–4.

"How Transfer Pricing Can Support Business Strategies." *Business International Money Report,* March 7, 1988, pp. 82–88.

"MNCs Face Tighter Net over Transfer Pricing Rules." *Business International,* October 31, 1988, pp. 337–38.

Samiee, Saeed. "Pricing in Marketing Strategies of U.S.- and Foreign-Based Companies." *Journal of Business Research,* 1987:15:1730.

"Seven Ways to Get an Edge in the Pricing Tug of War." *Business Latin America,* September 12, 1988, p. 284.

Product

"America's International Winners." *Fortune,* April 14, 1986, pp. 34–46.

"Europewide Plans Arise at Sara Lee." *Advertising Age,* June 5, 1989, p. 50.

Hill, John S., and Richard R. Still. "Adapting Products to LDC Tastes." *Harvard Business Review*, March–April 1984, pp. 92–101.

"How to Be a Global Manager." *Fortune*, March 14, 1988, pp. 52–58.

"How to Check the Quality of Customer Service and Raise the Standard." *International Management*, February 1987, pp. 34–35.

"Southern Europe Heats up for '92." *Advertising Age*, June 5, 1989, p. 6.

"The Year of the Brand." *The Economist*, December 24, 1988, pp. 95–96.

Public Relations

"IBM Lobbies for Freer European Market." *The Wall Street Journal*, April 20, 1988, p. 18.

"Making Company Disasters Less Disastrous." *The Economist*, January 31, 1987, pp. 55–56.

"MNC Image-Building Comes of Age as a Working Tool." *Business International*, January 13, 1986, p. 13.

Muskie, Edmund S., and Daniel J. Greenwood III. "The Nestlé Infant Formula Audit Commission as a Model." *Journal of Business Strategy*, Spring 1988, pp. 19–23.

"Nestlé Rejects Militant PR Plan to Combat Renewal of Boycott." *The Wall Street Journal*, April 25, 1989, p. B6.

"The Gall in Mother's Milk." *The Journal of Advertising* 1, 1982, pp. 1–10.

"Trend-Setting Companies Elevate PR to the Level of Strategic Weapon." *International Management*, June 1985, pp. 50–55.

Retailing

"Cable TV Shopping Service Now a Reality in Europe." *Business International Ideas in Action*, May 11, 1987, p. 11.

"Cherchez la Store." *Forbes*, January 9, 1989, pp. 311–14.

"Europe's Hypermarkets Making Waves Here." *Advertising Age*, May 4, 1987, pp. S18–19.

Kacker, Madhav. "Coming to Terms with Global Retailing." *International Marketing Review*, Spring 1986, pp. 7–19.

"Retailers Fly into Hyperspace." *Fortune*, October 24, 1988, pp. 150–52.

"The New Japan Goes Shopping." *The Economist*, August 13, 1988, pp. 55–56.

"U.S., European Retailers Are Becoming More Transnational." *Europe*, January/February 1989, pp. 20–54.

Sales Promotion

Boddewyn, J. J. *Premiums, Gifts, Competitions, and Other Sales Promotions*. New York: International Advertising Association, 1988.

Foxman, Ellen R.; Patriya S. Tansuhaj; and John K. Wong. "Evaluating Cross-National Sales Promotion Strategy: An Audit Approach." *International Marketing Review*, Winter 1988, pp. 7–15.

"How Companies Profit from Promotions in Italy." *Business Europe*, June 26, 1985, pp. 201–2.

"How Sumitomo Is Making Dunlop's Tires Profitable." *Business Europe*, June 7, 1985, pp. 177–78.

Service Marketing

"As World Shrinks, Nielsen Expands." *Advertising Age*, June 5, 1989, p. 52.

"At Your Service." *The Rotarian*, May 1989, pp. 20–25.

"Creativity with Discipline." *Forbes*, March 6, 1989, pp. 41–42.

"Services: U.S., EC Prepare for Talks." *Europe*, January/February 1986, pp. 16–18.

"The Bright Future of Service Exports." *Fortune*, June 8, 1987, pp. 32–38.

"The Ever-Bigger Boom in Consulting." *Fortune*, April 24, 1989, pp. 113–34.

Television

"Europe's Audiovisual Challenge." *Europe*, April 1989, pp. 28–30.

"Europe's Priorities." *The Economist*, December 20, 1986, pp. 16–18.

"How Companies Are Advertising on Pan-European Television." *Business International Ideas in Action*, June 9, 1986, pp. 13–18.

"Murdoch's Sky Channel Beams Strong Signal across Europe." *International Management*, March 1985, pp. 48–50.

"Profile of Sky-Watchers." *International Advertiser*, June 1986, pp. 22–23.

"Satellite Success." *Europe*, May 1989, p. 5.

"Satellite TV Becomes a Credible Advertising Medium." *Business International Ideas in Action*, April 14, 1986, pp. 2–9.

"The Appeal of China TV." *International Advertiser*, June 1986, pp. 37–41.

"Uncertain Future Plagues Marketers Planning for 1992." *Advertising Age*, June 5, 1989, pp. 1–42.

"U.S.-Style TV Turns on Europe." *Fortune*, April 13, 1987, pp. 96–98.

ENDNOTES

1. R&D is still highly concentrated in the home country, which means that at least the important product changes for the foreign markets must be made there. Foreign and domestic personnel compete for R&D time. Also, a product specification is rarely frozen (look at the minor changes in automobiles in a single model year). Notifying all of the production facilities worldwide about these modifications is difficult enough, but it is much more complex when the product is not internationally standardized.

2. "Multinational, not Global," *The Economist*, December 24, 1988, p. 99.

3. "Nestlé Shows How to Gobble Markets," *Fortune,* January 16, 1989, p. 75.

4. One of the writers went to pick up his car in a garage and asked the mechanic whether he had test-driven it after finishing his work. Much to his surprise, the mechanic answered that he had not—he didn't know how to drive!

5. At times, the obsolete products may find a market in developed countries. A large American tire company does a good business in the United States by importing tires for antique cars from its foreign subsidiaries, where these sizes are in regular production because the old cars are still on the road.

6. "Consumer Nondurables," *Business International,* June 16, 1986, p. 190.

7. "Whirlpool Is Gathering a Global Momentum," *The New York Times,* April 23, 1989, p. F10.

8. "A Global Comeback," *Advertising Age,* August 20, 1987, p. 146.

9. Other LDCs follow this practice also. The pharmaceuticals mentioned are those sold in the United States with a prescription. To our knowledge, there is no country other than the United States where prescription drugs are counted or weighed and then packaged and labeled by the pharmacist. Elsewhere, the manufacturers, many of which are American subsidiaries, package the prescription drugs in small packages containing dosages that are commonly prescribed by the physician. The patient takes a prescription written by the physician in the language of the country (no Latin) and hands it to the pharmacist. He or she reaches up on the shelf and gives the customer a package. The pharmacist does not count, does not fill a plastic vial, and does not type labels. Incidentally, each package carries an insert that describes the common dosage, symptoms of overdose, and precautions to take when using the drug. Interestingly, the American Medical Association and owners of pharmacies have striven to block the idea of inserts in the United States. Their reason: the American public, unlike people in other countries, is not well enough educated to understand the insert.

10. "Gillette Keys Sales to Third World Tastes," *The Wall Street Journal,* January 23, 1986, p. 36.

11. We believe but cannot prove that sales of flea powder per capita should be high there. All the Americans we knew used to douse their legs liberally with it before going to the movies. If not, they would be eaten alive.

12. "How to Be a Global Manager," *Fortune,* March 14, 1988, pp. 52–53.

13. Warren J. Keegan, "Multinational Product Planning: Strategic Alternatives," *Journal of Marketing,* January 1969, pp. 58–62, combines these alternatives to formulate five product strategies.

14. "No. 1 Dentsu Hits Lofty $1.2 Billion in Gross Income," *Advertising Age,* March 29, 1989, p. 70.

15. "Le Défi Disney," *Forbes,* February 20, 1989, pp. 39–40.

16. "Europe's Audiovisual Challenge," *Europe,* April 1989, pp. 28–30.

17. "U.S.-Style TV Turns on Europe," *Fortune,* April 13, 1987, p. 97.

18. "The Coming Profits from European TV," *U.S. News & World Report,* May 25, 1987, p. 52.

19. *Target 1992* (Brussels: Commission of the European Communities, November 1987), p. 8.

20. "Advertising," *The Wall Street Journal,* May 18, 1989, p. B8.

21. "U.S.-Style TV Turns on Europe," p. 97.

22. "Broader Horizons," *The Wall Street Journal,* December 12, 1987, p. 1.

23. Data from *Africa South of the Sahara* and *The Middle East and North Africa* (London: Europe Publications, 1988).

24. "Videotapes Are Common throughout Middle East," *International Advertiser,* February 1986, p. 31.

25. Various annual reports.

26. "More Freedom on French TV," *International Advertiser,* June 1986, p. 12.

27. "Women, Advertising, and Islam," *Chicago Tribune,* August 4, 1982, sect. 3, p. 2; and "No Women, No Alcohol: Learning Saudi Taboos before Placing Ads," *International Advertiser,* February 1986, pp. 11–12.

28. From various articles in *Advertising World* and *Business International.*

29. Robert S. Trebus, "Can a Good Ad Campaign Cross Borders?" *Advertising World,* Spring 1978, pp. 6–8.

30. "Global Advertising: Multinational versus International Pros and Cons," *International Advertiser,* February 1986, pp. 34–37.

31. D. Peebles, J. Ryans, and I. Vernon, "Coordinating International Advertising," *Journal of Marketing,* January 1978, pp. 28–34; and "Centralized International Advertising," *International Advertiser,* September 1986, pp. 35–36.

32. Telephone conversation with Avon headquarters.

33. "Why Direct Selling Is now a Crucial Tool for Big Business," *International Management,* March 1988, pp. 38–46.

34. J. J. Boddewyn, *Premiums, Gifts, and Other Sales Promotions* (New York: International Advertising Association, 1988), pp. 12–13.

35. "A Boycott over Infant Formula," *Business Week,* April 23, 1979, pp. 137–38; and "New Attack on Nestlé," *Advertising Age,* October 17, 1983, pp. 28–29.

36. "Nestlé Rejects Militant PR Plan to Combat Renewal of Boycott," *The Wall Street Journal,* April 25, 1989, p. B6.

37. "IBM Lobbies for Freer European Market," *The Wall Street Journal,* April 20, 1988, p. 18.

38. Arthur Adelberg, "Resolving Conflicts in Intracompany Pricing," *Accountancy,* November 1986, pp. 86–89.

39. Southland Corporation, *Annual Report, 1988,* p. 5.

40. "The New Japan Goes Shopping," *The Economist,* August 13, 1988, pp. 55–56.

41. "U.S., European Retailers Are Becoming More Transnational," *Europe,* January/February 1989, pp. 20–54.

42. The idea for this matrix came to one of the writers when he was working on the first edition of this book. It is a kind of checklist to help those working on the standardization of an element of the marketing mix to remember the impact of the uncontrollable forces. He wishes he had such a tool when he was an international marketing manager.

Chapter 16

Export and Import Practices and Procedures

At no other time in U.S. history has international commerce been as important to our domestic growth as it is today. . . . . America has been the world's market. Now it is time for the world to be our market.

President Bush

LEARNING OBJECTIVES

In this chapter, you will study:

1. Why large and small companies export.

2. The three problem areas of exporting.

3. The main elements of the export sales assistance program of the U.S. Department of Commerce.

4. The meaning of the various terms of sale.

5. The kinds of payment terms that are offered.

6. The kinds of export documents that are required.

7. Activities of a foreign freight forwarder.

8. Some sources of export financing.

9. Export documentation.

10. The important innovations in materials handling in sea and air transport.

11. Why it may be more advantageous to use air freight rather than ocean freight.

12. How to identify import sources.

13. The activities of a customhouse broker.

KEY WORDS AND CONCEPTS

- Accidental exporting
- District Export Council
- Terms of sale
- "Factory door" cost
- Letter of credit (L/C)
- Confirm
- Irrevocable
- Air waybill
- Pro forma invoice
- Export, sight, and time drafts
- Compensatory trade
- Factoring, Forfaiting
- Eximbank
- Overseas Private Investment Corporation (OPIC)
- Foreign Sales Corporation (FSC)
- Free trade zone, foreign trade zone (FTZ)
- Foreign freight forwarder
- Export licenses
- General Export License, Validated Export License
- Coordinating Committee on Multilateral Export Controls (COCOM)
- Export bill of lading (B/L)
- Insurance certificate
- Collection documents
- LASH (Lighter Aboard Ship)
- Demurrage charge
- RO-RO (Roll On–Roll Off)
- Customhouse broker
- Bonded warehouse

BUSINESS INCIDENT

Global corporations export . . .

Du Pont, the sixth largest U.S. exporter, has been able to remain a competitor in the tough chemical export market because it began to pay serious attention to exports back in 1978, when the dollar's value fell sharply. "We recognized that our business was changing from national to regional or global, so you didn't have a lot of options," says P. J. Roessel, Du Pont's director of international planning. "If you didn't participate in those foreign markets, your competitors would gradually get stronger and come and eat your lunch in the U.S."

Du Pont's marketing strategy is to promote the sale of U.S. exports by its overseas manufacturing subsidiaries. "We have plotted back for 25 years and have found that as we have invested and built abroad, exports have gone up in complete tandem," says Roessel. "Such subsidiaries are able to 'pull' products from the parent company to achieve real market synergy." A Japanese Du Pont subsidiary, for example, makes engineering plastics for autos and has developed markets for polyester and acetyl products made by Du Pont in the United States.

So do small companies . . .

Can a four-employee Tennessee manufacturer successfully sell its products in Japan?

Quality Control Instruments (QCI) of Oak Ridge, Tennessee, not only can—it is selling there: Japan is the largest of its 26 foreign-country markets. The company, which started six years ago in a one-room warehouse, makes products for the metal-plating and metallurgy industries that have a wide variety of applications, such as molds for Barbie dolls and instruments for the aircraft and electronic industries. It now exports one third of its production.

The Japanese business started with a QCI advertisement in a trade journal, spotted by executives of Nippon Steel. Three Nippon executives arranged to meet Roger

BUSINESS INCIDENT (concluded)

Derby, QCI president, at a trade show in Philadelphia in 1986. The meeting, which lasted three hours, led to regular orders, currently running on the scale of $5,000 a month. Derby says he likes doing business with the Japanese because they pay promptly and keep placing more orders.

Derby, confident that his products can compete technologically overseas, says the company now needs to emphasize marketing. It has sales agents in Japan, Hong Kong, South Korea, Singapore, the Philippines, and Taiwan and is looking for more. The company is exploring the Chinese market; to get ready, Derby is studying conversational Chinese.

Exporting caused QCI to develop a new product: a battery charger used for batteries in its products. Foreign battery chargers, made for different voltages overseas, do not work on batteries that QCI puts in its instruments without adjustments. For the convenience of its foreign customers, QCI makes it a practice to enclose battery chargers with shipments of its products. However, the company had trouble finding American-made battery chargers it considered reasonably priced and well made. So it developed its own battery charger. Now, QCI anticipates a new market for its charger: other U.S. instrument manufacturers that also want to send battery chargers with their overseas shipments for customers' convenience.

QCI uses U.S. Department of Commerce export services through the Nashville District Office of the International Trade Administration. The company participated in Matchmaker 85 in the United Kingdom, the Korea Trade Promotion Corporation (KORTA) U.S. Products Show in Seoul in 1987, and Analytical 87 in Mexico City.

Sources: "Smoother Sailing Overseas," *Business Week,* April 18, 1986, p. 289; "50 Leading U.S. Exporters," *Fortune,* July 18, 1988, p. 71; and "Exporting Pays Off," *Business America,* September 26, 1988, p. 18.

Du Pont is typical of the large firms that do considerable exporting even though they possess foreign production facilities. Of the 20 largest U.S. exporters listed in Table 16–1, only the aircraft manufacturers have no overseas plants.

WHY EXPORT?

We already have examined in Chapter 2 some reasons why companies go overseas, but we did not distinguish among them. Now let us look at some specific reasons for exporting.

Large Firms

No firm can produce every product in every market.   Many of these firms, like Du Pont, supply numerous foreign markets by exporting to them because no firm, no matter how large it is, can afford to manufacture in every country where its goods are sold. Markets that are too small to support local production are supplied by exports from either the home country or a foreign affiliate. In markets of sufficient size to justify the manufacturing of some, but not all, of the product mix, it is rather common to supplement the sales of local production with imports. Thus, an automobile plant in an LDC will produce the least expensive cars and, laws permitting, import the luxury models. A notable exception to this generality was Iran, where, because of the wealth generated from high crude oil prices, General Motors began its assembly operations with the Cadillac. Also, home country plants, which usually are more vertically integrated than overseas plants (discussed in Chapter 2), export semifinished products that are inputs for the less integrated subsidiaries.

■ **TABLE 16–1**
The 20 Largest U.S. Exporters

Company	Products	Exports ($ millions)	Total Sales ($ millions)	Exports as Percent of Sales
General Motors	Autos, locomotives	$8,731	$101,782	8.6%
Ford	Autos and parts	7,614	71,643	10.6
Boeing	Aircraft	6,286	15,355	40.9
General Electric	Aircraft engines, locomotives	4,825	39,315	12.3
IBM	Information systems	3,994	54,217	7.4
Du Pont	Chemicals, fibers, plastics	3,526	30,468	11.6
McDonnell Douglas	Aircraft, missiles	3,243	13,146	24.7
Chrysler	Autos and parts	3,052	26,258	11.6
Eastman Kodak	Photographic equipment	2,255	13,305	17.0
Caterpillar	Construction equipment	2,190	8,180	26.8
United Technologies	Aircraft engines, helicopters	2,071	17,170	12.1
Digital Equipment	Computers	1,921	9,389	20.5
Philip Morris	Tobacco, food	1,700	22,279	7.6
Hewlett-Packard	Computers	1,596	8,090	19.7
Allied Signal	Aircraft, chemicals	1,416	11,597	12.2
Occidental Petroleum	Agricultural products, coal	1,316	17,096	7.7
Motorola	Semiconductors, radio equipment	1,303	6,707	19.4
Unisys	Computers	1,198	9,713	12.3
Weyerhaeuser	Wood, pulp, lumber	1,159	6,990	16.6
General Dynamics	Tanks, aircraft, missiles	1,157	9,344	12.4

Source: "50 Leading U.S. Exporters," *Fortune,* July 18, 1988, pp. 70–71.

Exporting to some markets that are rather small and have local competitors was not important to many firms until regional economic groups were formed. But after the creation of the EC, EFTA, ASEAN, and others, managements realized that by setting up a plant in one member-nation, they could then market their products throughout the region.

The free movement of goods within the EC and similar groups has enabled companies to obtain greater economies of scale by dividing the production of components among their subsidiaries rather than requiring each foreign plant to produce all parts of the finished product. For example, Ford's engine plant in England supplies engines to its German plant, which in turn supplies various components to Ford's English plant. Each subsidiary must export and import so that assembly plants in both countries can produce an automobile.

Host government may require it. Increasingly, LDC governments are stipulating that the local affiliate must export. Some have gone so far as to insist that sufficient foreign exchange be earned by the affiliate to cover the cost of all its imports. For this reason, Ford located a radio plant in Brazil that exports to Ford assembly plants in Europe.[1] The new Mexican law on foreign investments stipulates that for investors to have 100 percent ownership of a Mexican company, they must at least balance their foreign exchange earnings and expenditures for the first three years of operation. Note that the exports do not have to relate to the firm's products; Nissan Mexicana exports coffee,

WORLDVIEW

The 12 Most Common Mistakes and Pitfalls Awaiting New Exporters

The following may be considered the 12 most common mistakes and pitfalls made by new exporters.

1. Failure to obtain qualified export counseling and to develop a master international marketing plan before starting an export business. To be successful, a firm must first clearly define goals, objectives, and the problems encountered. Second, it must develop a definitive plan to accomplish an objective despite the problems involved. Unless the firm is fortunate enough to possess a staff with considerable export expertise, it may not be able to take this crucial first step without qualified outside guidance.

2. Insufficient commitment by top management to overcome the initial difficulties and financial requirements of exporting. It may take more time and effort to establish a firm in a foreign market than in domestic ones. Although the early delays and costs involved in exporting may seem difficult to justify when compared to established domestic trade, the exporter should take a long-range view of this process and carefully monitor international marketing efforts through these early difficulties. If a good foundation is laid for export business, the benefits derived should eventually outweigh the investment.

3. Insufficient care in selecting overseas distributors. The selection of each foreign distributor is crucial. The complications involved in overseas communications and transportation require international distributors to act with greater independence than their domestic counterparts. Also, since a new exporter's history, trademarks, and reputation are usually unknown in the foreign market, foreign customers may buy on the strength of a distributor's reputation. A firm should therefore conduct a personal evaluation of the personnel handling its account, the distributor's facilities, and the management methods employed.

4. Chasing orders from around the world instead of establishing a basis for profitable operations and orderly growth. If exporters expect distributors to actively promote their accounts, the distributors must be trained and assisted and their performance must be continually monitored. This requires a company marketing executive permanently located in the distributor's geographical region. New exporters should concentrate their efforts in one or two geographical areas until there is sufficient business to support a company representative. Then, while this initial core area is expanded, the exporter can move into the next selected geographical area.

5. Neglecting export business when the U.S. market booms. Too many companies turn to exporting when business falls off in the United States. When domestic business starts to boom again, they neglect their export trade or relegate it to a secondary place. Such neglect can seriously harm the business and motivation of their overseas representatives, strangle the U.S. company's

honey, and horsemeat. This is also true in one form of countertrade, which you study in the next chapter.

Export to remain competitive in home market. One other reason why more foreign affiliates have engaged in exporting is that many companies need their exports to remain competitive in their home markets. Various firms either import labor-intensive components produced in their foreign affiliates or export the components for assembly in countries where labor is less expensive. The final product is then imported for sale in the home country. The Mexican-American twin plant arrangement discussed in Chapter 2 is based on this concept.

Test the market first with exports. This is a fairly common strategy employed by firms that want to test a market for product acceptance before going to the expense of establishing local production. A trial with exports also

own export trade, and leave the firm without recourse when domestic business falls off once more. Even if domestic business remains strong, the company may eventually realize that it has only succeeded in shutting off a valuable source of additional profits.

6. Failure to treat international distributors on an equal basis with domestic counterparts. Often, companies carry out institutional advertising campaigns, special discount offers, sales incentive programs, special credit term programs, warranty offers, etc., in the U.S. market but fail to make similar assistance available to their international distributors. This is a mistake that can destroy the vitality of overseas marketing efforts.

7. Assuming that a given market technique and product will automatically be successful in all countries. What works in one market may not work in others. Each market has to be treated separately to ensure maximum success.

8. Unwillingness to modify products to meet regulations or cultural preferences of other countries. Local safety and security codes, as well as import restrictions, cannot be ignored by foreign distributors. If necessary modifications are not made at the factory, the distributor must do them—usually at greater cost and, perhaps, not as well. It should also be noted that the resulting smaller profit margin makes the account less attractive.

9. Failure to print service, sale, and warranty messages in locally understood languages. Although a distributor's top management may speak English, it is unlikely that all sales personnel (let alone service personnel) have this capability. Without a clear understanding of sales messages or service instructions, these persons may be less effective in performing their functions.

10. Failure to consider use of an export management company. If a firm decides it cannot afford its own export department (or has tried one unsuccessfully), it should consider the possibility of appointing an appropriate export management company (EMC).

11. Failure to consider licensing or joint venture agreements. Import restrictions in some countries, insufficient personnel/financial resources, or a too limited product line cause many companies to dismiss international marketing as unfeasible. Yet, many products that can compete on a national basis in the United States can be successfully marketed in most markets of the world. A licensing or joint venture arrangement may be the simple, profitable answer to any reservations. In general, all that is needed for success is flexibility in using the proper combination of marketing techniques.

12. Failure to provide readily available servicing for the product. A product without the necessary service support can acquire a bad reputation in a short period, potentially preventing further sales.

Source: *Business America,* December 7, 1987, pp. 14–15.

enables them to test marketing strategies and make adjustments with less risk. If either the product or the strategy fails, the company can withdraw without having a costly production facility to sell at a loss.

Smaller Firms

Like the large firms, no smaller firm can afford to ignore the international marketplace. Increasingly, all companies must penetrate new markets overseas to sustain their growth; they can no longer depend on their competitive home markets for it. Smaller companies can gain significant sales by establishing overseas market niches.[2]

As you read in the business incident, a four-employee operation with superior products began exporting because it was asked to, and now it exports one third of its production. This **accidental exporting** is fairly common—

accidental exporting export business obtained through no effort of exporter

foreign buyers see an advertisement in an American trade journal, as the Japanese did, or, in searching for a source of supply for something unavailable locally, they come across a company name in the *Thomas Register*. This publication, which lists American suppliers for hundreds of products, is used in the United States by purchasing agents. Every American consulate, overseas library of the American Information Service, and local chamber of commerce (French-American, German-American, etc.) has a copy, which anyone can use.

Another reason for accidental exporting is the unfavorable trade balances that the United States has with such nations as Japan and Taiwan. Their governments have organized buying missions, which come to this country to see what they can buy. Amazingly, their requests for quotations have sometimes been turned down because "exporting is too much trouble."[3]

> Pressure to reduce trade surpluses creates export opportunities in other countries as well. One of the writers was working for General Tire-Chile when a Chilean government official asked him if his company made anything that could be sold to Bolivia. That government had promised to buy Chilean products for its tin mines to help reduce the trade imbalance, and the official was asking someone to visit them. The writer went and, with difficulty, made some sales. See a related incident on that trip in endnote 16 of Chapter 8.

Not all companies wait for customers to come to them, of course, and many actively seek export business as a means of increasing their sales. Still, if exporting is a means to increase sales and profits, why did the United States export only 5.4 percent of its GNP in 1988, when exports of some nations amounted to up to half of their total output?[4] The U.S. Department of Commerce estimates that 20,000 firms in this country sell exportable products but avoid foreign markets. Why don't they export?

WHY DON'T THEY EXPORT?

The two major reasons that U.S. firms give for not exporting are (1) preoccupation with the vast American market and (2) a reluctance to become involved in a new and unknown operation. When nonexporting firms are asked why they are not active in international markets, they generally mention the following as problem areas: (1) locating foreign markets, (2) payment and financing procedures, and (3) export procedures. Although considerable assistance is available from the federal and state departments of commerce, banks, Small Business Administration, Small Business Development Centers (does your school have one?), private consultants (your international business professor may consult), and numerous other sources, some of which we mentioned in Chapter 14, insufficient managers are taking advantage of this assistance. Let us examine the three problem areas.

LOCATING FOREIGN MARKETS

The first step in locating foreign markets, whether for export or foreign manufacturing, is to determine whether a market exists for the firm's products. The initial screening step described in Chapter 14 indicated a procedure to follow that will pose no problem for the experienced market analyst who is well acquainted with the available sources of information and assistance. However, newcomers to exporting, especially the smaller firms, may still be at a loss as to where to start, and for them, the U.S. Department of Commerce export assistance program, Export Now, can be especially helpful.

Department of Commerce Export Assistance Program

Foreign market research.   Probably the quickest and least expensive way for the inexperienced firm to begin is to contact the international trade specialist in the nearest Department of Commerce district office.

After a short discussion to learn about the company and its products, the specialist will usually suggest accessing the Foreign Traders Index, a Commerce Department data base in Washington, D.C. For a $25 access fee and $.25 per company name, the potential exporter can have immediately a Best Prospect List containing the names and addresses of potential distributors, the businesses they are in, the products they handle, and whom to contact. This list indicates the possibilities for representation and can serve as a mailing list if the exporter wishes to make a bulk mailing. The specialist can also select from a number of Commerce Department publications those that will provide additional information. The *Industry Sector Analysis,* for example, gives the exporter a feel for the market by country on an industry basis.

A relatively new service, *Export Statistics Profile,* shows the exports of specific U.S. products to individual countries. Each profile consists of an *Export Market Brief,* which gives a quick picture of the industry's export potential, including growth rate, fastest-growing items, leading foreign markets, and foreign competitors; a *Trade Opportunity Frequency Report,* which indicates the number of sales leads collected by the Department of Commerce for the last four years; and *Statistical Tables,* which show a five-year flow of exports for the industry.

Smaller number of potential markets.   At this point, the research may have identified a small number of potential markets. For those that are among the 14 countries for which the Department of Commerce has the Comparison Shopping Service, by paying $500 per market, the firm will receive a custom-tailored market research survey on a specific product of its choice. This service provides information on marketability, names of competitors, comparative prices, distribution channels, and names of potential sales representatives. Each study is conducted on-site by a U.S. commercial officer. For markets not included in the service, a Department of Commerce specialist may recommend such publications as *Country Market Surveys, Competitive Assessments,* and *Annual Worldwide Industry Reviews,* all of which are available on an industry basis.

There are still other helpful publications and services. *Foreign Economic Trends Reports* summarize the economic and commercial trends in a country and are a good source of information as to which American products are most in demand. A series of reports, *Overseas Business Reports (OBR),* provide basic background data on specific countries. Each *OBR* discusses separate topics on a single country, such as basic economic data, foreign trade regulations, market factors, and trade with the United States. The firm may subscribe to *Business America,* a biweekly magazine, whose "International Commerce" section contains announcements about (1) U.S. promotions abroad in which the firm can participate; (2) foreign concerns looking for licensors, joint venture partners, or distributorships; and (3) opportunities to make direct sales.

Direct or indirect exporting.   When it has been established that there is an existing or potential market for its goods, the firm must choose between exporting indirectly through U.S.-based exporters or exporting directly using its own staff. If it opts for indirect exporting as a way to test the market, the trade specialist can provide assistance in locating one of the types of exporters listed in Chapter 13. However, should the firm prefer to set up its own export operation, it must then obtain overseas distribution.

The exporter may, as we mentioned previously, try a broad-based mailing to solicit representatives or use the Department of Commerce Agent-Distributor Search service. Commercial officers of American embassies or consulates will, within 90 days, personally interview and identify up to six local prospects who have seen the company literature and expressed an interest in representation. The exporters may then obtain information covering their commercial activities and competence by asking the Department of Commerce to supply a *World Traders Data Report*. Credit reporting agencies, such as Dun & Bradstreet, FCIB (Finance, Credit, and International Business Association), and the exporter's bank, will also supply credit information.

The Foreign Agricultural Service of the U.S. Department of Agriculture offers similar services to potential exporters of agricultural products.

Show and sell.   The Department of Commerce also organizes trade events that are helpful in both locating foreign representatives and making sales.[5] There are four kinds:

1. *Trade fairs.* Commerce organizes exhibitions or American pavilions at international trade fairs, which are held regularly in major cities worldwide. At one time, the U.S. government owned 15 trade centers in which American industry periodically held exhibitions, but for budgetary reasons, these have been reduced to 4 (London, Mexico City, Seoul, and Tokyo).
2. *"Matchmakers" and trade shows.* Commerce representatives accompany groups of American businesspeople overseas to meet with qualified agents, distributors, and customers. Prior to their arrival, overseas consular officials make appointments with qualified agents, distributors, and customers. The Department of Commerce also sponsors state- and industry-organized trade missions.
3. *Foreign buyer program.* The Commerce Department annually sponsors about 20 domestic trade shows, which bring foreign buyers and U.S. manufacturers together. American consular officers promote these trade shows in over 60 countries to attract foreign business representatives.
4. *Catalog and video shows.* American manufacturers can gain market visibility without going overseas by participating in a catalog and video show. They merely give their literature and promotional videos to Commerce, which displays it for select audiences in several foreign countries.

Other Sources of Assistance

Other sources of assistance available to the exporter include the following:

World Trade Centers Association.   The World Trade Centers Association, another aid to marketing for the new exporter, was founded by the New York-New Jersey Port Authority, which has licensed over 60 centers worldwide. Through membership, exporters and importers have access to an online trading system called NETWORK. Exporters need only a computer and a modem to put offers to sell in an electronic data base, and importers anywhere can send messages to the exporters' mailboxes accepting advertised prices or initiating electronic negotiations. Access can be gained with a local telephone in 800 cities in 64 countries.

District export councils.   The Department of Commerce has 51 **district export councils** comprised of volunteer business and trade experts who assist in workshops and also arrange for consultation between experienced and prospective exporters.

district export councils groups of volunteer business-people in every state that are appointed by the U.S. Department of Commerce to assist exporters

State governments.   All states have export development programs, which offer assistance to exporters by providing sales leads, locating overseas representatives, and counseling. Twenty-two states also have export-financing programs, and more are setting them up.[6]

Export Marketing Plan

As soon as possible, an export marketing plan must be drawn up. The experienced firm will already have a plan in operation, but newcomers will usually need to wait until they have accumulated at least some of the information from the foreign market research.

Same as domestic marketing plan.   Essentially, the export marketing plan is the same as the domestic marketing plan. It should be specific about (1) the markets to be developed, (2) the marketing strategy for serving them, and (3) the tactics required to make the strategy operational. Sales forecasts and budgets, pricing policies, product characteristics, promotional plans, and details on the arrangements with foreign representatives are required. In other words, the export marketing plan will spell out what must be done and when, who should do it, and how much money will be spent.

Marketing mix.   Because the comments in Chapter 15 concerning the marketing mix are valid for exporters, there is no need for a detailed discussion here. Two aspects that do require some explanation, however, are *export pricing* and *sales agreements for foreign representatives*.

Pricing policies.   Pricing is a problem even for experienced exporters. Noncompetitive prices cause sales to be lost to foreign competitors, but incorrect pricing can also cause the exporter to lose money on a sale.

terms of sale conditions of a sale that stipulate the point where all costs and risks are borne by buyer

One new area of concern for many firms that are beginning to export is the necessity to quote **terms of sale** that differ from those normally used. For domestic sales, the company may be quoting FOB factory, which means all costs and risks from that point on are borne by the buyer. Foreign customers, however, may insist on one of the following terms of sale:

1. *FAS (free alongside ship), port of exit.* The seller pays all of the transportation and delivery expense up to the ship's side. The buyer is responsible for any loss or damage to the shipment from that point on.

2. *CIF (cost, insurance, freight), foreign port.* The seller quotes a price that includes the cost of the goods, insurance, and all transportation and miscellaneous charges to the named foreign port in the country of final destination. If the buyer requires an on-board bill of lading (the usual case), then it is responsible for any loss or damage to the goods after they are delivered on board the vessel.

3. *C&F (cost, freight), foreign port.* This is similar to CIF except the buyer purchases the insurance, either because it can obtain the insurance at a lower cost or because its government, to save foreign exchange, insists that it use a local insurance company.[7]

CIF and C&F terms of sale are more convenient for foreign buyers because, to establish their cost, they merely have to add the import duties, landing charges, and freight from the port of arrival to their warehouse.

However, these terms can present a problem for new exporters if they forget the miscellaneous costs—wharf storage and handling charges, freight forwarder's charges, and consular fees—incurred in making a CIF shipment and simply add freight, insurance, and export packing costs to the domestic selling price. The resulting price may be too low, but more often it will be too high, because the domestic marketing and general administrative costs that are included in the domestic selling price are frequently greater than the actual cost of making the export sale.

The preferred pricing method is the use of the **"factory door" cost** (production cost without domestic marketing and general administrative costs), to which are added the direct cost of making the export sale and a percentage of the general administrative overhead. This percentage can be derived from managers' estimates of the part of their total time spent on export matters. The minimum FOB price will be the sum of these costs plus the required profit. If research in a market has shown either that there is little competition or that competitive prices are higher, then, of course, the exporter is free to charge a high price in that market (price skim) or to set a low price to gain a larger percentage of the market (penetration pricing). The course of action taken will depend on the firm's sales objectives, just as it does in the domestic market.

Sales agreement.   The sales agreement should specify as simply as possible the duties of the representative and the firm. Most of what is contained in the contract for a domestic representative can be used in export also, but special attention must be given to two points: (1) designation of the responsibilities for patent and trademark registration and (2) designation of the country and state, if applicable, whose laws will govern a contractual dispute. To be absolutely safe, the firm should register all patents and trademarks. Policing them may be left to the local representative if management so chooses.

U.S. exporters would prefer to stipulate the laws of the United States and their home state, but many nations, especially those of Latin America, will not

factory door cost   production cost only; does not include domestic marketing or general administrative costs

permit this (Calvo Doctrine). The Calvo Doctrine, promulgated by Calvo, an Argentine jurist, holds that trying cases locally under foreign laws should not be permitted because it gives the foreign company an advantage over local firms, which must be tried under local laws. If an American state can be designated, its laws may be followed even though the dispute is adjudicated in a foreign country. The presiding judge will have the pertinent parts of the law translated or will call on witnesses who are known experts in the area of law involved.

PAYMENT AND FINANCING PROCEDURES

The second major problem area concerns payment and financing procedures.

Export Payment Terms

Payment terms, as every marketer knows, are often a decisive factor in obtaining an order. As a sales official of an international grain exporter put it, "If you give credit to a guy who is broke, he'll pay any price for your product." This is somewhat exaggerated, but customers will often pay higher prices when terms are more lenient. This is especially significant in countries where capital is scarce and interest rates are high. The kinds of payment terms offered by exporters to foreign buyers are (1) cash in advance, (2) open account, (3) consignment, (4) letters of credit, and (5) documentary drafts.

Cash in advance.   When the credit standing of the buyer is not known or is uncertain, cash in advance is desirable. However, very few buyers will accept these terms, because part of their working capital is tied up until the merchandise has been received and sold. Furthermore, they have no guarantee that they will receive what they ordered. As a result, few customers will pay cash in advance unless the order is either small or for a product of special manufacture.

letter of credit (L/C) document issued by the buyer's bank in which the bank promises to pay the buyer a specified amount under specified conditions

Open account.   When a sale is made on open account, the seller assumes all of the risk, and therefore these terms should be offered only to reliable customers in economically stable countries. The exporter's capital, of course, is tied up until payment has been received.

confirm act of a correspondent bank in the seller's vicinity by which it agrees to honor the issuing bank's letter of credit

Consignment.   This follows the procedure well known in the United States by which goods are shipped to the buyer and payment is not made until they have been sold. All of the risk is assumed by the seller, and such terms should not be offered without making the same extensive investigation of the buyer and country that is recommended for open account terms. WWCs frequently sell goods to their subsidiaries on this basis.

Letters of credit.   Only cash in advance offers more protection to the seller than an export **letter of credit (L/C)**. This document is issued by the buyer's bank, which promises to pay the seller a specified amount when the bank has received certain documents stipulated in the letter of credit by a specified time.

irrevocable a letter of credit that cannot be canceled

Confirmed and irrevocable.   Generally, the seller will request that the letter of credit be **confirmed** and **irrevocable**. Irrevocable means that once the credit has been accepted by the seller, it cannot be altered or canceled by the customer

■ FIGURE 16–1
Letter of Credit

THE MERCHANTS NATIONAL BANK OF MOBILE
MOBILE, ALABAMA

FOREIGN DEPARTMENT

Confirmed Irrevocable Straight Credit — Credit No. 0000

Smith & Company
P. O. Box 000
Towne, Alabama 36000

SAMPLE

Mobile, Alabama, April 1, 19__

DEAR SIRS:

WE ARE INSTRUCTED BY Banco Americano, Bogota, Colombia

TO ADVISE YOU THAT THEY HAVE OPENED THEIR IRREVOCABLE CREDIT IN YOUR FAVOR FOR ACCOUNT OF

Compañia Santandereana de Automotores Ltda. "Sanautos", Bucaramanga, Colombia

UNDER THEIR CREDIT NUMBER 111-222 FOR A SUM OR SUMS NOT EXCEEDING A TOTAL OF $40,000.00

(FORTY THOUSAND NO/100 U.S. DOLLARS)

AVAILABLE BY YOUR DRAFTS ON US AT sight FOR INVOICE

VALUE OF 100%

SAMPLE

TO BE ACCOMPANIED BY

1. Commercial Invoice: five copies signed by the beneficiaries with sworn statement regarding price and origin of merchandise.
2. Air Waybill: three non-negotiable copies, consigned to the order of: Sanautos, Carrera 15 Calle 29, Bucaramanga, for notification of same.
3. Consular Invoice: three copies.
4. Certificate of Origin: three copies
5. Copy of the airmail letter addressed to: Sanautos, Apartado Aereo No. 936, [redacted] Bucaramanga, Colombia, remitting original of shipping documents requested.
6. Packing List: three copies.
7. Copy of the airmail letter addressed to: Compañia de Seguros Bolivar, Calle 36, No. 17-03, Bucaramanga, Colombia, covering details of shipment of merchandise, for insurance purposes.

Evidencing shipment of: "Repuestos para vehiculos automotores, registro de importacion No. 67038 del 21 de Noviembre de 19—." Port of Shipment: any American port. Destination: Bucaramanga. Partial shipments are permitted.

ALL DRAFTS SO DRAWN MUST BE MARKED "DRAWN UNDER THE MERCHANTS NATIONAL BANK OF MOBILE CREDIT NO. 0000, Banco Americano No. L/C 111-222

THE ABOVE MENTIONED CORRESPONDENT ENGAGES WITH YOU THAT ALL DRAFTS DRAWN UNDER AND IN COMPLIANCE WITH THE TERMS OF THIS CREDIT WILL BE DULY HONORED ON DELIVERY OF DOCUMENTS AS SPECIFIED IF PRESENTED AT THIS OFFICE ON OR BEFORE June 27, 19__ : WE CONFIRM THE CREDIT AND THEREBY UNDERTAKE THAT ALL DRAFTS DRAWN AND PRESENTED AS ABOVE SPECIFIED WILL BE DULY HONORED BY US.

UNLESS OTHERWISE EXPRESSLY STATED, THIS CREDIT IS SUBJECT TO THE UNIFORM CUSTOMS AND PRACTICE FOR COMMERCIAL DOCUMENTARY CREDITS FIXED BY SEVENTH CONGRESS OF THE INTERNATIONAL CHAMBER OF COMMERCE AND CERTAIN GUIDING PROVISIONS, ALL AS ADOPTED BY CERTAIN BANKS AND OTHER CONCERNS IN THE U. S. A.

YOURS VERY TRULY,

SAMPLE

ASSISTANT MANAGER — John Doe, Vice President
VICE PRESIDENT, ASSISTANT CASHIER — Allen Jones, Vice President

cc Banco Americano, Bogota, Colombia

without the seller's consent. If the irrevocable letter of credit is *not* confirmed, the correspondent bank (Merchants National Bank of Mobile in Figure 16–1) has no obligation to pay the seller, Smith & Co., when it receives the documents listed in the letter of credit. Only the issuing bank, Banco Americano in Bogota, is responsible. If Smith & Co. wishes to be able to collect from an American bank, it will insist that the credit be confirmed by such a bank. This is generally done by the correspondent bank, as it was in Figure 16–1. In this case, when the Merchants National Bank of Mobile confirmed

■ **FIGURE 16-2**
Letter of Credit Transaction

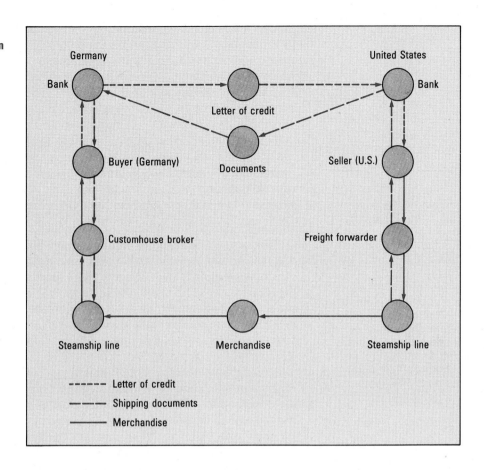

the credit, it undertook an obligation to pay Smith & Co. if all of the documents listed in the letter were presented on or before the stipulated date.

Note that nothing is mentioned about the goods themselves; the buyer has stipulated only that an **air waybill** issued by the carrier be presented as proof that shipment has been made. Even if bank officials knew that the plane had crashed after the takeoff, they would still have to pay Smith & Co. *Banks are concerned with documents, not merchandise.*

Prior to opening a letter of credit, a buyer frequently requests a **pro forma invoice.** This is the exporter's formal quotation containing a description of the merchandise, price, delivery time, proposed method of shipment, ports of exit and entry, and terms of sale. It is more than a quotation, however. Generally, the bank will use it when opening a letter of credit, and in countries requiring import licenses or permits to purchase foreign exchange, government officials will insist on receiving copies.

Letter of credit transactions. Figure 16-2 illustrates the routes taken by the merchandise, letter of credit, and documents in a letter of credit transaction.

When a German buyer accepts the terms of sale that provide for a confirmed irrevocable letter of credit, it goes to its bank to arrange for opening the required letter. The buyer will furnish the bank with the information contained in the pro forma invoice, specify the documents that the exporter must present to obtain payment, and set the expiration date for the credit.

air waybill a bill of lading issued by an air carrier

pro forma invoice exporter's formal quotation containing a description of the merchandise, price, delivery time, method of shipping, terms of sale, and points of exit and entry

The German bank then instructs its correspondent bank in the United States to confirm the credit and inform the seller that it has been established. The seller prepares the merchandise for shipment and notifies the freight forwarder, which books space on a ship, prepares the export documents, and arranges to have the merchandise delivered to the port. The documents, together with a sight or time draft drawn by the seller, are presented to the U.S. bank, which pays the seller and forwards the documents for collection to the German bank.

To obtain the documents that give title to the shipment, the buyer must either pay the *sight draft* or accept a *time draft*. Having done so, the buyer receives the documents, which are then given to the customhouse broker. The customhouse broker acts as the buyer's agent in receiving the goods from the steamship line and clearing them through the German customs.

Documentary drafts.   When the exporter believes the political and commercial risks are not sufficient to require a letter of credit, the exporter may agree to payment on a documentary draft basis, which is less costly to the buyer.

export draft an unconditional order that is drawn by the seller on the buyer to pay the draft's amount on presentation **(sight draft)** or at an agreed future date **(time draft)** and that must be paid before the buyer receives shipping documents

An **export draft,** shown in Figure 16–3, is an unconditional order drawn by the seller on the buyer instructing the buyer to pay the amount of the order on presentation **(sight draft)** or at an agreed future date **(time draft)**. Generally, the seller will request its bank to send the draft and documents to a bank in the buyer's country, which will proceed with the collection as described in the letter of credit transaction.

Although documentary draft and letter of credit terms are similar, there is one important difference. A confirmed letter of credit guarantees payment to the seller if the seller conforms to its requirements, but there is no such guarantee with documentary drafts. An unscrupulous buyer can refuse to pay the drafts when presented and then attempt to bargain with the seller for a lower price. The seller must then acquiesce, try to find another buyer, pay a large freight bill to bring back the goods, or abandon them. If the seller chooses the last alternative, customs will auction off the goods, and chances are the original buyer will be able to acquire them at a bargain price. The seller, of course, receives nothing.

compensatory trade any transaction that involves asset transfer as a condition of purchase

Compensatory trade.   A form of payment that has become increasingly popular is **compensatory trade**—any transaction that involves asset transfers as a condition of purchase, including local content requirements, licensing, and other performance requirements as well as the traditional forms of countertrade, which are described in detail in Chapter 18. For example, the government of a nation importing railway cars might insist that they be assembled locally as a condition of the purchase, or a construction company building roads might be asked to put up some low-cost housing as part of the deal.

Barter-type arrangements, which are estimated to comprise 5 percent of world trade ($150 billion), are occurring because (1) Third World and communist nations lack convertible currency and (2) these nations wish to exploit the marketing networks in the industrialized nations. However, even Australia is demanding offsets (a portion of the work on a project or product to be performed in that country) or a counterpurchase (the seller agrees to purchase goods in Australia equivalent in value to a minimum of 30 percent of the cost of goods sold).

Compensatory trade has become so important that a number of WWCs, such as General Motors and Volkswagen, have wholly owned subsidiaries to

■ **FIGURE 16–3   Sight Draft**

```
FIRST NATIONAL BANK
MOBILE          ALABAMA

$ 2,500.00                    MOBILE, ALA.,  July 6,              19 __

Sight D/P-------------------------------------------- PAY TO THE ORDER OF

_ Clayton Motor Company _____

Two Thousand Five Hundred ------------------------------------------ DOLLARS


VALUE RECEIVED AND CHARGE SAME TO ACCOUNT OF
                                            CLAYTON MOTOR COMPANY
To___ First National Bank of Mobile _____   }
       P. O. Box 1467                           BY_____
       Mobile, Alabama  36621                   John P. Clayton, President
```

handle such transactions. Smaller firms can contract with independent barter-switch companies, which will do the work for them. Figure 16–4 illustrates a countertrade operation by means of which Chrysler automobiles were exchanged for Jamaican bauxite.

Export Financing

Although exporters would prefer to sell on the almost riskless letter of credit terms, increased foreign competition and the universally tight money situation are forcing them to offer credit. To do so, they must be familiar with the available sources and kinds of export financing, both private and public.

Private source.   Commercial banks have always been a source of export financing through loans for working capital and the discounting of time drafts. A bank may discount an export time draft, pay the seller and keep it until maturity, or, if it is the bank on which the draft is drawn, "accept" it. By accepting a time draft, a bank assumes the responsibility for making payment at maturity of the draft. The accepting bank may or may not purchase (at a discount) the draft. If it does not, the exporter can sell a bank acceptance readily in the open market. In recent years, new types of financing have been developed—factoring and forfaiting.

Factoring.   This financing technique permits the exporter to be more competitive by selling on open account rather than by means of the more costly letter of credit method. Long used in the United States, factoring is now being employed in international trade.

factoring discounting without recourse an account receivable

    Factoring is essentially discounting *without* recourse because it is the sale of export accounts receivable to a third party, which assumes the credit risk. A factor may be a factoring house or a special department in a commercial bank.

    Under the export factoring arrangement, the seller passes its order to the factor for approval of the credit risk. Once the order has been approved, the exporter has complete protection against bad debts and political risk. The customer pays the factor, which, in effect, acts as the exporter's credit and

■ **FIGURE 16–4 Jamaican Countertrade**

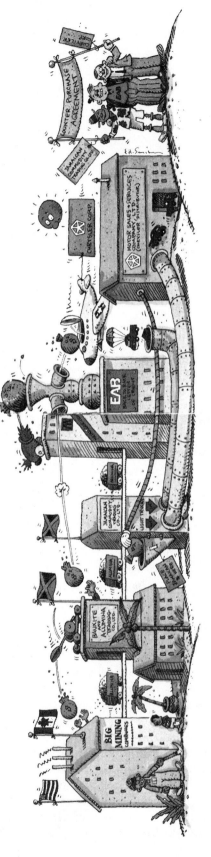

Countertrade made simple: If you think it's tough selling cars and trucks in the United States, this is what Chrysler went through to sell several hundred vehicles to credit-starved Jamaica. The American and Canadian mining companies (far left), which dig Jamaica's bauxite and refine it into alumina, hand over some 50,000 tons of alumina to the government's Bauxite & Alumina Trading Co. The trading company, in turn, gives the alumina to Metallgesellschaft, a German metals company. MG sells the alumina to a refiner, which converts it to aluminum. The money MG gets for the alumina goes to the European American Bank, Chrysler's adviser. EAB sends part of the money back to the Bauxite & Alumina Trading Co., which pays the mining companies. The balance goes to finance a letter of credit made out to Chrysler, which then ships trucks to Jamaica. Title is taken by another government firm, the Jamaican Commodity Trading Co., which sells the vehicles to Motors Sales & Services Co., Chrysler's local distributor. The dealer sells them to the public. The part you don't see—and the parties want to keep hidden—is what makes the convoluted deal click. Jamaica probably is shaving price to unload bauxite, while Chrysler is absorbing extra costs to make the sale.

Source:"The Explosion of International Barter," *Fortune*, February 7, 1983, pp. 88–89.

collection department. The period of settlement generally does not exceed 180 days.

Forfaiting.   **Forfaiting** denotes the purchase of obligations that arise from the sale of goods and services and fall due at some date beyond the 90 to 180 days that are customary for factoring. These receivables are usually in the form of trade drafts or promissory notes with maturities ranging from six months to five years.

Because it is sold without recourse, forfaited debt is nearly always accompanied by bank security in the form of a guarantee or aval. While the guarantee is a separate document, the aval is a promise to pay written directly in the document ("per aval" and the signature).

The forfaiter purchases the bill and discounts it for the entire credit period. Thus, the exporter, through forfaiting, has converted its credit-based sale into a cash transaction.

Although banks have traditionally concentrated on short-term financing, they have become involved in medium- and even long-term financing because numerous government and government-assisted organizations are offering export credit guarantees and insurance against commercial and political risks.

Export-Import Bank, FCIA, and PEFCO.   The U.S. Export-Import Bank (**Eximbank**) is the principal government agency responsible for aiding the export of American goods and services through a variety of loan, guarantee, and insurance programs.[8] Generally, its programs are available to any American export firm regardless of size.

Direct and intermediary loans.   The Eximbank provides two types of loans: (1) direct loans to foreign buyers of American exports and (2) intermediary loans to responsible parties, such as a foreign government lending agency that relends to foreign buyers of capital goods and related services (for example, a maintenance contract for a jet passenger plane). Both programs cover up to 85 percent of the value of the exported goods and services, with repayment terms of one year or more.

Working capital guarantee.   This program helps small businesses obtain working capital to cover their export sales. It guarantees working capital loans extended by banks to eligible exporters with exportable inventory or export receivables as collateral.

Guarantees.   Eximbank's guarantee provides repayment protection for private-sector loans to buyers of U.S. capital equipment and related services. The guarantee is available alone or may be combined with an intermediary loan.

Export credit insurance.   An exporter may reduce its financing risks by purchasing export credit insurance from the Foreign Credit Insurance Association (FCIA), the Eximbank's agent. FCIA insurance may be obtained for export sales, leasing of equipment, and consignments in foreign markets. The coverage may be comprehensive or limited to political risk only.

Since its inception in 1934, the Eximbank has supported nearly $200 billion in U.S. exports. Every industrialized nation and many that are industrializing have similar banks. Another government agency, the Small Business Administration, operates loan guarantee and direct loan programs to assist small-business exporters.

---

forfaiting purchasing without recourse an account receivable whose credit terms are longer than the 90 to 180 days usual in factoring; unlike factoring, political and transfer risks are borne by the forfaiter

Eximbank principal federal government agency that aids American exporters by means of loans, guarantees, and insurance programs

PEFCO.   PEFCO (Private Export Funding Corporation), a corporation owned by 54 commercial banks, 7 large manufacturers, and an investment bank, was established to be a supplemental lender. PEFCO makes financing available only in cases where other private-sector lenders will not provide sufficient financing on competitive terms. Although PEFCO's loans are mostly medium term (average seven years), some are made for as long as 20 years. All of its loans must be covered by an unconditional guarantee of the Eximbank.

OTHER GOVERNMENT INCENTIVES

Other government incentives for trade, although not strictly a part of export financing, are certainly closely related to it. These are the Overseas Private Investment Corporation (OPIC), the Foreign Sales Corporation (FSC), and the foreign trade zone (FTZ).

Overseas Private Investment Corporation (OPIC)

Overseas Private Investment Corporation (OPIC) government corporation that offers American investors in developing countries insurance against expropriation, currency inconvertibility, and damages from wars and revolutions

The Overseas Private Investment Corporation (OPIC) is a government corporation that was formed to stimulate private investment in developing countries. It offers investors insurance against expropriation, currency inconvertibility, and damages from wars or revolutions. OPIC also offers specialized insurance for American service contractors and exporters operating in foreign countries. Its connection with exporting stems from the fact that exports of capital equipment and semiprocessed raw materials generally follow these investments.

Foreign Sales Corporation

Foreign Sales Corporation (FSC)   special corporate form authorized by the federal government that provides tax advantages for exporting firms

The **Foreign Sales Corporation (FSC)** is a new entity authorized by the Tax Reform Act of 1984. It replaces the domestic international sales corporation (DISC), which was the object of complaints by U.S. trading partners that DISCs violated the General Agreement on Tariffs and Trade.

Unlike its DISC predecessor, an FSC must be located either in a U.S. possession other than Puerto Rico or in a foreign country that has an information exchange agreement with the United States. The FSC's shareholders' and directors' meetings must be held outside the United States, and its principal bank account must be maintained outside the United States.

The portion of the FSC's income that is exempt from U.S. corporate taxation is 32 percent if the FSC buys from independent suppliers or uses the Section 482* arm's-length pricing rule with related suppliers.[9]

Foreign Trade Zones

For centuries, various forms of duty-free areas have existed in many parts of the world to facilitate trade by lessening the effect of customs restrictions. These customs-privileged areas may be free ports, transit zones, free perimeters, export processing zones, or free trade zones. In each instance, a specific and limited area is involved, into which imported goods may be brought without the payment of import duties. At present, there are nearly 350 such

---

* See Chapter 15 for details on Section 482.

areas located in 72 countries. Of the five types, the free trade zone is the most common.

The **free trade zone** is an enclosed area considered to be outside the customs territory of the country in which it is located. Goods of foreign origin may be brought into the zone pending eventual transshipment, reexportation, or importation into the country. While the goods are in the zone, no import duties need to be paid.

The American version, called the **foreign trade zone (FTZ)**, has been growing in popularity, and there are now more than 240 of these zones in operation.[*] Many are situated at seaports, but some are located at inland distribution points.

Goods brought into the FTZ may be stored, inspected, repackaged, or combined with American components. Due to differences in the import tariff schedule, the finished product often pays less duty than what would be charged for the disassembled parts. Bicycles have been assembled in the Kansas City FTZ for that reason. Importers of machinery and automobiles improve their cash flow by storing spare parts in an FTZ, because duty is not paid until they are withdrawn.

Although the advantages of the FTZ to importers are well known, its benefits to exporters appear to have been overlooked. Foreign trade zones can provide accelerated export status for purposes of excise tax rebates and customs drawbacks. Manufacturers of such items as tires, trucks, and tobacco products are required to pay federal excise taxes when these items are produced, but the taxes are rebated if the items are exported. Firms including imported parts in their finished product must pay duty on the imports, but this duty is returned when the product is exported (customs drawback). The recovery of this money takes time, however, and meanwhile the exporter can have considerable capital tied up in excise taxes and import duties. Because a product is considered exported as soon as it enters an FTZ, the exporter can immediately apply for a rebate or a drawback while waiting to make an export sale. If assembly or manufacturing is done in the FTZ using imported components, no duties need ever be paid when the finished product is exported. This is also the purpose of the previously mentioned export processing zones in which firms use cheap local labor for assembly. There are various such zones in China, for example.

free trade zone an area designated by the government of a country for duty-free entry of any nonprohibited good

foreign trade zone (FTZ) American version of a free trade zone

EXPORT PROCEDURES

When nonexporters complain about the complexity of export procedures, they are generally referring to documentation. Instead of the two documents (the freight bill and the bill of lading) to which they are accustomed when shipping domestically, they are suddenly confronted by five to six times as many documents for a foreign shipment. According to an OECD study, the average overseas transaction needs 35 documents with a total of 360 copies. The study states that the "paper costs" of international trade come to between 1.4 percent and 5.7 percent of the value of the trade. "Exports move on a sea of documents" is a popular saying in the industry. Although the extra burden

[*] Includes subzones for individual plants.

may be handled by the traffic department, many firms give all or at least part of the work to a foreign freight forwarder.

Foreign Freight Forwarders

foreign freight forwarder independent business that handles export shipments for compensation

Foreign freight forwarders act as agents for exporters. They prepare documents, book space with a carrier, and in general act as the firm's export traffic department. If asked, they will offer advice about markets, import and export regulations, the best mode of transport, and export packing, and they will supply cargo insurance. After shipment, they forward all documents to the importer or to the paying bank, according to the exporter's requirements.

Export Documents

Correct documentation is vital to the success of any export shipment. For discussion purposes, we shall divide export documents into two categories: (1) shipping documents and (2) collection documents.

Shipping documents.   Shipping documents are prepared by exporters or their freight forwarders so that the shipment may pass through U.S. Customs, be loaded on the carrier, and sent to its destination. They include the domestic bill of lading, export packing list, export licenses, export bill of lading, and insurance certificate. Inasmuch as the first two documents are nearly the same as those used in domestic traffic, we shall limit our discussion to the export licenses, the insurance certificate, and the export bill of lading. Note, however, that a domestic bill of lading for goods to be exported must contain a statement by the seller that these goods will not be diverted to another destination. Export package marks and the latest allowable arrival date in the port of export should be noted. The export packing list differs from the domestic list in that it is much more detailed with respect to the weights and measurements of each package. The material in each package must be itemized.

export license government document that permits the exporter to export designated goods to certain destinations

General Export License any export license covering export commodities for which a validated license is not required; no formal application required

Export licenses.   All exported goods with the exception of those going to U.S. possessions or Canada (with a few exceptions) require **export licenses**—either a *General License* or a *Validated Export License.*

Most products can be exported under the **General License,** for which no special authorization is necessary. The correct General License symbol, which is obtainable from the Department of Commerce district office, is merely written in the *Shipper's Export Declaration.* This document, which must be filed with U.S. Customs, indicates that there is an authorization to export and also provides the statistical information for the *FT 410.* For strategic materials and all shipments to communist countries, a **Validated Export License** is mandatory. This is a special authorization for a specific shipment and is issued only on formal application to the Department of Commerce's Office of Export Administration for scarce materials, strategic goods, and technology or to the Department of State for war materials.

Validated Export License a required document issued by the U.S. government authorizing the export of specified commodities

Coordinating Committee on Multilateral Export Controls (COCOM) voluntary group of most NATO nations that administers a common set of export controls to prevent transfer of sensitive goods to Soviet-bloc nations

Exporters selling strategic and high-tech products overseas must be aware that the Department of Commerce checks very thoroughly license applications for these products, as do all member-governments of **COCOM (Coordinating Committee on Multilateral Export Controls),** a voluntary group comprising Japan and all NATO countries except Spain and Iceland. COCOM nations administer a common set of export controls intended to prevent the transfer of advanced technology to Soviet-bloc countries. Particular attention is given to dual-use items—those with both commercial and military applications. To enforce controls in this country, the Department of Commerce has an Office of Export Enforcement with armed agents in field offices located near high-tech production centers and in U.S. embassies in Vienna and Stockholm. Violators of diversion laws and export controls can be fined and imprisoned.

> Two brothers, secret owners of a West German helicopter firm that was a former distributor of Hughes Helicopters, pleaded guilty in Los Angeles to illegally exporting over 100 U.S. helicopters to North Korea. One was given three years in jail, and the other, one year. Each was fined $40,000.[10]

export bill of lading (B/L) contract of carriage between shipper and carrier: straight bill of lading is nonnegotiable; endorsed "to order" bill gives holder claim on merchandise

Export bill of lading.   The **export bill of lading (B/L)** serves a dual purpose. First, it is a contract for carriage between the shipper and the carrier, and second, it is evidence of title to the merchandise. Bills of lading are generally called *air waybills* (air shipments) or *ocean bills of lading* (steamships).

Ocean bills of lading may be either "straight" or "to order," but air waybills are always "straight." A straight bill of lading is nonnegotiable, and only the person stipulated in it may obtain the merchandise on arrival. An order bill of lading, however, is negotiable. It can be endorsed like a check or left blank. In this case, the holder of the original bill of lading is the owner of the merchandise. Sight draft or letter of credit shipments require "to order" bills marked "Clean on Board" by the steamship company, which means there is no apparent damage to the shipment and it has actually been loaded onto the vessel.

insurance certificate evidence that marine insurance has been obtained to cover stipulated risks during transit

Insurance certificate.   The **insurance certificate** is evidence that insurance coverage has been obtained to protect the shipment from loss or damage while it is in transit. Unlike domestic carriers, oceangoing steamship companies assume no responsibility for the merchandise they carry unless the loss is caused by their negligence.

Marine insurance on an international transaction may be arranged by either the exporter or the importer, depending on the terms of sale. The laws of a country often require the importer to buy such insurance, thus protecting the local insurance industry and saving foreign exchange. If the exporter has sold on sight draft terms, it is at risk while the goods are in transit. In this case, the firm should buy contingent interest insurance to protect it in the event that the shipment is lost or damaged and it is unable to collect from the buyer. We believe that the exporter selling on C&F terms (the buyer purchases the insurance) should also buy contingent interest insurance to protect itself in case the buyer's insurance does not cover all risks. The premiums are low because damages are paid only on what is not covered by the buyer's policy.

Broadly speaking, there are three kinds of marine insurance policies: (1) basic named perils, (2) broad named perils, and (3) all risks.

1. *Basic named perils* includes perils of the sea, fires, jettisons, explosions, and hurricanes.
2. *Broad named perils* includes theft, pilferage, nondelivery, breakage, and leakage in addition to the basic perils. Both policies contain a clause that determines the extent to which losses caused by an insured peril will be paid. The purchaser of the insurance may request either

(*a*) free of particular average (excluding partial loss) or (*b*) with particular average (covering partial loss). Obviously, the rates differ.

3. *All risks* covers all physical loss or damage from any external cause and is more expensive than the policies previously mentioned. War risks are covered under a separate contract.

For the sake of convenience, the occasional exporter will ask the forwarder to arrange for insurance, but when shipments begin on a regular basis, the shipper can economize by going directly to a marine insurance broker. The broker, acting as the shipper's agent, will draw up a contract to fit the shipper's needs by choosing appropriate clauses from among the hundreds that are available.

The premiums charged depend on a number of factors, among which are the goods insured, the destination, the age of the ship, whether the goods are stowed on deck or under deck, the volume of business (there are volume discounts), how the goods are packed, and the number of claims that the shipper has filed. Brokers will sometimes admit that in the long run it is preferable not to file numerous small claims, even if these are justified, because the higher premiums charged for future shipments will be greater than the money recovered.

Because neither the policies nor the premiums are standard, it is highly recommended that the exporter obtain various quotations.

collection documents all documents submitted to the buyer for the purpose of receiving payment for a shipment

Collection documents.   The seller is required to provide the buyer with these documents to receive payment. For a letter of credit transaction, the **collection documents** must be submitted to a bank, but to collect against documentary drafts, anyone may be designated to act on the seller's behalf. A few exporters send their drafts overseas to a representative or bank for collection, but it is preferable to have a bank in the exporter's country forward them to its correspondent bank in the city of destination.

First of all, the collection costs are usually less, because the correspondent bank charges the exporter's bank less than it would charge the exporter. Second, because of the correspondent relationship between the banks, the foreign bank will generally exert a greater effort to collect the money on time. Should the exporter wish to change instructions to the foreign bank, the private cable codes and tests of banks permit new instructions to be authenticated and acted on quickly, whereas a cable from the exporter to a foreign bank would probably be ignored until it had been confirmed by a letter with a signature that could be checked for authenticity.

The documents required for collection vary among countries and among customers, but some of the most common are (1) commercial invoices, (2) consular invoices, (3) certificates of origin, and (4) inspection certificates.

Commercial invoices.   Commercial invoices for export orders are similar to domestic invoices but include additional information, such as the origin of the goods, export packing marks, and a clause stating that the goods will not be diverted to another country. Invoices for letter of credit sales will name the bank and the credit numbers. Some importing countries require the commercial invoice to be in their language and to be visaed by their local consul.

Consular invoices.   A few countries require both the commercial invoice and a special form called the consular invoice. These forms are purchased from the consul, prepared in the language of the country, and then visaed by the consul.

Certificates of origin.   Although the commercial invoice carries a statement regarding the origin of the merchandise, a number of foreign governments require a separate *certificate of origin.* This document is commonly issued by the local chamber of commerce and visaed by the consul.

Inspection certificates.   Inspection certificates are frequently required by buyers of grain, foodstuffs, and live animals. These are issued by the Department of Agriculture in the United States. Purchasers of machinery or products containing a specified combination of ingredients may insist that an American engineering firm or laboratory inspect and certify that the merchandise is exactly as ordered.

EXPORT SHIPMENTS

Most newcomers are so preoccupied with making a sale and handling the extra paperwork needed when exporting that they fail to be concerned about the physical movement of their goods. Yet, if they knew about the advances in material-handling techniques, they might not only save money but also reach markets that they previously could not serve.

For example, do you want to reduce handling costs? Do you want to reduce pilferage, always a problem in both the port of exit and the port of entry?

> One of the writers, a crew member of a merchant ship docked in an American port to discharge cargo, was leaving the ship when he heard a tremendous thump. The stevedores who were unloading the ship were picking up a large crate with the ship's winch and dropping it on the ground to break it open. Obviously, they suspected that it contained valuable merchandise. Within a few hours of a ship's arrival to unload, you can see peddlers in the street offering merchandise that arrived on the ship. You can purchase bananas, for example, outside the dock area soon after their arrival.

One means of drastically reducing both theft and handling costs is to use containers.

Containers

Containers are large boxes—8 by 8 feet in cross-section by either 10, 20, or 40 feet in length—that the seller fills with the shipment in its own warehouse. Airlines also provide smaller containers with rounded cross-sections for a better fit in the fuselage. The containers are then sealed and opened only when the goods arrive at their final destination. Containers will be picked up by a tractor-trailer or a railroad for delivery to shipside, where they will be loaded aboard ship. From the port of entry, railroads or trucks will deliver them, often unopened even for customs inspection, to the buyer's warehouse. In most countries, customs officials will go to the warehouse to examine the shipment. This not only reduces handling time, but it also minimizes the risks of damage and theft because the buyer's own employees unload the containers. If the importer or exporter has a warehouse on a river too shallow for ocean vessels,

Container ship

Courtesy Lykes Brothers

it can save time and expense by loading containers on barges, which are towed to the harbor where a LASH vessel is anchored.

LASH

LASH (Lighter Aboard Ship)
specially designed ocean-
going vessel for carrying
barges

LASH (Lighter Aboard Ship) vessels give exporters and importers direct access to ocean freight service even though they are located on shallow inland waterways. Sixty-foot-long barges are towed to inland locations, loaded, and towed back to deep water where they are loaded aboard anchored LASH ships. Exporters who are not located in deep-water ports should check to see if this service is available. Not only will they decrease their risks, but they may gain from their competitors those customers facing the same problems because they too are located far from seaports. This is especially true in LDCs, where oceangoing vessels may wait in anchor a month or more for docking space. Not only do customers have to wait for the merchandise, but freight charges will be higher because the ship has a long, unproductive wait. All the expenses of operating the vessel, which can amount to thousands of dollars daily, are included in a **demurrage charge** added to the exporter's or importer's normal freight charge.

demurrage charge as-
sessed by a carrier on an
exporter or an importer for
excess time taken to unload
or load a vessel

RO–RO vessel

Courtesy California Photo Service

RO–RO

Another innovation in cargo handling is the **RO–RO (Roll On–Roll Off)** ship, which permits loaded trailers and any equipment on wheels to be driven onto this specially designed vessel. RO–RO service has brought the benefits of containerization that we discussed to ports that have been unable to invest in the expensive lifting equipment required for containers. Innovative exporters might be able to combine their container shipments with other exporters' shipments of rolling stock. Of course, they must first know that RO–RO vessels exist.

Air Freight

Air freight has had a profound effect on international business because it permits shipments that once required 30 days to arrive in 1 day. Huge freight planes carry payloads of 200,000 pounds, most of which goes either in containers or on pallets. Airlines guarantee overnight delivery from New York to many European airports and claim that their planes can be completely loaded or unloaded within 45 minutes.

Many newcomers to exporting use ocean freight rather than air freight because ocean freight is so much cheaper. But if they compare the total costs of each mode, they frequently find that air freight is less costly. Total cost components that may be lower for air freight include the following:

1. *Insurance rates*—less chance of damage.

A transport van brings lower deck containers to a Lufthansa Boeing 747 for loading.

Courtesy Lufthansa

2. *Packing*—can go in domestic packaging instead of the heavier, more costly export packing, which the exporter may have to pay to have done by an outside firm.

3. *Customs duties*—when calculated on gross weights.

4. *Replacement costs for damaged goods*—less chance of damaging shipment. Mercedes ships many of its automobiles to the United States by air freight.

5. *Inventory costs*—rapid delivery by air freight often obviates the need for expensive warehouses.

6. *Increased customer satisfaction*—receives shipment sooner with less chance of damage or delays caused by replacing damaged product.

Table 16–2 illustrates how the total cost of air freight may be lower than ocean freight.

Even when the total costs based on these items are higher for air freight, it may still be advantageous to ship by air when factors other than the conventional expense, inventory, and capital are considered:

1. *Production and opportunity costs,* although somewhat more difficult to calculate, are properly a part of the total cost. Getting the product to the buyer more quickly results in faster payment, which speeds up the return on investment and improves cash flow. The firm's capital is released more quickly and can be invested in other profit-making ventures or can be used to repay borrowed capital, thus reducing interest payments. Production equipment may be assembled and sent by air so that it goes into production sooner without the transit and setup delays associated with ocean shipments, a strong sales argument.

■ TABLE 16–2
Sea–Air Total Cost
Comparison
(Shipment of spare part)

	Ocean Freight (with warehousing)	Air Freight (no warehousing)
Warehouse administrative costs	$ 850	—
Warehouse rent	1,400	—
Inventory costs		
Taxes and insurance	630	$ 330
Inventory financing	240	160
Inventory obsolescence	1,500	0 (minimal)
Seller's warehouse and handling costs	1,550	950
Transportation	350	2,000
Packaging and handling	250	100
Cargo insurance	60	30
Customs duties	110	107
Total	$6,940	$3,677

2. *The firm may be air dependent;* that is, the exporter is in business only because of air freight. Suppliers of perishable food products to Europe, Japan, and the Middle East are in this category, as are suppliers of live animals (newly hatched poultry and prize bulls) and fresh flowers, a big, legal Colombian export. *Without air freight, these firms would be out of business.*

3. *The products may be air dependent* because the market itself is perishable. Consumer products with extremely short life cycles (high-fashion and fad items) are examples, but many industrial products also fit into this category. A computer, for example, is perishable to the extent that the time it loses between the final assembly and the installation at the customer's location is time in which it is not earning income (the leasing fee).

4. The sales argument that spare parts and factory technical personnel are available within a few hours is a strong one for the exporting firm that has to compete with overseas manufacturers.

IMPORTING

In one sense, importers are the reverse of exporters; they sell domestically and buy in foreign markets. However, many of their concerns are similar. As in the case of exporters, there are small firms whose only business is to import, and there are global corporations for which importing is just one of their functions.

How does the prospective importer identify import sources? In a number of ways:

1. If similar imported products are already in the market, go to a retailer that sells them and examine the product label to see where it is made. U.S. law requires the country of origin to be clearly marked on each product or on its container if product marking is not feasible (individual cigarettes, for example).

   Once you know where the product is produced, call the nearest consul or embassy of that country and request the names of

Two 10-foot "bungalows" and an outsized piece of cargo that is even longer than its pallet move to their loading positions on the main deck of Lufthansa's Boeing 747F.

Courtesy Lufthansa

manufacturers. One of the principal duties of all foreign government representatives is to promote exports. Some countries publish newsletters in which products are offered for export. Ask to be on their mailing lists. You can also call foreign chambers of commerce in your country (the German-American Chamber of Commerce in New York City is an example). The Japan External Trade Organization (JETRO), which provides information on Japanese exporters, has a number of offices in the United States and other countries. Foreign governments sponsor trade shows in many countries, as we mentioned in our discussion of how the U.S. Department of Commerce assists exporters. Visit these as well as industry shows in your home country. Once you have names and addresses of foreign manufacturers, you can write to them for quotations.

2. If the product is not being imported, you should contact all the sources listed in item 1. The only difference is that you will have to contact more countries. Banks may be another source of names.

3. Accidental importing also takes place. When you visit a foreign country, look for products that may have a market at home. Finding one could put you into a new business, one that makes foreign traveling tax deductible.

Let's look at some of the technical aspects of importing for which customhouse brokers can provide assistance.

Customhouse Brokers

customhouse broker independent business that handles import shipments for compensation

In every nation, there are **customhouse brokers** just as there are foreign freight forwarders; but instead of helping exporters to export (the function of foreign freight forwarders), they help importers to import. The functions of the two are very similar; in fact, a number of firms provide both services. In the United

States, both are licensed: customhouse brokers are licensed by U.S. Customs after passing an extensive examination, and foreign freight forwarders are licensed by the U.S. Maritime Administration.

Principal activity.   Acting as the agent for the importer, customhouse brokers bring the imported goods through customs, which requires them to know well the many import regulations and the extensive Tariff Schedule mentioned in Chapter 2. If a customs official places the import in a category requiring higher import duties than the importer had planned on paying, the importing firm may not be able to compete pricewise and still make a profit. Generally, customs evaluators everywhere use units for products that carry specific duties and the invoice price as the basis for ad valorem duties. As we explained in Chapter 2, there are some exceptions.

The practice of U.S. Customs is to use the transaction price, which appears on the commercial invoice accompanying the shipment, plus any other charges not included in the transaction price. These may be royalty or license fees, packing, or any assists. *Assist* is the U.S. Customs term for any item that the buyer provides free or at reduced cost for use in the production or sale of merchandise for export to this country. Examples are molds and dies sent overseas to produce the product, a common practice of importers that want the goods produced using their design, and components and parts that the buyer provides for incorporation in the finished article.[11]

American-made goods can be returned to this country duty free; if they have been improved in any way, however, the importers must pay import duties. Mexico's twin-plant concept would not exist if Congress had not passed a law exempting American firms from paying import duties on the American components in finished products that are assembled in Mexico and exported to the United States.

Other activities.   Customhouse brokers can also provide other services, such as arranging transportation for the goods after they have left Customs or even transportation for the goods from a foreign country if the exporter has not done so. Another important function is to know when imports are subject to import quotas and how much of the quota has been filled at the time of the import. No matter at which port the goods arrive, U.S. Customs, aided by a computer network to all American ports, knows immediately the quantity that has been imported. Merchandise subject to import quotas can be on the dock of an American port awaiting clearance through Customs; if the quota fills anywhere meanwhile, those goods cannot be imported for the rest of the fiscal year. The would-be importer must either (1) put them in a **bonded warehouse** or a foreign trade zone, where merchandise can be stored without paying duty and wait for the rest of the year, (2) abandon them, or (3) send them to another country. Importers of high-fashion clothing have lost millions of dollars because the quotas were filled and they could not sell the clothing until the following year—by then, it was out of fashion.

bonded warehouse authorized by customs authorities for storage of goods on which payment of import duties is deferred until the goods are removed

A prospective importer should follow these rules:

1. Disclose fully to the U.S. Customs Service all foreign and financial arrangements before passing the goods through Customs. The penalties for fraud are high.

2. Ask the advice of a customhouse broker *before* making the transaction. Frequently, a simple change in the product can result in much lower import duties. For example, if you are an importer of jeans, you will pay higher duties if the label is outside the back pocket instead of under the belt. If the words on the label are stylized, duties are more than if they are in simple block letters. Any clothing that is ornamented pays more duty. This is why one importer brings in plain sports shirts and sews on an animal figure after they are in the United States.

3. Calculate carefully the landed price in advance. If there is a doubt about the import category, the importer can ask Customs to determine the category in advance and to put it in writing—just as you can obtain advanced rulings from the Internal Revenue Service. At the time of importation, customs inspectors must respect this determination. Many customs procedures are like those of the IRS. Both have similar procedures for appealing their decisions, for example. This is no coincidence—both are under the secretary of the Treasury.

SUMMARY

Firms of all sizes export, including worldwide corporations that own overseas production facilities. You studied the reason why firms go overseas in Chapter 2, and, in this chapter, you saw some specific reasons why they export: completing product lines; exporting production inputs to affiliates; the host government requiring an affiliate to export; importing from their affiliates to be competitive in their home markets; or testing a new market or a new product first with exports.

Smaller firms, like the larger ones, export to increase sales. Some begin to export accidently, while others seek out foreign customers. Generally, companies choose not to export because of the perceived difficulties in (1) locating new markets, (2) payment and financing procedures, and (3) export procedures.

Market screening as described in Chapter 14 will enable the firm to locate foreign markets, and various Department of Commerce programs are also helpful. When preparing the export marketing mix, special attention must be given to export pricing and the preparation of sales agreements for overseas representatives.

The terms of payment offered in the export market are (1) cash in advance, (2) open account, (3) consignment, (4) letters of credit, and (5) documentary drafts. Although exporters would prefer to sell on letter of credit terms, the competitive situation in world markets forces them to offer credit. A number of sources and kinds of export financing, both private and public, are available. Government incentives to export trade include OPIC, Foreign Sales Corporations, and foreign trade zones.

Export procedures are considered a problem by newcomers because of the multiplicity of the documents required. Foreign freight forwarders are available to act as agents in the preparation of documents and in the booking of space on carriers. In addition to the documents required for domestic shipments, goods for export usually require export licenses and export bills of lading. Inasmuch as oceangoing steamship companies assume no responsibility for the merchandise they carry, the shipper must buy marine insurance. The documents required for collection vary among customers and destinations, but they commonly include (1) commercial invoices, (2) consular invoices, (3) certificates of origin, and (4) inspection certificates.

Innovations in transportation and materials handling, such as containerization, RO–RO, and LASH, are enabling exporters to reach new markets.

Importers sell domestically and buy overseas, the reverse of what exporters do. Like exporters, large and small firms import. Customhouse brokers are agents who help importers to import. They bring goods through Customs but also perform other duties, such as arranging for transportation after the goods have cleared Customs. They also know what products are subject to import quotas, a nation's import regulations, and its tariff schedule.

American importers should follow these rules: (1) disclose fully to U.S. Customs all foreign financial arrangements before passing goods through Customs, as penalties for fraud are high, (2) ask the customhouse broker for advice before making the transaction, and (3) calculate carefully the landed price in advance. Customs will examine a product and determine the import category in advance on request.

QUESTIONS

1. What are the major problem areas that nonexporting firms cite as reasons for not exporting?
2. What are the common terms of sale quoted by exporters? For each, explain to what point the seller must pay all transportation and delivery costs. Where does the responsibility for loss or damage pass to the buyer?
3. What two parts of a sales agreement with a foreign representative deserve special attention?
4. *a.* Explain the various export payment terms that are available.
   b. Which two offer the most protection to the seller?
5. What is the procedure for a letter of credit transaction?
6. What government and government-assisted organizations offer assistance in export financing?
7. The manager of the international department of the Modesto Bank learns on the way to work that the ship on which a local exporter shipped some goods has sunk. The manager has received all of the documents required in the letter of credit and is ready to pay the exporter for the shipment. In view of the news about the ship, the manager now knows that the foreign customer will never receive the goods. Should the manager pay the exporter, or should he withhold payment and notify the overseas customer?
8. What is a foreign trade zone? Check with a customhouse broker or a U.S. Customs official or do some research in the library to find out the advantages of a foreign trade zone over a bonded warehouse.
9. What are the purposes of an export bill of lading?
10. Air shipments can lower inventory costs in at least three ways. What are they?
11. An importer brings plain sports shirts to this country because the import duty is lower than it is for shirts with adornments. It then sews on a figure of a fox in this country. Should the importer do this operation in a foreign trade zone?
12. How would you find sources for a product that you want to import?
13. What does a customhouse broker do?

MINICASE 16–1

State Manufacturing Export Sales Price

State Manufacturing Company, a producer of farm equipment, had just received an inquiry from a large distributor in Italy. The quantity on which the distributor wanted a price was sufficiently large that Jim Mason, the sales manager, felt he had to respond. He knew the inquiry was genuine, because he had called two of the companies that the distributor said he represented, and both had assured him that the Italian firm was a serious one. It paid its bills regularly with no problems. Both companies were selling the firm on open account terms.

Mason's problem was that he had never quoted on a sale for export before. His first impulse was to take the regular FOB factory price and add the cost of the extraheavy export packing plus the inland freight cost to the nearest U.S. port. This price should enable the company to make money if he quoted the price FAS port of exit.

However, the terms of sale were bothering him. The traffic manager had called a foreign freight forwarder to learn about the frequency of sailings to Italy, and during the conversation she had suggested to the traffic manager that she might be able to help Mason. When Mason called her, he learned that because of competition, many firms like State Manufacturing were quoting CIF foreign port as a convenience to the importer. She asked him what payment terms he would quote, and he replied that his credit manager had suggested an irrevocable, confirmed letter of credit so as to be sure of receiving payment for the sale. He admitted that the distributor, however, had asked for payment against a 90-day time draft.

The foreign freight forwarder urged Mason to consider quoting CIF port of entry in Italy with payment as requested by the distributor to be more competitive. She informed him that he could get insurance to protect the company against commercial risk. To help him calculate a CIF price, she offered to give him the various charges if he would tell her the weight and value of his shipment FOB factory. He replied that the total price was $21,500 and that the gross weight, including the container, was 3,629 kilos.

Two hours later, she called to give him the following charges:

1. Containerization	$ 200.00
2. Inland freight less handling	798.00
3. Forwarding and documentation	90.00
4. Ocean freight	2,633.00
5. Commercial risk insurance	105.00
6. Marine insurance—total of items 1–5 × 1.1 = $27,858.60 at 60¢/$100*	167.15

*Total coverage of marine insurance is commonly calculated on the basis of the total price plus 10 percent.

During that time, Mason had been thinking about the competition. Could he lower the FOB price for an export sale? He looked at the cost figures. Sales expense amounted to 20 percent of the sales price. Couldn't this be deducted on a foreign order? Research and development amounted to 10 percent. Should this be charged? Advertising and promotional expense amounted to another 10 percent. What about that? Because this was an unsolicited inquiry, there was no selling expense for this sale except for his and the secretary's time. Mason felt that it wasn't worth calculating this time.

If you were Jim Mason, how would you calculate the CIF port of entry price?

MINICASE 16–2

Morgan Guaranty Trust Company Letter of Credit

MORGAN GUARANTY TRUST COMPANY
OF NEW YORK

INTERNATIONAL BANKING DIVISION

23 WALL STREET, NEW YORK, N. Y. 10015   March 5, 19*

Smith Tool Co. Inc.
29 Bleecker Street
New York, N.Y. 10012

On all communications please refer to

NUMBER IC - 152647

Dear Sirs:

    We are instructed to advise you of the establishment by
. Bank of South America, Puerto Cabello, Venezuela . . . .
of their IRREVOCABLE Credit No. 19845 . . . .
in your favor, for the account of John Doe, Puerto Cabello, Venezuela . . . .
for U. S. $3,000.00 (THREE THOUSAND U. S. DOLLARS) . . . .
available upon presentation to us of your drafts at sight on us, accompanied by:

Commercial Invoice in triplicate, describing the merchandise as indicated below

Consular Invoice in triplicate, all signed and stamped by the Consul of Venezuela

Negotiable Insurance Policy and/or Underwriter's Certificate, endorsed in blank, covering marine and war risks

Full set of straight ocean steamer Bills of Lading, showing consignment to the Bank of South America, Puerto Cabello, stamped by Venezuelan Consul and marked "Freight Prepaid",

evidencing shipment of UNA MAQUINA DE SELLAR LATAS, C.I.F. Puerto Cabello, from United States Port to Puerto Cabello, Venezuela

> Page 6
> Advice of irrevocable letter of credit issued by
> a foreign bank in favor of a U.S. exporter and
> confirmed by Morgan Guaranty, which is
> obliged to honor drafts drawn under credit.

Except as otherwise expressly stated herein, this credit is subject to the Uniform Customs and Practice for Documentary Credits (1974 revision), International Chamber of Commerce Publication No. 290.

    The above bank engages with you that all drafts drawn under and in compliance with the terms of this advice will be duly honored if presented to our Commercial Credits Department, 15 Broad Street, New York, N. Y. 10015, on or before March 31, 19* on which date this credit expires.

    We confirm the foregoing and undertake that all drafts drawn and presented in accordance with its terms will be duly honored.

                    Yours very truly,

                    Authorized Signature

Immediately upon receipt, please examine this instrument and if its terms are not clear to you or if you need any assistance in respect to your availment of it, we would welcome your communicating with us. Documents should be presented promptly and not later than 3 P.M.

1. Who issued the letter of credit?
2. Is it irrevocable?
3. Has it been confirmed?
4. If so, by whom?
5. Who is the buyer?
6. Who is the seller?
7. What kind of draft is to be presented?
8. What documents are required?
9. What are the terms of sale?
10. When does the letter of credit expire?
11. Where does the seller go for payment?
12. Who pays the freight?
13. Who pays the marine insurance?
14. Must the steamship company attest that the merchandise has been loaded on ship?
15. What is the reason for your answer to question 14?

MINICASE 16–3

Eckerd Manufacturing

Eckerd Manufacturing Company is a Los Angeles firm that sells pool tables and accessories in the United States and in various world markets. To be competitive pricewise, the firm sources the components worldwide. For example, it imports slate for the tables from Sicily, rubber bumpers from Taiwan, pool balls from Africa, and wood from Brazil. The tables are assembled in the Los Angeles plant. About half of the company's sales are for export.

Shirley Thomas, Eckerd's president, is searching for ways to lower the costs of the tables. She does apply for drawbacks on the duty that the company pays for imported components that are incorporated into the exported tables. However, she has to wait for these Customs rebates, which amount to 90 percent of all duties paid. Interestingly, the import duty on a finished pool table is less than the sum of the duties on all the components.

Based on what you have learned from Chapter 16, what do you recommend?

SUPPLEMENTARY READINGS

Export assistance

"District Export Councils." *Business America*, April 24, 1989, pp. 2–6.

Exporters' Guide to Federal Resources for Small Business. Rev. ed. Washington, D.C.: Interagency Task Force on Trade, 1988.

"Small Business: Obstacles to Exporting." *Business America*, May 8, 1989, pp. 5–11.

Export assistance, U.S. Department of Commerce

"Be Ready for 1992—Export to EUROPE NOW." *Business America*, August 1, 1988, pp. 14–16.

"Commerce Program Matches Foreign Buyers with Suppliers and Exhibitors at U.S. Shows." *Business America*, May 23, 1988, p. 20.

"Learning the Ropes." *INC*, August 1988, pp. 103–6.

"TOP Program Helps U.S. Firms Tap Foreign Markets." *Business America*, February 27, 1989, pp. 12–13.

Export licensing and control

"Export Enforcement Secures America's Technology." *Business America*, February 29, 1988, pp. 22–24.

"Export Licensing from A to Z." *Business America*, February 29, 1988. pp. 12–15.

"ITA's Export Control Automated Support System Cuts down Processing Time for Export Licenses." *Business America*, July 6, 1987, p. 6.

"The Electronic Age of Export Licensing." *Business America*, February 29, 1988, pp. 7–10.

"The New Bureau of Export Administration." *Business America*, February 29, 1988, pp. 3–6.

"Worldwide Survey of Trade Conditions." *Business International Money Report*, May 1987, pp. 158–59. It includes export and import controls.

Exporting, general

A Basic Guide to Exporting. Washington, D.C.: U.S. Department of Commerce, 1986.

"A Step-by-Step Approach to Market Research." *Business America*, March 16, 1987, pp. 4–5.

Axinn, Catherine N. "Export Performance: Do Managerial Perceptions Make a Difference?" *International Marketing Review*, Summer 1988, pp. 61–71.

"Export Strategies." *Small Business Reports*, May 1989, pp. 20–27.

"Good Follow-Up Is Vital to Export Success." *Business America*, October 26, 1987, pp. 14–17.

"How to Prepare Your Product for Export." *Business America,* May 25, 1987, pp. 10–11.

"The CEO's Role in a Successful Export Strategy." *Small Business Reports,* May 1989, pp. 28–32.

"The New Export Entrepreneurs." *Fortune,* June 6, 1988, pp. 89–102.

Importing

"Importing for Exporters." *Distribution,* October 1982, pp. 95–108.

Importing into the United States. Washington, D.C.: Department of the Treasury, 1986.

"New Tariff Code Streamlines Global Trading System." *Business America,* November 23, 1987, pp. 2–5.

Payments and financing

"Eximbank, TDP, and OPIC Are Active in South America." *Business America,* June 5, 1989, pp. 16–20.

"Letting Go of the L/C Security Blanket." *Northeast International Business,* September 1988, p. 12.

"The New and Improved Eximbank." *Small Business Reports,* November 1988, pp. 30–33.

ENDNOTES

1. Telephone conversation on June 19, 1989, with Al Chambers, Ford International.

2. "Export Strategies," *Small Business Reports,* May 1989, p. 20.

3. Wendell McCulloch, Jr., *American Exports: Why Have They Lagged?* (Washington, D.C.: Joint Economic Committee, Congress of the United States, May 14, 1985).

4. "U.S. Trade Facts," *Business America,* May 22, 1989, p. 12.

5. "Be Ready for 1992," *Business America,* August 1, 1988, pp. 14–16.

6. "States See Exports as a Tool for Local Business Expansion," *Business America,* February 27, 1989, pp. 7–11.

7. These and other terms have been codified in *INCO-TERMS, 1980* by the International Chamber of Commerce and in *Revised American Foreign Trade Definition—1941,* which has been adopted by the U.S. Chamber of Commerce, the National Council of American Exporters, and the National Foreign Trade Council. The point at which title and risk pass from the seller to the buyer is specified, as are the duties of each party.

8. "Other Federal Export Assistance," *Business America,* May 22, 1989, p. 18.

9. *A Basic Guide to Exporting* (Washington, D.C.: U.S. Department of Commerce, 1988), p. 56.

10. "Export Enforcement Secures America's Technology," *Business America,* February 29, 1988, pp. 22–23.

11. "Transaction Value," *Importing into the United States* (Washington, D.C.: U.S. Department of the Treasury, 1986), pp. 34–35.

Chapter 17

East-West Relations

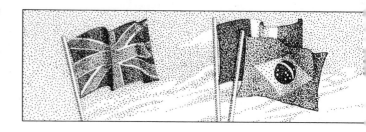

Soviet bottom line is that few people know what one is.

The Wall Street Journal, February 5, 1989, headline for an article about a new business school in the Soviet Union

One source told me that only 18 percent of the 30,000 students who have gone abroad to study have returned, thus producing a "brain drain" of China's best and brightest.

David L. Shambaugh, "Commentary," The Asian Wall Street Journal, January 18, 1988

LEARNING OBJECTIVES

In this chapter, you will study:

1. What countries are meant when you read or hear about "East-West relations."
2. The meaning of "centrally planned economy."
3. Why the People's Republic of China (PRC), with its huge population, has never become a large consumer market.
4. Why the United States and the PRC began to trade in the 1970s and recognized each other in 1979.
5. What the East wants most from the West.
6. Why the East cannot afford to pay for all its wants.
7. The bureaucratic labyrinth through which you must find your way in order to sell to the East.
8. Glasnost and perestroika.
9. Some departures by the PRC from the usual practices of the East in its dealings with the West.
10. How the East has paid and is trying to pay for imports from the West.
11. Common objections in the West to goods and services from the East.
12. Why some of those objections can probably be overcome, and why that process may make the other objections stronger and more forceful.
13. Some differences between the East and the West in the concepts of costs in determining how to price a product.
14. Changes occurring in the East.

KEY WORDS AND CONCEPTS

- Centrally planned economy
- East-West trade
- Joint venture
- Countertrade
- Dumping
- Glasnost
- Perestroika

BUSINESS INCIDENT

Joint ventures (JVs) between Soviet agencies and Western companies are favored by the Soviet government. The first American company to sign a JV surprised some people. Trenton, New Jersey, is Moscow's U.S. sister city, and in 1987 the mayor of the Lenin district of Moscow visited Trenton. While there, he sampled the pizzas of Roma Food Enterprises and immediately invited Roma's president, Louis Piancone, to visit Moscow and discuss a JV.

When Mr. Piancone got to Moscow, he encountered skepticism about the ability of Roma, which had never done export business, to handle the logistics of operating successfully in the world's biggest nation. The turning point came when an interpreter asked Mr. Piancone whether he had seen the world's largest pizza on television a few days earlier. "See it? I made it," he responded. When the Soviet negotiators realized Roma was the creator of a 15-ton pizza, they stood up and saluted, and a JV agreement was signed in short order.

Now Roma's Pizza van cruises Moscow, selling about 6,000 slices a day. The company plans to open 25 Italian restaurants in the Soviet Union by 1993.

Source: Patricia A. Dreyfus, "Negotiating the Kremlin Maze," *Business Month*, November 1988, pp. 55–63.

"**E**ast is east and west is west and never the twain shall meet" was not accurate when Rudyard Kipling wrote it, and it is even less correct today. Of course, *collide* may be a better verb than *meet* because the economic and political systems of the two groups are so different. We shall examine some most interesting economic and political changes currently being attempted in the People's Republic of China (PRC) and the Soviet Union.

We shall identify the countries of the West and the East and look very briefly at the background of their relationships. East Germany and the People's Republic of China are being treated differently by West Germany and the United States, and we shall show how.

Dumping by the East on markets of the West is not easily proved. We shall see why. Other East-West problems involve the competition of products from the East with products from LDCs with which West countries have historic relationships. Moreover, overhanging the entire subject of East-West trade are East-West political relations, which fluctuate between areas and times of détente to areas and times of shooting wars.

THE EAST COUNTRIES

"East," as used in this chapter, includes the centrally planned economies of the Union of Soviet Socialist Republics (USSR), its East European satellites (Poland, East Germany, Czechoslovakia, Hungary, Romania, and Bulgaria), and its other satellites, such as Cuba, Ethiopia, South Yemen, and Vietnam. It also includes Yugoslavia and the People's Republic of China (PRC), which occupies mainland China and is to be differentiated from the Republic of China, which occupies Taiwan.

centrally planned economies the government owns all the important factors of production and dictates how much of each product will be made

In the preceding paragraph, we spoke of **centrally planned economies**. In countries with such economies, the central, national government decides how much of what product will be made during each year or other planning period, such as a five-year plan. Yugoslavia—and, to a growing extent, the PRC—the USSR, and some of its Eastern European satellites have delegated some decision making to industries or factories. Historically in centrally planned economies, all major factors of production have been owned and controlled by the government, but changes are occurring. The PRC, USSR, and some other communist countries have begun to permit foreign companies to own parts of joint ventures (JVs). The PRC has gone even farther by permitting its own people to buy shares of Chinese companies. The labor factor is controlled, as the unions are essentially government agencies and workers must obtain government approval to move from one area or job to another.

THE WEST COUNTRIES

"West," as used here, includes the industrial countries of Western Europe and North America plus Japan and such other countries as Australia and New Zealand. For practical purposes, the Western countries are members of the Organization for Economic Cooperation and Development (OECD).

■ **TABLE 17–1**
OECD Exports to
Centrally Planned
Economies (US$ millions)

	1978	1979	1980	1981	1982	1983	1984	1985	1986	1987
USSR	$ 5,316	$ 6,399	$2,066	$2,025	$1,899	$1,871	$1,825	$1,748	$1,716	$1,746
East Germany	514	799	175	182	143	165	149	123	159	212
Poland	1,952	2,022	466	300	270	241	246	260	281	328
Czechoslovakia	806	922	267	227	179	162	158	181	228	276
Hungary	1,037	996	234	207	239	216	210	235	289	325
Romania	1,049	1,262	288	295	139	108	116	119	137	108
Bulgaria	386	413	82	71	129	130	122	153	183	195
China (PRC)	2,529	3,362	732	890	894	978	1,288	2,050	1,868	1,809
Total	$13,589	$16,175	$4,310	$4,197	$3,892	$3,871	$4,114	$4,869	$4,861	$4,999

Source: *Foreign Trade Monthly Bulletin* (Paris: Organizations for Economic Cooperation and Development), October 1980, October 1982, July 1986; and OECD, *Monthly Statistics of Foreign Trade,* September 1988.

EAST-WEST ECONOMIC RELATIONS

Prior to World War I and again in the 1920s and 30s, many American companies played important roles in the economic development of the USSR. During World War II (WW II), hundreds of American suppliers provided billions of dollars' worth of goods and services to the USSR.[1]

Following WW II, the hostilities of the Cold War succeeded the WW II alliance, and **East-West trade** dropped sharply. Even though it revived considerably in the 1960s and 70s, it has still not achieved the percentages of pre-WW II 1938. Then, East-West trade accounted for 74 percent of the total trade of Eastern countries and for 9.5 percent of that of Western countries. In 1987, 49 years later, Eastern countries' trade with the West was only 30 percent of their total trade, and Western countries' trade with the East was less than 3 percent of their total trade.

Tables 17–1 and 17–2 show the growth of trade between the OECD countries and those with centrally planned economies between 1976 and 1985.

East-West trade trade between the countries of the East and those of the West, as they have been identified above.

West Germany–East Trade

Even though East Germany is one of the economically strongest countries in Eastern Europe, you will observe that its trade figures in Tables 17–1 and 17–2 are relatively small. This is because its major Western trading partner, West Germany, considers trade with East Germany to be domestic, not foreign, trade and therefore does not report the large amounts involved as exports and imports.

West Germany is the largest trading partner of the Soviet-bloc countries, whose trading organization is called Comecon (Council for Mutual Economic Assistance), but some of Comecon's share of the West German market is being taken by the four Asian "tigers": Hong Kong, the Republic of China (Taiwan), Singapore, and South Korea. Comecon (minus East Germany) provided only 3.6 percent of West German imports in 1988, compared to 5.1 percent in 1985. Comecon's sales of machinery and other manufactured products have

■ **TABLE 17-2**
OECD Imports from Centrally Planned Economies (US$ millions)

	1978	1979	1980	1981	1982	1983	1984	1985	1986	1987
USSR	$ 4,853	$ 6,681	$1,800	$1,853	$2,175	$2,079	$2,161	$1,922	$1,696	$1,906
East Germany	485	545	208	207	198	202	194	193	206	216
Poland	1,489	1,705	542	381	278	275	332	327	352	410
Czechoslovakia	752	920	247	198	222	218	226	220	258	291
Hungary	655	1,767	273	266	188	194	212	217	249	307
Romania	808	1,084	326	246	215	231	309	288	299	338
Bulgaria	188	307	134	155	87	61	62	59	62	63
China (PRC)	1,383	2,013	1,107	1,065	1,898	875	1,041	1,195	1,320	1,793
Total	$10,613	$15,022	$4,371	$4,371	$4,261	$4,135	$4,537	$4,421	$4,442	$5,324

Source: *Foreign Trade Monthly Bulletin* (Paris: Organizations for Economic Cooperation and Development), October 1980, October 1982, July 1986, and July 1988.

fallen steadily in recent years, while the "tigers" are carving a West German market for their industrial wares.[2]

The People's Republic of China (PRC)

Often, images of trade with the PRC do not represent reality: The myth of the China market has persisted although consumer demand has never approached Western expectations. China, an agrarian nation, has always been desperately poor, surviving on a subsistence level except for a tiny wealthy elite. The Confucian class has now been replaced by the elitist Communist party.

After the communist armies forced the Nationalist forces off the mainland to Taiwan in 1949, American contacts with the mainland were almost nonexistent until 1970. By then the PRC leadership had apparently embarked on a fundamental reappraisal of policies that included a new perception of the military threat posed by the USSR.

During the early 1970s, the United States was winding down its Vietnam involvement while observing the USSR's growing military might. Both the PRC and the United States perceived each other as counterweights against the USSR, and they began political and trade relations based on mutual political advantage. In the matter of trade, the success of the changed relationship can be seen by comparing the U.S.–PRC trade figure of 1971, which was $4.9 million, to that of 1988, when the amount had grown to over $8 billion.

The PRC's trade with the world has undergone large swings, as illustrated by Table 17-3.

U.S. Trade with the East Other than the PRC

For a number of reasons, primarily political, the United States lagged behind Canada, Japan, and Western Europe in trade with the East. Despite a late start, however, U.S. trade with the East grew through 1979, as shown in Table 17-4.

Large consumer product sales to the East are unlikely, but the East is anxious to acquire Western technology and capital goods. Politics and bureaucracies permitting, these product areas represent huge market opportunities.

**■ TABLE 17–3
PRC Trade Figures
(US $ billions)**

	1979	1980	1981	1982	1983	1984	1985	1986	1987
Exports	$ 13.6	$ 18.1	$ 21.5	$ 21.9	$ 22.2	$ 24.8	$ 27.3	$ 30.9	$ 39.2
Imports	15.6	19.9	21.6	18.9	21.3	26.0	42.5	42.9	39.0
Balance	−2	−1.8	−0.1	+3.0	+0.9	−1.2	−15.2	−12.0	+0.2

Since 1984, devaluation of the renminbi (the PRC's currency) has gradually inflated U.S. dollar values by about 26%. In adjusted comparable terms, the figures would be approximately:

	1984	1985	1986	1987
Exports	$ 24.8	$ 24.0	$ 23.0	$ 32.6
Imports	26.0	37.0	32.0	31.1
Balance	−1.2	−13.0	−9.0	+1.5

Source: PRC Ministry of Foreign Relations and Trade, as quoted in Asian Development Bank's *Key Indicators*, July 1988.

**■ TABLE 17–4
U.S. Trade with
Communist Countries,
Excluding China (PRC),
Exports and Imports
(US $ millions)**

Country	1981	1982	1983	1984	1985	1986	1987
Total trade							
United States	$4,953	$4,248	$3,843	$5,977	$4,843	$3,786	$3,749
Albania	11	20	8	12	16	9	5
Bulgaria	295	137	96	75	143	158	136
Czechoslovakia	156	152	127	154	148	186	143
Germany	348	282	203	304	175	144	140
Hungary	218	213	282	330	336	345	400
Romania	1,116	604	749	1,218	1,159	1,090	975
USSR	2,809	2,840	2,378	3,884	2,866	1,854	1,950
Exports							
United States	3,657	3,315	2,567	3,869	2,978	1,840	1,961
Albania	6	17	4	9	12	5	3
Bulgaria	258	106	66	44	104	97	89
Czechoslovakia	83	84	59	58	63	93	57
Germany	296	223	139	137	73	48	44
Hungary	78	68	110	88	95	98	95
Romania	504	224	186	249	208	251	193
USSR	2,432	2,593	2,003	3,284	2,423	1,248	1,480
Imports							
United States	1,296	933	1,276	2,108	1,865	1,946	1,788
Albania	5	3	4	3	4	4	2
Bulgaria	37	31	30	31	39	61	47
Czechoslovakia	73	68	68	96	85	93	86
Germany	52	59	64	167	102	96	96
Hungary	140	145	172	242	241	247	305
Romania	612	380	563	969	951	839	782
USSR	377	247	375	600	443	606	470

Source: IMF, *Direction of Trade Statistics Yearbook*, 1988, p. 134.

Political tensions and U.S.—Soviet trade.   After a decade of rapid growth, U.S. exports of nonfarm goods to the Soviet Union hit a peak of over $700 million in 1979, and agricultural shipments reached $2.9 billion. After the Afghanistan assault in December 1979 and the tensions over unrest in Poland and Nicaragua, the U.S. government revoked and denied export licenses to Russia. In 1980, nonfarm exports slid to $313 million, and grain and other farm sales totaled only $1.2 billion. The American embargo on sales to the Soviet Union was lifted in 1981, and, as Table 17—4 illustrates, U.S. exports to that country revived, reaching over $2.5 billion by 1986. Something else you can note from Table 17—4 is that although both exports and imports to and from the Soviets declined dramatically in 1981, trade with the other Comecon countries seemed little affected by the Soviet—U.S. tensions.

Intra Comecon and Comecon-West trade.   East-West trade faltered in 1985. While the volume of world trade grew 6 percent in 1985, the trade of the West with the Comecon countries fell 5 percent, and that drop occurred before the gentle slide in oil prices became a tumble in 1986. Fuel accounts for nearly 30 percent of Soviet exports and 25 percent of East European exports. The growth in the value of the East's oil exports disguised the lackluster performance of East-West trade during the 1975—85 decade.

During the 1980s, efforts were made to make Comecon more self-sufficient and to encourage intraComecon trade. Some success was realized in the early 1980s as Western capital goods suppliers' share of the market fell to 36 percent from the 46 percent share they had enjoyed in 1975. And, at a summer 1988 Comecon summit meeting in Prague, Czechoslovakia, the lofty goal of "a unified market in the long term" was set.

To some observers, both inside and outside Comecon, it looks as if the term will be very long. The drop in the world price of oil, gas, and raw materials exposed the weakness of Comecon's archaic barter trading system. Moscow sends its allies fuel in return for Eastern European industrial goods, and lower world commodity prices have cut the quantity of industrial products Moscow can import. That is because the outside world prices are used as a measure of the value of the commodities the Soviets export to East Europe. In turn, that is because there is no convertible Comecon currency, and there are no meaningful market prices.

Dr. Alexander Bykov, deputy head of the World Socialist System in Moscow, says, "We say we want some kind of common market." But he feels they are doomed to failure without the reform of each country's price system and elimination of their endemic shortage of consumer goods.

Mikhail Gorbachev, General Secretary of the Communist Party and the Soviets' leader, has expressed his desire for closer integration with the Western economic system; and it is becoming clearer that many Comecon partners are unenthusiastic about trading with one another and would prefer Western trade partners. Two high obstacles to achieving such partnerships are the East's chronic shortage of convertible Western currencies and the East's inability to earn much of those currencies due to the noncompetitive quality of their industrial products. Dr. Bykov speaks of the "rubbish" Comecon countries sell to each other. Gird Biro, director general of the Hungarian Chamber of Commerce, described the vicious circle in which Hungarian producers dependent on the Soviet market were seldom able to produce competitive products for sale in the West.[3] Later in this chapter, we shall discuss Comecon's joint venture efforts to overcome these obstacles.

HOW TO SELL TO THE EAST

Selling to the East is not easy. The institutions, trading techniques, and behavior of the East in international trade are quite different than those of the West. This results from the centrally planned economies common to all the countries of the East. We shall look at the practices of the USSR; those of the other East countries are very similar.

Steps in East Countries' Purchasing Procedures

The decision on what to buy and whether to buy from a Western company is made by government agencies. Assume the desired product is petroleum-production equipment. An agency called the Gosplan is central to all Soviet procurement, and all procurement goes through it. The Soviet oil production agency informs Gosplan about the type and amount of equipment it wants to acquire. Thereupon, the procurement steps are: (1) The Gosplan, through the Ministry of Petroleum, consults various technical, research, and production organizations to determine specifications, requirements, and availability in the USSR or Comecon. If not available there, the equipment will be compared with other projects competing for scarce foreign convertible currency. At the same time, Gosplan and other ministries would be preparing a plan for export or other means to finance the desired import. (2) When all of that has been accomplished, the Ministry of Petroleum and Gosplan send a purchase order to the foreign trade organization (FTO) specializing in petroleum-production equipment. (3) That FTO consults with the Ministry of Petroleum on technical specifications. (4) The FTO solicits bids. (5) A non-Comecon company submits a proposal. (Of course, there may be competition between two or more bidders.) (6) The FTO, in consultation with the Ministry of Petroleum, prepares a contract. (7) The FTO and the non-Comecon supplier conclude a contract. (8) If a letter of credit is used, the Vneshtorgbank (Bank of Foreign Trade) opens a letter, usually with the suppliers' bank. (9) The equipment is delivered. (10) Documents, such as bill of lading, insurance, and inspection certificates, are sent to Vneshtorgbank. (11) The supplier is paid.

Will the System Be Simplified?

In 1986, Gorbachev began making changes in the Soviet trade bureaucracies. Some of the FTOs lost their monopoly, and some individual enterprises were given the right to deal directly with foreigners. In 1988, the government abolished the all-powerful Ministry of Foreign Trade, a move that was heralded as the cornerstone of reform.

The results were confusion instead of simplification. The enterprise managers were not prepared for their new responsibilities, and, partly as a result, government ministries have continued to impose binding instructions in the form of state orders covering up to (and sometimes more than) 100 percent of factories' output.[4]

The confusion is not only on the Soviets' side. Byzantine as it was, the pre-Gorbachev system of Soviet procurement had been learned by foreigners

■ FIGURE 17–1
East-West Broker

selling to the USSR, and the foreign suppliers had come to know the Soviet bureaucrats who ran the system. Now the suppliers have to learn a new system and deal with different people.

To bridge this confusion gap, a growing number of firms are offering to act as go-betweens. (See the advertisement for one such firm in Figure 17–1.) These are Western companies that have traded in the USSR, and there is at least one Soviet private consulting company, FAKT, offering its services. A

West German company, Varioline, and the accounting firm, Ernst & Young, linked up with a Soviet-Finnish company to get into the business. One rather unique entry in the field is Aldriedge & Miller, Inc., a company formed by two American women with long experience working in the USSR.[5]

How Western Companies Sell to the East

Completing the procedures listed above is usually extremely time consuming and complex. How do Western companies sell in the East? A minority of Western companies open and maintain representative offices in Moscow or some other city. Most Western companies utilize the services of companies that specialize in dealing with the East, such as Satra Corporation or Tower International, Inc. These companies have dealt in many sorts of products and services, including chrome, steel, grain, shoes, hotels, and soybean mills. Their clients have included such major firms as IBM, Borg-Warner, Caterpillar Tractor, and USX.

There are at least two other methods of selling to the East—trade fairs and personal visits.

Trade fairs.   Exhibits at fairs are important ways for Western companies to reach potential customers in both Eastern Europe and the People's Republic of China. Attendance at the Chinese fairs is by invitation only, and if you are not invited, it is unlikely that you can sell your product to the PRC. However, when a new exhibition is started, the Chinese may advertise it and offer to put your name on a mailing list. An example is the "China Develops" advertisement reproduced in Figure 17–2.

Common sense should probably indicate what to do and what not to do when your company has a stand at a trade fair. However, there have apparently been some unfortunate departures from common sense, so two UN officials have drawn up a checklist for "Manning a Trade Fair Stand." It is reproduced as Figure 17–3.

Personal visits.   Personal contacts are important, and when you are trying to sell products to the Chinese, Soviet, or East European governments, you should not rely too much on correspondence. Personal business visits to Moscow or other capitals, as appropriate, are almost always necessary if you hope to make sales. However, travel in China and Eastern Europe is expensive and not many sales are made, so a trip should not be made without some combination of the following conditions: (1) company personnel can meet key government officials; (2) the company is contemplating a long-term sales campaign or is at a crucial negotiating point near the end of a campaign; or (3) the volume and profitability of a potential sale warrants the trip.

The Chinese customer wants to scrutinize the Western executives personally and make assessments of their trustworthiness and goodwill. The Chinese want to feel they are dealing with a friend who will play fair and make possible a comfortable, long-term relationship.

Hugh P. Donaghue, vice president of Control Data Corporation, visited China carrying three large boxes stuffed with product brochures and other literature, which he expected to hand to his Chinese hosts at the first meeting. It didn't work that way. They first asked him about his philosophy of life and then about Control Data's business philosophy. For 10 days, they talked about all sorts of

■ FIGURE 17–2
Chinese Trade Fair

CHINA DEVELOPS 1

中國建築工程材料及設備技術交流展覽會
THE 1st INTERNATIONAL CONSTRUCTION MACHINERY & MATERIALS EXHIBITIONS & TECHNICAL EXCHANGE
at
GUANGZHOU, CHINA
from 8th July, 1980.
sponsored by
The Architectural Society of China & its Kwangtung & Guangzhou Chapter
&
Asian Consortium Exhibitions Limited

Scope of Exhibition:

- Building and Construction Machinery & Material
- New Building Methods, Systems and Knowhow
- Instrumentation for Detection and Survey
- Computer Application
- Cleansing and Maintenance and Protection Technology

Technical Exchange:

Exhibitors are required in principle to present their technology and products either on academic and commercial basis.

Rental:

- Indoor from U.S. $36.00 / sq. ft.
- Outdoor from U.S. $10.00 / sq. ft.
- Auxiliary charge of U.S. $20.00 / sq. ft.

For services rendered and expenses incurred by the organizers for arrangement of visa, publicity in China, customs, moving of exhibits, arrangements for translations, lighting & security etc.

Application to participate now open

Please telex or cable for application form and information:

Hongkong Office:
Telex: 73643 DORCE HX
Cable: ASIANSHOW

Asian Consortium Exhibitions Limited.
13th Floor, Stanhopa House, 734, King's Road, Hong Kong.

NOTE: *To prevent crowded lines, please telex during off office hours.*

1981-1982
Our other exhibitions and technical exchange in the near future in the field of:

- Production Machinery and Light Industries
- Electronics and Appliances
- Petroleum and Exploration
- Chemicals
- Textile
- Tourism and Hotel Supplies

If you wish us to retain your name in our mailing list,
please telex after 1st March, 1980 or write to us.

Source: *Los Angeles Times,* March 13, 1980, part 4, p. 7. Reproduced with permission of the publisher.

subjects except Control Data products. Finally, as Donaghue was about ready to carry the three boxes home still full, the Chinese finally asked him what he had to sell. Control Data made sales and has been doing increased business with China.

In Moscow and in Washington, the U.S. government has information for American businesses trying to sell in the USSR. It also has assistance for firms that want to enter the PRC market.

■ **FIGURE 17–3**
Manning a Trade Fair Stand

1. Company representatives should be knowledgeable about the company and its products, empowered to conduct business negotiations, and clear on its objectives in exhibiting.

2. Never ignore a visitor to your stand.

3. Approach visitors who seem interested in your display; do not wait for them to approach you.

4. Look interested. Do not sit about chatting with your colleagues. Do not position yourself so as to hide your products or to block access to them.

5. Start the conversation with a positive remark about your product or a question that will generate a discussion.

6. Identify as quickly as possible the visitor's business and specific interest and his importance as a prospect. Always keep your objective in mind.

7. Answer all questions as forthrightly and factually as possible.

8. Remember to sell your company as well as your products, and relate your remarks to the visitor's interests.

9. Use the conversation to elicit information about the market and reactions to your products.

10. Carry negotiations as far forward as you are empowered to, if you are convinced the visitor represents a solid prospect.

11. Use inquiry forms and supplementary notes to record details about the visitor's company, his interests, and follow-up action to be taken.

12. Allow time after the fair closes to continue important discussions.

13. Provide promised information as soon as possible.

14. Observe fair hours, and never leave your exhibit unattended.

15. Use slack periods to make contacts at other stands, provided your own is manned.

Source: Umphon Phanachet and Zhang Huixiang, *Guidebook on Trading with the People's Republic of China* (Trade Promotion Centre of ESCAP, 1982), p. 33.

As foreign companies have sold or tried to sell to the PRC over recent years, much experience has been acquired, and some checklists have been developed. One list is suggested by Ronald Wombolt, vice president and director of international operations of John Fluke Manufacturing Company, an American producer of electronic test and measurement instrumentation. Wombolt's checklist is:

> Do not always offer your most favorable price up front. The Chinese want to bargain and negotiate.
>
> Do not, without good cause, insist on selling on letter of credit terms. The Chinese are usually prompt payers.
>
> Do not make any statement you can't back up, because the Chinese record everything you say in negotiating sessions.
>
> Do not offer or accept any terms or conditions that you will not want in future transactions. Although the Chinese will constantly ask for something "this time only," it means every time.
>
> Offer training in China and abroad.
>
> Maintain a consistent pricing policy.
>
> To follow the rules listed above, have the same group in your company deal with the Chinese over time, at least one of whom understands the language.[6]

Information from the U.S. and PRC governments. The U.S. Commercial Office in Moscow is available to U.S. companies wishing to sell to the USSR. Interested firms can contact the Trade Promotion Division, Bureau of

■ **FIGURE 17–4**
Practical Information on Doing Business with the Soviet Union

Prepared by: USSR Division, Room 3414, International Trade Administration, U.S. Department of Commerce, Washington, D.C. 20230 (202) 377–4655

Source: U.S. Department of Commerce, International Trade Administration, April 1989.

East-West Trade, U.S. Department of Commerce, Washington, D.C. 20230, or the U.S. Commercial Office, U.S. Department of State–Moscow, Washington, D.C. 20520.

In April 1989, the U.S. Department of Commerce published the pamphlet "Doing Business with the USSR." It can be obtained from the U.S. Government Printing Office in Washington. To give you some idea of the type of information contained in the pamphlet, its contents page is reproduced as Figure 17–4.

In recognition of the bureaucratic, linguistic, and cultural difficulties for Americans attempting to sell in the PRC market, the Chinese government set up its first U.S. trade promotion office in Los Angeles in 1986. It is called the China–U.S. Trading Corporation, and it is operated by the Foreign Enterprises Services Corporation (FESCO), a government agency.

FESCO has helped guide several American companies into the PRC market. One of these companies, Bank of America Check Corporation, the traveler's check arm of Bank of America, has opened 40 outlets in China. Another company, International Matex Tank Terminals, a New Orleans-based builder of liquid bulk terminals, had fallen afoul of the PRC bureaucratic maze. FESCO stepped in to help it through the maze.[7]

Self-help. In 1989 a Soviet Trade Directory became available. It contains addresses of industrial branches of Soviet enterprises and information on how to make direct contact with factory managers and engineers. Addresses from which it may be ordered in several countries can be seen in an ad for the directory shown in Figure 17–5.

■ **FIGURE 17–5**
Soviet Trade Assistance

SOVIET TRADE DIRECTORY
Direct Contact with Soviet
Factory Managers and Engineers!

Soviet Trade Directory contains approximately 25,000 addresses of Soviet enterprises, all industrial branches, with relevant information.
£300.00 (Registered postage and packing included). This Directory is not available through book distributors or public libraries. All copies are numbered.

SOVIET TRADE DIRECTORY
can be ordered at the following addresses:
MOSCOW: The British-Soviet Chamber of Commerce, World Trade Centre, Office 1904, Krasnopresnenskaya Nab. 12, Moscow 123601. Telephone: 253 8263.
or
Information Moscow, Leninsky Pr.45 Kv.426, Moscow 117334
Telephone: 591 0479, 135 1164
TOKYO: Junnosuke Katayama, Iwato-Minami, 2-5-1-303, Komae-shi, Tokyo, 201.
PARIS: Maison du Livre Etranger, 9, Rue de l'Eperon, 75006 Paris,
Telephone: 43.26.10.60.
Compte cheque postal Paris 966-94 H sinon cheque bancaire à l'ordre de Maison du Livre Etranger.
MUNICH: Kubon & Sagner, Muenchen, 34, Hessstrasse 39/41,
Telephone: 089 522 027.
LONDON: The British-Soviet Chamber of Commerce, 2, Lowndes Street, London SW1X 9ET.
Telephone: 01 235 2423,
or direct from the publishers:
FLEGON PRESS,
37B, New Cavendish St. London W1M 8JR, Tel: 487-5348

A CAPITALIST PEOPLE'S REPUBLIC OF CHINA?

Although the PRC bureaucratic maze is probably second to none, some developments are now under way that would have shocked Chairman Mao.* The PRC is admitting foreign, private ownership of production facilities within the country, flirting with corporate stock issues, and investing abroad.

Joint Ventures (JVs)

joint venture (as used in this chapter) a West firm operating in an East country in some form of cooperation with an agency of the East country government

In 1979, the PRC published a **joint venture** law, and companies came from America, Europe, Japan, and elsewhere to try the Chinese market. At first the influx was slow due to vagaries in the law, so the Chinese released an implementing act in 1983 to clarify the law, and more foreign firms moved in.

JV difficulties in the PRC.   Although some 666 joint ventures were in place by 1986, the difficulties for foreigners operating in the PRC caused some failures, losses, and low-profit or low-quality products. As a result, the first nine months of 1986 saw a 40 percent decline in foreign investments. This so concerned the government that it began giving seminars featuring successful joint ventures. The profitable foreign venturers told others how they had done it. Some of the keys are:

Insist on the right to hire and fire employees and to reward good workers with bonuses or otherwise.

* Mao Tse-tung was the absolute dictator of the PRC until his death in 1976.

Establish good training programs.

Choose the right location even if the costs are higher.

Obtain the support of local as well as Beijing authorities.

Be prepared to invest in infrastructure, such as power cables and water pipes.

Keep quality standards high.

Establish reliable foreign suppliers, because PRC sources may be unreliable.

The best technology isn't necessarily the most advanced; the technology should be easy to learn and maintain.[8]

Specific difficulties for the foreign firm in a PRC JV include getting out profits or interest in convertible currency, finding qualified employees, and, even more difficult, firing employees. Both types of problems can be ameliorated by making clear, detailed agreements with the Chinese JV partner before investing. It is extremely important for these agreements to be approved by the highest appropriate PRC government agency; the Chinese partner—or local bureaucrats—may have inflated notions of their own power and fail to consult their superiors.[9]

The PRC is given to sudden policy shifts and zigzags, which make business management very difficult. In October 1988, China abruptly adopted stiff measures to slow economic growth, including import restrictions and a credit squeeze. JVs that needed some foreign source components and those that needed operating capital from PRC banks—which is virtually all of them— suffered.[10]

Corporate Stock

In 1983, the PRC authorized three enterprises to raise money by selling stock to private buyers. Many residents of the country, plus overseas Chinese and others, are potential buyers, but there are obstacles to the widespread, successful use of stock sales to raise capital for Chinese companies. Diehard communist cadres have to be convinced that stock issues are just a means of raising money and do not mean the PRC is giving up communism. Managers have to learn to report to a board of directors and be answerable to shareholders. The legal status of stock companies needs to be established in the PRC, and the mechanics of issuing and trading securities must be learned. Officials at the Bank of China's overseas branches and its 12 affiliates are probably ready to assist with the procedural problems.[11]

Until September 1986, there was no formal, legal method to trade the securities. Then, for the first time since the communists came to power in 1949, the government authorized the establishment of a stock and bond exchange, in Shanghai. Public interest and trading are growing, but there is opposition. A number of Communist party faithful complain that a stock exchange is capitalist. The banks complain that people withdraw their deposits to buy securities.[12]

It must be recognized that the PRC is engaged in a unique, historic experiment. It is attempting to liberalize the economy, and even to permit private ownership and operation of farms and factories, while maintaining rigid communist party control of the country.

Political Backlashes

The liberalization movement has been led by Deng Xiaoping, who was 85 years old in 1989, and many wonder whether his moderate, pragmatic policies will continue after his death or retirement. The American State Department feels there are enough like-minded leaders behind Deng to prevent reversal of his policies. However, others remember the "let a thousand flowers bloom" era under Mao Tse-tung. Mao encouraged playrights, poets, and writers to speak out without fear of government reprisal. Quite a number of people took him at his word, and there was an outpouring of works that could not have been published previously. Suddenly, Mao changed his mind and his policy. The people who had spoken out were imprisoned, sent to labor gangs, or otherwise punished.

During 1986, Chinese students from a dozen campuses began to march and demonstrate for political democracy, which is anathema to a communist government. After some hesitation, the government began to suppress the students, and the students returned to campus. One result was that the Communist party chief, Hu Yaobang, was forced to resign because of accusations that he encouraged the students' demands for democratization.

Hu's downfall began a six-month campaign against "bourgeois liberalism," and in March 1989, a reporter for the *Financial Times* stated, "The halcyon days of China's economic and political liberalism appear to be over." Xinhua, the official Chinese news agency, made an unusually strident attack on Western influence, stating, "The Chinese people suffered enough from foreign invasions. . . . The Chinese people have become masters of themselves . . . . Copying foreign political systems and experiences will not save China."[13]

Hu's death in April 1989 triggered an outpouring of student sympathy and renewed demands for political democracy. Despite government crackdown threats, the student marches and calls for "democracy" spread from campus to campus.[14]

As the students' demonstrations continued and grew while the government refused to talk with their representatives and failed to use force to disperse them, the students were joined by workers and others. Although demonstrations and marches occurred in many parts of the country, the ones that received the most attention were held in Tienanmen Square in the capitol, Beijing. The demonstrators, unarmed and peaceful, were requesting political freedoms to accompany the new freedoms being applied to the economy. The demonstrations and marches went on through May until the night of June 3, 1989.

Deng had encouraged economic liberalizations but would have no part of political freedom for China. Zhao Ziyang, the party general secretary, was the highest-ranking supporter of the students' goals and was ousted from power in May. Then, supported by other hardliners such as Li Peng, Deng ordered the "People's Liberation Army" to open fire and to use its tanks to crush—sometimes literally—the demonstrations and the demonstrators.

The army moved in during the nights of June 3rd and 4th, and according to observers—both Chinese and foreign—and the foreign press, thousands were killed. This action was followed by months of arrests of people who had been involved, many of whom were summarily executed.

The Chinese government dismissed the Tienanmen massacre, saying that because the demonstrators had attacked and killed many of the soldiers, the square had to be cleared and the demonstrators dispersed. The government invited foreign businesspeople, most of whom had fled the country, to return and resume business as usual. Those people and their companies had to make decisions involving safety, ethics, and finance.

Having observed the violence and realizing the depth of the Chinese people's discontent, a long period of unrest may be ahead. How safe would foreigners and their families be in such a society?

Ethically, do foreign companies want to do business with a government that ruthlessly butchers its own people? The fact is the PRC's civil rights record has been dreadful for years, yet foreign governments and firms have chosen to look the other way. Recently it seemed possible that civil rights might improve, particularly if Zhao took power when Deng retired or died. But, beginning on June 3, 1989, when the government's brutal suppression was televised for several days before the foreign media were evicted, the probability of a more humane PRC seemed far less likely.

With regard to financial considerations, because China is a huge potential market just beginning to open, a firm would not want to be beaten out by its competitors. Because change is constant in China, there is the possibility that Zhao or other like-thinkers could return to power, creating even greater business opportunities for foreign firms.

Investments Abroad

Since 1979, the PRC has invested in over 550 joint ventures outside China. These ventures were at first in trading houses, department stores, and servicing agencies, but in 1983, the emphasis changed to focus on manufacturing companies. The PRC wants overseas stakes in iron ore, aluminum, paper pulp, fertilizer, and fisheries projects and also wants to acquire technology and management skills.

In 1988, China invested $150 million abroad and, by the end of the year, had direct investments in 79 countries. The host countries ranged from LDCs to the most developed and included Australia, Canada, Hong Kong, Malaysia, Mauritius, Pakistan, the United States, and Zambia.[15]

Then, in April 1989, a PRC state-owned company, China National Metals and Minerals Import and Export Corporation (Minmetals), tried to make one investment abroad that was larger than all those of 1988. Minmetals outbid large Western industrial groups to gain control of New Zealand Steel. The bid was $244 million. Minmetals is one of China's largest import-export concerns, with an annual turnover of some $6 billion, and it carries on business with more than 150 countries.[16] In June 1989, in the aftermath of the Beijing massacre, it developed that Minmetals was unable to meet the preconditions for the purchase, and the sales agreement was terminated.[17]

Don't Forget the Bureaucratic Maze

The red tape is unbelievably costly and time consuming. It takes at least two years to start a business. In Shanghai, over 60 "chops" are required to get government approval of a project (chops are authorization stamps from various government bureaus—they even have a bureau governing the giving of prizes at parties). The bureaucracy created such obstacles that the mayor of Shanghai set up a new office—called the "one chop shoppe"—in an attempt to consolidate the bureaucratic maze.

Bribery of government officials is essential to get anything done. Even after government approval, there is a two-year wait to get a telephone, after which only 30 percent of local calls and 20 percent of long-distance ones make it through.[18]

The picture of the three men was drawn to illustrate the bureaucracy at "work." Each bureaucrat is indicating "not me" and pointing to another.

EAST-WEST TRADE PROBLEMS

Getting paid for goods sold to the East is not easy. The communist nations' demand for Western goods and technology has been far greater than Western demand for Eastern exports. Therefore, the Eastern countries have not been able to pay for their imports with their exports.

The East Owes the West a Lot of Money

To finance East-West trade gaps, the Comecon countries have borrowed heavily from Western banks and suppliers. The gross East European debt to the West at the end of 1988 was estimated to be almost $137 billion, and Western creditors must wonder how and when they will be repaid. As Table 17–5 illustrates, total debt of the eight countries increased each year from 1984 through 1986, although Romania managed to decrease the amount it owes. Romania reduced its foreign debt on the backs of its people as their consumption and standard of living dropped so the government could export more and decrease its debt. By 1988, the Romanian debt was down to about $3.8 billion. By contrast, the debts of the other countries had increased to approximately USSR, $40 billion; Poland, $38 billion; East Germany, $19 billion; Hungary, $16 billion; Czechoslovakia, $9 billion; Bulgaria, $6 billion; and Yugoslavia, $20 billion.[19]

Nonetheless, an OECD report stated some of the East European countries are able to finance higher debts. They are the USSR, Czechoslovakia, Romania, and East Germany. Creditors are less well inclined toward Bulgaria, Hungary, and Poland.[20]

	1984	1985	1986
Total gross debt	$101,070	$116,380	$136,760
USSR	21,500	28,200	36,700
Poland	26,800	29,300	33,500
East Germany	12,150	13,900	16,750
Romania	7,100	6,600	6,000
Hungary	8,840	11,760	15,090
Czechoslovakia	3,600	3,830	4,480
Bulgaria	2,260	3,610	4,880
Yugoslavia	18,820	19,180	19,360

Source: *Statistical Abstract of the United States, 1988*, p. 823.

The Eastern European countries are not the only communist countries whose debts to the West are growing. At the end of 1988, China's debt reached $40 billion, an increase of $5 billion from mid-1988. The PRC government is now taking steps to cut foreign borrowing, which has been growing at an annual rate of 38 percent during the past four years. The number of PRC entities permitted to borrow abroad has been limited to 10, and only the central bank (the People's Bank of China) can borrow from the IMF.[21]

The reasons for the East's trade deficits and resulting large debts are easily stated. The manufactured products of the East European countries are not of sufficient quality to compete in markets of the West against Western products. They do not export enough raw materials to pay for the imports they desire. In lower-technology or labor-intensive products in which their quality is competitive, they encounter protectionism due to pressure from labor unions in the Western countries.

Western Strategic Technology for the East?

Because of long-standing East-West hostilities—the Warsaw Pact countries versus NATO; the cold war, or communism versus capitalism—the Western countries have limited the strategically useful technology they would sell to the East. To be sure, the countries have applied the limits with varying degrees of rigor—German and Japanese limits have probably been the leakiest, but there have been leaks from all Western countries. And, successful Eastern espionage has stolen vast amounts of Western "secrets."

The Western agency charged with enforcing the limits is the Coordinating Committee on Multilateral Export Controls (CoCom), whose members are the NATO countries plus Japan and minus Iceland. Each member-country is responsible for enforcing the technology export limitations, and despite leaks and espionage, the consensus is that CoCom has prevented or at least delayed Eastern countries' receipt of militarily useful technology.

This situation is changing. CoCom restrictions on sales to China have been relaxed as its perceived strategic threat has abated. The Soviet Union has been making friendlier noises, and some CoCom members—notably the Germans—want more freedom to sell the East technology.[22]

Nevertheless, West Trades with East

So, as we see, the East has not been able to sell enough to the West to make the money to pay for what it wants to buy from the West. Nevertheless, there has been a large volume of trade between the West and the Soviet-dominated East, with the U.S. share shrinking after 1979. As the immense debts of the Soviet bloc to the West illustrate, a lot of that trade has been financed by credits from Western banks, suppliers, and governments. One method that the East favors to obtain goods and technology is **countertrade.** There are many varieties of countertrade, all of which involve the Western seller taking all or part of its payment in Eastern goods or services rather than in money. Still another device used by Western suppliers and Eastern customers is industrial cooperation between Western companies and Eastern factories through subcontracting, joint ventures, licensing, or other schemes to minimize the need for hard-currency payments East to West.

Both countertrade and industrial cooperation are important and growing means for maintaining trade between the industrial West and countries that are short of hard, convertible currency. Such countries include not only the East but also the many noncommunist developing countries, frequently called less developed countries or LDCs.

Another term used to identify those noncommunist LDCs is *Third World countries*. This means that in addition to the Third World there are two other "worlds" of countries, and those worlds are the East and the West.

Inasmuch as countertrade and industrial cooperation are as much applicable to West-LDC trade as they are to West-East trade, we will deal with those subjects in more detail in Chapter 18. There we deal with finance, and both countertrade and industrial cooperation are used as substitutes for money.

In the West, resistance has developed to countertrade and industrial cooperation. Some of that resistance is directed particularly at the East, and so we shall discuss that here.

Opposition to Countertrade and Industrial Cooperation

Resistance to Eastern goods is sometimes based on (1) the inferior quality of the goods and of Eastern technology, (2) damage to competing Western companies and their workers, or (3) damage to producers and their workers in friendly countries with which the West has trade agreements.

As to quality and technology, these may not be enduring problems. One need only remember the Japanese example. After WW II, Japanese products were dismissed as inferior. Within 20 years, Japan was a world leader in technology and exports. Furthermore, it has been estimated that as many as 25 percent of all the scientists in the world are now employed in the USSR.[23] There are technical areas in which the USSR leads the United States, and there has been an increase of Soviet patent registrations in the United States.[24]

Dumping.   Resistance to Eastern goods being imported into Western countries is sometimes based on damage to competing Western companies and their workers. Western companies and unions have begun to complain that Eastern products are being dumped in Western markets.

Dumping is selling in one export market at a price lower than prices charged in the domestic market or in third-country export markets. The sales prices

countertrade payment for imports at least in part with something other than money

dumping the selling abroad of products at prices lower than those charged in the producing country or in other national markets

may be lower than the production costs. *Predatory dumping* is dumping whose objective is to damage or destroy competitors in the country where the goods are dumped.

EC makers of steel, cars, chemicals, shoes, textiles, clothing, and electric motors are complaining loudly about unfair Comecon competition. Some of those EC producers, and related labor unions, are already getting protection from EC antidumping action, and others want more protection.[25]

In 1989, a dumping complaint was lodged against the Soviet Union for allegedly dumping the chemical, potassium permanganate, into the EC market. The complaint was on behalf of the Spanish company, Industrial Quimica de Nalon, which warned that its survival was threatened. It is the EC's only producer of this chemical.[26]

We mentioned above that the PRC exports products to the United States that are competitive with American products particularly sensitive to foreign competition. In addition to textiles, these products include footwear, watches, electronics, and glass products.[27]

Attitude of American labor.   One American labor union official said that he thought the idea of building factories for Eastern-bloc countries (industrial cooperation) was fine if production were for their home markets. But he pointed out that if an Eastern factory exported its products to the West in payment for the factory, it would be difficult for noncommunist trade unionists—"who have the right to bargain collectively and to strike"—to compete with the controlled and subservient labor of the East.[28]

The labor union official was talking about the cost of the labor factor, which is one determinant of the price of goods produced. He was complaining that the East had an unfair cost advantage because it had the power to keep labor under its thumb.

Is it dumping?   One aspect of deciding whether an exported product is being dumped is to determine whether the price charged by the producer covers all of its costs, including a profit and the cost of capital. In the East, the cost of labor is artificially low, compared to the West, because labor in the East is not free to bargain for higher wages and to strike for them if necessary. Other costs are differently conceived in the West than in the East. Profit is not an element in the East because production facilities in Eastern countries, unlike those in Western countries, are not required to make profits to continue operations. The elaborate cost accounting practices of Western business are not found in the East. Thus, costs are not comparable.

For another thing, comparisons of domestic prices with export prices as dumping criteria are misleading because no currency of the East is convertible. In addition, an East country can easily export at a loss by its own figures, for political purposes or to earn needed hard, convertible currencies.

Competition with traditional suppliers and allies.   As to damage to suppliers and workers in friendly countries, it is clear that many Comecon and PRC exports are competitive with products from other countries, particularly LDCs. For the U.S. market, there are traditional suppliers and allies, such as the Philippines, South Korea, Taiwan, Hong Kong, and Central and South American countries. For the EC countries, there are ex-colonies in Africa and Asia, with which they maintain relatively close economic ties.

In the United States, it has been suggested that some of these trading partners may exert some behind-the-scenes pressures to protect their American markets. The countries mentioned above—the Philippines and so forth—all have embassies or representatives in the United States and friends in Congress and the executive branch. These can be expected to lobby and pressure to protect their U.S. markets from the competition of Eastern countries.

PRC and USSR Reforms

Just as seemingly deep-seated forces are causing changes in the PRC, so also may changes in the USSR move it away from the rigid, centralized, communist-state condition that has characterized it for more than 70 years.

Differences.   Start with agriculture. Soviet agriculture has never recovered from the dual blow of the Bolshevik Revolution and Joseph Stalin's war against the kulaks, as Russia's farmers were called. Stalin forced the creation of huge state farms and starved, murdered, or deported the kulaks. The Soviet Union is a predominantly urban economy, and the people who work on the collectivized farms are nothing but hired hands with little interest in the output of the farms or the maintenance of their equipment. The tradition of an independent, self-employed farmer hardly survives, even as a folk memory, now, 60 years after eradication of the kulaks.

Thus Gorbachev's offer to lease land to the hired hands falls on uncomprehending and unenthusiastic ears. The farm workers are making low but living wages. Why give that up and take chances with their own plot of farmland?[29]

By contrast, China at the end of the 1970s was still an overwhelmingly agrarian economy, and the experience of farm collectivization was only a decade-and-a-half old. It was already breaking down at the roots before Deng proclaimed reform from the top.[30]

The results were startling as the Chinese farmers were given the freedom to grow and sell their own crops at market prices. Production soared, and many farmers became prosperous.

Not all Russian farmland was collectivized. Some 1.6 percent of its arable land is farmed by private farmers who can sell at market prices. That 1.6 percent of the land produces 30 percent of the food. About one third of the state farm crops never reach the consumer because of poor storage, poor transportation, poor roads, and poor refrigeration, but pests aplenty.[31]

So, cooperation and participation by the people who must make it work are the major reasons the Chinese agricultural reforms so far are much more successful than those of the Soviet Union.

The same seems to be occurring with industrial reforms. As with agriculture, the reforms began sooner in the PRC than they did in the USSR. Probably more important, the communist system was not imposed in China until after the communists won their civil war in 1949. The system was put in place in the Soviet Union after the 1917 revolution. Many Chinese had experienced private business and farming and noncommunist governments; not so for the people of the USSR.

Soviet intellectuals are delighted at the prospects of reform. They want to be free to research, write, compose, publish, and travel. However, as Gorbachev has said, the reforms will "bog down if we fail to rally the people to its cause." That is not proving easy.

Workers are willing to recognize that the number one problem is productivity, but the overwhelming majority tend to lay blame on almost anyone but themselves. Notably absent are references to the alcoholism, absenteeism, and general lethargy that continue to cripple production.

All this is scarcely surprising. Today's Soviet work force is born of a system that for generations treated the individual as little more than a meaningless cog in the wheel of production. The centralization of political and economic power has at best discouraged and at worst viciously punished individual innovation and initiative. Having endured decades of powerlessness and alienation from the basic decisions that effect their lives, the Soviet people seem numb.[32]

Glasnost and perestroika.   Recognizing that the Soviet economy is badly in need of new methods and new technology, Gorbachev set out to change old ways and encourage innovation. He has made two Russian words well known in the world: **glasnost** and **perestroika**. **Glasnost** connotes openness with information about the economy and other aspects of the USSR. **Perestroika** was to mean decontrol of prices and decentralization of management.

Joint ventures with foreign firms are a major Soviet objective. Gorbachev has also permitted some privately owned and operated small businesses, which they term **cooperatives**.

Joint ventures (JVs).   JVs are important to the Soviet Union. They are intended to bring foreign investment, technical know-how, hard-currency earnings, and consumer and capital goods to the domestic markets. Those benefits would be attained without adding to the level of foreign indebtedness.

There are bureaucratic and economic obstacles to starting and operating JVs, but the Soviet government has made some things a little easier. Bureaucratic decentralization, by moving responsibility for specific JVs away from the Ministry of Foreign and Economic Affairs to the industrial or trade ministry directly concerned, has helped create a more flexible environment. Foreign partners are finding they can set new conditions, such as running their own set of books. The Soviet practice of using 12–14 percent per year depreciation schedules appropriate for heavy industry can be negotiated to reflect the shorter economic lives of computers and other high-tech, modern equipment.

An economic difficulty that has not been solved is getting JV profits into hard currency and out of the USSR. Under the law, all dividends to the Western partner, as well as foreign currency expenditures, must be covered by hard-currency earnings.[33]

The Soviets' JV program received a major boost in March 1989, when six major U.S. companies signed an agreement that could result in as many as 25 JVs and bring in $5 billion to $10 billion over the next 15 years. The U.S. companies are Chevron, Eastman Kodak, Johnson & Johnson, RJR, Archer-Daniels-Midland, and Mercator (the group's merchant banker). A seventh member, Ford Motor Company, pulled out at the last minute because the Soviets could not ensure availability of hard currency for foreign procurement or dividends.[34]

Cooperatives.   Beginning in 1987, private companies were permitted to operate legally. At first, they were seen as a fast way to improve consumer

---

glasnost openness with information

---

perestroika (literally restructured as used by Gorbachev) decontrol of prices and decentralization of management

---

joint ventures (as envisioned by the Soviets as part of perestroika) bringing in Western companies with their capital and technology to work with and modernize Soviet industry and agriculture

---

cooperatives the term used in the Soviet Union to connote small private businesses now being permitted there

WORLDVIEW
Success for Perestroika?

Mikhail Gorbachev has taken bold steps to make perestroika work, and he and other communist party officials appear ready to go further. Vadim A. Medvedev, the party's secretary for ideology and a member of the politburo, said, "Until now, no tangible results in meeting the everyday needs of the people have been achieved." Without giving details, he suggested the leadership should try "major economic reforms."

Most Western political leaders hope perestroika succeeds. They feel a more open and prosperous Soviet Union may be more confident and less reliant on its immense military power for status as a superpower.

Western economists have serious doubts perestroika can succeed. The *Financial Times* reported on the "perils of perestroika":

> If the reform process is to succeed, three things have to be achieved, all of them rather swiftly: sterilization of the liquidity overhang,* a move to profit incentives combined with free market prices, and elimination of the fiscal deficit.
>
> To list these requirements is to demonstrate their im-

plausibility. A communist party whose claim on power is its special understanding of the forces of history is openly confessing it has flunked its specialist subject. The bureaucrats, whose *raison d'être* is interference in all aspects of economic and social life, are being asked to abandon that role voluntarily. A people that has been taught for more than two generations that markets are wasteful and profits exploitive is expected to change its beliefs while continuing to trust the teacher.

Dr. Martin Feldstein, professor of economics at Harvard and former chairman of the American President's Council of Economic Advisors, makes the same point. He concludes, "The contrast between political reforms and economic stagnation is a major challenge to the stability of the current Soviet regime. A nation that can now express its complaints in the press and even in the ballot box will not continue to suffer economic stagnation in silence. If the Soviet leaders don't find a way to restart perestroika and raise the standard of living, the recently achieved political liberties may be short lived."

Sources: Michael Parks, "Reforms Fail to Produce Economic Gains, Senior Soviet Official Says," *Los Angeles Times*, April 22, 1989, part I, p. 15; "The Perils of Perestroika," *Financial Times*, February 28, 1989, p. 16; and Martin Feldstein, "Why Perestroika Isn't Happening," *The Wall Street Journal*, April 21, 1989, p. A16.

*The liquidity overhang is the billions of rubles being held by the Soviet people because there is so little consumer products and food to spend them on.

services; but as they have grown in number, they have expanded into light industry and specialized services.

The cooperatives began providing products and services that were not available from government stores or were of better quality. Buyers from the cooperatives could avoid the long lines that are a way of Soviet life.

However, prices are higher, and the owners have been making very good incomes, which have aroused animosity and envy among the people and some government officials. This has resulted in three blows to the cooperative movement. In December 1988, the Soviet Council of Ministers banned cooperatives from dealing in a range of businesses, including medical supplies, publishing, and educational and video ventures. Second, price controls were approved by the politburo which could be used by government enterprises to throttle the cooperatives. Third, the politburo approved new tax legislation giving the 15 state governments in the Soviet Union a free hand as to the tax rates they may choose to impose on cooperatives. There are no ceilings, and the taxes will be imposed on "gross income" before allowing for wages and investment for future production.

The new laws were condemned by Lev Nikferov, a specialist in the cooperative sector at the Soviet Academy of Sciences Institute of Economics. Nikferov warned the laws could result in cooperatives being "completely eradicated" in some states where the authorities are hostile to the whole concept.[35]

DÉTENTE

Because a fundamental goal of communism is the spread of its system throughout the world, communist governments—particularly the USSR—have aggressively encouraged communist takeovers of noncommunist countries. That aggressiveness has alternated with periods of relative calm, and during the calmer periods, leaders speak of détente.

Détente is defined as an easing of discord among nations. Successive American, European, and Japanese governments have had détente with the communist bloc of countries as one of their major objectives.

In large part, it is because of the desire for détente in the West that East–West trade has grown. However, the USSR and its Cuban, East European, and Vietnamese allies continued to topple governments friendly to the West (or neutral), which alarmed a number of leaders in the West. The USSR used its own troops to invade Afghanistan, while the troops of its allies occupied countries in Africa, Asia, and the Middle East.

There has always been some anticommunist feeling in the West, and the belligerence of the Soviet Union and its allies reinforced that feeling. Among the results have been the embargoes placed by the U.S. president on the export of agricultural and high-tech products to the USSR.

It is extremely interesting to observe that at the same time that U.S. trade with the USSR declined for political reasons, trade between the United States and the PRC grew. The two trends are connected, as the United States and the PRC became closer politically—and therefore commercially—to counter the strength and aggressiveness of the mutually perceived danger from the USSR.

But things may be changing. Former President Ronald Reagan held summit meetings with Gorbachev, as has President Bush. A U.S.–Soviet arms control agreement was reached in 1988. Gorbachev met with Chinese leader Deng in 1989 after Soviet troops had withdrawn from Afghanistan. Elections of sorts were held in the Soviet Union, Hungary, and Poland, while ethnic minorities in the Soviet Union are agitating for autonomy, if not freedom.

Peter F. Drucker of the Claremont Graduate School says that within 25 years, the Russian empire will have disappeared. He points out that the Russian half of the population is growing at one third the rate of the country's central Asian people and says that one reason Gorbachev offered to reduce Soviet troop strength by 500,000 is that, lacking Russian youths to fill the ranks, he would have had to recruit and arm Asians.

Nevertheless, the Soviet Union remains a mighty military power. In 1989, U.S. Secretary of Defense Richard Cheney said Gorbachev's attempts to reform his economy would lead to his downfall. Cheney wasn't arguing for higher defense spending but rather cautioning against a hasty withdrawal of U.S. troops from Europe. He warns that Gorbachev's sweet talk could be replaced by tomorrow's growl of the Soviet bear.[36]

A major lesson for international business executives and students is that political forces and considerations are of paramount importance in East-West trade. As and if détente lives and prospers, so does trade.

SUMMARY

The Comecon countries and the PRC have huge populations, landmasses, and resources. In theory, they should be excellent trading partners for the OECD countries, but translation of theory to fact is proving most difficult.

Ideological differences reinforced by armaments have made for hostilities. Hostilities have been expressed in cold wars that have frequently become hot.

There is trade, but much of it has been unnatural from the points of view of both sides. The East has been unable to earn enough money to pay for what it desires to buy from the West, and therefore the East wants the West to take payment in the form of more Eastern goods and services.

But complaints are made about many Eastern goods in Western markets. The complaints are based on the grounds that Eastern goods are of inferior quality or that they are unfairly competitive with Western or traditional suppliers and labor. It seems quite possible that the quality problems will be solved. The problem of unfair competition will be more difficult to overcome.

Concepts of costs in the East are hardly comparable to those in the West. In the East, there are no significant free markets, so that a method of establishing value or cost does not exist. There is no profit motive, and the only production factor whose cost is considered is labor. But labor in the East is not free to bargain collectively or to strike, so even that cost is not comparable between Eastern and Western countries.

Finally, the political tensions between the communist East and the socialist or capitalist West relax or become more intense as armed conflict and other hostilities between East and West forces cool or heat. The PRC, the Soviet Union, and some European countries are trying joint ventures and other openings to the West, and Western countries are responding with varying degrees of caution.

QUESTIONS

1. *a.* When East-West is spoken of, what countries are included in "East"?
   b. "West"?

2. What is a centrally planned economy?

3. Why are the reported trade figures between East Germany and the OECD relatively small?

4. Why has the PRC never become a large market for consumer goods?

5. *a.* What is a major probable reason that the PRC recognized the United States in 1979 and wants to trade with the United States?
   b. What changes are occurring in the PRC's economic relations with foreigners?

6. What does the East want most from the West?

7. What are the major obstacles to the East getting what it wants?

8. How is the East getting—and trying to get means to pay for—imports from the West?

9. Why is the East having difficulties getting the West to accept its products?

10. *a.* Is the East likely to be able to improve the quality of its products?
    b. Why?

11. *a.* If the East succeeds in improving the quality of the products it exports to the West, will that end Western objections to imports from the East?
    b. Why?

12. What does cost have to do with determining whether an imported product is priced unfairly low, or being dumped?

13. Identify some differences between East and West in production cost computations.

14. *a.* What is the USSR trying to achieve with perestroika?
    b. Discuss its chances of success.

MINICASE 17–1

Marketing in the People's Republic of China

You are the CEO of a company that manufactures machine tools in American factories. Sales were low in 1985 and 1986 but began to pick up in 1987. Even with the increased order volume, your plant operations are well below capacity, and even though your technology is well advanced, import competition is tough.

You are beginning to consider export possibilities, and your marketing vice president suggests the PRC. She shows you academic studies, Department of Commerce publications, and PRC trade fair literature that convince you that the PRC market is worth a try.

What steps should your marketing vice president take to gain acceptance of your product by the PRC and to get orders? What should you and she avoid?

MINICASE 17–2

Joint Venturing in Eastern Europe

You are the vice president for planning of an American manufacturer of machine tools. You report to the president, and he calls you to his office one day.

When you get there, he starts talking about how tough it is to get new business and about how well the company's European and Japanese competitors have been doing in the American market. He then points out that the company has never made a sale in Eastern Europe, and he asks you why that is.

You reply that business has been good enough in the United States and in the several Latin American markets where the company's products are sold, so no sales efforts have been made in Eastern Europe. You can anticipate the president's next words, and they are not long in coming.

"Latin America has gone to hell in a hand basket! They are spending all their money paying back the greedy banks that lent them too much money, and they're broke when it comes to buying our stuff. We need new markets! Get out of here and see how we can get into Eastern Europe."

What steps are you going to take to try to get into that market—or those markets? To whom should you talk? Where can you turn for information? Does détente or perestroika have anything to do with the likelihood of your success? Discuss. Should you make a trip to the area? If so, when? If not, why not?

SUPPLEMENTARY READINGS

Hanson, Philip. *Trade and Technology in Soviet-Western Relations.* New York: Columbia University Press, 1981.

Hogberg, Bengt, and Clas Wahlbin. "East-West Industrial Cooperations: The Swedish Case." *Journal of International Business Studies,* Spring/Summer 1984, pp. 72–83.

Hungarian Chamber of Commerce. "Ideas for Joint Ventures." Budapest: Foreign Investment Promotion Service, 1989/1.

Kanet, Roger E., ed. *Soviet Foreign Policy and East-West Relations.* Elmsford, N.Y.: Pergamon Press, 1982.

Starr, Robert, ed. "Practical Aspects of Trading with the USSR." Montreux, Switzerland: Worldwide Information, 1989.

————."Joint Ventures in the USSR." Worldwide Information, Montreux, Switzerland: 1989.

Woolcock, Stephen. *Western Policies on East-West Trade.* Boston: Routledge & Kegan Paul, 1982.

ENDNOTES

1. Anthony C. Sutton, *Western Technology and Soviet Economic Development,* vols. 1 and 2 (Stanford, Calif.: Hoover Institution Press, 1968 and 1971).

2. Leslie Colitt, "Asian Oust Comecon in West German Market," *Financial Times,* April 20, 1989, p. 7.

3. Leslie Colitt, "Comrades Dream of a Single Market," *Financial Times,* September 28, 1988, p. 24.

4. "Every Step Hurts," *The Economist,* January 14, 1988, pp. 44–45.

5. Peter Gumbel, "Soviet Trade Awaits the Next Revolution," *The Wall Street Journal*, February 21, 1989, p. A14.

6. Robert McCluskey, "The Bottom Line," *International Management*, July 1986, pp. 49–50.

7. Nancy Yoshihara, "China to Open Office to Aid U.S. Firms," *Los Angeles Times*, April 13, 1986, part 4, p. 4.

8. Vigor Keung Fung, "China Flirts with a Basic Capitalist Tool: Stocks," *The Asian Wall Street Journal*, September 26, 1983, p. 14.

9. "Managing Money Matters in China Joint Ventures," *Business Asia*, June 13, 1988, pp. 194–96.

10. Julia Leung, "Foreign Companies in China Devising Plans to Weather Sudden Policy Shifts," *The Asian Wall Street Journal*, November 14, 1988, p. 22.

11. Vigor Keung Fung, "China Aims to Revive Foreign Interest," *The Asian Wall Street Journal*, December 8, 1986, p. 13; and "China, New Foreign Investment Incentives," *Standard Chartered Review*, November 1986, pp. 21–22.

12. Vigor Keung Fung, "Chinese Are Eager to Take the Plunge," *The Asian Wall Street Journal*, November 17, 1986, p. 22.

13. Peter Ellingsen, "China Shuts Door on Rapid Reform," *Financial Times*, March 20, 1989, p. 26.

14. Adi Ignatius, "Death of Ex-Party Chief Hu Is Viewed as Blow to China's Liberal Reformers," *The Wall Street Journal*, April 17, 1989, p. A7.

15. "No Order Too Small," *The Economist*, February 18, 1989, p. 34.

16. Dai Hayward and Colina MacDougall, "Cut and Thrust of Chinese Steel," *Financial Times*, April 18, 1989, p. 23.

17. "Sale of New Zealand Steel to Minmetals Is Scrapped," *The Asian Wall Street Journal*, June 19, 1989, p. 3.

18. Mark Skousen, "Bureaucratic Nightmare," *Forecasts & Strategies*, April 1989, p. 7.

19. "Debt," *The Economist*, December 24, 1988, p. 130.

20. "OECD Takes Gloomy View Of East-Block Debt Situation," *The Wall Street Journal*, March 1, 1989, p. A10.

21. "China Foreign Debt Swells," *Los Angeles Times*, April 24, 1989, part IV, p. 3.

22. Peter Montagnon, "Key Questions Raised," *Financial Times*, December 13, 1989, p. 36.

23. John W. Kiser III, "Technology Is Not a One-Way Street," *Foreign Policy*, Summer 1976, pp. 131–48.

24. Ibid.

25. *The Economist*, August 5, 1979, pp. 38–39.

26. William Dawkins, "Soviet Union Faces EC Probe on Chemical Pricing," *Financial Times*, August 1, 1989, p. 6.

27. Jay F. Henderson, Nicholas H. Ludlow, and Eugene A. Theroux, "China and the Trade Act of 1974," *U.S.-China Business Review*, January–February 1975.

28. Benjamin A. Sharman, in an interview reported in *Contemporary Perspectives in International Business*, ed. Harold W. Berkman and Ivan R. Vernon (Skokie, Ill.; Rand McNally, 1979), p. 142.

29. "The Missing Kulak," *Financial Times*, March 20, 1989, p. 24.

30. Ibid.

31. Henrik Bering-Jensen, "Stomachs Growl at Farm System," *Insight*, April 3, 1989, pp. 38–39.

32. Daniel J. Arbess and Marlene Greenberg, "Moscow's Puzzle Is How to Motivate the Soviet Worker," *Los Angeles Times*, March 13, 1989, part II, p. 5; see also, Nathan Gardels, "Communism: All That Is Sacred Is Profane," *The Wall Street Journal*, January 24, 1989, p. A18.

33. "Joint Ventures Move Centre Stage," *Euromoney*, September 1988, pp. 65–69.

34. Peter Gumbel, "Soviets, 6 U.S. Firms Reach Trade Accord," *The Wall Street Journal*, March 30, 1989, p. A2.

35. Quentin Peel, "Tax Threat to Soviet Cooperative Movement," *Financial Times*, April 27, 1989, p. 14.

36. James Flanigan, "World Economy Feels Impact of Perestroika," *Los Angeles Times*, May 7, 1989, part IV, p. 1.

Chapter 18

Financial Management

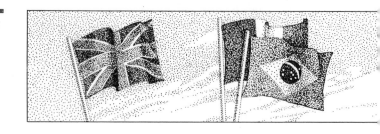

Ten minutes is a long-term outlook.

> Foreign currency dealers,
> Manufacturers Hanover Trust
> Company

In countertrading, companies sometimes let themselves get stuck with products they don't know anything about. A computer guy called me to help get rid of 30,000 tons of oranges he'd taken in a deal. I told him to squeeze them into orange juice and freeze the concentrate, or he would wind up with oranges good for nothing but penicillin.

> Takis Argentinis, director,
> Countertrade Operations, General
> Electric Company

LEARNING OBJECTIVES

In this chapter, you will study:

1. How the currencies of the main trading nations change in value in terms of each other.

2. How currency value changes affect international business transactions and the reporting of profits, losses, assets, and liabilities.

3. The tremendous importance of financial management to an international company.

4. How financial management can protect an international company from risks and create advantages as a result of currency value changes.

5. Financial management tools, including hedging, timing of payments, exposure netting, price adjustments, balance sheet neutralizing, and swaps.

6. Why the financial management of a worldwide company (WWC) encounters more problems and opportunities in raising capital than does the financial management of a domestic company.

7. Why international competition has forced exporters to customers in soft-currency countries to accept payment in forms other than money.

8. Why a foreign investor in a soft-currency country must sometimes accept dividends, interest, or repayment in forms other than money.

9. Why noncommunist less developed countries (LDCs) and soft-currency countries are usually more open about their economies than are communist countries.

10. Why noncommunist less developed countries are more likely to receive and accept financial and technological assistance from UN agencies and developed-country (DC) governments and companies.

11. International finance centers, which handle the entire intra-WWC invoicing procedure for some WWCs and may coordinate all international financial activities of the organization's parent and its affiliates.

KEY WORDS AND CONCEPTS

- Fluctuating exchanges rates
- Transaction risks
- Hedging
- Leads
- Lags
- Exposure netting
- Translation risks
- Neutralizing the balance sheet
- Swaps
- Equity capital
- Debt capital
- Countertrade
- Industrial cooperation
- International finance center

BUSINESS INCIDENT

David Edwards was born in Wichita Falls, Texas, but was intrigued by international business and finance. He worked his way up the ladder of Citibank's international operation, where he moved into a senior slot in Paris as head of *les cambistes,* as the fast-and-furious currency exchange traders are called. His boldness and quick mind equipped him well for this high-pressure operation, and he did very well for his employer and for himself. Occasionally, however, his Wichita Falls French got him in trouble. He tells of one occasion when Citibank's currency trader at the Bourse,* who was a Frenchman, phoned him and reported that the U.S. dollar bids were going down fast. Edwards shouted into the telephone, "Aw, shit!" and slammed down the receiver. A few seconds later, the trader called Edwards on another phone and reported proudly that he had bought a large block of U.S. dollars. "You did what?" Edwards yelled, to which the startled trader protested, "But you said, *'Achete.'* "† That evening, Edwards walked into his boss's office and said, "I've got a funny story to tell you, but it's going to cost you a quarter of a million dollars to hear it."

Source: Roy Rowan, *Fortune,* January 10, 1983, p. 46.

* *Bourse* is the French word for stock and currency markets.
† *Achete* means "buy" in French.

In Chapter 6, we spoke of some of the financial forces with which WWC management is confronted and of the financial problems it must try to solve. In this chapter, we shall examine some of the tools and methods that financial management uses to solve those problems. The forces or problems that we identified were fluctuating currency exchange rates, currency exchange controls, tariffs, taxes, inflation, and accounting practices.

One problem faced by the financial management of a WWC that can be turned into an opportunity is in what currency to raise capital. The company may need or be able to use two or more currencies. If so, its financial management can shop the many financial centers around the world to raise the currency it can use at the lowest cost.

A related problem results from payment for products sold internationally. If you are the seller, the buyer may pay you in your currency, which is the same as a domestic sale. But payment may be made in another currency. If it is a convertible currency, you can convert it to your currency, though there may be a currency exchange rate risk if payment is delayed—for example, if you extend credit to the buyer.

If the buyer has too little convertible currency, the seller may accept goods or services instead of money. Financial management must convert the goods or services to money, a growing phenomenon as international competition grows keener.

Elsewhere in the book, we deal with market assessment and analysis and with production planning. Early in their assessment, analysis, and planning, marketing and production management should bring in financial management to coordinate capital needs with capital availability.

The financial managers must examine the alternative ways of financing the marketing and production plans. How much capital of what sorts will be needed, and when? What are the best sources, and how long can the new operations be expected to need support before they are financially self-sufficient?

FLUCTUATING CURRENCY EXCHANGE RATES

fluctuating exchange rates currencies of different countries go up and down in value in terms of each other

Wherever the WWC does business, the financial manager must consider **fluctuating exchange rates**—the fluctuating values of currencies in terms of each other. Also to be considered is the value of each of those currencies in terms of the currency of the WWC's home or financial and tax-reporting country.

The fluctuations create currency value risks. These may be categorized as (1) transaction risks and (2) translation risks.

Transaction Risks

transaction risks in import/export transactions, the party that must pay or receive a foreign currency in the future takes the risk that the currency value will change to its disadvantage

Transaction risks usually involve a receivable or a payable denominated in a foreign currency.[1] These risks arise from transactions, such as a purchase from a foreign supplier or a sale to a foreign customer. There are several methods by which the financial manager can buy protection against these risks.[2] The company can engage in several types of **hedging,** in various ways, or if it is a buyer or a borrower, it may be able to accelerate or delay payments or provisions for payments. Within limits, price increases may be used.

hedging trying to protect yourself against losses due to currency exchange rate fluctuations

Forward hedge.   This is accomplished in the foreign exchange market, and it involves a contract. The WWC contracts with another party to deliver to that other party at an agreed future date a fixed amount of one currency in return for a fixed amount of another currency. Contracts in the major trading country currencies are generally available for 30- , 60- , 90- , or 180-day deliveries. Longer-term contracts can sometimes be negotiated.

5 Norwegian krone = 1 U.S. dollar.   An example could work as follows. An American exporter sells $1 million of goods to a Norwegian importer. The rate of exchange on the date of sale is 5 Norwegian krone to 1 U.S. dollar (NK5 = US$1) and therefore involves NK5 million. The agreement is that the importer will pay the exporter NK5 million in 180 days.

The risk of any change in the US$–NK exchange rate is now on the American exporter. If the NK loses value, say, to NK7 = US$1, during the 180 days, the NK5 million will buy only US$714,285.71 when received. But the American exporter's expectation was to receive US$1 milllion, and the exchange rate change causes a loss of more than $285,000.

The hedge involves a contract.   The U.S. exporter could use a forward hedge to protect against such a loss by contracting at the time of sale to sell NK5 million to be delivered to the buyer (the other party to the hedge contract) in 180 days in return for US$1 million, which the other party agrees to deliver to the WWC at the same time. The actual amount received by the exporter will be less than $1 million because the other party to the hedge contract will want compensation for the risk of a drop in the value of the NK during the 180 days. Assume the other party wants 1 percent and the exporter agrees. One percent would be $10,000, and the other party would deliver $990,000 in exchange for NK5 million.[3]

The $10,000 can be regarded as a sort of insurance premium that the exporter pays to be certain how much in US$s it will receive in 180 days. Of course, it must have made the business decision that $990,000 is an acceptable amount for the goods it is selling.

As with other prices in a free market society, there is no law or regulation that mandates 1 percent, or $10,000, as the cost for a $1 million hedge. In our example, the good financial manager for the exporter will shop around among banks and will find some prices lower than others. The NK is not traded on the International Monetary Market (IMM) in Chicago. If the currency of payment were one of the eight traded there, the financial manager should also get a quote for an IMM contract. The traded currencies are shown in Figure 18 – 1.

The IMM contract is a futures hedge.   If the financial manager uses IMM contracts, the hedge is with a futures, not a forward, contract. At the IMM, the traded currencies are treated as commodities (wheat, soybeans, sow bellies, and so forth) and traded as futures contracts. Futures contracts are traded by brokers, and the exporter must have a margin account with a broker. Futures contracts come in fixed amounts, such as BP25,000, and standardized delivery dates are used.

Currency options.   At the end of 1982, the Philadelphia Stock Exchange began dealing in options to buy or sell currencies. That offered another hedge opportunity, which has been expanded since then in at least two ways. First, other exchanges have begun dealing in currency options in, among other cities,

Traded Currency	Ticker Code
British pound	BP
Canadian dollar	CD
Deutsche mark	DM
Dutch guilder	DG
French franc	FF
Japanese yen	JY
Mexican peso	MP
Swiss franc	SF

London, Chicago, Amsterdam, and New York. Second, there now exists an over-the-counter currency option market involving banks, multinationals, and brokers.

Intra-WWC hedge. A rapidly growing practice is for multinationals to seek an internal hedge within their own network of parent, subsidiary, and affiliated companies. Suppose that in our NK–US$ case, the financial manager found that one of the WWC companies owed about NK5 million, payable about the same time as the NK5 million was receivable under the export contract. The NK payable by one unit of the WWC could then be hedged (netted) against the NK receivable carried by the other WWC unit. Thus, two hedges are achieved at no ouside cost, and the bank, option, or IMM fees are avoided.

A covered position. Even though the exporter in the above forward hedge example does not have any NKs at the time it enters the hedge contract, it does have the Norwegian importer's obligation to pay the NK5 million, which can be delivered to the other party to the hedge contract. If you either have the funds (NK5 million) when you enter the hedge contract or they are due from another business transaction on or before the due date under your hedge contract (as here), you are in a "covered" position.[4]

An uncovered position. A financial manager can also use the foreign exchange market to take advantage of an expected rise or fall in the relative value of currency. There will then be created an "uncovered" long or short position. For example, if the financial manager of an American company believes the NK will appreciate in value in the next few months, the procedure would be to go long on the NK at the spot rate, NK5 = US$1. This is a contract whereby the company buys, say, NK5 million for US$1 million, both currencies to be delivered at a future date. If the NK appreciates to NK4 = US$1, the financial manager was correct, and the NK5 million received by the company is worth $1,250,000. The company pays, as agreed, $1 million. If the financial manager believes the NK will depreciate in the next few months, the procedure would be to short NKs at the spot rate. To short money or any other commodity is to sell it without having it either on hand or due you under another business transaction.

Using the same rate (NK5 = US$1), and the same amount (NK5 million), the company agrees to deliver NK5 million at a future date in return for US$1 million. If, in fact, the NK depreciates to NK6 = US$1, the financial manager

■ **FIGURE 18–2**
Currency Futures Market

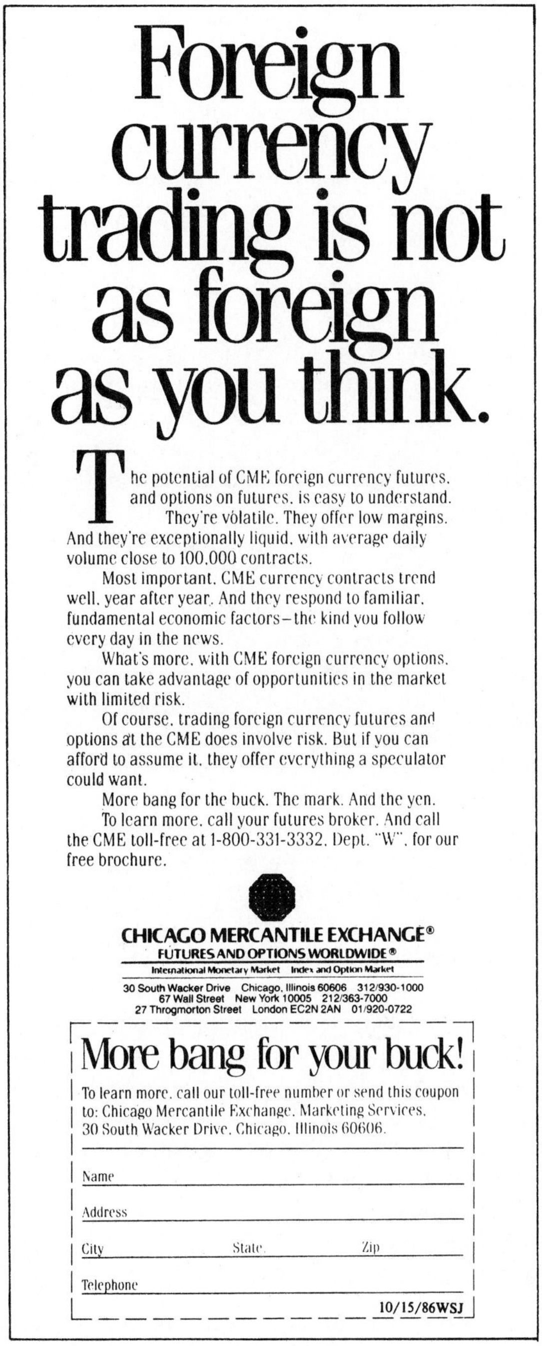

was again correct. The company can buy the NK5 million for approximately $830,000. The company will be paid, as agreed, $1 million.

Both of the above stories had happy endings for the company, but it exposed itself to risk. Short-term currency value movements are extremely uncertain in both direction and amount, and those company stories (and perhaps the financial manager) could have had sad endings if the currencies had moved in the other directions. People who study currency markets and deal in them daily tend to be modest in their forecasts of short-term movements.

We have interviewed and talked at length with foreign exchange market officers, bank traders, and bank economists in America and Europe. Almost all of them expressed definite views, opinions, and forecasts about long-term currency value changes. Not one of them would hazard more than a guess about tomorrow's prices.

Credit or money market hedge.   As indicated by its name, the credit or money market hedge involves credit—borrowing money. The company desiring a hedge is the borrower. The credit or money market hedge may be illustrated by the same data used above to discuss the forward exchange market hedge.

The American exporter will be paid NK5 million by the Norwegian importer for the goods in 180 days. With the money market hedge, the exporter will borrow NK5 million from an Oslo bank on the day of the sale to the Norwegian importer.* The exporter will immediately convert to US$s at the current NK5 = US$1 rate, giving the exporter the $1 million selling price, but it owes NK5 million to the Norwegian bank, due in 180 days. That will be repaid with the Norwegian importer's NK5 million payment.

The exporter has a variety of options for use of the $1 million. It can lend it, put it in certificates of deposit, use it in a swap (see below), or use it as internal operating capital. The financial manager will study all of the options to find which will be most beneficial.

Before the money market hedge is used, a comparison must be made of the interest rates in the exporter's and the importer's countries. If the interest on the exporter's borrowing in the importer's country is significantly higher than the amount the exporter can earn on the money in its country, the cost of this type of hedge may be too great.

Other comparisons and checks should be made before borrowing the NK from an Oslo bank. Even though the NK is not one of the most widely traded currencies, the financial manager should inquire of banks in major Eurocurrency centers (such as London, Paris, Zurich, and Frankfurt) to ascertain whether NKs could be borrowed at a lower interest cost. And in the case of NKs, other Scandinavian financial centers—Copenhagen, Helsinki, and Stockholm—should be checked for competitive bids.

Just as in the foreign exchange market hedge situation, a WWC should check its company units to learn whether any of them have an NK balance that could be lent internally, that is, from the unit with the balance to the unit with the NK foreign exchange exposure. Thus, interest payments to banks outside the WWC could be avoided.

Acceleration or delay of payment.   If you are an importer in a country whose currency is expected to depreciate in terms of the currency of your foreign supplier, you are motivated to buy the necessary foreign currency as soon as you can. This assumes the importer must pay in the currency of the exporter, the opposite of our assumption in the hedging discussions.

---

* Actually, the amount borrowed will usually be less than NK5 million. It will be an amount that, plus interest for 180 days, will total NK5 million at the end of that period. Thus, the NK5 million payment from the importer will exactly repay the loan, with no odd amounts plus or minus.

Which way will the exchange rates go?   If you have agreed to pay $1 million when the exchange rate was NK5 = US$1, your cost at that time would be NK5 million. If, before payment is due, the rate drops to NK6 = US$1, your cost will be NK6 million. You are tempted to pay early or, if possible, to make the currency exchange at once and use the foreign currency until the payment due date.

Of course, the opposite would be the case if you expect the NK to strengthen from the NK5 = US$1 rate at the time of the purchase contract. You are motivated to delay payment and to delay conversion from NKs to US$s. For example, if the rate goes to NK4 = US$1, the necessary $1 million will cost you only NK4 million. Payment accelerations or delays are frequently called **leads** or **lags**.

Unrelated companies.   Although independent, unrelated companies use acceleration or delay on each other, one may be doing so at the expense of the other. Usually, however, the exporter is indifferent as to the method used by the importer to protect itself against currency risk as long as payment is received on time in the agreed currency. The WWC, on the other hand, may be able to realize enterprise-wide benefit using payment leads and lags.

Within a WWC.   For purposes of examining potential payment accelerations or delays between different country operations of one WWC, we should differentiate two types of WWCs. At one extreme is the WWC that operates a coordinated, integrated worldwide business with the objective of the greatest profit for the total enterprise. At the other extreme is the independent operation of each part of the WWC as its own separate profit center.

As pointed out above, international payment leads and lags between independent companies are usually of no concern to the exporter as long as it receives payment as agreed. The same would be true of WWC units that operate autonomously. But an integrated, coordinated WWC can benefit the enterprise as a whole by cooperating in payment leads or lags. The overall WWC objective is to get its money out of weak currencies and into strong currencies as quickly as reasonably possible.

Thus, instead of incurring the hedging costs incurred by independent companies while awaiting the future day of payment, WWC units can make payment immediately if trading out of a weak currency or delay payment until the payment date if trading out of a strong currency. If the profit of the unit paying immediately suffers from loss of interest on the money or shortage of operating capital (manager compensation and promotion frequently depend on profit), adjustment can be made to recognize that the WWC gained as a result of the cooperation of that management's WWC unit. We shall deal with management performance measurements and compensation packages in Chapter 22.

Effects of leads and lags on foreign exchange markets.   When an importer in a weak currency country buys from an exporter in a strong currency country with payment in the future, the usual practice is to convert or hedge immediately. And by selling the currency expected to go down in value and buying the one expected to go up in value, the importer helps realize those expectations; the prophecies are self-fulfilling.

The opposite is done when the importer in a country with a strong currency buys from a country with a weak currency. Now the importer will hold onto

---

leads buying a foreign currency immediately to satisfy a future need because you believe it will strengthen vis-à-vis your own currency

---

lags waiting until the last moment to buy a foreign currency you will need in the future because you believe it will weaken vis-à-vis your own currency

its perceived strong currency until the last moment and not buy the weak currency till then. Again, this strengthens the perceived strong currency and weakens the other.

Purposes of intra-WWC payments. Payments between WWC affiliates or between them and the parent[5] are of the same kinds as any company makes. On the operations side, they may be for:

1. Services, such as management or consulting fees.
2. Rental or lease payments for land, buildings, or equipment.
3. Royalties under license agreements.
4. Receivables and payables for parts, components, or raw materials provided by one part of the WWC to another.

On the capital side, they may be for:

1. Dividends out of an affiliate's profit on stock owned by the parent.
2. Interest or principal repayment of a loan from one part of a WWC to another.
3. Investment of additional capital, usually by the parent in an affiliate.

Objectives of intra-WWC payments. Within the strictures of applicable laws and the minimum working capital requirements of the parent and affiliates, WWCs can maximize their currency strengths and minimize their currency weaknesses.[6] Their objectives are to:

1. Keep as much money as is reasonably possible in countries with high interest rates. This is done to avoid borrowing at high rates, or perhaps to have capital to lend at those rates.
2. Keep as much money as is reasonably possible in countries where credit is difficult to obtain. If the WWC unit in such a country needs capital, it may be able to generate it internally.
3. Maximize holdings of hard, strong currencies, which may appreciate in value in terms of soft, weak currencies. Minimize, as much as is reasonably possible, holdings of the latter. You may observe that this objective may conflict with the first objective because strong currencies are usually available at lower interest rates than are weak ones. Financial management must consider all of the conditions, needs, and expectations and make a balanced judgment.
4. Minimize holdings of currencies that either are subject to currency exchange controls or can be expected to be subject to them during the period in which the company will hold those currencies.

exposure netting taking open positions in two currencies that are expected to balance each other

Exposure netting. **Exposure netting** is the acceptance of open positions* in two or more currencies that are considered to balance one another and therefore require no further internal or external hedging. Basically, there are two ways to accomplish this: (1) currency groups and (2) a combination of a strong currency and a weak currency.

Currency groups. Some groups of currencies tend to move in close conjunction with one another even during floating rate periods.[7] For example,

---

* An *open* position exists when you have greater assets than you have liabilities (or greater liabilities than you have assets) in one currency. A *closed*, or *covered*, position exists when your assets and liabilities in a currency are equal.

some LDC currencies are pegged to the currency of their most important DC trading partner; and among European DCs, the European Monetary System is an effort to coordinate movements of the participating governments' currencies vis-à-vis other currencies. In this situation, exposure netting could involve the simultaneous long and short of, say the Belgian franc and the Dutch guilder; the financial manager would have a franc receivable and a guilder payable and would feel that they cover each other.[8]

A strong currency and a weak currency.   A second exposure netting possibility involves two payables (or two receivables), one in a currently strong currency, such as the deutsche mark, and the other in a weaker one, such as the Canadian dollar. The hope is that weakness in one will offset the strength of the other.[9]

An advantage of exposure netting is that it avoids the costs of hedging. It is also more risky; the currencies may not behave as expected during the periods of the open receivables or payables.

Price adjustments.   Sales management often desires to make sales in a country whose currency is expected to be devalued. In such a situation, financial management finds that neither hedging nor exposure netting is possible or economic. Within the limitations of competition and the customer's budget, it may be possible to make price adjustments—to raise the selling price in the customer's currency. The hope is that the additional amount will compensate for the expected drop in value of the customer's currency.

Price adjustments within a WWC group.   If a WWC is of the coordinated, integrated type, there is much opportunity to adjust selling prices on intra-enterprise transactions between the parent and/or affiliated companies. The selling prices are raised or lowered by billing rate adjustments in attempts to anticipate currency exchange rate changes, thereby maximizing gains and minimizing losses.

Government reactions to intraenterprise price adjustments.   Such intraenterprise pricing practices are often used for purposes of (1) realizing higher profits in countries with lower tax rates and harder currencies and (2) decreasing import duties. Tax and customs officials have become more knowledgeable about such practices and now have the power to disregard prices that they consider unreasonably low or high. They then levy taxes or tariffs on what they determine to be reasonable profits or prices. Therefore, such practices must be used carefully and with discretion; financial management should be able to substantiate its prices with convincing cost data. Some writers do not recommend aggressive use of transfer pricing* for foreign exchange management.[10]

The alternatives the financial manager for the American exporter should consider to reduce the risk of exchange losses are shown in Figure 18–3. We use the transaction discussed above, in which an American exporter sold $1 million of goods to a Norwegian importer. At the time of sale, the exchange rate was $1 = 5 Norwegian krone. The sales contract called for the Norwegian importer to pay the American exporter NK5 million in six months, which placed the currency exchange risk on the exporter.

---

* Transfer pricing is a term that means the price when one unit of a WWC buys from another. See discussion of transfer pricing in Chapter 15.

■ **FIGURE 18–3** Hedging Currency Risks

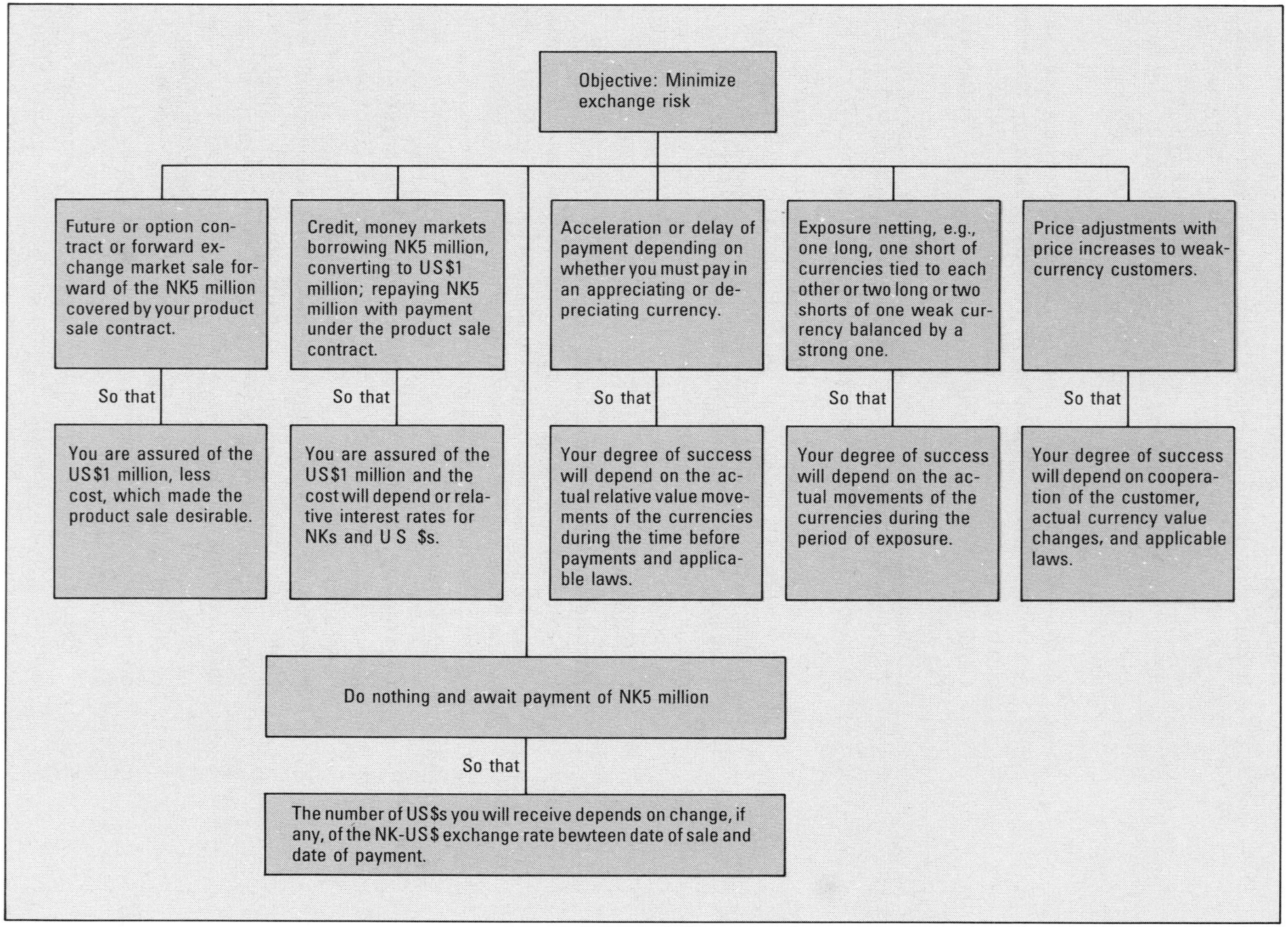

Objective: Minimize exchange risk

Future or option contract or forward exchange market sale forward of the NK5 million covered by your product sale contract.

So that

You are assured of the US$1 million, less cost, which made the product sale desirable.

Credit, money markets borrowing NK5 million, converting to US$1 million; repaying NK5 million with payment under the product sale contract.

So that

You are assured of the US$1 million and the cost will depend or relative interest rates for NKs and U S $s.

Acceleration or delay of payment depending on whether you must pay in an appreciating or depreciating currency.

So that

Your degree of success will depend on the actual relative value movements of the currencies during the time before payments and applicable laws.

Exposure netting, e.g., one long, one short of currencies tied to each other or two long or two shorts of one weak currency balanced by a strong one.

So that

Your degree of success will depend on the actual movements of the currencies during the period of exposure.

Price adjustments with price increases to weak-currency customers.

So that

Your degree of success will depend on coopera-tion of the customer, actual currency value changes, and applicable laws.

Do nothing and await payment of NK5 million

So that

The number of US$s you will receive depends on change, if any, of the NK-US$ exchange rate bewteen date of sale and date of payment.

Only for Big Business?

Generally, only larger companies can afford the expertise and deal in big enough amounts to make currency-risk hedging practical. However, a new development will bring some hedging within reach of medium and small businesses.

In January 1990, the U.S. Federal Reserve allowed American banks to hold foreign currency deposits in the United States. It is difficult or even impossible for a smaller firm to open a modest account at a foreign bank, but it is much less intimidating to deal with the firm's regular, local bank.

Now, to protect against a drop in the US$'s value, an importer from France can buy the number of French francs that will be needed to pay the French exporter. They can be held in its local account, earning interest until needed.

Translation Risks

We have just examined the risks that an international business incurs when it buys and sells between two or more countries and agrees to either make or receive a future payment in a foreign currency. The purchase or sale is a transaction, and the currency value change risk is called a transaction risk.[11]

Financial statements of multinationals must be stated in one currency, just as are the statements of any domestic business. The WWC may have businesses and assets in several currencies, such as German marks, French francs, and Japanese yen, but the financial statements would be meaningless for most people if all of those currencies were used. One must be chosen, and the values of the others must be translated to the chosen currency.

Sooner or later, companies with international operations will have assets, liabilities, revenues, and expenses in more than one currency. The financial statements of an American WWC must translate assets and so forth from the currencies of their locations into US$s.

translation risks the assets and liabilities/payables and receivables arising from investments abroad must be translated from the other currencies to your currency

The **translation risks** can be illustrated by assuming an American opens a Canadian dollar (C$) bank account of C$1 million at a time when the exchange rate is C$1 = US$1. If, one year later, the exchange rate has changed to C$1.10 = US$1 and the bank balance is still C$1 million, the American WWC still has its C$1 million. However, the company must report financially in US$s, and the Canadian bank account is now worth only about US$909,090.

FASB 8 and *FASB 52*

Due to significant variations in the translation methods used by American firms, the Financial Accounting Standards Board (FASB) issued a ruling called *FASB 8* in 1975 to establish uniform translation standards.

Foreign exchange reserves. U.S. companies once established foreign exchange reserves for their foreign subsidiaries to compensate for financial disclosure requirements of foreign exchange gains and losses. However, *FASB 8* put an end to those reserves. Accountants distrusted foreign exchange reserves because they felt that those reserves could be juggled, added to, or depleted, not so much to hedge exposure as to smooth corporate profits.

Some did not like *FASB 8*. Some argue that foreign currency gains and losses should not be translated and reported as required by *FASB 8* unless and until an actual gain or loss has been realized. They argue that unrealized gains or losses are only paper entries and that their translation and reporting distort actual business results. As reported in Chapter 6, *FASB 8* requirements were relaxed in 1981 to lessen the effects of translation on company financial statements. *FASB 52* replaced *FASB 8*.

Realistic information.   However, you should bear in mind that ongoing translating and reporting bring up to date the values in US$s of previously reported assets and so forth. Management must base important decisions, such as dividends, pricing, new investment, and asset location, on the consolidation of all such asset and earnings values. It is unrealistic for management to base key decisions on the assumption that exchange rates have not and will not change.

Previously used foreign exchange reserves gave management at least some cushion or leeway in making decisions regardless of changing exchange rates. Now, unable to use those reserves but required to translate and consolidate, management is taking action to hedge its balance sheets against translation losses.

Management fears.   Managers fear that translated and reported foreign exchange losses will be regarded as speculation, or worse, bad management, by shareholders and analysts. It is difficult to explain that reported losses are irrelevant or should be ignored. Even though reserves are not permitted under *FASB 52*, management is attempting to insulate financial statements from foreign exchange market fluctuations by other means.[12]

Some of the means for insulating financial statements from currency value fluctuations are the same as those discussed above in connection with transaction risks. Management can hedge, accelerate or delay payment, net exposures, or adjust prices. There are other means that can be used against transaction risks, but these are more often used in translation situations. Management can neutralize the company's balance sheet through the use of swaps.

neutralizing the balance sheet   having monetary assets in amounts approximately equal to monetary liabilities

Neutralizing the balance sheet.   In **neutralizing the balance sheet,** the procedure is to endeavor to have monetary assets in a given currency approximate monetary liabilities in that currency. In that condition, a fall in the currency value of your assets will be matched by the fall in your payment obligations; thus, the translation risk is avoided.

However, before financial management neutralizes its balance sheet to avoid translation risk, it must look to the business needs of the parent and subsidiary companies. The ongoing business flow of and need for capital, the cost of capital from country to country, payrolls, payables and receivables, optimum location for new investment, and dozens of other business considerations must be factored in before an attempt is made to neutralize the balance sheets of all subsidiaries. In other words, maximizing the profit of the enterprise should be more important than avoiding translation risk where they conflict.

Swaps

swaps   trades of assets and liabilities in different currencies or interest rate structures to lessen risks or lower costs

Swaps may be used to protect against transaction risks, are more likely to be used against translation risks, but are most likely to be useful as companies raise or transfer capital. Therefore, we shall treat swaps separately and examine several types: (1) spot and forward market swaps, (2) back-to-back

■ **FIGURE 18-4**
Back-to-Back Loans by
Two Parent Companies
(Each to the subsidiary of
the other)

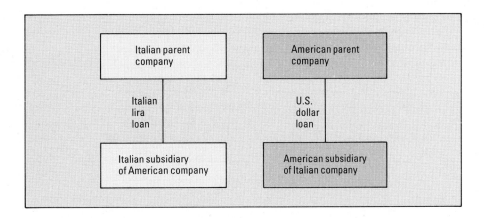

loans, and (3) bank swaps. Interest rate swaps are dealt with below in the "Capital Raising and Investing" section.

Spot and forward market swaps. Suppose an American parent wants to lend Italian lira (Il) to its Italian subsidiary and to avoid currency exchange risk. The parent will buy Il in the spot market and lend them to the subsidiary. At the same time, the parent will short the same amount of Il (buying US$s for forward delivery) for the period of the loan. The short Il position is covered with the Il repaid by the subsidiary, and the parent receives the dollars. The cost will depend on the discount rate in the forward market as compared to the spot market rate.

Back-to-back loans. Keeping the American parent and its Italian subsidiary of the previous example, let's add an Italian parent company and its American subsidiary. Assume each parent wants to lend to its subsidiary in the subsidiary's currency. This can be accomplished without using the foreign exchange market. The Italian parent lends the agreed amount in lira to the Italian subsidiary of the American parent. At the same time and the same loan maturity, the American parent lends the same amount (at the spot Il US$ rate) in US$s to the American subsidiary of the Italian parent. Figure 18-4 illustrates this.

As you see, each loan is made and repaid in one currency, thus avoiding foreign exchange risk. Each loan should have the right of offset, which means that if either subsidiary defaults on its repayment, the other subsidiary can withhold its repayment. This avoids the need for parent company guarantees.

This sort of back-to-back loan swap can be adapted to many circumstances and can involve more than two countries or companies. If a subsidiary in a blocked currency country has a surplus of that currency in its local operation, perhaps the local subsidiary of another WWC needs capital.[13] The other WWC would like to provide that capital but would not like to convert more of its hard currency into a soft currency. The subsidiary of the first WWC lends its surplus currency to the subsidiary of the second WWC. The parent company of the second WWC lends the parent company of the first WWC an equivalent amount in some other currency that it can use.[14] Figure 18-5 illustrates this.

Interest may or may not be charged on swaps. That usually depends on whether interest rates in the two countries were at similar rates or were widely different. In the latter situation, the borrower getting the higher-cost currency might pay an equivalently higher interest on repayment.

■ **FIGURE 18–5**
Back-to-Back Swap
(Where a soft currency is involved)

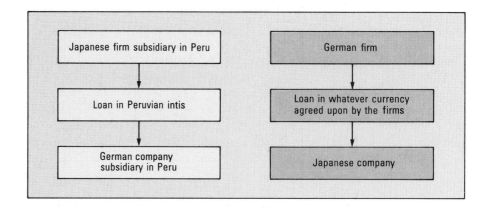

You may have observed that there has been no mention of banks in our discussion of swaps. These company-to-company loans are competition for commercial banks, but some banks will facilitate negotiations or act as a broker between clients in arranging swaps. Investment banks and other money brokers sometimes facilitate or even instigate swaps as a service to clients.

Bank swaps.   Historically, swaps of this kind have been between banks (commercial or central) of two or more countries for the purpose of acquiring temporarily needed foreign exchange, but in recent years companies have entered the field. A typical use of a bank swap is to finance expansion of a WWC subsidiary in an LDC whose currency is soft and nonconvertible or blocked.

The mechanics are simple. Assume a Swiss WWC wishes to expand a subsidiary's plant in Indonesia and, in doing so, to minimize foreign exchange risks and to avoid exchanging any more hard Swiss francs (Sfs) for soft Indonesian rupiahs (Irs).

The Swiss parent company may deal either with a commercial bank in Indonesia or with the Indonesian central bank. In either event, the Swiss WWC deposits Sfs in a Swiss bank to the credit of the Indonesian bank. In turn, the Indonesian bank lends Irs to the Indonesian subsidiary. At an agreed future date, the Indonesian bank repays the Sfs and the subsidiary repays the Irs.

You may have observed that in this example the Indonesian rupiahs are lent and repaid in Indonesia and the Swiss francs are lent and repaid in Switzerland, which eliminates the need to use the foreign exchange markets. Thus, exchange market costs are avoided while both parties obtain a foreign currency for which they have a use.

We have spoken of swaps as methods to lessen translation risks and raise capital. There are also more common ways to raise capital.

CAPITAL RAISING AND INVESTING

When a company wishes to raise capital, financial management must make a number of decisions. To cut the costs of capital, financial managers are increasingly exploring the uses of interest rate swaps and currency swaps. As these are relatively new and growing in popularity, we shall treat them separately.

Decisions

1. The currency in which the capital will be raised.
2. Long-term estimate of the strength or weakness of that currency.
3. Whether part or all of the capital should be raised by the sale of **equity** instead of **debt.**[15]
4. Whether the money should be borrowed from *(a)* a commercial bank by an ordinary loan; *(b)* a bank as part of a swap, discussed above; *(c)* another company as part of a swap or otherwise; *(d)* another part of the WWC; or *(e)* a public offering in one of the world's capital markets, for example, in the New York or Eurobond markets.
5. If the decision is made to use one of the world's capital markets, management must then decide in which of those markets it can achieve its objectives at lowest cost. The WWC can shop among the national markets in such diverse centers as New York, London, Paris, Zurich, Bahrain, Singapore, Tokyo, and the Cayman Islands. Or it can try the international, or Eurobond, Eurocurrency-type, markets in the above-named centers and elsewhere.[16]
6. How much money the company needs and for how long. For instance, if the company is moving into a new market or product, there will probably be a period during product introduction, plant construction, or whatever when the new venture will need more capital than it can generate.
7. Whether other sources of money are available. For example, if the company is forming or expanding a joint venture operation, the joint venturer may be a good source of money. Or if the move is into a country or area that wants the WWC's technology or management or the jobs that will be created, the government may be a source of low-cost funds. Under such circumstances, the company may also be able to negotiate tax reductions or holidays.*

To optimize the decision results, the company needs up-to-date, accurate information. It should also have good, ongoing relationships with international bank officers and with financial management at other firms.

We have been dealing with external sources of capital, that is, sources outside the company's operations. Of course, a successful company generates its own capital internally, but that subject is not included here.

Interest Rate Swaps

Interest rate swaps are a product of the advent and evolution of currency swaps, which were intended as an arbitrage between currency markets. Interest rate swaps are themselves a form of arbitrage but are between the fixed-rate and the floating-rate interest markets. An interest rate swap, in its most basic form, is nothing more than an exchange by two parties of interest rate flows on borrowings made in these two markets—fixed for floating and floating for fixed. The result: each party obtains the type of liability it prefers and at a more attractive rate.

equity capital capital raised by selling common stock representing ownership of the company

debt capital capital raised by selling bonds representing debt of the company

---

* A tax holiday is a period after an investment is made during which the government agrees not to tax the company's operations, profits, or executives.

Bank-intermediated "plain vanilla" swaps.   In a typical plain vanilla swap, a BBB-rated U.S. corporation is paired with an AAA-rated foreign bank. The BBB corporation wants to borrow at fixed rates but is discouraged from doing so by the high rates attached to its low rating. The company can borrow in the floating-rate market, however. The AAA foreign bank wants to borrow at floating rates, as its assets are tied to LIBOR. The bank normally pays LIBOR to obtain lendable funds. It is able to borrow at fixed rates, which are better than those the corporation could get.

When the swap is planned, the bank borrows at fixed rates in the Eurobond market, and the BBB corporation borrows at floating rates. With this done, the two then swap rates on their respective loans. The corporation entices the bank into doing this by discounting the floating rate to the bank by LIBOR minus 0.25 percent. In return, the bank gives the BBB corporation a fixed rate that is better than the one the corporation could acquire on its own. A hypothetical numerical example is shown below.

Assume the BBB firm can borrow fixed-rate at 12.5 percent.

1. AAA bank issues 11 percent fixed-rate debt.
2. BBB firm taps floating-rate market at LIBOR plus 0.5 percent.
3. BBB firm swaps floating-rate to bank at LIBOR minus 0.25 percent.
4. AAA bank swaps 11 percent fixed-rate to BBB firm.

Net result: the BBB firm saves 150 basis points and passes 75 of them on to the AAA bank; the bank saves 25 basis points on the normal floating rate.

There are nine basic advantages to interest rate swaps. First, swaps give the corporation the flexibility to transform floating-rate debt to fixed-rate, and vice versa. Second, there are potential rate savings, as illustrated previously. Third, swaps may be based on outstanding debt and may thus avoid increasing liabilities. Fourth, swaps provide alternative sources of financing. Fifth, swaps are private transactions. Sixth, there are no SEC reporting or registration requirements, as yet. Seventh, the swap contract is simple and straightforward. Eighth, rating agencies, such as Moody's and S&P, take a neutral to positive position on corporate swaps. Ninth, tax treatment on swaps is uncomplicated, as there are no withholding taxes levied on interest payments to overseas swap partners, and the interest expense of the fixed-rate payer is treated as though it were on a fixed-rate obligation.

The only drawback to swaps is the risk that one swap partner may fail to make the agreed payments to the other swap partner.

The impact of swaps on financial management practices is predicted to be great. It is foreseeable that corporations will use swaps to match assets to liabilities and to protect investments in capital assets, such as plant and equipment, from floating-rate interest fluctuations. Financial institutions also see swaps as a way to match receivables (loans made) to liabilities (investors' deposits). For example, to match a fixed-rate loan, the financial institution would sell a floating-rate CD and then swap it for a fixed-rate liability.

Many corporations and financial institutions have engaged in swaps. The Greyhound Corporation, for example, was involved in $80 million of swaps with Bank of America (three times) and Goldman Sachs (once). Transamerica, ITT Financial, Great Western Financial Corporation, and Consumer Power Company have also been involved in swaps.

"We need two hundred million bucks by Friday—any ideas?"

The Wall Street Journal, with permission of Cartoon Features Syndicate

Arranging swaps is quite lucrative. Fees for arranging swaps include a 0.5 percent charge on the fixed-rate payer, 1.87 percent as the front-end Eurobond spread, and 0.125 percent as a standard Eurobond expense. Thus, total front-end fees average 2.5 percent, or $2.5 million on the average $100 million, seven-year transaction. The top investment bankers in the area of arranging swaps are First Boston Corporation, Goldman Sachs & Co., Morgan Stanley & Co., Salomon Brothers, and Lehman Brothers Kuhn Loeb. The top commercial banks in this area are Morgan Guaranty Trust, Citicorp, Bankers Trust, Manufacturers Hanover Trust, and Continental Illinois. The difference between the two groups is that investment bankers stress their Eurobond expertise and their network of corporate contacts, while commercial banks emphasize "their larger coverage of the marketplace."[17]

"Synthetic swaps" with or without bank intermediation.   The "synthetic swap" is created by using interest rate futures markets to fix floating rates, or vice versa. For instance, a company with floating-rate debt could fix the interest charge by selling—or, more accurately, shorting—interest rate futures contracts. Now, if interest rates go up, the company must pay more on its floating-rate debt, but it will profit on the short futures position to offset the higher interest payment.

Going the other direction.   Suppose the company has fixed-rate debt and wants to go float. It would buy floating Euro currency or Treasury futures. In this case, if interest rates fall, the company is stuck with a fixed-rate primary loan on which interest payments remain at the same higher level. As the rates fall, however, the futures contracts would appreciate, and the fixed payments would be subsidized by futures profits.

Currency swaps.   Companies use the currency swap markets when they need to raise money in a currency issued by a country in which they are not well known and must therefore pay a higher interest rate than would be available to a local or better-known borrower. For example, a medium-size American company may have need of Swiss francs (SFs), but even though it is a sound credit risk, it may be relatively unknown in Switzerland.

If it can find—if a bank or broker can pair it with—a Swiss company that wants US$s, the swap would work as follows. The American company would borrow US$s in the United States, where it is well known and can get a low interest rate. The Swiss company would borrow SFs in Switzerland for the same reason. They would then swap the currencies and service each other's loans; that is, the Swiss company would repay the US$ loan, while the American company would repay the SF loan.

SALES WITHOUT MONEY

A number of countries desire goods and products for which they do not have the convertible currency to pay. That has not prevented efforts by many suppliers to sell to them anyway. Such countries are usually communist and/or less developed, and there are differences in dealings with a communist as compared to a noncommunist customer, although applicable to both are variations on the two main nonmoney trade themes—countertrade and industrial cooperation.

Communist Customers Are Different

As indicated above, there are some differences between the communist and noncommunist countries in terms of nonmoney trade. The differences can be important.

The noncommunist countries tend to be more open with their production, trade, employment, education, fiscal, and monetary statistics. Such statistics are not notably reliable in LDCs, but the noncommunist ones are more likely to let in and take advice from World Bank, International Monetary Fund, or national aid experts. The statistics are improving.

The noncommunist countries are more likely to get financial aid and technology from UN agencies.[18] They are also more likely to get aid and technology from the Western developed countries, which have the most to give.

Those differences noted, it is still necessary to utilize the barter, countertrade, compensation, coproduction, and switch devices to sell to the nonoil LDCs and the communist (LDC/C) countries.[19]

Countertrade

countertrade LDC/C countries' attempts to acquire DC goods and services by trading LDC/C goods

Countertrade usually involves two or more contracts, one for the purchase of DC products or services and one or more for the purchase of LDC/C products or services. A Mitsui study speaks of six varieties of countertrade.[20] They are called (1) counterpurchase, (2) compensation, (3) barter, (4) switch, (5) offset, and (6) clearing account arrangements. All involve to a greater or lesser degree the substitution of LDC/C goods, products, or services for scarce DC money. They may be relatively simple, involving only two countries or companies, or quite complex, calling for a number of countries, companies, currencies, and contracts.[21]

Counterpurchase.   In counterpurchase situations, the goods supplied by the LDC/C are not produced by or out of the goods or products imported from the DC. An example of counterpurchase is PepsiCo's arrangement with the USSR.

PepsiCo sells to the USSR the concentrate for the drink, which is bottled and sold in that country. In exchange, PepsiCo has exclusive rights to export Soviet vodka for sale in the West.

Compensation. Such transactions call for payment by the LDC/C in products produced by DC equipment. The products made in the LDC/C by the DC equipment are shipped to the DC in payment for the equipment. International Harvester has a compensation agreement with Poland for tractors. Poland is paying with components that International uses at its assembly plant in England.

Barter. Barter is an ancient form of commerce and the simplest sort of countertrade. The LDC/C sends products to the DC that are equal in value to the products delivered by the DC to the LDC/C.

Switch. Frequently, the goods delivered by the LDC/C are not easily usable or salable. Then a third party is brought in to dispose of them. This process is called *switch trading.*

Offset. The offset form occurs when the importing nation requires a portion of the materials, components, or subassemblies of a product to be procured in the local (importer's) market. The exporter may set up or cooperate in setting up a parts manufacturing and assembly facility in the importing country.

Clearing account arrangements. These are used to facilitate the exchange of products over a specified time period. When the period ends, any balance outstanding must be cleared by the purchase of additional goods or settled by a cash payment. The bank or broker acts as an intermediary to facilitate settlement of the clearing accounts by finding markets for counterpurchased goods or by converting goods or cash payments into products desired by the country with a surplus.

How important is countertrade? Frequently, countertrade agreements and their executions are not reported publicly. Indeed, the parties often prefer privacy and confidentiality for competitive reasons and to not set precedents for future deals. Therefore, estimates of the extent of countertrade vary widely. The U.S. Commerce Department estimates that between 20 and 30 percent of world trade is now subject to some form of countertrade and that the proportion could reach 50 percent in 15 years.

Major U.S. firms report transactions involving some form of countertrade. *Business Week* and General Electric each independently estimate the volume at 30 percent of world trade. By far the lowest estimate, 8 percent, was made by the General Agreement on Tariffs and Trade.

Regardless of which estimate is nearest the truth, the value of countertrade is very large. Apply any of the estimates to the over $2.5 trillion volume of world trade, and the result is big.[22]

U.S. government's positions on countertrade. We say "positions" because different agencies contradict each other, and Congress contradicts itself. The Treasury Department is flatly opposed to countertrade, the Commerce Department helps companies engage in it, and the Export-Import Bank has no policy for dealing with it. In Congress, legislation has been introduced both to curtail countertrading and to encourage countertrading of U.S. surplus agricultural commodities.[23]

Other governments' positions on countertrade.   The governments of most LDCs either encourage or require countertrade, but so also do such industrialized countries as Australia and New Zealand. No country forbids countertrade. For information about the attitudes and laws of individual countries on the subject, see *Business International* listings, such as the one in its July 14, 1986, issue, pages 220–21, which lists the positions of Asian and Pacific countries on countertrade.

Twin problems.   The age-old twin problems with goods coming from the LDC/C side of countertrade transactions are product quality and delivery reliability. In general, there are two ways the DC side is coping with those problems.

One solution is inspection of the goods before they leave the LDC/C plant by a reliable, third-party organization. Two such organizations are the Paris-based Bureau Veritas and the Societé Generale de Surveillance, whose main office is in Geneva.

Roger Gyarmaty of Veritas says, "We go back to the production process to see if the goods are being made to specifications. We see to it that delivery times and terms are being met. And we check the packaging and loading to be sure the goods are not damaged at those points. Companies can save up to two or three times the cost of our services just through fewer headaches when they receive the goods."[24]

A second solution is growing in popularity. The Eastern European banking structure is developing, and the DC countertrade party is increasingly getting a guarantee of quality and delivery from a bank in the LDC/C country. When such a guarantee has been given, the bank takes a stern interest in the product's production line to avoid having to come up with precious foreign exchange in the event of quality or delivery not in accordance with the contract.[25]

New directions.   Not all countertrade is between DCs and LDC/Cs. In 1988, there was trade of Angolan coffee for Soviet equipment, and developing countries frequently have agreements encouraging trade with each other, such as those between Argentina and Brazil and among the ASEAN member-countries.

Alan Linger, Lloyds Bank countertrade manager, believes such business could become triangular by including DCs. For example, DC goods would be exported to an Eastern European country, products of which would go to an LDC, which would complete the triangle by shipping its commodities to the DC.[26]

Industrial Cooperation

industrial cooperation
long-term relationships between DC companies and LDC/C plants in which some or all production is done in the LDC/C plant

Industrial cooperation, which is favored by the LDC/C, requires long-term relationships, with part or all of the production being done in the LDC/C.[27] Part of the resulting products is sold in the DCs or the Third World.

One writer, Ronald E. Hayt, speaks of five industrial cooperation methods.[28]

1. *Joint venture.* Two or more companies or state agencies combine assets to form a new and distinct economic entity, and they share management, profits, and losses.

2. *Coproduction and specialization.* The factory in the LDC/C produces certain agreed components of a product, while a company in the DC produces the other components. The product is then assembled at both locations for their respective markets.

3. *Subcontracting.* The LDC/C factory manufactures a product according to specifications of the DC company and delivers the product to the DC company, which then markets it.

4. *Licensing.* The LDC/C and DC parties enter into a license agreement whereby the LDC/C enterprise uses DC technology to manufacture a product. The DC company is paid a license royalty fee in money or in product. The latter method is preferred by the LDC/C.

5. *Turnkey plants.* The DC party is responsible for building the entire plant, starting it, training LDC/C personnel, and turning over the keys to the LDC/C party. Of course, the LDC/C wants to pay in products of the new plant.

Two threads run through countertrade and industrial cooperation. The first is that the LDC/C does not have enough hard, convertible currency to buy what it wants from the DC. That leads to the second, which is the effort of the LDC/C to substitute goods for currency.

INTERNATIONAL FINANCE CENTER

A number of new developments are forcing international companies to pay more attention to financial management. International financial management has become more and more different than domestic financial management, and in several such companies, the finance operation has become a profit center and is no longer merely a service. Some of the new developments are (1) floating exchange rates, whose fluctuations are sometimes volatile; (2) *FASB 52*, which requires translation of assets, liabilities, payables, and receivables from foreign currencies to the company's currency; (3) growth in the number of capital and foreign exchange markets where a WWC can shop for lower interest costs and better currency rates; (4) different and changing inflation rates from country to country; (5) advances in electronic cash management systems; and realization by financial managers that through innovative management of temporarily idle cash balances of the WWC units, they can increase the yields and the enterprise's profit. The WWCs have established **international finance centers.**

international finance centers handle most or all international financial transactions for all units of a WWC

Volatile, Floating Currency Exchange Rates

An international finance center can take advantage of volatile, floating currency exchange rates to make money for the WWC in several ways. It would be aware of which currencies are most susceptible to sudden weakness, avoid borrowing in undervalued currencies, and maximize short-term assets in strong currencies.[29] This is currency exposure management.

FASB 52

This rule introduced the concept of the "functional currency"—that is, the dominant currency of the economic environment of each WWC affiliate. If the functional currency is the local currency (for example, French francs for the French affiliate), *FASB 52* allows translations to flow to the equity section of the parent company's balance sheet, which is less visible and more desirable than putting them in the profit and loss statement, as was required by *FASB 8*. Nevertheless, it is better to minimize dramatic changes in equity, and the international finance center simplifies this in three ways.

1. *Intraenterprise trading.* Financial dealings of this kind are funneled through the center. It can net out open positions for each of the affiliates.

2. *Borrowing.* The center quickly spots exposed assets and receivables that cannot be netted. It can borrow or lend in the appropriate currency to cover those positions.

3. *Hedging.* Other positions that do not net out can be hedged, which the center can do quickly and efficiently.[30]

Capital and Exchange Markets

Like any company, a WWC needs to raise capital from time to time. Unlike most domestic companies, it needs to exchange currencies. Given the proliferation of capital and exchange markets, the international finance center should advise and direct the parent and affiliates where to raise and exchange money at the lowest costs.

Inflation Rates

Inflation goes up and inflation goes down, and while it's going up in one country, it's going down in another. The international finance center should be aware of all those trends and advise and direct the WWC system how to protect assets and profits from monetary erosion and other economic and political risks.

Electronic Cash Management

Currency exposure management is being simplified. New technology is permitting the creation of worldwide networks that enable firms to transfer funds electronically. The international finance center should evaluate and use the best of those developing systems. Some of them are Electronic Funds Transfer Network, Society for Worldwide Interbank Financial Telecommunications, Clearing House Automated Payment System, and Clearing House Interbank Payments Transfer.[31]

Other Uses of the International Finance Center

Mentioned above are only a few of the possible functions of an international finance center. Here are some others:

1. *Handle internal and external invoicing.* The center can make complex decisions about financing international trade among the WWC units and between them and outside suppliers and customers. All data on imports and exports can be channeled through the center, which can determine which currencies will be used and how the trades will be financed.[32]

2. *Help weak currency affiliate.* An affiliate with a weak currency could have difficulty obtaining needed imports. By placing itself in the trade chain, the center can arrange the financing needed by such an affiliate.

3. *Strengthen affiliate evaluation and reporting systems.* The center is in a unique position to understand and interpret the performance of affiliates in countries around the world. Inherent differences are exacerbated by volatile exchange rates, different inflation rates, varying tax laws and accounting rules, transfer price policies, and a host of environmental factors. WWC decisions about transfer pricing, choosing one subsidiary over another to compete for a contract, or adding capital to one subsidiary rather than another also complicate performance evaluations, with which the international finance center can assist.

A Racy Convertible from Toyota

Although Toyota, Japan's biggest automaker, was flush with cash during 1986, in that year it floated the biggest convertible yen bond that had ever been seen in Japan. In one go, it raised ¥200 billion (about $1.23 billion), twice as much as any other Japanese company had ever raised in this way. Why?

As the bluest of Japanese blue chips, Toyota commanded the finest of fine terms, and those convertibles carried a coupon of only 1.7 percent. The normal interest for other companies was around 2.5 percent.

Toyota reinvested the ¥200 billion in financial instruments on better terms than it paid and thus made more than it could have made from building and selling automobiles. In Japan, this practice is called *Zaiteku*, or "financial engineering," and numerous companies have been doing it.

For the 10 biggest earners from *Zaiteku*, it accounted for at least a third of their pre-tax profits in the first half of 1986. For Nissan, *Zaiteku* made the difference between a profit and a loss. But not all *Zaiteku* practitioners were as skilled as Nissan—some lost money at it.[33]

SUMMARY

The importance of financial management has so increased in the last few years that some WWCs have made financial management a profit center. Financial management is no longer just a service. Foreign currency exchange gains or losses on payables, receivables, assets, and liabilities can substantially alter profit and loss statements and balance sheets.

The chapter examined transaction and translation risks and the means used by multinational company managers to deal with these risks, such as hedges, acceleration or delay of payment, exposure netting, price adjustments, and swaps. It spoke of how *FASB 8* dealt with translation risks and of how *FASB 8* was replaced by *FASB 52*.

The chapter also dealt briefly with the raising and investing of capital and the decisions that financial management must make in connection with those activities. Other types of decisions are called for if a company wishes to do business with a customer that has little or no convertible currency. This involves some form of countertrade or industrial cooperation.

Relatively new and of growing importance are international finance centers. These represent an extension of the increasing recognition of financial management as a potential profit center.

The objectives of this chapter have been, not to identify all the problems of financial management nor all the tools and practices used to solve them, but to introduce you to the subject, to make you aware that international business presents more financial problems than does purely domestic business, and to assure you that most of these problems can be overcome. In fact, not only can they be overcome, but in some instances, they can be turned to the company's advantage.

Some of the big Japanese companies have such good credit ratings that they can borrow money at lower interest rates than are available to most Japanese companies. They are therefore able to borrow money and to lend the borrowed money at a profit. The Japanese call this process *Zaiteku*, which translates as "financial engineering."

QUESTIONS

1. Why is an exporter that is to be paid in six months in a foreign currency worried about fluctuating foreign exchange rates?

2. Are there ways that this exporter can protect itself? If so, what are they?

3. How does the credit or money market hedge work?

4. Why is acceleration or delay of payments more useful to a WWC than to smaller, separate companies?

5. How would you accomplish exposure netting with currencies of two countries that tend to go up and down together in value?

6. Why is the price adjustment device more useful to a WWC than to smaller, separate companies?

7. Some argue that translation gains or losses are not important so long as they have not been realized and are only accounting entries. What is the other side of that argument?

8. Is the back-to-back loan a sort of swap? How does it work?

9. What advantage does a WWC have over a single-country operation in raising capital?

10. How and why would a seller make a sale to a buyer that has no money the seller can use?

11. DC partners in countertrade contracts have had problems with quality and timely delivery of goods from the LDC/C partners. How are they trying to deal with those problems?

MINICASE 18–1

Dealing with the Transaction Risk Caused by Fluctuations of Relative Currency Values

You are the finance manager of an American multinational. Your company has sold US$1 million of its product to a French importer. The rate of exchange on the day of sale is US$1 = Ff5, so on that day the 1 million U.S. dollars equals 5 million French francs.

The contract calls for the French importer to pay your company Ff5 million six months from the date of sale. Therefore, your company bears the transaction risk of a change in the currency exchange rates between the US$ and the Ff.

Assume your company has no need for French francs and will want U.S. dollars no later than the payment date. Assume further that you do not wish to carry the transaction risk. Give two methods by which you might protect your company from that risk.

MINICASE 18–2

Countertrade

An American company and a Soviet foreign trade organization (FTO) have reached agreement on all the technical aspects of the product that the company wants to sell and the Soviet Union wants to buy. All export license problems have been cleared, but one obstacle remains. The Soviet Union is not willing to pay in a hard, convertible currency.

The product includes late technology, but it has some relatively simple components. The company has not sold previously to the East or to any customer for which U.S. dollar availability was a difficulty.

The company turns to you, an international business consultant with extensive experience in dealing with communist and Third World customers. What inquiries will you advise your client to make? What steps would you advise the client to take in efforts to consummate the sale and get the U.S. dollars it needs?

MINICASE 18-3

Countertrade

In your contertrade experience, you have encountered two serious problems. Sometimes the quality of the goods supplied by the LDC/C partner is not up to specifications. On other occasions, the LDC/C partner was late in making deliveries or delivered only part of the goods promised.

What are two methods you might try to avoid those problems in future contracts?

MINICASE 18-4

CFO Decisions When the Company Has a Temporary Surplus of Funds

You are the chief financial officer (CFO) of a WWC. The parent company has a temporary surplus of funds. You do not foresee an operating need for the money, $5 million, for about six months.

What are some possible uses for that money by the parent? What uses are possible within the WWC system? What considerations will govern your decision as to how best to utilize the money?

MINICASE 18-5

Using a Temporary Fund Surplus to Make Some Profit in Currency Forward Markets

Assume your decision in Minicase 18-4 was to use the $5 million to buy one or more open contracts in the currency forward markets. The first contract was long in British pounds at 1.5138 for 30 days with your $5 million.

How many pounds and pence is your company long?

In 30 days when you cover the contract, the price is 1.5347. Did you make or lose money for your company? How much? (For purposes of these minicases, ignore commissions.)

MINICASE 18-6

Short the French Franc

Use the same facts as in Minicase 18-5. Your decision is to invest the $5 million in a contract shorting the French franc at 8.0475 for 30 days. How many francs and cents are you short? In this instance, you cover at the end of the 30-day contract at 7.8992. Did you make or lose money for your company? How much?

SUPPLEMENTARY READINGS

Argy, Victor E. *Exchange Rate Management in Theory and Practice.* Princeton, N.J.: International Finance Section, Department of Economics, Princeton University, 1982.

Babbel, David F. "Determining the Optimum Strategy for Hedging Currency Exposure." *Journal of International Business Studies,* Spring–Summer 1983, pp. 133–39.

Batra, Raveendra N.; Shabtai Domenfeld; and Josef Hadar. "Hedging Behavior by Multinational Firms." *Journal of International Business Studies,* Winter 1982, pp. 59–70.

"Big Is Beautiful in Countertrade." *Euromoney,* January 1985, pp. 144–48.

Blin, J. M.; Stuart I. Greenbaum; and Donald P. Jacobs. *Flexible Exchange Rates and International Business.* Washington, D.C.: British-North American Committee, 1981.

Countertrade. Antwerp: Kredietbank, September 18, 1987.

East-West Trade: Recent Developments in Countertrade. Paris: Organization for Economic Cooperation and Development, 1981.

Fitzgerald, Bruce. "Countertrade Reconsidered." *Finance & Development,* June 1987, pp. 46–49.

Foreign Currency Translation. Stamford, Conn.: Financial Accounting Standards Board, 1981.

Gernon, Helen. "The Effect of Translation on Multinational Corporations' Internal Performance Evaluations." *Journal of International Business Studies,* Spring–Summer 1983, pp. 103–12.

Herring, Richard J., ed. *Managing Foreign Exchange Risk: Essays Commissioned in Honor of the Centenary of the Wharton School, University of Pennsylvania.* New York: Cambridge University Press, 1983.

Höberg, Bengt, and Clas Wahlbin. "East-West Industrial Cooperation: The Swedish Case." *Journal of International Business Studies,* Spring–Summer 1984, pp. 63–80.

Kenyon, Alfred. *Currency Risk Management.* New York: John Wiley & Sons, 1981.

Kettell, Brian. *The Finance of International Business.* Westport, Conn.: Quorum Books, 1981.

Kyung, Mo Huh. "Countertrade: Trade without Cash?" *Finance & Development,* December 1983, pp. 14–16.

Miramon, Jacques. "Countertrade: An Illusory Solution." *OECD Observer,* May 1985, pp. 24–29.

Mirus, Rolf, and Bernard Yeung. "Economic Incentives for Countertrade." *Journal of International Business Studies,* Fall 1986, pp. 27–40.

Mitsui's Countertrade Services. Mitsui Trade News, March/April 1987.

Rodriquez, Rita M. *Foreign Exchange Management in U.S. Multinationals.* Lexington, Mass.: Lexington Books, 1980.

Vinson, Joseph D. "Financial Planning for the Multinational Corporation with Multiple Goals." *Journal of International Business Studies,* Winter 1982. pp. 43–58.

Warren, Geoffrey. "Latest in Currency Hedging Methods." *Euromoney,* May 1987, pp. 245–64.

ENDNOTES

1. See the first illustration and accompanying discussion in Chapter 6.

2. There is almost always some cost for protection, and an important management function is to compare the magnitude of the risk with the cost of protection against it.

3. If you were dealing in a currency more actively traded than the krone, such as the British, Canadian, French, Japanese, Swiss, or West German currency, you would use the 180-day futures quotation for that currency.

4. Covered positions are also referred to as "square" or "perfect" positions.

5. In every WWC, there is one central company at the top of the organization. That company is called the parent company. The other companies are referred to as affiliated or subsidiary companies.

6. The power of WWCs to control the timing and currencies of payment and of asset accumulation has not been ignored by governments. In furtherance of their tax and exchange control policies, most countries have legal limits on acceleration, delays, and intra-WWC netting.

7. Currencies may be fixed in value in terms of each other by international agreement; if there are no such agreements, they are said to float.

8. The Netherlands and Belgium are both members of the European Monetary System.

9. Andreas R. Prindl, *Foreign Exchange Risk* (New York: John Wiley & Sons, 1976), p. 61.

10. Ibid., p. 65.

11. Alan C. Shapiro, *Foreign Exchange Risk Management* (New York: AMACOM, 1978), p. 12.

12. "Why a Reserve Is Cheaper," *Euromoney,* February 1979, p. 56.

13. A blocked currency situation arises either because there is no satisfactory market for the currency or because of a country's laws.

14. In such circumstances, the equivalent amount is subject to some negotiation, because a blocked, nonconvertible currency does not have a free market spot or other exchange rate, which would be used when dealing with two convertible currencies.

15. When equity securities (stock) are issued, part of the ownership is being sold. No money is being borrowed that must be repaid, as is the case when debt securities (bonds) are issued.

16. The international, or Euro-type, capital market has been created by national currencies being traded, borrowed, and lent outside their countries of origin. Thus, U.S. dollars outside the United States are Eurodollars, and West German deutsche marks outside Germany are Euromarks.

17. Beth McGoldrick, "The Interest Rate Swap Comes of Age," *Institutional Investor,* August 1983, p. 83.

18. See Chapter 4.

19. Nonoil LDCs are LDCs that are net petroleum importers.

20. *Mitsui Trade News,* March/April 1987, pp. 1–4.

21. Edward W. Stroh, "Countertrade: Not for Everyone, but Worth a Look," *International Business and Economic Studies,* November 1979, pp. 87–89.

22. Stephen S. Cohen and John Zysman, "Countertrade Deals Are Running out of Control," *Los Angeles Times,* March 23, 1986, part 4, pp. 3 and 7.

23. Ibid.

24. "Countertrade: Avoiding Problems with Suppliers," *Business Eastern Europe,* May 16, 1988, p. 155.

25. Alan Spence, "East-West Countertrade Entering New Era of Complexity," *Financial Times,* December 13, 1988, p. 38.

26. Ibid.

27. Karen C. Taylor, *East-West Trade: Managing Encounter and Accommodation,* ed. Lawrence C. McQuade, Atlantic Council of the United States (Boulder: Westview Press, 1977), pp. 72–79.

28. Ronald E. Hayt, "East-West Trade Growth Potential for the 1980s," *Columbia-Journal of World Business,* Spring 1978, p. 63.

29. "Defending against a Strong Dollar," *Business International,* July 16, 1982, p. 226.

30. Christopher Power, "RJR's Foreign Coup," *Forbes,* September 12, 1983, p. 226.

31. "Fine-Tuning Financial Management," *Business International,* January 14, 1983, p. 10.

32. For an account of one reinvoicing center, see "An Invoice Center that Juggles Currencies," *Business Week,* November 27, 1978, p. 128. For a more complete account of international finance centers and in-house banks, see "A Special Report: Global Finance and Investing." *The Asian Wall Street Journal,* October 6, 1986, p. 10.

33. *The Economist,* December 13, 1986, p. 84.

Chapter 19

Production Systems

There is a significant difference between the American and European philosophy of production and the Japanese philosophy of production. The Americans think stock is a necessary evil for smooth-running production, but the Japanese believe stock is an absolute evil.

Shigeo Shingo, dean of Japanese productivity and quality consultants

LEARNING OBJECTIVES

In this chapter, you will study:

1. Japanese efforts to improve quality and lower costs.

2. Problems with just-in-time (JIT).

3. Synchronized manufacturing.

4. American and European efforts to improve quality and lower costs.

5. Why multinational firms wish to standardize production processes and procedures on a worldwide basis.

6. The impediments to worldwide standardization of production processes and procedures.

7. The four principal factors involved in the efficient operation of the production system—plant location, plant layout, materials handling, and the human element.

8. The two general classes of activities, productive and supportive, that must be performed in all production systems.

9. Some of the reasons why a given production system may not perform as expected.

10. The principal supportive activities—purchasing, maintenance, and the technical function.

KEY WORDS AND CONCEPTS

- Total quality control (TQC)
- Just-in-time
- Quality circles (quality control circles)
- Taylor's scientific management system
- Preventive (planned) maintenance
- Synchronized manufacturing
- Bottleneck
- Manufacturing rationalization
- Backward vertical integration
- Intermediate technology
- Appropriate technology
- Export processing zones

BUSINESS INCIDENT

Allen-Bradley and Computer Integrated Manufacturing

Daily, the Milwaukee plant of Allen-Bradley produces between 1,000 and 4,000 controllers for electric motors. It prices them competitively, guarantees they will work, and promises they will be ready to deliver the day after the order is in. The company does this with only four people attending 26 machines, which use 180 components in producing 765 different configurations of controllers. A mainframe computer receives the customer's order and downloads manufacturing instructions to microcomputers that guide the production machinery. Products go through 3,500 checks during the process, and, when a product fails, it's rejected and the system automatically builds a new one so that the order is complete at the end of the day. Production lot sizes can be as small as *one*.

The plant was built to lower production costs because European manufacturers were taking some of Allen-Bradley's domestic market, although the company's president says it was also part of his plan to build international sales. How successful was the plan? Not only does the company compete pricewise in the United States with French and German manufacturers, but its overseas sales now make up 25 percent of its total sales. Ten years ago, overseas sales were only 3 percent. Based on its U.S. experience, the company has since installed two similar production lines in its English plant.

Source: "Allen-Bradley Tries to Fight Competition by Tooling Up," *Datamation*, March 15, 1988, pp. 33–36; and "Manufacturing's New Window of Opportunity," *The Wall Street Journal*, April 29, 1988, p. 29.

The quotation at the beginning of the chapter stated what had been a long-standing difference between the production philosophies of Japan and those of the other industrialized nations. There are a number of reasons for this difference.

After WW II, Japanese manufacturers realized that because of the limited size of Japan's economy, they would have to export to grow. They were also cognizant of the country's lack of natural resources.

To be competitive in world markets, Japanese companies would have to provide high-quality products at low prices. But "Made in Japan" meant poor quality and shoddy manufacture to the rest of the world. For example, Toyota's first export, the Toyopet, was a disaster, and the company withdrew from the export market. In the 1950s, Japanese firms brought in American consultants, such as Deming (a statistics professor, who showed them how to improve quality and productivity by "doing it right the first time"), Juran, and others, who were largely ignored by U.S. manufacturers. There are too many reasons for the Americans' attitude to describe here, but essentially, American products were better than those produced in other countries and were competing well in world markets.

JAPANESE EFFORTS TO LOWER COSTS AND IMPROVE QUALITY

Lower Costs

In examining the components of their costs, Japanese managers realized what all firms know: inventory costs are a major factor. Getting rid of inventory lowers labor cost by 40 percent, for example.[1] To operate without inventory, however, certain requirements would have to be met:

1. Components, whether purchased from outside suppliers or made in the same plant, had to be defect free, or else the production line would be shut down while the workers in all successive operations waited for usable inputs.

2. Parts and components had to be delivered to each point in the production process at the time when they were needed; hence the name **just-in-time.**

just-in-time   a balanced system in which there is little or no delay time and idle in-process and finished goods inventory

3. Customers everywhere want delivery when they make the purchase, so sellers maintain inventories of finished products. Sales often are made because one firm can supply the product from stock but a competitor cannot. How long do you want to wait for delivery of your car after you buy it?

To eliminate inventories of finished goods and still respond quickly to customers' orders required manufacturers to set up flexible production units, which necessitated rapid setup times. Toyota, for example, learned to change a punch press die in 12 minutes; the same operation required three to six hours at General Motors.

4. It was also necessary to reduce process time. One way is to lower the time to transport work in progress from one operation to the next. American and European preoccupation with economic order lots resulted in their grouping machines by function (all drill presses together, punch presses together, etc.), but transporting the machines' output to the next functional area takes time and costs money. Japanese firms grouped machines according to the workflow of a single product (an American invention—a separate

production line for each product), which virtually eliminated transport cost. Also, because parts were arriving immediately from one operation to the next, when the output of the preceding operation was defective, that operation could be stopped until the cause was rectified. Moreover, this too lowered production costs because fewer defective parts were produced.

5. Flexible manufacturing enables product changes to be made rapidly, but each change in the production line still costs money. So, the manufacturers simplified product lines and designed the products to use as many of the same parts as possible. This also contributed to the company suppliers' acceptance of the just-in-time concept because they received fewer but larger orders, which permitted longer, less costly (fewer production changeovers) production runs.

6. For just-in-time to be successful, manufacturers had to have the cooperation of their suppliers. They could not follow the common American practice of having numerous vendors, which buyers often play one against the other to get the best price. Japanese firms used fewer vendors and sought to establish close relationships with them, including calling them in during the design of the product.

7. To lower costs, improve quality, and lower production times, Japanese managements required product designers, production managers, purchasing people, and marketers to work as a team. They realized that something better than the American and European "bucket brigade" was needed. That term stems from an analogy between the ancient method of putting out fires and the process by which an idea becomes a product in many firms.

> The research laboratory gets an idea. It passes the idea to the engineering department, which converts it to a design with all parts specified. Manufacturing gets the specifications from engineering and figures out how to make the product. Responsibility for selling it is "dumped" on marketing.

8. Getting these people together enabled suppliers to suggest using the lower-cost standard parts that they regularly produce, manufacturing to indicate when a design change could simplify the production process, and marketing to contribute the customer's viewpoint, *all before the first product was produced.*[2]

Improve Quality

total quality control (TQC) a system that integrates the development, maintenance, and improvement of quality among all functional areas of the firm

To improve quality, Japanese managers had to use a different human relations approach than the one common in the United States and Europe (more about this in the next chapter). Everyone—from top management to worker—had to be committed to quality. Getting worker involvement was not especially difficult, thanks to the Japanese practice of lifetime employment and the social benefits that Japanese companies offer their employees.

The idea for **total quality control (TQC)**—quality control in all functions of the firm—originated, like many of the ideas that the Japanese adopted, with an American. Armand Feigenbaum first wrote about total quality control in 1951, and he suggested assigning quality control specialists to all functional areas of the firm. The Japanese interpreted the idea to mean that every functional area should think about quality control without the need for inspectors, an important difference.[3]

quality circles (quality control circles) small work groups that meet periodically to discuss ways to improve their functional areas and the quality of the product

A Japanese quality expert, Ishikawa, extended the TQC concept to include **quality circles (quality control circles).** Look at how the president of Komatsu,

Caterpillar's Japanese competitor, describes the use of quality circles in his company.

> The objective of the quality circle is to take part of the responsibility for the quality goal of each section. "Quality circle members are aware of the extent to which their achievement of their objectives will contribute to the results of their department, and also to the business of the company as a whole."
>
> A small group of employees, led by a foreman who has previously received quality control education, independently undertakes quality control activities. The circle's activities are divided among subdivisions of the circle led by a person junior to the foreman. Here is an example to illustrate that quality circles are used in all functional areas, not just in manufacturing.
>
> One day, telephone operators received complaints from outside callers regarding delays in answering telephones, so they surveyed company employees, who confirmed that the complaint was valid. They then studied the average time they were taking to answer a call and found that it was 7.4 seconds. They called the telephone company, who informed them that its standard was three seconds. The quality circle then discussed how to reach the three-second standard.[4]

Problems with Implementing the Japanese Just-In-Time System

Many American manufacturers rushed to Japan to study the just-in-time (JIT) "miracle" and mistakenly copied parts of it without realizing that it was a *total system* covering management of materials, people, and relations with suppliers. Another difficulty was the difference in attitudes (a cultural force) between Japanese and Western managers. American managers and unions still valued highly the specialization of worker functions based on **Taylor's scientific management system.** This system contradicts the principles of quality circles: (1) participative decision making and (2) problem-solving capabilities of workers. Americans, pressured for quick results, were disappointed when quality circles didn't offer immediate solutions for improvement. The practice of not guaranteeing long-term employment also made it more difficult to attain the company loyalty for JIT.[5]

Taylor's scientific management system a system based on scientific measurements that prescribes a division of work whereby planning is done by managers and plan execution is left to supervisors and workers

Problems with JIT

American production experts also realized that there were problems with JIT itself:

1. JIT is restricted to operations that produce the same parts repeatedly because it is a *balanced* system; that is, all operations are designed to produce the same quantity of parts. Yet, as Westinghouse saw when visiting Mitsubishi, repetitive operations may appear only in parts of the manufacturing process. It is far less useful for job shops (firms, or departments within larger firms, that specialize in producing small numbers of custom-designed products).*

2. Because JIT is a balanced system, if one operation stops, the entire production line stops—there is no inventory to keep succeeding operations working.

---

* Job shop also refers to a production system in which departments are organized around specific operations (grinding, drilling, etc.).

3. Achieving a balanced system is difficult because production capacities differ among the various classes of machines. It might require five lathes to keep one punch press busy, for example, and it takes dozens of tire-building machines to use the output of just one calendar, a huge machine (similar in size to a newspaper printing press) that rubberizes the fabric used in making tires. This problem is less severe for large production units, of course.

4. JIT makes no allowances for contingencies, so every piece must be defect free when it is received, and delivery promises must be kept. **Preventive (planned) maintenance** is crucial. A sudden machine breakdown will stop the entire production process.

5. JIT is a slow process to put into effect because it is the result of trial and error (it is evolutionary).[6]

Synchronized Manufacturing

The problems with JIT, especially the long time required for its installation in a production system, caused some American firms to realize that something else was needed if they were going to regain market share lost to the Japanese. Some turned to **synchronized manufacturing,** a production system whose output is set at the output of the operation (**bottleneck**) that is working at full capacity. Software was available that took into account such constraints as limited facilities, personnel, and machines when developing production schedules. This made installation much faster because production schedules and simulation could be done on a computer instead of having to arrive at solutions by trial and error, as is necessary with JIT.[7]

Instead of attempting to achieve a balanced system like JIT, in which the capacities of all operations are equal, synchronized manufacturing aims to balance the *product flow* through the system, which leaves output levels of the various operations *unbalanced.*[8] For example, with the bottleneck operation producing at full capacity, perhaps only 60 percent capacity is needed at another operation. Because there is no reason for this operation to produce over 60 percent of its capacity, it is stopped at that point; anything more would be unwanted inventory. Inasmuch as work is assigned to each operation rather than to the entire system, as in JIT, there is no need for more work in process than that which is actually being worked on. Inventory may also be placed near the bottleneck to avoid any shutdown in this crucial operation, and sometimes, unlike JIT, there may even be a quality control inspector to check the bottleneck operation's input.

Notice that management's attention is focused on the bottleneck rather than on the other operations, because a production increase at the bottleneck means an increase for the entire production system; an increase in a nonbottleneck operation only adds to that machine's idle time.

Note another important difference between JIT and synchronized manufacturing: a defective part or component at any point of the production process can shut down a JIT system. But because a synchronized manufacturing system has excess capacity in all operations except at the bottleneck, any defective part produced before the bottleneck can be remade, and thus the entire system is not stopped.

Incidentally, the deemphasis of the full utilization of resources is requiring a change in the use of some historical cost accounting measurements. Inventory

---

preventive (planned) maintenance   maintenance done according to plan, not when machines break down

---

synchronized manufacturing   an entire manufacturing process with unbalanced operations that emphasizes total system performance

---

bottleneck   operation in a production system whose output sets the limit for the entire system's output

is valued at the cost of the materials it contains; value added is ignored, for example.

AMERICAN AND EUROPEAN EFFORTS TO IMPROVE QUALITY AND LOWER COSTS

We all know how the Japanese efforts to improve product quality while reducing cost have changed world opinion about their products. There are exceptions, however, as the following Worldview illustrates.

Many companies, such as Allen-Bradley in the Business Incident, have successfully put into place the JIT system or have highly synchronized their manufacturing systems. Moreover, they have taken advantage of the capabilities of computers and robots to further improve productivity and quality. You recognize, of course, that neither robots nor computers are essential for the implementation of most of the concepts we have described.

Western Firms That Are Succeeding

General Motors, General Electric, Ford, IBM, Motorola—the list is long of American firms that have a synchronized manufacturing and total quality control (TQC) system. Corning, the glass manufacturer, has changed the way it designs and makes products to better compete with its Japanese and European competitors. It analyzed the 235 operations in its manufacturing process, eliminated 115 of them, and reduced production time from four weeks to three days. The company reduced the worker job classifications to two, so there is only a single management layer between workers and managers. Representatives from production, design, and marketing work jointly on new products; the result is that new product introduction, which used to take three years, is now done in one.[9]

General Electric consolidated its circuit-breaker unit at one automated plant and shut down five other plants. It also simplified the box's design, reducing the total parts from 28,000 to only 1,275. The computerized system it installed examines each production order and programs the production machinery automatically to make the specified boxes. General Electric also eliminated all line supervisors and quality inspectors and gave their responsibilities to production workers. Productivity jumped 20 percent while manufacturing costs declined 30 percent. It now takes three days, not three weeks, to fill an order.[10]

Service organizations are also applying many of the principles of synchronized manufacturing. American Financial Services, an international consumer finance and insurance company with $7 billion sales, asked its U.S. companies and subsidiaries in Canada, the United Kingdom, and Australia to develop their own programs. In only two years, the Canadian affiliate alone doubled its profits and saved $2 million. Management, recognizing that total decentralization was not the best way to manage the process globally, appointed a person to oversee its global operation and also appointed an international excellence steering committee.[11]

Examples of European worldwide firms using synchronized manufacturing systems are Electrolux (Swedish), Volkswagen (German), and Rover (English).[12] In France, Pechiney, the global aluminum producer, has 250

WORLDVIEW
"Made in Japan" Could Mean Made for Mischief

Tokyo—If you think "Made in Japan" means the world's best, come over to my house for a piece of toast.

If you're lucky, just the upper half will be black. More likely, your toast won't pop up until the smoke alarm screams. Or it won't stay down. Four years of breakfasts haven't produced a quality-controlled piece of toast from my Toshiba toaster.

Sure, everyone has evil-tempered-toaster stories. But Japanese goods aren't supposed to behave badly. Japan has a trade surplus because its products are flawless and Americans make junk, right?

Hogwash. Japan still churns out its share of schlock, and I'd swear it has all landed in my house.

Take my Japanese computer. With fine-tuned reliability, the NEC desk-top machine I'm using right now inserts uncalled-for letters into my text. I type "w-o-r" and get "w-o-j-r." "Wojrse" still is a bug lurking in the lap-top machine that I bring home from "wojrk." Every few months, the bug sneaks into the memory, devouring articles, letters, memos, everything. The bug is hungriest around deadline time.

Other Japanese junk abounds in the house's every corner. In my closet hang shirts whose buttons popped off on first wearing. The telephone picks up radio baseball broadcasts.

Our Japanese-made stereo is an assemblage of lemons. The Akai tape deck eats the Maxell tapes. The Kenwood compact disk player is persnickety about its music; it adores Mozart, but skips and stutters over Billie Holiday disks. And now that its warranty has run out, the machine flatly rejects Dire Straits, producing a sort of munching noise instead.

The Kenwood people say they can fix the machine—for nearly as much money as the price of a new one. Experience makes me wonder. Nikon specialists have "fixed" my Nikon camera three times, but it still doesn't work right.

Japanese junk has even caused minor tragedies in our home. His first day in Japan, my six-year-old nephew spent his hard-earned allowance on one of those tin toy helicopters that twirls its little plastic blades when you scuff its wheels along the floor. After 15 minutes of normal kid use, the propellers went limp, fatally crippled by some internal injury.

The dead chopper rests in pieces deep in toy box. Try explaining Japanese design superiority to my nephew.

Another demise was the ice cream maker my wife bought for my birthday. A "marvel" of Japanese engineering, it was designed so that salty ice water trickled into the motor. The electric coils turned into a hunk of rust that had to be overhauled on the kitchen table every time we dragged the thing out. It now rusts away in a landfill somewhere.

Then there's the house itself. Owned by an executive on transfer, it has the features of a typical, new Japanese upper-middle-class home: kitschy light fixtures made of fake-brass-colored tin, walls as thin as cardboard, and aluminum window frames that belong on a trailer home.

In fairness, I admit to having my share of Japanese wonders—like the vintage Sony Trinitron I picked out of the neighbor's trash heap four years ago. It still works perfectly, as do a score of other electronic gizmos around the house.

But I think I've found a solution to the other junk. I now buy Korean shirts, am switching to an IBM-compatible computer, and am eyeing a Swedish Hasselblad camera. We hand-crank ice cream in an American freezer we bought at a yard sale.

As for the toaster, a colleague has explained the problem to me. "The Japanese simply haven't gotten down the learning curve on toasters yet," he tells me.

In the meantime, I'm sending for my parents' old chrome General Electric toaster—the one that's worked since they got it as a wedding present in 1953.

Source: Stephen Kreider Yoder, " 'Made in Japan' Could Mean Made for Mischief," *The Wall Street Journal*, September 21, 1987, p. 24.

quality circles in 10 of its companies and 40 plants.[13] In a 1986 survey, the Australian Federation of Automotive Product Manufacturers found that 34 of 48 respondents were operating a full or pilot JIT system, and 8 more were planning to introduce it in 1987. Obviously, the fact that the local automakers were already using synchronized manufacturing influenced their decisions.[14]

REASONS FOR WORLDWIDE STANDARDIZATION OF PRODUCTION SYSTEMS AND FACILITIES

The advantages of synchronized manufacturing and TQC are compelling reasons why numerous global and multinational corporations are installing them worldwide. Certainly, customers everywhere want quality products at low prices. In large markets, such as the EC and Japan, some American firms are copying home country production systems (for example, Allen-Bradley in Scotland). Tecktronix, a leading American producer of oscilloscopes, introduced in its English plant a system similar to the one in its home plant.[15] Ford's German plant has installed a pilot just-in-time program, which will be adopted in its other European plants.[16] In addition to the advantages just mentioned, there are other important, although perhaps less obvious, advantages to worldwide standardization.

Organization and Staffing

Simpler and less costly when standardized. The standardization of production processes and procedures simplifies the production organization at headquarters because their replication enables the work to be accomplished with a smaller staff of support personnel. Fewer labor-hours in plant design are involved because each new plant is essentially a scaled-up or scaled-down version of an existing one. The permanent group of experts that worldwide companies maintain to give technical assistance to overseas plants can be smaller. Extra technicians who are accustomed to working with the same machinery can be borrowed from the domestic operation as needed.

Worldwide uniformity in production methods also increases headquarters' effectiveness in keeping the production specifications current. Every firm has hundreds of specifications, and these are constantly being changed because of new raw materials or manufacturing procedures. If all plants, domestic and foreign, possess the same equipment, notice of a change can be given with one indiscriminate mailing; there is no need for highly paid engineers to check each affiliate's list of equipment to see which ones are affected. Companies whose production processes are not unified have found that task of maintaining a current separate set of specifications for each of 15 or 20 affiliates to be both more costly (larger staff) and also more error prone.

Logistics of supply. Management has become increasingly aware of the greater profits that may be obtained by organizing all of its companies' production facilities into one logistical supply system that includes all of the activities required to move raw materials, parts, and finished inventory from vendors, between enterprise facilities, and to customers. The standardization of processes and machinery provides a reasonable guarantee that parts manufactured in the firm's various plants will be interchangeable. This assurance of interchangeability enables management to divide the production of components among a number of subsidiaries to achieve greater economies of scale and to take advantage of the lower production costs in some countries.

manufacturing rationalization division of production among a number of production units, thus enabling each to produce only a limited number of components for all of a firm's assembly plants

Rationalization.   **Manufacturing rationalization,** as this production strategy is called, involves a change from manufacturing by a subsidiary only for its own national market to producing a limited number of components for use by all subsidiaries. The Ford Escort car, for example, is sourced from a number of Ford factories. Figure 19–1 illustrates that the global car receives components from 15 nations.

SKF, a major bearing manufacturer with headquarters in Sweden, was able to reduce the types of ball bearings produced in five major overseas subsidiaries years ago from 50,000 to 20,000. Of the 20,000 remaining types, 7,000 have been rationalized among the five plants, and the other 13,000 are produced solely by one or another subsidiary for its local customers.[17]

These examples illustrate that for production rationalization to be possible, the product mix must first by rationalized; that is, the firm must elect to produce products that are identical worldwide or regionwide. Once this has been done, each subsidiary can be assigned to produce certain components for other foreign plants, thus attaining a higher volume with a lower production cost than would be possible if it manufactured the complete product for its national market only. Obviously, this strategy is not viable when consumers' tastes and preferences differ markedly among markets. For less differentiated products, however, manufacturing rationalization permits economies of scale in production and engineering that would otherwise be impossible. Nissan Motors has been able to employ the most modern methods, including CAM,* in its Mexican motor plant because of the high input it obtains through exports (80 percent of the total) to Tennessee, Japan, and Latin America. And Ford, as you read in Chapter 16, supplies engines for all Ford-Europe from one plant in England.[18]

Purchasing.   When foreign subsidiaries are unable to purchase raw materials and machinery locally, they generally look for assistance from the purchasing department at headquarters. Because unified processes require the same materials everywhere, buyers can handle foreign requirements by simply increasing their regular orders to their usual suppliers and passing on the volume discounts to the subsidiaries. However, when special materials are required, purchasing agents must search out new vendors and place smaller orders, often at higher prices.

Control

All the advantages of the worldwide standardization of production cited thus far also pertain to the other functions of management. Three aspects of control—quality, production, and maintenance—merit additional discussion, however.

Quality control.   When production equipment is similar, home office control of quality in foreign affiliates is less difficult because management can expect all plants to adhere to the same standard. The periodic reports that all affiliates submit can be compared, and deviations from the norm that require remedial

---

* CAM—computer-assisted manufacturing—generally includes automated materials handling and programmable robots.

■ **FIGURE 19–1   Global Manufacturing: The Component Network for the Ford Escort in Europe**

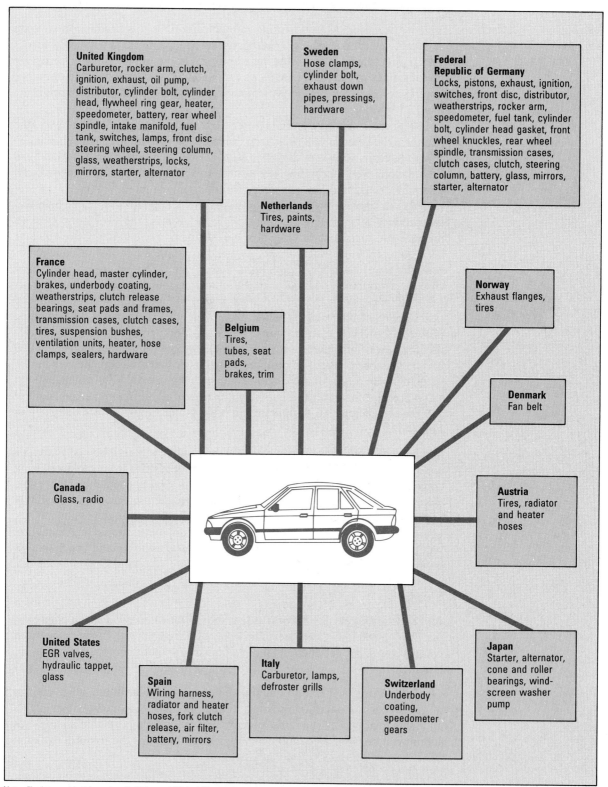

United Kingdom
Carburetor, rocker arm, clutch, ignition, exhaust, oil pump, distributor, cylinder bolt, cylinder head, flywheel ring gear, heater, speedometer, battery, rear wheel spindle, intake manifold, fuel tank, switches, lamps, front disc steering wheel, steering column, glass, weatherstrips, locks, mirrors, starter, alternator

Sweden
Hose clamps, cylinder bolt, exhaust down pipes, pressings, hardware

Federal Republic of Germany
Locks, pistons, exhaust, ignition, switches, front disc, distributor, weatherstrips, rocker arm, speedometer, fuel tank, cylinder bolt, cylinder head gasket, front wheel knuckles, rear wheel spindle, transmission cases, clutch cases, clutch, steering column, battery, glass, mirrors, starter, alternator

Netherlands
Tires, paints, hardware

France
Cylinder head, master cylinder, brakes, underbody coating, weatherstrips, clutch release bearings, seat pads and frames, transmission cases, clutch cases, tires, suspension bushes, ventilation units, heater, hose clamps, sealers, hardware

Norway
Exhaust flanges, tires

Belgium
Tires, tubes, seat pads, brakes, trim

Denmark
Fan belt

Canada
Glass, radio

Austria
Tires, radiator and heater hoses

United States
EGR valves, hydraulic tappet, glass

Spain
Wiring harness, radiator and heater hoses, fork clutch release, air filter, battery, mirrors

Italy
Carburetor, lamps, defroster grills

Switzerland
Underbody coating, speedometer gears

Japan
Starter, alternator, cone and roller bearings, wind-screen washer pump

Note: Final assembly takes place in Halewood (United Kingdom) and Saarlouis (Federal Republic of Germany).

Source: P. Dicken, *Global Shift: Industrial Change in a Turbulent World* (London: Harper & Row, 1986), Fig. 9.9, p. 304. Updated information from John Emmert, Public Affairs, Ford International, August 3, 1987.

action, such as a large number of product rejects, can be quickly spotted. Separate standards for each plant because of equipment differences are unnecessary.

Production and maintenance control.   A single standard also lessens the task of maintenance and production control. The same machinery should produce at the same rate of output and have the same frequency of maintenance no matter where it is located. In practice, there will be deviations because of the human and physical factors (dust, humidity, temperature), but at least similar machinery permits the establishing of standards by which the effectiveness of local managements may be determined. Furthermore, the maintenance experience of other production units as to the frequency of overhauls and the stock of spare parts needed will help plants avoid costly, unforeseen stoppages from sudden breakdowns.

Planning

When a new plant can be built that is a duplicate of others already functioning, the planning and design work will be both simpler and quicker because it is essentially a repetition of work that has already been done:

1. Design engineers need only copy the drawings and lists of materials that they have in their files.
2. Vendors will be requested to furnish equipment that they have supplied previously.
3. The technical department can send the current manufacturing specifications without alteration.
4. Labor trainers experienced in the operation of the machinery can be sent to the new location without undergoing special training on new equipment.
5. Reasonably accurate forecasts of plant erection time and output can be made based on the experience with existing facilities.

In other words, the duplication of existing plants greatly reduces the engineering time required in planning and designing the new facilities and eliminates many of the start-up difficulties inherent in any new operation. To be sure, a newly designed plant causes problems when it is erected domestically, but those problems are greater when the plant is located in a different environment at a great distance from headquarters. Just how important the savings from plant duplication are was emphasized in a study of the chemical and refining industries that indicated the cost of technology transfer was lowered by 34 and 19 percent for the second and third start-ups.[19]

Since the case for international standardization of production is so strong, why do differences among plants in the same company persist?

IMPEDIMENTS TO WORLDWIDE STANDARDIZATION OF PRODUCTION FACILITIES

Generally, it is easier for worldwide corporations to standardize the concepts of total quality control and synchronized manufacturing in their overseas affiliates than it is to standardize the actual production facilities. The fact that units of a multiplant operation are diverse with respect to size, machinery, and procedures stems from the intervention of the foreign environmental forces, especially the economic, cultural, and political forces.

Environmental Forces

Economic forces.   The most important element of the economic forces that impedes production standardization is the wide range of market sizes, which we examined in Chapter 14.[20] To cope with the great variety of production requirements, the designer generally has the option of selecting either a *capital-intensive process* incorporating automated, high-output machinery or a *labor-intensive process* employing more people and semimanual general-purpose equipment with lower productive capacity. The automated machinery is severely limited with respect to flexibility (variety of products and range of sizes), but once set up, it will turn out in a few days what may be a year's supply for some markets.[21] For many processes, this problem may be resolved by installing one machine of the type used by the hundreds in the larger home plant. However, sometimes this option is not available because for some processes, only one or two large machines are used even in production facilities with large output—as we mentioned in the discussion of standardized manufacturing. Until recently, when the option was not available, plant designers had to choose between the high-output specialized machinery and the lower-output general-purpose machines mentioned earlier.

However, a third alternative has become available, though its high cost and high technological content have limited its application to manufacturers in industrialized nations. *Computerized integrated manufacturing* (CIM) systems enable a machine to make one part as easily as another in random order on an instruction from a bar code reader of the kind used in supermarkets. This reduces to one the economic batch quantity—the minimum number of a part that can be made economically by a factory. There is a limit, nevertheless, to the variety of shapes, sizes, and materials that can be accommodated.

Another economic factor that influences the designer's selection of processes is the *cost of production*. Automation tends to increase the productivity per worker because with automation, less labor is used and output per machine is higher. But, if the desired output requires the machines to be operated only a fraction of the time, the high capital costs of automated equipment may result in excessive production costs even though labor costs are low. In situations where production costs favor semimanual equipment, the designer may be compelled to install high-capacity machines instead because of a lack of floor space. This is because, generally, the space occupied by a few high-capacity machines is less than that required for the greater number of semimanual machines to produce the same output. On the other hand, because the correct type and quality of process materials are indispensable for specialized machinery, the engineers could not recommend this equipment if such materials are unobtainable either locally or through importation. Occasionally, management will bypass this obstacle by **backward vertical integration;** that is, manufacturing capacity to produce essential inputs will be included in the plant design even though it would be preferable from an economic standpoint to purchase these materials from outside vendors. For example, a textile factory might include a facility for producing nylon fibers.

backward vertical integration establishing facilities to manufacture inputs used in the production of a firm's final products

The economic forces that we have described are fundamental considerations in plant design, yet elements of the cultural and political forces may be sufficiently significant to override decisions based on purely economic reasoning.

Cultural forces. When a factory is to be built in an industrialized nation where there is a sizable market and high labor costs, capital-intensive processes will undoubtedly be employed. However, such processes may also be employed in developing countries, which commonly lack skilled workers despite their abundant supply of labor. This situation favors the use of specialized machines because, although a few highly skilled persons are needed for maintenance and setup, the job of *attending* these machines (starting, feeding stock) can be performed by unskilled workers after a short training period. In contrast, general-purpose machinery requires many more skilled operators.[22]

These operators could be trained in technical schools, but the low prestige of such employment, a cultural characteristic, affects both the demand for and the supply of vocational education. Students do not demand it, and the traditional elitist attitude of the educational administrators in many developing nations causes resources to be directed to professional education instead of to the trades where they are needed.

Firms that attempt to reduce their requirements for skilled workers by installing automatic machinery, are, of course, left vulnerable to another cultural characteristic of the less developed countries—absenteeism. If the setup and maintenance crews fail to report to work, the entire production line may be shut down. Some managers resolve this difficulty by training a few extra people as backups. Having extra personnel is viewed as production insurance necessary to keep the plant in operation. This extra expense may be far less than the expense of handling the greater number of labor-management problems resulting from the larger work force in a nonautomated factory of similar capacity.

These economic and cultural variables, important as they are, are not the only considerations of management; the requirements of the host government must be met if the proposed plant is to become a reality.

Political forces. When planning a new production facility in a developing country, management is frequently confronted by an intriguing paradox. Although the country desperately needs new job creation, which favors labor-intensive processes, government officials often insist on the most modern equipment. Local pride may be the cause, or the cause may be that these officials, wishing to see the new firm export, believe only a factory with advanced technology can compete in world markets. They not only may be reluctant to take chances on "inferior" or untried alternatives, they may also feel that low-productivity technology will keep the country dependent on the industrialized countries. In some developing countries, this fear has been formalized by laws prohibiting the importation of used machinery.

Some Design Solutions

Hybrid design. More often than not, the resultant plant design will be a hybrid of capital-intensive processes when they are considered essential to ensure product quality and labor-intensive methods. As an example, machine welding rather than hand welding may be required, while the painting, packaging, and materials handling are performed with semimanual equipment.

Intermediate technology.   In recent years, the press of a growing population and the rise in capital costs have forced governments of developing nations to search for something less than highly automated processes. They are becoming convinced that there should be something midway between the capital- and labor-intensive processes that will create more jobs, require less capital, but still produce the desired product quality. Governments are urging investors to consider an **intermediate technology,** which, unfortunately, is not readily available in the industrialized nations. This means that the WWCs cannot transfer the technology with which they are familiar but must develop new and different manufacturing methods. It is also possible that the savings in reduced capital costs of the intermediate technology may be nullified by higher start-up costs and the greater expense of its transfer.

intermediate technology
production methods between capital- and labor-intensive methods

Appropriate Technology

One global corporation, Philips in the Netherlands, has worked systematically to match a country's markets with its resources and ability to produce certain components to obtain an optimal technological mix. A pilot plant devises commercially viable production patterns based on the factors that enable foreign subsidiaries to manufacture small volumes with processes that are less automated than those of the home plant.

Rather than search for an intermediate technology, the emphasis of Philips and others is on employing the **appropriate technology,** which can range from the most advanced to the most primitive, depending on the economic, sociocultural, and political variables. For some products, the superiority in productivity and product quality of the modern process is so marked that it makes the labor-intensive method totally inappropriate. Compare resource mapping by satellites with geologists on horseback, for example. Yet in the case of sugar refining, it was found in India that for the same amount of capital, either a large plant capable of producing 12,000 tons of sugar annually with 900 employees or 47 small plants with an output of 30,000 tons employing 10,000 workers could be built.[23]

appropriate technology
production methods—intermediate, capital-, or labor-intensive (or a mixture)—considered most suitable for an area according to its cultural, political, and economic situation

Does this mean the government should urge a company to adopt the second alternative? It may be that the cost per unit produced is higher with the less capital-intensive process. In this case, government administration must choose between (1) the use of the less capital-intensive technology to save scarce capital and create more jobs and (2) the more capital-intensive processes that will provide a less expensive product for its citizens. The choice obviously depends on government priorities.

These examples help substantiate a growing belief that there is no universally appropriate technology. In fact, proponents of this concept state that what may be suitable for the cultural, political, and economic situation in one region is not necessarily applicable even in another area of the same country. The concept's effect on attempts to standardize production facilities worldwide is obvious.

THE LOCAL PRODUCTION SYSTEM

Basis for Organization

The local production organization is commonly a scaled-down version of that found in the parent company. If at home the firm is organized by product companies or divisions (tires, industrial products, chemicals), the subsidiary will be divided into product departments. Manufacturing firms that use process organizations (departmentalized according to production processes) in the domestic operation will set up a similar structure in their foreign affiliates. In a paper-box factory, separate departments will cut the logs, produce the paper, and assemble the boxes. The only noticeable difference between the foreign and domestic operations is that in the foreign plant, all of these processes are more likely to be at one location because of the smaller size of each department.

Horizontal and Vertical Integration

The local production organization is rarely integrated either vertically or horizontally to the extent that the parent is. Some vertical integration is traditional, as in the case of the paper-box factory, and some will occur if it is necessary to assure a supply of raw materials. In this situation, the subsidiary might be more vertically integrated than the parent, who depends on outside sources for much of its inputs. However, the additional investment is a deterrent to vertical integration, as are the extra profits gained by supplying inputs to these captive customers from the home plants. In some countries, vertical integration is prohibited by law for certain industries. Mexico, for example, has not allowed automobile manufacturers to own parts suppliers. But in Mexico, Brazil, and numerous other nations, a percentage of local content in the finished product is required by law. When the subsidiary cannot meet the requirement by local outside sourcing, it may be forced to produce components that its parent does not.

Horizontal integration is much less prevalent in the foreign subsidiaries, although restaurant chains, banks, food-processing plants, and other industries characterized by small production units will, of course, integrate horizontally in the manner of the domestic company. Overseas affiliates themselves become conglomerates when the parent acquires a multinational. The many mergers and acquisitions of the late 1980s have turned various affiliates into conglomerates.

> European ITT affiliates found themselves in hotels (Sheraton), car rental (Avis), and electrical connectors (Cannon Electric) when these multinationals were bought by the parent. The affiliates themselves have acquired insurance companies, schools, and manufacturers of auto parts, cosmetics, and food products. When considered as a separate company, ITT Europe ranks 25th in sales among European firms.

Design of the Production System

A *production system* is essentially a functionally related group of activities for creating value. Although the production system as described below is basically one for producing tangible goods, nearly everything that is said applies equally to the production of services. Factors involved in the efficient operation of a production system include:

1. Plant location.
2. Plant layout.
3. Materials handling.
4. Human element.

Plant location.   Plant location is significant because of its effect on both production and distribution costs, which are frequently in conflict. The gain in government incentives and in the lower land and labor costs obtained by locating away from major cities may be offset by the increased expense of warehousing and transportation to serve these markets. Management will, after ascertaining that adequate labor, raw materials, water, and power are available, seek the least-cost location, or the one for which the sum of production and transfer costs is minimized. Management's first choice may then be modified by market requirements, the influence of competitors' locations, employee preference (climate, recreational facilities), and conditions imposed by the local authorities.

Governments that are anxious to limit the congestion of large urban areas may either prohibit firms from locating in the major cities or offer them important financial inducement to locate elsewhere.

> Businesses that establish plants in the Mezzogiorno (southern Italy) can obtain soft loans, tax exemptions, and outright grants of up to 40 percent of the fixed investment. Nearly all of the European nations and some nations in Latin America offer similar advantages. For example, since 1989, a foreign firm that wants a wholly owned subsidiary in Mexico must locate outside Mexico City, Monterrey, and Guadalajara, which, in the government's opinion, are already overcrowded.

Firms that have come to a country to take advantage of low labor costs and export their production have a limited selection of plant locations. They must locate in **export processing zones,** such as Mexico's in-bond manufacturing zones, most of which are on the Mexican–American border. Similar zones exist in South Korea, Taiwan, Singapore, and some 50 other nations.[24]

Plant layout.   Modern practice dictates that the arrangement of machinery, personnel, and service facilities should be made prior to the erection of the building. In this way, the building is accommodated to the layout that is judged most capable of obtaining a smoothly functioning production system.

The designer must attempt to obtain the maximum utility from costly building space while providing room for the future expansion of each department. Space can become critical very quickly if forecasts, especially for new products, prove to have been unduly pessimistic. Managements of plants located in developing countries may attempt to stint on space for employees' facilities, reasoning that the workers' standard of living in these countries is lower and that they will accept less just to have employment. Often, however, foreign labor laws are more demanding than those of the home country.

Materials handling.   Considerable savings in production costs can be achieved by a careful planning of materials handling, which, as you have seen, is a major consideration in synchronized manufacturing. What production managers often failed to appreciate is that inefficient handling of materials may cause excessive inventories of partly finished parts to accumulate at some work stations, while at others, expensive machinery was idle for lack of work (bottleneck). This concerned marketers too, because poor materials handling can result in late deliveries and damaged goods, which, in turn, lead to order cancelation and a loss of customers. Therefore, marketers must also be included in the total quality control approach we discussed earlier in this chapter.

Human element.   The effectiveness of the production system depends on people, who are, in turn, affected by the system. Productivity suffers when there is extreme heat or cold, excessive noise, or faulty illumination. Colors also influence human behavior—pale colors are restful and unobtrusive, whereas bright colors attract attention. Plant designers take advantage of this fact by painting the walls of the working areas pale blue and green but marking exits with a bright yellow and painting safety equipment red. This practice is accepted nearly everywhere, although, as we indicated in the sociocultural chapter, color connotations vary among cultures.

For reasons of safety and ease of operation, controls of imported machinery must frequently be altered to accommodate the smaller worker. Extra lifting devices, unnecessary in the home country, may be required. Where illiteracy is a problem, safety signs must include pictures. For example, a picture of a burning cigarette with a red line through it may substitute for a "No Smoking" sign. Plants in multilingual nations and plants that employ large numbers of foreign workers will require warnings in more than one language.

Because of the prohibitive cost of automobiles in many developing nations, employees ride bicycles to work, so bicycle stands must be provided in the parking lots. Special dietary kitchens are necessary when workers from more than one culture work together. These and other special conditions caused by environmental differences must be reckoned with in the design of the production system.

Operation of the Production System

Once the production system has been put into operation, two general classes of activities—*productive activities* and *supportive activities*—must be performed.

Productive activities.   After the initial trial period, during which the workers become familiar with the production processes, management will expect the system to produce at a rate sufficient to satisfy market demand. It is the function of the line organization—from production manager to first-level supervisor—to work with labor, raw materials, and machinery to produce on time the required amount of product with the desired quality at the budgeted cost.

Obstacles to meeting production standards.   Management must be prepared to deal with any obstacle to meeting the production standards. Among these obstacles are (1) low output, (2) inferior quality, and (3) excessive manufacturing costs.

Low output.   Any number of factors may be responsible for the system's failure to meet the design standards for output.

1. Raw materials suppliers may fail to meet delivery dates or may furnish material out of specification. This is a common occurrence in the sellers' markets of developing countries, but it is also occasionally a problem in the industrialized countries. The purchasing department must attempt to educate the vendor as to the importance of delivery dates and specifications, although the effectiveness of this strategy is limited when, as is often the case in developing nations, there is only one supplier. Increasing the price paid and sending technicians to assist the vendor generally improve this situation.

> When the automobile plants in Mexico were required to incorporate locally made parts into the product, they not only provided their own technical assistance to vendors but also arranged for licensing agreements from U.S. suppliers and even guaranteed bank loans enabling the vendors to buy production machinery. This tremendous assistance program, literally dumped in the laps of small local manufacturers, was a leading factor in creating the Mexican parts industry.

2. Poor coordination of production scheduling slows the delivery of finished products when, for example, completely assembled automobiles wait for bumpers. Scheduling personnel may require additional training or closer supervision. Often, scheduling personnel—or any production workers, for that matter—are unaware of the importance of their jobs because they have not been shown "the big picture." Firms that teach employees why they do what they do, as well as how, find that this pays off in creating a better attitude, which results in higher productivity. This has become crucial as firms strive for participative management, which is essential to synchronized manufacturing.

Remember from Chapter 9 the experience of the American manager who tried to introduce participative management in Peru? The cultural forces of attitude toward authority and great difference between the educational levels, common in many countries, establishes a gulf between managers and workers. In fact, this is one of the reasons why Japanese affiliates have had trouble introducing their production methods in the United States, where distances between managers and workers are much smaller than they are in most developing nations. Getting the participative management necessary for JIT and synchronized manufacturing will necessitate workers making sizable cultural changes, which, in our opinion, will require many years to attain.

Another cultural problem is the desire to please everyone and the aversion to long-range planning. You have seen the importance of planning for the success of JIT, and you also learned that firm production schedules at least a month long are requisite. The desire to please everyone prevalent in some cultures tends to cause neglect of the schedule while production stops to attend the latest request from a customer. Moreover, because the markets are smaller in developing countries than in industrialized nations, product variations will have to be pared even more, and production systems will have to be even more flexible, if possible.

3. *Absenteeism,* always a problem for production managers everywhere in meeting production standards, has become even more significant in a bottleneck operation of a synchronized manufacturing system. Imagine the problems that occur when an entire department is idled because workers are at home helping the extended family with the harvest. When poor transportation systems make getting to work difficult, companies frequently provide transportation. To counteract absences due to illness and injury, they subsidize

workers' lunches—prepared by trained nutritionists—and provide special shoes and protective clothing. Of course, management has the problem of educating workers not to remove the restraining apparel that they have never used before.

Low morale conducive to high absenteeism will result if foreign managers trying to introduce the participative management necessary for synchronized manufacturing fail to assume the role of *patron* that most workers in developing countries expect. When employees have personal problems, they presume that the boss, not the personnel office, will find a solution. Personal debts, marital problems, and difficulties with the police are all part of manager-employee relations.

All too often, expatriate managers accept high absenteeism and low productivity as the norm instead of attempting to correct them. Yet those who apply all of the corrective means used at home, making adjustments for the foreign environment when necessary, do achieve notable success. One corrective measure, the discharge of unsatisfactory workers, is frequently impossible to apply because of legal constraints; but a consistent, energetic program of employee training, good union and labor relations, and the use of such morale builders as employee recognition, company reunions, sponsorship of team sports, and even suggestion boxes with rewards can be as successful in a foreign location as in the domestic operation.

Inferior product quality. Good quality is relative. What passes for good quality in the industrialized nations may actually be poor quality where a lack of maintenance and operating skills requires looser bearing fits and strong but more unwieldy parts. If the product or service satisfies the purpose for which it is purchased, then the buyer considers it to be of good quality.

> In World War II, the American military found that the Japanese submachine gun, poorly finished except at the working surfaces, was as effective a weapon as the American Thompson, which was finely finished all over. A gun collector would consider the American weapon to be of higher quality, but was it of higher quality from the Japanese standpoint?

Production quality standards are not set arbitrarily. It is the responsibility of the marketers, after studying their target market, to choose the price-quality combination they believe is most apt to satisfy that market. On the basis of this information, the quality standards for incoming materials, in-process items, and finished products should be established.

When the headquarters of global corporations insist that all foreign subsidiaries maintain the high-quality standards of the domestic plants, a number of problems can occur. Production may have to accept inputs of poorer quality when there is no alternative source of supply and then rework them. As we have pointed out, quality tolerances are especially tight for automated machinery. Finished-product standards set by a home office concerned about maintaining its global reputation can cause a product to be too costly for the local market. Many globals resolve this problem by permitting the subsidiary to manufacture products of lower quality under different brand names. If they wish the local plant to be a part of a worldwide logistic system, they may require a special quality to be produced for export. In some areas, "export quality" still denotes a superior product. Quality control, by the way, is not left exclusively in the hands of the subsidiary.

Export-quality cigarettes

Courtesy R. J. Reynolds

Nearly all worldwide corporations require their foreign plants to submit samples of the finished product for testing on a regular basis.

Excessive manufacturing costs.   Any manufacturing cost that exceeds the budgeted cost is excessive and naturally is of concern to the marketing and financial manager as well as to production personnel. Low output for any of the reasons we have discussed may be the cause, but the fault may also lie with the assumptions underlying the budget. Overoptimistic sales forecasts, the failure of suppliers to meet delivery dates, the failure of the government to issue import permits for essential raw materials in time, and unforeseen water or power failure are a few of the reasons why output may be lower than expected.

Managements have always tried to limit inventories of raw materials, spare parts for plant machinery, and finished products, and those managements with synchronized production systems have a goal of almost complete elimination. But when there is an uncertainty of supply, as in most developing nations, stocks of these items can quickly get out of control. Production tends to overstock inputs to avoid the expense of changing production schedules when a given raw material has been exhausted. Maintenance personnel lay in an excessive stock of spare parts because they worry about not having something when they need it. Marketers, fearful of the frequent delays in production, overreact by building up finished goods inventories to avoid lost sales. When sales decrease, production may continue to produce finished products rather than lay off workers, because the labor laws in many countries, unlike American labor laws, make employee layoffs both difficult and costly. In countries where skilled workers are in short supply, management does not dare to lay them off even if the law permits, because these people will obtain employment elsewhere. The only alternative in the short run is to keep the factory running.

Finance, the one headquarters department that would ordinarily act to limit inventory building, will not move aggressively to stop this practice in countries afflicted with hyperinflation. It knows that under this condition, sizable profits can be made by being short in cash and long in inventory.

Supportive activities.   Every production system requires staff units to provide the **supportive activities** essential to its operation. Two of these, quality control and inventory control, were examined in the previous section. Let us look now at the purchasing, maintenance, and technical functions.

Purchasing.   Production depends on the purchasing department to procure the raw materials, component parts, supplies, and machinery it requires to produce the finished product. The inability to obtain these materials when needed can result in costly shutdowns and lost sales. If the buyers agree to prices that are higher than what competitors are paying, the firm must either sell the finished product at higher prices or price competitively and earn less profit. The quality of the finished product may suffer if the quality of the purchased materials is inadequate.

Even in the industrialized countries before JIT was introduced, purchasing agents rarely could satisfy all of their companies' needs by waiting for the suppliers' representatives to come to them. They had to seek out and develop suppliers by visiting their plants and arranging for their companies' production and technical personnel to discuss materiel problems with the vendors' counterparts. In the developing countries, where many suppliers do not retain a sales force because they can sell everything they produce, supplier development assumes greater importance. The ability to locate vendors can easily compensate for a lack of other skills that management would require of a buyer at home.

When the firm depends heavily on imported materials, the prime criterion for hiring will be the purchasing agents' knowledge of import procedures and their connections with key government officials. The purchasing agents must constantly monitor government actions that can affect the availability of foreign exchange. They will often buy as much as possible of regularly consumed materials because they know they can always sell the excess to others, possibly at a profit. Interestingly, a study has found that the use of locally available raw materials varies according to the company's ownership. Those owned by parents from other developing nations imported 39 percent of their raw materials, locally owned plants imported 65 percent, and factories owned by WWCs imported 76 percent.[25]

Whether to fill the critical position of purchasing agent with a local citizen or with someone from the home office is often the subject of considerable debate at headquarters. A native has the advantage of being better acquainted with the local supply sources and government officials, but there is a chance that he or she suffers from such cultural disadvantages as a tendency to favor members of the extended family or to accept as a normal business practice the giving (scarce supply) or receiving (plentiful supply) of bribes. The employee from the home office, on the other hand, will be experienced in company purchasing procedures and should be free of these cultural disadvantages. Managers are not so naive as to believe that belonging to a certain culture guarantees that an individual will or will not engage in unethical activities.

However, the tendency to commit these acts may be greater where there are no cultural constraints.

Maintenance.   A second function supporting production is the maintenance of buildings and equipment. The aim of the maintenance department is to prevent the occurrence of unscheduled work stoppages caused by equipment failures. Because of difficulty in obtaining imported spare parts and machinery, the machine shops of many maintenance departments actually manufacture these items.

> General Tire—Spain began building tire molds for its own use but became so proficient that it was soon selling them to other affiliates. General Motors subsidiaries are regularly supplied with tools and dies made by GM in Mexico.

It is common practice in the industrialized countries to establish preventive maintenance programs in which machinery is shut down according to plan and worn parts are replaced. Such programs are especially important for a synchronized manufacturing system, as you know. The production department with advance notice of a shutdown can schedule around the machine, or, by working the machine overtime, inventories can be built up temporarily, permitting the production process to continue during its overhaul.

This concept is not widely accepted in developing countries, where firms seem to take a fatalistic attitude toward equipment: "It it breaks down, we'll repair it." Furthermore, in a seller's market, maintenance personnel are pressured by production and marketing managers to keep machinery running. This short-term view allows no time for scheduled shutdowns. The subsidiaries that do practice preventive maintenance with overhaul periods based on headquarters standards frequently find these standards inadequate because of local operating conditions (humidity, dust, and temperature) and the manner in which the operators handle the machinery. When the amount of spare parts ordered with the machinery is based on domestic experience, it is often insufficient.

In one sense, proper maintenance is more critical than 100 percent attendance of workers. The absence of one worker from a group of six usually will not halt production, but if a key machine suddenly breaks down, the entire plant can be idled.

Technical function.   The function of the technical department is to provide production with manufacturing specifications. Usually, technical personnel are also responsible for checking the quality of inputs and the finished product. The task of the technical department in a foreign subsidiary is not simply one of maintaining a file of specifications sent by the home office, because difficulty in obtaining the same kinds of raw materials as those used by the home plants may require substitutions that necessitate the complete rewriting of specifications.

> When a synthetic rubber plant was established in Mexico to produce some kinds of synthetic rubber, the government banned imports of all synthetic rubbers. Technical departments worked day and night to produce specifications that enabled the tire companies to substitute the few types available locally for the many kinds formerly imported.

The affiliate's technical manager is a key figure in the maintenance of product quality and thus is extremely influential in selecting sources of supply.

Global and multinational companies go to great lengths in persuading host governments and joint venture partners of the need to place one of their people in this position. In this way, they are certain to keep the affiliate as a captive customer purchasing all of the inputs that the more highly integrated parent manufactures.

SUMMARY

After WW II, Japanese manufacturers believed that to be competitive globally, they would have to improve their product quality and lower costs. To achieve these goals, they created a production system based primarily on American production concepts. This system, now called just-in-time, required coordinated management of materials, people, and suppliers. JIT's goal was to eliminate inventories, reduce process and setup times, and use participative management to ensure worker input and loyalty to the firm. Total quality control (TQC) in all functional areas was necessary. Quality circles were an important component of TQC.

There were some problems with JIT. And American production experts, aided by computer software, developed synchronized manufacturing, whose goal is *unbalanced* production scheduling rather than the balanced scheduling of JIT; attention is focused on the bottleneck of the production system, and scheduling for the entire system is controlled by the output of the bottleneck operation.

Although many of the production processes and procedures employed by the parent can be transferred overseas, some must be altered or discarded because of environmental differences. Central managements' preference for worldwide standardization is based on the fact that unified methods simplify the execution of the management functions and are usually less costly.

Governments of developing nations, preoccupied with high unemployment and rising capital costs, are urging investors to consider an *intermediate technology* rather than the highly automated processes of the industrialized nations. The multinationals' response, in some instances, has been to search for an *appropriate technology,* which matches a country's market with its resources. Under this concept, the production processes used may vary from the most advanced to the most primitive, depending on the influence of the economic, sociocultural, and political variables.

A production system is essentially a functionally related group of activities for creating value. Factors included in the system's operations are (1) plant location, (2) plant layout, (3) materials handling, and (4) the human element. After the system is operable, two general classes of activities, productive and supportive, must be performed. Among the important supportive activities are purchasing, maintenance, and the technical function. The primary aim of both types of activities is to ensure that the system produces on time the required amount of product of the desired quality at the budgeted cost.

QUESTIONS

1. What are the trade-offs for a firm that uses a just-in-time production system?

2. What advantages does synchronized manufacturing have over JIT?

3. What does quality in a pickup truck mean to you? To a farmer in Africa?

4. What difficulties do you see for global firms when they implement synchronized manufacturing in their plants located in developing countries? Are there any advantages that are more valuable to them than to plants in industrialized nations?

5. What is the connection between manufacturers' insistence on receiving components with zero defects from outside suppliers and JIT?

6. What are the advantages to a worldwide firm of global standardization of its production facilities?

7. Discuss the influence of the uncontrollable environmental forces in global standardization of a firm's production facilities.

8. Why are plant location and materials handling important factors in the design of a production system?

9. Why might production costs be excessive?

10. Who should be in charge of the purchasing function of an overseas affiliate, a local person or someone from the home office? Why?

11. What is the importance of preventive maintenance? Why might it be difficult to establish a preventive program in an overseas plant?

12. What is the connection between quality circles and participative management?

MINICASE 19–1

Site Selection: Johnson Machine Tool Manufacturing (Europa)

A site selection committee was named by the president of a small company, Johnson Machine Tool Manufacturing (annual sales—$21 million), to recommend the location of Johnson's first plant in Europa. A subcommittee consisting of the managers of finance, marketing, and production has just returned from a two-week visit. Its members are in agreement that two locations in Europa are preferable to all others:

1. Carlsburg, the capital and largest city (2,300,000 population).
2. Andein (180,000 population).

Carlsburg, also a manufacturing center for the country, is located almost equidistant from the borders. Andein, on the other hand, occupies the southeastern corner of the nation, almost 350 kilometers away. There are some light manufacturing plants in Andein.

To reduce the time required to gather the information needed to choose a plant site, the subcommittee divided the work as follows:

1. Marketing manager:
   a. Confirmed desk study concerning the marketing analysis.
   b. Checked on the availability of freight carriers, especially carriers of motor freight, and on freight rates.
   c. Investigated the availability and rent of warehouse space in Carlsburg.

2. Production manager:
   a. Obtained information concerning wages and the cost of fringe benefits for various skill levels in Carlsburg and Andein. Checked both markets for labor supply.
   b. Obtained cost estimates for plant construction in Carlsburg and Andein.
   c. Visited the utility companies to learn about the supply and rates in both cities.
   d. Checked the availability and cost of housing in both cities.
   e. Inquired about cultural and recreational activities and schools in both cities.

3. Finance manager:
   a. Inquired about taxes in both cities—property, state, income, and payroll taxes.
   b. Visited the national development office to confirm the amount and kinds of assistance to be

obtained from the national government for establishing a manufacturing plant in Europa.
   c. Obtained prices on tracts of land in Carlsburg and Andein.

The results of the investigation are as follows:

1. Monthly rent of warehouse and office space in Carlsburg—$1,500. This is necessary if the plant is set up in Andein. Warehousing and offices will be at the plant site if the company locates at Carlsburg.

2. Annual transportation costs for incoming raw materials and component parts should average $160,000 if the plant is located in Carlsburg and $270,000 if it is established in Andein. Transportation costs for finished goods will be $270,000 for the Carlsburg location and $390,000 if the plant is set up in Andein. Service is adequate to both locations.

3. Labor costs are somewhat higher in the capital. With fringe benefits included, the cost should be $1,100,000 for Carlsburg and $970,000 for Andein. The supply of labor is adequate at both locations.

4. Annual depreciation of building and equipment will amount to $160,000 in Carlsburg and $100,000 in Andein. It is planned to use straight-line depreciation over a 10-year period.

5. To include differences in land costs, the treasurer has recommended that 10 percent of the value of the land purchase be included under the heading of Implied Interest. This amounts annually to $90,000 for Carlsburg and $50,000 for Andein.

6. Power and heat are expected to cost $76,000 annually in both Carlsburg and Andein because the same power company supplies both areas. The power supply is adequate at both locations.

7. Water will cost $15,000 annually in Carlsburg and $12,000 in Andein. The supply is adequate in both cities.

8. Insurance is slightly higher in Andein—$39,000 annually versus $36,000 for Carlsburg.

9. Property values are lower in Andein, as are the tax rates. Property taxes are expected to be $27,000 in Carlsburg and $14,000 in Andein.

10. State income taxes are also lower in Andein—$14,000 versus $27,000 in Carlsburg.

11. Although the payroll tax is a federal tax with the same rate in all parts of the country, Andein's

lower wage rates cause its payroll to be lower than that of Carlsburg. Payroll taxes are $15,400 in Carlsburg and $13,600 in Andein.

12. The federal government is urging companies to locate away from the capital and offers a 10-year exemption equal to 50 percent of federal income taxes to those that do. The financial manager estimates that by the second year, the subsidiary would have taxable earnings of approximately $750,000. The tax rate is 40 percent.

13. There are state parks within an hour's drive from each city. Carlsburg has an opera company, a symphony orchestra, and various golf courses and tennis courts. The major university of the nation is located in Carlsburg. There is also an English-speaking school with grades K through 12.

14. Andein is near two lakes and a forest. Fishing and hunting are permitted. A regional university is in the city. Although there is no English-speaking school for grades K through 12 in Andein, the U.S. Army base 15 miles away does have such a school for army dependents, some of whom live in Andein. There is a daily bus service from Andein to the school on the base, and American children who are not army dependents are permitted to attend if they pay an $80 monthly tuition.

In light of these results:

1. Which city do you recommend as a plant site?
2. Show all of your calculations.
3. In addition to costs, what other factors are you considering?

MINICASE 19–2

Maquinas para el Hogar Penwick

Maquinas para el Hogar Penwick is a manufacturing subsidiary of Penwick Home Appliances in Boston. It is located in El Pais, a nation with 25 million inhabitants whose GNP/capita is $1,480. The country's annual inflation rate is about 30 percent, but the local company makes a good profit, in part because it keeps large stocks of components and raw materials purchased as much as 12 months before they are needed for production. The finished products are sold at prices set as if the raw materials and components had been purchased recently; hence the high profits. Penwick's competitors use the same strategy.

Penwick–El Pais has three competitors, none of which produces as complete a product mix or as many variations in each of the product lines of refrigerators, kitchen stoves and washing machines as does the local Penwick plant. José Garcia, the local marketing manager, is proud of the fact that Penwick–El Pais makes as many kinds of products and variations of products as the much larger home plant, and he has told the managing director of the local company that it is the wide product mix that maintains Penwick–El Pais's number-one position in sales. It is true that Manuel Cardenas, the local production manager, and Garcia frequently have heated discussions, because Cardenas wants to make fewer product variations. Garcia accuses him of wanting to make black stoves like Henry Ford made black cars, but Cardenas claims he could double his production if he could make fewer kinds of products and less variations. Cardenas knows the value of long production runs and tries to get them. Garcia retorts that if Cardenas would pay attention to what he wants instead of making what Cardenas wants to make, he could sell more.

This is a sore spot with Cardenas, because he tries hard to produce a new product according to Garcia's written request. If Garcia's memo says he wants a new size refrigerator in three colors to be available with or without beverage coolers or ice cube makers, these are the models that Cardenas asks the product design department to design and make production specifications for. True, Garcia at one time or other has asked to attend meetings with Cardenas and his staff, but Cardenas considers this a waste of time. After all, he doesn't waste the design department's time by asking to attend their meetings; why should a salesperson attend his meetings? He has enough problems with the high prices for parts that the purchasing department gives him. When he complains, they tell him that everything he orders is special manufacture for the vendors. That's their problem; this is what the design department specifies, and this is what he has to use to build the product.

Cardenas has more pressing problems. Headquarters has adopted a new production system, synchronized manufacturing, and now wants him to do the same. In fact, he had to send his assistant manager to Boston for a month's training. Now she and the design manager, who also went, are back, and they brought one of the home office experts with them. They're all going to have a long meeting with him this afternoon. Cardenas has read about synchronized manufacturing in technical journals, and it does seem to have some advantages. But, all of them have been in highly industrialized nations, and there are a lot of cultural and economic differences between El Pais and those countries.

You might role-play this case. Imagine you are one of the group of three that has come from Boston. Even though you know the local plant has orders to convert to synchronized manufacturing, you still have to win over the local personnel.

1. What will you say?
2. Can you think of any advantages that might be even more important for the local plant than they are for the larger home plant?
3. What problems do you foresee in putting synchronized manufacturing in place?

SUPPLEMENTARY READINGS

Global manufacturing

Ferdows, Kasra; J. G. Miller; J. Nakane; and T. E. Vollmann. "Evolving Global Manufacturing Strategies: Projections into the 1990s." *International Journal of Operation and Production Management* 6, no. 4 (1986), pp. 6–16.

"How Ford Used Videoconferencing to Solve Production Problems." *Business Europe*, April 13, 1987, pp. 6–8.

"How Levi Strauss Achieves Maximum Flexibility with Local Manufacturing." *Business Europe*, February 16, 1987, p. 12.

"The Hollow Corporation." *Business Week*, March 13, 1986, pp. 57–74.

JIT and synchronized manufacturing

"Allen-Bradley Tries to Fight Competition by Tooling Up." *Datamation*, March 15, 1988, pp. 33–34.

Chase, Richard B., and Nicholas J. Aquilano. *Productions and Operations Management*. 5th ed. Homewood, Ill.: Richard D. Irwin, 1989.

"Factories that Turn Nuts into Bolts." *U.S. News & World Report*, July 14, 1986, pp. 44–45.

"How Hewlett-Packard Combines Just-In-Time with Quality Control." *Business International*, April 18, 1988, pp. 113–15.

" 'Just-In-Time' Inventories Putting Australian Firms on More Competitive Footing." *Business Asia*, November 9, 1987, p. 360.

"Manufacturing's New Window of Opportunity." *The Wall Street Journal*, April 19, 1988, p. 29.

Schonberger, Richard J., and Edward M. Knod, Jr. *Operations Management*. 3rd ed. Plano, Tex.: Business Publications, 1988.

Shingo, Shigeo. *Non-Stock Production: The Shingo System for Continuous Improvement*. Cambridge, Mass.: Productivity Press, 1988.

"Smart Factories: America's Turn?" *Business Week*, May 8, 1989, pp. 142–48.

"The Vital Elements of World-Class Manufacturing." *International Management*, May 1986, pp. 76–78.

"The Export of a Japanese Idea." *The Economist*, April 25, 1987, p. 68.

"White Goods Empire: 400 Villages Crown Electrolux King." *Business International*, August 11, 1986, pp. 250–51.

Manufacturing rationalization

"A BI Checklist: Points to Consider in Rationalization Plans." *Business International*, January 29, 1982, pp. 35–37.

"Cutting Production Costs: Seven Ways to Check When Auditing Operations." *Business International*, February 1, 1988, p. 30.

"Rationalization Planning Is Becoming a Must for International Companies." *Business International*, December 19, 1980, pp. 401–02.

New accounting for synchronized manufacturing

Chase, Richard B., and Nicholas J. Aquilano. *Production and Operations Management*. 5th ed. Homewood, Ill.: Richard D. Irwin, 1989, pp. 796, 814–24.

"How the New Math of Productivity Adds Up." *Business Week*, June 6, 1988, pp. 103–12.

McNair, Carol. "Timely Information for High Tech." *New Accountant*, November 1988, pp. 4–9.

Quality and quality circles

"Armand Feigenbaum: Making Quality a Way of Life." *International Management*, January 1984, pp. 16–18.

Deming, W. Edwards. *Out of the Crisis*. Cambridge, Mass.: MIT Press, 1986.

"French Quality Circles Multiply." *International Management*, December 1986, pp. 30–32.

"How AVCO's Quality System Boosts Profits Worldwide." *Business International*, January 18, 1988, pp. 9–11.

Ishikawa, Kaoru. *Guide to Quality Control*. 2nd ed. Tokyo: Asian Productivity Organization, 1982.

"Marketers Discover What 'Quality' Really Means." *Business Marketing*, April 1987, pp. 58–72.

"Motivation Systems for Small-Group Quality Control Activities." *The Japan Economic Journal*, June 28, 1983, pp. 33–35.

"Quality Circles." *Kredeitbank Weekly Bulletin*, October 21, 1983, pp. 1–5.

"Quality Control at Toyota Motor Corporation." *The Wheel Extended,* Special Supplement, July–September 1982.

Shimada, Justin Y.; Kenneth M. Jenkins; and Lewis N. Goslin. "Quality Circles Can Meet the Challenge." *Business Forum,* Spring 1983, pp. 18–21.

Strier, Franklin. "Quality Circles in the United States: Fad or Fixture?" *Business Forum,* Summer 1984, pp. 19–23.

"What American Makes Best." *Fortune,* March 28, 1988, pp. 40–53.

ENDNOTES

1. Shigeo Shingo, *Non-Stock Production: The Shingo System for Continuous Improvement* (Cambridge, Mass.: Productivity Press, 1988), p. 36.

2. "Innovation," *Business Week,* Special Issue, June 1989, p. 107.

3. Richard J. Schonberger and Edward M. Knod, Jr., *Operations Management,* 3rd ed. (Plano, Tex.: Business Publications, 1988), p. 544; and Shingo, *Non-Stock Production,* p. 320.

4. "Motivation Systems for Small-Group Quality Control Activities," *The Japan Economic Journal,* June 28, 1983, pp. 33–35.

5. Franklin Strier, "Quality Circles in the United States: Fad or Fixture?" *Business Forum,* Summer 1984, pp. 19–23.

6. Richard B. Chase and Nicholas J. Aquilano, *Production and Operations Management* (Homewood, Ill.: Richard D. Irwin, 1989), pp. 736–68.

7. Ibid., p. 792.

8. Ibid., p. 797.

9. "A Select Few Poised to Lead Business in the 90s," *The Wall Street Journal,* Centennial Edition, June 23, 1989, p. A3.

10. Ibid., p. A22.

11. "How AVCO's Quality System Boosts Profits Worldwide," *Business International,* January 18, 1988, pp. 9–11.

12. "The Export of a Japanese Idea," *The Economist,* April 25, 1987, p. 68.

13. "French Quality Circles Multiply," *International Management,* December 1986, p. 31.

14. " 'Just-In-Time' Inventories Putting Australian Firms on More Competitive Footing," *Business Asia,* November 9, 1987, p. 360.

15. "Export of a Japanese Idea," p. 68.

16. "Ford Tests Just-In-Time Parts Delivery at German Plant," *Automotive News,* October 17, 1988, p. 40.

17. Yves L. Doz, "Managing Manufacturing Rationalization within Multinational Companies," *Columbia Journal of World Business,* Fall 1978, pp. 82–93.

18. Conversation with Ford International representative, June 19, 1989; and "Gearing Up to Export Three Million Engines to Auto Plants Abroad," *R&D Mexico,* February 1982, pp. 20–23.

19. D. J. Teece, "Technology Transfer by Multinational Firms," *Economic Journal,* June 1977, pp. 242–61.

20. A number of studies confirmed by personal experience have shown that the foremost criterion for plant design is the output desired. Once this is known, the engineering department of a multiplant operation will check to see whether a factory already built has a capacity similar to the output specified. If so, this facility will serve as a design standard for the new plant, though modifications may be made to eliminate problems encountered in the original design. Many large multiplant firms actually have standard designs for large, medium, and small production outputs.

21. A highly automated machine might make only one or two sizes or types of a product, whereas a general-purpose machine may be capable of producing not only all sizes of a product but other products as well. Its output, however, may be as little as 1 percent of that of a specialized machine.

22. The skill level required of general-purpose machine operators is much higher than that required of operators attending automated machinery, but it is lower than that needed to set up and maintain this equipment.

23. This does not mean that unit production costs are lower in the small plants, and certainly the coordination of their activities will be formidable. The example does illustrate the extreme range of possibilities when capital costs are a primary consideration. From Colin Norman, *Soft Technology, Hard Choice* (Washington, D.C.: Worldwatch Institute, June 1978), p. 14.

24. *Transnational Corporations in World Development* (New York: United Nations, 1988), p. 170.

25. Louis T. Wells, *Technology and Third World Countries,* ILO Working Paper, Geneva, 1982.

Chapter 20

Labor Relations Policies and Management

You can get an assembly robot today for $20,000. Compared to a person, that's cheap. A robot also shows up every day. It doesn't have to have a raise. You've got it for life. It releases the manufacturer of geographical limitations on the availability of labor.

Vincent M. Altamuro, robotics consultant

LEARNING OBJECTIVES

In this chapter, you will study:

1. The importance of thoroughly analyzing the available labor force before a company makes an investment requiring workers in a foreign country.

2. Employee recruitment and selection methods, which may vary depending on whether the host country is in a developed or a developing state.

3. The necessity and methods of training new employees and upgrading training for existing employees.

4. Some precautions managers from industrialized countries should observe when recruiting, selecting, and training employees in nonindustrialized countries.

5. Changes in American compensation and incentive practices.

6. Japanese labor management practices.

7. Labor unions, which may be parts of an industry's disciplinary system and which negotiate all sorts of other matters, such as wages and working conditions, with employers.

8. Laws that mandate working conditions and other labor matters, such as severance pay when workers are fired.

9. Codetermination, which puts worker representatives on company boards of directors.

10. Quality circles and why they might or might not work.

11. Robotics.

12. How faster, cheaper computers together with robotics are creating the factories of the future.

13. The importance for a WWC of coordinating labor relations among the parent, subsidiary, and affiliated companies.

14. Some labor relations' differences between LDCs and industrialized countries.

KEY WORDS AND CONCEPTS

- Fringe benefits
- Skilled labor
- Unskilled labor
- Employee facilities
- In-house training programs
- On-the-job training
- Apprenticeship programs
- Off-premises training
- Incentive pay plans
- Quality circles
- Robotics
- Collective bargaining
- Codetermination

BUSINESS (LABOR) INCIDENT

How do you make an American worker as enthusiastic, loyal, and hardworking as a Japanese? A few years ago, the fashionable answer was to copy Japanese ways, such as quality circles and suggestion boxes. Monsanto seems to have found better ways, as illustrated in its Luling, Louisiana, agricultural chemicals plant.

It is making employees feel "ownership" for their company by allowing them to use their brains as well as their hands. Monsanto's main organizational change has been to do away with most of its foremen, supervisors, and quality inspectors and instead to have plant workers oversee themselves. To assist them, it now gives the workers financial information about their part of the operation, which had previously been kept secret.

Another step was to encourage them to form teams and look for measurable improvements, big or small. The 30-year-old Luling plant leaks. Instead of calling for expensive outside repair people, the workers formed a team and plugged the leaks, saving Monsanto some $155,000 a year.

A further successful change was to put workers in touch with distributors and customers so they know where the product goes and how it is used. One result was that a Luling team redesigned the packaging when they saw what was really needed. Also, quality control improved markedly based on feedback from vendors and customers. Complaints were halved in 1988.

Source: "No Blues on the Mississippi," *The Economist,* January 7, 1989, p. 56.

In Chapter 12, we saw some of the labor forces with which international business management is faced from country to country. Are there enough bodies present? Do the persons in the bodies possess the skills your operation needs? Even if there are sufficient bodies and skills, will they work for your operation? If there are insufficient bodies, skills, or willingness to work, can you find and train other labor?

In this chapter, we shall not concern ourselves with the problems of executive-level personnel, which are dealt with in Chapter 22. The problems of lower-level management and the workers are the ones we shall attempt to solve here.

The effectiveness of every organization depends to a great extent on how well its human resources are utilized. Their effective use is dependent on management's policies and practices. Management of a company's human resources is a shared responsibility. The day-to-day supervision of people on the job is the duty of the operating managers, who must integrate the human, financial, and physical resources into an efficient production system. However, the formulation of policies and procedures for (1) estimation of work force needs, (2) recruitment and selection, (3) training and development, (4) motivation, (5) compensation, (6) discipline, (7) relations with employee associations, and (8) employment termination is generally the responsibility of personnel managers working in cooperation with executives from marketing, production, and finance as well as the firm's lawyers.

The St. Gobain minicase at the end of the chapter is an example of a lack or failure of cooperation—and perhaps communication—between financial and personnel management. The personnel people should have been able to warn of the possible adverse labor relations results caused by sudden revelations of previously secret financial information.

PERSONNEL NEEDS, AVAILABILITY, AND LABOR LAWS[1]

Analysis of the Labor Force

Because of the labor force's influence on the choice of plant site, factory design, and production processes, data on the available labor force must be gathered prior to making final decisions in these areas. Labor laws, going wage rates, and the characteristics of workers, such as their skills, work attitudes, and prejudices about gender and caste, as well as their propensity to join labor organizations and to strike, all weigh heavily in these decisions. All too often, failures to obtain such information result in costly mistakes. Managements, attracted by low wage rates, have set up plants only to learn later that the labor costs are considerably higher than expected because of the existence of **fringe benefits,** which are usually government requirements. Such errors could have been avoided by consulting local experts.

fringe benefits benefits for employees over and above base wages, including bonuses, maternity leaves, education leaves, sick leaves, and medical payments

A simple reading of the labor laws by a layman, and particularly a foreign layman, will almost never give a complete or accurate understanding of their exact meaning or of how they are applied and enforced by the authorities. Sometimes laws are enforced very stringently and in surprising ways, but often they are ignored. In addition, firms frequently pay and give more than the legally required minimums. A study by the American Chamber of Commerce in Mexico showed that 19 percent of the 121 companies surveyed gave punctuality and attendance bonuses averaging 20 percent of monthly wages. Death benefits paid by the firms averaged 15 months' wages for natural deaths and 26 months' wages for acciden-tal death. One company gave a 100-minute coffee break. In all, more than two dozen types of benefits were offered that were not required by law.

Another costly omission is the failure to ascertain the availability of **skilled labor** or of **unskilled labor** willing to work on an assembly line. Establishing a plant solely because of an abundance of low-cost labor can be a big mistake if the cost and time required to train for necessary skills have not been factored into the cost analyses and start-up plans.

Of course, the employer may try to bring from abroad the skilled personnel who are unavailable locally, but that effort usually meets with host country government hostility and resistance; the host country wants its own people hired and trained. Less host country resistance may be encountered if a labor shortage is due to its people's unwillingness to work on an assembly line or if there is very low unemployment.

Those situations led to the northern European guest worker programs we discussed in Chapter 12. You recall that when unemployment grew among the local people, the guest workers were no longer welcome.

Employee Facilities

Another element of personnel planning is that of **employee facilities** on and off the job. For example, will a first-aid dispensary be sufficient, or must a hospital and dental clinic be provided either because the law demands it or because there are no satisfactory facilities nearby? If an appreciable number of foreign workers will be employed, special dietary kitchens and recreation equipment may be needed. When women are employed, provision must be made to care for children, and the firm may build a nursery (required by law in some countries) or contract private nurseries to provide the services. In Germany, a number of firms subsidize privately operated day nurseries in exchange for guaranteed numbers of places for their employees' children. Local authorities in Italy provide nurseries financed by part of the employer's social security payments.

In situations where the plant is located some distance from the nearest city, the firm may construct a "company town." However, in extended family-type societies, this may be a trap for the well-intentioned employer. Employee dissatisfaction and unrest may develop as the employee's extended family moves into housing designed for only the immediate family, causing over-crowding and shortages of water, sewage facilities, medical facilities, or schools. Alternatives to the company town are for the employer to provide or subsidize transportation to and from the nearest communities or to subsidize local government housing. Using these alternatives, the workers are less likely to blame their employers for problems that arise with their living quarters.

skilled labor labor that has learned job-useful skills through training and/or experience

unskilled labor has not learned such skills

employee facilities not directly job related, but may be necessary to attract and keep employees; include rec-reational or medical facilities, child day-care center, or spe-cial dietary kitchens

RECRUITMENT AND SELECTION

Recruitment

Once it has been determined how many of what types of employees will be needed, the personnel department can begin to recruit. Various kinds of labor recruitment sources are available. Suitable candidates may be found within the hiring unit of the company if it is already in operation, within other units of the company, or from the outside.

Internal sources.   The use of internal sources, the company's present employees, can be an effective recruitment method. The cost is relatively low, morale benefits from inside promotions, and each applicant is already known to the employer. Where labor is organized, the company-union contract may require members to be given the first opportunities to apply for vacant positions.

Employees as recruiters—Advantages.   The use of a firm's present workers to locate new employees can be efficient and low cost. Such practices can build morale.

Employees as recruiters—Disadvantages.   It is human nature that the employees will try to help family and friends. Thus, considerations of family, similar social status, caste, geographic origin, culture, or language are usually more important than qualifications for the vacant position. Such considerations exist in any country, but they are especially prevalent in less developed countries, where an employed member of the extended family is under pressure to help the other members find work. More than one foreign managing director has been shocked to find that the local personnel director has filled the plant with relatives or people from the same hometown. Such a work force can be expected to be more loyal to the personnel director than to the firm.

External sources.   Overseas, WWCs tend to employ the same kinds of external recruiting methods and sources as are used in their home countries. These may include (1) newspaper advertising, (2) trade schools, (3) radio advertising, (4) labor unions, and (5) employment agencies. However, there are important differences between their use in the industrialized countries and their use in the developing countries.

Unskilled workers.   Because of high unemployment in most LDCs, the WWC subsidiaries there generally have no difficulties in filling jobs calling for little or no skill. Furthermore, such companies usually have a recruiting advantage over indigenous concerns because of the WWCs' reputations for on-the-job training plus higher wages and other benefits.

Skilled workers.   The recruitment of skilled workers is more difficult because they are generally in short supply in developing countries. Some walk in, attracted by the knowledge that advancement may be more rapid in foreign-owned firms than in locally owned ones, but managements will try to utilize other methods and sources as well. Newspaper advertisements will not have the effectiveness to which foreign managers are accustomed, because in the LDCs, many workers who learned their skills on the job can neither read nor write. A solution to this difficulty is to announce the jobs on the radio.

Employment agencies are utilized much less in the LDCs than in the industrialized countries. The job applicants frequently cannot afford to pay the agency's fee even if that were legal, which it often is not. In cases where the companies pay the fee, it is not unusual for the agencies to connive with the applicant to split the payment. The applicant takes the job, and the company pays the agency's fee, which it splits with the hired applicant, who then quits. The agency and the applicant can repeat this as many times as they can get away with it.

Selection

By means of the selection processes, management chooses those applicants whose qualifications seem most nearly to match the job requirements.

Industrialized countries.   Most companies in the industrialized countries follow rather standard procedures of requesting personal information, including work experience, to be given on an application form and during interviews. In some countries, the worker carries an identification book, which must be presented when seeking employment. The book entries constitute a record of employment, including jobs, wages, and employer comments. If the worker has a prison record, the book will include information about that. The hiring company may give prospective employees a physical examination and aptitude or psychological tests.

Developing countries.   In LDCs, the hiring process is usually less formal. Less testing is done, and when it is done, the results are likely to be used somewhat superficially. As has been mentioned before, family ties, social status, caste, language, and common origin are more likely to be elements of hiring decisions in LDCs than in other countries.

Recruiting and selecting employees are the initial steps in building an effective work force. Once the workers are hired, they must undergo training and development.

TRAINING AND DEVELOPMENT

Most new employees need to be trained and developed to fit into the employer firm's specific operations. In addition, because of technological or market changes, employees sometimes need to have their skills upgraded or need to be taught new ones. The preparation and supervision of training and development programs, both in-house and off-premises, are normally the responsibility of the personnel department after it ascertains operating department needs.

In-House Programs

in-house training programs training programs developed by the employer on its premises

Several kinds of **in-house training programs** are offered by firms in both the developed and developing nations. Among these programs are on-the-job training, apprenticeship training, classroom sessions, conferences, and simulation. The programs frequently overlap.

on-the-job training worker learns by doing the job under the supervision of an experienced employee

On-the-job training.   **On-the-job training** methods make either a supervisor or an experienced operator responsible for training new or promoted employees. Probably the most significant difference between the developed and developing countries as to on-the-job training is the utilization in the former of more training aids. The use of audiovisual equipment and simulation training on identical equipment set up in an area away from the actual production space enable the learning workers to master the job more quickly than they could on the production line. Because of the high cost of many training aids and shortages of experienced trainers, these methods have been slow to appear in the less developed nations. However, this is changing as many multinationals are transferring the methods to their LDC subsidiaries with excellent results.

One of those results is the recruiting edge that good training gives the WWC subsidiaries in attracting needed employees. This works both ways, however, as the locally owned firms regularly hire away workers who have been trained by foreign-owned companies—one of the benefits that LDCs derive from multinational operations within their borders.

> Managers of WWC subsidiaries in Mexico have been heard to complain that "they must be training half the machinists in Mexico."

Labor trainers in developing nations have found that the people learn industrial skills rapidly. More difficult is teaching new workers who come from farms and villages how to adjust socially and psychologically to factory life. Some of these workers must be taught not only job skills but also the concept of time. They are not accustomed to reporting to work at the same time and place each workday or to meeting production schedules.

They must be introduced to factory teamwork and to an industrial hierarchy. Frequently, the company must compromise and not attempt to change customary farm and village practices too quickly and completely.

> A Spanish company opened a factory in Guatemala, hired local people, and tried to operate as if it were in Europe. The Spanish management installed work hours and production routines and schedules that had worked efficiently in Spain. They were nearly disastrous at that stage of development in Guatemala.
>
> *Reactions.* The people refused to work and became hostile. Guatemalan troops were necessary to protect the factory. Management at last considered local needs and compromised, and mutually satisfactory solutions were found.
>
> *Solutions.* The solutions included four-hour breaks between two daily work periods. During the breaks, the male employees took care of their farms and gardens and the female employees attended to household needs and cared for their children. As another part of the solution, the employees were willing to work Saturdays to make up production lost during the breaks.[2]
>
> Through compromise and patience, European management, operating in a preindustrial setting, was able to achieve satisfactory production. It studied, negotiated, and adapted to local needs. The alternatives were low production or perhaps even a destroyed factory.

Apprenticeship programs.   **Apprenticeship programs** are a special kind of on-the-job training for skilled tradespeople, such as plumbers, electricians, and toolmakers, that has existed for many years. Young workers called apprentices assist experienced craftsmen for periods of two to five years, until the apprentices are capable of doing the job without supervision.

apprenticeship programs beginning workers work under the direction of skilled workers for a minimum period of two to five years

In the more developed nations, the majority of the trades require the apprentices to pass examinations before they are certified as skilled craftspeople. Europe's apprenticeship training is especially good. It is a highly formalized part of a nation's educational system, and it includes classroom instruction as well as on-the-job training.

> The combination of classroom and on-the-job training is utilized in the United States by some firms, but the practice has not been incorporated into the national educational system to the extent that it has in Europe. Some vocational schools and community colleges do offer cooperative programs with industry that approach the European system, and many community and city colleges and high schools have a wide variety of vocational and trade courses that workers can take on their own.

Managers coming from countries with formal training programs to a developing nation must be careful when they hire persons claiming to have a skilled trade; the types of training programs with which the manager is familiar are extremely rare in the LDCs. Even if the applicant is truly skilled, the skill may be narrowly limited to what was learned on the job.

Off-Premises Training and Development

Sending workers and supervisors off the company's premises has become an accepted practice in the United States and other developed nations. Personnel managers have learned that training and development by skilled educators working in an educational setting are often less costly and more effective than training and development done in-house with company employees. France has a particularly innovative law that permits workers to apply for a one-year leave of absence to enroll in an approved training program if they have been employed for at least two years. The French government and the employers share the expenses, which include the employees' salaries while they are in training.[3]

off-premises training sending employees out of the plant to a school or other training site

Off-premises training is far less common in the developing nations, but beginnings are being made as multinationals' subsidiaries in LDCs are cooperating with the host governments and inaugurating such programs. In addition, schools and universities in the LDCs, aided by their counterparts from the industrialized countries, are offering training and development programs to local industry.

MOTIVATION

Regardless of how well employees are selected and trained, they will not perform satisfactorily unless they are properly motivated. Effective personnel management requires an understanding of the motivational processes, including human needs. Without an understanding of those needs, managers cannot determine the kinds of employee motivation needed to induce employees to work toward the organization's goals.

Bonuses, Salaries, and Wages

Not long ago in the United States, the compensation hierarchy was clear cut; executives received bonuses on top of their salaries, middle and lower management were paid salaries only, and the other employees got wages. Those days are gone.

incentive pay plans forms of worker compensation in addition to basic wages with the purpose of improving quality and productivity

To motivate workers and give them greater incentive to improve productivity and meet international competition, American firms are making sweeping worker compensation changes. For example, base wage increases are replaced by bonuses or gain-sharing plans to reward improvements in quality or productivity. At other plants, pay-for-knowledge plans reward workers for the job-useful skills they master in addition to paying for the work they perform. Figure 20–1 offers a guide to these **incentive pay plans.** It comments on how they work and how to make them effective, and then it presents their advantages and disadvantages.

■ **FIGURE 20-1   A Guide to Incentive Pay Plans**

Plan Type	How It Works	What It Requires to Be Effective	Advantages	Disadvantages
Profit sharing	Employees receive a varying annual bonus based on corporate profits. Payments can be made in cash or deferred into a retirement fund.	Participating employees collectively must be able to influence profits. Owners must value employees' contributions enough to be willing to share profits.	The incentive formula is simple and easy to communicate. The plan is guaranteed to be affordable: It pays only when the firm is sufficiently profitable. It unites the financial interests of owners and employees.	Annual payments may lead employees to ignore long-term performance. Factors beyond the employee's control can influence profits. The plan forces private companies to open their books.
Gain sharing	When a unit beats predetermined performance targets, all members get bonuses. Objectives often include better productivity, quality, and customer service.	Objectives must be measurable. Management must encourage employee involvement. Employees must have a high degree of trust in management.	The plan enhances coordination and teamwork. Employees learn more about the business and focus on objectives. Employees work harder and smarter.	Plans that focus only on productivity may lead employees to ignore other important objectives, such as quality. The company may have to pay bonuses even when unprofitable.
Lump-sum bonus	Instead of a wage or salary increase, employees get a one-time cash payment based on performance or a union contract. The bonus does not become part of base pay.	Employees must have a sense that their prosperity mirrors the company's. Management must have a good relationship with employees.	The plan lets companies control fixed costs by limiting pay raises and attendant benefit increases.	Management sometimes awards bonuses subjectively, so employees may resent awards they consider unfair.
Pay for knowledge	An employee's salary or wage rises with the number of tasks he can do, regardless of the job he performs.	Skills must be identified and assigned a pay grade. The company must have well-developed employee assessment and training procedures.	By increasing flexibility, the plan lets the company operate with a leaner staff. The plan gives workers a broad perspective, making them more adept at problem solving.	Most employees will learn all applicable skills, raising labor costs. Training costs are high.

Source: *Fortune*, December 19, 1988, p. 52. Courtesy of *Fortune*.

Incentive Pay Plans

These plans not only encourage workers to produce more and better, they also hold down fixed wages and wage-related benefits and let compensation costs rise and fall with the company's profits.

Not all such plans succeed. They need a well-defined business strategy, and when installed for no clear reason, they usually fail. Profit is a business objective, but profit-sharing plans for workers may not be effective motivators because most employees have little influence on profits. Too many decisions and forces affect profit but are beyond the workers' control. Such decisions and forces include pricing policy, marketing strategy, assumption of debt or taxes, or market competition.

How to make an incentive plan succeed is the subject of the list below.* It begins with a clear strategy and recognizes that sometimes a plan must be phased out:

1. **Start with a clear strategy.**   Think hard about your goals. Focusing just on customer service, for example, could also raise costs.

*Source: *Fortune*, December 19, 1988, p. 54. Courtesy of *Fortune*.

2. **Focus on jobs that can be measured.**   Make sure managers know what constitutes peak performance and how to value it.

3. **Decentralize incentives.**   Allow individual business units to tailor reward plans to their specific situations.

4. **Separate incentives from base pay.**   Deliver incentive rewards in a lump sum to highlight the link between rewards and performance.

5. **Create a "sunset" provision.**   State conditions, such as the introduction of new technology or a change in business plans, under which the program will be modified or terminated.

Is the plan working?   Look again at the business incident, and you can see that Monsanto's plan was succeeding. Costs and customer complaints were down—measurable results. Before such results are in, management should be able to get indications of the plan's progress. Listen to the workers: are they interested and beginning to try it? Talk to the workers: do they understand the plan? Is the listening and talking more effective? In other words, are worker-management communications improving? Are the incentives being paid for the targeted results, and are they being withheld when targets are not hit? And finally, are desired end results being achieved, such as lower costs, better quality, higher productivity, fewer customer complaints, and more profit?[4]

For incentive plans to be successful, they must be reviewed and updated regularly. Conditions change. One company instituted an incentive system for its word processing personnel. They were expected to produce a certain number of pages for their regular wages, and if they exceeded that number, they could earn a bonus of up to 10 percent of their wages. After a time, management noticed that employees were sitting idly at their desks for most of the afternoons, even though they were turning in at the end of each day the number of pages needed to earn the maximum bonus. It developed that although the employees had been given new, faster word processors, no one had thought to change the bonus structure.

Motivation Japanese Style

In the sections above, we spoke of the flexible bonus in addition to employees' wages as an incentive. Some 25 percent of Japanese workers' compensation is in the bonus form, as opposed to only about 1 percent in the United States, although the practice is growing in America.[5]

Japanese-owned-and-directed manufacturing plants are in place and growing in America, notably in the automobile industry. Japanese automakers are inculcating American workers with different attitudes.

Instead of narrow job classifications, the companies give production workers broad titles. They are called "technicians" at Nissan, "associates" at Honda, and "team workers" at Mazda and Toyota.* Even the new hires are made to feel important by participating in decisions that most American and

---

* Of course, the Americans and Japanese are not alone in recognizing the importance of titles. One of the authors remembers a baggage handlers' strike at Heathrow Airport in London. He had to crawl into the hold of the plane with other passengers and airline employees to get the baggage out. Talking to a striker later, he was told that money was no longer the issue; the baggage handlers wanted a dignified title. The strike was settled when Heathrow agreed to recognize them as "baggage engineers."

"Today we'll be talking about some new approaches"

European companies vest in managers, such as scheduling overtime or rotating jobs.

Employees work in small groups, and those on the production line have responsibility both for assuring quality and improving productivity. An egalitarian atmosphere creates cooperation between workers and management. Executives have open, unassuming offices, no one has a reserved parking space, and everyone lunches in the same cafeteria.

Many American workers are enthusiastic boosters of their Japanese employers. One who came from the Volkswagen plant in Pennsylvania said the main difference was in the training, which he found superior at the Toyota plant in Kentucky. Another—who is new to manufacturing, having previously been a hairdresser—says getting her Toyota job was like winning a lottery. She was sent for four weeks' training in Japan and is making 50 percent more than in her old job.

Honeymoon ends?   Maintaining the team spirit is already a struggle at Nissan after five and a half years in Tennessee. For one thing, workers were subjected to an intense organizing drive by the United Auto Workers (UAW).

One reason the UAW hoped to succeed was demonstrated by Nissan production line employees' complaints that the production pace was burning them out. Although Japanese lines don't move faster than Detroit's, the Nissan workers are responsible for more tasks in addition to monitoring quality.

There are two sides to the Japanese system. One includes better efficiency, increased quality, and worker involvement. The other is increased pressure and stress in a tightly strung manufacturing process. For example, Japanese plants do not provide a relief worker to replace an ill employee, so it is up to the other team members to do the absent member's tasks on top of their own.[6]

The national leadership of the UAW remains committed to the team program, but elections in May 1989, for officers of a new UAW local at a Mazda plant near Detroit were won by dissidents. However, the UAW lost the July 1989 election at the Nissan factory in Tennessee by a vote of 1,622 to 711. In spite of the loss, one observer said, "It was odder, in fact, that one third of the carefully chosen 'technicians' dared to challenge the established order."[7]

WORLDVIEW
The *Shinjinrui* of Japan

The emergence of the *shinjinrui* is one development that seems to indicate a weakening of loyalty to employers in Japan. A growing sector of Japan's young people are doing the minimum amount of work necessary to keep from being demoted or fired. They are unwilling to work overtime, and they prefer to socialize with their friends rather than make the expected after-hours rounds of bars with bosses and co-workers. They are called "shinjinrui" (pronounced *sheen jeen roo ee*), which, literally translated, means "new human species."

Traditional Japanese are contemptuous of the *shinjinrui*, saying, for example, "These Japanese are not Japanese. They all want to live in California. You know, roller skating and surfing," or "Go to hell *shinjinrui*." One commentator, Tetsuya Chikushi of the *Asahi Journal*, urged something be done to discipline the new breed before they bring about the ruin of Japan. Chikushi unflatteringly compared Japan's *shinjinrui* with Americans, whom he described as lazy and unwilling to work.

Employees at Nippon Steel bow on command to company president.

Photo by Shigehieko Togo, *The Washington Post.*

American supervisors to blame?   Workers interviewed after the Mazda elections said the vote did not represent a rejection of the Mazda theory but was a protest over the way in which the theory had been implemented by the plant's American supervisors. One worker said "I don't think the Japanese are causing the problems, but I think the American supervisors are running the place like a traditional American car plant. They took the worst of both the Japanese and American systems and put them together here."[8]

QUALITY CIRCLES (QCs)

Quality circles are treated apart from the subject of employee motivation because although motivation is one objective of quality circles, there are others. As the name indicates, one of these objectives is improving product quality. Others are productivity, employee involvement, communications

■ **FIGURE 20–2**
Quality Circle

Definition:
A small group of people from the same work area who meet on a regular basis to identify, analyze, and solve product quality and other problems in their area.

Participants:
Leader—train, maintain records, motivate, lead, resource.
Facilitator (part- or full-time)—train, resource, group dynamics.
Member—identify problems, contribute ideas, develop solutions, implement solutions when feasible.
Management—obtain ownership support, furnish prompt responses, deal with issues and problems that surface, share information, provide resources.

---

quality circles employees in a part of the production process who work as a team to improve quality and productivity

improvement, team building, professional and personal growth opportunities, and better company profits.

"Quality circles are a raging disease in America and in many other countries," said Dr. W. Edwards Deming in a keynote lecture to the 1982 International Convention on Quality Circles in Seoul, Korea. A recent New York Stock Exchange survey bears him out; it found that 75 percent of manufacturing companies with over 10,000 employees had begun QCs. However, Dr. Deming feels that management in non-Japanese companies expects quick fixes from employee QCs but is not doing its part to permit these QCs to be successful. He says that management must research and experiment with engineers, designers, and production people and must listen to and act on QC suggestions.

At the same convention, Dr. Kaoru Ishikawa said of American management that it had "long experience and high pride, so it doesn't listen to others." Dr. Ishikawa became a leader in the Japanese QC movement after learning a great deal about the subject from Dr. Deming.[9]

The Idea behind Quality Circles

The idea behind quality circles is that it is cheaper to prevent rejects than to cure them. Quality control has a big effect on costs; in too many companies, it is the task of a few managers isolated from the shop floor. Dr. Deming taught, and his Japanese students learned, that workers ought to be made responsible for meeting quality targets. This helps motivate the workers and permits problems to be tackled early in production.

Jill H. King* suggests the outline of a QC as shown in Figure 20–2. She has identified a number of problems and issues in the QC movement. A few of them are middle-management resistance, unclear goals, little or no union involvement, and inadequate training. Another problem she identified is lack of top-management commitment, which brings us to the subject of company-wide quality control.

Companywide Quality Control (CWQC)

Companywide quality control (CWQC) is not a new system or scheme. According to one writer, it is a holistic approach to achieving objectives more effectively for an entire company.[10]

---

* King is manager, personnel training and development, Human Resources, Radar Systems Group, Hughes Aircraft Company.

■ FIGURE 20–3
The Buildup of Quality in Seven Stages

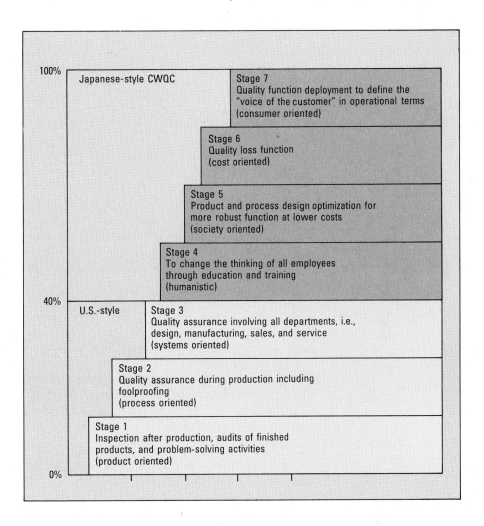

Companywide.   With CWQC, quality control begins with the product design in the production process and, equally important, applies to every job in the company. In Japan, all the employees in every aspect of their jobs are thought of as being components of CWQC. In the United States, by contrast, quality control grew out of inspecting the end product to ascertain whether it met engineering specifications. In many American companies, that is still all it means.

Quality.   In Japan, quality means user satisfaction. The Japanese believe the American definition of quality as meaning conformance with engineering specifications is too narrow. For the Japanese, the user may be the ultimate customer, but in a multiple-procedure manufacturing process, the user is the next department of the company, and the work done at each production stage must satisfy each succeeding stage. Some American departments regard the next department as a "policeman" or even as an "enemy."

A good comparison between the American and Japanese approaches to quality control can be seen in Figure 20–3 which illustrates the additional stages employed in Japan. Control is approached from more points of view in Japan than in the United States.

■ **FIGURE 20–4**
Quality Effort by Activity

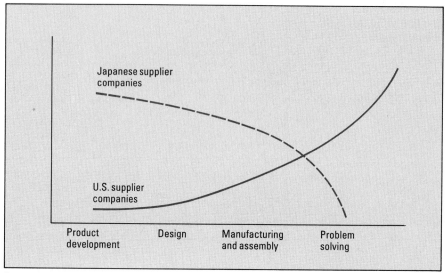

Source: *Quality Progress*, May 1986, p. 78.

Figure 20–4 shows that Japanese manufacturers involve their suppliers in the production process at the product development and design phases. That is much sooner than is the usual American practice, and the American suppliers are much more likely to be involved in later problem solving than are their Japanese counterparts.

CWQC and quality circles.   We are brought back to the idea expressed earlier that management—from top to bottom—must be involved for QCs to be truly and lastingly effective. QCs must be only one part of companywide quality control activities.

To envision the top-to-bottom and bottom-to-top nature of CWQC, see Figure 20–3. It illustrates that quality control must be the concern of everyone in the company, from the CEO down, with ideas and suggestions for improvement originating at every level.

The lessons of "Old Image—New Image" presented in Figure 20–5 may be summarized as follows: Concerns about a product's quality must begin at the product's design stage. Cooperate with suppliers to ensure the quality of the components coming from them. Quality consciousness is the responsibility of every worker, and when a nonconformance is spotted, the production line should be halted and the quality error corrected immediately. Workers should participate in management of their part of the operation, and the executives should work closely with the employees to resolve problems permanently.

One lesson from Figure 20–5 taught by Dr. Deming and learned by his Japanese students is the establishment of close, long-term relationships with the company's suppliers. Such relationships result in understanding and trust between the company and its supplier, and they improve the quality of the materials supplied. This practice, now prevalent in Japan, is attacked by would-be exporters to Japan as a nontariff barrier to trade.[11]

Now some Americans are listening to Dr. Deming. They include Chevron, Ford, Campbell Soup, Hewlett-Packard, Kaiser Tech, Lockheed, and Varian

■ FIGURE 20–5
Implementing a New
Image of Quality Control

The Old Image of QC	The New Image of QC
Low quality is caused by low performance of people. Automation is the key to higher quality.	Low quality is caused by poor management of people. Respect for people is the key to higher quality.
Loss of work ethic causes poor quality in the United States. The Japanese maintain a quality edge due to their ethical and cultural values.	American workers, when properly managed, are as good as or better than any others, particularly in their commitment to jobs.
Some defects are acceptable. Lots are accepted if they meet minimum quality standards on average.	Zero defects is the goal. There is not a minimum average acceptable quality. All units should be free of defects.
Inspect for product problems regularly, then rework. Rework is done at a later and separate stage.	Inspect for process problems; and fix problems so they do not recur. Any repair work is done on the line with no delay.
Higher quality means higher costs and therefore lower profits. Quality is expensive and a burden for manufacturing.	Higher quality is a means to higher profits. Quality is the goal; it is not the burden for manufacturing.
Quality is inspected into the product. Nonconforming units are continuously discovered, reworked, or scrapped.	Quality is designed and built into the product. A nonconformance is a means for resolving the problems permanently.
A quality control organization, as a separate department, inspects the output of manufacturing and evaluates the quality of production.	Quality is everyone's job. Total quality control includes all functions and individuals and all stages of manufacturing.
Quality is secondary to profits. To maximize profits, the sum of prevention, inspection, and failure costs is minimized.	Initial investment in quality is key to long-term profits. The book value of nonconformances is not simply deducted from profits.
Catch mistakes and fix them. Units are routed to manufacturing and inspection several times to pass the requirements.	Do it right the first time. Quality at the source is the key. Do not make mistakes. Quality is free if produced for the first time.
Suppliers are adversaries and thus suspect. All products must have at least a second source. Order as needed and expedite.	Suppliers are trusted members of our team. Work with a primary source to ensure reliability and quality.
Buy from the lowest bidder. Competition among the suppliers will reduce the total cost.	Buy for quality and reliability. Information and profits may be shared with suppliers.
Quality is a function of manufacturing. The products have high quality if they are manufactured properly.	High quality depends on all stages, from design to shipping, and is reached only if all functions work properly together.
Errors will be caught by the inspectors. Keep the production line moving by keeping a safety stock.	Do not pass on nonconformances. Stop the line if there is a quality problem. A safety stock of work in progress is a waste.
Produce as many units as possible in the shortest possible time to increase efficiency and utilization.	Produce effectively only what is needed and only when it is needed for the quality requirement of the internal or external customers.
Use specialized workers on operations to reduce the time needed for training. Produce units on an assembly line with highly specialized, single-operation–type workers. Do not rotate workers; rotation may reduce efficiency.	Train workers for diversified jobs and high flexibility. Promote cross-training and job sharing among workers.
The quality department is responsible for quality. Problems need not be communicated to and from manufacturing.	Quality consciousness is the responsibility of everyone involved. Suggestions and discussions are particularly welcomed.
Management must discern quality problems and delegate responsibility for improvement. Employees should carry out the plans.	Management depends on employees to identify and solve problems. Management works closely with employees to resolve problems permanently.
The worker is responsible for most quality problems. He should be disciplined and trained to perform properly.	Management systems are the cause of most quality problems. Workers should be allowed to participate in management.
Statistics are an exotic tool for quality engineers. Control charts are used to highlight the problems.	Every employee should have an understanding of statistical quality control, which is used to highlight areas for improvement.

(continued)

■ FIGURE 20–5
(concluded)

The Old Image of QC	The New Image of QC
Additional inventory is maintained to keep workers utilized. The workers' idle time is a waste.	Inventory is a waste. The workers may spend their nonproductive time in other productive functions.
Large lot sizes are produced to increase quality and to reduce production cost and average setup time.	Setup should be reduced to allow for lot sizes of one. Lower lot size means lower lead time, higher flexibility, and less rework.

Source: Mehran Sepehri, "Quality Control Circles: A Vehicle for Just-In-Time Implementation," *Quality Progress,* July 1985, p. 23.

Associates. Stripped of the jargon, Deming's philosophy is threefold: give workers chances to make more decisions, listen carefully to the customer, and use statistical analysis to detect and repair flaws.[12]

ROBOTICS

robotics the use of machines to replace people in the work force

Robotics is the industry of machines that work with humanlike skill. Robots are substitutes for human workers, and American management has concluded that is must use many more robots to improve productivity. Japan is in the lead in the use of robots, but American and European plants are moving aggressively into the field. In 1987, about 80,000 industrial robots were flexing their muscles around the clock in Japan; the number in Europe was some 27,000; and there were approximately 20,000 in the United States. In every country, robots are replacing human workers.

On the subject of robots taking the jobs of human laborers, robotics consultant Vincent M. Altamuro (see the quotation at the beginning of this chapter) makes several points. For one, the cost of robots is going down while the cost of labor is going up. For another, managers consider robots to have an advantage over people in workplaces with dangerous or noxious situations. Employers don't have to worry about a robot being killed, injured, or having its health impaired.[13]

Steel-Collar Migrant Workers

As members of management have been termed *white-collar workers* and members of the labor force have been termed *blue-collar workers,* some writers refer to robots as *steel-collared workers,* and these workers are migrating. Japan sold over 50 billion yen worth of robots to the world in 1985, and in 1986 the export value of Japanese robots rose to almost 60 billion yen. The United States was the biggest market, followed by West Germany.

However, neither the Japanese nor the American robot manufacturers made much profit in 1985 or 1986. The Westinghouse subsidiary, Unimation, was a loser in the robotics field, as was General Electric. Cincinnati Milacron and Sweden's ASEA made small profits, and the most profitable robot manufacturer was GMF Robotics, a joint venture between General Motors and the Japanese robot company Fanuc. Two thirds of GMF Robotics' 1985 sales were to GM, which slowed its robot purchase program in the years 1986 through 1988.

The reason for the losses or low profits of robot manufacturers is that you cannot simply wind up a robot in the morning and send it out to do a person's work. Robots require complex software to do even the simplest tasks, and they must be taught to communicate with the other machines working beside them on the shop floor. Great expense is involved in creating the necessary software and communication links, not to mention training and paying the people needed to service and maintain the entire complex. However, the software is being created, and the people are being trained.

Factories of the Future

As computers become more powerful and less expensive, they are reshaping the factory. Computer-aided design (CAD), robotic tools, sensors, and improved telecommunications techniques are forging the factory of the future.

Using computers instead of people costs 8,000 times less today than in 1950. Electronic transactions can be made 80 million times faster now than then. Errors occur in modern computers at the rate of 1 in 3 million, compared with 1 in 30 when humans do similar calculations.[14]

New future directions.   Businesses adopting computer-aided management methods may find themselves heading in a variety of new directions. These directions include:

1. *Production disbursement.* Production is moving into even smaller manufacturing units.

2. *Labor costs less important.* As computer-controlled robots become less expensive and more efficient, labor costs will shrink as a percentage of total costs. Manufacturers may become less attracted to low-wage countries.

3. *Engineering centralized.* Characteristic of high-tech engineering is centralized design. Product blueprints are likely to be transmitted from the head office via long-distance telephone lines to computer-aided manufacturing (CAM) plants in the company's principal market regions and countries.

4. *Manufacturing flexibility.* A wider variety of products can be produced at no greater costs. The plants could break even at 30 to 35 percent of capacity, compared to 65 to 70 percent in conventional operations.

5. *Plug-in repairs.* Product faults can usually be diagnosed by plugging the product into a computer. General Motors plans to use computerized diagnostics in its U.S. repair shops.

6. *Economies of scale.* The conventional assembly line economies of scale will be diminished. That could be counteracted by economies in such areas as marketing research and development.

7. *Consultants and contractors.* Small businesses with the latest computer-aided designs and techniques are beginning to sell services to the bigger companies. Some of those companies may decide to subcontract production.[15]

Fears.   Many managers are hesitant to adopt computerized manufacturing systems. Their concerns include potential misuse, reliability, security, difficult maintenance, and cost. Perhaps kicking and screaming, they will probably be forced to go along by competition.[16]

COMPENSATION

Financial compensation is not the only motivator, but it is a pervasive one that affects people at every economic level. In addition to satisfying basic wants, money satisfies social and esteem needs. Personnel managers must formulate compensation plans that combine employee needs satisfaction with incentives to result in satisfactory work performance for the employer.

Wages and Salaries

Employees are paid on the basis of productivity, time spent on the job, or a combination of the two unless union contracts or government laws specify otherwise. In the industrialized countries, the time unit for which pay is established is generally the hour, whereas a daily rate is most common in developing countries. The piece rate* pay method is quite common. In some countries, of which Japan is a good example, seniority is an important element in determining employees' pay rates.

When the subsidiaries of multinationals commence operations in a foreign country, they usually set their pay scales at or slightly higher than the prevailing wages paid by indigenous companies. The foreign-owned subsidiary does not want to be accused of exploiting the local workers. Although it might seem that paying wages higher than the going rate would be welcomed by the host government, usually the opposite is true. Local firms are quick to complain that such wages will cause unrest and disruption in the labor force. The foreign manager—even in developed countries—is repeatedly counseled by local managers, "Don't spoil our people."

Benefits

The types and sizes of the supplementary benefits† that workers receive vary considerably among nations and are frequently higher as a percentage of wages than the U.S. average of 35 percent. A study conducted a few years ago revealed such benefit percentages to be Belgium, 55 percent; France, 70 percent; Germany, 45 percent; Italy, 92 percent; Luxembourg, 41 percent; and the Netherlands, 50 percent. The benefit percentages tend to increase as labor unions negotiate new contracts or as governments legislate more and higher benefits.

Benefits: Contractual or legislated.   In the United States, many—but by no means all—benefits result from labor contracts. The opposite is true of many other countries, where most benefits are legislated and ordered by the governments. In France, for example, the following are mandated by law: (1) profit-sharing, (2) year-end bonuses, (3) paid holidays, (4) paid vacations of two days for each month worked, (5) three days' leave for the father when his child is born, (6) severance pay, (7) 70 to 90 percent of medical and dental expenses, (8) disability benefits, (9) retirement insurance, and (10) payments to relatives on the employee's death. In addition, the law requires allowances for

---

* Piece rate is payment per unit produced; for example, $1 per basket woven or 25 cents per button sewn on.

† Frequently called fringe benefits.

maternity, housing, moving, and children. Similar benefits and allowances are required by the laws of all European countries.

Europe is not alone in such requirements. Brazilian law includes most of the benefits listed for Europe, plus an extra one—a grant paid to the dependents of a worker who has been sent to prison. An unusual benefit called for in Mexican law is up to three scholarships for workers or their children.

Additional voluntary benefits.   Some employers grant benefits greater than those required by law. Japanese firms are notable in this regard and typically pay such things as commuting expenses and housing allowances as well as providing resort housing for employee vacation use. Some American banks make low-interest loans to employees to purchase housing or an automobile.

DISCIPLINE

Although an effective personnel program of selection, training, motivation, and compensation is essential for the attainment of the organization's goals, there always will be occasions that require employee discipline. Employees' job performance may be poor, or safety, time, or other rules may be broken. Such rules can be especially difficult to enforce if the employees are unaccustomed to working in an industrial organization.

Less Developed Countries (LDCs)

When managers from industrialized nations start factory operations in developing countries, they frequently encounter different practices, attitudes, and cultures. If the safety shoes hurt the workers' feet, the workers take them off, just as they did on the farm, and if the workers are tired, they rest when they want to and not when the rules permit. Usually they do not set out to break the rules deliberately; they just fail to understand or see any sense in them. This is why, as we have mentioned previously, workers without industrial experience must be taught not only how to do the job but also how to work in an industrial setting.

The extended family encountered in some LDCs can cause discipline problems. Loyalty tends to be more to one another than to the employer, and the supervisor member of the family may hesitate to discipline other members who are workers. Companies have tried to avoid situations of this kind by bringing in young, nonfamily, technical graduates as supervisors. The workers will generally accept the authority of such supervisors unless they regard the new supervisor as belonging to a lower caste or having a lower social status than their own. As we have indicated, such problems exist in certain developing countries.

One other cultural difference leading to disciplinary difficulties in some LDCs is leadership style. Managers from Europe or North America, especially those who practice participative leadership, may view the local supervisor's authoritarian approach as too tough or cruel. However, those managers should change the local supervisor's approach slowly and cautiously—and maybe not at all. In cultures accustomed to a strong father figure, the workers regard a supervisor who attempts participative leadership as weak and indecisive.

With the growth of industry in LDCs and perhaps with a second generation of workers in the factories, the attitudes of workers, including those toward authority, change, and management, must be sufficiently flexible to adapt to these changes. In addition, the managers will be working to create change. Concepts and methods of supervisory training and practices developed in industrialized nations are exportable and should be utilized.[17]

Developed Countries

In industrialized nations, the rules and expected performance must be communicated to employees, but, unlike the situation in some LDCs, the reasons for them will be understood and accepted by the employees. When they are not, management must take corrective steps, such as (1) clearer explanation of the rules, (2) docking of some pay, (3) demotion, and (4) discharging the worker.

In nonunion plants, management selects the corrective steps, subject to the constraints that it wants a productive, efficient work force and must select, train, motivate, and compensate well enough to achieve that.

In industrialized nations, however, management is quite likely to encounter labor unions. They have great impact on the whys, hows, and whens of discipline but are sufficiently important to be treated separately.

UNION RELATIONSHIPS

Labor unions can be a force for discipline because (1) they should require their worker members to adhere to agreed rules and (2) they establish with management a set of disciplinary procedures through collective bargaining.

Collective Bargaining

collective bargaining the process of negotiations between employers and the labor union(s) representing the employees

Of course, disciplinary procedures are not the only subjects of bargaining between labor and management. In the United States, some other subjects of **collective bargaining** are wages, retirement plans, union shop, work rules, and management rights. Elsewhere, as has been pointed out, in both developed and developing countries, many of those subjects and others are legislated or decreed by the government.

Labor's Political Influence

Labor has considerable political influence in the United States, as the large unions have powerful lobbying operations in Washington and the state capitals and support friendly candidates in their political campaigns. However, labor in European and other countries is sometimes even more powerful politically, and it sometimes merges with a major political party. One of the two largest political parties in Britain is called the Labour party; and the Histadrut, the general trade union in Israel, has a powerful influence in the formation of Israeli governments.[18]

Even when collective bargaining takes place, the governments in some countries are deeply involved. Their involvement often stems from the fact that large parts of industry are nationalized. For example, at Renault, the French government-owned automobile manufacturer, unions make use of political pressures in their bargaining with managers, who are essentially government employees. The resulting agreement terms then set the standards for other firms.

A number of developing nations require a government official to be present during the bargaining process because they fear that the generally weak unions with relatively uneducated leaders will lack the capacity to bargain with the skilled management representatives. In addition to government help, union negotiators in LDCs sometimes get help from the union that organized the employees of the parent company in its home country.

Home Country Assistance

Industrial country labor unions that have organized the parent company occasionally send their negotiators abroad to bargain with its subsidiaries. They may do this to help both the local unions and themselves. A more costly contract will increase the subsidiary's labor expense and thus may impede the transfer of production from the home plant to overseas facilities. This sometimes produces an odd situation, such as the one that occurred at an American subsidiary in the Caribbean. Company negotiators from the home office were surprised to find themselves face to face with the same union officials who had negotiated the union's contract with the parent company in the United States.

Localize labor relations.   Until subsidiary management becomes skilled in labor contract negotiation and union relationships, the WWC headquarters should send negotiators and consultants from the home country. However, recognizing that each country presents a unique set of labor conditions, types of unions, attitudes, and laws, most multinational enterprises hold local management of foreign subsidiaries responsible for labor relations in their own country.

In the first place, this is done because the subsidiary's management should be much better informed about conditions and trends in its country than parent company management would be. Second, the subsidiary's management will have to live with its labor agreement, so it should have the authority to negotiate and agree with labor. Without such authority, the prestige of the subsidiary's management would be lowered, and it would have much more difficulty developing and implementing the long-term personnel policies necessary for the subsidiary's successful operation.

Before the home headquarters would entrust subsidiary management with the scope of authority suggested above, headquarters would want to be satisfied that the subsidiary managers are thoroughly trained and capable. The WWC should also exercise some coordination.

Coordination of labor relations.   Coordination of labor relations can be important because labor contracts made in one country might provide precedent in other countries. This will be more and more the case as unions develop international cooperation.*

---

* Remember the examples given in Chapter 12 of the European unions' international actions against ITT and of the Coca-Cola boycotts in Europe and elsewhere because of alleged anti-labor practices in Guatemala.

If WWC headquarters is to carry out its coordinating duties intelligently, it must require a continuing flow of labor relations information from each subsidiary. This gives headquarters' management the facts needed to use labor conditions as one important component in investment or reinvestment decisions. Such facts are also necessary to permit management evaluations among the subsidiaries.

Not only has union activity become international, thus requiring management to coordinate labor policy worldwide, but labor has also entered the boardroom and become a part of management. One name for this process is **codetermination**.

codetermination the participation of labor in the company management up to and including the board of directors

Labor in Management: Codetermination

Like it or not (most managements do not), there is a growing movement toward granting workers some voice in management. Participatory management is required by law in various countries; companies must comply if they wish to do business there. In other countries, worker participation is being brought about voluntarily by management. As was mentioned in Chapter 12, in 1980 Chrysler Corporation elected the president of the United Automobile Workers to its board of directors.

The oldest legal requirement for codetermination was the 1951 German law calling for a 50–50 management-labor membership on the board of directors of the iron, coal, and steel industries. In 1951, the Germans passed another law calling for a one-third representation for labor on the boards of other German industries of certain sizes. In 1976, the labor representation was increased to 50 percent. Other European countries and Japan have similar legislation.[19]

Most managements have objected and resisted. At least one German firm, Volkswagen, has had difficulties with new investment decisions because of codetermination.[20] On the other hand, some reporters find more labor peace in countries with labor participation in management (sometimes referred to as "industrial democracy") than in those without it.

Some students of international business operations foresee possibilities that intraenterprise cooperative projects could become difficult or impossible because of codetermination. If labor board members of an important subsidiary in Europe believe a parent-ordered project is not in the best interest of the subsidiary's labor force, they can block it. The possibility has been referred to as "mutiny on the multinational."[21]

Management is learning to live with codetermination, industrial democracy, or whatever it is called because, in most cases, it must. Among the measures that management has adopted for this purpose have been opening and improving lines of communication and improving relationships between labor and management board members. There has been some inclination to lessen dependence on a subsidiary that might "mutiny" against the system. One management function that has been complicated by codetermination is the firing of workers.

EMPLOYMENT TERMINATION

As we have mentioned, Volkswagen and other firms have faced delays in decisions to invest in new plants in other countries because of labor fears of job losses in the home country. When labor is represented on a company's board of directors, it has the power to delay or even prevent actions that it feels will cause layoffs among the work force. In addition, labor has the power to strike, and labor unions negotiate labor contracts with employers.

Labor Contracts

One subject probably covered in every labor contract is the termination of employment. Standards of work performance are established, and when managers feel that a worker is not performing up to the standards, management must consult with union representatives before firing the worker. The union representatives may agree that the worker is not performing adequately and should be discharged, or they may suggest a transfer to a different job. If management and the union disagree, the contract contains a provision for grievance procedures or arbitration to resolve their differences. In most countries, many aspects of labor relations, including worker discharge, are covered by laws and government regulations.

Labor Laws

A number of countries have laws that oblige firms to give severance pay to terminated employees who have obtained permanent status, usually after a 60- to 90-day trial period. In Mexico, workers who have been employed for even one day after the trial period must be paid three months' wages if they are discharged. That amount is increased by 20 days' wages for each additional year of employment.

Because of laws requiring that sizable sums be paid to permanent workers on discharge, some companies have striven to keep a large part of their work force as temporary workers by firing them one day before the temporary period expires and then rehiring them. Many governments have amended their laws to prevent that sort of practice.

A number of multinationals and other employers have complained of the excessive labor costs imposed by labor laws, and some countries have changed their laws to make employee discharge easier. Peru now requires a worker to be employed for three years instead of 90 days before becoming a permanent employee. Chile has eliminated the requirement that allowed permanent workers to be fired solely for legally recognized causes. Now the firm need give only 30 days' notice or 30 days' severance pay.

Other Termination Conditions

Of course, not all employees are union members, not all companies are organized by unions, and not all countries have laws dealing with employment termination. Under such circumstances, the discharge of employees is at the discretion of the employers, subject to any agreements between the employees as individuals and their employers. The employees' skills and the availability of replacements would affect the relative bargaining positions of the employees and the employers.

SUMMARY

Because of the importance of an adequate labor force, a would-be employer must carefully study how to find it, hire it, train it, and—if necessary—fire it. Who is available, and how do host country laws and practices limit the employer's freedom?

Motivation of workers is important to get productivity and quality products from them. There are a number of incentive pay plans, each with advantages and disadvantages. Pay and incentive practices in the United States have changed considerably in the last few years. Japanese practices—many of which they learned from the American, Deming—are in some ways different and are now being tried in the United States, with mixed results.

Deming advocated quality circles and companywide

quality control. Quality is every employee's business, from the floor worker to the CEO.

Computerized robotics are leading to the factories of the future. More and more work will be done by machines and less by laborers.

Discipline of the work force is necessary. It differs somewhat between LDCs and industrialized countries.

The same can be true of company relationships with labor unions. The unions are making efforts to cooperate internationally. Under codetermination laws or practices, labor unions have seats on many companies' boards of directors.

Termination of employment may be governed by the union-company agreement. In some countries, it is covered by law.

QUESTIONS

1. Before making an investment that will involve hiring employees in a foreign country, what are some questions concerning labor in that country to which management should get answers?

2. What are some advantages and disadvantages of using present employees to recruit new employees?

3. Why have many firms begun to utilize off-premises training and development programs?

4. What are quality circles? How do they relate to companywide quality control?

5. Describe and explain changes in American compensation and incentive practices in recent years.

6. What are some common fringe benefits?

7. Discuss the changes in the types of factories and production being brought about by faster, cheaper computers and more efficient robots.

8. What is collective bargaining?

9. Why is it important for a multinational to coordinate labor relations?

10. What is codetermination? What are some contrasting attitudes toward it?

11. The Japanese have opened manufacturing plants in the United States. How well are their personnel practices working?

MINICASE 20–1

Philippine Pesos for a New Plant

The company for which you work manufacturers a product that is sold in the home market and exported. The manufacturing process calls for semiskilled and skilled labor.

To assure itself of a production facility within the ASEAN market, which your company forecasts will grow and raise trade barriers to outside products, the company has decided to invest in the Philippines. Research and negotiations by your representatives in Manila and elsewhere in the country have led to decisions not to build the plant in Manila but in a rural area on an island near Luzon, where Manila is located.

The chosen area is depressed economically, with high unemployment and low literacy. Most of its people have few industrial skills.

The Philippine government induced the company to locate there by offering an array of enticements. There will be a 10-year tax holiday for the company and for the foreign management and technical personnel it employs. The government will donate the land site chosen by your company for its plant. The government will improve the ferry and air transport and the telephone and telegraph service between the island and Luzon.

The government has other funds available to help your company set up and get into successful operation.

You are the personnel manager for the new Philippine operations. What problems should you anticipate? What solutions should you consider? The government has asked your suggestions as to how it can best spend the funds it has available for helping your company—Philippine pesos only—to assist you in solving personnel problems you foresee. How will you suggest that the pesos be spent?

MINICASE 20–2

Keep It Top Secret*

Management of the French multinational enterprise St. Gobain opposed the efforts of another company to acquire control of it. As part of its opposition campaign, the management appealed to St. Gobain's stockholders not to sell their stock and revealed to them much of the previously secret financial data about the company. Its profitability (larger than had been publicly admitted previously) and its use of a Swiss holding company to reduce taxes were told to stockholders to induce them to hold their shares.

At that time, St. Gobain also had labor relations difficulties with unions in France, Italy, the United States, and West Germany. Of course, the unions got their hands on the previously confidential information.

The unions coordinated their collective bargaining in all four countries. St. Gobain was hit by strikes and finally made large concessions to settle. As a result, St. Gobain made little profit during the late 1970s.

1. Would you have handled this situation in the same way that St. Gobain's management did? Discuss.
2. Now that the damage has been done, what labor relations steps should St. Gobain take? Explain.
3. What is your guess as to why management made the revelations?

*Source: David A. Ricks, M. Fu, and Jeffrey S. Arpan, *International Business Blunders* (Columbus: Grid, 1974), pp. 59–60.

SUPPLEMENTARY READINGS

Albano, Debbie. "British Miners Strike—Seek World Support." *Labor Today,* January 1985, p. 1.

Bhatt, Bhal J., and Edwin L. Miller. "Industrial Relations in Foreign and Local Firms in Asia." *Management International Review,* Summer 1984, pp. 62–73.

Busch, G. K. *The Political Role of International Trade Unions.* London: Macmillan, 1983.

Dreyer, Peter H. "European Unions on the Defense." *Journal of Commerce,* March 12, 1986, p. 4A.

Ebrahimpour, Malig. "An Examination of Quality Management in Japan: Implications for Management in the United States." *Journal of Operations Management,* August 1986, pp. 4–9.

Enderwick, Peter. "Ownership Nationality and Industrial Relations Practices in British Non-Manufacturing Industries." *Industrial Relations Journal,* January 1986, pp. 50–62.

Foreign Labor Trends in a number of separate countries. These are released by the U.S. Department of Labor, Bureau of International Labor Affairs. Each is prepared by the American embassy in the subject country.

Gordon, William I. "Gaining Employee Commitment to Quality." *Supervisory Management,* November 1985, pp. 30–38.

Harnett, Donald C., and L. L. Cummings. *Bargaining Behavior: An International Study.* Houston: Dame Publications, 1980.

Hutchins, Dave. "Quality Is Everybody's Business." *Management Decision,* Winter 1986, pp. 3–10.

Jacoby, S. M. "The Future of Industrial Relations in the United States." *California Management Review,* Summer 1984, pp. 90–94.

Jones, Sam L. "Quality Circles Can Enhance Firm's Communication." *American Metal Market,* September 7, 1984, pp. 6–11.

Kaha, Helen. "Cooperation Is Focus of Labor Study." *Automotive News,* June 23, 1986, p. 1.

Landon, David N., and Steve Moulton. "Quality Circles: What's in Them for Employees?" *Personnel Journal,* June 1986, pp. 23–29.

Matsuura, Nanthi. "Japanese Management and Labor Relations in U.S. Subsidiaries." *Industrial Relations Journal,* Winter 1984, pp. 38–44.

Poole, Michael. "Industrial Relations in the Future." *Journal of General Management,* August 1985, pp. 38–48.

Reitsperger, Wolf D. "Japanese Management: Coping with British Industrial Relations." *Journal of Management Studies,* January 1986, pp. 72–86.

Siberman, David. "Labor Law Turned Upside Down." *American Federationist,* July 6, 1985, pp. 5–11.

Trever, Malcolm. "Quality Control—Learning from the Japanese." *Long-Range Planning,* October 1986, pp. 46–54.

Zahasin, Gretchan. "Quality Control: It's Money in the Bank." *ABA Banking Journal,* December 1986, pp. 22–27.

ENDNOTES

1. Some experts refer to the subject we shall cover here as human resources planning. However, that appears to us to include all the functions numbered in the introduction, and we wish to limit the material in this section to the analyses of the company's personnel needs, the availability of the needed personnel, and applicable laws.

2. Manning Nash, "The Interplay of Culture and Management in a Guatemalan Textile Plant," in *Culture and Management*, ed. Ross A. Webber (Homewood, Ill.: Richard D. Irwin, 1969), p. 317–24.

3. Denis Debost, *Summary of French Labor and Social Security Laws* (Paris: French Industrial Development Agency, 1972), p. 7.

4. Nancy J. Perry, "Here Come Richer, Riskier Pay Plans," *Fortune*, December 19, 1988, pp. 50–58. This article gives numerous examples of incentive pay plans in action.

5. Ibid.

6. Louis Kraar, "Japan's Gung-Ho U.S. Car Plants," *Fortune*, January 30, 1989, pp. 97–108.

7. "Battle at Smyrna," *The Economist*, August 8, 1989, p. 27.

8. James Risen, "Japanese Labor Policies Stirring U.S. Rebellion," *Los Angeles Times*, May 20, 1989, pp. A1 and 18.

9. Davida M. Amsden and Robert T. Amsden, "ICQCC Seoul 82," *Quality Circle Journal*, September 1983, pp. 12–14.

10. Wayne S. Rieker, "QC Circles and Companywide Quality Control," *Quality Progress*, October 1983, pp. 14–17.

11. *The Economist*, November 23, 1985, p. 81.

12. Jeff Pelline, "Hero of Japan Tones up Chevron," *San Francisco Chronicle*, January 10, 1989, p. C1.

13. George Melloan, "Robots Talk back to Product Designers," *The Wall Street Journal*, May 26, 1987, p. 29.

14. M. E. Porter and V. E. Millar, "How Information Gives You Competitive Advantage," *Harvard Business Review*, July–August 1985, pp. 75–83.

15. "Management in the 1990s Research Program," Organizational Reform Workshop, Sloan School of Management, January 1986.

16. For a comprehensive look at American, European, and Japanese approaches to the factory of the future, see Nicholas Valery, "The Challenge," *The Economist*, May 30, 1987, a survey.

17. W. Skinner, *American Industry in Developing Economies* (New York: John Wiley & Sons, 1968), p. 65.

18. *Trade and Investment in Israel* (Tel Aviv: Bank Leumi Le Israel, 1978), p. 67.

19. Robert J. Kuhne, "Codetermination: A Statutory Restructuring of the Organization," *Columbia Journal of World Business*, Summer 1976, pp. 17–25.

20. Alfred J. Thimm, "Decision Making at Volkswagen, 1973–1975," *Columbia Journal of World Business*, Spring 1976, pp. 94–103.

21. Robert J. Kuhne, "Statutory Codetermination: Mutiny on the Multinational?" Paper presented at the annual national meeting of the Academy of International Business, Orlando, Florida, August 1977.

Chapter 21

Strategic Planning and Organizational Design

Corporate planning is a little like marriage: it is a commitment to a long-term relationship that is of vital interest to all the parties involved. Like marriage, it should not be entered upon lightly or wantonly but discreetly and soberly.

Roy Forman, CEO of a British
private health insurance firm

LEARNING OBJECTIVES

In this chapter, you will study:

1. The benefits of global strategic planning.

2. The steps in a global strategic planning process.

3. What a planning staff does.

4. Various examples of corporate mission statements, objectives, quantified goals, and strategies.

5. New directions in strategic planning.

6. Various organizational forms.

7. Some newer organizational forms.

8. The characteristics of the "right" organization.

KEY WORDS AND CONCEPTS

- Watch list
- Mission statement
- Corporate strategy
- Scenario
- Contingency plan
- Top-down planning
- Bottom-up planning
- Iterative planning
- International division
- Hybrid organization
- Matrix organization
- Matrix overlay
- Strategic business unit (SBU)

BUSINESS INCIDENT

A Global Strategic Planner

Minnesota Mining & Manufacturing (3M), known as one of the best-managed and most innovative American worldwide companies, was founded in 1902. However, it was in business for nearly 50 years before it established an international division and began to export. Yet, by 1988, about 40 percent of its total sales ($10.6 billion) were coming from foreign markets; nearly $1 billion were from U.S. exports. Managers of its overseas subsidiaries operate with a high degree of autonomy and finance their own expansion. But corporate culture is worldwide; in fact, many managers are third-country nationals (citizens of neither the home nor the host country who work in a host country affiliate).

Structured strategic planning was not adopted until 1981, after a new CEO joined the firm. He felt that although cross-functional teams at the product level were doing a good job of decision making, they weren't steering the company. Despite the long-term nature of many of its product developments, the company's planning was essentially short term. The president recognized that 3M could continue to innovate on a large scale only if its technological resources were shared among its units, and he wanted to operate on a planned global strategic basis without losing the autonomous, entrepreneurial ability of the product divisions. The result was a reorganization of the company's 200 organizational units worldwide into 20 strategic business centers (SBCs).

Within each SBC, planning starts with the operating managers of the various subsidiaries, who analyze internal strengths and weaknesses and external forces, such as new technology and government regulatory changes; make a competitor analysis; and determine the company resources they will need to achieve their objectives. Their plans go to the SBCs for review and consultation. SBC plans then go to a strategic planning committee consisting of vice presidents at headquarters who represent the four sectors into which the 20 SBCs are divided. The

BUSINESS INCIDENT (concluded)

■ **FIGURE 21–1**
3M Strategic Planning Cycle

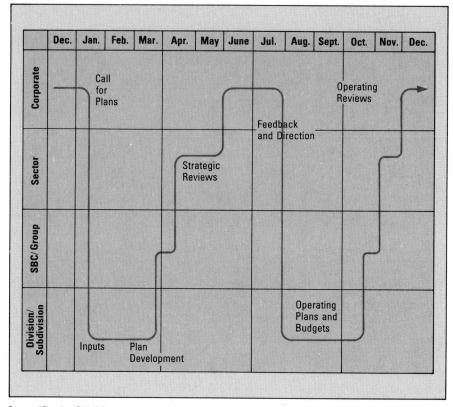

Source: "Planning Global Strategies for 3M," *Long-Range Planning,* February 1988, p. 15.

plans are reviewed with at least two members of the strategic planning committee present, and results of this review are discussed with SBC managements. Any differences between SBC managements and sector management are reconciled.

Two months later (July), the corporate headquarters' 34-person management committee, to which the 12 strategic planning committee members belong, reviews the plans and votes on spending priorities. Feedback and direction are given to the operating units, who then prepare operating plans and budgets by December and submit them to headquarters. There, they are finalized jointly with corporate worldwide plans.

A few days before the December operating reviews, the management committee holds brainstorming sessions to discuss trends and developments over the coming 15 years. The general manager of each business unit presents the best picture possible for that industry for the period. The outcome of this meeting is a broad guide for strategic planning. The company's strategic planning cycle is diagrammed in Figure 21–1.

Although planning is done by operating managers, the director and staff of a planning services and development unit provide an analysis of 3M's 20 principal competitors worldwide and any other information the units require. They also try to identify opportunities and new products.

Allen Jacobson, who became CEO in 1986, says, "When you get a new chief executive and strategic planning together, people expect a dramatic change. I'm not the least bit interested in drama, I'm interested in seeing our business progress. Our company is multiproduct, multitechnology, multinational, and multimarket. We probably sell to a greater variety of commercial, industrial, and consumer markets than anybody else. Now with that diversity, you can't make all the important decisions on the 13th or 14th floor [offices of top managements] of this building. You have to have a system that depends on your people, or on the people closest to the job, the technology, and the customer." He admits that there is more headquarters involvement in seeing (1) that business plans are consistent with overall strategy and (2) that the company is exploiting all of the opportunities in an area.

Source: Based on Carol Kennedy, "Planning Global Strategies for 3M," *Long-Range Planning,* August 1988, p. 63.

GLOBAL STRATEGIC PLANNING

Why Plan Globally?

Numerous worldwide firms like 3M have found it necessary to institute formal global strategic planning to provide a means for managers to identify opportunities and threats, formulate strategies to handle them, and stipulate how to finance the strategies' implementation. Strategic plans not only provide for consistency of action among managers but also encourage the participants to consider the ramifications of their actions on the other geographical and functional areas of the firm.

Standardization and Planning

Historically, more aspects of production than of marketing have been standardized and coordinated worldwide. This is because many top executives believe marketing strategies are best determined locally due to differences among the various foreign environments. Yet, you have seen that there is a growing tendency to standardize not only marketing strategies but also the total product, which leads to their inclusion in the global strategic planning process. Of course, you realize that their standardization can also be the *result* of strategic planning as managements search for ways to lower costs and to present a uniform company image as global producers of quality products. We mentioned in Chapter 19 that many Japanese firms have adopted this strategy. Let us look at the planning process.

Global Strategic Planning Process

Global strategic planning, as you know, is the primary function of managers, and the manager of strategic planning and strategy making is the firm's chief executive officer. The process of strategic planning provides a formal structure in which managers (1) analyze the company's external environments, (2) analyze the company's internal environment, (3) define the company's business and mission, (4) set corporate objectives, (5) quantify goals, (6) formulate strategies, and (7) make tactical plans. You will note that this planning process, illustrated in Figure 21–2, has the same format as the planning process for a purely domestic firm. As you know by now, most activities of the two kinds of operations are that way. It's the variations in values of uncontrollable forces that make the activities in a worldwide corporation more complex than they are in a purely domestic firm.

Analysis of domestic, international, and foreign environments. Because the firm has little opportunity to control these forces, its managers must know not only what the present values of the forces are but also where the forces appear to be headed. An environmental scanning process similar to the market screening process described in Chapter 14 can be used for a continuous gathering of information.

Is there a planning staff?   If the firm has a planning staff, as 3M does, it will have the prime responsibility for this step of the process and will also be the repository for information sent from the various functional areas of the firm. It probably will have an environmental data base. Planning personnel may also

■ **FIGURE 21–2**
The Global Strategic
Planning Process

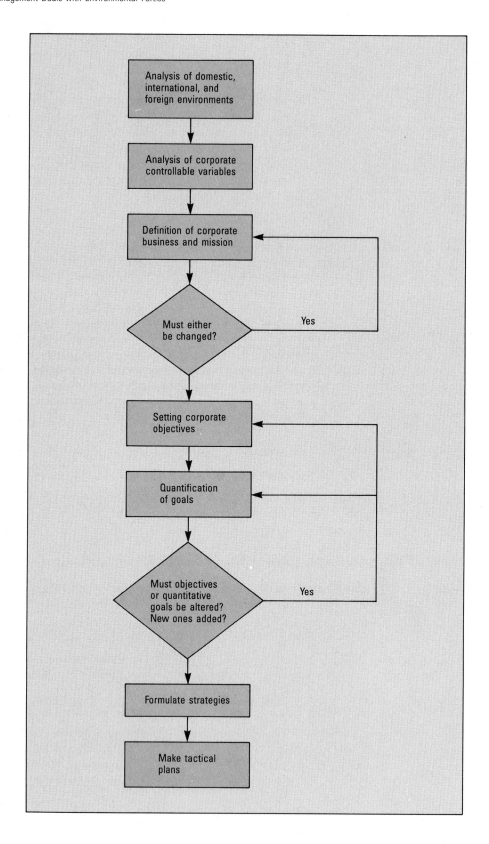

do the competitor analysis with input from R&D, marketing, and perhaps other departments, or they may gather information from the competitor intelligence system (if there is one) for integration into their analysis. They probably will subscribe to services that specialize in political risk assessment, such as *Business Environment Risk Index, Business International's Country Ratings,* and Frost & Sullivan's *World Summary* and 60 *Country Reports.* We mentioned several sources of information in Chapter 14.

The planning staff may use global **watch lists**, which contain items pertinent to certain aspects of the uncontrollable environmental variables that top management has indicated are of special interest to the firm. Petroleum refiners are interested in anything having to do with oil spills and the use of methanol in automobiles, for example. Information for the global watch lists of international construction firms will come from the lists of loans made by the World Bank and other international lending agencies.

watch list list containing items of interest concerning the uncontrollable variables that are of special interest to the firm

Analysis of corporate controllable variables.   An analysis of the forces controlled by the firm will also include a situational analysis and a forecast. The various functional areas will submit input to the planning staff (if there is one), who will in turn prepare a report for the strategy planning committee. This committee must answer questions such as the following: What are our strengths and weaknesses? What are our human and financial resources? Where are we with respect to our present objectives? Have we uncovered any facts that require us to delete goals, alter them, or add new ones? After completing this internal audit, the committee is ready to examine its business and **mission statements.**

mission statement a broad statement that defines the organization's scope

Defining the corporate business and mission statements.   These broad statements, communicate to the corporation's stakeholders (employees, stockholders, governments, suppliers, and customers) what the company is and where it is going. Some firms have both statements, whereas others combine them into one. In either case, these statements must be evaluated against changing realities uncovered in the external and internal analyses and then altered when necessary.

Some examples.   Look at Coca-Cola's combined statement: "The Coca-Cola Company is the worldwide soft-drink leader, as well as one of the world's leading producers and distributors of filmed entertainment and the leading U.S. marketer of orange juice and juice products."[1] PepsiCo, its competitor in soft drinks, says, "PepsiCo has achieved a leadership position in three major domestic and international markets: soft drinks, snack foods, and restaurants."[2] Mitsubishi Corporation, the *sogo shosha* of the Mitsubishi Group, states that it is "a global enterprise engaged in general trade and diversified services." Its mission: "We are committed to facilitating trade and enhancing worldwide commercial development. In addition to handling an enormous volume of domestic, import, export, and offshore trading transactions, we also organize business ventures, arrange technology transfers and resource development, and provide financing.[3] Once the corporate business and mission are defined, management must then set corporate objectives.

Set corporate objectives.   Objectives direct the firm's course of action, maintain it within the boundaries of the stated mission, and ensure its continuing existence. The Campbell Soup Company says, "Our goals are to maximize long-term profitability and shareholder value."[4] But how does Campbell's management know if it is achieving this objective?

Quantify the objectives.   When objectives can be quantified, they should be converted to quantified goals. What does Campbell Soup's management consider to be long-term profitability and shareholder value? The company's annual report states, "In fiscal 1987, we established new financial objectives, which call for the company to achieve a 13 percent return on invested capital by 1992; a 5 percent unit growth rate; and a sales increase of 5 percent a year, plus inflation."[5]

Despite the strong preference of most top managers for verifiable objectives, they frequently do have nonquantifiable or directional goals. One of PepsiCo's objectives, for example, is to accelerate profitable growth. Although this goal is not quantified, it does set the direction for managers and requires them to formulate more specific strategies to attain it. Incidentally, objectives do tend to be more quantified as they progress down the organization to the operational level, because, for the most part, strategies at one level become the objectives for the succeeding level. Up to this point, only *what, how much,* and *when* have been stipulated. *How* these objectives are to be achieved will be determined in the formulation of strategies.

Formulate the corporate strategies.   Generally, participants in the strategic planning process will formulate alternate **corporate strategies**, or action plans, that seem plausible considering the directions the external environmental forces are taking and corporation's strengths and weaknesses. Suppose (1) their analysis of the external environment convinces them that the Japanese government is making it easier for foreign firms to enter that market and (2) the competitor analysis reveals that a Japanese competitor is preparing to enter the United States (or wherever the home market is). Should the firm adopt a defensive strategy of defending the home market by lowering its price there, or should it attack the competitor in its home market by establishing a subsidiary in Japan? Management may decide to pursue either strategy or both, depending on its interpretation of the situation.

> **corporate strategy** action plan to enable an organization to reach its objectives

When choosing among strategies, management must consider corporate culture.[6] If it decides to put into effect a quality control system that includes quality circles, and heretofore there has been little employee participation in decision making, the strategy will have to include the cost of and time for training the employees to accept this cultural change.

Strategies may also be general.   At the corporate level, strategies, like objectives, may be rather general. PepsiCo states that to achieve its objective of accelerating growth, it is "executing these strategies of (1) segmenting the market to reach more people with more products, (2) expanding through existing and new distribution channels, (3) staying contemporary to attract new generations of customers, and (4) strengthening and expanding our infrastructure to make us more competitive in existing markets and to reach new markets."[7] You can be sure that the marketing function, which receives these strategies as its objectives, will be required to quantify as many as possible.

Scenarios.   Because of the rapidity of environmental changes, many managements have become dissatisfied with planning for a single set of events and

scenario description of a possible future, often most likely, worst, and best cases

contingency plan ·plan for the best- or worst-case scenarios or for critical events that could have a severe impact on the firm

have turned to "what if" **scenarios**, descriptions of possible alternative futures. Scenarios help managers become aware of the critical elements of the external and internal forces and often are the basis for preparing stand-by, or contingency, plans.

Contingency plans.   Most managements prepare **contingency plans** for worst- and best-case scenarios and for critical events as well. Every operator of a nuclear plant has contingency plans, as do most producers of petroleum and hazardous chemicals since such ecological disasters as the Valdez oil spill and the tragic Bhopal gas leak occurred.

Prepare tactical plans.   Because strategic plans are fairly broad, tactical (also called operational) plans are a requisite for spelling out in detail how the objectives will be reached. In other words, very specific, short-term means for achieving the goals are the object of tactical planning. For instance, if the British subsidiary of an American producer of prepared foods has as a quantitative goal a 20 percent increase in sales, its strategy might be to sell 30 percent more to institutional users. The tactical plan could include such points as hiring three new specialized sales representatives, attending four trade shows, and advertising in two industry periodicals every other month next year. This is the kind of specificity found in the tactical plan.

Strategic Plan Features and Implementation Facilitators

Sales forecasts and budgets.   Two prominent features of the strategic plan are *sales forecasts* and *budgets*. The sales forecast not only provides management with an estimate of the revenue to be received and the units to be sold but also serves as the basis for planning in the other functional areas. Without this information, the production, financial, and procurement plans cannot be formulated. Budgets, like sales forecasts, are both a planning and a control technique. During planning, they coordinate all of the functions within the firm and provide management with a detailed statement of future operating results.

Plan implementation facilitators.   Once the plan has been prepared, it must be implemented. Two of the most important plan implementation facilitators that management employs are policies and procedures.

Policies.   Policies are broad guidelines issued by upper management for the purpose of assisting lower-level managers in handling recurring problems. Because policies are broad, they permit discretionary action and interpretation. The object of a policy is to economize managerial time and promote consistency among the various operating units. If the distribution policy states that the firm's policy is to sell through wholesalers, marketing managers throughout the world know that they should normally use wholesalers and avoid selling directly to retailers. The disclosure of the widespread occurrence of bribery prompted company presidents to issue policy statements condemning this practice. Managers were put on notice by these statements that they were not to offer bribes.

Procedures.   Procedures prescribe how certain activities will be carried out, thereby ensuring uniform action on the part of all corporate members. For instance, most corporate headquarters issue a procedure for their subsidiaries to follow in preparing the annual budget. This procedure assures corporate management that all budgets will be prepared using the same format, which will facilitate their comparison.

Kinds of Strategic Plans

Time horizon.   Although strategic plans may be classified as short, medium, or long term, there is little agreement as to the length of these periods. For some, long-range planning may be for a five-year period. For others, this would be the length of a medium-term plan; their long range might cover 15 years or more. Short-range plans are usually for one to three years; however, even long-term plans are subject to review annually or more frequently if a situation requires it. Furthermore, the time horizon will vary according to the age of the firm and the stability of its market. A new venture is extremely difficult to plan for more than three years in advance, but a five- or six-year horizon is probably sufficient for a mature company in a steady market.

Level in the organization.   If the corporation has three organizational levels, as 3M does, there will be three levels of plans, each of which will generally be more specific and for a shorter time frame than it is at the level above. In addition, the functional areas at each level will have plans and sometimes will be subject to the same hierarchy, depending mainly on how the company is organized.

Methods of Planning

top-down planning planning process that begins at the highest level in the organization and continues downward

Top-down planning.   In **top-down planning**, corporate headquarters develops and provides guidelines that include the definition of the business, the mission statement, company objectives, financial assumptions, the content of the plan, and special issues. If there is an international division, its management may be told that this division is expected to contribute $5 million in profits, for example. The division, in turn, would break this total down among the affiliates under its control. The managing director in Germany would be informed that the German operation is expected to contribute $1 million; Brazil, $300,000; and so on.

Disadvantages of top-down planning are that it restricts initiative at the lower levels and shows some insensitivity to local conditions. Furthermore, especially in a worldwide company, there are so many interrelationships that consultation is necessary. Can top management, for example, decide on rationalization of manufacturing without obtaining the opinions of the local units as to its feasibility?

The advantage of top-down planning is that the home office with its global perspective should be able to formulate plans that ensure the optimal corporatewide use of the firm's scarce resources.

bottom-up planning planning process that begins at the lowest level in the organization and continues upward

Bottom-up planning.   **Bottom-up planning** operates in the opposite manner. The lowest operating levels inform top management of what they expect to do, and the total becomes the firm's goals. The advantage of bottom-up planning is that the people responsible for attaining the goals are formulating them. Who knows better than the subsidiaries' directors what and how much the subsidiaries can sell? Because the subsidiaries' directors set the goals with no coercion from top management, they feel obligated to make their word good. However, there is also a disadvantage. Each affiliate is free to some extent to pursue the goals it wishes to pursue, and so there is no guarantee that the sum total of all the affiliates' goals will coincide with those of headquarters. When discrepancies occur, extra time must be taken at headquarters to eliminate them. Bottom-up planning is the almost invariable method used by Japanese managements because they strive for a consensus at every level.

Iterative planning. It appears that **iterative planning**, which 3M practices, is becoming more popular, especially in global companies which seek to have a single global plan while operating in many diverse foreign environments. As you saw, iterative planning combines aspects of both top-down and bottom-up planning.

iterative planning repetition of the bottom-up or top-down planning process until all differences are reconciled

New Directions in Planning

Planning during the 60s and early 70s commonly consisted of a company's CEO and the head of planning getting together to devise a corporate plan, which would then be handed to the operating people for execution. Changes in the business environment, however, caused changes to be made in three areas: (1) who does the planning, (2) how it is done, and (3) the contents of the plan.

Who does it. By the mid-70s, strategic planners had become dominant figures in their companies. They were accustomed to writing a blueprint for each subsidiary, which they would then present to the management of each operating unit. The planners' power grew and the operating managers' influence waned, and of course there was hostility between the two groups. Roger Smith, chairman of GM, says, "We got those great plans together, put them on a shelf, and marched off to do what we would be doing anyway."[8]

But a number of factors were acting to upset this pattern. It became clear that world uncertainty made long-range planning in detail impossible, so corporate plans had to be short and simple. With huge, detailed plans no longer as useful as they had been, there was less need for professional planners. Stronger competition required as essential input to strategic planning a practical knowledge of the company and the industry. This brought senior operating managers into the planning process, enabling firms to change the role and reduce the size of their planning staffs. General Electric, for example, reduced its corporate planning group from 58 to 33, and GM decreed that "planning is the responsibility of every line manager. The role of the planner is to be the catalyst for change—not to do the planning for each business unit."[9]

How it is done. By the 1960s, firms were using computer models and sophisticated forecasting methods to help produce the voluminous plans we mentioned above. These plans were not only huge but also very detailed. As a Texas Instruments executive put it, "The company let its management system, which can track the eye of every sparrow, creep into the planning process, so we were making more and more detailed plans. It became a morale problem because managers knew they couldn't project numbers out five years to two decimal points."[10]

The heavy emphasis on these methods tended to result in a concentration on factors that could be quantified easily. However, the less quantifiable factors relating to sociopolitical developments were becoming increasingly important.

Also, the rapid rise in the levels of uncertainty made it clear to top managers that there was no point in using advanced techniques to make detailed five-year forecasts when various crises were exposing the nonsense of many previous forecasts. (Prior to 1973, for example, there had been a great discussion as to whether the price of crude oil would ever go above $2 per barrel.)[11]

Because of these problems, there has been a decided move among many firms toward a less structured format and a much shorter document. General Electric chairman J. F. Welch says, "A strategy can be summarized in a page or two."[12]

Contents of the plan.   The contents of the plan are also different. Managements of many companies say they are much more concerned now with issues, strategies, and implementation. The planning director of Shell Oil, the British-Dutch transnational, says,

> The Shell approach has swung increasingly away from a mechanistic methodology and centrally set forecasts towards a more conceptual or qualitative analysis of the forces and pressures impinging on the industry. What Shell planners try to do is identify the key elements pertaining to a particular area of decision making—the different competitive, political, economic, social, and technical forces that are likely to have the greatest influence on the overall situation. In a global organization, the higher level of management is likely to be most interested in global scenarios—looking at worldwide developments—while the focus becomes narrower as one proceeds into the more specialized functions, division, and business sectors of individual companies.[13]

Summary of the Planning Process

Perhaps a good way to summarize the new direction in planning is to quote Frederick W. Gluck, a director of the multinational management consulting firm McKinsey & Co., and a principal architect of its strategic management practice. Gluck says that if major corporations are to develop the flexibility to compete, they must make the following major changes in the way they plan:

1. Top management must assume a more explicit strategic decision-making role, dedicating a large amount of time to deciding how things ought to be instead of listening to analyses of how they are.
2. The nature of planning must undergo a fundamental change from an exercise in forecasting to an exercise in creativity.
3. Planning processes and tools that assume a future much like the past must be replaced by a mind-set that is obsessed with being first to recognize change and turn it into a competitive advantage.
4. The role of the planner must change from being a purveyor of incrementalism to that of a crusader for action and an alter ego to line management.
5. Strategic planning must be restored to the core of line management responsibilities.[14]

ORGANIZATIONAL DESIGN

Organizing normally follows planning because the organization must implement the strategic plan. The planning process itself, because it encompasses an analysis of all the firm's activities, often discloses a need to alter the organization. Changes in strategy may require changes in the organization, but the reverse is also true. A new CEO joins the firm, or an important customer changes its method of operating—adopts a synchronized manufacturing process, for example. Planning and organizing are so closely related that normally the structure of the organization is treated by management as an integral part of the planning process.

In designing the organizational structure, management is faced with two concerns: (1) finding the most effective way to departmentalize to take advantage of the efficiencies gained from the specialization of labor and (2) coordinating the firm's activities to enable it to meet its overall objectives. As all managers know, these two concerns run counter to each other; that is, the gain from the increased specialization of labor may sometimes be nullified by the increased costs of greater coordination. It is the constant search for an optimum balance between them that causes the organizational structure to change continually. However, as one critic of this frantic search for the suitable organization points out, "The companies I studied have *not* continually reorganized their operations. Each has retained for years a simple structure built around an **international division**—a form of organization that many management theorists regard as embryonic, appropriate only for companies in the earliest stages of worldwide growth."[15] IBM and Ford are two examples of global firms that have international divisions.

international division a division in the organization that is at the same level as the domestic division and is responsible for all non-home country activities

Evolution of the Global Company

You will remember reading in Chapter 2 that companies often enter foreign markets first by exporting and then, as sales increase, forming overseas sales companies and eventually setting up production facilities. As the firm's foreign involvement changed, its organization frequently changed. It might first have had *no one* responsible for international business; each domestic product division may have been responsible for filling export orders. Next, an export department might have been created, and, when the company began to invest in various overseas locations, it might have formed an international division to take charge of all overseas involvement. Note that the international division itself is usually organized on a regional (geographical) basis. This is how IBM and Ford organize their international divisions. IBM's corporate organization is shown in Figure 21-3.

As their overseas operations increased in importance and scope, most managements, with some exceptions, felt the need to eliminate international divisions and establish worldwide organizations based on *product, region,* or *function.* In rarer instances, customer classes are also a top-level dimension. Some service companies and financial institutions are organized this way. At secondary, tertiary, and still lower levels, these four dimensions—plus (1) process, (2) national subsidiary, and (3) international or domestic—provide the basis for subdivisions.

Managements who changed to these types of organizations felt they would (1) be more capable of developing competitive strategies to confront the new global competition, (2) obtain lower production costs by promoting worldwide product standardization and manufacturing rationalization, and (3) enhance technology transfer and the allocation of company resources.

Global corporate form—product. Frequently, this structure has been a return to preexport department times in that the domestic product division has

■ **FIGURE 21–3** International Division—IBM Corporate Organization

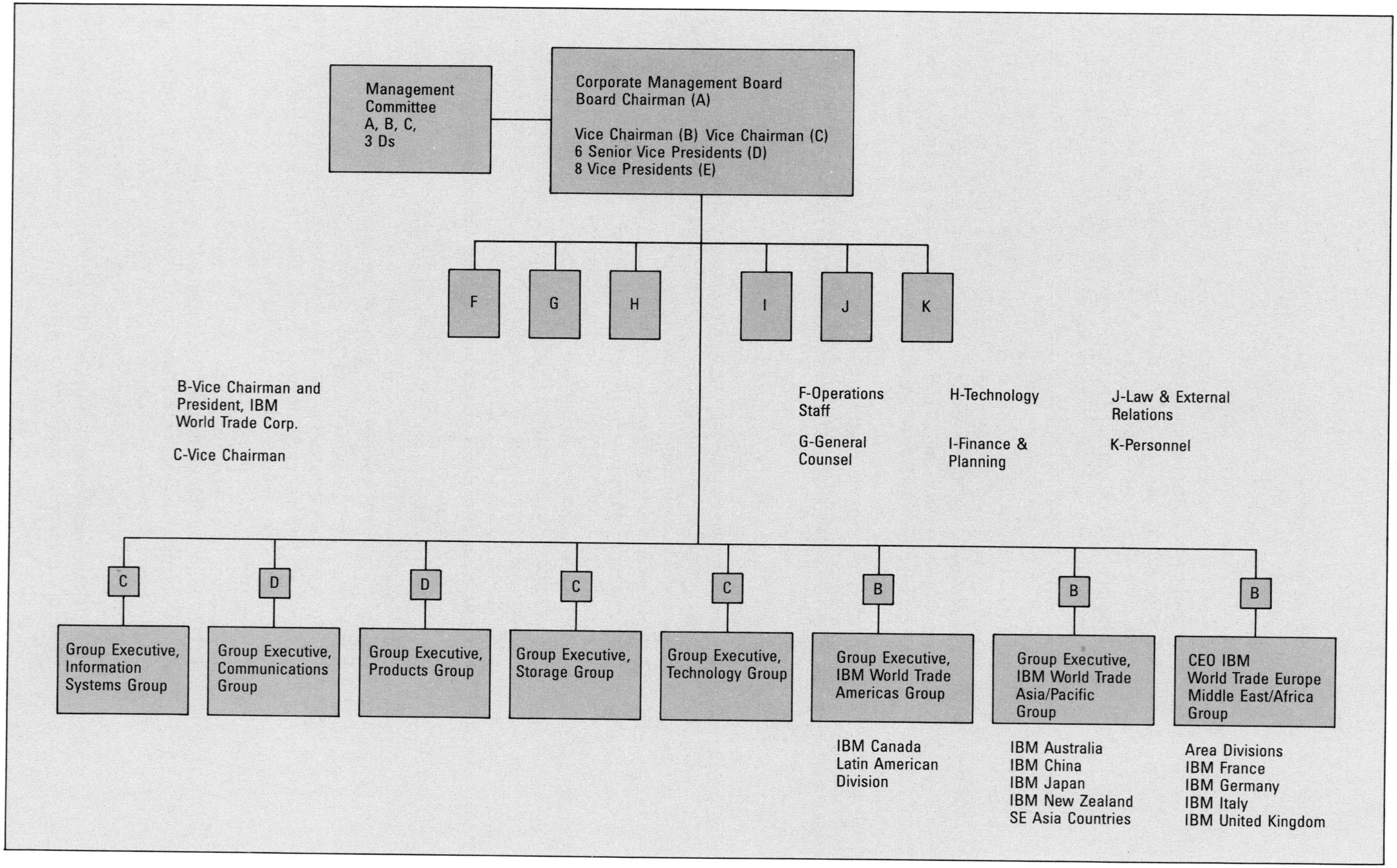

Management Committee
A, B, C,
3 Ds

Corporate Management Board
Board Chairman (A)

Vice Chairman (B) Vice Chairman (C)
6 Senior Vice Presidents (D)
8 Vice Presidents (E)

F—Operations Staff
G—General Counsel
H—Technology
I—Finance & Planning
J—Law & External Relations
K—Personnel

B—Vice Chairman and President, IBM World Trade Corp.
C—Vice Chairman

Group Executive, Information Systems Group

Group Executive, Communications Group

Group Executive, Products Group

Group Executive, Storage Group

Group Executive, Technology Group

Group Executive, IBM World Trade Americas Group

IBM Canada
Latin American Division

Group Executive, IBM World Trade Asia/Pacific Group

IBM Australia
IBM China
IBM Japan
IBM New Zealand
SE Asia Countries

CEO IBM World Trade Europe Middle East/Africa Group

Area Divisions
IBM France
IBM Germany
IBM Italy
IBM United Kingdom

■ **FIGURE 21–4   Global Corporate Form—Product**

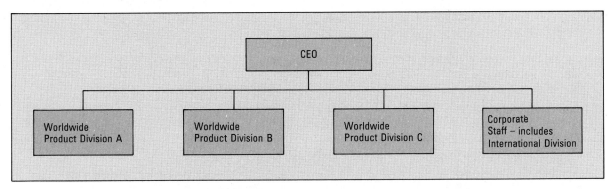

■ **FIGURE 21–5   Global Corporate Form—Geographic Regions**

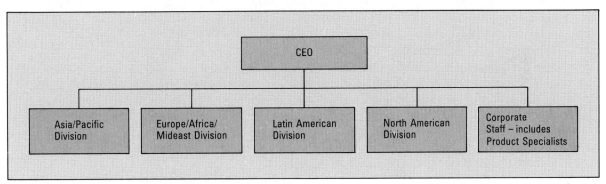

Source: Adapted from *New Directions in Multinational Corporations, 1981,* Business International Corporation.

been given responsibility for global line and staff operations. To be able to operate overseas, each product division generally has regional experts; so, while this organizational form avoids the duplication of product experts common in the company with an international division, it creates a duplication of area experts. Occasionally, to eliminate placing regional specialists in each product division, management will have a group of regional specialists in an international division that advises the product divisions but has no line authority over them (see Figure 21–4).

Although organization by product is most favored by global companies, the organization alone does not guarantee that the firm is a global one. The Worldview describes the attempt of Japanese companies organized by product to change from multinational to global companies.

Global corporate form—Geographical regions.   Firms in which geographic regions are the primary basis for division put the responsibility for all activities under area managers who report directly to the chief executive officer. This kind of organization simplifies the task of directing worldwide operations, because every country in the world is clearly under the control of someone who is in contact with headquarters (see Figure 21–5).

WORLDVIEW
Japanese Firms Formulate Global Strategies

Many Japanese firms are striving to become global companies. Although they have had foreign factories and sales offices for decades, their product development, marketing, financing, and investment plans have been directed from Japan; they are Japanese multinationals whose management philosophy is decidedly ethnocentric (home country does it better). Why should long-established firms like Toyota, Matsushita, and Hitachi, all of which are convinced of the superiority of the "Japanese way," change their methods of operating which have been so profitable for so long?

The main reason is that their overseas manufacturing operations are becoming so large and diversified that they are beyond effective centralized control from the home offices. Governments, especially those of EC members, are enacting stricter local-content laws requiring local manufacture, not just assembly. NEC, for example, has formulated a new global strategy of manufacturing in "optimum locations." A network of regional manufacturing operations now does work for each other, with or without support from NEC plants in Japan. Matsushita is rearranging its 69 overseas plants in a "global localization" plan to supply four "major poles"—North America, Europe, Japan, and the rest of Asia. It now has regional headquarters for each area. To get the latest technology needed to remain competitive worldwide, Japanese companies have established research centers in the United States and Europe. These too are becoming difficult to manage from Japan.

For many Japanese companies accustomed to strict control from headquarters, it is going to be difficult to give responsibility and authority to distant operations and leave it to their local managers to adjust to the cultures, tastes, and business practices of their markets. Also, they are not particularly skilled in dealing with minorities (which they don't have at home), as their records in the United States and other countries show. They have the same problem with unions as well.

The role model for many of the Japanese companies trying to become global is IBM. They are impressed by the more than 30 research facilities IBM has around the world. Of course, IBM's global success is not due solely to a worldwide network of research centers; one of the ingredients of its success is that IBM-Germany is a true German company, as IBM-Japan is a Japanese company. An executive of a large Japanese publisher, when asked which firm had written the software his firm uses for computer translation, said it could only have been a Japanese company—IBM.

Source: "The Multinational, Eastern Style," *The Economist*, June 24, 1989, pp. 63–64.

Of course, this organizational type is used for both multinational (multidomestic) and global companies. Global companies that use it consider the division in which the home country is located as just another division for purposes of resource allocation and a source of management personnel. Some U.S. global companies have created a North American division that includes Canada, Mexico, and Central American countries in addition to the United States, possibly in part to emphasize that the home country is given no preference.

The regionalized organization appears to be popular with companies that manufacture products with a rather low or, at least, stable technological content that require strong marketing ability. It is also favored by firms with diverse products, each having different product requirements, competitive environments, and political risks. Producers of consumer products, such as prepared foods, pharmaceuticals, and household products, employ this type of organization. The disadvantage of an organization divided into geographic

■ **FIGURE 21–6   Global Corporate Form—Function**

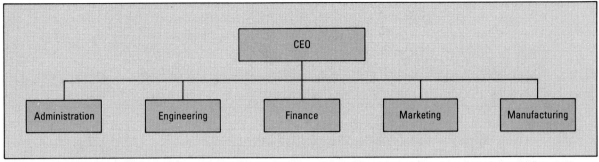

Source: From *New Directions in Multinational Corporations, 1981,* p. 19, with the permission of the publisher, Business International Corporation (New York).

regions is that each region must have its own product and functional specialists so that although the duplication of area specialists found in product divisions is eliminated, a duplication of product and functional specialists is necessary.

Product coordination across regions presents difficult problems, as does global product planning. To alleviate these problems managements often place specialized product managers on the headquarters staff. Although these managers have no line authority, they do provide input to corporate decisions concerning products.

Global corporate form—function.   Few firms are organized by function at the top level. Those that are obviously believe worldwide functional expertise is more significant to the firm than product or area knowledge. In this type of organization, those reporting to the CEO might be the senior executives responsible for each functional area (marketing, production, finance, etc.), as in Figure 21–6.[16] The commonality among the users of the functional form is a narrow and highly integrated product mix, such as that of aircraft manufacturers. For example, Sun Co., a petroleum company that also mines coal, has three group heads reporting to the CEO: (1) refining and marketing, (2) exploration and production, and (3) energy minerals.[17] Because of the presence of this last group, Sun really has a mixed, or **hybrid, organization.**

Hybrid forms.   In a hybrid organization, a mixture of the organizational forms is used at the top level and may or not be present at the lower levels. Figure 21–7 illustrates a simple hybrid form.

Such combinations are often the result of having introduced a new and different product line that management believes can best be handled by a worldwide product division. An acquired company with distinct products and a functioning marketing network may be incorporated as a product division even though the rest of the firm is organized on a regional basis. Later, after corporate management becomes familiar with the operation, it may be regionalized.

A mixed structure may also result from the firm's selling to a sizable, homogeneous class of customers. Special divisions for handling sales to the military or to original equipment manufacturers are often established at the same level as regional or product divisions.

hybrid organization structure organized by more than one dimension at the top level

■ **FIGURE 21–7   Hybrid Organizational Form**

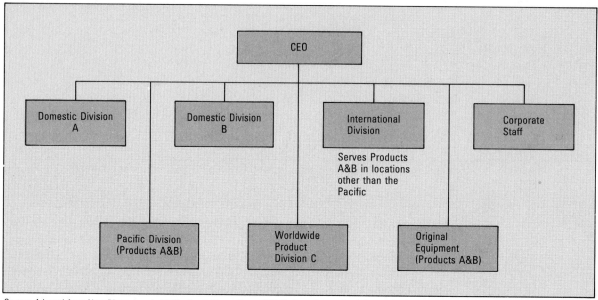

Source: Adapted from *New Dimensions in Multinational Corporations, 1981,* Business International Corporation.

---

matrix organization an organizational structure composed of one or more super-imposed organizational structures in an attempt to mesh product, regional, functional, and other expertise

Matrix organizations.   The **matrix organization** has evolved from management's attempt to mesh product, regional, and functional expertise while still maintaining clear lines of authority. It is called a matrix because it superimposes an organization based on one dimension on an organization based on another dimension. In such an organization, both the area and product managers will be at the same level and their responsibilities will overlap. An individual manager—say, a marketing manager in Germany—will have a multiple reporting relationship, being responsible to the area manager and, in some instances, to an international or worldwide marketing manager at headquarters. Figure 21–8 illustrates an extremely simple matrix organization based on two organizational dimensions. Note that the country managers are responsible to both the area and the product line managers.

Ciba-Geigy, the Swiss chemical and pharmaceutical multinational, has an organizational structure based on a matrix of *three* dimensions: (1) product, (2) function, and (3) geographic region. Lines of communication flow both horizontally and vertically across these main dimensions. However, final authority rests with the executive committee, which is the highest executive body in the parent company. The task of this committee is to maintain two-way communication between the home office and the lower units. Committee members are not supermanagers of the divisions.

Problems with the matrix.   Although at one time it seemed that the matrix organizational form would enable firms to have the advantages of the product, regional, and functional forms, the disadvantages of the matrix form have kept most worldwide companies from adopting it. One problem with the matrix is that the two or three managers (if it is a three-dimensional matrix) must agree on a decision. This can lead to less-than-optimum compromises, delayed

■ **FIGURE 21–8   Regional–Product Matrix**

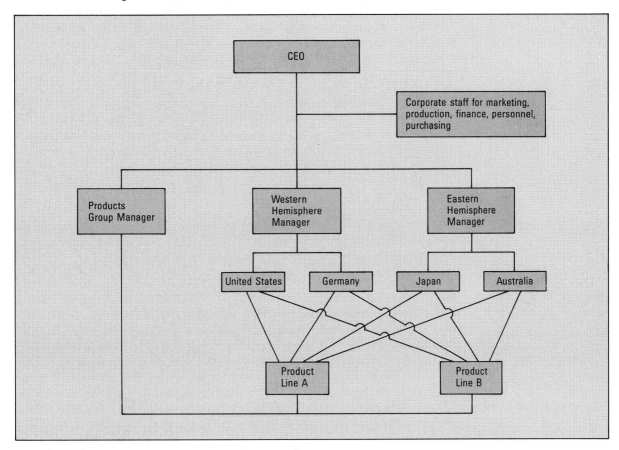

responses, and power politics where more attention is paid to the process than to the problem. When the managers cannot agree, the problem goes higher in the organization and takes top management away from its duties.[18] Because of these difficulties, many firms have maintained their original organization based on product, function, region, or international division and built into the structure accountability for the other organizational dimensions, called by some a **matrix overlay.**

matrix overlay   an organization in which top-level divisions are required to heed input from a staff composed of experts of another organizational dimension in an attempt to avoid the double-reporting difficulty of a matrix organization but still mesh two or more dimensions

Matrix overlay.   We have mentioned previously some of the steps that managements have taken to try to avoid the problems inherent in each organizational form. A company organized by product may have regional specialists in a staff function with the requirement that they have input to product decisions. They may even be organized in an international division, as we mentioned. A regional organization would have product managers on its staff, who provide input to regional decisions.

Other solutions.   Planning is a way to get both product and regional managers involved in decision making. At General Electric, each country executive develops a comprehensive country opportunity plan covering all products and strategies that is then compared with plans of the product groups. Conflicts are identified and solutions proposed.[19] A regionalized organization might follow the same procedure using worldwide product committees. Another solution is to transfer product managers to regional divisions, and vice versa, so they have a better appreciation for the need to coordinate their decisions.

The "Right" Organizational Form

Four facts concerning organizational forms should have become evident from our discussion: (1) there is not one "right" way to organize; (2) generally, organizations are not "pure," but mixed; (3) the greater the specialization of the organization's units, the more difficult it is to coordinate their activities; and (4) organizational structures are never permanent.

Changing Forms

Managements are constantly searching for an organizational form that will be more responsive to the firm's needs. Not only have they mixed the standard forms, but they have conceived some entirely new ones.

strategic business unit (SBU) business entity with a clearly defined market, specific competitors, the ability to carry out its business mission, and a size appropriate for control by a single manager

Strategic business units.   **Strategic business units (SBUs),** which originated with General Electric, are a relatively new organizational form in which product divisions have been redefined as though they were distinct, independent businesses. They are commonly defined as a business entity with a clearly defined market, specific competitors, the ability to carry out its business mission, and a size appropriate for control by a single manager. Most SBUs are based on product lines, and if a product must be modified to suit different markets, a worldwide product SBU may be divided into a few product/market SBUs serving various countries or groups of countries. Strategic business units do not determine how a company as a whole will organize its internal operations.

Sectors or operating units.   Companies with numerous SBUs (Gillette calls them *product groups*) frequently group them into an another unit, called *sector* by 3M and *operating unit* by Gillette. Other firms use other names. The heads of these organizations are just under the CEO and carry such titles as company vice president or, in Gillette's case, vice chairman.

Free-form management design.   This structure, which began in the 1960s, may become popular again, especially for conglomerates or holding companies, because it encourages entrepreneurship. Local managers are free to do almost anything they wish as long as they meet profit or ROI requirements set at headquarters, which offers assistance through task forces and project teams. The free-form management design is also useful for companies involved with rapidly changing technological innovations, such as computers and robots.

The choice of form primarily depends on the managerial philosophy of the chief executive officers and on what they perceive to be their firms' requirements. But these requirements change, and so must the organization. The emergence of worldwide competition (especially from the Japanese), the promise of lower costs by manufacturing rationalization and synchronized manufacturing, Europe 1992, and the worldwide convergence of consumer preferences have all motivated corporate reorganization.

Managerial Talent

The managerial talent available to the corporation has been and will continue to be extremely significant both in the choice of organizational form and in the transition from one form to another. Evidently, the lack of global orientation on the part of product managers was a strong factor in Bristol-Myers' decision to revert to an international division after having had a global product organization.

The importance of capable managers cannot be underestimated. They can make a less-than-optimum organization function well. There is less need for a matrix organization, for example, if area managers work well with managers having global responsibility for products. By their personal capabilities, these managers can overcome the problem of other organizational forms in getting the needed cooperation and coordination, which is usually achieved through a matrix. Product managers who are able to generate support and enthusiasm for their product lines do not require a dotted line to be drawn on a chart. In fact, such actions are often formalized by management after observing what actually takes place.

Characteristics of the "Right" Organization

Regardless of the form, the right organization should, according to Peter Drucker, have the following characteristics:

1. *Clarity,* as opposed to simplicity. (The Gothic cathedral is not a simple design, but your position in it is clear; you know where to stand and where to go. A modern office building is exceedingly simple in design, but it is very easy to get lost in one; it is not clear.)
2. *Economy* of effort to maintain control and minimize friction.
3. *Direction* of vision toward the product rather than the process—the result rather than the effort.
4. *Understanding* by each individual of his or her own task as well as that of the organization as a whole.
5. *Decision making* that focuses on the right issues, is action oriented, and is carried out at the lowest possible level of management.
6. *Stability,* as opposed to rigidity, to survive turmoil, and *adaptability to* learn from it.
7. *Perpetuation* and *self-renewal,* which require an organization to be able to produce tomorrow's leaders from within, helping each person develop continuously; the structure must also be open to new ideas.

Corporate Survival into the 21st Century

Boards of directors and chief executive officers are realizing the necessity to view the world as both their marketplace and the source of competitors. To become global companies, they cannot be governed solely by local interests, of course; but neither can they be so enveloped in the struggle for globalism that they fail to consider them. Successful global company managements will have a worldwide perspective and a national competence.[20] In the words of Roberto Goizueta, chairman of Coca-Cola, "Think globally, act locally."

SUMMARY

Many worldwide companies have instituted formal worldwide strategic planning to identify opportunities and threats, formulate strategies to handle them, and stipulate the means to finance those strategies. Global strategic planning provides a formal structure in which managers (1) analyze the company's external environments, (2) analyze the firm's internal environment, (3) define the company's business and mission, (4) set corporate objectives, (5) quantify goals, (6) formulate strategies, and (7) make tactical plans.

Operating managers do the planning; the planning staff assists them primarily by providing information on the environments. Statements of the corporate business and mission communicate to the firm's stakeholders what the company is and where it is going. Its objectives direct its course of action, and its strategies enable management to reach its objectives. Scenarios and contingency plans help management prepare for critical events. Tactical plans are detailed plans for implementing the strategies. Planning may be top-down or bottom-up, but iterative planning, a combination of both, is

becoming more popular. Plans are becoming shorter and more concerned with issues, strategies, and their implementation instead of the voluminous, detailed forecasts of the past.

Organizational design usually follows strategic planning, and, because of the close relationship between the two functions, both are commonly done during the strategic planning process. Companies may (1) have an international division, (2) be organized by product, function, or region, or (3) have a mixture of them (hybrid form). To attain a balance between product and regional expertise, some managements have tried a matrix form of organization. Its disadvantages, however, have caused many managements to put a matrix overlay over the traditional product, regional, or functional form instead of using the matrix. Strategic business units (SBUs) and sectors are newer organizational forms that companies are using to become global companies. Managerial talent is extremely significant in the choice of organizational form. To survive into the 21st century, managers will have to *think globally* and *act locally*.

QUESTIONS

1. Why have many worldwide firms found it necessary to institute global strategic planning?

2. Prepare a watch list for Exxon.

3. Suppose the competitor analysis reveals that the American subsidiary of your firm's German competitor is about to broaden its product mix in the American market by introducing a new line against which your company has not previously had to compete in the home market. The environmental analysis shows that the dollar-mark exchange rate is going to continue to make American exports expensive in Germany. Do you recommend a defensive strategy, or do you attack your competitor in its home market? How will you implement your strategy?

4. You have been employed by the Brazilian subsidiary of an American multinational corporation whose primary interest is in the financial performance of its subsidiaries. A Japanese firm is setting up a Brazilian subsidiary and has offered you a salary that you cannot refuse. What cultural adjustments will you probably have to make in your new job?

5. You are the CEO of the Jones Petrochemical company and have just finished studying next year's plans of your foreign subsidiaries. You are pleased that the Israeli plan is so optimistic because that

subsidiary contributes heavily to your company's income. But OPEC is meeting next month. Should you ask your planning committee, which meets tomorrow, to construct some scenarios? Of so, about what?

6. The planning perspective should be benefit oriented rather than solution oriented. Please explain the meaning of this statement.

7. Your firm has used bottom-up planning for years, but the subsidiaries' plans differ with respect to approaches to goals and assumptions—even the time frames are different. How can you, the CEO, get them to agree on these points and still get their individual input?

8. Your matrix organization isn't working; decisions are taking too long, and it seems to you that, instead of best solutions, you're getting compromises. What can you, the CEO, do?

9. You are the CEO of Mancon Incorporated, and you have just acquired Pozoli, the Italian small-appliance maker (electric shavers, small household and personal care appliances). It has been in business 30 years and has manufacturing plants in Italy, Mexico, Ireland, and Spain. Its output is sold in more than 100 markets worldwide, including the United States.

Your company is now organized into two product groups—shaving, personal care, and an international division at the top level. How are you going to include Pozoli in your organization?

10. It is obvious that in formulating new strategies, management may uncover a need to change its organization. Can you give some situations where the reverse may be true?

11. Can a worldwide company with an international division be a global company?

12. What does Coca-Cola's chairman mean by "think globally, act locally"?

MINICASE 21–1

What Organizational Form Should Gillette Have?

"The Gillette Company, founded in 1901, is an international consumer products firm engaged in the development, manufacture, and sale of a wide range of products for personal care or use. Major lines include blades and razors, toiletries and cosmetics, stationery products, Braun electric razors and small appliances and Oral-B oral care products." Braun and Oral-B are former independent companies that were acquired by Gillette. It has also acquired Jafra, a California firm that operates in 14 countries—including the United States—with 130,000 independent representatives visiting the homes, as Avon does. Jafra's management has reorganized to emphasize Latin American sales, which are growing rapidly. Its worldwide sales in 1988 were $120 million. Jafra products are made in California and Spain.

Sales of blades and razors amounted to $1.147 billion in 1988 and contributed 60 percent of Gillette's profits. In most major markets worldwide, Gillette blades and razors continue to outsell all competitive brands combined. Although worldwide sales of double-edged blades dropped slightly, the company retained its leadership in this category. Disposable razors registered a substantial sales increase internationally. Since the early 1970s, Gillette has begun blade manufacturing in over a dozen developing countries, including Egypt, China, India, and Pakistan. Companies in these last two countries are joint ventures.

Sales of stationery products (such as Paper Mate, Flexgrip, and Liquid Paper), which amounted to $385 million in 1988, were assisted by sales from Waterman, a French manufacturer of premium pens and pencils acquired in 1987, and Sylvapen, an Argentine manufacturer of coloring sets and writing instruments purchased in 1986. Both product lines are now marketed internationally.

In 1988, sales of toiletries and cosmetics amounted to $1,019 billion. The recent acquisitions of La Toja Cosmeticos, a Spanish maker of bath products (1986); UNISA, a Chilean skin care manufacturer (1987); and Antica Erboristeria, an Italian producer of herbal toiletries (1988) contributed to a 10 percent increase over 1987 sales. Jafra's sales are included in this total. Interestingly, Gillette now has seven different manufacturing plants in Spain, far more than in any other European country.

Braun, a German manufacturer of electric shavers and small household and personal care appliances, was founded in 1921 and acquired by Gillette in 1967. Its household appliances include hand mixers, coffeemakers, juice extractors, and electric alarm clocks; cordless curlers, electric toothbrushes, and water jets are some of its personal care appliances. Its hand mixers are first in sales in the United States, Canada, and most European countries, and its cordless curlers are the top seller worldwide.[1] The company's market share of cord shavers in Japan, where it has had a sales company for 25 years, is 60 percent.[2] Total sales in 1988 were $824 million. Braun has manufacturing facilities in Germany, Mexico, Ireland, and Spain and employs 8,200 people worldwide in production and sales. Its products are sold in more than 100 countries. The name Gillette does not figure prominently in Braun's advertising.

Gillette acquired Oral-B, another California company, in 1984. It has 1,450 employees worldwide who sell a broad range of oral care products to dentists and consumers in 30 countries. Its most important product, toothbrushes, is the top seller in the United States and several foreign markets. Sales in 1988 were $202 million. Oral-B manufactures in the United States, Ireland, and Australia.

Gillette distributes its products in over 200 countries and territories and has 62 manufacturing facilities in 28 countries. These include 3 plants in the United States for blades and razors, stationery products, and personal care products; 2 plants in Canada for the above-mentioned product lines; and 8 plants of Braun, Oral-B, and Jafra; and 28 plants in the rest of the world, *excluding* Europe. Worldwide, total sales were $3.58 billion in 1988, a 13 percent gain over 1987. Management's goal is sustained profitable growth, which the company achieves by emphasizing strong technical and marketing efforts in existing lines and selective diversification, both internally and through acquisition.[3] The company is known as one of the industry's top innovators and now has an equally important goal of shortening new product development to prevent competitors from rushing to copy a new product that appears in one market and getting their copies in other markets before Gillette.[4] The company is ready for Europe 1992. In 1983, management standardized its European marketing mix.

Due in part to takeover threats, Gillette reorganized its entire organization in 1987 to lower operating costs.

How would you have organized the company?

(To the instructor: There is a current chart of the company in your I.M.)

---

[1] Sales information from the Gillette Company, *Annual Report 1988.*

[2] "Braun: Cutting into Japan's Shaver Market," *Journal of Japanese Trade & Industry,* November 2, 1984, p. 45.

[3] *Annual Report 1988,* inside cover.

[4] "The Innovation Strategy That Keeps Gillette in the Pink," *International Management,* September 1984, p. 90.

MINICASE 21–2

Name Those Objectives—H. J. Heinz Co.

Can you determine three broad objectives of Heinz's president from these 1988 results?

1. Acquired Champion Valley Farms, an East Coast manufacturer and distributor of dog foods, from Campbell Soup Company.

2. New products launched in Weight Watchers' English subsidiary, whose sales have tripled in two years. Soup reformulations have increase Heinz's share to 60 percent of the English market.

3. Five low-calorie salads introduced by Weight Watchers in Germany.

4. Bought California Home Brands, producer of Skippy and Vet dog food, Petuna brand cat food, and a large private-label canned pet food business.

5. Nationwide launch of Heinz-Japan's canned dog and cat foods. It also introduced a new line of cooking sauces.

6. Added a Mississippi manufacturer of cat foods.

7. Acquired the popular "Marie Elizabeth" trademark and two canneries from Portugal's leading exporter of branded sardines.

8. Began producing ketchup, mayonnaise, margarine, and corn oil in Seoul-Heinz joint venture.

9. Introduction of a new line of convenience foods containing tuna and sardines by the French subsidiary of Star-Kist, a Heinz company.

10. Started a joint venture in Thailand.

11. Entered Spain by acquiring Orlando S.A., maker of the leading brand of spiced tomato sauce.

12. Completed its $10 million expansion program in American Samoa, making it the world's second-largest tuna plant.

13. Launched Mexican ketchup for French, Belgian, and Dutch consumers, who like spicy condiments.

14. Heinz-China received recognition from the Chinese government for contributions to improving nutrition among 6 million children in Guangdong Province; Instant Nutritious Rice Cereal and Instant Nutritious Hi-Protein Cereal received endorsements from three Chinese industry and medical associations.

Source: H. J. Heinz Co., *Annual Report, 1988.*

SUPPLEMENTARY READINGS

Company examples

"Companies That Compete Best." *Fortune,* May 22, 1989, pp. 36–44.

Herbert, Ira C. "How Coke Markets to the World." *The Journal of Business Strategy,* September/October 1988, pp. 4–7.

Kennedy, Carol. "Planning Global Strategies for 3M." *Long-Range Planning,* February 1988, pp. 9–17.

Pink, Alan I. "Strategic Leadership through Corporate Planning at ICI." *Long-Range Planning,* February 1988, pp. 18–25.

"Survival and Growth in This Age of Global Competition." *Business International,* January 13, 1986, pp. 9–11.

Competitive strategy planning

Attanasio, Dominick B. "The Multiple Benefits of Competitor Intelligence." *The Journal of Business Strategy,* May/June 1988, pp. 16–19.

David, Fred R. "A Framework for Conducting an External Strategic Management Audit." *Journal of Business Strategy,* Spring 1986, pp. 22–33.

Porter, Michael, ed. *Competition in Global Industries.* Boston: Harvard Business School, 1986.

Shanks, David C. "Strategic Planning for Global Competition." *The Journal of Business Strategy,* Winter 1985, pp. 80–89.

Issues analysis

Kharbanda, Om P., and Ernest A. Stallworthy. "Planning for Emergencies—Lessons from the Chemical Industry." *Long-Range Planning,* February 1989, pp. 83–89.

McConkey, Dale D. "Planning for Uncertainty." *Business Horizons,* January–February 1987, pp. 40–45.

Nigh, D., and P. L. Cochran. "Issues Management and the Multinational Enterprise." *Management International Review,* 1987/1, pp. 4–12.

Preble, John F., and Pradeep A. Rau. "Combining Delphi and Multiple Scenario Analysis for Planning Purposes." *Journal of Business Strategy,* Fall 1986, pp. 12–21.

Organization design

"Are Regional Headquarters Worthwhile?" *Business Europe,* December 21, 1987, pp. 2–5.

"ASEA Brown Boveri Organizes for 1992." *Business Europe,* May 9, 1988, pp. 14–20.

Bartlett, Christopher A. "MNCs: Get off the Reorganization Merry-Go-Round." *Harvard Business Review.* March–April 1983, pp. 138–46.

Bartlett, Christopher A., and Sumantra Ghoshal. "Organizing for Worldwide Effectiveness: The Transnational Solution." *California Management Review,* Fall 1988, pp. 54–74.

"Facing up to the Globalization Challenge." *The McKinsey Quarterly,* Winter 1986, pp. 52–68.

"Global Organization: Square D Managers to Compete Globally." *Business International,* September 21, 1987, pp. 297–302.

Gluck, Frederick W. "Strategic Planning in a New Key." *The McKinsey Quarterly,* Winter 1986, pp. 18–41.

"How Decentralization Sparked a Revival for Campbell Canada." *Business International,* January 25, 1988, pp. 20–21.

Kriger, Mark P., and Patrick J. J. Rich. "Strategic Governance: Why and How MNCs Are Using Boards of Directors in Foreign Subsidiaries." *Columbia Journal of World Business,* Winter 1987, pp. 39–45.

New Directions in Multinational Corporate Organization. New York: Business International, 1981.

Ohmae, Kenichi. "Why Companies Must Reorganize in the Age of Global Products." *International Management,* September 1985, p. 117.

Pitts, Robert A., and John D. Daniels. "Aftermath of the Matrix Mania." *Columbia Journal of World Business,* Summer 1984, pp. 48–54.

Restructuring and Turnaround: Experiences in Corporate Renewal. New York: Business International, 1987.

"The Issues Globalists Don't Talk About." *International Management,* September 1987, pp. 37–42.

"The Multinational, Eastern Style." *The Economist,* June 24, 1989, pp. 63–64.

Strategic planning

Chakravarthy, Balaji S., and Howard V. Perlmutter. "Strategic Planning for a Global Business." *Columbia Journal of World Business,* Summer 1985, pp. 3–10.

"Corporate Strategy for the 1990s." *Fortune,* February 29, 1988, pp. 34–42.

David, Fred R. "How Companies Define Their Mission." *Long-Range Planning,* February 1989, pp. 90–95.

Gluck, Frederick W. "A Fresh Look at Strategic Management." *The Journal of Business Strategy,* Fall 1985, pp. 4–19.

Hamel, Gary, and C. K. Prahalad. "Do You Really Have a Global Strategy?" *The McKinsey Quarterly,* Summer 1986, pp. 34–50.

King, Elizabeth M.; Wayne Norvell; and Dan Devine. "Budgeting: A Strategic Managerial Tool." *Journal of Business Strategies,* Fall 1988, pp. 69–75.

Maddox, Nick; William P. Anthony; and Walt Wheatly, Jr. "Creative Strategic Planning Using Imagery." *Long-Range Planning,* October 1987, pp. 118–24.

Mintzberg, Henry. "Strategy-Making in Three Modes." *California Management Review,* Winter 1972, pp. 44–53.

Naylor, Thomas H. "The International Strategy Mix." *Columbia Journal of World Business,* Summer 1985, pp. 11–19.

Porter, Michael. "The State of Strategic Thinking." *The Economist,* May 29, 1987, pp. 17–22.

Quinn, James Brian. "Strategical Change: Logical Incrementalism." *Sloan Management Review,* Fall 1978, pp. 7–21.

Reed, Richard, and M. Ronald Buckley. "Strategy in Action—Techniques for Implementing Strategy." *Long-Range Planning,* June 1988, pp. 67–73.

Strategies

Ackerman, Laurence D. "Identify Strategies That Make a Difference."*The Journal of Business Strategy,* May/June 1988, pp. 28–32.

Gilbert, Xavier, and Paul Strebel. "Strategies to Outpace the Competition." *The Journal of Business Strategy,* Summer 1987, pp. 28–36.

Lei, David. "Strategies for Global Competition." *Long-Range Planning,* February 1989, pp. 102–9.

Shrivastava, Paul. "Integrating Strategy Formulation with Organizational Culture." *The Journal of Business Strategy,* Winter 1985, pp. 103–11.

Vernon-Wortzel, Heidi, and Lawrence H. Wortzel. "Globalizing Strategies for Multinationals from Developing Countries." *Columbia Journal of World Business,* Spring 1988, pp. 27–35.

Ward, John L., and Stanley F. Stasch. "How Small-Share Firms Can Uncover Winning Strategies." *The Journal of Business Strategy,* September/October 1988, pp. 26–31.

ENDNOTES

1. The Coca-Cola Company, *Annual Report,* 1986, inside cover.

2. PepsiCo, *Annual Report,* 1987, p. 6.

3. Mitsubishi Corporation, *Annual Report,* 1988, inside cover.

4. The Campbell Soup Company, *Annual Report,* 1987, p. 1.

5. Ibid., p. 4.

6. Paul Shrivastava, "Integrating Strategy Formulation with Organizational Culture," *The Journal of Business Strategy,* Winter 1985, pp. 103–11.

7. PepsiCo, *Annual Report,* pp. 12–13.

8. "The New Breed of Strategic Planner," *Business Week,* September 17, 1984, p. 62.

9. Ibid., p. 62.

10. Ibid., p. 64.

11. P. W. Beck, "Corporate Planning for an Uncertain Future," *Long-Range Planning,* August 1982, p. 14.

12. "New Breed of Strategic Planner," p. 66.

13. "Corporate Planning for an Uncertain Future," p. 17.

14. Frederick W. Gluck, "A Fresh Look at Strategic Management," *The Journal of Business Strategy,* Fall 1985, p. 6.

15. Christopher A. Bartlett, "MNCs: Get off the Reorganization Merry-Go-Round," *Harvard Business Review,* March–April 1983, p. 138.

16. *New Directions in Multinational Corporate Organization* (New York: Business International, 1981), pp. 1–6.

17. Sun Co., *Annual Report,* 1987, p.49.

18. Robert A. Pitts and John D. Daniels, "Aftermath of the Matrix Mania," *Columbia Journal of World Business,* Summer 1984, p. 51.

19. *New Directions in Multinational Corporate Organization,* p. 41.

20. Christopher A. Bartlett and Sumantra Ghoshal, "Organizing for Worldwide Effectiveness: The Transnational Solution," *California Management Review,* Fall 1988, p. 71.

Chapter 22

Control and Staffing

There's no great difference in managing a small or large company. In both cases, it's simply a matter of having more money at the end of the day than when you started in the morning.

Rune Andresson, managing director of Trelleborg A. B.

How does it work out when there is a woman manager in the family? There is no solution because there is no problem in Japan. Management is for men only.

William A. Cohen, in a review of Mitsuyuki Masatsugu

As I saw it, here was a sector of the economy crying out for the application of good management skills.

Sydney Biddle Barrows, descendant of the Mayflower pilgrims, describing her decision to create and manage a profitable New York call girl network

As a general matter, we [Americans] pride ourselves on our pioneering traditions. But outside the publicly funded defense area, we underinvest in research and development. Some high-priced managers seem to spend less time developing R&D budgets than they spend reviewing golf scores.

Richard G. Darman, director, Office of Management and Budget

KEY WORDS AND CONCEPTS

- Subsidiaries
- Affiliates
- Subsidiary detriment
- Information glut
- Geocentric
- Expatriate
- Allowances
- Bonuses
- International status

BUSINESS INCIDENT

Michel Thomas's foreign language centers in Beverly Hills and New York charge pupils up to $12,000 for 10 days' intensive instruction in French, German, or Spanish. Until recently, his star students were show business celebrities, such as Woody Allen, Ann-Margret, and Donald Sutherland. Today his best customers are executives from Boeing, Chase Manhattan, General Electric, Shearson Lehman Hutton, Westinghouse, and the like. Why the boom? "The answer's simple," says Thomas. "1992."

Source: "Le defi is back" *The Economist,* May 13, 1989, p. 70.

The planning that is the necessary foundation for all aspects of any successful business was dealt with in the preceding chapter. The control activities of which we shall speak here are the efforts to (1) put the plans into effect, (2) learn whether the plans are working as intended (they rarely do), and (3) make whatever corrections seem called for and practicable.

In Chapter 20, we discussed labor relations policies and practices of a worldwide company (WWC) with regard to the workers and their supervisors in the operation. To complete the picture, we must examine WWC policies and practices covering selecting, training, and compensating executive personnel.

The business incident illustrates one aspect of the training as managers rush to become proficient in other languages. The languages offered by Michel Thomas's schools are European, but becoming equally important for businesspeople are Asian languages, notably Chinese and Japanese.

CONTROL

Every successful company uses controls to put its plans into effect, evaluate their effectiveness, make desirable corrections, and evaluate and reward or correct executive performance. Matters are more complicated for an international company than for a one-country operation. In earlier chapters, we have brought out the complicating causes. They include different languages, cultures, and attitudes; different taxes and accounting methods; different currencies, labor costs, market sizes; different degrees of political stability and security for personnel and property; and many more. For these reasons, multinational companies need controls even more than do domestic ones.

Subsidiaries, 100 Percent Owned

subsidiary a company controlled by another company through ownership of enough voting stock to elect a board of directors majority

The words **subsidiaries** and **affiliates** are used interchangeably, and we shall examine first the control of those in which the parent has 100 percent ownership. This avoids for now the additional complications of joint ventures or subsidiaries in which the parent has less than 100 percent ownership. We shall deal with those later in the chapter.

Where Are Decisions Made?

affiliate sometimes used interchangeably with "subsidiary," but more forms exist than just stock ownership

There are three possibilities. Two of them are that all decisions are made at either the WWC headquarters or at the subsidiary level. Theoretically, all decisions could be made at one or the other location. As common sense would indicate, they are not; instead, some decisions are made at one place, some are made at the other place, and some are made cooperatively.[1] Many variables determine which decision is made where. Some of the more significant variables are (1) product and equipment, (2) the competence of subsidiary management and reliance on that management by the worldwide headquarters, (3) the size of the WWC and how long it has been one, (4) the detriment of a subsidiary for the benefit of the enterprise, and (5) subsidiary frustration.

Product and equipment.   As to decision location, questions of standardization of product and equipment and second markets can be important.

Standardize?   An easily made argument is that the product and the equipment with which to make it should be tailored to fit each national market. The other side is that overall enterprise gains from worldwide uniformity may more than compensate for individual country losses. Standardization of equipment may result in lower purchasing costs of the equipment as well as savings in equipment operation training, maintenance, and spare parts.[2]

As to the product, uniformity gives greater flexibility in its sourcing. For example, if the product is made in two or more countries and such difficulties as strikes, natural disasters, political upheavals, or currency problems affect one country, the product can be delivered from the other.

In determining whether equipment and product should be standardized worldwide or tailored to different national markets, a multinational should gather opinions from each affected subsidiary. If any subsidiary can demonstrate that the profit potential that can be realized from tailoring to its own market is greater than the profit potential that the enterprise will realize from standardization, the subsidiary should be permitted to proceed. Elements of profit potential would include the size of the subsidiary's market, the competition there, and the possibilities for exporting to areas with similar characteristics. Of course, the decision in such a case is cooperative in that the parent has the power to veto or override its subsidiary's decisions.

Second markets.   A product may be introduced by the parent company in its largest market, and by the time that product is offered in smaller markets, it may have been adapted to eliminate "bugs" or improve performance. The parent would want to ensure that the mistakes already discovered and corrected would not be repeated in later markets.[3] Even though some subsidiaries may wish to alter the product, second-market situations would indicate WWC central decision making. Such decision making would be necessary to ensure uniformity of quality and performance as well as market timing and product improvement.

Competence of subsidiary management and reliance on subsidiary management by parent headquarters.   Reliance on subsidiary management can depend on how well the executives know one another and how well they know company policies, on whether headquarters management feels that it understands host country conditions, on the distances between the home country and the host countries, and on how big and old the parent company is.

Move the executives around.   Some WWCs have a policy of transferring promising-looking management personnel between parent headquarters and subsidiaries and among subsidiaries. Thus, the manager learns firsthand the policies of headquarters and the problems of putting those policies into effect at subsidiary levels.[4]

A result of such transfers, which is difficult to measure but nevertheless important, is a network of intra-WWC personal relationships. This tends to increase the confidence of executives in one another and to make communication among executives easier and less subject to error.[5]

Another development is that some WWCs have moved their regional executives into headquarters. The reasons are to improve communications and reduce cost.[6]

Does parent headquarters understand host country conditions?   One element in the degree of headquarters' reliance on subsidiary management is the familiarity of headquarters with conditions in the subsidiary's host country. The less familiar or the more different conditions in the host country are perceived to be, the more likely headquarters is to rely on subsidiary management.

How far away is the host country?   Another element in the degree of headquarters' reliance on subsidiary management is the distance of the host country from home headquarters. Thus, an American parent is likely to place more reliance on the management of an Indonesian subsidiary than on the management of a Canadian subsidiary. This would be for two reasons: management conditions in Canada would be perceived by American management as more easily understood than conditions in Indonesia, and Indonesia is much farther from the United States than Canada is.[7]

Size of the WWC and how long it has been one.   As a rule, a large company can afford to hire more specialists, experts, and experienced executives than can a smaller one. The longer a company has been a WWC, the more likely it is to have a number of experienced executives who know company policies and who have worked at headquarters and in the field. Successful experience builds confidence.

In most WWCs, the top positions are at headquarters, and the ablest and most persistent executives get there in time. Thus, over time, headquarters of a successful company is run by experienced executives who are confident of their knowledge of the business in the home and host countries and in combinations thereof.

It follows that in the larger, older organizations, more decisions are made at headquarters and fewer are delegated to subsidiaries. The smaller company, in business for a shorter period of time, tends to be able to afford fewer internationally experienced executives and will not have had time to develop them internally. The smaller, newer company has no choice but to delegate decisions to subsidiary management.[8]

The generality that the larger, older WWCs delegate fewer decisions is subject to exceptions, and there seems to come a point in growth where the centralization trend reverses. Studies by Robbins and Stobaugh show that as WWCs become very large and complex, a tendency to decentralize appears. There come to be too many decisions for headquarters to deal with each one. At that point, the companies develop policies and guidelines for the subsidiaries. Headquarters reserves decision authority only for the most important matters and establishes processes to monitor the others.[9]

> **subsidiary detriments** a small loss for a subsidiary results in a greater gain for the total WWC

Decisions that may benefit the enterprise to the detriment of a subsidiary.   A WWC has opportunities to source raw materials and components, locate factories, allocate orders, and govern intraenterprise pricing that are not available to a non-WWC. Such activities may be beneficial to the enterprise yet result in **subsidiary detriments**.

Move production factors.   For any number of reasons, a WWC may decide to move factors of production from one country to another or to expand in one country in preference to another. Tax, labor, market, currency, or political stability are a few possible reasons.

The subsidiary from which factors are being taken would be unenthusiastic. Its management would be slow, at best, to cut the company's capacity. Such decisions would be made by headquarters.

Which subsidiary gets the order?   Similarly, if an order—say, from an Argentine customer—could be filled from a subsidiary in France or another in South Africa or a third in Brazil, parent headquarters might decide which subsidiary gets the business. Among the considerations in the decision would be transportation costs, production costs, comparative tariff rates, customers' currency restrictions, comparative order backlogs, and taxes. One reason for having such a decision made by WWC headquarters is that this would avoid price competition among members of the same multinational.

Multicountry production.   Frequently, the size of the market in a single country is too small to permit economies of scale in manufacturing an entire industrial product for that one market. An example is Ford's production of a light vehicle for the Asian market.

In that situation, Ford negotiated with several countries to the end that one country would make one component of the vehicle for all of the countries involved. Thus, one country makes the engine, a second country has the body-stamping plant, a third country makes the transmission, and so forth. In this fashion, each operation achieves the efficiency and cost savings of economies of scale.[10] Of course, this kind of multinational production demands a high degree of WWC headquarters' control and coordination.

Which subsidiary books the profit?   In certain circumstances, a multinational may have some choice of two or more countries in which to declare profits. Such circumstances may arise where two or more units of the WWC cooperate in supplying components or services under a contract with a customer unrelated to any part of the multinational. Under these conditions, there may be opportunities to allocate higher prices to one unit or subsidiary and lower prices to another within the global price to the customer.

If the host country of one of the subsidiaries has lower taxes than the other host countries, it would be natural to try to maximize profits in the lower-tax country and minimize them in the higher-tax country. Other differences between host countries could dictate the allocation of profit to or from the subsidiaries located there. Such differences could include currency controls, labor relations, political climate, or social unrest, and it is sensible to direct or allocate as much profit as reasonably possible to subsidiaries in countries with the least currency controls, the best labor relations and political climate, and the least social unrest.

The intraenterprise transaction may also give a company choices of profit location. Pricing between members of the same enterprise is referred to as transfer pricing and while WWC headquarters could permit undirected, arm's-length negotiations between itself and its subsidiaries, that might not yield the most advantageous results for the enterprise as a whole.[11]

Price and profit allocation decisions like these are usually best made at parent company headquarters, which is supposed to maintain the overall view, looking out for the best interests of the enterprise.[12] Naturally, decisions to accept lower profits are not gladly made by subsidiary management, largely because its evaluation may suffer. We shall discuss management evaluation further on in this chapter.

An illustration of how the enterprise might profit even though one subsidiary makes less is given in the following two tables. Assume a cooperative contract by which two subsidiaries are selling products and services to an outside customer for a contract price of $100 million. The host country of WWC Alpha levies company income taxes at the rate of 50 percent, whereas WWC Beta's host country taxes its income at 20 percent. The customer is in a third country, has agreed to pay $100 million, and is indifferent to how Alpha and Beta share the money. The first table below shows the multinational's after-tax income if Alpha is paid $60 million and Beta, $40 million.

	Receives (in $ millions)	Tax (in $ millions)	After Tax (in $ millions)
Alpha	$60	$30	$30
Beta	40	8	32
			$62

Thus, after tax, the enterprise realizes $62 million.

The second table shows the multinational's after-tax income if Alpha is paid $40 million and Beta, $60 million.

	Receives (in $ millions)	Tax (in $ millions)	After Tax (in $ millions)
Alpha	$40	$20	$20
Beta	60	12	48
			$68

Thus, after tax, the enterprise realizes $68 million.

These simple examples illustrate that the WWC would be $6 million better off if it could shift $20 million of the payment from Alpha to Beta, while the customer is no worse off, as it pays $100 million in either case. Alpha, having received $20 million less payment, is $10 million worse off after taxes, but Beta is $16 million better off and the enterprise if $6 million ahead on the same contract. Given the number of countries and tax laws in the world, there are countless combinations of how such savings can be accomplished. Financial management awareness and control are the keys.

We do not mean to leave the impression that the host or home governments are unaware of or indifferent to transfer pricing and profit allocating by WWCs operating within their borders. The companies must expect questioning by host and home governments and must be prepared to demonstrate that prices or allocations are "reasonable." This may be done by showing that other companies charge comparable prices for the same or similar items or, if there are no similar items, by showing that costs plus profit have been used reasonably to arrive at the price. As to allocation of profits, the WWC in our example would try to prove that the volume or importance of the work done by Beta or the responsibilities assumed by Beta, such as financing, after-sales service, or warranty obligations, justify the higher amount being paid to Beta. Of course, the questioning in this instance would come from the host government of Alpha if it got wind of the possibility of more taxable income for Beta and less for itself.

Subsidiary frustration.   An extremely important consideration for parent company management is that the management of its subsidiaries be motivated and loyal. If all the big decisions are made, or are perceived to be made, at the WWC headquarters, the managers of subsidiaries will lose incentive and will lose prestige or face with their employees and the community.[13] They may grow hostile and disloyal.

Therefore, even though there may be reasons for headquarters to make decisions, it should delegate as much as is reasonably possible. Management of each subsidiary should be kept thoroughly informed and should be consulted seriously about decisions, negotiations, and developments in its geographic area.

Joint Ventures and Subsidiaries Less than 100 Percent Owned

A joint venture may be, as defined in Chapter 2, a corporate entity between a WWC and local owners or a corporate entity between two or more companies that are foreign to the area where the joint venture is located, or it may involve one company working on a project of limited duration (constructing a dam, for example) in cooperation with one or more other companies. The other companies may be subsidiaries or affiliates, but they may also be entirely independent entities.

All the reasons for making decisions at WWC headquarters, at subsidiary headquarters, or cooperatively apply equally in joint venture situations. However, headquarters will almost never have as much freedom of action and flexibility in a joint venture as it has with subsidiaries that are 100 percent owned.

Loss of freedom and flexibility.   The reasons for that loss of freedom and flexibility are easy to see. If shareholders outside the multinational own control of the affiliate, they can block efforts of WWC headquarters to move production factors away, to fill an export order from another affiliate or subsidiary, and so forth. Even if outside shareholders are a minority and cannot directly control the affiliate, they can bring legal or political pressures on the WWC to prevent it from diminishing the affiliate's profitability for the enterprise's benefit. Likewise, the local partner in a joint venture is highly unlikely to agree with measures that penalize the joint venture for the WWC's benefit.

How the Japanese do it.   Japanese companies used the joint venture method abroad earlier and more extensively than did American or European companies. In attempting to control their joint ventures, the Japanese companies use several devices.

The Japanese partner provides and controls the technology and the management expertise. It furnishes key components and parts for the finished product. It tries to put its Japanese personnel into the important executive positions of the joint venture.[14]

As might be expected, the Japanese have encountered resistance to putting Japanese in the important executive positions from their joint venture partners or from host governments. The natural desire of these partners and governments is that their own nationals have at least equality in the important positions and that they get training and experience in the technology and management.[15]

Reporting

For controls to be effective, all operating units of a WWC must provide headquarters with timely, accurate, and complete reports. There are many uses for the information reported. Among the types of reporting required are (1) financial, (2) technological, (3) market opportunity, and (4) political and economic.

Financial.   A surplus of funds in one subsidiary should perhaps be retained there for investment or contingencies. On the other hand, such a surplus might be more useful at the parent company, in which case payment of a dividend is indicated. Or perhaps another subsidiary or affiliate needs capital, and the surplus could be lent or invested there. Obviously, parent headquarters must know the existence and size of a surplus to determine its best use.

Technological.   New technology should be reported. New technology is constantly being developed in different countries, and the subsidiary or affiliated company operating in such a country is likely to learn about it before WWC headquarters hundreds or thousands of miles away. If headquarters finds the new technology potentially valuable, it could gain competitive advantage by being the first to contact the developer for a license to use it.

One study indicates that most reports emphasize financial and market data. Technological information was in third place.[16]

Market opportunities.   The affiliates in various countries may spot new or growing markets for some product of the multinational. This could be profitable all around, as the WWC sells more of the product while the affiliate earns sales commissions. Of course, if the new market is sufficiently large, the affiliate may begin to assemble or produce the product under license from the parent company or from another affiliate.

Other market-related information that should be reported to WWC headquarters includes competitors' activities, price developments, and new products of potential interest to the WWC group. Also of importance is information on the subsidiary's market share and whether it is growing or shrinking, together with explanations.

Political and economic.   Interestingly, reports on political and economic conditions have not been found to be frequent.[17] This is probably changing as a result of the revolutions, terrorism, coups, and other political unrest of the 1970s and 80s. For example, the American bank, Citibank, had a representative office in Tehran, Iran, during the 1970s. Even though some government intelligence services were said to be surprised when the Ayatollah Khomeini threw out the shah of Iran in 1979, the Citibank Tehran office had become aware of potential danger as early as the summer of 1978. The office first lowered the ceiling on Iranian loans and then froze any new business, even to existing customers, in the autumn of 1978.[18]

Management Evaluation

One important use of reports is to evaluate and compare management performance in every unit of the multinational. The raw financial figures are not adequate for this, nor do they give a fair, comparative evaluation.

Parent headquarters' decisions may have awarded an export order to one subsidiary in preference to a second even though the second might have gotten the order if competition had been permitted. Through no skill or fault of theirs, management of the first subsidiary looks good in comparison with management of the second.

Or, in an intraenterprise transaction, a larger profit may be left in a low-tax country and a smaller profit in a high-tax country. This is done for the benefit of the enterprise, and management in the high-tax country should not be penalized in its comparative evaluation because it has been done.[19]

Efforts should be made to factor out of management evaluations conditions beyond management control. These conditions include price controls, currency controls, inflation, political upheaval, terrorism, and changes in currency exchange values.

Information Glut

information glut a situation in which more information has been gathered than can be intelligently or efficiently used

A large multinational, with many far-flung operating units, could find itself overwhelmed by reports. The solutions suggested for such an **information glut** have included centralized data banks at information centers. Information can be coded as to type and be available on call to management at WWC headquarters and at the subsidiaries.[20]

STAFFING

Finding the right people to manage an organization can be difficult under any circumstances, but it is especially difficult to find good managers of overseas operations. In a survey taken of 166 senior-level international executives, more than one third mentioned the shortage of qualified management personnel as an important problem. A computer manufacturer put it this way: "The shortage is so serious that more than anything else, this may slow our expansion in key markets."[21]

The difficulties in finding the right people for foreign management positions stem from the fact that such positions require more and different skills than do purely domestic executive jobs. The right persons need to be bicultural, with knowledge of the business practices in the home country plus understanding of business practices and customs in the host country. The successful manager of a foreign affiliate must be able to operate efficiently in one culture and to explain operations in that culture to executives in another culture. Such managers exist, and they may be found in (1) the home country, (2) the host country, or (3) a third country.

Sources of Managers

Home country.   Most multinationals utilize citizens of their own countries in many foreign management and technical positions even though at first such personnel are usually not knowledgeable about the host country culture and language. Many such expatriates have adapted, learned the language, and become thoroughly accepted in the host country. Of course, it would not be necessary for a host country citizen to undergo all of that adapting, but for a variety of reasons, WWC headquarters frequently needs or wants its own nationals in executive or technical positions abroad.

Host country nationals unavailable.   A foreign subsidiary often cannot find suitable host country personnel for management jobs, and in such instances, parent headquarters will send out its people to manage until local personnel can be found and trained. Those are full-time jobs, but other circumstances call for temporary help from headquarters. Labor negotiators, mentioned in Chapter 20, and other specialists may be sent to troubleshoot such problems as product warranty, international contracts, taxes, accounting, or reporting. Teams may be sent from the home country to assist with new plant start-up, and they would probably stay until subsidiary personnel were trained to run and maintain the new facilities.

Training for headquarters.   Another reason for using home country citizens abroad is to broaden their experience in preparation for becoming high-level managers at headquarters. Firms with large parts of their earnings from international sources require top executives who have a worldwide perspective, business and political.[22] It is difficult to impossible to acquire that sort of perspective without living and working abroad for a substantial time.

Headquarters' representatives.   Some firms, although their policy is to employ host country nationals in most positions, want at least one or two home country managers (commonly the general manager or the finance officer) in their foreign subsidiaries. If new technology for the subsidiary is involved, the parent company will probably station at least one of its technologically qualified experts at the subsidiary until its local personnel learn the technology. In this way, the home office can be confident that someone is immediately available to explain headquarters' policies and procedures, see that they are observed, and interpret what is happening locally to the WWC's management. Positions that a WWC must take or demands that it must make are sometimes not popular with a host government. It can seem unpatriotic for a host country national to do such things, whereas the host government can understand—and sometimes accept—such positions or demands from a foreigner who is a citizen of the parent company's home country.

> One of the authors remembers the relief expressed by the Argentinean executives of an Argentine subsidiary of an American WWC because an American manager was present to press the Argentine government for what seemed to be unusually extensive payment guarantees by the Argentine government. The contract was for a product partly manufactured and assembled in Argentina but mostly manufactured in the United States and imported into Argentina from the United States.

Host country.   When host country nationals are employed, there is no problem of their being unfamiliar with local customs, culture, and language. Furthermore, the first costs of employing them are generally lower (as compared to the costs of employing home country nationals), although considerable training costs are sometimes necessary. If there is a strong feeling of nationalism in the host country, having nationals as managers can make the subsidiary seem less foreign.

The government development plans and laws of some countries demand that employment in all sectors and at all levels reflect the racial composition of the society. In other words, more skilled and managerial slots must be given to the local people. If foreign-owned firms in Indonesia fail to hire enough *pribumi* (indigenous Indonesians), the firms are likely to encounter difficulties with reentry permits for foreign employees as well as with other government licenses and permits that the firms need. Bribery requests have been known to increase until more pribumi were hired and promoted. Malaysia threatens to revoke the operating licenses of foreign-owned firms that fail to have a satisfactory number of *bumiputra* (indigenous Malays) in sufficiently elevated jobs.[23]

A disadvantage of hiring local managers is that they are often unfamiliar with the home country of the WWC and with its policies and practices. Differences in attitudes and values, as discussed in Chapter 9, can cause them to act in ways that surprise or displease headquarters. Also, local managers may create their own upward immobility if, because of strong cultural or family ties, they are reluctant to accept promotions that would require them to leave the country to work at parent headquarters or at another subsidiary.

A new problem has developed for foreign-owned companies that hire and train local, host country people. The best of these people may be pirated away by local firms or other WWC subsidiaries, as local executive recruiters are constantly on the lookout to make raids.[24]

Finally, there can be a conflict of loyalty between the host country and the employer. For example, the host country national may give preference to a local supplier even though imported products may be less expensive or of better quality. Local managers might oppose headquarters' requests to set low transfer prices in order to lower taxes payable to the host government.

Third country.   The disadvantages often encountered when using employees from the home or host countries can sometimes be avoided by sending nationals from a third country to fill management posts. A Chilean going to Argentina would have little cultural or language difficulty, but WWC headquarters should be careful not to rely too heavily on similarities in language as a guide to similarities in other aspects of the cultures. Mexicans, for example, would have to make considerable adjustments if they were transferred to Argentina, and they would find a move to Spain even more difficult. This is because the Mexican culture is far less European than that of either Argentina or Chile. While the latter two cultures are certainly not identical, they do have many similarities. A fair generalization is that after an executive has adapted once to a new culture and language, a second or succeeding adaptation is easier.

An employer should not count on cost savings in using third-country nationals. Although they may come from countries where salary scales are lower, in such countries as Brazil and most of the nations of northwestern Europe, salaries may be higher than American companies are paying at comparable position levels. Furthermore, many multinationals give international status* to both home country nationals and third-country nationals,

---

*   International status is discussed later in this chapter.

who then receive the same perquisites and compensation packages for the same job.

Selection and Training

The selection and training of managers varies somewhat, depending on whether the candidate is from the home country, the host country, or a third country.

Home country. Relatively few recent college graduates are hired for the express purpose of being sent overseas. Usually they spend a number of years in the domestic (parent) company, and they may get into the company's international operations by design and persistence, by luck, or frequently by a combination. Those who make it into the international side may be assigned to the firm's international division, where they handle problems submitted by foreign affiliates and meet overseas personnel who are visiting WWC headquarters.

If it seems likely to the company that it will be sending home country employees abroad, the company frequently encourages those employees to study the language and culture of the country to which it expects to send them.[25] Such employees will probably be sent on short trips abroad to handle special assignments and to be exposed to foreign surroundings. Newly hired home country nationals with prior overseas experience may undergo similar but shorter training periods.

It is increasingly possible for American WWCs to supplement their in-house training for overseas work with courses in American business schools. In recognition of the growing importance of international business, those schools are expanding the number and scope of international business courses. In addition, a number of university-level business schools are now operating in other countries.[26]

One large problem that has plagued employers is caused by the families of executives transferred overseas. Even though the employee may adapt to and enjoy the foreign experience, the family may not, and an unhappy family may sour the employee on the job and split up the marriage. In either event, the company may have to ship the family back home at great expense—seldom less than $25,000. Consequently, many companies try to assess whether the executive's family can adapt to the foreign ambience before the executive is assigned abroad.

Host country. The same general criteria for selecting home country employees apply to host country nationals. Usually, however, the training of host country nationals will differ from that of home country nationals in that host country nationals generally lack knowledge of advanced business techniques and of the company.

Host country nationals hired in the home country. Many multinationals try to solve the business technique problem by hiring host country students on their graduation from home country business schools. After they have been hired, these new employees are usually sent to WWC headquarters to receive indoctrination in the firm's policies and procedures as well as on-the-job training in a specific function, such as finance, marketing, or production.

Host country nationals hired in the host country.   Because the number of host country citizens being graduated from home country universities is limited, multinationals must also recruit locally for their management positions. To impart knowledge of business technique, the company may do one or more things. It may set up in-house training programs in the host country subsidiary, or it may utilize business courses in the host country's universities. The WWC may also send new employees to home country business schools or to parent company training programs. In addition, employees who show promise will be sent repeatedly to the parent company headquarters and divisions and to other subsidiaries to observe the various enterprise operations and meet personally the other executives with whom they will be communicating during their careers. Such visits are also learning experiences for the home office and the other subsidiaries.

Third country.   Hiring personnel who are citizens of neither the home country nor the host country is often advantageous. Third-country nationals may accept lower wages and benefits than will employees from the home country, and they may come from a culture similar to that of the host country. In addition, they may have worked for another unit of the WWC and thus be familiar with its policies, procedures, and people.

The use of third-country nationals has become particularly prevalent in the LDCs because of shortages of literate, not to mention skilled, locals. It can be an advantage to get someone already residing in the country inasmuch as such an individual already has necessary work permits as well as knowledge of local languages and customs.

Host country attitudes.   If the host government is emphasizing employment of its own citizens, third-country nationals will be no more welcome than home country people. Actually, third-country nationals could face an additional obstacle in obtaining necessary work permits. For example, the host government can understand that the German parent company of a subsidiary would want some German executives to look after its interest in the host country. It may be harder to convince the government that a third-country native is any better for the parent than a local executive would be.

Generalizations difficult.   We must be careful with generalizations about third-country personnel, partly because people achieve that status in different ways. They may be foreigners hired in the home country and sent to a host country subsidiary either because they have had previous experience there or because that country's culture is similar to their own. Third-country nationals may have originally been home country personnel who were sent abroad and became dissatisfied with the job but not with the host country. After leaving the firm that sent them abroad, they take positions with subsidiaries of multinationals from different home countries. Another way in which third-country nationals can be created is by promotion within a WWC. For instance, if a Spanish executive of the Spanish subsidiary of an Italian multinational is promoted to be general manager of the Italian firm's Colombian subsidiary, the Spanish executive is then a third-country national.

geocentric   to hire and promote based on ability and experience without considering race or other factors

As multinationals increasingly take the **geocentric** view toward promoting (according to ability and not nationality), we can be certain to see greater use of third-country nationals. This development will be accelerated as more and

WORLDVIEW
Women and Foreign Postings

When Carla Hills was first nominated for her job as U.S. trade representative, some people had doubts.

Philip Grub, a George Washington University professor of multinational management, told a conference that among concerns about Hills herself, he questioned the cultural sensitivity of sending a woman to negotiate with the Japanese. Senator Steven Symms wondered whether she would appear as rigorous as the "tough men, warriors" who preceded her.

Such anxieties go to the heart of the debate over who should be doing America's business overseas. In choosing their emissaries, companies are often daunted by stories of submissive Asian wives, racist remarks by Japanese leaders, and laws barring Saudi women from driving. The result is that women and minorities, although making small gains, are even rarer among managers abroad than they are at home.

But the few women and minority executives who have worked overseas say many companies are clinging to false notions about other cultures. Although the executives acknowledge that hurdles exist, they say misguided attitudes leave companies unreasonably pessimistic about overcoming them.

"It's a classic case of projection," says Lennie Copeland, a producer at Copeland Griggs Productions, Inc., in San Francisco, which makes films on cultural issues in business. "The American company has a problem accepting women, so they assume it's going to be worse overseas."

Women account for only 5 percent of American expatriate managers, although many more are sent on brief assignments, according to a survey by Moran, Stahl & Boyer, Inc., a New York consulting firm. Of the companies polled, 80 percent said there were disadvantages to sending women overseas.

"Clients refuse to do business with female representatives," one company told Moran. Another explained: "The desired expatriate is a 30-ish married man with preschool-age children. This is to project our image as a conservative institution with good moral fiber. . . . Many of our potential female expatriates are single, and a swinging single is not the right image."

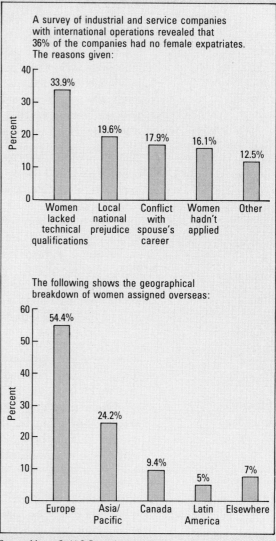

A survey of industrial and service companies with international operations revealed that 36% of the companies had no female expatriates. The reasons given:

Women lacked technical qualifications — 33.9%
Local national prejudice — 19.6%
Conflict with spouse's career — 17.9%
Women hadn't applied — 16.1%
Other — 12.5%

The following shows the geographical breakdown of women assigned overseas:

Europe — 54.4%
Asia/Pacific — 24.2%
Canada — 9.4%
Latin America — 5%
Elsewhere — 7%

Source: Moran, Stahl & Boyer, Inc.

Even some executives with international experience agree that there are practical limits. They cite Saudi Arabia and Pakistan, for example, as places where it doesn't make sense to send a woman.

But Stephen J. Kobrin, a professor of international management at the University of Pennsylvania's Wharton

School, contends that many cautionary arguments echo those once made by corporations against hiring women at home. "If you follow this to its logical conclusion," he says, "you're back in 1954."

Women executives who have worked abroad also complain that companies often fail to differentiate among nations in given parts of the world—ruling out, say, all of Asia for women. "People lump all those countries together," says Anna Ball, president of Ball Seed Company in West Chicago, Illinois. Ball adds that while she works comfortably in Japan, she finds South Korea and especially Taiwan much more accepting of business-women.

Conversely, many Americans assume England is the closest thing to home outside North America (the Moran survey showed that almost 24 percent of the female expatriates were posted there). But Americans find that many British men are uncomfortable with female managers.

Robert Petzinger, managing director of AT&T's international communications services in London, recently chose an American woman to head a sales force there. He says five of the men she will manage immediately let him know they thought he had "made the wrong choice." Petzinger adds that he has told the woman she faces a challenge.

Even where a culture puts several restraints on its own women, outsiders may be treated differently, notes Nancy Adler, associate professor at McGill University in Montreal. "You are seen as a foreigner first and then as a woman," she says. "The best predictor of success isn't how they treat their own women, but how they treat other Americans."

Pat Burns, director of industrial development for Madison Public Relations Group, Inc., in Washington, D.C., has been doing business in northern Africa and the Mideast since the mid-1970s. On one occasion in Sudan, she was invited into the home of a businessman, who brought her a cushion, served her food, and washed her arms with rose water after the meal—all things a man normally would never do for a woman. After the meeting,

Burns asked her local agent how the man could have violated accepted rules of conduct. "Oh, it's no problem," she recalls being told. "Women do not do business; therefore, you are not a woman."

Ironically, many women feel they have an advantage in business overseas for the same reason they have trouble in business at home: their different upbringing. Consultants say women are generally more patient than men and more interested in creating harmony and consensus.

"That's considered wimpy here," says Marlene L. Rossman, a New York marketing consultant, "and considered very appropriate overseas."

As companies address the "glass ceiling" problem at home, more are pushing the boundaries abroad as well. AT&T, for example, last year commissioned a 22-country study by Moran to evaluate how women are received in various places and what barriers they might face. A few of the findings are illustrative: Chinese businessmen seem less threatened by American women than by American men; there is less *machismo* in Argentina than in other Latin countries.

Daniel McCabe, manager of human resources for AT&T's international communications services, says he wanted to have a "defensible study behind us" when encouraging managers to send women farther afield.

Amid such efforts, though, one of the hardest parts of an overseas assignment for women remains: in showing respect and understanding for the local culture, they may have to tolerate attitudes they wouldn't brook at home. Burns says she has gone out of her way in the Mideast to express respect for a business partner's wife or daughter, or to praise women executives and officials. Still, she says, when a Saudi general recently invited her to visit and asked whether she minded using the women's entrance, she replied, "Not at all."

Source: Jolie Solomon, *The Wall Street Journal*, June 2, 1989, p. B1.

more executives of all nationalities gain experience outside their native lands. Another, and growing, source for third-country nationals is the heterogeneous body of international agencies. As indicated in Chapter 4, these agencies deal with virtually every field of human endeavor, and all member-countries send their nationals as representatives to the headquarters and branch office cities all over the world. Many of those people become available to, or can be hired away by, multinational companies.

Women

The subject of staffing the executive offices of modern American companies is not completely covered without a look at the growing role of women. About half of the students in American business schools are now women; they have moved into the managements of banks, businesses, and government agencies and have been at least as successful as their male counterparts. Old-girl networks are now in place alongside the old-boy networks, providing role models and helping younger female managers.

Most observers agree that these are positive developments for American management. They are developments, however, that cannot be transferred intact out of the United States to every other country of the world. As was indicated in Chapter 12, attitudes toward and treatment of women differ vastly from one culture or religion to another. A review of material in Chapter 12 could be helpful at this point.

Résumés Can Mislead

The résumés of most job applicants are probably reasonably accurate, although people are taught how to put their best foot forward and present themselves in the best light. Sometimes that light distorts reality.

The case of Friedrich von Braun was reported by the press in 1986. He was the managing director of Commodity Fundsters, a British company that was in financial difficulty.

Von Braun said that his claim to be the third son of a German baron was based on tales his mother had told him. He could not explain why he was brought up in Warrington, England, and was known to the locals as Fred.

His claims to have been educated at Eton were based on a one-day trip to Windsor in the summer of 1955; he said he had learned a lot about history at that time. He did spend two weeks at Oxford—in a squat on the Iffley Road.

As for his listed hobbies (opera and observing art), he admitted that his work had allowed him no time for either in the past 18 years.

He worked not for the famous banking firm Morgan Stanley, as listed in his résumé, but for Stanley Morgan, a Welsh farmer. His "brilliant" banking career was not with the American bank First Interstate but with a Panamanian financial company known to its liquidators as First Into Straits.

Von Braun said that his career details were misleading because of some "insignificant" typographical errors. He maintained that the mistakes were irrelevant to his ability to look after the interests of "wise" investors who entrusted their money to him.

People's Republic of China Different

An American banker sitting in his cramped hotel office in Beijing said, "Foreigners coming to China had better be prepared for the bleakness of Chinese life." China is an especially tough assignment for Western managers; for one thing, Western-style housing is unavailable, so most Western managers must spend their entire stays in a hotel room.

A study was made of the assets that a Westerner needed to succeed in China. Knowledge of Chinese business customs, negotiating style, and social practices was ranked as most important, but not much more so than Chinese language, politics, and culture.

One manager quoted in the study remarked on "a general sense of uncertainty" in his business dealings. He noted the "vagueness of the Chinese system. You think something will be a problem, and it's not, and vice versa." Another stressed that Westerners in China should understand that despite the recent economic reforms, "communism and the bureaucratic system are number one."[27]

Selection Do's and Don'ts

Executives who should know better sometimes assume that all nationalities work within a framework of common cultures and business practices. Instant communication of information, supersonic travel, and the emergence of international financial institutions have created a global economy.

Yet, this economic interdependence does not translate into a common "business culture." Business standards and practices reflect the cultures in which they are rooted. Their nuances very widely by continent, by country, and even by region.

An executive with no cross-cultural experience can, regardless of other professional credentials, unwittingly wreak havoc with corporate plans abroad. The ability of a company to succeed in another country rests heavily on the managers' abilities to function in that country's culture. An executive search firm has drawn up a checklist of do's and don'ts in selecting executives for foreign operations.

   Do promote from within. All other things being equal, selecting a known employee reduces risk. The employee knows the company and the company knows the employee's strengths and weaknesses. The weaknesses of a new person may not be evident at first.

   Don't promote an insider if the outsider is clearly better qualified. "John's been doing a good job in New York, and he's always liked London" is not good enough. It can be a costly approach.

   Don't be blinded by language fluency. Just because a candidate is fluent in the host country's language does not mean he or she is the best person for the job. Unless your business is the local Berlitz franchise, the candidate must have the requisite technical and managerial skills.

   Do assess the total person. Functional skills, language proficiency, and knowledge of the international business environment are all important. With regard to international business savvy, third-country nationals are sometimes better qualified than people born in the host country who have not lived and worked aboard. It has been noted that Scandinavians, Dutch, and Swiss are disproportionately represented in international business management positions. They come from small countries with limited markets, so their education and business experience have been geared to the outside world. As a group, these executives have an outlook that is more cosmopolitan than nationalistic.[28]

COMPENSATION

Establishing a compensation plan that is equitable, consistent, and yet does not overcompensate the overseas executive is a challenging, complex task. The method favored by the majority of American multinationals has been to pay a base salary equal to that paid to a domestic counterpart and then, in the belief that no one should be worse off for accepting foreign employment, to add a variety of allowances and bonuses.

Salaries

The practice of paying home country nationals the same salaries as their domestic counterparts are paid permits worldwide consistency for this part of the compensation package. Because of the increasing use of third-country nationals, those personnel are generally treated in the same way.

Some firms carry the equal-pay-for-equal-work concept one step further and pay the same base salaries to host country nationals. In countries that legislate yearly bonuses and family allowances for their citizens, a local national may receive what appears to be a higher salary than is paid the **expatriate,** although companies usually make extra payments to prevent expatriates from falling behind in this regard. In Great Britain, it is the practice to pay executives relatively lower salaries and to provide them with expensive perquisites, such as chauffeured automobiles, housing, or club memberships. A number of American companies follow British practices in compensating their executives working in Britain.

expatriate a person living outside of his or her country of citizenship

Allowances

Allowances are extra payments made to compensate expatriates for the extra overseas costs that they must incur to live as well abroad as they did in the home country. The most common allowances are housing, cost-of-living, tax differentials, education, and moving.

allowances employee compensation payments added to base salaries because of higher expenses encountered when living abroad

Housing allowances.   Housing allowances are designed to permit executives to live in houses as good as those they had at home. Typically, the firm will pay all of the rent that is in excess of 15 percent of the executive's salary.

Cost-of-living allowances.   Cost-of-living allowances are based on the differences in the prices paid for food, utilities, transportation, entertainment, clothing, personal services, and medical expenses overseas as compared to the prices paid for these items in the headquarters city. Many WWCs use the U.S. Department of State index, which is based on the cost of these items in Washington, D.C., but have found it is not altogether satisfactory. For one thing, critics claim this index is not adjusted often enough to account for either the rapid inflation in some countries or the changes in relative currency values. Another objection is that the index does not include many cities in which the

■ TABLE 22–1
BI's Executive Cost of
Living in Major Cities

Ranking/City	BI Index* (NY = 100) April 1988	BI Index* (NY = 100) Oct. 1988	Annual Inflation† (Percent increase from April 1987–April 1988)
1. Tokyo	221	190	3.24%
2. Osaka/Kobe	219	189	3.20
3. Tehran	192	174	13.00
4. Libreville	182	171	4.75
5. Brazzaville	168	172	13.80
6. Lome	154	133	24.00
7. Oslo	152	139	9.50
8. Abidjan	151	142	8.60
9. Dakar	143	134	5.00
Zurich	143	128	3.90
10. Geneva	141	127	3.50
11. Helsinki	140	127	5.87
12. Taipei	137	130	4.50
13. Copenhagen	135	119	8.50
14. Vienna	133	122	4.20
15. Munich	126	113	3.70
16. Hamburg	125	113	3.50
Paris	125	113	4.40
17. London	123	108	5.20
Stockholm	123	110	8.40
18. Dublin	122	—	5.40
19. Berlin	121	—	3.00
20. Tel Aviv	120	107	25.00

Notes: *The weighted index is based on the following items: shopping basket of food items, alcoholic beverages, household supplies, personal care items, tobacco, utilities, clothing, domestic help, recreation, entertainment, and transportation.
†This annual inflation indicator is based solely on the price movements of the items included in the BI Index and should be considered to be "Inflation for Executive Living Costs" as it takes into account the purchasing habits of this particular group.
Source: Business International, July 11, 1988, p. 215.

firm operates. As a result, many companies take their own surveys or use data from the United Nations, the World Bank, the International Monetary Fund, or private consulting firms. Figures and comparisons on costs of living, prices, and wages can also be found in private publications. (See Table 22–1.)

Allowances for tax differentials.   WWCs pay tax differentials when the host country taxes are higher than the taxes that the expatriates would pay on the same base salary at home. The objective is to ensure that expatriates will not have less after-tax take-home pay in the host country than they would at home. This can create a considerable extra financial burden on an American parent company because, among other things, the U.S. Internal Revenue Code treats tax allowances as additional taxable income. There are other tax disincentives for Americans to work abroad.*

* For more on this subject and other effects of U.S. tax laws on American WWCs, see the taxation section of Chapter 11.

Education allowances.   Expatriates are naturally concerned that their children receive educations at least equal to those they would get in their home countries, and many want their children taught in their native language. Primary and secondary schools with teachers from most industrialized home countries are available in many cities around the world, but these are private schools and therefore charge tuition. Multinationals either pay the tuition or, if there are enough expatriate children, will operate their own schools. For decades, petroleum companies in the Mideast and in Venezuela have maintained schools for their employees' children.

Moving and orientation allowances.   Companies generally pay the total costs of transferring their employees overseas. These include transportation for the family, moving household effects, and maintaining the family in a hotel on a full expense account until the household effects arrive. Some firms find it less expensive to send the household effects by air rather than by ship because the reduction in hotel expenses more than compensates for the higher cost of airfreight. It has also been found that moving into a house sooner raises the employee's morale.

Companies may also pay for some orientation of the employees and their families. Companies frequently pay for language instruction, and some will provide the family with guidance on the intricacies of everyday living, such as shopping, hiring domestic help, and sending children to school.

Bonuses

bonuses expatriate employee compensation payments in addition to base salaries and allowances because of hardship, inconvenience, or danger

Bonuses (or premiums), unlike allowances, are paid by the firm in recognition that expatriates and their families undergo some hardships and inconveniences and make sacrifices while living abroad. Bonuses include overseas premiums, contract termination payments, and home leave reimbursement.

Overseas premiums.   Overseas premiums are additional payments to the expatriates and are generally established as a percentage of the base salary. They range from 10 to 25 percent. If the living conditions are extremely disagreeable, the company may pay larger premiums for hardship posts.

Contract termination payments.   These payments are made as inducements for employees to stay on their jobs and work out the periods of their overseas contracts. The payments are made at the end of the contract periods only if the employees have worked out their contracts. Such bonuses are used in the construction and petroleum industries or by other firms that have contracts requiring work abroad for a specific period of time or for a specific project. They may also be used if the foreign post is a hardship or not a particularly desirable one.

Home leave.[29]   Multinationals that post home country—and sometimes third-country—nationals in foreign countries make it a practice to pay for periodic trips back to the home country made by such employees and their families. The reasons for this are twofold. One reason is that the companies do not want the employees and their families to lose touch with the home country and its culture. The other reason is that the companies want to have the employees spend at least a few days at company headquarters to renew relationships with headquarters' personnel and to catch up with new company policies and practices.

Some firms grant three-month home leaves after an employee has been abroad about three years, but it is probably a more common practice to give two to four weeks' leave each year. All transportation costs are paid to and from the executive's hometown, and all expenses are paid during the executive's stay at company headquarters.

Compensation Packages Can Be Complicated

One might think from the discussion to this point that compensation packages, while costly—the "extras" may total 50 percent or more of the base salary—are fairly straightforward in their calculation. Nothing could be further from the truth.

What percentage?   All allowances and a percentage of the base salary are usually paid in the host country currency. What should this percentage be? In practice, it varies from 65 to 75 percent, with the remainder being banked wherever the employee wishes. One reason for these practices is to decrease the local portion of the salary, thereby lowering host country income taxes and giving the appearance to government authorities and local employees that there is less difference between the salaries of local and foreign employees than is actually the case. Another reason is that expatriate employees have various expenses that must be paid in home country currency. Such expenses include professional society memberships, purchases during home leave, or tuition and other costs for children in home country universities.

What exchange rate?   Inasmuch as most of the expatriate's compensation is usually denominated in the host country currency but is usually established in terms of the home country currency to achieve comparable compensation throughout the enterprise, a currency exchange rate must be chosen. In countries whose currencies are freely convertible into other currencies, this presents no serious problem, although the experienced expatriate will argue that an exchange rate covers only international transactions and may not present a true purchasing power parity between the local and home country currencies. For instance, such items as bread and milk are rarely traded internationally, and living costs as well as inflation rates may be much higher in the host country than in the home country. Multinationals attempt to compensate for such differences in the cost-of-living allowances.

More difficult problems must be solved in countries that have exchange controls and nonconvertible currencies. Without exception, those currencies are overvalued at the official rate, and if the firm uses that rate, the expatriate employees are certain to be shortchanged. Reference may be made to the free market rate for the host country currency in free currency markets in, for example, the United States or Switzerland or to the black market rate in the host country, but these do not give the final answers. In the end, all companies must pay their expatriate employees enough to enable them to live as well as others who have similar positions in other firms, regardless of how the amount is calculated.

Compensation of Third-Country Nationals

Although some companies have different compensation plans for third-country nationals, there is a trend toward treating third-country nationals the same as home country expatriates. In either event, there are areas in which problems can arise. One of these areas is the calculation of income tax differentials when

We offer executives

a much better position.

After those other airlines' San Francisco-to-Tokyo flights, you can be left feeling so bent out of shape that you half expect to be dumped off on the baggage carousel!

Not when you fly Philippine Airlines' new nonstops to Tokyo. Beginning August 2.

We offer First Class passengers the only beds between San Francisco and Tokyo. Honest-to-goodness, full-length beds! 14 of them. Tucked quietly upstairs on our 747's where no one will disturb you — even during take-offs and landings.

So catch our new nonstops to Tokyo; catch our First Class, 5-star service from your seat downstairs; then catch all the sleep you need in your very own Skybed upstairs.

And arrive in Tokyo feeling like a million. Not like excess baggage.

Philippine Airlines now to Tokyo.

an American expatriate is compared with an expatriate from another country. This results from the unique American government practices of taxing U.S. citizens even though they live and work abroad and of treating tax differential payments made to those citizens as additional taxable income. No other major country taxes its nationals in those ways.

Another possible problem area is the home leave bonus. The two purposes of home leave are to prevent expatriates from losing touch with their native cultures and to have them visit WWC headquarters. A third-country national must visit two countries instead of only one to achieve both purposes, and the additional costs can be substantial. Compare the cost of sending an Australian employee home from Mexico with that required to send an American from Mexico to Dallas.

International Status

international status enti-
tles the expatriate employee
to all the allowances and
bonuses applicable to the
place of residence and employment

In all of this discussion, we have been describing compensation for expatriates who have been granted **international status**. Merely being from another country does not automatically qualify an employee for all of the benefits we have mentioned. A subsidiary may hire home country nationals or third-country nationals and pay them the same as it pays host country employees. However, managements have found that although an American, for example, may agree initially to take a job and be paid on the local scale, sooner or later bad feeling and friction will develop as that person sees fellow Americans enjoying international status perquisites to which he or she is not entitled.

Another use for international status is to promote host country employees to that status even without transferring them abroad. This is a means of rewarding valuable people and of preventing them from leaving the company for better jobs elsewhere.

So international status means being paid some or all the allowances and bonuses we have discussed, and there can be other sorts of payments as individual circumstances and people's imaginations combine to create them. The Philippine Airlines ad shows two sleeping men. The one in the bottom picture is clearly the one with international status. The executives' compensation package is sufficiently important and complicated to have become a specialization in the personnel management field; at one firm, the title is "International Employee Benefits Consultant."[30]

Help is becoming available from outside the WWC. For one example, Ernst & Young publish an International Series, pamphlets advising about transfer to specific countries.[31] Some comparisons of white-collar pay in various countries can be seen in Figure 22–1.

Perks

These originated in the perquisites of the medieval lords of the manor, whose workers paid parts of their profits or produce to the lords to be allowed to continue working. Today, perks are symbols of rank in the corporate hierarchy and are used to compensate executives while minimizing taxes. Among the most common perks are

Cars, which higher up the organization ladder come with chauffeurs.

Private pension plan.

Retirement payment.

Life insurance.

Health insurance.

Company house or apartment.

■ **FIGURE 22–1 Executive Pay**

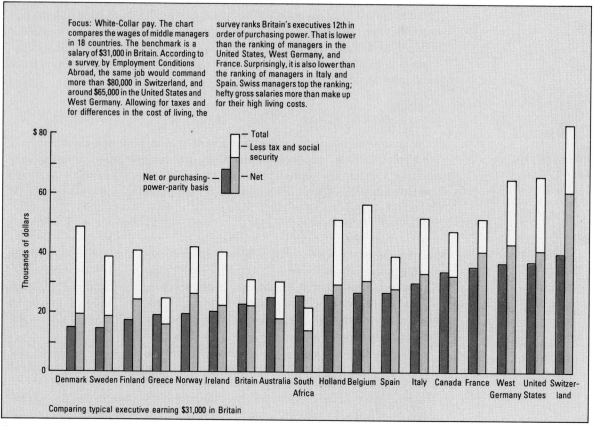

Focus: White-Collar pay. The chart compares the wages of middle managers in 18 countries. The benchmark is a salary of $31,000 in Britain. According to a survey by Employment Conditions Abroad, the same job would command more than $80,000 in Switzerland, and around $65,000 in the United States and West Germany. Allowing for taxes and for differences in the cost of living, the survey ranks Britain's executives 12th in order of purchasing power. That is lower than the ranking of managers in the United States, West Germany, and France. Surprisingly, it is also lower than the ranking of managers in Italy and Spain. Swiss managers top the ranking; hefty gross salaries more than make up for their high living costs.

Comparing typical executive earning $31,000 in Britain

Source: *The Economist,* September 27, 1988, p. 111. Based on information from Employment Conditions Abroad, Ltd.

Directorship of a foreign subsidiary.

Seminar holiday travel.

Club memberships.

Hidden slush fund (such funds are illegal, but some corporations are said to have them).

What's Important to You?

While working abroad as an executive of an American multinational, one of the authors had a colleague who was an American expatriate married to a French woman. They had raised a family in several countries where they had been assigned by the company. Together with some other cosmopolites, they devised a table of items deemed important to at least one of them in choosing a city for location of a company facility that employs foreigners.

The list included the usual items, such as cost of living, safety of personnel, medical facilities, housing, and schools. It also included such other items as availability of good wine at reasonable prices, quality of theater and whether it was live or cinema, number and type of one-star or better (*Michelin Guide*)* restaurants, type and accessibility of sports facilities for both participants and viewers, and shopping facilities for fashionable clothes.

The table of items was circulated informally throughout the multinational's many locations, and many cities in its network were graded as to each item on a 1-to-10 scale. When the New York headquarters saw the table, there was much mirth and merriment; suggestions—perhaps not all of them serious—were made as to additional items about which they would like information when they visited the cities.

However, the mirth and merriment subsided as more and more executives being assigned or reassigned abroad used the table to demand better compensation packages. Some even refused transfers because of the ratings given a city.

* *The Michelin Guide* rates restaurants and hotels in France and neighboring countries.

SUMMARY

Intraenterprise controls must be effective if a WWC is to maximize success and minimize problems. Such controls include guidelines as to where decisions will be made, which may be at the parent company level, at the subsidiary company level, or cooperatively at both levels. Among the factors that affect intraenterprise controls are product and equipment introduction, improvement, and standardization; the competence of subsidiary management; the distance of the host country from the home country and the differences in their cultures; and the size of the WWC and how long it has operated multinationally. Guidelines as to where decisions will be made are affected by circumstances in which some detriment to a subsidiary will result in greater benefit for the enterprise as a whole. Such detriment/benefit situations arise in intraenterprise transactions wherein profit can be maximized in lower-tax countries and minimized in higher-tax countries or tariffs can be minimized by intraenterprise transfer price decisions. Also, where a customer order can be filled by more than one unit of a WWC, having the parent decide which unit gets the order can avoid intraenterprise competition and can ensure that such considerations as order backlogs, labor problems, and comparative tariffs are taken into account.

It is easier for a parent company to exercise control over a subsidiary if it owns 100 percent of the subsidiary than if it owns less than 100 percent. And control of a joint venture with a separate entity in which the parent company has no ownership is more difficult than control of a subsidiary in which it has less than 100 percent

ownership. In such instances, control is sought through control of the capital and technology as well as by holding strategic joint venture executive positions.

For controls to work, all operating WWC units must provide headquarters with timely, accurate, and complete reports. These reports should cover such subjects as finance, technology, market opportunities, new products, competitor activities, price changes, market share, and political and economic information.

A very important use of reports is as a means for evaluating and comparing management performance. For this purpose, the raw figures are inadequate and may be misleading. The parent company must factor in such elements as decisions it made that penalized one subsidiary while benefiting another and conditions beyond the subsidiary management's control, such as inflation or political instability.

It is difficult to locate effective executives for multinational operations. Two or more cultures are involved, and usually two or more languages. The WWC may find employees in its home country, the host country, or elsewhere, and the nationalities of those employees may be home country, host country, or third country. The types of training that employees should receive and the adaptation that they should undergo depend on their nationality and previous experience. The home country national needs to learn about the host country culture and language, while the opposite is true of the host country national. Frequently, third-country nationals are hired because they have experience with both—and sometimes other—cultures and languages.

WWC headquarters often sends specialists to assist foreign subsidiaries with problems that have multinational ramifications, such as taxes, labor, or product sales contracts. In addition, headquarters usually likes to have one or two of its nationals in such key positions as general manager or financial manager.

Moving employees from country to country among subsidiaries and the WWC home operations can develop and mature those employees and provide learning experiences for the subsidiaries and home operations. Such moves can be for temporary duty or longer-term assignments. One result desired from such moves is the formation of personal relationships among WWC personnel that will facilitate intraenterprise communication and understanding.

Company loyalties and nationalistic attitudes must be taken into account. Host country employees may place host country interests above those of the company and may be reluctant to press their governments for unpopular concessions even though the company would benefit. However, all countries have rules and limitations on the number of foreign employees who can be brought in.

Most executives sent from their home countries take families, and the difficulties of cultural and linguistic adaptations may be more severe for the families than for the executives. Most companies now make efforts to evaluate whether the families can and will adapt before sending executives abroad. Failure to adapt causes broken families, poor employee morale, and expensive relocation of families back to the home countries.

Expatriate employees are generally paid the same basic salary as their domestic counterparts. However, additional expenses and hardships are frequently encountered abroad, and the expatriates receive additional payments in the forms of allowances and bonuses or premiums. Among the allowances commonly given are those for housing, cost of living, tax differentials, schooling, moving, and orientation. The bonuses include overseas premiums and contract termination payments, which are used if living conditions are difficult or if a specific term or project must be completed. Another bonus is home leave for employees and families, whose purpose is to prevent expatriates from losing touch with their native cultures and to permit them to visit WWC headquarters at least periodically.

Compensation packages for expatriates are complicated because there are so many variables to consider. In addition to home country salary levels, the types and levels of compensation of equivalent executives in the host country must be considered. Comparative taxes, costs of living, and inflation rates must be factored in, as must difficulties of living conditions. An additional set of complications can arise from the currencies utilized, because although some currencies are freely convertible, most are not, and currencies fluctuate in value in terms of each other.

The expatriate who is paid some or all of the bonuses and allowances we have discussed is said to be on international status. From time to time, firms will promote subsidiary host country nationals to international status. Their motives for doing so may be to reward such employees for meritorious service or to keep them from leaving to work for a competitor.

Women are moving in increasing numbers onto and up corporate executive ladders. With regard to assignment and promotion abroad, they are encountering the same obstacles and glass ceilings they meet at home, although the excuses for not sending and promoting women abroad are sometimes different. The excuses are variations of the theme that the host country cultures do not accept women executives. Nevertheless, women are overcoming the obstacles and moving up.

QUESTIONS

1. In determining whether decisions will be made by the parent company or by its subsidiaries, what are the considerations when equipment and products are standardized worldwide rather than tailored to individual national circumstances and markets?

2. *a.* In a WWC, what are some decisions that could result in detriment for a subsidiary but greater benefit for the enterprise?
   b. In such circumstances, where will the decision be made—at WWC headquarters or at the affected subsidiary?

3. What measures can be utilized to control subsidiaries that are less than 100 percent owned by the firm or joint venture partners in which the firm has no ownership?

4. What are the roles of reporting in multinational controls?

5. *a.* When subsidiaries report net profits, must parent management look behind the reported numbers to evaluate subsidiary managements fairly?
   b. Why?

6. When staffing a multinational organization for service outside the WWC home country, what are some advantages and disadvantages of hiring home country personnel?

7. Why has there been an increasing use of third-country nationals in the foreign operations of WWCs?

8. Why are expatriate employees frequently paid more than their colleagues at equivalent job levels in the home office?

9. Why are compensation packages for expatriates more complicated than those for domestic employees?

10. What is international status? Who gets it? Why?

11. Women executives face obstacles to assignment and promotion both in the home country and in host countries. What additional obstacle applies to the latter?

MINICASE 22-1

Female Executives in International Business

For a number of reasons, women are being hired and promoted as executives by American business. The United States is almost alone in this development. Some Western European countries are moving slowly toward more female executive development, but elsewhere in the world, notably Latin American, Africa, Asia, and Eastern Europe, women are given very few executive opportunities.

Suppose you are the chief executive officer (CEO) of an American multinational. On your staff and in the U.S. operating divisions of your company are several bright, able, dedicated female executives. They are also ambitious, and in your company, international experience is a must before an executive can hope to get into top management.

An opening comes up for the position of executive vice president in the company's Mexican subsidiary. One of the women on your staff applies for the position, and she is well qualified for the job, better than anyone else in the company. Would you give her the position? What are the arguments pro and con?

Another position becomes available, this one as treasurer of the Japanese subsidiary. The chief financial officer of the company's California division applies for this job. She has performed to everyone's satisfaction, and she seems thoroughly qualified to become the treasurer in Japan. In addition, she speaks and writes Japanese. She is the daughter of a Japanese mother and an American father, and they encouraged her to become fluent in both English and Japanese.

Would you give her the job? Why or why not?

SUPPLEMENTARY READINGS

Adler, Nancy J. "A Typology of Management Studies Involving Culture." *Journal of International Business Studies,* Fall 1983, pp. 29–48.

Bacchus, I. William. "Staffing for Foreign Affairs: A Personnel System." *Public Personnel Management,* Fall 1985, pp. 315–30.

Dymsza, William A., and Anant R. Negandhi. "Introduction to Cross-Cultural Management Issue." *Journal of International Business Studies,* Fall 1983, pp. 15–16.

Gates, Stephen R., and William G. Egelhoff. "Centralization in Headquarters–Subsidiary Relationships." *Journal of International Business Studies,* Summer 1986, pp. 71–92.

Guisinger, S. E., and associates. *Investment Incentives and Performance Requirements.* New York: Praeger Publishers, 1985.

Harvey, Michael C. "The Other Side of Foreign Assignments: Dealing with the Repatriation Dilemma." *Columbia Journal of World Business,* Spring 1982, pp. 53–59.

Hill, Ray. "Women-Owned Companies Finally Start Making Their Mark." *International Management,* May 1986, p. 66.

Kale, S. H., and D. Sudharshan. "A Strategic Approach to International Segmentation." *International Marketing Review* 5, Summer 1987, pp. 60–70.

Lecraw, J. D. "Performance of Transnational Corporations in Less Developed Countries." *Journal of International Business Studies* 14, Spring/Summer 1983, pp. 15–33.

Murray, Robin, ed. *Multinationals beyond the Market: Intra-Firm Trade and the Control of Transfer Pricing.* New York: John Wiley & Sons, 1981.

Packard, P., and J. Slater. "Staff Appraisal: A First Step to Effective Leaders." *Journal of Occupational Psychology,* September 1985, p. 261.

Tomoda, Shizna. "Measuring Female Labor Activities in Asian Developing Countries: A Time Allocation Approach." *International Labor Review,* November–December 1985, p. 661.

Turbeyz, Peggy. "International Organization Helps Women Overcome Barriers to Obtaining Credit." *American Banker,* September 6, 1985, p. 16.

Weigand, L. T. "Social Cost/Benefit Analysis for MNCs." *Harvard Business Review,* July–August 1983, pp. 146–52.

ENDNOTES

1. David P. Rutenberg, "Organizational Archetypes of a Multinational Company," *Management Science,* February 1970, pp. B337–49.

2. Richard N. Farmer and Barry M. Richman, *International Business,* 3rd ed. (Bloomington, Ind.: Cedarwood Press, 1980), chap. 12.

3. Warren J. Keegan, "Multinational Marketing Control," *Journal of International Business Studies,* Fall 1972, pp. 34–47.

4. Ulrich Weichmann, "Integrating Multinational Marketing Activities," *Columbia Journal of World Business,* Winter 1974, pp. 13–14.

5. William K. Brandt and James M. Hulbert, "Patterns of Communications in the Multinational Corporation: An Empirical Study," *Journal of International Business Studies,* Spring 1976, pp. 17–30.

6. *Business International,* July 30, 1976, p. 247.

7. Jacques Picard, "How European Companies Control Marketing Decisions Abroad," *Columbia Journal of World Business,* Summer 1977, pp. 113–21.

8. R. J. Aylmer, "Who Makes Marketing Decisions in the Multinational Firm?" *Journal of Marketing,* October 1970, pp. 27–29.

9. Sidney M. Robbins and Robert B. Stobaugh, *Money in the Multinational Enterprise* (New York: Basic Books, 1973), pp. 140–51.

10. Farmer and Richman, *International Business,* pp. 285–86.

11. James M. Fremgren, "Transfer Pricing and Management Goals," *Management Accounting,* December 1970, pp. 25–31.

12. Itzhak Sharov, "Transfer Pricing: Diversity of Goals and Practice," *Journal of Accountancy,* April 1974, pp. 56–62.

13. James Shulman, "When the Price Is Wrong—by Design," *Columbia Journal of World Business,* May–June 1967, p. 74.

14. Stefan H. Robock and Kenneth Simmonds, *International Business and Multinational Enterprises,* 4th ed. (Homewood, Ill.: Richard D. Irwin, 1989), pp. 526–28.

15. Wendell H. McCulloch, Jr., "Japan's Trade and Investment with the Less-Developed Countries," *The Wall Street Journal,* October 3, 1980, p. 19.

16. Hans Schollhammer, "Organization Structures of Multinational Corporations," *Academy of Management Journal,* September 1971, pp. 360–63.

17. Millard H. Pryor, Jr., "Planning in a Worldwide Business," *Harvard Business Review,* January–February 1965, pp. 131–32.

18. Richard F. Janssen, "U.S. Lenders Taking New Looks at Risks from Political, Social Upheavals Abroad," *The Wall Street Journal,* March 13, 1979, p. 7.

19. V. Mauriel, "Evaluation and Control of Overseas Operations," *Management Accounting,* May 1969, pp. 35–39.

20. Leland M. Wooton, "The Emergence of Multinational Information Centers," *Management International Review,* Winter 1977, pp. 21–23.

21. Michael G. Duerr and James Greene, *The Problems Facing International Management* (New York: Conference Board, 1968), p. 25.

22. Farmer and Richman, *International Business,* chap. 10.

23. *Business International,* July 2, 1983, pp. 209, 211.

24. *Business International,* July 22, 1983, pp. 228–29.

25. One study of U.S.-based WWCs showed that about one half required some language training. Burton W. Teague, *Selecting and Orienting Staff for Service Overseas* (New York: Conference Board, 1976), p. 16.

26. Shawn Tully, "Europe: Best Business Schools," *Fortune,* May 23, 1988, pp. 106–10.

27. John Frankenstein, "Training Experts to Manage in China," *The Asian Wall Street Journal,* August 26, 1985, p. 17.

28. Fortunat F. Mueller-Maerkl, "Do's and Don'ts in Selecting Managers for Foreign Operations," in *U.S.-German Economic Survey* (New York: German/American Chamber of Commerce, 1984), pp. 123–25.

29. Some writers regard paid home leave as an allowance, but our experience convinces us that it is a premium, because WWCs consistently give more frequent or longer home leaves to employees working in less desirable assignments.

30. G. W. Hallmark and Charles W. Rogers III, "The Challenge of Providing Benefit and Compensation Programs for Third-Country Nationals," in *The International Essays for Business Decision Makers,* vol. 3, ed. Mark W. Winchester (New York: AMACOM for the Center for International Business, 1978).

31. *Handbook for Employees Transferring to France,* Ernst & Whinney, International Series, March 1980; *to the United States,* March 1980; *to Belgium,* April 1980; *to the United Kingdom,* April 1980; *to Italy,* June 1980; *to Hong Kong,* October 1980; *to Luxembourg,* October 1980, *to Denmark,* October 1980; *Abroad,* November 1980; and more. They are updated periodically.

Chapter 23

Trends and New Directions

The old model of the multinational enterprise has become obsolete.

> Kenichi Ohmae, director,
> McKinsey & Co., Tokyo office

There is a joke about buying a huge ship, equipping it with the CAD–CAM automated production capability, and dropping anchor on the shore of whatever country at the moment offers the best currency exchange opportunity.

> Gerrit Jeelof, vice chairman,
> N.V. Philips
> Gloeilampenfabrieken

It can bring jobs and development to China or anyplace else it locates. And, if a government pushes it around, it can move its computer-aided manufacturing elsewhere. Its real assets are its brains and its access to world money markets.

> Patrick Wang, managing director,
> Johnson Electric Industrial Manufactory, Ltd.

LEARNING OBJECTIVES

In this chapter, you will study:

1. A day in the life of tomorrow's manager.
2. Changes in multinationals' home countries.
3. Changing attitudes toward multinationals.
4. Meanings of globalization.
5. Growing flexibility and versatility of production.
6. American free trade area agreements (FTAs).
7. FTAs, EC 1992, and GATT.
8. How political developments affect business.

A DAY IN THE LIFE OF TOMORROW'S MANAGER: HE OR SHE FACES A MORE DIVERSE, QUICKER MARKET

6:10 A.M. The year is 2010, and another Monday morning has begun for Peter Smith. The marketing vice president for a home-appliance division of a major U.S. manufacturer is awakened by his computer alarm. He saunters to his terminal to check the weather outlook in Madrid, where he'll fly late tonight, and to send an electronic-voice message to a supplier in Thailand.

Meet the manager of the future.

A different breed from his contemporary counterpart, our fictitious Peter Smith inhabits an international business world shaped by competition, collaboration, and corporate diversity. (For one thing, he's just as likely to be a woman as a man and—with the profound demographic changes ahead—will probably manage a work force comprising mostly women and minorities.)

Comfortable with technology, he's been logging on to computers since he was seven years old. A literature honors student with a joint M.B.A./advanced-communications degree, the 38-year-old joined his current employer four years ago after stints at two other corporations—one abroad—and a marketing consulting firm. Now he oversees offices in a score of countries on four continents.

Tomorrow's manager "will have to know how to operate in an anytime, anyplace universe," says Stanley Davis, a management consultant and author of "Future Perfect," a look at the 21st-century business world.

Adds James Maxmin, chief executive of London-based Thorn EMI PLC's home-electronics division, "We've all come to accept that organizations and managers who aren't cost-conscious and productive won't survive. But in the future, we'll also have to be more flexible, responsive, and smarter. Managers will have to be nurturers and teachers, instead of policemen and watchdogs."

7:20 A.M. Smith and his wife, who heads her own architectural firm, organize the home front before darting to the supertrain. They leave instructions for their personal computer to call the home-cleaning service as well as a gourmet carryout service, which will prepare dinner for eight guests Saturday. And they quickly go over the day's schedules for their three- and six-year-old daughters with their nanny.

On the train during a speedy 20-minute commute from suburb to Manhattan, Smith checks his electronic mailbox and also reads his favorite trade magazine via his laptop computer.

The jury is still out on how dual-career couples will juggle high-pressure work and personal lives. Some consultants and executives predict that the frenetic pace will only quicken. "I joke to managers now that we come in on London time and leave on Tokyo time," says Anthony Terracciano, president of Mellon Bank Corp. in Pittsburgh. He foresees an even more difficult work schedule ahead.

But others believe more creative uses of flexible schedules, as well as technological advances in communications and travel, will allow more balance. "In the past, nobody cared if your staff had heart attacks; but in tomorrow's knowledge-based economy, we'll be judged more on how well we take care of people," contends Robert Kelley, a professor at Carnegie Mellon University's business school.

8:15 A.M. In his high-tech office, which doubles as a conference room, Smith reviews the day's schedule with his executive assistant (traditional secretaries vanished a decade earlier). Then, it's on to his first meeting: a conference via videoscreen between his division's chief production manager in Cincinnati and a supplier near Munich.

The supplier tells them she can deliver a critical component for a new appliance at a 10 percent cost saving if they grab it within a week. Smith and the production manager quickly concur that it's a good deal. Although they'll have to immediately change production schedules, they'll be able to snare a new customer who has been balking about price.

Today's manager spends most of his time conferring with bosses and subordinates within his own company, but tomorrow's manager will be "intimately hooked to suppliers and customers" and well versed in competitors' strategies, says Stanley Davis, the management consultant.

The marketplace will demand customized products and immediate delivery. This will force managers to make swift product-design and marketing decisions, which now often take months and reams of reports. "Instant performance will be expected of them, and it's going to be harder to hide incompetence," says Ann Barry, vice president of research at Handy Associates, Inc., a New York consultant.

10:30 A.M. At a staff meeting, Smith finds himself refereeing two subordinates who disagree vehemently on how to promote a new appliance. One, an Asian manager, suggests that a fresh campaign begin much sooner than initially envisioned. The other, a European, wants to hold off until results of a test market are received later that week.

Smith quickly realizes this is a cultural, not strategic, clash pitting a let's-do-it-now, analyze-it-later approach against a more cautious style. He makes them aware that they're not really far apart, and the European manager agrees to move swiftly.

By 2010, managers will have to handle greater cultural diversity with subtle human relations skills. Managers will have to understand that employees don't think alike about such basics as "handling confrontation or even what it means to do a good day's work," says Jeffrey Sonnenfeld, a Harvard Business School professor.

12:30 P.M. Lunch is in Smith's office today, giving him time to take a video lesson in conversational Chinese. He already speaks Spanish fluently, having learned during a work stint in Argentina, and he wants to master at least two more languages. After 20 minutes, though, he decides to go to his computer to check his company's latest political risk assessment on Spain, where recent student unrest has erupted into riots. The report tells him that the disturbances aren't anti-American, but he decides to have a bodyguard meet him at the Madrid airport anyway.

Technology will give managers easy access to more data than they can possibly use. The challenge will be to "synthesize data to make effective decisions," says Mellon's Terracciano.

2:20 P.M. Two of Smith's top lieutenants complain that they and others on his staff feel a recent bonus payment for a successful project wasn't divided equitably. Bluntly, they note that while Smith received a hefty $20,000 bonus, his 15-member staff had to split $5,000, and they threaten to defect. He quickly calls his boss, who says he'll think about increasing the bonus for staff members.

With skilled technical and professional employees likely to be in short supply, tomorrow's managers will have to share more authority with subordinates and, in some cases, pay them as much as or more than the managers themselves earn.

While yielding more to their employees, managers in their 30s in the year 2010 may find their own climb up the corporate ladder stalled by superiors. After advancing rapidly in their 20s, this generation "will be locked in a heated fight with older baby-boomers who won't want to retire," says Harvard's Sonnenfeld.

4 P.M. Smith learns from the field that a large retail customer has been approached by a foreign competitor promising to quickly supply him with a best-selling appliance. After conferring with his division's production managers, he phones the customer and suggests that his company could supply the same product but with three slightly different custom designs. They arrange a meeting later in the week.

Despite the globalization of companies and speed of overall change, some things will stay the same. Managers intent on rising to the top will still be judged largely on how well they articulate ideas and work with others.

In addition, different corporate cultures will still encourage and reward divergent qualities. Companies banking on new products, for example, will reward risk takers, while slow-growth industries will stress predictability and caution in their ranks.

6 P.M. Before heading to the airport, Smith uses his videophone to give his daughters a good-night kiss and to talk about the next day's schedule with his wife. Learning that she must take an unexpected trip herself the next evening, he promises to catch the SuperConcorde home in time to put the kids to sleep himself.[*]

CHANGES AND NEW DEVELOPMENTS

Worldwide companies (WWCs)—including multinational companies (MNCs), multinational enterprises (MNEs), globals, or transnationals, as the multicountry banking and business organizations are variously called—are undergoing several types of change. For one thing, many companies with home countries other than the United States have grown more rapidly than U.S.-based companies. For another, the number of companies whose home countries are developing countries is growing.

The companies' relationships with the EC and the UN are changing, and the attitudes and policies of less developed countries (LDCs) as host countries are becoming more hospitable.

Many people are speaking of different sorts of organizations and operations when they refer to MNCs and globals/transnationals. A number of national laws requiring minimum local-manufactured content and/or investment control are inhibiting the globalization of some MNCs. Differing national consumer tastes are also causing some companies to tailor their products, at

[*] Source: Carol Hymowitz, "Day in the Life of Tomorrow's Manager," *The Wall Street Journal*, March 20, 1989, p. B1.

least partially, to individual markets, and flexible manufacturing systems are making the tailoring faster and less costly.

Some of the organizations are structuring themselves to globalize as much as is profitable under control of a home country headquarters, while maintaining flexibility to tailor for national or regional markets where that approach is more profitable or legally necessary. In the tailoring instances, there is more autonomy for management in the host countries.

There are those who want and others who fear the creation of trade blocs of countries with free trade within the bloc but protectionism against the rest of the world. Such blocs are forming or are under discussion; whether they will cooperate or compete with each other remains to be seen.

World business is strongly affected by politics. East-West trade and other commercial and investment activities increase during times of détente and decrease when political relations deteriorate. The USSR, Hungary, and Poland seem to be opening their political systems to some extent.

In Tienanmen Square in Beijing, the capital of the People's Republic of China (PRC), thousands of students, intellectuals, and workers demonstrated for days and nights, demanding negotiations with the government for "democracy." In early June 1989, China's People's Liberation Army used tanks and infantry to massacre apparently thousands of demonstrators and clear the square. Such a massacre was denied by the PRC government, although it had been reported by both Chinese and foreign news correspondents and other observers. Not disputed was the subsequent hunt for and arrest of demonstration leaders, some of whom were condemned to death. These developments will surely affect American, European, and Japanese efforts to start and successfully operate businesses in the PRC.

Let us now discuss briefly the trends and new directions we see as they regard those matters. Of course, trends frequently change directions; being proved wrong is a risk the writer of this sort of chapter must accept.

WORLDWIDE COMPANIES BASED IN INDUSTRIAL COUNTRIES: TRENDS AND REACTIONS

The United States got a head start with foreign investments that resulted in worldwide companies, and many WWCs—but a diminishing percentage of the total number—are still American owned (that is, the United States is the home country of the parent company). You need only compare Table 23–1 with Table 23–2 to see this trend. The first shows standings as of June 30, 1986, while the second is as of June 30, 1988.

As you can see, the Japanese Nippon Telephone and Telegraph (NTT) replaced the American IBM as number one. We should point out that NTT was not a public company in 1986; it was entirely government owned until shares were sold to the public in 1987.

Sumitomo Bank moved up to third from sixth. General Electric dropped from 3rd to 14th. Comparing the number of companies in the biggest 25 based in America, Europe, and Japan, we see the following changes from 1986 to 1988: The number of U.S.-based companies declined from 11 to 5, while European-based companies went from 4 to 3; the number of Japanese-based companies increased from 10 to 17.

■ **TABLE 23–1**
The World's 25 Largest Public Companies
(By market value on June 20, 1986, converted into US$s at the closing exchange rate on that date)

Company Name	Country	Market Value (in millions)
1. IBM	U.S.	$87,697
2. Exxon	U.S.	44,015
3. General Electric	U.S.	36,820
4. Tokyo Electric	Japan	32,421
5. AT&T	U.S.	27,138
6. Sumitomo Bank	Japan	25,962
7. Toyota Motor	Japan	25,197
8. General Motors	U.S.	24,751
9. Dai-Ichi-Kangyo Bank	Japan	23,729
10. Nomura Securities	Japan	23,151
11. Royal Dutch Petroleum	Netherlands, U.K.	21,592
12. Mitsubishi Bank	Japan	21,461
13. Fuji Bank	Japan	21,460
14. Daimler-Benz	West Germany	20,874
15. British Telecom	U.K.	20,430
16. Du Pont	U.S.	20,093
17. BellSouth	U.S.	19,246
18. Industrial Bank of Japan	Japan	19,092
19. Sanwa Bank	Japan	18,346
20. Philip Morris	U.S.	17,813
21. Sears Roebuck	U.S.	17,659
22. British Petroleum	U.K.	16,651
23. Matsushita Electric Industrial	Japan	16,210
24. Coca-Cola	U.S.	16,147
25. Amoco	U.S.	15,588

Source: *Forbes Magazine,* July 26, 1986 © Forbes Inc. 1986.

The relative growth in the size of Japanese banks has been even more impressive. Compare Table 23–3 with Table 23–4.

The U.S.-based Citicorp was the world's biggest in 1985; but by 1987, Citicorp was in eighth place. The seven biggest were Japanese. Of the largest 25 banks based in America, Europe, and Japan, by 1987 the 4 U.S. banks had dwindled to 1, European banks were down from 9 to 7, while Japanese-based banks increased from 12 to 17.

Reasons for the greater relative growth of Japanese-based companies and banks are several. Among the most important must be included the single-minded and highly successful export policies of Japanese business and government. They have made deep penetration into North America, Europe, and most other markets—and grown rapidly in the process.

The resulting trade surpluses have provided huge amounts of dollars and other currencies for business expansion and for Japanese banks to lend and grow. At the same time, American and, to a lesser extent, European banks were

■ TABLE 23–2
The World's 25 Largest
Public Companies
(By market value on
June 30, 1988, converted
into US$s at exchange
rates on December 31,
1987)

Rank				
1988	1987	Company Name	Country	Market Value (in millions)
1	1	NTT	Japan	$276,840
2	2	IBM	U.S.	76,049
3	4	Sumitomo Bank	Japan	65,335
4	3	Exxon	U.S.	62,572
5	8	Dai-Ichi Kangyo Bank	Japan	61,971
6	9	Fuji Bank	Japan	59,746
7	6	Tokyo Electric Power	Japan	57,318
8	10	Mitsubishi Bank	Japan	53,934
9	5	Industrial Bank of Japan	Japan	52,170
10	7	Nomura Securities	Japan	51,154
11	13	Royal Dutch/Shell	Netherlands, U.K.	49,312
12	14	Toyota Motor	Japan	46,334
13	12	Sanwa Bank	Japan	46,136
14	11	General Electric	U.S.	39,617
15	23	Matsushita Electric	Japan	34,852
16	77	Nippon Steel	Japan	32,252
17	32	Hitachi	Japan	31,721
18	27	Tokai Bank	Japan	31,288
19	16	Long-Term Credit Bank	Japan	30,078
20	20	Mitsui Bank	Japan	29,351
21	17	AT&T	U.S.	28,855
22	24	Ford Motor	U.S.	28,585
23	15	British Petroleum	U.K.	27,441
24	22	British Telecom	U.K.	26,612
25	19	Mitsubishi Trust	Japan	25,621

Source: *The Wall Street Journal,* September 23, 1988, p. 18R.

lending less as they concentrated on collecting the billions they had poured out to Latin American, African, Asian, and East European borrowers during the 1970s and early 80s.

These trends have not reversed. Japan continues to run very large balance-of-trade surpluses. Moreover, as Japan begins to collect interest and profits on its foreign loans and investments, its balance-of-payments surpluses will swell.

Countervailing trends are trade protectionist measures in Europe and North America. In 1988, the United States passed a new trade act, the centerpiece of which is Section 301, which required the Bush administration to name countries that are guilty of "unfair" trade practices against the United States. In June 1989, three countries were identified, and the main target was Japan. If, after 18 months of negotiations, the United States is not satisfied that the unfair practices are ended, the law requires sanctions against imports from the offending country.

■ **TABLE 23–3**
The World's 25 Largest Banks
(Ranked by assets, converted to US$s at the end of each company's fiscal year 1985)

Company	Country	Assets (in US$ millions)
1. Citicorp	U.S.	$173,597
2. Banque Nationale de Paris (BNP)	France	123,074
3. Dai-Ichi Kangyo Bank	Japan	122,895
4. Credit Agricole	France	122,884
5. Fuji Bank	Japan	121,384
6. Bank America	U.S.	118,541
7. Sumitomo Bank	Japan	113,985
8. Credit Lyonnais	France	111,452
9. Mitsubishi Bank	Japan	105,819
10. National Westminster Bank	U.K.	104,677
11. Sanwa Bank	Japan	102,731
12. Société Generale	France	97,621
13. Deutsche Bank	West Germany	96,383
14. Barclays	U.K.	94,169
15. Chase Manhattan	U.S.	87,685
16. Mitsubishi Trust & Banking	Japan	86,668
17. Norinchukin Bank	Japan	85,199
18. Industrial Bank of Japan	Japan	84,932
19. Midland Bank	U.K.	83,860
20. Sumitomo Trust & Banking	Japan	80,813
21. Tokai Bank	Japan	77,669
22. Dresdner Bank	West Germany	76,652
23. Manufacturers Hanover	U.S.	76,526
24. Mitsui Trust & Banking	Japan	75,982
25. Yasuda Trust & Banking	Japan	75,028

Source: Worldscope, 1986.

OTHER WWCs

Companies based in a number of developing or communist countries have ventured overseas. Six very big ones are Hyundai of South Korea, Walsin Lihwa of the Republic of China, and the state oil companies of Brazil, Kuwait, Mexico, and Venezuela, which have become multinationals with factories and holdings abroad.

As mentioned in Chapter 17, the People's Republic of China is investing in several foreign countries. Many Indian companies operate multinationally, as do companies based in Hong Kong and Singapore. Other companies call Indonesia, the Philippines, Malaysia, Argentina, and Thailand their home country.

The motives of WWCs based in nonindustrial countries tend to differ somewhat from the motives of those based in industrial countries. WWCs from advanced countries speak of exploiting experience with high-tech production and using marketing expertise. Those from other countries stress diversifica-

■ TABLE 23–4
The World's 25 Largest
Banks
(Ranked by assets,
converted to US$s at
exchange rates on
December 31, 1987)

Rank 1987	Rank 1986	Company	Country	Assets (in US$ millions)
1	1	Dai-Ichi Kangyo Bank	Japan	$319,006
2	3	Fuji Bank	Japan	287,245
3	5	Sumitomo Bank	Japan	286,249
4	4	Mitsubishi Bank	Japan	268,041
5	6	Sanwa Bank	Japan	264,453
6	8	Industrial Bank of Japan	Japan	221,175
7	7	Norinchukin Bank	Japan	218,118
8	2	Citicorp	U.S.	198,388
9	13	Tokai Bank	Japan	190,267
10	15	Mitsui Bank	Japan	181,559
11	18	Mitsubishi Trust & Banking	Japan	181,358
12	9	Banque Nationale de Paris	France	181,660
13	12	Credit Agricole	France	177,843
14	19	Sumitomo Trust & Banking	Japan	169,968
15	10	Deutsche Bank	W. Germany	166,562
16	11	Credit Lyonnais	France	166,487
17	17	Barclays Bank	U.K.	163,062
18	14	National Westminster Bank	U.K.	161,653
19	23	Mitsui Trust & Banking	Japan	157,232
20	22	Taiyo Kobe Bank	Japan	156,897
21	21	Long-Term Credit Bank of Japan	Japan	152,620
22	16	Société Generale	France	151,334
23	20	Bank of Tokyo	Japan	149,914
24	31	Yasuda Trust & Banking	Japan	138,913
25	29	Daiwa Bank	Japan	134,397

Source: *The Wall Street Journal,* September 23, 1988, p. 19R.

tion of risk, high local return, exploiting experience with labor-intensive production, relatives or countrymen business associates in the host country, and small home markets.[1] There are also similarities; both groups are abroad primarily to get and defend markets.

Regardless of the WWC's home country, it must deal with a variety of entities other than the home government. Among them are host countries, the European Community, the United Nations, and the World Bank.

CHANGING ATTITUDES TOWARD WORLDWIDE COMPANIES

In the European Community (EC), at the United Nations (UN), and in the host, less developed countries (LDCs), the WWCs are being treated with more respect and given warmer welcomes. One notable exception to this is India, which in 1989 was making it difficult for Coca-Cola and Du Pont to make substantial investments.

As the EC moves along with its Project 1992, European companies are merging with each other and with firms from outside Europe to achieve sufficient size to compete in the new 320-million-consumer market. Competition is expected from other European companies as well as from American and Japanese firms. The EC Commission is encouraging the mergers.[2]

WWCs once seemed fated to succeed colonial powers as the bogeymen of UN agencies and their LDC clients. Now they look nicer than bank loans. Of course, part of the reason for this is that bank loans are much scarcer than they were in the 1970s and early 1980s, but there is much more to it than that. Third World governments are coming to appreciate the technology, employment, skills, exports, and import substitutes that WWCs deliver.

TREND TOWARD GLOBAL?

Yes and no. As one writer puts it, "There's no place to hide as global companies build, buy, and sell across borders. But why hide? Wealth is multiplying, along with the markets it sustains."[3] Politicians and labor leaders, unlike businesspeople, take a parochial view of global investment, fearing loss of sovereignty and jobs. But foreign-owned companies account for more than 20 percent of West German industrial production and more than 50 percent of Canadian. In Brazil, $30 billion of foreign investment is largely responsible for that country's growing automotive, office equipment, farm machinery, and pharmaceutical industries, and foreign investment in the United States is booming. None of these countries has experienced a resulting sovereignty loss. As to jobs, the foreign owners hire locals for all but the very top executive positions—and sometimes for them, too.[4]

Product Globalization

This can mean two different things. First, it can mean the same, standardized product for markets everywhere in the world. Standardization has become highly important in electronics because so many electronic products must interface with items made by other firms. The stand-alone character of many electronic products is disappearing. It is always interfaced with software, or the program, or the network. One of the most promising global products for the years ahead is high-definition TV.[5]

Second, product globalization sometimes means a product whose design and components come from several countries. The design and parts for one "American" automobile—the 1989 Pontiac LeMans—come from eight countries.[6] See Table 23–5.

The French company, Peugeot, set up a joint venture with an Indian company to produce French-designed pickup trucks near Bombay in 1989. Chrysler unveiled a double-barreled plan not only to link up with Renault of France but Hyundai of South Korea as well. In January 1989, Toyota announced it is planning to build passenger cars in Britain. Cadillac builds its Allante bodies in Turin, Italy, and flies them each day to the United States.

But there are skeptics. Some analysts and auto executives disagree that all the interlocking ventures have led to a high level of cooperation between the automakers. Maryanne Keller, automotive analyst with Turman, Selz, Dietz &

■ **TABLE 23–5**
The "American" Pontiac
Is a Melting Pot

Design—West Germany

Final assembly—South Korea

1.6-liter engines—South Korea

2.0-liter engines—Australia

Transmission and automatic transaxle—Canada, United States

Manual transaxle—South Korea

Brake components—France, United States, South Korea

Tires—South Korea

Electrical (wiring) harness—South Korea

Sheet metal—Japan

Stamping of exterior body parts—South Korea

Fuel-injection system—United States

Rear axle components—United States, South Korea

Fuel pump—United States

Radio—Singapore

Steering components—United States

Windshield glass—South Korea

Battery—South Korea

Birney, a New York investment firm, says, "I don't see these joint ventures as anything but extremely opportunistic relationships. They are, for the most part, one-shot events. These companies are, in fact, major competitors and will try to limit the amount of confidential information they exchange."[7]

Product Differentiation

The concept of product globalization hit the academic journals, books, and popular press around the end of 1983, and much has been written about it. Especially in America, managers have been told to emulate the Japanese by producing standardized, global products and by shifting decision-making power from their far-flung, autonomous subsidiaries to the head office.

According to some authors, the advice is not just formula-like, imitative, and therefore inappropriate, but it is also based on a badly outdated view of Japanese strategy and organization structure. The Japanese are much more sensitive to the flip side of globalism and have been focusing on the growing demands of host governments for local investments, the emerging resistance of consumers to standardized global products, and the arrival of manufacturing technologies that are making small-scale production and tailored products much more feasible than in the past.[8]

A similar point of view is that some multinational manufacturers and suppliers of consumer goods and services have been "taken in" by the notion that most markets in the industrialized world are undergoing an irrevocable process of homogenization and that national differences are declining. The "reality," it is said, is different.

Powerful competitors, such as Nissan in cars and Matsushita in consumer electronics, have realized that although some market segments are globalizing, others are shifting the opposite way toward fragmentation either on regional or national grounds. There is no single, correct strategy; the best approach varies from one product and one market to another.[9]

Flexibility and Versatility

So we see that for a variety of reasons, some major firms are limiting or reversing product globalization. In this process, they are sacrificing the economies of scale that result from producing a standard product for the world. One way they are coping with that loss is through use of flexible manufacturing systems (FMSs).

Difficult to design and produce, FMSs are finally producing healthy results for many manufacturers. Small-batch production provides the flexibility needed for just-in-time manufacturing to customer order and eliminating inventory.

The problem with small batches is the setup time of the machine tools involved, which can be many hours or several days. The function of an FMS is to avoid this delay by separating the setup operation from production. For example, while an operator at one station is preparing a pallet for machining, machine tools at other stations are cutting the prepared components. To keep production going continuously, an FMS has to incorporate tool stores, pallet stores, and an automated cart that transfers the pallets between the different stations and stores. The whole operation is computer controlled. Computer assisted design (CAD) and computer assisted manufacturing (CAM) systems are making production more efficient and speeding design and production of goods to fulfill the customer's order.

One French company says that from the moment a customer places an order by telex, it takes only 30 minutes before the FMS starts machining the component—provided it is already "known" to the system. A British firm, speaking of orders for products not already known to the system, has reduced the time between ordering and delivering from three months to five weeks. Its target is 20 days.[10]

In meeting competition, some versatility can help. A successful American high-tech firm suddenly began losing business to a Japanese competitor. A key difference was that the U.S. company's sales team just wrote up orders, while the Japanese firm sent engineers to make sales. They made changes for the customer, solved problems, and addressed customer concerns.

The American company responded by involving its salespeople in seeking solutions, and they decided they must become problem solvers. That was achieved by giving them laptop computers, which linked them not only with the company's engineers but also with finance, legal, and sales managers as needed.[11]

Personnel Globalization

The ability to maximize global opportunities while being sensitive to national or regional markets or requirements is dependent on executives who are world-wise and WWC-wise. The companies that are succeeding move executives between parent and foreign subsidiaries on both long- and short-term assignments. Third-country nationals frequently are high in management.

Of the American motor companies, Ford is the most global, which some of its management assignments demonstrate. The managing director of Ford-Italy is French. A Norwegian runs the Ford sales company in Spain. A Belgian is in charge of the U.K. body and assembly shop. The head of Ford-U.K. is English, but before that assignment he was chief of the Brazilian operations. And so it goes throughout the company, including the movement of Europeans to senior management posts in the United States.

Ford hires M.B.A.s from business schools, who are usually given jobs outside their native countries. For its existing managers, Ford presents an international outlook at its Executive Development Center, where executives from all over the world attended sessions at least once every two years.[12]

Of course, Ford is not alone in its efforts to globalize its managers. Texas Instruments requires managers with global responsibility to meet with their overseas colleagues every quarter to set worldwide strategy.[13]

TRADE BLOCS/FREE TRADE AREAS

Groups of nations around the world are banding together to increase trade and investment within the group. Other nations are considering beginning negotiations aimed at creating such groups.

In 1985, the United States signed a Free Trade Area (FTA) agreement with Israel that is taking effect gradually over a decade. Under the agreement, all tariffs will be phased out, as will all quotas except on certain agricultural products. Israel agreed to cease subsidizing exports to the United States. Protection of intellectual property rights were reaffirmed, and liberal investment policies have been maintained.[14]

An FTA between Canada and the United States went into effect in 1989. Those countries are each other's largest trading partners, and their two-way trade volume of some $125 billion makes it the world's biggest bilateral trade relationship. As with the Israeli agreement, the FTA with Canada will be phased in over a 10-year period.

America's Possible Future FTA Partners

Senator Phil Gramm and others in the U.S. Congress have called for a North American FTA to include the United States, Canada, Mexico, the Caribbean, and Central America. Countries in Asia and South America that have expressed interest in FTAs with the United States include Singapore, Thailand, the Republic of China (Taiwan), the Association of South East Asian Nations (Brunei, Indonesia, Malaysia, the Philippines, Singapore, and Thailand), and Uruguay.

Project EC 1992

Not to be outdone, the European Community is nearing culmination of its own bloc, which will result in a market of 320 million relatively—or very—affluent consumers. We dealt with EC 1992 in Chapter 4.

FTAs versus EC 1992?

A potential conflict exists between the current and possible future American FTAs and EC 1992. In other words, they could lower trade and investment barriers among members while maintaining or raising them against outsiders. This would damage all the countries and lower their citizens' standards of living.

That should not and need not happen, but at least one author recommends using FTA leverage to discourage EC 1992 from becoming a Fortress Europe.[15] Of course, the leverage would work both ways.

FTAs and the GATT

The General Agreement on Tariffs and Trade (GATT) has over 90 member-countries, and some argue that GATT would be a better forum for trade liberalization than FTAs. However, there need be no conflict between GATT reforms and FTAs. If FTA members recognize and enjoy the economic benefits of open markets, it makes no sense for them to forgo those benefits because other nations are not as wise.

It has been pointed out that FTAs could help in the GATT process. As the GATT Uruguay Round is dealing with trade problems not touched in earlier rounds, such as subsidies, services, government procurement, and intellectual property, solutions negotiated in an FTA could provide guidance for the GATT solutions.[16]

Outsider Worries

As Japan watches the United States forming FTAs with other countries and observes the development of EC Project 1992, it is concerned that the exports on which it depends may be affected. Japan and Japanese companies are taking steps to protect themselves, and they are considering other moves. They are investing in Canada, Europe, and the United States to produce inside those markets.

Some Japanese are suggesting negotiating an FTA with the United States. Others want to revive the pre-World War II idea of an Asian trading bloc, with Japan as the dominant member.

Partly in reaction to EC 1992 and the FTAs, Prime Minister Bob Hawke of Australia has proposed a "consultative" group of Asian-Pacific nations to examine regional trade and economic issues. The Association of South East Asian Nations is planning to negotiate as a bloc to get the best possible terms of entry for their products into the EC 1992 and FTA countries.[17]

POLITICAL DEVELOPMENTS AFFECT BUSINESS

In Beijing, in June 1989, popular demonstrations for "democracy" were crushed by the People's Liberation Army tanks and guns. Most Western business executives fled the country, and China began a propaganda campaign against the United States. It is probable that most of the executives will return but that business will be more restricted by the new hard-line PRC government.

Some voting was permitted in the USSR, Poland, and Hungary, and non-Communist parties have begun to share some government power in the latter two countries. The Soviet Union is experiencing nationalist stirring in Estonia, Latvia, and Lithuania and ethnic violence in Uzbekistan and other southern provinces. At the same time, the Soviet leader, Gorbachev, is courting Western business for investment and joint ventures in the USSR. The political unrest added to the Soviet Union's economic difficulties—caused largely by communist policies—will make his success doubtful.

Surprising and seemingly fundamental developments have seen thousands of East Germans pouring into West Germany, first through Hungary or Czechoslovakia, and then directly through the Berlin Wall. They are mostly young, well-trained people whose loss will be a blow to the East German economy and a boost for labor-short West Germany.

East Germany has formed a new government, and the West has offered major financial assistance if a democratic government results. These developments, plus those in Hungary and Poland, could offer potentially rich opportunities for trade and investment in East Europe. As events unfold, it is probable that the other East European countries will also open to the West.

Central America may not be a good site for business in the near future. The Arias plan to bring free, democratic elections to Nicaragua may not work. A conservative party—not supported by the United States—won the 1989 presidential elections in El Salvador, and the civil war there continues.

Democracies—although fragile—are the rule in South America. However, most governments lack the political will to control inflation, which is rampant except in Bolivia and Chile. High inflation creates an unhealthy atmosphere for business.

In Japan, the ruling Liberal Democratic Party (LDP) has been shaken by the Recruit scandal, which involved company stock given to party members just before the stock's value soared on the market. When the LDP finally found a prominent member not tainted by Recruit, it made him prime minister in May 1989. Less than a month later, a Japanese woman told a magazine, which published her story, that the newly minted prime minister, Sosuka Uno, had paid her the equivalent of $30,000 to be his lover in 1985 and 1986. The woman said she went public with the affair because she thought Uno was too selfish to be a good prime minister.[18]

Japan has been accustomed to its politicians taking and giving bribes and keeping mistresses, but the 1989 scandals aroused more public resentment than usual. Uno's predecessor was forced to resign, and Uno resigned in disgrace. The LDP continued to suffer sex scandals, and one leader of the party insulted Japanese women by stating they are unsuited to government leadership and should stay home. In the July 1989 elections, the LDP for the first time in its history lost control of the upper house of the Japanese diet (parliament). The Socialist Party which won the election was headed by a woman. The LDP has been close to Japanese business, which may get less government support if the party is weakened.

South Africa's apartheid policies have caused the U.S. Congress to pass laws restricting trade with that country. Church and school groups have pressured American companies to sell their South African assets, and many have done so. Some European countries have also restricted their South African trade and investments. There seems little prospect of much change in that situation in the near future, although new South African leaders are trying to make changes in their system.

SUMMARY

Although U.S.-based companies began large-scale foreign investment before those based in Europe and Japan, the latter flourished in the 1980s and are still growing. Japanese companies and banks have grown particularly rapidly due in part to their huge trade surplus with the United States. The 1988 American trade law caused the Bush administration to single out Japan for retaliation if that country does not cease "unfair" trade practices.

The EC, the UN, and LDC host countries have become more friendly and hospitable toward WWCs. They have realized that WWCs bring technology, capital, jobs, exports, and other benefits.

Globalization is being sought by many companies. That can mean a standardized product for every market or a product whose design and components come from several countries.

But globalization has limits. Some host countries require minimum amounts of locally manufactured components and/or local ownership of subsidiaries. And some of the big companies are tailoring products for regional or national markets after encountering consumer resistance to standardized, global products.

The new and improving flexible manufacturing systems (FMSs) are making smaller-batch production runs for smaller markets economical. FMSs are significantly reducing machine tool setup times as a plant shifts from production of one product to another.

The ability to maximize global opportunities while remaining sensitive to national or regional markets or requirements is dependent on executives who are worldwise and know their company well. Successful WWCs move their executives among parent and subsidiary companies so that they can make personal relationships throughout the WWC and understand its parts. A number of companies hold periodic meetings or seminars attended by managers from all parts of the WWC. The managers thus come to know each other and the company.

Free trade areas (FTAs) are coming into effect between the United States and Israel and the United States and Canada. Others are being discussed. Project EC 1992 is under way, and the GATT is trying to liberalize world trade. These developments could result in trade wars between blocs of nations or in freer trade, depending on how they are managed.

Political events have great impact on business. Managers must be aware of the political climate as it changes.

QUESTIONS

1. Why have Japanese banks grown more rapidly than those based in Europe or the United States?
2. Is that growth trend continuing? Why?
3. What does Section 301 of the 1988 U.S. trade act provide?
4. Why are WWCs becoming more popular with the EC, the UN, and LDC host countries?
5. What are the two meanings of product globalization?
6. Are some products being tailored for national or regional markets? Why?
7. What is a flexible manufacturing system (FMS)?
8. Why are FMSs being introduced?
9. How and why are WWCs globalizing their managements?
10. What are free trade areas (FTAs)?
11. Will FTAs necessarily conflict with GATT processes? Discuss.
12. Will FTAs necessarily conflict with EC 1992? Discuss.
13. *a.* Read your newspapers and periodicals, and discuss how political events are affecting business in the PRC.
    b. Do the same concerning the Soviet Union.
    c. Choose some other area of the world and do the same.

MINICASE 23–1

Competition within the Multinational

MC is a multinational with subsidiary manufacturing plants in several countries around the world. MC has just won a very large contract to supply locomotives to Paraguay, which is modernizing its entire railway system with financing from the World Bank.

MC's home country is the United States, and it could

manufacture parts or all of the locomotives in its U.S. plants. MC subsidiary companies in Spain, Mexico, and Australia could also manufacture parts or all of the locomotives. The managers of all those subsidiaries know about the big new contract, and each is eager to get the work involved in performing it.

A meeting of the subsidiary chief executive officers (CEOs) is called at MC's headquarters in New York to discuss which plant or plants will get the work. The manager of the American locomotive plant is also at the meeting, and she makes a strong case for giving her plant the work. It has laid off 1,000 workers, and this big job would permit it to recall them. In addition, the American plant has all of the latest technology, some of which has not been supplied to the subsidiary companies.

The subsidiary CEOs each argue that there is unemployment in their countries too, and that as responsible citizens they must hire more local people. Each CEO also points out that hiring local people would reduce hostility toward the subsidiary in the host country and give it defenses against left-wing attacks on foreign-owned companies. One CEO suggests that each plant enter competitive bids and let Paraguayan Railways make the decision.

You are the CEO of MC, and you have the authority and responsibility to allocate parts or all of the work to one or more of the plants. List and explain the considerations that will govern your decisions.

SUPPLEMENTARY READINGS

Bartlett, Christopher A., and Sumantra Ghoshal. "Organizing for Worldwide Effectiveness: The Transnational Solution." *California Management Review,* Fall 1988, pp. 54–74.

Blank, Stephen. *Assessing the Political Environment: An Emerging Function in International Companies.* New York: Conference Board, 1980.

Blin, J. M.; Stuart I. Greenbaum; and Donald P. Jacobs. *Flexible Exchange Rates and International Business.* Washington, D.C.: British–North American Committee, 1981.

Bussing, Rezu. *Power vs. Profit: Multinational Corporation–Nation State Interaction.* New York: Arno Press, 1980.

Byrne, A. John, and G. David Wallace. "For More and More Foreign Companies, America Isn't Paved with Gold." *Business Week,* February 3, 1986, p. 84.

Casson, Mark. *Multinational and World Trade Vertical Integration and the Division of Labor in World Industries.* London: Allen & Unwin, 1986.

Caves, Richard E. *Multinational Enterprise: Economic Analysis.* New York: Cambridge University Press, 1982.

Davidson, W. H., and D. G. McFetridge. "Recent Directions in International Strategies: Production Rationalization or Portfolio Adjustment?" *Columbia Journal of World Business,* Summer 1984, pp. 95–101.

Eaker, R. Mark, and Loan Lenowitz. "Multinational Borrowing Decisions and the Empirical Exchange Rate Evidence." *Management International Review,* Winter 1986, pp. 24–35.

Eiteman, David K., and Arthur I. Stonehill. *Multinational Business Finance.* 4th ed. Reading, Mass: Addison-Wesley Publishing, 1986.

Erdilek, Asim. "Multinationals in Mutual Invaders: Intra-Industry Direct Foreign Investment." *Journal of International Business Studies,* Summer 1986, pp. 182–91.

Fisher, Bart S., and Jeff Turner, eds. *Regulating the Multinational Enterprise: National and International.* New York: Praeger Publishers, 1983.

Flamn, Kenneth, *The Global Factory: Foreign Assembly in International Trade.* Washington, D.C.: Brookings Institution, 1985.

Gamwall, C. C. "Maximizing Cash Flow in Multinational Benefit Plans." *Risk Management,* October 1984, pp. 50–66.

Ghosh, Pradip K., ed. *Multinational Cooperation and Third World Development.* Westport, Conn.: Greenwood Press, 1984.

Grosse, Robert. "Financial Transfer in the MNE: The Latin American Case." *Management International Review,* Winter 1986, pp. 33–42.

Hall, R. Quane. *Overseas Acquisitions and Mergers: Combining for Profits Abroad.* New York: Praeger Publishers, 1986.

Hennast, Jean. *A Theory of Multinational Enterprise.* Ann Arbor: University of Michigan Press. 1982.

Hladik, Karen F. *International Joint Ventures: An Economic Analysis of U.S.–Foreign Business Partnerships.* Lexington, Mass.: Lexington Books, 1985.

Kester, Carl, and Timothy A. Luehrman. "Why Dollar Bashing Doesn't Work: Effect of Cheapening Currency on Manufacturers." *Fortune,* October 27, 1986, pp. 137–39.

Kettell, Brian, *The Finance of International Business.* Westport, Conn.: Quorum Books, 1981.

Kim, Suk H. *International Business Finance.* Richmond, Va.: R. F. Dame, 1983.

Kong, Leo Edwin. *The International Transfer of Commercial Technology: The Role of Multinational Corporations.* New York: Arno Press, 1980.

Lachenmayer, Hubert. "The Effect of Currency Exchange Risks on the Cost of Equity Capital of the International and Multinational Firm." *Management International Review,* Spring 1984, pp. 28–36.

Linsberry, Gary. "American Insurance Companies Help Overseas Corporate Subsidiaries to Comply with Pension Legislation." *Barron's,* November 3, 1986, p. 50.

Pratten, Cliff. "The Importance of Giant Companies." *Lloyds Bank Review*, January 1986, p. 33.

Rahman, M. Zubaidus, and Robert W. Scapins. "Transfer Pricing by Multinationals: Some Evidence from Bangladesh." *Journal of Business Finance and Accounting*, August 1986, pp. 383–90.

Sesit, R. Michael. "Dollar's Drop Helps Most Multinational Firms: Currency Approach to Decline Varies Widely." *The Wall Street Journal*, September 3, 1986, p. 6.

Shapiro, Alan C. *Multinational Financial Management*. 2nd ed. Boston: Allyn & Bacon, 1986

Sprinivasan, Venkat, and Yong H. Kim. "Payments Netting in International Cash Management: A Network Optimization Approach." *Journal of International Business Studies*, Summer 1986, pp. 1–11.

Swanson, E. Peggy. "Portfolio Diversification by Currency Denomination: An Approach to International Cash Management with Implications for Foreign Exchange Markets." *Quarterly Review of Economics and Business*, Spring 1986, pp. 95–106.

Szala, Ginger, "How Multinational Firms Use Futures and Options: Currency Trading One Way to Curb Risk." *Futures*, September 1985, pp. 54–61.

Wilson, Elizabeth. "The Impact of the Dollar on High-Tech Multinationals." *Electronic Business*, May 15, 1985, pp. 59–66.

ENDNOTES

1. Louis T. Well, Jr., *Third World Multinationals: The Risk of Foreign Investment from Developing Countries* (Cambridge, Mass.: MIT Press, 1983).

2. John Robinson, "The European Commission: A New-Found Friend of Business," *International Management*, September 1986, pp. 70–74.

3. Richard I. Kirkland, Jr., "Entering a New Age of Boundless Competition," *Fortune*, March 14, 1988, pp. 40–48.

4. Ibid.

5. George Melloan, "Global Manufacturing Is an Intricate Game," *The Wall Street Journal*, November 29, 1988, p. A19.

6. James Risen, "Buying American Becomes Increasingly Difficult as Car Makers Globalize Operations," *Los Angeles Times*, February 12, 1989, part IV, pp. 1, 4.

7. Ibid.

8. Christopher Lorenz, "An Outdated View of Globalisation," *Financial Times*, December 12, 1988, p. 13. For a more complete discussion, see Christopher A. Bartlett and Sumantra Ghoshal, "Organizing for Worldwide Effectiveness: The Transnational Solution," *California Management Review*, Fall 1988, pp. 54–74.

9. "The Limits of Globalisation," *Financial Times*, May 24, 1989, p. 22.

10. Nick Garnett, "The Healthy Results of a Little Flexibility," *Financial Times*, May 31, 1989, p. 33. See also "Design It Yourself," *The Economist*, July 28, 1989, pp. 13–14.

11. Patrice Apodaca, "Learning to Manage Rapid Change Is Vital," *Investor's Daily*, March 7, 1989, p. 1ff.

12. Michael Skapinker, "Ford's Cosmopolitan Carousel," *Financial Times*, May 12, 1989, p. 9.

13. Andrew Kupfer, "The Long Arm of Jerry Junkins," *Fortune*, March 14, 1988, p. 28.

14. Edward L. Hudgins, "Free Trade Areas: Removing Trade Obstacles and Bucking Protection," *Backgrounder*, no. 587, The Heritage Foundation, June 17, 1987.

15. Wendell H. McCulloch, Jr., "Europe 1992: Ensuring A Fair Deal for the U.S.," *Backgrounder*, no. 705, The Heritage Foundation, May 5, 1989.

16. Hudgins, "Free Trade Areas."

17. Steven Jones, "Protectionism or Partnership?" *The Asian Wall Street Journal*, June 12, 1989, pp. 22, 27.

18. Elisabeth Rubinfien, "Sex Scandal Rocking Japan's Premier Shows Traditional Attitudes Changing," *The Wall Street Journal*, June 20, 1989, p. A12.

Three Diversified Cases

In closing, we offer three cases, each quite different than the others. They present factual situations, problems, and the solutions decided on by the people involved. You might want to consider whether you would have approached and solved them the same ways.

The first case involves optimizing the management information system(s) of a WWC on a global basis. The second is about how three companies set up operations in Germany. The third case is about how political policy change can affect business plans.

CASE 1 THE NEED TO OPTIMIZE MIS ON A GLOBAL BASIS

Over the past decade, the consumer products division of a French multinational, Bazaar Maison SA, has spent more than FF60 million (8.5 million ECUs) trying to create a centralized management information system (MIS) that would satisfy the needs of national and regional operating units while also meeting headquarters' requirements for timely data for strategic planning and global forecasting.

The MIS originally envisaged by Information Technology Vice President Michel Badar would have provided a daily global overview of the division's production, distribution, marketing, and finance data. Successive changes in top management, however, with differing views on the need for such an elaborate MIS, stymied the development of a true on-line system. Instead, Badar had to be satisfied with the piecemeal development of a

system that had become unusable for top management.

One critical shortcoming—a consequence of the lack of direction from the top—was that the operating units went on to choose their own hardware and software and develop their own information systems. Tailored to meet local needs, the data fed by these units to headquarters varied widely in sophistication and reliability.

Manual and semimanual operations often had to be performed to comply with corporate information requests. These prolonged the data-gathering process, increased errors, and meant that much of the information was obsolete when it arrived at headquarters.

One major repercussion of obsolete data was the recurrent shortage of newly launched household appliance models. Determined to solve the problem, recently appointed divisional CEO Simon Goulet, a strong advocate of the benefits of information technology (IT), summoned Badar to his office and asked:

"What's the cost of setting up a consolidated global management decision support system?"

"We're talking big money, because we're virtually going to have to start from scratch," said Badar. "None of our operating units provides an identical set of data. To have an integrated on-line forecasting system, we would need to modify every part of the existing network to produce the same data. The cost could be as much as we've already spent on a corporate system that is less than adequate."

"The cost would be shared with the operational units," Goulet explained.

"That's sure to cause conflict," Badar remarked. "Most of them have their own systems to provide local solutions and would object to paying for a new one that would mainly benefit headquarters."

"No problem," said Goulet. "To justify the cost, you'll just have to convince them of such benefits as improved marketing and customer service, faster communications, and more accurate forecasting."

"In view of the ramifications and the cost, I believe this is a job for the CEO," replied Badar.

To resolve conflicting needs, Badar is right to insist that his CEO has a crucial role to play in the success of Bazaar Maison's new management information system. It is of primary importance to have timely global information at headquarters to detect critical problems at an early stage and to optimize worldwide materials planning and management.

On the other hand, the introduction of a centralized MIS can become extremely heavy-handed and time consuming if it is set up at the expense of existing systems that already successfully meet specific local requirements. Above all, local units must retain the ability to make "quick fixes" to meet user demand, rather than having to join a queuing system for resolution at the centre.

Headquarters will naturally try to justify its control by demonstrating cost savings through economies of scale and various synergies. But how can this be measured against the loss of motivation at the local level, where IT personnel are reduced to an administrative role?

Although his status is typical of that of IT directors in many companies, Badar's inability to resolve conflicts by consensus within his peer group justifies Goulet's intervention. Regional managers defend the needs of their local units, while the functional managers refuse to compromise on their central information requirements. The CEO must arbitrate these disputes. He should also participate in the definition of the new MIS, because subordinates will often demand data that they think he might ask for.

To preserve the integrity of the new MIS, a few basic rules must be observed, and Badar will probably need Goulet's support to enforce strict adherence to them. Only systems that communicate reasonably well can be purchased. Data required by the centre should be easy to extract from local systems. Locally, only MIS managers who have a "broader view of the world" should be hired to evolve the vital dialogue between headquarters and local units.

Finally, though everything might appear very civilized during the planning state of the new MIS, infighting is sure to begin during the long implementation phase. To avoid major confrontations, the CEO should preside over a monthly review committee involving the key players.

For Goulet, taking such an active part in setting up a new management information system might appear a mundane job compared to masterminding glamorous product development or marketing

strategies. But he cannot afford to delegate such a vital task, considering the competitive edge that a state-of-the-art MIS could give Bazaar Maison—or the huge, hidden costs of a malfunctioning one.

Source:

"Dilemma & Decision," *International Management*, May 1989, p. 16.

CASE 2 THREE FOREIGN COMPANIES MOVE INTO GERMANY—DIFFERENTLY

You are the head of a company that wants to expand abroad, and your eyes have lit eagerly on Western Europe's biggest market.

With a population of 61 million, West Germany seems an obvious magnet for your operation and an ideal route for deeper export penetration. Its hardworking, prosperous people demand the best in what they buy and are prepared to pay for it.

But wait a moment! Isn't the German language one of Western Europe's most difficult? And what about the infuriating German thoroughness and addiction to rules and bureaucracy? Then there are the country's tightly hedged labour laws—making it hard to fire people whose work is not up to scratch—and its high wages.

Are you ready to cope with all this?

When you have weighed these aspects, you can then consider whether your product or service will really appeal to fussy German consumers, how you can find this out, and how you should get your message across.

Clearly, you will need to think long and hard about setting up in Germany.

Once the decision has been made, however, the results can be well worth the effort. For as well as being the world's biggest exporter, the Federal Republic is also a sizable importer. Its flourishing export surpluses have added hugely to purchasing power, though Germans are also champion savers.

When talking to companies that have recently established themselves in Germany and to those who advise them, several things become apparent. Although it may not seem easy at first glance, forming a subsidiary need not be that difficult.

Follow the rules—there are plenty of them—use all the expert help you can get, and the way becomes smoother.

"Compared with other countries, it's not that difficult to establish subsidiaries here," says Patrick Manon, commercial attaché at the French consulate in Frankfurt. "It's easier than in France. It's a matter of will." This is important, as psychological brick walls can easily appear in Germany.

Setting up and surviving in Germany can be a bit of a shock, particularly for the unprepared small firm, according to Roger Thomas, U.K. commercial consul in the city. Such preparation can be made much easier by seeking help from consulates, local development bodies, or specialist advisers.

He warns: "The rules, regulations and procedures for buying a car, getting a resident's permit, setting up a business, or even opening a bank account and obtaining credit are all quite normal to German citizens who have grown up with the system, but they can be quite horrific for the easygoing Brit who is used to doing all that in an afternoon back home."

Although Germans are mostly helpful and friendly as well as diligent, they are not, as a rule, easygoing.

For this case, the experiences of three very different companies have been looked at: Psion, a small but fast-growing U.K. maker of hand-held personal computers; Toys "R" Us, a big U.S. toy retailer that is expanding worldwide; and Cisi, a French software concern specializing in defense, electronics, and aerospace applications.

Looking back, all admit that getting started in Germany took some effort but was ultimately worthwhile. There is no substitute for actually being in the market. "The name of the game is to think German, act German, and, above all, be in Germany," asserts Thomas.

The market can be both tough and rewarding. It can be a mistake for companies to think they can simply transfer their product and marketing from their home market to Germany.

"The German market is completely different," believes Rolf Kannenberg, Psion's general manager in Germany. "It is even different from Austria and Switzerland. It is certainly different from France and Belgium and much more different from operating in the English-speaking area."

Germans tend to be perfectionists. "There's no doubt," says David Elder, Psion's export manager in London, "that Germans require everything working and perfect from day one. In the U.K. and France, you can get away with 90 percent."

Thus, out of a total staff of 10 in Germany, it has 3 technical people rather than the 2 it might need elsewhere. One works on a full-time hotline service to ensure a rapid follow-up to problems.

"You have to invest in technical support," says Elder. "You have to carry that overhead earlier than you would otherwise have done." Also, no matter how good the product—and Psion's business is growing in Germany, with a planned annual turnover of up to DM5m—people will not buy it if the marketing is not right.

So Kannenberg has made a determined assault on large, specialized dealers and distributors, aiming to line up around 30 across the country. These, in turn, serve local outlets.

Previously, its business was handled by a Hanover-based dealer, whose reach was too small for Psion's ambitions in Germany. The specialized trade dealers are the most important sales route for Psion, says Kanneberg, followed by individual firms or retailing groups like Computerland, and then by store chains like Kaufhof and Karstadt and mail-order concerns. A portable Psion computer costs nearly DM500 in Germany, excluding add-on equipment.

Potential buyers with specific professional needs want to be convinced of the product's value and will feel best served by a specialized dealer who can explain and demonstrate its advantages fully.

"People are more critical here," notes Kannenburg. "They're more demanding on quality and the price-performance relationship."

The challenges Psion faces now in Germany are those of a company on the move. Getting started was another matter. Like many other foreign—mainly British and U.S.—companies, it used the services of Lairco, which specializes in helping foreign businesses start up in Germany. Lairco provides space, telephones, secretaries, and friendly advice at a cost much lower than the expenses of setting up a new office alone.

This is where Psion began, with Sheila Hartley, now office manager, as its first employee. "Without Lairco, Psion in England would have had to invest a lot more money. They couldn't have just started with me." Lairco, run by an American husband-and-wife team, Alexander and Bernadine Lairo, charges around DM45,000 a year ($24,300), including 500 hours of secretarial use, for one of its offices—compared to an estimated DM150,000 for a company starting with no local support.

"They helped with translators and things like letterheads; they even found us a butcher to supply a party when we left them," says Hartley. Today, Psion operates from smart new offices in Bad Homburg. This enables it to skirt another potential snag—high city rents. Being just outside Frankfurt, its rents are only DM19 a square metre, compared with DM45 in central Frankfurt.

Once out of the Lairco fold, she found the biggest hurdle was the bureaucracy. "I saw it as a challenge. I took it in my stride. All the requirements have got to be adhered to, and it is important to do them correctly. It became a matter of egoism."

Actually establishing the subsidiary—the most common form is the GmbH (Gesellschaft mit beschrankter Haftung), a limited company—is the least of the obstacles. That requires a minimum capital of DM50,000 ($27,000) and can be done, with the necessary lawyers' signatures and official registration, in under two months.

More frustrating are practical matters like telephones, accommodation, furniture, cars, and, not least, staff.

Here Hartley has a few words of warning. Furniture can take up to 10 weeks to arrive, because suppliers work to orders. "So at first, it was a bit sparse here." For cars, too, the German practice can be frustrating. The leasing company insisted on bank guarantees for Psion's first three cars.

Taking on staff may also be a headache. A top bilingual secretary can cost DM5,000 a month. "Just hiring a secretary can be such an important first step," says Alexander Lairo. "Some look for foreign companies because they know how to take advantage of them."

Under strict labour laws, inefficient staff cannot easily be fired. On the other hand, many Germans are skeptical about working for foreign, especially small, companies—wondering how long they will last.

"We employ people at the start of each quarter," says Hartley. This is normal German practice. "In England, people tend to come and go." In Germany, most employees want security and are thinking of their pension rights at a young age. "We wanted to employ one woman as a secretary, and her husband wanted to know all about our parent and its activities." In the end, she decided the job was too risky.

To guard against disappointments on both sides, a probationary period of three months is usual for most staff, with six for managers. Also, employees expect to be paid a 13th month, though this does not necessarily mean the total sum is any different than what they would receive on a 12-month basis.

Germans are also used to better working conditions that those existing in may other countries. Comments John Brennan, head of Access Business Services, a similar operation to Lairco: "Germans expect bigger offices than maybe their chairman would occupy in the United States."

That may be the least of the differences, however. At the German headquarters of Toys "R" Us in Cologne, Joseph Baczko, president of its international division, explains how a raft of objections was thrown up by outsiders when the group considered coming to Germany: "We were told the Germans like wooden toys and are keen on technical things. Well, we sell a lot of plastic, we are self-service, and we sell both technical and nontechnical items."

Some local manufacturers also thought Toys "R" Us would be better advised to go for 5,000 square feet instead of its usual 45,000-square-foot stores. It ignored this.

"We were told we wouldn't get the permission," adds Baczko, "Our management has to come face to face with the conventional wisdom every day and challenge it."

The U.S. concern has done so to the extent that it now has 7 stores in Germany and will have 12 by the end of 1990. Its goal is 50.

Because busy young German mothers are used to hypermarkets and supermarkets, says Baczko, they have taken to the all-embracing Toys "R" Us concept, where a host of products is offered all year round and not just at Christmas.

Even the limited shopping hours in Germany are not seen as a hindrance, though Baczko does not regard them as immutable. "We didn't come to Germany just to get market share. We aim to be number one, and we will be. In that way, restrictive trading practices work in our favour. We are the point of convenience for the customer."

To obtain the edge-of-town sites it requires, Toys "R" Us is prepared to argue with local authorities for as long as it takes. "There's not one site yet that we've abandoned." Where sites are not zoned for retailing, the company has to do a lot of badgering, especially where local competitors have strong influence. "We have to fight; we continue to do that every day."

Within the company, Toys "R" Us strives for harmony and informality. All staff have stock options, which is unusual in Germany—"a bit of sweet equity underscores the entrepreneurial drive," says Baczko.

Staff are also encouraged to call each other by first names, definitely a rarity in German operations where titles and surnames are used. "To us, the culture is very important. If they're all going to be entrepreneurs, you can't have that type of hierarchy."

With typical American energy, Toys "R" Us has managed to both work with the German system and implant its own concept onto the retail landscape. "There's been nothing put forward as an obstacle or as a reason for not being here that has not proved to be false," insists Baczko.

Its managers clearly have to be untypical, gung-ho types. Speaking as distant revelers rolled through Cologne's streets, he concluded: "If you're not ready to be here on carnival day in Cologne, you probably don't belong here."

Few newcomers have the resources or the fiercely can-do approach of Toys "R" Us. But all face basically the same problems in Germany. Dieter Glotzel, general manager of Cisi Engineering, part of Cisi Software of France, agrees with Psion that distribution is a major hurdle, especially for specialized products and services. So is finding the right staff, blending both technical and sales expertise. He reckons French engineers are much better educated in information technology than Germans are.

Overcoming many Germans' aversion to risk taking is also not easy. "A lot of people strive for security and would never join a small firm. Others have the pioneer spirit, and those are the ones we want." Cisi is still small in Germany, with turnover of around DM1m. But like Toys "R" Us at the other end of the scale, it is breaking new ground in a market that can pay handsome dividends if well nurtured.

Source:
The Financial Times, March 15, 1989, p. 19.

CASE 3   NEW GOVERNMENT DEMANDS QUICK PROFIT

The postal services of Durbania were not as efficient as they should have been—mail was delayed and sometimes lost—and it was running seven-digit losses, which were increasing. In desperation, the minister for postal services turned to the private sector for a management and organization expert and hired Jason McNab, one of the best. McNab took over as chairman of postal services.

He found the following state of affairs. The equipment was old, out of date, and subject to frequent malfunction. As with all postal services, this one is required to pick up and deliver mail throughout the whole country, including the sparsely populated mountains and rural areas. It cannot shut down those loss-causing services and concentrate on the profitable business and urban customers.

Competition was growing from such profitable, private communications methods as electronic mail, facsimile transmission, and UPS-type services. Durbania's postal service offered none of those services.

After two years in the job, McNab had ended the long history of increasing postal service losses, and they were stable along with the government subsidy necessary to keep services going. He was well along with a multimillion-dollar investment program that was on track to make postal services break even within five years.

At this time, Durbania held elections, and the Reform party won in a landslide over the Labor party, which had governed for eight years. McNab expected a period of uncertainty followed by a cost-saving exercise that would pay lip service to promises to lower inflation and speed up privatization of public services.

To his surprise, the Reformers acted quickly, as the central bank raised discount rates 2 percent as an inflation-fighting measure. That would make the financing for his modernization of the postal service equipment more expensive.

Then, barely a week after the new postal minister's appointment, McNab was summoned to her office. She got straight to the point by announcing to a stunned McNab that his government subsidy would be withdrawn at the end of the next fiscal year, which was only 20 months in the future. "We've got to reduce public spending next year, and I don't think we can afford you. We should see a return on assets—perhaps 2 percent—in three years," she told McNab. Her goal was to privatize the postal service before the end of Reform's four-year term.

McNab explained his schedule, which projected an end of losses and at least a break-even in five years. He pointed out that higher interest rates were already hampering his modernization efforts and how difficult it would be to cut costs sufficiently to offset loss of the subsidy.

"That's your problem," said the minister. "If you don't think you can meet the new government's goals, then I'm sure we'll be able to find someone who can."

Poor McNab rushed back to his office and called a must meeting of the top postal service managers for that night. He had no time to spare. They worked through the night and until noon the next day; when the meeting ended, they were tired but enthusiastic. They had decided on the only strategy bold enough to have any reasonable chance of success.

They decided they must increase revenue and cut unit costs, which are the only ones that reasonably can be cut back given the large fixed-cost base of the postal system. They must maintain output if revenue is to rise.

The revenue increases required to have any chance of profitability in three years must come from the high-income parts of the market. These are premium services for which customers are willing to pay for quality service. The postal service must move into competition with private companies and offer electronic mail, facsimile, and UPS-types of services.

Its fixed assets, which it must maintain to remain a postal service for all the people, will give it excellent bases from which to offer the premium services. They decided they could not afford to cut the investment program. Not only will it increase quality of services, it will also result in a more salable asset at privatization time.

Source:

Adapted from "Dilemma & Decision," *International Management,* December 1988, p. 22.

Appendix A

Sources of Economic and Financial Information

I. WORLD
   A. *Abecor Country Reports*—Barclays Bank, 54 Lombard Street, London EC3P 3AH. Free to educators and prospective customers.
   B. *Business International*—Business International, One Dag Hammarskjold Plaza, New York 10017.
   C. *Balance of Payments Statistics* (annual with monthly supplements)—Should be in your library. Order from Publication Services, IMF, Washington, DC 20431.
   D. *Culturegrams*—Publications on individual countries with information for businesspeople. Write David M. Kennedy Center for International Studies, Brigham Young University, Provo, Utah 89602.
   E. *Direction of Trade Statistics* (monthly and annual yearbook)—Information on exports and imports for about 140 countries. IMF publication.
   F. *Doing Business in . . .*—Books on 16 major markets. Explain local business customs and how to negotiate. Published by SRI International, Menlo Park, California. Call (415) 859–4600.
   G. *Economic Review*—Public Information Dept., Federal Reserve Bank of San Francisco, P.O. Box 7702, San Francisco, California 94120. Free.
   H. *Ernst & Young International Series*—Ernst & Young, 153 East 53rd Street, New York 10022. Free to educators and prospective customers.
   I. *Europa Yearbook* (two volumes)—Covers international organizations and provides information on the political, sociocultural, and economic conditions on a country-by-country basis. Published by Europa Publications, 18 Bedford Square, London WC1B 3JN, which also publishes four regional yearbooks with additional information on regional organizations and each country in the region.
   J. *International Executive*—Periodical that publishes abstracts of selected articles and books about international business. Published at American Graduate School of International Management in Glendale, Arizona 85306.

K. *Eximbank Record*—Exim Bank, Washington, D.C. 20571. Free.

L. Extebank—Banco Exterior de España; Carrera de San Jeronimo, Madrid. Free to educators and prospective customers.

M. *Finance & Development*—International Monetary Fund, Washington, D.C. 20431. Free to educators.

N. *Foreign Exchange Review*—Manufacturers Hanover Trust Company, New York 10022.

O. *IMF Survey*—IMF, Washington, D.C. 20431. Free to educators.

P. *International Economic Conditions*—Research and Public Information, Federal Reserve Bank of St. Louis, P.O. Box 442, St. Louis, Missouri 63166. Free to educators.

Q. *International Finance*—The Chase Manhattan Bank, New York.

R. *International Management* (monthly)—Good articles on international business. Published by Reed Business Publishing, Oakfield House, West Sussex RH16 3DH, England.

S. *International Marketing Data & Statistics* (annual)—Marketing data on about 100 countries. Published by Euromonitor, London. Your library can order from Gale Research in Detroit.

T. International Publications Service—Sells trade directories, business guides, and reference books. Has good selection on Japan and China. Call 1–800–821–8312 for free catalog.

U. *OPEC Bulletin*—Public Information Department, Organization of the Petroleum Exporting Countries, Obere Donaustrasse 93, 1020 Vienna, Austria. Free.

V. *Overseas Business Reports*—U.S. Department of Commerce, Washington, D.C.

W. *Prospects*—Swiss Bank Corporation, CH–4002, Basel. Free to educators and prospective customers.

X. *Review* (bimonthly)—Good articles on international financial matters. Free from Federal Reserve Bank of St. Louis, P.O. Box 442, St. Louis, Missouri 63166.

Y. *Transnational Corporations in World Development*—A 600-page study that is periodically updated. Has useful information about worldwide companies. Their relationship with governments is discussed. Published by the United Nations Centre on Transnational Corporations, it is available on microfiche from Index to International Statistics as well as in hard copy.

Z. *UNESCO Statistical Yearbook*—Information on educational systems, research expenditures, and radio and TV stations. Contact the UN.

AA. *U.N. Statistical Yearbook*—United Nations.

BB. *UNU Newsletter*—1911 Kenbar Court, McLean, Virginia 22101.

CC. *World Development Report* (annual)—Publications, The World Bank, 1818 H Street, N.W., Washington, D.C. 20433; $12.95. This is an invaluable data source. Ask for World Bank publication list.

DD. *World Statistics in Brief*—United Nations.

EE. *World Tables* (annual)—Data for 140 countries. Contact Publication Sales Unit, World Bank, Washington, D.C. 20433. The World Bank says it should be on diskettes by 1990.

FF. *Yearbook of Labor Statistics*—International Labor Organization, Geneva, Switzerland.

See the appendix in Chapter 14 for additional data sources.

II. AFRICA
   A. Region.
      1. *Business Europe*—Business International, see above.
      2. *Middle East & North Africa*—Information on regional organizations and more data on countries in the region than *Europa* has. Published by Europa. See item I(I) above.
      3. *Africa South of the Sahara*—Same kind of information as in item II2 above. Another Europa publication.
   B. South Africa.
      South African Digest—Department of Information, Private Bag X152, Pretoria 0001.
   C. Tunisia.
      Tunisia Industrial News—Tunisia Investment Promotion Agency, 630 Fifth Avenue, Suite 862, New York 10020.

III. ASIA
   A. Region.
      1. *ABD Development Review* (biannual)—Asian Development Bank, P.O. Box 789, Manila, The Philippines. Free to educators.
      2. *Business Asia*—Business International, see above.
      3. *Pacific Basin Economic Indicators*—Federal Reserve Bank of San Francisco, P.O. Box 7702, San Francisco 94120. Free.
      4. *The Far East and Australasia*—Another Europa publication. See item IIA2.
   B. India. *United Commercial Bank Review*—United Commercial Bank, 10 Brabourne Road, Calcutta.
   C. Indonesia.
      Indonesia Development News—National Development Information Office, Hill and Knowlton, Inc., 633 Third Avenue, New York 10017. Free.
   D. Japan.
      1. *Japan Banking Briefs*—Fuji Bank, C.P.O. Box 148, Tokyo. Free.
      2. *Japan Report, Consulate General of Japan*—280 Park Avenue, New York 10017. Free.
      3. *Jetro Business Information Series*—Japanese Trade Organization, 1221 Avenue of the Americas, New York. Free to educators.
      4. *Sell in Japan*—U.S. Department of Commerce, Washington, D.C. 20230.
      5. *Sumitomo Bank Review, Economic Survey*—Sumitomo Bank, 3–2, 1–Chome, Marunouchi, Chiyoda-ku, Tokyo. Free.
      6. *The Wheel Extended*—Toyota Motor Sales, Public Relations Department 2–3–18, Kudan-Minami, Chiyodo-ku, Tokyo 102. Free.
      7. *Japan Periodicals*—This is a listing of 225 business periodicals in Japan, some of which are free. Write Keizai Koho Center,

6–1, Otemachi 1-Chome, Chiyoda-ku, Tokyo 100. Tell them you are a professor of international business.

8. *Speaking of Japan*—Same address as 7.

9. *Economic Eye*—Same address as 7.

E. Korea.

1. *Monthly Bulletin*—The Bank of Korea, Seoul.

2. *Monthly Economic Statistics*—The Bank of Korea.

3. *Quarterly Economic Review*—The Bank of Korea.

F. Middle East.

Middle East Executive Reports (monthly)—Middle East Executive Reports, 1115 Massachusetts Avenue, N.W., Washington, D.C. 20005. $300 annually ($145 to universities).

G. Taiwan.

1. *Economic Review*—International Commercial Bank of China, Taipai, **Taiwan**. Free.

2. *Taiwan Industrial Panorama*—Industrial Development and Investment Center, Taipai, Taiwan. Free.

3. *Monthly Economic Survey*—The International Commercial Bank of China, Head Office, Taipai, Taiwan. Free.

H. Thailand.

Monthly Review—Public Relations Dept. Bankok Bank, 23 Surawong Road, Bankok. Free.

I. Turkey.

1. *Bulletin Mensuel*—Banque Centrale de la Republique de Turquie, Ankara. Free.

2. *Turkey, An Economic Survey* (annual)—Turkish Industrialists and Businessmen's Association, Cumhuriyet Cadessi, Dortler Apt. 18/2 Elmadag, Istanbul. Free.

3. YAPI ve KREDI BANKASI, Economics Department, P.O. Box 250, 250 Beyoglu, Istanbul. Free.

IV. EUROPE

A. Region.

1. *A Selective Study Guide to the European Community*—A list of books, bibliographies, and periodicals on the European Community. Free from Commission of the European Communities, 2100 M Street, N.W., Washington, D.C. 20037.

2. *Bulletin*—Crédit Suisse, 8021 Zurich, 8 Paradeplatz, Switzerland.

3. *Business Europe*—Business International. One Dag Hammarskjold Plaza, New York 10017.

4. *Business Facts and Figures*—Union Bank of Switzerland, Zurich.

5. *EFTA Bulletin*—EFTA, 9–11 Rue de Varembé CH–1211, Geneva 20.

6. *EuroBusiness*—A monthly publication. Write 21 Gold Street, Saffron Walden, Essex CB10 1EJ, England.

7. *European Marketing Data & Statistics* (annual)—Published by Euromonitor and distributed by Gale Research in Detroit.

8. *Europe*—European Community, 2100 M Street, N.W., Washington, D.C. 20037. Ask for EC publication list.

9. *OECD Economic Indicators* (annual)—OECD.

10. *OECD Economy Surveys*—OECD.

11. *OECD Observer*—OECD, 1750 Pennsylvania Avenue N.W., Washington, D.C. 20006. Ask for publication list.

12. *Prospects*—Swiss Bank Corporation, Aeschenvorstadt 1, Basel.

B. Austria.

Landerbank Report, Landerbank, A-1010 Vienna, Am Hof 2, Austria.

C. Belgium.

Weekly Bulletin—Kredietbank, Opzichterstraat 41, B-1020, Brussels.

D. Denmark.

1. *Main Features of the Danish Economy*—Den Danske Bank, AF 1871 Aktieselskab, Holmens Kanal, Dk-1092 Copenhagen K.

2. *Quarterly Review*—Copenhagen Handelsbank, 2, Holmens Kanal, Dk-1091 Copenhagen K.

E. Finland.

1. *Economic Review*—Kansallis–Osake–Pankki, Box 10, SF-00101, Helsinki 10.

2. *Monthly Bulletin*—Bank of Finland, Helsinki.

F. Germany, East.

GDR Economics Service, Chamber of Foreign Trade of the GDR, DDR-108 Berlin, Schadowstrasse 1.

G. Germany, West.

1. *German–American Trade News*—German–American Chamber of Commerce, 666 Fifth Avenue, New York 10019.

2. *Monthly Report*—Deutsche Bundesbank, P.O. Box 2633, D6000, Frankfurt am Main 1.

3. *Deutsche Bank Bulletin*—Deutsche Bank, Frankfurt (Main).

H. Great Britain.

1. *Economic Progress Report*—H.M. Treasury, Parliament Street, London SW1P3AG.

2. *Quarterly Bulletin*—Bank of England, London, EC2R8AH.

3. *Lloyds Bank Review*—The Editor, Lloyds Bank Review, 71 Lombard Street, London EC3P 3BS.

4. *Quarterly Review*—National Westminster Bank Limited, 41 Lothbury, London EC2P 2BP.

5. *Midland Bank Review*—Midland Bank plc, P.O. Box 2, Griffin House, Silver Street Head, Sheffield, S1 3GG.

I. Italy.

1. *Italian Trends*—Banca Nazionale del Lavoro, Via Veneto 119, Rome.

2. *Review of the Economic Condition in Italy*—Banco di Roma, Via del Corso, 207, 00186 Rome.

3. *The Italian Economy*—Economic Research Dept., Banca Commerciale Italiana, Milan.

J. Netherlands.

1. *Bank Mees and Hope NV,* P.O. Box 95, 3000 AB Rotterdam.

2. *Economic Review*—ABN Bank, 32 Vijzelstraat, Amsterdam.

3. *Holland Info*—Economic Information Service, The Hague.

K. Norway.
1. *DNC Monthly Survey*—Den Norske Creditbank, Oslo.
2. *Economic Bulletin*—Norges Bank, P.O. Box 336, Sentrum, Oslo 1.
3. *Economic News*—Bergen Bank, Oslo.
4. *Financial Review*—Norwegian Bankers' Association, P.O. Box 1489, Vika, Oslo.
5. *Norway Information*—Norwegian Information Service, 825 Third Avenue, New York 10022.

L. **Spain.**
Noticiario Economico—Banco de Vizcaya, Gran Via, 1, Bilbao.

M. Sweden.
Newsletter from Sweden—Swedish-International Press Bureau, Skeppargatan 37, S–11452, Stockholm.

N. Switzerland
SwissBusiness (bimonthly)—Swiss Office for Development of Trade, Case Postal 1128, CH–1001, Lausanne.

V. WESTERN HEMISPHERE
A. Region.
1. *Andean Group*—Junta de Cartagena, Casilla 3237, Lima, Peru (official organ of the Andean Group).
2. *BOLSA Review*—Bank of London and South America, 40–66 Queen Victoria Street, London EC4P 4EL.
3. *Business Latin America*—Business International, One Dag Hammarskjold Plaza, New York 10017.
4. *Caribbean Basin Economic Survey*—Federal Reserve Bank of Atlanta GA 30303.
5. *Comercio Exterior*—Banco Nacional de Comercio Exterior, Avenue Chapultapec, 230; Mexico 7, D.F., Mexico. In Spanish.
6. *IDB News*—Inter-American Development Bank, 303 17th Street, N.W., Washington D.C. 20577.
7. *Lateinamerkia*—Deutsche Bank, Frankfurt (Main), Germany. In English.
8. *Notas Sobre la Economia y el Desarrollo de America Latina*—Cepal, Casilla 179 D. Santiago, Chile. In Spanish.
9. *South America, Central America and the Caribbean*—A Europa publication. See IIA2.

B. Argentina.
Economic Information on Argentina—Ministerio de Economia (prensa), Hipolita Yrigoyen 250, piso 6, oficina 625, Buenos Aires.

C. Brazil.
1. *ML Monthly Letter*—Banco do Brasil, 550 Fifth Ave., New York, N.Y. 10036.
2. *Trends and Perspectives of the Brazilian Economy*—Quarterly from Banco Lar Brasileiro, caixa Postal, 221–Zc–00, 20,000, Rio de Janeiro, R.J. Brazil.
3. *Brasil*—Comercio e Industria, SIG, Q4–No. 217, 70.610-Brasilia, D.F., Brazil. Free.

D. Canada.
1. *Business Review*—Bank of Montreal, P.O. Box 6002, Montreal, P.O., H3C, 3B1. Free to educators.

       2. *Monthly Review*—The Bank of Nova Scotia, 44 King Street, W., Toronto, Canada M5H 1H1. Free to educators.

  E. Caricom.

    Caricom Perspective—The Caricom Secretariat, Bank of Guyana Building, P.O. Box 10827, Georgetown, Guyana, S.A.

  F. Chile.

    Economic News—Corfo, One World Trade Center, Suite 1551, New York 10048.

  G. Colombia.

    Colombia Today—Colombia Information Service, 144 E. 57th Street, New York 10022.

  H. Costa Rica.

    Información Economica Semanal—Banco Central de Costa Rica, San Jose, Costa Rica.

  I. Mexico (all the following are free).

       1. *El Mercado de Valores*—Nacional financiera, see 6 below.

       2. *Mexican–American Review*—Camara de Comercio Americano, Lucerna 78, Mexico 6, D.F.

       3. *Mexico Statistical Data*—Banco Nacional de Mexico; Isabel la Catolica, 44; Mexico 1, D.F.; Mexico.

       4. *Panorama Economico*—Bancomer, S.A., V. Carranza 44, Mexico 1, D.F.

       5. *Review of the Economic Situation in Mexico*—Banco Nacional de Mexico.

       6. *Statistics on the Mexican Economy*—Nacional Financiera, Isabel la Catolica, 51; Mexico 1, D.F.; Mexico.

VI. OCEANIA

  A. Region.

       1. *The Far East and Australasia*—See IIIA4.

       2. *Pacific Islands Yearbook*—Historical, cultural, and business information on Pacific island countries. Write Pacific Publications, 76 Clarence Street, Sydney, Australia.

  B. Australia (all are free to educators and prospective customers).

       1. *ANZ Bank Business Indicators*—Australia and New Zealand Banking Group Limited, 55 Collins Street, Melbourne, 3000, Australia.

       2. *Australian Investment and Economic Newsletter*—The National Bank of Australasia, Ltd., P.O. Box 84A, Melbourne, Victoria 3001.

       3. *Monthly Summary*—National Australia Bank Limited, 500 Bourke Street (PO Box 84A), Melbourne, Victoria 3001.

  C. New Zealand.

       1. *Bulletin*—Reserve Bank of New Zealand, Wellington.

       2. *New Zealand News Review*—Reserve Bank of New Zealand, Wellington.

VII. EASTERN BLOC

  A. Region.

       1. *Business Eastern Europe*—Business International, One Dag Hammarskjold Plaza, New York 10017.

       2. *Newsletter*—East–West Trade Expansion Committee, 600 New Hampshire Ave., N.W., Washington, D.C. 20037.

B. Bulgaria.
    Bulgarian Foreign Trade—Bulgarreklama Agency, 42 Parchevich Street, Sofia.
C. Hungary.
    1. *Hungarian Foreign Trade* (quarterly)—Hungarian Chamber of Commerce, Kultura, P.O. Box 149, H 1389 Budapest.
    2. *Marketing in Hungary* (quarterly)—Same as above.
    3. *The Hungarian Economy* (quarterly)—Same as above.
D. Romania.
    Publications of the Chamber of Commerce of the Socialist Republic of Romania, 22, N. Balcescu Boulevard, Bucharest.
E. Russia.
    Soviet Business and Economic Report—Porter International, 1776 K Street, N.W., Washington, D.C. 20006.
F. Yugoslavia.
    Statistical Pocket Book of Yugoslavia—Federal Institute for Statistics, Beograd, Kenza Milosa 20, Yugoslavia.

VIII. DATA BASES
    A. *Dialogue*—Many data bases on Dialogue have information on foreign and domestic operations for specific industries. Call 1–800–334–2564 for information.
    B. *PTS Index* and *Trade & Industry Index*—Predicast data bases. Call 1–800–321–6388 for information.
    C. *ABI Inform*—Call 1–800–626–2823 for information.

Appendix B

International Organizations

ACM Andean Common Market

ADELA Adela Group

AID Agency for International Development

ASEAN Association of South East Asian Nations

BMSE Baltic Mercantile and Shipping Exchange

BIS Bank for International Settlements

CACM Central American Common Market

CCM Caribbean Common Market, Caribbean Community

COMECON Council for Mutual Economic Assistance

EEC European Economic Community, generally referred to as the Common Market and frequently as EC for European Community

ECOWAS Economic Community of West African States

EFTA European Free Trade Association

ESA Department of Economic and Social Affairs

FAO Food and Agriculture Organization

GATT General Agreement on Tariffs and Trade

IAEA International Atomic Energy Agency

IBRD International Bank for Reconstruction and Development, commonly called World Bank

ICAO International Civil Aviation Organization

IDA International Development Association

IFAD International Fund for Agricultural Development

IFC International Finance Corporation

ILO International Labor Organization

IMCO Inter-Governmental Maritime Consultative Organization

IMF International Monetary Fund

ITU International Telecommunication Union

LAAD Latin American Agribusiness Development Corporation

LAAI Latin American Association for Integration

NAFTA New Zealand–Australia Free Trade Agreement

OECD Organization for Economic Cooperation and Development

OPEC Organization of Petroleum-Exporting Countries

PICA Private Investment Company for Asia

SIFIDA   Societé Internationale Financiere pour les Investissements et Developpement en Afrique S.A.

UN   United Nations

UNCITRAL   UN Conference on International Trade Law

UNCTAD   UN Conference on Trade and Development

UNDP   UN Development Program

UNESCO   UN Educational, Scientific, and Cultural Organization

UNICEF   UN Children's Fund (formerly UN International Children's Emergency Fund)

UNIDO   UN Industrial Development Organization

UNITAR   UN Institute for Training and Research

UPU   Universal Postal Union

WFP   World Food Program

WHO   World Health Organization

WMO   World Meteorological Organization

Glossary

absolute advantage   The advantage enjoyed by a country because it can produce a product at a lower cost than can other countries.

accidental exporting   Export business obtained through no effort of the exporter.

accounting exposure   The total net of accounting statement items on which loss could occur because of currency exchange rate changes.

adjustment assistance   Financial and technical assistance to workers, firms, and communities to help them adjust to import competition.

ad valorem tariff or duty   Literally "according to the value." A method in which customs duties or tariffs are established and charged as a percentage of the value of imported goods.

advertising, paid   Nonpersonal presentation of ideas, goods, or services by an identified sponsor.

advising bank   The bank that notifies the beneficiary of the opening of a letter of credit. The advising bank makes no payment commitment.

aesthetics   A culture's sense of beauty and good taste.

affiliated company   May be a subsidiary or a company in which a WWC has less than 100 percent ownership.

A.G.   Aktien-Gesellschaft. A joint stock company in Germany.

agency office   An office of a foreign bank in the United States that cannot accept domestic deposits. It seeks business for the bank when U.S. companies operate internationally.

air waybill   For goods shipped by air, performs the functions of a bill of lading in land surface transport or of a marine bill of lading in water transport.

allowance   Extra payments to expatriate employees to meet the higher costs they incur abroad.

American depository receipt (ADR)   Stock of a foreign corporation is deposited at an American bank. The bank issues an ADR, not the corporation's stock certificate, to an American investor who buys shares of that corporation. The stock certificate is kept at the bank.

antiboycott law   An American law against complying with the Arab countries' boycott of Israel.

antitrust laws   Laws to prevent business from engaging in such practices as price-fixing or market sharing.

appreciation   An increase in the value of one currency in terms of another currency.

apprenticeship program   Enables a person to learn a job skill by working with a skilled worker.

appropriate technology   The technology—advanced, intermediate, or primitive—that most fits the society using it.

arbitrage   The simultaneous purchase and sale of something in two (or more) markets at a time when it is selling (being bought) at different prices in the markets. Profit is the price differential minus the cost.

arbitration   The settlement of a dispute between parties by a third, presumably unbiased, party.

arm's-length transaction   A transaction between two or more unrelated parties. (A transaction between two subsidiaries of a WWC would not be an arm's-length transaction.)

associations   Social units based on age, sex, or common interest, not on kinship.

back-to-back letter of credit (L/C)   A paying bank that will pay the exporter opens a back-to-back L/C based on the underlying L/C the exporter's supplier (a manufacturer, for example) may be paid.

back-to-back loans   A unit of one WWC lends to a unit of a second WWC; and at the same time and in equivalent amounts, another unit of the second WWC lends to another unit of the first.

backward vertical integration   Establishing facilities to manufacture inputs used in the production of a firm's final products.

balance of payments (BOP)   A financial statement that compares all reported payments by residents of one country to residents of other countries with payments to domestic residents by foreign residents. If more money has been paid out than received, the BOP is in deficit. If the opposite condition exists, the BOP is in surplus.

banker's acceptance   A draft drawn, for example, by an exporter on an importer's bank. If the bank accepts the draft, the bank has agreed to pay in accordance with its terms.

bank swaps   To avoid currency exchange problems, a bank in a soft-currency country will lend to a WWC subsidiary there. The WWC or its bank will make hard currency available to the lending bank outside the soft-currency country.

barter   The exchange of goods or services for goods or services. No money is used.

bill of exchange (draft)   An unconditional written order calling on the party to whom it is addressed to pay on demand or at a future date a sum of money to the order of a named party or to the bearer. Examples are acceptances or the commercial bank check.

bill of lading (B/L)   A receipt given by a carrier of goods received and contract for their delivery. Usually a B/L is made to the order of someone and is negotiable. The B/L is also a document of title with which the holder may claim the goods from the carrier.

blocked account   Financial assets that cannot be transferred into another currency or out of the country without the government's permission.

bonded warehouse   Warehouse authorized by customs authorities for storage of goods on which payment of import duties is deferred until the goods are removed.

bonds: Eurobond   A long-term bond marketed internationally in countries other than the country of the currency in which it is denominated. The issue is not subject to national restrictions. **zero-coupon bonds**   Pay no periodic interest (hence their name), so the total yield is obtained entirely as capital gain on the final maturity date. **dual-currency bonds**   Denominated in one currency but pay interest in another currency at a fixed rate of exchange. Dual-currency bonds can also pay redemption proceeds in a different currency than the currency of denomination. **floating rate bonds**   The most commonly issued instrument, the interest coupons on which are adjusted regularly according to the level of some base interest rate plus a fixed spread.

bonuses   Extra payments to expatriates because of hardships and inconveniences encountered in some foreign postings.

boomerang effect   Refers to the fact that technology sold to companies in another nation may be used to produce goods that will then compete with those of the seller of the technology.

bottleneck   Operation in production system whose output sets limit for entire system's output.

bottom-up planning   Planning process that begins at the lowest level in the organization and continues upward.

brain drain   The loss by a country of its most intelligent and best-educated people.

branch office   An office or department of a company at a location away from headquarters. It is a part of the company and not a separate legal entity, as is a subsidiary, an affiliate, or a joint venture.

Bretton Woods   A resort in New Hampshire at which bank and treasury officials of the major Allied powers met near the end of World War II. There they established the international monetary system that, in some parts, still endures. It is known as the Bretton Woods system.

bribes   Gifts or payments to induce the receiver to do something illegal for the giver.

buffer stock   A supply of a commodity that the executive of a commodity agreement tries to accumulate and hold so that when the price of the commodity begins to rise above desirable levels, sales can be made from that stock to dampen the price rise.

Canadian Shield   A massive land area of bedrock covering one half of Canada's land mass.

capital intensive   Describes processes that require a high concentration of capital relative to labor per unit of output and products produced by such processes. The opposite is labor intensive.

capitalism   All possible activities are performed by private business or persons rather than by a government.

cartel   An organization of suppliers that controls the supply and price of a commodity. To be successful, a cartel should have relatively few members who control most of the export supply of the commodity; the members must observe the cartel rules; and the commodity must be a necessity with a price-inelastic demand.

caste system   An aspect of Hinduism by which the entire society is divided into four groups plus the outcasts, and each is assigned a certain class of work.

central banks   Government institutions with authority over the size and growth of the national monetary stock. Central banks frequently regulate commercial banks and usually act as the government's fiscal agent.

central reserve assets   Gold, SDRs, ECUs or hard foreign currencies held in a nation's treasury.

centrally planned economy   Governments plan and direct almost all economic activity and usually own the factors of production.

centrally planned markets   Markets in which there is almost no free market activity and the government owns all major factors of production, controls labor, and tries to plan all activity.

certificate of review   Legal document issued by U.S. Department of Commerce that grants immunity from state and federal antitrust prosecution to export trading companies.

chaebols   The large South Korean business conglomerates that have succeeded worldwide in such fields as computers, construction, shipbuilding, textiles, and steel.

CIF (cost, insurance, and freight)   A term used in the delivery of goods from one party to another. The price includes the costs of the goods, the maritime or other appropriate transportation, the insurance premium, and the freight charges to the destination.

climate   The meteorological conditions, including temperature, precipitation, and wind, that prevail in a region.

cluster analysis   Statistical technique dividing objects into groups so that the objects within each group are similar.

COCOM   Voluntary group of most NATO nations that administers a common set of export controls to prevent transfer of sensitive goods to Soviet-bloc nations.

codetermination   A system in which representatives of labor participate in the management of a company.

collection documents   All documents submitted to a buyer for the purpose of receiving payment for a shipment.

collective bargaining   Bargaining between an employer and a labor union about employee wages and working conditions.

commodity agreement   An agreement between the producers and consumers of a commodity (for example, tin, cocoa, or rubber) to regulate the production, price, and trade of the commodity.

common external tariff   Under an agreement reached by a group of nations, such as the EC, the same level of tariffs is imposed by these nations on all goods imported from other nations.

communism   A theory of a classless society conceived by Marx. Lenin, Stalin, and others developed it differently.

comparative advantage   Unless a country has the same absolute advantage in producing all goods and services, there would be some goods and services in which it had less relative advantage. It would gain by importing those and exporting the ones in which it had an absolute advantage, or the greatest relative advantage.

compensation   A form of countertrade involving payment in goods and cash.

compensatory financing   A program to assist countries in financial difficulties due to drops in export earnings because of natural causes, such as drought, or because of international market price decreases. The IMF and the EC have compensatory financing programs.

compensatory trade   Any transaction that involves asset transfer as a condition of purchase.

competitive alliance   Cooperation between competitors for specific purposes.

competitive analysis   Process in which principal competitors are identified and their objectives, strengths, weaknesses, and product lines are assessed.

competitor intelligence system   Procedure for gathering, analyzing, and disseminating information about a firm's competitors.

compound duty   A form of import duty consisting of an ad valorem duty and a specific duty.

confirm   Act of a correspondent bank in the seller's vicinity by which it agrees to honor the issuing bank's letter of credit.

confirmed letter of credit (L/C)   An L/C confirmed by a bank other than the opening bank. Thus, it is an obligation of more than one bank.

confiscation   Seizure by a government of foreign-owned assets that is not followed by prompt, effective, and adequate compensation.

Confucian work ethic   Same as the Christian work ethic. The term is used in Asian nations where Confucianism is a major religion.

conservative   In American political usage, a conservative advocates minimum government activity.

contingency plan   Plan for the best- or worst-case scenarios or for critical events that could have a severe impact on the firm.

contract manufacturing   Manufacturing of a product or component by one company for anther company. The two companies may or may not be related by stock ownership, common parent, or otherwise.

controllable forces   The forces internal to the firm that management administers to adapt to changes in the uncontrollable environmental forces.

convertible currencies   Currencies that may be changed for or converted into other currencies, at least for current account payments, without government permission.

cooperative exporters   Established international manufacturers who export other manufacturers' goods as well as their own.

coproduction   A form of industrial cooperation in which two or more factories produce components for a final product.

corporate strategy   Action plan to enable an organization to reach its objectives.

cottage industry   Production away from a central factory, typically in the worker's own home or cottage. Workers are paid on a piece-rate basis, or so much for each unit produced.

counterfeiting   Illegal use of a well-known manufacturer's brand name on copies of the firm's merchandise.

countertrade   A transaction in which goods are exchanged for goods. Payment by a purchaser is entirely or partially in goods instead of hard currencies for products or technology from other countries.

countervailing duty   An additional amount of tariff levied on an import that is found to have benefited from an export subsidy.

country risk assessment   Evaluating the risks before lending or investing in a country.

covered investment or interest arbitrage   Investment in a second currency that is "covered" by a forward sale of that currency to protect against exchange rate fluctuations. Profit depends on interest rate differentials minus the discount or plus the premium on a forward sale.

covering   Buying or selling foreign currencies in amounts equivalent to future payments to be made or received. A means of protection against loss due to currency exchange rate fluctuations.

credit or money market hedge   Hedging by borrowing the currency of risk, converting it immediately to the ultimately desired currency, and repaying the loan when payment is received.

cross investment   Foreign direct investment made by oligopolistic firms in each other's home country as a defense measure.

cross rate   The exchange rate between two currencies, which is determined by means of the U.S. dollar. For example, if someone wants to sell Japanese yen and buy Swiss francs, the procedure is to buy dollars with the yen and then buy Swiss francs with the dollars.

culture   The benefits, rules, techniques, institutions, and artifacts that characterize human populations.

currency area   The group of countries whose currencies are pegged to any one DC currency. Many LDCs peg the value of their currency to that of their major DC trading partner.

currency exchange controls   A government's controls over how much foreign currency its residents or visitors can have and how much they must pay for it.

currency swap   The exchange of one currency into another at an agreed rate and a reversal of that exchange at the same rate at the end of the swap contract period.

customhouse broker   Independent business that handles import shipments for compensation.

customs union   An arrangement between two or more countries whereby they eliminate tariffs and other import restrictions on one another's goods and establish a common tariff on the goods from all other countries.

debt capital   Money raised by selling bonds, the principal and interest on which must be repaid.

debt default   When a debtor fails or refuses to pay a debt.

debt rescheduling   Defaulted debt is renegotiated, giving the debtor a longer time to pay and/or a lower interest rate.

demonstration effect   The result of having seen others with desirable goods.

demurrage   Charge assessed by a carrier on an exporter or an importer for excess time taken to unload or load a vessel.

depreciation of a currency   A decline in the value of a currency in terms of another currency or in terms of gold. "Depreciation" and "devaluation" are used interchangeably.

devaluation   Depreciation of a currency by official government action.

developed   A classification for all industrialized nations; that is, those that are more developed technically.

developed countries (DCs)   Industrialized countries.

developing   A classification for the world's lower-income nations that are less technically developed.

development banks   Banks that aid less developed countries (LDCs) in economic development. They may lend or invest money and encourage local ownership. They may be worldwide, regional, or national.

direct exporting   The exporting of goods and services by the firm that produces them.

direct investment   Sufficient investment to obtain at least some voice in management. The U.S. government considers 10 percent or more equity in a foreign company to be direct investment.

dirty float   A currency that floats in value in terms of other currencies but is not free of government intervention. Governments intervene to "smooth" or "manage" fluctuations or to maintain desired exchange rates.

discretionary income   The amount of income remaining after paying taxes and making essential purchases.

disposable income   The amount of income remaining after taxes.

distributors   Independent importers who buy for their own account for resale.

district export councils   Groups of volunteer businesspeople in every state that are appointed by the U.S. Department of Commerce to assist exporters.

documentary drafts   Drafts accompanied by such documents as invoices, bills of lading, inspection certificates, and insurance papers.

domestication   Term used to indicate process in which a host government brings pressure to force a foreign owner to turn over partial ownership to the host country government or host country citizens.

domestic environment   All the uncontrollable forces originating in the home country that surround and influence the firm's life and development.

domestic international sales corporation (DISC)   A

subsidiary corporation of a U.S. company that is incorporated in a state of the United States for the purpose of exporting from the United States. DISCs are given certain tax advantages. Generally, they have been superseded by foreign sales corporations.

drafts (bills of exchange)   Orders drawn by a drawer that order a second party, the drawee, to pay a sum of money to a payee. The payee may be the same party as the drawer.

drawback   The reimbursement of the tariff paid on an imported component that is later exported. When a component is imported into the United States, a tariff is levied on it and paid by the importer. If that component is later exported, the exporter is entitled to get 99 percent of the tariff amount from U.S. Customs.

drawee   See *drafts.*

drawer   See *drafts.*

dumping   Selling abroad at prices lower than those charged in the home or other markets.

duties (tariffs)   Amounts charged when goods are imported into a country. If such duties are based on the values of the goods, they are called ad valorem. If they are based on the number of items imported, they are called specified.

earned income   Income derived from efforts, labor, sales, or active participation in business. Salaries, wages, bonuses, and commissions are examples, Unearned income is a return on investment of money or time. Examples are interest, dividends, and royalties. The distinction is important for purposes of U.S. taxation of American residents abroad.

East-West trade   Trade between the centrally planned economies of the communist block (East) and the more market-oriented economies of the OECD nations (West).

Edge Act corporation   A subsidiary of a U.S. commercial bank that operates in a foreign country. The Edge subsidiary, operating abroad, is free of restraints of U.S. law and may perform whatever services and functions are legal in the countries where it operates.

employee facilities   Schools, cafeterias, housing, recreation, or other employer-provided facilities.

environment   All the forces surrounding and influencing the life and development of the firm.

environmental scanning   Procedure in which a firm scans the world for changes in the environmental forces that might affect it.

equity capital   Money raised by selling corporate stock that represents ownership of the corporation.

equity-related bonds   Bonds that are convertible at the option of the holder into other securities of the issuer, usually common stock-type equity. Called convertibles in the United States.

escape clause   A legal provision concerning products whose tariffs have been reduced. If, thereafter, imports increase and threaten the domestic producers of those products, the escape clause permits the tariffs to be put back up.

estimation by analogy   Using a market factor that is successful in one market to estimate demand in a similar market.

ethnocentricity   A belief in the superiority of one's own ethnic group.

Eurobonds   Bonds that are issued outside the restriction applying to domestic offerings and are syndicated and traded mostly from London. Most of these bonds are denominated in U.S. dollars.

Eurocurrency   A currency being used or traded outside the country that issued it.

Eurodollar   The U.S. dollar is the most widely used Eurocurrency.

European Currency Unit (ECU)   A currency unit established by the European Monetary System. Its value is determined by reference to the value of a "basket" of currencies. The currencies in the basket are those of the system's member-countries.

European Economic Zone   The European Free Trade Zone consisting of the EC and EFTA.

European Monetary Cooperation Fund (EMCF)   Lends assistance to EMS member-countries that have difficulties in keeping their currencies within the agreed value relationships.

European Monetary System (EMS)   A system, established in 1979, under which West European countries agreed to keep their currency values within an established range in relation to one another.

exchange rate   The price of one currency stated in another currency.

exchange rate risk   In activities involving two or more currencies, the risk that losses can occur as a result of changes in their relative value.

Eximbank (Export-Import Bank)   Principal federal government agency that aids American exporters by means of loans, guarantees, and insurance programs.

export bill of lading   Contract of carriage between shipper and carrier. Straight bill of lading is nonnegotiable; an endorsed "to-order" bill gives the holder claim on merchandise.

export draft   An unconditional order drawn by the seller on the buyer to pay the draft's amount on presentation (sight draft) or at an agreed future date (time draft) that must be paid before the buyer receives shipping documents.

export incentives   Subsidies or tax rebates paid by governments to companies to encourage them to export.

export licenses   A government document that permits the exporter to export designated goods to certain destinations. In the United States, the export license will be either a General Export License or a Validated Export License.

export management company   A company that acts as the export department for other companies. It performs all export-related services for its customers except supplying the product.

export processing zones   Specific and limited areas into which imported components may be brought for further processing. The finished product must be reexported to avoid payment of import duties.

export trading company   A firm established principally to export domestic goods and services and help unrelated companies export their products.

exposure netting   An open position in two or more currencies whose strengths and weaknesses are thought to balance one another.

expropriation   Seizure by a government of foreign-owned assets. Such seizure is not contrary to international law if it is followed by prompt, adequate, and effective compensation. If not, it is called confiscation.

extended family   Includes relatives beyond the parents and children.

extortion   Payments made to keep the receiver from causing harm to the payer.

extraterritorial application of laws   Attempts by a government to apply its laws outside its territorial borders.

factor   A buyer, at a discount, of a company's receivables with short-term maturities of no longer than a year.

factor endowment   A country is or is not endowed with one or more of the factors of production, capital, labor, and natural resources.

factoring   Discounting without recourse an account receivable.

"factory door" cost   The production cost of a good or service to which marketing and general administrative costs have not been added.

firm surveillance   The IMF has the power to monitor the exchange rate policies of member-nations.

fiscal policies   Government policies about the collection and spending of money.

fixed exchange rates   A system under which the values of currencies in terms of other currencies are fixed by

intergovernmental agreement and by governmental intervention in the currency exchange markets.

fixed interest rate   An interest rate that is set when a loan is made and remains the same for the life of the loan regardless of whether other interest rates rise or fall.

floating exchange rates   A system in which the values of currencies in terms of other currencies are determined by the supply of and demand for the currencies in currency markets. If governments do not intervene in the markets, the float is said to be "clean." If they do intervene, the float is said to be "dirty."

floating interest rates   A loan situation in which the interest rate set when a loan is made may rise or fall as the interest rates of some reference, such as LIBOR or the prime rate, vary. Sometimes called variable rates.

floating-rate notes or bonds   Debt instruments with floating or variable interest rates. The interest rates are pegged to a fluctuating interest rate, such as the six-month LIBOR rate.

fluctuating exchange rates   See *floating exchange rates*.

Foreign Corrupt Practices Act of 1977   An American law against making questionable payments when American companies do business abroad.

foreign exchange   The exchanges of the currency of one country for that of another country.

foreign exchange rates   Prices of one currency in terms of other currencies.

foreign exchange reserves   Gold, SDRs, U.S. dollars, and other convertible currencies held in a nation's treasury.

foreign financing   Occurs when a foreign company or other borrower comes to a nation's capital market and borrows in the local currency; for example, when an Italian company borrows U.S. dollars in New York or French francs in Paris.

foreign freight forwarder   Independent business that handles export shipments for compensation.

foreign national pricing   Local pricing in another country.

foreign sales corporation (FSC)   A corporation provided for in the Tax Reform Act of 1984. The FSC replaces the domestic international sales corporation (DISC) as a tax incentive for exporters.

foreign tax credit   The credit an American taxpayer may take against American income tax for tax levied on the same income by a foreign government.

foreign trade organization (FTO)   An organization involved in procurement from foreign suppliers. The USSR and other communist countries have a number of FTOs, each specializing in an industry.

foreign trade zone (FTZ)   American version of a free trade zone. In an FTZ, goods may be imported and manufactured or handled and changed in any way. No tariff need be paid unless and until the goods are removed from the FTZ into the country where the FTZ is located.

forfaiting   Has the same purposes and procedures as factoring, which is the sale by an exporter of its accounts receivable for immediate cash. However, there are two important differences: (1) factoring involves credit terms of no more than 180 days, while forfaiting may involve years; (2) factoring does not usually cover political and transfer risks, while forfaiting does.

forward contract   A contract to exchange one currency for another currency at an agreed exchange rate at a future date, usually 30, 60, or 90 days. May be used to hedge. See *forward rate*.

forward rate   The cost today for a commitment by one party to deliver to or take from another party an agreed amount of a currency at a fixed or future date. This rate is established by the forward contract. See *forward tract; spot rate*.

Fourth World   The poorest of the world's countries.

franchising   A franchisee pays a franchisor for the right to use the franchisor's logo, procedures, materials, and advertising.

free trade zones   An area designated by the government of a country for duty-free entry of any nonprohibited goods.

friendship, commerce, and navigation (FCN) treaties   The basic agreements between nations about such matters as treatment of each others' citizens or companies.

fringe benefits   Payments or other benefits given to employees over and above base wages.

general export license   Any export license covering export commodities for which a validated license is not required. No formal application is required.

generalized systems of preference (GSP)   An agreement under the auspices of GATT under which many products of developing nations are provided duty-free access to most developed nations.

general trading companies   Exist in many countries, including the United States, though the Japanese versions of these companies, called sogo shosha in Japanese, are the best known. For many years, the sogo shosha have imported and distributed commodities and products for use by Japanese industries and consumers, sought foreign customers for Japanese companies, and exported to other companies.

geocentric   As used in this book, hiring and promoting employees because of their abilities without reference to their nationality or race.

gilts   Technically, British and Irish government securities, though the term also includes issues of local British authorities.

glasnost   A word popularized by Gorbachev meaning openness of information.

global company   A company that markets a standardized product worldwide and allows only minimum adaptations to local conditions and tastes from country to country. Its financial, marketing, and advertising strategies are global with little differentiation among countries or areas as to product. Other authors, particularly when writing about the automobile industry, mean the company's ability to source parts and components from subsidiaries in several countries for assembly in the market country or area.

GmbH   Gesellschaft mit beschrankter Haftung (organization with limited ability). A German form of business organization.

GNP/capita   The gross national product of a nation divided by its population (an arithmetic mean).

gold exchange standard   The system established at Bretton Woods whereby the value of one currency (the U.S. dollar) was set in terms of gold. The United States held gold and agreed that when another country accumulated U.S. dollars, it could exchange them for gold at the set value.

gold standard   A system under which currency values are set in terms of gold and each country agrees that if a second country accumulates more of a first country's currency than it wants for other purposes, the second country can exchange the first country's currency for that amount of the first country's gold.

gold tranche   The amount of gold paid by a country as its contributed capital in the International Monetary Fund.

Gosbank   Central planning agency for the USSR.

gray market   Where goods are sold, that are either legal but unauthorized imports bearing domestic manufacturers' trade names or are exports diverted to the domestic market.

gross domestic product (GDP)   The market value of a country's output attributable to factors of production located in the country's territory. It differs from GNP by the exclusion of net factor income payments, such as interest and dividends received from, or paid to, the rest of the world. See *gross national product (GNP)*.

gross national product (GNP)   The market value of all the final goods and services produced by a national economy over a period of time, usually a year.

Group of 5   The term used for meetings of the finance ministers and central bank governors of France, the Federal Republic of Germany, Japan, the United Kingdom, and the United States.

Group of 7   The Group of 5 plus Canada and Italy.

Group of 10   The Group of 7 plus Belgium, the Netherlands, and Sweden.

Group of 77   Had its origins in the caucus of 75 developing countries that met in 1964 to prepare for UNCTAD. After the first UNCTAD meeting, the caucus grew to 77.

guest workers   Foreign workers who are brought into a country by legal means to perform needed labor.

hard currency   A currency that is freely convertible into other currencies.

hard loans   Loans that must be repaid in a hard currency at market interest rates.

hedging   Selling forward currency exchange, borrowing, or using other means to protect against losses from possible currency exchange rate changes that affect the values of assets and liabilities.

hierarchy   A system in which there are several layers of authority between the lowest rank (say, the peasant or untouchables) to the highest rank (say, king, commissar, or brahmin).

hit list or super 301   Refers to Section 301 of the U.S. 1988 Trade Act, which requires the U.S. trade representative to prepare a list of countries that systematically restrict access of American products to their markets.

hollowing out   Refers to the practice of firms that close their production facilities and become marketing organizations for other producers, mostly foreign.

home country   The country where the parent company's headquarters are located.

host country   The country in which foreign investment is made.

human needs approach   A way to economic development that includes the elimination of poverty and unemployment as well as an increase in income.

hybrid organization   A structure organized by more than one dimension at the top level.

hypermarkets   Huge combination supermarkets and discount stores where soft and hard goods are sold.

import substitution   An industrialization policy followed by some developing nations by which the government encourages the local production of substitutes for imported goods. High import duties protect local producers from import competition.

incentive pay plans   Plans that pay employees more for achieving certain goals.

income distribution   A measure of how a nation's income is apportioned among its people. It is commonly reported as the percentage of income received by population quintiles.

INCOTERMS   A publication of the International Chamber of Commerce setting forth recommended standard definitions for the major trade terms used in international trade.

indexing   Taking into account the effect of inflation on assets and liabilities and adjusting the amounts of these items to preserve their original relationships.

indicative planning   Planning done by governments in collaboration with industry. It is essentially a forecast of the direction the economy is expected to take. The indicative plan does not control economic activity as in the centrally planned economies, and firms are free to make their own decisions.

indirect exporting   The exporting of goods and services through various types of home-based exporters.

industrial cooperation   A long-term relationship with a company in the West in which a Comecon country or an LDC produces products for its own market and/or export to the West.

industrial espionage   Stealing trade, process, customer, pricing, or technology secrets from a business.

industrial targeting   Government practice of assisting selected industries to grow.

information glut   There is too much information to absorb or it is not properly classified or organized.

infrastructure   The fundamental underpinnings of an economy—roads, railroads, communications, water supplies, energy supplies, and so forth.

in-house training programs   Programs provided by an employer on its own property.

instability   As used in this book, occurs when a government is likely to be overthrown by a revolution or coup.

insurance certificate   Evidence that marine insurance has been obtained to cover stipulated risks during transit.

interest arbitrage   Lending in another country to take advantage of higher interest rates. Such arbitrage tends to equalize interest rates.

Interest Equalization Tax (IET)   From 1963 to 1974, a tax that U.S. residents were required to pay on the purchase of foreign securities. The IET was a device to combat U.S. BOP deficits.

interest rate swap   A transaction in which two parties exchange interest payment streams of differing character based on an underlying principal amount. The three main types are coupon swaps (fixed rate to floating rate in the same currency), basis swaps (one floating rate index to another floating rate index in the same currency), and cross-currency interest rate swaps (fixed or floating rate in one currency or fixed or floating rate in another currency).

intermediate technology   Production method between capital- and labor-intensive methods.

internalization theory   An extension of the market imperfection theory, which claims that to obtain a higher return on its investment, a firm will transfer its superior knowledge to a foreign subsidiary rather than sell it on the open market.

international division   A division in the organization that is at the same level as the domestic division in the firm and is responsible for all nonhome country activities.

international environment   The interaction between the domestic and foreign environmental forces.

international finance center   A multinational's or global's office that handles the great majority of international money transactions for all the firm's units.

international financing   Occurs when a borrower raises capital in the Eurocurrency or Eurobond markets, outside the restrictions that are applied to domestic or foreign offerings. *See foreign financing.*

international law   A body of principles and practices that have been generally accepted by countries in their relations with other countries and with citizens of other countries.

international management information system   Organized process of gathering, storing, processing, and disseminating information about international operations to managers to assist them in making business decisions.

international monetary system   The agreements, practices, laws, customs, and institutions that deal with money (debts, payments, investments) internationally.

international product life cycle   A theory that helps explain both trade flows and foreign direct investment on the basis of a product's position in the four stages of (1) exports of an industrialized nation, (2) beginning of foreign production, (3) foreign competition in export markets, and (4) import competition in the country where the product was introduced originally.

international status   Confers extra perquisites and privileges on a multinational's top employees.

intervention currency   A currency bought or sold by a country (not necessarily the one issued by it) to influence the value of its own currency.

intraenterprise transaction   A transaction between two or more units of the same WWC.

irrevocable letter of credit (L/C)   Refers to a letter of credit that cannot be canceled.

Islam   A religion found primarily in North Africa and the Middle East. Moslems believe the future is ordained by Allah (God). The Koran, a collection of Allah's revelations to Muhammad, the founder of Islam, is accepted as God's eternal word.

iterative planning   Repetition of the bottom-up or top-down planning process until all differences are reconciled.

J curve   A curve illustrating the theory that immediately after a country devalues its currency, its imports become more expensive and its exports cheaper, thus worsening a BOP deficit. As the country's exports increase, it earns more money and the deficit bottoms out and becomes a surplus up the right side of the J.

just-in-time   A balanced system in which there is little or no delay time or inventory.

joint venture   May be (1) a corporate entity between a WWC and local owners, (2) a corporate entity between two or more WWCs that are foreign to the area where the joint venture is located, or (3) a cooperative undertaking between two or more firms for a limited-duration project.

key currencies   Those held extensively as foreign exchange reserves.

labor force composition   The different sorts of available laborers, differentiated in terms of skill, age, race, or gender.

labor intensive   Describes products whose production requires a relatively large amount of labor and a relatively small amount of capital. Also describes the manufacturing process.

labor market   The labor available in an area.

labor mobility   The willingness of labor to move from one location to another.

labor productivity   How much a labor force produces in a given time period.

labor quality   The skill and industriousness of labor.

labor quantity   The number of available laborers.

labor unions   Organizations of laborers that represent and negotiate for workers.

lags   As used in this book, delaying conversion when payment is to be made in another currency in the belief the other currency will cost less when needed.

landlocked   Refers to a nation bordered on all of its frontiers by land.

LASH   Specially designed ocean-going vessel for carrying barges.

leads   As used in this book, converting immediately when payment is to be made in another currency in the belief the other currency will cost more when needed.

left wing   Extremely liberal, in the American sense of the word.

less developed countries (LDCs)   Countries with low per capita income, low levels of industrialization, high illiteracy, and usually political instability.

letter of credit (L/C)   A letter issued by a bank indicating that the bank will accept drafts (make payments) under specified circumstances.

liberal   In American political usage, a liberal advocates extensive government intervention in business and society.

licensing   A contractual arrangement in which one firm, the licensor, grants access to its patents, trademarks, or technology to another firm, the licensee, for a fee, usually called a royalty.

lingua franca   A foreign language used to communicate among a nation's diverse cultures that have diverse languages.

linkage   In international marketing, the creation of demand in a second national market by movement of the product and/or the customer into that market.

Lombard rate   The interest rate that a central bank charges other banks on loans secured by government and other selected securities.

Lomé convention   An agreement between 66 African, Caribbean, and Pacific states and the EC by means of which 99.2 percent of the former group's exports are admitted duty-free to the EC.

London Interbank Offered Rate (LIBOR)   The interest rate the most creditworthy banks charge one another for loans of Eurodollars overnight in the London market. LIBOR is a cornerstone in the pricing on money market issues and other short-term debt issues by both government and business borrowers. Interest is often stated to be LIBOR plus a fraction.

long position   The position taken when a party buys something for future delivery. This may be done in the expectation that the item bought will increase in value. It may also be done to hedge a currency risk.

managed float   See *floating exchange rates*. "Managed" is a more decorous word than "dirty."

managed trade   Trade managed in some way(s) by governments.

management contract   An agreement by which a foreign firm provides management in all or specific areas to a local company for a fee.

management information system (MIS)   The computerized system through which multinational or global executives get timely, relevant information about all the company's units.

manufacturers' agents   Independent sales representatives of various noncompeting suppliers.

manufacturing rationalization   Division of production among a number of production units, enabling each to produce only a limited number of components for all of a firm's assembly plants.

market economies   Economies that are characterized by a relatively large, free (nongovernmental) market sector. There is no such thing as a totally free market; all governments regulate, tax, and intervene in various ways.

market factors   Economic data that correlate highly with market demand for a product.

market indicators   Economic data used to measure relative market strengths of countries or geographical areas.

market method to correct BOP deficit   Deflate the economy and devalue the currency.

market screening   A version of environmental scanning in which the firm identifies desirable markets by using the environmental forces to eliminate the less desirable markets.

Marshall Plan   The U.S. aid program that helped European countries reconstruct after World War II. Cooperation among the European countries was a forerunner of the EC.

material culture   Refers to all manmade objects and is concerned with how people make things (technology) and who makes what and why (economics).

matrix organization   An organizational structure composed of one or more organizational structures superimposed over one another in an attempt to mesh product, regional, functional, and other expertise.

matrix overlay   An organization whose top-level divisions are required to heed input from a staff composed of experts of another organizational dimension. It attempts to avoid the double-reporting difficulty of a matrix organization but still mesh two or more dimensions.

mercantilism   The economic philosophy that equates the possession of gold or other international monetary assets with wealth. It also holds that trade activities should be directed or controlled by the government.

merchant banks   Combine long- and short-term financing with the underwriting and distributing of securities.

minorities   As used in this book, a group of people of one race or religion living in an area populated by a larger number of people of a different race or religion.

mission statement   A broad statement defining the organization's scope.

mitbestimmung   German for "codetermination." The Germans pioneered codetermination, and their word for it is frequently used.

monetary policies   Government policies regulating whether the country's money supply grows and, if so, how fast.

money markets   Places where currencies are traded or capital is raised.

monopolistic advantage theory   The idea that foreign direct investment is made by firms in oligopolistic industries that possess technical and other advantages over indigenous firms.

most favored nation (MFN)   The policy of nondiscrimination in international commercial policy, extending to all nations the same customs and tariff treatments as are extended to the most-favored nation.

multinational economic union   A group of nations that have reduced barriers to intergroup trade and are cooperating in economic matters. It may be in the form of a (1) free trade area, (2) customs union, (3) common market, or (4) regional cooperation group.

multinational, multinational company, or multinational enterprise (MNC or MNE)   Terms used by some authors to mean an organization consisting of a parent company in a home country that owns relatively autonomous subsidiaries in various host countries.

national (macro) competition   Ability of a nation's producers to compete successfully in the world markets and with imports in their own domestic markets.

national economic plans   Plans prepared by governments that state their economic goals and means for reaching them for periods of usually up to five years.

nationalism   A strong attachment to and support of one's country.

nationalization   Government takeover of private property.

national tax jurisdiction   Taxation on the basis of nationality regardless of where in the world the taxpayer's income is earned or where the activities of the taxpayer take place.

natural resources   Anything supplied by nature on which people depend.

net negative international investment position   Residents of a country have less investments abroad than nonresidents have in the country.

neutralizing the balance sheet   Having the assets in a given currency approximate the liabilities in that currency.

newly industrializing countries (NICs)   A group of middle-income nations with high growth in manufacturing. Much of their production goes to high-income, industrialized nations.

nonmarket economy   The World Bank designation for a communist nation.

nonmarket measures   Use of currency controls, tariffs, or quotas to correct a BOP deficit.

nonrecourse financing   Financing in which the factor assumes the full responsibility and all the risk of collecting from a third party. See *forfaiting*.

nonrevenue tax purpose   Use of a tax to encourage some perceived socially desirable end, such as home ownership, or to discourage something undesirable, such as tobacco.

nontariff barriers (NTBs)   Constraints on imports other than import duties, such as quotas, product standards, orderly marketing arrangements, customs and administrative procedures, and government participation in trade.

note issuance facility (NIF)   Medium-term arrangements that enable borrowers to issue paper, typically of three- or six-months' maturity, in their own names. A group of underwriting bank guarantees the availability of funds to the borrower by purchasing any unsold notes or by providing standby credit.

off-premises training   The employer sends workers away from its property to a school or other site to be trained.

offshore banking   The use of banks located in other countries, particularly tax havens like the Caymans and the Bahamas.

offshore funds   Investment funds whose shares are usually denominated in U.S. dollars but located and sold outside the United States. There are tax and securities-registration reasons for such funds.

on-the-job training   Employees learn a job by performing it under supervision.

opening bank   The bank that opens a letter of credit (L/C). This bank will honor (pay) drafts drawn under the L/C if specified conditions are met.

orderly marketing agreements (OMAs)   Compacts negotiated between two or more nations under whose terms the exporting nation or nations agree to limit exports of specified goods to the importing nation. They are sometimes called voluntary export agreements (VEA).

Overseas Private Insurance Corporation (OPIC)   A U.S. government corporation that offers American investors in developing countries insurance against expropriation, currency inconvertibility, and damages from wars and revolutions.

overvalued currency   A currency whose value is kept higher by government action than it would be in a free market.

paper gold   See *special drawing rights (SDRs)*.

parallel importer   Wholesaler who imports products independently of manufacturer-authorized importers or buys goods for export and diverts them to the domestic market.

parallel importing   The importing of a product by an independent operator that is not part of the manufacturer's channel of distribution. The parallel importer may compete with the authorized importer or with a subsidiary of the foreign manufacturer that produces the product in the local market.

parent company   A company that owns subsidiary companies.

par value   The value that a government, by agreement or regulation, sets on its currency in terms of other currencies. At Bretton Woods, other currencies were assigned par values in terms of the U.S. dollar.

paternalism   A system in which a chief, sheik, or other authority figure cares for all the people as if he were their father.

pegged exchange rate   An exchange rate in which a country's currency is fixed in terms of another country's currency. Frequently, the other country is a major trading partner or a country with which there was a colonial relationship.

perestroika   A word popularized by Gorbachev meaning modernizing the economy and devolving decision power from the central government.

peril point   In U.S. law, a point below which a tariff cannot be lowered without causing or threatening serious injury to U.S. producers of competitive products.

physical product   The basic physical product produced by a firm's production system. It does not include attributes added after production, such as packaging, brand name, service, or financing.

political risks   The risks to a business and its employees that stem from political unrest in an area. As a result of such unrest, the markets or supplies of the business may be disrupted or the business may be nationalized and its employees may lose their jobs or be kidnapped, injured, or even killed.

population density   A measure of the number of inhabitants per area unit (inhabitants per kilometer or mile).

population distribution   A measure of how the inhabitants are distributed over a nation's area.

polymetallic deposits   Deposits that contain a number of metals.

portfolio investment   The purchase of stocks and bonds to obtain a return in the money invested. The investors are not interested in assuming control of the firm.

preindustrial societies   A designation that can signify anything from traditional societies up through societies in the early stages of agricultural and industrial organization.

preventive maintenance (planned maintenance)   Maintenance done according to plan, not when a machine breaks down.

price and wage controls   Government limits on prices that may be charged and wages that may be paid.

privatization   When a government transfers ownership and/or operation of a government-owned enterprise to private owners/operators.

product liability   Liability of a product's manufacturer for damage caused by the product.

pro forma invoice   Exporter's formal quotation containing a description of the merchandise, price, delivery time, method of shipping, terms of sale, and points of entry.

programmed-management approach   A middle-ground advertising strategy between globally standardized and entirely local programs.

promotion   All forms of communication between a firm and its publics.

promotional mix   A blend of the promotional methods a firm uses to sell its products.

Protestant work ethic   The duty of Christians to glorify God by hard work and the practice of thrift.

public relations   Various methods of communicating with the firm's publics to secure a favorable impression.

purchasing power parity   The relative ability of one unit of two countries' currencies to purchase similar goods. From this relative ability is derived an indication of what the market exchange rate between the two currencies should be.

quality circles (quality control circles)   Small work groups that meet periodically to discuss ways to improve their functional areas in the firm and the quality of the products.

questionable or dubious payments   Bribes.

quota   (1) A limitation on imports by number or by weight; for example, only so many of a given item or only so many pounds or kilos may be imported. (2) At the IMF, each member-nation has a quota that determines the amount of its subscription and how much it can borrow.

regional dualism A situation in which some regions of a nation have high productivity and high incomes while, other regions of the same country have little economic development and lower incomes.

regression analysis Statistical technique that utilizes a linear model to establish relationships between independent variables and the dependent variable.

reinvoicing Centralizing all international invoicing by a WWC. The reinvoicing center decides which currencies should be used and where, how, and when.

repatriation The transfer home of assets held abroad.

representative office An office of an out-of-state or foreign bank that is not permitted to conduct direct banking functions. The purpose of such an office is to solicit business for its parent bank, where it can conduct such functions.

restrictive trade practices legislation The European versions of American antitrust laws.

revaluation of a currency An increase in a currency's value in terms of other currencies. See *devaluation*.

reverse engineering Also called "benchmarking": Dismantling a competitor's product to learn everything possible about it.

reverse imports Products made by a multinational's overseas subsidiaries that are exported to the home country.

revocable letters of credit (L/Cs) L/Cs that the opening bank may revoke at any time without notice to the beneficiary.

Rhine waterway A system of rivers and canals that is the main transportation artery of Europe.

right wing Extremely conservative politically.

robotics Machines, usually computer controlled, doing work previously done by human workers.

RO-RO Specially designed ocean-going vessel that permits any equipment on wheels to be rolled on board.

rural-to-urban shift Describes the movement of a nation's population from rural areas to cities.

S.A. Société Anonyme, Sociedad Anomina, or Societa Anomina. Joint-stock companies (in French, Spanish, and Italian, respectively).

safe haven The currency of a country that is politically secure is called a safe haven currency.

sales company A corporate entity established in a foreign country by the parent company to sell goods or services imported from the parent company and other foreign affiliates.

sales promotion Selling aids, including displays, premiums, contests, and gifts.

S.A.R.L. Société à Responsibilité Limitée.

scenario Description of a possible future. Managers often use most-likely, worst, and best cases for the purpose of planning.

securitization The term is most often used to mean the process by which traditional bank assets, mainly loans or mortgages, are converted into negotiable securities. More broadly, refers to the development of markets for a variety of new negotiable instruments.

self-reference criterion Unconscious reference to one's own cultural values when judging behavioral actions of others in a new and different environment.

shale A fissile (capable of being split) rock composed of laminated layers of claylike, fine-grained sediment.

short position The position of a party when it has sold something it does not own and to which it has no contractual right. This is for future delivery in the expectation that the item sold will decrease in price. It is also done to hedge a currency risk.

sight draft A bill of exchange that is payable immediately on presentation or demand. A bank check is a sight draft.

skilled labor Employees trained in needed skills.

Smithsonian agreement New agreements on currency par values, the value of gold, and tariffs reached by the major trading countries at the Smithsonian Institution in Washington, D.C., in December 1971. When the United States closed the "gold window" in August 1971, the world currency exchanges were thrown into turmoil, and such agreements became necessary.

snake During the 1970s, several West European countries agreed to keep the values of their currencies within established ranges in terms of one another. The currencies would all float in value in terms of other currencies—for example, the U.S. dollar and the Japanese yen.

socialism A theory of society in which the government owns or directs most of the factors of production.

soft currency A currency that is not freely convertible into other currencies. Such a currency is usually subject to national currency controls.

soft loans Loans like those granted by the IDA. These loans may have grace periods during which no payments need be made; they may bear low or no interest; and they may be repayable in a soft currency.

sogo shosha The Japanese term for general trading companies.

sovereign debt The debt of a national government.

sovereign immunity   The immunity of a government from lawsuits in the courts of its own country or other countries unless it submits voluntarily. Such immunity is particularly likely to exist if the government limits itself to "governmental" functions as opposed to economic ones.

sovereignty   The power of each national government over the land within its border and over the people and organizations within those borders.

special drawing rights (SDRs)   Accounting entries at the IMF. SDRs are treated as reserve assets and are credited or debited to member-countries' accounts. Sometimes called paper gold, they permit liquidity to be created by agreement at the IMF rather than having it depend on the U.S. BOP deficit.

specific tariff or duty   A method of measuring customs duties or tariffs by number or weight instead of by value. Thus, the amount of the tariff or duty is based on how many units or how many pounds or kilos are imported, regardless of their value. See *ad valorem tariff or duty*.

spot rate or spot quotation   The rate of exchange between two currencies for immediate delivery, one for the other. See *forward rate*.

stability   As used in this book, occurs when a government is not likely to be overturned by a revolution or a coup.

standardization of the marketing mix   The utilization of the same pricing, product, distribution, and promotional strategies in all markets where the firm does business.

straight bonds or notes   Issues with a fixed (not floating) coupon or interest rate.

strategic business unit (SBU)   Business entity with a clearly defined market, specific competitors, the ability to carry out its business mission, and a size appropriate for control by a single manager.

subcontracting   Prime manufacturers purchase of components from other suppliers. Used in industrial cooperation.

subsidiaries   Companies owned by another company, which is referred to as the parent company.

subsidiary detriment   A subsidiary is deprived of a potential advantage so that the multinational as a whole may enjoy a greater advantage.

subsidies, export   Financial encouragement to export. Such subsidies can take the form of lower taxes, tax rebates, or direct payments.

superstores   Name given to hypermarkets in Japan and in some parts of Europe and the United States.

swaps   Are of two basic kinds: interest rate swaps and currency swaps. Interest rate swaps typically exchange floating-rate payments. Currency swaps are accords to deliver one currency against another currency at certain intervals.

swing   In a bilateral trade agreement, the leeway provided for mutual extension of credit.

switch trade   A type of countertrade utilized when a country lacks sufficient hard currency to pay for its imports. When it can acquire from a third country products desired by its creditor country, it switches shipment of those products to the creditor country. Its debt to the creditor country is thereby paid.

synchronized manufacturing   An entire manufacturing process with unbalanced operations. Total system performance is emphasized.

takeoff   A phase in the development of an LDC when its infrastructure has been sufficiently developed, enough interacting industries have been established, and domestic capital formation exceeds consumption, so that the country's own momentum carries the development process onward.

tariff quota   A tariff that has a lower rate until the end of a specified period or until a specified amount of the commodity has been imported. At that point, the rate increases.

tariffs   See *duties*.

tax haven   A country that has low or no taxes on income from foreign sources or capital gains.

tax incentives   The tax holidays that LDCs sometimes give companies and their managements if they will invest in the country, or that DCs sometimes give them to induce investment in an area of high unemployment.

tax treaty   A treaty between two countries in which each country usually lowers certain taxes on residents who are nationals of the other, and the countries agree to cooperate in tax matters like enforcement.

Taylor's scientific management system   A system based on scientific measurements that prescribes a division of work whereby planning is done by managers and plan execution is left to supervisors and workers.

technological dualism   The presence in a country of industries using modern technology while others employ more primitive methods.

terms of sale   Conditions of a sale that stipulate the point where all costs and risks are borne by the buyer.

terms of trade   The real quantities of exports that are required to pay for a given amount of imports.

territorial tax jurisdiction   The levying of tax on taxpayers while living and working in the territory of the taxing government. Income earned while living and working elsewhere is not taxed or is taxed at a lower rate.

terrorism The use by nongovernment forces of murder, kidnapping, and destruction to publicize or gain political goals.

third-country nationals Citizens of neither the home nor the host country who work in a host country affiliate.

Third World The Eastern-bloc countries dominated by the USSR are considered one world. The countries of the West, primarily the OECD countries, are considered another world. All other countries are sometimes referred to as Third World countries.

tied loans or grants Loans or grants that the borrower or recipient must spend in the country that made them.

time draft An unconditional order drawn by the seller on the buyer to pay the draft's amount at an agreed future date.

top-down planning Planning process that begins at the highest level in the organization and continues downward.

topography The surface features of a region, such as mountains, deserts, plains, and bodies of water.

total product What the customer buys, i.e., includes physical product, brand name, after-sale service, warranty, instructions for use, company image, and package.

total quality-control system A system that integrates the development, maintenance, and improvement of quality among all functional areas of the firm.

trade acceptance A draft similar to a banker's acceptance, the difference being that no bank is involved. The exporter presents the draft to the importer for its acceptance to pay the amount started at a fixed future date.

trade block A group of countries with special trading rules among them, such as the EC or Comecon.

trade deficit/surplus A trade deficit is an excess of merchandise imports over exports. A trade surplus is the opposite.

trade fair A large exhibition generally held periodically at the same place and time at which companies maintain booths to promote the sale of their products.

trade mission Group of businesspeople and/or government officials (state and federal) that visits a foreign market in search of business opportunities.

trading at a discount When a currency costs less in the forward market than the spot cost.

trading at a premium When a currency costs more in the forward market than the spot cost.

trading companies Firms that develop international trade and serve as intermediaries between foreign buyers and domestic sellers, and vice versa.

traditional economy An area in a most rudimentary state. In such an economy, the people are typically nomadic, agriculture is at a bare subsistence level, and industry is virtually nonexistent.

traditional hostilities When nations, races, or religions have been in conflict for long periods.

transaction risk The risk run in international trade that changes in relative currency values will cause losses.

transfer price The price charged by one unit of a WWC for goods or services that it sells to another unit of the same WWC.

translation risk The apparent losses or gains that can result from the restatement of values from one currency into another, even if there are no transactions, when the currencies change in value relative to each other. Translation risks are common with long-term foreign investments as foreign currency values are translated to the investor's financial statements in its home currency.

transnationals Used by the UN and some others to connote organizations variously called global, multinational, or worldwide companies.

Treaty of Rome Established the EC.

trend analysis Statistical technique by which successive observations of a variable at regular time intervals are analyzed for the purpose of establishing regular patterns that are used for establishing future values.

twin plants Along the Mexican-American border, the plant on the U.S. side does the high-tech, capital-intensive part of production, while the Mexican plant does the labor-intensive part. Also called maquiladoras.

unbalanced growth theory The idea that economic growth can be attained by deliberately creating an imbalance in the economy through investment in an industry that will require further investment in supporting industries to reduce the imbalance.

uncontrollable environmental forces The external forces in the domestic and foreign environments over which management has no direct control.

underground economy The part of a nation's income that, underreported or unreported is not measured by official statistics.

undervalued currency A currency that has been oversold because of emotional selling, or a currency whose value a government tries to keep below market to make its country's exports less expensive and more competitive.

unit labor costs The labor cost to produce one unit of output.

unskilled labor Employees without needed skills.

unspoken language Refers to nonverbal communication, such as gestures and body language.

untouchables Lowest-caste Indians. Mahatma Gandhi called them harijans, the children of God.

Uruguay Round The round of GATT negotiations that held its first meeting in Uruguay in 1986.

validated export license A required document issued by the U.S. government authorizing the export of specified commodities.

value-added tax (VAT) A tax levied at each stage in the production of a product. The tax is on the value added to the product by that stage.

variable levy Import duties set at the differences between world market prices and local government-supported prices. Used by the European Community on grain imports to ensure that they have no price advantage over locally grown grains.

vehicle currency A currency used in international transactions to make quotes and payments. The U.S. dollar is the currency most often used.

venture capital Money invested, usually in equity, in a new, relatively high-risk undertaking.

vertical mobility An individual's opportunities to move upward in a society to a higher caste or a higher social status.

Vneshtorgbank USSR state bank for foreign trade.

voluntary export agreements (VEA) See *orderly marketing agreements.*

voluntary export restraints (VERS) Export quotas imposed by the exporting nation.

watch list List containing items of interest concerning the uncontrollable variables of special interest to the firm.

Webb-Pomerene Act Exempts from U.S. antitrust laws those associations among business competitors engaged in export trade. They must not restrain trade within the United States or the trade of any other U.S. competitors.

worldwide companies Used by some authors to connote the organizations referred to by others as globals, multinationals, or transnationals.

zaibatsu Centralized, family-dominated, monopolistic economic groups that dominated the Japanese economy until the end of World War II, at which time they were broken up. As time passed, however, the units of the old zaibatsu drifted back together, and they now cooperate within the group much as they did before their dissolution.

zero-coupon bonds Bonds that are issued at a heavy discount and pay no interest but are redeemable at par at a future date.

Name Index

Company Index

Subject Index

Cultural forces; *see* Sociocultural forces
Culture
  definition, 257
  language, 281–82
  significance for international business,
    257–59
Currencies
  bid and asked prices, 170
  convertible, 136
  fixed (hard) exchange rate, 136, 144
  fluctuating exchange rates; *see*
    Fluctuating (floating) exchange rates
  intervention, 166
  vehicle, 166
Currency areas, 145–46
Currency conversion, 90–91
Currency exchange controls, 171–73
  laws governing, 340–41
  worldwide, 172–73
Currency exchange rates; *see* Exchange
    rate
Currency exposure management, 587
Currency markets, 149
Currency swaps, 583
Currency values, fluctuating, 166, 170
Current account, 140
Custom house broker, 530–32

D

Debits and credits in international
    transactions, 138
Debt capital, 581
Debt default, 115
Debtor countries, 180–84
  LDCs, 180–83
  United States, 183–84
Debt rescheduling, 115
Deficit, U.S., 137, 141–43
  fundamental, 141
  market and nonmarket measures of
    dealing with, 138
  temporary, 141
Deflation, 142
Demonstration effect, 263
Demurrage charge, 526
Department of Commerce, U.S.
  East-West trade, 549–50
  export assistance programs, 509–10
  Foreign Trade Report, FT 410, 437
  market assessment aids, 438, 442
  Office of Export Enforcement, 523
Deserts as marketing influence, 230–32
Détente, 562–63
Devaluation of currency, 76
Developed countries, world trade, 29
Developing countries, 29, 88
  characteristics of, 92
  trade and competition, 403–6

Development finance companies (DFCs),
    112
Development risks as defense to product
    liability suits, 339
*Digest of Commercial Laws of the
    World* (Oceana), 442
Direct exporting, 53, 416–17
Direct imports, 418
Direct investment, 35
  contemporary theories, 95–96
  definition, 140
  direction, 36–38
  volume, 36
Dirty currency float, 144–45
DISC (domestic international sales
    corporation), 349, 520
Discipline of work force, 641–42
Discretionary income, 197
Disposable income, 196
Distribution channels; *see* Channels of
    distribution
Distribution strategies, 489–93
  standardization, 492–93
Distributive structure, 411
Distributors, 417
District Export Council, 511
Documentary drafts, 516
Dollar, U.S.
  central reserve asset, 137, 138, 153
  gold exchange standard, 142–43
  safe haven aspect, 167
Domestication, 336
Domestic environment, 15
Domestic International Sales
    Corporation (DISC), 349, 520
Double taxation of profits, 392
Dumping, 81, 557–58
Duties, 82, 174

E

East countries, 540
Eastern bloc, economic and financial
    information, 735–36
East European debt, 555
East Germany, 540, 541
East-West trade, 538–63
  détente, 562–63
  problems, 555–62
  selling to the East, 545–51
  technology, 556
EC; *see* European Community
EC Commission, restrictive trade
    practice, 333
EC 1992; *see* Europe 1992
Economic analysis, 191–212; *see also*
    Economic forces
Economic development, 88
  GNP/capita as indicator, 89–92

Economic development—*cont.*
  human needs approach, 92
Economic forces, 190
  dimensions of the economy, 193–204
  impediment to standardization, 606–7
  industry dimension, 212
  international economic analysis, 191–
    212
  market screening, 436–42
  national economic plans, 211–12
  product strategies, 470
  socioeconomic dimensions, 204–11
The Economist, 438, 443
Economist Intelligence Unit, 190, 212
ECU; *see* European currency unit
Education, 276–80
  allowances, 696
  brain drain, 278–79
  women's, 280, 281
  yardsticks, 276–78
Electronic Funds Transfer Network, 588
    588
Employee facilities, 625
Employer-employee relationships; *see*
    Labor relations
EMS; *see* European Monetary System
Entry barriers, 442
Environmental scanning, 436
Environment of business, 14–17
  controllable forces, 15
  decision making, 17
  domestic, 15
  external or internal, 14–15
  foreign, 16
  international, 17
  uncontrollable forces, 14
Equity capital, 581
Ernst and Ernst International Services,
    442
Estimation by analogy, 440–41
Euromonitor, 439
European Central Bank, 154
European Common Market, 124
European Community, 7, 9, 15, 42, 317,
    398
  antitrust enforcement, 333
  background of, 123–24
  central banker groups, 119
  export subsidy, 86
  Fortress Europe concept, 126–27
  versus Hoffman-La Roche, 333–34
  labor unions, 381
  Project 1992; *see* Europe 1992
  relations with United States, 65, 126
  Swiss government, 334
  trade retaliation, 80
  trade volume, 28
European currency unit (ECU), 128,
    136, 145, 154, 155–58